THE END OF THE OLD

AND

THE BEGINNING OF THE NEW

COMMENTS ON

REVELATION

Comments and Studies Based Upon

The Jonathan Mitchell New Testament

by

JONATHAN MITCHELL, M.A.

DEDICATION

This work is dedicated to my friend and brother, Walter Daniel Kaplan, in appreciation for his constant support of, and insightful input into, the entire process of creating this commentary. Dan's wealth of knowledge of the Scriptures, from a lifetime of study, and his spiritual insight, from "hearing" the Lord, have enriched the content of this book. The first-draft comments on each verse of the Unveiling were immediately sent to Dan for his response and input. His encouragement to me, throughout the months of writing, have been priceless. He, with the continuous support and technical expertise of his wife, Nancy, has been an invaluable research assistant in bringing the threads of the old into the pictures in the new, as we present the beautiful tapestry that was given to John, in the 1st century AD.

ACKNOWLEDGEMENTS

I want to give special acknowledgement to Kenneth Earl, who first introduced me to non-literal reading of the Scriptures, in 1962, and then to the works and teachings of Ray Prinzing, Malcolm Smith and J. Preston Eby who over the past decades have continued being instrumental in opening my understanding to the symbolic figures and language that comprise the apocalyptic work commonly called *Revelation*. These teachers guided me and set me on a good Path, for which I am continuously grateful.

I also want to acknowledge the friends and scholars who are listed in the Bibliography and Sources, below. Without them this work would have never come into being. This journey has had many turns with necessary adjustments to my understanding of this ancient visionary letter from John.

I am grateful of my wife, Lynda, for her feedback and the postings from the book on Facebook, and for her creative work on our book covers. I am indebted to my sister, Rebecca Mitchell, and my wife, Lynda Mitchell, for their faithful efforts at proof reading the texts. I am blessed by our son, Joshua Mitchell, for his commitment to this ministry and for his technical support in IT, as well as for being the technical creator of our book covers, our webmaster and our publisher.

We are also thankful for those who have financially supported our work, thus making it all possible.

Jonathan Mitchell
Surprise AZ, USA, 2017

> "The task of interpretation that gives contemporary access to the scriptural text is an ongoing one that is never finished. It requires, moreover, venturesome imagination that is always risky; those risks, however, are not as great as the risk of flat, one-dimensional reiteration that does not connect'" (Walter Brueggemann, *Journey to the Common Good*, Westminster John Knox Press, 2010 p ix)

TABLE of CONTENTS

DEDICATION and ACKNOWLEDGEMENTS
CONTENTS
INTRODUCTION
BIBLIOGRAPHY and SOURCES
ABBREVIATIONS and APPARATUS

Chapter 1	1
Chapter 2	26
Chapter 3	62
Chapter 4	87
Chapter 5	106
Chapter 6	125
Chapter 7	155
Chapter 8	175
Chapter 9	191
Chapter 10	215
Chapter 11	236
Chapter 12	305
Chapter 13	350
Chapter 14	395
Chapter 15	430
Chapter 16	438
Chapter 17	458
Chapter 18	482
Chapter 19	506
Chapter 20	545
Chapter 21	574
Chapter 22	623
What is the Timeframe of Acts 3:21?	665
You Will Love God	672

Copyright 2018 Harper Brown Publishing
ISBN 978-1-7321205-0-1

Cover Photo: Mishara Mitchell

New Testament text:
The New Testament, God's Message of Goodness, Ease and Well-Being, Which Brings God's Gifts of His Spirit, His Life, His Grace, His Power, His Fairness, His Peace and His Love, translated by Jonathan Mitchell; Copyright 2009, 2015 and 2018, all rights reserved; ISBN 978-1-4507-0505-9

Front Cover design and creation: Lynda Mitchell, Joshua Mitchell, Jessica Mitchell and Mishara Mitchell
Cover productions: Joshua Mitchell, Volcano Studios LLC

INTRODUCTION

According to the critical analysis of John A.T. Robinson (*Redating the New Testament*, The Westmister Press, 1976), this work was originally written circa A.D. 68-70. This seems confirmed by the internal evidence, if taken at face value, for in chapter 11 we find that the temple is still standing, along with a prophecy of the destruction of Jerusalem. Milton S. Terry instructs us,

> "It is worthy of note that the 'Muratorian Fragment,' a very ancient and important document (A.D. 170), declares that 'the blessed apostle Paul, *following the manner of his predecessor John*, wrote in like manner to seven churches expressly by name.' This testimony clearly puts John before Paul in writing epistles to the churches, and tends to confirm the position taken above that Gal. 4:25, 26, is an allusion to John's picture of the heavenly Jerusalem" (*Biblical Apocalyptics, A Study of the Most Notable Revelations of God and of Christ in the Canonical Scriptures*, Wipf and Stock Publishers, 2001 [originally in1898], p 267; emphasis original).

The purpose for writing another commentary on Revelation (or: An Unveiling) is to offer an interpretation that points out the significance of the frequent use of the Greek present tense (which tells us that the author is speaking of lineal or durative action, which can be construed as continuous, or habitual, or repeated, or progressive action). The context will also, at times, indicate that this action is presently ongoing. With this work being based upon *The New Testament, God's Message of Goodness, Ease and Well-Being Which Brings God's Gifts of His Spirit, His Life, His Grace, His Power, His Fairness, His Peace and His Love* (Harper Brown Publishing, 2015 Edition), another reason for this work is to uncover what light an expanded translation (having multiple renderings) will shed upon our understanding of what John was communicating to his listeners. We will consider the views of a variety of scholars, gathering their insights, but this endeavor will be a fresh interpretation of the text. My comments, and those of some of my friends, will be a kind of *midrash*: reflections on the story (the drama set forth in the visions) to communicate all of its underlying messages, as we currently perceive them.

Marcus J. Borg makes some insightful observations in, *Reading the Bible Again for the First Time* (HarperSanFrancisco, 2001). In his Preface, p ix, he states,

> "Conflict about the Bible is the single most divisive issue among Christians in North America today.... The conflict is between two very different ways of reading the Bible... between a 'literal-factual way'... and a 'historical-metaphorical' way of reading it.... The latter has been taught in seminaries of mainline denominations for the better part of a century. Most clergy have known about it for a long time. In the last few decades, the historical-metaphorical way of reading the Bible has become increasingly common among lay members of mainline churches."

It is this "historical-metaphorical way" that will be followed in this present work, allowing the Scriptures that the first century author would have drawn upon and alluded to, which was the Hebrew Bible (i.e., the OT), to supply the meanings of the apocalyptic symbolism, while also turning to the writings of other first century authors to inform our understanding of the text.

In the Introduction to chapter 10 ("Reading Revelation Again"), of this same work, Borg observes concerning the canonical placement of Revelation at the end of the NT, that "the Bible moves from 'paradise lost' [i.e., the opening chapters of Genesis] to 'paradise restored" (ibid p 267; brackets added). He, along with most scholars, reads Revelation as apocalyptic literature, which he instructs us, "flourished in Judaism from about 200 BCE to 100 CE," and points out that, "it is also a letter addressed to seven Christian communities in seven cities in Asia Minor," then also remarks that,

> "as many as 65 percent of the verses in Revelation echo or allude to passages from the Hebrew Bible" (ibid p 268).

William Barclay shares that apocalyptic literature is,

> "representative of a kind of literature which was the commonest of all between the Old and the New Testaments.... the product of an indestructible Jewish hope.... History for the Jews was a

catalogue of disasters from which it became clear that no human deliverer could rescue them.... [they] looked for the direct intervention of God.... All apocalyptic literature deals with these events.... It is entirely composed of dreams and visions of the end. That means that all apocalyptic literature is necessarily cryptic. It is continually attempting to describe the indescribable, to say the unsayable, to paint the unpaintable" (*The Revelation of John*, Vol. 1, The Daily Study Bible Series, Westminster Press, 1976 pp 2-4; brackets added).

For an in-depth introduction to the various ways that this book has been interpreted, I recommend *The New International Greek Testament Commentary, The Book of Revelation*, G.K. Beale, William B. Eerdmans Publishing Company, 1999. The author of this present volume will present a primarily preterist (Latin *praeter* means "before") interpretation which views Revelation as speaking of events that were to happen, and that were fulfilled or inaugurated, in the first century A.D. Added to this will be comments on what this means to us in our day, and what it can mean to folks who read Revelation in future days. The author sees this Unveiling of and from Jesus, the Messiah, as an apocalyptic "gospel." It is filled with good news: Jesus Christ reigns! Jesus is Lord! He is,

> "**presently making all things new** (or: habitually creating everything [to be] new and fresh; progressively forming [the] whole anew; or, reading παντα as masculine: periodically making **all humanity** new; progressively creating **every person** anew; constantly constructing [as corporate being] all people fresh and new; continuously renewing **everyone**)!" (Rev. 21:5)

The book begins with a figurative vision of the resurrected Jesus Christ and presents the introduction to the entire book, chapter 1, then in chapters 2-3 John is told what to write to seven of the called-out, covenant communities in Asia Minor. Following this John experiences a series of visions concerning which, in 1:19, he is told to write of "**the things you see** (or: saw), **and the things presently existing** (or: what they are), **as well as which things are progressively about to occur** (or: are now impending to be coming into existence) **after these things**." What is often overlooked is that some of the visions which John saw might be speaking of the first category, "the things presently existing." Borg notes that, "in the book as a whole, 'I saw' is used about fifty-five times" (ibid p 270). So in considering the things that were disclosed to John, care must be taken in order to discern between what spoke of the realities of the present time in which John was living, and the forecasts of what would soon take place after his having received the visions.

The structure of the visions which compose the rest of the book (following the letters to the called-out folks in chapters 2 and 3) has been seen in a variety of ways (*Cf* Beale's Introduction), but here will be presented as different symbolic pictures of the scenarios that presently exist in God's new creation (e.g., chapter 4 and chapter 22), and of things that would culminate in the destruction of Jerusalem in AD 70. The book speaks to historical situations concerning those seven communities to which this letter was to be sent, it affirms various aspects of the new creation, describes the relationship between Jerusalem and the Roman Empire, together with judgment of both of these, and ends with a glorious picture of Christ's body as the New, Heavenly Jerusalem and its ministry to the nations – right here on earth.

> "Revelation is a narrative within a letter, introduced as an apocalypse. It is not strictly chronological. When Christ unleashes the great eschatological events, they take place in two great cycles of visions that cover some of the same ground from different angles. This is called recapitulation. Having a grasp of Revelation's structure will help us to keep track of what is going on as we read the book" (Frederick J. Murphy, *Apocalypticism in the Bible and Its World*, Baker Academic, 2012, p 97).

Beale offers other views than what Murphy has just said, and I invite you to keep an open mind regarding how the book is structured, but Murphy's description will be a good starting point for our journey. Chapter 1:1-3 provides John's descriptive title. On the history of this genre of literature, S. MacLean Gilmour posits:

> "Jewish apocalyptic had its roots, then, in OT prophecy, but its development was in the main the

consequence of alien influence. The literature of Babylonia and of Iran reveals at an earlier date than does the OT the chief apocalyptic traits.... It is no accident that apocalyptic ideas became naturalized within Judaism after the exilic period, for it was then that the Jews were vassals of the Persians.... Apocalyptic literature reflects the historical situation at the time of writing" (*The Interpreter's One-Volume Commentary on the Bible*, Abingdon Press, 1971, p 945).

A.E. Harvey shares:

"The Revelation. So far as we know, this had never before been the title of a book. The idea behind the title is of course as old as religion itself: there have always been certain men and women who have claimed that in the course of some supernatural experience divine mysteries were 'revealed' to them; and the religions of Greece and Rome, as of Palestine and Egypt, produced numerous books in which the writer (whether under his own or an assumed name) claimed to have fallen into a trance, to have seen inexpressible visions, and to have been instructed by heavenly voices, apparitions or angels in the meaning of the mysteries he had seen and heard.... The ultimate mystery, for the Jews, was the future – the state of affairs for which creation had been destined by God, and which alone gave meaning to the present.... For Christians, on the other hand, this kind of writing assumed great importance. The conditions... were now dramatically altered. The new age... was now inaugurated by Jesus Christ... There existed now... an authoritative and final revelation. The claim contained in the first words of the book was as new as the religion which made such a book possible" (A.E. Harvey, *The New English Bible Companion to the New Testament*, Oxford University Press, 1970, pp 787-8).

David H. Stern observes,

"Moreover, the book of Revelation is highly distinctive in the way it uses the *Tanakh* [OT]. There are very few direct quotations, but no less than five hundred allusions to the *Tanakh* [OT], especially the books of Exodus, Isaiah, Jeremiah, Ezekiel, Zechariah and Daniel.... But the overall effect of so many *Tanakh* [OT] references and allusions is to anchor every part of the book in the God-inspired words of Israel's Prophets" (*Jewish New Testament Commentary*, Jewish NT Pub, Inc, 1999, p785; brackets added).

Jean-Louis D'Aragon points out that, "It has been influenced, in varying degrees, by three literary forms: (a) apocalyptic, (b) prophetic, and (c) epistolary" (*The Jerome Biblical Commentary*, Vol. II, Prentice Hall, Inc., 1968, p 467).

Bruce M. Metzger states,

"The book of Revelation is unique in appealing primarily to our *imagination* – not, however, a freewheeling imagination, but a disciplined imagination. This book contains a series of word pictures.... Many of the details of the pictures are intended to contribute to the total impression, and are not to be isolated and interpreted with wooden literalism.... In any case, it is important to recognize that the descriptions are *descriptions of symbols, not of the reality conveyed by the symbols*" (*Breaking the Code, Understanding the Book of Revelation*, Abingdon Press,1999, pp 11, 14; emphasis original). He further points out that "Of the 404 verses that comprise the 22 chapters of the book of Revelation, 278 verses contain one or more allusions to an OT passage" (*Breaking the Code, Understanding the Book of Revelation*, Abingdon Press,1999 p 13).

Beale (ibid p 51-2, 56) notes the use of the Greek verb σημαινω (to indicate by signs or symbols) in Dan. 2 (especially vs. 45) and Rev. 1:1, and thus affirms,

"The symbolic use of σημαινω in Dan. 2 defines the use in Rev. 1:1 as referring to symbolic communication and not mere general conveyance of information.... Hence, the predominant manner by which to approach the material will be according to a nonliteral interpretative method.... The OT and Judaism are the primary background against which to understand the images and ideas of the Apocalypse."

As we will see, this is the key to understanding the figures and symbols throughout this letter. A major symbolic feature is the use of numbers. As Beale attests, "... these numbers receive their figurative significance from the OT.... The frequent repetition of the numbers underscores the notion that nothing is random or coincidental" (ibid p 58, 63). In considering the format of the letter, 1:1-8 can be viewed as a prologue, with 22:6-21 as the epilogue. Between these, some see the body of the letter divided into

seven sections, while others see eight sections, and some see only two. Metzger suggests "seven parallel sections divided at 3:22; 8:2; 11:19; 14:20; 16:21; and 19:21," and gives us the insightful admonition that, "There is, however, no reason to assume that the order in which John received his visions must be the order in which the contents of the visions are to be fulfilled.... he repeats his messages more than once from differing points of view" (ibid pp 18-19). The first section begins with John's vision of, and instructions from, the risen Christ, seen in a symbolic form, and then continues with the letters to seven of the called-out communities in 1st century Asia Minor. D'Aragon informs us,
> "Symbolic numbers acquire a considerable importance: *Seven* (54 times) signifies fullness, perfection; *twelve* (23 times) recalls the 12 tribes of Israel and indicates that the people of God has reached its eschatological perfection; *four* (16 times) symbolizes the universality of the visible world; also worth mentioning: *three* (11 times), *ten* (10 times) and *a thousand* (6 times in ch. 20; often in multiples)" (ibid).

Metzger adds,
> "John is fond of sevens; he mentions seven golden lampstands, seven stars, seven flaming torches, seven spirits of God, seven eyes, seven seals, seven angels, seven trumpets, seven thunders, seven heads on the dragon, seven plagues, seven bowls, seven mountains and seven kings... as well as the seven-fold praise presented to the Lamb (5:12)" (ibid p 18 n 5).

Borg adds to these, "seven beatitudes, seven hymns of praise, seven categories of people, seven references to the altar..." (ibid p 270).

Beale concludes that, "the focus of the book is exhortation to the church community..." (ibid p 33).

The author of this Unveiling identifies himself as John.
> "A tradition that goes right back to the 2nd century A.D. identifies him with the author of the gospel and letters of John.... The most which the evidence allows us to say is that the work was written.... by a Jewish Christian who was familiar with some of the ideas contained in John's gospel, who was held in respect by certain churches in Asia Minor..." (Harvey, ibid p 788-9).

In the Foreword to, *The Consummation of the Ages, A.D. 70 and the Second Coming in the Book of Revelation* (Kurt M. Simmons, Bimillennial Preterist Association, 2003, p xvi), Todd Dennis quotes Origen,
> "I challenge anyone to prove my statement untrue if I say that the entire Jewish nation was destroyed less than one whole generation later... For it was, I believe, forty-two years from the time when they crucified Jesus to the destruction of Jerusalem" (A.D. 250: Origenes, *Contra Celsum*, 198-199).

Beale identifies two forms of the preterist perspective: (1) "Revelation as a prophecy of the fall of Jerusalem in 70 A.D.;" (2) "a prophecy of the fall of the Roman Empire, 'Babylon the Great,'... in the fifth century A.D." (ibid p 44, 45). But there are more forms of this perspective, among them being "partial preterism" (i.e., some, but not all of the prophecies have been fulfilled) and "full preterism" (i.e., all has been fulfilled, including the resurrection) – along with other variations of these two categories.

"The OT and Judaism are the primary background against which to understand the images and ideas of the Apocalypse.... [it] contains more OT references than any other NT book" (Beal, ibid pp 56, 77; brackets added). Terry maintains,
> "... the prophecies of this book are an apocalypse of the fall of Jerusalem and the rise and triumph of Christianity.... [it] is but an enlargement of our Lord's eschatological sermon on the Mount of Olives.... The corrupt and outcast Jerusalem, guilty of 'all the righteous blood shed on the earth [or: land]' (Mat. 23:35), is called Sodom, and Egypt and Babylon; but the heavenly kingdom which shall never be destroyed is appropriately called 'the holy city, new Jerusalem'" (ibid p 269-70; brackets added).

Gilmour states, "Apocalyptic literature reflects the historical situation at the time of writing.... written for their own day and generation" (ibid p 945, 949).

Lynn Hiles brings us another perspective to investigating this book:
> "[T]his book is Covenantal because the Book of Revelation is about the church moving from the

Old Covenant to the New Covenant in its understanding. And it is Christological because it is a study of the Head and His Body being unveiled.... As you look into the Word of God, not only do you see the Head, but also the members of His body" (*The Revelation of Jesus Christ, An Open Letter to the Church from a Modern Perspective of the Book of Revelation*, Destiny Image Publishers, 2007, p 16).

Another overview that Hiles has on offer is seeing the patterns in play between Israel's annual religious calendar, and the visions here in Revelation:

> "We first saw the lamb slain, shadowed for us in the Feast of Passover. Now we see in Rev. six and seven a picture of the Feast of Pentecost where angels seal God's servants on their foreheads.... It is no coincidence that in chapter eight we see seven angels with seven trumpets, preparing to sound. By looking at Israel's feasts in the OT, we find the Feast of Pentecost followed by the Feast of Trumpets.... After each angel sounds in Rev. eight, there is an outpouring of seven vials (literally, bowls of blood) symbolizing the great Day of Atonement. This day follows the Feast of Trumpets in the Hebrew calendar. In Revelation's closing, the Feast of Ingratherings is pictured. Using the sickle, the angel reaps the first fruits of the people, 'for the harvest is ripe' (Rev. 14:15). I think you will agree that this is a great conclusion.... We can see that Revelation is a book painting the complete picture from all the glimpses given to us throughout the OT" (ibid pp 34, 36).

Hiles' perceptions regarding the structure and plan of the book find currency in the three-fold division of "seals, trumpets and bowls (vials)" as being allusions to the annual cultic calendar of OT Israel. We will find the repeated recapitulations as picturing different aspects of God's eschatological deliverance in Christ. These will be seen to frequently echo Israel's Exodus and the ensuing establishment of its cultus that the NT writers present as disclosures pointing to the work of the Messiah. Furthermore, we can keep in mind the many and varied comparisons that Jesus used to describe God's (or: heaven's) sovereign activities and influences within His reign (or: kingdom dominion). Like the figures and prophecies in the OT, here in the Unveiling their counterparts spoke of literal, existing and soon-coming, realities of the 1st century AD, yet also pointed above to the spiritual realities of the inaugurated new age of the Messiah.

As we read through the book, we will be able to observe inter-relating threads that combine to form a unified tapestry. When reading the letters to the called-out communities, we will note some correlations in the descriptions of the visions that follow. As we consider the visions we will observe themes from the OT tabernacle and temple, such as lampstands (1:12, 13, 20; 2:1, 5; 11:4), the throne (figured by the ark of the covenant), the sea of glass (figured by the brass laver) and the four living beings (figures associated with the cherubim embroidered into the curtains and on the mercy seat) in chapters 4 and 5. We find the altar of sacrifice in 6:9, and the throne (ark) again in 7:9-17. The incense altar comes on the scene in 8:3-4, and an altar (probably the one in the outer court) is seen again in 11:1. The temple itself is specifically cited in 2:12, 7:15, 11:1-2, 19, 14:17 and in chapters 15-16. The temple is the center from which the 7 plagues are sent out (15:6) and one of the living beings comes on the scene again in 15:7. The settings change with chapter 17, and the rest of the visions move from the temple out into the two cities which are the main topics for the remainder of the book. As we read, and encounter all these visions, it may be helpful to keep in mind the short, apocalyptic picture presented to us in Heb. 12:

> 22. **But to the contrary, you folks have approached so that you are now at Mount Zion – even in a city of a continuously living God; in "Jerusalem upon heaven"**
> > (or: in a Jerusalem pertaining to and having the character and qualities of a superior, or added, heaven and atmosphere; or: in Jerusalem [situated] upon, and comparable to, the atmosphere) – **also among ten-thousands** (or: myriads) **of agents and messengers**
> (people with a/the message)**:**
> 23. **[that is] in** (or: to) **an assembly of an entire people** (or: an assembly of all; a universal convocation) **and in** (or: to) **a summoning forth** (or: a called-out and gathered community) **of firstborn folks having been copied** (from-written, as from a pattern; or: enrolled; registered) **within [the; or: various] atmospheres** (or: heavens), **and in** (or: to; with) **God, a Judge** (an

Evaluator and Decider) **of all mankind, even among** (or: to; with) **spirits of just folks** (or: breath-effects from those who are fair and equitable and in right relationship within the Way pointed out) **having been brought to the destined goal** (perfected; finished; matured; made complete),

24. **and in** (or: to) **Jesus, a Medium** (or: an agency; an intervening substance; a middle state; one in a middle position; a go-between; an Umpire; a Mediator) **of a new and fresh** (young; recently-born) **arrangement** (covenant; settlement; a deposit which moves throughout in every direction; a placing through the midst; a will and testament), **and to and in blood of sprinkling, and to One continuously speaking something superior to** (or: stronger and better than) **Abel**.

Furthermore, we should keep in mind that the temple-associated symbols in the visions will correspond to the new creation situation, i.e., the "temple" and its furniture would spiritually represent the corporate body of Christ that has been,

"**jointly roused and raised** (or: suddenly awakens and raises) **[us] up, and caused [us] to sit** (or: seats [us]; = enthroned [us]) **together within the things situated upon** [thus, above] **the heavens within and in union with Christ Jesus**" (Eph. 2:6).

One of the traditions that will be challenged in this work is the assumption that there is a reference to, or a depiction of, a "final" judgment in the letters to the communities, or in any of the visions in Revelation. A corollary of this view is that this Unveiling speaks about "the end of human history." This view will be disregarded, from being unsupported by the text. I suggest that we will find that the visions involve aspects that attended the change from the previous age of the Law into the age of the Messiah and the inauguration of the reign of the resurrected Jesus Christ as King of kings and Lord of lords. A central focus of the entire book is the new creation, which encompasses all the metaphors in the book. Paul informed us,

"**Consequently, since someone [is] within Christ** (or: So that if anyone [is] in union with [the] Anointed One; or: And as since a Certain One [was] in Christ), **[there is] a new creation** (or: [it is] a framing and founding of a different kind; [he or she is] an act of creation having a fresh character and a new quality)**: the original things** (the beginning [situations]; the archaic and primitive [arrangements]) **passed by** (or: went to the side). **Consider! New things have come into existence** (have been birthed; or: It has become new things; or: He has been birthed and now exists being ones of a different kind, character and quality)" (2 Cor. 5:17).

In this overarching phrase, "new creation," which Paul affirmed here as having already come into existence, "is the 'center' of NT theology, comprehending within itself all other *major* themes and doctrines (e.g., covenant, temple, Israel, Jerusalem, justification, reconciliation and sanctification), though the ultimate goal even of new creation is seen to be God's glory" (Beale, ibid p 173 n 7; emphasis original).

In describing John's methods of expression as being the "literary form of symbolic parable," Beale instructs us that,

"Parables function in the same manner in Ezekiel and in Jesus' ministry. Therefore, the appearance of parables in redemptive history signals judgment on the majority of the covenant community" (ibid p 176). He insightfully points us to the "repeated use of the hearing formula, 'the one having ears, let him hear,'" and referencing Isa. 6:9-10; Ezk. 3:27; 12:2, along with Mat. 13:9-17, suggests that this, "is not novel but in line with the prior prophetic pattern.... intended both to open the eyes of the true remnant and to blind counterfeit members of the covenant community." He goes on to inform us that, "The hearing formula at the end of each letter anticipates the visionary parables in chs. 4-21," and that, "This means that the symbolic visions in chs. 4-21 are parabolic portrayals of the more abstractly expressed material in chs. 2-3. Therefore, the letters broadly interpret the symbolic visions, and vice versa.... John has patterned the series of trumpets and bowls after the Exodus plague signs, which functioned both to harden the Egyptians, and to give insight and redemption to Israel" (ibid p 177).

As Barclay points out,
> "Paul received his gospel... by an *apokalupsis* from Jesus Christ (Gal. 1:12). In the Christian assembly the message of the preacher is an *apokalupsis* (1 Cor. 14:6). It is used of God's revealing to me of his own mysteries, especially in the incarnation of Jesus Christ (Rom. 16:25; Eph. 3:3)" (ibid p 22).

Nik Ansell concludes,
> "God's judgment on Israel, carried out by the Romans, is acted out by Jesus in his 'cleansing' of the Temple and his cursing of the fig-tree (see Mk. 11:12-25 and 13:28-31). In the coming destruction, he said, the Son of Man would be vindicated (see Mk. 13:40). This judgment / vindication, which is described in terms of de-creation and enthronement, is also a main theme of the Book of Revelation" ("Hell: 'The Nemesis of Hope?' in "Afterword," *Her Gates Will Never Be Shut, Hope, Hell, and the New Jerusalem*, Bradley Jersak, Wipf & Stock, 2009 p 202-3).

Dan Kaplan alerts us to the use of "creatures" and "animals" here, and throughout all metaphorical passages in Scriptures: they all represent people or domination systems created by people. This is a key to unlocking the visions in *An Unveiling*.

As we have seen with the writings of Paul, this Unveiling that was given to John is deeply rooted in Israel's story. Keeping this in mind will facilitate our comprehension. In his Introduction to Martin Heidegger's, *What is Called Thinking?* (Harper & Row, Pub., 1968) J. Glenn Gray observes, "There is always a struggle to advance a new way of seeing things because customary ways and preconceptions about it stand in the way" (p x). In this same work, Heidegger makes these cogent remarks:
> "[The] multiplicity of possible interpretations does not discredit the strictness of the thought content. For all true thought remains open to more than one interpretation – and this by reason of its nature.... multiplicity of meanings is the element in which all thought must move in order to be strict thought.... Therefore, we always must seek out thinking, and its burden of thought, in the element of its multiple meanings, else everything will remain closed to us" (ibid p 71).

Much emphasis is given to the meanings of words, in this work, and many words are used to unpack the *Unveiling*. But let us not be, in the words of John O'Donohue, "impatient of words that carry with them histories and associations" (*Anam Cara, A Book of Celtic Wisdom*, Perennial, Harper Collins 2004 p 67). The *Unveiling* from Jesus Christ begins with Himself, and then seven called-out, covenant communities (seven being a symbol of the "complete" body of Christ in John's day), and ends with a picture of this same entity in its developed, world-wide form that represents the resurrected, reunited Israel: a City with twelve gates, but that is now founded upon the twelve original disciples of Jesus, and ministers Life to all humanity. The drama that will unfold in the following pages has its roots in the Tanakh, from the Torah, to the Prophets and the Writings, and it finds its fruition in the Words of Jesus, as well as in the writings of Paul, Peter, Jacob, Judah and John – and now by John in a sparkling array of apocalyptic symbols, figures and visionary metaphors. The time of its fulfillment was in John's day, but it contains levels of interpretation that have applied to humanity ever since that time. As to the nature of this *Unveiling*, although it is quite different from other NT letters that were written to the called-out communities, we should keep in mind that these 1st century cities received knowledge about Jesus as the Anointed One through means of a "disclosure" of the Good News. Their eyes were "unveiled" concerning the nature of the true, Creator God, and His Son, Jesus – known as "the Christ," or, "the Messiah (for the Jews)." Through the teachings of Jesus, Paul, John, Peter, and others, all covenant communities of that period were expecting some sort of "coming" of Christ, in their day. In the words of Jaroslav Pelikan (*Whose Bible Is It?*, Viking, 2005 p 226), each group was, "an apocalyptic community." So it would not have been strange for those in Asia Minor to receive this *Unveiling* from John.

The information divulged in the *Unveiling* came through the divine **Logos** laying its message out for the called-out, covenant communities in Asia Minor. In 1:2, below, we are informed of John "**who witnessed** (or: gives testimony and evidence of) **the Word of God** (or: God's **Logos**)." Then in 1:9, John tells us that he, "**was within the island called Patmos because of God's Word** (or: the **Logos**, which is God)."

We find a similar statement in 20:4, below, and in 19:13 John sees a vision of the Christ-figure, and, "**His Name is being called "The Word of God** (God's **Logos**)." The use of this term, *Logos*, may be an allusion to the Prologue of John's Gospel, "In [the **Logos**] was Life, and that Life was the light of human beings" (Jn. 1:4). In Jn. 1:11, we see that, "**It** (or: He) **came into Its** (or: His) **own things** (possessions, or people), **and Its own** (or: His own) **people did not receive It** (or: Him) **and take It** (or: Him) **to their side**." Upon citing this verse, Niels Henrik Gregersen observes, "What is said here [in Jn. 1:11] eventually is that the Logos is 'at home in the universe'" [brackets added]. Then referencing Jn. 19:30, where Jesus said, "It is accomplished," Gregersen concludes that,

> "The process of incarnation was not fulfilled until the end of the life of Jesus on the cross.... The death of Jesus, then fulfills the self-divesting nature of the divine Logos for all sentient and suffering beings, human or animal. And the Logos would be Light not only for every human being entering the world, but also the 'Light of the world' and the 'Light of life' (Jn. 8:12).... Seen from this historical context and applied to today's context of an informational universe, the divine Logos could be seen as the informational resource active in the world of creation.... The 'flesh' of the material world is by John seen as saturated by the presence of the divine Logos, who has united itself with the world of creation..." (*Information and the Nature of Reality; From Physics to Metaphysics*, edited by Paul Davies and Niels Henrik Gregersen, Cambridge University Press, 2010 p 343-46).

I share this quote to encourage the reader to look for the divine *Logos* (Christ) throughout the entire *Unveiling*, just as Jesus, "**beginning from Moses, and then from all the prophets, continued to fully interpret and explain to** (or: for) **them the things pertaining to** (or: the references about) **Himself within all the Scriptures**" (Lu. 24:27). The divine Logos now inhabits His temple (us) and continues being the informational resource that lives within us, which can unlock for us the symbols and figures of the *Unveiling*. Don K. Preston writes, "Revelation is a book of Hebraic Apocalyptic language. The Western reader wants to think prosaically, while the Hebraic world was one of metaphor, poetic imagery and hyperbole" ("Objection Overruled!, *Fulfilled! Magazine*, Vol. 12, Issue 1 p 18).

The fresh, expanded translation of the Greek text, below, will not only provide the reader with more information from the grammar of the Greek, in the *Unveiling*, but, as Pelikan said, in reference to the New English Bible of 1970, may it be found, "in the freshness of a new translation, and stop speaking in clichés and begin to address the reader directly" (my paraphrase; ibid p 229). To ease the reading of the many quotes from my translation of other NT books that have been inserted into my comments, I have shortened, or eliminated some of the parenthetical expansions that appear in that volume. May this work inform our reading of the text as we investigate this *Unveiling*. "Only the book of Revelation provides a fitting conclusion to the story begun in Genesis. With its bookends of Genesis and Revelation the Bible takes us from creation to new creation" (Brian Zahnd, *Sinners in the Hands of a Loving God*, Waterbrook, 2017 p 185).

Jonathan Mitchell

Other Bible translations used in this work:
A New English Translation of the Septuagint; *Concordant Version of the Old Testament*; *Concordant Literal New Testament*; *English Standard Version*; *New American Standard*; *New International Version*; *New Revised Standard Version*; *Tanakh*; *The Emphasized Bible* (J.B. Rotherham); *The Emphatic Diaglott*; *The Holy Bible in Modern English* (Ferrar Fenton); *The New English Bible*; *The New Testament, An Expanded Translation* (K. Wuest); *The Septuagint Bible*; *Young's Literal Translation*

BIBLIOGRAPHY and SOURCES

Nik Ansell, "Hell: 'The Nemesis of Hope?' in "Afterword," *Her Gates Will Never Be Shut, Hope, Hell, and the New Jerusalem*, Bradley Jersak, Wipf & Stock, 2009
Gary Amirault, "The History of the Doctrine of Eternal Torment," www.tentmaker.org
Mark Austin, in a personal conversation
William Barclay, *The Revelation of John*, Vol. 1 and 2, The Daily Study Bible Series, Westminster Press, 1976
R.J. Bauckham, *Climax of Prophecy: Studies in the Book of Revelation*, 1993 (cited in Beale)
G.K. Beale, *The New International Greek Testament Commentary, The Book of Revelation*, William B. Eerdmans Publishing Company, 1999
G.R. Beasley-Murray, *The New Bible Commentary, Revised*, W.B. Eerdmans Pub., 1970
Marcus J Borg, *Reading the Bible Again for the First Time*, HarperSanFrancisco, 2001
John L. Bray, booklets: "The Millennium;" "The Rapture of Christians"
Walter Brueggemann, *The Land, Place as Gift, Promise and Challenge in Biblical Faith*, Fortress Press, 1977
E.W. Bullinger, *The Companion Bible*
Rudolf Bultmann, *Theology of the New Testament*, Charles Scribner & Sons, 1951
James H. Charlesworth, Editor, *The Old Testament Pseudepigrapha*, Vol. 1 & 2, Hendrickson Pub, 2013
David Chilton, *The Days of Vengeance, An Exposition of the Book of Revelation*, Dominion Press, 1987
Judson Cornwall, *Elements of Worship*, Bridge Publishing, 1985
John Dominic Crossan, *The Historical Jesus, The Life of a Mediterranean Jewish Peasant*, HarperSanFrancisco, 1991; *Who Killed Jesus?*, 1996
Paul Davies and Niels Henrik Gregersen, editors, *Information and the Nature of Reality; From Physics to Metaphysics*, 2010
Jean-Louis D'Aragon, *The Jerome Biblical Commentary*, Vol. II, Prentice Hall, Inc., 1968
Alain Decaux, *Paul, Least of the Apostles, The Story of the Most Unlikely Witness to Christ*, Pauline Books and Media, 2006
T. Everett Denton, *Pertinent Parousia Passages, Second-Coming Scripture Studies*, 2016
Kenneth Earl, teachings and writings
J. Preston Eby, *The Gospel in the Stars*; and, *From The Candlestick to the Throne, Studies in Revelation*
Alfred Edersheim, *The Life and Time of Jesus the Messiah*, Wm. B. Eerdmans Pub. Co., Vol. 1, 1953
Arthur Eedle, "The Wellspring, #23"
J. M. Ford (*Revelation: Introduction, Translation and Commentary*, Doubleday, 1975 (cited in Chilton)
Francis Frangipane, article in "The Morningstar Journal"
Cameron Fultz, personal email
John Gavazzoni, personal communication
John Gill, *Exposition of the Bible*, from BibleStudyTools.com
S. MacLean Gilmour, *The Interpreter's One-Volume Commentary on the Bible*, Abingdon Press, 1971
Peter Goodgame, "Only An Entrance," a Facebook post
J. Glen Gray (in Heidegger)
Heinrich Greeven, *TDNT*, Vol. 6
Henry H. Halley, *Bible Handbook*
Everett F. Harrison, *The Wycliffe Bible Commentary*, Moody Press, 1962, 1990
A.E. Harvey, *The New English Bible Companion to the New Testament*, Oxford University Press, 1970
George Hawtin, booklet: "Mystery Babylon"
Martin Hengel, *Crucifixion*, 1997 (cited in Crossan, *Who Killed Jesus?*)
E.W. Hengstenberg, *The Revelation of St. John*, vol. 2, Mack Pub. Co (cited in Chilton)
Matthew Henry, *Commentary on the Whole Bible*
Martin Heidegger, *What is Called Thinking?*, Harper & Row, Pub., 1968
Peter Hiett, *Eternity Now!, Encountering the Jesus of Revelation*, Integrity Publishers, 2003
Lynn Hiles, *The Revelation of Jesus Christ, An Open Letter to the Church from a Modern Perspective of the Book of Revelation*, Destiny Image Publishers, 2007; "A Redemptive Look at the Book of Revelation," Vol. 1 pt 19, audio rec.
Mark Hillmer, *NIV Study Bible*, Zondervan, 1995
Larry Hodges, "The Shofar Letters"
Dean Hough, "Unsearchable Riches," Vol. 88, #6
Hannah Hurnard, *Steps to the Kingdom*, Harper & Row, 1985 [originally, *The Secrets of the Kingdom of Heaven*, 1959]
Jamieson, Fausset and Brown, *Commentary on the Whole Bible*, Zondervan Publishing House, 1961
Bradley Jersak, *Her Gates Will Never Be Shut; Hope, Hell, and the New Jerusalem*, Wipf & Stock, 2009
Josephus, *Josephus, Complete Works*, Kregel Pub., 1960, William Whiston translation
Walter Daniel Kaplan, personal communications

Max R. King, *The Cross and The Parousia of Christ, The Two Dimensions Of One Age-Changing Eschaton*, Writing and Research Ministry – The Parkman Road Church of Christ, 1987
A.E. Knoch, *Concordant Commentary on the New Testament*, Concordant Publishing Concern, 1968
Catherine Mowry LaCugna, *God For Us: The Trinity and Christian Life*, HarperSanFrancisco, 1991, quoted in Richard Rohr's "Daily Meditations"
Witness Lee, *The Recovery Version of the New Testament*
R.C.H. Lenski, *The Interpretation of St. John's Revelation*, Augsburg Pub. House, 1943, 1963 (cited in Chilton)
Adam Maarschalk, "Pursuing Truth," adammaarschalk.com
Burton Mack, "The Kingdom Sayings in Mark," *Forum*, 1987, cited in Crossan
Brian D. McLaren, *A New Kind of Christianity, Ten Questions That are Transforming the Faith*, Harper One, 2010
Bruce M. Metzger, *Breaking the Code, Understanding the Book of Revelation*, Abingdon Press, 1999; *A Textual Commentary on the Greek NT*, 2nd Ed, UBS, 1994
Robert Mounce, David O'Brien, NIV Study Bible, Zondervan Pub., 1995, "Introduction" to Revelation
Frederick J. Murphy, *Apocalypticism in the Bible and Its World*, Baker Academic, 2012
Ken Nichols, personal communications
John Noē, *The Creation of Evil, Casting Light into the Purposes of Darkness*, East 2 West Press, 2015
John O'Donohue, *Anam Cara, A Book of Celtic Wisdom*, Perennial, Harper Collins 2004
Randall E. Otto. *Coming in the Clouds, An Evangelical Case for the Invisibility of Christ at His Second Coming*, University Press of America, 1994
J. H. Paton, from an article published in "The World's Hope," 1907 (reprinted by Savior of All Fellowship)
Michael Phillips, *The Commands of Jesus*, Sunrise Books, Pub., 2014
Don K. Preston, *Fulfilled! Magazine*, Vol. 12, Issue 1, 2017
Ray Prinzing, *Revelation, A Positive Book*
K.H. Rengstorf, *Theological Dictionary of the New Testament*, Vol. 2
Gregory J. Riley, *One Jesus, Many Christs*, HarperSanFrancisco, 1997; *The River of God, A New History of Christian Origins*, HarperSanFrancisco, 2001
John A.T. Robinson, *Redating the New Testament*, The Westmister Press, 1976
Richard Rohr, *Daily Meditations*
Jean-Pierre Ruiz, *The New Oxford Annotated Bible*, 2001
James Stuart Russell, *The Parousia*, Kingdom Publications, 1996
Kurt M. Simmons, *The Consummation of the Ages, A.D. 70 and the Second Coming in the Book of Revelation*, Bimillennial Preterist Association, 2003
Malcolm Smith, recorded teachings on Revelation
David H. Stern, *Jewish New Testament Commentary*, Jewish NT Pub, Inc., 1999
Edward E. Stevens, booklet: "What Happened in AD 70?"
Milton S. Terry, *Biblical Apocalyptics, A Study of the Most Notable Revelations of God and of Christ in the Canonical Scriptures*, Wipf and Stock Publishers, 2001, originally in 1898
J.P.M. Sweet, *Revelation*, 1979 (quoted in Chilton)
Paul Tillich, *Systematic Theology*, Vol. 3
J.M. Vogelgesang, *Interpretation of Ezekiel in Revelation*, cited in Beale
Marvin Vincent, *Vincent's Word Studies in the New Testament*, Vol. 2, Hendrickson Pub, 1985 (1887)
Foy E. Wallace, Jr., *The Book of Revelation*, Richard E. Black Pub., 1997
Lance Wallnau, from his website and webinar
Benjamin Wilson, *The Emphatic Diaglott*
Walter Wink, *When The Powers Fall, Reconciliation in the Healing of Nations*, Fortress Press, 1998
Michael Wise, Martin Abegg, Jr. & Edward Cook, *The Dead Sea Scrolls, A New Translation*, HarperSanFrancisco, 1996
Ben Witherington III, *Conflict and Community in Corinth, A Socio-Rhetorical Commentary on 1 and 2 Corinthians*, Wm. B. Eerdmans Pub. Co., 1995
John Wood, prof. of philosophy, Northern Arizona University; course in *Ethics*
Ronald Youngblood, *NIV Study Bible*, Zondervan Publishing House, 1995
Brian Zahnd, *Beauty Will Save the World*; Charisma House, 2012; brianzahnd.com; *Sinners in the Hands of a Loving God*, WaterBrook, 2017
Spiros Zodhiates, *The Hebrew-Greek Key Study Bible*, AMG Pub., 2008

ABBREVIATIONS and TEXTUAL APPARATUS

ABBREVIATIONS:
CVOT: *Concordant Version of the Old Testament*
CLNT: *Concordant Literal New Testament*
DSS: Dead Sea Scrolls
JM: translations of the LXX by the author
LXX: The Septuagint – Greek version of the Old Testament
MS: manuscript; MSS: manuscripts
MT: Masoretic Text (Hebrew text of the Tanakh)
NETS: *A New English Translation of the Septuagint*, A. Pietersma, B. Wright, Oxford Univ. Press, 2007
n: note
OT, NT: Old Testament, New Testament
Gen., Ex., Mat., Rom., etc.: commonly accepted indicators of the books of the Bible
Aleph, A, B, C, D, Ψ, etc.: indicate an individual codex or MS
p: signifies that the MS is a papyrus MS
TR: *Textus Receptus* (the "Received Text;" the "Majority Text")
cf: confer or compare
TDNT: *Theological Dictionary of the New Testament*, Ed. Gerhard Kittle, W.B. Eerdmans, 1977

APPARATUS:
Brackets, [ ]'s, have been used for the following situations:
    to give a reading based upon other MSS
    to insert notes or comments into the text
    to insert words to aid in the reading of the English version
    to indicate the reference of a quote from the Old Testament
    to insert explanations
Parentheses, ( )'s, have been used for the following situations:
    to give other possible meanings of a Greek word
    to give alternate renderings of phrases or verses
    to give a potential idiomatic translation
    "=" has been placed before words for the following situations:
    to signify that the following is a potential idiomatic translation, or paraphrase; to give another spelling of a name or a suggested equivalent name; to give a Hebrew equivalent of a word or name; to give an explanatory note

OTHER PUBLISHED WORKS BY THE AUTHOR

THE NEW TESTAMENT, Expanded, Amplified and with Multiple Renderings
PETER, PAUL & JACOB, Comments on First Peter, Philippians, Colossians, First Thessalonians, Second Thessalonians, First Timothy, Second Timothy, Titus, Jacob (James)
JOHN, JUDAH, PAUL & ?, Comments on First John, Second John, Third John, Judah (Jude), Hebrews, Galatians
JUST PAUL, Comments on Romans
PETER'S ENCORE & LATER PAUL, Comments on Second Peter & Ephesians

Available from Harper Brown Publishing, www.jonathanmitchellnewtestament.com

AN UNVEILING OF AND FROM JESUS CHRIST
(REVELATION)

The Prologue (1:1-20)

Chapter 1

1. **An unveiling of, and which is, Jesus Christ** (or: A disclosure from Jesus [the] Anointed; A revelation which pertains to Jesus [the Messiah]) **which God gave by Him** (in Him; for Him; to Him) **to point out to His slaves that which continues necessary to come to be** (or: be birthed; happen) **in swiftness** (= speedily; or: shortly) [note: this phrase means either the manner in which events will happen, or that it is quickly going to happen]. **And sending [Him] as an emissary** (or: representative), **through means of His agent** (or: messenger) **He indicated [it] by signs** (or: symbols) **to** (or: in; for) **His slave John,**

The first word of this letter describes the nature of its overall contents: an unveiling; a disclosure; a revelation. It speaks of something that had been veiled, undisclosed and not previously seen – but now would be. The genitive case of the Name, "Jesus," and the title, "Christ (= Messiah)," can be rendered according to the different functions of the case:
      a) **of Jesus Christ**: it is an unveiling of Him
      b) **which is Jesus Christ**: the unveiling itself (via words; in the form of visions) is Jesus Christ
      c) from Jesus [the] Anointed: Jesus is the immediate source of this disclosure to John
      d) which pertains to Jesus [the Messiah]: the revelation has reference to Him; He is the main topic and the main message – the Lamb rules: the old has passed; the new has come.
With this in mind, and being aware of what lies ahead in this *Unveiling*, consider Jesus' words in Lu. 17:
      29. "**but on the day in which Lot came** (or: at one went) **out from Sodom, it suddenly rained fire and sulphur from [the] sky and atmosphere** (or: fire – even deity and the divine nature – from heaven), **and at once destroyed them all.**
      30. "**Down from and in accord with the very same things will it proceed being – on the Day in which the Son of the Man** (= Adam's Son; = the eschatological messianic figure) **is being progressively UNVEILED** (or: continues being revealed and disclosed).

God is the author of this unveiling disclosure. He gave it **by** the resurrected Christ. The unveiling occurred "in Christ." The revelation was for Jesus, and it was a gift **to Him**. Barclay (ibid p 23) points us to the words of Jesus in Jn. 7:16, "**My teaching is not My own, but rather belongs to and comes from the One sending Me**." *Cf* Jn. 12:49. The purpose here was for Him **to point out to His slave** events and situations that were going **to come to be** – be birthed into existence, happen, or occur. It was binding and **necessary** for these things to happen – necessary to God's "plan of the ages" (Eph. 3:11). The events would happen swiftly, and as many interpret the Greek phrase, *en taxei*, they would occur shortly, or soon.

The next statement has **God** as the antecedent of the participle **sending**, with Jesus Christ being the One that God sent (indicated by **[Him]** in my translation). Next we see that Jesus **indicated [the unveiling/revelation/disclosure] by signs** (and symbols) **through means of His agent** (or: messenger). That is, Christ used His agent to disclose the information **to, in** or **for His slave, John**. Any of the functions (to, in or for) of the dative case of this final phrase seem to fit the context. The messages are given to John, but this could have happened in him. The entire complex of disclosures was for John so that they could be written down by him.

You will observe that I do not transliterate the Greek word *angelos* with the word "angel," for this is misleading. Rather, I translate the word, which means, "an agent; a messenger." This term is used in different ways in the book, sometimes as being part of a vision, sometimes as someone speaking with John. Here, in vs. 1, it could even be seen as referring to Jesus Christ, as God's agent to John in the prologue. We must look to the context of each occurrence of the word. In chapters 2 and 3, below, we find the word used enigmatically with reference to each called-out, covenant community. As noted in the introduction, we need to be alert to the use of signs and symbols in this apocalyptic letter, else we may be misled into literalistic interpretations which are contrary to this genre of literature.

Metzger concludes that, "The purpose of the revelation is to show 'what must soon take place'.... The word *soon* indicates that John intended his message for his own generation" (ibid p 21; emphasis original). Beale, referencing the LXX, instructs us that, "the whole of Rev. 1:1 is patterned after the broad structure of Dan. 2:28-30... where the verb *apokaluptō* ('reveal') appears five times... the phrase... (what must come to pass') appears three times... and... ('signify') appears twice" (ibid p 181). With this in mind, we can see that **in swiftness** here would refer to "the definite, imminent time of fulfillment, which likely has already begun in the present," since, "Daniel 2 must be understood as referring only to the temporal aspect of the prophecy's fulfillment and not to the rapid manner in which it is to be fulfilled" (ibid p 181-2).

> "But in contrast, there is a God in heaven [that is] continually unveiling (revealing; disclosing) secrets (or: mysteries), and He is making known to King Nabouchodonosor what must happen upon (or: at) the last parts (or: times) of the days" (Dan. 2:28, LXX, JM)

Here Beale rightly points us to Lu. 20:18 (Mat. 21:44) that, "quotes Jesus as equating the 'stone' of Dan. 2:34-35 with his own ministry" (ibid n 6). These spoke to specific historical events that involved world kingdoms, as well as the kingdom of God. While Dan. 2 spoke to the time period of the 1st century, which we will see alluded to in some of the visions, below, I suggest that a framework structured around the temple and Jerusalem (both being figures of the corporate body of Christ) will be a guiding principle for understanding what John has presented to us in the *Unveiling*.

2. **who witnessed** (or: gives testimony and evidence of) **the Word of God** (or: God's Logos; the ideas of and thoughts from God; the expressed message about God), **even the witness** (or: evidence) **pertaining to Jesus Christ** (or: the testimony from [Messiah] Jesus; the martyrdom of Jesus [the] Anointed) – **as many things as he saw** (or: as much as he perceived [of it]).

The semantic range of the verb and the ambiguity of the aorist tense combine to offer different readings of the first clause. Was John saying that he had **witnessed the Word**, i.e., God's Logos (Jn. 1:1ff) in the form of **Jesus Christ**, prior to His death and resurrection, as in 1 Jn. 1:1,

> "**The One whom we have listened to, and still hear; the One whom we have seen, and now yet perceive with our eyes** (or: in our eyes); **the One whom we gazed upon as a public spectacle** (as an exhibit in a theater) **and our hands handled** (felt about for and touched) – **groping around the Word of the Life**,"

or, is John the one who now "gives testimony and evidence" of the Word of God that is the content of this letter? Either reading makes sense. John's listeners may well have seen the parallel of these connected phrases, in vs. 2, with the "witness" that John had given to the many layers presented in Jn. 1:1-14, which made a direct presentation of the Logos being incarnated in, or as, Jesus Christ. Here, the Word is **the witness, testimony and evidence [that is] pertaining to Jesus Christ**, for this is the Good News that was proclaimed by His emissaries. But the noun *marturia* that begins this last phrase had also become a technical term, "martyr" – one that had been killed for the witness that she or he gave. Thus John may have been saying that he had witnessed the death of Jesus [the] Anointed One (i.e., the Messiah). If he was referring to the content of this letter, then he is saying that he "gave evidence (etc.) of the ideas and thoughts from God (or: God's **Logos**)" – as much as he perceived in the visions that follow. Or, again, he gives testimony to... the evidence pertaining to Jesus Christ, i.e., **as many things as he saw** during the earthly ministry of Jesus, or in the visions that he experienced and recorded, below. Reading Jesus Christ as an ablative, we have, "the testimony from [Messiah] Jesus."

Terry suggests that, "The aorist tense here used suggests that this title and superscription were written, in the manner of a preface, after the rest of the book was completed..." (ibid p 276). These opening verses inform the listeners of this book's origin, the genre in which it will be presented, what it concerns and the overall purpose of its disclosure to the nearby called-out, covenant communities.

3. **Happy and blessed is the person constantly reading [it] aloud** (or: retrieving knowledge from [it in the midst of an assembly]), **and those constantly hearing** (or: listening and paying attention to; = observing and obeying) **the words of the prophecy** (or: the messages contained in the light and understanding seen ahead of time) **and habitually keeping watch over** (guarding; observing) **the things having been written within it, for the situation is close at hand** (or: for you see, the season, fertile moment and appointed occasion is near – close enough to touch).

These first three verses comprise the introduction to this work, followed by John's greetings to the intended recipients which include a statement about the Lord and a quote from Him (vss. 4-8), an explanation of John's situation when he received this disclosure (vss. 9-10), and then the initial vision designating the source and authority of the content that will be shown to John, and then John's first instructions (vss. 12-20). We should note that John calls this book **the prophecy**: "it has the weight of the words of the prophets of the OT" (Metzger, ibid p 22). Beale observes that the references to **constantly hearing** and **habitually keeping watch over** embody "obedience," and comments that,
> "Therefore, προφητεια ('prophecy') in vs. 3 is primarily a reference not to predictive revelation but to divine disclosure demanding an ethical response, in line with OT 'prophecy,' which primarily addresses present situations and only secondarily foretells" (ibid p 184-5).

This verse contains the first of 7 "beatitudes" ("**Happy and blessed**") that are found in this book. The others are in 14:13; 16:15; 19:9; 20:6; 22:7, 14. This alerts us to the tone of the content: the person **reading [it] aloud** (meaning, to the congregation) and those listening will be happy and blessed. But note the expansion on **hearing**: "listening and paying attention; = observing and obeying." This book was more than mere information. The letters in chapters 2 and 3 will make this clear. Here we should also reflect upon the happy/blessed pronouncement given by Jesus in Mat. 5:3ff that led off with, "**The destitute folks [are] happy in spirit and attitude, because the reign of the heavens is continually belonging to, and made up of, them**." This should alert us to a correlation between "the sermon on the mount" and things that will be encountered in this book. The "messages contained in the light and understanding seen ahead of time" are **things** that they (the entire group) should be **habitually keeping watch over** (guarding; observing): these things will affect them. And the reason for this is because, **the situation is close at hand** (or: for you see, the season, fertile moment and appointed occasion is near – close enough to touch). The visions and proclamations concerned 1st century events. It was the season of the Messiah and the new age. The word "close at hand (etc.)" is a cognate of the verb that Jesus used pertaining to God's kingdom (*cf* Lu. 10:9; *et al*). He used a similar expression in Mk. 1:15,
> "**The season and appointed situation has been fulfilled** (The fertile moment has been filled up and now continues full and is now ripe) **and God's kingdom** (the reigning and ruling of God as King; God's activity of exercising sovereignty) **has approached and is now near at hand and is close enough to touch** (= has arrived and is now accessible)!"

It is the same word that He used in regard to the time of the destruction of Jerusalem in Mat. 24:32-3 and Lu. 21:30-1. We also find the same clause at 22:10, below. If we consider that in this same introduction

John has used in vs. 1 a phrase (**in swiftness**, etc.) that can be a temporal expression that indicates imminence, it would seem unwarranted – in light of these two verses that describe the setting of what will follow – to assume that the visions from chapter 4, on, speak to a distant future. In 1:9, below, he indicates that "**the pressure** (squeezing; affliction; tribulation; oppression)" is already occurring. *Cf* 2:9, 22; 3:10. The last phrase of vs. 3, here, may be an echo of Dan. 7:22,

> "… the Ancient of days came, and He presented the effect of the Decision by the set-apart folks belonging to the Highest One (or: He gave the judgment-results to the sacred people who correspond to the Most High), and the season (fitting situation and fertile moment) outstripped [the former situation] and arrived, being close at hand, and then the set-apart folks possessed the kingdom (fully held the reign; held fast the sovereign influence and royal action)" (LXX, JM).

This letter begins by addressing covenant communities and ends saying that the book is a witness to, and a testimony for, these same called-out groups (22:16, below).

4. **John, to the seven called-out communities** (covenant congregations; summoned forth assemblies) **within Asia: grace and peace to you** (or: favor and [the] harmony [= shalom] of the joining [are] for and among you) **folks from** [TR adds: God,] **the One continuously existing** (or: unceasingly being; Who continuously IS), **even the One Who was, and continued being, and the One Who is continuously** (or: repeatedly; habitually; progressively) **coming or going – even** (or: and; also) **from the Seven Spirits** (or: Breath-effects; Attitudes) **which [are] in front of His throne –**

"The salutation thus indicates that the entire book, not merely the portion containing the seven letters (chapters 2 and 3), is intended for the churches of Asia" (Metzger, ibid p 22).

We observe that the **grace and peace** come from **the One**, but also **from the Seven Spirits**. The figure of this latter phrase is usually thought to be an echo of Isa. 11:2, which in the LXX reads,

> "the spirit of wisdom and understanding, the spirit of counsel and might, the spirit of knowledge and godliness, the spirit of the fear (reverence) of God…"

The parenthetical rendering of the second clause (supplying "[are]" for the ellipsis) renders two other functions of the dative form of the pronoun **you**. It has been the habit of translators to assume that the form of the salutation of a letter conforms to our modern way of writing and thinking, i.e., "**to you**." While this makes sense of the Greek and the context, the frequent occurrence of omitting the copulative verb (a form of the verb "to be," e.g.: is; are) should also be considered in these ancient documents. The greeting does not necessarily need to be seen as a wish (as in our day), but this "blessing" can be seen as an affirmation of the existent reality in Christ. Thus, "favor and [the] harmony [= shalom] of the joining [are] for and among you folks," as rendered in the parenthetical expansion.

The stylized three-part form used to describe God in the last clause has been expanded to show the meanings of the verb forms. The first is a present indicative, the second is an imperfect indicative, and the third is a present participle. Each of these indicates continuous action (especially in the first two). The last, since it is not a verb of "being," can be rendered with an auxiliary which indicates that the action is **continuous**, repeated, habitual or progressive. Since this last verb means either "to come" or "to go," I have conflated these two meanings in the present participle: **coming or going**. The picture in the "formula" is that of God – via His Spirit or His Christ – making constant, or repeated, or habitual, or even progressive special involvements with His creation and with His people. Note the bracketed addition of the word "God" in the later scribal tradition represented by TR (Majority, or Byzantine, Text). A survey of the OT will find Yahweh periodically coming (which implies periodic goings). It is a symbolic picture of involved interaction. This does not, therefore, speak of some final (or, "end of time") coming, nor of the erroneous, unscriptural term, "second coming." This speaks of a God who is present. We read in Ps. 68: 4 about singing to, "Him that rideth through the waste plains... Yah is His Name." Isa. 19:1 proclaimed, "Lo! Yahweh riding upon a swift cloud, and he will enter Egypt, and the idols of Egypt shall shake at His presence..." We have the imagery of Ps. 104:3, "Who maketh clouds His chariot, and Who passeth along on the wings of the wind" (readings from Rotherham's *Emphasized Bible*). This phrase is often seen as an allusion to Ex. 3:14, where in the LXX the phrase, "**the One continuously existing**," is used twice in giving an explanation of God's Name to Moses. The Greeks spoke of "Zeus who was, Zeus who is and Zeus who will be" (Barclay, ibid p 30). Remember Heb. 13:8, "**Jesus Christ [is] the same yesterday and today and on into the ages**."

The final compound phrase is rendered as another descriptive clause of God, in an apocalyptic form crafted to the repeated "7-theme" found throughout this book: **the Seven Spirits** (Breath-effects; Attitudes) **which [are] in front of His throne**. This speaks of the full and complete aspects and qualities of God which one would encounter when approaching God's throne (ark; mercy seat, in the Tabernacle). They also speak of the effective attributes of His sovereign activities and presence. This symbol corresponds to the 7-branched lampstand of the holy place in the OT Tabernacle (the oil and the fire that provided light were both figures of His Spirit). This is our first allusion to Zech.4:3ff, where we read of a lampstand with 7 lamps. The holy place, where the lampstand was situated, was **in front of** the innermost chamber of the tabernacle which contained the ark, which was God's **throne** in the midst of Israel. Note 7 lampstand in 1:12, 20, below, and in 4:5, "**seven shining ones** (or: lamps; lights; torches) **of fire**... **before the throne**." In 5:6, below, we have another picture of these Seven Spirits, and are there told something of their function:

> "**I saw a little Lamb standing, as one having been slaughtered, having seven horns and seven eyes – which are the Seven Spirits of God** (or: God's seven Breath-effects/Attitudes)**: the Ones having been and still being sent forth as envoys** (representatives) **into all the Land** (or: earth)." This same verse informs us that the Lamb (Christ) is, with Yahweh, "**within the midst of the throne**." These Seven Spirits are parts (horns and eyes) of the risen Christ, and as we shall see below, are a part of His temple (the 7 called-out, covenant communities) which is also His body. The Christ (here, the little Lamb) is Jesus plus the Anointing by God's Spirit (human + Spirit = Christ, the Anointed One); the body of Christ is also composed of humans Anointed by God's Spirit, and thus become the 7 lampstands (1:20, below).

In Heb. 2:4 we read of "divisions of [the] Holy Spirit," along with expanded renderings,
> "**God joining with added corroborating witness, both by signs and wonders and a full spectrum of** (or: various; multi-faceted) **powers and abilities, and by** (or: in) **divisions** (partings; distributions) **of set-apart Breath-effect** (or: of [the] Holy Spirit; from a sacred attitude), **corresponding to His willing [it] and exercising His purpose**."

The number 7 should be seen as an "idea" in this book. It points to the full-spectrum, or the complete influence, or the full development, or a complete representation, or a complete and finished act or work. The 7 horns on the slaughtered Lamb present a picture of the full power of the work of the cross. It is a little Lamb that has overcome death and now reigns. See the treatment on this number by K.H. Rengstorf (*TDNT* II, p 627-35). E.g.,
> "The Sadducees refer to 7 brothers who each married the same wife, six in fulfillment of the appropriate law (Mat. 22:23; Deut. 25:5ff). The implication is that they have in view an infinite series.... In Mat. 12:45; Lu. 11:26, it is said of the backslider that with the exorcised spirit seven worse spirits return into him.... the number 7 points to the fact that there could be no worse state of corruption" (ibid p 630).

5. **and from Jesus Christ, the faithful Witness** (or: reliable Evidence; loyal Martyr), **the First-born of** (or: pertaining to; from among; or: belonging to) **the dead folks: even the Ruler** (or: Prince; Leader, Beginner; Originator; One in first place) **of the kings of the earth – by** (or: in) **the One continuously loving us by loosing** [other MSS: washing] **us from** [other MSS: out of] **our failures and deviations** (or: sins; errors; situations and results of where we missed the target or fell short of the goal) **within His blood** (or: in union with the blood which is Him),

Here we see that **grace and peace** also come **from Jesus Christ**. Identifying markers are next given to describe His place in God's family, His resurrected status, His political and authoritative position in God's reign, all of which are qualified by His relationship to humanity as being **the One continuously loving us** (*cf* Jn. 3:16) and **loosing us from, and out of, our failures and deviations** (a description identifying Him as our Rescuer, Deliverer and Savior) **within His blood** (signifying His sacrifice, the giving of His life to us -- i.e., the work of the cross and His death).

The person **Jesus** is **the faithful Witness** and **reliable Evidence** that God loves humanity. In Jn. 3:11 Jesus tells Nicodemus,

> "**Certainly it is so, I am now saying to you, that which we have seen and thus know** (or: perceive), **we are constantly speaking** (or: telling; chattering [about]), **and what we have caught sight of and seen we repeatedly bear witness of** (constantly give testimony to)." And

in Jn. 18:37 He tells Pilate,

> "**I Myself have been born, and I have come into this System** (world and culture; social arrangement) **and continue being present: to the end that I could and should bear witness to Reality** (or: give testimony to and evidence of the Truth)."

The reference to **the dead folks** is a phrase that includes all humanity, for we read of the past state of people, before their resurrection into Christ, that,

> "**you folks [were] continuously existing being dead ones by** (or: to; with; in) **the results and effects of your stumblings aside** (offenses; wrong steps) **and failures to hit the mark** (or: mistakes; errors; times of falling short; sins; deviations)" (Eph. 2:1). So here, Christ is the first of

the resurrection, and we find in Rom. 6:4b that,

> "**just as** (or: in the same manner as) **Christ was roused and raised forth from out of the midst of dead folks THROUGH** (through means of) **THE GLORY** (the glorious manifestation of splendor which calls forth praise; the notion; the renown; the reputation; the imagination) **of The Father** (or: which is the Father), **thus also we can walk around** (or: we also should likewise conduct ourselves and order our behavior) **within newness of life** (in union with life characterized by being new in kind and quality, and different from that which was former)."

The designation of the titles, **Firstborn** and **Ruler** (or: Prince; Leader; Beginner; Originator) both refer to first positions: 1) in the new generation of a family, 2) the head of a clan or ruler of a nation. There may also be in both of these an allusion to Adam, God's firstborn human (Lu. 3:38), the Beginner of the human race. A correlation with these has been seen in Ps. 89:26-29,

> "He will continue calling upon Me [saying], 'You are My Father, My God, and a Supporter (Assistant; One who takes hold on the opposite side in order to help) which is (or: pertaining to) My deliverance (rescue; salvation; wholeness).' And so I, Myself, will proceed placing (setting; establishing) Him: a Firstborn, higher than the kings of the land (or: earth). And I will continue keeping, watching over and guarding My peace and joining in, for and with Him, on into the midst of the Age; and My arrangement/covenant reliably faithful, certain and secure in Him (or: with Him; to Him; for Him; by Him). So I will proceed placing (setting; establishing) His Seed on into the Age of the age (or: the unseen time period of the Age; or: the Age arising from this age), and

His throne as the days of the heaven (or: related to that uplifted sphere; or: from that atmosphere)" (LXX, JM).

Barclay informs us that, "the first-born was the son who inherited his father's honor and power... *one who occupies the first place...*" (ibid p 32; emphasis original). This is one who had the means to act as a kinsman-redeemer. In Col. 1:15b we are instructed that He is,
> "**the Firstborn of all creation** (or: of every creature; or: of every framing and founding; of every act of settling from a state of disorder and wildness; or: pertaining to the whole creation; or: = the Inheritor of all creation Who will also assume authority over and responsibility for every creature)."

We will see the phrase "**the kings of the earth**" again, below, in 6:15; (16:14 is similar); 17:2; 18:3, 9; 19:19 and finally in 21:24 where we find that, "**the kings of the Land** (or: earth) **continually carry** (bring; bear) **their glory** [Codex Vaticanus adds: and honor] **into her**." So here, in 1:5, the end is proclaimed from the beginning: the total victory of the little Lamb.

The second half of the verse, which I set off with a dash, begins with the definite article followed by two participles in the dative case (which shows their relation to the article). So I began with the instrumental function, and parenthetically inserted the location function: "**by** (or: in) **the One continuously loving us by loosing** [other MSS: washing] **us from** [other MSS: out of] **our failures and deviations** (or: sins; errors; situations and results of where we missed the target or fell short of the goal)." The **grace and peace** of vs. 4 come to us "by and in" **the One**, Jesus Christ, Who by and in **continuously loving us** (by His death) created the new reality of **loosing us from out of our failures and deviations**. The MS tradition that reads "washing us" arises from a reading that has the word *lousanti* instead of *lusanti* (which to a scribe hearing the text read aloud, both words would sound the same – and each makes sense to the text). My bold reading reads with the earlier MSS. The ideas in both verbs are allusions to the Day of Atonement in Israel's OT cultus. In Lev. 16:14-19 we find the high priest sprinkling the **blood** of the sacrifice 7 times upon the mercy seat. So in the term, **within His blood**, the minds of John's listeners would be carried to the death of Jesus, as well as to it being the fulfillment of the final major sacrifice which "cleansed" the entire people (and loosed them from the preceding year's sins, mistakes (etc.), and which had its setting in the tabernacle (a theme that we shall repeatedly encounter in the visions). It is also an allusion to the release from slavery, accessing Israel's Exodus story with the original Passover and the blood of the lamb on the doorposts (Ex. 12:13). We also have the metaphor in 1 Jn. 1:7b,
> "**the blood of Jesus, His Son, keeps continually and repeatedly cleansing us** (or: is progressively rendering us pure) **from every sin** (or: from all error, failure, deviation, mistake, and from every [successive] shot that is off target [when it occurs])."

We should note the present tense of the participle **loving**, and the aorist (point of time or "snapshot" tense) participle **loosing**, this latter one agreeing in tense with the aorist tense of the next verb (which begins the first clause of 1:6, below) that speaks to the new creation aspect of the Christ event (cross and resurrection). Here Barclay explains that this, "tells of one act completed in the past and it means that in the one act of the Cross our liberation from sin was achieved... one availing act in time which was an expression of the continuous love of God" (ibid p 34). The "loosing" was at the same time that which "**made**, formed, created and produced" the next phase of God's plan of the ages, as described in the following verse.

6. **and made us [to be] a kingdom** [with other MSS: constructed **of us** a kingdom of sovereign influence; formed **in us** a sovereign reign; created **for** us a kingship; produces **with us** {His} sovereign

activities and royal rule]: **priests in** (or: by; for; with) **His God and Father. In Him [is] the Glory** (or: For Him [is] the good reputation; By Him [is] the manifestation of that which calls forth praise; With Him [is] the appearance which affects the opinion of the whole of human experience) **and the Strength** (or: Might), **on into the ages** (or: indefinite time periods [some MSS add: of the ages])! **It is so** (Count on it; Amen).

Again, note the aorist tense of the verb "**made**, constructed, formed, created," which speaks to the past action of the resurrected Christ in forming the new creation (2 Cor. 5:17), but also note the "fact" sense of this tense, rendered as a simple English, "produces," for as folks are one-after-another born into this physical world, at some point He produces them as a part of His "**kingdom**, or, sovereign reign, influence, activities and royal rule." There are significant MSS which have the pronoun **us** in the dative, and thus on offer are these potential readings:
    a) formed **in us** a sovereign reign
    b) created **for us** a kingship
    c) produces **with us** [His] sovereign activities and royal rule; other MSS read:
    d) constructed **of us** a kingdom of sovereign influence.

John Dominic Crossan (*The Historical Jesus, The Life of a Mediterranean Jewish Peasant*, HarperSanFrancisco, 1991, p 287) in commenting on the phrase "kingdom of God" being understood (in the Gospels) as sapiential rather than apocalyptic, in the ears of the hearers in that day during the Greco-Roman period, notes that:
> "But what is actually at stake is not kingdom as place, be it here or there, but rule as state, be it active or passive. The problem in plain language, is power: who rules and how one should."

He quotes Burton Mack ("The Kingdom Sayings in Mark," *Forum*, 1987),
> "Discourse about *basileia* ('rule'; [kingdom]) during the Greco-Roman period was not limited to circles of Jewish apocalypticists, nor, for that matter, to those with specifically Jewish interests. *Basileia* was a common topic of far-reaching significance throughout Hellenistic culture…. the critical issues now centered on power and privilege, and on the rights and duties of those who had it…. 'King' became an abstract representation of *anthropos* ('human being') at the 'highest' level imaginable…" (Crossan, ibid; parentheses original; brackets added).

George Lamsa's rendering of the Peshita (Aramaic) MSS renders this phrase, "a spiritual kingdom" (*The Holy Bible from Ancient Eastern Manuscripts*, A.J. Holman Co, 1957) which captures the essence of what the Greek phrases are offering.

The allusion is generally taken to be from Ex. 19:6a, which reads, "Now you people, yourselves, will continue being (existing as) a royal, kingly priesthood and a set-apart ethnic group (sacred nation; holy cultural multitude)" (LXX, JM). Peter also picked up this description,
> "**you yourselves are, as living stones, continuously being erected** (or: progressively constructed and built up), **[being] a spiritual house** (a building with its source being the Spirit, with the characteristics of a Breath-effect), **into a set-apart** (or: holy; sacred; different-from-the-ordinary) **priesthood to bear up spiritual sacrifices** (or: offerings) **well** (or: most) **acceptable in God** (or: by God; to God; with God), **through Jesus Christ…. a picked-out** (selected; chosen) **offspring** (family; kin; lineage; race; species; breed) [Isa. 43:20; Deut. 7:6], **a royal** (kingly; palace) **priesthood** [Ex. 19:6; Isa. 61:6], **a set-apart** (holy; different) **multitude** (company; nation; body of people living together; swarm; association; ethnic group; caste; [Ex. 19:6; note: implies a sacred life]), **a people constructed into an encirclement** (made into a surrounding structure; set as a perimeter; made into a performance about [Him]; formed around as an acquisition; gathered into a surrounding [flock]) [Isa. 43:21; Ex. 19:5] **– so that you may tell forth the message of** (or: out-message; publish; declare abroad) **the excellencies and qualities of**

nobleness (virtues of braveness, courage, good character, quality, self-restraint, magnificence, benevolence, reliability) **of and from the One calling you out of darkness** (gloomy dimness; the realm of shadows and obscurity) **into the midst of His wonderful** (marvelous; amazing) **light** [*p72* reads: into the wonderful Light], **[you] who [were] once** (or: formerly) **'not a people,' but now [are] 'God's people;' [formerly] being the ones having 'not been given mercy,' yet now [are] 'folks being merced** (being given mercy)'" (1 Pet. 2:5, 9-10; *cf* Hos. 2:23).

Peter's quote of Hos. 2:23 informs us that the prophecy made by Jesus had come to pass,
"**Because of this, I am now saying to you men that God's reign** (or: the kingdom of God; the influence and activity of God's sovereignty) **will be progressively lifted up away from you folks, and it** (or: she) **will proceed being given to an ethnic multitude** (or: nation; people group) **consistently producing its** (or: her) **fruit!.... so, upon hearing His illustrations** (parables), **the chief and ranking priests – as well as the Pharisees – knew by this experience that He had been speaking about them**" (Mat. 21:43, 45).

And then in Lu. 12:32, Jesus told His disciples, "**Stop fearing** (or: Do not continue being wary), **little flock, because it delights the Father** (or: because the Father thought it good, and thus, approved) **to give the rule** (reign; kingship; kingdom; sovereign influence and activities) **to you folks**," which answers to what he said to the "sheep" in Mat. 25:34b,
"**At once come into possession of the inheritance of, and enjoy the allotment of,** [the period of, place of, or realm of] **the reign** (or: kingdom; influence and activity of sovereignty) **having been prepared and made ready from a founding** (a casting down [as of a foundation; or: of seed]) **of a system** (or: of [the] adorned arrangement; of an arranged order; of [the] world)."

Jacob (aka: James) passes this good news along:
"**Did not God at one point choose** (call and speak out; pick out; select) **for Himself the poor folks in the System** (or: Does not God Himself lay out and collect the beggars and those who slink and cower with wretchedness in the world of society, culture, religion and government) – **rich folks in faith, trust, loyalty and conviction, and also heirs** (those who possess by distribution of an allotment) **of the reign and kingdom which He promised to and assured for those continually loving Him?**" (Jas. 2:5).

We also can hear Paul in Rom. 11:17,
"**Now since some** (or: if certain ones) **of the branches are broken off** (or: were at one point broken out of [the tree]), **yet you yourself, being a wild olive tree of the field or forest, you are** (or: were) **grafted in within** (or: among) **them, you also came to be** (are birthed; are become) **a joint-participant** (a partner taking in common together with; a co-partaker) **of the Root and of the Fatness** (= sap) **of The Olive Tree** (or: of the oil of the olive)."

This is echoed in 5:9b-10, below,
"**You were slaughtered, and bought us by God** (for God; in God; with God), **within Your blood, from out of the midst of every tribe and tongue and people and ethnic multitude. And then You made** (or: make) **them kings and priests in, for and by our God -- and they continue reigning upon the Land** (or: earth)."

In Col. 1:13 Paul gives us another picture of what John has just said here:
"**He who drags us out of danger** (or: rescued us) **forth from out of the midst of the authority of the Darkness** (from Darkness's jurisdiction and right; from existing out of gloomy shadows and obscure dimness; = the privilege of ignorance), **and changes [our] position** (or: transported [us], thus, giving [us] a change of standing, and transferred [us]) **into the midst of the kingdom and reign of the Son of His love**

> (or: into the midst of the sovereign influence of the Son Who has the characteristics and qualities of His accepting love; into union with the sovereign activities of the Son Whose origin is His love; or: into the sphere of the reign of the Son of the Love which is Him; into

the center of the kingdom of the Son, which is His love)." This is our present situation. Then in 1 Thes. 2:12 Paul speaks of, "**the God** (= living your lives in a manner equal in value with regard to the God) **[Who is] continuously calling** (or: repeatedly inviting) **you people into His own kingdom** (or: reign; sovereign influence and activity) **and glory** (or: a manifestation which calls forth praise; or: reputation; or: opinion and imagination; or: = manifest presence)."

Paul instructs us in Rom. 14:17 that,
> "**you see, God's kingdom** (or: the reign-and-dominion which is God; the expression, influence and activity of God's sovereignty) **is not** (or: does not exist being) **solid food and drink, but rather, eschatological deliverance into fair and equitable dealing which brings justice and right relationship in the Way pointed out** (being turned in the right direction; rightwisedness; also = covenant inclusion and participation), **peace** (and: harmony; = shalom) **and joy** (or: happiness; rejoicing) **within set-apart Breath-effect** (or: in union with and amidst a dedicated spirit and a sacred attitude; or: in [the] Holy Spirit)."

When speaking of proper demeanor and the way of life within the called-out communities, Paul instructed, "**Old** (or: Aged; Older) **women, similarly** (or: likewise), **[are to be] women in a state and resultant condition proper and fitting for being engaged in the sacred** (suitable in demeanor for serving the temple; or: = living a life appropriate [for] a person [being] a temple)" (Tit. 2:3). And in 1 Cor. 3:16 he reminded them,
> "**Have you folks not seen, to now know, that you people continuously exist being God's Temple** (Divine habitation; holy place and holy of holies; inner sanctuary), **and God's Spirit is constantly dwelling** (God's Breath is making Its home; the Wind which is God is housing Himself; the Attitude from God is progressively co-habiting) **within the midst of you folks?**" Cf 1 Cor. 6:19; 2 Cor. 6:16; Eph. 2:21; 2 Thes. 2:4; Rev. 3:12.

In 7:15, below, we find one of the elders (older people) instructing John that the folks he had been viewing in the vision, "**are constantly before** (in the sight and presence of) **God's throne, and they habitually do public service to** (in; by; for) **Him, day and night, within the midst of His Temple**." Service in the temple (which was "before God's throne," i.e., in the "holy place," which was the first chamber of the temple) was done by the priests. So these folks are performing as priests, in this vision. Recall, also, that Jesus referred to His body in the new covenant – the resurrected body – in John 2:19, and John explains this there in vs. 21, "**Yet that One** (= He) **had been speaking about the Sanctuary** (or: inner Temple; Divine habitation) **which is His body**" – and we learn from Paul that upon resurrection Jesus became the Head and Source of a corporate body, the called-out group (Col. 1:18; Eph. 4:15; 5:23).

Where under the Law of the old covenant only the chief priest, once a year, could enter the holy of holies in the tabernacle/temple, now, under the new covenant,
> "**We should, then, be repeatedly and habitually coming to the throne of Grace** ([= mercy seat and place of Grace's authority]; or: the throne which is grace; the throne that is marked by grace and whose source is joyous favor) **with freedom in speaking and outspoken boldness as a citizen who has no fear of reprisal, so that we can at once receive and take mercy as well as grace and favor into a timely** (seasonable; well-suited) **response to a cry for help**" (Heb. 4:16).

We have another picture of this in Heb. 10:
> 19. **Therefore, having freedom, openness and boldness of speech which comes from being citizens, brothers** (= fellow members), **with a view to the Entrance of the set-apart places** (or: into the Pathway-into the midst, pertaining to the Holiest Place, which is the separated

ones and which pertains to the sacred folks) – **within and in union with the blood of Jesus;**
20. **a Way** (Path; Road) **which was done anew** (or: which He innovates and makes new in species, character or mode, within and in the midst) **for us and in us, recently slain and yet living, through the veil that is His flesh** (or: which way through the veil He did anew for us – that is, His flesh (= His body): recently slain, and now living) –
21. **along with a Great Priest [enthroned] upon God's House** (or: the house from God) –
22. **we can be continuously and progressively approaching with a true heart in union with full-assurance from the completed act of faithfulness** (or: centered within [the] full-carrying from [His] loyalty and fidelity), **the hearts having been sprinkled from a misery-gushed consciousness of what is evil or unserviceable** (or: a joint-knowledge full of labor; a conscience in a bad condition), **and then the body having been bathed in and by clean water.**

The "doxology" which comprises the second half of the verse begins with the personal pronoun "Him" (as a reference to God) in the dative case, and so we have on offer the following options: "**In Him [is] the Glory** (or: For Him [is] the good reputation; By Him [is] the manifestation of that which calls forth praise; With Him [is] the appearance which affects the opinion of the whole of human experience) **and the Strength** (or: Might), **on into the ages** (or: indefinite time periods [some MSS add: of the ages])!" Rather than saying what "we" might do (reading the dative as: To Him [be]...) are the far greater affirmations:
> In Him (i.e., in Christ; in God) [is] the glory
> By Him [is] the manifestation (the crucifixion and resurrection) which calls forth creation's praise
> With Him [is] the appearance (God's image reflected to the world) which affects the opinion of the whole of human experience.

7. **Consider** (or: Look; Behold)! **He is continuously** (or: presently; repeatedly; habitually; progressively) **coming with the clouds, and every eye will progressively discern and perceive** (or: continue recognizing; or: repeatedly see) **Him, even whichever of you folks pierced** (or: pierce) **Him. And all the tribes** (people-groups) **of the Land** (or: territory; earth) **shall beat themselves** (strike their breasts in grief, mourning or repentance) **upon** (= because of) **Him. Yes, it is true** (amen)! [Dan. 7:13; Zech. 12:10-14; *cf* Lu. 3:6]

The previous verse ends with "**It is so** (Count on it; Amen)." This would alert John's listeners to expect a change of topic, or for something different to be said, or a different line of communication. So the first clause of this verse reminds them of Yahweh's past activities over the period of Israel's history: **He is continuously** (or: presently; repeatedly; habitually; progressively) **coming with the clouds**. This is what He does; He is quite involved with His creation – but we should recognize the apocalyptic language of this entire verse. This clause is an allusion to Dan. 7:13-14, and so take note of the setting and means of Daniel seeing this coming, as he describes it in the first clause:
> "I was continuing in watching in the visions of the night (or: the night visions) -- and consider this -- One like a son of man (or: like a human being) repeatedly coming and going (or: progressively coming) with the clouds of the sky (atmosphere; heaven); and then at one point He arrived as far as the Ancient of Days (or: the Old One from the days), and so He was brought toward (or: carried to be face-to-face with) Him. Next the beginning (or: rule; headship) and the honor and the reign (kingship; kingdom; sovereign influence) were given to Him, and so all the peoples, tribes and tongues will continue performing as slaves for Him. His right and privilege from out of Being (or: His authority) [is] an eonian right (a privilege associated with the Age; an indefinite authority) which will not pass away, and His reign (kingship; kingdom; sovereign influence) will not proceed in being thoroughly decayed, corrupted, ruined or spoiled throughout" (LXX, JM).

It is suggested by Beale that this verse begins a "midrash" on Dan. 7 and 10, i.e., "an interpretative expansion of one text that draws in other texts to supplement its meaning" (ibid p 220), which continues on through vs. 20. But this clause would also bring to mind Jesus' words concerning the destruction of Jerusalem and the temple, in Mat. 24:30-31,

> "**And at that time, the 'sign' which is the Son of the Man** (= Adam's son; the son who has the [true] character and qualities of humanity; or: = the expected Messianic figure; the Human Being) **will be made progressively visible** (be brought to light and made to shine), **in union with heaven** (or: within the midst of [the] atmosphere), **and at that point 'all the tribes of the land** (or: earth) **will continue beating themselves** (= a figure of striking one's breast in grief and remorse; or: as when grain is being threshed; or: give themselves to wearisome toil; or: cut themselves off, as when harvesting grain),' **and they will proceed in seeing for themselves 'the Son of the Man progressively coming upon the clouds of the atmosphere** (or: sky),' **with power and ability, as well as much glory** (= many manifestations which call forth praise; an extensive good reputation). **And then He will continue sending His agents** (messengers; folks with the message) **off on a mission 'with a great trumpet** (perhaps: = a large shofar; or: = a loud trumpet blast; [note: a figure of a publicly proclaimed message or instruction]),' [Isa. 27:13] **and they will progressively be fully** (or: additionally) **gathering together His picked out and chosen folks from out of the four winds – from [the] heavens'** (or: atmospheres') **extremities: until their farthest points** (= from the four quarters of the land, from one end of the sky to the other)!"

We will see more of "agents" and "trumpets" in what follows below. The context of "the Son of man coming in a cloud" is found again in Lu. 21, where, in vs. 20, Jesus spoke of His disciples seeing, "**Jerusalem being continuously surrounded by encamped armies, at that time realize and know from that experience that her desolation has drawn near and is now present**." So from this introduction in the Unveiling, we can see the time-frame of the historical setting of this apocalyptic prophecy. It began with the advent of Jesus as Israel's Messiah, continued into His resurrection and enthronement, and then the giving of the Holy Spirit at Pentecost with Peter affirming that this (Acts 2:17-20) was fulfilling Joel's prophecy (Joel 2:28-32), and here we can note that Joel 2:2 speaks of this day as being a "day of clouds," and Joel 2:30-32 sounds like what is seen here in the visions, below.

The second clause fits the picture of the setting of the first clause, but it, too, must be understood symbolically as part of the apocalyptic description. The inclusiveness of this book eventually applying to the whole of humanity (in the last, or *eschatos*, Adam – 1 Cor. 15:45) is seen in the qualifying phrase, **every eye**. Yet its immediate application (1st century Palestine) is speaking of "every eye" of the folks within the picture that is being figuratively painted, with Jerusalem being the central focus of His coming on the clouds of judgment, as we will see. On offer are three renderings from the semantic range of the verb: **will progressively discern and perceive** (or: continue recognizing; or: repeatedly see). Jesus used this same verb in Jn. 14:9b, "**The one having discerned and seen Me has seen, and now perceives, the Father! How are you now saying, 'Show us the Father'?**" He also said, in Mat. 13:16, "**your eyes [are] happy** (blessed and prosperous, and thus, privileged), **because they continue seeing**." The idea of "seeing" often meant "perception." These folks would perceive and recognize the fulfillment of Jesus' prophecy to the chief priest, in Mk. 14:

> 61. **Yet He continued silent and from considered decision did not respond anything. Again, the chief priest continued inquiring of Him and proceeds saying to Him, "Are you the Christ** (the Anointed One; = the Messiah), **the son of the Blessed One?**"
> 62. **Now Jesus said, "I am** (or: I, Myself, am [He]) [some later MSS and quotes by Origen, read: You are saying that I am])! **And furthermore, YOU MEN will proceed seeing the Son of the Man** (the human's son; the Human Being) **by habit** (or: continue) **sitting at** (or: forth from the midst of) **[the] right [hand; section] of the Power, and progressively** (or: repeatedly; as by

habit) **coming** (or: coming and going) **with the clouds of the atmosphere** (or: the sky; the heaven)." [Dan. 7:13; Ps. 110:1]

We also have Lu. 3:6 quoting Isa 40:5, "'**Then all flesh will proceed in seeing God's Deliverance** (Salvation; Rescue; health and wholeness; Returning [all; things] to the original state and condition)**!**'"

The aorist (indefinite, fact tense) is used in the next clause: **even whichever of you folks pierced** (or: pierce) **Him**. This could be referring to the chief priest (as a representative of the Jewish leadership), in Mk. 14:62, above, or to the Romans (signifying the Empire from the one soldier who thrust a javelin into Jesus' side when He was on the execution pole). Either of those can be seen in the simple past tense, "**pierced**." But just as Heb. 6:6b affirms that, "**[they are] continuously suspending back up** (or: hanging on a pole; crucifying) **again in, with, to, for and by themselves the Son of God, and [are] constantly exposing [Him] to public shame/disgrace**," the fact/point-in-time rendering, "pierce," can speak to any who do as the passage of Heb. 6 describes.

The last half of this verse is an allusion to Zech. 12:10-14, where the setting is Jerusalem, and in vs. 10b we read, "and they shall look upon Me whom they have pierced, and they shall mourn..." Even though this passage in Zech. is speaking of the land and families of Israel (and thus is my bold rendering here, **Land**), there, in vs. 9, it speaks of destroying "all the nations that come against Jerusalem," which prophesies of the future demise of the Roman Empire, following the destruction of Jerusalem in AD 70.

So we can see literal, historical fulfillments referred to in both the apocalyptic picture of the first clause of this verse, and then, similar to the predictions made by Jesus of a literal destruction of the temple and Jerusalem, we can see allusions to OT prophets who spoke concerning the same thing, and the same historic context. Here is an example of the need to discern the kind of speech that is being used, whether apocalyptic symbolism, or simply prophecy.

The final clause of the verse contains ambiguities due to the terms that it uses: **shall beat themselves** (strike their breasts in grief, mourning or repentance) **upon** (= because of) **Him**. Just what is this picture saying to the folks in Asia Minor? The allusion to Zech. 12 would seem to indicate the grief of mourning, or, perhaps it indicates repentance. The literal rendering of the last phrase, "**upon Him**," could be taken as meaning "because of Him" (whether referring to His death, or the realization of impending judgment), or perhaps, "on account of Him," which could be speaking of sorrow either for what they had done, or for what will now be the consequences. It may depend upon who these folks are. "**All the tribes**" could refer to the whole of Israel; or, it may be a reference to all of humanity (the tribes of "the earth"). Each layer of perception is probably correct. And as John says, "**Yes, it is true** (amen)."

8. "**I am continuously** (or: repeatedly) **the Alpha and the Omega,**" **says the Lord** [= Christ or Yahweh] **God, "the One continuously being, even the One Who was and continued being, and the One presently and continuously** (or: progressively) **coming and going, the Almighty."**
    (or: The Owner is laying out these thoughts: "I Myself exist being the Alpha and the Omega – the continuously existing God, even the One Who continued existing [as] Being, as well as the One habitually being on the go and repeatedly moving about – the All-Strong.")

There were no quotation marks in the early MSS, so some translations give only the first clause in quotes, since the verb is in the first person. The second half of the verse has only participles, and thus some read these as a tri-part formula that modifies the Name, "**the Lord God**." Others, as I do here, read the string of participles as part of the predicate of the first clause (modifying "**I am**") and thus make these as part of what "the Lord God" was saying. John introduces this quote without any introduction, except perhaps as an allusion to Isa. 41:4; 44:6 and 48:12, where the clauses are, "I am the First and the Last."

We find the A and the Ω again in 21:6, below, with allusions to "First and Last" in the formulation, "**I am the Alpha and the Omega: The Beginning** (Origin; Source; Headship; First Principle) **and The End** (The Goal; Consummation; The Finished Product; The Destiny; The Purpose)," and this is repeated in 22:13. The "first and last" placement of these declarations virtually "bookend" the entire Apocalypse. When the Lord speaks of Himself in a certain way, and then says it three times in a single message (an Unveiling), we should pause and give this expression focused thought.

We suggest that Paul articulated the same idea in Rom. 11:36a,
> "**Because, forth from out of the midst of Him, then through the midst of Him** (or: through means of Him), **and [finally] into the midst of Him, [is; will be] the whole** (everything; [are] all things; or: = Because He is the source, means and goal/destiny of all things – everything leads into Him)!"

"The Alpha and the Omega" is an example of a traditional rhetorical technique where "polar opposites" are stated "in order to highlight everything between the opposites" (Beale, ibid p 199). "Under Hellenistic influence, the symbolic value of the alphabet was gradually assimilated by Judaism; the first letter associated with the last signified totality" (D'Aragon, ibid p 472). So when God says this of Himself, and we realize that as in Rom. 11, quoted here, He is speaking of the A and the Ω – and everything in between – that came "from out of the midst of Him," we see a snapshot of creation and the ages. We read of Christ, in Heb. 1:2, "**a Son whom He placed** (or: sets) **[as; to be] Heir of all** (or: One who receives all humanity as an allotment; or: heir of all things; or: One who received everything as his allotted inheritance) **through Whom He also made the ages.**" And Paul proclaims an apocalyptic A to Ω in Col. 1:16,
> "**within Him was created the whole** (or: in union with Him everything is founded and settled, is built and planted, is brought into being, is produced and established; or: within the midst of Him all things were brought from chaos into order) **– the things within the skies and atmospheres, and the things upon the earth** (or: those [situations, conditions and/or people] in the heavens and on the land); **the visible things, and the unseen** (or: unable to be seen; invisible) **things: whether thrones** (seats of power) **or lordships** (ownership systems) **or governments** (rulers; leadership systems; sovereignties) **or authorities – the whole has been created and all things continue founded, put in order and stand framed through means of Him, and [proceeds, or were placed] into Him** (or: = He is the agent and goal of all creation)."

I suggest this inclusive picture is what the Lord God is indicating in the first clause of this verse. The string of participles starts with the present tense describing "**continuous being,**" then moves to the imperfect tense of the second one – giving a glance back to His existence (and implied activities) in the past of creation's history, and then focuses the final participle on His "**presently and continuously** (or: progressively) **coming and going**" – constantly involved with everything between the A and the Ω.

The final attribute, **the Almighty** (the All-Strong), is an affirmation of God's sovereignty over creation, and throughout the ages. We find the risen Jesus Christ proclaiming the right to use all of God's Strength and Might: "**All authority** (or: Every right and privilege from out of Being) **is** (or: was) **given to Me within heaven and upon the earth** (or: in sky and atmosphere, as well as on land)!" (Mat. 28:18). We will see this pictured, below, when John sees, "**within the midst of the throne and of the four living ones, and within the midst of the elders, I saw a little Lamb standing, as one having been slaughtered, having seven horns** [a figure of complete, or total, power] **and seven eyes** [complete vision: sees all]." This union of power is also seen in 3:21b where Christ says to those in Laodicea, "**as I also conquer** (or: conquered; overcome; overcame and was victorious) **and sit** (or: sat down) **with My Father within His throne.**" Putting the name, **the Lord God**, with the ending designation, **the Almighty**, forms the complete expression that is found in Hos. 12:5 and Amos 9:5, in the LXX (which is the translation of the Hebrew, "Yahweh, God of Hosts").

9. **I, John, your brother and joint-participant** (or: sharer of common-being/partnered-existence) **within the pressure** (squeezing; affliction; tribulation; oppression) **and kingdom** (or: reign; sovereign rule and activity) **and persistent remaining-under** (steadfast, humble and supportive endurance), **in union with** (or: within; [Griesbach and other MSS: of; originating in; pertaining to]) **Jesus Christ** (= [the] Messiah),

Both John and the covenant communities were experiencing "the tribulation," i.e., **the pressure**, the squeezing affliction and the oppression that was coming from their surrounding environments in 1st century Asia Minor. This introductory statement sets the scene and context of both the letters and the visions which follow. The oppression was likely coming from the Roman Empire, the pagan cults in their areas, as well as from the local synagogues (e.g., 2:9, below).

The word "**join-participant**" is built from *koin* (common) plus *ōn* (present participle of *eimi*: to be, to exist) plus the preposition *sun-* (with; joined together). It is a word of holding both a common being and a partnered existence with other people. John's common-being is being a fellow member (a brother) of Christ's body; his common-existence and joint-participation within God's reign -- which includes the pressure (etc.). Jesus told his followers,
> "**Within the System** (controlling world of culture, religion, economy and government) **you normally have pressure and stress** (or: continually have squeezing; repeatedly have tribulation and oppression), **but nonetheless, be confident and take courage! I Myself have overcome and conquered the System** (dominating world; organized arrangement of religion and society; aggregate of humanity) **so that it stands a completed victory!**" (Jn. 16:33)

His followers remembered this, and in Acts 14:22 Paul and Barnabas (and others) affirmed that, "**It continues binding and necessary for us to enter into the reign of God** (or: God's kingdom; the sovereign activities which are God) **through the midst of many pressures, squeezings, tribulations, afflictions and oppressions**." Just prior to saying this, "certain Jews from Antioch" had come into Lycaonia, "and [with other MSS: from their repeated arguments, publicly] **persuaded the crowds** [other MSS add: to separate from them, saying that they were not even speaking truth, but rather were all constantly lying]. **And so, after stoning Paul, they proceeded to be violently dragging [him] outside of the city, continuing in presuming him to have died**" (Acts 14:19). It is likely to this sort of behavior that John refers here in 1:9.

There are three nouns that follow a single definite article, **the**, and so there is reason to interpret these three nouns as being in close association: **pressure, kingdom** and **persistent remaining-under** (i.e., steadfast, humble and supportive endurance). God's reign, sovereign rule and activity brings affliction and oppression to the followers of Jesus. Thus, His reign in our lives – and recall that Jesus said in Lu. 17:21, "**God's reign** (kingdom; royal rule; sovereign influence and activity) **continually exists inside you folks** (or: is on the inside of you people; or: = within your community)" – requires "steadfast, humble and supportive endurance," and thus involves **persistent remaining-under** whatever situations come along. This is a literal rendering of the noun which the parenthetical expansion explains. We endure when we remain under a hard situation, but the kingship aspect is remaining there for the sake of others – or as Jesus said, "lay down our life for a friend." We persist in order to give support, to help carry the burden and to proclaim solidarity with others who are in the same situation. In this we join our Master, Who "**remained under a cross** (an execution pole for suspending a body) **– despising shame** (or: thinking nothing of [the] disgrace)" (Heb. 12:2).

But all of this (including His kingdom and reign) occurs **in union with Jesus Christ**, or, the sphere of our lives is "within" the resurrected, corporate Messiah – of which Jesus is the Head and Ruler. Of the preposition (*en*) forming this phrase, Beale (ibid p 201) remarks that it, "can designate both sphere and incorporation with respect to Christ, as it does in 14:12," which reads:

> "**In this place** (or: Here) **exists** (or: is) **the persistent and patient endurance** (the steadfast, humble remaining-under for support) **of the set-apart folks** (or: from the saints) **– the people continually keeping watch upon** (guarding, observing, having custody over) **God's implanted goals** (impartations of the finished product within; inward purposed directives and inner destiny) **and the faith of Jesus**."

Watching, guarding, observing and keeping custody over what the Spirit has imparted to us give definition to how we are to respond to the pressures (etc.), and this way of life which arises from the indwelling Christ both guides and empowers our endurance. Verse 9, here, is also an allusion to Dan. 7:27a,

> "And the kingdom (or: reign and sphere of sovereign influence) and the authority (or: right from out of being)… were given to **the set-apart folks** of, and which correspond to and represent, [the] Most High (or: were presented by holy and sacred people from [the] Highest One)…" (LXX, JM).

10. **was within the island called Patmos because of God's Word** (or: the Logos of God; the message which is God; the thoughts and ideas from God) **and because of the testimony** (witness; evidence) **pertaining to and having the characteristics of Jesus Christ. I came to be** (or: birthed myself; happened to be) **within spirit** (or: in union with [the] Spirit; in the midst of a Breath-effect) **within the Day which pertains to or has the characteristics of the Lord** (the Lord's Day; = the Day of Yahweh; or, = the Day of Christ; = Christ's Day), **and I heard behind me a great voice** (or: = a loud sound), **as of a trumpet, saying** (or: = like that of a trumpet sounding a command or a message),

Patmos, located near Asia Minor and close to Ephesus, was known to be a place where Rome deposited political exiles. John simply tells us that he was there **because of the testimony** (witness; evidence) **pertaining to and having the characteristics of Jesus Christ**. We do not know whether he means because of the witness that he was proclaiming, or because of the testimony that had been spread abroad about the focus of his life or concerning his character, or perhaps more pertinent to what he writes, he was there to receive this Unveiling, and receive the mission of sharing this with the called-out communities. In all of these possibilities, he was there **because of God's Word** (or: the Logos of God; the message which is God; the thoughts and ideas from God). *Cf* 1:2, above, 19:13; 20:4; and Jn. 1:1-14.

That he was "in union with [the] Spirit, or, in the midst of a Breath-effect **within the Day which pertains to or has the characteristics of the Lord**" sets the scene as a spiritual experience. Some interpret the phrase "the Lord's Day" as a day of the week, but more in sync with the apocalyptic genre of this writing, we may be more advised to read this in the sense of "the Day of Yahweh" – an allusion to the oft-used expression in the OT prophets. In other words, "in the midst of a Breath-effect" he was transported into the very setting that is the main theme of the letter.

The second statement begins with a setting that calls to mind Ezk. 2:2, "Then a spirit (or: [the] Spirit) came upon me…" (LXX, JM) and raised Ezekiel up from having fallen on his face from his experience of the Lord's glory. This was a typical response of prophets receiving a vision, in the OT.

The **great voice**, or "loud sound," and **a trumpet** echo the setting on Mt. Sinai in Ex. 19:16; and the blowing of trumpets which began the 7th month and the Feast of Tabernacles, in Lev. 23:24; then the celebration of the year of Jubilee in Lev. 25:9; the two silver trumpets for calling assembly in Nu. 10:2ff, and especially the 7 trumpets used in the siege of Jericho, in Josh. 6:4. Such an opening, here, would have alerted John's listeners to prepare to hear a message of great significance for them. Trumpets will play key parts in the visions, below. This description of what John heard calls to mind Paul's words in 1 Thes. 4:16,

> "**the Lord** [= Yahweh or Christ] **Himself will continue habitually descending** (or: repeatedly descend) **from [the] atmosphere** (or: heaven) **within the midst of** (or: in union with) **a shout of command, within the midst of [the] Chief Agent's** (or: in union with an original messenger's or a chief and ruling agent's) **voice, and within the midst of** (or: in union with) **God's trumpet**..."

John's experience, here, may be one of many fulfillments of the apocalyptic words in this 1 Thes. text.

11. **"What you are presently observing** (or: continue seeing) **write into a scroll and send [it] to the seven called-out communities** (or: summoned-forth congregations): **into Ephesus, and into Smyrna, and into Pergamos, and into Thyatira, and into Sardis, and into Philadelphia, and into Laodicea."**

This is the first message of the Voice that was like a Trumpet. The entire book, that follows, was to be sent to each of these 7 communities. That 7 communities were chosen out of the greater number that were in Asia Minor bears consideration. Perhaps John is indicating that the messages and visions comprise "the last trumpet" (1 Cor. 15:52): the message of the Good News that Christ reigns.

The instruction to **write into a scroll** echoes Ex. 17:14, "And so the Lord [= Yahweh] said to Moses, 'Write this down into a scroll, with a view to a memorial...'" (LXX, JM). Then in Isa. 30:6 he is told, "Now then, after sitting down, write these upon a tablet, and into a scroll..." (LXX, JM). Jer. 37:2 records, "Write upon a scroll all the words (thoughts; ideas) which I usefully communicated to you" (LXX, JM). And in Hab. 2:2 we find,

> "And from discernment [the] Lord [= Yahweh] decisively responded to me, and said, 'Write [the] vision -- and [write it] plainly and clearly into a tablet -- so that the person presently reading it can progressively take flight (or: may continue running; or: would habitually pursue). Because [the] vision [is] yet unto the midst of a season (fitting situation) and it progressively shoots up (or: continues rising again) into a bounded limit (a concluded extremity) -- and not in vain (or: into emptiness) -- even if it [i.e., the season] (or: He) should delay (or: may lack or fail; come after [a time]), remain under it (or: patiently endure and support Him), because in steadily coming it will progressively reach the time and take place (or: He will have reached the point, and arrive), and will by no means be late or delay" (LXX, JM).

Cf also Isa. 8:1ff, with its prophecies against Syria, Israel and Judah (including vs. 14, "He will become... a Stone of stumbling and a Rock of offence to both the houses of Israel, for a Trap and for a Snare to the inhabitants of Jerusalem"). Cf further Jer. 36:1ff [in the LXX] and the prophecy concerning the 70 years in vs. 10, there.

Here the writing is to be sent to the called-out communities, and the content of each letter is judgment: pronouncements that are positive, along with pronouncements that are negative. The word "judgment" means a situation has been divided out in its parts in order to evaluate and make the appropriate decision. The letters (chapters 2-3) are pronouncements of such decisions (judgments) based upon what the risen Christ has observed as He continuously walks around within those communities (2:1, below). It is with this perception of a present and ongoing activity of judging that we should approach the visions of the scrolls being opened and rightwising decisions being made (e.g., the "great, white throne" in 20:11ff, where the "second death" is mentioned, correlated with this same "second death" being brought into view in the letter to Smyrna, in 2:11). The judgments that will later be observed in relation to the opening of the 7 seals are in the context of opening a scroll.

As to the reason for the order in which this verse (along with chapters 2-3) lists these communities, Metzger suggests a simple, practical explanation: "it is the order in which, starting from Ephesus (the city closest to Patmos), a messenger carrying the book would travel, somewhat in a semicircle, going successively to each of the churches" (ibid p 26).

The first, introductory vision, below, follows the typical pattern of visions in the OT and Jewish apocalyptic literature: first we have the initial vision (vss. 12-16) followed by the seer's response (vs. 17a) and then an interpretation of the vision (vss. 17b-20).

12. And so I turned upon the Voice, to see who spoke with me. And upon fully turning around, I saw seven golden lampstands,

Notice that Christ's voice comes from within the midst of the **7 golden lampstands** – His called-out, covenant communities (vs. 20, below). Bringing these together with the 7 lamps of fire before the throne (see discussion on vs. 4, above) that in 5:4 are equated with the **Seven Spirit of God**, and recalling the scene on the Day of Pentecost where we read of "**tongues as if of fire**" that "**sat down upon each one of them**" (Act 2:3), we can see a picture developing that depicts the joining of the 7 Spirits to the 7 congregations – and the setting of the holy place of the tabernacle also comes in view, which will be revisited in chapter 4, below.

Our first reference to a golden lampstand, in Israel's story, is found in Ex. 25:31-37, where it is a single lampstand (figure of a unified Israel) with 7 lamps (vs. 37; *cf* Ex. 37:17-23; Nu. 8:2-4). But a prophetic and apocalyptic picture is found in Zech. 4:2-14 (which will also be alluded to in the context of 11:4, below). Zech. 4:2-3 opens with, "an entirely gold lampstand... and 7 lamps upon it.... and two olive trees upon it, one from the right of its bowl for the lamp-oil (or: torch) and one from out of [the] left." Then in Zech. 4:12, 14,
> "... What [are] the two branches of the olive trees, in the hands (or: handles) of two gold tubes continuously pouring on and then constantly leading back up again upon the golden pouring vessels (or: oil funnels)?.... These two sons of fatness (or: = anointed sons) stand alongside, by (or: with; for) the Lord (or: Owner) of all the earth (or: land)" (LXX, JM).

Historically, these two anointed sons were Joshua the chief priest (Zech. 3), and Zerubbabel (Zech. 4:6-10), the governor of Yehuda (when Judea was a vassal state of the Persian Empire). Paul picked up the olive tree metaphor, with its fatness, in Rom. 11:17, and the theme is the anointing of the oil that is a figure for the Spirit that gives Light through burning the oil in the lampstand (now the called-out communities, vs. 20, below). This Unveiling draws strongly upon Israel's temple cultus and the messianic prophecies in Zech. and other prophets.

John's response to the Voice calls us back to Saul, on the road to Damascus in Acts 9, where instead of turning (since Saul had been knocked to the ground), and instead of the Voice from heaven announcing at the beginning Who it was that was speaking in apocalyptic terms (vs. 8, above), Saul was asked a question, in vs. 4, " **Saul... Saul... Why do you continue pursuing and persecuting Me?**" When Saul asks who He is, He gave His identity with His human name and at the same time affirms His identity with His followers: "**I, Myself, am Jesus... Whom you continue pursuing and persecuting!**" But as with John, here in this Unveiling, what follows for Saul are instructions regarding what the Lord wants him to do. But instead of being struck with blindness (as Saul was), John begins seeing visions. It is instructive to note that the first thing that he lists as having seen are **7 golden lampstands**. This establishes the setting and context for the called-out, covenant communities as being one of the central themes of the book – along with the next thing of which he writes (in vs. 13), **like a Son of Man**. We will read in vs. 20, below, that these lampstands represent the 7 communities that are listed in vs. 11. But what is emphasized, by its position in the list of what he sees, is that he is looking into a figure of the holy place of the tabernacle, which contained the 7-branched lampstand, the table for the loaves that represented (corporately) the 12 tribes of Israel, and the altar of incense that represented prayers and thanksgiving that were offered to God. This setting was the place where the priests offered daily service to God, and as representatives of the entire people. So we should keep this place and this service (which are now located in and performed by the covenant communities) in mind as we proceed through the book.

13. and within the midst of the lampstands, One like a Son of Man (or: a son of mankind; = [the] son of Adam; = like a human being; [or: an eschatological symbol referring to such as in Dan. 7:13 and 10:5-6]), **being clothed** (or: invested) **[with a garment] reaching to the feet; being girded about at the breasts with a golden belt.**

This description calls to mind Dan. 10:5, "And I raised my eyes and saw, and lo, there was one person clothed in linen and girded with gold around the waist by gold of Ophaz" (LXX, with Theodotion version, NETS, Oxford Univ. Press, 2007). But here, this **One** is within the midst of the communities (God's temple). The picture being painted is that of Christ's eschatological presence, in visionary (or, apocalyptic) symbolism, that will inform the listeners concerning the manner and effect of His presence within the new creation environment that is the "heaven" (Eph. 2:6) where they now dwell.

The clothing is that of a priest or a king, which tells us that this **Son of Man** functions in both roles. But just as the phrase "son of man" can also refer to "a human being" or a "son of Adam" (Ezk. 2:1, 3, 6, 8) we find a similar description of the garments of the priests of the new creation temple (i.e., the members of the called-out, covenant communities) in 15:5-6, below,

> "**Later, after these things, I saw, and the Temple** (Divine habitation; sanctuary), **which equates to the Tabernacle of the Witness** (or: whose source and origin was the tent of testimony and evidence), **was opened up within the midst of the atmosphere** (or: centered in, and in union with, heaven), **and the seven agents – those continuously holding the seven plagues** (smitings) **– came out of the Temple, being clothed with bright, clean** (unsoiled, pure) **linen, and having been bound with a girdle around the breasts [with] golden girdles.**"

Christ's body (the members that serve as His agents, messengers, priests and kings here on earth) has the same clothing as Jesus, e.g.,
"**may thus clothe himself in white garments**" – 3:5, below; also, 3:18; "**and upon the thrones, twenty-four elders** (or: old people) **continuously sitting, having been clothed in white garments. And upon their heads [were; are] golden wreaths**" – 4:4; "**And a brilliant white robe was given to each of them**" – 6:11; "**A vast crowd** (great multitude), **which no one was able to number, from out of every ethnic group** (or: nation) **– even of tribes and of peoples and of tongues** (languages) **– standing before** (in the sight of) **the throne, and before** (in the sight of) **the little Lamb, having been clothed with bright white robes** (or: equipment; uniforms) **– who are they and whence came they?.... they habitually do public to** (in; by; for) **Him, day and night, within the midst of His Temple**" – 7:13, 15; "**Then it was** (or: is) **granted** (or: given) **to her to the end that she may clothe herself with bright and clean fine cotton** (or: she may cast bright, pure, fine linen around her) **– for the fine cotton** (or: linen) **represents the effects of right relationship and equity in the life of the Way pointed out**
> (or: the results of being rightwised; the actualizations of justice; consequences of justice rendered from being turned in the right direction; the effects of having been eschatologically delivered and placed in the Path pointed out; or: the just awards) **of the set-apart folks** (pertaining to the saints; from the sacred people)" – 19:8, below.

We find Jesus in the transfigured state (Mat. 17:2) where "**He was transformed** (changed in external form and appearance) **and His face radiated light, like a lamp, and shone like the sun. His outer garments also turned white – bright as the light!**" The description of the clothing here in vs. 13 may also be an allusion to Jesus (LXX; MT: Joshua), the great priest, in Zech. 3:4b-5a, "Remove the filthy clothes from him.... And clothe him with a full-length robe, and put a clean turban on his head" (NETS, ibid p 815). Relating 1:7 & 13, here, to the texts in Zech. 3 and 12, as well as *The Epistle of Barnabas* 7:6-12, Crossan makes an interesting observation,

> "The advantage of that combination's intensive intertextuality is that passion (piercing) and parousia (looking/mourning) from Zech. 12:10-14 is expanded by passion (disrobing) and parousia (re-robing, crowning) in Zech. 3:1-5" (ibid p 379).

14. Now His head and hairs [are] white, as white wool – as snow – and His eyes as a flame of fire,

The **head**... **white**... **as snow** answers to Mat. 17:2, above. The **hair** being **white** is an allusion to the "Ancient of days" in Dan. 7:13. **His eyes as a flame of fire** echoes Dan. 10:6, "eyes like torches of fire" (NETS, ibid). Clearly, this figure is the eschatological, resurrected Christ that is both King and Chief Priest (Heb. 4). We see His eyes described the same way in 19:12, below.

15. and His feet [are] like white brass (or: bronze; fine copper) **as having been set on fire in a furnace, and His Voice [is] as a roar** (or: sound; voice) **of many [rushing or crashing] waters.**

Dan. 10:6, "his arms and feet like dazzling (Theodotion: gleaming) bronze, and the sound of his talking (Theodotion: words) like the sound of a throng (Theodotion: crowd)" (NETS, ibid). So once again we have references to imagery from Daniel's visions. Here, the **feet** are symbols of both His stance (Eph. 6:13b), and His walk (or, manner of living): **white brass as having been set on fire in a furnace**. The brass is an allusion to the brazen altar of sacrifice (His path dealt with sin), to healing from the effects of sin (Gen. 3:15b; Nu. 21:9, the serpent on the pole; Rom. 16:20) and to judging (Deut. 28:23). There is also an allusion in this brass/bronze element to Ezk. 40:3 and the vision of, "a man, and his appearance was like an appearance of flashing bronze, and in his hand was a builder's cord and a measuring reed, and he stood by the gate" (NETS, ibid; *cf* 11:1ff, below). The word **furnace** calls back to Dan.3:19-25, and looks ahead to 14:10, below.

We find this description repeated in 2:18, in the letter to Thyatira, to which He speaks of coming to them in judgment. A symbolic Agent is seen in 10:1, below, where we read of, "**His face as the sun, and His feet as pillars of fire**." Christ is unveiled throughout the book.

Ezekiel's first vision is of four living beings (see the Unveiling's version of these introduced in 4:6ff, below) in 1:5ff. There, in vs. 24, it is said of them,

> "Then I heard the voice (or: sound) of their wings, in the midst of the [situation for] them to pass from one place to another -- as a voice (or: sound) of much (or: abundant) water, as the voice (sound) of the Mighty (or: Worthy; Fit; Sufficient) One... a voice (sound) of the Word as the voice (sound) of an encampment of an army" (LXX, JM).

In his vision in Ezk. 43, vs. 2 speaks of the coming of the glory of the God of Israel, "and a voice (or: sound) of the encampment of an army, as a voice (sound) of many repetitions [perhaps: of ranks]" (LXX, JM). So in this apocalyptic vision, the **many waters** might be signifying that this symbolic picture represents a corporate Being: the body of Christ, or of Christ's agents. We see the same picture in different figures (but with some similarities) in 19:11-16, below, where the armies that follow Him are "**ones having been clothed with** (invested with; entered within) **clean** (or: pure) **bright, white fine cotton**," (not in the garb of normal soldiers). The pictures in this book are symbols of ideas, not depictions of physical entities or of literal situations, even though they may speak concerning literal fulfillment of their prophecies that would soon take place. The symbols must be interpreted in accord with the traditions and meanings of this genre of literature: Jewish apocalyptic; visionary, with OT allusions.

16. Furthermore, [He is] constantly holding (or: having; possessing) **seven stars centered in** (or: within the midst of; in union with) **His right hand, and a sharp two-mouthed** (= double-edged) **broadsword is continuously** (or: repeatedly) **proceeding** (issuing forth) **from out of His mouth. And His appearance** (countenance; sight) **continually shines as the sun, in its power.**

This description is visionary, apocalyptic symbolism. Both the **broadsword** and the **seven stars** are parts of the whole picture, just as are the other parts. They describe qualities, abilities, equipment, and potentiality. Just as the sword (coming out of **His mouth**) is a figure, so are the 7 stars. The number 7 is an idea that is seen repeatedly throughout the book. In vs. 20, below, we find these stars identified as "agents" or "messengers" or "folks with a or the message." Instead of the sword being in His right hand (i.e., in the place of power, authority, or if in the hand, the threat of judgment) we find it in His mouth, signifying that His Word is His only weapon, but that it is an effective one -- as we see in Heb. 4:12,

> "**For the Word of God** (or: God's thought, idea and message; or: the expressed Logos from God; or: the Word which is God) **[is] living** (or: alive), **and active** (working; operative; energetic; at work; productive) **and more cutting above every two-mouthed sword, even passing through** (penetrating) **as far as a dividing** (or: parting; partitioning) **of soul and spirit** (or: of inner self-life and breath-effect), **both of joints and marrows, even able to discern** (separate; judge; decide) **concerning thoughts** (ponderings; reflections; in-rushings; passions) **and intentions** (notions; purposes) **of a heart** (= core of the being)."

And we see from this exactly where He uses it, and its purpose: divine surgery on the hearts of people. In Eph. 6:17b Paul admonished his listeners to receive and retain for themselves, "**the Spirit's sword** (the short sword from the Attitude; or: the dagger which is spirit; the dirk which is the Breath-effect) **– the one being God's gush-effect**

> (or: which is the result of the flow from God; the one existing [as] a result of a flux or an effect of a continuous movement, the source of which is God; or: which is a spoken Word of God; or: that being an utterance or declaration which is God)."

In Isa. 11:4b we observe in the Heb. text, "He shall strike the land (or: earth) with the rod (or: club; scepter) of His mouth...," but the LXX translates this, "... with the Word of His mouth." Isa. 49:1-2 reads, "He made my mouth like a sharp sword.." (in both the Heb. and the LXX). This metaphor is picked up again in 2:16, below, where Christ warns that He may use this sword against the community in Pergamos,

> "**You must change your mind** (your way of thinking), **therefore! Yet if not, I am repeatedly** (habitually) **coming swiftly in you** (to you; for you) [again: you, singular], **and I will proceed waging war** (doing battle) **with them within the broadsword of My mouth**."

In Gen. 37:9-10, Jacob interprets the moon in Joseph's dream as being Joseph's "mother." We should keep this idea in mind when we come to the vision of 12:1, below. Jacob interpreted the "eleven stars" as being Joseph's brothers (which, with Joseph, became the twelve tribes of Israel). In Dan. 12, Daniel is informed:

> "And so, within the midst of that season, Michael -- the great Ruler (Beginning One): the One having stood and still standing upon the sons of your People -- will proceed raising Himself back up again (will progressively resurrect Himself) and re-establish Himself, and yet there will progressively be a season (or: fitting and appointed situation) of pressure (tribulation; affliction; oppression).... Within the midst of that season your People will be progressively rescued and will continue being delivered -- every person [other MS add: found] being written within the scroll. And then (or: so) many of the folks continuously sleeping within a mound of soil (or: centered in an embankment of earth) shall proceed being awakened and raised out from the midst: these into the midst of eonian life (life pertaining to the Age of the Messiah), and those (= others) into the midst of insult (reproach; verbal abuse; scorning; scolding) and into an age-lasting disgrace (or:

eonian shame; shame pertaining to the Age of the Messiah). And then the intelligent folks (the people being able to progressively put things together) will progressively shine and continue giving light, as the brightness of the firmament (or: will proceed lighting up like the luminaries of the heaven), and from among the many just folks who were put right in the Way pointed-out (the rightwised ones) as the stars, on into the midst of the ages, and beyond (or: yet still)" (vss. 1-3, LXX, JM).

We will come upon this apocalyptic figure "Michael" again in 12:7, below.

Instead of the sword being in His right hand, we find His agents there – folks through whom He accomplishes His work and delivers His messages. But these should be seen as an extension of this picture, and thus, and extension of the resurrected Christ. Beal points out that **hand** should be understood as metaphorical for "sovereignty" (ibid p 211). The **stars** should be interpreted christo-centrically, as part of the vision of the Christ, in the same way that the sword is seen as His Word. We find the stars, again, in vs. 20, below, where they are defined as "folks with the message." In 10:1, below, we will see a vision of an Agent which, by its very description, will be perceived to be another apocalyptic representation of the exalted Christ.

That **His appearance** (countenance; sight) **continually shines as the sun, in its power** may be an echo of Jud. 5:31, "as a going forth (exodus; = rising) of [the] sun in its power [other MS: dominance]" (LXX, JM), but we see a more current parallel in Mat. 17: 2, "**all of a sudden, He was transformed** (changed in external form and appearance) **and His face radiated light, like a lamp, and shone like the sun. His outer garments also turned white – bright as the light**" (*cf* Mk. 9:2; Lu. 9:28). Again, this calls to mind the bright light from the risen Jesus that blinded Saul when on the road to Damascus (Acts 9:3).

17. **And so when I saw Him, I fell toward His feet, as dead. And He placed His right hand upon me, saying, "Do not be** (or: Stop) **fearing** (Don't be terrified)**! As for Me, I am the First and the Last** (or: I Myself continuously exist being the first one as well as the Last One),

Dan. 10:9, "I fell on my face to the ground" (NETS, ibid). Dan. 10:10 (Theo.), "And lo, a hand touching me, and it roused me to my knees" (NETS, ibid). Dan. 10:12, "Do not be (or: Stop) fearing" (LXX, JM). We can recall Jesus saying the same thing to His apprentices out on the lake, in Mat. 14:27, and then when in the high mountain we find a similar situation to vs. 17, here:

> "**the disciples fell** (= flung themselves) **upon their faces and then were made extremely afraid** (or: became terrified). **So Jesus approached and, upon touching – and as it were kindling – them, said, "Be aroused, get up and stop being made afraid. Now, upon lifting up their eyes, they saw no one** (or: not even one person) **except Him – only Jesus**" (Mat. 17:6-8). *Cf* Ezk. 2:1b; 2:2.

This designation of **the First and the Last** is a redundant parallelism of **the Alpha and the Omega** in vs. 8, above. He is affirming to John that the One that he now sees is the same One that he heard interject that exclamation into John's introductory remarks. But this second Witness as to just Who He is should be marked as being a very important disclosure. John does not need ask, as did Saul, "Who are you, Lord?" The second half of vs. 8 is now repeated in different form, in vs. 18. This last clause is considered to be taken from Isa. 44:6; 48:12. But the Heb. word for "last" can also mean "latter," and the CVOT designates this word as more literally meaning, "after." Now the LXX for Isa. 44:6 reads, "I Myself [am] First, and I Myself [am] after these," and 48:12 reads, "I Myself am (exist being) First, and I Myself am (exist being) on into the midst of the Age" (JM). In both texts, in the Heb., it is Yahweh who is speaking, thus this is His self-designation. So it would seem that the risen Christ has assumed these aspects or attributes that in the OT were self-references of Yahweh.

18. **"even The Living One** (or: and now, the One continuously living), **I also brought Myself to be** (or: birthed Myself) **a dead one** (or: I also came by Myself to be dead), **and now, Look and consider! I am living on into the ages of the ages** (or: the unspecified and indefinite time periods of the eons), **and I constantly hold the keys of and pertaining to the Death and of and pertaining to the Unseen**
> (or: have the keys, which are Death and Hades [= *sheol*; perhaps: "the grave"]; possess the keys from the Death and from the unseen "realm/state of the dead"; hold the keys belonging to death and shadowy existence).

The Voice of the resurrected Christ that began speaking in 17b continues the identification of Himself in this verse, giving John further information about His present condition (**The Living One**), about His past recent experience (**I also brought Myself to be** {or: birthed Myself} **a dead one** {or: I also came by Myself to be dead}), and about the fact that He is **living on into the ages of the ages**. The rendering, "**brought Myself** (birthed Myself; came by Myself to be)" is from the fact that the verb is a middle deponent: the subject is understood as acting upon itself. Recall that Jesus said,
> "**I Myself am constantly placing** (or: repeatedly setting; or: progressively laying [down]) **My soul** (inner life or being; or: = the whole self), **to the end that I may take it in My hand** (or: receive her) **again. No one at any point lifts it** [with other MSS: Not one person is presently lifting her] **up and carries it away** (or: proceeds to remove her) **from Me; on the contrary, I Myself continue putting** (placing; setting; laying) **it** (or: her) **away from Myself**..." (Jn. 10:17b-18a).

He thus affirms that He is the Jesus Christ who was crucified, but is now resurrected and will continue living on into the unspecified and indefinite time periods of the oncoming eons. But this experience has revealed that He possess **the keys of and pertaining to the Death and of and pertaining to the Unseen**.

The parenthetical expansion on the last, compound phrase offers three more functions of the two genitive nouns: "which are" (which would mean that both the Death and the Unseen are keys to the plan of the ages), or "belonging to" (which would mean that these two – personified – possessed keys to either themselves, or to God's plans). Read, instead, as ablatives produces: "from" (which would mean that Jesus either took or received these keys, or found the keys that had their origins in the Death and the Unseen). Each noun has the definite article, so these can be interpreted in the following ways:
> 1) personifications, as in 20:14, below,
> 2) the death state of separation and estrangement that resulted from Adam's disobedience, and "**through The Sin** (failure; the mistake; the miss of the target; the deviation) **The Death, [and] in this way The Death thus also passed through in all directions** (or: came through the midst causing division and duality; went throughout) **into all mankind** (or: into the midst of humanity; or: to all people)" (Rom. 5:12),
> 3) the second death, which the One Man (Christ), the Second Human, experienced for all, so "**that** [some MSS add: since] **One Person** (or: Man) **died over [the situation of] all mankind** (or: for the sake of all); **consequently all people died** (or: accordingly, then, all humanity died)" (2 Cor. 5:14b), which Paul explains in Rom. 6:3b, "**we who are immersed** (or: were at one point soaked or baptized) **into Christ Jesus are immersed** (or: were then baptized) **into His death**,"
> 4) the Death, and its location: the Unseen (the state or condition of blindness) of which Paul spoke in Eph. 2:1, "**And you folks [were] continuously existing being dead ones by** (or: to; with; in) **the results and effects of your stumblings aside** (offenses; wrong steps) **and failures to hit the mark** (or: mistakes; errors; times of falling short; sins; deviations)."

"Hades for this author is not the Greek place of punishment but the Hebrew Sheol.... the place of the dead, and both are personified in 6:8; 20:13. Since they have been overcome by Christ, he can be pictured as holding **keys** with which at the time of the end he can release..." (Gilmour, ibid p 950). Metzger instructs us,

"No distinction is to be drawn here between Death and Hades; they combine to express one idea, the realm of the departed. Because Christ has the 'keys,' the time and manner of the death of each person are under his control" (ibid p 28).

Instructive here are the apocalyptic words of Jesus in Mat.16:18-19 where we find **the Unseen** – and **keys**:

> "**And now I Myself am saying to you that you are Peter** (or: that you continue being an isolated stone). **And you see, [it is] upon this, this rock-mass** (or: bedrock), **[that] I will progressively be constructing and building up My house – the called-out community. And even gates of [the] Unseen** (or: gates of an unseen place; [= boulders on the entrances of graves; = {the prison} gates of the 'house of death'; or: the bars enclosing the realm of the dead]) **will not continue bringing strength down against it** (or: will not proceed to be coming to their full strength in relation to it; or: will not continue overpowering it or prevail in resisting it). **I will continue giving to you the keys** [note: = means of locking or unlocking] **which have their origin and source in the reign and activities of the heavens**
>> (or: which pertain to and have the characteristics of the kingdom of the heavens; or: which belong to the sovereignty from the atmospheres; or, as a genitive of apposition: the keys which are the sovereign reign of the heavens). **And so, whatever you can** (or: may; should) **bind upon the earth will continue being [something] having been bound, and still remaining bound, within the midst of the heavens** (or: in the atmospheres). **Also, whatever you can** (or: may; should) **loose upon the earth will continue being [something] having been loosed** (unbound; untied), **and remaining free of bonds, within the midst of the heavens** (or: in the atmospheres)."

The keys, "which are the sovereign reign of the heavens" are also **keys of and pertaining to the Death and of and pertaining to the Unseen**. This is true because of what was revealed to Paul in 1 Cor. 15,

> "**The Death was drunk down and swallowed into Victory** (or: overcoming)!" [Isa. 25:8] **Where, O Death, [is] your victory** (or: overcoming)**? Where, O Death, [is] your stinger** (sharp point; sting; goad; spur)**?"** [Hos. 13:14; note: TR reads "O Unseen (Hades)" in the second line, following the LXX and Heb.].... **But grace and joyous favor [is] in God** (or: by God) **– the One presently and progressively giving the Victory** (or: the overcoming) **to us, in us and for us through our Lord** (Owner; Master), **Jesus, [the] Christ!**" (vss. 54b-55, 57)

In Acts 2:27 Peter quotes Ps. 16:10,

> "**You will not continue leaving my soul** (my interior self; my existential life) **down in** (or: abandon me into) **[the] Unseen** (or: Hades, the unseen abode of the dead), **neither will You proceed giving Your loyal one** (a person sanctioned by God's law, and by nature; a pious and devout person) **to see** (= experience) **corruption** (thorough ruin, rot and decay)."

Because of His imminent death and resurrection, Jesus could now say to the criminal being suspended on the execution stake next to Him,

> "**Truly it is so** (or: Count on it!)**... I am now saying to you** (D adds: Be of good cheer and take courage)**... Today** (This very day) **you will proceed being** (continue existing) **with Me within the midst of Paradise** (= in the Garden [note: used in the LXX for the Garden of Eden])!" (Lu. 23:43).

Jesus had the keys of death and of the realm/state of the dead, and promised to use them, and we find His kingdom's keys referenced in 3:7, below, where David is a symbol for the Messiah's kingdom, and now the risen Christ is, "**the One having** (continuously holding) **David's Key, the One habitually opening – and no one keeps on shutting** (or: locking) **– and He is repeatedly shutting (locking) – and no one keeps on opening –** [cf Isa. 22:22]." We see another key in 9:1, below, which may be related to our present verse: "**a Star – having fallen from out of the sky** (or: heaven) **into the Land** (earth) – **and the key of the well** (cistern; shaft; pit) **of The Deep was given to Him.**" (*cf* comments, below). *Cf* 20:1-3, below; I suggest that these are all pictures of the same event: the work of the Christ.

19. "**So then, write what things you see** (or: saw; perceived), **and then what things are presently existing** (or: what they are; what they mean or represent), **as well as which things are progressively about to occur** (or: what is now impending to be coming into existence) **after these things.**

The first clause echoes Isa. 30:8, "Now then, sit down and write these things upon a tablet, and into a little scroll, because these things shall progress to be into the midst of a day, in a season (or: appointed situation) even until into the midst of the Age" (LXX, JM). The context of this passage of Isa. was a proclamation of judgment against Israel. A different echo comes from Ex. 34:27, "And the Lord said to Moses, Write these words for yourself, for you see, upon these Words I have set a covenant and established an arrangement with and for you, as well as with and for Israel" (LXX, JM). The word to Isaiah in 8:1 is more apropos to what John is given here: "Take for yourself a leaf from a large new scroll and write on it with a man's pen, 'In order to take plunder from the spoils quickly, for it is near'..." (NETS). *Cf* Hab. 2:2-3.

In reading this verse as "an allusion to the eschatological text of Dan. 2:28ff," Beale suggests that, "John's present is part of Daniel's latter days" (ibid p 163).

The ambivalence of the tense of the verb in the first clause (which is the aorist, the fact or "snap-shot" tense) leaves us to read this as a simple present tense "**what things you see**," or, as more commonly rendered, "what things you saw, or perceived." In other words, the speaker could be pointing forward, or back to what John had just seen. But the plural relative pronoun, "**what things**," at the beginning of each of the three clauses, points to it not being limited to the 1:12-18, above, but rather to the entirety of the book. Vs. 11, above, has this same verb in the present tense.

Once we read the visions, below, we will see things that refer to John's past, things that are present realities for John, and things which prophesy about events of John's future.

20. "**The secret of the seven stars which you saw upon My right hand, and the seven golden lampstands: the seven stars are agents of** (or: messengers pertaining to, belonging to, or having the qualities and characteristics of; or: folks with the message from) **the seven called-out communities, and the seven lampstands are the seven covenant communities** (or: summoned-forth congregations).**"**

The first clause opens with the word **secret**, which also means "mystery," and is another allusion to the book of Daniel, where in 2:28 we read, "there is a God in heaven (the atmosphere) continually unveiling (habitually disclosing; from time to time revealing) secrets (or: mysteries)..." (LXX, JM). But Paul also spoke of,

> "**preaching and public heralding of the message of and from Jesus Christ – down from** (in accord with; in line with) **an unveiling of a secret** (or: a revelation and a disclosure of a mystery) **that had been being kept silent** (or: quiet) **in eonian times** (or: for time periods of the [preceding] ages; to [the] times [that would] pertain to the Age [of Messiah]), **but now is being brought to light and manifested, and through prophetic Scriptures, down from** (in accord with, on the level of and in line with) **a command of the eonian God**
>> (from the God Who exists through and comprises the ages; of God in relation to the ages; or: = from the God who created, inhabits, owns and rules the ages), **[which leads] into hearing obedience from faith as well as a humble listening and paying attention belonging**

to trust, pertaining to confidence and which comprises loyalty – suddenly being made known unto all the ethnic multitudes (nations; Gentiles; pagans; non-Israelites) **by God**" (Rom. 16:25b-27a).

And then, in Eph. 3:3, he informed them,

"**in accord with an unveiling** (or. down from and in line with a revelation; in keeping with a disclosure), **the secret** (or: mystery) **was made known to me**."

So the audience should now be fully convinced concerning the nature of this book, and how to interpret the secrets that are yet to come. This verse gives an opening explanation of the "**secret**" symbols: "**stars**" and "**the seven lampstands**." The **agents** are an extension of His hand: His sovereign influence and activities – or, they manifest His kingdom and glory. This calls to mind Ps. 19:1,

"The heavens are progressively narrating a story, continuously leading through a description of God's glory and reputation; and the firmament habitually brings back a message and repeatedly announces again a performing of His hands (or: a creation from His hands; [the] working and constructing of His hands)" (LXX, JM).

Note the parenthetical expansion of the genitive/ablative phrase "**the seven called-out communities**," where, "**the seven stars are**:

a) messengers pertaining to, belonging to, or having the qualities and characteristics of; or,

b) folks with the message from **the seven called-out communities**."

All of these grammatical options fit the context, and give us pause for reflection.

Although the planets and constellations of the physical universe indeed fulfill this Psalm, when we consider that the tabernacle/temple was constructed to represent the heavens (God's dwelling place in the midst of Israel), and that the stars (and later, the 12 signs of the ancient zodiac) represented the 12 tribes of Israel, we can discern the story of humanity and the Christ in the symbols of the tabernacle. Israel was given the job of displaying God's glory to the world, and now the called-out communities (the resurrected Olive Tree of the one new, combined humanity – Eph. 2:15 – the new creation) is called to narrate the message of God's glory, the Christ, and to describe the outcome of His infinite grace. We will see this story intertwined within the visions of this book. In the letters of chapters 2 and 3, the figure "agent" stands in this apocalyptic drama as a corporate symbol of the covenant assembly, and it is the agent that is addressed, or for which the message pertains, and you will observe that the pronouncements (evaluations and decision – or, judgments) are mainly presented in the singular and pertain to the group, as a whole.

The Letters (Chapters 2 and 3)

Chapter 2

As we read through the next two chapters, the seven letters can be seen as having similar literary structures. Following the address to each particular community is the instruction for John to "write." Next, each letter takes a specific part of the apocalyptic description of the risen Christ that John has seen in the "Son of Man Vision" of chapter one, and inserts this as the identity of the Author of the letter. This is normally followed by an acknowledgement of the good things that the community has been doing, which is then followed by noting each community's particular area(s) of failure to live the Christ life as they had been taught. Admonitions to change their way of thinking and feeling are followed by warnings of corrective measures that will otherwise be taken by the risen Christ, Who is constantly within their midst (2:1). Then comes an exhortation to hear what the Spirit has been saying – both through the letter that has just been read to them, and what He habitually speaks in their hearts. A promise of reward for those overcoming the difficulties which they face, or who conquer in their inner battles is given as incentive.

Some have compared the form of these letters to what they have called "covenantal form," citing allusions to Deut. 4:2 and 22:16-20 (*cf* Beale, ibid p 227, who references works by Shea, Aune and Strand). Borg observes,

> "His messages to the individual groups commend some for their faithfulness to Jesus and reprove others for their accommodation to the culture and values of empire, calling them back to what they first heard" (ibid p 288).

Metzger points out that, "The literary structure of the seven letters discloses a certain uniform pattern. Each message is prefaced with an identification of the heavenly Christ" (ibid p 29).

1. **"To the agent which is** (or: For the messenger belonging to; In the person with the message which corresponds to; For the agent of and from) **the called-out community within Ephesus, write:**

The apocalyptic imagery in the opening phrases of this verse, and of the "address lines" to the following six communities, has raised questions about the significance of the noun **agent**, or, "messenger." How are we to understand this term? I have only given translations of the Greek *angelos*, refraining from following the tradition that transliterates the word into English (i.e., as "angel") instead of translating it in its proper meaning: an agent; a messenger; a person with a message.

Although the normal way to translate a dative case that is the opening word of an address line that begins a letter is to render it, "To...," since this letter is part of a visionary experience that John is having, and since the genre of this "Unveiling" is apocalyptic literature, I have on offer other functions of the dative: "For, or In." This letter is "for" the entire community. John's reason for communicating Christ's words and thoughts are so that they will end up "in" the entire community.

I have first (in the bold rendering) given the next prepositional phrase, which modifies "**agent** (etc.)," as apposition: "**which is the called-out community**." Since the text of the letter is to the entire community, this seems to be the best reading. However, the parenthetical expansion gives four other genitive-form renderings: "belonging to; which corresponds to; of; from." The first, "belonging to," could refer to a representative of the group who was able to read, or who was a recognized leader of the community. The second, "which corresponds to," could be seen as either a teacher, a leader, or to the corporate entity. The third, "of," is the simple genitive of relation. The forth, "from," expresses the ablative but can be understood in the senses of any of the foregoing renderings.

The expanded renderings also offer alternative renderings of *angelos*: "the messenger," which would seem to indicate an intermediary or a representative; "the person with the message" would indicate either those who understood "the Good News of Jesus Christ," or, perhaps, to teachers who had internalized the "message." Yet, "the agent which is" seems to best fit the structure of these seven, individual letters.

Ephesus was the closest city to Patmos, so it was a logical starting point for these letters. The folks there would have received Paul's circular sermon ("Ephesians") at least ten years earlier. The area of Asia Minor was not new to the "Gospel." As with all the NT letters, they were written both to address problems and to encourage or remind.

> **'The One continuously holding in His strength** (or: the One being constantly strong in) **the seven stars residing within His right hand, the One continuously walking about within the midst of the seven golden lampstands, continues saying these things:**

This apocalyptic identification of the Author of this letter reaches back to 1:20, above. The picture of Christ "holding in His strength the seven stars" calls to mind Paul's words that, "**you folks died, and your**

life has been hidden so that it is now concealed together with the Christ, within the midst of God (or: in union with God)" (Col. 3:3). This proclaims a promise of protection and direction, but also indicates the potential of restraint being exercised upon the communities.

The "right hand" speaks of strength, authority, power and potential action. The second identification of the Speaker describes His location and His area of activity: **within the midst of the seven [called-out, covenant communities – i.e., the "lampstands"]**. So although He is sending these messages through John, He continues being within their midst. He normally uses people to bring His messages to people.

The present tense ("**continues saying**") tells us that this is an ongoing or habitual activity of Christ. We should continually expect to hear from Him. He has not left us alone and on our own. He is involved with His body, as we see laid out through all these seven letters. We live *corem Deo*, in the presence of God. Christ is here now, and His glory is within us (Col. 1:27). Recall that Jesus said,

> "**You see, where there are two or three people that have been led and gathered together into My Name, I am there** (in that place) **within the midst of and among them**" (Mat.18:20).

We are not waiting for Him to return; He is here, for He never left. We are with Him on Mt. Zion, as we read in Heb. 12:22ff, "**you folks have approached so that you are now at Mount Zion – even in a city of a continuously living God**… **and in** (or: to) **Jesus, a Medium of a new and fresh** (young; recently-born) **arrangement** (covenant)." Also, Paul wrote to Colossae,

> "**Since, therefore, you folks were awakened and are raised up together in the Christ** (or: If, then, you are aroused and raised with the Anointed One), **be constantly seeking and trying to find the upward things** (or: the things being above), **where the Christ is** (exists being)…" (Col. 3:1).

Let us keep this in mind as we read through this Unveiling of His presence.

2.   *I have seen, and thus know, your* [note: the pronouns and verbs are singular] **works** *(acts; deeds),* **and your exhausting labor, and your remaining-under to give support** *(or: patient endurance),* **and that you are not able** *(have no power)* **to bear up** *(lift up to carry; or: put up with)* **worthless people** *(folks who are not as they ought to be; evil men; ugly situations of bad quality),* **and you put to the proof those declaring themselves to be envoys** *(representatives; "apostles") –* **and they are not – and you found them false** *(liars; deceivers);*

I inserted the note concerning the message being written with singular pronouns and verbs to alert the reader that the community was being addressed as a whole, as a single unit: Christ's representative (agent) in Ephesus. Christ is within their midst and knows of their "**exhausting labor**" and how they, as a congregation, are "**remaining under to give support**" in difficult situations, displaying patient endurance both to their fellow members and to folks within the surrounding city.

He has observed that they "have no power," and so are "**not able to bear up worthless people**, or folks who are not as they ought to be." Neither can this community put up with evil men, nor can it "lift up and carry (i.e., support or handle) ugly situations of bad quality." This community lacks ability to deal with such people, possibly because of being exhausted. But if we take the verb as meaning "put up with" (an extended application of the verb), then this can be seen as a compliment: they deal with such folks or these ugly situations. This same verb is used in the next verse, but seemingly with a different application.

Christ also noted that this community followed John's advice in 1 Jn. 4:1,

"**Beloved ones, stop believing** (or: you must not continually believe or put trust in; being loyal or pledging allegiance to) **every spirit** (or: expression of some influence; breath-effect; attitude), **but rather, you folks must constantly examine, test and prove the spirits** (influences; attitudes) **to assay** (or: prove) **if they are existing from out of God, because many false prophets have gone** (or: come) **out into the ordered System** (world of societal culture, government, economy and religion) **and continue there**."

Apparently these lying representatives did not have Christ's spirit or attitude, but perhaps came with a spirit of religion. Paul dealt with this in Galatia and wrote to the community in Rome to warn them of the same. Dealing with such folks had exhausted them.

Paul had given similar advice in 1 Cor. 14:29,
"**Now let two or three prophets be speaking, one after another, and let the other folks continue thoroughly sifting and sorting so as to fully evaluate and reach a decision**."
Those in Ephesus had obviously done this and found that some, probably Judaizers who wanted to bring Christians back under the Law, had come as though Christ had sent them. They presented "another gospel" (Gal. 1:6-12). It is also possible that these false envoys were trying to bring the Ephesian community under control of the called-out group in Jerusalem. In Acts, 20:29-30, when Paul is saying goodbye to the elders at Ephesus, he foresaw what would later happen there,

"**Now I myself have seen and am aware that, after** (or: with) **my spreading forth as dust and ashes** (= going away, so as to be out of reach), **heavy** (= burdensome and oppressive) **wolves will enter into the midst of you folks – folks by habit not sparing** (or: treating with tenderness or forbearance) **the flock, and men from among you yourselves** (= from your own community) **will of themselves proceed standing up, repeatedly speaking things having been thoroughly turned and twisted** (things that are distorted and not straight), **to progressively drag** (or: draw; [D & p41 read: turn]) **away the disciples behind** (thus: after) **themselves**."

What he had predicted had come to pass.

3. ***and you constantly have patient endurance*** *(habitually hold to remaining-under),* ***and you bore up*** *(lifted; carried-on)* ***because of My Name, and are not wearied.***

Christ affirms again that the community "**constantly has patient endurance**" and is "habitually holding [together] to remain under" these situations. Such a repeated compliment must have really encouraged the group. Knowing that God has seen, and is aware of, all their "exhausting labor" must have meant a lot to them. They had done this because of His **Name**. This phrase takes us back to the commission that was given to Christ's apprentices, in Mat. 28:19, to immerse all ethnic groups "**into the Name**" – and we see here that this was Christ's Name. In Acts 3:6b, Peter told the lame man, "**Within, and in union with, the Name of Jesus Christ the Nazarene, start walking, and then keep on walking about** (around)!" Then in Acts. 3:16 he explained,

"**by the faith from** (or: in the trust which has its source in; with the loyalty and reliability of) **His Name, His Name at once made this person firm, solid and stable**."

Despite their exhausting labor, Christ affirms that the group is "**not wearied**." They remained faithful to His Name. We see His Name associated with "His faithfulness" in vs.13, below, and His Word (Idea; message) connected with His Name in 3:8, below.

4. ***But on the other hand, I hold*** *(or: have)* ***[this] down against you: you*** *[note: still singular]* ***sent away*** *(or: left; abandoned)* ***your first love*** *(urge toward reunion; unambiguous acceptance of others as being on the same ground; participating in the others; movement toward overcoming existential separation from another being – Tillich).*

This community is standing before "the judgment seat of Christ" as He sits on the mercy seat in the holy of holies within their midst (remember: they are God's temple; the ark of the covenant was God's throne when He spoke through Moses to the people of Israel and made observations about them and rendered decisions concerning them). The next verse explains how they had "**sent away, left and abandoned [their] first love**." We understand this by what He instructs them to change and do. John is not told about specifics, but just that they had "**fallen**" (vs. 5) by abandoning their "**first urge toward reunion**" – either reunion with God, or with other people. Following Paul Tillich's expanded definitions of *agapē*, we see that they "**sent away unambiguous acceptance of others as being on the same ground**" as they are: they had turned back to the Jews' position of "us-and-them," perhaps from the influence of Judaizers. They left the practice of "participating in others" – living in the true union of the joining that Christ had accomplished (Eph. 2:15), where all are now one New Humanity, the last (*eschatos*) Adam (1 Cor. 15:45). They had abandoned their "movement toward overcoming existential separation from another being." We find this situation addressed in 1 Jn. 2:

> 10. **The person habitually loving** (seeking accepting reunion with) **his brother constantly abides** (remains; dwells; = has his home) **within and in union with the Light, and there exists no snare** (trap-spring; stick upon which bait is put; = cause for stumbling) **within him.**
> 11. **But the person habitually hating** (or: repeatedly having ill-will toward) **his brother** (or: = fellow believer or fellowman) **constantly exists within the Darkness** (the obscure dimness of the realm of the shadows, lacking of the light of the Day) **and so continuously walks about amidst the Darkness, and has not seen so is not aware where he is progressively departing** (or: habitually going away), **because that Darkness blinds** (or: blinded) **his eyes.**

He addressed this topic a second time in 1 Jn. 4:

> 7. **Beloved ones, we are** (or: can and should be) **continuously loving one another, because love** (or: the urge toward reunion and acceptance) **exists continuously** (or: is) **from out of the midst of God, and every one continuously loving has been born, and exists being a born-one, from out of the midst of God, and constantly experiences intimate knowledge of God** (or: comes to know by experiences from God; gains knowledge and insight by the experience which is God).
> 8. **The one not habitually loving has not come to know God by intimate experience, because God continuously exists being Love** (or: for God is Love and Acceptance).

It is possible that this abandoning of love was connected to what Jesus said in Mat. 24:12,

> "**because the lawlessness is to be multiplied and increased, the majority of the people's love** (or: the love of many folks; = acceptance from the masses) **will be progressively caused to blow cold** (or: will continue cooling off from the Breath blowing on it)."

5. *You [assembly]* **must be remembering, then, whence you** *[as a single entity]* **have fallen, and you must change your way of thinking and feeling** *(change your frame of mind and your perceptions),* **and you** *[group]* **must do** *(perform; construct)* **the first works** *(deeds; actions).* **Yet if not, I am continuously** *(repeatedly; habitually)* **coming to you** *[as a group],* **and I will proceed removing** *(or: moving)* **your lampstand out of its place, if ever you** *[as a group]* **may not change your way of thinking** *(your mind-set and paradigm).*

The Lord is not telling them something new, He is reminding them. This opening remark of His corrective admonition calls to mind 2 Pet. 1:12-13,

> "**Wherefore** (or: For this cause) **it will always continue being my intent to be constantly reminding you concerning these things – even though [you are] being folks having seen**

and thus knowing, and ones being set and firmly established within the truth and reality [that is] being continuously present (existing alongside) **[with and in you]. But I am continuously considering it right, and in accord with the Way pointed out – as long as I continue existing within this tent-effect** (or: tabernacle) **– to keep on arousing and to progress in fully awakening you folks with a reminder.**"

Again, He points out that they "**have fallen.**" Paul used a strengthened form of this verb in Gal. 5:4,
"**You people who in union with** (or: centered in; [remaining] within) **Law continue being liberated and rightwised, from grace** (or: placed in the Way pointed out and included in the new covenant of grace; being given an eschatological transformation, which is favor), **were at once discharged** (made inactive, idle, useless, unproductive and without effect; or: voided, nullified, exempted) **away from Christ – you at once fell out from [the grace and favor]!**"

It was through God's grace that they became able to love, and this very love, which was an impartation of God Himself into them and which was the Love that birthed them into Christ, was the "first love" that they had abandoned. They continued working and being true to His Name, but they had abandoned Him in all their religious works. Jesus pointed out how without thought or awareness His sheep would just automatically feed, clothe, welcome or visit others in need (Mat. 25:34-40) – and He said that in so doing they had done it to Him: they had **loved** Him. But Ephesus had become religious. The Judaizers had apparently produced an unconscious affect upon them. They were being "good Christians" but were no longer accepting the stranger or the foreigner. They were no longer seeking to embrace the demonized. Tillich also described *agapē* as "acceptance of the object of love without restriction, in spite of the estranged, profanized and demonized state of the object" – *Systematic Theology III*, pp 134-138.

Christ calls the entire community to "**change your way of thinking and feeling** (change your frame of mind and your perceptions)." Since we see that they had abandoned love, then this change of thinking and feeling, the change of their frame of mind and perceptions, would seem to suggest that it was in regard to how they thought about "others." They were being called back to non-dualistic thinking and feeling – of seeing that the new creation had joined and reunified all into the One. This was a call to return to the perception of the "other" as a "brother." It meant to frame their corporate mind to see the stranger as a sister, even if she was yet existentially but an ovum in the Jerusalem which is above, and to see her destined end as being a member of the body of Christ.

"**Doing the first works**, performing the first deeds, and constructing the first actions" means (in this context) living out works, performance and deeds that are Love. Jesus told His hearers:
"**Be constantly loving your enemies** (urging toward reunion with, and accepting as persons standing on the same ground, those folks hostile to you; [comment: this could have applied to the Romans, as well as to personal enemies]), **and be habitually praying goodness over the people continuously persecuting you** (constantly thinking and speaking on behalf of the folks repeatedly pursuing you to have ease and well-being)" (Mat. 5:44).

I think that the Spirit (vs. 7, below) is still saying that to the covenant communities. In Jn. 15:13 we find Jesus describing a "first work":
"**No one continues holding** (or: having) **greater love than this: that someone should place** (set; lay; lay down) **his soul** (or: soul-life; inner being; self; person) **over [the situation or circumstances of]** (or: on behalf of) **his friends.**"

Another instruction that came through John is found in 1 Jn. 4:16b-18,
"**God exists continually being Love** (God is Love), **and the person continuously remaining** (dwelling; abiding) **within, and in union with, the Love, is continuously remaining** (dwelling; abiding) **within, and in union with, God – and God constantly dwells** (remains; abides) **within him and in union with him. Within this the Love has been brought to its goal, been**

matured, reached its destiny and is now perfected with us, to the end that we may continuously have confident freedom of speech (the boldness of a citizen to speak publicly without fear of punishment) **within the day of sifting and separation** (distinction, evaluation and decision; judging; judicial proceeding; or: administering of justice), **because just as That One is, we also continuously exist being: within the midst of this ordered System**
> (or: because in this world of culture, religion, economy and government, even we, ourselves, progressively exist – correspondingly as, and to the according level as, That One continuously exists and is progressively being). **Fear does not exist within the Love, but rather perfect love** (mature love; love having reached its goal) **repeatedly** (habitually; progressively) **throws the fear outside, because the fear constantly has and holds a pruning** (a curtailment; a checking; restraint; a lopping off – thus, a correction). **But the one habitually fearing or dreading has not been perfected within the Love** (has not been brought to the destined goal of maturity – in union with love)."

Another beautiful text comes through the hand of Paul in 1 Cor. 13:7,
> "**[Love] continuously covers all mankind; it is habitually loyal to all humanity; it constantly has an expectation for all mankind; it is continuously remaining under and giving support to all people.**
> (or, since "all" can also be neuter: It [i.e., unambiguous acceptance] progressively puts a protecting roof over all things; it is habitually trusting in, and believing for, all things; it is continually hoping in or for all things; it keeps on patiently enduring all things.)"

The last half of this verse instructs us that Christ is, "**continuously** (repeatedly; habitually) **coming to [them,** as a group]." We have no reason to think that He has ever stopped visiting His called-out communities, both to bless and to correct. Here, because of the abandonment of the core essence of being a covenant community, He warns of an action that will disqualify them as being folks that are "the light of the world" (Mat. 5:14). He tells them that He, "**will proceed removing** (or: moving) **your lampstand out of its place**." Bruce Metzger observes here,
> "The presence of Christ departs when well-intentioned people, zealous to find the right way, depart from the ultimate way, which is love" (ibid p 32).

Being a religious community that does not reflect what God is turns that community into a club that has rules concerning their own views of morality. For many in the 1st century, this would have been a falling back into Judaism with its "us-and-them" mentality. It would be an echo of 1 Sam. 4:21,
> "Ichabod… The glory is departed…"

There it was due to the departure of the ark of God; here it would be the departure of the lampstand from the holy place. What would be left would be darkness. History has born this out. What happened to the leadership in Jerusalem could also happen in Ephesus,
> "**God's reign** (or: the kingdom of God; the influence and activity of God's sovereignty) **will be progressively lifted up away from you folks, and it** (or: she) **will proceed being given to an ethnic multitude** (or: nation; people group; swarm of people) **consistently producing its** (or: her) **fruit!**" (Mat. 21:43).

As Beale points out (ibid p 231), "That the primary meaning of lampstand is that of witness is confirmed in Rev. 11:3-7, 10…" *Cf* Mk. 4:21 and Lu. 8:16.

In regard to the warning of purposeful, repeated, or habitual, coming to them, Simmons points out that "Five times in chapters two and three Christ says he is coming (Rev. 2:5, 16, 25; 3:3, 11)" (ibid p 78).

The symbol of the lampstand is an echo of Zech. 4, which presents a temple setting that this letter again echoes and expands in 11:3-12, below, and is also a reference to Isa. 42:6b, where Israel was "called" to be "a light of the nations (Gentiles; non-Israelites)." This is the same mission into which the Gentile communities were grafted (Rom. 11:17ff). It was not a call into a "bless me club." Isa. 49:6 repeats this call where His Servant, and servants, are given "for a light of the nations (ethnic multitudes), for you to become deliverance, rescue and healing unto the ends of the land/territory/earth." Jesus picked up this theme in Mat. 5:14-16,

> "**You folks, yourselves, exist being** (are) **the light of the ordered System** (the world of culture, religion, politics, government, and secular society; = the human sociological realm; or: the aggregate of humanity). **A city located up on a mountain** (or: situated on top of a mountain range) **continues unable to be hidden or concealed. Likewise, people are not normally lighting a lamp and then placing it under the measuring bowl** (or: a one-peck grain-measuring basket), **but rather upon the lampstand – and it continues shining and giving light for all those within the house. In this way, let the Light, which you folks possess** (or: which has a source in you folks; or: which you people are), **shine in front of mankind** (before humans), **so that people can see your fine works** (or: the beautiful works that you are; the ideal acts which come from you folks) **and they can give glory to** (or: and [these deeds; or: these works of beauty] will bring a good reputation for) **your Father – the One in union with the atmospheres [that surround you folks]** (or: within the midst of the heavens)!"

Yet we should also recall that Jesus gave a warning of losing what one has, as is stated in Mat. 13:12; 25:29, Mk. 4:25 and Lu. 8:18; 19:26. What should be especially observed in this warning to Ephesus is that the risen Christ promises to historically invade their existential existence with a judgment (a decision and a resultant action). Throughout these letters we see Him presently involved with these communities, constantly present among them, and ready to act on their behalf. He is not an absent Head of the body.

6.   *But still, this you do have, that you are constantly hating the works (acts; deeds) of the Nicolaitans, which I also continuously hate (detach from; regard with ill-will).'*

He now graciously ends with another compliment to lift their hearts. We are not told what the "**works, acts or deeds of the Nicolaitans were**," but He tells them that He **hates, detaches from and regard with ill-will** these activities. The term Nicolaitans comes from *nikaō*, which means "to conquer, be victor and overcome," and *laos*, which means "the people." There is speculation as to whether this referred to the followers of an actual person, Nicholas, or that this term is symbolic. Those of the latter persuasion – and keep in mind that this is a book of symbols and figures, as are the names Balaam and Jezebel (vss. 14, 20, below) – view this phrase as indicating the doctrine which instituted a separation within the body of Christ and created a hierarchy: the "rulers" later known as the clergy, while those of the communities who were not professionals, or were persons who did not hold an office within this hierarchy, became known as the laity. Whether this is the meaning of the word, or not, this latter situation did in fact develop in the Catholic Church, and continues on in Protestantism. However, this may be reading history back into our text. But if we look at the meaning from the Greek elements of the word, we see that the Lord hates a teaching which results in people being conquered. This can come without any formal hierarchy, as from peer pressure to do whatever a group leader, or their "prophet," tells them to do. 1 Pet. 5:2-3 comes to mind where Peter admonishes,

> "**you folks shepherd** (i.e., lead to pasture, feed, tend, protect, care for) **God's little flock [that is] among you folks, constantly watching over [them], not in a forced manner** (not by exercising compulsion or constraint; or: not unwillingly), **but to the contrary, without compulsion** (engendering volunteering; yieldingly; or: voluntarily; willingly), **in accord with** (or: in line with and corresponding to; in the sphere of) **God; neither with eagerness for dishonest gain** (greedily; for the low reason of what you can get out of it), **but rather, readily rushing toward it with passion. Nor yet as ones constantly exercising down-oriented lordship** (acting as owners or masters, bearing down with demands) **of the members of the inheritance** (of those who are the allotments of the heritage; or: of those considered to be small objects to be

used in assigning positions or portions), **but to the contrary, progressively becoming beaten models** (types made by the strike of a hammer; examples) **for the little flock.**"

Christ came to set us free from the rule of any priesthood or professional scholar (as were the "scribes" among the Jews of that period) or religious elite (as the Pharisees). He hates a teaching that establishes or supports such a system or arrangement.

The Nicolaitans are also in Pergamum (vs. 15, below). Barclay suggests that the name "Balaam" (vs. 14, below), "can be derived from the two Hebrew words, *bela*, to *conquer*, and *ha'am*, *the people*. The two names, then, are the same and both can describe [a]… teacher who has won victory over the people and subjugated them…" (ibid p 66; emphasis original; brackets added). Rather than being a name, this term may be a figure for the false emissaries referred to in vs. 2, above. By leaving some ambiguity, the admonition can refer to any false leader who does not truly represent Christ.

7. "Let the person having an ear listen and hear what the Spirit is repeatedly saying to, in and by (or: the Breath-effect is continuously laying out for) **the called-out communities:**
> '**In and by the one** (or: To or for the person) **continuously overcoming** (habitually conquering; normally victorious) **I will continue giving by and in him** (or: to him; for him) **to eat from out of the substance of the tree** (wood; log; post) **of the Life which continuously is** (exists being) **within the midst of God's paradise.**' [note: same word in Gen. 2:8, LXX; Luke 23:43; a garden of fruit trees]

The admonition of the first clause calls to mind the teaching style of Jesus, as in Mk. 4:9 when He had finished the parable,
> "**The one continually in possession of** (habitually having) **ears to continue hearing, let him continue to listen and be hearing!**"

Metzger comments, "Of course everyone has ears, but the sense here is that everyone who has spiritual perception should listen" (ibid). In discussing Jesus' statements in the Gospels about folks who have ears, John Dominic Crossan takes a different view:
> "The enigmatic injunction should be interpreted in the simplest possibly way. It means, on the lips of the historical Jesus, 'You have ears, use them; what I say is as clear and obvious as I can make it; all you have to do is listen'…" (*The Historical Jesus, The Life of a Mediterranean Jewish Peasant*, HarperSanFrancisco, 1992 p 349).

We should also point out the present tense of the verb "**saying**." The Spirit is repeatedly speaking to the called-out communities. The Breath-effect is continuously laying things out for the group to hear. From the phrase "the person having an ear" we can conclude that not all are given this "ear" (or, ability to hear), and thus cannot hear the effect of the Breath of God. Recall Heb. 5:14,
> "**But solid food belongs to perfected ones** (complete and mature ones; ones who are fully developed and have reached the goal of their destiny) **– those, because of HABIT, having ORGANS of PERCEPTION trained as in gymnastic exercise and thus being skilled, because of practice, and disciplined with a view to a discerning** (or: when facing the act of separating, making a distinction and then a decision about)…"

In Rom. 10:17, Paul informs us about how "hearing" comes to us,
> "**Consequently, the faithfulness** (or: the trust and faith; confidence; loyalty) **[comes or arises] from out of the midst of, or from within, hearing, yet the hearing [comes] through a gush-effect of Christ, even through the result of a flow which is Christ** (or: through Christ's utterance; through something spoken concerning Christ; or: by means of a declaration which is anointed, or from Christ; through a word uttered which is Christ; [other MSS: God's speech])."

We also need to be aware of the functions of the dative case that are on offer in the plural noun "called-out communities." What the Breath-effect lays out is not just for one particular group. But the Spirit repeatedly speaks TO the communities, speaks IN the communities, and speaks BY the communities.

Here, John Gavazzoni instructs us:
> "Spiritual verities are translated into human, existential experience by the Logos. 'The words I speak to you are spirit and life,' otherwise they become and remain mere metaphors and intellectual conceptual constructs. I've been deeply impacted by the consideration that the very dynamic of the Christ Event, for instance, by the apostolic heralding (not with enticing words of man's wisdom, but in the demonstration of spirit and power) was translated into human experience, and the hearers had co-crucifixion and co-resurrection imparted to them via human language – and that, even in a way maintaining the personality of the speaker – which became the very speaking of God to man by and as the communion of the Holy Spirit. This very moment, I'm seeing how [the] translation option of 'Sacred Breath-Effect' helps clarify this divine action. It's not just the Sacred Breath, it's that Breath's EFFECT.
>
> "If there is preaching that does not reach the level of the above, then we have mere religious mind-trips that provide an artificial satisfaction to the soul, but there is no regeneration and no true renewing of the mind. God's Word is truly 'living and operative.' It's not that human intellect is bypassed; it's instead a matter of heaven and earth becoming one. The truth that God's thoughts can become our thoughts by the action of His Word strikes me with awe" (from a personal email).

In 1 Cor. 15:57 Paul informs us in the Good News:
> "**But grace and joyous favor [is] in God** (or: by God) **– the One presently and progressively giving the Victory** (or: the overcoming) **to us, in us and for us through our Lord** (Owner; Master), **Jesus, [the] Christ!**"

Jesus said in Jn. 16:33b,
> "**Within the System** (controlling world of culture, religion, economy and government) **you normally have pressure and stress** (or: continually have squeezing; repeatedly have tribulation and oppression), **but nonetheless, be confident and take courage! I Myself have overcome and conquered the System** (dominating world; organized arrangement of religion and society; aggregate of humanity) **so that it stands a completed victory!**"

We find light regarding **the one continuously overcoming** from 1 Jn. 5:4-5,
> "**everything having been born from out of the midst of God continuously overcomes** (habitually conquers and is progressively victorious over) **the controlling System** (ordered world of religion, secular culture, economy and government). **And this is the victory** (or: conquest) **at once overcoming** (conquering; victorious over) **the controlling System** (ordered world of religion, culture, economy and government)**: our trust, confidence and faith! Now who is the person continuously overcoming** (or: progressively conquering) **the ordered System** (world; secular realm; religious arrangement) **if not the one continuously believing, progressively trusting and being constantly loyal to [the fact] that Jesus is** (continuously exists being) **the Son of God** (God's Son; or: the Son who is God)**?**"

We are also instructed by Paul in Rom. 12:21,
> "**Do not be habitually conquered under** (or: Stop being overcome by) **the worthless** (the bad of quality; the ugly and unsound; the evil), **but to the contrary, be constantly conquering** (overcoming; victorious over) **the worthless** (the unsound, the bad and the ugly; the evil) **[by being] in union with The Good One** (or: [a participant] within what is profitable; or: in the midst of virtue)."

As we read of "overcoming" or "being victorious" in these letters, we must keep in mind that we can only do this by "abiding in the Vine" (Jn. 15:1ff). It is our participation in Him and our drawing nourishment from Him (Who is the tree of the Life) that we live in His garden.

I have on offer in vs. 7, here, four functions of the dative case of the present participle, *nikōnti* (overcoming, etc.), and of the dative personal pronoun *autō* (him). The functions "in" and "by" can be seen as references to Christ and His work on the cross, even though the Spirit is speaking to the community. These functions can speak of Christ as the Overcomer functioning within His body (the community) so that what He gives to others comes "in" and "by" the community. The functions "to" or "for" would speak to us, and our work of love, in Christ, to which John spoke in vss. 4-5, above. In these latter functions, Christ might be alluding to the Ephesians overcoming (*nikōnti*) the *niko-laitōn* (the Nicolaitans) who were attempting to "overcome" the "people" of the Ephesian community. We also find in 12:11, below,

> "**And they at once overcame** (or: at some point overcome; conquer) **him because of the blood of the little Lamb, and** (or: even) **because of the word** (or: message; Word; Logos) **of their witness** (evidence; testimony) – **and they love not** (or: did not love) **their soul** (soul-life; inner self; personhood) **even to** (or: until) **death**."

And now to the promise that the risen Christ offers. Here is the first allusion to the Garden of Eden setting of Gen. 2:8-9ff. We will find the Unveiling returning to this setting in 22:2, below, as John finished this work. The end returns to the beginning, as in Rom. 11:36a. As to "**eating**" of this "**tree of THE Life**," (note the definite article: this refers to "the Christ Life"), recall that Jesus spoke of our eating Him in Jn. 6:48-57. There in vs. 48 He said, "**I Myself am** (or: continuously exist being) **the 'Bread of the Life'** (or: the bread which is life and which gives life)." Then He said, in vs. 56, "**The person habitually eating** (constantly chewing [on]) **My flesh and repeatedly drinking My blood is continuously remaining** (abiding; dwelling) **within, and in union with, Me – and I Myself within, and in union with, him**." Then in vs. 58b He closes with, "**The person habitually eating** (continually chewing and feeding [on]) **this Bread will continue living** [*p*66 & others read middle: will in (or: of) himself continue living; D reads present: is continuously living] **on into the Age**." When some were offended at His words, He gave further explanation in vs. 63, "**The declarations** (gush-effects; spoken words; sayings; results of the Flow) **which I Myself have spoken to you folks are** (or: continue to be) **Spirit** (or: spirit; Breath-effect; attitude) **and they are** (or: continue being) **Life**." No wonder we are admonished to "**listen and hear what the Spirit is continuously saying**. This is a source of continuous life in Him, just as the branch continuously receives life from the Vine. We find Jesus describing our partaking of Him, via table fellowship, in Mk.14:

> 22. **And during their continued eating, Jesus, taking a loaf of bread [and] saying a good word** (or: expressing the goodness, ease and wellbeing of the Word; or: speaking a blessing), **breaks [it] and gives [it] to them, then said, "You men take** (or: grasp) **this. It is My body."** (or: "Get hold of and receive [it]. This is My body.")
> 23. **Then, taking a cup – while speaking of the goodness and wellbeing of grace, and expressing gratitude [for it] – He gave [it] to them and all the men drank from out of it.**
> 24. **Then He said to them, "This is the blood – pertaining to My arrangement** (My covenant; or: My will; [with other MSS: This is My blood which is the source of the New Covenant]) **– the [blood] being now progressively poured, scattered and diffused out over many [folks; peoples].**

The figure of the "**tree**" bears consideration. The word for tree is literally "wood," and can denote a tree, timber, a log or pole, a staff, or just the material "wood." Benjamin Wilson says, "May here denote an aggregation of *dendra*, or trees, commonly called a wood, or forest" (*The Emphatic Diaglott*). This is the word used in the LXX version of Gen. 1:11, 29; 2:9, 19; 3:4, 9; 6:15; 22:3; Ex. 7:19; 15:25; 25:5; 26:15, etc. Meditation upon this fact has given rise to connecting this "tree" to Christ's execution pole, and by extension, to Christ Himself. We find this picture of paradise in 22:1-2, below, where both a river of life and the tree, or a forest, of life is on both sides of the river, and we are informed that "**the leaves of the tree** (wood; timber) **[are given] for** (or: into) **service** (nurture, care; healing or medical service; a body of household attendants) **of the multitudes** (nations; Gentiles; non-Jews; ethnic groups)." [*cf* Ezk. 47:1-12]

Observe the note that I inserted into the translation regarding the word **paradise** in the last clause of the verse. Here John uses the same Greek word that the LXX used in Gen. 2:8. This is a symbolic reference but it is not mythical. God's people – those who were chosen to be a light to the world – were often described by agricultural metaphors. There are many metaphors in Scripture that are taken from the plant kingdom: seeds, vines, agricultural field crops, trees, fruit, branches, leaves, roots. They all are usually a figure to share some truth regarding humanity and God's relationship to humanity. Ps. 1 describes an upright person who is in right relationship with God. Vs. 3 tells us, "He is like a tree planted by streams of water, which yields its fruit in season and whose leaf does not wither." Song of Songs 4:12 says, "You are a garden locked up, my sister, my bride..." Ps. 80:8, speaking of Israel says, "You have brought a vine out of Egypt; You have cast out the heathen, and it filled the Land." Isa. chapter 5 is a song of God's vineyard, and vs. 7 tells us, "The vineyard of the Lord Almighty is the house of Israel, and the men of Judah are the garden of His delight." A vineyard or a garden both speak of land that is tended by its owner. In 1 Cor. 3:9b Paul tells the community there, "**You folks are God's farm** (or: field under cultivation)." A "garden of delight" well describes a "paradise." In Rom. 11:17, Paul compares the life of Israel to an olive tree. Jer. 11:36 says, "a green olive tree, fair with goodly fruit, did Yahweh call your name... and the branches thereof shall be broken." Ps. 128:3, "... your children [are] like plantings of olive trees." In Prov. 3:13-18 we see that, "Wisdom... is a tree of life to those laying hold on her... by Wisdom Yahweh founded the earth..." Prov. 11:30, "The fruit of justice (fairness; equity; rightwised relationship) is a tree of life;" 13:12, "But a tree of life is desire fulfilled;" 15:4, "Gentleness of the tongue is a tree of life." From these OT expressions, the tree of life speaks of community and relationships.

In the garden story of Gen. 3, the Garden/Paradise was a place of communion with God. So we have the statement by Jesus, in Lu. 23:43, "**Today you will be** (or: be existing) **with Me in the midst of Paradise**." If we connect this with 22:1-2 and 21:2-10, below, we realize that Jesus was telling the dying criminal that he would join Jesus in the new Jerusalem, which Paul referred to as "the Jerusalem which is above" (Gal. 4:26) and which the writer of Hebrews described in Heb. 12:22-24. In the 1st century *Odes of Solomon* we find believers admonished:
> "But put on the grace of the Lord generously, and come into his Paradise, and make for yourself a crown from his tree" (20:7, translated By J.H. Charlesworth; *The Old Testament Pseudepigrapha*, Vol. 2, Hendrickson Publishers, 2013 p 753).

As we are led full circle in 22:14, below, we find this same tree of the Life associated with the City, the New Jerusalem, and also connected with the cleansing work of Christ:
> "**Blessed** (Happy) **folks [are] the ones** (folks; people) **continually washing their garments** (equipment) [other MSS: continually doing His inner goals], **to the end that their authority** (or: right from out of Being; privilege) **will continue being over** (or: upon) **the tree** (pole) **of The Life, and they may enter into the City by the gates**."

D'Aragon points out, "The decree that excluded man from the tree of life (Gen. 3:22f) is now abrogated by Christ..." (ibid p 473). In 22:2b, below, we are given the purpose for having access to this Tree of the Life:
> "**the leaves of the tree** (wood; timber) **[are given] for** (or: into) **service** (nurture, care; healing or medical service; a body of household attendants) **of the multitudes** (nations; Gentiles; non-Jews; ethnic groups)."

Christ's firstfruits of His harvest, His "elect," have been chosen to minister healing life to the rest of the harvest. In the *Psalms of Solomon* 14:3 (considered to be written in the 1st century AD) we read, "the Lord's paradise, the trees of life, are his devout ones" (translated by R.B. Wright, *The OT Pseudepigrapha*, Vol.2, ibid p 663). Simmons insightfully points out that in the New Jerusalem, "the tree of the knowledge of good and evil is not present" (ibid p 81).

8. **"And in and for the agent which is** (or: For the messenger belonging to; In the person with the message which corresponds to; For the agent of) **the called-out community within Smyrna, write:**
> **'The First and the Last, the One Who came to be** (was birthed) **a dead one, and yet lives** (or: lived; or: came to life), **is presently saying these things:**

The introduction of this letter takes another piece of the Son of man vision of chapter 1, giving a description of the risen Christ that is similar to 1:8, 17-18. Here the tense of the verb "live" is aorist, the fact tense indicating that He "**lives**," or, it can be used as a simple past, "lived," speaking in reference to His resurrection. That He came to be a "**dead one**" indicates the literalness of His death on the cross, but also can be a reference to His taking the form of a servant, as we are instructed in Phil. 2:7-8,

> "**He empties Himself** (or: removed the contents of Himself; made Himself empty), **receiving** (or: taking; accepting) **a slave's form** (external shape; outward mold), **coming to be** (or: birthing Himself) **within an effect of humanity's** (mankind's; people's) **likeness. And so, being found in an outward fashion, mode of circumstance, condition, form-appearance** (or: character, role, phase, configuration, manner) **as a human** (a person; a man), **He lowers Himself** (or: humbled Himself; made Himself low; degrades Himself; levels Himself off), **coming to be** (or: birthing Himself) **a submissive, obedient One** (one who gives the ear and listens)…"

He came to be one of us, and lived among those who were, "**continuously existing being dead ones by** (or: to; with; in) **the results and effects of your stumblings aside** (offenses; wrong steps) **and failures to hit the mark** (or: mistakes; errors; times of falling short; sins; deviations)" (Eph. 2:1).

The proclamation here calls to mind the promise in Rom. 8:11,

> "**Now since the Breath-effect** (or: Spirit; Attitude) **of the One arousing and raising Jesus forth from out of the midst of dead folks is continuously housing Itself** (making His abode; residing; making His home; by idiom: living together as husband and wife) **within, and in union with, you folks, the One raising Christ Jesus forth from out of dead ones will also continue progressively giving Life to** (or: will even habitually make alive) **the mortal bodies of you folks** (or: your mortal bodies) **through the constant indwelling of His Spirit** (or: the continual in-housing of His Breath-effect; the continuous internal residing of the Attitude, which is Him,) [other MSS: because of His habitually-indwelling Spirit] **within and among you folks.**"

Hyles (ibid p 116) points out that the meaning of Smyrna is "suffering or bitterness." Death may come to them, but because He is the resurrection, and as He told Martha, "**The one progressively believing and habitually putting trust into Me, even if he may die-off** (or: die-away), **will continue living** (or: will proceed being alive)!" (Jn. 11:25). Furthermore, Paul instructs us in Rom. 6:

> 5. **For since** (or: You see, if) **we have been birthed** (have become; have come to be) **folks engrafted and produced together** (or: planted and made to grow together; brought forth together; congenital) **in, by, to and with the result of the likeness of** (or: the effect of the similar manner from) **His death, then certainly we shall also continue existing [in and with the effects of the likeness] of The Resurrection**....
>
> 8. **Now since we died** (or: if we die) **together with Christ, we are continuously believing** (relying; trusting) **that we shall also continue living together in Him** (by Him; for Him; to Him; with Him).

9. ***I have seen, and thus know** (am aware of) **your works** (deeds; actions) **and pressure** (squeezing; tribulation) **and poverty – but rather, you are rich – and the blasphemy** (slanderous speech; hindering of light) **of those declaring themselves to be Jews – and yet they are not – but rather [are] a gathering-together** (a synagogue) **of the adversary** (Greek: of satan; or: which is satan; or: from the adversary).*

Here He declares His awareness of their activities, the tribulation and pressure which they are experiencing, and the fact of their poverty. Yet He declares that they are rich – quite the contrast to what He says of the 7th church (3:17, below). This paradox of being in poverty, yet being **rich**, should be understood to apply to two different realms: the first to the material realm; the second to the realm of spirit and God's kingdom, reign and sovereign influence/activities. Their riches were described by Paul in Col. 1:27, "**the riches of the glory of this Secret within the multitudes** (among the nations; in the Gentiles; IN UNION WITH the swarms of ethnic groups), **which is Christ within [them]**." Then in Col. 2:2-3, Paul explained,

> "**all the riches pertaining to the state of having been brought to fullness from the comprehension** (or: which is the joint-flow of discernment) **[leading] into full, accurate, intimate and experiential knowledge and added insight of God's Secret: Christ, within Whom are all the hidden-away treasures of the wisdom and experiential, intimate knowledge and insight.**"

Now what about those who falsely claim to be Jews? Who, in the 1st century, would claim to be Jews but those who were actually Jews by natural birth – or perhaps converts to the Jewish religion? Yet the Lord either calls this claim blasphemy, or refers to some blasphemy or slanderous talk which this group speaks. Either way, the Lord says that THEY ARE NOT JEWS, and goes farther to say what they are: the congregation, or, "**a gathering-together** (or: a synagogue) **of the adversary** (or: of *satan*; or: which is *satan*; or: from the adversary)." What does this mean?

1) Consider the situation in Jn. 8:37-47,
> Jesus said, "**I am aware that you are Abraham's seed** (vs. 37).... **They answered and said to Him, 'OUR father is Abraham'** (vs. 39).... **They said to Him, '...we have one Father: God!'** (vs. 41). Jesus then said, '**You folks, in particular, are** (exist and have your being) **from out of, and have your source in, the ancestor who cast [an object] through [someone]** (or: the father, the devil; or: the devil father; or: the father – the one thrusting [words or issues] through [folks/groups] and dividing them)...' (vs. 44a).

How did He mean that? Is this not a parallel passage? They claim to be Jews (i.e., descendants of Abraham); He said they were descendants of the devil – that the devil was their father, or ancestor! Here in vs. 9 He is saying that they are not Jews, but **rather** are of the congregation **of the adversary** (or: *satan*). I suspect that in both cases they were literally Jews, in the flesh. I also suggest that the Lord in both cases is making a distinction between the flesh and the spirit; between a natural kingdom and a spiritual kingdom; between a natural people and a spiritual people. Historically, "Smyrna was also the center of a large Jewish population with a strong influence on the Roman authorities" (Peter Hiett, *Eternity Now!, Encountering the Jesus of Revelation*, Integrity Publishers, 2003 p 35).

2) Rom. 9:6-8 informs us,
> "**... for all those who [are] from out of Israel, these [are] not Israel, neither that they are seed of Abraham [are they] all children; but in Isaac shall a seed be called to you. That is, the children of the flesh THESE [are] NOT the children of God, but THE CHILDREN of the PROMISE He is reckoning a seed.**"

So it is those who are of the promise who are Israel, and Abraham's seed. In Rom. 8:14 Paul defines those who are existentially God's people:
> "**For as many as are being continuously led by God's Spirit** (or: habitually brought or conducted in [the] Breath-effect which is God; progressively driven along with an attitude from God), **these folks are God's sons** (or: = folks with the character and qualities of God)."

Then Gal. 3:29 tells us, "**And if you [are] Christ's consequently you are Abraham's seed, and heirs according to PROMISE.**" And Gal. 3:7 says, "**Be assured, consequently, that the folks [springing] forth from out of the midst of faithfulness** (or: whose source is faith, trust and confident loyalty), **are sons of Abraham**." So it is of promise, of being led by God's Breath-effect, and of faithfulness and trust. It is not of flesh. Thus, those who are not of Christ's faith, and are not born of spiritual birth (i.e., of promise, as was Isaac; or as Jn. 1:13 puts it, "**Who were born not out of bloods [natural genealogy, like literal Jews in the flesh], nor out of flesh's will, nor out of a man's will, but rather, out of God**") – these are of their father, the devil, and belong to a congregation of satan. In other words, they are adversaries of the called-out community – be they Jews, or pagans. Obviously these would be religious people, but they are trying to be and claiming to be something that God says they are not. The final phrase of the verse is offered in apposition, which would make the last affirmation read: "*a synagogue which is satan*." This may be giving us a definition of what the term *satan* means, in the Unveiling. By rendering that same phrase as an ablative, we would have, "*a gathering-together from the adversary*," which would be referring to a particular group that was set in opposition to the covenant community and was bringing "*pressure (squeezing; tribulation)*." These may possibly have been literal Jews who had joined the Caesar cult (idolatry was far from unknown in Israel's history); they may have been from the Jewish religion; or they may have been Judaizing Christians.

Although this letter contains no criticism of the Smyrna called-out folks, it is instructive to become aware of their environment of not only a large population of Jews (Simmons, ibid p 81; Hiett, p 35), but that it had a renowned loyalty to Rome and its ritual worship of the emperor. Almost three hundred years earlier, "the first temple in the world dedicated to the goddess Roma was built in Smyrna," (Metzger, ibid p 33). Also in the first century a "magnificent temple in honor of the Emperor Tiberius" was dedicated, so that the city became "a center of worship of both Rome and Caesar" (ibid).

10.   ***Do not be habitually fearing things which you are about to experience*** *(or: to suffer; in which you are about to have sensible experience).* ***Consider: the one who thrusts-through*** *(the one who casts adversity through your midst; the devil)* ***is about to thrust some from among you into prison*** *(or: jail),* ***so that you may be tried*** *(put to the proof),* ***and you will continue having pressure*** *(squeezing; tribulation)* ***[for] ten days.***

        Progressively come to be a faithful and reliable person *(or: You must be being birthed a trusting and loyal one)* ***until death, and I will continue giving Life's wreath to you*** *(or: for you the wreath of The Life; or: the victor's symbol, which is life in you).*'

This is an admonition to fear nothing of their continual experiences. This applies to us all. He has not given us a spirit of fear, for, "**perfect love thrusts fear outside**" (1 Jn. 4:18). "**Since God is for us, who or what can be against us?**" (Rom. 8:31). What we are not to fear involves all of our experiences – not just suffering.

A specific word of knowledge is given concerning certain folks of the called-out in Smyrna: their upcoming 10 days of pressure in the local prison, or jail. Simmons (ibid p 85) looks to OT examples of testings, frustrations or predicaments that were associated with the number 10: In Gen. 31:7,41, Laban changed Jacob's wages "ten times." Then,

> "the children of Israel tempted God 'ten times' (Nu. 14:22); and Job complained that his friends had reproached him 'these ten times' (Job 19:3); Zech. 8:23 says ten men of the nations would take hold of the skirt of him that is a Jew, saying 'We will go with you: for we have heard that God is with you.' There were ten plagues visited upon Pharaoh (Ex. 7:19-12:30.... Finally, Daniel and his fellows were tested ten days (Dan. 1:12, 14)."

So we can see the number ten had a history in OT writings of being associated, symbolically, with trial, predicament or hard times. But at the same time, it speaks of something of short duration.

Now for us, reading this later, we can see the kinds of thrusts we can expect to encounter: pressure and imprisonment – whether physical, emotional and/or spiritual. Then we read, "**Progressively come to be a faithful and reliable person** (or: You must be being birthed a trusting and loyal one) **until death**..." The statement is in the imperative voice, but it is a verb of coming into existence, or, being born. The bold rendering is an empowering directive, the Voice of creation; the parenthetical alternative speaks of a process that must be brought upon us: birthing. We are called into continuous transformation, which can often be compared to a born-again experience. This is the work of His love in us. Faithfulness and loyalty are the equivalence of what He refers to as "overcoming." It is the life of Christ living Himself in us. The result is "the wreath of THE Life" – the life of the Christ. Life itself is a gift (Rom. 6:23) – not a prize. But this victor's symbol is THE Life of the Christ being lived out IN us. This "wreath" symbolizes the uppermost realm of "the LIFE" which all are destined to some time live, because of His overcoming in them.

We read in Jas. 1:12,

> "**Happy and blessed is the adult male** [A and other MSS: person] **who is continuously remaining under a proving** (a putting to the proof; or: a trial; an ordeal), **because upon being birthed approved** (or: growing and becoming proved and accepted) **he will continue laying hold of the circle of the life** (or: life's crown; life's encirclement; the encirclement from this living existence; or: the wreath which is the Life) **which He** [some MSS: the Lord (= Yahweh or Christ)] **Himself promised to those continuously loving Him**."

Peter gave a similar promise which says the same thing as 2:10 does here,

> "**and so, with the Chief Shepherd** (or: the Original and Ruling Shepherd) **[thus] being made visible** (being shown in clear light), **you folks will continue bringing to yourselves – with care and kindly keeping – the unwithering and unfading wreath of the glory** (or: the enduring recognition of achievement which comes from this good reputation)," (1 Pet. 5:4).

There may be here an allusion to the "contests" referred to where Virtue tested and presided over the perseverance of the Maccabee brothers (4 Mac. 17:12-18). The reward of victory (overcoming) meant "incorruptibility (soundness in lack of decay) in a long-lasting life (or: in union with a life of much time)" (vs.12). Upon their death, it was said, "Through which, also, in and by God they now continue standing beside [Him, and others] in the throne and live a life of the happy (or: blessed) age" (vs. 18) (LXX, JM).

11. "**Let the person who has an ear listen and hear what the Spirit is presently and continually saying to the called-out communities** (the summoned forth covenant assemblies)**:**
> '**The person habitually overcoming** (or: repeatedly victorious; progressively conquering) **may by no means be injured or harmed from the midst of the second death.'**

This again calls us to listen and to hear what the Spirit is presently and continually saying. What does this promise mean: The person wearing the wreath of the Life and being repeatedly victorious or progressively conquering "**may by no means be injured or harmed from the midst of the second death**?" In 20:14, below, we find the definition of this symbol, "**This is the second death: the lake of the Fire** (or: the basin which is fire)." Also, in 21:8, "... **the lake** (or: basin; artificial pool; marshy area) **continuously burning with Fire and Deity, which is the Second Death**." Are we to infer that one who is not **habitually overcoming** will experience **injury and harm** from this **death**? Paul may have answered this question in his fire metaphor (1 Cor. 3:10-17): "**he will incur a loss** (sustain the damage)," yet, "**he himself will be saved** (rescued and delivered; healed and restored to health; returned to his original state and condition), **and as in this way – through Fire!**" (vs. 15). Let us consider some allusions that may shed light on this enigmatic statement, keeping in mind that this pronouncement is a symbol. Isa. 33:14-15 says, "... who among us can sojourn with a fire that devours? Who among us can sojourn with age-lasting (eonian; that which pertains to the Age [of the Messiah]) burning? He that walks righteously and speaks uprightly..." This last phrase describes the overcomer – this person can sojourn with that fire, for "**even our God [is] a continuously all-consuming Fire** (or: our God [is] also a progressively fully-devouring fire)" (Heb. 12:29). As a physical example of this spiritual experience, consider the story of the three faithful Hebrews in the book of Daniel who were cast into the furnace (Dan. 3). We see that "the Son of man" is there in that fire, and the fire burns up that which binds whoever is cast into it. From this example, we see that overcomers also pass through this "baptism (immersion) of the Holy Spirit" – as John the baptizer put it in Lu. 3:

> 16. **John gave a decided response, repeatedly saying, "I, myself, on the one hand am in the process of immersing** (baptizing) **you folks in** (or: with) **water. Yet on the other hand, the Person stronger than I is now progressively coming – the lace** (or: strap; thong) **of Whose sandals I am not competent** (fit; sufficient) **to loosen or untie. He, Himself, will proceed immersing** (or: baptizing) **you folks within the midst of set-apart Spirit** (or: set-apart spirit; sacred attitude; Holy Breath-effect) **and** (or: even) **Fire –**
> 17. "**Whose winnowing shovel** (or: fork) **[is] in His hand to thoroughly clean** [other MSS: and He will thoroughly cleanse] **His threshing floor and to gather together** [with other MSS: He will collect] **the grain into His storehouse** (granary; barn) **– but then He will progressively burn down** (or: up) **the chaff** (husks and straw; = the useless remains of the dead plants) **with** (or: in) **an inextinguishable Fire.**" [comment: the same fire as in the previous verse; *cf* 1 Cor. 3:7-17].

Isa. 4:2-4 spoke to this same situation:
> "In that day the Branch of Yahweh will be beautiful and glorious.... When Yahweh has washed away the filth of the daughters of Zion, and has purged the bloodshed (or: blood-guilt) of Jerusalem from her midst, by a spirit of judgment, even (or: as well as) in and by a Spirit of burning."

In Isa. 6:6-7, Isaiah is given a visionary experience that described him being made an overcomer:
> "Then one of the burning ones flew to me and in his hand was a glowing (burning; live) coal that he had taken with tongs off the altar. He touched it to my mouth and then said, 'Now consider: This has touched your lips, and it will progressively take away your qualities and activities of lawlessness (or: violations of the Law) and will continue sweeping all around to fully cleanse, purify and remove, as with the scapegoat, your times of failure (areas of error; situations of missing the goal; incidents of sin; qualities of deviation; experiences of sin)." (6a from MT; 6b-7, LXX, JM)

Isa. 43:2b informed Israel what it would be like to be with Yahweh,
> "When you go through the fire, you shall not be scorched, and the blaze, it shall not consume you" (CVOT).

This is a description of experiencing the "**second death**" – the lake of His Fire. Yahweh describes this process in Isa. 48:10b, "I have tested you in a smelting-pot of affliction" (Rotherham). And in Jer. 23:29a we read, "Is not My word a scorching Fire...?" (CVOT). The vision of the Ancient of Days offers this picture: "His throne [was] ablaze with flames; its wheels [were] a burning fire. A river of fire was flowing and coming out from before Him" (Dan. 7:9b-10a, NASB). The "basin of Fire," which is later defined for John as being "the second death," and other visions of fire here in this Unveiling are allusions to OT texts such as these quoted, above. So when we encounter Fire here, these texts should instruct our interpretation of the visions. These OT and NT passages imply an experience of purification through an encounter with God. The overcomer will not be hurt by these experiences – just as the bush, which Moses encountered, was not burned up by the Flame of God's presence.

The second death can be seen as the end of death, i.e., the death of the death which is the carnal, flesh-oriented inner nature of the first Adam within us. Paul informed us, in Rom. 8:6, that,
> "**For the result of the thinking** (mind-set; effect of the way of thinking; disposition; result of understanding and inclination; the minding; the opinion; the thought; the outlook) **of the flesh** (= the human condition or the System of culture and cultus; or: = outward Torah ceremony) **[is; brings] death, yet the result of the thinking** (mind-set; disposition; thought and way of thinking; outlook) **of the spirit** (or: the Spirit; the Breath-effect; the Attitude) **[is; brings] Life and Peace**."

We will further explore this metaphor when we discuss 19:20ff, below. It seems significant that this topic is mentioned in the letters to the called-out communities, thus establishing an association between them and the "lake of Fire," and that the recipients of this Unveiling are alerted to this figure early on in the document.

12. **"And in** (or: to; for) **the agent which is** (or: For the messenger belonging to; In the person with the message which corresponds to; For the agent of) **the called-out community within Pergamos** (or: Pergamum), **write:**
> **'The One constantly holding** (having) **the sharp, two-mouthed broadsword is presently laying out and saying these things:**

That He stresses that He is the one with the sharp sword would suggest His readiness to use it – to do battle, to slay the adversary, to cut off our flesh, to overcome on the community's behalf, as He states in vs. 16, below. We should keep in mind Eph. 6:17b, that,
> "**the Spirit's sword** (the short sword from the Attitude; or: the dagger which is spirit; the dirk which is the Breath-effect) **– [is] the one being God's gush-effect**
>> (or: which is the result of the flow from God; the one existing [as] a result of a flux or an effect of a continuous movement, the source of which is God; or: which is a spoken Word of God; or: that being an utterance or declaration which is God)."

"As we consider **the Spirit's sword** (note the genitive of possession; it is God's sword), observe that the 'sword' is a response to a 'flow from God'; it is '**God's gush-effect**' and God gushes Love to His adversaries, His useful kindness converting them. This "dirk" is the Breath-effect, a blowing of the essence of God. The 'short sword from the Attitude [of God]' is 'a result of a flux or an effect of a continuous movement, the source of which is God.' This can be manifested as a 'spoken Word of God,' or, 'an utterance or declaration which is God.' Once again, it is the result or effect of a movement that God makes. The only sword that we handle is something that gushes forth from God Himself. We see this in the apocalyptic symbolism that is pictured as, '**a sharp two-edged broadsword [that] repeatedly goes out** (issues forth; proceeds) **from His mouth**' (Rev. 19:15a), which is a figure of His speaking. Paul may again be echoing Isa. in these last phrases. Isa. 11:4-5 promised, concerning the Branch and Root from Jesse (King David's father) upon Whom the Spirit of God would rest (vss. 1-2),
> 'He will progressively administer justice to [the] low person (make decisions in and for a humble or depressed one) and will continue testing (or: working conviction from a proof

for) the low and humbled folks of the Land (or: earth). And then He will proceed to strike the Land (or: the earth; the ground) with the Word of His mouth, and in a Breath by means of (or: through) His lips He will continue lifting up (or: taking back; choosing again) the impious person that lacks shame and awe. And so He will continue being girded (tied or belted around the waist) with eschatological deliverance into rightwised relationships in the Way pointed out, and with [His] sides (ribs) wrapped with Truth and Reality.' (LXX, JM)....

"In 2 Thes. 2:8 Paul offers another situation where the **Spirit's sword** is effective,

'the lawless person (the unlawful one; the one without law; the man who violates the Law; the person being contrary to custom) **will be uncovered** (unveiled; disclosed), **whom the Lord Jesus will take back up again** (or: lift up; [reading αναιρεω with Nestle, Tasker & Concordant texts; Griesbach & other MSS read αναλισκω: consume, use up, expend]) **by the Spirit of** (or: the Breath-effect from) **His mouth, and will deactivate** (render inoperative and useless; make inert) **by the manifestation** (the bringing of light upon and setting in full and clear view, causing an appearance) **of his** (or: its; or: His) **presence.**'" (from the author's commentary: *Peter's Encore & Later Paul, comments on Second Peter & Ephesians*, Harper Brown, 2016, pp 252-3)

13. ***I have seen, and thus know** (am aware of) **where you are continually dwelling** (settling down for an abode) – **where satan's seat** (or: the adversary's throne and place of power) **[is]! – and yet you are constantly strong in** (or: getting into your power) **My Name, and did not deny** (disown; contradict; say, 'No,' to) **My faithfulness** (or: trust), **even in the days in which Antipas, My faithful witness who was killed alongside you folks: where satan presently dwells** (or: days of opposition from everyone against the loyal testimony about Me, and faithful witness from Me, which was killed at your side: the place the adversary continuously has an abode).*

We see here that He is also aware of the company that they were keeping, i.e., where they were residing – living their lives – and it is a place, or realm, where satan's influence, or control/domination, is being exercised: "**the authority of the Darkness**" (Col. 1:13). Now that community in Pergamos had been transported out of that authority and into the reign/kingdom of the Son of His love, just as the community in Colossae had been: what had happened? Just as some of the company of Israel in the desert wished to return to Egypt, had Pergamos fulfilled that type and returned to dwell where satan's throne is – under the influence of the System of culture, politics, government and religion (perhaps by Judaizing)? Apparently so. This would no doubt be a place of bondage, as well.

But this verse continues with His noting: "**and yet you are constantly strong in** (or: getting into your power) **My Name, and did not deny** (disown; contradict; say, 'No,' to) **My faithfulness**." To deny Christ's faithfulness is to live one's life without trust in Him or to doubt the effectiveness of the work of the cross (which was His **faithfulness** to the will of His Father). To disown suggests a further stepping away from alignment with the Way that He has pointed out. It implies a way of life that is not joined to the Vine. To contradict His faithfulness, is to take a position that is both hostile to Christ and which would be siding with the Jews, that Jesus was not the Messiah. To "say, 'No,' to" His faithfulness is to either take an attitude of refusal of acknowledging His Lordship or to endeavor to block the effects of His reign. Saul would have been the paradigm of all of these.

The adversary had slain at least one of their brothers there. We are not told who, or what group, had killed Antipas, or whether this name, also, is a symbol or code. It may not even be a name. If we read the text as *anti pas*, i.e., as separate words, we could read the last clause: "even within those days of opposition from everyone against My faithful testimony (or: the loyal witness about Me), which was killed at your side: the place the opponent continuously has an abode!"

The situation calls to mind Lot in Sodom (2 Pet. 2:7-8). This is a remarkable description of a church! It is *satan's* home and headquarters. Note that *satan's* work is normally in the realm of the religious. Even so, they had not denied His faithfulness – which speaks of His work of faith in enduring His cross. Consider the marked parallelism in this verse between the first clause, where He says, "**I have seen, and thus know where you are continually dwelling**," and the last clause, "**where satan presently dwells**." The death of His witness in this context suggests that both are dwelling in the same place. Let us remember, as we today look around at similar situations, that these folks were still His called-out community – just as Israel was still His people even while dwelling in Babylon.

14.   ***But still I am holding down a few things against you: you have there those continuously strong to be retaining the teaching of Balaam, who instructed Balak to thrust a snare in the sight of the sons of Israel to eat things offered to forms*** (or: sacrificed to idols), ***and thus, to commit prostitution*** (= idolatry).

As we move to vs. 14 we can see why the adversary ruled and lived in their environment. Those holding Balaam's teachings would then be like Balak: enemies of God's people. Why else would they want to ensnare the believers to bring God's judgment upon them as in the days of Balaam? (see Num. 25:1-9; 31:15-16; 2 Pet. 2:15; Jude 11) The introduction of idolatry (as in the days of Balaam) was through the bringing into Christianity elements of pagan religions. This echoes Isa. 1:21, "How is the faithful city become a prostitute! It was full of judgment; righteousness lodged in it; but now murderers." God had termed Israel's turning to pagan idolatry as committing prostitution. This brings spiritual death – it murders the inner life of the people.

Borg instructs us,
> "The communities in Pergamum and Thyatira are charged with eating food that has been sacrificed to idols, a symptom of accommodation…. Cumulatively, John's negative indictments portray communities that no longer differentiate themselves from the world of empire" (ibid pp 288-290).

But what is today's counterpart? What are the forms or external appearances (which is the root meaning of the word for "idol") that the adversary holds out for the called-out to partake of, or to co-habit with, in place of the Holy Spirit or in place of Christ's teachings? With Pergamos the problem was false teachings. It would be wisdom to challenge traditional teachings of the institutional church, to see if they align with what is revealed about God in Jesus Christ, and to assess their congruence with His teachings as we follow Paul's teaching:
> "**For though habitually walking about and ordering our behavior within [the] flesh** (= in a physical body; or: = in the human condition), **we are not waging warfare** (or: performing military service) **in correspondence and accord to flesh** (= on the level of estranged or enslaved humanity, or in line with the human condition; or: = in the sphere of old covenant Jewish reasonings), **for you see, the tools and weapons of our military service and warfare [are] not fleshly** (= do not pertain to our human condition; ["are not the weapons of the Domination System" – Walter Wink]), **but rather, [are] powerful ones and capable ones in God** (or: by God), **[focused] toward [the] pulling down** (demolition) **of effects of fortifications** (or: strongholds; strongly entrenched positions [of the "Domination System" – Walter Wink, *Engaging the Powers*]), **progressively tearing down and demolishing conceptions** (concepts; the effects of thoughts, calculations, imaginations, reasonings and reflections) **and every height** (or:

high position; high-effect) **and lofty [attitude, purpose or obstacle] that is habitually lifting itself up against** (or: elevating itself up on so as to put down) **the intimate and experiential knowledge of God, and then taking captive every thought – one after another – and leading them prisoner into the hearing obedience of the Christ** (or: the humble attentive listening, which comes from the Anointed One; or: the submissive paying attention, which is the Anointing), **even continuously holding [them] in a ready state and prepared condition to support fairness and equity, while maintaining rightwised relationships from out of the Way pointed out, for every mishearing** (or: hearing-aside; setting of our attention to the side; or: disobedience) **– whenever your hearing obedience may be made full** (or: as soon as the humble attentive listening and submissive paying attention has been brought to full measure, from, and with regard to, you folks)!" (2 Cor. 10:3-6).

15. *Thus, you also constantly have those being continuously strong in, and retaining, the teaching of the Nicolaitans, likewise.*

These folks also had the teachings of the Nicolaitans, as we saw in vs. 6, above. It is apparent that this teaching had spread in Asia Minor during the 1st century. D'Aragon suggests that, "The Nicolaitans and the disciples of Balaam probably made up a single group" (ibid p 473). From the very beginning, false prophets and false teachers (with their false concepts and flat, literal readings of Scripture) have been the adversaries (the *satans*, the opponents) of the message of the Christ. And they have brought controlling domination in their systems of theology which have engendered division and hate in the place of unity and love. We can hear in this verse what must have frustrated the risen Christ, just as the Judaizers had frustrated Paul. If this name is symbolic, the teaching that had "conquered the people" would have taken their freedom in Christ (Gal. 5:1). I second the admonition of Brian D. McLaren when he says,

"In the tradition of Menno Simons and the Anabaptists, we can learn to proceed less by loud disputation and bitter polemics and more by quietly building communities of peace and practice rooted in the teaching and example of Jesus.… In the tradition of the early Pentecostals, we can experience the fire of the Holy Spirit so powerfully that the dividing walls between races, classes and denomination will burn away" (*A New Kind of Christianity, Ten Questions That are Transforming the Faith*, Harper One, 2010, p 227-8).

Let us have no more Nicolaitans.

16. *You must change your mind (your way of thinking), therefore! Yet if not, I am repeatedly (habitually) coming swiftly in you (to you; for you) [again: you, singular], and I will proceed waging war (doing battle) with them within the broadsword of My mouth.'*

So of what are they to change their mind and way of thinking? First it would be regarding where they were living their lives (or dwelling, vs. 13) – away from where *satan* (some adversary) is having influence over them. Perhaps this would mean leaving a particular congregation (or, perhaps it was in their day a synagogue). Second, it might suggest a change in their thinking concerning having leaders in their fellowship who promote the teachings of Balaam and the Nicolaitans. Keep in mind that these statements are made to the corporate assembly. Thus they should cease to have a tolerant attitude toward these teachings, and toward the fact that such teachings are being given out. We can see that the Lord came swiftly to the leaders and rebels in Jerusalem "with the broadsword of His mouth" directing the Romans to judge them (which judging was concluded in AD 70) and bring an end to the old ways. Israel's history repeated itself. In our day, sometimes the life of the "church" is simply dried up, and sometimes that fellowship disappears, as we have observed or experienced throughout our lives. We should mark the fact that He is **repeatedly** (habitually) **coming** to the called-out, covenant communities. His coming brings His active work among the group. We should also mark the fact that since He **will proceed waging war** (doing battle) **with them** that He has come to be an Adversary to the situations which He has been unfavorably critiquing. But His judgments are always with the intent of bringing folks, and humanity, to a higher level. He takes away the old to establish the new (Heb. 10:9).

The **broadsword of [His] mouth** is a figure for His Word to them, and for any corrective measures which He will announce. We find this sword metaphor used in Heb. 4:12-13,

> "**For the Word of God** (or: God's thought, idea and message; or: the expressed Logos from God; or: the Word which is God) **[is] living** (or: alive), **and active** (working; operative; energetic; at work; productive) **and more cutting above every two-mouthed sword, even passing through** (penetrating) **as far as a dividing** (or: parting; partitioning) **of soul and spirit** (or: of inner self-life and breath-effect), **both of joints and marrows, even able to discern** (separate; judge; decide) **concerning thoughts** (ponderings; reflections; in-rushings; passions) **and intentions** (notions; purposes) **of a heart** (= core of the being). **And no creature** (thing formed, framed or created) **is** (or: exists being) **out of sight** (not manifest; concealed) **in His** (or: in Its – i.e., the Word's) **presence, but all things [are] naked and have been gripped and bent back at the neck** [thus, exposing the face and throat] **to** (or: in; by) **His** (or: Its) **eyes, face to face with Whom** (or: Which) **in us** (or: to us; for us; with us) **[is] this Word** (or: with a view to Whom by us [is] the message and the account; or: toward whom, for us and among us, [comes] the Idea and the Reason)."

I cite this verse again to point to the living, interior work of God's thoughts, ideas and message (e.g., Christ) as He deals with wrong thinking, wrong concepts, wrong attitudes that arise for a wounded or distorted heart. The "warrior" image is an allusion to OT history where Yahweh worked decisively (usually through human agents) to bring correction. Correction is what was needed in Pergamos. That is why He admonished them to **change [their] mind and way of thinking**. The infection of non-Christ-like teaching would destroy the community, and a change, away from the thinking of the Nicolaitans, needed to happen.

17. "**Let the one having an ear hear what the Spirit is now saying to the called-out community:
    'By and in the one** (or: To the person) **habitually overcoming** (repeatedly conquering), **by and in him** (or: to him; for him) **I will continue giving manna having been hidden, and I will proceed to give in him** (or: to or for him) **a white pebble, and upon the pebble a new** (different in character) **name having been written which no one has seen, so as to know, except the one presently receiving it.'**

In this verse comes again the call to listen to the Spirit, Who is constantly speaking to the communities. Here the "hidden manna" is an allusion to the pot of manna which was laid up in the ark, in the holy of holies. We are informed of this in Heb. 9:3-4,

> "**But after the second veil, a tabernacle being called the set-apart of the set-apart ones** (the Holy of Holies; the separated one of the separated ones; = the most set-apart), **having the ark of the arrangement** (or: chest pertaining to the covenant), **having been covered round about by gold, in which [was] a golden pot** (or: urn) **continuously holding** (or: having) **the manna, and Aaron's rod – the one sprouting** (budding) **– and the tablets of the arrangement** (disposition; covenant)."

The concept of "manna from on high" being available "**when the effect of the filling of the time came** (or: that which was filled up by time reached full term)" – Gal. 4:4a – was, among some Jewish groups of this era, understood as an eschatological gift from God at the time of the "consummation." We read in the Syriac Apocalypse of *2 Baruch* 29:3, 6-8 (written in the early 2nd cent. AD) the following:

"And it will happen that when all that which should come to pass in these parts has been accomplished, the Anointed One will begin to be revealed.... And those who are hungry will enjoy themselves... For winds will go out in front of me every morning to bring the fragrance of aromatic fruits and clouds at the end of the day to distill the dew of health. And it will happen at that time that the treasury of manna will come down again from on high, and they will eat of it in those years because these are they who will have arrived at the consummation of time" (translated by A.F.J. Klijn, *The OT Pseudepigrapha*, Vol. 2, ibid pp 630-31).

The *Sibylline Oracles* (dated from the 2nd cent. BC) spoke, in book 7, of the restoration of the world. In 7:148-49 we read:

"There will be no vine branches or ear of corn, but all, at once will eat the dewy manna with white teeth" (translated by J.J. Collins, *The OT Pseudepigrapha*, Vol. 2, ibid p 413)

These early and current prophetic writings may well have informed John's readers about how to interpret the symbol of "manna" in this verse. It was obviously a figure of blessing and provision.

On offer for the first phrase of the proclamation are three functions of the dative case, represented by three different prepositions that express these functions:

"**By** the one habitually overcoming" would indicate the Christ would use this person or group to "**continue giving manna having been hidden**" to those with whom they have contact. Through them the families of the land are to be blessed. This calls to mind the words of Jesus in Jn. 7:38, "**Rivers** (or: Floods; Torrents) **of living water will continuously flow** (or: gush; flood) **from out of the midst of His cavity** (His innermost being or part; or: the hollow of his belly; [used of the womb])" – which would apply to His corporate body, as well as to Himself.

"**In** the one habitually overcoming" states that Christ will provide this manna within the person or within the group.

"**To** the one habitually overcoming" simply identifies the recipient of the gift.

The present tense of the participle, "overcoming/conquering," indicates that this is a way of life: habitual or repeated action. The present tense of the verb, "giving," indicates Christ's continual action of continued giving – a figure of constant provision of spiritual food from Christ. The personal pronoun, "**him**," is also in the dative case, so again on offer are expressions of the potential functions of this case:

"by him" indicating again the instrumentality of the overcomer (e.g., the community) in the giving;
"in him" indicating the sphere where the gift is received;
"to him" would mean that this one receives the gift;
"for him" suggests that the gift of food will be to nourish and bless the receiver.

The ark, within which the manna was hidden, is a figure of both God's throne and also of the body of Christ. Thus we can see both God's provision in Christ, and the nourishment from the true bread from heaven – the Lord (Jn. 6:31-35; 48-51). One must enter into the holy of holies (the reality of heaven, of spirit) to have access to this. We must also be joined to Christ, "**within Whom are** (continually exist) **all the hidden-away treasures of the wisdom and experiential, intimate knowledge and insight**" (Col. 2:3). "**Now we presently and continuously hold** (have and possess) **this treasure within containers** (jars; pots; vessels) **made of baked clay**" (2 Cor. 4:7) – the body of Christ.

"It is the glory of God to conceal a thing: but the honor of kings is to search out a matter" (Prov. 25:2). "**For you folks died, and your life has been hidden so that it is now concealed together with the Christ, within the midst of God** (or: in union with God)." (Col. 3:3). "But we are speaking God's wisdom which has been hidden within a secret, which God previously marked out before the ages, unto our glory" (1 Cor. 2:7). "But decorate the hidden man of the heart with what is incorruptible: a meek and quiet spirit..." (1 Pet. 3:4).

Ray Prinzing, in *Revelation, A Positive Book*, lists five things that a white stone signified: 1) acquittal, at a trial; 2) given to a winner of a race; 3) used in casting of lots in election for "yes;" 4) sometimes handed to a guest as a token of hospitality and a right to all that is in the house; 5) used in the allotting of and for inheritance. Peter Hiett instructs us that, "To control the mob, Rome gave out white stones as tickets to the coliseum to get free bread and watch people die" (*Eternity Now!, Encountering the Jesus of Revelation*, Integrity Publishers, 2003 p 44). Beale notes that the OT describes the manna "as resembling white bdellium stone" (ibid p 253). The LXX of Nu. 11:7 reads, "the appearance was the appearance of rock-crystal." The color "white" also speaks of purity or righteousness. With all these uses as a background for the metaphor, it can be seen that to receive a white stone was a good thing.

In the Scriptures a name signifies a person's character (e.g., Gen. 49, as Jacob blesses his sons; also recall the times God changed a person's name). Receiving a new name (e.g., Simon now being called Peter) would mean to receive a new character – either prophetically, as with Peter, or as the result of overcoming the old character/nature (recall Jacob wrestling with the agent, and the new name Israel). A new name also represented a new relationship to God, or an aspect of a person's calling (e.g., Mat. 16:18). The fact that no one else knows what the new name is suggests that this is a personal thing between God and the overcomer, perhaps that this is an interior event, in one's spirit. We find an almost identical phrase concerning a name in 19:12, below:

> "**having a name having been written** [other MSS: having names written, and a name] **which no one knows except Himself**,"

which is amidst a reference to, and a description of, the risen Christ. We find a similar sense of intimate secrecy in reference to the Father and the Son in Lu. 10:22,

> "**All mankind and All things were given over and transferred to Me by, and under, My Father, and yet no one is in constant, intimate, experiential knowledge of Who the Son is** (exists being), **except the Father, nor Who is the Father, except the Son – and whomsoever the Son is now wanting and continuing intending to at some point unveil** (uncover; reveal; disclose) **[Him]**."

In 19:16, below, a displayed "name" is written upon His outer garment and upon His thigh. This Name is a title: "**King of kings and Lord of lords**." We also find the promise of an apparently displayed name written on "the overcomer" in 3:12b, below:

> "**and I will proceed to write upon him My God's Name, and the name of the City of My God: 'The New and different Jerusalem' – the one habitually descending from out of the atmosphere** (or: heaven), **from God – and My Name, the one new in character and quality** [others MSS: and the new name]."

The writing of these names seems to signify the identity of the one receiving the name. It connects first the overcomer with the "New and different Jerusalem," and then with the risen Christ, who is speaking. This idea is again seen in 14:1, below, "**folks continuously having His Name, and** (or: even) **His Father's Name, having been written upon their foreheads**." Beale offers one view, that the name, here in vs. 17, is "a name that the whole Christian community knows together" and points out that, "all the letters speak… in the singular but with a collective intention…" (ibid p 257). Beale further points out that to receive a new name signifies "membership in the community…" (ibid p 255).

Hiett (ibid p 43) cites Isa. 62:1-2 here, where God says, "For Jerusalem's sake I will not rest…. The nations shall see your vindication, and all the kings your glory; and you shall be called by a new name, which the mouth of the LORD will give." In fact, allusions to Isa. 62:1-5 can be seen throughout Rev. *Cf* Isa. 65:15b.

18. "**And to** (or: in; for) **the agent and message-bearer of, and which is, the called-out community in Thyatira, write:**

'The Son of God, the One having His eyes as a flame of fire and His feet like burnished (or: white) **brass** (bronze; fine copper)**, presently says these things:**

Again, it is obvious that it is Christ speaking here. But why these particular descriptions of Himself? Eyes like a flame of fire emphasize the purifying vision, intensity, and the seeing with the eyes of God. Feet – symbolizing His walk, His path, His way of moving among the called-out communities – that have the character of God's judgment and corrective justice. Both of these elements would let this "church" know that the Speaker is serious, and is a person to be reckoned-with. He walks in judgment – constantly evaluating, making separations and decisions. But all this is for our purification. Recall Mal. 3:3-4,

> "Yet who will endure the Day of His coming? And who will stand up when He appears? For He is like a refiner's fire, and a cleanser of silver. And He will cleanse the sons of Levi, and refine them like gold and like silver. And they will come to be for Yahweh, bringing close [the approach] present in righteousness" (CVOT).

"Thyatira was the smallest and least consequential of the seven cities to which the Revelation was written… but [it] gets the longest letter" (Hiett, ibid p 50; brackets added).

19. *I have seen, and thus know* (am aware of) *your* [singular] *acts* (deeds; works), *and love* (urge toward reunion; participating acceptance), *and faith* (loyalty; reliability), *and service, as well as persistent remaining-under for support* (relentless, humble endurance); *and your last acts* (works) *[are] more than the first ones,*

He commends how they are living – His eyes have seen it all – and He acknowledges an improvement: more works now than at the beginning. His noting their works and actions calls to mind Paul's words in Eph. 2:10.

> "**the fact is, we are** (continually exist being) **the effect of what He did** (or: His creation; the thing He has constructed; the result of His work; His achievement; His opus; the effect of His Deed)**: people being founded from a state of disorder and wildness** (being framed, built, settled and created; being changed from chaos to order)**, within and in union with Christ Jesus; [founded and built] upon good works** (virtuous actions; excellent deeds) **which God made ready** (prepared; or: prepares) **beforehand, to the end that we may, could, should and would walk about** (= live our lives) **centered within and in union with them.**"

Again, notice the singular pronoun "**your,**" for He is speaking to them as a group. He selects four aspects of the life of the community that He is commending: **love,** which is the urge toward reunion with people, which leads to "participating acceptance" of them; **faith,** which can also be understood as a life of trust in God, loyalty to Christ and His mission, and reliability to be counted upon when there is a need; **service,** which describes the way of life for a follower of Christ (Lu. 22:26, 27b); all of which leads to **persistent remaining-under [a situation] for support,** or relentless, humble endurance within difficult circumstances. In all these things, the Thyatiran community had prospered and grown. Notice that He is not commending their "systematic theology" or their "justification theory" or their "Christology" or their "eschatology" or their "hermeneutics" or even their "world view." No, it's all about living the Christ-life, as Jesus described the actions of the sheep in Mat. 25. Or, as Paul emphasized in 1 Cor. 13, it's all about love.

20. *but still, I continue holding* (having) *much down against you, because you are constantly letting-off* (tolerating; allowing; pardoning) *your wife* [other MSS: the woman] *Jezebel – she is habitually calling herself a prophetess – and she is continually teaching and deceiving* (seducing; leading astray) *My slaves to practice*

prostitution *(adultery; fornication)* **and** *(or: that is,)* **to eat things sacrificed to idols** *(things offered to forms and outward appearances).*

Yet we see that there was a problem. Verse 20 addresses the situation figured by Jezebel (1 Ki. 18 & 19) of Israel's history. Ahab's marriage to her was the first instance of a marriage of a heathen princess with a king of the northern kingdom of Israel. Marvin Vincent (*Word Studies in the NT*, Vo. 2, Hendrickson Pub., 1985) pointed out that this alliance was a turning-point in the moral history of Israel. She brought the worship of Baal from Sidon. She tried to destroy all God's prophets in Israel, while installing prophets of Baal and Asherah (the Phoenician "Venus"). Both her name and her activities in Thyatira speak of the introduction of idolatry and elements of pagan religion into the called-out community. The corruption of the message of goodness in Christ began with the called-out's very beginning. Paul fought the re-introduction of Judaism and legalism. Here John writes of Christ speaking out against paganism and idolatry in the covenant communities of Christ. This allusion to Israel's one-time queen, and her idolatry, might also be a subtle reference to the Emperor-worship in Asia Minor, but it also sets the scene for Babylon in 17-18, below.

And further, Jezebel of old exercised control over the weak leadership in Israel (i.e., Ahab, her husband). In 2 Ki. 9:22 Jehu refers to her prostitutions and witchcrafts as being "many." The most basic form of witchcraft is to exercise control by means of a wrong spirit – one that is not holy or that does not spring from love. A church, or a person, that gives-in to a spirit of control – instead of being led by the Holy Spirit – is placing the influence of that spirit (which can come through an individual or an organization) above the leadership of God, and is thus practicing both adultery (for God is our Husband-Lord) and idolatry. We must discern what spirit is trying to influence us – is it God, or that of another? "**Beloved, do not believe [or, obey] every spirit, but test the spirits to see if they are of God, for many false prophets have come** (or: gone) **out into the ordered system** (of religion, culture and government)" (1 Jn. 4:1).

The "Jezebel spirit" – which is manifested through either an individual or a group – is a false representative of God (she merely "**calls herself**" a **prophetess**) and is allowed (tolerated) to operate by the community. This need not be so: the prophetic ministry (figured by Elijah and Elisha) and the anointed leadership (figured by Jehu in 1 Kings 19:16 and 2 Kings 9) can put this to an end. Thyatira is now the third called-out community to be infested with the spirits which lead to immorality, idolatry and false teaching: the Nicolaitans, the Balaamites, and those following Jezebel. By calling Jezebel the **wife** of Thyatira, her connection to the times of Israel's kings (in 1 and 2 Ki.) makes clear the relationship between "the woman" and the community: control of the leadership; persecution of those truly anointed among the community; idolatry and false religion; and accommodation to the surrounding religions.

J. Preston Eby comments on Jezebel prophesying:
> "This should help us see how it is that when the soul speaks – Jezebel prophesies! The soul is always prophesying! The soul is just bubbling over with all kinds of revelations out of the tree of knowledge! The soul wants to serve God just as Jezebel wanted to run the kingdom of Israel, but always in a manipulative, carnal, perverted way. The soul is assertive, aggressive, creative, articulate, seductive, controlling, and demanding. The soul will invent a thousand ways to serve God, none of which are sanctioned by the spirit, born of the spirit, or led by the spirit. Eve and Jezebel are both cut from the same cloth and instead of living by the tree of life they live by the tree of knowledge. The soul wants to serve God independent of the spirit and always quenches the spirit in favor of carnal means and methods" (*Kingdom Bible Studies:* From the Candlestick to the Throne, part 46).

Recall Paul's admonitions to the community in Corinth,

> "**Have you folks not seen so as to know that your** [other MSS: our] **bodies are members** (body parts) **of Christ? Upon lifting up and carrying off the members** (body parts) **of the Christ, will I proceed then in making** (or: could or should I at any point yield) **[them] members** (body parts) **of a prostitute? May it not come to be or happen** (= No way)**! Or, have you folks not seen so as to know that the man continually joining himself** (or: being habitually glued in intimate union) **to** (or: in) **a prostitute exists being one body [with her]? For, He says, "The two will continue existing, being [joined] into one flesh."** [Gen. 2:24] **Now the person continually joining himself** (or: being habitually glued in intimate union; in himself being continuously welded) **to** (or: in; with) **the Lord exists being one spirit** (or: one Breath-effect)**. Constantly flee the prostitution**" (1 Cor. 6:15-18a).

In his second letter to Corinth, Paul made similar, corporate admonitions (2 Cor. 6):

> 14. **Do not of yourself continue** (or: Stop) **becoming yoked differently** (or: unevenly yoked; yoked with ones of a different sort) **with folks without faith** (or: by those without trust; to unbelievers; with disloyal people), **for, what mutual holding** (sharing; partnership; communion; membership) **[have] rightwised living and lawlessness** (or: fairness/equity, and a lack of following rules; [covenant membership] in right relationship which accords with the Way pointed out, and wrong which come from violation of law), **or what common existing** (participation; partnership; sharing) **[is] in light [directed] toward, or face to face with, darkness?**
> 15. **And what joining of voice** (concord, agreement and harmony of sound) **has Christ [when faced] toward Belial** [Hebrew word for "worthlessness"]**? Or what part for one full of faith and trust** (or: portion in a believer) **[corresponds] with one who lacks faith** (an unbeliever; one who is not trustworthy or loyal)**?**
> 16. **Now what mutual deposit** (or: concurrence or agreement arrived by group decision) **[does] God's Temple [have] with idols** (or: external forms or appearances; or: phantoms of the mind; unsubstantial images or forms)**? For, you see, we continuously exist being** (we/you are) **a temple of [the] living God, just as God said,**
>> **"I will proceed to make My home and will continue walking about within and among them** (= I will habitually reside and live My life within and among them)**, and I will proceed existing being** (or: I will continue being) **their God, and they will proceed existing being** (or: will continue being) **My people."** [Lev. 26:12; etc.]
> 17. **On which account [the] Lord says,**
>> **"Instantly go forth from out of their midst and be instantly marked off by boundaries so as to be defined and restricted – and do not continue** (or: stop) **touching what is unclean** (= ceremonially defiled)**,** [Isa. 52:11] **and then I, Myself, will constantly admit you folks and receive you into [Myself; My family],** [Ezk. 20:41]

On this latter passage, Ben Witherington III states, "Paul has in mind not merely participation in idol worship, but rather the problem already broached in 1 Cor. 8 and 10 – that of eating in idol temples" (*Conflict and Community in Corinth, A Socio-Rhetorical Commentary on 1 and 2 Corinthians*, Wm. B. Eerdmans Pub. Co., 1995, p 403). As with Israel's ancient history, associations involving idols were (and still are) a widespread problem for Christians living in the midst of a world of un-Christ-like notions and behaviors.

> 21. *And I give time to her, to the intent that she may change her mind (way of thinking), and habitually she is not intending (or: willing) to change her thinking out of her prostitution (= idolatry, or, association with idol temples).*

This indicates that this spirit (figuratively symbolized as "Jezebel") has no intention of leaving or changing, but must be destroyed from out of the midst. God gives individuals and groups time to change their thinking from this error, and it is in the realm of "thinking" and "attitudes" from which such negative spirits (within individual or groups) arise. This is the reason for the call "**to change her thinking**." We also need to realize that these historical figures that are being employed to describe current situations are not gender-driven metaphors. In Israel's history they happened to be men or women, but the application of these "types" apply to anyone. Today we would refer to this situation as "an addiction," and addictions come in many forms (pun intended: an idol is a form).

From the days of John the baptizer, to Jesus, to Paul, and now to the risen Christ we find the call for us to change our minds and our ways of thinking – for our thinking affects our behavior and way of life.

22. *Consider: I am presently casting her into a bed, and those habitually committing adultery with her into great pressure (tribulation; squeezing) if ever they may not change their minds out of her works (activities; deeds).*

That Christ is "**presently casting her into a bed**" may speak in the metaphor of prostitution/adultery. However, others suggest that this could refer to a "bed of sickness." In the very situation in which this error is operating is the situation in which His correction will come. All involved in this will experience His pressure and trouble – unless they change their thinking on this matter, and refuse to be influenced by the actions and works of this spirit. As with His warnings to Israel, of old, He always gives space and time for folks to adjust to what is right. Adultery is a figure for participating in that which is neither loyalty nor love. It always brings pain. In our day it could be participation in the spirit of nationalism, or racism, or unjust capitalism, or dualism in its many forms. All these attitudes are not the Spirit of Christ, so to participate in them is what the resurrected Christ calls "adultery," as also Paul infers in the quote from 1 Cor. 6, and 2 Cor. 6, above.

The admonition to **change** their mindsets and their focus **out of her** "deeds and activities," calls to mind the words of Jesus, in Mat. 7:22-23,
> "**Within** (or: On) **That Day many will repeatedly say to Me, 'Lord! O Lord! do** (or: did) **we not prophesy in** (or: by) **Your Name? And do** (or: did) **we not cast out demons** (Hellenistic concept and term: = animistic influences) **in** (or: by) **Your Name? And do** (or: did) **we not perform many works of power and ability in** (or: by) **Your Name? And at that time I will repeatedly confess assuredly to them, 'I never came to know or became acquainted with you folks** (or: I not even once had intimate, experiential knowledge of you). **Those people habitually working** (performing; or: making a trade of; making a living in) **the lawlessness are now to go off to a space** (or: territory) **away, and proceed in giving way to Me and making room for Me.'** [Ps. 6:9]

Eby, commenting on the **working the lawlessness** in this Mat. passage, just quoted, paraphrases what Jesus meant, then summarizes:
> "'You did things you wanted to do and you did it as by my authority and at my word – but I had nothing to do with it!.... Nothing that you did led to sonship!.... you worked iniquity, lawlessness, unauthorized activities!' Can we not see by this that within these folks the religious soul is acting independent of the spirit. It is the spirit of Jezebel!" (ibid).)

23. *And I will proceed killing her children within death, and all the called-out assemblies shall know that I am the One continuously searching the kidneys and hearts, and I will continue giving to each one of you down from (in accord to; in the sphere of; to the level of) your [plural] actions (deeds; works).*

Now the judgment given in vs. 23 is, like the rest, a figure. "**Her children**" may refer to her "spiritual descendants," and be an allusion to Ahab's sons being killed, in 2 Ki. 10:7 (D'Aragon, ibid p 474), or, to those of John 1:13 who were born "**forth from the will of flesh**," or "**out of the will** (purpose; intent) **of an adult male**," and not "**from out of the midst of God**." Jesus said in Matt. 15:13, "**Every plant, which My Father – the heavenly One** (or: the One Who inhabits, and can be compared to, the atmosphere) – **did not plant, will be pulled out by the roots**." In this birth/plant metaphor, keep in mind that Jezebel's children are mindsets, perceptions, doctrines and attitudes – not the people, themselves. In the plant metaphor, the people are the soil, the field; the plant is a teaching or a doctrine. Those born of spiritual prostitution would be in this category. But what does this mean? It refers to the inner spiritual condition, for vs. 23 goes on to say that all the called-out groups would know that He Himself is carefully **searching** to see the CONDITION of the **hearts** and the seats of folks emotions (the **kidneys** – a Hebrew figure of speech), and that He knows what kind of birth has taken place. Many folks are "birthed" via an "evangelistic crusade," but few of these were engrafted into the Vine or the Olive Tree. Many are persuaded by human reasoning and become members of some religious organization, but have not been born from Above.

Eby says of this prophesied judgment,
> "The Father is never more close to you, my beloved, than when He is reaching in and taking out of your heart and life those things that hinder the development of HIS LIFE and the manifestation of HIS NATURE.... He casts her into a bed of trouble rather than pleasure.... This is the judgment which will redeem Zion! This is the judgment which washes away the filth of the daughters of Zion and the blood of Jerusalem! This is a revelation of the Lord which starts at the house of God (1 Pet. 4:17) and then flows out from that house to all creation! The sons are the firstfruits – every other man must at God's appointed time pass through the same dealings, the same revelation and purpose of the Father. When the process is completed God will be ALL IN ALL, everything to everybody, the indwelling and controlling factor of every life (1 Cor. 15:28, Amplified)" (ibid part 47).

The purpose clause that finishes this verse is an allusion to Jer. 17:10,
> "I [am] Yahweh [Who] continually investigates [the] heart, [Who] repeatedly tests [the] kidneys (= innermost being; seat of affection) so as to give to each [one] according to his ways; according to [the] fruit of his actions (works; deeds)."

Not only is the resurrected Christ speaking like Yahweh, this allusion would seem to identify Him as Yahweh. In 1 Sam. 16:7b we read, "Yahweh is continually seeing into the heart." This is why Christ characterizes Himself as, "**the One having His eyes as a flame of fire**," in 2:18, above. In Ps. 7:9b Yahweh is described as the God, "testing hearts and kidneys (innermost beings; seats of affection)."

Cf Jer. 11:20; 20:12a; 1 Thes. 2:4b. We also read in Jn. 2:24b, concerning Jesus, and "**the [situation for] Him to be continuously** (habitually; progressively) **knowing all people by intimate experience and through insight**." Then in Rom. 8:27 we are instructed of God's constant, beautiful work on our behalf,
> "**But the One continuously searching** (tracing; exploring; trying to find out [concerning]) **the hearts has seen, and thus knows and is aware of, what [is] the effect of the mind-set and way of thinking of the Breath-effect** (or: the Spirit's opinion and thinking; or: the frame of mind and thought of the [person's] spirit and attitude), **that** (or: because) **down from God** (or: in accord with God; on the level of and commensurate with God) **it** (or: It; He) **continually hits on target within** (encounters and falls in union; obtains within while interceding), **over [the situation of] and for the sake of [the] set-apart folks** (saints; holy ones; sacredly different people)."

The final phrase, "**and I will continue giving to each one of you down from** (in accord to; in the sphere of; to the level of) **your actions** (deeds; works)," when He came to Thyatira, calls to mind the picture of this given in 20:11-13, below, where the same pronouncement is made:

> "**And they are judged** (evaluated) **according to their works** (in correspondence with their actions; in line with their deeds)."

Jesus' actions in Thyatira are an example of "**the great** (= God's) **white** (= pure) **throne**" decisions. The evaluations and judgments are His gift to them, which accord to their deeds and which are in the sphere of their actions. This equates to Rom. 14:10b,

> "**For you see, we will all continue standing in attendance alongside on God's elevated place** (platform or stage which is ascended by steps, from which one speaks in a public assembly; or: we will all repeatedly present ourselves at the seat, dais or throne which is God [some MSS: Christ])."

Note the durative future tense: this predicts that what is happening now will continue happening. He does not change, but continues as a faithful Father, correcting His children.

And in 2 Cor. 5:10,

> "**for it continues** (or: is repeatedly) **necessary for us – the all** (= the whole of humanity) **– to be manifested in front of Christ's elevated place** (a step, platform, stage, or place ascended by steps to speak in public assembly in the center of a city; or: = an official bench of a judge or public official), **to the end that each one may himself take into kindly keeping, for care and provision** (= be responsible for), **the things [done] through** (or: by means of; or: [during our] passing through [with]) **the body – [oriented] toward what things he practices** (or: she accomplished), **whether good or bad, whether serviceable or inefficient, whether fair or foul, whether capable or careless.**
>
>> (or: for you see that it continues binding for us all to be set in light so as to be clearly seen in the presence of the judgment seat which is Christ, so that each should keep and provide for the things performed through the body, with a view to, and face to face with, what things [were practiced], whether virtuous or vile)."

As to their acts,

> "**the person continually sowing into the flesh of himself** (= his estranged inner being), **will progressively reap corruption** (spoil; ruin; decay) **forth from out of the flesh** (= the estranged inner being);
>
>> (or: the one habitually sowing into the flesh [system], of himself will continue to reap decay from out of the flesh [system])
>
> **yet the one constantly sowing into the spirit** (or: the Breath) **will be progressively reaping eonian life** (life having the characteristics of the Age [of Messiah]; or: life from the Age that lasts on through the ages) **forth from out of the spirit** (or: the Spirit; the Breath; that attitude)." (Gal. 6:8).

Cf Mat. 16:27; 2 Cor. 11:15b; 1 Pet. 1:17; Rev. 22:12. God's evaluated decisions (judgments) all pertain to our actions and deeds – not to our belief systems or to what we think about Him. It is about how we live our lives.

24. *Now I am saying to you, to the rest (the remaining) within Thyatira – whoever are not holding this teaching – who do not know "the depths of satan (from the adversary)," as they are laying it out, I will be casting no other burden (weight) upon you.*

The remaining discourse to Thyatira is to those not involved with Jezebel, her idolatry, or her adultery, nor have they known by experience **the depths** of the adversary. To what does this last part refer? Vincent (ibid) thought that this was a reference to the Gnostic sect of the Ophites (the word *ofis* means serpent; known in Hebrew as Naasenes, "serpent-worshipers"). Justinian passed laws against it as late as AD 530, so we can see that it was around for a long time. The serpent was thought to be an instrument of higher wisdom, thus the Gnostics would boast of their insights and knowledge of divine or spiritual things.

Reading the prepositional phrase as an ablative, we have, "the depths FROM the adversary." Now observe that these **depths of** *satan*, may be describing what Jezebel has been **teaching** (vs. 20, above). These teachings may be coming from the adversaries of the covenant community. They may be the dualism from Persian Zoroastrianism that influenced the post-Exile Jews, or they may have come from other mystery-religions of the temples that some had been visiting, joining in the temple feasts. Another possibility is the adversary which was elements of Judaism, or the Judaizers. Paul warned about this in Tit. 1:14,

> "**not habitually holding to** (having [a propensity] toward; heeding and clinging in the direction toward) **Jewish myths** (or: fictions; or, possibly: oral traditions) **and to implanted goals** (inward directives) **whose source and origin is people** (or: human commandments) **[thus] continually being twisted and turned away from the Truth** (or: reality)."

In 1 Tim. 1:4a, he admonished: "**nor yet to constantly hold toward myths** (or: stories; fictions) **and unbounded** (= endless) **genealogies**…" He brought this up again in 2 Tim. 4:4b, speaking of those who "**will be progressively turned out** (have their [steps] turned out of [the Path] into a direction) **upon the myths**." This was, and has continued to be, an ever-present problem because of the human desire for esoteric wisdom, or higher knowledge (Gen. 3:1-6): the innate desire to be more than we are, fueled by our pride. Peter made it clear that, "**You see, we did not experientially or intimately make known to you the power and presence** (or: ability and [the] being alongside; *parousia*) **of our Lord, Jesus Christ, by following forth in** (or: by) **wisely-made myths**" (2 Pet. 1:16).

In contrast, Paul spoke of "**the depth of [the] riches** (wealth; resources) **and wisdom and intimate, experiential knowledge and insight of God** (or: from God)" (Rom. 11:33), and said that "**the spirit** (or: the Spirit; the Breath-effect) **constantly and progressively searches, examines and investigates all mankind, and all things – even the depths of God!**" (1 Cor. 2:10). Matthew Henry compared the depths of satan and darkness to "the secret (mystery) of iniquity," in 2 Thes. 2:7. Mystery cults were common before, during and after the 1st century. Today satanism is common, but is more of a fringe religion. We should not have an "us-and-them" attitude toward these folks, but should love and accept them, while shining Christ's Light. What Christ was addressing here was a situation within His own called-out, covenant community. His corrective words were addressed to them, not to the world-at-large. They were called to bear His image to the world, not the image of something negative, or distorted, or as in John's day, exclusionary (the mystery cults tended to be elitist and exclusive). The particular adversary (*satan*) is not identified, but the context of "teaching" points back to "Jezebel," in vs. 20. However, by leaving the term "**adversary**" ambiguous, His admonition can refer to anything that is adversarial to Christ or His reign. It suggests refusal to become entangled in any system of one's world – be it the Empire, in the 1st century, or any system of religion whose "depths" of doctrine or philosophy become like weeds that overgrow a field and "choke out" the teachings of Christ.

I have purposely retained the transliteration of the term "*satan*" in these passages, so that the reader may reflect upon the traditional personification of this term (which should have been translated instead of made into a proper name). A mythical, dualistic reading of these texts will obscure their meanings. Gregory J. Riley explains the source and process of a dualistic worldview which changed the Jews during their Babylonian-Persian exile:

"The Persians brought not only release from exile to Israel; they also brought an old and highly influential view of the spiritual world. The Persians were an Indo-European culture whose religion was based on a view of the world very different from the monistic cultures of the ancient Near East: theological dualism.... Zoroastrianism... included much more than merely a dualism of God and the Devil. That dualism had consequences... Before creation, both God and the Devil had each emanated armies of archangels and angels, archdemons and demons. God then formed the world as a battleground on which the Devil could be defeated. As soon as it was completed, the dark forces attacked and defiled creation, resulting in this present 'evil age' of mixture of good and evil. The Two – God and the Devil – now had to fight over the loyalty of humans" (*The River of God, A New History of Christian Origins*, HarperSanFrancisco, 2001, pp 94-95).

This same Zoroastrian worldview was picked up by much of Christianity, and persists even to this day. Even in the called-out communities of our day (the "churches," or, home groups) over-emphasis of *satan* or his "power" (which virtually is non-existent, since Christ has authority over it: all authority in heaven and on earth was given to Jesus – Matt. 28:18), or a focus on demonology and the actions of evil spirits, can ensnare people, taking them away from the focus on, and praise of, God, and away from His purposes.

The promise of "**casting no other burden** (weight) **upon you**" may be an allusion to Acts 15:28 and the letter sent from the Jerusalem leaders to the Gentiles in Antioch, Syria and Cilicia. It might also reach back, as a contrast, to what the Torah lawyers were accused by Jesus of doing to the people (Lu. 11:46).

25. *Moreover, what you have (hold) you must get into your power (be strong in; lay hold of), until of which [time or situation] whenever I may arrive (or, as a future: will proceed to be arriving).*'

The phrase "**get into your power** (be strong in; lay hold of)" calls to mind Eph. 6:13,
"**On account of this, you folks receive back again** (or: at once take up) **the full suit of armor** (panoply; implements of war) **which is God** (or: which belongs to and has its source in God), **to the end that you would have power** (or: be able) **to withstand and resist** (to stand opposite, over against as facing an opponent; or: stand in [other folks'] place, instead of [them]) **within the harmful day** (the day of bad conditions), **and accomplishing all** (achieving and effecting everything [the whole]), **to stand firm**."

The last clause of vs. 25 is awkward in the Greek. Vatican MS #1160 and others read "until whither I shall open." Perhaps a good paraphrase would be, "hang in there until I change things for you." But take note of the immanent sense of this clause – He would seem to be indicating to Thyatira that He would soon be with them. The form of the verb **arrive** is either an aorist subjunctive, or a future indicative; thus the two renderings.

26. "'**And [to] the one habitually conquering** (repeatedly overcoming; progressively victorious) **and keeping watch over** (guarding; maintaining observance of) **My acts** (works; deeds) **until completion** (down to a final act; as far as [the] purposed and destined goal; until an end), **I will continue giving to him authority** (right and privilege from out of Being) **upon the multitudes** (the nations; the ethnic groups; the Gentiles).

Once again we find a prize being offered to the victor: **authority**. But consider the literal meaning in the parenthetical expansion of this noun: "right and privilege from out of Being (*ex-ousia*)." As we abide in the Vine, His BEING provides us with privilege and authority. This **habitual overcoming** may have had reference to overcoming the influence of Jezebel within their community. In 1 Cor. 9:24, where Paul said, "**those running in a racecourse indeed all run, but one receives the prize**," he was not referring to salvation, but to a goal to be attained, once the life of the "gift" is realized. The figure of "authority over the multitudes/nations" is echoed in 3:21, below: **"to sit down with Me in My throne."**

As noted, above, "all authority" was given to the risen Christ. So here He shares this with those who abide in Him. The allusion is to Ps. 2:8-9. It calls to mind the apocalyptic picture given by Paul in Eph. 2:6,
> "**He jointly roused and raised** (or: suddenly awakens and raises) **[us] up, and caused [us] to sit** (or: seats [us]; = enthroned [us]) **together within the things situated upon** [thus, above] **the heavens**
>> (or: in union with the full, perfected heavenlies; or, although neuter: among those comprising the complete and perfected heavenlies; among the ones [residing] upon the atmospheres; in union with the celestials; among the folks [residing] upon the atmospheres) **within and in union with Christ Jesus**."

But let us note the purpose for this, which is given in Eph. 2:7,
> "**to the end that within the continuously oncoming ages** (the indefinite time periods continually and progressively coming upon and overtaking [us]) **He may exhibit** (display; point out; give proof of) **the continuously transcending** (being cast beyond; overshooting) **riches and wealth of His grace and favor, in useful goodness** (beneficial kindness) **[flooding] upon us, within Christ Jesus** (or: in union with [the] Anointed Jesus)."

Our "authority" is to be the Light of the aggregate of humanity (the world) – Mat. 5:14. Our authority is to be an **exhibit** (display; a pointed-out example; a proof that has been given) **of the continuously transcending** (being cast beyond; overshooting) **riches of His grace**. Notice that this "right and privilege is "**upon the multitudes** (the nations; the ethnic groups; the Gentiles)." The old nation of Israel was to soon pass away, and Christ had made Jew and non-Jew into one NEW humanity (Eph. 2:15). It is the privilege and right of Christ's followers to act on the instructions of Mat. 28:19,
> "**Therefore, while going on your way, instruct and make disciples** (students and apprentices) **of all the ethnic multitudes** (the pagans; the Gentiles; the nations; the non-Israelites), **habitually immersing them** (baptizing them to the point of infusion and saturation) **into the NAME which has reference to, belongs to, has its origin and character in, and which represents, the Father and the Son, as well as the Set-apart Breath-effect**."

This began happening on the Day of Pentecost (Acts 2). To His disciples He said,
> "**You folks will progressively receive power and will continue taking to yourselves ability [at, or with, the] added, full coming of the Set-apart Breath-effect** (the Holy Spirit and Sacred Attitude) **upon you folks – and you will keep on being My witnesses, both within Jerusalem and within all Judea and Samaria... even as far as [the] end of the Land** (or: a farthest point of the earth)" (Acts 1:8).

What are we to make of the second half of the stipulation: "**keeping watch over** (guarding; maintaining; observing) **My acts** (works; deeds) **until completion**"? In Jn. 5:19, Jesus said of Himself:
> "**the Son continues unable to do anything from Himself** (or: the Son, from Himself, habitually has no power to be doing anything [independently]) **except He can continue seeing something the Father is in process of doing** (or: if not something He may presently observe the Father making, producing, constructing, or creating), **for what things That One may likely be progressively doing** (making; constructing; creating; producing), **these things, also, the Son is likewise habitually doing** (or: is in like manner constantly making, producing, creating)."

He made a similar statement in Jn. 5:30, adding the sense of hearing:
> "**I, Myself, am continually unable** (or: As for Me, I habitually have no power or ability) **to be doing anything from Myself: correspondingly as I am continuously hearing, I am habitually sifting, separating, evaluating and deciding** (or: judging), **and My deciding** (separating and

evaluating; judging) **is right and just** (continues being in accord with the Way pointed out and is turned in the right direction of fairness, equity, justice and right relationship), **because I am not seeking my own will** (intent; purpose), **but rather the purpose** (intent; will) **of the One sending Me**."

So His **acts, works and deeds** were things corresponding to what He saw the Father doing, and what He heard the Father, or the Spirit, saying. In Jn. 5:27 Jesus said that the Father, "**gives in Him** (or: to Him; by Him) **authority** (or: the right, etc.) **to be habitually separating and deciding** (to be constantly sifting and evaluating; to continuously do [the] judging)." So here we have "**authority**" connected with His acts. This may be what "**keeping watch over**" and "observing" is signifying. His life was a pattern for His disciples to observe and follow. These are examples of the life to which Paul referred, in Rom. 8:14,

"**For as many as are being continuously led by God's Spirit** (or: habitually brought or conducted in [the] Breath-effect which is God; progressively driven along with an attitude from God), **these folks are God's sons**."

Now in Acts 10:38 it is reported about Jesus that He,

"**went throughout repeatedly doing works bringing goodness, ease and well-being, as well as constantly healing all the folks being continuously held down under power** (tyrannized and oppressed) **by the one that casts things through folks** (the accuser, slanderer, adversary)**... because God was with Him**."

Recall that in Jn. 14:12 Jesus said to His listeners,

"**I am saying to you folks, the person habitually trusting and progressively believing into Me, the works** (actions; deeds) **which I Myself am constantly doing** (habitually performing; progressively making, constructing, creating, forming) **that one also will proceed doing** (performing; making; creating), **and he will progressively be doing greater than these, because I Myself am progressively journeying** (traveling; going from this place to another) **toward** (or: facing) **the Father**."

Pulling all these statements together may create for us a picture to help us understand the intent of His words to Thyatira. Paul explained that, "**God is the One habitually operating with inward activity, repeatedly working within, constantly causing function and progressively producing effects within, among and in union with you folks**" (Phil. 2:13). Jesus informed us that, "**My Father is continuously working and keeps on being in action until the present moment** (or: up to right now); **I, Myself, also am continually working**" (Jn. 5:17). With this in mind, it behooves us to "habitually maintain observance of [His] acts."

Now let us consider the next phrase: **until completion** (down to a final act; as far as [the] purposed and destined goal; until an end). This is a very general qualifier which refers to any of His acts, deeds or works. It is an ongoing call to faithfulness and remaining under life's burdens with others, in order to give them support. It speaks to laying down our lives for our friends. God continues working in and with people. He has a good end in mind for them, and we are called to participate with Him. As Paul put it:

"**For we are God's fellow-workers** (or: we are co-workers of and from God; we exist being co-workers who belong to God). **You folks are God's farm** (or: field under cultivation), **God's building** (or: construction project; structure, or act of building)" (1 Cor. 3:9).

So "His acts and works" are, in fact, His PEOPLE. We are called to watch over, guard and maintain them.

Another layer of interpreting the meaning of the phrase, "My works," may be seen in His prayer to the Father in Jn. 17:4,

"**I Myself glorify** (or: brought a good reputation and a manifestation which called forth praise to) **You upon the earth** (or: the Land), **finishing and perfecting** (bringing to its goal, purpose, destiny and fruition) **the Work** (the Deed; the Act) **which You have given to** (or: in; for) **Me, to the end that I could do** (or: would perform) **[it]**."

It may be the work of the cross and the resurrection that Christ now instructs His community to "guard." We, by our lives, actions and words, are called to maintain these Works of Christ within His ongoing reign in the earth, today. He has given to us this "right" and "privilege," from "out of His Being."

Our authority is to represent Him by being the servants of all, as He was and is – for He is the same (Heb. 13:8); He does not change into a "warrior god;" the vision of Him in 19:11ff, below, must be understood in light of this instruction from the book of Hebrews, as well as from the following verse, here:

27. "'**and so he will continue shepherding** (i.e., feeding, tending and guarding) **them with a staff made of iron, as he is being continuously broken [like] pottery vessels,** [Ps. 2:9] **as I also have received from My Father.**

This explains that this authority is given so that we can feed His sheep (Jn. 21:15-18). It shows His heart, and His purpose for us "ruling" or "judging the 12 tribes of Israel" (Matt. 19:28): to be shepherds; to feed, protect, guide and care for His sheep – even at the expense of the shepherd laying down his life (or, being broken) for his sheep (Jn. 10:11). The staff made of iron symbolizes a strong defense for, or correction of, the sheep. The verb "**broken**" is in the 3rd person, singular, present PASSIVE, with no pronoun – thus my translation, above. It means that "**the one habitually conquering**," which is still the subject of this verse, will be broken, as was our Shepherd. Jesus spoke of this, about Himself, in Mk. 14:27,

> "**It has been written,**
> '**I will proceed to strike** (smite; hit) **the shepherd, and the sheep will continue being thoroughly scattered and dispersed throughout.**'" [Zech. 13:7] *Cf* Mat. 26:31

As noted in the verse, this is a quote of Ps. 2:9 (LXX) which uses the verb "to shepherd," as opposed to the Heb. MT which reads "smite; break." Beale notes that the Syriac Peshitta, the Vulgate, and Jerome agree with the LXX (ibid p 267), and obviously John understood this to be the correct meaning of the psalm. Let us see where this verb is used once again in regard to the nations: in 19:15a, below,

> "**Also, a sharp two-edged broadsword repeatedly goes out** (issues forth; proceeds) **from His mouth, to the end that in it He may smite** (or: strike) **the multitudes** (nations; ethnic groups). **And He will continue shepherding them with an iron staff**."

So the nations are now a part of His flock, and the "smiting" or "striking" is a corrective measure, as a shepherd might use his staff to sternly redirect a rebellious sheep. We already saw that the sword coming out of His mouth represents a decisive word, or message. The symbolism of 19:15 is a picture of one who has conquered and overcome. It speaks of Christ dealing with the ethnic multitudes in a manner that overcomes their "free will." This verb, "to shepherd," is also used in 12:5, below,

> "**And so she brought forth a Son – an adult man** (or: male; masculine one) **Who is about to continuously shepherd** (tend and protect) **all the multitudes** (ethnic groups; nations) **in the sphere of and with relying on the use of an iron staff** (or: rod)."

Therefore, now "**the multitudes** (the nations; the ethnic groups; the Gentiles)" can say with the psalmist:

> "**[The] LORD** (= Yahweh) **continually shepherds** (habitually cares for and tends, repeatedly leads to pasture and constantly protects) **me [as a part of the flock], and He will continue causing me to lack nothing. Into a place of [the] tender shoot** (or: Into the midst of a verdant place), **there** (in that place) **He encamped me; upon water of rest** (or: at restful water; on a water of ceasing) **He nourishes and rears me. He turned my soul around** (or: He turns upon my whole being; He restored my self-life; He turned-about my inner being): **He leads and guides me upon the well-worn Path of the Way pointed out, in righted covenant-participation,**

because of and for the sake of His Name... **You are, and continue being, with me: Your rod and your staff – these, from a call to be at my side, give me aid and impart relief, encouragement and comfort** (these are paracletes to help me)" (Ps. 23:1-3, LXX, JM).

The covenant communities were instructed:

"**You folks shepherd** (i.e., lead to pasture, feed, tend, protect, care for) **God's little flock [that is] among you folks, constantly watching over [them], not in a forced manner** (not by exercising compulsion or constraint; or: not unwillingly), **but to the contrary, without compulsion** (engendering volunteering; yieldingly; or: voluntarily; willingly), **in accord with** (or: in line with and corresponding to; in the sphere of) **God**..." (1 Pet. 5:2).

And in Eph. 4:11, "**He Himself at one point gave**... **the shepherds**..."

Now the work has been broadened and extended to include all the ethnic multitudes and nations. Jesus spoke of this new situation in Jn. 10:16,

"**And I constantly have** (hold; possess) **other sheep which do not exist** (or: are not) **from out of this fold** (or: sheep pen), **and it is binding** (or: necessary) **for Me to progressively lead those also, and they will continue listening to** (will habitually hear and pay attention to [implying: obey]) **My voice, and they** [other MSS: it; there] **will progressively become One Flock, One Shepherd**."

Those "overcoming" will not only exercise His shepherding authority over the ethnic multitudes, but they, themselves, will continue to experience His shepherding of them:

"**because** (or: seeing that) **the little Lamb – the One back up amidst the throne** (or: the One again in the midst of the throne) **– will continue shepherding** [other MSS: is continuously shepherding] **them, and will continue guiding** [other MSS: is continuously guiding] **them upon springs of waters of life** [other MSS: living springs of water]. **And God will continue anointing** (or: wiping and smearing) **every tear shed from out of their eyes**" (7:17, below) [cf Isa. 49:10; Jer. 2:13; Ezk. 34:23; Ps. 23:1-2; Isa. 25:8]

They receive in order to give.

The "breaking" that Christ received from His Father was the part of God's plan for Him to be the loaf of bread that was broken so that it (He) could be shared with us for our nourishment and strength. We are to "follow Him" in this path, as well. Recall that Paul informed us that "**we are one loaf of bread**" (1 Cor. 10:17), just as we are one body, with Christ as our Source and Head. We, too, will be broken so as to be given to others – to give them Life.

28. "'**and thus I will continue giving to him** (or: bestowing in him; granting for him; delivering up with him) **the morning star**.'

The meaning of the symbol "**the morning star**" is given in 22:16, below, "**I, Jesus**.... **am the root and offspring of David: the light-emitting** (Shining; Radiant) **Morning Star**." Back in 1:20, above, we saw that a star is a figure of a messenger or an agent: it gives light (a message; knowledge; understanding), and together with others, can tell a story.

One thing that can be drawn from this is that the overcomer will be given the message, or knowledge, pertaining to the dawn of the New Day, the Age of Messiah. That Jesus identifies Himself as this light-giving morning star would mean that He Himself will be given to the victor – what more could be given, as a prize? In Dan. 12:3 it is said, "and those justifying many are as stars, for the eons and further" (CVOT). Rotherham renders it thus: "and they who make wise (the instructors) shall shine like the shining of the expanse (= atmosphere) – and they who bring the many to righteousness, like the stars, to times age-abiding and beyond." I also like NEB's phrase, "... and those who have guided the people in the true path shall be like the stars..."

In Joseph's dream (Gen. 37:9), we see the sun, the moon and the eleven stars bowing themselves to Joseph. Verse 10 reads, "... do WE certainly come – I and thy mother and thy brothers – to bow down to thee, to the earth?" (Young). So here are a couple examples of a star being a figure of a person. Then in Job 38 Yahweh asked Job about the time "when the morning stars sang together, and all the sons of God shouted for joy." Vincent comments that the star was the ancient emblem of sovereignty. Num. 24:17 says, "There has marched forth a star out of Jacob, and arisen a scepter out of Israel." Matt. 2:2 says of the baby Jesus, "we saw His star in the east..."

The woman in 12:1, below, has a crown of 12 stars. Judges 5:20 says symbolically, "the stars from their highways fought with Sisera." The figure seems to speak of ruling and of an exalted position, like that of Joseph, who functioned as a savior with provision for the nation of Egypt. Beale (ibid p 269) instructs us that "the morning star" had been associated with Roman emperors, and that their legions carried its sign on their standards. So one inference might be that this verse speaks to the kingdoms of the System becoming the kingdom of our Lord and His anointed (11:15, below).

The "morning star" is found in the LXX of Isa. 14:12, "How is the Morning Star fallen from out of the heaven (or: the sky) – the one normally rising up…?" (JM). The Heb. text of this verse reads the title as, "O Shining One" (Rotherham); "light-bringer *and* day-star" (Amplified OT). Here is a speculation, based upon an allegorical interpretation of the Isa. 14 passage, for your consideration:
> If interpreters are correct that this passage in Isa. 14 (also connected to Ezk. 28) was a symbolic look back to the "fall of Adam" from out of a "spiritual" Garden of Eden, then the symbol here may point to Jesus being the Last Adam (1 Cor. 15:45), that rose up again, figuratively taking the Second Humanity (1 Cor. 15:47) back to Paradise.

29. "So let the person having an ear at once listen, and hear (= pay attention and obey) **what the Spirit is now continuously saying to** (or: in; for; among) **the called-out, covenant communities!**

Again we encounter the formulated imperative to listen, hear, and thus obey what the Breath-effect (Spirit) continues saying to the called-out communities. It does not say, listen to the doctrines of the theologians, or to the traditions of your particular group. It speaks of a living relationship which acknowledges His authority and direction in His involvement with humanity.

Chapter 3

1. "Next, to (or: in; for) **the agent which is** (or: messenger from; person with the message of, or pertaining to) **the called-out community within Sardis, write:**
> **'The One having** (or: holding; possessing) **the seven spirits and attitudes of God – and** (or: even) **the seven stars – is presently saying these things,**

Compare 1:4, above, where the 7 spirits were positioned in front of His throne – the place of authority and power. Here it says that the Christ Figure of this book is holding (or: possessing; having) these 7 spirits – or the fullness of the Breath-effect; the full cycle and completeness of the Spirit of God. Might we connect this description of the risen Christ with what we find in 2 Jn. 9b?
> "**the person remaining** (dwelling; abiding; staying) **within that teaching, this one continuously has** (or: holds; possesses) **both Father and Son** (or: the Father and the Son)."

In 2 Jn. 3 we can observe five "spirits" referenced, along with the Father and the Son:

"**Grace** (or: Joyous favor), **Mercy [and] Peace** (Joining) **will continuously be with us from beside** (or: in the presence of; along with) **God the Father, and from beside** (or: in the presence of; along with) **Jesus Christ, the Father's Son, within Truth** (or: in the midst of reality) **and Love**."

Now 1 Jn. 4:16b tells us that,

"**God exists continually being Love** (God is Love, which is Unrestricted Acceptance), **and the person continuously remaining** (dwelling; abiding) **within, and in union with, the Love, is continuously remaining** (dwelling; abiding) **within, and in union with, God – and God constantly dwells** (remains) **within the midst of him and abides in union with him**."

So since God is Love, and God is Spirit, spirit or Breath-effect (Jn. 4:24), can we extrapolate to say that Grace, Mercy and Truth are also spirit/Spirit, along with the Father and His Son (Gal. 4:6)? This seems to point to a conclusion that God is more than just "trinity." John Gavazzoni has described God as Family (via a personal email). When we experience any of the "Spirits" of God (figuratively numbered here as "**the seven spirits and attitudes of God**," it seems logical to surmise that we have encountered God.

Isa. 11:1-2 says, "And a Rod has come out from the stock of Jesse, even a Branch from his roots is fruitful. Rested upon Him has (1) the Spirit of Yahweh, (2) the Spirit of Wisdom and (3) Understanding, (4) the Spirit of Counsel, and (5) Might, Valor and Mastery, (6) the Spirit of Knowledge and (7) Reverence from (or: Fear with respect to) Yahweh." This is an example of personification of various aspects, or qualities, of God's Spirit.

> *I have seen, and thus know (am aware of) your works (actions; deeds) [and] that you have a name (= reputation) that you are living, and yet you are dead!*

He states to this community, as well, that He is aware of what they are doing. He knows their reputation, but He speaks truth that invalidates their reputation before people. They have a name, or reputation, that they are a real "live church!" But He pronounces them dead. Both being alive and being dead, here, are figures of speech. One is from the human view; the other is God's view – this latter referring to the realm of their spirit. As the prodigal son was dead to his father (Lu. 15:24), so this covenant community is dead to the Father. We can look to Mat. 23:27-28 for a parallel case,

"**Tragic will be the fate of you Law scholars and Pharisees – you who recite a front of your own opinions and answers** (or: overly-critical folks)! **[It will be] because you continue closely resembling whitewashed** (i.e., smeared or plastered with lime) **tombs** (sepulchers; grave sites), **which indeed, from outside, continue being made to appear in the prime of beauty, for a time – yet inside they contain a full load of bones of dead folks, as well as every uncleanness. In this way you, yourselves, also on the one hand are continually made to outwardly appear to people [to be] just** (fair, righteous, in right relationships, and in accord with the way pointed out) **– yet inside you continuously exist being men glutted and distended, full of opinionated answers** (or: perverse detail-oriented scholarship; hyper-criticism and judgmentalism; well-sifted wicked interpretations) **and lawlessness** (= practice which is contrary to the Law [Torah])."

Another use of death as a metaphor is found in Rom. 8:6a, "**For the result of the thinking** (mind-set; effect of the way of thinking; disposition; result of understanding and inclination; the minding; the opinion; the thought; the outlook) **of the flesh** (= the human condition or the System of culture and cultus; or: = outward Torah ceremony) **[is; brings] death**." It may well be that this had inwardly slain them. Another metaphorical situation is 1 Tim. 5:6,

"**the woman continuously indulging herself in riotous luxury** (excessive comfort; sensual gratification), **while continuing being alive** (or: [though] living), **she is dead** (or: she has died)."

If this community has regressed into Judaism, or paganism, it is possible that their condition that is described here is that which Paul described in Eph. 2:1, 5,

> "**And you folks [who were] continuously existing being dead ones by** (or: to; with; in) **the results and effects of your stumblings aside** (offenses; wrong steps) **and failures to hit the mark** (or: mistakes; errors; times of falling short; sins; deviations).... **even us, being continuously dead ones by** (or: in; to; with) **the results and effects of stumblings aside** (wrong steps; offences)..."

2.   ***Come to be** (Be birthed) **awake ones** (watchful people) **and establish** (set fast) **the remaining things which were about to die** (or: rot), **for I have not found your works** (acts; deeds) **being fulfilled** (being made full) **in front of and in the sight of My God** (or: before God – which is Me).*

They are dead, so they must "be birthed" once more. Paul said to those in Galatia,

> "**O my little children** (born ones), **with whom I am progressing, again, in childbirth labor** (travail; labor pains) **until Christ may be suddenly formed** (= until the Anointing would be at some point birthed) **within you folks!**" (Gal. 4:19).

They are asleep (often a figure of death); they must come to be **awake** and watchful. Birth and death are often simply metaphors of going from one realm to another, within the mind or spirit. In Rom. 13:11 Paul says,

> "**being folks having seen and thus knowing the season** (the fit of the situation; the appointed fertile moment) – **that [it is] by this time** (or: already) **an hour to be aroused** (or: awakened) **out of sleep**..."

And in Eph. 5:14 he makes this statement,

> "**Wherefore He is now** (or: it keeps on) **saying,**
>> "**Let the sleeper** (the person continuously down and being fast asleep) **be waking up, continue rousing, and then stand up** (arise) **from out of the midst of the dead ones, and the Christ will continue shining upon you** (progressively enlightening you)!"

The community of Sardis were in the spiritual state of being that which was the same as some of the folks in Rome, and some of those in Ephesus. It is often just a condition of being unaware of God – either within an individual, or within one's environment or situation. It can be like being blind to how God is active in one's world, or like being oblivious to the reality that God's kingdom is at hand: close enough to touch; accessible!

In Mat. 26:41a, Jesus admonished His disciples,

> "**You folks continue awake and keep on watching. And continue praying to the end that you folks may not enter into a test** (a trial; a putting to the proof)."

Michael Phillips, citing Mat. 16:6; 24:42; 25:13; 26:41; Lu. 11:35; 12:1 and 17:13, makes these cogent observations:

> "A serious examination of the Gospels reveals three surprising combinations of injunctions emerging as the most frequent given Commands of Jesus.... All three [are] commanded upon us by Jesus *more* often than the Commands to love, pray, believe, trust or have faith. Jesus speaks but *once* about the necessity of being born again. But these three groups of Commands (toward *watchfulness, fearlessness*, and *mental diligence*) are urged upon the disciples a combined *seventy* times! Yet an entire theology of salvation has grown up around Jesus' conversation with Nicodemus in the third chapter of John, while these far more frequently given Commands lay beside the road virtually unnoticed" (*The Commands of Jesus*, Sunrise Books, Pub., 2014 p 16-17; emphasis original; brackets added).

In Mk. 8:15, we read of Jesus:

> "**Then He began instructing, and continued to be fully setting things in order for them, saying, 'Be continuously looking and observing, so as to be seeing with perception! Be constantly taking note of and look out for so as to beware of the leavening agent** (or: the yeast; = the pervading elements of fermentation and fomentation) **of the Pharisees as well as the leavening agent of Herod** [i.e., = the pervading doctrines and theology of the structured and organized religion, as well as current governmental politics].'"

Phillips, of course, expands upon these observation in very practical terms from other NT passages. But we see here in vs. 2 that Christ must again call them to alertness, and in vs. 3, below, He says, "**Continuously keep watch**." How easy it is to be lulled to sleep, or to be distracted. God was doing things in their day, but He has continuously been active in human affairs, and is still so today. Our eyes should be on Him (Heb. 12:2), observing what He is doing – not worrying about what some cabal is doing. Or, as Phillips puts it, "Jesus did not command us to beware of the leaven of Caesar, but of the Pharisees and Sadducees.... [and] in Lu. 11:35: 'Be careful lest what you think is light within you is actually darkness.'" (ibid; brackets added). He *will proceed arriving* (vs. 3) and we *will continue walking with [Him]* (vs. 4, below). We need to be watchful as we are following Him, so that we can observe where His Path (Way) is leading us, daily.

We are not told what it is that those in Sardis must establish, only that they were things that were **about to die** and rot. Perhaps it was their first love – something that was not outwardly apparent, for they had a name of being alive. Perhaps it was Christ's way of thinking (Phil. 2:5, "**You see, this way of thinking** {this attitude and disposition} **is continuously within and among you folks** {or, as an imperative: So let this minding be habitually within you folks} **– which [is] also within Christ Jesus**,") which had been displaced by "**the disposition** (way of thinking) **of the flesh**."

Furthermore, their **works** were not **fulfilled**, or completed, **in God's sight**. Was this like fruit that never ripened? Was the fruit of the Spirit (love, joy, peace, forbearance, kindness, goodness, faithfulness/loyalty, meekness, self-control – Gal. 5:22) not come to maturity? Did the vine dry up (Joel 1:12); did the fig tree produce no fruit (Mark 11:13)? "**This is the work of God: that you would be trusting and believing into the One Whom He commissions**" (John 6:29). Perhaps it was their trusting and believing which did not come to fruition.

The final prepositional phrase is first offered as a possessive genitive, "… of My God," which is the common rendering. But in vs. 1 it is the risen Christ (the speaker) who says, "**I have seen**…" So on offer in the parenthetical expansion is the appositional rendering of the genitive, "before God – which is Me."

3. *Remember, then, how you have received* (or: taken with the hand) *and heard! Continuously keep watch* (or: Guard [it]) *and change your way of thinking, [and turn to God]. If ever, then, you should not be watching, I will proceed arriving* (or: may arrive) *upon you as a thief, and under no circumstances would you know what hour I will* (or: may) *be arriving upon you.*

How had they received? "**For you see, by** (or: to; in; for; with) **the grace and joyous favor you are** (you continuously exist being) **folks having been delivered** (rescued; kept safe; saved; made whole; restored to your original state and condition) **so as to now be enjoying salvation through** [some MSS add: the] **faithfulness** (or: loyalty; trust; faith; confidence), **and even this not forth from out of you folks, [it is] the gift of and from God** (or: the gift which is God; or: the gift pertains to God)," (Eph. 2:8).

> "**Being, then, folks that were eschatologically delivered and rightwised** (placed in the right relationship of [covenantal] solidarity in the Way pointed out and made fair, equitable, just, free

from guilt and turned in the right direction) **from the midst of [His] faithfulness, out of trust and from conviction, we continuously hold and progressively have** [other MSS: let us (or: we can and should) habitually retain and enjoy] **peace and harmony face to face with God** (or: [directing and conducting us] toward God), **through our Owner and Lord, Jesus Christ** (or: Master, [the] Anointed Jesus), **through Whom, also, we have had and now hold the conducted approach and access** (or: the act of bringing toward to gain entrée), **by [His] faithfulness** (or: in this trust; with that confidence; for loyalty), **into this grace and joyous favor within which we have stood and in union with which we now stand, and so we keep on celebrating, speaking loudly and boasting upon the expectation** (or: expectant hope) **of God's glory** (the manifestation from God which calls forth praise; from the splendor, which is God; and: from God's good reputation; of the opinion from God; from the imagination which has the quality of God)." (Rom. 5:1-2)

"**Yet to the contrary, [it is] not in the same way [with] the effect of grace** (result of favor; the thing graciously given) **as [it was with] the effect of the fall to the side** (or: = the result of the stumbling aside and the offence is not simply balanced out by the result of the joyful gift of grace – the gratuitous favor). **For you see, since** (or: if) **by** (or: in) **the effect of the fall to the side** (the result of the stumbling aside and the offense) **of the one THE MANY** (= the mass of humanity) **died, MUCH MORE** (= infinitely greater) **[is] the Grace of God** (God's Grace; favor which is God), **and the gift** (or: gratuitous benefit) **within Grace – a joy-producing act of Favor – by that of the One Man, Jesus Christ, surrounded** (or: encircles) **into encompassing superabundance** (extraordinary surplus and excess) **into THE MANY** (= the mass of humanity)." (Rom. 5:15).

The Lord charges them to **remember** all this, and to hear. They are then told to **continuously keep watch**. The sense here may be to guard what they had received, as one guards a possession against thieves (folks or organizations which present contrary views that may take away their expectation or steal their freedom in Christ and lead them back into the bondage of religion). It may also be to watch over in the sense of tending a crop so that there will be a harvest of fruit, or of tending the sheep of the community. To do this they must change their frame of mind – **their way of thinking**. Their thinking had resulted in their becoming dead to God's sovereign activities among them; dead by employing the way of thinking from the flesh realm, instead of from the Spirit. If they fail to make this change, He promises to come unexpectedly to them (***arriving upon [them] as a thief***), to bring needed correction.

In the last part of this verse, judgment is inferred in the aspect of His coming – a decision from Him that will take one by surprise – if His community does not comply with His instructions. Note the close, interactive relationship between Christ and His covenant community that is implied in the language of this verse! There is also the sense of the possibility of loss of what they have received – for this is what a thief does; he comes to steal and to destroy (John 10:10 – and considering the context which follows vs. 10 there, could it be that He might come to them via a hireling that is sent to them?) Lu. 12:39 also speaks of a situation of not knowing what hour the thief would come. Usually we don't think of this as being a coming of the Lord, but we see here that it is. He comes to us in all things – and they are all for our ultimate good.

Christ's coming to Sardis (which would take them by surprise, if they are not watching for Him) is a coming that ties chapters 2 and 3 with the rest of the book. Consider what He says in 16:15, in the vision of the bowls (or: cups):

"**Consider! I continually** (or: repeatedly) **am coming as a thief! The one continually watching** (or: in wakeful vigilance) **and keeping guard upon his garments [is; will be] blessed** (or: a happy person), **to the end that he may not be continually walking about** (or: roaming; =

living his life) **naked so that they may continually see** (or: observe) **his indecency** (condition of being without proper form, shape or character; shame; ungracefulness)." [*cf* 1 Thes. 5:2; Matt. 24:43; 2 Pet. 3:10; 2 Cor. 5:3]

Beale cites two occasions from Israel's history where the Jews had been caught by surprise: "years before Cyrus's attack (549 BC), and then later that of Antiochus the Great (218 BC), caught the city off guard because of its lack of vigilance" (ibid p 276). The last clause, here, "**what hour I will** (or: may) **be arriving upon you**," should be noted: it does not say "what year, or what day." He was speaking of an imminent arrival, bringing corrective measure that would end in their being "alive" again. Jesus said,

"**I, Myself, come so that they can progressively possess** (would continuously have; could habitually hold) **Life, and may continue possessing [it] in superabundance** (or: and may have a surplus surrounding them in excessive amounts). **I, Myself, am the Ideal Shepherd. The Ideal** (Fine; Beautiful) **Shepherd continually places His soul over the sheep** (or: habitually sets [*p45* & others: gives] His soul-life and His entire being for, and on behalf of the situation of, the sheep)" (Jn. 10:10b-11).

But He also comes to purify His priests, and His temple (Mal. 3:1-3, 5-6; 4:1-3, 6). Paul spoke of the same thing in 1 Cor. 3:10b-17. In Mat. 3:12, John told his listeners, concerning Jesus:

"**Whose winnowing fork** (or: shovel) **[is] within His hand, and He will proceed thoroughly cleaning up** (clearing, scouring and cleansing) **His threshing floor and then will progressively gather** (bring together) **His grain into the storehouse** (granary; barn), **yet the chaff** (straw and husks; i.e., that which is no longer of use in folks' lives) **He will continue completely burning, in an inextinguishable Fire**."

The grain was the purpose of growing the crop, not the chaff. He would soon come to Jerusalem and do this very thing, in AD 70. Following Christ's resurrection, all nations and races are treated the same; what He would later do in Jerusalem, breaking out the unbelieving branches (Rom. 11:17), in AD 70, He would also do in Sardis or any other covenant community (Rom. 11:18-22).

4. ***But still, you have a few names in Sardis which do** (or: did) **not stain** (soil; pollute) **their garments, and they will continue walking with Me in white [garments] because they are worthy ones** (folks of corresponding value).'*

Here the word "**names**" refers to people. In this case it refers to a few folks to whom the previous complaints do not apply. **Staining** (polluting; soiling) the **garments** is a metaphor for allowing the impure aspects of the profane life of our environment, or just common everyday living, to detract from our life in the spirit (typified here by **walking** with Christ **in white garments**), or to bring things from the estranged system into the higher life in God. Being **worthy**, or "of corresponding value," means that they live their lives in the realm of having been cleansed by His blood (see 7:9, 13, 14, below – another tie-in of these letters to the communities with the rest of the book) so that their lives are compared to **white** robes – a rightwised life that has been transformed by the work of Christ, so that it is focused in the right direction. *Cf* 3:18 and 4:4, below, for other instances of this metaphor. 19:8, below, gives an explanation of the white garment symbol:

"**Then it was** (or: is) **granted** (or: given) **to her to the end that she may clothe herself with bright and clean fine cotton** (or: she may cast bright, pure, fine linen around her) **– for the fine cotton** (or: linen) **is the effects of fair and equitable deeds and way of life** (or: just awards; the results of rightwised behavior; the actualizations of justice; consequences of justice rendered; the effects of living in right relationship which accords with the Way pointed out) **of the set-apart folks**."

The reference to the "white" may be an allusion to Dan.11:35, "Some from among the intelligent shall stumble, to refine and to purify and to **whiten** them until the era of the end…" Then in Dan. 12:10 we have a similar statement, "Many shall purify and **whiten** themselves and be refined…" Also, Mal. 3:2b.

Jesus said, "**And the person who is not taking his cross and following after Me is not worthy of Me**" (Mat. 10:38). Mat. 10:32-42 is instructive for understanding these letters to the seven communities. Paul said, "**For I consider that the sufferings and experiences of the current season are not worthy** (of equal value) **to the glory about to be revealed** (unveiled) **into us, indeed**… **the unveiling of the sons of God**" (Rom. 8:18, 19). For the metaphor of clothing we have Gal. 3:27, "**For whoever are baptized into Christ put on [as a garment] Christ**." It is Christ Himself who is our white garments.

5. "'**The person habitually conquering** (repeatedly or progressively overcoming) **may thus clothe himself in white garments, and under no circumstances will I proceed to erase his name from out of the scroll of The Life** (or: Life's scroll; the scroll which signifies life), **and I will continue speaking in accordance to his name** (saying the same thing as his name; confessing and avowing his name) **in front of My Father, and in front of His agents** (or: messengers; folks with the Message).'

This continual overcoming through the One who indwells us allows us to be constantly dressing ourselves with Christ, our "**white garment**." With this continual union with Christ a person's name will by no means be **erased** from the scroll of **The Life** – a figure for participation in the Christ-Life, or as elsewhere termed, have their name written in, "**The Scroll of the Life of the Lamb**" (13:8, below; *cf* Dan. 12:1b; Mal. 3:16). It is HIS LIFE that is being referred to; our name being written there just means that we are abiding in the Vine and His sap (life/Spirit) is flowing into and through us. Just as in John 15 there is potential for the branch to not abide in the Vine, so here there is potential not to remain in union with the Christ Life, and wither spiritually just like the branch that does not abide in the flow of the life of the Vine. The Lamb, the scroll of The Life, and the Vine are parallel metaphors. Having one's name in Christ's scroll may be an allusion to Ex. 32:32 where Moses uses the phrase when speaking to Yahweh, "Yet if not, wipe me, I pray, from Your scroll which You have written." But Yahweh's answer to him was, "Anyone who has sinned against Me, I shall wipe him from My scroll. And now, go, guide the people…. and in the day of My visitation, then I will visit on them their sin" (32:33-34). Note first of all that it was their sin that would come upon them in the day of His visitation (which meant, "when He would come to judge them"). In the OT, such visitation was temporal, in this life. It did not apply to an "after-death" experience. That concept did not infiltrate the Jews until they incorporated it from Persian Zoroastrianism. If these Exodus verses were indeed being referenced, then this might have been a subtle allusion to what would come in Jerusalem's "day of visitation" that happened in AD 70, recalling Jesus' words in Lu.19:41-44,

> "**And then, as He came near, upon seeing** (or: viewing and perceiving) **the City, He wept** (or: wailed; or: lamented; or: cried, shedding tears as an expression of grief) **upon it** (= over its condition and situation), **then saying, 'If you, even you yourself, knew by intimate experience or had discerned in this day the things [leading, moving or tending] toward peace** (= shalom; [other MSS: your peace])! **– but at this time it is** (or: has been) **hidden from your eyes – that days will proceed arriving upon you, and your enemies will be progressively setting up an encampment beside you and will continue casting up a mound beside [you and] a staked fortification** (or: rampart) **on** (or: next to) **you, and next will proceed to encircle and surround you, then continue bringing and enclosing pressure on you from every side! Later, they will proceed in dashing you to the ground and razing you, as well as your children within the midst of you – then they will continue not leaving stone upon stone** (or: a stone on a stone) **within you – in return for what things? Because you do not know the season** (or: had no intimate or personal awareness so as to recognize the occasion; have no insights about the fertile moment) **of your visitation and inspection.'"**

Our verse, here, may also be an allusion to Ps. 69:28, where David seeks reprisal for his persecutors:
> "Let them be wiped from the scroll of life [note: a poetic way of saying, 'let them die, or be killed'], and let them not be written with the righteous [which is a poetic way of saying, 'let them not be blessed or be included in what You are doing with us!']."

Jerusalem and its temple cultus were removed from the book of the Life of the little Lamb with the end of the age of the Law (AD 70). Neither would continue to participate in His reign, but individuals would be grafted back in, in their own time and class (Rom. 11:23-26; 1 Cor. 15:22-23a).

The metaphor of "overcoming" or "**conquering**" is parallel to what Paul referred to as "running a race" and "winning the prize" which pertains to the upward invitation in Christ (Phil. 3:14). We can be disqualified from this by not abiding in Him, and thus by not being victorious. This passage is not talking about being a child of God, but about pursuing God in this upward call – once we have been born back up again into the reign and kingdom of God. If we do not abide in Him, we will wither. The potential for this is what Paul referred to when he said,
> "**To the contrary, I am repeatedly "striking my face below my eyes and beating my body black and blue"** (= treating my body severely by discipline and hardship) **and continually leading [it] as a slave** (or: causing it to lead the life of a slave), **lest somehow, while proclaiming** (heralding; preaching; [note: at the games it means to announce the rules of the game and call out the competitors]) **to** (or: for) **others, I myself should** (can; may; would) **come to be one that does not stand the test** (or: unproved; or: without the approval which comes from testing; or: disapproved and disqualified)." (1 Cor. 9:27).

In 1 Cor.9:26 Paul had just said, "**So now, I myself am constantly running** (racing) **in this manner,**" and this is the context of "**those progressively running, on the race-course within a stadium**," (vs. 24). Also in vs. 26 he says, "**thus I am habitually boxing**." This all refers to how a person leads his life in the spirit.

In 13:8, below, we read of a category of folks who "**dwell upon the earth**," i.e., not in the heavens or atmospheres (vs. 6), i.e., in God's realm, and who worship the beast, "**whose name[s] [have] not been written in the scroll of the Lamb' Life**..." Here we have the contrast via the figures of living "**upon the earth**" versus "**in the heavens**." Those whose lives are lived in the spirit, in heaven, in union with Christ are like citizens of ancient cities, who were registered as living in that city. Paul uses the metaphors of "**the Jerusalem which is above**" in contrast with the then existing physical Jerusalem on earth (Gal. 4:25, 26). To have one's name in the book of the Lamb's life, is to actively, existentially participate in the Christ life – the upward invitation – and to be a part of the first-fruits, and thus, live in the anointing. Paul made a similar statement in Phil. 4:3,
> "**O genuine and legitimate yokefellow, be consistently taking these women together to yourself to aid and assist them – which women toil together with me** (or: compete [as] in the public games along with me, and contend on my side) **within the message of goodness and well-being, with Clement and the rest of my fellow workers, whose names [are] within Life's Book** (or: in a book of life; a book which is Life; [comment: = participation in life])." Cf 21:27, below.

That He will speak before the Father and His agents in accord to the overcomer's name, would suggest a tribute to the conqueror's accomplishments – perhaps that he built with gold, or with silver, or with precious stones (1 Cor. 3:12), rather than with the disqualifying materials which would not withstand the test of the Fire (God). Notice that those whose work did not stand the test suffered a loss, regarding their work on God's temple, but this did not affect their ultimate situation:

> "**If anyone's work will be burned down, he will incur a loss** (sustain the damage; forfeit [it]), **yet he himself will be saved** (rescued and delivered; healed and restored to health; returned to his original state and condition), **and as in this way – through Fire!**" (1 Cor. 3:15).

Christ will confess the character that has been built into the overcomer, and give praise for their service to others (e.g., Mat. 25:34-36), or His assessment of their life may be that they failed to exhibit Christ's character – they had not remained "joined to the Vine" (Jn. 15:1ff). They had not been living like a citizen of the New Jerusalem, but rather either like the old covenant Jerusalem, or like a citizen of the world. They would need to be re-connected to the Vine, begin using kingdom materials that are compared to gold, silver and precious stones, or perhaps be returned to the dealings of God's refining Fire (Mal. 3:2-3). Having one's name in the scroll of the Lamb's Life symbolizes existentially and presently living the cruciform life, following Christ as a disciple (Mat. 16:24-27). Not all believers live this kind of life. One must "**walk worthy of our calling**" (Eph. 4:1) to be assessed as "living **the Life of the Lamb**." As Dan Kaplan has said, "The Lamb submits to its death." That was Christ's pattern for us.

This can also be compared to the time where Jacob blessed his sons, confessing their names and characters (Gen. 49). Our understanding of the last clause of vs. 5, here, may be enhanced by considering the passage of Jesus' teaching in Mat. 10:16-42. There, in vss. 26-31, He tells them not to fear what might come against them, and speaks of their value to God. Then, in vs. 32-33, He explains,

> "**Everyone, then, that will keep on acknowledging union with Me and speaking in accord with Me in front of** (before and in the presence of) **humans** (mankind), **I, Myself, also will continue to acknowledge union with him and will keep on speaking of him in the same way** (saying the same thing of him) **in front of** (before and in the presence of) **My Father – the One within and in union with the heavens** (or: in the midst of the atmospheres). **Yet, whoever may refuse [to acknowledge] Me, or can disown and deny Me, in front of humans** (mankind), **I, Myself, also will continue refusing [to acknowledge] him, and will keep on disowning and denying him, in front of My Father – the One within and in union with the heavens** (or: in the midst of the atmospheres)."

The context of these words was the 1st century ministry of Jesus, when He was sending out the twelve, who were only to go to "the lost sheep of the house of Israel" (10:6). So the negative response just quoted in vs. 33 would refer to those Jews who did not accept His disciples nor Him, which was one of His many subtle statements about what would soon happen to the leadership in Jerusalem.

Kaplan also reminded me of Paul's metaphor of the olive tree in Rom. 11:17-21. The warning, there, in vss. 18-21, shed light on the possibility of a believer having his name "**erased from out of the scroll of The Life**." There we are warned not to boast against the branches that were broken out of the tree (figure of the unbelieving Jews of Paul's time). Verse 21 completes this warning:

> "**For you see, since** (or: if) **God spares not** (or: was not thrifty with) **the natural branches** (the branches down from, or, in accord with, nature), **neither will He continue sparing you!**"

Being broken out of Israel's olive tree is equivalent to having one's name erased from the scroll of the Christ-Life. Here we should note the parenthetical expansion: "the scroll which signifies life." If a believer, or a community, does not have its name in this scroll it means that he, she or they are dead. Paul said, in Rom. 8:6,

> "**the result of the thinking** (mind-set; effect of the way of thinking; disposition; result of understanding and inclination; the minding; the opinion; the thought; the outlook) **of the flesh** (= the human condition or the System of culture and cultus; or: = outward Torah ceremony) **[is; brings] death**."

An example of a community that would not have had their name written in "the scroll that signifies life," was Sardis, in 3:1, above; note: even though they "**were dead**," Christ was still writing to them, admonishing them.

Just as this Unveiling, written down by John, often has allusions to Israel's ancient past, I suggest that we should understand some of these enigmatic statements by the risen Christ as pertaining primarily to the 1st century setting into which this writing was to be sent. But having one's name in the scroll of the Life of the Lamb (indicating those who live a cruciform life in Christ) does not speak about their ultimate destiny, nor of their final end. It speaks to how they are living in this life, here and now.

6. **"Now let the one having an ear continuously listen, and hear what the Spirit** (or: Breath-effect; Attitude) **is normally and presently saying to the called-out, covenant communities.**

This repeats the "admonition formula" given to all the covenant communities: to **listen** and **hear** what God is **presently** or **normally** saying to us. This repetition is like saying, "Now don't let your eyes glaze over: this is important. Listen with the perception provided by the Spirit that is within you, so that you will understand these messages!"

7. **"And so to the agent and message-bearer which is** (or: of; from; with regard to) **the called-out community in Philadelphia, write:**
> **'The Set-apart One** (The Holy One; The Saint), **the True One, the One having** (continuously holding) **David's Key, the One habitually opening – and no one keeps on shutting** (or: locking) **– and He is repeatedly shutting (locking) – and no one keeps on opening –** [Isa. 22:22] **He, is presently saying these things,**

Consider the continued identification of Himself by attributes of His character (e.g., holy, true) or of His power and authority (having David's key; the 7 spirits in vs. 1; the two-edged sword in His mouth, etc.). If such things are important to God, should they not also be so to us? Do we relate to ourselves, or to others, as being a holy one (one **set apart**), a **true one**, etc.? That first phrase, "**The Set-apart/Holy One**, may be an allusion to Isa. 6:3, "Holy, holy, holy [is] Yahweh of hosts; his glory is the fullness of the whole earth!" If so, the risen Christ is again identifying Himself with Yahweh. In Acts 3:14 we read,
> "**But then you yourselves renounced** (disowned; denied) **the set-apart and fair Person** (the Holy and Just One Who personified the Way pointed out; this consecrated and rightwised One)..."

Cf my comments on Mat. 10, in vs. 5, above. Peter here, in Acts, affirms the ones of whom Jesus was speaking in Mat. 10: 33.

That He is **the True One** is affirmed in vs. 14, below, "**the Faithful** (or: Trustworthy, Reliable) **and True Witness**." Cf also Jn. 14:6. And we have Jn. 1:9,
> "**It was** (or: **He** was, and continued being) **the True and Genuine Light which** (or: Who) **is continuously** (repeatedly; progressively) **enlightening** (giving light to) **every person** (or: human) **continuously** (repeatedly; progressively; constantly; one after another) **coming into the world** (or: the ordered system of culture, religion, economics and government; or: the universe)
>> (or: It was the real Light, progressively coming into the world {organized system}, which is progressively enlightening {or: shedding light on} every human)."

And then we have the beautiful affirmation in 1 Jn. 5:20,
> "**yet we have seen and thus know that God's Son has arrived and is continuously here, and He has given thorough understanding** (comprehension; faculty of thought; intelligence; intellectual capacity; input throughout the mind) **to the end that we would constantly know** [other MSS: so that we do constantly know] **by experience the True One** (or: the true, the real and the genuine), **and we constantly exist within and in union with the True One** (or: in the real [situation]; in the midst of Reality): **within His Son, Jesus Christ. This One is the True**

(Real; Genuine) **God, and Life pertaining to and having the qualities of the Age** (or: life having its source in the Age [of Messiah]; eonian life; Life of, for and on through, the ages)."

He is continuously, or repeatedly, opening things for us, and presumably, for others. Yet, as He so chooses, He is also constantly and repeatedly shutting (presumably doors, perceptions or opportunities). Can we accept this from one who loves us? We love having opportunities (open doors), but do we just as much love closed opportunities and doors being shut to us? He is telling us that **He is set-apart** in this context, so can we assume that His decisions about opening or closing are made objectively, from His overarching purposes and goals? With our limited views and perspectives, can we thank Him for what He chooses in these situations? If we trust Him, if we have placed our faith into Him, then we can say, "Yes," and give thanks to Him for both open doors and locked ones?

David's key is a figure for control to access, for ability to be coming into or going out of situations, and for security; it's a figure for the Messiah's kingdom and sovereign activities. He is able to unlock secrets of the universe, and of His plans, for us. It is a symbol of His being in authority in His City, and, in this case, in His called-out community in Philadelphia.

Yet further, the Lord is citing a reference to Eliakim in Isa. 22:20-25, who in turn was the spokesman for king Hezekiah when Rabshakeh and the hosts of Assyria came against Jerusalem (2 Ki. 18:16-37). In this latter passage, this Assyrian general says to Eliakim, "Am I now come up without Yahweh against this place, to destroy it?" (vs. 25). The Lord's paraphrase of Isa. may be a veiled reference to the upcoming destruction of Jerusalem by the Romans in AD 70. And through the figure Eliakim in Isa. 22:22 (upon whose shoulder is laid "the key of the house of David"), we see that it is the Lord who now holds the key to the gates of the city of David (this city also being a symbol for the people of Judea) – and its/their fate is in His hands. So too is the situation for those of the "synagogue of satan" who are calling themselves Jews (vs. 9, above). His decision for them will stand. *Cf* Lu. 1:32. Could "David's Key" be synonymous with "**the keys of, and pertaining to, the Death and of, and pertaining to, the Unseen** (or: which are Death and Hades [= *sheol*; perhaps: 'the grave']; from the Death and from the unseen 'realm/state of the dead'; belonging to death and shadowy existence)," in 1:18, above? Or, Mat. 16:19,

> "**I will continue giving to you the keys which have their origin and source in the reign and activities of the heavens**
> > (or: which pertain to and have the characteristics of the kingdom of the heavens; or: which belong to the sovereignty from the atmospheres; or, as a genitive of apposition: the keys which are the sovereign reign of the heavens). **And so, whatever you can** (or: may; should) **bind upon the earth will continue being [something] having been bound, and still remaining bound, within the midst of the heavens** (or: in the atmospheres). **Also, whatever you can** (or: may; should) **loose upon the earth will continue being [something] having been loosed** (unbound; untied), **and remaining free of bonds, within the midst of the heavens** (or: in the atmospheres)."

8. *I have seen, and thus know (am aware of) your* [note: pronouns & verbs are singular] *actions (works; deeds). Consider! I have given before you an open door (or: a door having been opened in your sight) which no one is able (or: has power) to shut, because you continue holding a little power (having a little ability), and you keep watch over (guarded) My Word (Idea), and you do not contradict (deny) My Name.*

Now in addressing Philadelphia, He announces an **open door** (= access or opportunity into something, or, escape out of a bad situation) for them. *Cf* 2 Cor. 2:12. It could apply to group situations, or, an individual leading by the Holy Spirit. Recall the saying of Jesus, "**knock and keep on knocking,**

and it will be opened" (Matt. 7:7). That He has the power to keep the door open for them would give hope and courage to proceed. But this **open door** may symbolize access to spiritual vision, and entrance into viewing reality from God's viewpoint, as John was granted in 4:1, below. It is possible that the "**open door**" is an enigmatic symbol, rather than a figure of speech. What might be on offer is access to the sphere of the New Jerusalem, whose "**gates shall by no means be closed**," (21:25, below). *Cf* Isa. 45:1.

He recognizes even the **little power and ability** which they do have, and this opens opportunity to them: "to him who has shall more be given" (Mat. 13:12; 25:29). He values having His Word kept and nurtured, and our being loyal to His **Name** – which implies to Him, to His character and qualities, and to His reputation.

The verb **watch over** means to guard, and also to maintain and preserve. It is in the aorist (fact) tense, so I have offered both a simple present rendering and a simple past rendering. Since the Greek *logos* means both "word" and "idea," the implication of "preserving His Idea (i.e., His plan and purpose)" lends a larger perspective of Christ's acknowledgement of the stance which this congregation holds. They know His Message of goodness, ease and well-being.

The last clause, "**you do not contradict My Name**," suggests that this community did not live in a way that contradicts Who He is, and that their concepts and words do not contradict His character. The idea of denial, here, would also suggest succumbing to either the Jews or the pagan pressures (such as the Emperor cult, or, the trade union deities). John Gavazzoni pointed us to what Paul said in Gal. 2:19-20, in regard to this phrase,

> "**You see, I myself through [the] Law died by [the] Law** (or: to [the] Law; in [the] Law; with [the] Law), **to the end that I could and would live by God, in God, for God, to God and with God! I was crucified together with Christ** [= the Messiah], **and thus it remains** (or: I have been jointly put on the execution stake in [the] Anointed One, and continue in this state)... **yet I continue living! [It is] no longer I, but it is Christ continuously living and alive within me!** (or: No longer an "I" – now Christ constantly lives in the midst of, and in union with, me). **Now that which I, at the present moment, continue living within flesh** (= a physical body), **I am constantly living within [His] faithfulness – in and by that [faithfulness] which is the Son of God** (or: in union with the trust and confidence that is from God's Son; [with other MSS: in the faith and fidelity belonging to God and Christ])*,*"

Keep in mind the singular pronouns and verbs: this message applies to the entire community as a corporate entity. They, collectively, are His agent in Philadelphia. This should speak to the connectedness that we enjoy because of His Spirit within and among us. We are a City; we are a People.

9.   *Consider! I am [other MSS: could be] **constantly giving to those from out of the synagogue of satan** (the assembly of the adversary; the congregation which is the adversary) – **the ones repeatedly saying [that] they themselves are Jews, and yet they are not, but are lying – Consider! I will continue forming, constructing and making them so that they will proceed arriving, and then they will proceed worshiping in front of your feet and can know that I, Myself, love and accept you!***

This is the second city where He mentions there being a synagogue of the adversary there, but it is the fourth community whose message from Him speaks of something regarding *satan* (2:9; 2:13; 2:24). Does He mean that those folks have an adversarial spirit that characterizes their group? Or is this a figure of the Judaizers who try to reintroduce keeping the Law? Or, does it symbolize the Jewish opposition to

Christianity that was present? Whichever it is, it is obvious that *satan's* realm is the religious community, and its (or, "their" – the opponent may be a group) main activity is in relation to the called-out groups.

The present tense verb, "**constantly giving**," in the first clause has two textual traditions. One has the verb in the indicative, the other in the subjunctive (the bracketed reading). Neither tradition has a direct object of the verb. We find this same situation in 11:3, below. So we might ask, What is He giving, or could He be giving? Perhaps the answer lies in the latter part of the verse, where He promises to "***continue forming, constructing and making them***." I.e., He will continue giving (a durative future tense) them whatever they need to bring His desired end, which we find in the last clause of the verse. What a beautiful picture of reconciliation that HE is in the process of creating, as He continues forming the community's adversaries! THIS is what God is **constantly giving**. They will proceed to be doing obeisance to God within the presence of Philadelphia's called-out assembly! This is an example of what Paul referred to Phil. 2:10-11a,

> "**within The Name: Jesus! every knee** (= person) – **of the folks upon the heaven and of the people existing upon the earth and of the folks dwelling down under the ground** (or: on the level of or pertaining to subterranean ones; [comment: note the ancient science of the day – a three-tiered universe]) – **may bend** (or: would bow) **in prayer, submission and allegiance, and then every tongue** (= person) **may speak out the same thing** (should and would openly agree, confess, avow and acclaim) **that Jesus Christ [is] Lord**…"

So the second half of the verse is a picture of the removal of estrangement and enmity in these folks. So here we see the goal and the end for "**the synagogue of *satan*.**" His gift is grace to them. It is also a picture of folks coming to seek forgiveness and reconciliation. In judgment He remembers mercy (Hab. 3:2).

What does He mean where He identifies these folks as, "***repeatedly saying [that] they themselves are Jews, and yet they are not, but are lying***"? We read in Rom. 2:28-29a,

> "**for you see, the Jew is not the one in the visibly apparent or outwardly manifest** (or: For not he in the outward appearance is a Jew), **neither [is] circumcision that [which is] visibly apparent** (outwardly manifest) **in flesh** (= in body), **but rather, a Jew [is] the one within the hidden [place]** (or: [that which is] in the concealed [realm]) **and circumcision [is] of [the] heart** (= core of our being) – **in union with Breath-effect** (or: within [the] spirit; in attitude), **not in letter**."

Cf the comments on 2:9, above, where He made a similar statement. This calls to mind the branches that were broken out of the olive tree, in Rom. 11:17ff. Those broken out branches were no longer "Jews," in God's economy.

This may be an allusion to Isa. 60:14, "The sons also of them that afflicted you shall come bending unto you; and all those that despised you shall bow themselves down at the soles of your feet; and they shall call YOU 'The city of Yahweh, the Zion of the Holy One of Israel.'" Then there is Isa. 49:23, "And kings shall be your nourishing fathers, and their queens your nursing mothers: they shall bow down to you with their face to the ground, and then lick up the dust of your feet, and thus you shall know that I am Yahweh – for they shall not be ashamed that wait for Me." In both cases, those people or those adversarial spirits who/which were previously enemies now acknowledge both God's people, and God Himself. They have been transformed. *Cf*, also, Isa. 45:14.

Another echo of this figure comes from Gen. 37:5-11, where Joseph had dreams of his parents and his brothers bowing down to him. His brothers became adversaries to him and he winds up a slave in prison in Egypt. Then Yahweh creates a situation where they "arrive" and worship at his feet.

10. *Because you keep watch over (observe; preserve; guard)* **the Word of My patient endurance** *(of My remaining-under),* **I, also, will continue keeping watch over** *(observing; preserving; guarding)* **you from out the midst of the hour of the putting to the proof** *(or: trial; test)* **which is presently about to be progressively coming upon the whole territory where folks normally dwell** *(or: inhabited land; = Roman Empire),* **to put to the proof** *(to test, try and put through an ordeal)* **those continually dwelling down in houses upon the Land** *(or: inhabiting the territory).'* [*cf* 1 Pet. 4:12]

Here we come to the phrase "**the Word of My patient endurance** (of My remaining under)" which they keep and watch over. Is this the message of His bearing the cross? Heb. 12:2-3 says, "**Who, in the place of the joy continuously lying before Him, remained under** (endured) **a cross – despising shame and disgrace.... the One having remained under** (having endured) **such contradiction by those missing the mark**..." 2 Tim. 2:10 speaks of Paul constantly enduring all things because of the chosen folks. We also see an affirmation of His personal involvement with our lives, and a corresponding participation with us: *Because you keep watch over… I, also, will continue keeping watch over.* They guarded and preserved "**the Word of [His] remaining-under,**" and He "**will continue guarding and preserving [them]**" as they pass "**through the midst of Him**" (Rom. 11:36).

The promise to keep, observe, preserve and guard is echoed in 2 Pet. 2:9,
"**[The] Lord** [=Yahweh], **having seen, thus knows to** (or: knows how to) **continuously drag out of danger** (or: rescue) **a reverent person** (one standing in devout goodness, in awe and in virtuous conduct with ease and well-being from relationship with God) **from out of the midst of a trial** (or: ordeal; [other MSS: trials]), **yet to constantly keep in custody, guard, watch over and maintain unjust folks** (people who live contrary to the Way pointed out; unrightwised folks) **[who are] being repeatedly pruned** (or: being progressively corrected), **[which is leading] unto a day of evaluating for making a decision [about their progress]** (or: of judging [condition])."

Here, we should also recall Jesus' words in Jn. 16:33,
"**Within the System** (dominating and controlling world of culture, religion, economy and government; or: among and in union with the aggregate of humanity) **you normally have pressure and stress** (or: continually have squeezing; repeatedly have tribulation and oppression), **but nonetheless, be confident and take courage! I, Myself, have overcome and conquered the System** (dominating world; organized arrangement of religion and society; aggregate of humanity) **so that it stands a completed victory!**"

Putting these verses together, we see that vs. 10, here, is not promising to keep us from hard experiences, as the common rendering "keep you from" tends to imply. Rather, the expanded rendering, "***keeping watch over*** *(observing; preserving; guarding),*" speaks of attentive care. By expanding the rendering of the preposition *ek* to its core idea, "***from out of the midst,***" it explains that the attentive care and preservation which He gives comes from "the midst" of the situation – for He is there with us, in the midst of the very test and trial. He does not leave us or forsake us. Recall 2:1, above: He is "**the One continuously walking about within the midst of the seven golden lampstands,**" i.e., within the called-out communities. You see, we are intended to go through the same tests and trials that others go through, so that He can give attentive care to them – through us.

The clause, "***the putting to the proof*** *(or: trial; test)* ***which is presently about to be progressively coming upon the whole territory,***" shows that this was, on the first level, speaking about a 1st century situation: a relatively local area (within the Empire) and that it was about to happen, at the time of John writing this letter. We see that Peter later wrote that these tests and trials were indeed happening to these folks (1 Pet. 4:12), in his first letter to this same region (1 Pet. 1:1). T. Everett Denton points this out, and remarks that there it was, "indicating, of course, that Revelation was penned before 1 Peter" (*Pertinent Parousia Passages, Second-Coming Scripture Studies*, 2016, p 217). We should also take note that this trial is qualified by Him with the term, "*the hour.*" It was to come soon, like Jesus said in Mk. 14:41, "**The hour comes. Look, and consider** (See, and understand), **the Son of the Man** (the human son) **is being progressively given over**..."). *Cf* Jn. 16:32. But it was also to be a short season. We read in 7:14b, below, that folks were, "**continuously coming forth from out of the midst of great pressure** (squeezing; ordeal; tribulation)."

The last clause, "*those continually dwelling down in houses upon the Land,*" is seen as a technical term (*cf* Beale, ibid p 290). It is found again, below, in: 6:10; 8:13; 11:10; 12:12; 13:8, 12 14; 14:6; and 17:2, 8. Its literal, historic meaning would refer to those living in the Roman Empire, in the 1st century. But as a figurative symbol, it would speak of those who were not living the Christ-life (as those who were seated in the spiritual realm with Christ – Eph. 2:6), i.e., in the realm of the Spirit, but, to the contrary were living with their thinking in the natural, or carnal, realm (e.g., Rom. 8:6). This is the same way in which the repeated metaphor "overcoming" is used in these letters: winning at the games, or overcoming obstacles.

11. "**I am repeatedly** (habitually; constantly) **coming and going swiftly** (or: = progressively coming soon)! **You must be continuously strong in what you have** (or: you must constantly hold in your power that which you possess) **to the end that no one may take your winner's wreath** (your emblem of victory; or: your encirclement).

This affirms once again that He is continually, repeatedly, progressively (or, at that time, presently) **coming** (the Greek present tense). The Greek verb means either "to come," or, "to go." Since the tense of the verb indicates that the action may be habitual, it stands to reason that "habitual coming" also indicates "habitual going," as with someone constantly, or **repeatedly**, coming to visit, then departing until the next visit. This language suggests dynamic interaction between the risen Christ and His communities. Before, He said that He comes as a thief; here He says that He comes swiftly – the opposite of a slow or gradual approach. It would seem that Philadelphia did not have long to wait for His "progressively coming soon." Then He tells them to **continue being strong** so as not to lose their **victor's emblem**. Paul, in Eph. 6:10, says, "**you must continuously empower yourselves within the Lord, and within** (in union with) **the strength of His might**." He say a similar thing in 2 Tim. 2:1, but there he was to do it "**in union with the grace which is within Christ Jesus**."

The possibility of the loss of the winner's wreath is a metaphor from the games, where an opponent will always try to throw us down and beat us, so that we lose the contest. We should keep in mind that the games happened here, in this life, and often annually. This is just another metaphor for having diligence as we live the Christ life among those whose lives can be abrasive or hard to deal-with. Both Paul and John are given pictures which represent life as a contest. In life we find that there is often a struggle to survive – in one situation or another. This being the case, we should always look to the Lord for our strength, and for our ability to overcome adversity. This admonition is not speaking about some "final outcome of our life." It should be seen with the same understanding as where Paul is using his own life as an encouragement for others, as in Phil. 3:13b-14,

> "**habitually forgetting, on the one hand, the things behind** (or: in the back), **and on the other hand constantly reaching and stretching myself out upon the things in front** (or: ahead), **I am continuously pressing forward, pursuing down toward** [the; or: an] **object in view** (a mark on which the eye is fixed)**: into the awarded contest prize of God's** (or: the award which is God's) **invitation to an above place** (or: the prize from, and which is, the upward calling from, and which is, the God) **within the midst of and in union with Christ Jesus**."

When John's listeners heard this admonition from Christ, they would have understood that it meant that they should put all their effort into bringing Christ's reign to others, to reach out in accepting love for others, and to strive to live in the peace from the joining of all people into one new humanity (Eph. 2:15). This is a call to **strong** and healthy living within the brotherhood of Christ, gathering strength from Christ to remain under the normal burdens of living together in love. It is a symbolic presentation of all the imperatives that we find in Jesus' teachings, Paul's epistles, and the rest of the NT writings.

12. **"'The one habitually conquering** (repeatedly overcoming so as to be the victor) **– I will continue making** (forming; constructing; creating; producing) **him [to be] a pillar** (or: column) **in the Temple that is My God, and he** (or: it) **may nevermore** (by no means any more) **come** (or: go) **out** (outside)**, and I will proceed to write upon him My God's Name, and the name of the City of My God: "The New and different Jerusalem"** – **the one habitually descending from out of the atmosphere** (or: heaven), **from God – and My Name, the one new in character and quality** [other MSS: and the new name].'

This tells us, as before, that there is a prize for this **overcoming**. We are formed into being part of the supporting structure (**a pillar**) in the body of Christ. It is the Lord that is building His called-out groups (Matt. 16:18), and recall Paul's words that we are **the temple of the living God** (2 Cor. 6:16). Those in Asia Minor were growing together into a set-apart temple – God's dwelling place, in spirit (Eph. 2:19-22). Always being a part of the temple is like having your name in the story (the scroll) of the Lamb's life. *Cf* Gal. 2:9 for another use of the "pillar" metaphor; also 1 Pet. 2:5. Note that I have rendered the genitive phrase, following the word "**pillar**," as appositional: "**in the Temple that is My God**." For affirmation of this, *cf* 21:22, below.

Next we come to having **God's Name** and "**the New Jerusalem**" written upon the conqueror. We are identified with God, and with the New Jerusalem (the one constantly descending out of heaven; "the Jerusalem above is free, who is our mother" – Gal. 4:26. This indicates that we have been born back up from above again – John 3:3, and corresponds to Eph. 2:5-6 where Paul tells us that "**He aroused [us] together and caused [us] to sit together within heavenly places within Christ Jesus**"). We have God's and Jerusalem's character – what a promise. Then He stresses that we ourselves have **His new Name**: thus we are either married to Him, or we are His body, a part of Him. In all this we also represent God, the New Jerusalem and Christ, for we bear His Name. In *Odes of Solomon* 42:20 (late 1st century) we read:
> "And I placed my name upon their head because they are free and they are mine" (translated by J.H. Charlesworth, *The OT Pseudepigrapha*, Vol. 2, Hendrickson, 2013 p 771).

But this idea goes back to the forming of Israel, where in Nu. 6:27 Yahweh instructs Moses that Aaron should bless Israel,
> "Thus they will place My Name upon the sons of Israel – and I Myself will bless them!"

And we see in Deut. 28:10, "All the peoples of the land/earth shall see that you are called by the Name of Yahweh." The LXX reads, "the Name of the LORD has been called upon you (or: surnamed to you)."
And Isa. 43:7 speaks of, "Everyone who is called by My Name…" Then Dan. 9:19b reads, "Because Your own Name has been called upon Your city, and upon your people."

As with Christ, it is the nature of the heavenly folks to descend to those of low position ("**continuously leading yourselves away together to the low folks**" – Rom. 12:16). Thus is the New (Heavenly) Jerusalem continuously descending from God, out of heaven, taking the form of a servant. Beale cites G.B. Caird, *Revelation*, 55, and M.R. Mulholland, *Revelation*,130, stating, "Caird and Mulholland conclude that the present participle *katabainousa* ('descending') means that the New Jerusalem is a present reality descending throughout history" (ibid p 296; note: Beale does not accept this view).

The new name has its roots in Isa. 62:2 "and you shall be called by a new name, which the mouth of Yahweh will specify." Also Isa. 65:15, "and He will call His servants by another name." Again, recall the name changes of Abram, Jacob, and Simon. *Cf* 14:1 and 22:4, below. It's about our taking on His identity, as Paul described it in Gal. 2:20,

> "**I was crucified together with Christ** [= the Messiah], **and thus it remains... yet I continue living!** [It is] **no longer I, but it is Christ continuously living and alive within me! Now that which I, at the present moment, continue living within flesh** (= a physical body), **I am constantly living within [His] faithfulness – in and by that [faithfulness] which is the Son of God, the One loving me and giving Himself over to another for the sake of me.**"

We find descriptions of **The New and different Jerusalem** in Heb. 12:22-24,

> "**But to the contrary, you folks have approached so that you are now at Mount Zion – even in a city of a continuously living God; in "Jerusalem upon heaven"**
> (or: in a Jerusalem pertaining to and having the character and qualities of a superior, or added, heaven and atmosphere; or: in Jerusalem [situated] upon, and comparable to, the atmosphere) – **also among ten-thousands of agents and messengers** (people with a/the message): **[that is] in** (or: to) **an assembly of an entire people** (or: an assembly of all; a universal convocation) **and in** (or: to) **a summoning forth** (or: a called-out and gathered community) **of firstborn folks having been copied** (or: registered) **within [the; or: various] atmospheres** (or: heavens), **and in** (or: to; with) **God, a Judge of all mankind, even among** (or: to; with) **spirits of just folks having been brought to the destined goal** (perfected; finished; matured; made complete), **and in** (or: to) **Jesus, a Medium** (or: an Umpire; a Mediator) **of a new and fresh** (young; recently-born) **arrangement** (covenant), **and to and in blood of sprinkling...**"

This is definitely a different, NEW Jerusalem. *Cf* also 21:2, below.

13. "Let the person having an ear listen to and hear what the Spirit (Breath-effect) **is repeatedly** (or: progressively) **saying to the called-out, covenant communities!**

Verse 13 repeats the admonition to listen and to hear. The Spirit is repeatedly and continuously saying things to us. Perhaps this relates to what Jesus said in Jn. 16:12-13,

> "**I still have** (or: hold) **many things to be progressively telling you folks, but yet, you continue not yet being able** (or: having no power) **to habitually or progressively pick it up and carry** (or: bear) **it right now** (at present). **Yet, whenever that One – the Spirit of the Truth** (or: the Breath-effect from Reality) **– should come, It** (or: He) **will constantly be a Guide and will progressively lead you on the Path directed toward and proceeding on into all Truth and Reality...**"

14. "And then, to (or: in; for) **the agent which is** (or: messenger from; person having the message of, or with regard to) **the called-out community within Laodicea, write:**
> '**The Amen** (The It-is-so), **the Faithful** (or: Trustworthy, Reliable) **and True Witness, the Beginning of God's Creation** (or: the Prime Source of God's creation; the First Place or Chief of God's Framing; the Origin of God's act of building and founding; the Starting Point from God's act of reducing from a state of wildness and disorder) **is presently saying these things,**

Once again, the Lord identifies Himself with aspects of His character. In Isa. 65:16 we are told that **Yahweh** is "the God of truth, or, faithfulness," but in the Hebrew it reads "the God of the **Amen**" (Rotherham, n "c"; Strong, #543; Young: So it is; It is so). The enthroned Christ uses language that was used to describe Yahweh. This also calls to mind J. Wash Watts' translation of the last phrases of Gen.

1:7, 9, 11 and 24, "... and gradually it came to be **so**" (*A Distinctive Translation of Genesis*, Wm B Eerdmans Pub., 1963). Jesus frequently used the Greek version of this word (*Amēn*) in His teachings. There is here an association with Yahweh, and with promises that can be relied upon. Paul used this word in 2 Cor. 1:20,

> "**So you see, as many as [be] God's promises, [they are] the "Yes," within and in union with Him. Wherefore also, through Him [is] The Amen** (or: the affirmation; the "Count on it!;" the "It is so") **in** (or: by; with) **God [directed] toward and face to face with glory, a good opinion or reputation, and a manifestation which calls forth praise, through us**."

That He is **the Faithful** (or: Trustworthy; Loyal) **and True Witness** also calls to mind the teaching manner of Jesus: we can count on what He tells us; His evidence which He presents to us is trustworthy, and He is loyal in His taking a stand for us – witnessing to the truth of our situation. We might have an allusion to Isa. 55:4 in this verse:

> "Lo! As a Witness to the peoples have I given Him; as a Leader and Commander to the peoples."

Next He calls Himself "**the Beginning of God's Creation** (or: the Origin of God's creation; the First Place or Chief of God's Framing; the Beginning of God's act of building and founding; the Starting Point from God's act of reducing from a state of wildness and disorder)." The phrase, **the Beginning of God's Creation**, can have a double reference: back to the very beginning of creation, in Gen. 1-2, or, back to the new creation in Christ (2 Cor. 5:17; Eph. 2:14-16; 1 Cor. 15:22, 44-49). The Greek word for "beginning" is the same word which John used in the first verse of his gospel, "**In [the] beginning was, and continued being, the Word** (etc.)..." Many shy away from translating it this way for fear of portraying Christ as a created being. They emphasize the idea of His being in first place, i.e., the Ruler, or the first cause – the Originator. The Concordant Version reads, "God's creative Original." All of this may be true, and the Greek "*archē*" allows it, but if we see that He is not only God, but He, in this unveiling, represents the corporate Christ, then He, being the Head/Source of the Body, is the beginning of The Christ: God's New Creation – the Last Adam – God's construction plan of the Ages! He is the beginning of everything that God does. He is the beginning of God's purpose. He is the beginning of the New Humanity that was/is created in Him. To paraphrase Preston Eby, He is "God (Who is Spirit) through Himself (the Word) and out of Himself expressing Himself on another dimension (the realm of form, and 'things')."

Paul put it this way, in Col. 1:15,

> "**It is [this Son] Who is the Image** (portrait; the Exact Formed Likeness; the Figure and Representation; visible likeness and manifestation) **of the not-seen God** (or: the unable to be seen God; the invisible God), **the Firstborn of all creation**
>> (or: of every creature; or: of every framing and founding; of every act of settling from a state of disorder and wildness; or: pertaining to the whole creation; or: = the Inheritor of all creation Who will also assume authority over and responsibility for every creature [note: this is the duty of the firstborn])."

Standing behind vss. 12 and 14, here, are the prophecies in Isa. 65:16b-18,

> "For the former distresses are forgotten, and indeed they are concealed from My eyes. For behold Me creating new heavens and a new earth, and the former shall not be remembered (or: mentioned), nor shall they come up on the heart. But rather be elated and exult in the futures of the future which I shall be creating, for behold me creating Jerusalem an exultation, and her people an elation (or: a joy)" (CVOT; my additions).

Some scholars maintain that the phrase, "**the Beginning of God's Creation**," is dependent upon Prov. 8:22, 30, which speaks about Wisdom. But Paul's revelation seems to color in the picture in bright hues, in Col. 1:17-20,

"**And He is before** (or: maintains precedence of) **all things and all people, and the whole has** (or: all things have) **been placed together and now continues to jointly-stand within the midst of and in union with Him, and so He is the Head** (or: Source) **of the body – which is the called-out community – Who is the Beginning, a Firstborn forth from out of the midst of dead folks, to the end that He would be birthed** (or: could come to be) **within all things and in all people: He continuously holding first place, because WITHIN Him all – the entire contents** (the result of that which fills everything; all the effect of the full measure [of things]) – **delights to settle down and dwell as in a house and THROUGH Him at once to transfer the all** (the whole; = all of existential creation), **away from a certain state to the level of another which is quite different** (or: to change all things, bringing movement away from being down; to reconcile all things; to change everything from estrangement and alienation to friendship and harmony and move all), **INTO Him – making** (creating) **peace** (harmonious joining) **through the blood of His cross: through Him, whether the things upon the earth** (or: land) **or the things within the atmospheres and heavens!**"

Although the original creation described in Gen. 1 and Paul's referencing the first Adam, in 1 Cor. 15:45, find correlations and show continuity, I suggest that both the immediate and the general contexts of these verses (12 and 14) speak here of the new creation (e.g., 21:5, below; 2 Cor. 5:17) that was formed through, and within, the resurrection of Christ. As Beale points out (ibid p 301), the titles given in this verse must relate to this particular letter to Laodicea, and, I suggest, to the entire Unveiling, as a whole.

15. *I have seen, and thus know* (am aware of) *your* [singular] *works* (acts), *that you are* (continue being) *neither cold nor boiling hot* (or: zealous): *O that you were being cold, or boiling hot* (zealous)!

He has witnessed their works, and gives faithful testimony about their condition: they are **lukewarm, neither hot nor cold**. He is speaking of extremes and the hyperbole is obvious – they are neither passionate and zealous, nor uninterested and indifferent. They are somewhere in the middle, a mixture, perhaps turning one way then another. But He wishes them to be the one extreme or the other! We can easily discern this condition in the masses of Christianity today – and often within ourselves. But the reminder of just Who He is, given in vs. 14, above, should inject a Fire, and renewed life, into their community.

We can understand His wanting His called-out folks to be burning with zeal, but why this either/or? If the figure is of a drink, then we can see the pleasure of either a hot drink, or the refreshing of a cold one. Cold food is good; hot food is good; but food that has been sitting out for hours breeds salmonella and can make us sick, and we might throw up. But again, why not just say that He wants His people to be zealous? One would be boiling hot when he is being baptized in the Holy Spirit's Fire. The three Hebrews were zealous for Yahweh even in the fiery furnace (Dan. 3) – and that was where the Son of Man made His appearance. The tongues of Fire on the day of Pentecost might have been a sign that those folks were "boiling hot." Being hot speaks of being in God's presence; it can also speak of being purged in a lake of Fire.

But what about being cold? The word is *psuchros* (**cold**) and comes from the same root as *psuchē* (soul). Perhaps this is a metaphorical comparison between the soul and the spirit. When Saul was persecuting the church he was zealous, even if it was a zeal of soul. Some have presented the idea that to be "cold" meant to be away from God and in the "world." To be tepid and lukewarm would refer to those who would think, "I'm saved, and that's enough." Their **works** and "acts" were only "half-way" in their faithfulness to Christ's teachings (*cf* Mat. 25:42-43).

16. ***Thus, because you continue being lukewarm** (tepid), **and are neither boiling hot nor cold, I am about to vomit you out of My mouth.***

It is curious that the water supply of the city (brought via an aqueduct from Hierapolis) was "lukewarm and distasteful" (Hiett, ibid p 74).

If we look back to the Gospels, we see that Jesus hung out with those that the Pharisees would have called cold: the outcasts and sinners. They knew their condition and of their need for mercy (Lu. 18:13), and they welcomed Him. Yet, it would seem that it was the Pharisees whom He would have vomited out (Mat. 23:2-39). They were the whitewashed tombs (Mat. 23:27) – good appearance; foul contents. The "form" of piety, but denying God's Power. Here, in the covenant group in the city whose name means "the people of the right path," we see this same condition as was seen in the Pharisees. Jesus indicated that the Jewish leadership would be thrown out into the outer darkness (Mat. 8:10-12) – a place where they would be unable to participate in what God was doing, at that time. Another metaphor of being tossed out of the position of reigning in Christ's kingdom was the man not properly clothed to participate in the wedding feast (Mat. 22:11-14). But folks out in the cold of darkness become people who desire the heat and the Light. Christ spews out in order to bring folks to a place of receptivity – and to be clothed with Christ. His earthly mission was, "**to seek after, and then to save, deliver and restore what is existing being lost and destroyed**" (Lu. 19:10). He keeps on doing what He IS (Heb. 13:8), so those tossed into a "lost" and "cold" condition will be sought out by Him (Lu.15:4-7).

In a personal email, my friend Ken Nichols shared the following, in regard to this verse:
> "Cold, as in realizing their need for the gospel 'good news.' They might be lost in sin, but they KNOW they need help. They FEEL lost. They are 'poor in Spirit.'
> Hot, as in the one's PREACHING the 'good news' of a savior searching for those who are lost with means to rescue and heal them.
> Lukewarm, as those who BELIEVE they are 'saved' (in/going to heaven) because of their religious efforts (though they may not recognize these), and who are now 'partially blinded' to the truth. They know who Jesus is but have not translated that to change their thinking (repent) of their impure (sinful) view of the Father. They are still seeking to put others in bondage to a wrathful, retributive God. So, they THINK they are HOT, but they have 'missed the mark' of Jesus' revelation. I was DEFINITELY 'lukewarm' three years ago. I was sure I had it ALL figured out, every 'jot' and 'tittle' of my theology was squared away, and everyone who 'deserved' hell would get it (and I had VERY liberal ideas of who would escape it - or so I thought). Anyway, I'm so happy the Spirit choose to peel that blindfold from my eyes."

Hannah Hurnard, in *Steps to the Kingdom*, observed:
> "[Jesus] was a man of intensely strong emotions, all completely under his control… In him they were holy passions, and they were the conductors along which his holy power was transmitted to others… when he was 'moved with compassion' he could heal the sick, cleanse lepers, and raise the dead. When he was 'on fire with zeal' he could overawe and completely master crowds of angry people. When he was burning with love, he could cast out devils and evil spirits. And because he was aflame with forgiveness, he could conquer the cross and rise from the dead. He taught us that when emotion is absent, nothing superhuman or supernatural can be done, but heavenly emotions can produce miracles. Lukewarmness and indifference he could not bear…. Heavenly works cannot be accomplished without holy emotion and passion" (Harper & Row Pub., 1985 [originally, *The Secrets of the Kingdom of Heaven*, 1959] p 62-63).

The above applications of the term **lukewarm** are valid, and insightful. However, I think that Lynn Hiles has the best understanding of what Christ meant by this term, concerning the community in Laodicea. He sees this condition as being "half-way between the covenants; a mixture of Law and grace" ("A Redemptive Look at the Book of Revelation," Vol. 1, audio recording, part 19). This would align with Paul's messages against Judaizing: bringing the Mosaic Law into the life of the covenant communities. The figurative language, "***vomit you out of My mouth***," would correspond to Jesus' parables about **casting** the "**unprofitable servan**t" (a figure of the scribes and Pharisees) "**into outer darkness**," where they would then be **cold** (Mat. 25:30). Christ is suggesting that Laodicea had become like the Pharisees who were not cold (they were attempting to keep the Law), but neither were they **boiling hot** with Zeal for the Christ Life that was typified by "tongues as of Fire" sitting upon folks (Acts 2:3), nor were they burning with the Spirit's Fire, lighting up the surrounding darkness, as Christ's Lampstand. When water is ***boiling hot***, it gives off steam, the "spirit" form of water.

17. ***Because you are habitually saying, "I am rich and have acquired wealth and continuously have need of nothing," and you have not seen so as to know*** (or: are not aware) ***that you continue being wretched*** (or: miserable; in hardship) ***and pitiful and poor and blind and naked,***

It has been noted that of the 7 called-out communities addressed in this book, this is the only one of which Christ has nothing good to say: there is no redeeming feature. In the material realm, they were probably the most prosperous city in Asia Minor. The evaluation that they are poor, wretched, pitiful and naked would refer to their spiritual condition before the Lord. Scholars have compared this critique to that of Ephraim in Hosea 12. Despite the prophet's noting their emptiness, i.e., "grazing on wind," and their "daily increase of lies" (vs. 1), we read in vss. 7-8,

"A trafficker – in his hand are scales of deceit; he loves to exploit: hence Ephraim is saying, Yea, I am rich; I find virility for myself in all my labor…" (CVOT).

Beale (ibid p 305) notes how the material wealth with spiritual poverty in Laodicea contrasts to the material poverty with spiritual riches in Smyrna. That these "mirror opposites" have been emphasized may be a purposeful allusion to Jesus' teaching,

"**It is so** (or: Truly; Count on it), **I am now saying to you men, it is with things that are disagreeable and difficult for those who are hard to please that a rich and wealthy person will progressively enter into the reign of the heavens** (or: the heavens' kingdom; or: the sovereign rule pertaining to the atmospheres)" (Mat. 19:23).

Returning to Hos. 12, again, where Ephraim claimed to be rich, vs. 9 instructed them that Yahweh would, "cause [them] to dwell in tents," symbolizing a return to a nomadic life that was divorced from merchandising and riches. Perhaps the Lord was calling Loadicea to consider what happened to Ephraim, in Israel's history. Judgment always begins with God's people (1 Pet. 4:17a).

Hiles points us to the parable of the "Rich Man and Lazarus," in Lu. 16:19-31. There, the rich man is a figure of the Jews (who had the covenant and the promises, figured by Abraham being his father and his brothers having Moses, in the story) and the destitute Lazarus was a figure of Israel's hungry outcasts (Lu. 6:21a), and the Gentiles – to whom the kingdom was being given (Lu. 6:20b). Jesus addressed their respective conditions and their sudden reversal of situations in the parable, where Lazarus (the outcasts, Samaritans and Gentile nations) winds up being included in Abraham's bosom (Lu. 16:23b), but the rich man did not at that time enter into the realm of Abraham's seed, so as to be an heir of the Promise (Gal. 3:29). *Cf* Mat. 5:3ff, the "beatitudes," which Hiles interprets as "the attitudes needed to receive the kingdom" (ibid).

May the Lord open our eyes if indeed we are **blind** to our true condition. Recall Matt. 23:16-28, "Woe to you, blind guides (vs. 16).... stupid and blind (17&19).... blind guides (24).... blind Pharisees! (26)." Of this they were unaware! Like Laodicea, those folks thought that they were rich in Yahweh's kingdom, and yet they were not. They were only rich in material goods.

What did Christ mean when He said that they were **naked**? This may be an allusion to the Garden story, but in that situation both Adam and Eve had seen that they were naked. The tree of the Law (knowledge of good and evil; right and wrong) had showed them this fact. Here, they are blind, so they do not see their nakedness. Their blindness indicates that they were not even in the place of walking by the dim light of the Law. They had become like the Pharisees and scribes who, although having the Law, were not walking in its light. Neither were they hot from the Fiery Light of the Christ Life – which provides the **white garments** (vs. 18, below). They apparently had no righteousness at all – they were not living in accord with either the old covenant, or the new. They felt that they "had it all," but from the perspective of Christ's reign, they were "**wretched** (or: miserable; in hardship) **and pitiful and poor**." Their condition is an allusion to Ezk. 16:2-10, the wretchedness of Jerusalem before Yahweh gave her life, washed her, clothed her, and "entered into a covenant with [her]" (vs. 8b); before that, she was "**naked** and bare" (vs. 7b). But later, she "trusted in [her] own beauty and "played the prostitute" (vs. 15). Here, Laodicea would seem to be close to mimicking Jerusalem, which we will encounter in chapters 17-18, below.

18. ***I continue advising you** [singular] **to buy from Me gold having been refined** (set ablaze) **forth from out of fire, to the end that you may become rich; and white garments, to the end that you may clothe yourself and the shame** (disgrace) **of your nakedness may not be manifested** (brought to light; caused to appear)**; and eye-salve to anoint** (rub in) **your eyes, to the end that you may be continuously observing** (or: progressively seeing).'*

Laodicea is said to have prided itself in its financial wealth, its extensive textile industry, and in is famous **eye-salve**. Plainly, the Lord is saying that what they have of themselves, what they can do for themselves, will not fill their real needs. They are poor, naked and blind – and in fact, they are wretched and pitiful. This calls to mind Jesus' hard words to the Pharisees and other Jewish leaders. What this community needs it must **buy** from God. But how can we buy from God? Why buy gold? What is the medium of exchange when buying something from God? Keeping in mind that the messenger was sent to make things known by signs and symbols, what does gold signify?

We are not told how to buy from God, but an allusion to buy from Him is found in Isa. 55:1,
> "Ho! All who are thirsty, come (or: go) to the Water! Yes, he who has no money, come (or: go), purchase and eat!"

Purchase, when you have no money? This is a picture of Grace!

Gold is spoken of in the Bible more than any other metal. It was used to make the furniture of the tabernacle and to gild the boards which formed its walls. It was also used to make idols. It was the most precious metal of those days. It was used to make the most precious objects. From these we can see that gold represents 1) something of highest value; 2) the qualities, character, realm and presence of God; 3) the act or qualities involved with worship; 4) the attributes or position of a king [cf Dan. 2:38]; 5) it represents wealth. Another clue may be found in Ps. 12:6,
> "The words of Yahweh [are] pure (clean) words: [like] silver refined with a flame in a kiln and [CVOT adds: fine gold] cleansed from its earth seven times" (CVOT and Fenton).

And we have Mal. 3:3,

"Like a fire He is to refiners, and like the soap to a fuller, He sits down to fuse and refine out the dross from the silver, and Levi's sons He will cleanse, and refine like to silver and gold" (Fenton).

But how can we buy these, as He says here, in vs. 18? In those days, when one had nothing to give in trade for something, or to pay a debt, he could trade himself: he could sell himself into slavery. Was this perhaps why Paul called himself a slave of Christ (Rom. 1:1)? The Laodiceans were wretched and poor. What else could they give to God for this burning gold of His – except themselves? Perhaps this gold was to be used in the construction of His building (1 Cor. 3:9-15). Peter used gold as a comparison to faith, trust and loyalty,

"**the examined and tested approval of your faith** (of the trust and faithfulness of you folks) – **[being] of much greater value and worth, and more precious, than of gold that constantly loses itself away** (perishes of itself) **despite being progressively tested and examined through fire – might be found [progressing] into praise** (approval; commendation) **and glory** (or: a good reputation) **and honor** (value; worth) **within an unveiling of Jesus Christ**" (1 Pet. 1:7).

Perhaps it is our "Amen; make it so" to "the examined and tested approval of [our] trust and faithfulness" that is the currency that buys His fire-purified **gold**. Perhaps it is our, "Nevertheless, not my will, but Yours be done." Submission and obedience were core qualities needed for discipleship.

God's **eye-salve** is the anointing of His Holy Spirit. This too is something that He advised us to buy – to give our all for, or as Paul said, "**forgetting those things which are behind**... **press** (pursue) **toward the mark, for the prize which is the upward invitation from God, in union with Christ Jesus**" (Phil. 3:13-14). In vs. 8 of that same chapter, Paul had said,

"**I even am habitually considering all things to be a loss because of the thing that is constantly holding things above and thus having all-surpassing value and superiority: that which pertains to and comes from the experience of the intimate knowledge of my Lord, Jesus Christ – because of, on account of and for the sake of Whom I undergo loss of all things and I continue considering them to be [either] a lot of refuse and filth [or] things that are cast away from the table to the dogs** (garbage), **to the end that I may have the advantage of Christ**."

So deeming personal gain as refuse is one way of buying from God. This anointing with God's Spirit is that which enables us to see.

19. "**Whosoever, if I may be having affection for them** (regard them as fond friends), **I constantly put to the proof** (or: expose; reprove) **and I continuously educate** (discipline; give child-instruction). **Therefore be hot** (zealous) **and change your mind** (your way of thinking; your attitude and frame of mind)!

This declaration calls to mind Heb. 12:5-11 where the Lord speaks of the necessity of a son being educated and disciplined, if one is a true son. Also, Job 5:17-18, informs us, "Behold, happy is the mortal whom God corrects; Thus you must not reject the admonition of Him-Who-Suffices. For He Himself causes pain, and He shall bind up; He smites through, and His hands shall heal." Ps. 94:12 affirms, "Happy [is] the master whom You are disciplining, O Yah." Then in Prov. 3:12, we see:

"For whom Yahweh loves, He corrects, and He [gives] pain [to the] son He holds dear" (CVOT). These statements may sound harsh to our modern, western ears, but they represent the language and culture of the ancient world, and we see that the INTENT of the discipline had its source in LOVE for the one being harshly disciplined. This was still true in the 1st century Roman Empire, so John's listeners would not have been offended or confused about a loving Christ using such words to them. Recall Paul's words concerning unbelieving Jews, in Rom. 11:

22. **Observe, perceive and consider, then, God's useful kindness** (benevolent utility) **and abruptness** (sheer cutting-off; rigorous severity) – **on the one hand upon those falling: abruptness** (sheer cutting-off); **on the other hand** (or: yet) **upon you: God's useful kindness** (benign, profitable utility), **provided** (or: if) **you should persistently remain in** (or: with; by) **the useful kindness** (or: = continue to be kind and useful). **Otherwise you, also, will proceed in being cut out!**

23. **Now they also, if they should not persistently remain in the lack of faith and trust** (or: unbelief), **they will proceed in being grafted in, for God is able** (capable; is constantly powerful) **to graft them back in again!**

Paul put it this way, in 1 Cor. 11:32,

"**Yet, being folks habitually being sifted, separated, evaluated and judged by, and under, the Lord** [= Christ or Yahweh], **we are being continuously child-trained, educated and disciplined [by the Lord or His agent], to the end that we should not at any point be correspondingly evaluated or commensurately decided about** (separated-down or condemned; or: = have sentence passed on us) **together, and in company with, the organized and controlling System** (the world of culture, religion, economy and government)."

Again we have here the advice to be **hot** (zealous), as in vss. 15-16, above. Thus, of the hot/cold choices in those verses, He prefers the **hot**! To do this there must be an accompanying **change in attitude and way of thinking**, which (in Hiles' view, ibid) is: "Change the way you think, from old covenant thinking to new covenant thinking!" What Christ says to this community, in the last clause, is the instruction with which Jesus began His earthly ministry. He is beginning all over again, with them. The need for "child-instruction" reveals their spiritual condition, and reminds us of Paul's frustration with Corinth (1 Cor. 3:1-2). They were obviously not being "led by the Spirit" (Rom. 8:14).

20. "**Consider! I have stood, and continue standing, upon** (= at) **the door** (entrance), **and I am constantly knocking; if ever anyone may** (or: can) **hear My voice** (or: sound) **and would open the door, I will proceed entering** (coming or going in) **toward him, and then I will continue eating the evening meal with him, and he with Me.**

Now we see that His position was that of being outside the community, seeking entrance. There is no mention of a lampstand in this group, and obviously His presence is outside. It is supper time, so perhaps He is in the outer darkness of the city street. Yet, despite their wretched condition, He presents Himself to them, calls to them, knocks at their entrance and promises to share communion with them. He asks for even **one** to open the door, and **He will re-enter**. Notice that He is **constantly knocking**. He is always there, ready to enter. This call was made to Jerusalem, of old:

"Lift up your heads, gateways, and be lifted up, portals eonian, that the King of glory may come in!" (Ps. 24:7, 9, CVOT).

This was happening in the 1st century, and I believe it has been happening in some "church" ever since. The conditions of each of these seven communities speaks of the conditions of the entire corporate and universal called-out body: some individual groups being represented by one of these listed here, other groups being represented by another of these symbolic (though real) communities. Through all of these 7, i.e., the entire "called-out," He is continuously walking (2:1, above) with feet of burnished brass (figure of judgment and cleansing at the brazen altar), yet He also stands at the door and continuously knocks. Those represented by this 7th community feel that they have need of nothing – not even His manifest presence, for I do not think that they are aware that He is not within their group, for you see, they are blind.

Let us consider the last clause: **then I will continue eating the evening meal with him, and he with Me**. First of all, this is speaking about the community table-fellowship that was characteristic of the early called-out groups. Next, it represented the Messianic banquet that Jesus attempted to have with Jerusalem, by entering her gates, but they were unaware of the Day of their visitation (Lu. 19:41-44). Then, it represents a situation for Middle Eastern hospitality, and being taken in as a stranger (Mat. 25:35, 43). And the picture in these words is that of intimacy with Christ. Hiles (ibid) connects this offer of an **evening meal** with Lu. 14:16-24, where "**A certain person** (human) **was in the process of preparing** (making) **a great dinner** (main meal of the day), **and he [had] invited many people**." Those invited (figure of the Jewish leadership) gave excuses for not coming. The parable ends:

> "**So the owner** (lord; master) **said to the slave, 'At once go out into the roads and fenced areas** (or: hedgerows; boundary walls), **and at once compel** (force; oblige) **[them] to come in, so that my house may be filled to capacity!**'" (vs. 23)

This was an allusion to Gentile inclusion, in the new covenant's messianic banquet. So Christ is once again offering a "great dinner" of intimacy with Himself to this Gentile-based community.

How does a person, or an assembly, or a community, "**open the door**"? In 3:8, above, He said, "*I have given before you an open door*." We have all be GIVEN an open door to Him; the veil in the temple was ripped apart, we now have access to His intimate presence. So have we, at times "closed the door to Him"? Relationships can be like that, when the old "self" is reigning in our midst. We (as individuals and as groups) at times deny free access to others. Is Christ perhaps there, at our door, in the form of the person in need (Mat. 25:42)? We may be waiting for a "revival," or a "reformation," or "His coming," when He is at our door (Lu. 16:20). Here, Richard Rohr's statement seems appropriate:

> "This new Realm is based on a relationship with a God who can be experienced personally, presently, and existentially" ("To Know God is to Love God," Daily Meditation, 1/19/18).

21. "'**To** (or: In; For) **him who is habitually conquering** (repeatedly overcoming; normally victorious) **I will continue giving** [the right? the ability? the honor?] **to sit** (or: be seated) **with Me within My throne, as I also conquer** (or: conquered; overcome; overcame and was victorious) **and sit** (or: sat down) **with My Father within His throne.**'

Even to this 7th church we still find Him offering the challenge and opportunity to be an **overcomer**. He holds before them the prize of **sitting with Him within His throne**. The ancient, eastern throne was more like a couch than a single seat. But the emphasis is on shared ruling (or, shepherding – 2:27, above), and the oneness of Christ and His body (John 17:21).

Another point to note is the parallel case between the disciple and the Master: they are to **conquer** and overcome "**as I also conquer**." He overcame. He overcame through the cross; they are to take up their crosses, follow Him, and thus also overcome (Mat. 16:24-26). But as Paul said,

> "**You see, the message** (the word; the Logos) **of the cross** (or: the idea from, and the concept pertaining to, the execution-stake/suspension-pole) **is and continues being, on the one hand, stupidity** (nonsense; foolishness) **to** (or: for; in) **those folks presently and progressively destroying themselves** (or, as a passive: being habitually lost or progressively undone); **yet, on the other hand, it is and continues being God's power** (or: the ability of and from God; the power which is God) **in us, to us and for us: in the folks being presently delivered**
>> (or: for those being continually rescued, repeatedly saved and progressively restored to health and wholeness; or: to the ones being now salvaged and progressively restored to their original state and condition)" (1 Cor. 1:18).

When we are abiding in the Vine (Jn. 15:1ff) we are existentially **sitting with Him** in His throne (Ep. 2:6).

22. "Let the one who has an ear listen to and hear what the Spirit (Breath-effect) **is presently saying to these called-out, covenant communities."**

Finally, we see the call to anyone who has an ear to hear the knock. This one will be able to hear the noise (whether the sound of a mighty rushing wind, or the still small voice), and will recognize that it is the Lord seeking entrance. Each letter, to each called-out community, finishes with these words of listening to what the Spirit is saying. Note that He says this to the "communities," plural. All the messages are to each community. Barclay points out that this "generalizes the message of the letters" (ibid p 149) – indicating that the messages are not confined to just those folks, but rather that they are speaking to every person in each generation – but also this closing individualizes the message: for whoever can hear, "All these things are meant for *you*" (ibid). Another insight to the repeated admonitions, which were given to each community, is that the following visions, which begin in ch. 4, are the Spirit speaking to these communities through all of the following visions. We read in 22:16 Jesus saying,

> "**I, Jesus, sent** (or: send) **My agent to bear witness to you people [concerning] these things [being imposed] upon the called-out communities** (or: to testify these things to, by or in you, over the [situation of the] summoned-forth assemblies)."

Before we leave this first vision, where John saw the risen Christ amidst His communities, let us consider a couple points. Notice how many times He emphasizes His presently, habitually, continuously or repeatedly coming to His called-out communities. Borg observes: "The book itself indicates that John was thinking of his own time. Seven times in his prologue and epilogue, he tells his audience that he is writing about the near future" (ibid p 276).

In a personal email, Cameron Fultz offered these insights on the situations of these called-out communities, and on their need for this *Unveiling*:

> "I've been pondering Rev 1:1 a little more and wonder if the 'Revelation' is what the seven churches needed to happen or be birthed quickly before Jesus pulled away their lampstands. I means, it may be that this opening verse speaks directly into their situations. They originally knew Him in a revelatory formation process, but it had faded away like Paul had discovered with the Galatians. In that situation I think they allowed a slick salesman of religion to convince them that circumcision was spiritually profitable. And so Paul recognized this lack of discernment as a lack of their establishment in the revelatory life of Christ as their freedom. Thus, Paul travailed for this birthing again for them that Christ would be formed in them. In Jude (Judah's) case I think the stealthy people with sensuality problems were not Gnostics, but Christ-followers who wanted a practical religion and wanted to be "like" Christ through the sense-realm: see, hear, taste, touch, smell. I suspect that early on people arose that did not value the 'mystical' Presence of Jesus being Himself in the human soul. There is a forming process where the lost life of Adam is usurped by Christ as Life (Col. 3:4)."

The Visions (Chapters 4 through 22)

Chapter 4

"Unlike chapters 2 and 3, which are focused on the conditions of seven churches located in western Asia Minor, the focus of chapters 4 and 5 is heaven [or, the realm of spirit]" (Metzger, ibid p 47; brackets added). I suggest that the setting of this chapter is God's spiritual temple, of which the tabernacle and temple in the OT were types.

1. After these things I saw (or: perceived) **– and now consider this! – A door** (or: gate; entrance; portal), **having been opened** (thus: standing open) **within the atmosphere** (or: heaven; sky). **And the first sound** (or: voice) **which I hear** (or: heard) **[is; was] as a war-trumpet talking with me, saying,**
> **"Come up here** (Ascend to this place), **and I will proceed showing you what things it is necessary** (binding) **to birth** (to come to be in existence) **after these things."**

In Jn. 10:7, Jesus instructed us,
> "**I tell you, and it is certainly true** (amen, amen), **I Myself am the Door for the sheep** (or: the sheep's Gate and Entrance)."

Then in vs. 9 He repeats this idea,
> "**I Myself am the Door** (or: Gate; Entrance); **if anyone should enter in through Me he will be constantly kept safe and protected** (made whole and returned to his original condition; rescued; delivered; saved), **and he will be habitually going in** (entering) **and going out** (exiting), **and he will continue finding pasture** (something to feed on)."

So we may assume that this is another symbolic representation of the risen Christ: the Door into the atmosphere of the kingdom of God. He is our entrance into the realm of God's Spirit. We were just told that the Lord stands at the door and is knocking (3:20). He set a door of opportunity before the Church within Philadelphia (3:8a) – or was that also a door of access into a higher realm? In any case or situation, Jesus is always our Way (Jn. 14:6) of entry or passage.

Here we have a **door** having been **opened** to John, within heaven (or: **the atmosphere**). Metzger points out that, from the perfect tense of the verb, this door remains open (ibid). Borg comments that, "He then looks through that door into another level of reality" (ibid p 271). There are other "openings" in this Unveiling: in 19:11, below, we see heaven itself "opened" (cf Matt. 3:16 where Jesus sees the heavens opened, at His baptism). In 9:2, below, we find "opened" the well (or, pit, shaft) of the abyss (the bottomless; the deep – this word was used in the LXX in Gen.1:2; 7:11; Isa. 44:27; 51:10; 63:13; Amos 7:4; Jonah 2:5); then in 12:16, below, the earth "opens" her mouth to swallow up a river. There are openings of scrolls and seals. In 11:19, below, God's temple (which is the Body of Christ – 2 Cor. 6:16) is "opened" within heaven (which is a figure for His body being in the realm of the "spirit," i.e., in heaven); then in 15:5 the temple pertaining to the tabernacle of witness is also "opened" within heaven (does this speak of "the body of Moses" [cf Jude 9; 1 Cor. 10:2; Heb. 3:2]? We find the term "tabernacle of witness" used in the O.T. for the tabernacle in the wilderness – Num. 9:15; 17:7; 18:2). These "openings" seem to speak of access, of things released or consumed, and of revelation. What has been opened signifies that "the way is clear for others, as well as the seer" (Metzger, ibid). The allusion is to Ezk. 1:1, "the heavens were 'opened,' and I saw visions of God." It also reaches back to Jacob's dream in Gen. 28:12-15, where, in vs. 17b, he referred to the place where he had the dream as, "the gate of heaven."

In this second vision John heard the voice of the same person Who spoke to him in the first vision: again, it was the voice as of **a war-trumpet** (1:10, above). We think it safe to conclude that this speaker is the Lord.

The message to John was to come up to where the speaker was: "**Come up here**." Recall this:
> "**Within My Father's house** (or: household) **are many abodes** (dwelling places; homes; rooms). **Now if not, I would at once tell you folks, because I am progressively passing** (or: traveling) **along to prepare and make ready a place in you** (or: for you; with and among you folks). **Even if I should journey on and prepare** (make suitable, fit and appropriate) **a place** (or: a spot; a position; a role) **in you folks** (or: with you; for you), **I am now presently** (or: progressively; repeatedly; habitually) **coming again, and then, I will progressively take you folks in My arms and receive you to Myself, directing you toward Myself so as to be face to face with Me, to**

the end that where I, Myself, am (or: exist) **you folks also can continue being** (or: may and would ongoingly exist). **And to the place under where I, Myself, am progressively leading the way** (or: where I am submissively going), **you have seen and know the Way** (or: path; road)" – Jn. 14:2-3.

In these visions, the Lord has come again to John and has invited him to come into the realm where He continuously exists. This also calls to mind the words of Paul in Phil. 3:14, "the high call," "the upwards invitation," "God's calling above within Christ Jesus." The door into heaven, access to the place where the Lord is, has been opened to John, and now he has been invited to ascend into this place. It was the place where John would be shown this vision: a vision about things that must be birthed into existence. It is a holy place that is set-apart from the Land.

What John will see in this ascended realm will be, "**what things it is necessary** (binding) **to birth** (to come to be in existence) **after these things**." The idea of these upcoming events being **necessary**, or "binding," suggests that these occurrences are what God has decided to do. God's plan is behind what we will see through John's testimony. There is no duality expressed in the Unveiling. God rules; His will prevails.

2. And then, immediately, I in myself came to exist within spirit (or: in myself I came to be within [the] Spirit; I birthed myself in union with a Breath-effect) – **and now consider this! – A throne being laid down and lying within the atmosphere** (or: heaven; sky), **and upon the throne [was] One continuously sitting** (or: as well as [One] being permanently seated on the throne).

It would seem that the sound, or voice, that John just heard, both had an effect on him and also prompted him to inwardly move from the "natural" (soul or sense?) realm on into "spirit." These verses parallel 1:10, above,

> "**I came to be** (or: birthed myself; happened to be) **within spirit** (or: in union with [the] Spirit; in the midst of a Breath-effect) **within the Day which pertains to or has the characteristics of the Lord** (the Lord's Day; = the Day of Yahweh; or, = the Day of Christ; = Christ's Day), **and I heard behind me a great voice** (or: = a loud sound), **as of a trumpet, saying** (or: = like that of a trumpet sounding a command or a message)."

The order of events: "sound/voice," and "being within spirit," are reversed in these two instances. Perhaps the first experience prompted John to immediately direct his focus into the realm of spirit upon both seeing the vision and hearing the sound/voice. It is also quite possible that this present vision came at a later time – thus the need to once again be birthed within spirit. The first clause qualifies what will follow. What he will see will be in the realm of **spirit**, and so must be "spiritually" interpreted (1 Cor. 2:10-16). This should alert the reader not to look for a literal interpretation of the symbols. The **Throne** that he sees in the next clause is not a literal throne, but a symbol of God's reign and the realm of His kingdom and sovereign activities.

The call to John implied action on his part, similar to Jesus' call, "Follow Me." He was not transported, but was told to come up. The verb in the first phrase is in the middle voice, which means that the subject (John) was acting upon itself (i.e., himself). Thus it would seem from this that to come to be "within [the] spirit" requires something from us. John's response was immediate; it was like Matthew immediately leaving the tax station to follow Jesus. Once he had "come up" into the spirit realm (heaven) he could see what was there, and what the Lord wanted to show him. Like Moses climbing up Sinai to meet with Yahweh, John ascends into the spiritual realm of Mt. Zion (Heb. 12:22ff).

"Yahweh is in His holy TEMPLE; Yahweh - His throne is in the heavens" (Ps. 11:4, CVOT). From this association we can see the ark as a symbol of His throne, and the Holy of Holies (the Most Holy place of the tabernacle/temple) is a type of the upper atmospheres of the heavens, which are figurative of the higher realms of spirit. This reminds us of what Paul said:

> "**I am acquainted with a person** (or: a man; a human) **in Christ**... **being snatched away** (dragged off; seized and taken) **as such, as far as [the; or: a] third heaven** (or: atmosphere).... **into the Paradise and heard inexpressible gush-effects and utterances**" (2 Cor. 12:2, 4a).

"Thus says Yahweh, 'The heavens are my throne, and the earth is my footstool'" (Isa. 66:1, Rotherham). So the entire creation is His "throne room." This figure shows contrast between the two realms, defines the place of ruling, shows the subservient place of earth, and establishes the place of His throne. I would also point out that God is continuously sitting upon the throne: He always rules; He is always in control. Isaiah had a vision similar to this one that John here describes. I would suggest reading Isa. 6. It would also be good to compare what Ezekiel was shown in chapter 1 of his book. We read in Jer. 17:12,

> "A glorious THRONE, exalted from the first (or: beginning), [is; has been] the PLACE of the rising and standing of our SANCTUARY (place set-apart)."

The LXX reads: "An exalted **throne** of glory [is] our **Sanctuary** (effect of set-apartness; or: holy precinct)." Or, this could read, "A throne of exalted reputation [is] a result of our state of being set-apart" (JM). This concept is tied to Ex. 25:8, where Yahweh instructed Moses, "Thus they will make for Me a **Sanctuary**, and I will **tabernacle** in their midst." We see an echo of this in 21:3, below. Also, the same word family is used in Ex. 3:5 where Yahweh instructed Moses that, "the place on which you are standing, this is holy ground (or: a ground of set-apartness)." This was a revelation that established the fact that it was God's presence that made something or someone "holy," or, set-apart. From all of this, we can see a connection between God's tabernacle/temple in the OT being termed His Sanctuary (place that has been set-apart from common use). And Jeremiah, above, instructs us that THIS is the place of His **throne**. From these pronouncements we see that the Tabernacle, and Temple, represented "heaven" in OT symbology.

Micaiah "**saw** the Lord sitting on His throne and all the host of the heavens standing beside Him, on His right hand and on His left" (I Ki. 22:19). Micaiah said that he "saw" this, which indicates that it was a vision, and symbolic in nature, or his description was a parable which metaphorically brought the prophecy that followed. [Now consider: In that context a spirit came forward and stood before the Lord and volunteered to become a lying spirit (a spirit of falsehood) in the mouths of all His prophets (vs. 21-23). Is this a parallel of the first two chapters of Job?]

But for a moment, let's consider the discussion in Heb. 8:1-5. We have Jesus, the new Chief Priest, within the right part of the **throne** in the heavens (the same place as we see described here in Rev. 4), and He is a Servant of the Holy Things (or: Places) and of the True **Tabernacle** which the Lord pitched [i.e., in the heavenlies, our atmosphere]. Verses 3 and 4, there, compare Him to the earthly priests, showing the differences and how they rendered service for "an example," and BY A SHADOW, of the upper heavens, accordingly as Moses had been instructed, being about to finish the Tabernacle. Verse 5 ends saying,

> "**Continue to observe so as to see that you make** (or: construct) **all things down from and in accord with the pattern** (the type; the impress made by a strike; the mark of the wound inflicted) **shown to you** (presented to your sight) **on** (or: in; in the midst of) **the mountain**." [cf Ex. 25:40]

Can we conclude, then, that what Moses saw when he ascended into the mountain (a type of heaven, and a counterpart of Mt. Zion in Heb. 12:22) was the same scene that John here sees, and that the **Tabernacle** contains a type (in the Holy of Holies) of God's **throne room**? Are the cherubim on the veil and on each side of the mercy seat (throne) the same symbol as we will be seeing here in vss. 6-8, below? If so, then it may be helpful to keep the shadows of the Tabernacle in mind as we consider this present scene of the new reality (new creation). What will be seen here is a figure of the spiritual aspect of the covenant communities, which are His temple.

3. And the One continuously sitting [was; is] for appearance (or: to [my] vision) **like a jasper stone and a carnelian. And a rainbow, similar in appearance to an emerald, [was; is] around the throne.**

> "One thing is certain; these were typical of the most precious stones ... they were a part of the rich array of the king or Tyre (Ezk. 28:13); they were among the precious stones on the breastplate of the High Priest (Ex. 28:17); they were among the stones which were the foundation of the Holy City (Rev. 21:19)." (Barclay, Vol. 1, ibid p 151)

Thus, the OT referents are unmistakeable, and the tie-in with the end of the story (the latter chapters of the Unveiling) is clear. The setting of this vision is the holy of holies, in the Tabernacle/Temple. This description is an allusion to Ezk. 1:26-27a, amidst a description of the four living beings,

> "Above the atmosphere that was over their head, like the appearance of sapphire stone, was the likeness of a throne. And on this likeness of a throne was a likeness like the appearance of a human (*adam*) on it, upward. And I saw what was like the sparkle of amber, like the appearance of fire enclosed round about it..." (CVOT; addition mine)

Similarly, Ezk. 10:1, "on the atmosphere which was over the head of the cherubim [there was something] like a sapphire stone; an appearance like a **throne** over them" (CVOT).

John, and his audience, were obviously supposed to connect the present vision with that which was given to Ezekiel, and thus to draw from those OT symbols and images. Since Ezk. was part of the "Bible" which the early Christians read, we can assume that they would have made these connections. Another allusion may be to Ex. 24:10, "And they saw the God of Israel, and beneath His feet as it were a work of sapphire tiling (or: a pavement of sapphire stones), even like the substance of the very heavens/sky, for brightness and purity." *Cf* 21:11, 18, below. This chapter also has allusions to Dan. 7 and its visions.

We find the word **rainbow** used only one other place in the NT: in 10:1, below, where it is upon the Head of the Strong Agent of that vision. The word also means "iris," the flower. It is used only once in the LXX, in Ex. 30:24, where it is used as an ingredient of the holy anointing oil. But the rain-bow is normally associated with Gen. 9:13-16, where God placed His "bow" in the cloud (a symbol of His covenant with Noah). The Hebrew word used for bow, in that passage, is the same word used for a "bow" that shoots arrows – which is its normal use in the OT. But the rainbow has taken on a traditional meaning of the Gen.9 promise: mercy in judgment. We find the word "bow" used of a rainbow in the description of the throne, and the One upon it, in Ezk. 1:27b-28:

> "And [there was] a bright [light] round about Him, like [the] appearance of the bow which comes in [the] cloud on the day of downpour, so [was the] appearance of the bright [light] round about. It [was the] appearance of [the] likeness of Yahweh's glory..." (CVOT).

The precious **stones** mentioned in this verse are an allusion to the stone and color described in Ezk. 1:26-27, along with Ex. 24:10, and prefigure those found in chapter 21, below. They are nuances of glory and sovereignty.

4. Next, around (or: encircling) **the throne, [were; are] twenty-four thrones** (or: seats; chairs), **and upon the thrones** (seats; chairs), **twenty-four elders** (or: old people) **continuously sitting, having been clothed in white garments. And upon their heads [were; are] golden wreaths** (symbols of having won in a contest, or of festal celebration).

This setting is likely an allusion to what some scholars have suggested as being a "divine-council scene," such as described in 1 Ki. 22:19-22, Job 1:6-12; 2:1-6, Ezk. 28:2-19, Zech. 3:1-10, and possibly Gen. 1:26. Just as the Unveiling is a collection of visionary images that tell a story by symbols, it is likely that the OT passages, just cited, were also metaphorical pictures attesting to God's sovereignty and control over the earth – set in pictures from familiar royal/kingdom situations on earth.

The Greek word *thronos* corresponds to our English word "throne" when used in connection with a king or ruler. But the Greek word also means just a "seat," or a "chair." In this verse the definite article is used with the first use of the word here, but not with the second. Thus, I have added the parenthetical options in the second use, since in vs. 10, below, we see these elders giving obeisance to "**the One continuously sitting upon the throne**" that is referred to in vs. 9.

The 24 Elders: Here Smith says that "numbers" in the book of the Rev. are "ideas," not arithmetic. 24 is an idea. The idea is 12+12, as noted above. 12 is 3 (God in His "triunity") X 4 (the complete coverage of the world; the 4 corners or directions of the earth; the totality of the universe). Thus, 12 = the triune aspect of God working out His purpose in the whole world. "When God was working out the totality of His purpose in the OT, you had the nation of Israel. When unfolding His purposes to man in the NT, He did it through 12 apostles" (Malcolm Smith, ibid). We find one of these 24 elders speaking with John in 5:5, and one again in 7:13-17. Then the 24 are making a proclamation in 11:16-18, below – they are a part of the setting for the eschatological play that these visions produce. The 144,000 sing their song before these same elders in 14:3, then these elders are brought back to the stage in 19:4 to add their chorus, "**Amen** (Make it so; So be it). **Praise Yahweh** (Hallelujah)!" Some scholars have pointed to the 24 renowned individuals in Israel's history that received special mention in Sirach (Ecclesiasticus), chapters 44-49, as a possible source for this figure of "24." The *Gospel of Thomas* 52 reads, "His disciples said to Him, 'Twenty-four prophets have spoken in Israel, and they all spoke about you.'" In the Unveiling we find a number of themes that repeatedly recur, as threads in a tapestry. I would also suggest that since 24 is also 6X4, and since the number 6 is identified with humanity, it could represent God's universal plan for mankind, if we take into account all the use of numbers in the OT – especially in religious dimensions (e.g., the tabernacle/temple) and the prophecies, such as Ezekiel's.

So this picture may well represent the universal covenant community that is ruling and reigning with Christ. These 24 may be one figure of the old and new covenant overcomers – since we see that they are wearing **golden wreaths**, "symbols of having won in a contest," i.e., an "overcomer." Notice that they are seated:
> "**and He jointly roused and raised** (or: suddenly awakens and raises) **[us] up, and caused [us] to sit** (or: seats [us]; = enthroned [us]) **together within the things situated upon [thus, above] the heavens**
>> (or: in union with the full, perfected heavenlies; or, although neuter: among those comprising the complete and perfected heavenlies; among the ones [residing] upon the atmospheres; in union with the celestials; among the folks [residing] upon the atmospheres) **within and in union with Christ Jesus**" (Eph. 2:6).

They are clothed in white garments (a promise to the overcomer – 3:5, above). It echoes the picture in Job 1:6 and 2:1 where God's sons meet with Him. Ps. 122 is titled "A song of Ascents," which refers to "the house of Yahweh" (vs. 1), Jerusalem (vs. 2) which vs. 4 locates as "where the tribes ascend… to acclaim the Name of Yahweh," and then we read in vs. 5, "For **there** are located thrones of judgment, the thrones for the house of David," with vs. 6 stating, "Ask for Jerusalem's well-being…" This picture lends more evidence that Jerusalem, the temple and God's people are the echo for this present vision. Furthermore, we find thrones again in 20:4, below,

"**And I saw thrones** (or: seats; chairs) – **and they sit** (or: sat; are seated) **upon them, and judgment-effect** (decision-result; judicial process and verdict) **is given by them** (or: authority to judge was given to them; decisions and separations are made by them) – **and souls** (inner lives) **of those being ones having been cut with an axe** (= beheaded) **because of the testimony** (witness) **of** (or: pertaining to; from) **Jesus, and because of the Word of and from God – even those** (or: also the ones) **who do not** (or: did not) **worship the little wild animal** (or: beast), **nor its image, and do not** (or: did not) **take** (or: receive) **the imprinted mark** (engraving; carve-effect; result of sculpting) **upon their forehead and upon their right hand – and they live and reign** (or: lived and reigned) **with the Christ** (the Anointed One) **one thousand** [other MSS: the thousand] **years**."

Also, in 5:10, below, we have an allusion to sitting on a throne,

"**And You made** (or: make; form; construct; produce) **them** [minuscule 792, the Clementia Vulgate (1592) and Primasius (6th century) read: us] **kings** [other MSS: a kingdom] **and priests in** (for; to; by) **our God, and they** [the Armenian, Clementia Vulgate (1592) and Primasiua read: we] **continue reigning** [reading with Westcott & Hort (following A); other MSS: they will continue reigning] **upon the Land** (or: the earth)."

In early Israel, and on through to the 1st century, the "elders" – the old people – were considered to be the leaders of the communities. *Cf* Ex. 12:21; 24:9 and Nu. 11:16-17; also: 1 Pet. 5:1-5, which in vs. 5 admonishes, "**you younger people be humbly placed, arranged and aligned by and with** (or: subjected for support to and among) **older folks**."

This vision may also be picturing a fulfillment of Isa.24:23b,

"For Yahweh of hosts will reign in Mount Zion and in Jerusalem, and in front of His elders will He be glorified" (CVOT).

Heb. 12 describes this scene from another perspective:

22. **But to the contrary, you folks have approached so that you are now at Mount Zion – even in a city of a continuously living God; in "Jerusalem upon heaven"** [*cf* 11:16, above] (or: in a Jerusalem pertaining to and having the character and qualities of a superior, or added, heaven and atmosphere; or: in Jerusalem [situated] upon, and comparable to, the atmosphere) – **also among ten-thousands** (or: myriads) **of agents and messengers** (people with a/the message):

23. **[that is] in** (or: to) **an assembly of an entire people** (or: an assembly of all; a universal convocation) **and in** (or: to) **a summoning forth** (or: a called-out and gathered community) **of firstborn folks having been copied** (from-written, as from a pattern; or: enrolled; registered) **within [the; or: various] atmospheres** (or: heavens), **and in** (or: to; with) **God, a Judge** (an Evaluator and Decider) **of all mankind, even among** (or: to; with) **spirits of just folks** (or: breath-effects from those who are fair and equitable and in right relationship within the Way pointed out) **having been brought to the destined goal** (perfected; finished; matured; made complete), [*cf* Rev. 3:12; 21:1-2; Eph. 2:6; Phil. 3:20; Rev. 14:1-5; Ex. 4:22; Gal. 3:19]

Another possibility for the significance of 24 is the 24 different courses of the priests, 1 Chron. 24:7-18. Each course had an "elder" (called princes or governors of God's house in vs. 5, there). The Levites were also divided into 24 courses for the work in the Temple, and they praise God with harps & cymbals (1 Chron.25:6-31; see also 5:8, below). David Chilton notes Ezk. 8:16 where 25 men were engaged in sun worship: "the representatives of the twenty-four courses of the priesthood, plus the High Priest" (*The Days of Vengeance, An Exposition of the Book of Revelation*, Dominion Press, 1987 p 152). Recall that God's people are called a kingdom of priests (1:6, above). Beale (ibid p 326) notes that some identify these 24 with the names given as part of the construction of the new Jerusalem, in 21:12-14, below.

In 19:8, below, we read,

> "**Then it was** (or: is) **granted** (or: given) **to her to the end that she may clothe herself with bright and clean fine cotton** (or: she may cast bright, pure, fine linen around her) – **for the fine cotton** (or: linen) **represents the effects of right relationship and equity in the life of the Way pointed out**..."

In Jn. 20:12 we find, "**two agents** (or: messengers) **in brilliant, shining white** (as being in a bright light), **remaining sitting down**." *Cf* Acts 1:10. In 3:18, above, **white garments** were needed to cover one's nakedness (*cf* Gen. 3:10ff); in 6:11, below, the souls under the alter were given **white robes**; in 7:9 those before the throne and before the little Lamb are **clothed in white robes**. White robes seem to be the apparel for being in the temple, and in God's manifested presence. Does this relate to what Paul said in 2 Cor. 5:2,

> "**within this one we are continuously groaning, utterly longing and constantly yearning to fully enter within and to clothe upon ourselves** (to dress upon ourselves) **our dwelling-house** (habitation) – **the one [made] out of heaven** (or: the one from, or made of, atmosphere; the [dwelling-house, or habitation] from out of the midst of [the] sky)"?

Or, how about Rom. 13:14,

> "**you folks must clothe yourselves with** (or: enter within and put on) **the Lord, Jesus Christ**"?

Similarly, see: Rom. 13:12; 1 Cor. 15:53, 54; Gal. 3:27; Eph. 4:24; 6:11; Col. 3:10, 12; 1Thes. 5:8, where in each case the same verb is used. "**White garments**" are a symbol of the purity of Christ.

5. Also – forth from out of the throne – lightnings and voices (or: sounds) **and thunders repeatedly** (or: continuously) **proceed out. Furthermore, [there were] seven shining ones** (or: lamps; lights; torches) **of fire, which are the Seven Spirits of God** (or: God's seven Breath-effects), **being continuously caused to burn before the throne.**

The figure of the **thunde**r & **lightning**, the **voices**, or, "sounds" (e.g., call of the trumpet) all call to mind the scene in Ex. 19:16-20 where Moses met with God and received the pattern, then later built the model, i.e., the Tabernacle. We find these visionary symbols again in 8:5, 11:19 and 16:18, below. Beale (ibid p 326) suggests that it is God, from His throne, that is the source of what happens in these later passages. The ark represents God's throne (the Mercy Seat). Ps. 99:1, "The LORD, enthroned on cherubim, is king." (Tanakh), or, in the CVOT, "Yahweh reigns; ... He is dwelling between the cherubim."
The **seven shining ones** (lamps; lights; torches) are an allusion to Zech. 4:2 where he sees, "a lampstand... and seven lamps on it." This image is taken up in 1:12, 20 and 2:1, above. Putting these together, we can discern that the setting in chapter 4, here, is the same setting as chapters 2-3, i.e., the called-out covenant communities, which are the "new covenant" temple.

The seven Spirits of God (the shining ones, the torches) correspond to the seven lamps (flames of fire) of the lampstand in the Holy Place. Remember, a number in this book is an idea. Seven signifies completeness or the full extent. These speak of the fullness of God's Light that He has placed in His temple (the called-out communities). *Cf* 1:4, above. The setting of this vision is taken from the temple: the holy place now joined to the holy of holies by the removal of the veil that had separated those chambers, in the old covenant arrangement (Heb. 9:1ff). The worship and praise which the 24 elders offer to God in Rev. 4:9-11, below, correspond to the altar of incense that was in the holy place, just outside the ark chamber – God's throne. In that first chamber was the table of "the bread of the presence," having one loaf for each tribe, representing the whole of Israel, God's people. This corresponds to the 24 elders in this vision (a figure of the combined 12 patriarchs and the 12 apostles; God's universal called-out groups with the old covenant now pictured in a joined continuity to the new: one olive tree – Rom. 11:17; Eph. 2:15). The rainbow around the throne is represented in the colors woven into the veil, in the old arrangement (Ex. 36:35). The sea of glass can figure 1) the brazen sea which Solomon made – 1 Chron. 18:8, and speak of the washing of the water by the Word (Eph. 5:26), the cleansing aspect of the work of Christ; 2) a host of mankind – the sea being often a figure of people – having been calmed (no longer raging – Jude 13) by the sacrifice of the Lamb being slain (Who we meet in chapter 5, below) at the brazen altar.

> "Read through chapters 4 and 5 in one sitting & you will see that what John saw was what Moses saw." (Malcolm Smith, from an audio teaching on Rev. 4)

The **lightnings** and the light of the **shining ones** echoes 1 Tim. 6:15, 16, "**The King of those reigning as kings, and Lord of those ruling as lords**... **the One continuously making inaccessible** (or: unapproachable) **light His home** (or: dwelling)." Also, Ps. 104:2, "Putting on light as a robe, stretching out the heavens as a curtain."

6. And before the throne [is; was] a sea as of glass (or: as a glassy sea), **like clear ice** (or: crystal). **Then, within the middle** (or: centered in the midst) **of the throne, and in a circle around the throne [were; are] four living ones** (or: living beings) **continuously being full of eyes in front and behind:**

In 1 Ki. 7 we find descriptions of Solomon's temple. Beginning with vs. 23 we find the "**sea**" that he had built, which was located in the court, just outside the holy place of the Sanctuary:

> "He made the sea out of cast metal, ten cubits from its one lip unto its other lip, circular round about.... It was standing on twelve oxen, three facing north, three facing west, three facing south and three facing east. The sea was above, upon them.... It contained two thousand bath measures. He made the ten bases of bronze; four cubits, the length of each base; four cubits its width and three cubits its rise. This was the workmanship of the bases: they had insets... On the insets... [were] lions, oxen and cherubim" (vss. 23-29a; CVOT).

In vs. 25 of this passage, we see that the twelve oxen (a figure of the 12 tribes of Israel) that supported the "sea" were set in groups of three with each group facing one of the four directions, in a pattern that represented the proscribed encampments of the twelve tribes "from a distance around the tent of appointment (= the tabernacle)" – Nu. 2:2, 3, 10, 18, 25. An allusion to these oxen is seen in the "**resemblance of a young calf** (or: bullock)," in vs. 7, below. A discussion on the "**four living ones (living beings)**" will follow after the next verse, but here let us note that the imagery of "**a sea**" was a part of the temple complex, which in the new covenant is a picture of the called-out communities (2 Cor. 6:16; Eph. 2:19-22; 1 Pet. 2:5). In 2 Chron. 4:6, following the description of the sea, we find its use, and a possible explanation of its use as a ready source of water for the ten lavers, these latter being used, as follows:

> "He also made ten lavers... to wash in them; they rinsed out in them the implements for the ascent offerings; but the sea was for the priests to wash in it" (CVOT).

This place of "washing" calls to mind Jesus washing the feet of His disciples (Jn. 13:5-14), who became priests of the new covenant (1:6, above; *cf* 1 Tim. 5:10; also: Acts 22:16; 1 Cor. 6:11), and the explanation in 7:14, below. The fulfillment of this OT figure is likewise found in Eph. 5:26,

> "**that He may set her apart** (separate her; consecrate and make her holy), **cleansing** (purging) **[her] by the bath of the Water [that is] within a result of a flow** (or: in union with a gush-effect; or: in the midst of a spoken word, a declaration, or an utterance),"

as well as in the picture described in Tit. 3:5b,

> "**a bath of, and from, a birth-back-up-again** (or: [the] bathing of a regeneration; note: can = a ritual immersion pool of rebirth) **and a making back-up-new** (of a different kind and quality) **again from a set-apart Breath-effect**
> (or: of a renewal and renovation whose source is [the] Holy Spirit; or: a set-apart spirit's creating or birthing [us] back-up-new-again; a renewal which is a holy attitude)."

When we visualize the "throne" as being "the ark of the covenant," located in the holy of holies, we can see that this "sea" was "**before the throne.**" So, our interpretation of this present chapter as being set in "temple imagery," is hereby supported. This sea is "**as of glass**" because it is in a set-apart place, where there is peace and calm. The little Lamb, which we encounter in the next chapter, created this peace:
> "**THROUGH Him at once to transfer the all** (the whole; = all of existential creation), **away from a certain state to the level of another which is quite different**
>> (or: to change all things, bringing movement away from being down; to reconcile all things; to change everything from estrangement and alienation to friendship and harmony and move all), **INTO Him – making** (constructing; forming; creating) **peace** (harmonious joining) **through the blood of His cross** (execution stake/pole): **through Him, whether the things upon the earth** (or: land) **or the things within the atmospheres and heavens**" (Col. 1:20).

The figure of "the sea" outside of this temple/heaven context, i.e., in the "world" of tribal religions, governments, economies and cultures, is a picture of turbulent, lost humanity that produces the dominating control systems which are pictured as "beasts," or, "little wild animals," as in 13:1, below. But here, folks are "**like clear ice, or crystal.**" Here people are transparent, having been purified by the work of Christ's life. They are the ones of whom Jesus spoke,
> "'**Rivers** (or: Floods; Torrents) **of living water will continuously flow** (or: gush; flood) **from out of the midst of His cavity** (His innermost being or part; or: the hollow of his belly; [used of the womb]).' [cf Isa. 58:11; Ezk. 47:1; Joel 3:18; Zech. 13:1; 14:8] **Now this He said about** (or: with regard to) **the Breath-effect** (or: Spirit; Attitude; [other MSS: Holy, or set-apart Spirit; Sacred Wind]) **of which** (or: of Whom as a source; [other MSS simple read: which]) **they – those trusting and believing into Him – were about to be continuously and progressively receiving**" (Jn. 7:38-39a).

In Ps. 28:3 we read "The voice (or: sound) of Yahweh is upon the waters." Then in Ps. 28:10, "The LORD will continue settling and dwelling down on the water-flood" (LXX, JM); or, "The Lord will cause that which was deluged to be inhabited" (*The Septuagint Bible*, translated by Charles Thomson). Rotherham renders the Heb., "Yahweh, at the Flood, was seated (or: enthroned)," and the CVOT reads, "Yahweh, He sat [enthroned] above (Heb., for) [the] deluge." I offer all these renderings to emphasize God's involvement and close association with his called-out communities (figured by the temple complex), and also with humanity at large. He does not hold Himself back from human experience.

Beale (ibid p 328) points us to the Quran, Sura 27.44, which speaks of the Queen of Sheba entering into Solomon's reception hall, before his throne,
> "It was said unto her, 'Enter the pavilion.' But when she saw it, she supposed it to be an expanse of water and bared her legs…" (*The Study Quran*, HarperOne, 2015 p 934-6)

Now if we connect "**a sea as of glass** (or: as a glassy sea), **like clear ice** (or: crystal)" with 15:2-3a, below, our understanding will be enlightened:
> "**And I saw as it were a glassy** (crystalline) **sea having been mixed with Fire, and the folks** (or: those) **continually overcoming** (being progressively victorious; presently conquering) – **from out of [the power and influence of] the little wild animal** (creature; beast), **and from out of [the nature of] its image, and from out of [the identity of] the number of its name – standing** (or: having made a stand) **upon the glassy** (crystalline) **sea, continuously holding God's lyres** (harps). **And they repeatedly sing the song** (or: ode) **of Moses, God's slave, as well as** (or: even) **the song** (or: ode) **of the little Lamb…**"

Connecting this passage in chapter 15 with our present setting of the temple court, the place of the Lamb's sacrifice, we can see how it is that they "overcome" the influence of the wild, untamed nature, and

the dominating "beast" system that demands compliance. Both the song of Moses and the song of the little Lamb are songs of deliverance – the former from Egypt, the latter from Rome and the estranged human nature. Note that these in 15:2 "make a stand." This calls to mind Rom. 12:1,
> "**Consequently, brothers, I am repeatedly calling you folks alongside to advise, exhort, implore and encourage you, through God's compassions to stand your bodies alongside** (or: to set or place your bodies beside) **[the] Well-pleasing, Set-apart** (Holy; Different-from-the-usual), **Living Sacrifice by God** (or: in God; for God; to God; with God), **[this being] your sacred service which pertains to thought, reason and communication** (or: your reasoned and rational service; the logical and Word-based service from you folks; or: = temple service)."

That the living ones within and around the throne are cherubim is confirmed in Ezk. 10:15, "Then arose the cherubim - the same was the living one which I had seen by the river Chebar." (Rotherham) See also vs. 20. Note Ezk. 1:14, "And **the living ones** ran and returned – like the appearance of a **flash of lightning**." Ezk. 1:13 in the LXX reads,
> "And in the middle of the living beings was an appearance like burning coals of fire, as the look of torches coming together between the living beings, and a radiance of the fire, and lightning was issuing from the fire" (NETS).

We will see, below, how these **living ones** correspond to the cherubim. Not only were they a part of the mercy seat (throne), as described in Ex. 37:6-9, Solomon put two cherubim in the holy of holies (2 Chron. 3:10-13). *Cf* Lu. 17:33, "**will bring [his soul] forth as a living being** (engender it as a living creature)."

The **eyes** will be discussed below. But as to their location, **in front and behind**, this suggests having perceptions from the past (Israel's roots and history, e.g., Rom. 11:16-18; the OT) while looking into the glories of the future. The picture: **full of eyes** suggests full vision and seeing everything; nothing would be missed; the whole picture would be seen. Metzger suggests that this would indicate "watchfulness" (ibid p 51). Milton Terry suggests that these descriptions are, "symbols of remarkable intelligence" (ibid p 318). This is an obvious allusion to Ezk. 1:18; 10:12, or Zech. 4:10, and in 2 Chron. 16:9 we read:
> "For, [as regards] Yahweh, His eyes go to and fro through all the earth to reinforce the heart of those who are at peace with Him" (CVOT).

These visions repeatedly bring the types and shadows of the OT into their fulfillments within the new creation reality. But we must read them metaphorically, and through the lens of the new arrangement (covenant) formed through the resurrection of Christ. The old was the roots, but the new life is the plant that lives above, in the atmosphere (a figure of "heaven," or the life of the Spirit). *Cf* 1 Cor. 15:36-38. Before we leave this verse, we should consider the implications of the phrases, "**within the middle** (or: centered in the midst) **of the throne, and in a circle around the throne**." Why these contrasting, yet complimentary, descriptions of the locations of these **four living ones**? "Within the middle of" suggests being seated together with Christ. "In a circle around" suggests close attendance and a universal aspect which has the throne at its center. Could this suggest both ruling authority and full-spectrum influence? Both "kingdom authority" and participatory involvement in His influence and the activities of His reign? Perhaps the best rendering of the first phrase is the parenthetical one, "centered in the midst of the throne," indicating that the throne is their "center," their place of grounding. The picture in verse 6, here, is a close allusion to Isa. 6:2,
> "And seraphim [in Heb., 'burning ones'] had taken a stand, and now stood, in a circle round about Him (or: in His circle)" (LXX, JM).

This picture, here in vs. 6, is unpacked in 1 Pet. 2:9a,
> "**Yet you folks [are] "a picked-out** (selected; chosen) **offspring** (family; kin; lineage; race; species; breed) [Isa. 43:20; Deut. 7:6], **a royal** (kingly; palace) **priesthood** [Ex. 19:6; Isa. 61:6], **a set-apart** (holy; different) **multitude** (company; nation; body of people living together; swarm; association; ethnic group; caste; [Ex. 19:6; note: implies a sacred life]), **a people constructed**

into an encirclement (made into a surrounding structure; set as a perimeter; made into a performance about [Him]; formed around as an acquisition; gathered into a surrounding [flock])." [cf Isa. 43:21; Ex. 19:5]

How many folks are "in the midst" of God's throne? In 3:21, above, we find the promise,
"**To** (or: In; For) **him who is habitually conquering** (repeatedly overcoming; normally victorious) **I will continue giving** [the right? the ability? the honor?] **to sit** (or: be seated) **with Me within My throne.**"
The Isa. 6 setting of the "burning ones" (seraphim) may correspond to the "**shining ones** (or: lamps; lights; torches) **of fire**" of vs. 5, above. If this is connected to the lampstands of 1:20 and 2:1, above, and we then connect these to the "tongues of fire" sitting upon Christ's followers (the first called-out community) in Acts 2:3, the setting of this chapter (the temple) may point us to the conclusion that these visionary images are figures of Christ's "priests," the ministering body of Christ.

7. the first living one resembling a lion, the second living one resembling a calf (or: young bullock), **the third living one has a human's face, and the fourth living one resembles a flying vulture** (or: eagle). [Ezk. 1:5-10]

To begin our consideration of what these symbols mean, Beale cites information from L. Gizberg (*Legends of the Jews*) and J.A. Seiss (*Apocalypse*) that lends insights from ancient Jewish tradition in regard to the four groupings of Israel in the wilderness:
"According to *Targum Palestinian* Num. 2, each group had a standard with the colors of the stones representing their tribes on the priest's breastplate and with an insignia on it: a lion, a stag (originally an ox), a man, and a serpent (which tradition changed to an eagle).... If this material has a link with earlier tradition, it could suggest further that the living creatures in Rev. 4:8ff represent humanity..." (Beale, ibid p 331).
As to the original figure of a serpent, to which Beale refers (and which, being the last one, corresponds to the last listing of the groups, in Nu. 2:25, which was represented by the tribe of Dan), let us recall Jacob's blessing of his son Dan, in Gen.49:17,
"Dan shall be a serpent by the way, an adder in the path, that bites the horse's heels so that his rider shall fall backward."
Dan Kaplan reminded me that the name Dan means "judge," in Hebrew. And in Gen. 49:16 Jacob says of him, "Dan shall judge (or: adjudicate) his people..." I find it curious that the tribe of Dan is missing from the list of the twelve tribes of those who are sealed by the agent, in 7:2-8, below. Could this be an allusion to the truth given us by Paul, in 2 Cor. 5:19b, that God is, "**not accounting to them [i.e., the aggregate of humanity; the world]** (not putting to their account; not logically considering for them; not reasoning in them) **the results and effects of their falls to the side** (their trespasses and offenses)"? And then there is Jesus' admonition in Mat. 10:16,
"**Therefore, habitually come to be thoughtful, prudent, cautious and discreet** (or: = wary and on the alert; = observant, decisive and timely) – **as the snakes** (or: serpents) **[are]; and yet [still] unmixed** (pure; = without negative characteristics added) – **as the doves [are].**"
Is the serpent being transformed into a dove, in His followers?

Kaplan also pointed out that during the wilderness march of Israel, Nu. 10:25 informs us that it was the tribe of Dan that brought up the rear, acting "as rear guard for all the camps," while Judah was in first place in the procession. With Christ at our Head, the "tail" of the judges is no longer necessary. We have arrived at Mount Zion (Heb. 12:22) and need no "rear guard," and the new covenant Israel (figured by the twelve disciples: the 12 foundations of the New Jerusalem – Christ's body) "**continue sitting down,**

upon twelve thrones, continuously separating [issues], making decisions and administering justice for the twelve tribes of Israel" (Mat. 19:28b).

The resemblances listed here in vs. 7 correspond to what Ezekiel saw in Ezk. 1:10,
> "As [for the] likeness of their faces, [each had the] face of a human, and the four of them had the face of a lion to the right, and the four of them had the face of a bull on the left, and the four of them had the face of a vulture (or: eagle)."

But in Ezk. 10:14, the face of the bull was replaced by, "the face of a cherub." Also, in Ezk. 10:3 we see the context of the cherubim, there, which is, again, the temple:
> "Now the cherubim were standing on the right side of the House [= Temple] when the man entered, and the cloud filled the inner court."

Then in vs. 7, there, we see another clue: "Then a cherub put forth his HAND from among the cherubim to the fire which [was] among the cherubim, and he lifted it and gave it into both hands of the [man] clothed in linen." This calls to mind the temple setting of Isa. 6, where in vs. 6 one of the "burning ones" takes a hot coal from the altar and uses it to purge Isaiah's sin and iniquity (vs. 7).

So the **Four Living Ones** also correspond to the 4 cherubim. The number 4, recall, signifies the complete coverage of the earth, or land. In 7:1, below, we read of "**four agents** (or: messengers; folks with the message) **standing upon the four corners of the Land** (or: earth), **continuously holding in their power** (or: restraining) **the four winds of the Land** (or: earth), **so that wind may not be blowing upon the Land** (or: earth; soil)," and in 20:8, below, we read of "**nations** (multitudes; ethnic groups) **within the four corners of the Land** (or: earth)." So these "living ones" are symbolic of the whole Land (corresponding to the square encampment of Israel, in Nu. 2), or the whole earth (seen poetically as four-cornered, corresponding to the four cardinal directions).

But for what is a cherub a symbol? According to Young's Concordance the word *cherub* means, "one grasped, held fast." The plural, *cherubim*, means "those grasped; those held fast." Now imagine if the translators had "translated" these words instead of "transliterating" them. We would realize that when Ezekiel described the living ones, he would have been describing those who are grasped and held fast by God. I suggest the same applies here. Paul, in Phil. 3:12-14, says, "Yet I am pursuing, if I may be grasping also that for which I was grasped also by Christ Jesus . . . stretching out . . . toward the goal am I pursuing for the prize ..." (CLNT). Again, in 1 Cor. 9:24,
> '**Have you folks not seen, so as to know, that those progressively running, on the race-course within a stadium, are indeed all progressively running** (or: constantly and repeatedly racing), **yet one normally** (= each time) **grasps** (takes; receives) **the contest prize** (victor's award)? **Be habitually running** (progressively racing) **so that you folks can** (may; would) **seize and take [it] down in your hands!**"

Here I see grasping and being grasped both associated with being "apprehended or seized [by God] (Phil. 3:12)," but also with winning, overcoming your opponents. I would thus suggest that the grasped ones, the cherubim, are another picture of the overcomers. Let us consider their description.

The cherubim are mentioned first in Gen. 3:24 where they are caused "to dwell at the east of the garden of Eden [Paradise]" along with "the flame of the sword which is turning itself round to guard the Way of the Tree of the Life." (Young) This setting would seem to be at the entrance of the garden. It would correspond to the entrance of the temple which also faced with its entrance to the east. I suggest that that entrance corresponds to the door of vs. 1, above.

Next we see the cherubim in Ex. 25, and there are two of them, one on each end, as a part of the ark in the Tabernacle. They each face toward the presence of God (upon the Mercy Seat), and face "a man towards a brother" (Ex. 37:9, literal Heb.). Here they each have two wings. Two is the number of witness. In Ex. 26 we also find them in the curtains (the entrance) of the Tabernacle.

Now let us move to Ezk. 1:5 to see, "... a likeness of four living ones, — and this was their appearance, the likeness of A MAN (Heb., Adam)." (Rotherham) "And they had four faces each, and four wings each" (vs. 6). Here the faces are of a man, a lion, an ox, and a vulture (or, eagle).

When John saw these living ones, the faces are the same as Ezk. 1, but they now have six wings apiece (vs. 8, below). In Ezk. 1:9, the wings were joined "a woman to a sister" (Heb., literal). These are balanced beings, having both masculine & feminine qualities; having four faces speaks of their universal aspect, they face the cardinal directions, they cover the earth, or with regard to Israel, the Land. Six wings speaks of humanity (his number is 6) having attained to the heavenlies, the realm of spirit. We see no wheels here (wheels are used upon the earth) for Christ has lifted those of His body above the heavens and has given them access to the heavens (Eph. 2:6).

Historically, the four faces have been associated with the four gospels, each face representing the central aspect, or focus, of one of the gospels, but there is no textual evidence for this. See also Bullinger's *Companion Bible* notes on Num. 2:2, 32, where he cites the *Targum of Jonathan* in regard to the tribal standards corresponding to the twelve constellations of the ancient Zodiac. J. Preston Eby has written a series of studies on "The Gospel in the Stars," which is excellent. Joseph A. Seiss wrote a book, *The Gospel in the Stars* (Kregel Pub., [1882] 1972).

Chilton (ibid p 158) makes some interesting observations:
> "The faces of the cherubim, in both Ezk. And Rev., are the middle signs in the four quarters of the Zodiac: the Lion is Leo; the Bull is Taurus; the Man is Aquarius, the Waterer; and the Eagle... is Scorpio [figured as an Eagle, according to the Chaldean system then in vogue]." (brackets also Chilton).

He also observes (ibid p 159):
> "The arrangement of the twelve tribes of Israel around the Tabernacle (Nu. 2) corresponded to the order of the Zodiac; and, like the cherubim, four of the tribes represented the middle signs of each quarter: Judah was the Lion, Reuben the Man, Ephraim the Bull, and Dan is the Eagle."

[Cf Gen. 37:9 for Jacob, Rachael, and Joseph's brothers interpreted as "the sun, the moon and stars."]
In contrast to these traditions, let us consider the symbolism as it would relate to God's people, specifically to the body of Christ. The lion, most readily associated with the Lion of the tribe of Judah, speaks of the kingly, or ruling, aspect of the living ones. The calf, or ox, speaks of the sacrificial nature of this calling, and perhaps one of the qualifying factors, and speaks of those who, having His great love, lay down their lives for their friends. This animal also is a figure of strength for long endurance. The man speaks of the last Adam, humanity in Christ's image restored to Paradise (the realm of the spirit; heaven). The vulture, or eagle, signifies their access to, and movement in, the heavenlies (atmospheres), their ability to rise above the realm of earth, and symbolizes the divine nature having been implanted in their hearts. It also suggests long-range vision, able to see details on earth from a "heavenly" perspective. Terry adds these insights: "The elders and the cherubs may therefore represent, not different orders of created beings, but the whole body of the redeemed..." (ibid p 319).

8. And the four living ones (or: living beings), **each one of them having six wings apiece** [Isa. 6:2], **are continuously full of eyes in a circle around and internally; and day and night they continuously have no rest** (or: intermission), **constantly** (or: repeatedly) **saying,**
> **"Set-apart, Set-apart, Set-apart** (Consecrated; Holy; Sacred)! **O Lord [= Yahweh] God, The All-strong** (the Almighty; the Strong Holder-of-all) [Isa. 6:3; Amos 3:13; 4:13] **– the One Who**

was and continued being, the continuously Existing One, even the One continuously (habitually; repeatedly; progressively) **coming or going** (= the One constantly on the move)."

The **six wings** is an allusion to the *seraphim* (burning ones) of Isa. 6:2, and the number 6 associates these with humanity. The **eyes** speak of vision, the ability to see and perceive. The circle of eyes and the internal eyes signify total vision, both internally and externally. That the eyes are "in front and behind" describes their ability to prophetically discern the future and that which lies before them, and also understand the past and the purposes of those ages and events. Jesus instructed us that,

> "**The eye is the lamp of the body. If, then, your eye may continue being single-fold** (or: simple and uncompounded; perhaps: single-focused and suggest being straightforward; may = healthy; may suggest generosity), **your whole body will continue being** (will continuously exist being) **illuminated** (enlightened; or: lustrous; luminous; radiant; shining)" (Mat. 6:22).

Then in, Eph. 1:18, Paul prays that,

> "**the eyes of the heart of you folks** (= the insights and perceptions of the core of your [corporate] being) **having been and continuing enlightened into the [situation for] you folks to have seen and thus perceive and know what is the expectation of His calling** (or: from the invitation which is Him) **and what [is] the wealth and riches from the glory** (or: of the imagination and opinion; pertaining to the reputation) **of and from the enjoyment of His lot-acquired inheritance within, in union with, and among the set-apart, sacred people**,"

that is, among those same ones whose very being and existence continuously says, "Holy, Sacred, Set-apart, O Lord God, the Strong Holder-of-All," in vs. 8, below. This is the true opening of the eyes which counteracts what Eve was told, and what happened, in Gen. 3:5,

> "**your eyes will progressively be fully opened wide** (or: be constantly opened throughout the midst) **and then you folks will continue existing** (or: being) **as** (or: in the same way as; like; as it were) **gods, continuously and progressively knowing – by intimate, existential experience and insight – [the] beautiful** (fine; ideal) **as well as of, and from, [the] misery-gushed** (painful; anguished; harmful; unsound; worthless; useless; unprofitable; disadvantageous; malevolent; wrong; bad; evil; laborsome; malignant)." (LXX, vs. 6; JM)

Eyes speak of perception, awareness and experience – all of which lead to understanding.

Note that the living ones have not rest or intermission DAY & NIGHT in their continuous praise. Although they are in the heavens within, they must be on earth without, for earth is the place where there is day and night. This ceaseless action by these symbolic figures calls to mind Paul's admonitions to the called-out communities,

> "**we ourselves also continuously give thanks to God** (or: affirm the goodness of the grace and favor in God) **by an unvarying practice** (or: incessantly; unintermittingly)" – 1 Thes. 2:13
> "**Continuously think, speak and act with a view toward having well-being and goodness – unceasingly** (or: By habit be praying unintermittingly)" – 1 Thes. 5:17. Elsewhere he says,
> "**[I] do not pause** (or: cease; stop myself) **in continuously giving thanks over you folks** (or: speaking good favor on your behalf; or: expressing the well-being of grace because of your [situation or condition])" – Eph. 1:16a.

This picture speaks of our daily living a life of thanksgiving in an attitude of gratitude. In the first clause of the repeated statement, we see a proclamation that everything is sacred. Metzger suggests that this picture of constant activity represents "their constant disposition – their every action is an expression of adoration…. the threefold repetition of 'holy' designates the superlative degree" (ibid p 51). All that they see is now perceived to be "set-apart" for God's specific purpose for everything. All these eyes perceive His sovereignty and complete power; they perceive and acknowledge that Yahweh (note that this is a quote from the OT, where the Hebrew is literally God's Name, not just "Lord") is "**the One Who was and continued being, the continuously Existing One, even the One continuously** (habitually; repeatedly;

progressively) **coming or going** (= the One constantly on the move)." Here Metzger instructs us that, "the use of the definite article with each of the three nouns in the Greek indicates totality" (ibid). We should not miss the fact that in 1:8, above, it is the symbolic manifestation of the risen Christ who says this same thing about Himself. An unbiased reading of these passages should conclude an identity between the risen Christ and Yahweh. He has always been "the One constantly on the move," in His repeated "**coming or going**" – the Greek present participle has both meanings. We can observe Yahweh "coming and going" all through the OT, and in His letters in chapters 2 and 3, above, we see His promises to do the same with them. Only God is the "**continuously Existing One**," when compared to our short-term existence here in this life.

Terry (ibid p 318-19) points out that where Isa 6:3 gives the "Holy! Holy! Holy! Yahweh of hosts!" with the affirmation, "The fullness of the whole earth (or: Land) [is] His glory" (Rotherham), or, with the CVOT, "… [manifests] His glory!," here in 4:8 there is a kind of "enlarged" parallelism: "**was and continued being, the continuously Existing One, even the One continuously** (habitually; repeatedly; progressively) **coming**," which describes Him, rather than referring to His glory, or to its relationship to the earth – or, perhaps more specifically, to the Land of Israel. That particular Land is no longer in view in the new creation and the new covenant.

9. And whenever the living ones will repeatedly give glory and honor (or: value; respect) **and thanks** (gratitude; good favor) **to the One continuously sitting upon the throne – to the One continuously living on into the ages** (or: indefinite time periods; most important eons) **of the ages**.

Note that not only do the living ones give glory and honor, but also thanks to God; they express their gratitude. Why? I suggest it is because of what He has done for them. They are thanking the One Who is continuously living. Jesus said to His disciples, "**Because I, Myself, am continuously living, you folks will also continue living**." (John 14:19). And we see that these, too, are living ones.

The word "whenever" indicates that John was observing this scene for a period of time, and also suggests the habitual activity of the covenant communities, spread throughout the four directions of the Roman Empire, expressing their gratitude to God for the work of the Christ. Paul spoke of this in Col. 3:17,
> "**And everything – whatsoever you may be habitually doing, in word or in action** (within a thought or message, or within a work or deed) **– [do] everything** (all; all things) **within and in union with [the] Name of [the] Lord, Jesus** [other MSS: of Jesus Christ; others: of {the} Lord, Jesus Christ], **constantly giving thanks** (expressing gratitude) **to Father God** (or: in union with God, [the] Father) **through Him**."

Then in Heb. 2:9 we read,
> "**But yet, we are continuously seeing Jesus – having been made inferior for a brief time beside agents – having been encompassed with glory** (or: crowned by a good reputation) **and with honor** (or: in value) **on account of** (or: through) **the effect of the experience of death so that by the grace of and from God** (or: in the favor which is God) **He might taste of death over [the situation and condition of] all mankind** (or: for and on behalf of everyone)."

The writer of Hebrews speaks of a continuous vision of the resurrected Christ – or, he is describing an ongoing perception that is seen with "**organs of perception trained as in gymnastic exercise and thus being skilled, because of practice, and disciplined with a view to a discerning**" (Heb. 5:14b). But we find a striking parallel to vs. 9, here, in 1 Tim. 4:17 which should enlighten us regarding the meaning of the symbolic vision here,
> "**So, to [the] King of The Ages** (or: eons; indefinite time periods), **to [the] incorruptible** (undecayable; unspoilable), **invisible** (unseen; not-able-to be seen) **One, to [the] only God**

[some MSS add: wise; so: only wise God], **[be] honor** (value; worth) **and glory** (reputation which calls forth praise), **on into the ages** (or: indefinite time periods) **of the ages. It is so** (Amen)!
(or: Now in and by the King to Whom belongs the ages – in and by the imperishable, invisible [and] only One – in and by God [is] honor and glory, [leading] into the [most important] eons of the eons. So it is!)"

What these four living ones are doing in this vision is what Paul does in his letter to Timothy. Peter also unpacks this in 1 Pet. 2:9b,

"**that you may tell forth the message of** (or: publish; declare abroad) **the excellencies and qualities of nobleness** (virtues of braveness, courage, good character, quality, self-restraint, magnificence, benevolence, reliability) **of and from the One calling you out of darkness into the midst of His wonderful** (marvelous; amazing) **light** [p72 reads: into the wonderful Light]."

The final phrases of these two verses (vs. 9, here, and in 1 Tim. 1:17) are identical in the Greek: **into the ages** (or: indefinite time periods; most important eons) **of the ages**. The parenthetical expansions offer other readings that illumine the Greek for us. The final phrase, "of the ages," speaks of the totality of God's creation program. It speaks of the whole tapestry from the Beginning of this particular opus until its conclusion, which may well be open-ended. Paul spoke of this overarching program in Eph. 3:11,

"**a purpose of the ages** (a fore-designed aim, plan and object [which He is bent on achieving] of the unspecified time-periods) **which He formed** (forms; made; constructs; creates; produced) **within the Christ by our Lord and Owner, Jesus** (or: in union with Jesus the Anointed One [= Messiah], within the midst of and for our Lord and Master)."

The same idea in speaking of an indefinite future expanse of time is given in the LXX of Dan. 4:31b, "His right from out of Being (or: privilege and authority) [is] an age-lasting (eonian) right of Being (privilege and authority), and His reign (kingly sphere of influence and sovereign activity) [is] into generation upon generation" (JM). But the phrase in Dan. 12:7 (LXX) reads, "the One continuously living on into the Age [of the Messiah] (or: into the indefinite future or time period of the eon)" (JM).

10. the twenty-four elders (or: older people) **will repeatedly fall before the One continuously sitting upon the throne, and will continue worshiping** (bowing; kissing toward) **the One continuously living on into the ages** (or: indefinite time periods; most important eons) **of the ages, and they will proceed casting their wreaths** (symbols of victory or celebration) **before the throne, repeatedly saying,**

This "**falling before**" and "**worshiping**" (the combined actions describe "doing obeisance") by the 24 older people is also a symbol: a visionary figure, which like most of the other symbols in this book derive from OT imagery. Such an action was a cultural way of acknowledging someone of a higher rank or social status, and was not necessarily a religious action. It is a physical picture of expressing honor and gratitude which demonstrates what the four living ones said, in vs. 9, above. We do not find this behavior as a normal part of Jesus' teachings, nor is it taught of in any of the letters by Paul or mentioned by the other NT writers, except Hebrews 1:6, which is a quote from the OT, and 11:21, which is speaking of Jacob. Other than quoting the OT, Jesus' only reference to "worship" (Jn. 4:21-24) spoke of a change from the old, and of a prostrating one's self "**in union with spirit and Truth** (in Breath-effect and Reality; within the midst of [the] Spirit and [the] Fact; centered in [life]-attitude and genuineness/actuality)." This speaks of a life-attitude of submission to, along with honor and respect for, God – not some form of religious behavior. The picture given by Paul in Eph. 2:6, is that of the Lord raising us up to His level and of participating with Him. It does not displace honor or respect, but it describes a new arrangement. We find the risen Christ saying virtually the same thing in 3:21, above. Paul referred to Christ as our firstborn **Brother** in Rom. 8:29b. Jesus called His disciples, "**friends** (beloved associates)" in Jn. 15:14-15. God is now relating to us as **family**; Christ is the Head of us, His body; He is the **Bridegroom**, and we are His **bride**. He has brought us up to His level, and at the same time has come down to live among us. We are His temple (which is the home of a deity) and He lives in us. All of this describes "union" and "oneness," rather than separation and duality. So the old pictures and "worldviews" have to change. The old has passed away and the new has come (2 Cor. 5:17).

In Lu. 22:27b, Jesus explained the new order and told His followers, "**I Myself am in your midst as the person constantly giving attending service.**" Jesus' life demonstrated God's relationship to us. In contrast to the behavior and social stratification where "**kings of the nations and ethnic multitudes are habitually acting as their lords and owners, and those exercising authority**" (vs. 25), He presented the new social order of God's reign: "**Yet you men [are] not [to be] thus** (or: [are] not [to behave] in this way), **but to the contrary, let the greater among you come to be like** (or: as) **the younger; and the one normally leading like** (or: as) **the person normally giving attending service** " (vs. 26). Jesus lived and manifested the personality and the character (and thus, the desires and expectations) of the Father. In Jn. 14:7, He told them, "**Since you men have personally and experientially known Me** (or: If you folks had insight of Me or were acquainted with Me), **you also will continue personally and experientially knowing and perceiving My Father**," then adding in vs. 9,

> "**I continue being (I am) with you folks so much time, and you have not come to intimately and experientially know Me, Philip? The one having discerned and seen Me has seen, and now perceives, the Father! How are you now saying, 'Show us the Father'?**"

All of this is an expansion of what He had just said in 14:6, "**I, Myself, am** (exist being) **the Way** (or: Path), **the Truth** (the Reality) **and the Life** (or: = I am the way to really live)." The Way is explained in Lu. 22:26, above, which describes the obliteration of social stratification and functional hierarchy in God's kingdom. He is One who washes our feet (Jn. 13:4-20)! And Jesus is a picture of God, in this act. Consider His instruction in Lu. 12:36-37,

> "**and you, yourselves, [be] like people habitually focused toward anticipating, welcoming and receiving their own master** (lord; owner) – **whenever he can untie [himself], loosen up [his involvement] and break loose from the midst of the marriage banquet – so that, upon coming and knocking, they might immediately open up to** (or: for) **him. Those slaves [are] happy and fortunate whom the master** (lord; owner) – **upon coming – will proceed to find being continuously awake, alert and watchful. Truly** (or: It is so)! **I say to you folks that he will proceed to gird himself about** (as with an apron) **and will continue in causing them to recline [at a meal]. Then, coming alongside, he will give attending service to them!**"

Walter Wink offers us the following insights on these verses in Lu. 12, and elsewhere,

> "These are the words and deeds, not of a minor reformer, but of an egalitarian prophet who repudiates the very premises of which domination is based: the right of some to lord it over others by means of power, wealth, shaming, or titles…. His followers are not to take titles: 'But you are not to be called rabbi, for you have one teacher, and you are all students…..' (Mat. 23:8-10). His followers are to maintain domination-free relationships in a discipleship of equals that includes women. The hierarchal relationship… is not to persist" (*When The Powers Fall, Reconciliation in the Healing of Nations*, Fortress Press, 1998 p 7).

Are we just to forget all this because of our religious traditions and perceptions? We need to change our thinking – and this is the point of my critique of "worship" in the Christian culture, as well as in the culture of other religions. But let me again emphasize that praise and thanksgiving remain high on our list of social behaviors toward God and toward our fellow humans. Expressions and acts of honor are always in order.

The restatement of the descriptive title of the One is given for emphasis, "**living on into the ages** (or: indefinite time periods; most important eons) **of the ages**." He sits enthroned (vs. 9) and continuously lives throughout all the ages. For the original listeners of this message, this would have been a stark contrast to the Roman emperors who obviously did not live on throughout the ages. The function of the four living creatures, who are mentioned fourteen times in the book, seems to be that of leading everyone else in vocal recognition of the value, and now the reputation (or: glory), of God and what He has done in the Christ.

The casting of the wreaths is a figure to say that He is the one Who did the overcoming in them, that He gets the credit for these victories. Metzger instructs us: "In typical oriental fashion they lay down their crowns [more literally: wreathes] as a sign of their homage, and as a dramatic demonstration of their acknowledgment of God's sovereignty" (ibid p 51; brackets added). Foy E. Wallace, Jr., saw this as "a sign of surrender to God's will" (*The Book of Revelation*, Richard E. Black Pub., 1997 p 130). This could also be a picture of the old order (including the time of the disciples, prior to Christ's resurrection), the former arrangement and covenants, submitting and yielding priority to the reign of Christ. This scene may reflect the firstfruits of what Paul describes in Phil. 2:10-11,

> "**to the end that within The Name: Jesus!** (or: in union with the name of Jesus), **every knee** (= person) – **of the folks upon the heaven** (or: [situated] upon the atmosphere) **and of the people existing upon the earth and of the folks dwelling down under the ground** (or: on the level of or pertaining to subterranean ones; [comment: note the ancient science of the day – a three-tiered universe]) – **may bend** (or: would bow) **in prayer, submission and allegiance, and then every tongue** (= person) **may speak out the same thing** (would openly agree, confess) **that Jesus Christ [is] Lord** (Master; Owner) – **[leading] into [the] glory of Father God** (or: unto Father God's good reputation and a manifestation which calls forth praise)!"

11. "**You are constantly worthy** (or: of equal value), **our Lord [= Yahweh] and God, to receive** (or: take) **the glory** (or: the reputation; 'the opinion which is based on the whole of human experience' – Paul Tillich), **and the honor, and the power, because You create all things** (or: You brought the whole from chaos, disorder and wildness to framed and founded order), **and because of Your will, intent and purpose, they were existing, and continued being, and they are** (or: were) **framed and created.**"

Thus do they say that He is worthy to receive the glory and the honor, because He is the one that brought them to these seats, and that it was His **power** that has done all. Then they acknowledge that it was He Who created every situation, formed all circumstances, created all the ages and everything within them, and did it all for His own purpose,

> "**in keeping with** (or: down from; corresponding to; in accord with) **a before-placed** (or: destined) **aim, design and purpose of the One continuously operating** (effecting; energizing) **all things** (or: the whole) **in accord with** (or: down from; in line with; in correspondence to; following the pattern of) **the deliberated purpose** (intent; design; plan; determined counsel) **of His will** (or: resultant decision of His resolve; effect of His desire)," (Eph. 1:11).

Everything and everyone exists because it is His will and purpose for them to exist! Terry (ibid p 320-1) sees the threefold "glory... honor... power" as a literary design. It could be echoing the Holy, holy, holy of 8b, above. Terry also considers the last half of this verse as, "a pledge of the final glorification of the creation of God..." (ibid). This part of the verse may be an allusion to Gen. 1:1ff, or Ex. 20:11. But if it is speaking of the new creation (2 Cor. 5:17a), then we should consider Col. 1:16,

> "**because within Him was created the whole** (or: in union with Him everything is founded and settled, is built and planted, is brought into being, is produced and established; or: within the midst of Him all things were brought from chaos into order) – **the things within the skies and atmospheres, and the things upon the earth** (or: those [situations, conditions and/or people] in the heavens and on the land); **the visible things, and the unseen** (or: unable to be seen; invisible) **things: whether thrones** (seats of power) **or lordships** (ownership systems) **or governments** (rulers; leadership systems; sovereignties) **or authorities – the whole has been**

created and all things continue founded, put in order and stand framed through means of Him, and [proceeds, or were placed] into Him (or: = He is the agent and goal of all creation)."

This is similar to Eph. 3:9,

"**to illuminate all people** (give light to everyone) **[as to] what [is] the execution of the detailed plan and household administration of the secret** (or: mystery) **pertaining to that having been hidden** (concealed) **away, apart from the ages** (or: disassociated from the [past] periods of time), **within the midst of God – in the One forming and founding** (framing, building and settling from a state of disorder and wildness; creating) **all things** (the Whole; everything)."

Then in Eph. 4:24, we are instructed to,

"**enter within** (or: clothe yourselves with) **the new humanity** (or: the Person that is different and innovative in kind and quality) **– the one in accord with and corresponding to God** (or: the person at the Divine level) **– being formed** (framed, built, founded and settled from a state of disorder and wildness; **created**) **within the Way pointed out** (or: in union with fair and equitable dealings with rightwised relationships, justice, righteousness and covenant participation; centered in [His] eschatological deliverance) **and reverent dedication** (or: benign relationship with nature) **pertaining to the Truth** (or: in intrinsic alignment with reality, which is the Truth)." Cf 10:6, below.

In reading this apocalyptic writing of the *Unveiling* (Rev.) it is helpful to keep in mind the "unveilings" given to others on the same or similar topics regarding God's new arrangement in Christ. This chapter has been a prelude to what will take place in Chapter 5, and vs. 11 is echoed in 5:12, below.

Chapter 5

1. Then, upon the [open] right [hand] of the One continuously sitting upon the throne, I saw a little book (or: scroll; perhaps: codex) **having been written within and behind** (i.e., written on both sides), **having been sealed with** (or: by) **seven seals.**

Terry remarks that, "The division of chapters at this point is unfortunate, and tends to mislead the common reader" (ibid p 321), i.e., what John now sees is a continuation of what has gone immediately before in chapter 4. As John continues to describe the scene, the first thing he notes is a scroll which is "**upon**" the hand of **the Enthroned One**. This term would suggest that the hand was perhaps extended, but specifically that it was open, palm up. Were it closed around the scroll, it would have been "in" His hand. The significance of this is that the scroll is being offered, presented to whomever is found worthy to open its seals. In vs. 7, below, the Little Lamb takes the scroll which has been presented.

A similar situation is seen is Ezk. 2:9-10. There, however, the scroll is not sealed, but is spread before Ezekiel. It, also, is written on both sides, and contains dirges, a soliloquy, and woe. He is commanded to eat this scroll (a figure for taking its words into himself and "digesting" its contents) and then to go and speak these words to the house of Israel. A scroll is also used in Zech. 5 as a symbol of a curse which is going forth over the face of all the Land (or, earth). However, in Ps. 40:7 it says, "Then I said, Behold, I have come. In the roll of the scroll it is written concerning me." Thus, unless specified here, let us not presume that this scroll in this Unveiling signifies woe or a curse. I think that the scroll is a figure of a message from God: a revelation; a disclosure. Let us remember here that we are reading and studying *An Unveiling of, and from, Jesus Christ*.

That it is written on both sides (not an everyday procedure) might tell us that it was a lengthy production: it contains a lot of information, or speaks of a subject of vast and detailed process. In Ex. 32:15 we see that the tablets of the Testimony were inscribed on both sides, front and back. Verse 16, there, tells us that these tablets were the work of God.

But this is classified information and there is only One in the entire universe Who is worthy to open its secrets to us. Seven seals is an idea. "The one ordinary document sealed with seven seals was a will. Under Roman law the seven witnesses to a will sealed it with their seals, and it could only be opened when all seven, or their legal representatives, were present" (William Barclay, ibid p 166). Another thought is that this means that it was completely sealed; "indicating absolute inviolability" (NIV Study Bible). The fact that there were seven seals, may signify that it is completely inaccessible for being read (vs. 3, below), or that its contents are a complete secret, or are hidden (*cf* Metzger, ibid p 52). Paul spoke of that which was secret and had been hidden:

> "**we habitually speak God's wisdom within the midst of a secret** (or: we normally speak – in [the form or realm of] a mystery which only the initiated understand – the wisdom which is God)**: the [wisdom] having been hidden away and remaining concealed, which God before marked out and set its boundaries** (or: previously designed) **– before the ages – [leading] into our glory** (our manifestation which calls forth praise; our good reputation)" (1 Cor. 2:7).

And in 1 Cor. 4:5 he instruct us,

> "**do not be constantly evaluating** (or: stop judging, making decisions about or critiquing) **anything before [its] season** (before a fitting, due or appointed situation; prior to a fertile moment)**: until the Lord** [= Yahweh or Christ] **would come – Who will continue giving light to** (or: shine upon and illuminate) **the hidden things of the Darkness** (or: the hiding things which are things in the shadows and dimness of obscurity), **and will progressively set in clear light** (or: keep on manifesting) **the intentions and purposes** (designs, dispositions, motives and counsels) **of the hearts – and then the praise and applause from God will repeatedly be birthed** (happen; come into being) **in each human** (or: for every person)!"

It is possible that what Paul has said, here, pertains to the contents of these visions.

Perhaps Isaiah gives the best answer: "So the entire vision shall become to you like the words of a sealed scroll, which, when they give it to one acquainted with script, saying, 'Please read this,' he says, 'I cannot, for it is sealed'" (Isa. 29:11; CVOT). Or, Dan. 12:4,

> "Now you, Daniel, obstruct the words (bar passage of the messages; shut up the ideas) and seal the scroll until a season of ends joining together (or: fertile moment of completion; fitting situation from a consummation), until many can (or: would; may) be taught (instructed; trained) and then the intimate, experiential knowledge and insight can be multiplied to the full." (LXX, JM)

In chapter 6, below, we will begin to see what happens when the seals are opened, but not specifically what is written in the scroll. Some have suggested that this scroll contains the remainder of the revelations of this book. Others have suggested that it contains the plan and purposes of the ages which the Little Lamb opens to us. What do you think this scroll meant to the church of the first century? What does it now mean to us? Does it contain prophesies of the future? Is it the timeless Word of God? Does it contain the Good News of the Kingdom, i.e., the Gospel? Terry suggests that, "The unsealing of the book is the apocalypse itself, 'the revelation of Jesus Christ,'... (4:1)" (ibid). Metzger suggests that the scroll is "the book of the... decrees of God" (ibid). Let the Spirit speak to your heart, concerning this.

Judson Cornwall, in his book, *Elements of Worship* (BridgePublishing,1985), suggests that the scroll here in chapter 5 should be understood with a view to the Jewish laws of redemption. On pp 28-29 he maintains that this scroll concerned a forfeited inheritance, saying,

> "There was an automatic redemption and there was an intermediary redemption. Their property would be returned to them automatically in the year of Jubilee, or, a kinsman-redeemer could buy back their lost estates at any time.... The terms of redemption were established at the time the property was sold. When an inheritance was sold, encumbered, or transferred away, there were two scrolls, or instruments of writing, made of the transaction. One was open; the other was sealed. The unsealed one stated the right of possession to the purchaser; basically it was the

> public record of the transaction. The second scroll, however, contained both the details of the sale and the terms of redemption. This scroll had the signatures of witnesses written on the back side, and then it was rolled up and sealed."

The seals would be opened when redemption was paid, according to the specifications written within the scroll (*cf* Jer. 32:6-15). Cornwall continues,

> "A sealed scroll, then, became a demonstrable sign of an alienated inheritance which could be recovered at Jubilee or through a *goel* [kinsman-redeemer] according to the terms specified inside the sealed copy" (ibid).

2. **Next I saw a strong agent** (or: messenger; person with a message) **repeatedly proclaiming** (announcing a message openly and publicly) **in a great** (= loud) **voice,**

> **"Who is worthy** (of equal value) **to open the little book** (or: scroll; codex), **and to loose** (or: destroy) **its seals?"**

The idea of "**worthy**" or of being "of equal value" is answered in vs. 3, below: it would be one who, "**had power or was able**." In the book of Ruth we see that the right, or "ability," to redeem a person was first given to the person who was the closest kinsman (Ru. 3:9-4:11a), and of course this person would have needed to have the purchasing power (possess corresponding value), as well.

Apparently it is God's desire to have the scroll opened. This is not something done in secret. There follows, in vs. 3, an open quest for one who is worthy, and the search covers first heaven, then earth, then down under the earth. The idea suggested by calling the proclaimer of this public question a "**strong agent**" may be to show how he or she would be able to "**proclaim in a great voice**." This suggests that the message was going far and wide – to the extent described in vs. 3, below. There is nowhere that this question was not to be heard, or contemplated. Even the realm of the dead (**down under the earth**, vs. 3) would hear it. Jesus spoke of such a situation in Jn. 5:25, 28-29,

> "**I am presently continuing to say to you folks that an hour is progressively** (or: presently in process of) **coming, and even now exists** (or: = is now here), **when the dead folks WILL be repeatedly hearing the voice of God's Son** (or: the Voice from, and which is, the Son of God), **and the ones hearing WILL proceed to be living!.... an hour is progressively** (or: presently; or: repeatedly) **coming within which all the people within the memorial tombs** (or: graves) – **will be continuously or repeatedly hearing His voice, and they will proceed journeying out: the ones doing virtue** (producing, making or constructing good) **into a resurrection which is Life** (or: of, from and with the quality of Life); **the ones practicing careless** (base, worthless, cheap, slight, paltry, inefficient, thoughtless, common or mean) **things into a resurrection of separating and evaluating for a decision** (or: a resurrection which is a judging)."

We will find echoes of this, below, in the visions of this book.

From 1:10, above, through 21:3, below, voices play a significant role in this book. John the baptizer was a voice that was crying out in the wilderness (Jn. 1:23). In Jn. 3:29 he rejoiced at hearing the Voice of the Bridegroom. A voice always suggests a message, and the question here may be to point out that throughout the coming of the Messiah and the message of goodness, ease and well-being there were great voices proclaiming this message, and the unveiling of God's plan for mankind. One of those "people with a message" was Paul, who indeed had a "great voice."

Dan Kaplan has suggested that this "strong messenger" (One with a message) might be a visionary symbol for the Holy Spirit. We need to keep in mind that it is not only the book or the seals that are figurative in this spiritual play. Might not this "**repeatedly proclaiming** (announcing a message openly and publicly) **in a great** (= loud) **voice**" be an instance of what was repeatedly instructed to the seven called-out communities, beginning with 2:7, above, "**Let the person having an ear hear what the Spirit is repeatedly saying to, in and by** (or: the Breath-effect is continuously laying out for) **the called-out communities**"?

Kaplan pointed to Jn. 14:26 where Jesus told us,
> "**Now the Helper** (the One called alongside to aid, comfort, encourage and bring relief; the Paraclete), **the set-apart Spirit** (or: the Sacred Breath; the holy Breath-effect; the holy attitude), **which the Father will proceed sending within, and in union with, My Name, that One will be progressively teaching you all things** (everything) **and will continue reminding you of** (calling to your mind and causing you to think about) **everything** (all things) **which I, Myself, said to you**."

The "teaching" which the **set-apart Spirit** brings to us is a "message," and thus He is a Messenger. Jesus also spoke of God's Sacred Breath-effect, the Spirit of the Truth, in Jn. 15:26,
> "**Whenever the One called alongside to aid, comfort, encourage and bring relief** (the Helper; the Paraclete) **should come – the Spirit of the Truth** (or: the Breath-effect of, and which is, reality) **Which** (or: Who) **is constantly** (habitually; progressively) **proceeding and traveling out from beside the Father** (= emanating from the Father's presence; or: from a presence which is the Father), **[and] Which** (or: Whom) **I, Myself, will continue sending to you from the Father's side** (or: from the presence which is the Father) **– that One will continue bearing witness** (giving testimony; showing evidence) **about Me**."

It will be worthwhile to read what Jesus further said in Jn. 16:7-14, concerning the Spirit's role within the called-out, covenant communities:

> 7. "**Nevertheless, I, Myself, am telling you the Truth** (or: speaking reality to you). **It progressively bears together for you people** (It continues being expedient and advantageous in you; It is now for your benefit) **to the end that I should go away. For if I should not go away, the One called alongside to aid, comfort, encourage and bring relief** (the Helper; the Paraclete) **will not come** [other MSS: may by no means come] **to you and be face to face with you folks. Yet if I should journey on** (or: would travel on to another place) **I will habitually send Him to you.**
>
> 8. "**And upon coming, that One will be progressively testing and putting the System** (the world of culture, society, religion, economy and politics) **to the proof** (or: exposing and presenting convincing arguments about the aggregate of humanity) **concerning error** (failure; deviation; missing the target; sin) **and about fairness and equity in rightwised relationships which comprise the Way pointed out** (or: concerning eschatological deliverance that produces covenant inclusion) **– and about dividing and separating for evaluation and decision** (or: judging). [comment: thus, the Paraclete replaces the Law]
>
> 9. "**About error** (failure; missing the mark; sin; deviation), **on the one hand, because they are not constantly trusting or progressively believing into Me.**
>   [comment: this now defines sin and failure to hit the Target (Christ)]
>
> 10. "**About fairness and equity in rightwised relationships** (or: concerning eschatological deliverance that produces covenant participation) **on the other hand, because I am progressively leading [everything] under control by withdrawing toward** (or: to; [to be] face to face with) **the Father, and so you folks are no longer continually gazing upon and contemplatively watching Me.**
>
> 11. "**And about dividing and separating for evaluation and decision, because the ruler** (one in first place; chief) **of this System** (world of culture, economics, religion or politics) **has been sifted, separated, evaluated and decided about, and now stands judged**

(or: Yet concerning judging, because the Prince and Leader of this universe and the aggregate of humanity has had a decision made about Him, and He now stands judged [by the System]).

12. "**I still have** (or: hold) **many things to be progressively telling you folks, but yet, you continue not yet being able** (or: having no power) **to habitually or progressively pick it up and carry** (or: bear) **it right now** (at present).

13. "**Yet, whenever that One – the Spirit of the Truth** (or: the Breath-effect from Reality; the attitude which is genuineness) **– may come** (or: Nonetheless, at the time when that spirit which is truth and reality should come), **It** (or: He) **will constantly be a Guide and will progressively lead you on the Path** (or: it will continue leading the way for you) **directed toward and proceeding on into all Truth and Reality** (or: into the midst of every truth and genuine reality) – **for It** (He; it) **will not habitually speak from Itself** (or: Himself), **but rather, as many things as It** (He; it) **continuously hears, It** (He; it) **will proceed speaking, and will continue reporting back to you the things presently and progressively coming, as well as those that are habitually coming and going.**

14. "**That One will glorify Me** (will give Me a good reputation; will give a manifestation of Me which calls forth praise), **because It** (He; it) **will constantly take from out of what is Mine** (or: receive from the one from, and which is, Me) **and will repeatedly report back to you folks** (or: will continue announcing to and informing you).

We see another figurative Agent described in 10:1-3, below, which many scholars have rightly interpreted to be a symbol of the risen Christ:

"**Next I saw a Strong Agent** (other MSS: another Agent, a Strong One) **progressively descending** (stepping down) **from out of the atmosphere** (or: sky; heaven) **– having been clothed with a cloud, and the rainbow upon His head, and His face as the sun, and His feet as pillars of fire – and constantly holding in His hand a tiny scroll having been opened up**…. **Then He uttered a cry with** (or: by) **a great Voice, even as a Lion is roaring**...."

Thus, as we come across the various "players" in this cosmic opera, let us listen to what the Spirit is saying to us through the designation of each character within each vision.

3. **And yet no one** (or: not one person) **within the atmosphere** (or: heaven; sky), **neither upon the land** (or: earth; ground) **nor down under the land** (earth; ground), **had power or was able to open the little book** (or: scroll; codex) **nor to see or observe it.**

The three realms mentioned in this verse are also spoken of in Ex. 20:4, "Thou shalt not make to thee an image, or any form, that is in the heavens above, or that is in the earth beneath, or that is in the waters beneath the earth (ground)." (Rotherham) Also, we read in Phil. 2:10b,

"**of the folks upon the heaven** (of those belonging to the super-heaven, or [situated] upon the atmosphere) **and of the people existing upon the earth and of the folks dwelling down under the ground** (or: on the level of or pertaining to subterranean ones; [comment: note the ancient science of the day])…"

In the Exodus reference it is likely that the third level referred to the creatures in the sea or in lakes, etc. But here in 5:3, 13, and in Phil. 2:10, above, the reference to a level, or realm, down under the earth (or: ground) seems to be a separate category. Terry understood that the three locations mentioned denoted the entire universe (ibid p 322), i.e., what scholars today refer to as a "three-tiered universe," which was the worldview of the 1st century, in the Middle East.

One obvious reference is to the grave. In Gen. 50:5, Joseph quotes Jacob as saying, "in my grave which I dug for myself, in the land of Canaan, there shall you bury me." The old prophet, in 1 Kings 13:30, "laid his [the man of God's] dead body in his own grave." Jonah speaks figuratively of his situation in the bowels of the great fish as "the belly of the unseen (sheol; hades)." Then in 2:6 he said, "the earth, [with] its bars, are about me for the age, yet You will bring up my soul from ruin, Yahweh, my God."

In Ps. 88:3 we read, "For my soul is sated with misfortunes, and my life has drawn near unto the unseen (*sheol; hades*)." Then in vs. 4, "I am counted with them who descend into the pit." Verse 5: "Among the dead I am free, like the slain that lie in the grave." Jacob, speaking of his dying says, "Surely I will go down mourning towards the unseen (*sheol; hades*), unto my son" (Gen 37:35; *cf* Gen. 42:38; 44:29, 31). 1 Sam. 2:6 records, "Yahweh doth kill, and makes alive – He takes down to the unseen (*sheol; hades*) and brings up." So what does the Lord mean here in 5:3? We see in the verses above that the unseen is associated with (although not identical to) the grave. Obviously, those in a grave are no longer seen. But is this what the Lord is speaking of here? Is he referring to the dead as a state of existence? Or, is this referring to those (being dead) located, existing, in hades (the unseen)? We get more views, during OT times, in the following Psalms:

    9:17, "The wicked shall return to the unseen (*sheol; hades*)"
    16:10, "For You shall not forsake my soul in the unseen (*s.; h.*)"
    18:4, "The cables (meshes; Rotherham) of death have enveloped me, ..."
    18:5, The cables (meshes; Rotherham) of the unseen (*s.; h.*) surrounded me;"
    55:15, "May death lure them away; may they descend to the unseen (*s.; h.*) alive."
    86:13, "... and You have rescued my soul from the unseen (*s.; h.*) beneath."
    139:8, "And should I make my berth (couch) in the unseen (*s.; h.*), You are there."

Then in Pr. 15:11, "The unseen (*s.; h.*) and destruction are before Yahweh" and in Pr. 15:24, "The way of life is upwards to the prudent, that he MAY DEPART from the unseen (*s.; h.*) beneath," then in Pr. 23:13, 14, "Withhold not from a youth correction ....You with the rod shall smite him, and you shall deliver his soul from the unseen (*s.; h.*)."

Some of these verses would seem to refer to a literal death and subsequent entrance into *sheol*, the unseen, which is referred to as being "beneath." What we must consider is whether the term "beneath" is literal or figurative. Tradition has said that it is literal. Yet God continually sits upon His throne; His throne is in the heavens (which are "above"); but David says that if he makes his bed in the unseen (*sheol; hades*) that God is there. Of course God is everywhere – that was David's point. But, this seems to suggest that the unseen (*sheol; hades*) is a condition rather than a place. David was speaking figuratively, but in what way? Did he mean that if he made a mess of things in his life that God was still there to help him? Or, did he mean that if he ordered his life and lived in such a way that he would be judged as wicked (Ps. 9:17) and end up in the unseen, that even in that condition (or, place; or, sphere) God would still be present and even, perhaps, there to help him?

Let's look at another scene. Turn to Isa. 14. Let me begin by saying that most scholars agree that Ezk. 28 is a parallel passage to this, and I agree, so I may make occasional reference to it while considering the subject of Isa. 14. This is a subject all its own, but perhaps a short review of it will shed some light upon our current discussion. The setting is when Israel is given rest upon their own soil (which is also Yahweh's – vs. 2) and they are taking captive their captors. [Can we see a figure here of entering into His rest and overcoming?] They are to take up a taunt (Rotherham; "proverb"- CVOT; "simile" - Young) concerning the king of Babylon. It begins in vs. 4: The oppressor has ceased; Yahweh has broken the staff of the wicked and the sceptre of rulers. In vs. 9, since he was laid low, the unseen (*sheol; hades*) beneath is disturbed at him and, among other things, makes all the kings of the nations to rise from their thrones. [Do we get the sense that this is a figurative piece?] In vs. 10 we see that he has been made weak (without strength, ill) like the kings of the earth! [this could not possibly be describing a spirit, a principality of the heavenlies, or "Satan"] His pride is brought down to the unseen (*sheol*; *hades*), "the maggot is berthing under you, and the worm is covering you" (vs. 11, CVOT). Maggots eat flesh; worms eat flesh & earth.

Then in vs. 12, "How you have fallen from the heavens [Eden, God's paradise – Ezk. 28:13]!"
> "So here we have a fall from one place (realm, or, condition): the heavens, to another place: the unseen, the recesses of the pit (vs. 15), yet, these verses [16-20a] seem to take place on earth, not in the realm of the dead (Sheol)" (Herbert Wolf and John H. Stek, NIV Study Bible, 1995).

This is also the place of maggots and worms. Ezk. 28:2 says, "Because your heart is lofty (haughty), and you have said, 'I am a god (or, I am God),' ....whereas you are Adam (a man) and not God." This last phrase is repeated in vs. 9, then in vs. 17 it says, "Upon the earth did I cast you," and in vs. 18, "And I turned you to ashes [Heb. also means "dust"] on the ground (earth)."

Without diverging to a lengthy study on this subject, let me just point out that it would seem that there are really only two conditions, places, or realms in the view of this context: heaven and earth. These two are contrasted throughout the Scriptures. The unseen, from our look at Isa. & Ezk., above, seems to be upon (or, in a figure, within) the earth. Death and corruption are the conditions of one who is in the unseen - be these literal, or figurative. Both lack light and life.

Now let's look at 1 Pet. 3:18-20, where we read of Christ,
> "**because even Christ** (or: considering that Messiah also) **died** [other MSS: suffered], **once for all, concerning and in relation to failures to hit the target** (about errors and mistakes; around and encompassing sins [some MSS: our failures; other MSS: your failures]) **– a Just One** (a rightwised One; One in accord with the Way pointed out; a fair and equitable individual) **over [the situation of]** (or: for the sake of) **unjust ones** (capsized folks; those out of accord with the Way pointed out; unfair and inequitable people) **– to the end that He at once may bring** (or: can lead; would conduct) **you folks** [other MSS: us] **to** (or: toward; to be face to face with) **God. [He], on the one hand, being put to death in flesh** (= a physical body), **yet on the other hand, being made alive in spirit** (or: indeed, being put to death by flesh {or: = the estranged human condition}, yet, being engendered a living one by Breath-effect {or: [the] Spirit}), **at one point journeying** (going from one place to another; passing on) **within which** (or: in union with Which), **He also proclaimed** (published; preached; heralded) **the message to and for** (or: among) **the spirits in prison** (within a guardhouse): **to and for those being at one time unconvinced** (unpersuaded; disobedient; noncompliant) **within [the] days of Noah...**"

Where was this prison? The text does not say. We can presume, I think, that the prison was (or, was in) the unseen, whether this is understood as an existential condition (expressed metaphorically) here in this life, or a sphere of existence after an earthly life, prior to the advent of Jesus, the Messiah.

From all of this, I think the term "down under the earth" of 5:3, here, refers in figure to the unseen: the *sheol* of the Hebrew; the *hades* of the Greek. How we interpret this depends upon our worldview. That no one "**had power or was able to open the little book nor to observe it**," was this not the state of humanity (the former "shining one" of Isa. 14) before the emergence of the Lamb of God on the earth?

4. And so I was greatly weeping, that no one was or is found worthy (of equal value) **to open the little book** (or: scroll; codex) **nor even to see or observe it.**

We are reminded of Jn. 11:35, "**Jesus sheds tears** (let tears flow; gave way to tears; or: bursts into tears)." Yet He also told His followers, "**Happy and blessed [are] the folks presently crying! – because you will proceed to be laughing**" (Lu. 6:21). Perhaps John was so caught up in the drama of this cosmic opera that he momentarily forgot about the work of the Christ. One of the old people remind him of this, in the next verse. That no one else could **see or observe it** suggests a state of general blindness, perhaps an allusion to 2 Cor. 3:14-16, "**the results of their mental conceptions, intellectual workings and thought processes were petrified.... a head-covering** (veil) **continues lying upon their heart** (= the innermost being of the group)." Jesus referred to such folks,

> "**They exist being blind guides of the Path** (or: blind leaders of the Way). **Now if a blind person should ever lead or guide [another] blind person, both people will proceed to be falling into a pit**" (Mat. 15:14b).

Only in Christ can we observe and see, as Paul instructs us in 1 Cor. 2,

> 9. **But to the contrary, according as it has been and stands written,**
> > "**Things which an eye has not seen and an ear does not hear, neither does it ascend** (climb up) **upon [the] heart of a human, so as to conceive – so many things God prepares and makes ready in, for and by the folks habitually loving** (accepting and urging toward reunion with; fully giving themselves to) **Him.**" [Isa. 64:3; 52:15]
> 10. **Yet** [other MSS: For] **God unveils [them] in us** (reveals [them] to us; uncovers [them] for us; discloses [these] among us) **through the spirit** (or: the Spirit; the Breath-effect), **for you see, the spirit** (or: the Spirit; the Breath-effect; the Attitude) **constantly and progressively searches, examines and investigates all mankind, and all things – even the depths of God!**

The focus of opening the book/scroll is an allusion to Dan. 7:10b, where, "a tool for evaluating and a standard for deciding was installed (or: He seated a tribunal) and the books were opened." (LXX, JM) That context speaks to the Unveiling, here, and 20:12, below.

> 5. **Then one forth from among the elders** (or: old people) **is saying to me,**
> > "**Do not continue weeping! Consider! The Lion out of the tribe of Judah, the Root of** (from) **David, overcame to open the little book, and to loose** (or: destroy) **its seven seals** [with other MSS: He conquers! He is presently opening the scroll, as well as its seven seals]."

This picture (figure) of the visionary **elder** reaching out with encouragement to John may be a parable for the older folks of the called-out communities, who have insight like this elder, to encourage others when the picture looks hopeless to carnal perceptions. This quote alludes Isa. 11:1, "Then a Branch will shoot out from the Stock of Jesse and a Shoot from his roots will spring up, and upon Him the Spirit of Life will remain..." (Ferrar Fenton). Jer. 23:5 picks up this theme: "I will raise for David a righteous offshoot, and royal king, who will govern and do justice and right in the land" (Fenton). Paul's address to the Jews in Antioch references Jesse and David, connecting this lineage to Jesus, in Acts 13:22-23, concluding in vs. 22,

> "**From the seed of this one** (or: From this person's descendant) – **corresponding to and in accord with [the] promise – He brought to** (or: for; in; by) **Israel a Deliverer** (Savior; Rescuer; Restorer to health and wholeness), **Jesus.**"

In 22:16, below, the risen Jesus proclaims, "**I am** (I continuously exist being) **the Root and the Offspring of** (Family from; Race which is) **David**," which is to say, "the Alpha, or Source, and the Omega, or Final Product," of the Davidic prophecies; the origin and the product of what David represented.

Paul presented the expanded unveiling which includes the Gentiles, the ethnic multitudes of the nations, by quoting Isa. 11:10 in Rom. 15:12,

> "**There** (or: He) **will continue being The Root** (or: the Sprout from the root) **of Jesse, even the One habitually standing up** (placing Himself back; raising Himself up) **to continue being Ruler** (being The Chief; to repeatedly be the Beginner) **of multitudes**

(ethnic groups; of nations; of Gentiles). **Upon Him ethnic multitudes** (non-Jews; nations) **will continue placing their expectation** (will rely; will hope)."

This corresponds to the picture in vs. 6, below, where we note that the little Lamb is "**standing**" within the midst of the throne. And from Isaiah we see the universal reach of this little Lamb.

"Stop crying!" (vs. 5, Barclay translation) This means that there is a solution:
> "Swete has an interesting comment on this. John was weeping and yet his tears were unnecessary. Human grief often springs from insufficient knowledge. If we had patience to wait and trust, we see that God has his own solutions for the situation which brings us tears" (Barclay, ibid p 169).

The title, **Lion out of the tribe of Judah**, goes back to Gen. 49:9, where Jacob prophetically blesses his sons. Note that this is also one of the faces (identities, characters, aspects) of the living ones. This title speaks of the royal, kingly quality of Christ and affirms Christ as being in the continued line of God's people. There is one continuous plan. Scholars have seen this figure as an allusion to the late 1st century, AD, 4 Esdras 12:31-32,
> "And as for the lion that you saw rousing up out of the forest and roaring and speaking to the eagle and reproving him for his unrighteousness, and as for all his words that you have heard, this is the Messiah whom the Most High has kept until the end of days, who will arise from the posterity of David, and will come and speak to them…" (*The OT Pseudepigrapha*, Vol. 1, Hendrickson Pub., 1983, p 550, trans. by B. Metzger).

He **overcame** (conquered) - or, as this is the Gk. aorist tense, "overcomes (conquers)" – and His work still applies; He is still overcoming in us. Now He has the power to open the scroll and loose, or destroy, its seals.

6. **And then within the midst of the throne and of the four living ones, and within the midst of the elders, I saw a little Lamb standing, as one having been slaughtered, having seven horns and seven eyes – which are the Seven Spirits of God** (or: God's seven Breath-effects/Attitudes)**: the Ones having been and still being sent forth as envoys** (representatives) **into all the Land** (or: earth) –

Imagine John's surprise: expecting to see a lion, he sees a **little Lamb**. The Jews had expected a Messiah that would be like a lion, but they found Jesus to be a non-violent man who did not resist the Roman Empire (Isa. 53:7) or liberate Judea from its dominating system of rule. He laid down His life (Jn. 10:18) for His friends (Jn. 15:13). And yet John, here, might have quickly recalled John the baptizer's proclamation,
> "**The next day** (or: On the morrow) **he is looking at and observing Jesus** [= Yahshua] **progressively coming toward him, and he begins saying, "Look!** (Pay attention, see and perceive)**! God's Lamb** (or: the Lamb from God; the Lamb having the character and qualities of God; or, in apposition: the Lamb which is God)**, the One continuously lifting up and progressively carrying away the Sin of the world, and removing the sin which belongs to and is a part of the System**
>> (or: habitually picking up and taking away the failure and error brought on by the organized system; progressively removing the falling short and the missing of the goal from the world of culture, religion, economy and government, society, and from the aggregate of humanity)" (Jn. 1:29).

The present participle here in Jn., "continuously lifting up and progressively carrying away," corresponds to the perfect participle "**having been slaughtered**" in vs. 6, above, for the perfect tense "expresses an abiding condition as a result of the past act of being slain" (Beale, ibid p 352).

In 1 Pet. 1:18-19 Peter makes a similar reference to the crucifixion of Jesus, and the effects it had upon humanity:
> "**having seen, and thus knowing, that you folks were not unbound and released by a ransom of corruptible things** (things that are perishable and subject to spoiling)… **but rather by Christ's precious blood** (or: in valuable blood, which is [the] Anointed One; by costly blood from [the Messiah]) **– as of a flawless** (unblemished) **and spotless Lamb**."

The same imagery is seen in Heb. 9:1-28, where in vs. 14 we read,
> "**to how much greater an extent shall the blood of the Christ** (Anointed One; [Messiah]) **– Who through means of a spirit** (or: attitude; [the] Breath-effect) **pertaining to the Age offers Himself** (or: brought Himself face to face and offers Himself) **without blemish by and with God** (or: in, to and for God) **– continue cleansing and pruning your conscience and shared consciousness from works of death** (or: dead procedures and activities; deeds of dead folks) **[leading] into [the situation] to be continuously rendering sacred service, as well as habitually doing the business and duties of life, for, in, by, to and with the living, as well as true and real, God?**"

Then in vs. 24 we are informed:
> "**Christ did not enter into set-apart places made by hands** (= by humans) **– representations** (things formed after a pattern) **of the true and real things – but rather into the atmosphere and heaven itself, now to be manifested** (exhibited to view; caused to appear in clear light; made apparent) **by the presence of God over us** (or: in God's face and countenance [being] on our behalf)."

And then in vs. 26b we are told,
> "**Yet now** (at this time), **once, upon a conjunction** (a joined destiny; a bringing of [two] ends together ["denoting the joining of two age-times" – E.W. Bullinger]) **of the ages, He has been and remains manifested** (has been brought to light and continues visible) **into a displacement of the failure** (from the error, sin and deviation from the target) **through the sacrifice of Himself** (or: through His sacrifice; or: by means of the sacrificial altar-offering which was Himself)." [cf Rom. 6:9-10]

The Gospels portray Christ as a new Moses, and His crucifixion was at the time of the Passover festival, which was a memorial of Israel's deliverance from slavery in Egypt. But that festival was not about a cleansing of Israel from their mistakes and sins, rather this was annually accomplished for all of Israel on the Day of Atonement, when the chief priest entered, only once a year, for the cleansing of Israel, and the bearing away, out of the community of Israel, of all Israel's sins by the scapegoat. Hebrews chapter 9 is about the Day of Atonement, as we see in these verses, quoted above – especially vs. 24.

Now look again at the proclamation of John the baptizer, quoted above: "**continuously lifting up and progressively carrying away the Sin of the world, and removing the sin which belongs to and is a part of the System**" seems to picture the Day of Atonement, but now he applies it not to just Israel, but to "the world of culture, religion, economy and government, society, and from the aggregate of humanity." The entire world was cleansed by Christ's sacrifice. Peter's reference to "**a flawless and spotless Lamb**" has a similar allusion. The Heb. 9 theme, from vss. 1 to 28, also speaks of the Day of Atonement.

Peter's description, "**unbound and released by a ransom**," sounds like a reference to Passover, and Israel's release from the **bondage** in Egypt. So it was all accomplished by the "**little Lamb standing, as one having been slaughtered**."

Where this little Lamb is standing is in the center of all that John is seeing. He is the center of the universe (just as He is in the center of this temple imagery, for the temple was a figure for the heavens, and the people of Israel were a figure of the Land, or, the earth). So in this picture, above, we see everyone else surrounding the throne and the little once-slain Lamb, in the temple's holy of holies.

Now let us consider the second half of vs. 6: "**having seven horns and seven eyes – which are the Seven Spirits of God** (or: God's seven Breath-effects/Attitudes)**: the Ones having been and still being sent forth as envoys** (representatives) **into all the Land** (or: earth)." Horns were OT symbols representing power, or the strength of a nation (cf Deut. 33:17; 1 Ki. 22:11; Ps. 89:17; Dan. 7:7-8:24). That the Lamb has *seven* horns signifies the fullness of his strength. In this verse these horns would be a symbolic representation of what the risen Jesus said in Mat. 28:18,
> "**All authority** (or: Every right and privilege from out of Being) **is** (or: was) **given to Me within heaven and upon the earth** (or: in sky and atmosphere, as well as on land)!"

It seems best to understand "**seven horns and seven eyes**" together, as a paired unit depicting aspects "**which are the Seven Spirits of God**." Recall the previous characterization of the "fullness of His Spirit" in 4:5, above, where we see the same thing pictured as "**seven shining ones** (or: lamps; lights; torches) **of fire**." The phrase, "**the Ones having been and still being sent forth as envoys** (representatives)," is another perfect participle, thus my rendering, "and still being sent forth." The participle is a form of the verb *apostellō*, and the noun form is the word commonly transliterated "apostle," which really means an envoy or a representative. The verb carries the sense of being sent with a commission, or being sent as a missionary. To connect all this to the traditional term "apostle," we would have a transliterated phrase for the participle: "sent forth as apostles." We bring up this tradition (even though it is not a proper rendering of the Greek term) to suggest that these "horns and eyes" can be seen as figures of the Lamb's body, i.e., His commissioned communities.

The figure of "**eyes**" is an allusion to Zech. 3:9, "For behold the stone that I have laid (or: set) before Joshua; upon one stone are seven eyes… and I will remove (take away) the iniquity of the Land (or: earth) in one day." And of course what comes to mind is Christ, the Rock, as well of the Stone that becomes a great mountain (i.e., a kingdom) and fills the whole earth, in Dan. 2:34, 35, 44, 45. Back in Zech., we read of Judea's governor, concerning the rebuilding of the temple, in 4:10, "And they will rejoice and see the stone [of the] plumb [line] in the hand of Zerubbabel; these seven [are] the eyes of Yahweh; they [are] going to and fro in the entire land (or: whole earth)." These seven Spirits represent God's awareness and activities in the earth, which are often through members of humanity. We are God's co-laborers. We are Christ's sent-forth envoys and representatives.

7. **and it came** (or: went), **and it has taken** (or: received) **so that it has the scroll** (or: book; codex) **from out of the right [hand] of the One continuously sitting upon the throne.**

Standing behind this picture which depicts the little Lamb approaching God's throne is Dan. 7:13-14,
> "I was observing, and continued noticing and contemplating, within the night vision, and then, consider this: One as a son of a human (or: [the] Son of man; = a human being) progressively coming with the clouds of the sky (or: atmosphere; heaven), and He overtook as far as, and so arrived at, the Ancient of days (or: the Old One, from the days [gone by?; having passed?]), and He was brought near toward Him (or: he was carried to be face-to-face with Him; he was presented to Him; he was borne along by Him). Then the beginning (or: the primacy; or: the headship and rule) was given to Him, along with the honor and the reign (or: kingship; kingdom), and so the peoples, tribes and languages continuously perform as (do the duties of) slaves for (or: to) him. His right from out of Being and Existing (or: his privilege and authority) [is] an eonian

right from Existing (or: a privilege pertaining to the Age of the Messiah; an age-lasting authority) which will not pass away – and His reign (kingship; kingdom; sovereign activities) will not be ruined, corrupted or destroyed" (LXX, JM).

Was it from this passage in Daniel that Paul regarded himself as a "slave of Jesus Christ" (Rom. 1:1)? And did Christ's reign play out according to how Daniel understood that it would? In vs. 10, below, the living ones and the twenty-four elders sing a song that states that Christ made them (or: us) to be kings and to continue reigning. This follows what Jesus told the poor, in Mat. 5:3,

> "**The destitute folks [are] happy in spirit and attitude, because the reign and dominion of the heavens is continually belonging to, and made up of, them**."

We, represented by the 4 and the 24 in this passage, regard Christ as the One that "**is worthy** (of value) **to take** (receive) **the power and ability, as well as wealth and riches**..." (vs. 12, below), but as we saw earlier, He brings us up to His level and seats us with Him. He did away with social stratification in His reign, but WE always know Who is the Head.

This scene calls to mind the words that opened this book, in 1:1a,

> "**An unveiling of, and which is, Jesus Christ** (or: A disclosure from Jesus [the] Anointed; A revelation which pertains to Jesus [the Messiah]) **which God gave by Him** (in Him; for Him; **to** Him) **to point out to His slaves that which continues necessary to come to be** (or: be birthed; happen) **in swiftness** (= speedily; or: shortly).

God gave it to Him, for Him and by Him. So it is with this little scroll. Here Metzger comments, "In short, Jesus does not change the divine plan; he unfolds its eternal and unchangeable nature by his obedience, even unto death on the cross" (ibid p 53).

So the Little Lamb went and took the scroll. The call of the strong messenger of vs. 2 has been answered. One who humbled Himself to become a servant (Phil. 2:7) now possesses all power and moves to the place of God's power (**the right hand**) and takes control of this most significant scroll. He now has the ability to loose the seals and to begin the process of bringing forth His life into the universe.

8. **Now when it took** (or: received) **the little book** (or: scroll; codex), **the four living ones and the twenty-four elders** (older folks) **fell before the little Lamb – each one constantly holding lyres** (or: harps) **and golden, shallow bowls being continuously brimming full of incenses** (things passed off in fumes), **which are the thoughts and speech toward having things going well and being at ease** (or: prayers) **of, and from, the set-apart folks** (or: holy ones; saints; sacred people).

The action of taking the scroll causes **the four living ones** and the **24 elders** to **fall before the little Lamb** (vs. 8) and **sing a new song** (vs. 9, below). My sister, Rebecca, remarked about the resulting mess of burning incense all over the floor; the clang of the golden bowls hitting the sea of glass (4:6, above); and the cacophony from the crash of 24 lyres adding to the din – IF this scene were interpreted literally! Selah. The word "**fell**," here, is not the normal Greek word for "worship" or for "giving obeisance." It simply mean that they fell. If we look back to the types and shadows of the O.T. we will find that praise, worship and prayer before the throne only happened in the Tabernacle of David, which he set up to house the Ark of the Covenant (2 Sam. 6:17, "And they brought in the Ark of the Lord, and set it in His place, in the midst of the Tabernacle that David had pitched for it; and David offered burnt offerings and peace offerings before the Lord"). Prior to this, when the Ark was in the Tabernacle of Moses, only the high priest could enter into the Holy of Holies (a type of this present scene here in Rev. 4 & 5) once a year on the Day of Atonement. In David's tent there was no veil and he was neither a priest nor a Levite, yet he had access to the Mercy Seat (the Throne of Grace - Heb. 4:16).

See 1 Chron. 25:1-7 where David set up 24 Orders of Singers "for song in the house of the Lord, with cymbals, psalteries, and harps, for the service of the house of God ..." (vs. 6). We see here in Rev. that the 24 elders have instruments for praise and **bowls brimming** with things **offered** in sacrifice, and they sing a new song. The Tabernacle of David was a type of the heavenlies, the realm of spirit and praise (Jn. 4:24), in which Christ is the Priest-King after the Order of Melchisedec (typified by David), and in which the called-out communities offer up praise and acknowledgement for what He has done (vs. 9, below) and sing the new song, while having or speaking **"thoughts and speech toward having things going well and being at ease."**

Note that what the 24 elders figuratively offer (the bowls of incenses) are defined here as "**the PRAYERS of, and from the set-apart folks** (or: holy ones; saints; sacred people)." This identifies who these 24 elders represent: they are priests; this scene is a picture of the sacred communities of Christ, whose lives answer to the past figure of the work of the priests in the physical temple. "Let my prayer be before Thee counted as incense; and the lifting up of my hands as an evening sacrifice." (Ps. 141:2) And in Lu. 1 we see the priestly work of Zacharias doing the course of Abiah, where in vss. 8b-10 we observe:

> "**in his arranged order and appointment of the daily [service division] within the presence of and facing before God, [and] corresponding to and in accord with the custom of the priesthood, he obtained by lot the [duty] to burn incense, after entering into the [holy place] of the inner sanctuary of the Temple of the Lord. Also, during the hour of the incense offering, all the full capacity, of the people normally praying, was outside.**"

Also, in Eph. 5:2, Paul admonishes,

> "**keep on walking** (= progressively living and maintaining your life) **within, and in union with, Love** (self-giving acceptance and the urge for union), **according as the Christ also loves** (or: to the same level and commensurately as the Anointed One loved, accepted and achieved reunion with) **you folks, and also gives** (or: gave) **Himself over in our behalf: a bearing toward and a bringing to be face to face, even an offering by** (or: in; with; or: to; for) **God [turning] into a fragrant odor** (or: and unto a sweet-smelling incense-sacrifice amid God)."

9. **And they repeatedly sing a new song** (an ode or hymn different in character), **constantly saying, "You are worthy to take** (of equal value to receive) **the scroll** (or: codex; book) **and to open its seals, because You were** (or: are) **slaughtered and bought us by God** (for God; in God; with God), **within Your blood** (or: in union with the blood which is You), **from out of the midst of every tribe and tongue** (or: language) **and people and ethnic multitude** (or: nation).

Now see that the community of Christ, His separated ones, continuously, or habitually, sings **a new song** (representative of the new deliverance from bondage, the new creation and the New Covenant, or arrangement) of praise to Christ for what He has done: He was slaughtered, and thus bought us for God. This purchase was transacted "**within Your Blood**" and was made "**from out of the midst of every tribe and tongue** (or: language) **and people and ethnic multitude** (or: nation)." This shows that the work of Christ went beyond the Jews and Israel and that this scene is representative of the universal body of Christ, of which the covenant with Israel was the type. He gave His life a ransom for MANY (Mk. 10:45). Also, " **Christ bought us [back] out** (or: redeems and reclaims us out [of slavery] and liberates us) **from the midst of the curse** (or: adversarial prayer; imprecation) **of and from the Law**..." (Gal. 3:13)

We find here a very strong allusion to Ps. 98:1,

> "You folks should in celebration sing to, for, in and with the LORD (= Yahweh) a new song (a celebrative ode that is different in character), because the LORD (= Yahweh) has done (made; formed; created; produced) marvelous and wonderful things. His right hand and His sacred, set-

apart arm rescued, brought deliverance (or: saved) and restores to health and wholeness" (LXX, JM).

In Ps. 33:2-3 we read, "Praise Yahweh with a harp…. Sing unto him a new song; play skilfully with a loud noise." And in Ps. 144:9-10,

"O Elohim, let me sing a new song to You; On a zither of ten strings let me make melody to You [Who are] giving salvation… setting loose…" (CVOT). *Cf* Isa.42:10; Ps. 149:1a.

Ps. 96:1-3 is another witness:

"Sing to Yahweh a new song; sing to Yahweh, **all the earth!**…. Bear the tidings of His salvation day after day! Recount His glory among the nations; among all the peoples, His marvelous works" (CVOT).

We should note the dative form of the word **God**, here (as with Ps. 98:1, above). There is no expressed preposition in the text, so we must consider the functions of the dative that will make sense to the verse and the larger context. Only MS A omits the word **us**, following the word **bought**, but many translations follow A. These then have to add a word either after "bought" or before the complex phrase beginning with "**from out of**," which is usually a limited term, like "persons" (NWT) or "saints" (NRSV) or "men" (NIV). The reading "**us**" solves the problem without having to add a word to the text. Those singing the song are representative (a symbol) of all that He bought and set free. The 24 and the 4 represent people from all four directions and times. So now we consider the options of the preposition that is to follow **us**: **by** shows that this purchase was done "**by God**." "For" indicated that we were bought "for God." "In" indicated the realm and sphere in which this transaction took place. "With" tells us that God was the currency used. It was God's life that bought us out of slavery to failure and sin. Thus, it makes sense that it happened "**within [His] blood**;" it was God's blood, through His Son's life; it happened within the sphere of His life and "in union with the blood which [was Him]." Here the blood is also an allusion to the blood on the door posts when Israel was set free from Egypt. And so, what seems to be an ambiguous reading actually fits all the functions of the dative case, and we have a fuller picture of what took place on the cross.

The last long phrase is as complete a statement as could be made to express the universality of the effect of His sacrifice: tribe, tongue, people and ethnic multitude (or: nation). This is like saying "in all four directions of humanity" or, from all the world. This speaks of the cross proclaiming the ultimate end of all domination systems, and calls to mind Jesus' words,

"**And so then I, if I should be lifted up from out of the earth** (or: when I can be exalted forth from the midst of this Land), **I will progressively drag** [note: drag as with, or in, a net; or: draw, as drawing water with a bucket, or a sword out of a sheath] **all mankind** (or: everyone) **to Myself**" (Jn. 12:32).

But in John's day, the called-out communities were just the beginning, as we read in Jn. 1:18,

"**from being pregnant He gave birth to us** (brought us forth; prolifically produced us) **by a Word** (in a collected thought; for an expressed idea; with a message) **of Truth and from Reality – into the [situation for] us to be** (or: to continuously exist being) **a specific** (or: a certain; some) **firstfruit of His created beings**."

A "firstfruit" implies a harvest that will come later.

10. **"And You made** (or: make; form; construct; produce) **them** [minuscule 792, the Clementia Vulgate (1592) and Primasius (6th century) read: us] **kings** [other MSS: a kingdom] **and priests in** (for; to; by) **our God, and they** [the Armenian, Clementia Vulgate (1592) and Primasiua read: we] **continue reigning** [reading with Westcott & Hort (following A); other MSS: they will continue reigning] **upon the Land** (or: the earth)."

This continues the song, saying that those whom He bought He **makes** (forms into) **kings and priests**, and that these are to rule as kings upon the earth. This also shows a break from the old covenant, for under the old both kings and priests had to descend from the blood line of either a king or a priest, respectively. These are taken from every tribe, tongue & nation, or ethnic group. This is no longer just about Israel. Yet the type is followed, in the sense that this purchase was made within His blood. Thus we, being placed within His blood, are into His blood line, but it is a blood line of the last Adam, the Second Humanity (1 Cor. 15:45-48). We are born again and are made sons of God; His sons. He being a priest & king, His sons are priests & kings. He, the Last Adam, has joined us to Himself and to the place of caretaking for which the first Adam was created: to reign in love upon the earth. This is restoration, but into a new creation (2 Cor. 5:17a).

Once again, background OT allusions are seen here. An echo of vss. 9b-10 is found in Ex. 19:5-6,
> "For, in, to and with, Me you folks will continue existing a people being encircled around [Me], laid up as a super-abounding acquisition of property [*cf* Tit. 2:14b], [separated] from all the ethnic multitudes (nations), for you see, all the earth is Mine. But further, you folks will continue existing for Me, in Me, and with Me, a royal effect of a body of priests..." (LXX, JM).

In Dan. 7:22b, the LXX reads, "then the season came on and the set-apart folks fully possessed the reign of sovereign influence," and 7:27 reads, "And the reign (sovereign influence)… was given to the set-apart folks belonging to the Most High," and in 7:18b, "and so set-apart folks belonging to the Most High shall receive alongside and take to themselves the reign (sovereign influence), and they shall continue holding down and fully possessing it as far as an Age of the ages" (JM).

But keep in mind that this kingdom does not look like other kingdoms or systems of rule. It is not a domination system, but a life of serving, healing and giving life. *Cf* the teachings of Jesus, in the Gospels.

Notice the present tense, **continue reigning**. That was happening in the 1st century, and has continued through those who have remained joined to the Vine (Jn. 15:1ff) since Jesus was enthroned and was given "all authority" (3:21, above; Mat. 28:18). Furthermore, this reigning is not in some far off "heaven," but right here, **upon the Land** (meaning the Land of Israel and the habitable regions of the Roman Empire, in the 1st century), or, "upon the earth" (in our day).

11. **Next I saw and also heard a sound** (or: a voice) **of many agents forming a circle around the throne, the living ones, and the elders. And the number of them [is; was] innumerable groups of innumerable groups** (myriads of myriads), **even thousands of thousands,**

The next phase of this vision is the perception by John of countless multitudes of messengers (**agents**) **forming a circle around the throne**, and around those about the throne. They, too, continuously give witness of the worthiness of the little Lamb (vs. 12), but they say something a little different than what the new song said, above, as we see in the next verse. The **number** echoes Nu. 10:36 (LXX), "Turn again (or: Turn back), so that they are changed, O LORD (= Yahweh), [the] thousands – [the] innumerable thousands (myriads) – within the midst of Israel" (JM). But a closer allusion is in Ps. 68:17,
> "The chariot of God [is] ten thousand-fold: thousands of progressively thriving and continuously prospering folks: [the] LORD (= Yahweh) [is] among them – [as] in Sinai, [so] centered within the midst of the holy place (= the temple; or: in the set-apart place)" (LXX, JM)

Then, of course, is Dan. 7:10a,
> "A river (or: stream) of Fire was continuously and progressively drawing, in His presence [other MSS: progressively passing along forth from before Him; continuously went out from in front of Him]; a thousand thousands were continuously ministering and serving as priests for Him, and

ten thousand ten thousands (a myriad of myriads) having taken a stand alongside in His midst, and remaining standing with and for Him" (LXX, JM).

The different MS readings in Dan. 7:10a give varying pictures. The "drawing" by the river of Fire sketches a scene of all returning into the midst of Him (Rom. 11:36); the "passing along forth from before Him" draws a picture of His fiery love on the move into His creation, purifying as it goes. *Cf* Heb. 12:22

The picture described by the phrase "**forming a circle around the throne**," calls to mind a similar picture found in 1 Pet.2:9-10,

> "**Yet you folks [are] 'a picked-out offspring** [Isa. 43:21; Deut. 7:6], **a royal priesthood, a set-apart multitude, a people constructed into an encirclement** (made into a surrounding structure; made into a performance about [Him]; gathered into a surrounding [flock])'.... **[you] who [were] once** (or: formerly) **'not a people,' but now [are] 'God's people;' [formerly] being the ones having 'not been given mercy,' yet now [are] 'folks being mercied** (being given mercy).'" [Hos. 2:23]

Paul uses a corresponding word picture,

> "**a freedom of the encircling acquisition, which is that which has been constructed as a perimeter around [Him]; into the praise and approval from** (or: which is) **His glory**" (an alternate rendering from Eph. 1:14).

And in 2 Thes. 2:14, "**He also called you folks** [other MSS: us] **into an encompassing** (or: forming an encirclement; establishing a perimeter; creating a surrounding) **of the glory** (or: which is the glory) **of our Lord, Jesus Christ**."

12. **repeatedly saying with a great voice,**
> "**The little Lamb, the One having been slaughtered, is worthy** (of value) **to take** (receive) **the power and ability, as well as wealth and riches, and wisdom and strength and honor and glory** (or: reputation) **and blessing** (a word and message of goodness, ease and well-being)."

The elders & living ones say that He is worthy to take the scroll and to open its seals, but these say He is worthy "to take **THE POWER**, even **wealth** and **wisdom** and **strength** and **honor** and **glory** and **blessing**." Is this perhaps an expansion, or an explanation, of the significance of the scroll and its being opened? Does this eulogy perhaps describe the characteristics of His reign and God's kingdom? Is the scroll not only the plan and purpose of the ages, the plan of redemption, the Word pertaining to Christ, but also the power, ability, authority and blessings of the Kingdom of God? Notice that this proclamation comes "**with a great voice**," like that of the agent/messenger in vs. 2, above.

The eulogy of this verse may be an allusion to 1 Chron. 29:11-13, spoken of Yahweh:
> "Yours, O Yahweh, are greatness, mastery, beauty, permanence and splendor; indeed, everything in the heavens and on the earth. Yours, O Yahweh, is the kingship, lifting Yourself up as Head over all. Riches and glory, [come] from before You, and You are ruling over all... And now, our Elohim... we are acclaiming You and praising Your beauteous Name" (CVOT).

The LXX of this passage uses the same word, "power and ability," "wealth and riches," "strength," and "glory" that are found in our text, here, in 5:12.

Only a **slaughtered lamb** can be worthy of such honor, and be entrusted with this **power and ability**. The symbol refers, of course, to Jesus, but it also applies to His followers who have taken up their execution stakes. We read these qualifications, given by Jesus, in Mat. 16:24-27,

> **24. At that point Jesus said to His disciples, "If anyone continues intending** (purposing; willing; wanting) **to come on behind Me, let him at once deny, reject and disown himself, and**

then in one move lift up his execution stake and after that proceed to be by habit continuously following after Me!

25. "You see, whoever may intend** (or: should purpose; might set his will; happens to want) **to keep his soul-life safe** (to rescue himself; to preserve the interior life that he is living) **will continue loosing-it-away and destroying it. Yet whoever can loose-away and even destroy his soul-life** (the interior self) **on My account, he will continue finding it!**

26. "For what will a person** (or: mankind) **proceed being benefited, or in what will he** (or: they) **continue helped or augmented, if he can or would advantageously procure [for himself** (or: themselves)**] and gain the whole ordered system of society: government, economy, culture, religion – even the whole universe, yet would be undergoing the loss of, receive damage to, or be made to forfeit, his soul-life** (his interior self [in its reality])**? Or what will a person** (or: mankind) **continue giving, as a price paid to change his** (or: its) **soul back** (or: to effect the interior transformation of himself/itself, back again to make himself/itself other than he/it is)**?**

27. "You see, the Son of the Man is presently about to continue progressively coming within the glory** (the manifestation which calls forth praise) **of His Father, with His agents** (messengers). **And at that time, He will proceed giving back** (or: repaying; recompensing) **to each one in corresponding accord with his practice, behavior and operation of business."**

We should keep this passage in mind as we read the rest of this *Unveiling*.

13. **And then all creation** (or: every creature) **which exists within the sky** (or: atmosphere; heaven), **and on the earth, even down under the earth** (or: ground; soil), **as well as which is upon the sea – even all things** (the whole; everything) **within them – I heard repeatedly saying,**

> **"The blessing** (word of goodness and well-being) **and the honor and the glory** (good reputation) **and the strength** (might) **[are] in** (by; for; to; with) **the One continuously sitting upon the throne, and in** (by; to; for; with) **the little Lamb, on into the ages of the ages."**

In this next scene, **all creation** in every realm and in all places echo a witness back to God, and to those described in this scene, the last part of the eulogy just pronounced by the countless groups of agents. This is a universal pledge of allegiance by all creation to God and to Christ. "Wherefore, also, God highly exalts Him, and graces Him with the Name that is above **every name**, that in the Name of Jesus **every knee** should be bowing, celestial and terrestrial and subterranean, and **every tongue** should be acclaiming that Jesus Christ is Lord, for the glory of God, the Father" (Phil. 2:9-11, CLNT). Paul apparently had the same vision that John had. NONE are left out. He also gave us an expanded version of vs. 13 in Eph. 3:20-21,

> "**But by** (or: Now in) **the One being continuously able and powerful to do** (make; form; create; produce) **above and beyond all things – surpassingly above, over and beyond things which we are repeatedly asking for ourselves or are normally grasping with the mind** (apprehending; imagining; considering; conceiving) **– in accord with** (or: down from; corresponding to; in the sphere of and along the line of) **the power and ability [which is] continuously operating** (making itself effective; energizing itself; working and developing) **within us, and in union with us, by Him** (to Him; for Him; in Him; with Him) **[is] the glory** (the manifestation which calls forth praise) **within the called-out community** (the summoned-forth congregation) **as well as within Christ Jesus: unto** (or: [proceeding] into) **all the generations** (births; progenies) **of the Age of the ages** (= the most significant, or crowning, Age of all the ages)**!"**

This is one of the most universal confessions of God and of Jesus that can be found in all of Scripture. Nothing, and no one, is left out: **all creation**; every creature. The whole universe affirms God and the little Lamb **on into the ages of the ages**, i.e., into the unforeseeable future, and beyond! The Christ event inaugurated cosmic transformation which resulted in what is recorded here.

The first clause is the common, 1st century view of the universe. Those who had been buried were considered to be **down under the earth**. But the message is not about their state or condition, but that all who ever lived will be a part of this praise for God. Every conceivable realm (**all things**; the whole; everything), whether now dead, or living, proclaims **blessing, honor and glory** to God.

Metzger observes that in the Greek of verses 12 and 13 there are, "The seven terms [which] symbolize the fullness of praise" (ibid p 54; brackets added): power/ability, wealth/riches, strength, wisdom, honor, glory/reputation, and blessing/words-of-goodness.

14. **And then the four living ones say** (or: said), **"It is so (Amen)!" And the elders fall** (or: the older people fell [forward]) **and worship** (or: worshiped; kissed the hand toward [the throne] and paid homage).

The question is: did John see something that then existed in heaven, in the spirit realm? did he see something that existed then and continued to exist into the present? did he see something that would exist in the future? Was this a case of God "calling the things not being (existing) as being (existing)" (Rom. 4:17)? Perhaps the answer is "Yes" to all these questions. If we agree that what John saw here was what Moses saw and of which he built a pattern, or that he saw the shadow of this at least, then what John saw perhaps existed from the foundation of the world, for Jesus was

> "**the little Lamb**" – **the One having been slaughtered from a casting-down of [the; an] ordered arrangement** (or: on account of [the] establishing of [the] world of culture, religion, government and economics; or: from [the] world's founding; or: from a disrupting, down-casting of [the] aggregate of humanity)" (13:8, below).

This is His unveiling, and He is the same yesterday, today and on into the ages (Heb. 13:8). So, in regard to the little Lamb and the One on the throne, we can say that this is a timeless scene. But the event (universal redemption, vss. 9, 13, above) which is the subject of the song, that these four living ones and the 24 elders sing (vs. 9), has its origin at the cross. Thus, this scene existed in John's time, and yet we can conclude that the situation continues to exist since it pictures the spiritual atmospheres. What can we say about the innumerable groups of agents surrounding this inner circle? This picture calls to mind Heb. 12:22-24, quoted above. We would suggest that this passage in Hebrews is talking about the same group, describing them first as agents, next as an assembly of an entire people, then as a called-out community of firstborn folks who are the spirits of just folks that have been brought to the goal.

The pronouncement by the four living ones, that "**It is so**," speaks of the accomplishment, and the present existence of what has just been said in vs. 13. We observe the "**until now**" time-frame given by Paul in Rom. 8:22,

> "**You see, we have seen, and thus know and are aware, that all the creation keeps on sighing, groaning or querulously moaning together, and yet progressively travailing together as in childbirth** (continues suffering common birthing pains) **until now** (to the point of the present moment)."

What we read in vs. 13, above, does not sound like **sighing, groaning or querulously moaning together**; it does not sound like **travailing together as in childbirth**. It sounds like the praise and rejoicing of the accomplished work of Christ, as seen from the view of being seated with Christ in the spiritual realm (Eph. 2:6). But there is an existential factor to Rom. 8:18-25 because people are still being born into this earth-existence, and must walk out their human journey. This whole creation was still groaning in Paul's day, and I think that most of it is still groaning today. Rom.8:23-24a records,

"**Yet not only [this], but further, even we ourselves – constantly holding** (or: having; possessing) **the firstfruit of, and which is, the Spirit** (or: the Firstfruit whose source is the Breath-effect; or: the first offering, or first portion, which is spirit and breath, and is from the Attitude) **– we ourselves also continually sigh and groan within** (in the center of) **ourselves, continuously accepting and with our hands taking away from out of a placing in the condition of a son** (or: [the] deposit of the Son; a setting in place which is the Son; a constituting as a son; a placing in the Son)**: the process of the release of our body from slavery**
> (or: [and] the loosing from destruction pertaining to the [corporate] body, which is us; or: = the unbinding and release of the body [of Adam; of humanity], which belongs to us).
For in the expectation and with hope we are suddenly made whole and healthy
> (or: You see, by the expectation we are delivered and saved; or: For we were at one point rescued to expectation; or: To be sure, we were kept safe for this expectation)!"

Where vs. 13, above, shows us a picture of the final goal and end of all people and of the entire creation, this praise for the gift of the Christ-life comes to us, "**each person within the result and effect of his or her own class** (or: ordered place; appointed position [in line]; arranged time or order of succession; = place in a harvest calendar, thus, due season of maturity)" (1 Cor. 15:23a). The work in view, in vs. 13, above, is the completed work of Christ. But the ages keep rolling on. As a part of His firstfruits, we can join in with the praise for His death and resurrection. But the rest of the harvest still groans until their crop (or: class) has matured to the ripeness described in Eph. 4:13,

> "**until we – the whole of mankind** (all people) **– can** (or: would) **come down to the goal** (or: attain; arrive at; meet accordingly; meet down face-to-face)**: into the state of oneness from, and which is, The Faithfulness** (or: the unity of, that belongs to and which characterizes that which is faith; or: the lack of division which has its source in trust, confidence and reliability, has the character of and is in reference to the loyalty and fidelity), **even which is the full, experiential and intimate knowledge** (or: and from recognition; and of discovery; as well as pertaining to insight) **which is** (or: of; from; in reference to) **the Son of God, [growing] into [the] purposed and destined adult man** (complete, finished, full-grown, perfect, goal-attained, mature manhood) **– into** (or: unto) **[the] measure of [the] stature** (full age; prime of life) **of the entire content which comprises the Anointed One**."

In this verse, **the four living ones** only speak, but **the twenty-four elders do obeisance** (as it were, being overwhelmed) from the effect of the praise that all levels of creation and every creature give forth to God and to the little Lamb, which they just heard, in vs. 13. The elders, being figures both of tribal cultures and tribal religions, cannot remain seated in their normal positions, nor continue enthroned as the heads of human religions. We find the twelve tribes (corporate Israel) as entry points to the new city (figured as "gates" in 21:12, below) and the twelve sent-forth representatives symbolically figured as the foundations of the city (21:14), this latter being an echo of Eph. 2:20,

> 19. **Consequently then** (or: Thereupon), **you folks no longer continuously exist being strangers** (foreigners) **and sojourners** (folks being or living beside a house; temporary residents in a foreign land), **but in contrast, you continually exist being fellow-citizens of those set apart to be sacred people** (or: folks residing together in a City belonging to, and composed of, the holy ones)**: even God's family** (members of God's household),
> 20. **being fully built as a house upon the foundation of the sent-forth representatives** (or: emissaries) **and prophets** (folks who had light ahead of time), **Jesus Christ continuously being a corner-foundation [stone] of it** (or: there being an extreme point and head of the corner, or, capstone/keystone: Jesus Christ Himself),
> 21. **within and in union with Whom all the home-building** (all the construction of the house; or: = every house that is constructed, or, the entire building), **being continuously fitted [and] progressively framed together** (closely and harmoniously joined together; made a common

joint by a word), **is continuously and progressively growing into a set-apart temple** (or: separate, different and holy inner sanctuary) **within [the] Lord** [= Christ, or, Yahweh]:
22. **within the midst of** (or: in union with) **Whom you folks, also, are continuously and progressively being formed a constituent part of the structure** (or: being built together into a house) – **into God's down-home place** (place of settling down to dwell; abode; permanent dwelling) **within [the] Spirit** (or: in spirit; or: in the midst of a Breath-effect and an attitude).

If we can see both the Christ event and the called-out covenant communities (figured by those of chapters 2 and 3) as the subject of chapters 4 and 5, then we might conclude that Dan. 7 was fulfilled in the 1st century. More on this conclusion will be seen in the following visions. We can see a comparison between the concluding portions of 4:11, above, and 5:9-13. We can observe the same connection both in Rom. 5:12-21 and 1 Cor. 15:42-49.

This chapter has been interpreted by many as the risen Christ's enthronement scene, following His ascension (Acts 1:9). But we should keep in mind that chapters 4 and 5 are figures of the "holy of holies" in the midst of God's temple, which is the body of Christ, the called-out covenant communities. The mercy seat, God's throne from which Christ now reigns, is in the heart of the temple: the heart of the corporate communities, and the core of each individual's being. So may we "**let the peace, which is God, act as the umpire in our hearts**" as we play the games of this life and run our course.

Chapter 6

The following scenes, of the vision that continues from chapters 4 and 5, begin showing John apocalyptic action, as viewed from the realm of the Spirit, to where John was caught up, in 4:2, above. So what we will be considering is still a spiritual vision of this cosmic opera that is being shown to John. This compares to what Moses saw when he ascended into the top of Sinai, to receive the pattern for the Tabernacle. The setting is the atmosphere, or, heaven, and it is similar to the disciples seeing Moses and Elijah speaking with Jesus on the "mount of transfiguration" (Mat. 17:15). As with the visions in the OT that had a literal application to the lives of ancient Israel, these too have a first-layer application to the folks living in the 1st century. The literal message was not for the distant future, but for their time and location. In the following visions, you will note that I normally translate the Greek word *gē* as "Land," referring either to Palestine or to the areas defined by the Roman Empire. When you read each verse that has this word, think of that first, and then, to receive the message that can apply to us, think of this word as "ground" or "earth" in the sense of being in distinction to "the atmosphere," or, "heaven," i.e., the realm of the Spirit. Keep in mind Acts 17:28, "**in Him we live, and are moved, and exist**." Our God is ever present, and so is the realm of His life and His activities.

So, following a 1st century application, which corresponds to the Preterist interpretation, I will share a more "timeless" application that applied to all who have read this Unveiling ever since the 1st century.

We will also share the varying viewpoints of other scholars who have written about these visions. For example, Metzger understands:
> "With the sixth chapter, the main action of the book may be said properly to begin. The section extending from chapter 6 to the end of chapter 11 is intended to bring before the reader not only the struggle of the church amid conflict and persecution, but also the judgments of God upon the church's enemies" (ibid p 55).

He interprets the first four seal-openings as "opened at once, and will together make up one picture." Also, he states:

> "Then the fifth and sixth seals will be opened together making up one picture…. The seventh seal, in turn, is really the introduction to a new series of visions…. The trumpets more or less repeat the revelation of the seven seals, though they present it more from God's standpoint…. Thus, the seven seals and the seven trumpets essentially tell the same thing, each time emphasizing one or another aspect of the whole" (ibid p 55-56).

This provides us with a good framework for a basic understanding of what we will be shown. Beale, as well, considers the opening of the four seals as being "simultaneous," noting that,

> "(1) the fourth seal summarizes the prior three (see below on 6:8); (2) the models of Ezk. 14:12-13; Zech. 6:5-8, and the Synoptic eschatological discourse, on which Rev. 6:1-8 is based, portray events of tribulation occurring simultaneously…" (ibid p 370-1).

As we read these visions, it is imperative to keep in mind the "unveiling" given to Paul, concerning our existential situation, in Eph. 1:

> 9. **[This occurred] while making known to us** (acquainting us by intimate, experiential knowledge) **the secret** (mystery; hidden knowledge) **of His will** (determined purpose; resolve) – **in accord with** (or: down from and following the pattern of; corresponding to; in line with) **His good thought which He before placed within Himself**
>> (or: – corresponding to the measure of His pleasing imagination and intent of well-being which He designed beforehand and determined by setting it forth in union with Himself),
>
> 10. **[leading] into an administration, implementation and realization from a detailed plan of the effects of that which fills up the appointed seasons and fertile moments** (or: unto a dispensing of the entire contents of the opportune situations; into an administration of the full effect from the eras), **[designed] to itself bring back again all things up under one Head** (or: to gather everything around the main point and sum it all up in unity; to unite and return all things to the Source) **within and in union with the Christ: those things upon** [other MSS: within] **the heavens** (or: the atmospheres) **and the things upon the land** (earth) – **centered in, within the midst of, and in union with, Him!**

What Paul described about "**bring[ing] back again all things under one Head within and in union with the Christ**" is the same as the little Lamb, here in the Unveiling shown to John, being enthroned within God's Temple (His people). Notice that Paul also included "**the heavens** (or: the atmospheres) **and the things upon the land** (earth)," a shortened version of "the universe of creation." Here in chapter six, the little Lamb is opening "**the secret** (mystery; hidden knowledge) **of His will** (determined purpose; resolve)" – pictured as being contained in a sealed scroll, or book.

D'Aragon's view, which is similar to Metzger's, concerning verses 6:1-8 is, "This homogeneous group [of the first four seals] forms a unit expressed in a literary parallelism formed by the repetition of the same expressions: 'When the Lamb had opened,' 'I heard,' 'Come!'" (ibid p 476; brackets added). He further understands that,

> "The riders, who personify these misfortunes, symbolize a conquering power and the three evils that follow from it: war, famine and pestilence" (ibid p 476-7).

This interpretation fits the historical, 1st century application that Preterists embrace, who see the "war" as the Jewish war against Rome, with the famine and pestilence that followed the devastation of that war. Here Chilton suggests,

> "[T]he Seals are not meant to represent a progressive chronology. It is more likely that they reveal the main ideas of the Book's contents, the major themes of the judgments that came upon Israel during the Last Days, from AD 30-70" (ibid p 181).

He also points us to the apocalypses in the Gospels: Mat. 24:6-31; Mk. 13:1-6 and Lu. 21:9-27. It will be fruitful for the reader to review those passages before proceeding in our present chapter, here.

Before continuing into the chapter itself, let us read from Zech. 6:1-8 in order to directly observe this OT background imagery:
> "And I turned and lifted my eyes and saw, and behold, four chariots coming out from between two mountains, and the mountains were bronze mountains. On the first chariot were red horses, and on the second chariot black horses, and on the third chariot white horses, and on the fourth chariot various shades of dapple-gray horses. And I answered... "What are these, lord?' And the angel [literally: agent; messenger] who talked with me answered and said, 'These are the four winds of the sky; they go out to attend on the Lord of all the earth.... And he said [to them], 'Go, and patrol the earth [or: Land].' And he shouted and spoke to me, saying, 'Behold, those who go toward the north country have caused my rage [or: rushing passion] to rest in the north country'" (LXX, N.E.T.S., p 815-16; brackets mine).

In Zech. 1:8, 10b, we read,
> "In the night I have seen, and behold, a man riding on a red horse! And this one stood among the shaded mountains, and behind him were red and gray and spotted and white horses.... And the man who stood among the mountains answered and said to me, 'These are those whom the Lord has sent to patrol the earth'" (ibid p 814).

The next OT passage which we should review is Ezk. 14:12-23,
> "The word of Yahweh came to me, saying: 'Son of humanity, the land, when it is sinning against Me by offending with offense, then I will stretch out My hand against it and break its staff of bread, and send famine upon it and cut off from it human and beast.... Or... bring a sword on that land.... Or... send a plague upon that land.... My four evil judgments, sword and famine and wild animal and plague I send against Jerusalem, to cut off from it human and beast..." (CVOT)

Notice that the recipient of the four judgments was Jerusalem, not Rome. And in Ezk. 14:1-11 it was the elders of Israel, and their idolatry (the "offense" of vs. 13), that brought the judgment upon all the inhabitants of that Land.

Other allusions for this next section in chapter 6, below, can be found in Lev. 26:21-33,
> "And if you [Israel] walk contrary unto Me, and will not hearken unto Me, I will bring seven times more plagues upon you, according to your sins. I will also send wild animals among you.... I will bring a sword upon you.... [break] the staff of your bread.... also, in fury, I, even I, will chastise you seven times for your sins... I will destroy your high places [pagan temples or idol locations] and cut down your images.... make your cities waste and bring down your sanctuaries unto desolation.... bring the Land into desolation.... And I will winnow and scatter you among the nations..." (brackets added).

This is a picture of Jerusalem and Judea, in AD 70. So while the echoes from Zechariah seem mystical and quite figurative (though with a literal, historical reference and meaning), the allusions from Ezekiel and Leviticus are narratives, with promises of judgment. These four pictures of 6:2-8, below, refer, in their first application, to contemporary historical events.

However, we shall also investigate a second layer of interpretation that speaks to events in our lives that God brings to His followers as they bear their execution stakes. Thus it is that Ray Prinzing titled his book: *Revelation, A Positive Book*, and I consider *The Unveiling* (Revelation) to be the NT's fifth Gospel. We will share some of Prinzing's comments, below. If we see, from the OT allusions, that God is the source of what follows, we may ask: "Where is grace and mercy in all of this?" If the Preterist view is correct, the following visions would be a picture of Yahweh's final judgment on Israel, under the Mosaic covenant, which would fulfill the prophecies given by Jesus and end the old temple cultus, along with the termination of the Law. They predict the fall of Jerusalem in AD 70 (*cf* 11:2, below), which demonstrated that God had ushered in a new arrangement with humanity – a new covenant that has its source in Christ, through the Holy Spirit. So let us now read on.

1. **Then I saw when the little Lamb opened one from out of the seven seals; and I heard one from out of the midst of the four living ones repeatedly saying, as a sound** (or: voice) **of thunder,**
> "**Come** (or: Be coming; or: Go; Pass on; [TR, with Aleph, add: and see])**!**"

"In the first section of the visions, 6:1-8, the AV consistently follows a form of the Greek text which makes each of the four living creatures say: 'Come and see!' (vss. 1, 3, 5, 7). In all the best Greek manuscripts it is simply, 'Come!' as translated in the RSV. This is not an invitation to John to come and see; it is a summons to the four horses and their riders one by one to come forward ..." (William Barclay, ibid, Vol. 2, p 1).

Simmons disagrees, favoring the TR reading of the later Majority Text tradition,
> "In the present case, manuscripts, version, and fathers all testify to the veracity of the present [TR] words; Victorinus, bishop of Petau, martyred in AD 304, quotes them in his commentary at this place." (ibid p 143; brackets added).

This reading would remove **the living one** from directing the action, having them only call John to a place where he can view what is taking place. John is called in this way in 17:1 and 21:9, below, but the text uses a different Greek word *Deuro*, "**Come here!**" while in this chapter the Greek word used is *Erchou*, "Come," or, "Go!" Also, if we consider the text of Zech. 6:7 to which our present verse seems to allude, the agent (or: one) is quoted as directing the four chariotreers, saying, "You [four] be progressively and continuously going, passing on from one place to another: travel about and patrol the Land (territory)" (LXX, JM). This seems to lend evidence to the older MS's shorter readings, "**Come** (or: Go; the Greek verb has both meanings)!"

The message given in the opening of the seven seals is normally concluded to be a message of Divine judgement. Of what or whom is a much debated subject. But let us return to the question, To whom was this message first delivered? Did this vision have significance to their situation? The "Preterist" viewpoint would see this "exclusively in terms of its first century setting, claiming that most of its events have already taken place" (NIV Study Bible). I think that those who first read this chapter would have seen practical applications of these figures in their lives and times. "We note that the origin of this vision is in Zech. 6:1-8. Zechariah sees four horses which are let loose upon the earth to deal out vengeance on Babylon and Egypt and the nations which have oppressed God's people." (Barclay, ibid p 2). This setting is the allusion, a "type": but what is its meaning here in the Unveiling?

When Zechariah first sees the various colored horses in chapter 1:8, and then in vs. 9 says, "What are these, my lord?" As we saw, above, the messenger tells him in vs. 10, "These are those whom Yahweh sends to walk to and fro in the Land." They report to the Messenger of Yahweh, "We walk in all the Land (earth), and behold! all the earth is sitting still and is quiet (or: at rest)" (vs. 11). The setting is at the end of the seventy years of judgement & exile of Judah (vs. 12), "the time of the Jewish restoration from Babylonian captivity" (NIV Study Bible). Now, in vs. 16, "Therefore thus says Yahweh: I return to Jerusalem with compassions; My house shall be built in it, (averring is Yahweh of Hosts), and a tape shall be stretched out on Jerusalem." This picture of measuring is echoed in 11:1-2, below. We heard a similar description of the report given to Yahweh in Zech. 1:10 by one of God's agents in Job 1:7,
> "And Yahweh said unto the adversary (Heb., *satan*), 'From where have you come?' Then the adversary (*satan*) reported, 'From going to and fro in the Land (or: on earth), and from walking up and down in it.'"

This should give us pause, to consider these parallel reports, and those who made them.

Zech. 2:1-2 continues this same theme of measuring (seen in Zech. 1:16, which also spoke of building His house) with the figure of a man with a measuring line in his hand, obviously one of the craftsmen of chapter 1:20-21. Thus, we see that the Lord's purpose is to build His house, His body, and that the horses have been involved. The building theme is seen in Zech. 4:10 when it speaks of the plumb line in the hand of Zerubbabel. Paul picks up the building theme in 1 Cor. 3:9-17 where he identifies us as God's building, God's temple. He references it again in Eph. 2:20-22,

> "**you folks… exist being… God's family, being fully built as a house upon the foundation of the sent-forth representatives and prophets, Jesus Christ continuously being a corner-foundation [stone] of it, within and in union with Whom all the home-building** (all the construction of the house; or: the entire building), **being continuously fitted [and] progressively framed together** (closely joined together; made a common joint by a word), **is continuously and progressively growing into a set-apart temple within [the] Lord: within the midst of** (or: in union with) **Whom you folks, also, are continuously and progressively being formed a constituent part of the structure** (or: being built together into a house) **– into God's down-home place** (or: permanent dwelling), **within [the] Spirit**."

Zechariah spoke concerning the literal temple; new covenant building concerns Christ's body: the heavenly temple, the called-out folks gathered in God's atmosphere and Spirit.

Returning to the horses, Zech. 6:1-3 presents four chariots coming out from between two mountains made of brass (brass is often a figure of judgement). The horses pulling the chariots are of similar color to here, but the order is different: 1st) fiery red, 2nd) black, 3rd) white, and the 4th) diversely colored (e.g., dappled, or iron-gray). These are identified in vs. 5 as "four spirits of the heavens faring forth from stationing themselves with the Lord of the entire earth." (CVOT). These horses are sent out in the four cardinal directions, "so they went throughout the Land (territory; earth)" (vs. 7). The Lord's Spirit was given rest when the black horses brought judgement in the land of the north (primarily Babylon), vs. 8. If we keep in mind that God's main purpose – the theme that threads through these eight verses in Zech. 6 is the restoration of His people from Babylonian captivity, and the rebuilding of Jerusalem and His temple – then we will have a clue to the purpose of the judgement and dealings of the four horses in Rev. 6. With this in mind, let us return to the Unveiling and consider its context.

2. **And so I saw; now consider: A bright-white horse, and the One** (or: He) **continually sitting upon it is constantly holding a bow. And a victor's wreath was given to Him, and He came forth** (or: went out; passed on) **repeatedly overcoming** (continuously conquering), **even to the end that He may overcome** (conquer; be Victor).

Here the picture is One riding a white horse, and His purpose is stated: "**and He came forth** (or: went out; passed on) **repeatedly overcoming** (continuously conquering), **even to the end that He may overcome** (conquer; be Victor)." The bow He is holding is a symbol of battle. "In the O.T., the bow is always the sign of military power. In the final defeat of Babylon her mighty men are taken and their bows – i.e., their military power – are destroyed (Jer. 51:56). God will break the bow of Israel in the valley of Jezreel (Hos. 1:5)" (Barclay, ibid p 4). "Your arrows, sharpened, [pierce] the breast of the King's enemies; peoples fall at Your feet" (Ps. 45:6, Tanakh). Paul spoke of Christ in similar terms,

> "**after Himself causing the sinking out and away of** (or: stripping off and away [of power and abilities]; undressing [them of arms and glory]; putting off and laying away [of categories and classifications]; or: divesting Himself of) **the governments and the authorities** (or: the ruling folks or people of primacy, and the privileged folks). **And then He made a public exhibit, in a citizen's bold freedom of speaking the truth, leading them in a triumphal procession within it [i.e., the cross/suspension-pole]**" (Col. 2:15).

Then in I Cor. 15:25,
> "**For it is binding and necessary for Him to be continuously reigning** (ruling as King; exercising sovereignty) **until which [time or situation]** (or: until where) **He would put** (or: may place; could set) **all the things that have or hold ruin** (or: the enemies) **under His feet**."

Recall 3:21, above, "**To** (or: In; For) **the person who is habitually conquering** (repeatedly overcoming; normally victorious)... **as I also conquer** (or: conquered; overcome; overcame and was victorious)." The identity of this Rider here in 6:2 is made completely clear in 19:11-12, below, for as Malcolm Smith says, "the code must be consistent." Here we have the Rider of the white horse identified:
> "**Then I saw the atmosphere** (or: sky; heaven), **having been opened – and consider! A bright, white horse. And the One continually sitting upon it being constantly called 'Faithful** (Full of Faith; To Be Trusted; Trustworthy; Loyal) **and True** (or: Real),' **and He is continuously judging** (making decisions and evaluations) **and battling** (making war) **in eschatological deliverance** (within equitable dealings; in justice, fairness and righted relations which accord with the covenantal Way pointed out). **And His eyes [are] a flame of fire; and upon His head [are] many diadems** (kingly bands), **having a name having been written** [other MSS: having names written, and a name] **which no one knows except Himself**."

Verse 2, here, together with 19:11-12, may be an allusion to Ps. 45:3-5,
> "Gird your sword upon [Your] thigh, O powerful One, with your glory and your majesty, and in your majesty ride and draw [the bow] prosperously on behalf of truth and humility and righteousness... Your arrows being whetted, peoples beneath You shall fall, [struck] in the heart..." [MT and LXX]. The reign of God is within, and among, us.

In 19:15, below, we see that, "**He will continue shepherding them with an iron staff**," which calls us back to 2:27, above, where this same thing is spoken in regard to the overcomer (victor). And in 19:16 we read that on His thigh (a part of His body) a Name is written, "**King of kings and Lord of lords**," which might be considered to be His new Name (3:12, above) since we see in 11:15, below, that,
> "**The reign of the ordered System** (of the world of religion, culture, government and economy; or: of the realm of the religious and secular) **suddenly came to belong to our Lord** [= Yahweh or Christ] **and to the anointed of Him**
>> (or: The kingdom of the arranged system at once became our Lord's and His Christ's; The rule as king which pertains to the world, was birthed to be the possession of [Yahweh], as well as of His Anointed), **and so He will continue reigning**..."

But now the question before us is: Who is this Victor riding out to conquer? Is it Israel, or in the 1st century, the Jews, as we look back to Lev. 26 and Ezk. 14, cited above? Or is it Rome, as Barclay, above, interprets Zech. 6 to be describing Yahweh's judgment on Babylon and Egypt, back in Zechariah's day? Or, is it us (humanity), as Prinzing suggests, below? Perhaps it is all of these, each in their own time and situation. The book of Job contrasts God's sovereignty (prologue, Job's assessment, and epilogue) to the wisdom of his day (figured by the discourses of Job's "friends"). In Job 6:4 is his statement that echoes into our text, here:
> "For the arrows of the Breasted-One (*Shaddai*; = the One Who Supplies and Suffices; the All-bountiful) [are] in me; my spirit has been drinking their venom. Frightening [things] from God are arrayed [toward] me." (JM)

Then in Ps. 38:2, "Your arrows stick fast in me; Your hand presses down on me."

The OT book of Lamentations is "a series of laments over the destruction of Jerusalem in 586 BC.... Orthodox Jews customarily read it aloud... [on] the date of the destruction of Herod's temple in AD 70" (Ronald Youngblood, NIV Study Bible, ibid p 1207; brackets added). There, in 3:12-13, we read,
> "He positions His bow and is setting me as [a; the] target for arrows; He pierces my innermost being [with the] sons of His quiver" (CVOT).

Allusions to these OT texts suggest a similar context for the imagery of chapter 6, here in the Unveiling.

"HE IS REIGNING NOW! HE IS RIDING NOW!" (Ray Prinzing; emphasis original) We see a time reference to Christ's righting of things in 1 Pet. 4:
> 17. **because** [it is; this is; now is] **the** [other MSS: a] **fitting situation and fertile moment of the appointed season for the result of the judgment** (the effect of the separating for evaluation and decision) **to begin** (to start) **from God's house. Now if first from us, what [will be] the closing act** (the final stage; the end; the consummation; the outcome; the finished product) **pertaining to those continuing unpersuaded and unconvinced by** (or: uncompliant to; disobedient to; stubborn in) **God's message of goodness and well-being** (or: good news)?
> 18. **"And if the rightwised one** (the fair and just person in right relationships in accord to the Way pointed out) **is repeatedly delivered** (rescued; brought to safety; made healthy and whole) **with difficult labor, then where will the irreverent** (the person without pious awe) **and the failure** (the one who makes mistakes and cannot hit the target; the sinner; the outcast) **proceed in making an appearance?"** [Prov. 11:31]
> 19. **So then, also, let those repeatedly feeling the effects of experiences and of suffering which correspond to, and [are] in the sphere of, God's will** (intent; purpose) **continuously commit their souls to a Faithful Former** (or: Loyal Founder; Trustworthy Creator), **within [the] producing of good** (in union with making of virtue; in construction of excellence; within the midst of performing goodness).

Note that He is given a victor's wreath! Prinzing continues with a second layer of interpretation – a spiritual one:
> "GOD IS PREPARED TO DO BATTLE IN YOU! Whatever warfare is necessary, still He purposes to redeem you, to cleanse, purify, transform, until IN YOU He hath 'made all things new.' He who wrestled with Jacob 'until the breaking of the day,' (Gen. 32:24) will wrestle with you for however long it is necessary, until HE WINS.... It is essential that first He RIDES IN YOU, before you ride WITH Him.... All of this is working to bring forth 'a revelation of Jesus Christ' to us, in us, and through us. 'It pleased God ... to reveal His Son in me ...' (Gal. 1:15-16)" (Ray Prinzing, ibid).

Thus, where the literal events of AD 70 involved war, famine and destruction, they were part of the transition of the kingdom from Israel to Christ's followers (Mat. 21:43), and so have a positive outcome.

Ps. 110:1 reports, "Yahweh said unto my Lord, 'Sit at My right hand (= join Me in My reign) until I make Your enemies Your footstool (= a support for Your feet)." This is quoted three times in the NT: Mat. 22:44; Lu. 20:43; Acts 2:34-35. In Isaiah we read:
> "When Your judgments are in the Land (or: earth; territory), the inhabitants of the world will learn righteousness!" (26:9b).
> "Look unto Me and be saved, all the ends of the Land (or: earth)" (45:22).

When we tie all this in to Paul's unveiling regarding God's program of reconciling all mankind to Himself (2 Cor. 5:19), the insights from Walter Wink apply: "Reconciliation is a process.... the issue is complex" (ibid p 28). It involves the death of the old (Jn. 12:24), in order to produce germination of the new; it involves crosses in peoples' lives (Mat. 16:24ff). And thus we will see the process acted out by these four horsemen, below, as the end of the old is "opened" to us as the prelude to the beginning of the new. But for us in the "new," we should be guided by Paul's admonitions in 2 Cor. 10:3-6,
> 3. **For though habitually walking about and ordering our behavior within [the] flesh** (= in a physical body; or: = in the human condition), **we are not waging warfare** (or: performing military service) **in correspondence and accord to flesh** (= on the level of estranged or enslaved humanity, or in line with human condition; or: = in the sphere of old covenant Jewish reasonings),

4. **for you see, the tools and weapons of our military service and warfare [are] not fleshly** (= do not pertain to our human condition; ["are not the weapons of the Domination System" – Walter Wink]), **but rather, [are] powerful ones and capable ones in God** (or: by God), **[focused] toward [the] pulling down** (demolition) **of effects of fortifications** (or: strongholds; strongly entrenched positions [of the "Domination System" – Walter Wink, *Engaging the Powers*]),
5. **progressively tearing down and demolishing conceptions** (concepts; the effects of thoughts, calculations, imaginations, reasonings and reflections) **and every height** (or: high position; high-effect) **and lofty [attitude, purpose or obstacle] that is habitually lifting itself up against** (or: elevating itself up on so as to put down) **the intimate and experiential knowledge of God, and then taking captive every thought – one after another – and leading them prisoner into the hearing obedience of the Christ** (or: the humble attentive listening, which comes from the Anointed One; or: the submissive paying attention, which is the Anointing),
6. **even continuously holding [them] in a ready state and prepared condition to support fairness and equity, while maintaining rightwised relationships from out of the Way pointed out, for every mishearing** (or: hearing-aside; setting of our attention to the side; or: disobedience) **– whenever your hearing obedience may be made full** (or: as soon as the humble attentive listening and submissive paying attention has been brought to full measure, from, and with regard to, you folks)**!**

As for the color of this horse, Barclay instructs us,
"When a Roman general celebrated a triumph… his chariot was drawn by white horses, the symbol of victory" (ibid p 5).
Concerning the colors of all of the horses, Metzger notes that this vision, "borrows [from Zech. 6] only the symbol of the horses and their color…" (ibid p 56; brackets added). Metzger also observes that the riders say nothing, and, "We do not know in which direction they ride, because the Greek word that has been traditionally 'Come!' may also be translated 'Go!' Do they ride from heaven to earth, or from one place on earth to another place on earth?" (ibid p 57). Apparently these details were not considered important. The important message is that God sends them on their missions.

3. Next, when He opened the second seal, I heard the second living one repeatedly saying, "Come (or: Go; [other MSS add: and see])**!"**
4. **And so another horse, fiery** (fiery-red; of the character or color of fire), **came forth** (or: went out), **and to the One continually sitting upon it, to Him it was given to take the peace out of the Land** (or: earth; territory; ground) **so that they would slaughter** (kill) **each other. And a great sword was given to Him.**

With the opening of the second seal we see a fiery-red horse. This color is from the root *pur* which means "fire." Call to mind that "**our God is a consuming fire**" (Heb. 12:29). And,
"**He, Himself, will proceed immersing** (baptizing) **you folks within the midst of a set-apart Breath-effect and Fire** (or: will repeatedly submerge you to the point of saturation, in union with [the] Holy Spirit, even to the permeation of a Sacred Attitude, as well as with [the] Fire).... **yet the chaff** (straw and husks) **He will continue completely burning, in an inextinguishable Fire**." (Matt. 3:11, 12)
"For, lo, Jehovah as fire cometh, and as a hurricane His chariots, to refresh in fury His anger and His rebuke in flames of fire. For by fire and by His sword doth Jehovah do judgment with ALL FLESH and many have been Jehovah's pierced ones" (Isa. 66:15-16, Young). See also Mal. 3:2-3, "He is like a refiner's fire …He shall purify … and purge."

"Remember, all of this serves to bring forth another expression of 'the revelation of Jesus Christ.' And He said, 'Think not that I am come to send peace on earth: I came not to send peace, but a sword. For I am come to set a man at variance against his father, and the daughter against her mother ... and a man's foes shall be they of his own household' [Matt. 10:34-36]." (Prinzing, ibid).

So to this One on the fiery horse it was given to take the peace out of our personal earth (our bodies): He was given the great sword to use on us. There is a season in our lives when He swears "they shall not enter [His] rest" (Heb. 3:11 & 4:3) "because of [our] incompliance (disobedience, unbelief)" (Heb. 4:6) and because we may be "hardening [our] hearts, as in the incitement to bitter feelings from the day of the putting to the proof in the desert" (Heb. 4:8). As Israel in their desert testing, sometimes we are "led astray (caused to wander) by the heart" (Heb. 3:10). So He ruffles our nest and removes peace from our situation [remember we are to "let the peace of Christ be arbitrating (presiding) in your hearts," Col. 3:15] and then He, the living Word of God becomes "operative and more cutting above every two-edged sword" (Heb. 4:12). Eventually this same sword will be beaten (transformed) into a plowshare (Isa. 2:4) to plow up our hard earth so that a new crop can be planted (the Seed of the Word) on our burned-over field (Heb. 6:4-8). It all depends upon what He sees that is needed in our lives to make us "good soil" (Matt. 13:8).

This vision is an echo of Mat. 10:34-36,

> 34. **"You folks should not assume from custom or infer from the Law that I come** (or: came) **to throw peace** [= shalom] **upon the Land** (or: earth). **I do** (or: did) **not come to throw peace, but to the contrary, a sword** (a curved weapon for close combat)!
> 35. **"You see, I come** (or: came) **to disunite** (to make to be two and then pit):
> 'a man against his father, and a daughter against her mother, and a bride against her mother-in-law,'
> 36. **"And so,**
> 'a person's enemies [are/will be] those of his own household.' [Micah 7:6]

We may also see here an allusion to Jer. 16:5b-6a,

> "I have taken away My peace from this people…. Both the great and the small shall die in the Land…"

From the writings of Josephus, we find that this actually happened in the Jewish Wars, ending in AD 70. But there was another meaning to Jesus' words. He called His followers out of the old system of religion and into the reign of God. His sword is the "sword of His mouth," i.e., His Word, as we read in Heb. 4:12,

> "**For the Word of God** (or: God's thought, idea and message; or: the expressed Logos from God; or: the Word which is God) **[is] living** (or: alive), **and active** (working; operative; energetic; at work; productive) **and more cutting above every two-mouthed sword, even passing through** (penetrating) **as far as a dividing** (or: parting; partitioning) **of soul and spirit** (or: of inner self-life and breath-effect), **both of joints and marrows, even able to discern** (separate; judge; decide) **concerning thoughts** (ponderings; reflections; in-rushings; passions) **and intentions** (notions; purposes) **of a heart** (= core of the being)."

His teachings separated His followers from those who could not receive Him. He turned custom and tradition on their heads. The disciples' enemies came to be those of Israel's household. He came to bury the old covenant in order to resurrect it with new life, in a different form (or, body – Jn. 12:24; 1 Cor. 15:37-38).

Their Messiah came in peace bringing a new kind of Peace (literally: a Joining; Jn. 14:27), in the order of Melchisedec (Heb. 7:11, 15, 17), and thus as "**King of Peace and of Harmony from the Joining**" (Heb. 7:2b). When the Jewish leadership rejected His peace/joining and had Him crucified, and God's reign of, "**eschatological deliverance into fair and equitable dealing which brings justice and right relationship in the Way pointed out** (being turned in the right direction; rightwisedness; also = covenant inclusion and participation), **peace** (harmony from the joining; = shalom) **and joy** (or: happiness; rejoicing) **within set-apart Breath-effect** (or: in union with and amidst a dedicated spirit and a sacred attitude; or: in [the] Holy Spirit)" (Rom. 14:17),

was given to a people who would produce its fruit, they soon rose up in rebellion against Rome and began to slaughter one another in that rebellion. *Cf* Joseph, *Wars*. But before that, Saul of Tarsus began to rage against Christ's covenant communities, and then other Jews tried numerous times to kill him. God's Word (Christ, His message and Paul's unveilings) did the work of Heb. 4:12, cited above. It was a dividing between covenants, and between ages. That sword ushered in "eschatological deliverance, justice and equity," and a new creation. The spirit exemplified by this **fiery red horse** brought first the lampstands of chapters 2 and 3, above, and also the later burning of Jerusalem. In both cases, it took **the peace out of the Land**. Still, they had the promise given by Jesus in Mat. 10:29b, "**And yet not one from among them** [i.e., the sparrows] **will proceed falling upon the ground without being with** (or: being away from) **your Father.**" Then He follows with vs. 31, "**You folks continuously carry on through so as to excel and be of more consequence than** (be superior to and thus of more value than) **whole flocks of sparrows.**"

So on the natural level, the sword carried by this rider was a figure of the coming war with Rome. But on the spiritual level, the level of the kingdom within and among us, it has been used to trim off the old flesh nature that saw itself as estranged from God, and from other people.

5. **Then, when He opened the third seal, I heard the third living one repeatedly saying,**
   "Come (or: Go; [other MSS add: and see])**!"**
And I saw; and so consider! A black horse, and the One continually sitting upon it [is] constantly holding a pair of balances (or: a balance bar) **in His hand.**

With the opening of the 3rd seal we see the emergence of a **black horse** whose Rider holds a set of **balances** in His **hand**. One obvious purpose that can be seen here is that He intends to bring balance into our lives.

"Why does He 'set men in depression'? (Ps. 90:3, Fenton). Why this BLACK MOOD that settles upon some? Why the dark night of the soul? Because in divine wisdom He incorporates the night with the light, and calls it 'a day.' 'And THE EVENING and the morning were day one' (Gen 1:5). And the sequence is most proper — for however dark the night might be, yet the process ends with the dawning light of that perfect day. 'For His anger endures but a moment; in His favor is life: weeping may endure for a night but joy cometh in the morning' (Ps. 30:5). Through it all He brings a balance to the inner man." (Prinzing, ibid)

"HE RIDES WITH A BALANCE IN HIS HAND — 'Every valley shall be filled, and every mountain and hill shall be brought low; and the crooked shall be made straight, and the rough ways shall be made smooth; and all FLESH shall see the salvation (deliverance) of the Lord.' (Luke 3:5-6). ...The black horse rides for this!" (Prinzing, ibid; emphasis original)

"Even darkness, it is not darkening to You, and the night, as the day, is giving light; darkness is as light." (Ps. 139:12, CVOT)

The called-out folks in the first century would likely have seen this Rider on a black horse as being sent to accomplish the same thing as did the symbolic black horses in Zechariah's day: to bring judgment in the land of the north – Babylon. But now, in their day, once again the "Faithful City" (Isa. 1:21) had become a prostitute (with Rome, politically, and by incorporating the concepts of "eternal punishments" from the pagan religions of the countries with which they had been in contact: Egypt, Persia, Greece, etc. – See Gary Amirault's "The History of the Doctrine of Eternal Torment" at tentmaker.org – their traditions had made His Word to them to be ineffectual and lifeless, not producing children of the kingdom), and we later find her called "Secret (Mystery) Babylon" in 17:5, below. Thus would they see here a prophecy of the destruction of Jerusalem and the Jewish polity that was persecuting them. Yet we should not presume that they could not also see the need for setting things right (judgment) internally, within themselves, and would not see that this was the fierceness of His love, for His judgment to begin in them who had now become the House of God.

The symbol of the balances had another meaning, for the natural level of interpretation. Ezk. 4 has the prophet mimic a siege of Jerusalem, and in vs. 10 he is told to weigh his food. This is explained in vs. 16 where God told him, "I will break the staff of bread (or: cut off the supply of food) in Jerusalem: and they shall eat bread by weight, and with care; and they shall drink water by measure, and with astonishment." Lev. 26:26 gives a similar picture, "they will deliver your food again by weight: you shall eat, and not be satisfied." *Cf* 2 Ki. 7:1. We should remember the proximity of this chapter in Ezekiel to the four living ones in Ezk. 1. The overall setting there is similar to the setting here.

Another allusion for the sword and scales can be found in Ezk 5:1-4,
> "Now, son of man, take a sharp sword and use it as a barber's razor to shave your head and your beard. Then take a set of scales and divide up the hair. When the days of your siege come to an end, burn a third of the hair with fire…. For I will pursue them with drawn sword…. A fire will spread from there to the whole house of Israel."

Once again, these allusions point to 1st century Jerusalem, and its destruction by Rome. But for the communities to which this picture was sent, the **balances** would remind them:
> "**for it continues** (or: is repeatedly) **necessary for us – the all** (= the whole of humanity) **– to be manifested in front of Christ's elevated place** (a step, platform, stage, or place ascended by steps to speak in public assembly in the center of a city; or: = an official bench of a judge or public official), **to the end that each one may himself take into kindly keeping, for care and provision** (= be responsible for), **the things [done] through** (or: by means of; or: [during our] passing through [with]) **the body – [oriented] toward what things he practices** (or: she accomplished), **whether good or bad, whether serviceable or inefficient, whether fair or foul, whether capable or careless.**
>> (or: for you see that it continues binding for us all to be set in light so as to be clearly seen in the presence of the judgment seat which is Christ, so that each should keep and provide for the things performed through the body, with a view to, and face to face with, what things [were practiced], whether virtuous or vile)" (2 Cor. 5:10). *Cf* Rom. 14:10b-14

Now let us look for keys to unlock the meaning of the color black. In vs. 12, below, the sun becomes **"black as sackcloth made of hair."** This may be an allusion to Isa. 50:3, where Yahweh says,
> "I clothe the skies (or: heavens) with blackness, and I make sackcloth their covering."

That came following His arguments that His people should trust Him (vs. 2). But in Jer. 4:27-29a we see a different picture:
> "For thus has Yahweh said, 'The whole Land shall be desolate; yet I will not make a full end. For this shall the Land mourn, and the skies above be black: because I have spoken, I have purposed (or: resolved), and I will neither regret nor turn back from it: the whole City will flee from the noise of the horsemen and bowmen…'"

Jeremiah gives us another picture of this color in 8:21, "For the hurt of the daughter of my people am I hurt; I am black; astonishment has taken hold on me." This is the opposite of a "bright countenance."

From hurt and astonishment, we see black describing pain and fear on the people facing a fierce army, in Joel 2:6, "Before their face the people will be much pained: all faces shall gather blackness." In Nahum 2:10b he describes the desperate situation of Nineveh, saying, "much pain [is] in all loins, and the faces of them all gather blackness." Then we find another use in Lam. 5:10, "Our skin was black, like an oven, because of the terrible famine." These all describe what we would metaphorically call "dark days." Black seems to speak of hard times, and especially when one's city is under siege. Josephus, in *Wars of the Jews*, reported famine during the time of the Roman siege – especially in the City.

But even when all is outwardly well, emotional losses or concerns, as well as psychological stress, can bring a personal "dark night of the soul," as many have attested. Yet, David comforts us in Ps. 23:

> 4. **For you see, even if I may** (or: should; would; could) **be caused to journey** (travel; pass from place to place) **within the midst of a shadow of death** (or: death's shadow; a shadow, from death), **I will continue not being caused to fear bad [times]** (will not be repeatedly frightened by worthless [situations or people]; will not be habitually afraid of misfortunes, harmful [experiences] or base [schemes]), **because You are, and continue being, with me: Your rod and your staff – these, from a call to be at my side, give me aid and impart relief, encouragement and comfort** (these are paracletes to help me). (LXX, JM)

6. **And I heard a voice within the midst of the four living ones repeatedly saying, "A small measure** (a *choenix*: about a quart) **of wheat [for] a denarius** (a silver coin equivalent to a day's pay), **and three small measures of barley [for] a denarius; and you may not act unjustly to** (wrong; harm; violate; injure) **the olive oil and the wine."**

This voice does not seem to come from the four living ones, but rather from the One on the throne, around which they have been positioned. The allusion is that God, as in OT times, has decreed this situation. We also see the little Lamb (Christ) within the midst of the throne, in 7:17, below, as well as in 5:6, above.

So now we have wheat and barley being sold. This, like most things in this book, has been seen in various, and opposing, ways. One view is that this speaks of famine, for the small measure of grain is sold for the equivalent of a day's wage, for the working man. A man's daily earnings would only buy enough **wheat** to feed just himself, or, if he bought **barley** (a cheaper, though less nutritious grain) he could feed himself plus two others. A picture of survival, but nothing more. A prediction of AD 70. Metzger instructs us,

> "Usually a denarius could purchase eight to sixteen times more grain than the amounts mentioned/ here. In other words, warfare is followed by inflation and famine" (ibid p 58).

An opposing view is presented by Malcolm Smith: 1) there are luxury items – **oil and wine**; 2) there is **wheat** and **barley** – if you've got the money!; 3) care is to be taken not to injure or do injustice to these luxury items. His conclusion: this is economical persecution. Jesus' teaching-prayer comes to mind,

> "**Repeatedly give** (or: Keep on giving) **to us our bread – the one that has been made upon being and has reference to existence** (or: the dole that is sufficient for today and the coming day), **the one that corresponds to and accords with [the] day**" (Lu. 11:3).

In 2 Ki. 6:24-25 the king of Aram laid a siege to Samaria which lasted so long that there was a great famine. The 7th chapter gives Elisha's prophesy that "about this time tomorrow, a seah [about 7 qts.] of flour will sell for a shekel [about the normal cost of flour] and two seahs [14 qts.] of barley for a shekel at the gate of Samaria" (vs. 1, NIV). This figure of the end of the famine, and thus the end of the siege, was literally fulfilled the next day (vs. 16). This would seem to lend weight to the "famine" interpretation of the situation in 6:6, here, but let us remember that this is a book of figures. Consider Amos 8:11, "Behold! the days are coming (averring is my Lord Yahweh), that I will send a famine into the land, not a famine for bread, nor a thirsting for water, but rather for hearing the Word of Yahweh." Here, then, is a word to us.

Ray Prinzing sees another aspect to this picture, "Jesus said to Peter, 'Satan hath desired to sift you as wheat: but I have prayed for thee that thy faith fail not'" (Lu. 22:31, 32). Why the sifting? To sift out all the uneven particles – the doubt, the unbelief, the self-will, etc. until only 'fine flour' remains. We get so tossed and shaken we think all balance is gone – but all of this is working that He might bring us into HIS balance" (ibid).

Consider also Dan. 5:26-27, "an accounting has God made of your kingdom and He balances it; ... weighed are you on the scales and found lacking" (CVOT). But Prinzing brings out that "'He maketh peace thy borders, and fills you with the finest of wheat.' (Ps. 47:14). He is the One that 'binds up our wounds, pouring in oil and wine' (Lu 10:34)" (ibid).

If we consider all of the above aspects of the black horse: the set of balances, the cost of food, and the protection of the oil and the wine, we can draw a few more conclusions:

    1) The black horses in Zech. seemed to speak of God's judgment of His people's enemies. His enemy within us is the minding (disposition) of the flesh (Rom. 8:7). His judgment is for purification and cleansing (Mal. 3:3, 5). The Jewish leadership had positioned themselves as enemy of Christianity, until AD 70. Rome became Jerusalem's enemy in order to crush the Zealots' rebellion; prior to that they maintained peace and order as an occupying domination system. The Jewish leadership approved of this arrangement and situation (Jn. 11:48).

    2) If the weighing out of food speaks of famine, or oppression, then perhaps we can see something in the type of the Law: Lev. 26:21-26, "If you go contrary to Me ... then I will add smitings to you sevenfold according to your sins. I will send the animal of the field against you .... I will bring the sword on you .... I will send the plague .... When I break the stock of bread for you then ten women will bake your bread in one stove and return your bread BY WEIGHT so that you will eat and not be satisfied." So the balances weighing out the wheat and the barley could speak of the Lord's judging His people, His house (1 Pet. 4:17): the Jews, then, by Rome in AD 70; the covenant communities, now, by oppressive domination systems. So for the first level of interpretation, this could apply to the destruction of Jerusalem in AD 70.

    3) That the oil and the wine are to be protected would speak of His concern for the healing of His people (Lu. 10:34, binding up the wounds). Further, it could suggest that the anointing of the Spirit is yet present, and that new life (the new wine) will come of this. As an OT allusion, Joel 1:10 describes severe famine as lacking both oil and wine (as well as a lack of grains, vs. 11). So if this description speaks of famine, it is not as severe as it could be. The phrase, "**you may not act unjustly to** (wrong; harm; violate; injure) **the olive oil and the wine**" could speak of dishonest marketing, or cheating folks (suggested by Giblin, cited in Beale, ibid p 381) – which would support Smith's view, cited above. Chilton cites J. M. Ford (*Revelation: Introduction, Translation and Commentary*, Doubleday & Co., 1975, p 107) who "mentions an order by Titus during the siege of Jerusalem that olive groves and vineyards were not to be disturbed" (ibid p 191).

    4) The idea of "a pair of balances" is only suggested in the text, for the Greek is only "a balance beam, or bar." This lends weight to the presentation by Ray Prinzing that His main purpose is to bring us into balance. This could also speak to the balance and equity that has progressively

come from His reign and constant sovereign activities in the affairs of humanity. Justice has always been one of God's priorities.

7. And when He opened the fourth seal, I heard the voice of the fourth living one repeatedly saying, "Come (or: Go; [other MSS add: and see])**!"**

It is noteworthy that each horse-and-rider has been called upon the scene, or sent out, by one of the **four living ones**, by number. The first one, corresponding to the white horse and Rider, resembled a Lion (of the tribe of Judah?); the second, corresponding to the fiery-red horse and Rider, resembled a calf (or, young bullock – a sacrificial or servant figure?); the third, corresponding to the black horse and Rider, has the face (identity; personality; character) of a human (the Son of man figure?); the fourth, corresponding to pale, yellowish-green horse and Rider, resembled a flying vulture (the creature that consumes dead flesh) – as we read in 4:7, above. In Ezk. 1:5 the four living ones each "had the likeness of a man (Hebrew: *adam*; a human; Adam?)," but there vs. 6 tells us that each one had four faces, and vs. 10 identifies these as a face of a human (*adam*; Adam), of a lion, of a bull (or: ox) and a vulture.

The fourth one, here in vss. 7-8, is associated with Death (personified, by giving it a name), which leads dead folks to the Unseen (figured, especially in the OT, by the grave and those buried in the dust). This is the final state of one who has been conquered by the Lion's horse, then passed through the fires of the sacrifice, with the Calf/Bullock's horse, and slain by His Word (sword), then brought into balance by the impartation of the new humanity of the Son of man's horse, to finally experience the death that came when the One died (2 Cor. 5:14) and through Him we were,

> "**immersed** (or: were then baptized) **into His death**.... **were buried together** (entombed together with funeral rites) **in Him** (or: by Him; with Him), **through the immersion** (baptism) **into the death**.... [and thus] **our old, former humanity is crucified together** (or: was simultaneously and jointly impaled and put to death on an execution stake) **with [Him]**" (Rom. 6:3, 4, 6).

Although a natural interpretation of these figures can be related to the Jewish rebellion that ended in AD 70, with this final horse speaking to the death of the many who were killed, a second layer of interpretation can speak to the work of Christ in all of these images, which all happened together as He once-for-all completed His work on the cross. Christ rode this pale colored horse to end the reign of death (Rom. 5:21) by taking Death to His grave. So in experiencing "death," Rom. 5:18b explains:

> "**through one just-effect and the result of one right act which set [all humanity] right and in accord with the Way pointed out** (through the result of one act of justice, equity and solidarity; through a single decree creating rightwised relationships; through one effect of rightwising which turns [people] in the right direction) **[it comes] into ALL MANKIND** (all humanity; all people; = the whole race) **[bringing them] into a setting right of Life and a liberating rightwising from Life [including them in covenant community]**
>> (or: Life's turning [folks] in the right direction resulting in right relating, equity and justice which is in accord with the Way pointed out; a making of situations and conditions to be right, which pertain to Life; an expressing of fairness and equity, which is LIFE; a rightly directed solidarity coming from Life; a just-acting deliverance having the qualities of life)."

8. And I saw, and consider! A pale, yellowish-green (pallid; ashen; colorless) **horse, and the name for Him [Who is] continually sitting upon it [is] Death, and the Unseen** (Greek: *hades*; or: = the grave) **has been following with Him. And authority** (privilege; jurisdiction; right from out of Being) **was given to** (or: by) **Him** [other MSS: them] **upon the fourth of the Land** (or: earth) **to kill within broadsword, and with famine, and within death, even by the little animals of the Land** (or: earth).

The color, or lack thereof, would seem to suggest the sickness and fading of life which precedes death. Thus we are told that Death rides this horse, and the Unseen (*Hades*) follows with Him. As stated above, the natural application of this verse would fit the context of the Jewish rebellion, which ended in the death of Israel as a political entity, with the physical death of most of those who challenged Rome's dominion. Taken literally, these descriptions, from **broadsword** to **little animals of the Land**, speak of that war and its aftermath. But what does this verse say to us, on another level of interpretation? This is the ultimate call of the cross, for on this we die, and in this we experience oblivion and can see nothing until His morning awakes us. Note that only 1/4 of our land is killed with the Sword of the Spirit: He doesn't do it all at once. Crucifixion is a drawn-out process! And each person has this existential experience in his or her own, appointed time (1 Cor. 15:22-23).

Now famine is mentioned specifically, but I think this is when He restricts His voice from us, and on our cross we too cry, "Father, why have You forsaken me?" We experience this state to the full within the particular metaphorical death that we are allotted by this Rider. We experience emptiness, nothingness. Even the little animals He sends to torment us (like barking dogs or infestations, etc.) – remember Lev. 26, above – or the mean spirits in people, their carnal, un-Christ-like attitudes and behaviors, e.g. as in Ps. 49:20, "A human (Adam), though wealthy, who does not discern has made himself a by-word: he is compared to senseless cattle and is like them."

We see here in 8b that **authority** – literally "that which is out of being," or, "right from out of Being" – **was given to**, or **by** Him (the dative case, with no expressed preposition in the text). So either God gives this Rider authority, or this Rider gives authority to others, to do what follows. The Majority Text [TR] tradition has this reading, **Him**, but Nestle-Aland reads, "them." If **Him** is the correct reading, then the authority was given to the Rider; if "them" is the correct reading, then this may be referring to all four horsemen, and this last half of the verse is a summation of the work of all of them. The reading "**Him**" seems to better fit the pattern seen in vs. 2 and vs. 4, above.

Prinzing suggests that where it mentions that "the fourth part of the earth" is killed (this being the fourth & final horse of this scene) that this is the concluding blow which finishes His process in us. That this dealing is really of Him, remember 1:18, above, "I ... **continuously hold the keys** [hold & control the power] **of Death and the Unseen**." Furthermore, we have the unveiling concerning both of these in 1 Cor. 15:

> 53. **For it continues being necessary** (it is habitually binding) **for this perishable and corruptible to at some point plunge** (or: sink) **in and clothe itself with** (or: slip on; put on) **incorruption and imperishability, and for this mortal** (one that is subject to death) **to at some point plunge and sink in and clothe itself with** (or: put on; slip on as a garment) **immortality** (or: the absence of death; deathlessness; undyingness).
> 54. **Now whenever** [other MSS add: this corruptible would (or: may) put on incorruption and] **this mortal would** (or: may) **plunge, sink in and clothe itself with** (or: slip on; put on) **the Immortality, then will continue taking place** (or: proceed being birthed; successively come into existence) **the word** (the thought; the message; the saying) **which has been written,**
>   "**The Death was drunk down and swallowed into Victory** (or: overcoming)!" [Isa. 25:8]
> 55.   "**Where, O Death, [is] your victory** (or: overcoming)?
>   **Where, O Death, [is] your stinger** (sharp point; sting; goad; spur)?" [Hos. 13:14; note: TR reads "O Unseen (Hades)" in the second line, following the LXX and Heb.]
> 56. **Now the sharp point and stinger of** (or: the sting, thus, the injection from) **the Death [is] the Sin** (the mistake; the error; the failure), **and the power and ability of the Sin [is] the Law.**

> 57. **But grace and joyous favor [is] in God** (or: by God) – **the One presently and progressively giving the Victory** (or: the overcoming) **to us, in us and for us through our Lord** (Owner; Master), **Jesus, [the] Christ!**

Take note that the **Victory**, which Isa. 25:8 describes as being the **swallowing of Death**, has been **given to us**. And because Christ has swallowed down Death, He has also ingested **the Unseen** (*hades*). Beale notes:

> "The LXX uses 'death' (*thanatos*) and 'Hades' (*hades*) in combination almost synonymously in reference to the region of the dead (e.g., Ps. 6:6[5]; 48[49]; Prov. 2:18; 5:5; Cant. 8:6; Job 17:13-16; 33:22)" (ibid p 382).

In 20:13-14, below,

> "**And the sea gives** (or: suddenly gave) **[up; back] the dead folks within it, and death and the Unseen give** (or: = the grave gave) **[up; back] the dead folks within them…. Next the Death and the Unseen** (or: = the grave) **are cast** (or: were thrown) **into the lake** (or: basin; artificial pool) **of the Fire** (or: the marshy area where there is fire). **This is the second death: the lake of the Fire** (or: the basin which is fire)."

Verse 14, there, describes the death of death, the swallowing up of the Unseen (*hades*), as Paul described in 1 Cor. 15:54, above. The basin of the Fire is a symbol of God in His purging action. *Cf* Mal. 3:2-3. This picture answers to Rom.11:36 where ALL THINGS return "**into the midst of God**."

Dan Kaplan insightfully pointed to the scribes and Pharisees as examples of the realm of the dead:

> "**you Law scholars and Pharisees… you continue closely resembling whitewashed** (i.e., smeared or plastered with lime) **tombs** (sepulchers; grave sites), **which indeed, from outside, continue being made to appear in the prime of beauty, for a time – yet inside they contain a full load of bones of dead folks, as well as every uncleanness**" (Mat. 23:27).

He also suggested a metaphorical interpretation of Mat. 27:52-53, suggesting that this picture represented folks who had been dead (like the scribes and Pharisees, cited above) and experienced the inner resurrection of the Christ-life (as did Abraham, who "saw Christ's day"):

> 52. **Later, the memorial tombs were opened up, and many of the bodies of the set-apart** (holy; sacred) **people – of the folks who had fallen asleep and continued sleeping – were aroused and raised up!**
>
> 53. **Then, upon going forth out of the memorial tombs – after His arousal and resurrection – they entered into the set-apart** (holy) **City and they were made visible in the midst of many people** (or: were made to inwardly shine to many folks; or: were made to appear in association with many).

Now a literal interpretation of this event would have these folks entering Jerusalem, "**the present Jerusalem**" (Gal. 4:25) which in Paul's day, "**continue[d] in slavery** (or: bondage) **with her children;**" a metaphorical interpretation would have them entering, "**the Jerusalem above [which] continues being free, [and] who is** (or: which particular one continues being) **our mother**" (Gal. 4:26). This latter is the New Jerusalem that we meet in 21:2, below.

Consider the following OT texts:

> "See now that I, I am He, and there is no other god with (beside) Me: I Myself put to death, and I make alive, I have smitten, and I heal …" (Deut. 32:39). "Go, and we will return to Yahweh, our God, for He tore to pieces, and He will heal us: He was smiting, and He will bind us up" (Hos. 6:1). "Fire and hail, snow and fume, tempestuous wind, performing His word" (Ps. 148:8). "[There is] no glorifying of negative forces – because HE IS IN CONTROL" (Prinzing, ibid; brackets added; emphasis original). Again, he continues, "It is by death that death is rendered powerless, and there shall arise a new life – His:

> **'in order that through means of death He might render useless** (or: deactivate; idle-down; discard) **the one normally having the strength** (or: the person presently holding the force) **of death** (or: which is death; or: whose source is death), **that is, the adversary**
>> (or: that which throws folks into dualism with divided thinking and perceptions; or: the one that throws something through the midst and casts division; the one who thrusts things through folks; the slanderer who accuses and deceives; or, commonly called: the 'devil')'
>
> (Heb. 2:14b).
>
> He is able to marshal the bestial nature of men about us, so that they are His instruments to put to death in us that which is not pleasing to Him. They might well be termed 'vessels of wrath fitted to destruction.' (Rom. 9:22), but they are under His control. 'For You, O God, have proved us: You have tried us, as silver is tried. You brought us into the net; You laid affliction upon our loins. YOU CAUSED MEN TO RIDE OVER OUR HEADS; we went through fire and through water: but You brought us out into a wealthy place'" (Ps. 66:10; – Prinzing, ibid).

Recall Dan. 4:16, "let the heart of a beast be given unto him." As to Prinzing's quote of Ps. 66:10, wild animals were used in Dan. 7 to represent kings and kingdoms – folks who had ridden over Israel, in the past. We should also note that here, in vs. 8, the Greek word for "wild animals" is in the diminutive form, thus they are **little animals**. They are not formidable, in God's view. They may simply eat the carrion, the dead flesh, leaving us as Israel in the valley of dry bones (Ezk. 37). But recall that when the Breath from the "four winds" breathed upon those bones, they lived and stood on their feet: they were resurrected (vss. 9-10).

First the natural (i.e., pertaining to the old covenant), afterwards that which is spiritual (i.e., the new; cf 1 Cor. 15:46). First the historical death at AD. 70, now they become a type and shadow for us. If the first four seal-openings are seen as a unit, we might see an allusion to Ezk. 14:21,
> "For thus says my Lord Yahweh: Indeed, then, My four evil judgments, sword and famine and wild animal and plague I send against Jerusalem, to cut off from it human and beast." (CVOT)

Note to whom they were sent. In AD 70 He sent them to her again. Ezk. 14:13 started this passage, "When the Land (a metaphor for the people living in that Land) sins against Me…" The Land had done this again, in the 1st century. The destruction of AD 70 was the final judgment upon Israel: it was the final act of bringing the death of the first creation. In Christ's new economy, Jew and Gentile were joined to be **"one new humanity"** (Eph. 2:14-15). But we should keep in mind what Paul said in Rom. 11:20b-21, **"Stop being haughty** (Don't constantly have high opinions; Do not continually think lofty things), **but to the contrary, [be constantly having] an attitude and mindset of respectful awe** (or: [Godly] fear; healthy respect)! **For you see, since** (or: if) **God spares not** (or: was not thrifty with) **the natural branches** (the branches down from, or, in accord with, nature), **neither will He continue sparing you!"**

A thought on the opening of the little scroll: a scroll when closed is rolled up. Before it can be unrolled, all the seals (7 in this case) must be broken. So what we see here in the opening of the seals is a process of breaking. The 7 seals being opened, or broken, is one process which will allow the scroll to be opened. Remember that 7 is an idea in this book: completeness; an entire process. As the visions of this book are not necessarily successive on some time-line, let us consider that the same may be true of the opening of these 7 seals. They may each simply describe a specific aspect of the entire process. Beale considers this fourth horseman as a summary of the first three, noting that it only affects **the fourth of the Land**. Others have seen this fraction as a symbol of God's mercy: a partial dealing that is not completely overwhelming. It is the Father giving measured discipline to His children (Heb. 12:5-9).

9. **Then when He opened the fifth seal, I saw, down under the altar of burnt-offering, the souls of the folks having been slaughtered [as in sacrifice] because of the Word of God** (or: God's message), **and because of the witness** (testimony; evidence) **which they were holding** (or: continued to have).

With the opening of the 5th seal we have a change in the metaphor. No longer do we see horses proceeding into our earth, we see the result of the work of those four. The picture is the brazen altar of sacrifice, the temple setting:
> "That picture is taken directly from the sacrificial ritual of the Temple. For a Jew the most sacred part of any sacrifice was the blood; the blood was regarded as being the life and the life belonged to God (Lev. 17:11-14, 'the soul of the flesh is in the blood'). Because of that, there were special regulations for the offering of the blood. 'The rest of the blood of the bull the priest shall pour out at the base of the altar of burnt offering' (Lev. 4:7). That is to say, the blood is offered at the foot of the altar. This gives us the meaning of our passage here. The souls ... are beneath the altar" (Barclay, ibid pp 10-11)

In Phil. 2:17 Paul said,
> "**But even more, since** (or: if) **I am also repeatedly poured out as a drink offering upon the sacrificial offering and public service pertaining to your faith** (or: which comes from your trust; in regard to the faithful loyalty which comprises you people), **I am constantly rejoicing** (or: glad) – **even continually rejoicing** (glad) **together with all of you!**"

Then in 2 Tim. 4:6a he said, "**You see, I, myself, am already being progressively poured out as a drink offering**..." Rom. 12:1 instructs us:
> "**Consequently, brothers, I am repeatedly calling you folks alongside to advise, exhort, implore and encourage you, through God's compassions to stand your bodies alongside** (or: to set or place your bodies beside) **[the] Well-pleasing, Set-apart** (Holy; Different-from-the-usual), **Living Sacrifice by God** (or: in God; for God; to God; with God), **[this being] your sacred service which pertains to thought, reason and communication** (or: your reasoned and rational service; the logical and Word-based service from you folks; or: = temple service)."

Also, in Phil. 3:10, Paul speaks of his own desires:
> "**to intimately and with insight experientially know Him, and the ability – even the power – of His resurrection and also the** [other MSS: a] **common existence** (participation; partnership, sharing and fellowship) **of the results and from the effects of His experiences** [note: these include good times/feelings and passions, as well as sufferings] – **being a person that is being continuously conformed by** (being progressively brought together with the form of; being habitually configured to) **His death**."

In regard to the particular context of 1 Cor. 15:31, Paul shares, "**Daily I am repeatedly facing death** (or: progressively dying)!" And we have Mat. 16:24, 25,
> "**At that point Jesus said to His disciples, "If anyone continues intending** (purposing; willing; wanting) **to come on behind Me, let him at once deny, reject and disown himself, and then in one move lift up his execution stake** (pole for suspending a corpse; cross), **and after that proceed to be by habit continuously following after Me! You see, whoever may intend** (or: should purpose; might set his will; happens to want) **to keep his soul-life safe** (to rescue himself; to preserve the interior life that he is living) **will continue loosing-it-away and destroying it. Yet whoever can loose-away and even destroy his soul-life** (the interior self) **on My account, he will continue finding it!**"

With these allusions to Paul and Jesus, it might be that the deaths, described as sacrificial slaughters, should be taken metaphorically, and thus could have multiple applications. The last sentence of Mat. 16:25 shows that Jesus was speaking figuratively. The **altar**, here in vs. 9, is the equivalent of the cross. These folks had taken up their metaphorical execution stakes and had taken their stand (Rom. 12:1). So, following Jesus on His Path, their next place would be inside the "holy place," as "lampstands" (1:20b, above), or as priests in the temple (7:15, below), i.e., His body, offering the incense of prayers and eating from the "loaves of the Presence" as they serve. (I owe this picture to Dan Kaplan, in a private conversation). The slaughter/offering of these folks need not be interpreted literally, although in the 1st century, and on to our present time, physical death may likely have attended their **sacred service**.

These have been slaughtered **because of God's Word** (or, Message), and because of the witness and testimony which they were continuously holding. They were His WITNESSES, and as we see from Paul and Jesus, above, their situation can also apply to us. It of course had a 1st century application, as we see from 1:9, above, as well as in 13:15, 18:24 and 20:4, below, where we see these folks again. Simmons views these folks as the OT martyrs, citing Mat. 23:35,

> "**so that upon you, yourselves, can** (or: should) **come all [the] just** (equitable; rightwised) **blood being continuously poured out** (or: spilled) **upon the Land – from the blood of rightwised** (just; fair; in-right-relationship) **Abel, until the blood of Zechariah, the son of Barachiah** (or: Baruch), **whom you people murdered between the Temple and the altar**."

We see reference to the NT martyrs in 12:11, below,

> "**And they at once overcame** (or: at some point overcome; conquer) **him because of the blood of the little Lamb, and** (or: even) **because of the word** (or: message; Word; Logos) **of their witness** (evidence; testimony) **– and they love not** (or: did not love) **their soul** (soul-life; inner self; personhood) **even to** (or: until) **death**."

Metaphorical statements such as in Mat. 10:38, "**he who is not habitually taking his cross** (execution-stake; hanging-pole) **and then constantly following after** (behind) **Me, is not suitable for Me** (worthy of Me)," and the likely situations described in Rom. 8:35, "**pressure** (squeezing; affliction; tribulation; oppression), **or confinement in a narrow, tight place** (distress; difficulty; trouble), **or pursuit** (the chase of persecution), **or famine** (or: hunger; deprivation of food), **or nakedness** (lack of sufficient clothing; deprivation of necessities), **or danger** (peril; risk), **or sword** (or: large butcher knife; or: curved weapon for close combat)," apply for all Christ's followers, in every generation. And Rom. 8:36, quoting Ps. 44:22, certainly fits our context here:

> "**Accordingly as it has been written,**
>> '**On Your account** (For Your sake; By reason of You) **we are progressively being put to death the whole day! We are logically considered** (accounted) **as sheep which belong to slaughter** (are associated with slaughter).'"

But Paul's unveiling in Rom. 8:37 cinches the connection with the Unveiling given to John:

> "**But rather** (or: On the contrary), **within all these things we are habitually over-conquering** (we are remaining completely victorious; we continue more than overcoming) **through the One loving, urging toward reunion with, and giving Himself to, us**."

Amidst a later vision, in 14:13, below, an echo of our verse here is heard:

> "**Write: 'From the present moment** (from this time; from now; henceforth) **the dead ones [are] blessed** (happy) **folks – those continuously dying within the Lord!' 'Yes, indeed,' the Spirit continues saying, 'to the end that they may rest themselves from out of their wearisome labor** (travail; toilsome exhaustion), **for their works** (actions; deeds) **are continually following together with them.'"**

10. **And they uttered a cry with a great** (or: by a loud) **voice, repeatedly saying,**

"Until when (How long), **O Absolute Owner** (Sovereign Lord; Master), **the Set-apart** (Holy) **and True One, are You not deciding** (separating, evaluating and judging) **and maintaining right for** (operating out of the way pointed out for; or: avenging) **our blood, out of those habitually having an abode** (dwelling) **upon the Land** (earth)?"

The cry which they uttered here was a cry from their souls. "How long?" "Till when?" Chilton observes,
> "**How long?** is a standard phrase throughout Scripture for invoking divine justice for the oppressed (cf Ps. 6:3; 13:1-2; 35:17; 74:10; 79:5; 80:4; 89:46; 90:13; 94:3-4; Hab. 1:2; 2:6). The particular background for its use here, however, is again in the prophecy of Zechariah (1:12): After the Four Horsemen have patrolled through the earth the angel [lit.: agent] asks, 'O Lord of Hosts, how long wilt Thou have no compassion for Jerusalem?'" (ibid p 194; brackets added).

He makes another insightful comment:
> "If the martyrs' blood is flowing around the base of the altar, it must be the priests of Jerusalem who have spilled it" (ibid).

The two witnesses in 11:3-12, below, were slain, and then,
> "**their fallen dead body will be upon** [other MSS: And their fall will be into] **the broad place** (street; square; plaza) **of The Great City – whatever, spiritually, is normally being called** (or: named) **"Sodom" and "Egypt" – where also their Lord was crucified** (or: where their Lord, also, was hung on a pole: suspended and executed on a torture stake)" (vs. 8).

And, of course, the City where Christ was crucified was Jerusalem.

And so, what are these martyrs crying for? The separating, the judging, and the maintaining right – operating out of the way pointed out – for their blood, their lives, their souls; and this, out of the ones who live their lives in the earth realm, the carnal. Do not we also cry out for His judgements to come in the land? "For [only] when Your judgments are in the earth [will] the inhabitants of the world learn righteousness" (Isa. 26:9, AOT). Our hearts cry out for this for our world, and for ourselves. And what is the Righteousness that is learned?
> "**Now you folks are, and continuously exist being, forth from out of the midst of Him – within and in union with Christ Jesus, Who came to be** (or: is birthed) **wisdom in and among us** (or: to us; for us), **from God: both a rightwising, eschatological deliverance into righted, covenantal existence in fair relationships of equity in the Way pointed out** (or: likewise a just Act from God) **and a being set-apart to be different, even a redemptive liberation**" (1 Cor. 1:30)

Yes, when His judgements come, the inhabitants of the world will learn Christ. We too, as He sits to refine us, to burn out of us that part of us which is still dwelling upon the earth – instead of in the heavenlies – we also "come to know Him by experience" as we are formed together (constructed) by His death (Phil. 3:10, above). Another aspect of the cry is given by D'Aragon:
> "This cry does not express a desire for vengeance, which would not be in accord with the teaching of Christ (Lu. 6:27f). The martyrs call for the securing of justice" (ibid p 477).
> Domination systems always remove justice from the areas of their influence and control.

11. **And a brilliant white robe was given to each of them, and it was declared to them that they may, and should, rest themselves** (permit themselves to cease from any movement or labor in order to recover strength; [other MSS: will continue resting up]) **a little time longer** (yet a short time) **while** (or; until) **also [the number of] their fellow-slaves, even their brothers – those continually being about to be killed, even as they [were] – would be fulfilled** (made full; other MSS: can fill or fulfill [it; all]).

What is the significance of the white robes given to each of them? This is one of the rewards of the overcomer in 3:5, above, and in 7:9, below, we read,

> "**After these things I saw** (or: perceived), **and consider! A vast crowd** (great multitude), **which no one was able to number, from out of every ethnic group** (or: nation) **– even of tribes and of peoples and of tongues** (languages) **– standing before** (in the sight of) **the throne, and before** (in the sight of) **the little Lamb, having been clothed with bright white robes** (or: equipment; uniforms), **and palm trees** (or: branches) **[are] in their hands**."

It would seem that overcomers, slain followers, and this vast crowd are all clothed in white robes. In 7:14, below, it is explained about the great multitude:
"**These are the ones continuously coming forth from out of the midst of great pressure** (squeezing; ordeal; tribulation), **and they washed their robes** (uniforms; equipment) **and made them bright and white within the little Lamb's blood**."
Note the differences: in 6:11, here, the white robe was given to them; in 7:14, they washed their robes in the Lamb's blood. In 3:18, above, they are advised to "buy" white garments. In 19:14 we see "**the armies in the atmosphere** (or: heaven) **– ones having been clothed with** (invested with; entered within) **clean** (or: pure) **bright, white fine cotton**." In Mat. 17:2, Jesus' garments become white. In mat. 28:2-3, the agent wore a white garment. Although it is not called "white," the garment description in 19:8, below, has traditionally been correlated to these references of "white garments":
"**it was** (or: is) **granted** (or: given) **to her to the end that she may clothe herself with bright and clean fine cotton** (or: she may cast bright, pure, fine linen around her) **– for the fine cotton** (or: linen) **represents the effects of right relationship and equity in the life of the Way pointed out**
(or: the results of being rightwised; the actualizations of justice; consequences of justice rendered from being turned in the right direction; the effects of having been eschatologically delivered and placed in the Path pointed out; or: the just awards) **of the set-apart folks** (pertaining to the saints; from the sacred people)."
D'Aragon (ibid) understands a white robe to mean "the victory of the martyrs," and cites 7:13-17, below, as an extended explanation of what this means. It might be a sort of badge or uniform which shows that they have completed the course.

Note that these have entered into rest, for they are to **rest** themselves a little time longer. This rest is something that we, too, should be endeavoring to enter into (Heb. 4:11; 11:39-40). This short time of resting is while their fellow-slaves and brothers are being fulfilled, or made full, or, as Vincent says, "shall have fulfilled their course." The phrase "**[the number of]**" is supplied as a potential meaning which would make sense with the final clause, "**would be fulfilled** (or: made full)." The alternate MS reading has the verb of that clause in the active voice. Thus, the last half of the verse could read, "**while, or until, also their fellow slaves can fill [it], or fulfill [it; all]**." With this reading I have supplied "**[it]**" with the rendering "fill," and "**[it; all]**" with the rendering "fulfill," for the potential meanings, since there is no expressed object of this active verb. Other suggestions, rather than "the number of," is that the filling or fulfilling refers to their sufferings or to their destinies, or that Vincent's suggestion, above, is correct. All things must be done according to His plan and purpose. There is "**the Father's previously set** [time or situation]" (Gal. 4:2) for all things. All appointments must run their courses, "to know experientially the love of the Christ which surpasses experiential knowledge in order that you may be filled up to the measure of all the fullness of God" (Eph. 3:19, Wuest).

Why the waiting, the time delay? It is referred to as, "**a little time longer** (yet a short time) **while**," so, historically, it probably referred to the 1st century, or possibly even until the end of the Jewish rebellion in AD 70. We can only assume that, "**their brothers – those continually being about to be killed**" might be a reference either to the War, or to other persecutions that were "**about to**" happen.

12. **Next I saw when He opened the sixth seal, and there came to be a great shaking. And the sun became black as sackcloth made of hair. And the whole moon became as blood.**

When the 6th seal is opened God brings a great shaking. This calls to mind Heb. 12:26,
> "**Still once [more; or: for all] I am shaking not only the land** (or: earth), **but also the heaven** (or: atmosphere; sky)." [Hag. 2:6; cf Heb. 12:19; Ex. 19:18; Joel 3:16-17]

He explains this in the next verse (27b): "**to the end that the things not being repeatedly** (or: continuously) **shaken may remain**" [cf 2 Cor. 3:7-13]. Heb. 12 continues:
> 28. **Therefore** (or: Because of which), **continuously taking to our sides** (or: progressively receiving alongside) **an unshaken Reign** (or: Kingdom; Sovereign influence), **we are constantly holding** (or: progressively having; [other MSS: can be now having]) **grace and joyous favor, through which we are** [other MSS: can be] **continually serving, well-pleasingly, in God** (or: for God; by God; to God), **with modesty** (an unseen behavior and manner) **in taking hold easily of goodness and well-being, as well as discretion and awe as to what is proper,** [cf Jn. 1:17]
> 29. **for you see, "even our God [is] a continuously all-consuming Fire** (or: our God [is] also a progressively fully-devouring fire)." [cf Deut. 4:24; 9:3; Isa. 33:14]

Shakings, in the physical manifested as earthquakes, are a "move" of God upon His creation. A shaking can be a sifting to remove the chaff. It can be a destruction to remove a structure or a kingdom. It definitely changes the status quo. It interrupts our routine and gets our attention.

Next we see signs in the heavenly realm, or sky, and on the earth. In verses 12 - 14 we have:
> 1) the sun became black as sackcloth made of hair
> 2) the whole moon became as blood
> 3) the stars of the heaven fell into the earth, as fruit falls from a tree in a storm
> 4) the heaven was parted away, as a scroll being rolled up
> 5) every mountain (or, hill) and island was moved out of its place.

Chilton comments on this whole section, from vss. 12-14:
> "The Lamb reveals the next great aspect of His covenantal judgments, in a symbol often used in Biblical prophecy: *de-creation*. Just as the salvation of God's people is spoken of in terms of creation (cf 2 Cor. 4:6, 5:17; Eph. 2:10; 4:24; Col. 3:10), so God's judgments… are spoken of in terms of de-creation, the collapse of the universe – God ripping apart and dissolving the fabric of creation…. First, destabilization: **a giant earthquake** [shaking, in my rendering, above] (cf Ex. 19:18; Ps. 18:7, 15; 60:2; Isa. 13:13-14; 24:19-20; Nah. 1:5). Second, the eclipse and mourning of Israel: **the sun became black as sackcloth made of hair** (Ex. 10:21-23; Job. 9:7; Isa. 5:30; 24:23; Ezk. 32:7;Joel 2:10, 31; 3:15; Amos 8:9; Mic. 3:6). Third, the continued image of an eclipse, with the idea of *defilement* added: **the whole moon became like blood** (Job 25:5; Isa. 13:10; 24:23; Ezk. 32:7; Joel 2:10, 31). The fourth judgment affects the stars, which are images of government (Gen. 1:16); they are also clocks (Gen. 1:14), and their fall shows that *Israel's time has run out*: **the stars fell to the earth, as a fig tree casts its unripe figs when shaken by a great wind** (Job 9:7; Eccl. 12:2; Isa. 13:10; 34:4; Ezk. 32:8; Dan. 8:10; Joel 2:10; 3:15); the **great wind**, of course, was brought by the Four Horsemen, who in Zechariah's original imagery were the Four Winds (Zech. 6:5), and who will be reintroduced to St. John in that form in 7:1; and the **fig tree** is Israel herself (Mat. 21:19; 24:32-34; Lu. 21:29-32). Fifth, Israel now simply disappears: **the heaven vanished like a scroll when it is rolled up** (Isa. 34:4; 51:6; Ps. 102:25-26; on the symbolism of Israel as 'heaven,' see Isa. 51:15-16; Jer. 4:23-31; cf Heb. 12:26-27). Sixth, the Gentile powers are shaken as well: **every mountain and island was moved out of its place** (Job. 9:5-6; 14:18-19; 28:9-11; Isa. 41:5, 15-16; Ezk. 38:20; Nah. 1:4-8; Zeph. 2:11). God's 'old creation,' Israel, is thus to be de-created, as the Kingdom is transferred to the Church, the New Creation (cf 2 Pet. 3:7-14)" (ibid p 196-7; emphasis original; brackets added).

This is a classic synopsis of the Preterist interpretation of what the Unveiling presents in its visions. When Rome destroyed Jerusalem in AD 70, the world of Judea came to an end – economically, politically, and in its temple-centered religion. The last fragments of Israel, as a nation, lost their identity. But beyond this historical interpretation, those of Christ's followers could look beyond the end of the old age of the Law and apply the lessons and covenant faithfulness that can be discerned here. We should always keep in mind the warnings and admonitions given to the seven churches in chapters 2-3, above, and both the provisional warning to individual Gentiles, in Rom. 11:19-24, as well as the promise to individual Israelites that Paul includes:

> 19. **You will say then, "Branches are broken off** (i.e., out of [the tree]) **to the end that I may be grafted in."**
> 20. **Beautifully [put]! In lack of faith or trust** (or: By unbelief; Because of lack of allegiance) **they are broken off, yet you yourself stand in trust and with confidence. Stop being haughty, but to the contrary, [have] an attitude and mindset of respectful awe!**
> 21. **For you see, since God spares not the natural branches, neither will He continue sparing you!**
> 22. **Observe, perceive and consider, then, God's useful kindness and abruptness** (sheer cutting-off; rigorous severity) **– on the one hand upon those falling: abruptness** (sheer cutting-off); **on the other hand upon you: God's useful kindness, provided you should persistently remain in** (or: with; by) **the useful kindness** (or: = continue to be kind and useful). **Otherwise you, also, will proceed in being cut out!**
> 23. **Now they also, if they should not persistently remain in the lack of faith and trust** (or: unbelief), **they will proceed in being grafted in, for God is able to graft them back in again!**
> 24. **For since you yourself were cut out of the olive tree [which is] wild by nature, and then to the side of nature** (or: contrary to, nature) **you are grafted in – into a fine olive tree – to how much greater an extent will these, the ones in accord with nature, proceed in being engrafted into their own olive tree!**

These are OT images, so let's look more closely at some of these, beginning with Joel 2:28-32. The context preceding these verses says the God will "repay you for the years which the locust devoured, the grub and the beetle and the larva, MY GREAT ARMY which I sent among you.... and you shall praise the name of Yahweh.... you shall know that within Israel am I.... and My people shall not be ashamed for the eon" (vss. 25-27, CVOT). So here we see a time of God's people, having gone through one of His periods of judgment, and now entering a period of His blessing ("He will bring down ... the former rain and the latter rain as at first," vs. 23) and also promising an age with no shame (vss. 26-27). Then the passage continues in vss. 28-32:

> "And it comes to be afterward, I shall pour out My Spirit upon all flesh; and your sons and your daughters shall prophesy .... in those days shall I pour out My Spirit. And I will give signs in the heavens above and signs on the earth: blood, and fire, and pillars of smoke, the sun shall be turned to darkness, and the moon to blood, before the coming of the great and manifest (clearly viewable, LXX) day of Yahweh. And it comes to be that everyone who shall call on the Name of Yahweh shall be delivered (saved), **for in mount Zion and in Jerusalem, deliverance shall come to be**, just as Yahweh says; and among the survivors are those whom Yahweh is calling."

Now keep in mind Heb. 12:22ff, **"you folks have approached so that you are now at Mount Zion – even in a City of a continuously living God; in 'Jerusalem upon heaven'."**

In this context it would seem that the signs, though ominous, are associated with blessings, the outpouring of the Spirit, deliverance and calling upon God. This all follows the period of devastation which He had sent among His people. The figures of blood, fire and the pillars of smoke are echoes of the Tabernacle in the wilderness: the sacrifices and the presence of God, along with how He led Israel during that time.

We read in Joel 2:10-11 (LXX),
> "Before them the earth shall be confounded and the heaven shall be shaken: the sun and the moon shall be darkened, and the stars shall withdraw their light, and the Lord shall utter His voice before His powerful ones, for His camp is very great, because the deeds of His words are strong (mighty); in as much as the day of the Lord is great; exceedingly illustrious! And which one shall be fit for it?"

Here we have the stars mentioned as part of the signs in the heavenlies, and it is in association with the actions of God's army (i.e., a conquering nation that He is using, most likely Babylon) and the workings of His words.

Now in Isa. 13 we see a pronouncement against Babylon where we find the same heavenly signs associated with God's passion, anger and judgment:
> "Behold and consider! A day of Yahweh [or: from {the} LORD] comes, fierce with wrath [rushing emotion] and heat of [passion and] anger, to make the Land [habitable region] become a desolation. Yes, its sinning ones He destroys from it. For the stars of the heavens and their constellations shall cause their light not to shine. The sun has been darkened in its going out and the moon is not brightening with its light, and I will visit [a bad situation on] and check [or: impart a directive for] all inhabitants for its evil and worthlessness... and I eradicate the pomp of the arrogant, and the pride of the terrifiers (or: tyrants) am I abasing" (vss. 9-11; Young, CVOT, Rotherham; brackets: LXX readings).

The prophet Zephaniah gave this description of such a time as we find in the Unveiling:
> "Near is the great day of Yahweh! Near, and exceedingly swift! The sound of the day of Yahweh [will be] bitter! There the master shall raise the battlecry! A day of rage [will be] that day, a day of distress and constraint, a day of thunderstorm and ruination, a day of darkness and gloominess, a day of cloud and murkiness, a day of trumpet and shout against the fortressed cities" (1:14-15, CVOT).

So we should see the visions of the Unveiling as standing in the prophetic traditions of Israel, and thus be historically applied to Jerusalem, in the days of the 1st century called-out, covenant communities of Christ. Simmons shares,
> "With the breaking of the sixth seal, that day was come. The blackening of the sun may refer to the dust and thick smoke of siege, funeral pyres, and burning of towns and villages by the legions of Rome. The same smoke that blackens the sun by day causes the moon to be red by night. Both are tokens of the coming destruction" (ibid p 153).

Concerning the figure of sackcloth, in Matt. 11:21 Jesus used it of repenting, changing their minds. In Jonah 3:5 the people of Nineveh used it for the same reason. In this context I suggest that it is a figure of a time of grief, mourning or despair, which may then lead to a change of thinking and to believing the Word of the Lord. It is a day of humility and situations that are the extreme opposite of glory.

13. And the stars of the sky (or: heaven) **fell into the Land** (or: earth), **as a fig tree is casting her winter** (i.e., unseasonable) **figs, while being continuously shaken by a great wind.**

14. And then the sky (or: atmosphere; heaven) **was parted away** (severed off and caused to recede, so as to disappear) **as a little scroll being progressively rolled up, and every mountain** (or: hill) **and [every] island were moved out of their places.**

The prediction of this time and situation, made by Jesus in Mat. 24, is a good place to start, here:

28. **"Wherever the carcass** (corpse) **may be, the vultures** (or: eagles) **will be progressively led together and gathered.**
29. **"Now immediately after the pressure** (constriction; tribulation) **of those [particular] days, 'the sun will be progressively made dark and the moon will not continue giving its diffused radiance,'** [Isa. 13:10; Ezk. 32:7; Joel 2:10] **and then the stars will, one after another, be falling from the sky** (or: heaven) – **'and so, the powers and abilities of the heavens will be progressively shaken** (made to rock so as to be ready to fall).' [Isa. 34:4; Hag. 2:6, 21]
30. **"And at that time, the 'sign' which is the Son of the Man** (or: = the expected Messianic figure) **will be made progressively visible** (be brought to light), **in union with heaven** (or: within [the] atmosphere), **and at that point 'all the tribes of the land** (or: earth) **will continue beating themselves** (= a figure of striking one's breast in grief and remorse; or: as when grain is being threshed; or: give themselves to wearisome toil; or: cut themselves off, as when harvesting grain),' [Zech. 12:10, 14] **and they will proceed in seeing for themselves 'the Son of the Man progressively coming upon the clouds of the atmosphere** (or: sky),' [Dan. 7:13-14] **with power and ability, as well as much glory** (= many manifestations which call forth praise).
34. **"It is true** (Count on it), **I now say to you folks, that this generation can by no means pass by until all these things can happen** (should occur; may be come to be).
35. **"The heaven and the earth** (or: The atmosphere and sky, as well as the land,) **will pass on by, yet My thoughts and words** (or: ideas and messages) **can by no means pass on by**.

This, of course, was in the context of the destruction of the Temple (24:2ff), and Lu. 21:20 adds His words, "**Now later, when you folks see Jerusalem being continuously surrounded by encamped armies, at that time realize and know from that experience that her desolation has drawn near and is now present.**"

Simmons notes: "In prophecy, stars are symbolic of rulers (Nu. 24:17; Isa. 14:12; Dan. 8:10)" (ibid p 153). Isa. 14:12 had a literal reference to the king of Babylon, "How are you fallen from heaven, O day star…?" The "male goat" of Dan. 8:5ff "grew as high as the hosts of heaven. It threw down to the earth some of the host and some of the stars, and trampled on them" (8:10). In vs. 15 a man appeared to Daniel and in vs. 17 told him that the vision was "for the time of the end," then in 20-21 explained that the ram (vs. 3ff) represented "the kings of Media and Persia," while the male goat was "the king of Greece." So we see that Daniel's vision had historical significance for the times of those three empires. In Joseph's dream (Gen.37:9ff) the stars represented his brothers, who would become the leaders of the twelve tribes of Israel. *Cf* Mk. 13:25.

In reference to the imagery of the fig tree being shaken, Nah. 3:12 spoke of Nineveh:
> "All your fortresses [are] fig trees with firstfruits: if they are swayed to and fro (or: shaken), then they will fall into the mouth of the eater" (CVOT).

Isa. 34:4 uses the figure of a scroll being rolled up, "Then shall be dissolved all the hosts of the heavens, and the heavens shall roll up as a scroll – yea all their hosts shall fade [decay] – like the fading and falling of a leaf from a vine, and like what fades and falls [or: like a decaying leaf] from a fig tree" (Rotherham; brackets: CVOT). This is in a context of a word of strong emotion and indignation to all the nations and races (vs. 1-3) – the promise of judgment soon coming to them. The use of the term "heavens" is clearly figurative, in this context – as Chilton pointed out, above. The LXX of the first clause of Isa. 34:4 reads, "all the powers of the heavens shall progressively melt, and the sky will coil up like a scroll." In regard to a figurative interpretation of these verses, Beale observes the following OT examples:
> "the defeat of Babylon (Isa. 13:10-13), Edom (Isa. 34:4), Egypt (Ezk. 32:6-8), Israel's enemies (Hab. 3:6-11), Israel itself (Joel 2:10, 30-31…)" (ibid p 379 n 79).

He concludes, "as in the OT, these cosmic descriptions are metaphors for God's judgment…" (ibid p 398).

So what did these figures and pictures mean to the 1st century Christians? Did the sun and the moon and the stars speak to them of their fathers, mothers and brothers – as they did to Joseph and his family (Gen. 37:9, 10)? Or did these folks see their worlds falling apart or their families dying? Or, did it simply mean that a change in the order of their world was coming – that there was coming a fall of that which had ruled their society? The preterist view would see this as prophetic of the fall of Jerusalem in AD 70. Some see this as pointing to everything changing in the realm of spirit. Are there new seasons coming with nothing to give direction (provided in that day by the celestial bodies in the sky, or by the traditions of their societies)? Now there is only faith, hope and love (1 Cor. 13:13), along with His Spirit and His Word, as an anchor to the soul. Kingdoms were to be disrupted (mountains moved). Private worlds (islands) were to be moved into a new place by the hand of God.

In Heb. 1 we have a quote of Ps. 102 that may shed some light on the end of the old and the beginning of the new:

10. **And further**,
    "O Lord [= Yahweh], **down from beginnings** (or: in accord with ruling [principle]s; corresponding to controlling [pattern]s), **You founded** (or: laid the foundations of) **the earth** (or: land), **and the works of Your hands are the heavens** (or: atmospheres).
11. **"They shall progressively destroy themselves** (or: ruin, or lose, themselves) – **but You continue remaining throughout**.
12. **"And all people, as a garment, shall progressively be made** (or: grow) **old. Then like that which is thrown around [as a cloak], You will roll or wrap them up as a garment, and so they** (or: the same people) **will progressively be made another** (be altered; be changed; be transformed), **yet You are the same, and Your years will not fail."** [Ps. 102:25-28]

We will quote from the author's commentary on the book of Hebrews, since there we consider points that apply to vss. 13-14, above, and our passage, in general:

"These verses are quoted from the LXX (Greek OT). By citing this psalm, the author uses verse 10 to access the creation story, recalling for the readers that the story of the Messiah in this letter had its roots in the very creation itself, and in Yahweh (in the Heb. version), the Creator. In vs. 19 of this psalm, just before this quote, it is stated that Yahweh will look from the heavens,

'To hear the groaning of the prisoner, to unloose the sons of death, [so] that the Name of Yahweh [would be] recounted in Zion, and His praise in Jerusalem, when the peoples are convened together and the kingdoms come to serve Yahweh' (vs. 20-22, CVOT).

The recipients of this letter must have had a considerable length of time being Christians, for the author calls them to consider the former times,

'**days in which, being enlightened** (illuminated), **you at one point remained under** (patiently endured while giving support in) **a great conflict** (contest or athletic combat) **of the effects of sense-experiences** (results of emotions, passions, sufferings and things that happened to you)' (Heb. 10:32).

I bring this up again to point out that these folks would most likely have been quite familiar with the immediate context in Ps. 102 (vs. 19-22) which led up to vss. 25-28, quoted here. It was the context of the mission of the Messiah. Verses 23-24 can be viewed as a foreshadowing of the cross.

"In vs. 11, above, can be seen first a contrast between the impermanence observed in creation, and the fact that He '**continue[s] remaining throughout**.' He can be depended upon, and looks from the heavens with the intent to send a Deliverer. Verse 12 is a restatement of vs. 11, except that the subject has changed from '**the earth**' (or: 'Land') – which throughout the OT was a symbol for the people of Israel (*cf* Walter Brueggemann, *The Land, Place as Gift, Promise, and Challenge in Biblical Faith*, 2nd Ed., Fortress Press, 2002) – to '**all people**' (*pantes*: masculine, plural, nominative). ALL people! '**He will roll** (or: wrap) **them up as a garment, and so they** (or: the same people) **will progressively be made another** (be altered; be changed; be transformed)!' This was more than the psalmist could see. It is God's new thing. This is humanity's destiny, because He is '**the same**' – *cf* Heb. 13:8.

"Dan Kaplan (in a phone conversation) pointed me to some OT passages about Yahweh's dealings with Israel that shed light on verses 11 and 12, above:

    Isa. ch. 24 speaks of His judgments upon the Land (= people) of Israel, in these vss.:
    1. Behold Yahweh making the Land void and evacuating it...
    3. That Land shall be voided, yes voided...
    4. The Land is mournful, it decays; the habitance is wasted away, it decays;
    12. There remains for the City, desolation, and the gate shall be pounded to decimation.
    18. And the foundations of the earth (Land) shall quake,
    19. The earth (Land) will be smashed, yes smashed...
    21. And for many days they shall be called to account.
    23. For Yahweh of host will reign in Mt. Zion and in Jerusalem, and in front of His elders will He be glorified.

This is an example of apocalyptic descriptions of the use of the word 'land (earth)' as a figure for people, and in this case God's judgment upon His people. Dan points us to another example of symbolic language in Isa. 34 that echoes the language of vs. 12, above:

    4. And the vales shall be putrefied; all the host of the heavens shall decay, and the heavens will be rolled up like a scroll. All their host shall decay as a leaf decays from the vine...
    5. When My sword has been satiated in the heavens, behold, on Edom it shall descend...

"This is all history and judgments of people surrounding Israel in OT times. Jamieson Fausset and Brown refer to this as 'judgment on Idumea.' Of vs. 4 they say, 'Violent convulsions of nature are in Scripture made the *images* of great changes in the human world...' (*Commentary on the Whole Bible*, Zondervan Publishing House, 1961, p 550, emphasis original). Next Dan leads us to places where '"garments"' are used symbolically of people. Isa. 50:9b speaks of the rebellious (vs. 5) and that,

    '... all of them shall wear out like a cloak; the moth shall devour them.'

And then there is Job 13:28,

    'A man, like a rotten thing, he is disintegrating like a cloak when a moth has eaten it.'
    Garments are also used metaphorically in the following verses to which Dan leads us:
    Isa. 59:17b 'He shall put on garments of vengeance for clothing and shall muffle Himself with jealousy as a robe.' (note: all OT quotes from the CVOT)
    1 Pet. 2:16 '**continually holding** (or: having) **the freedom as a covering** (or: a veil) **of worthlessness** (bad quality; evil; poorness of situation)...'
    1 Thes. 2:5 '**For neither did we at any time come to be flattering in word, according as you saw and are aware, neither within pretense** (a held-forward specious cloak) **from greed: God is witness!**'
    John 15:22 '**But now** (at this time) **they continue holding nothing which like a specious and deceptive cloak appears in front around their sin**
        (or: they are not continuing to hold that which is put forward to hide the situation concerning their failure; they are not habitually having an excuse or pretense about their deviation, error and miss of the target).'

"'Jesus was wrapped up in the Law (His grave clothes, the wrapping, were the preparation for burial which was according to their custom – or, law). It was the Law that killed Him. But when He was raised from the dead, those grave clothes (figure of the Law) remained in the tomb, buried. After His resurrection, the stone (figure of the tablets of the Law and the stony heart of the old covenant) was rolled away' – paraphrase of Dan Kaplan.

"In considering the clause, above, '**shall be made** (or: grow) **old,**' Heb. 8:13, comes to mind, in regard to the old covenant and the Law which bound folks up,
> '**In thus to be saying "new," He has made the first** (or: former) **"old," and that [which is] progressively growing old and obsolete** (failing of age), **[is] near its disappearing** (vanishing away).'

It was the old relationships, the old way of living and thinking, the old heart and the old 'dead' existence under the Law that was wrapped about humanity in the body of Jesus, and was then buried with Him to rise no more. The grave clothes remained behind. It was a new humanity, a new creation that,
> '**He jointly roused and raised** (or: suddenly awakens and raises) **up, and caused [us] to sit** (or: seats [us]) **together within the things situated upon** [thus, above] **the heavens** (or: in union with the full, perfected heavenlies; or, although neuter: among those comprising the complete and perfected heavenlies; among the ones [residing] upon the atmospheres; in union with the celestials) **within and in union with Christ Jesus**' (Eph. 2:6)." (*John, Judah, Paul & ?*, Harper Brown, 2013, p 98-99)

Simmons explains the general significance of the term "heaven(s)" in prophetic or apocalyptic imagery:
> "'Heaven' is the abode of ruling powers.... When a nation comes to an end, its heaven departs as a scroll; there is a complete cessation and dissolution of all governmental powers and function. Mountains are symbolic of landed nations; hence, Zion stands for Judea, the hill of Samaria for Israel, etc. (1 Ki. 16:24).... Islands represents the Gentile nations inhabiting the isles of the Mediterranean Sea. Ezekiel describes the fall of Tyre, saying 'the isles shall shake at the sound of thy fall (Ezk. 26:15; *cf* 27:35)" (ibid p 153). *Cf* Isa. 41:15.

He also cites Lam. 2:1 as another example:
> "How in His anger Yahweh has covered the daughter of Zion with a thick cloud! He flung from the heavens to the earth the beauty of Israel; He did not remember His footstool in the day of His anger" (CVOT) – note that Zion is called His "footstool."

All these apocalyptic symbols could be used for personal applications of what God is doing to prepare us for the destiny He has recorded for us which has been written within the tiny scroll, but first the seals must be broken. That which we looked at in Joel 2, Peter quoted in Acts. 2:17-21 and applied to the move of God upon the called-out at that time. Perhaps the Spirit is here speaking through John to the 1st century communities in the same way – to remind them that what they were then experiencing (and us, of what we may be now) is the work of the same Spirit. Jesus spoke in similar terms in Matt. 24:29 in prophesying about what was to come in AD 70. But if these signs speak of judgment, let us again recall Isa. 26:9, "For when Your judgments are wrought on earth, the inhabitants of the world learn righteousness" (Tanakh). Furthermore, remember:
> "For a little while I forsook you, but with vast love I will bring you back. In slight anger, for a moment, I hid My face from you; but with kindness everlasting I will take you back in love.... for the mountains may move and the hills be shaken, but My loyalty shall never move from you, nor My covenant of friendship be shaken – said the LORD, Who takes you back in love" (Isa. 54:7-8,10, Tanakh).

Tradition has viewed this passage as speaking of "the final judgment" (and nowhere in Scripture does it speak of a "final" judgment) or of "the end of the world (planet earth)." But if you consider all the links to the OT that we have observed, it becomes apparent that this is another judgment on Israel – it has all the markings of those other judgments that happened in Israel's history. It was the Jewish world of 1st century Palestine that came to an end. And it opened a new age – called in 2 Cor. 5:17 "a new creation." We find a similar clause about "heaven and earth" in 20:11, below,

> "**Next I saw a great bright, white throne, and the One continuously sitting upon it from Whose face the Land** (or: ground; earth) **and the atmosphere** (or: sky; heaven) **flee** (or: at once fled). **And a place is not found for them** (or: And then no position was discovered by them or found in them or for them)."

If we read this verse as speaking of the Land of Israel, and its atmosphere, we can see that the judgments in the Unveiling had the effect upon Jerusalem and Judea that, "no position was discovered by them or found in them or for them." That nation, and its economy, came to an end. Heaven, in the context of Israel, was God's dwelling place: the temple; and thus also was a reference to the priesthood and Jerusalem's leadership. The Land was, by comparison, a reference to the common people.

15. And the kings of the Land (or: earth), **and the great ones, and the commanders of thousands, and the wealthy** (rich) **folks, and the strong ones, and every slave, and every free one, [all] hid themselves into the caves and into the midst of the rocks of the mountains,**

These kings and all the others are those of the Roman Empire, and specifically, Palestine. Here we see human reactions to what has happened in vs. 12-14. No matter one's status in life, during times of pressure the flesh can want to hide or even seek self-destruction. The paradox of "swelling emotion" or "wrath" from a little Lamb (in the next verse) cannot be faced: they **hid themselves**. Here He is more like what we saw in the first chapter of this book. Who is able to stand? Job felt this way and even cursed his very existence – even though recognizing it being the hand of God as the source of his miseries.

> "Judgment is God's strange work. He uses it as a tool in His redemptive and restorative processes. Men make it the end. But judgment is always a MEANS to an end – never THE END!.... All judgments are limited – confined to a day, or to the limitations of prescribed ages. 'Because He hath appointed A DAY, in the which He will judge the world in righteousness by that Man whom He hath ordained' (Acts 17:31). 'And the smoke of their torment [literally: hard times and testing] doth go up to AGES of AGES [or: indefinite time periods pertaining to the ages]; and they have no rest DAY and NIGHT [time periods, here on earth], who are bowing before the beast and its image...' (Rev. 14:11, Young's Literal; brackets added).... God's great goal lies BEYOND THE AGES.... the wrath of the LAMB [Who takes away the sin of the World].... is that stern and tender hand of God which makes the Lion and the Lamb dwell together in the saints" ("Looking for His Appearing: Part 37 – Coming in Judgment," J Preston Eby; brackets added).

It is interesting to observe the symbolic number 7 (for completeness) that is embedded in this verse: the list contains seven classes of humanity.

The last part of this verse has an allusion to Isa. 2:10, 19,

> "Enter into the rock, and bury yourself in the soil from the face of the awe [inspiring] Yahweh, and from the effulgence of His augustness, when He rises to terrify the earth (or: Land).... People will enter into caves of the rocks and into tunnels of the soil..." (CVOT).

The context of Isa. 2 is Judah and Jerusalem; the house of Jacob and the house of Yahweh, on Zion. Now note in vs. 6b that "they are full of divinations from the East, and of consulting clouds like the Philistines." Verse 7 speaks of horses and chariots, and vs. 16 speaks of the ships of Tarshish. The setting was primarily for the time of Isaiah. During Elijah's days even those who were faithful to Yahweh are remembered in Heb. 11:38,

> "**of whom the System** (the ordered arrangement; the world or culture, secular society, religions and government) **was not worthy** (was not of equal value) – **being continually deceived** (led astray; caused to wander) **in deserts and mountains and caves and the holes of the earth** (or: ground)."

But the prophecy was about "the last days" (vs. 2) of Jerusalem and Judea, which finally came upon that area in the 1st century. This was the time that Isa. 2:2-4 began to happen, and thus, also, why vss. 10 and 19 are echoed here, in vs. 15. In Isa. 2:2 we read that, "The Mount of the House of Yahweh shall be established on the summit of the mountains... and all the nations will stream into it." This happened when Christ became King of kings, and we see the picture of spiritual Zion and the heavenly Jerusalem in Heb. 12:22ff. Paul spoke of the nations streaming into it, in Rom. 11:17ff (the grafting into the olive tree), and in Eph. 2:11-22 we read where the Gentiles and the Jews are joined to be **one new humanity** that are built into God's dwelling place through the Spirit. It is now that the law of love goes forth from out of this spiritual Zion (Isa. 2:3) and in the Unveiling, here, we see Him "judging between the nations and arbitrating for many peoples" (Isa.2:4). *Cf* Josephus, *Wars of the Jews*, VI, 7.3.

16. **repeatedly saying to the mountains and to the rocks,**
    "Fall upon us and hide us [Hos. 10:8] **from the Face of the One continuously sitting upon the throne, and from the inherent fervor** (natural impulse and propensity; internal swelling and teeming passion of desire; or: anger, wrath and indignation) **of the little Lamb."**

Barclay observes, "In the Garden of Eden Adam and Eve sought to hide themselves (Gen. 3:8).... But the wrath of God is the wrath of love, which is not out to destroy but even in anger is out to save..." (ibid p 17). We have an almost identical phrase, for trying to escape God's corrective measures, in Hos. 10:8,
> "And they will say to the mountains, 'Cover us!' And to the hills, 'Fall on us!'"

Jesus quoted this verse in Lu. 23:30, when He was referring to what would soon happen to Jerusalem.

17. **Because the great Day of their** [other MSS: His] **inherent fervor** (internal swelling emotion, teeming and passionate desire; impulse; or: anger, wrath and indignation; or: natural bent) **comes** (or: came), **and who** (which one) **is continuously able** (or: continues having power) **to be made to stand** (or: to be established)**?**

Here is an allusion to Nah. 1:6, "who can stand before His indignation? And who shall rise in the heat of His anger? His fury is poured forth like fire, and the rocks are thrown down by Him." Another allusion is to Mal. 3:2-3,
> "Yet who will endure the day of His coming? And who will stand when He appears? For He is like a refiner's fire and a cleanser of silver. And He will cleanse the sons of Levi, and refine them like gold and like silver [in His lake, or basin, of Fire]."

You see, this is all about cleansing and purification – in and by God, Himself.
In Ps. 76:7b we read: "Who can stand before You when once your anger is aroused?" But in 76:10 we find, "Surely the wrath of humanity shall praise You; the remainder of wrath You will restrain (or: bind around You)."

Terry, speaking of all the OT allusions in this passage describing the sixth seal, says,
> "[It] shows how freely our author appropriates the older scriptures to suit the purpose of his own book of prophecy.... as the language of the older scriptures referred to impending judgments of Jehovah on wicked men and nations, so these verses 12-17 are to be understood as a like description of fearful judgment impending at the time when this book was written.... The first four

[seals] find fulfillment in the war which began about AD 66, swept over Galilee and Samaria, laid waste all the cities and villages of Palestine… [to a] final overthrow of Jerusalem by the Romans…. These are all apocalyptic disclosures of things which were to 'come to pass quickly'" (ibid pp 332-3).

This 1st century time of judgment may have what Judah had in mind in Jude 6. *Cf John, Judah, Paul & ?*, ibid).

Here, Chilton makes the conclusion: "This passage is not speaking of the End of the World, but of *the End of Israel* in AD 70" (ibid p 198; emphasis original). D'Aragon comments, "It would be a mistake to interpret these images literally; they stand rather for social upheavals" (ibid). The picture described in vss. 13-14, above, has often been seen as connected to 2 Pet. 3:12, so let us examine that verse, together with my commentary on it:

> 12. **– while constantly being receptive toward** (or: continuing with expectation with regard to) **and eagerly speeding along** (or: progressively hastening after) **the presence of God's Day** (or: the presence, which is God's day; or: the presence of the day which has the quality and character of God and which is God), **through which skies and atmospheres** (or: heavens) **– being continuously on fire – will continue being loosed** (or: untied)! **And so [the body of] elements** (rudimentary principles and assumptions; component parts of the system), **now being continuously intensely hot and burning, [are] presently being progressively melted down** (or: liquefied).

"Their lives should be instruments that **eagerly speed God's presence** (that is within them and among them, since they are God's temple) to those around them. As Paul spoke of running a race (Phil. 3:14) they should "progressively hasten after" the presence of **God's Day** – a day "which has the quality and character of God, and which is God." They were "children of the Day" (1 Thes. 5:5) – even though "**the days** (= present times) **are of a bad quality** (or: a gush of misery; unsound; harmful; or: in a sorry plight; or: toilsome)" – Eph. 5:16.

"The apocalyptic picture of **skies and atmospheres being continuously on fire** and rudimentary assumptions, component parts of the religious and political arrangements being **progressively melted down**, is describing the Jewish world (as they presently knew it) coming to an end. This description is an expansion of the picture given in 2 Pet. 3:10" (*Peter's Encore & Later Paul, comments on Second Peter & Ephesians*, Harper Brown, 2016 p 56).

The social upheavals of the Jewish rebellion brought the end of the old on the social and political level, but the cross and resurrection brought the end of the old covenant that was with a single people-group. Christ's coming ushered in the new – an atmosphere (heaven) and a reign (heaven's; God's) with sovereign activities that are "new in kind and quality," that are making people (the land) "new in kind and quality (2 Pet. 3:13)."

Chapter 7

Terry comments on this chapter: "The martyr scene of the fifth seal [6:9-11, above] is here enlarged so as to take in all the servants (*douloi*) of God, and brethren who have been 'partakers in the tribulation and kingdom and patience which are in Jesus' (1:9, above), and who 'washed their robes and made them white in the blood of the Lamb' (vs. 14, below)" (ibid p 334; brackets added). He then makes an astute observation concerning the method displayed in this unveiling: "seven instances in which the writer introduces such visions of triumph and glory between appalling scenes of woe":

> 1) fifth seal, above; 2) sealing and salvation in this chapter, between the 6th and 7th seals; 3) triumph and ascension of the two witnesses in 11:3-12, below, between the 6th and 7th trumpets; 4) 144K with the little Lamb on Mt. Zion, between the persecution of the two beasts of ch. 13, and

the fall of Babylon, etc., in 14:1-6; 5) the victorious company singing the song of Moses and the Lamb, between the bloody scene of 14:17-20, and the seven last plagues (15:2-4); 6) the great singing multitude, between the fall of Babylon and the last great battle with the beast and his followers (19:1-10); 7) the vision of the enthroned martyrs between the binding and imprisonment of satan and his release for final war (20:4-6).

Terry concludes, "Thus again and again, in the midst of scenes of tribulation and judgment, we are lifted up by some corresponding picture of glory and triumph. This feature… is part of the plan and method…. guided so as to set the several revelations in most telling form" (ibid). He further posits that, "The contents of this 7th chapter are, in fact, an answer to the question with which the 6th chapter ends, 'Who is able to stand?'…. The entire picture of the 7th chapter seems also to correspond to the words of Jesus in Mat. 24:31" (ibid p 334-5). *Cf* a quote of this verse, below.

1. **After this I saw** (or: perceived) **four agents** (or: messengers; folks with the message) **standing upon the four corners of the Land** (or: earth), **continuously holding in their power** (or: restraining) **the four winds of the Land** (or: earth), **so that wind may not be blowing upon the Land** (or: earth; soil), **nor upon the sea, nor upon any tree** (or: all tree and shrub).

The opening phrase, "**After this**," refers to what John saw next, and does not mean that the scenes in this chapter follow a chronological sequence of happening after the events described in chapter 6. Note the three uses of the number 4, here. It is like pointing to the four cardinal directions, indication a complete coverage of the setting for this vision. This verse demonstrates a good example of why the Greek *angelos* is often preferably rendered "**agent**" in these visions: they are active participants, not just messengers, although they also do perform as messengers.

Since the Greek word *gē* means "earth, soil, land, a tract or region of land, thus, a territory," we should first consider the picture that John was seeing. He saw four of God's agents standing on the four corners of the Land. Was he seeing the entire earth, or did God simply show him a picture of his own country, or of the then known earth (perhaps the Roman Empire, or Palestine, or Asia Minor) which apparently was then considered to be flat, and thus have four corners?

Remember that this is a book of symbols and figures. With this in mind, I first chose the word "**Land**" to translate the Gr. *gē*, since it seems appropriate to the picture being described. This also would have spoken to the situation and understanding of those first century Christians to whom this was written. Whether the picture was global or localized, the message is the same. The figure "**four corners**" corresponds to the description of the New Jerusalem: "**the City is lying** (or: is continually being laid) **square** (four-angled; four-cornered)" – 21:16, below.

> "And thou, son of man, Thus said the Lord Jehovah to the ground [Adamah] of Israel: An end, come hath the end on the four corners of the land (earth). Now is the end unto thee, and I have sent Mine anger upon thee, and judged thee according to thy ways, and set against thee all thine abominations" (Ezk. 7:1-3, Young).

Here, the Lord's judgement was against all of Israel, typified by the phrase "the four corners of the land." He was judging "the ground of Israel," typifying their Adamic nature. Ezekiel continues, "For thy ways against thee I do set," (vs. 4) speaking of one of the means of His judgement. Again in, Ezk. 7:9,
> "And not pity doth Mine eye, nor do I spare; according to thy ways unto thee I give, and thine abominations are in thy midst, and ye have known that I am Jehovah the Smiter" (Young).

Jer. 49:34-39 presents a message from the Lord concerning Elam. In vs. 36 He says, "Then will I bring in against Elam four winds, from the four quarters of the heavens, and will scatter them to all these winds -

and there shall be no nation whither the outcasts of Elam shall not come." And in vs. 37-38, "and will send after them the sword, until I have made an end of them; and I will set my throne in Elam - and will destroy from thence king and princes, declares Yahweh." But note the turn-around in vs. 39, "But it shall come to pass, in the after part of the days, that I will bring back the captivity of Elam, declares Yahweh" (Rotherham). An interesting picture. He sets His throne (rule, dominion) in a Gentile nation – after He scatters them – then in the end He brings them back. A similar story to that of His judgements upon Israel. He holds to His pattern! Also, the book of Daniel "uses similar imagery to describe the succession of world empires in the Mediterranean world" (Simmons, ibid p 157):

> "I saw a vision, in the visions of the night, and noted the four winds of the sky rush out upon the Great Sea! And four Great Beasts arose from the sea, different from one another" (Dan. 7:2-3, Fenton).

Simmons (ibid p 158) connects the following OT passages for us: Yahweh's word in Jer. 51:1-2 was, "I will raise up against Babylon... a destroying wind... and shall empty her land..." In that same chapter, in vs. 6 He told them, "flee out of the midst of Babylon," and we find a similar admonition here in the Unveiling (18:4, below). Similar imagery was spoken against Jerusalem, in Jer. 4:11-13,

> "At that time shall it be said to this people and to Jerusalem, 'A dry wind of the high places in the wilderness toward the daughter of My people, not to fan, nor to cleanse; a full wind from those [places].... he shall come up as clouds, and his chariots, as a whirlwind; his horses are swifter than eagles... we are spoiled! O Jerusalem, wash your heart from wickedness so that you may be saved!"

John the baptizer gave the 1st century Judeans similar warning of purifying judgment in Mat. 3:11-12,

> "**the One progressively coming close after me is** (exists being) **stronger than me** (or: I)... **He, Himself, will proceed immersing** (baptizing) **you folks within the midst of a set-apart Breath-effect and Fire** (or: will repeatedly submerge you to the point of saturation, in union with [the] Holy Spirit, even to the permeation of a Sacred Attitude, as well as with [the] Fire) – **Whose winnowing fork** (or: shovel) **[is] within His hand, and He will proceed thoroughly cleaning up** (clearing, scouring and cleansing) **His threshing floor and then will progressively gather** (bring together) **His grain into the storehouse** (granary; barn), **yet the chaff** (straw and husks) **He will continue completely burning, in an inextinguishable Fire.**"

The chaff was the old-covenant religion, which was necessary for the growth of the Plant (Israel), but when it produced the Seed, the harvest came and the Seed was planted, as well as eaten. Then the chaff was burned.

Zech. 6:5, in the LXX reads, "And the agent (messenger) that talked with me answered and said, 'These are the four winds of heaven: they are continually going forth to stand before the Lord of all the earth." The Tanakh reads similar, here translating the Heb. *ruach*, spirit, as "wind." Then we have Matt. 24:31,

> "**And then He will continue sending His agents** (messengers; folks with the message) **off on a mission 'with a great trumpet** (perhaps: = a large shofar; or: = a loud trumpet blast; [note: a figure of a publicly proclaimed message or instruction]),' [Isa. 27:13] **and they will progressively be fully** (or: additionally) **gathering together His picked out and chosen folks from out of the four winds – from [the] heavens'** (or: atmospheres') **extremities: until their farthest points** (= from the four quarters of the land, from one end of the sky to the other)!"

Also, Isa. 11:12, "And He will lift up a standard ['a Root of Jesse,' vs. 10] to the nations, and will gather the outcasts of Israel, and the dispersed of Judah will He collect, from the four corners of the earth." (Rotherham)

So we see that the four winds are in service to the will of the Lord, to scatter those whom the Lord is judging; to bring up beasts out of the sea of humanity; to apparently hold and/or gather His chosen whom He has all over the heavens. But the obvious purpose for which He is using them in chapter 7 of the

Unveiling, is to bring judgement upon the Land. God had His agents controlling these powers. Now if no wind at all were allowed to blow upon the land, there would be serious weather problems.

In verse 1 we see the winds being restrained. They cannot blow upon the Land (a figure of Israel, as a whole), nor upon the sea (a figure of the rest of humanity), nor upon any tree (a figure of the specific planting of the Lord; the occupants in His Garden; that which brought perpetual harvest to His people). "Trees are variously employed to symbolize men, governments and nations in the scriptures" (Simmons, ibid). *Cf* Jud. 9:8; Isa. 14:8; Mat. 3:10; Jude 12

There may be an association between the 4 agents and the 4 winds, as Heb. 1:7, quoting Ps. 104:4, seems to indicate:

> "**And then, on the one hand, to the agents** (messengers; folks with the message) **He is saying, "He is the One making His agents** (messengers; folks with the message) **spirits** (or: Breath-effects), **and His public servants a flame of fire.**" [Ps. 104:4]

This is an example of Hebrew parallelism – the second line being a restatement of the first, but in a different figure; the figure is a reference both to the priests, as "public servants," and to the called-out community, figured as the lampstand in the Tabernacle in 1:20, above, and referencing Acts 2:3 – there being "tongues as if of fire" burning on the lamps in the one case, and upon the people in the second case; the agents speak a message of words that are "spirit," the effect of the Breath. In Jn. 14:12, Jesus said, "**the person habitually trusting and progressively believing into Me, the works** (actions; deeds) **which I Myself am constantly doing** (habitually performing; progressively making, constructing, creating, forming) **that one also will proceed doing** (performing; making; creating)." Paul said to the called-out community in Corinth, "**we are God's fellow-workers** (or: we are co-workers of and from God; we exist being co-workers who belong to God)" – 1 Cor. 3:9. Let us keep this in mind as we proceed investigating these symbolic visions.

2. **And then I saw** (or: perceived) **another agent** (or: messenger; person with a message) **progressively ascending** (stepping up) **from [a; the] rising of the sun** [i.e., from the dawn or the east], **continually holding a seal** (or: signet ring; [Vatican MS 1160: seals]) **of the continuously-living God. And he uttered a cry with** (or: by) **a great** (= loud) **voice – to the four agents** (or: messengers), **to whom it was** (or: is) **given for them** (to them; in them; by them) **to act unjustly to** (to violate, injure, wrong or hurt) **the Land** (earth; soil) **and the sea –**

The agent with the Lord's seal is progressively ascending, coming onto the scene, with the coming of Light. As we see, this actor on the stage does not descend from "heaven," but ascends from the sunrise, with the coming of "the Day." We are, "**sons of** (= associated with and having the qualities of) **Light and sons of** (= associated with and having qualities of) **Day!.... being of Day** (belonging to and having characteristics of [the] Day; having [the] Day as our source)" (1 Thes. 5:5, 8). This symbolic action also calls to mind Mat. 24:27-28,

> "**You see, just as the brightness** (the brilliant beam; the bright shining) **is habitually and progressively coming forth from [the] rising in the eastern parts** [= a figure of the sunrise] **and then is progressively and habitually shining and giving light as far as [the] western parts** (or: until the [recurring] settings), **in this way will proceed being the presence of the Son of the Man** (the Son from humanity; = Adam's son; or: = the eschatological Messianic figure; the Human Being). **Wherever the carcass** (corpse) **may be, the vultures** (or: eagles) **will be progressively led together and gathered.**"

We may also have, here, an allusion to Mal. 4:1-2,

"See, the day is coming, burning like an oven.... But for you who revere My name the sun of righteousness shall rise, with healings in its wings..." (NRSV).

Lu. 1:78-79 picks up this same theme:

because of our God's inner organs which are composed of mercy (= His tender compassions which have the character and quality of mercy), **in union with and amidst which an upward performance and a rising** (= a daybreak) **from out of the midst of an exaltation** (or: from on high) **to at once 'shine upon the people continuously sitting within the midst of darkness** (the realm of the shadow and obscurity; dimness and gloom)' [Isa. 9:1] **– even within death's shadow; to cause our feet to be fully straight and to [walk] in correspondence to straightness, into the path** (way; road) **of peace** (a joining)."

He operates in the realm of our hearts, until:

"**within and in union with Whom also, upon trusting and believing, you people are stamped** (or: were **sealed**; marked for acceptance, or with a signet ring; = personally authorized) **by the set-apart Breath-effect of The Promise** (or: with the holy attitude of assurance; in the sacred essence from the promise; or: for the Holy Spirit which is the Promise) **– Which is continuously a pledge and guarantee of our inheritance** (or: Who remains being an earnest deposit, a security and the first installment of our portion which was acquired by lot)" (Eph. 1:13b-14a).

The seal also was a sign of ownership,

"**Nevertheless** (or: However), **God's firm and solid deposit which is placed down** (a deposit of money; treasure; or: a foundation; basis) **stands, continuing to hold** (or: have) **this seal:**

'**[The] Lord** [= Yahweh] **knows** (or: knew) **by intimate experience those being of Him** (or: the ones that belong to Him; those having Him as their source),' [Nu. 16:5; Na. 1:7]

and:

'**Let everyone repeatedly naming the Name of [the] Lord** [= Yahweh or Christ] (or: by habit using the Lord's name) **stand away from** (withdraw from; keep away from) **injustice** (that which is unfair and inequitable, which negates relationship and does not correspond to the Way pointed out)'" [Num. 16:26] (2 Tim. 2:19).

The idea that this agent with the seal may be a figure of Christ's body ("sons of the Day," the called-out communities that are sent-forth emissaries who bring Christ to people through the Holy Spirit) may find its source in Hag. 2:23,

"In that day, says Yahweh of Hosts (or: the armies), 'I will take you, O Zerubabel, My servant... and I will make (or: place) you as a signet [ring], for I have chosen you...'"

We see in the second half of the verse that it is the **four agents** to whom it **was given** (i.e., by God – the "divine passive" of the verb) "**to act unjustly to** (to violate, injure, wrong or hurt) **the Land** (earth; soil) **and the sea.**" In other words, to bring God's corrective effects upon the Land of Palestine, as well as upon the masses of humans (i.e., the non-Jews, figured by "**the sea**"), at that time and in the context of this vison. We saw this same verb, also in the passive voice, in 6:2 and 4, above. In the vision of chapter 11, below, we find these same masses used to trample Jerusalem: "**it was given to the multitudes** (ethnic groups; nations), **and they will proceed treading** (advance by setting the foot upon) **the set-apart city** (or: the Holy City) **forty-two months**" (11:2b). Then in 11:3 we read, "**I will continue giving to My two witnesses,**" and then 11:6 says of these witnesses, "**they continue holding authority upon the waters, to continuously turn them into blood; and to smite** (beat, strike) **the Land** (or: soil; earth) **within every plague as often as they may will – if they intend** (purpose) **to.**" In these visions, God is giving both the nations and His witnesses the direction and the ability to perform His will upon the Land, and upon Jerusalem (i.e., upon the Jews, as a nation, and upon the Jewish leaders who have led the nation astray) during this period of judgment, in the 1st century. The "**four winds of the Land**" (vs. 1) are a symbol of what these four agents are using to act against what is just, to violate, to injure, to wrong or to hurt the inhabitants of Palestine, at that time. The figure of "four winds" would imply a complete surrounding – coming from all directions – and sweeping across the entire land. Beale (ibid p 406) suggests that these winds are a symbolic reference to the four horsemen of the previous chapter, and thus concludes that the sealing of the 144K (vss. 4-8, below) would have happened before the events of 6:1-8, above, were called forth and sent into the Land.

In the background imagery of Zech. 6, cited above, the four chariots, having the four variously colored horses, of vss. 1-3, are identified in vs. 5 as being, "**four winds** (or: spirits) of the skies (or: heavens; atmospheres) going forth from stationing themselves before the Lord of the entire earth (or: Land)." These visions of the Unveiling use these apocalyptic elements differently, but we can discern the correlations between how these elements are used here, and how they were used there in Zechariah. Here they are not just patrolling, but are bringing judgment.

3. **repeatedly saying,**
> **"You may not act unjustly to** (hurt; injure; wrong; violate) **the Land** (earth; soil), **nor the sea, nor the trees, until we may seal** (impress with a signet ring) **the slaves of our God upon their foreheads."**

Here we see why this judgment is being restrained: "**until we may seal the slaves of our God upon their foreheads**." So the delay is only temporary: it seems obvious that once the sealing is complete, then the winds will begin to blow and bring injustice, hurt, injury, violations. Is this God's pattern, which is the same yesterday, today and into the ages, that He will first complete His work in His chosen firstfruit of each generation and land before He allows those winds to blow?

"The origin of this picture is very likely in Ezk. 9" (Barclay, ibid p 23). Here we have a man clothed in a linen robe with the writing kit of a scribe (vs. 2), and he is to "Pass through in the midst of the city, in the midst of Jerusalem, and you will mark a mark on the foreheads of the mortals who are sighing and groaning over all the abhorrences being done in her midst" (vs. 4, CVOT). Then six mortals, each with "his shattering weapon in his hand" (vs. 2) were to pass through the city and smite (vs. 5), "Yet to any man on whom is the mark, you must not come close. Now from My sanctuary shall you start" (vs. 6, CVOT). Terry sees here an allusion to Ex. 12:7, 13, and "the mark of the blood of the paschal lamb on the dwellings of Israel [that] turned away the destroying angel from the door" (ibid p 336).

The result of the sealing here, in chapter 7, is seen in 14:1, below, "**and with Him [are] one hundred forty-four thousand: folks continuously having His Name, and** (or: even) **His Father's Name, having been written upon their foreheads.**" It would seem, then, that the **seal**, or imprint, is equivalent to the Name. The forehead is a figure for the mind. These have the identity (His Name) and the mind of Christ. They belong to Him. Another allusion, here, could be to Ex. 28:11, describing the high priest's garments,
> "With the handiwork of lapidary, as the engravings of a seal, shall you engrave the two stones with the names of the sons of Israel" (CVOT).

Then another facet of the seal is seen in Ex. 28:36-38,
> "You will make a blossom of pure gold and engrave on it like engravings of a seal: Holy [or: Set-apart] to Yahweh. You will place it on blue twine, and it will come to be on the turban; on the forefront of the face of the turban shall it come to be. It will come to be on the forehead of Aaron; thus Aaron will bear the depravity of the holy things which the sons of Israel shall sanctify for all their holy gifts; and it will come to be on his forehead continually for their acceptance before Yahweh" (CVOT; brackets added).

So an engraving of a seal was upon the forehead of the High Priest.

In the *Psalms of Solomon* (written in the 1st century, BC) we read in 15:6, 9, two contrasting uses for a mark,

> "For God's mark is on the righteous for [their] salvation.... on their forehead [is] the mark of destruction" (*The OT Pseudepigrapha*, Vol. 2, Hendrickson, 2013, trans. by R.B. Wright).

We find contrasting "marks," of the little animal (= the beast nature), and the number of its name in 13:16-17 and 14:9-11, below. These must be "burned out" through God's fires of purification (14:10).

The use of the word **slave**, which John also used in 1:1, above, in the opening lines of this Unveiling, shows how Christ's 1st century followers regarded God as being their Sovereign Owner (or: Lord). *Cf*, also, 2:20, above, and 19:5; 22:3, below, and, Rom. 1:1.

4. **Then I heard the number of the people having been sealed** (impressed; imprinted)**: one hundred forty-four thousand – folks having been sealed** (imprinted; certified; identified for ownership) **from out of every tribe of the sons of Israel.**

Here Malcolm Smith reminds us that a number is "an idea." Vincent refers to this number as "the number symbolical of fixedness and full completion." Barclay says, "The number 144,000 stands, not for limitation but for completeness and perfection. It is made up of 12 multiplied by 12 - the perfect square - and then rendered even more inclusive and complete by being multiplied by 1,000" (ibid p 24). Metzger concurs that it stands for completeness. Smith goes into more detail on the number, noting that it is 12 X 12 X 10 X 10 X 10. He explains that 12 was the number of Israel, both of which represented God's plan and purposes in the world (12 being 3 [God in His triune aspect] X 4 [the worldwide aspect of the 4 directions]). The 12 X 12 would be a picture of the "universal church": the 12 of the old covenant and the 12 of the new covenant. 10, he says, is the perfection of number: number completed. 1000 is 10 cubed (used three times: Triune). Thus, this number (144,000) signifies the perfect, completed called-out of God.

Terry notes the number 12, here, and brings to mind both its use in 14:1, below, and its repeated use in the description of the New Jerusalem in 21:12, below:
> "12 gates... the names of the 12 tribes; it measures 12 thousand furlongs and its walls are 144 cubits (21:16, 17). Compare the '12 pillars, according to the twelve tribes of Israel' (Ex. 24:4), the 12 cakes of showbread (Lev. 24:5), the 12 memorial stones ... (Josh. 4:5), and the '12 bullocks for all Israel' (Ezra 8:35)" (ibid p 336-7).

I would like to point out that the dimensions of the Holy of Holies was 10 X 10 X 10. So, when we see the number 1000 in this book, let us think of the Tabernacle; let us think of God's presence, His mercy, His ruling His people, His dwelling within the camp of His people, the place of fullness and maturity, the 100-fold harvest, the place of entering into His rest: the high call - all symbolized by the holy of holies in the Tabernacle.

Smith (ibid) points out that this listing is not a listing of natural Israel for the following reasons:
1) Reuben is always listed first in a listing of the natural tribes of Israel
2) Ephraim is left out. Ephraim was next in importance to Judah, and was often used to speak of all of Israel, apart from Judah
3) Dan is left out - you can't have an official listing of the tribes & leave a tribe out
4) Levi is included - this tribe was not usually included in the list of tribes
5) There was no tribe of Joseph – he gave his inheritance to his sons, and THEY became the tribes of Ephraim and Manasseh.

Notwithstanding Smith's assessment regarding the tribe of Dan, we find the tribe of Dan missing from the lists in 1 Chron. 4 through 8, although he is mentioned in 2:1, in that book. Also, Simeon is omitted in Deut. 33, although present in the listing of Deut. 27:12-13. But this Unveiling is a symbolic book, not a genealogy, so Smith's point deserves consideration, and we might ask, "Why was the tribe Dan, whose name meant "judge" and who was called a "serpent" by his father, omitted from this list? Is this sending us a message in regard to this Unveiling from Jesus Christ? All judgment and wisdom are now in Him. In Nu. 2:2-3ff, the tribe of Judah is listed first in the list of tribal encampments, and was to pitch their encampment, "on the east side [in front of the entry of the Tabernacle complex] toward the rising of the sun." He is also listed first in Nu. 34:19, and in 1 Chron. 12:23-37, so there is precedence for this tribe leading the list. The prophecy in Ezk. 37 speaks of a messianic David being king over the future "Israel," when they will have "one Shepherd" (vs. 24; cf vs. 17, below), which essentially repeats Ezk. 34:23 (cf also vs. 25).

Simmons (ibid p 163) notes that in vs. 4 John only "**heard the number of the people having been sealed** (impressed; imprinted)," while in vs. 9, below, he "**saw... a vast crowd**." The numbers are symbols, and can be taken into the mind without seeing the people: they represent an idea. Seeing the crowd leads to a description of their makeup and the diversity of their origins. Each vision has its own purpose, its own message.

5. **Out of Judah's tribe: twelve thousand sealed** (imprinted; certified; identified to the Owner)
   Out of Reuben's tribe: twelve thousand
   Out of Gad's tribe: twelve thousand
6. Out of Asher's tribe: twelve thousand
   Out of Naphtali's tribe: twelve thousand
   Out of Manasseh's tribe: twelve thousand
7. Out of Simeon's tribe: twelve thousand
   Out of Levi's tribe: twelve thousand
   Out of Issachar's tribe: twelve thousand
8. Out of Zebulon's tribe: twelve thousand
   Out of Joseph's tribe: twelve thousand
   Out of Benjamin's tribe: twelve thousand sealed (imprinted; certified; identified to the Owner).

Smith gives the list together with the meaning of their names, and sees, here, a description of the qualities and experiences of one who follows the Little Lamb:
> Judah -- "praise," the first thing in a Christian's experience is praise centered in the Lion of the Tribe of Judah. "Enter His courts with praise..." (Ps. 100:4)
> Reuben -- "behold, a Son" This is a company of the sons of God
> Gad -- "a great company; a troop" The many sons being brought to glory (Heb. 2:10)
> Asher -- "happy, joyful" Filled with the joy of the Holy Spirit
> Naphtali -- "to wrestle and overcome" The overcomers; those who wrestle against principalities, authorities, and the system strength of this darkness
> Manasseh -- "forgetting" These forget all their troubles & the things done to them (as did Joseph); their sins which have been forgiven; and, like Paul, the things which are behind (Phil. 3:13)
> Simeon -- "hearing" These are sheep who hear His voice; they are blessed with ears to hear; they also obey
> Levi -- "joined" These are joined unto the Lord; they are branches which abide in the vine; they are One Spirit (1 Cor. 6:17)

Issachar -- "a price was paid; a reward" These have been redeemed; they have also received the prize of the high call; they've run the race and won
Zebulon -- "a dwelling place" This company is the dwelling place of God (Eph. 2:22)
Joseph -- "add; increase; fruitful" The Spirit of God has been added to them, and they produce the fruit of the Spirit, bearing much fruit (John 15:8,16); their branches run over the wall (Gen. 49:22) to bring His fruit to those not yet in God's vineyard
Benjamin -- "son of My right hand" They have attained sonship, and are at the place of His power, authority and trust.

These all are sealed, imprinted with God's character and identity, and the mark of His ownership also provides security through trials (ordeals), tests and judgements which He brings upon His Land. With the breaking of the 7 seals on the little scroll – on something that was previously written, perhaps the vision that Daniel was told to seal up (Dan. 9:24), or the scroll that he was told to shut up and seal (Dan. 12:4), or, "the words [that were] closed up and sealed till the time of the end" (Dan. 12:9) – but here are new, living scrolls that are being sealed with God's seal, for,

> "**[We ourselves] are and continue being [His] letter – being one having been written** (inscribed; imprinted; engraved) **within our hearts; one progressively being experientially known and continuously read** (or: periodically recognized and experienced again) **by all people** (mankind).... **being one having been written** (inscribed; imprinted; engraved), **not in black** (= not with ink), **but rather, by** (or: in; with) **God's Spirit: One continuously living** (or: in a Breath-effect which has its origin in God, Who is constantly living)... **within tablets which are hearts made of flesh** (or: on tablets in hearts composed of flesh)." (1 Cor. 3:2, 3b).

In order for people to read us, our seals have to be broken so that we can be opened up to the world. As Prinzing said, His horses have to ride through us. Only the little Lamb is of equal value to do this for us, and in us. Once our seals are broken, then He puts His seal upon us and we represent Him to the world. And so, viewing these "sealings" as a figure of what happens to each individual, we might then correlate the little scroll in the hand of the agent, whose 7 seals must be broken, as a symbol for what has been written about the life of each person, up to the time of the opening of the seals. An interesting perspective from early Christian thinking about being "**sealed**" is found in *The Shepherd of Hermas*, dated by John. A.T. Robinson as written before AD 85. Both Origen and Irenaeus cited it as "Scripture," but others disagreed and considered it as simply Christian literature. In Parable 9.16.3 we read:

> "For before a man... bears the name of the Son of God, he is dead; but when he receives the seal, he lays aside his deadness and receives life."

Then in 9.17.1-.4,

> "These twelve mountains are twelve tribes that inhabit the whole world.... [they] are twelve nations.... all the nations... when they heard and believed, were called by the name of the Son of God. So when they received the seal, they had one thought and one mind, and one faith and one love became theirs..." (*The Apostolic Fathers*, 2nd Ed., Baker Book House. 1989 [1891], trans. by J.B. Lightfoot & J.R. Harmer, p 276-7)

Once again, the question is, did this sealing of Christ's followers happen in the 1st century, in the period when this letter was written to those specific churches? Does it repeatedly happen, to individuals or to new called-out groups? Is it something which will happen during, or at the supposed end of the "church age"? Will it happen in the next age? Or, is the answer to all these questions, "Yes!"? Is this a principle of Christ that is being unveiled to us here? Recall the words of Jesus when He prayed for His followers in John 17:15,

> "**I am not now making a request to the end that You should pick them up and carry** (or: remove; take) **them out of the System** (world system; ordered arrangement of culture, religion and government; secular society), **but rather that You should observe, guard, protect,**

maintain, care for and keep them out of the worthless or bad situation, the sorry plight, the effect of the knavish and good-for-nothing person, the oppressive toil and the base or evil influence."

Has not this been an observation of history? Remember the three Hebrew men in the fiery furnace? Daniel in the lion's den? He has made a promise to His people:
> "When you pass through water, I will be with you; through streams, they shall not overwhelm you. When you walk through fire [perhaps a sea, or lake of fire?], you shall not be scorched; through flame, it shall not burn you." (Isa. 43:2, Tanakh)

Here in Rev. 7, the act of sealing would seem to indicate that this will protect His chosen from the effect of the four winds. However, Beale cites R.J. Bauckham (*Climax of Prophecy: Studies in the Book of Revelation*, 1993 p 217-229), concluding that:
> "[T]he numbering of Rev. 7:4-8 suggests that those numbered are an army.... The reason for a census in the OT was always to determine the military strength of the nation (e.g., Num. 1:3, 18, 20; 26:2, 4; 1 Chron. 27:23; 2 Sam. 24:1-9).... Those counted in the OT were males of military age, and the 144K in Rev. 14:1-4 are 'male virgins'" (ibid p 422).

But we must keep in mind that "**[there is now] a new creation: the original things** (primitive [arrangements]) **passed by. Consider! New things have come into existence**" (2 Cor. 5:17). Also,
> "**He [is] also the One completely** (or: instantly, in one point in time) **sealing us** (stamping us with an identity-mark; imprinting us for ownership; or: validating/guaranteeing our genuineness), **even** (or: and) **completely giving the advance transaction of the agreement** (or: the pledge and down payment guaranteeing full payment for purchase; or: a dowry) **of the Spirit** (or: which is the spirit; or: having its source and origin in the Breath-effect; or: which belongs and pertains to the spirit; from the Attitude) **within the midst of our hearts**" (2 Cor. 1:22).

9. **After these things I saw** (or: perceived), **and consider! A vast crowd** (great multitude), **which no one was able to number, from out of every ethnic group** (or: nation) **– even of tribes and of peoples and of tongues** (languages) **– standing before** (in the sight of) **the throne, and before** (in the sight of) **the little Lamb, having been clothed with bright white robes** (or: equipment; uniforms), **and palm trees** (or: branches) **[are] within their hands.**

The second clause, "**which no one was able to number**," is an allusion to the promises to Abraham,
> "And I will make your seed like the soil [grains] of the Land, so that, if a man were able to count the soil [grains] of the Land, then your seed too might be counted" (Gen. 13:16, CVOT).

And in Gen. 15:5,
> "Then He brought him forth outside and said: 'Now look up toward the heavens and count off the stars, if you can number them.' And He promised him: 'Thus shall become your seed'" (CVOT).

Then in Gen.32:12,
> "... and I will make your seed like the sand of the sea **which cannot be numbered**, for multitude."

This is a clue that vs. 9, here, is speaking of the same group, the Seed of Abraham, and we should remember that Yahweh had promised him, "In you shall all families of the earth (or: Land) be blessed" (Gen. 12:2), and here we see the descriptive phrases, "**every ethnic group... tribes... peoples... tongues**" – which are a way of saying "everyone," not just Israel. This is a broadly inclusive picture – not just a "remnant." It is the same picture that Paul described in Eph. 2:15-16,
> "**rendering useless** (nullifying; rendering down in accord with inactivity and unemployment) **the Law** (or: the custom; = the Torah) **of the implanted goals** (or: concerning impartations of the finished product within; from commandments; which was inward directives) **consisting in decrees** (or: prescribed ordinances), **to the end that He may frame** (create; found and settle

from a state of wildness and disorder) **The Two** [i.e., the two classifications: 'uncircumcision' and 'circumcision'—vs. 11] **into One qualitatively New and Different** [p46 & others: common] **Humanity centered within the midst of, and in union with, Himself, continuously making** (progressively creating) **Peace and Harmony** (a joining; = shalom), **and then should fully transfer, from a certain state to another which is quite different, The Both – centered in, and within the midst of, One Body in God** (or: make completely other, while moving away from what had existed, and fully reconcile The Both, in one Body, **by, to,** with and for **God**), **through the cross** (execution stake) **– while in the midst of Himself killing the enmity and discordant hatred** (or: killing-off the characteristics of enemies within it)."

We saw in 5:6, above, that,

"**the Seven Spirits of God** (or: God's seven Breath-effects/Attitudes): **the Ones having been and are still being sent forth as envoys** (representatives) **into ALL the Land** (or: earth),"

and recall, in 5:9, that the four living ones and the 24 old folks affirmed that they had been bought,

"**by God, within [His] blood from out of the midst of every tribe and tongue** (or: language) **and people and ethnic multitude** (or: nation)."

Below, in 11:9, "**tribes and tongues and ethnic groups** (nations; multitudes; pagans; non-Jews)" are included in that vision. Then, "**authority was given to [the little animal] upon every tribe and people and tongue and multitude** (nation; ethnic group)," in 13:7; and in 14:6 an agent flies through the sky "**to proclaim the good news upon those situated** (or: habitually sitting down) **upon the Land** (or: earth), **and upon every multitude** (nation; ethnic group), **tribe, tongue, and people.**" And, in 17:15 (similar to 13:7), we read that, "**The waters which you saw** (or: see), **where the Prostitute continually sits, are peoples and crowds** (mobs) **and multitudes** (nations; ethnic groups) **and tongues** (languages)." The visions of the Unveiling were set in, and first pertained to, 1st century Palestine and the Roman Empire, but they also had a humanity-wide message.

So this presents a new picture, but it is an expansion, a further unfolding of the same scene which began to be unveiled in ch. 4 and continued in ch. 5. Metzger's view is that,

"The two visions in this chapter stand in strange contrast to each other, as to location as well as in other respects. In the first vision the throng can be counted; in the second, it is incalculably numerous. In the first, it is drawn from the twelve tribes of Israel; in the second, from every nation; in the first, it is being prepared for imminent peril; in the second, it is victorious and secure. The two visions are correlative and refer to the same people distinguished only by their location" (ibid p 61).

These folks are **standing before the throne, and before the little Lamb**. Verse, 15, below, also locates this vast throng as being "**before God's throne.**" In the vision of 4:5b, above, recall that John saw, "**seven shining ones** (or: lamps; lights; torches) **of fire, which are the Seven Spirits of God** (or: God's seven Breath-effects), **being continuously caused to burn before the throne.**" Now while we are speaking of the location of these folks, which has just been established, note vs. 15-17, below, where they will have God pitch a tent upon them, shepherd them, and guide them upon springs of waters of life. They serve as priests within His temple, Christ's body; they are protected from the elements and their needs are supplied. Putting all this together, we see that the 7 "shining ones" – the fullness of God's Spirit – are among, or in the presence of, His called-out communities. They, along with the 4 "living ones," are all in the same place: **before the throne**, which corresponds to "the holy place" of the temple, the location of the **lampstand** (figure of the called-out).

As being another picture of the same group just sealed in vs. 4-8, above, let us consider more clues to their identity:

1) They are out of every nation (or, ethnic group), tribe, people, and language. Was this not where Israel was scattered? (Matt. 24:31; Isa 11:12, noted above)
2) They are clothed in bright white robes: the identity of the overcomer
3) They have been delivered (saved) and attribute this glory to God (vs. 10)
4) They have been in great pressure (tribulation) – perhaps caused by the 4 winds?
5) They have the righteousness (white robes) which comes via the Lamb's blood
6) They are His sheep – is that not what one "shepherds"? (vs. 17)
7) They are within His temple – are not we His temple? (1 Cor. 3:16; 2 Cor. 6:16). If they are within His temple, are they not a part of His body?
8) They, again, are before the throne and before the Lamb: in His sight and presence.

I would conclude that these are a picture of the ones who have just been imprinted with God's seal, and it was the symbolic pressure of this seal, as it imprinted His character and identity into them, that was the great pressure which they had just undergone. Here we have unveiled another aspect of Christ: the process, pressure, cleansing requisite to becoming a part of the body which has the character and identity of Jesus Christ. Of these I think it could be said, "It is no longer [them], but Christ" (*cf.* Gal. 2:20).

The tears they shed are anointed tears (vs. 17, below). "As they pass through the Valley of Weeping, they make it a place of springs, as if the early rain had covered it with pools of blessings." (Ps. 84:6)

We notice that this group is carrying palm trees, or, perhaps, palm branches. What would this signify?
"Palms are characteristic of oases and watered places (Ex. 15:27; Nu. 33:9) .... Jericho was known as the City of Palms (Deut. 34:3; Jud. 1:16; 3:13). The judge Deborah rendered her decisions under a palm bearing her name (Jud. 4:5). The palm was a symbol of both beauty (Song. 7:7) and prosperity (Ps. 92:12) .... were used in the decoration of the Temple (1 Ki. 6:29, 32, 35; 7:36) and were part of Ezek.'s vision of the new Temple (Ezk. 40:16, 22, 26). Palms were used in the construction of the booths for the festival of booths (Lev. 23:40; Neh. 8:15). In John 12:13, the crowd used palm branches to welcome Jesus to Jerusalem" (Holman Bible Dict.).
All of these references bring interesting significance to the symbolism of their carrying palm trees (or, fronds):
1) they are now come to a watered place, or are in an oasis by comparison to their surroundings;
2) they have "crossed the Jordan" into "the promised land";
3) they are now qualified to judge as did Deborah;
4) they have been given "beauty for ashes (or, dust)" (Isa. 61:3, KJV), and have come to a prosperous place;
5) they are a part of the Temple;
6) they are celebrating the triumph of the Little Lamb, Who is the King that has come to the heavenly (spiritual) Jerusalem;
7) they are preparing to celebrate, or are signifying that this is the time of, the Feast of Tabernacles (Lev. 23:40; Neh. 8:14-15; Beale concurs – ibid p 428).
Barclay instructs us that, "The palm is also the sign of victory" (ibid p 26). *Cf* 2 Mac. 10:7. Terry suggests that they are "emblems of triumphant peace and joy" (ibid p 338). *Cf* Jn. 12:13.

The term **standing** deserves our attention. Let us recall from Paul's writings:
"**You folks must** (or, as a subjunctive: can; should) **stand** (or: at once take your stand), **then, after girding yourselves around your waist** (or: loins) **in union with Truth and within the midst of Reality**... **entering within** (putting on; clothing yourself with) **the breastplate armor** (cuirass; corslet) **of fair and equitable dealing of the eschatological deliverance**
(or: which is the rightwised relationships of inclusion in the Way pointed out)" (Eph. 6:14).

> "**[To] the end that you can stand [as] mature folks** (or: those having reached the purposed goal and destiny) **and people having been brought to fullness** (or: carried to the full measure) **within, and in union with, all God's will, intent, design and purpose**" (Col. 4:12b).
> "**Being, then, folks that were eschatologically delivered and rightwised** (also: made fair, equitable, just, free from guilt and turned in the right direction) **from the midst of [His] faithfulness, out of trust and from conviction, we continuously hold and progressively have peace and harmony face to face with God, through our Owner and Lord, Jesus Christ through Whom, also, we have had and now hold the conducted approach and access** (or: the act of bringing toward to gain entrée), **by [His] faithfulness** (or: in this trust; with that confidence; for loyalty), **into this grace and joyous favor within which we have stood and in union with which we now stand, and so we keep on celebrating, speaking loudly and boasting upon the expectation** (or: expectant hope) **of God's glory** (the manifestation from God which calls forth praise; and: from God's good reputation; of the opinion from God; from the imagination which is God)" (Rom. 5:1-2). *Cf* 1 Cor. 15:1.

The scene of this verse may correspond to one aspect of the great composite presented in Heb. 12:22b-24,

> "**ten-thousands** (or: myriads) **of agents and messengers** (people with a/the message), **[that is]... an assembly of an entire people and in** (or: to) **a summoning forth** (or: a called-out and gathered community) **of firstborn folks having been copied** (or: enrolled; registered) **within [the; or: various] atmospheres** (or: heavens), **and in** (or: to; with) **God, a Judge** (an Evaluator and Decider) **of all mankind, even among** (or: to; with) **spirits of just folks having been brought to the destined goal** (perfected; finished; matured; made complete), [*cf* Rev. 3:12; 21:1-2; Eph. 2:6; Phil. 3:20; Rev. 14:1-5; Ex. 4:22; Gal. 3:19] **and in** (or: to) **Jesus, a Medium** (or: one in a middle position; a go-between; an Umpire; a Mediator) **of a new and fresh** (young; recently-born) **arrangement** (covenant; settlement; a deposit which moves throughout in every direction; a placing through the midst; a will and testament), **and to and in blood of sprinkling, and to One continuously speaking something superior to** (or: stronger and better than) **Abel**" *Cf* Mat. 17:1-5; Gal. 4:22-26; Rev. 21:1-2; 9b-22:5; Jn. 4:21; Ps. 46:4; 132:13; Isa. 28:16; 33:5.

10. **And they are uttering a cry** (or: are exclaiming) **with a great** (= loud) **voice, repeatedly saying, "The deliverance** (Wholeness and health; The salvation) **[is] by our God** (in our God) – **by** (or: in) **the One continuously sitting upon the throne, even** (or: and) **by** (or: in) **the little Lamb!"**

In translating the dative case in vss. 10 and 12, I have chosen the word "**by**; in; for or with," instead of the usual rendering "to." All these words are legitimate renderings of the dative, but to me it seems more appropriate to indicate that God is the source and instrument (Dana & Mantey refer to this as "The Instrumental Dative") of their deliverance, and that the agents recognize that the blessing is by God; the glory is by God; the wisdom is by God; even the thanksgiving comes forth by His Spirit; honor is by God; and obviously power, ability and strength are by God. This is not to say that in so saying this they are not all attributing these things "to" God, for obviously they are. But further, the rescue, wholeness and salvation reside "**in God**." He is the realm of our deliverance and preservation. But the dative can also be rendered "for God." Here, Brian Zahnd gives us a beautiful insight:

> "... it is the *Lord's* salvation, for it is *God* who has suffered loss in the ruin of human civilization. In a world where Cain keeps killing Abel, it's not only Abel who suffers loss; God himself suffers loss" (*Beauty Will Save the World*; Charisma House, 2012, p 121; emphasis original).

Now we may tend to look to the future, to a time when we, or some, will utter the same exclamation as does this crowd in vs. 10. But should this not be "repeatedly" happening now? When the description of this great multitude is taken figuratively, can we not see that this is us now, and has been so of the Elect ever since the time that John wrote this? Was he not wanting those of communities in Asia to see themselves in this and take hope and courage?

The Greek for "**robe**" (used in vs. 9, 13, 14) is *stolē* and is from the verb *stellō* which can mean "to equip; to arrange; to place in set order." Thus did I expand the meaning of robe to "equipment, uniforms," to give the sense that they had been equipped ("...the equipping of the saints for the work of service..." Eph. 4:12, NASB), arranged by His hand, and put in their own order (1 Cor. 15:23).

The proclamation of this verse may be an allusion to Ps. 3:8a,
> "The deliverance (The wholeness and health; The salvation) [is] the LORD's ([= Yahweh's]; or: [is] of and from the LORD)..." (LXX, JM).

Also Ps. 3:3a affirms, "Yet You, O Yahweh [have been and are] a shield about me." Here, for the word "shield," the LXX (JM) reads, "the One Who takes or receives [a blow; an arrow; an assault] instead of me (or: in my place)." Jonah, "from out of the belly of the Unseen (*hades*)," also affirms, "rescue, salvation and deliverance [is] by and in the LORD (= Yahweh)" (2:3, 10b; LXX; JM).

In Acts 4 we read,
> "**in** (within and in union with) **the Name of Jesus Christ** (or: of [the] anointed Jesus), **the Nazarene…. the rescue and deliverance – the restoration to health and wholeness, the safety and salvation, and the return to our original state and condition – is in absolutely no other person**" (vss. 10, 12).

Appropriate to our present context is Peter's use of the noun "deliverance, etc." in 1 Pet. 1:
> 3. **Well-spoken of** (or: Eulogized; Blessed; or: Well-gathered, laid-out with ease, and worthy of praise) **[is] the God and Father of our Lord, Jesus Christ** (or: Who is our Owner, Jesus Christ), **the One bringing us to birth again** (regenerating us; begetting us back up again; causing us to be born again) **down from, in line with and in correspondence to His abundant mercy** (or: the much-existing sympathizing and active compassion which is Him) **– through Jesus Christ's resurrection forth from out of the midst of dead folks. [We are born again]:
> into a progressively living expectation** (or: into the midst of continuously living hope);
> 4.   **into the midst of an incorruptible** (unspoilable; imperishable; unruinable; undecayable), **unstained** (undefiled), **and unfading** (or: unwithering) **inheritance** (or: enjoyment of and participation in an allotted portion as a possession) –
>> **one having been kept in view, watched-over, guarded, and which continues being maintained and kept intact within the midst of [the, or our] atmospheres** (or: in union with heavens; = in realms of spirit);
> **– [which things were and are being birthed and entering] into the midst of you folks,**
> 5. **the ones being continuously garrisoned within** (or: kept under watch and guarded in the center of) **God's power, in union with an ability which is God, through [His] faithfulness, into a deliverance** (a rescue which brings health, wholeness; salvation) **[which is now] ready to be unveiled** (revealed; disclosed) **within the midst of and in union with [this] last season** (or: resident within a final fitting situation; in a final fertile moment; on [this] last occasion),
> 6. **within which [season and deliverance] you folks are presently feeling constant joy and happiness and are continuing to rejoice exceedingly – though for a little while, at present, since** (or: if) **it continues being binding and necessary, being pained** (distressed; grieved; sorrowed) **within various tests** (or: different trials and ordeals) **to put you to the proof.**

11. **And all the agents** (or: messengers) **had stood and continued standing in a circle around the throne and the elders** (or: older folks) **and the four living ones. And then they fell on their faces before the throne and worshiped** (did obeisance to and kissed toward) **God, repeatedly saying,**

The circle of agents and their eulogy in vs. 11-12, were already seen in 5:11-12, above, where they gave a similar eulogy. So, once again, we can see that this is part of the same scene. The action of these folks is a sudden, physical response to what was just proclaimed in vs. 10, and their action is followed by their own outburst, evoked by this proclamation, which we read in vs. 12. They are simply overwhelmed by the full realization of God's sovereignty and its resultant goodness. John had a similar physical response in 22:8, below. Note, there, that it was one of the 7 agents who had the shallow bowls (21:9) who had been showing John all those things – and he revealed to John that he was John's,

> "**fellow-slave, even of** (belonging to; from among) **your brothers – of** (or: belonging to and from among) **the prophets and of those continuously keeping and observing the words of this scroll**" (22:9).

This scene has often been interpreted as being liturgical, in some sort of "worship service" in heaven, but this is a symbolic vision that comes amidst many OT, and thus, old covenant, images. But this Unveiling was written to new covenant communities, and thus, should be interpreted from the viewpoint of the new arrangement in Christ, along the line of what Paul expressed in Eph. 2:6 – that of our being presently seated with Christ, and "**situated upon** [thus, above] **the heavens**." We are now "joined" to the Lord, and are "one spirit/Spirit" with Him (1 Cor. 6:17). All "physical worship" is simply bearing His image and living "joined to the Vine," i.e., BEING in Christ. Since we are His temple, all that we now do replaces the old covenant "forms" of "worship." It is all now a matter of Spirit and Truth (Christ) – Jn. 4:23-24.

12. **"It is so** (Amen)! **The blessing** (or: The word of goodness), **the glory** (reputation), **the wisdom, the gratitude** (thanksgiving), **the honor** (the value; the pricing), **the power** (the ability), **and the strength [is] in** (by; for; with) **our God, on into the ages** (eons) **of the ages! So it is** (Amen)!"

Seven words of affirmation and praise are found in 5:12, above, six of which are the same as here. It is again a symbol of viewing God as the source and example of complete worth, virtue and admirable qualities. All that we value is found in Him. Although we know that justice (among humans) and corrective judgment are important to God, despite what these **agents** and **elders** and **living ones** have been commissioned to execute, as seen in these visions, it is noteworthy that neither "justice" nor "judgment" are mentioned in this affirming response to the proclamation given in vs. 10: **deliverance**. Neither is the word "teeming emotion" or "anger" or "wrath." This book involves judgment, but its message is the Gospel (the good news; the message of goodness, ease and well-being), which is the characteristic and final end of all. All returns into union with God (Rom. 11:36).

13. **And one from out of the elders** (or: among the older people) **answered, saying to me, "These – the ones having been clothed with the bright, white robes** (or: uniforms; equipment) **– who are they and whence came they?"**

Terry points us back to Zech. 1:19, 21 and 4:11-13 for a comparison with the format that we have here and in vs. 14, below. He suggests, "This form of question and answer serves to give dramatic life to the description" (ibid p 339). It also shows the reader that one who sees a vision may also need it to be explained.

Barclay explains that, "The white robes always stand for two things. They stand for *purity*, for the life cleansed from the taint of past sin, the infection of present sin and the attack of future sin. They stand for victory.... in his life and in his death" (ibid p 32; emphasis original).

The semantic range of the word "**robes**" indicates that this picture has a broad application to a variety of walks of life and vocations. Also, we see that these have come from somewhere, or something. Either a battle, or from enduring persecution, and perhaps death. Probably from many existential situations, all of which vs. 14 describes as "**great pressure, squeezing, ordeal and tribulation**, but all from death into life.

14. **And I had spoken to him, "O, my lord, you have seen, and thus know," and so he said to me, "These are the ones continuously coming forth from out of the midst of the great pressure** (squeezing; ordeal; tribulation; oppression), **and they washed their robes** (uniforms; equipment) **and made them bright and white within the little Lamb's blood.**

The present participle, **continuously coming**, implies an ongoing process, in individual lives (each one in his or her own class – 1 Cor. 15:23), or in corporate ethnic, or community, experiences. The definite article tells us that he is speaking of a particular **pressure**, not generalized ordeals. It is "**the great tribulation**," most likely referring to the 1st century Jewish rebellion from AD 66-70. That was indeed a prolonged season of pressure and squeezing, not an instantaneous event. But the **little Lamb's blood** was sufficient to the task of cleansing. We can see an inference to this period in 3:10, above,
> "**the hour of the putting to the proof** (or: trial; test) **which is presently about to be progressively coming upon the whole territory where folks normally dwell** (or: inhabited land; = Roman Empire)." *Cf* Mat. 24:21.

Jesus forewarned His followers of this in Jn. 16:33,
> "**I have spoken these things to you so that you may continuously have** (hold; possess) **peace centered in, within the midst of and in union with Me. Within the System** (dominating and controlling world of culture, religion, economy and government; or: among and in union with the aggregate of humanity) **you normally have pressure and stress** (or: continually have squeezing; repeatedly have tribulation and oppression), **but nonetheless, be confident and take courage! I, Myself, have overcome and conquered the System** (dominating world; organized arrangement of religion and society; aggregate of humanity) **so that it stands a completed victory!**"

Furthermore, we are instructed in Acts 14:22,
> "**It continues binding and necessary for us to enter into the reign of God** (or: God's kingdom; the sovereign activities which are God) **through the midst of many pressures, squeezings, tribulations, afflictions and oppressions.**"

We again quote from Beale,
> "Bauckham notes that the saint's washing of their robes fits the narration of 'victory in a holy war, since the washing of garments was part of the ritual purification required after shedding blood (Nu. 31:19-20, 24; *cf* 19:19)'…. According to this view, 'the blood of the Lamb' refers to the saints' suffering, which is like Christ's…" (ibid p 423, with n 141).

This interpretation might relate the scene here to the aftermath of 19:11-16, below.

In the ancient world, people were prevented from approaching a god, or entering a temple, while wearing unclean garments. Isa. 64:6 says: 'We are becoming like [the] unclean, all of us, and all our cult-proscribed deeds (virtues; acts of righteousness) like a filthy rag (polluted garment); we are decaying like a leaf, all of us, and our depravities/iniquities, as a wind, carry us away)" (CVOT, Rotherham, and mine). In Ex. 19:10, Yahweh instructs Moses, "Go to the people, and you will hallow them… and they shall wash their clothes." Zech. 3:3 tells us, "Joshua was clothed in filthy garments… And He answered and spoke to those standing before him, saying, 'Take away the filthy garments from him.' And He said to him, 'See, I cause your depravity (or: guilt; iniquity) to pass from you, and will clothe you with fine outfits (rich, festal

apparel; robes of state).'" In Isa. 1:16, Yahweh says, "Wash; purge yourselves!" and in 1:18, "If your sins become like scarlet, as snow shall they be white; if they are red as crimson, as wool shall they become." Then in Ps. 51:7,
> "Expiate and cleanse me with hyssop, and I shall be clean; rinse me, and I shall be whiter than snow."

Hyssop is an allusion to Ex. 12:22, and the original Passover. It was used to apply the blood to the lintel and side posts of the doors. In Lev. 14 it was used in the cleansing rites for a leper. And Heb. 9:19 recalls that Moses,
> "**taking the blood of calves and he-goats, with water, scarlet wool and hyssop, he sprinkled both the scroll and all the People**."

This was an explanation of Heb. 9:14,
> "**to how much greater an extent shall the blood of the Christ** (Anointed One; [Messiah]) – **Who through means of a spirit** (or: attitude; [the] Breath-effect) **pertaining to the Age offers Himself** (or: brought Himself face to face and offers Himself) **without blemish by and with God** (or: in, to and for God) – **continue cleansing and pruning your conscience and shared consciousness from works of death** (or: dead procedures and activities; deeds of dead folks) **[leading] into [the situation] to be continuously rendering sacred service, as well as habitually doing the business and duties of life, for, in, by, to and with the living, as well as true and real, God?**"

So we see these two ideas of cleansing in the mixing of the metaphors of "washing" and "blood." Barclay further points us to Gen. 9:4 where the soul, or life, is equated with the blood. Then John informs us,
> "**the blood of, from, and which is Jesus, His Son, keeps continually and repeatedly cleansing us** (or: is progressively rendering us pure) **from every sin** (or: from all error, failure, deviation, mistake, and from every shot that is off target [when it occurs])" (1 Jn. 1:7).

And Paul instructs us, in Rom. 5:9,
> "**Much more, then – being NOW** (at the present time) **eschatologically delivered and rightwised** (turned in the right direction; placed in right relationships of solidarity; righted and made fair within the Way pointed out; or: justified and made free from guilt; or: = placed in covenant) **within His blood** (or: in union with the blood from, and which is, Him) – **through Him we will continue being rescued** (saved; delivered; made healthy and whole; returned to our original state and condition; kept safe), **away from the [conditions or situations of] personal emotion** (inherent fervor; natural mental bent or disposition; teeming passion and swelling desire; or: [our] anger and [human] wrath)."

Eph. 1:6b-7 explains,
> "**He graced us** (or: favors and gifts us with joyous grace) **within the One having been, and continuing being, loved** (or: in the midst of the Beloved One; or: in union with the One having been given and now expressing the essence and qualities of love; [some MSS: within His beloved Son]), **within and in union with Whom we continuously have** (constantly hold; progressively possess) **the release into freedom from slavery or imprisonment** (the liberation from our predicament) **through His blood – the sending away** (causing to flow off; forgiveness; dismissal) **of the effects and results of the fallings-aside** (the stumblings by the side; wrong steps; offences; transgressions), **in accordance with** (or: down from; corresponding to; in keeping with; to the level of; commensurate with) **the wealth of, and which is, His grace and the riches of the joy-producing act of His favor**" (or: of the favor/grace which is Him)."

Eph. 5:26-27 expands this,
> "**that He may set her apart** (separate her; consecrate and make her holy), **cleansing** (purging) **[her] by the bath of the Water [that is] within a result of a flow** (or: in union with a gush-effect; or: in the midst of a spoken word, a declaration, or an utterance), **so that He Himself could**

> place beside Himself (or: should present to and make to stand alongside in and with Himself) **an inwardly-glorious and honorable** (or: held in honor and high esteem; in-glorious-array; or: inwardly-reputable; centered-in-glory) **called-out community – [which] is continuously having neither spot** (or: stain), **nor wrinkle, nor any of such things, but to the contrary – to the end that she would continuously exist being set-apart** (holy; different from the 'ordinary and profane') **and flawless** (unblemished; or: unblamable)." *Cf* 22:14, below.

And in Col. 1 we read:
> 20. **and THROUGH Him at once to transfer the all** (the whole; = all of existential creation), **away from a certain state to the level of another which is quite different**
>> (or: to change all things, bringing movement away from being down; to reconcile all things; to change everything from estrangement and alienation to friendship and harmony and move all), **INTO Him – making** (constructing; forming; creating) **peace** (harmonious joining) **through the blood of His cross** (execution stake/pole)**: through Him, whether the things upon the earth** (or: land) **or the things within the atmospheres and heavens!**

Finally, here, let us allow Peter to fill in the picture, from 1 Pet. 1:
> 18. **having seen, and thus knowing, that you folks were not unbound and released by a ransom of corruptible things** (things that are perishable and subject to spoiling) **– by little coins of silver or gold – from out of your fruitless behavior** (vain conduct; idle and foolish way of life) **handed down by tradition from the fathers** (= your ancestors),
> 19. **but rather by Christ's precious blood** (or: in valuable blood, which is [the] Anointed One; with honorable blood of anointing; by costly blood from [the Messiah]) **– as of a flawless** (unblemished) **and spotless Lamb.**

These voices should clearly unpack the idea of "washing" our garments in Christ's blood. We find reference to this once again, in 22:14, below.

15. **"Because of this they are constantly before** (in the sight and presence of) **God's throne, and they habitually do public service to** (in; by; for) **Him, day and night, within the midst of His Temple. And the One continuously sitting upon the throne will continue pitching a tent** (spreading a covering or tabernacle) **upon them.**

This **day and night** service is an allusion to 1 Chron. 9:33, concerning the Levites:
> "they were on duty in the work by day and night."

The idea of Christ's followers being priests "for" God is a theme begun in 1:6, above, then continued in 5:10, and here. These are all allusions to Ex. 19:6,
> "As for you, you shall become Mine, a kingdom of priests and a holy nation" (CVOT).

The concept of being a priest "for" God means that we are His representatives, bringing His life to people who have not yet been existentially joined to the Lord, as a part of His anointed body. But our **public service** is **to Him**, because when we have done it to others, we have done it to Him (Mat. 25:40). We perform "in" Him, because we exist "in" Him (Acts 17:28). But our service is "by" Him, because He is the One constantly working within and among us (Phil. 2:13).

This vast multitude performs public service "within God's Temple," and they do it DAY and NIGHT. "Day and night" speaks of the realm of the earth, for it is the turning of the earth that creates day and night. So although the scene is "before God's throne," and speaks of the heavenly, or spiritual, realm, this company is serving His body (temple) which is, as Jesus was (John 3:13), in heaven and on earth at the same time. Because there is both day & night, we are given the clue that this scene takes place in time, not in the timeless realm of the spirit, or outside of the creation, or in what many call "eternity." It is in the "here and now." Terry (ibid p 339) suggests that this description is echoed in what is recorded in 11:19, below, **"the Temple of God – the one within, or in union with, the atmosphere** (or: centered in the heaven) –

was opened." There, we discern that this is indeed the new covenant temple, where the veil has been ripped away, for, "**the ark of the covenant** (or: arrangement) [other MSS read: ark of the covenant of the Lord; or: ark from God's covenant] **was seen** (or: is seen) **within the midst of His Temple**." Terry also points us to 21:22, below, where "this temple is identified with 'God the Almighty and the Lamb'."

The last clause, "**pitching a tent** (spreading a covering or tabernacle) **upon them**," shows His personal care for their needs, and the intimacy of His presence. We see a similar picture in 21:3, below, and is an allusion to Ex. 29:42-45. In Lev. 26:11-12a, Yahweh tells Israel, "I will set my tent (tabernacle) among you (in your midst), and My soul shall not loathe you, and **I will walk about** in your midst…"

The picture here may also answer to Isa. 4:4-6,
> "When Yahweh has washed away the filth of the daughters of Zion, and has rinsed out the bloodguilt of Jerusalem from within it by a spirit of judgment and by a spirit of consuming, then He will come and there will be over every site of Mount Zion and over all its common lands, a cloud by day and smoke and the brightness of a blazing fire by night. For over all, the glory will be a canopy, and a booth… for concealment from storm and from rain" (CVOT).

Terry concludes, "This mention of *throne, temple* and *tabernacle* in one verse is suggestive, and shows how all three are virtually one… [and] point out how God will dwell with men and men with God" (ibid p 340).

16.   **"They will no longer continue hungering, neither will they continue thirsting, nor may the sun repeatedly fall upon them, nor any scorching or burning heat,**

Now we see that they will not thirst. This would be because they drink of the water that He gives them:
> "**Yet whoever may** (or: would) **drink from out of the water which I, Myself, will be continuously giving to him will not repeatedly become thirsty, on into the age, but further, the water which I shall constantly give to** (or: in) **him will progressively come to be** (or: repeatedly become; continuously birth itself) **within him a spring** (or: fountain) **of water, constantly bubbling up** (continuously springing and leaping up) **into a life having the source, character and qualities of the Age** (life of and for the ages; eonian life; = the life of the Messianic age)" (Jn. 4:14).

As to their no longer hungering, they have now passed through the dealing of the Rider of the 4th seal, the Pale-horse Rider, Who killed them with hunger for God and His Word; Who brought in the famine of the hearing of the Word of the Lord. They have passed through their wilderness experience, and the burning heat of the baptism of fire, the scorching of the desert wind, as the burning of the desert sun did its work on their flesh. They were left as a valley of dry bones (Ezk. 37), with nothing of the flesh left upon them, but now they have been revived and are continuously before God's throne. They dwell with Him, within His tabernacle – and are His tabernacle – and He is continuously shepherding them and guiding them upon the springs of the waters of life (vs. 19, below). They not only drink of the water of life, but they are upon these waters, as Jesus and Peter walked upon the water, having authority over it.

This verse is an allusion to Isa. 49:10,
> "They shall not hunger nor thirst, and the parching wind or sun shall not smite them. For He Who shows them compassion shall lead them, and to founts of water shall He conduct them."

Ps. 121:5b-6 is also echoed here: "Yahweh is your Protecting Shade at your right hand; by day the sun shall not smite you, nor the moon by night" (CVOT). Such promises would have greatly encouraged those undergoing suffering from the war. We should remember that verses 16-17 are still symbols, figures representing the situation for those who are dwelling in Christ, seated with Him in the heavens (Eph. 2:6). In this realm they will not be touched by "all plague and pestilence, and such calamities as were about to come at the sound of the first four trumpets of woe (8:7-12)" (Terry, ibid p 340).

17. "**because** (or: seeing that) **the little Lamb – the One back up amidst the throne** (or: the One again in the midst of the throne) **– will continue shepherding** [other MSS: is continuously shepherding] **them, and will continue guiding** [other MSS: is continuously guiding] **them upon springs of waters of life** [other MSS: living springs of water]. **And God will continue anointing** (or: wiping and smearing) **every tear shed from out of their eyes.**" [Isa. 49:10; Jer. 2:13; Ezk. 34:23; Ps. 23:1-2; Isa. 25:8]

The need for **shepherding** suggests an earthly environment. The continual **guiding** calls to mind our present situation of being God's sons who are continually guided by His Spirit (Rom. 8:14). This setting calls to mind Ps. 23. This is not describing a life without tears, but one that is closely tended by our Shepherd. He anoints our eyes and wipes away our tears, when they come. He keeps us refreshed and hydrated by the flow of His life within us, and in our environments. This is a good place, comparable to an oasis or a Garden. Note the OT referenced in the brackets at the end of this verse. This picture is also an allusion to Ezk. 37:24-28, where a "David" will shepherd them and God will dwell with them.

This chapter is seen by some (including Malcolm Smith) to be parenthetical, being inserted between the opening of the sixth seal and the opening of the seventh (8:1, below). The 6th seal brings the signs in the heavens, with resulting effects upon the earth (Land). Similar occurrences are taken up again during the blowing of the trumpets in 8:8--9:2 (during the 1st, 3rd, 4th and 5th trumpets). This latter lends support to Smith's views that chapter 8 and the 7 trumpets begins the 3rd Vision, which, in his view, repeats the same message in a different scene and uses different figures to expand the message. He sees the half-hour of silence in 8:1 as a pause between scenes in this cosmic opera! As to whether chapter 7 is parenthetical, another view is that it may be something which happens within the opening of the 6th seal, for the next verse (which editors put as the first verse of chapter 8, although this verse could be the last verse of chapter 7) says, "**And when He opened the seventh seal, silence was birthed** (came into existence; came to be) **within the heaven as it were** (or, 'as') **half an hour.**" I wonder if this half-hour of silence is a figure (remember, we're reading a book of symbols) of "rest." Do these 7 seals correspond to the 7 days of creation? There were 6 days filled with activity, then on the 7th nothing happens. Is this the significance of the silence? Is this the entering into His rest, His Seventh Day?

Amidst all the ordeals and trials in this life, there remains the secret place:
> "The one who is dwelling in the secret place (or: the concealment) of the Most High (the Supreme) will lodge in (or: under) the shadow of the Almighty (*shaddai*, the Breasted One; Who-Suffices). I will say of Yahweh: My Refuge and my Fortress, My God in Whom I trust. For He Himself shall rescue you from the snare of the trapper; from the plague of woes (or: destructive pestilence).... A thousand may fall at your side... it shall not come close to you..." (Ps. 91:1-7)

And the witness of Jesus in Jn. 10 brings the beautiful promises which are echoed here,
11. "**I, Myself, am the Ideal Shepherd** (the Beautiful Protector of, and Provider for, the sheep). **The Ideal** (Fine; Beautiful) **Shepherd continually places His soul over the sheep** (or: habitually sets [*p45* & others: gives] His soul-life and His entire being for, and on behalf of the situation of, the sheep).
12. "**The hireling** (hired hand working for wages) **– not even being a shepherd [and] the sheep are not his own – continues attentively watching the wolf progressively coming, and proceeds to abandon the sheep and to take flight – and the wolf continues ravenously snatching them away and progressively scattering and dispersing them –**
13. "**because he is a hireling and it is not a concern to him about the sheep.**
14. "**I, Myself, am the Ideal Shepherd, and I intimately know Mine by experience, and Mine are now intimately coming to know Me by experience,**

> 15. "**just as the Father has continuous, intimate knowledge of Me, and I have continuous, intimate knowledge of the Father, and I am constantly placing My soul over the sheep.**
> 16. "**And I constantly have other sheep which do not exist** (or: are not) **from out of this fold** (or: sheep pen), **and it is binding** (or: necessary) **for Me to progressively lead those also, and they will continue listening to** (will habitually hear and pay attention to) **My voice, and they** [other MSS: it; there] **will progressively become One Flock, One Shepherd.**"

Terry notes that the wiping (literally, **anointing**) of **every tear**, not "all tears," is "more expressive and tender" – which calls to mind 1 Pet. 5:7,

> "**throwing** (or: tossing) **your entire concern** (whole worry; every anxiety) **upon Him, because He constantly cares about and takes an interest around you folks!**"

Isa. 25:8 informs us that, after swallowing up death (seen in its being tossed into the "lake, or **pond**, of **Fire** – 20:14, below), "the Lord God will wipe away tears from off all faces..." The association of swallowing up death with the wiping of tears is echoed in this same association, in 21:4, below:

> "**He will continue anointing** (or: progressively smear or repeatedly wipe away) **every tear from their eyes. And death will no longer continue existing.**"

Isa. 35:10 speaks of sorrow (or: affliction) and sighing fleeing away, after rejoicing overtakes them. These, in vss. 15-17, above, would seem to be in the same situation as those of 22:1-5, and 14, below. This theme of our present situation and final destiny continues being woven into His tapestry of the ages. Of this present chapter, Terry concludes, "If now we interpret 7:4-8 in the light of 14:1-5, and 7:9-17 in the light of what is seen in chapters 21 and 22 to constitute the new Jerusalem, we need not suppose the sealed and numbered Israelites of the first vision [above] to be excluded from the greater multitude of the second" (ibid p 341; brackets added])."

Chapter 8

1. **And when He opened the seventh seal, silence** (a hush) **was birthed** (or: occurred; came to be) **within the atmosphere** (or: heaven) **for about** (or: something like; as) **half an hour.**

From Israel's Scriptures we have the following about **silence**:
> Ex. 14:14, "Yahweh, He shall fight for you; as for you, you shall be silent." (CVOT).
> Ps. 94:17, "Were not the LORD my Help, I should soon dwell in silence." (Tanakh)
> Ps. 115:17, "The dead thank not the LORD, nor all who go to silence." (Fenton)
> Hab. 2:20, "But the LORD [is] in His holy Abode – be silent before Him all the earth!" (Tanakh)
> Ps. 62:2, "Truly my soul waits quietly for God; my deliverance comes from Him." (Tanakh)
> Zeph. 1:7, "Hush (Be silent) at the presence of My Lord, Yahweh." (Rotherham/Tanakh)
> Zech. 2:17, "Be silent, all flesh, before the LORD! For He is roused..." (Tanakh)
> Wis. of Sol., 18:13b-15a, "For whereas they would not believe anything by reason of the enchantments (magical practices), upon the destruction of the firstborn, they acknowledged this people to be a son of God. For while all things were in quiet (peaceful) silence, and that night was in the midst of her swift course, Your all-powerful Word leaped from heaven out of Your royal throne, as a stern warrior, into the midst of a land marked for destruction." (LXX)

There is also Ps. 31:18, "Let the lying lips be put to silence..." God is about to do something about them.

Matthew Henry comments that it may be "a silence of expectation." Barclay says that it might be either "a kind of breathing-space in the narrative" (ibid p 40). Perhaps this is indicating that in this realm – the Temple realm – people don't speak until they hear from the Lord:

> "**correspondingly as I am continuously hearing, I am habitually sifting, separating, evaluating and deciding** (or: judging)" (Jn. 5:30b).

"**what I hear from His side, these things I constantly speak and utter into the System** (into the world; into the ordered arrangement; or: unto the systems of control; or: to the aggregate of humanity)" (Jn. 8:26).

I appreciate the insights given to Prinzing:
> "One of the difficult tests in the life of the believer is that of 'silence,' and yet it is used of God in preparation for greater things to come. 'Be silent, O all flesh, before the Lord.' (Zech. 2:13) The more we are stripped of all flesh-works, the more inner Christ-life can find expression through us. Silence is a vital part of the in-working of redemption – it is a proving time whether we will seek for 'other voices,' or wait until He speaks to us again. A time of silence will test our ability to keep focused on Him. Thus it is also a mark that we are His: 'The sheep follow Him: for they know His voice... for they know not the voice of strangers.' (John 10:4-5) .... So purified, so becoming one with the Spirit, the soul is now silent before Him. A ceasing from all self-motion and noise. Trusting in HIS GRACE alone, to 'rest (be silent) in the Lord, and wait patiently for Him.' (Ps. 37:7) No longer [is there] the agitation of the mind, with thoughts in a turmoil, for the mind is renewed into oneness with the mind of Christ.... 'Praise waits (IS SILENT) for You, O God, in Zion.' (Ps. 65:1) The highest order of anything is to BECOME that thing — and when PRAISE is silent before the Lord, it signifies that we have BECOME HIS PRAISE, and in this state of being we stand before Him — what we are IS a praise to Him." (*Revelation, A Positive Book*, by Ray Prinzing).

Terry suggests recognizing here a rhetorical element: in 6:1, 3, 5, 7, 9, 12, 16, those preceding seal openings "were accompanied by voices... this last one is distinguished by the contrast of silence" (ibid p 343). He further points to 2 Chron. 29, the time when Hezekiah cleansed the temple and had the priests perform solemn sacrifices. Following these, the king and those with him bowed their heads, stooped down and did obeisance (likely being prostrate). This may have continued for a short time. *Cf* vss. 28-29.

But why for about "half an hour"? If this be, as some suggest, an interlude, then it is a short one. If it be a time of rest, then that too is a short one. But let us most of all keep in mind that this is a unit of "time." Even though it is "within the heaven (sky; atmosphere)," it pertains to the earth, for earth is where time exists – within His creation. In the Theodotion edition of Dan. 4:16 (LXX) we read that Daniel "was mute for about one hour, and his thoughts troubled him" (NETS). Perhaps John, being yet "in spirit" in the vision, is simply indicating that the visions stopped for this period of time, and there was a hush in this atmosphere as he awaited for what was next to come in this cosmic opera.

2. **Next I saw the seven agents** (or: messengers; or: folks with a message) **– the folks having stood and now standing before** (in the presence and sight of) **God. And seven trumpets** (or: = shofars; rams horns) **were given to them.**

This next scene – whether a part of the opening of the 7th seal, or the beginning of the next vision – is one that involves God's **agents**, His messengers. This is a transition scene which functions as an introduction to what will begin in vs. 6, below. John was shown seven agents who **were given** (the divine passive, again, meaning that God is behind this action) **seven trumpets**. The scene immediately changes, momentarily, and in vs. 3, below, we see another agent in another scene – or, in a separate part of the same vision. Let us keep in mind that this is a vision: using symbols, figures. What does each agent, or **messenger**, in this vision represent? Remember, in chapters 2 and 3, that the 7 agents (who were to receive those letters) could be identified AS BEING those 7 communities. An agent signifies one who represents, works for, and handles the power and authority of, God.

Trumpets were used in the OT days as a means of communicating a message, so here, these 7 trumpets may symbolize the fullness of the message that was coming into the Jewish world of the 1st century, through the proclamations of Christ's sent-forth representatives and messengers (the folks with THE Message). Notice that everyone who acts in this atmosphere of God's temple **stands before God**, or before His throne (symbol of authority and power). A first level of interpretation indicates that the messages of these agents concerned judgment and correction of 1st century situations in Palestine.

Israel's annual religious calendar had a Feast of Trumpets as a part of their third and final major feast, the Feast of Tabernacles (also called: Booths; Ingathering; Lev. 23:24; Nu. 29:1ff), which, interestingly, happened in the 7th month. But trumpets were also blown when Israel's encampments were to journey on (Nu. 10:8-9), as well as in "your gladness, and in your solemn days, and in the beginnings of your months... over your burnt offerings and over the sacrifices of your peace offerings" (Nu. 10:10). The blowing of a trumpet was an ongoing part of Israel's communal life. These trumpets may fit into any one or more of these aspects corresponding to daily living among His called-out communities. They announce an intention of God's Spirit, so may relate to the groups being "led" by the Spirit.

3. **Then another agent** (messenger) **came and was stationed** (or: was set; is made to stand) **upon** (or: = at) **the altar, continuously holding a golden censer. And there was given to him many incenses** (or: much incense), **so that he may give [them, or, it] by the words toward having goodness** (or: would offer [it] in the prayers; that he could impart [them] to the prayers) **of the set-apart folks** (from the holy ones), **upon the golden altar which is before the throne.** [comment: this would be in the holy place of the temple, in front of the holy of holies (within which is the ark of the covenant: = the throne)]

We saw "**another agent** (messenger)" enter the scene in 7:2, above, as well. Each agent is an actor on the stage that John is viewing. Each has his or her part to play in symbolically presenting the message. Here we see an agent who was stationed upon the altar, acting the part of an officiating priest.
> "And [Aaron] shall take a censer full of burning coals from the fire from off the altar before Yahweh, and with his hands full of sweet incense beaten small, and bring [it] within the veil. Then he shall put the incense upon the fire before Yahweh so that the cloud of the incense may cover the mercy seat that [is] upon the testimony..." (Lev. 16:12-13).

We should keep in mind, that we are now God's temple. The OT types, such as this verse just quoted, are patterns and references for the reader to be aware of the setting of the messages that were being delivered to the called-out communities in the 1st century. John was seeing something acted out that was in the temple setting, and the temple was still standing (cf 11:1ff, below) in his day. This gives us a background view of what is happening in the temple sphere and the activities of the called-out assemblies as they participate with God in both the end of the old and the beginning of the new.

The agent continues holding a golden censer. He is given many incenses – many prayers (5:8, above; in that vision it is the elders who had the bowls brimming with incenses "which are the prayers of the set-apart ones") – that he may offer these, by means of the prayers of the set-apart ones, upon the golden altar which is before the throne. Note the indirect object, "**by the words**, etc.," which expresses that the incenses were given by this instrument of "prayer." But the expansion shows other functions of the dative case: "in the prayers," or, "to the prayers" – i.e., adding fragrance to their prayers. Another possibility would be the dative of accompaniment, "with the prayers."

The setting has not changed: it is the "holy place," the location of the **golden incense-altar** within the tabernacle (or, later, the temple). It was stationed just before the ark, a figure of God's throne of mercy (Ex. 25:21-22), with the beautiful veil (with cherubim [which corresponds to the "living ones" of 4:6ff, above] hand-worked into it – Ex. 26:31ff) separating the two chambers (Ex. 30:6). *Cf* Heb. 9:1ff.

This scene may be an allusion to Amos 9:1, "I see Yahweh stationed over the altar, and He is saying, 'Smite the sphere-like capital, and the thresholds shall shake'..." Simmons suggests that the agent here, in this scene, "may represent Christ, for he would be fulfilling the role of the high priest, which prefigured Christ (Heb. 5:5; 7:26; 8:1; 9:11)" (ibid p 174). He further points out, "Since Christ is come, the types are abolished (Col. 2:16-17; Heb. 10:1)" (ibid p 175).

We suggest that this agent represents the praying aspect of the set-apart ones, the function of the body which as priests offer prayer, and praise. The phrase, here, is the same as we saw in 5:8b, above. In Ps. 141:2 we read, "May my **prayer** be established **as incense** before You; the lifting of my palms as the evening approach present." This agent represents the body of Christ in **prayer** (which literally means: a thought, word or deed having a focus toward, or an impartation of, goodness, ease and well-being to a person or situation). We are made to stand (are set, or **stationed**) **upon the altar** of incense. We are given, by the Spirit, many prayers (projections of goodness and well-being) to offer upon this altar before God, and in His presence. The smoke that ascends from this altar is a figure of the cloud of God's presence and leadership – as was the cloud of the Holy Spirit that guided Israel in the wilderness.

Our **thoughts toward having goodness, ease and well-being** (or: our prayers) are **given** to us. Recall Rom. 8:26,

> "**we have not seen, and thus do not know nor are aware of, the thing which we should think, speak or do toward having things go well unto goodness – to accord with what must be** (or: can pray commensurately to what is necessary and down from what is binding), **but rather the Spirit Himself** (the Breath-effect Itself; this Attitude itself) **from above constantly and repeatedly hits the target within us** (or: falls in on our behalf; instead of us hits within; falls in for and over us; or: makes hyper-intercession) **with unexpressed, unutterable or inexpressible groanings**
> > (or: in sighs too deep for words; with wordless and inarticulate battle cries of deep emotion; in shouts of victory from the core of His Being)."

We **continuously hold** this **golden censer**, for we are instructed by Paul to,

> "**Continuously think, speak and act with a view toward having well-being and goodness – unceasingly** (or: By habit be praying unintermittingly)" (1 Thes. 5:17).

The clause that begins, "**so that he may give**," has no direct object, so I have supplied the ellipsis with two potential options: **[them, or, it]**, i.e., either supply those praying **with** the good words, or may give the incense **by the words**. It is an awkward construction in the Greek, leaving some ambiguity. But, in this picture, note the connection between the agent with the censer and **the set-apart folks**, i.e., the covenant communities.

4. **And the smoke of the incenses ascended – by and in the prayers of the set-apart folks – from out of the agent's hand, before God** (or: in God's sight and presence).

The **smoke ascended by and in the prayers** of the called-out people. We see smoke ascending in other visions, below, for there were two altars associated with the temple. Outside the holy place, in the "outer court," was the altar concerned with sin-offerings and the cleansing offerings on the Day of Atonement. Smoke would have ascended there. This may be connected to the smoke that ascends in 14:10, below, where a cleansing and purification process is described as taking place "**in the presence of** (before; in the sight of) **the set-apart agents** (sacred folks with the message; holy messengers – corresponding to the priests, in the old covenant), **and in the presence of** (before) **the little Lamb**," i.e., in the presence of the holy place (where the agent-priests served) and the holy of holies (the throne room, where the little Lamb is seated on the Mercy Seat).

In a personal conversation, Dan Kaplan has pointed to the following statements by Paul, regarding our prayer, that should be considered as we unpack this scene of the vision:

"**By means of all thought, desire, imparted message or action toward having things be well** (or: Through every prayer) **and request regarding need, [be] folks continuously thinking, speaking and acting toward goodness and well-being** (or: praying) **within every season** (in union with every fitting situation; on every occasion; in the midst of every fertile moment) **within and in union with [the] Spirit, while maintaining a constant alertness** (or: in spirit being constantly vigilant), **also, to that end, in all focus to unremitting and stout continuance** (or: in union with every view to resolute, potent perseverance which brings control) **and request regarding need concerning** (or: surrounding) **all of the set-apart folks** (holy ones)" (Eph. 6:18).

"**Do not be habitually worried, anxious or overly concerned about anything! On the contrary, in everything by thinking and speaking toward having goodness and having things go well and with ease** (or: in prayer) **and in expression of need – together with thanksgiving – repeatedly let your requests be made known to God**" (Phil. 4:6).

"**Consequently I am habitually calling you alongside to encourage, counsel and exhort you to first of all be constantly making petitions for needs, speaking, thinking and doing toward things being well, encounters** (or: intercessions; meetings within situations to converse or hit and obtain the objective), **[and] expressions of gratitude** (or: of the goodness of grace) **over** (or: on behalf of) **all humans** (mankind) **– over** (or: for) **kings and all those being folks within a position of holding control over [others]** (or: being in superiority or high station), **to the end that we may continuously lead** (or: carry through) **a course of life that is still – at rest** (free from all agitation or disturbance with tranquility arising from without), **and also quiet – peaceable, in all reverence** (devout relations with everything) **and majestic seriousness** (dignity which inspires awe). **This [is] beautiful** (ideal) **and welcomingly received from the presence of, and in the sight of, God, our Deliverer** (our Savior; the One Who heals us, makes us whole and keeps us safe) **Who is constantly willing** (intending; purposing) **all humans to be saved** (delivered; made whole), **and** (or: even) **to come into a full, accurate, experiential and intimate knowledge and insight of Truth** (or: a complete realization of reality)" (1 Tim. 2:1-4).

These **prayers of the set-apart folks** are an integral part of "the Temple of God" and its service to and for people, and in this present scene the incense altar and the action of the agent are a symbol of the called-out communities. It is not only the "temple" that is a figure of the body of Christ, but the furniture within the temple speaks to various functions of the body. Consider the altar of burnt offerings, just outside the tabernacle in the outer court, where the bodies of animals were burned. Ex. 27:1-2 informs us that it was made of wood that was overlaid with bronze. The boards and bars that formed the walls of the tabernacle were also made of wood, then the boards were overlaid with gold (Ex. 26:26-29). Kaplan reminds us that "wood," in the OT types," is a figure of humanity. The gold is a figure of God's spirit overlaying (or, coming upon) a person, making him or her a part of the tabernacle/temple. The bronze was a figure of God's judgment which caused the offering (figure of the people) to ascend to God via the smoke (i.e., the flesh is transformed into spirit).

Both the olive tree and the fig tree were figures of Israel, just as was the vine. Ps. 1:3, "he shall be like a tree," is a typical example. The tree of life is a well-accepted symbol of Christ (the Christ being a human that is "anointed" with God's Spirit). Putting these symbols together, Kaplan pointed out that the fire on the altar of burnt offerings was a wood fire which burned down into coals. It was these coals that were brought into the tabernacle/temple and put onto the altar of incense, upon which the incenses were placed to make the incense rise in smoke, symbolizing the prayers of the people. All is connected.

The wood, being a figure of our first-Adam humanity, is burned up on the bronze altar, which is a figure of the place of Christ's sacrifice, and His being hung on the cross (a pole; a tree – on wood; on us) was a figure of His death and His blood covering us, taking our "dead (carnal)" humanity to the grave, then raising us up in Him as the corporate, last Adam – the second Humanity (1Cor. 15:44-48). Another symbol seen in the cross and wood is that what is burned up is the tree of the knowledge of good and evil, which brought death. [Mat. 3:10, "**the ax is already continuing lying [focused] toward the root of the trees**."] Its death, in the sin offering, brought an end to the death that its fruit had brought to Adam and Eve. The wood being burned, a figure of the cross, "is the beginning of the lake of fire" (Kaplan). But keep in mind the words of Jesus, on the cross,
> "**O Father, let it flow away in them** (or: send it away for them; forgive them), **for they have not seen, so they do not know or perceive, what they are now doing**" (Lu. 23:34).

The **agent's hand** is mentioned because he is holding the censer, but also because the hand speaks of actions, deeds and works that we are given to do, for we are,
> "**people being founded from a state of disorder and wildness** (being framed, built, settled and created; being changed from chaos to order), **within and in union with Christ Jesus; [founded and built] upon good works** (virtuous actions; excellent deeds) **which God made ready** (prepared; or: prepares) **beforehand, to the end that we may, could, should and would walk about** (= live our lives) **centered within and in union with them**" (Eph. 2:10b).

5. **Then the agent had taken the censer and filled it full out of the fire of the altar, and he threw [fire; or, the censer] into the Land** (or: earth; soil). **And thunders and sounds** (or: voices) **and lightnings and shakings birthed themselves** (or: of themselves came into being).

This may be an allusion to Ezk. 38:19,
> "My rushing emotion and My burning zeal shall ascend (step back up, again, and arise). In a fire of My inherent fervor and engorged passion I speak and proclaim: Surely, in that Day, there will proceed being a great shaking upon the Land of Israel" (LXX, JM).

So fire may simply represent the fervor and passion of God to correct and transform us. He comes to end one old, worn-out world, and to create a new one from the ashes, with "glory in place of ashes" (Isa. 61:3, LXX).

Here we see that the agent (His sons; His body) had taken the censer and filled it full out of the Fire (a symbol of God) of the altar. As our God is a consuming fire, these embers energize their prayers from filling their vessels with the burning presence and being of God Himself. These prayers (for His kingdom to come, for His will to be done on earth) are cast, or **thrown**, **into the Land** (the earth: the realm which is to be ruled by heaven; in the 1st century, this Land was Judea). The **thunders**, voices (or, **sounds**) and **lightnings** and **shakings** are a figure of the power, presence, Word, illumination, and activity of God, and here are a fourfold sign that indicates that it is time for the judgments to commence, that the agents with the trumpets should proceed. These may be an allusion to Ps. 77:18-20, which is a remembrance of Israel's exodus. Again, keep in mind the end of the old, the beginning of the new.

These sounds break the half-hour of silence. Once again we see an echo of the scene of God's presence manifested at Mt. Sinai. In David's Psalm of Thanksgiving (2 Sam. 22:15) lightning is used as a figure for God troubling and routing the enemy. In Ezk. 1:13, lightning came from out of the fire which moved among the living creatures (figures of the body of Christ, in Ezekiel's vision). Here it is His agent (the body) which He uses to express Himself. The signs of His presence, etc., accompany these fire-empowered prayers which they throw into the Land.

Another interesting point is that "in the Temple incense was burned and offered before the first and after the last sacrifices of the day" (Barclay, ibid p 40). Is this characteristic of the "Day of the Lord"? Barclay further points out that this picture is similar to the vision in Ezk. 10:2, "in which the man in the linen-cloth takes coals from between the cherubim and scatters them over the city." Simmons suggests that, "The phenomena that follow [the action of the agent] serve to underscore the divine origin and nature of the judgments thus visited upon the Jews…" (ibid p 175; brackets added). Beale sees here an allusion to Sinai (which is also referenced in Heb. 12:18-21). That was the time of Israel's creation as a nation. The lightning and earthquake encountered at Sinai thus become "creation" imagery. The prayers of the saints – speaking goodness (as an echo of the "good" recorded in Gen. 1) – contribute goodness into God's new creation in Christ. But the new creation began with the destruction of the old, which began with the death and burial of the Messiah, Who took the old covenant to the grave, and as Israel's representative, also took Israel to the grave. The action of the agent, here in vs. 5, shows that the destruction of the old began from within the Temple. Peter spoke of this:

> "**because [it is; this is; now is] the** [other MSS: a] **fitting situation and fertile moment of the appointed season for the result of the judgment** (the effect of the separating for evaluation and decision) **to begin** (to start) **from God's house**" (1 Pet. 4:17a).

The "**censer filled full of the fire of the altar, and thrown into the Land**" is a symbolic act of what will begin in vs. 7, below. The action here, with the censer, is within the "holy place," within the Temple. Beale may be right that vss. 3-5, here, serves as "an 'interlocking' function" which joins the conclusion of the seals, above, with the trumpets, below, serving as an introduction to the latter. (ibid).

Ex. 3:7-9 may be a background for the following trumpets, and may provide a response to the request of 6:9-11, above. In that OT passage, we read:

> "And Yahweh said: I see – completely see – the humiliation of My people who are in Egypt [the Roman Empire, in the 1st century], and I hear their crying… for I know their pains. I have descended to rescue them from the hand of Egypt [both Rome, and Jerusalem – 11:8, below]…. A cry of Israel's sons! It has come to Me, and indeed, I have seen the oppression with which Egypt [now Rome/Jerusalem] has been oppressing them" (CVOT; modified; brackets added).

This, in the Unveiling, would be an example of the NT using the historical of the OT to speak of the historical of the 1st century, while at the same time presenting a timeless message against all domination systems, including those strongholds within our minds and spirits. Jesus said that He was fulfilling Isa. 61:1b-2a,

> "**to publicly proclaim, as a herald, to** (for; among) **captives a release and liberation** (a letting go away) **and to** (for; among) **blind folks a seeing again** (a recovery of sight), **to send away with a mission those having been shattered by oppression, in a state of release and liberation, to publicly and loudly proclaim [the] Lord's** [= Yahweh's] **year which is characterized by being welcomed, favorably received and approved…!**" (Lu. 4:18b-19).

Isa. 61:2b would be fulfilled later, but in that same generation (Lu. 21:22, cf the context, there).

6. **Next the seven agents** (or: messengers) **– the folks holding the seven trumpets – prepared themselves** (made themselves ready), **so that they may sound the trumpets.**

The sounding of these **7 trumpets** comprises the rest of this chapter and on through chapter 9. We will see that just like the opening of the 7 seals, the first four trumpets form a group, with the last three being different. The message of the 7 trumpets is essentially the same as the message of the 7 shallow bowls that will be seen in chapter 16, below. As we approach these scenes, we should keep in mind Jesus' words in Lu. 21:25-26,

> "**Also, there will keep on being signs: in sun and moon and stars** [comment: a figure of a disruption of father, mother and brothers, i.e., social organization and leadership – Gen. 37:9-10], **and upon the Land** [comment: of Israel?] (or: earth; ground; soil)**: a constraint from [the] non-Jews** (or: with a character pagans; which is nations) **in the midst of a perplexity in which there seems no way out – [like being in the] roar and surging of a sea – pertaining to humans progressively breathing away and cooling off** (= fainting, or dying) **from fear and apprehension** (thoughts about what is going to happen) **pertaining to the things progressively coming upon the homeland** (the place being inhabited) **– for you see,**
>> **'the abilities of the heavens** (or: the powers of the sky and atmosphere; [note: may = folks normally in charge of things]) **will be progressively shaken.'**" [Hag. 2:6, 21]

Terry (ibid p 346) reminds us that the fall of Jericho involved 7 priests blowing 7 ram's horns (Josh. 6:4, 6, 20).

Next, John noted that **the seven agents** (messengers) **prepared themselves** to sound forth their messages. In God's program there is always preparation needed. The types in the sacrifices and worship portrayed in the Law attest to this. There was even designated a "Day of Preparation" before the festival of Passover. Were this not important, it would not have been necessary to include this fact in order to give the message of this scene.

Characteristic of this book, there are seven agents. Remember, 7 is an idea. This book is a complete message: from Alpha to Omega. Each agent, or messenger, gives a specific aspect of the message of this vision. Each one has his own message, but each is but a part of the whole. Ezekiel 33:3 points out that Israel sometimes had watchmen on their walls so that,

> "when he sees the sword come upon the Land, he [shall] blow the trumpet and warn the people."

And apropos to our scene here is Amos 3:6,

> "Shall a trumpet be blown in the city, and the people not be afraid? Shall there be evil in a city, and Yahweh have not done it?"

A trumpet's use as a warning is seen in Hos. 5:7-10. And Joel 2:1ff is another classic warning:

> "Blow the trumpet in Zion! And raise a shout [of alarm] in My holy mountain!.... For coming is the day of Yahweh! For it is near! A day of darkness and gloominess, a day of cloud and murkiness..." (CVOT).

7. And so the first one sounded a trumpet. Then hail and fire mixed in blood was birthed (came to be; or: hail and fire came to be mixed with blood), **and it was thrown into the Land** (earth; soil). **And the third of the trees was burned down, and all pale-green pasture** (or: grass) **was burned down.**

The vision begins (vs. 2-3, above) by "entering His gates with thanksgiving and His courts with praise" (Ps. 100:4). Next the burning prayers are thrown **into the Land** (vs. 5a), a symbol of beginning the vision of the trumpets. Now when **the first** agent **sounds** forth his message [recall that a trumpet was used as a means of communicating a message; see comments on vs. 2, above] the result is that **hail and fire mixed in blood is thrown into the Land**, answering to 5a. This is reminiscent of the "miraculous signs" of God in Ex. 10:1. Perhaps this is a description of the ministry of the two witnesses as described in chapter 11, below, where in vs. 6 one characteristic of their ministry echoes the plagues brought upon the land of Egypt through God's agent, Moses. These seven messages may be an amplification of that ministry, set in the conjunction of the ages (the Christ event and Jerusalem's destruction, in the 1st century). There may also be an allusion to Isa. 28:17, "And I will make [right] judgment... Then hail will scoop away the refuge of [the] lie" (CVOT). Here Eby comments on God's personal corrections within us:

"He will send the *hailstorms* into our lives to beat down and destroy all the refuge of lies, all the false messages, doctrines, opinions, ways, and every false thing in which we trust and every tree and all the grass that grows out of our carnal mind and earthy nature!" (ibid, pt 106).

As to the **fire**, Eby observes: "The New Testament manifestation of God as a consuming fire began on the day of Pentecost when tongues of fire rested upon the waiting disciples" (ibid).

Notice here that part (**the third**) of **the trees** and **all pale-green pasture** were destroyed: an echo of the plagues in Egypt (Ex. 9:23-26). There we saw "**hail and fire mixed**," but here is an addition of **blood**. This may speak to the beginning of God's work: Passover – judgement upon the world (figure of the flesh nature and of domination systems) and deliverance of God's people (our personal experience of Passover; the corporate deliverance of humanity through Christ's death and resurrection). The addition of **blood** in this present picture may be a combining of the 7th plague with the last, in Egypt's context. Simmons cites Josephus (*Wars of the Jews*, III, 4.1, Whiston ed.) who describes the literal fires and blood, where, "Galilee was all over filled with fire and blood" (ibid p 177). But Eby brings out another layer of interpretation. Since the LIFE is in the **blood**, "God mingles *His life* with His *purifying fire* so that we are not destroyed, just changed and transformed!" (ibid).

What is the significance of **the trees**? Many OT allusions could be cited. In Ps. 1 a tree is used for a metaphor of a person. Both the fig tree and the olive tree were used of figures of Israel. Ezk. 17 employs the cedar tree as a metaphor for God's judgment upon Zedekiah, prior to Jerusalem's invasion by Babylon. The last verse of that chapter concludes:
> "And all the trees of the field shall know that I, Yahweh, have brought down the high tree, have exalted the low tree; have dried up the green tree, and have made the dry tree to flourish."

Like the rich man in the parable with Lazarus (Lu. 16), Jerusalem suffered a reversal of positions in Israel's ancient history. This would happen again in AD 70. But there is also a personal application, for, once again, as Eby points out: "TREES represent those deeply rooted things that grow out of our human nature" (ibid). *Cf* Jude 12: "**These folks are… wasted autumnal trees – unfruitful, twice-died, uprooted.**" In Mat. 12:33, Jesus said,
> "**You folks either make the tree ideal** (fine and beautiful), **and thus its fruit ideal** (fine and beautiful), **or make the tree rotten, and its fruit [will be] rotten** (decayed). **You see, the tree is habitually being known and experienced from out of the [or: its] fruit.**"

He was speaking about people. So in this trumpet, the message is about judgment of people: many fig trees and olive trees would be **burned**, or branches of "the olive tree" would be broken out (Rom. 11:17).

What about "**all pale-green pasture** (or: grass)"? Perhaps 1 Pet. 1:24 gives us a clue:
> "**All flesh [is] like grass** (or: vegetation), **and all its glory [is] like a flower of grass** (of vegetation): **the grass is caused to dry out and wither, and the flower falls off…**" *Cf* Isa. 40:6

This allusion may be to the "flesh" nature of humans, or to the minding of the flesh realm (Rom. 8:6-7). Once again Eby adds light to this symbol: "GRASS represents those surface coverings and masks in our lives which hide the nature beneath from being seen for what it is…. When the fleshly mindset that governed our view of ourselves and our actions has been burnt up by the fire of the Spirit, the wonderful work of God has begun to bring forth the life of the Son of God as our *only reality!*" (ibid).

Hail and a storm wind were symbolic elements of judgment against the work of false prophets, in Ezk. 13:10-16. Fire was an element in the prophecy of Amos 7:4, and in Joel 1:19 we read,
> "O Yahweh, to You will I cry, for the fire has devoured the pastures of the wilderness and the flame has burned all the trees of the field."

But in our present passage, it is not so bad, for the fractions (here "the third") that we will see speak to God's mercy in judgment, and how He always left a remnant to carry on and be the seed of the next phase of His plans.

The "hail with fire [lightning?] flashing in the midst of it" which Yahweh "rained over the land," was the 7th plague in Egypt. It "smote all herbage in the field," even breaking the branches of the trees (Ex. 9:22, 25), which would have meant that it would have ruined the crops. Might the prophetic message of this trumpet have been, "harvest the crop, before this storm comes"? Might it mean that the coming judgment which culminated in AD 70 was the "night" (a figure of the coming "storm") to which Jesus referred in Jn. 9:4?

> "**It is constantly necessary** (or: binding) **for Me** [other MSS: us] **to be habitually performing the works** (accomplishing the deeds; active in the acts; doing the business) **of the One sending Me** [other MSS: us] **while it is day; night** (or: a night; = darkness; cf Gen. 1:5) **progressively** (repeatedly; habitually) **comes, when no one is able** (or: has power) **to continue performing work** (accomplishing deeds; doing business)."

He also said,

> "**On the one hand, the harvest [is] much** (or: vast; = it is a very good crop); **on the other hand, the workers are few. Therefore, at once urgently ask** (or: beg) **the Owner** (or: Lord; Master) **of the harvest so that He would** (or: should) **put out workers into His harvest**" (Lu. 10:2).

In 7:1, 3, above, the winds were to come against the Land (Israel) and the sea (the rest of humanity in the target area). Here, and in vs. 8, below, we see the Land and the sea targeted in this second view of that which was involved in the breaking of the 7 seals. Note the three normally-associated objects grouped together: here (land, trees, grass), and the three associated objects grouped together in vs. 9, below, (sea, sea creatures, ships). Cf Terry, ibid p 347. These are representative of the respective worlds of both the Jews (the land elements) and the rest of the population in the Empire (the sea elements). It would have likely been the case of the Roman army to have traveled to Palestine by sea, in ships.

8. And then the second agent trumpeted. Then something like a great mountain, continuously being burned in fire, was thrown into the sea. And the third of the sea came to be blood.

This is the second message. A figure of **a great mountain continuously burning with fire**. This figure has had opposing interpretations. Smith sees this as a symbol of the kingdom of God being plunged into the sea of humanity: a picture of the main message of this Unveiling – The little Lamb rules! Perhaps there is merit to this view. The allusion may be to the Stone that became a great Mountain that filled the earth (Dan. 2:34-35, explained in vss. 44-45 as being God's kingdom) and consumed the land's domination systems. The **third of the sea** becoming **blood** speaks to another of the signs in Egypt, and Egypt (an example of "the sea," i.e., the non-Israelite nations) was a domination system and answers to Rome, in the 1st century.

The opposing view is that this mountain is an allusion to Babylon (another captor of God's people) and that this scene is a reference to Jer. 51, the judgment of Babylon, and specifically vs. 25,

> "Behold, says Yahweh, 'I [am] against you, O destroying mountain, which destroys all the Land. I will stretch out My hand upon you, and then roll you down from the rocks and will make you a burnt-out mountain."

In 18:21, below, we read,

> "**And then, one strong agent lifts** (took up; carried away) **a stone as great as a millstone, and casts** (or: cast) **[it] into the sea, saying,**
>> "**Thus, by violence** (or: impetuous motion) **Babylon the Great City will be cast** (thrown) **and can by no means any longer be found** (or: be yet found)."

We read in Isa. 57:20, "the wicked [are] like the troubled sea, when it cannot rest, whose waters cast up mire (foulness) and mud." Jude refers to the "**dreaming ones** (folks continuing in sleep, or with imaginary experiences)" of verse 8 as, "**wild waves of the sea, continuously foaming out** (or: vomiting forth) **their shames** (or: disgraces)," in vs. 13. Another reference is Zech. 4:7, "What are you, great mountain? Before Zerubbabel you are to be a level plain." (CVOT).

Mountains in the Scriptures speak of kingdoms. Mount Zion was a frequent reference to first Israel, as a unified people, then later to the southern kingdom of Judea. The phrase "the mountain of Samaria" was an expression used to signify the northern kingdom of Israel (e.g., Amos 6:1). The "mount of Esau" was a designation for the kingdom of Edom (Oba. 8). The poetic imagery of Isa. 2:14 speaks of the Day of Yahweh being, "upon all the high mountains, and upon all the hills [that are] lifted up."

Perhaps it was this mountain that Jesus spoke of in Mat. 21:21 where He said,
> "**you can also say to this mountain range** (or: hill country; mountain), '**Be uplifted, and then be flung** (cast) **into the midst of the lake** (or: **sea**)!' **It will progressively come to pass** (It will proceed in birthing itself and happening)."

Was this mountain perhaps Jerusalem (Mount Zion), and the "kingdom" of the Jews? AD 70 brought it down, and the Jews were dispersed into the nations (figured by the sea). The third of the sea becoming blood could also be a figure of the deaths from the Jewish rebellion that was crushed by Rome.

Does the **sea** turned to **blood** also symbolize the fact that humanity must drink His blood (John 6:55-56)? Was this an allusion to the deaths in Egypt, and the Red Sea, during Israel's exodus? The great mountain may also look back into Israel's history,
> "The horse and its rider He has thrown into the sea" (Ex. 15:1) *Cf* Ex. 15:19.

The allusion to Moses, Aaron and the plagues is seen in Ex. 7:20-25, where the river was turned to blood, and "there was blood throughout all the land of Egypt" (vs. 21b).

The sea speaks of humanity (*cf*, above: 4:6; 5:13 comments). So whichever kingdom this represents, it is cast into humanity. That the 3rd of the sea came to be blood seems a reference to the plagues in Egypt, so I would conclude that this speaks of a judgment on mankind which will work into the good (deliverance) for God's people. His kingdom coming into humanity would do this. The fall of Babylon would also fit this scene. This could obviously prefigure the fall of Jerusalem and the blood which flowed there.

9. **And the third of the creatures within the sea – the ones** (or: things) **having souls – died. And the third of the ships was thoroughly ruined** (decayed; destroyed).

The allusion is to Ex. 7:21a, "And the fish that was in the river died, and the river stank." What do the **creatures within the sea** represent? In Gen. 1:21 we see, "And creating is the Elohim (God) great monsters and every living moving SOUL, with which the water roams .... and blessing them is the Elohim, saying, 'Be fruitful and increase and fill the water of the seas'" (CVOT). Here in vs. 9 it is specified that the third of the ones **having souls** are the ones in the sea that **died**. Is He speaking of fish, dolphins, etc.? If He were, do these have souls? Yes, see Gen 1:20 (in the Heb.). Or is the specification of "having souls" a key to tell us that He is speaking of people, because this is symbolic, not literal? Recall that Jesus used the metaphor of fishing in reference to capturing people for the kingdom (Mat. 4:19). People were also figured as "fish" in Jer. 16:16. The death of **the third** of **the sea creatures** is also figurative – remember, this is an apocalypse. In the Jewish wars, many of the Roman army would also have died. But on the interior level, this death may speak of those who were existentially taken into

Christ's death (Rom. 6:3-6). Does this speak of their being "**freed from sin**" (Rom. 6:7)? If the burning mountain of vs. 8 refers to the Fire of His reign, then these results might be seen as good.

That some of **the ships** were ruined would speak of the means of transportation used on the sea. It would affect their means of commerce. It would limit their ability to escape or to be about the things one does on the sea – meaning that their lives and way of life would be impacted. God invading our lives can have disastrous outward effects, in order to bring inner Life. That some would die could symbolize their no longer being a part of, or involved in, the world figured by "**the sea**." In using the figure of **the sea**, it would seem that this is speaking of those not at that time considered to be in "the called-out communities," or God's firstfruits. The thrusting of the burning kingdom into humanity is having direct results. If the messages of these trumpets are associated with the pattern of Israel in relation to Egypt, then later to the nations encountered on their journeys and the entering of Canaan, could this burning mountain be a figure of the kingdom of Israel as it was taken from Egypt and cast into the nations? They sure had an effect upon those nations and their ways of life. His Fire definitely impacts us. This final clause may prefigure the effects involving **ships** in the fall of Babylon, in 18:17-19, below.

10. **Next the third agent sounded a trumpet. And a great star, continuously burning as a lamp** (or: a shining one), **fell out of the sky** (or: heaven), **and it fell upon the third of the rivers and upon the springs of the waters.**

Now the third message is given to John. Here we see **a great star**. It is continuously burning as a lamp (or, a shining one). It **fell out of the sky**, or, heaven. Coming from "heaven" would mean that it came from the realm of God in His ruling as King, but vs. 11 informs us that it comes in judgment. It fell upon part of the **rivers** and **springs**. The OT background for this picture begins with Ex. 7:19,
> "Then Yahweh said to Moses: 'Say to Aaron [notice: he later became a tabernacle agent], Take your rod, and stretch out your hand over the waters of Egypt, over their streams, over their waterways, over their ponds and over every confluence of their waters...'" (CVOT).

Ps. 78:43-44, recalls this incident from their history,
> "He had worked His signs in Egypt... and had turned their rivers into blood; and their floods so that they could not drink."

4 Ezra 6:19-24 contains similar imagery to our present context:
> "when the **humiliation of Zion** is complete, and when the seal is placed upon the age which is about to pass away... the trumpet shall sound.... And the springs of fountains shall stand still..." (*The OT Pseudepigrapha*, Vol. 1, ibid p 535).

The rivers and springs were sources of life, in the Land. Eby speaks of the significance of springs and fountains in the symbology here:
> "The 'fountains of waters' represent the *sources* of the ideas, concepts, philosophies, teachings, precepts, creeds, doctrines, traditions, ideologies, observances, customs, laws — all the intellectual, moral, political, and religious influences of *this world* which are the sources from which men draw their life, their natural joy and refreshment, their ways of thinking, their image of themselves, their understanding of the world, their vocations, life-styles, their hopes, dreams, and ambitions, and their relationships" (ibid, pt 108; emphasis original).

Verse 11, below, shows that folks drank from these **waters**. This judgment may be symbolic of its coming against the life of Israel, and may be an allusion to Yahweh's judgment in Amos 6, because in 6:12b He makes this accusation:
> "You have turned the sentence of justice into poison, and the fruit of righteousness (i.e., that which is right) into wormwood."

In place of the metaphorical rivers of Israel that had become polluted, we find in 22:1, below,
> "**a river of 'water of, and from, life'** (or: Life's water; or: water which is Life), **bright** (resplendent, glistening, clear, sparkling) **as crystal** (clear ice), **continuously flowing** (issuing) **forth from out of God's – even the little Lamb's – throne**."

This is an allusion to Ezk. 47:1-12,
> "water coming forth from under the sill of the House [=Temple].... a torrent which could not be crossed.... It will come to be that every living soul that swarms wherever the watercourse is coming shall live.... along its shore... every food tree... for its waters are they which go forth from the Sanctuary; its fruit will be for food and its leaf for healing."

After the cleansing out of the polluted, He makes all things new (21:5, below). Having the end in view aids us in understanding the journey.

Terry suggests that, "The star in this plague served the same purpose as the burning mountain in the previous plague" (ibid p 347). Simmons (ibid p 181) reminds us that, "Stars are symbolic of governmental leaders and powers," citing Isa. 14:12, in the proverb against the king of Babylon, and then points us to Joseph's dream of the stars symbolizing his brothers who became the leaders of the 12 tribes of Israel (Gen. 37:9-10). Dan. 8:10 is another example of stars used in apocalyptic literature.

11. Now the name of the star is called Wormwood (or: Absinth). **And so the third of the waters are being birthed** (or: are coming to be) **wormwood. Then many of the people died from out of the waters, because they were embittered** (made bitter).

Wormwood first appears in Deut. 29:18 in a warning against idolatry where Moses ends the verse,
> "[beware] lest there should be among you a root being fruitful with poison and wormwood."

In Prov. 5:4, the warning against "a strange woman" (a euphemism for a prostitute) may fit the context of the judgment of Mystery Babylon, below. This wisdom text says of such a woman, "her end is bitter as wormwood."

In Jer. 9:11 Yahweh says, "I will make Jerusalem heaps... and the cities of Judah desolate." Then in vs. 13-14 His accusation is that "they have forsaken My Law... walked after the imagination of their own heart, and after Baalim." So, God says, in vs. 15, "I will feed them – THIS People – with wormwood and give them poisoned water to drink." Jeremiah 23:14-15 is significant because of the promised judgment of wormwood, and the fact that Yahweh compares the prophets of Jerusalem to Sodom (*cf* 11:8, below).
> "But among the prophets of Jerusalem I see a horrible [thing]: adultery and walking in falsehood. They reinforce the hands of evildoers... to Me they have become like Sodom.... I shall feed them wormwood, and I will give them poisoned water to drink, for from the prophets of Jerusalem pollution has gone forth to the entire Land" (CVOT).

The OT references should enlighten the metaphor of verse 11.

Here, the drinking waters of the Land become what the star is: absinth or wormwood (bitterness). What had once quenched the thirst of the Jews (i.e., the Law) had now been made bitter and caused death. What they must now turn to is Christ, the source of the water of Life. But, as we read in 22:17, below,
> "**And now the Spirit and the Bride are continuously saying, 'Be repeatedly coming!' Then let the one continuing to listen and hear say, 'Be continuously coming!' And so let the person constantly thirsting continuously come; let the one habitually willing at once receive Water of Life freely**"
>> (or: "And so the Breath-effect and the Bride are constantly laying it out: 'Be progressively going!' Also, let the now hearing say, 'Be progressively going!' Then, let the one

repeatedly being thirsty habitually come and go. Let the person desiring and intending take the Water from Life for a free gift [to others]").

This call goes out to all; this commission is for all His followers! The psalmist put it this way:

"A river! – whose channels (or: canals) shall gladden the City of God…" (Ps. 46:4a; Rotherham).

If we can reconstruct the scene which John saw, I suspect that he saw what we would call a meteorite, fall from the sky and land upon the springs and rivers – but let us further investigate its meaning. Recall the journey of Israel after they had passed through the sea and went three days into the wilderness and came to Marah (bitterness). They had found no other water, but the waters at Marah were too bitter to drink. The solution was: "Yahweh directed him (Moses) to a tree. So he flung it into the waters, and the waters were sweet. There He made for them a statute and a judgment, and there He probed them …" (Ex.15:22-26, CVOT). The Tree (the Cross of Christ; the tree of Life) turns our bitterness into sweetness!

The communities to which this letter was written would have remembered this story and would have made the association. Israel's next step is recorded in Ex. 15:27, "Then they came to Elim; there were 12 springs of water and 70 palms there. So they encamped there by the waters." The message is clear: although the heavens decree and send down bitterness into that from which we draw our life and refreshing, we should turn to the cross. He will then move us to the life and refreshing of the whole household of God (figured by the 12 tribes) and sustain us with fullness of prosperity (7X10 palms) and sustenance. Bitterness of heart or soul can bring death to spirit, soul, and eventually to the body. This is true of a community, or, corporate body, as well.

Remember that a star is an agent, or messenger (1:20, above). This one comes from heaven – the realm of the Spirit – to bring a negative situation into the lives of mankind. But remember the lesson of Ex. 15. The bitterness need not be the end. Absinth (wormwood) is an herb (related to sagebrush) that is very bitter. That the star is named Wormwood signifies the quality or character of its message and dealing:

"Bitter as the wormwood might be that is used to purge out the error of tradition, carnal concepts, the false self-image, etc., yet when He has finished this tremendous judgment, 'The earth shall be filled with the knowledge of the glory of the Lord, as the waters cover the sea' (Hab. 2:14). God has appointed HIS CLEANSING AGENTS and they shall be most effective in their working, and though bringing death to the old, it also bespeaks of the preparation for the birthing of the new" (Prinzing, ibid)

Terry observes, "The star in this plague served the same purpose as the burning mountain in the previous plague" (ibid p 347).

12. **And the fourth agent trumpeted. So the third of the sun and the third of the moon, and the third of the stars were struck** (or: received a blow, or plague), **to the end that the third of them may be darkened, and the day may not shine [for] the third of it – and the night in like manner.**

This brings the 4th message. The **third of the sun, moon** and **stars** were **darkened**. Part of the day and part of the night are not allowed to shine, to have light. This would seem to parallel the opening of the 6th seal (6:12, 13, above). Once again we see the things that govern their lives, the things that give light and instruction and guidance, come under restraints. For the people of God, there come times and dealings from God where faith and hope must carry us through dark nights of the soul and situations where we can see nothing.

Isa. 24 speaks of judgments upon the Land of Israel: verse 19 describes the Land as "utterly broken down, completely dissolved and exceedingly moved – all of which sounds a lot like our Unveiling. In vs. 23, "The moonbeams will be abashed, and the sunshine will be ashamed, for Yahweh of hosts will reign in Mount Zion and in Jerusalem, and in front of His elders will He be glorified" (CVOT). The picture is of the previous world and life that were diminished, when Yahweh's reign (in the 1st century, Christ's reign) came into the Land. Note the fraction that was affected: one **third**. It came on gradually, in those days. This was the proclamation of John the baptizer, Jesus and Paul – and it is what we have seen, here, in these visions.

Isa. 13 is a pronouncement against Babylon. In vss. 10-11 we have,
> "The stars and constellations of heaven shall not give off their light; the sun shall be dark when it rises, and the moon shall diffuse no glow. And I will requite to the wicked their iniquity; I will put an end to the pride of the arrogant and humble the haughtiness of tyrants."

Jesus prophesied about His generation, which would bring an end to the old world of Israel (which took place in AD 70), saying,
> "**Now immediately after the pressure** (constriction; tribulation) **of those [particular] days, 'the sun will be progressively made dark and the moon will not continue giving its** (or: her) **diffused radiance,'** [Isa. 13:10; Ezk. 32:7; Joel 2:10] **and then the stars will, one after another, be falling from the sky** (or: heaven) **– 'and so, the powers and abilities of the heavens will be progressively shaken** (agitated; stirred up; made to rock so as to be ready to fall).'" (Mat. 24:29; *cf* Isa. 34:4; Hag. 2:6, 21; Lu. 21:25).

Mark 13:29-30 quotes Jesus concluding the above quote by saying,
> "**Thus also, whenever you folks, yourselves, should see these things progressively occurring** (happening; coming into existence), **you will continue knowing from experience that it** (or: He) **progresses to be near – upon** (or: at) **the gates** (or: doors; entrances)! **Truly I am now saying to you folks that this generation may under no circumstances pass on by until which [time; situation] all these things should come to be** (occur; happen; be birthed)."

The literal fulfillment of the Unveiling's visions pertained to, and happened in, AD 66-70. It is the spiritual interpretations of these metaphors that have spoken to Christianity ever since that period. Here, Prinzing adds light:
> "and with the extinguishing of earth's lights, comes the forth-shining of God's luminaries of the new creation order. HE IS 'the True Light, which lights every man that comes into the world' (John 1:19). And He is also 'The Father of lights...' (Jas. 1:17). He births after His own kind. 'Now are you light in the Lord' (Eph. 5:8). To the new order He speaks, 'Arise, shine; for thy light is come, and the glory of the Lord is risen upon thee. For, behold, the darkness shall cover the earth, and gross darkness the people: [as the earth's lights are diminished] but the Lord shall arise upon thee, and His glory shall be seen upon thee. And the nations shall come to thy light, and kings to the brightness of thy rising' (Isa. 60:1-3; brackets added)" (ibid).

In Ex. 10:21-23, the ninth plague, we see that, "Moses stretched out his hand toward the sky, and total darkness covered all Egypt for three days .... yet all the Israelites had light in the places where they lived." But over the centuries this situation had changed, so that, when Christ came to Israel,
> "**the Light [was] constantly shining in the dim and shadowed places, and [kept] on progressively giving light within the gloomy darkness where there is no light** (or: within the midst of the obscurity of The Darkness where there is no light of The Day; or: = in the ignorant condition or system). **And yet the darkness [did] not grasp or receive it on the same level**
>> (or: Furthermore, the Darkness did not take it down, so as to overcome it or put it out; or: = the ignorant condition or system would have none of it, nor receive it down into itself [in order to perceive it]; But that darkness does not correspondingly accept It nor commensurately take It in hand so as to follow the pattern or be in line with Its bidding)" (Jn. 1:5; brackets altered the verb tense to locate the statement in Christ's history).

Now this plague has come upon Jerusalem, bringing darkness and spiritual blindness (*cf* Mat. 13:11-15; 2 Cor. 3:14-16) and it is the new covenant community which has the Light. We read in Mat. 6:23b,
> "**If, then, the light [which is] within the midst of you is darkness** (or: continually exists being dimness and lack of Light), **how thick [is] the darkness** (or: how great and extensive [will be] the obscurity and gloom of that area of shadows)!"

See 6:1-8, above, for the parallels to this passage.

13. **Next I saw and heard one vulture** (or: eagle; [Aleph with Maj. text, *Koine* proper; Maj. text, Andreas reads: agent; messenger]), **constantly flying within mid-heaven, repeatedly saying by a great voice,**
> "**W**oe (or: Tragic will be the fate)! **W**oe (or: Alas)! **W**oe (or: Tragedy)! **for those** (or: to or in the folks) **constantly dwelling upon the Land** (or: soil; earth), **from out of the midst of the remaining sounds** (voices) **of the trumpets of the three agents who are about to be one after another sounding a trumpet!**"

Hos. 8:1 is clearly the object of this allusion:
> "To your mouth [with the] trumpet! One like a vulture is over the House of Yahweh, because they trespass against My covenant and against My law they transgress" (CVOT).

Deut. 28:49 may also be a reference,
> "Yahweh shall lift up against you a nation from afar, from the end of the earth, just as the vulture swoops [down]..." (CVOT). *Cf* Deut. 32:11; Jer. 4:13; Ezk. 17:3ff.

Hab. 1:8, "their horsemen are coming from afar; they are flying, like a vulture hurries to devour" (CVOT). Then, in Lu. 17:37, Jesus informs them,
> "**Where the body [is], there in that place the eagles will also proceed being gathered together on [it]** (or: there, too, the vultures will continue assembling)."

The Greek *aetos* can be rendered either "eagle" of "vulture;" if the latter, then it means that the judgment has already come to pass. We see an eagle with a message in the 2nd century Syriac Apocalypse (trans. by A.F.J. Klijn): there Baruch wrote a letter and "sent [it] by means of an eagle to the nine and a half tribes... And I called an eagle and said to him these words.... But now go... over the breadth of the many waters of the river Euphrates... to the people that live there and cast down to them this letter" (2 Baruch 77:19-22, *The OT Pseudepigrapha*, Vol. 1, ibid p 647).

This seems to mark an interlude: **one vulture** (or, eagle) continuously flying in the sky with a message of three **woes**, which are the messages to be sounded out by the remaining three agents. The message comes from the heavens. The woes are to those who continuously dwell upon the Land, the earth realm. As Ray Prinzing points out, the woes are in every realm: spirit, soul and body. God brings His judgments (woes) to the earth to prepare men to live in the heavens, i.e., the realm of spirit, even while our natural lives are on earth (when His judgments are in the earth, the people learn righteousness).

Both vultures and eagles are often seen flying alone. The vulture is searching out the dead flesh — perhaps that of those who died from the bitterness of the wormwood. So, once they are consumed, the vulture will do its work until only dry bones are left. All flesh gone and bones separated one from another, then will they be ready for the Spirit of God to blow upon them (Ezk. 37:1-14).

"Who hath woe? who hath sorrow? who hath wounds without cause? who hath redness of eyes? They that tarry long at the wine ..." (Prov. 23:29-30). The old wine of Mat. 9:17? Woe in the O.T. was an indication that judgment was to come. And so it does here. Simmons observed that "Jesus pronounced 7 woes upon the Pharisees and rulers of Jerusalem (Mat. 23:13-39)" (ibid p 187).

Chapter 9

Our challenge here is to determine both the significance of the symbolism in this picture, and also whose forces are here being described: God's, or the devil's. Is this chapter with its trumpets a continuation of the same judgment/deliverance by the hands of God's agents as we saw in the previous four trumpets, or are the messages of these trumpets the work of "*demons*," under the command of *satan*? The latter is the view of traditional interpretation, but let's look at some OT passages to see if God has done similar things Himself.

We know how God used *satan*, through both men and nature, to bring Job to a greater understanding and relationship with Himself: to further perfect him (Job 1 and 2).

> "The book of Job, like all Scripture, directs our attention to God. The evil that came upon Job could be directly traced to boils and Sabeans, Chaldeans, fire and storm and then further back to satan as recorded in chapters 1 and 2. But behind it all was the hand of God, as Job himself declared in his crucial question to his wife, 'Indeed should we receive good from the One, Elohim, and should we not receive evil?' (Job 2:10)" (Dean Hough, Unsearchable Riches, Vol. 88, #6).

We also have seen how God used the nations – e.g. Babylon – to judge Israel, and how Paul used *satan* to teach Hymeneus and Alexander, "... **that they may be trained not to blaspheme**," (1 Tim. 1:20), and also judged, and instructed Corinth:

> "**[you are] to hand over such a man, with the adversarial [spirit]** (or: in the adversary; by the opponent; or: to *satan*), **into a loss of the flesh** (or: an undoing and destruction of this [estranged human nature]; a loss of [his "dominated existence" – Walter Wink]) **– to the end that the spirit may be saved** (rescued; delivered; restored to health, wholeness and its original state and condition): **within the midst of and in union with the Day of** (or: in this day from, or, which is) **the Lord** " (I Cor. 5:5).

So, is that the case here in ch. 9, or is this chapter a picture similar to the judgment brought by the hand of Moses in Egypt, and of the ministry of the two witnesses in chapter 11, below? We saw the bitterness brought by the star (agent) Wormwood, in 8:11, above. Jeremiah, in lamenting what the Babylonians had done to Jerusalem, said,

> "The ways of Zion are mourning ... it is bitter for her" (Lam. 1:4).
> In vs. 8 he gave the reason, "Jerusalem hath grievously sinned, for this cause unto exile hath she been delivered."

He then personalizes God's dealings with His people,

> "From on high He sent fire among my bones and laid them prostrate. He spread out a net for my feet, He made me turn back, He made me desolate, all the day faint.... all my foes – having heard of my calamities – have rejoiced, because YOU have done it." (Lam. 1:13, 21)

Then, in Lam. 2 we read,

> (vs. 2) "My Lord has swallowed up – without pity – all the PASTURES of Jacob [*cf* the 1st trumpet, in 8:7, above] .... (vs. 3) and He has kindled against Jacob a very fire of flame, devouring round about. (vs. 4) He bent His bow as an Enemy: stood has His Right Hand as an Adversary ... He has poured out AS FIRE His fury. (vs. 5) The LORD has been as an Enemy, He has swallowed up Israel ..."

> "A Bear lying in wait He is to me, a LION in secret places. My ways has He turned aside and has torn in pieces, has made me desolate. He has bent and positions His bow, and set me up as a mark for the arrow. He has caused to enter my vitals (kidneys) THE SONS of His quiver.... HE

has filled me with bitter things, has drenched me with WORMWOOD.... remember my humiliation and my feelings, the WORMWOOD and POISON" (Lam. 3:10-15, 19).

But Jeremiah has hope, "Surely THOUGH HE CAUSED GRIEF, yet HE WILL have compassion .... Out of THE MOUTH of the Most High proceed there not EVIL and BLESSINGS? ....We have trespassed and rebelled, You have NOT PARDONED [*cf* Heb. 6:4-8]" (Lam. 3:32, 38, 42). There, in vs. 47, Jeremiah uses a figure for the exile of Judah as being "Terror and a pit." Then, in ch. 4:11, he speaks of this judgment and gives us an example of God's completed indignation, the glow of His anger, and His fire,

> "Yahweh has completed His indignation, has poured out the glow of His anger, and has kindled a fire in Zion which has devoured her foundations."

Yet we know that this was not the end of His people, for He later restored them.

In Amos 3:6 we read, "WOULD THERE COME TO BE EVIL IN A CITY, AND YAHWEH NOT HAVE DONE IT?" (CVOT). And in Jer. 6:19, "Hear, O earth [or: Land], lo I AM BRINGING EVIL on THIS people, THE FRUIT OF THEIR DEVICES, for to My Words they gave no attention, and My law – they kicked against it" (Young; emphasis and brackets added). So with this OT background to guide us, we should see the agent of 9:1 as God's agent.

1. **And then the fifth agent** (messenger) **sounded a trumpet, and I saw a Star – having fallen from out of the sky** (or: heaven) **into the Land** (earth) **– and the key of the well** (cistern; shaft; pit) **of The Deep** (Abyss) **was given to Him.**

Here, at the message of **the fifth agent**, John saw another **Star** which had fallen **out of HEAVEN into the Land**. Recall the sounding of the 3rd agent (8:10, above) and the star named Wormwood. So John sees another sign in the heavens – another meteorite? – signifying a move of the heavens upon earth. To this **agent** is given (i.e., by God: the "divine passive") **the key** (access and control) of **the Well of the Deep**. Here, Terry points out that the **Star**, therefore (being given the key) is to be interpreted as being an "agent," Himself.

Contrary to the traditional view that this Star/Agent is not a "good agent" (as per Terry, ibid p 349) because of the perfect tense phrase, "**having fallen**," or that it represents "sinful humanity" (as per Beale, ibid p 493), or that the fall means "its loss of *dominion*" (as per Simmons, ibid p 188), let us entertain the possibility that It/He is playing a role in this scene that fulfills the plan of God to bring judgment to Jerusalem, and figuratively, to all whom He deems in need of a "course correction" in their lives. We will discuss, below, the nature and identity of the King over the swarm of "locusts" which this Star releases, below. We suggest that a dualistic world view, and the traditional preconceptions concerning "*demons*" that we find in the institutional Church, have been imported into the text of the Unveiling from Persian Zoroastrianism, via its assimilation by Second Temple Judaism (*cf.* Riley, *The River of God*, ibid p 90ff).

When John sees this Star, it is already in **the Land** (we learn this from the perfect tense of the participle), but further, the participle is in the active voice, meaning the subject (**the Star**) **did the action**. The emphasis is not about a "fall," but about a Star coming from the sky (or: heaven) to the earth, and remaining on earth during this scene of the vision. It probably looked to John like a meteor. This is a heavenly Agent that has come to the location of access to **the Deep**, here on earth. He has a mission:

> "**for neither is the Father presently** (progressively; constantly) **separating and making a decision about** (evaluating; judging) **anyone, but rather, He has given ALL sifting and decision-making in the Son** (or: has granted ALL judging by the Son; has handed over ALL evaluating of issues to the Son)" (Jn. 5:22).

In this same passage we read that **the Father**,

> "**gives in Him** (or: to Him; by Him) [i.e., the Son] **authority** (or: the right; the privilege; or: out of [His] essence and being) **to be habitually separating and deciding** (to be constantly sifting and evaluating; to continuously do [the] judging), **because He is a son of mankind** (= because He is human – a member of the human race [= Adam's Son]; or: = because He exists being the eschatological Messiah). **Don't you folks be constantly amazed at this, because an hour is progressively** (or: presently; or: repeatedly) **coming within which all the people within the memorial tombs** (or: graves) **– will be continuously or repeatedly hearing His voice, and they will proceed journeying out: the ones doing virtue** (producing, making or constructing good) **into a resurrection which is Life** (or: of, from and with the quality of Life); **the ones practicing careless** (base, worthless, cheap, slight, paltry, inefficient, thoughtless, common or mean) **things into a resurrection of separating and evaluating for a decision** (or: a resurrection which is a judging)" (Jn. 5:26-29).

The word translated **well** is used in John 4:11, 12, and numerous places in the O.T. to speak of a well having water; a source of water. But if the well is dry, it could be considered a pit. Thus, the Greek *frear* means a well, a cistern, a pit, or a shaft. I chose the word "**well**" because of its frequent connection with water in the LXX. However, the word "pit" also finds both literal and metaphorical currency in the OT. Walter Brueggemann observes "the 'pit' as the wrong place," in his book, *Praying the Psalms*:

> "*The speech of the wrong place*, is, of course, found in the prayers of disorientation. In the laments, there is a great deal of talk about the *pit*... the pit has concrete reality as a place in which to put people to render them null and void. In the pit, people are effectively removed from life. Historically, this is the device used for Joseph by his brothers (Gen. 37:22, 28) and for the prophet Jeremiah by his enemies (Jer. 38:6-9). The pit is used against enemies. It means to deny to a person all the resources necessary for life. It is therefore not difficult to see how the specific reference became an embracive symbol for death. The pit reduces one to powerlessness.... In [Ps.] 28:1, to 'be like those who go to the Pit,' means to be silent, forgotten, dead. This is clearly a cry of disorientation, for the speaker fears losing the old relation with Yahweh, knowing then that everything is lost. In Ps. 88, the language is fuller. The speaker is characterized (vs. 4-5) as having no strength and as being forsaken, among the dead, slain, not remembered, cut off. The image is repeated in vs. 6, expressed as dark and deep, and in vs. 7, there is reference to the flood waters of chaos that will overwhelm.... Thus there is the wish that the ones who have created the pit should be in it ([Ps.] 9:15, *cf* 94:13). In addition to the concrete word for *pit*, there is use of the word *Sheol*. This word has been mistakenly translated 'hell.' It does not refer to anything like that, for classical Israelite thought did not envision a place of ultimate punishment. Rather, the term refers simply to a place of undifferentiated, powerless, gray existence where one is removed from joy, and discourse with God. There is the wish that the troublemakers would go there ([Ps.] 31:17; 55:16; 141:7).... The image [of the pit] suggests also that there is real movement in its use. Those who stay with the image are able to speak not only in *prospect* of the pit or in the *midst* of trouble, but also *after* the trouble, in a mood of joy. The image occurs not only in songs of disorientation but in Psalms of thanksgiving which sing of reorientation:
>
>> 'O Lord, thou hast brought up my soul from *Sheol*,
>> Restored me to life from among those gone down to the *Pit*' ([Ps.] 30:3).
>> 'He drew me up from the desolate *pit*, out of the *miry bog*' ([Ps.] 40:2).
>> 'For thou dost not give me up to *Sheol*, or let thy godly one see the *Pit*' ([Ps.] 16:10).
>> 'Thou hast delivered my soul from the *depths of Sheol*' ([Ps.] 86:13)....
>
> The motif of pit enables the speaker to present every posture of life to God. Clearly the metaphor of pit in itself is of no interest to the Psalms, but it is a way of bringing life to God to have it dealt with.... These Psalms attest to us that the life of faith does not protect us from the pit. Rather, the

power of God brings us out of the pit to new life which is not the same as pre-pit existence" (Saint Mary's Press, 1986 pp 41-44; *italics* original; brackets added).

We should keep in mind the metaphor of "well" and "pit" in 9:1-2, here, as potential allusions to its use in the Psalms, along with the use of *Sheol* that we find in Jonah 2:2 coupled with the use of *pit* in Jonah 2:6.

The next term we need to investigate is the word "**deep**," also being translated by the word "abyss," and "bottomless." This last term arose from the concept that some places on earth (such as places in the oceans, some lakes, etc.) were so deep that their bottom could not be discerned, and so were thought to perhaps be "bottomless." The term "abyss" is merely a transliteration of the Greek *abussos*. It, too, means something very deep. Thus, the most correct translation of the Greek phrase in vss. 1 and 2 is "**the well of the Deep**." Simmons suggests that this term is used interchangeably with "the sea" in the Unveiling – e.g., 11:7 and 13:1, below (ibid p 189). To come to an understanding of the Scriptural meaning of this figure, let us first look at the historical (OT) usage of the word "**The Deep**."

Its first use is in Gen. 1:2, "But the earth was invisible (unseen) and un-built (unprepared; not ready), and darkness [was] up upon (over) **the Deep**, and God's Spirit (Breath-effect) was bearing (conducting) Himself over upon the water." (LXX, JM). The next occurrence of the word is in conjunction with the flood in Gen. 7:11, "...on this day all the springs (fountains) of **the Deep** were broken up..." (LXX).

In Gen. 8:2 we find that, "And the fountains of **the Deep** were closed up, and the flood-gates of heaven, and the rain from heaven was withheld." (LXX).

We next see the word used in Deut. 8:7, "For the Lord thy God will bring you into a good and extensive land, where there are torrents of waters, and springs (fountains) of **the Deeps** (pl.) issuing through the plains and through the mountains" (LXX). Here it would seem that **the Deep** was considered to be the source for the springs and rivers of the land.

In Deut. 33:13 we see that the Deeps (again pl.) are part of the blessings with which Moses blessed Joseph, "And to Joseph he said, 'His land is of **the blessing** of the Lord of the seasons of sky and dew, and from springs of **the Deep** below.' " (LXX).

"But whence has wisdom been discovered? .... it has neither indeed been discovered among men. **The Deep** said, 'It is not in me.' And the sea said, 'It is not with me.'" (Job 28:12-14, LXX) So here the sea and the Deep are put in parallel association. The Lord asks Job, "But have you come upon the spring of the sea, or walked about in the footsteps (tracks) of **the Deep**?" (Job 38:16, LXX).

"He makes the Deep boil like a brazen caldron; and He regards the sea as a pot of ointment and the subterranean part (Tartarus) of **the Deep** like a captive: He counts (regards, reckons) **the Deep** unto a range **for walking about**." (Job 41:22, 23, LXX).

Ps. 33:7, "...Who lays up **the Deeps** in treasuries." "...Thy **judgments** are as a great **Deep**." (Ps. 36:6, LXX). Ps. 42:7, "**Deep calls upon Deep**, unto the Voice of Thy cataracts: all Thy billows and thy waves have gone over me."

In Ps. 71:20-21, we see the term used figuratively and applied to events in this life:

"What afflictions many and sore have You showed me! Yet You turned and quickened me, and **brought me again from the Deeps** of the earth. You did multiply Your righteousness, and did turn and comfort me, and brought me again out of the Deeps of the earth." (LXX).

Here it is used of a place of afflictions (pressures, tribulations), but it is not the final place, for when the tribulations were finished he was QUICKENED (made alive).

In Ps. 76:16 we see that the Deeps can be agitated and troubled when they see God, even as the waters see Him and fear. Are these speaking figuratively of mankind, and the deep places within him?

In Ps. 104 we see some interesting descriptions, "Who robes Yourself with light as a garment ....Who covers His chambers with waters; Who makes the clouds His chariot ....**The Deep, as a garment**, is His covering..." (vs. 2, 3, 6, LXX).

Ps. 106:9, "...so He led them through **the Deep** as through the wilderness."

Ps. 107:23-26, "They that go down to the sea .... these have seen the works of the Lord, and HIS WONDERS IN **THE DEEP**....They go up to the heavens, and go down to the Deeps; their soul melts because of troubles."

Ps. 135:6, "All that the Lord willed, He did in heaven, and on the earth, in the sea, **and in all the Deeps**."

Ps. 148:7, 8, "Praise the Lord from the earth, you serpents (dragons), **and all Deeps**. Fire, hail, snow, ice, stormy wind: THE THINGS CONTINUALLY PERFORMING HIS WORD."

Prov. 3:20, "By understanding were **the Deeps** broken up ..."

Prov. 8:22-24, "The Lord made Me [Wisdom] the beginning of His ways, unto His works. He established Me before the Age, in the beginning, before He formed the earth, even before He constructed **the Deeps**"

Isa. 51:10, "Art Thou not It [the Arm of the Lord, vs. 9] that dried the sea, the water, the abundance of the Deep, that made the depths of the sea a way of passage for the delivered and the redeemed?"

Isa. 63:13, "He led them through the Deep, as a horse through the wilderness ..."

Ezk. 26:19, "For thus says the Lord God, when I shall make you **a desolate city** ... **when I have brought the Deep up upon you**."

Ezk. 31:4, 15, "The water nourished him, **the Deep** made him grow tall ....In the day wherein he went down into the Unseen, the Deep mourned for him."

Amos 7:4, "Thus has the Lord showed me; and behold, the Lord called for judgment by fire, and it devoured **the great Deep**, and devoured the Lord's portion [i.e., Jacob, vss. 2, 5]."

Jonah 2:6, "Water was poured around me to the soul: **the last Deep** compassed me..." All the above OT references were from the Septuagint (LXX, Bagster ed.) and use the same Greek word *abussos* that is used here in chapter 9.

The only occurrence of this word in the Gospels is in Lu. 8:31. Here, the situation is where Jesus came to the region of the Gerasenes (some MSS read "Gadarenes") and was met by the man who claimed that he was host to a legion of *demons*. "And they entreated Him to the end that He would not order (arrange upon) them to go away into **the Deep** ....that He would permit them to enter into [the herd of hogs], and He permitted them." (vs. 31, 32) In vs. 33 we see that once the *demons* were in the hogs, the whole herd rushed over a precipice into **the lake**, and the hogs drowned. Interesting to note in vs. 29 that when they were in the man that, "he was driven by the *demon* (singular) into the deserts." This would be a place away from water, or the Deep. Something about the Deep apparently held fear for them. Vs. 29 states that Jesus had commanded them to come out from the man, and thus he was continually asking that He would not examine (test, as with metals, by use of the touchstone) him. We are not told what happened to the *demons* when the hogs cast them, and themselves, into "the deep" of the lake at hand. Whatever the case, vs. 31 tells us that the *demons* did not want to go into the Deep. Thus it would not appear that this was their home, their origin, or the normal realm of their existence. To thus assume that it is *demons* that come out of the Deep in Rev. 9, seems inconsistent. The Deep here in Luke seemed to spell their doom to them.

One of the most interesting statements involving **the Deep** – and the only other place it is used in the NT outside of The Unveiling – is found in Rom. 10:7. "The quotation in 6-8 is a free citation from Deut. 30:11-14. Paul recognizes a secondary meaning in Moses' words, and thus changes the original expressions so as to apply them to the Christian faith-system. His object in the change is indicated by the explanatory words which he adds." (Vincent) "Or, who shall descend into **the Deep**? that is, to lead Christ back up from out of dead ones." (Rom. 10:7) Again quoting Vincent, "[The] Septuagint [reads], 'Who shall pass through to beyond the sea?' Paul changes the phrase in order to adapt it to the descent of Christ into Hades. The two ideas may be reconciled in the fact that the Jew conceived the sea as the abyss of waters on which the earth rested. Compare Ex. 20:4 ['... the waters under the earth']. Thus the ideas 'beyond the sea' and 'beneath the earth' coincide in designating the realm of the dead."

In 11:7, below, the two witnesses are killed by the little animal (little wild beast) that " – **the one repeatedly climbing up** (or: ascending) **out of the Deep** (or: the Abyss)." In 17:8, below, the scarlet little animal "**is about to repeatedly climb up** (or: progressively ascend) **out of the Deep, and to repeatedly lead under** (or: go away; [other MSS: then it progressively withdraws]) **into loss** (destruction; state of being lost)."

What then can we conclude from these references to "**the Deep**"? 1) it is a place where *satan* is bound; 2) *demons* don't want to go there; 3) an agent from heaven controls it; 4) Christ can descend to the dead there and then captivate the captivity there (Eph. 4:8, 9); 5) it can encompass a person, but one can be brought out of it again; 6) the children of Israel were led through it – it is compared to a wilderness; 7) it is a source of springs of water; 8) it is a source of blessings and prosperity; 9) it is a source of God's judgment; 10) it brings praise to the Lord; 11) His wonders are seen in it; 12) it is His covering, as a garment; 13) it was covered with darkness until God bore Himself (brooded) upon it; 14) it was a blessing in the promised land; 15) they are in His treasuries; 16) they call upon one another; 17) they were collected together into synagogues (Gen. 1:7, LXX); 18) they have footsteps; 19) they are places where God does His will; 20) a little beast continually rises up out of it.

Now, in Rev. 20:1, please note that **the agent** with **the key of the Deep** is descending out of heaven (is this another view of the same scene that John saw here, in 9:1?). There, in vs. 3, this **agent** (who in vs. 2 has seized and bound the dragon, "the original serpent that has been from the beginning," who is a devil and an adversary {a *satan*}) cast the adversary **into the Deep**, then closed and sealed over it. The Deep, where he is bound for 1000 years, is referred to as **his prison** (or, ward; place of custody where he is watched), from whence he is to be loosed for final use before being cast into the lake of Fire.

2. **And he opened up the well** (shaft; pit) **of The Deep and smoke ascended out of the well** (shaft), **as smoke of a great furnace** (or: kiln – for smelting, firing earthen ware or baking bread), **and the sun and the air were darkened from out of the smoke of the well** (or: shaft).

Smoke is a symbol; it was evidence of God's presence on Mt. Sinai,
> "And Mount Sinai smoked all over, because Yahweh had come down thereon, in fire, and the smoke went up as the smoke of a furnace, and all the mountain trembled exceedingly" (Ex. 19:18, Rotherham).

The first time "smoke" is used in Scripture was in Gen.15:17, when Yahweh cut a covenant with Abram,
> "So it came to pass, when the sun had gone in, and a thick darkness had come on, that lo! There was a smoking hearth (stove – CVOT; furnace – KJV) and torch of fire which passed through between these pieces" (Rotherham). For an example of judgment *cf* Gen. 19:28.

In Isa. 4:5 we read the promise:
> "Then will Yahweh create – over all the home of Mount Zion and over her assembly – a cloud by day and a smoke and the shining of a fire-flame by night" (Rotherham).

This promise represents the new creation, following the destruction of the old world of the Mosaic age. God's presence in the temple was indicated by smoke in the vision of Isa. 6:4, "the house [i.e., temple] was filled with smoke." Here, in this passage of the Unveiling, the smoke indicated His presence coming in judgment: in AD 70 Jerusalem was burned, becoming an "oven" in places (*cf* 18:9, below).

Note the semantic range of the word **furnace**: a kiln (for firing pottery – make vessels for Himself); a kiln for smelting ore (e.g., Mal. 3:2-3); an oven, for baking bread. These are all constructive, creative processes. There is no textual indication that this is speaking of a mythological "hell," or even that this furnace should be equated with the "lake of fire." The many references for **the Deep**, cited above, should give pause about too quickly assigning elements of this vision to traditional eschatology. See first its historical interpretation, then look for "timeless" lessons that folks can apply, figuratively, to their own time, and receive a blessing (1:3, above).

The "**sun and the air [being] darkened**" may be an echo of Isa.13:10.

3. **Next locusts came out of the smoke [and went] into the Land** (earth). **And authority** (or: the right; permission) **was given to them – as the scorpions of the land** (or: earth) **have authority** (permission; license) –

The **locusts** are an allusion to the plague in Ex. 10:12-15. There also may be seen here an allusion to Nah. 3:14-15, which also speaks to vs. 2, above: "make strong the brick-kiln…. There the fire shall devour you… Make yourself teeming (many) as the locust."
> "All through the O.T., locust is the symbol of destruction; and the most vivid description of them and of their destructiveness is in the first two chapters of Joel [that].... should be read in full and set beside the description in the Revelation." (Barclay, ibid p 49)

So, let us read, then list some excerpts from these chapters in Joel, to gain insights for the prophetic images of our present text (chapter 9).

From Joel, chapter 1 (Rotherham) we read:
> 4. That which was left by the creeping locust hath the swarming locust eaten, and that which was left by the swarming locust hath the grass locust (Heb. the devourer) eaten and that which was left by the grass locust hath the corn locust (the browser) eaten.
> 6. For a nation hath come up over My land, bold and without number – his teeth are the teeth of a lion, and the fangs of a lioness hath he.
> 7. He hath turned My vine to a waste, and my fig-tree to splinters...
> 15. Alas for The Day! For near is the Day of Yahweh, and as a veritable Destruction from The Destroyer (*cf* Rev. 9:11) shall it come.

Let me insert here Isa. 13:5,
> "They are coming in from a land far away, from the utmost bound OF THE HEAVENS – YAHWEH – with His WEAPONS of indignation, to destroy the Land."

Back to Joel 1:18-19,
> "How do the beasts groan! (*cf* Rom. 8:22) Perplexed are the herds of oxen, because there is no pasture for them – even the flocks of sheep are destroyed! ... for a fire has consumed the pastures of the wilderness and a flame has set ablaze all the trees of the field."

And now, Joel 2:
> 1. Blow ye a trumpet in Zion, sound an alarm in My Holy Mountain. Let all the inhabitants of the land tremble – for coming is the day of Yahweh, for it is near!
> 2. A day of obscurity and deep gloom; a day of cloud and thick darkness, AS DAWN spread over the mountains (*cf* Ex. 10:22, 23; 14:19, 20), a PEOPLE, numerous and mighty ...
> 3. Before him (or, it – the people) is a consuming fire, and after him is a flame kindled; as the garden of Eden is the land before him, but after him a desert most desolate...
> 4. Their appearance is as the appearance of horses; and as horsemen, so shall they run (pursue).

> 5. As the sound of chariots ... as the sound of a flame of fire devouring stubble, like a people bold, arrayed for battle.
>
> 10-11. Before him (it) the land (earth) quaked, the heavens tremble (*cf* Heb. 12:26), the sun and the moon have become dark and the stars have withdrawn their shining; and YAHWEH gives forth His Voice before HIS ARMY for exceedingly great (numerous) is HIS CAMP, for MIGHTY is THE DOER of HIS WORD, for great is the Day of Yahweh.

Here, let us consider Obad. 18-21,

> "And the house of Jacob shall become a fire, and the house of Joseph a blaze, and the house of Esau [comment: a type of the flesh, or of human endeavor] for stubble ... and there shall not be a survivor for the house of Esau .... and SAVIORS (DELIVERERS; rescuers) shall come up in mount Zion to judge mount Esau, and the kingdom shall become Yahweh's."

The purpose statement of all this judgment in Joel is the same as the purpose statement here in 9:20-21. In Joel 2:12-14 He says,

> "Even now, **therefore**, urges Yahweh, **Return unto Me** with all your heart ... tear your heart and not your garments, and **return** to Yahweh, your God, for **gracious and compassionate is He**, slow to anger and of great kindness, and He regrets over the evil. Who is knowing, if He will return and regret, **and let a blessing remain** behind Him..."

In 9:20-21, below, the purpose statement of the chapter was for them to "**change their mind** (change their perceptions or ways of thinking) **from out of the works** (actions; deeds) **of their hands, SO THAT they may not worship the demons** (Hellenistic concept and term: = animistic influences) **and the idols** (forms)..." This would not be the purpose of *satan* or his *demons*, else he is divided against himself. With a paradigm that this chapter portrays the purpose and work of God's army, let us continue to look at the specifics of the symbolism. Another purpose here may be that which is stated in Ezk. 38:22-23,

> "And I will PLEAD against him with pestilence and with blood ... and great hailstones, fire, and brimstone. THUS WILL I MAGNIFY MYSELF, and SANCTIFY MYSELF ... AND THEY SHALL KNOW THAT I AM Yahweh."

The picture here in chapter 9 reminds us of an erupting volcano: a **furnace** pouring out **smoke**. But this is God's kiln, His smelting pot that He has made to "boil as a caldron" (Job 41:31). It is the source of His transforming judgments. His presence is evidenced by the pillar of smoke (as with Israel of old). Once again we see His **army of locusts**, as in Joel, bringing judgment that the people of the land may learn righteousness.

The comparison to "**scorpions on the Land**," may be an allusion to the invasion of the Romans, as the Midianites and Amalekites has been: "as numerous as locusts" (Jud. 7:12). Simmons (ibid p 191) correlates this situation to Dan. 9:27 ("the abominations") and Mat. 24:15 ("abomination of desolation") and points us to Lu. 21:20,

> "**Now later, when you folks see Jerusalem being continuously surrounded by encamped armies, at that time realize and know from that experience that her desolation has drawn near and is now present.**"

4. **and yet it was declared to them that they may not be acting unjustly to** (be harming, injuring or violating) **the enclosed pasture** (or: grass) **of the Land** (earth; soil), **nor any green thing, nor any tree, except the humans** (the people): **those not having the seal** (or: imprint) **of God upon their foreheads.**

These are unusual locusts, for they do not eat vegetation (unlike Ex. 10:15 and Ps. 105:33-35), but rather they return man's injustice back upon himself. This is an apocalyptic device to indicate figurative use of the symbol of "locusts." They represent God's invasion into people's lives – be it through an invading army, such as with the passages quoted from Joel, above, or through personal dealings, as with Job – with the intent of turning them to Him.

The **humans** that did not have **the seal** (or: imprint) **of God upon their foreheads** (equivalent to "within the heavens; union with the atmospheres; in the skies" in Lu. 10:20, cited below) have a different mark on their foreheads: "**the imprinted mark-effect** (engraving; carve-effect) **or the name of the little animal, or the number of its name**" (13:17b, below). With a domination system controlling one's thinking, one is susceptible to whatever such locusts God sends into our lives. Such folks are lacking the full armor of God (Eph. 613-18).

5. **Now this was granted** (or: given) **to** (or: for) **them, not that they should be killing them, but rather so that they** [= the humans] **will be periodically examined** (or: continuously tried as metals by the touchstone; progressively distressed) **[for] five months. And their examination [is; was] as the distress** (metal testing) **of a scorpion whenever it may strike a human.**

The "**granting**" is equivalent to a "commissioning." Here again we have "the divine passive;" God has done the granting. As with the limitations that God put on His adversarial agent (*satan*) in Job 1:12 and 2:6, these locusts have limits put upon what they can do. God remains in control. The time-frame (correlated to the life cycle, or swarming period, of literal locusts) is also limited.

This is not for their death, but to test and **examine** them as metal is tested, and this for only a short period. They bring the pressure and discomforts which make men long for death (Job 3:21-23; Jer. 8:3). Observe that I did not use the word "tormented" for the Greek verb *basanizō*, but rather, rendered it "**examined** (tried as metals by the touchstone; distressed)." This verb strictly means "rub on the touchstone (*basanos*), a Lydian stone used to test the genuineness of metals; hence *test or make proof of* anything, or to examine its inherent composition." This is analogous to God testing Job through adversity, loss and physical/psychological pain. It represents the whole spectrum from mild irritations in life, to serious challenges. It was used in Mat. 8:6 to describe the discomforts of having the palsy. In Mat. 14:24 it referred to the disciples' boat being tossed by the waves of the sea (also, in Mk. 6:48). In 2 Pet. 2:8 it referred to Lot's soul being vexed by the unlawful acts of his neighbors. In 12:2, below, it describes a woman experiencing the pain of childbirth. So its uses in 11:10, 14:10 and 20:10, below, should be read with this understanding. Likewise with the use of the noun in 14:11 and in 18:7, 10, 15.

We see a similar use of the noun *basanos* in Wis. 3:1, 5-6,
> "The souls of the righteous are in the hand of God, and no torment (*basanos*) will ever touch them.... and having been disciplined a little, they will be greatly benefited, because God tested them and found them worthy of himself, as gold in the furnace, He tested them... accepted them" (NETS).

Note that this passage in Wis. 3 characterizes *basanos* as "disciplined a little" and "tested."

The sting of **a scorpion** can be like the sting of a bee or a wasp (I live in Arizona; I have been stung by them), or, it can be more serious. But here it is explicitly not to kill people. But this is all "in this life," and the literal interpretation of this metaphor referred to the invading Roman legions in the 1st century. Jesus told His disciples,
> "**So look, and realize – I have given to you folks the authority to habitually step on and trample snakes** (serpents) **and scorpions – as well as upon all the power and ability of the enemy** (or: the hostile or adversarial person) **– and nothing will proceed in any circumstance causing you folks harm** (or: wronging you or treating you unjustly).... **be constantly rejoicing that your names have been written on and stand engraved** (or: inscribed; [other MSS:

were/are written]) **within the heavens** (or: in union with the atmospheres; in the skies)" (Lu. 10:19-20).

The prophecy of Deut. 28:27, that was part of what would come on Israel for failure to observe the commandments of the Law, was that Yahweh would strike them "with the boil of Egypt," and, in vs. 60, "Thus He will bring back to you every disease of Egypt from the presence of which you shrank away, and they will cling to you." But, in referring to the period of Israel's wilderness journey, Wis.16:5-7 reminds us,
> "For even when the terrible rage of wild animals came upon them and they were perishing through the bites of twisted snakes [Nu. 21:6-9], Your anger did not continue to the end; for a short while they were troubled as a warning, possessing a symbol of salvation to remind them of the command of Your Law. For the one who turned was not saved because of what was beheld, but because of You, the Savior of all" (NETS; brackets added).

6. **And in those days the people** (humans) **will proceed seeking** (searching for; pursuing) **death, and will continue by no means** (or: under no circumstances) **finding it. And they will continue setting their desire to die, and death will continue fleeing** (or: escaping) **from them.**

The anticipated reaction of **the people**, in **seeking, searching and pursuing death**, shows the psychological aspect of the progressively distressing **examination** (vs. 5) that humans will undergo. We see examples of this desire to no longer continue living in the following situations:
 a) Elijah, when Jezebel endeavored to kill him (1 Ki. 19:1-4).
 b) Job, during his testing by Yahweh, (Job 3:1-26; 6:8-9; 7:15-16))
 c) The prophecy against Judah and Jerusalem, "death shall be chosen rather than life" (Jer. 8:3)
 d) Jeremiah's response to his persecution (Jer. 20:14-18)
 e) Jonah's reaction to God's graciousness to Nineveh (Jonah 4:3), then to the loss of shade from the death of the gourd (4:8).

This verse echoes the prediction made by Jesus, regarding the people of Jerusalem in His day,
> "**days are progressively coming in which they will proceed declaring, 'Happy [are] the sterile and barren women, and the wombs which do not give birth, and breasts which do not nourish!' At that time,**
> > '**They will begin saying to the mountains, "Fall at once upon us!" and to the mounds** (or: hills), **"At once veil** (cover; = hide) **us!"'**"

Jesus was quoting Hos. 10:8, referring to Israel's "high places" of idolatry. This "anticipates the siege of Jerusalem under Titus" (Simmons, ibid p192).

But we should keep in mind that all this was for "**not having the seal** (or: imprint) **of God upon their foreheads**" (vs. 4b, above). For those who possess God's imprint,
> "**God's peace** (= shalom; or: and so the joining-harmony which is God), **which is continuously having a hold over** (is habitually holding sway over; or: is constantly being superior and excelling by having it over) **all mind and inner sense** (or: every intellect; all power of comprehension; or: all process of thinking), **will continue garrisoning** (guarding; standing sentinel over) **your hearts and the results of thinking** (thoughts; reasonings; understandings; effects from directing the mind on something; or: dispositions; designs; purposes; effects of perceptions; [p16 adds: and bodies]), **within, and in union with, Christ Jesus**" (Phil. 4:7).

We also find it written concerning the 1st century martyrs, in 12:11b, below: "**they love not** (or: did not love) **their soul** (soul-life; inner self; personhood) **even to** (or: until) **death.**" This shows the dramatic contrast between those who do and those who do not have God's imprint in their minds – which is also known as, "**Christ's mind** (a mind which is Anointed, and which is Christ)," 1 Cor. 2:16.

7. **Now the representation-effects** (resultant likenesses and figures) **of the locusts [were] like** (similar to) **horses having been made ready** (or: prepared) **unto battle. And upon their heads [were] something like golden wreaths, and their faces [were] as human faces,**

What John saw were "**representation-effects** (resultant likenesses and figures)" that were "**like** (similar to).... **as**;" in other words, it did not look exactly like what he goes on to describe: **battle horses with human faces**. The horses are an echo of the horses and riders in 6:2-8, above. Their faces give their identities: they are humans. The picture is of a human army that is ready to attack Jerusalem. The **golden wreathes** on their heads tell us that these are those who have overcome in battles: they are victors who, like locusts, will compass the Land and bring God's judgment to pass.

Beale (ibid p 499) suggests that what is portrayed here, and through vs. 9, is based upon Joel 1-2. Now the beginning of this fulfillment was proclaimed by Peter on the Day of Pentecost:
> "**this is the thing** [= oracle; prophecy] **having been spoken through the prophet** (one who had light ahead of time and spoke before folks) **Joel**.... **Later I will keep on giving miracles** (wonders; omens; portents) **within the sky** (or: atmosphere; heaven) **above, and signs upon the Land below – blood and fire and vapor [pillars] of smoke; the sun will proceed being converted into darkness and the moon into blood**.... **everyone – whoever can** (or: may in any single situation) **call upon the Name of [the] Lord** [= Yahweh's name]! **– will proceed being rescued** (or: kept safe; healed and restored to wholeness; delivered; saved)" (Acts 2:16-21; quoting: Joel 2:28-32).

On the Day of Pentecost, they were living in vss. 17-18 of Acts 2; our passage here, in chapter 9, reflects Acts 2:19-21. As seen in vss. 20-21, below, so we see in Joel 2:18-30: the purpose of all this is a change of thinking and a turning to the Lord to be "rescued, or kept safe; to be healed and restored; to be delivered and saved."

The symbol of **locusts** also suggests a resulting famine, which was true for those in Jerusalem, during the Roman siege in AD 70. But another layer of understanding, regarding how this can apply to readers in the following centuries, is considering this judgment as an allusion to Amos 8:11,
> "Behold, the days are coming, averring is my Lord Yahweh, that I will send a famine into the Land; not a famine from bread, nor a thirsting for water, but rather, for hearing [the] words of Yahweh" (CVOT).

These locusts (devourers) are like battle horses: remember the opening of the first four seals. They are crowned with golden wreaths: symbol of overcomers. Remember, again, their faces: they are **humans**.

8. **and they were having hair as the hair of women, and their teeth were as those of lions.**

So are these locusts God's army?
> "Awake, awake clothe yourself with splendor, O Arm of the Lord! Awake as in days of old, as in former ages! It was You that hacked Rahab in pieces, that pierced the Dragon. It was You that dried up the Sea, the waters of the great Deep; that made the Abysses of the Sea a Road (Way) the REDEEMED might walk." (Isa. 51:9-10, Tanakh).

Do these also have the glory of women (a woman's hair is her glory – 1 Cor. 11:15)? Are these restored to completeness, having the qualities of male and female, as did Adam before the separation (Gen. 2:21-22)? Or does this speak of the Jewish rebels, adopting the image of Absalom (2 Sam. 14:25-26; 15:1-18:14)? Is "**hair as the hair of women**" an allusion to Samson, or a Nazarite's vow (Jud. 13:5)? Does this simply mean that they are uncivilized barbarians? Or, do they have the power of the Lion of the Tribe of Judah in their words (Lion's teeth in their mouths)? This image is likely drawn from Joel 1:6, "a nation is come upon my Land, strong and without number, whose teeth [are] the teeth of a lion, and he hath the cheek teeth of a great lion."

In a conversation about this verse with Dan Kaplan, he suggested that the symbol of "women's hair" might be an allusion to the mystery of the Bride of Christ (Eph. 5:24-32; composed, of course, of literal men and women). Here it is a picture of beauty and strength, performing His kingdom activities.

9. **And they were having breastplates – as breastplate armor made of iron – and the sound of their wings [was] as the sound of chariots of many horses continuously running into battle.**

Their armor is strong as the **iron** staff of the overcoming shepherds (2:26-27, above). The **sound of their wings** identifies them: "... behold, the mountain was **full of horses** and **chariots** of fire round about Elisha." (2 Kings 6:17) Recall Joel 2:5, above. Job 29:19-25 gives a description of a war horse, where vs. 25 speaks of it responding to the trumpet. In Jer. 51 we read of God's pronouncement of judgment against Babylon (here, below, in the Unveiling, this represents 1st century Jerusalem). There, in vs. 27 we read:

> "Blow a trumpet among the nations! Hallow nations against her! Summon kingdoms against her… Bring up horses like the bristling young-**locust**!" (CVOT)

There may also be an allusion to Isa. 33:2-4, where Yahweh is called upon for favor: to be their Arm, their Salvation in the time of distress. At the noise of His tumult, peoples retreated; nations were scattered when He lifted Himself up,

> "Then shall Your spoil be gathered, as the gathering of the caterpillar – as the swift running of **locusts** is **He** about to run upon them" (vs. 4, Rotherham).

In AD 70, the Roman army was God's instrument of judgment upon Jerusalem, for the final time. As Simmons terms it: "the final crisis of the Mosaic age and economy is here in view" (ibid p 196). But as Prinzing brought out about the horses of chapter 6, above, riding through our lives, so here, too, may this be a metaphor for the spiritual "house of Israel." Everyone needs correction, from time to time.

10. **And they continue having tails like scorpions, and stings** (goads; sharp points), **and in their tails [is] their authority** (permission; license) **to act unjustly to** (to harm or injure) **the humans [for] five months.**

John's continued description shows that these visionary locusts have **tails like scorpions**, with stingers, and that it is with these that they are commissioned to hurt those who do not have God's imprint in their foreheads, i.e., the mind, identity and character of Christ. The **sting** can be translated "goad," or, "sharp point." Keeping in mind the purpose statement of vss. 20 and 21, along with the fact that their purpose was not to be killing these men (vs. 5) but rather to be testing and examining them, is this pain from the stings meant to "goad" them toward repentance? This feature calls to mind Paul's words in 1 Cor. 15:56,

> "**Now the sharp point and stinger of** (or: the sting, thus, the injection from) **the Death [is] the Sin** (the mistake; the error; the failure), **and the power and ability of the Sin [is] the Law.**"

It was the Law that brought death to Jerusalem, in AD 70. It was the fulfillment of Deut. 28:15-68.

On a historical note, Simmons instructs us (and on p 307 shows a drawing) that the Romans used siege machinery (that hurled huge darts or stones) which roughly resembled, and was called, a "scorpion." He also informs us that "five months answers to the length of the siege of Jerusalem" prior to penetrating her walls (ibid p 196).

In 1 Ki. 12, when Rehoboam succeeded Solomon as king, Jeroboam and the assembly of Israel went to Rehoboam and asked him to lighten the load that Solomon had put upon them. Part of his ultimate reply to Israel was, "My Father scourged you with whips; I will scourge you with scorpions." (vs. 14) Thus we see the scorpion used as a metaphor for increased pain, discomfort, and a heavier burden to bear.

Scorpions were a part of the environment of the wilderness journeys that the Lord brought Israel through (Deut. 8:15). Thus, as God processes His people through their interior wilderness, the testing and examinations can bring pain and discomfort. But it is only for a time, and has the element of grace present (5 months: 5 being a numeric symbol for grace – Prinzing). In those areas of our lives where He has overcome us and we now have the victory, this "second death" will no longer hurt us and He will give us authority in that area, "**to habitually step on and trample snakes** (serpents) **and scorpions – as well as upon all the power and ability of the enemy** (or: the hostile or adversarial person) **– and nothing will proceed in any circumstance causing you folks harm** (or: wronging you or treating you unjustly)" (Lu. 10:19).

God uses the scorpion as a metaphor for irritating or abusive people, casting them in the same category as briers and thorns ["Vivid images of those who would make life difficult for the prophet" – Mark Hillmer, NIV Study Bible, ibid p 1225] in Ezk. 2:6, "And you, son of man, do not be afraid of them or their words. Do not be afraid, though briers and thorns are all around you and you live among scorpions."

So here, in vs. 10, their tails are compared to scorpions, while in vs. 19 the tails of the horses are compared to serpents. Note that the locusts – which were compared to horses in vs. 7 – have power to hurt in both the head (having lions' teeth, vs. 8) and the tail (having stings in their tails, vs. 10). The metaphor is changed a bit when the picture is seen of the four agents being loosed (vs. 15, below), and there we have two vast cavalries whose purpose is to be killing the third of the people. What started as pain and discomfort now intensifies to the point of death. But the tail metaphor is picked up again, and these troops are described as horses (vs. 17). These, like the locusts, have authority that "exists in their mouth and in their tails" (vs. 19). The staff (rod) of Moses, symbolizing his power and authority, became a serpent when God had him cast it to the earth (Ex. 4:2-4). It is interesting to note that God had him pick it up "by the tail," which is not the normal or safe way to pick up a snake. It is by the tail, the "least" part of the body (the opposite of the Head, as it were, the lowest position in the body), that God brings His judgments to people. The Head did not come to judge, but to give His life a ransom for many. Recall how God judged Israel with burning serpents (seraphim serpents), and how the bronze serpent that Moses put on the pole – which only had to be looked at and seen for them to live – was a type of Christ lifted up upon the cross (Num. 21:4-9; John 3:14). The serpent was created to be our adversary.

11. They habitually have a King (or One who reigns) **upon them: the Agent** (or: Messenger) **of the Deep. The name for Him in Hebrew [is] Abaddon** (Destruction; [note: see Ex. 12:23; in verb form, speaking of Yahweh, in Deut. 11:4; Ps. 5:6; Ps. 9:5; Jer. 15:7]), **and in the Greek He has the name Apollyon** (Destroyer; A Destroying One; or: One who makes folks lost; [verb form used in Lu. 17:33 and, of Yahweh, in Jude 5]).

Here we are told that the locusts have **a King** over them. The only king over natural locusts is God. Here, the King of these symbolic locusts is Destruction, A Destroyer. The name Abaddon comes from the Heb. root "Abad," or, "Avad." "It is used to describe the downfall of nations, the withering away of crops, and the fading away of strength, hope, wisdom, knowledge and wealth. It is applied to the destruction of temples, images, and pictures" (Lexical Aids to the O.T., Spiros Zodhiates – *The Hebrew-Greek Key Study Bible,* 2008). Behind all these is God. God was the Power that brought the various forms of His creation as plagues against Egypt. In speaking of the final one, Moses writes, "And Jehovah has passed on TO SMITE the Egyptians, and has seen the blood on the lintel, and on the two side-posts, and JEHOVAH has passed over the opening, and does not permit THE DESTRUCTION to come into your houses to smite." (Ex. 12:23, Young). In the same chapter, vs. 13, He said, "when I see the blood I will pass over you, so that no plague will destroy you WHEN I STRIKE THE LAND OF EGYPT" (Tanakh). Then in vs. 29, "And it came to pass at midnight that YAHWEH smote every firstborn in the land of Egypt ..." (Rotherham).

The Heb. verb "Abad" is used in the following passages (shown in *italics*):
> Deut. 11:4, "And what He did unto the forces of Egypt ... in that He caused the waters of the Red Sea to flow over their faces ... and so Yahweh *destroyed* them ..."
> Ps. 5:6, "You will *destroy* them who speak falsehood ..."
> Ps. 9:5, "You have *destroyed* the lawless one ..."
> Jer. 15:7, "Therefore have I winnowed them ... I have bereaved – I have *destroyed* My people: from their own ways have they not returned."
> Ezk. 6:3, "And say, 'You mountains of Israel ... Behold Me! I am bringing upon you a sword, and I will *destroy* your high places.' "
> Deut. 28:63, "And it shall come to pass that as Yahweh rejoiced over you to do you good and to multiply you, SO will Yahweh rejoice over you, to cause you to perish and to *destroy* you ... "
> Jer. 1:10, "See! I have set you in charge this day ... to uproot and to break down and to *destroy* and to tear in pieces, -- to build and to plant." [the work of a prophet].

From what we saw regarding God's control over **the Deep**, is it not logical that this "**Agent of the Deep**" would be a **figure** of the Power and Authority of God? Remember Who has the keys of the Unseen and death (1:18, above)?

As to the name Apollyon, which is a participle form of the Greek *apollumi*, which means "to lose, be lost, to destroy, be destroyed," let us look at a couple places where this verb is used. Matt. 16:25, "**For whoever may want to save his soul will destroy** (lose) **it; but whoever may destroy** (*apollumi*; active voice) **his soul on My account will find it**." Here it is those who are wanting to come after Jesus (vs. 24) that must become Destroyers of their own souls via their own crosses. A similar statement is recorded in Lu. 17:33, "**Whoever may seek to build a perimeter around** (construct a protecting shelter around) **his soul will destroy it; but whoever will destroy it will bring it forth** (birth it) **a living one**" (a living creature – *cf* 4:6ff, above). This verb is also used in Jude 5 where it speaks of what Yahweh did to those in the wilderness who did not believe. He is the Destroyer. But is the destruction by this One an end of the one destroyed? Let's let the Word speak for Itself: "But He answering, said, 'I was not sent with a commission EXCEPT UNTO THE DESTROYED (*apollumi*) SHEEP of THE HOUSE OF ISRAEL" (Mat. 15:24). "For the Son of Man has come to seek and TO SAVE THE ONE HAVING BEEN DESTROYED (*apollumi*)" (Lu. 19:10).

We should note that His body – those with His imprint within their minds – are not affected by this first woe. This is reminiscent of Israel in Goshen who were exempt from the plagues in Egypt.

12. **The one woe** (or: tragedy) **passed away. Consider – two woes are yet coming after these things** (or, with other MSS: Look and perceive! He {or: It} continues coming still! Two woes after these).

The MSS vary on the verb of the second clause. The bold reading represents the plural form of the verb; the parenthetical reading is of the third person singular, with no expressed subject. The reading "He" suggests that God continues coming in judgment. The reading "It" speaks of the judgment still coming, in two more woes. Some scholars suggest that the phrase "**after these things**" introduce the sixth trumpet: "And after these things, the sixth agent…" This latter would seem to speak more of "these things" being what John had been seeing (i.e., this section of the vision), while the reading expressed above would have "these things" refer to the "things" that comprised the first woe.

This verse may simply be a word from John to his listeners. It signals a changing of the scenes, but also says to those having this letter read to them: "Keep listening, there is more to come."

13. **And then the sixth agent** (or: messenger) **sounded a trumpet, and I heard one voice from out of the four horns of the golden altar [which is] before** (in the sight and presence of) **God** [note: a reference to the altar of incense which was in front of the innermost chamber in the Tabernacle],

Now we come to the sounding of the 6th agent's trumpet. The scene has moved back to the Tabernacle (or, Temple). It is the Holy Place, the location of the **golden altar** of incense. Now **one voice** is heard from out of **the 4 horns** of this altar. This speaks of a unity of the prayers of the universal (worldwide) body of Christ – they pray in "one voice," from, or to, the four directions of the heavens. What is their prayer? To "**loose the four agents: the ones having been bound upon the great river Euphrates**," vs. 14. This prayer (toward the goodness that the following judgment will cause) comes from the place of power and strength (the **horns**) of this altar (the body of Christ).

The **voice** may also refer to the voice of the agent at the altar of incense (8:3, above). The location of this altar is important, so it was mentioned where it is. What is happening takes place "in the sight and presence of **God**." We see a similar picture in 14:10, below, where the "second death" takes place: "**Fire and Deity** (or: in union with Fire, even Divine qualities) **in the presence of** (before; in the sight of) **the set-apart agents** (sacred folks with the message; holy messengers), **and in the presence of** (before) **the little Lamb**" (*cf* 2:11, above; 19:20; 21:14, below). In the Unveiling we see many different pictures of the same corrective judgment and transformation.

14. **presently saying to the sixth agent,**
    "**Loose the four agents: the ones having been bound upon the great river Euphrates.**"

Jer. 46 speaks of the conquest of Egypt by Babylon. There, vs. 2 locates the setting at the Euphrates, and in vs. 6 we read, "northward, by the side of the stream Euphrates they stumble and fall." In the LXX (there, ch. 26) vss. 2 and 10 reads as our text here: "upon the river Euphrates." Beale points out that, "Mention of the Euphrates here anticipates the battle of the sixth bowl, where the Euphrates is again mentioned" (16:12, below; ibid p 507). The imagery, here, is that of a conquering army about to come.

Terry instructs us that, "it is a well-attested fact that the Euphrates formed the eastern boundary of the Roman empire at the time of the Jewish war, and four legions of soldiers were station there (Tacitus, *Annals*, 4.5; Dio Cassius, 4.23); and Josephus states that Titus was followed by 'three thousand drawn from the river Euphrates' (*Wars*, 5.1.6)" (ibid p 356). This would have been the literal, historical interpretation of this verse, as we look back on the 1st century. But we should take care not to try to find a historical correlation to every detail of these visions. They were meant to tell a story; we need to watch the entire play to fully understand the message. Apocalyptic visions had reference to people and to history, but they were not meant to be history or even to correspond to factual realities (such as "living beings" with four different faces). The river Euphrates is a symbol, as are **the four agents**.

15. **And the four agents were loosed – those having been made ready** (or: being prepared) **unto the hour and day and month and year – so that they may be constantly killing the third of the humans.**

We see that the **4 agents** were loosed at a specific time, down to the very hour of a specific day of a specific month of a specific year. This detail of information locates the event at a specific time in history. Their purpose for being loosed is clearly stated: "**so that they may be constantly killing the third of the humans**." Which humans? I suggest that these are the same people as those in vs. 4, above: "**those not having the seal** (or: imprint) **of God upon their foreheads**." Throughout the history of ancient Israel, when God brought judgment to Israel, some men were usually killed. But as this is a book of symbols, is this then speaking of a physical death? Or is this judgment, this death, the **second death** spoken of elsewhere in this book and mentioned in the comments of vs. 13, above? Is it the enforcement of the "baptism of fire" spoken of by John the baptizer: the baptism in "**the lake of fire**" spoken of in this book? The literal, historical fulfillment would refer to the physical deaths of the Jews during their war against Rome, in AD 70. But the metaphorical death would come as the called-out communities were carrying their figurative crosses, on behalf of others, in laying down their inner lives, or even their physical lives, for the sake of their friends.

These being **four** agents, it represents a four-directional, complete coverage of the Empire, as God used the Roman soldiers to bring about His corrective judgments, the destruction of Israel's temple cultus, as an end of the old, while fully inaugurating the beginning of the new, with resurrection life following both physical and metaphorical deaths.

These 4 agents (messengers) have been prepared for this, and they are now made ready. The time has come, and they are finally loosed. But what is the significance of where they have been bound? It was upon the northern and eastern border of the land of Israel, the great Euphrates River (cf Deut. 11:24; Josh 1:4). What is the significance of the Euphrates? It speaks of the historical place of bondage of God's people. It was the border of their enemies, such as Babylon – which we see as a symbol again later in this book, where also it is said,

> "**Come out of her** (or: Go forth from out of her midst) **My people, so that you may not jointly participate with** (be a partner with; fellowship together with) **her sins** (failures; occasions of missing the mark), **and so that you may not receive from out of her plagues** (blows)" (18:4, below).

This, we will later see, has a physical application to the called-out folks coming out of Jerusalem before its destruction. In the centuries that have followed, it speaks of those who are actively following the little Lamb, coming out of the controlling systems of the Christian religion, and other religions, as well. These may be a figure of the sons of God, who up to this hour have been bound at the very border of symbolic Babylon, who have not fully come out of her, and have remained in bondage in her, at the very border of the Promised Land (the realm of the Spirit, in Christ – Eph. 2:6; agents serving in His temple/body). Though they have not been able to operate within her system and may not have yet been birthed by the mother which is above (12:5, below; Gal. 4:26 – cf vs. 25: "the Jerusalem which is now is **in bondage with her children**") into the land of the promise, part of their ministry is to bring adjustments and corrective judgment to God's house (1 Pet. 4:17).

Another aspect of the significance of the Euphrates River is that it is one of the 4 rivers of Eden (Gen. 2:14) and, according to Holman's Dictionary, this word means "bursting, sweet." Being bound upon this river of life/death is sweet, but within us is a bursting to be loosed!

As in 8:7-12, above, they are only able to kill a portion of the people: **one third**. The locusts, above, were only allowed to examine and test humans who did not yet have the mind of Christ (God's imprint), but no numerical limit was placed upon them. These four **agents** may answer to the four **winds** of 7:1, above. Recall that in Job's testing, it was a "great wind from the wilderness (the place where locusts breed –

Barclay, p 49) that struck the four corners of the house, and it fell upon the young men, and they [died]" (Job 1:19). This scene with its reference to the river may be an allusion to Isa. 8:6-8,

> "Because this people has rejected the waters of Shiloah that flow so gently [a figure of Christ – Jn. 7:37-38], and has given elation to Rezin and Remaliah's son [prophetic of the Jewish leadership colluding with Rome], now therefore behold, Yahweh is bringing up over them the waters of the Stream, staunch and abundant, the king of Assyria and all his glory. It will ascend over all its channels and go over all its banks; it will pass on into Judah… filling the width of your Land, O Immanuel! Know, peoples, and be dismayed…" (CVOT; brackets added).

16. Now the number of the troops (armed forces) **of the cavalry [was] two vast multitudes of innumerable groups** (or: myriads of myriads) **– I heard the number of them** (or: their number).

The number of **the troops of the cavalry** informs John's listeners that this is a huge army. What is the idea of this number? The significant number is TWO. There are literally two groups, which I believe correspond to the TWO witnesses of chapter 11, below. These groups are transliterated as "myriads." Another place where this word is used is in the book of Judah (Jude), vs. 14-15, where he quotes Enoch as having said,

> "**Behold, the Lord** [=Yahweh] **came** (or: comes and goes) **within His set-apart myriads** (or: in union with innumerable holy multitudes, which are Him), **to form a separation** (or: make a decision; construct a distinction; perform a sifting and a judging) **which corresponds to and falls in line with all people** (to the level of everyone), **and to test** (or: search thoroughly) **the irreverent folks concerning all their irreverent works** (activities; deeds) **which they irreverently did, and concerning all THE HARD THINGS which irreverent outcasts** (folks in error; sinners; failures; folks who make mistakes and miss the target) **SPOKE AGAINST Him**."

This quote from Judah affirms that, just as during Israel's history God came "within" invading armies, this present passage, speaking of the 7 trumpets, is describing a coming of the Lord to judge His people. The literal fulfillment in AD 70 was the final judgment and termination of Israel as a nation and as a separate people of God. In Christ He has now joined the two categories (Jew and Gentile; circumcision and uncircumcision) into one new humanity (Eph. 2:14-16). But as we noted in chapters 2 and 3, above, Christ spiritually judges His called-out communities, and these purging measures usually come through other people. We are all stones in His polishing tumbler.

"The chariots of God are two myriads – thousands repeated; My Lord is among them …" (Ps. 68:17, Rotherham).
In 7:4, above, John "heard the number" of those who were sealed. Numbers continue having symbolic significance; he again "hears the number of them." Like the locusts, above, there are too many to count or number. The idea in this number is that they will make a complete conquest that cannot be thwarted.

17. And thus I saw the horses in the vision: and the ones sitting upon them habitually having breastplates of Fire, even resembling hyacinth (or: amethyst) **stone, and being divine in character** (θειος: deity; divinity; divine nature or character; the fire of God; brimstone or sulphur). **And the heads of the horses [are] as heads of Lions. And Fire, Smoke and Deity** (divine nature and character) **continuously issues forth from out of their mouths.**

This begins a description of these groups. Recall how Joel 1 spoke of locusts, then Joel 2 spoke of troops and horses to describe God's army? Note that this first part of this scene (the message of the 5th agent) used the figure of locusts; now in this 6th message the figure changes to troops and horses. The description of the behemoth in Job 40:15ff, is called "the chief of what the Lord created," in the LXX. In Job 41:1 we have the beginning of leviathan (rendered "dragon" in the CVOT). In the LXX, 41:12 says,

"From its nostril proceeds smoke," and in 41:13 we read, "a flame proceeds from its mouth." The description of the war-horses, here in 9:17, may be allusions to these OT texts. (*cf* Beale, ibid p 516-17).

Let's consider the specifics of their description. The riders have breastplates of FIRE: fire is a symbol of God; in God's complete armor the breastplate is referred to as "righteousness and eschatological deliverance, etc." (Eph. 6:14). This is a figure of their being armed with God's righteous judgment, His "righting" of situations to conform them to the new creation in Christ. This armor has the appearance of a precious stone and is a foundation stone of the Jerusalem which is above (21:19-20, below). This armor also has the qualities of the Divine Character (*theios*) covering their hearts (the core of their beings) and lungs (the interchange and mingling of Breath-effects {or: exchange of spirit/Spirit}).

These horses are identified as being of the tribe of Judah, their heads symbolizing their Leader, the Lion of the tribe of Judah. What they say (what continuously issues forth from their mouths) is the same as the TWO WITNESSES of 11:5, below. They speak God's Word (Fire), with the evidence of God's presence (Smoke – *cf* Ex. 19:18), and express God's Character and Nature (Deity).

As in the exodus of Israel from Egypt, these two companies bring plagues to smite this same third of the people not having God's imprint. His presence and nature brings death to the carnal man (as it has been doing in His firstfruits company who are now judging the twelve tribes of Israel, Matt. 19:28).

18. **From these three plagues** (blows; smitings) **the third of the humans were killed – from out of the Fire, and from the Smoke, and from the Deity which is constantly issuing out of their mouths,**

From 8:7, above, on through this verse, and finally in 12:4, below, the expression "**the third**" is used fourteen times. Dan Kaplan pointed this out to me, relating it symbolically to the three divisions of the Tabernacle: the outer court, the holy place and the holy of holies (these three symbolizing the three-tiered universe of the Jews in ancient times). Then he related these to a person: the body (outer court), the soul (holy place, with its lampstand, loaves of bread and altar of incense: priestly service), and the spirit (the holy of holies: the place of God's throne, the mercy seat, and His intimate presence where we are one spirit/Spirit with Him – 1 Cor. 6:17). There are also three general stages of a person's life: childhood, youth/young adult, and being an elder. God deals with, and relates to, each of these areas and stages of development. The Way (or: Path) is the journey from the outer court, through the holy place, both of which lead to the Father. The death of the cross must come to each of these. In all phases of our life we must come to a cruciform expression of the One who died and was raised again into the higher realms of His creation (the sky; heaven) where through participating in His overcoming, we become overcomers and sit enthroned with Him (3:21, above; Eph. 2:6). The three things that issue from the horses' mouths also relate to the three sections of the Tabernacle: **Fire** (figure of the second death that God brings to us as a prelude to resurrection) in the altar of burnt offerings (outer court); **Smoke** (figure of His presence as the Light of the world) which rises from the 7-branched lampstand, and which rises with the prayers from the incense altar (both being in the holy place), and **Deity** – the One who dwells in the Holy of holies.

A literal interpretation of these metaphors could see this as a picture of the invading cavalry, on fierce war horses, coming against Jerusalem. As we have seen above, the "smitings" (**Fire, Smoke and Deity**) are all manifestations of God. Taken as a description of war-horses, Simmons (ibid p 201) points us to Job 39:19-25 where the passage ends,
> "With stamping and rage he drinks up the ground – he will not stand still when the horn sounds…
> from afar he scents the battle – the thunder of commanders and the war-cry" (Rotherham).

In Lev. 26:21 God tells Israel,

"And if you people walk contrary to Me, I will bring seven times more plagues upon you – in accord with your failures (sins; deviations)."

In the LXX, Lev. 26:25b reads, "And I will send out death against you, and you shall be delivered into the hands of your enemies." That is what we see here, which happened in AD 70. But it is whatever that is adversarial to us that He will use to keep us humble, or otherwise adjust us, as He did with Paul,

"And now, in the excess of the unveilings (or: with the transcendence of the revelations), **through this [situation] and for this reason – so that I could not be progressively exalted** (or: would not continue being overly lifted up [in myself or by others]) – **something with [its] point in [my] flesh is given in me** (or: an impaling-stake for the human nature was given for me; or: a thorn to the natural realm, and a splinter by alienated humanity, was assigned to me): **an agent of** (or: a messenger from) **the adversary, to the end that he** (or: it) **could** (or: would) **repeatedly beat me in the face with his** (or: its) **fist. I called the Lord alongside for relief, ease and comfort, and entreated [Him] three times over** (or: about) **this, so that he** (or: it) **would at once stand away and withdraw from me, and yet He has said to me – and His declaration stands, "My grace is continuously sufficient in you** (or: My joyous favor is constantly adequate to ward [it] off for you), **for you see, ability** (or: the [other MSS read: My] power) **is habitually brought to its goal** (or: finished; perfected; matured) **within the midst of weakness** (or: in union with lack of strength and infirmity)" (2 Cor. 12:7-9).

19. **for the authority** (the right, permission and license from out of Being) **of the horses exists in their mouth and in their tails, for their tails [are] like serpents, having heads, and within them they constantly inflict injustice** (harm; injury).

Now we see that their **authority** – i.e., their right, permission and license from out of Being (existence, or God) – exists in their **mouth** (symbolizing the Words which they speak; and also figuring their Head, Who originates these Words) and in their **tails** (a figure of the final part of the Body – the "time of the end of the Mosaic age" aspect of the ministry).

These end-time groups are "like" serpents – they bring judgment, as did the burning (Heb.: *seraphim*) serpents in Num. 21:6-9. The tails of these horses have **heads**: a figure of the many sons – the corporate Christ – the body which speaks this fire which inflicts injustice: the return of their own works upon them – the work of the Law, in its eye-for-an-eye system which brings death and injures them. The quelling of the Jewish rebellion by the Roman army was not through justice, but by the force of the sword – utter domination. Their soldiers inflicted "injustice" upon their subjects – which, of course, brought harm and injury. There was nothing "just" about either the rebellion or its being crushed. It was all about the power of the sword. So, too, have been the situations experienced by God's communities from then until now. This apocalyptic picture is one of devastation. But in this vision, it shows only the beginning.

20. **And yet the remaining ones** (or: the rest) **of the humans, those who were not killed in these blows** (or: wounding strikes; impacts; plagues), **did not change their mind** (change their perceptions or ways of thinking) **from out of the works** (actions; deeds) **of their hands, so that they may not worship the demons** (Hellenistic concept and term: = animistic influences) **and the idols** (forms): **the gold ones, and the wooden ones, which are able** (or: have power) **neither to see nor to hear, nor to walk about.**

We have already discussed vss. 20-21. This is the purpose statement of this entire vision. It speaks of "**blows** (or: wounding strikes; impacts; plagues)" that are corrective or instructive (as was done in child training, in that time and culture: Heb. 12:5-11; Prov. 13:24; 22:15; 23:13-14). The purpose is to impact them. It is to bring about a **change** in **their mind**, in their way of thinking, in their perception. It is to change it away from out of the works of their hands – from what they DO – to the end that they may not worship the demons (Hellenistic religious concepts) and idols (forms) i.e., all the things that they are involved in, in their daily lives: the material and the religious. The reference to **idols**, and the following description, is a reference to Ps. 115:4-7. Ps. 135:15-17 is similar. Appropriate to the theme of Babylon, in the judgments of the Unveiling, is Dan. 5:23, with its accusation against the king of Babylon:

> "Against the Lord of the heavens [you] have uplifted yourself, and the vessels of His house have they brought before you, and you and your nobles, your wives and your concubines have been drinking wine therein, and gods of silver and gold, of bronze, iron, wood and stone, which see not nor hear nor know, you have praised – whereas God, in whose hand is your breath and whose are all of your ways, HIM you have not glorified!"

Moses prophesied about this end of the age, in Deut. 31:29,

> "for I know that after my death you shall bring ruin, yes ruin on yourselves; you will withdraw from the way that I enjoined on you and the evil visitation will befall you in the latter days..."

In considering the 1st century context of this describing the people of Jerusalem and others of the old covenant who did not accept God coming to them in Jesus, as their Messiah, the failure to "**change their mind** (change their perceptions or ways of thinking) **from out of the works** (actions; deeds)" may refer to their continuing in the temple cultus and holding to the purity codes as were exemplified by the Pharisees to whom Jesus said,

> "**Blind 'guides and leaders' of the way: constantly filtering and straining [out] the gnat, yet habitually gulping** (drinking; swallowing) **down a camel! How tragic is the fate in you people – scribes and Pharisees: overly-critical interpreters! For you folks are habitually cleansing the outside of the cup and of the fine side dish – yet inside they continuously contain a full load from snatching** (plunder; pillage; = the fruits of forceful greed) **and lack of strength** (or: self-indulgence). **Blind Pharisee, first cleanse the inside of the cup and of the fine side dish – so that its outside can also come to be** (be birthed) **clean!**" (Mat. 23:24-26).

He continues His polemic against them in these following verses of that chapter:

> 29. "**It will be a tragic fate for you, theologians** (scholars of the Law) **and Pharisees [who are also] overly judging and critical** [see 6:2, above]. **Because, [you see], you are repeatedly building the tombs** (sepulchers) **of the prophets, and are constantly adorning and decorating the memorial grave monuments of just and rightwised folks,**
> 30. "**and you are habitually saying, 'If we had been existing in the days of our fathers** (= ancestors), **we would not have been participants** (partners; ones who shared in common and took part) **in [spilling] the blood of the prophets.'**
> 31. "**As a result, you are continually giving evidence in yourselves** (testifying to and for yourselves) **that you exist being sons of those that were murdering the prophets,**
> 32. "**And so, you, yourselves... Fill full the measure of your fathers!**
> 33. "**[You] snakes! [You] offspring** (brood) **of vipers** (poisonous serpents)**! How can you flee and escape from the judging which has the qualities, character and significance of the valley of Hinnom** (= the sentence to the city dump [Greek: *Gehenna*; = the Valley of Hinnom]; the deciding which pertains to the waste depository of the city)**?** [*cf* Jer. 19:1-15]
> 34. "**Because of this – look and consider! – I, Myself, am continuing in commissioning and sending off to you people prophets, wise people and scholars** (scribes; theologians of the Law). **Of them, [some] you folks will proceed to be killing, and [some] you will proceed to crucify** (hang and put to death on stakes). **Further, of them [some] you people will continue severely whipping** (scourge; lash) **within your synagogues, and then you, yourselves, will continue pursuing and persecuting [them] from city to city** (or: town to town),
> 35. "**so that upon you, yourselves, can** (or: should) **come all [the] just** (equitable; rightwised) **blood being continuously poured out** (or: spilled) **upon the Land – from the blood of**

rightwised (just; fair; in-right-relationship) **Abel, until the blood of Zechariah, the son of Barachiah** (or: Baruch), **whom you people murdered between the Temple and the altar.**
36. **"Assuredly, I am now saying to you people, it will progressively move toward this point, and then arrive – all these things! – upon this generation!**
37. **"O Jerusalem, Jerusalem! The one repeatedly killing the prophets, and habitually stoning the people sent off with a mission to her. How many times** (or: How often) **I wanted** (intended; purposed; longed) **to progressively gather your children together upon [Myself] in the manner in which a hen normally gathers her chicks together under [her] wings – and you did not want [it]** (or: you do not intend [it]). [cf Ruth 2:12; Ps. 17:6; 36:7; 57:1]
38. **"Look, and think about this! 'Your House is progressively left [to be] a wilderness** (desert; desolate place) **for you people** (or: is now abandoned to you).' [Jer. 22:5]
39. **"You see, I now say to you, you should by no means perceive** (or: see) **Me from this time on, until you folks should at some point say,**
> **'The One periodically coming in [the] Lord's** [= Yahweh's] **Name is One having been given – and still having – words of ease and wellness** (or: having been given the Blessing)**!'"** [Ps. 118:26]

1 Tim. 4:1-2 adds to these dire predictions:
"**Now the Spirit** (or: Breath-effect) **is explicitly saying that within subsequent seasons** (in fitting situations and on appropriate occasions which will be afterwards) **some of the faith** (or: certain folks belonging to this trust) **will proceed standing off and away [from the Path, or from the Community]** (or: some people will progressively withdraw from this conviction and loyalty), **habitually holding toward** (having a propensity to) **wandering and deceptive spirits** (or: straying and seducing breath-effects and attitudes) **and to teachings of demons**
> (to teachings about and pertaining to, or which are, demons [note: a Hellenistic concept and term: = animistic influences]; or: to instructions and training which come from animistic influences [= pagan religions]),

within perverse scholarship of false words from folks having their own consciences cauterized (seared; branded) **as with a hot iron**."
Another picture of Paul's day, and his prediction of the end of that age is found in 2 Tim. 3:
1. **Now progressively come to know this and continue realizing it, that within [the] last** (or: final) **days hard seasons** (difficult occasions and situations; irksome, perilous or fierce seasons) **will progressively set themselves in** (take a stand within; put themselves in place),
2. **for the people will continue being folks that are fond of themselves** (selfish), **fond of silver** (= money or things of monetary value), **empty pretenders** (impostors; ostentatious self-assumers), **haughty and arrogant, blasphemers** (abusive slanderers; folks who defame with a false image; or: light-hinderers), **uncompliant and disobedient to parents, ungrateful** (or: unthankful), **undutiful** (disloyal; without regard for divine or natural laws),
3. **without natural affection, unwilling to make a treaty** (not open to an agreement), **devils** (adversarial slanderers; folks who throw or thrust something through people to hurt or cause divisions), **without strength** (without [self-] control), **uncultivated** (wild; ferocious), **without fondness for expressions of good or aspects of goodness** (or: unfriendly; averse to virtue),
4. **pre-committers** (or: ones who give-over in advance, or who abandon), **rash** (reckless), **folks having been inflated with the fumes of conceit** (or: ones being beclouded in smoke), **pleasure-lovers rather than friends of God,**
5. **continuously having a form of reverence** (virtuous conduct) **yet being folks having refused** (or: turned their back on) **and now denying its power and ability! And so, be habitually turning your steps in a direction away from these folks and avoid them,**

> 6. **for you see, forth from out of the midst of these folks are the people repeatedly slipping-in, into the houses,** (or: households) **and habitually leading into captivity little women – those having been piled on and now being heaped up with failures** (errors; misses of the target; deviations from the goal; sins), **being constantly, or from time to time, led by** (or: in; to) **various** (diverse) **over-desires** (or: full passions; wants and wishes that are rushed upon),
> 7. **at all times folks that are constantly learning, and yet not at any time being able or having consistent power to come into a full, accurate experiential and intimate knowledge of Truth** (or: which is reality).

The charge of this verse in chapter 9 may also be an allusion to Isa. 65:3,
> "The people... burn incense on bricks to demons – which do not exist" (LXX, JM).

Verse 11 of that same chapter reads, "But you folks are they that have left Me, and forget My set-apart mountain, and prepare a table to (or: for) the demon, and fill up the drink-offering to (or: for) Fortune (or: Fate)" (LXX, JM). Here, again, is an association of the term "demon" with mythology and idolatry – worship of gods that do not exist. Israel played the prostitute:
> "How is the faithful city become a prostitute! It was full of judgment (or: justice); righteousness (doing what was right) lodged in it; but now murderers" (Isa. 1:21).

Yahweh continues with a promise of correction, in Isa. 1:25,
> "I will turn (or: restore) My hand upon you and purge away and refine your dross in a crucible; and I will take away all your tin [alloy; = that which is substandard or impure which lessens its value]."

This is what the Unveiling is about: the Fires (God's involvements in history) of purification and transformation.

21. **Also, they did not change their mind** (attitude and way of thinking) **from out of their murders, nor from out of their employment of drugs** (or: sorceries; enchantments), **nor from out of their prostitution** (fornication; [other MSS: worthless, misery-gushed {life}]), **nor from out of their thefts.**

This lists some of their acts: murder, sorceries (employment of drugs), prostitution, and thefts.
> "Everyone constantly hating (or: regarding with ill-will or detaching from) his brother constantly exists being a person-slayer (a murderer), and has not seen so as to be aware that every person-slayer does not presently have (or: is not continuously holding) life having its source in, or having the quality of, the Age (or: eonian life) presently remaining within him (or: continuously dwelling and abiding in union with him)" (1 John 3:15).

This was also written to the called-out by John in his first letter. As to sorceries, this too was a charge against Babylon in 18:23, below, an echo of Isa. 47:9 and 12. Prostitution was a problem in the community at Thyatira (2:20, above) and at Pergamos (2:14, above). We tend to think of such things only among the "heathen;" the "unsaved." Paul, in Rom. 2:21 chides the Judaizers, "**You, the one constantly preaching, 'Do not steal,' are habitually stealing!**" Those things common in "the world" (outside the covenant communities) are also common among God's people. This book, "*An Unveiling of Jesus Christ*," is written to, and applies to, the church. God's messages (here figured by the blowing of a trumpet) usually came to God's people, or to the leadership in Babylon, when God's people were in captivity there. As Peter stated in 1 Pet. 4:17, God's judgments begin at God's house.

The alternate MS reading, "worthless; misery-gushed," has good witnesses. This word is broader in its semantic range and so is a more general term than "prostitution/fornication." Either word works in the context.

A situation that probably involved "**employment of drugs**" is recorded in Acts 19:19. Following Paul's preaching in Ephesus,

"a considerable number of the folks practicing the meddling arts (= sorcery or magic arts), **after bringing together the scrolls, began burning [them] down** (= up) **in the sight of all**."

In our local gathering here, as we were first sharing regarding the significance of "the Deep," our son Joshua received the insight that this could be applied to "the Deep" within each of us. Just as the horses of the first 4 seals were seen as riding through us, so too we can see application here of the inward working of the Forces directed by His Spirit to cause us to repent from the works of our hands, that we, the first-fruits, may not be worshiping demons and idols "which we have made" (Lev. 19:4; 26:1). Outwardly, God uses other people, or nations, to bring judgment to His people (.e.g. the Babylonians in the OT; the Romans, here, in the NT). The Jews were branches that were broken off of the olive tree by God (via the Romans) in AD 70. But keep in mind that they can be grafted back in again (Rom. 11:17-26). In our lives He also uses other people to bring His fiery trials to purge His threshing floor (the inward work upon our self-lives).

As the literal Jerusalem was judged because it had departed from God, may we not now, in this present age, as the New Jerusalem, need to be corrected? Consider the conditions in the many "churches." Does not the "New Babylon," the church system which has man and man's structures and programs as the head, instead of Christ, also need to fall? Will there be a "spiritual" army that will destroy the current abomination which makes His people desolate? Selah!

In *The Days of Vengeance*, David Chilton, in considering chapters 8-14, says that this section,
> "dealt with the sanctions (curses and blessings) of the covenant (*cf* Deut. 27:1-26). In Deut., these sanctions are set forth in the context of a ratification ceremony, in which the Covenant between God and the people is renewed. Moses instructed the people to divide into two groups, six tribes on Mt. Gerizim (the symbol of blessing) and six at an altar built on Mt. Ebal (the symbol of cursing).... Moses made it clear that this Covenant oath involved not only the people who swore to it, with their wives, children, and servants, but also with the generations to come (Deut. 29:10-15).
>
> "Deut. 28 is practically the paradigmatic blessing/curse section of the entire Bible.... When the days of vengeance finally came to that generation, they were cursed in every aspect of life (Deut. 28:15-19); smitten with pestilence of every sort (Deut. 28:20-26); visited with plague, violence, and oppression (Deut. 28:27-37); struck by poor harvests, economic reversals, and the loss of their children (Deut. 28:38-48); besieged by enemies and starved into cannibalistic practices (Deut. 28:49-57); enslaved and scattered throughout the nations of the world, living in fear and despair night and day (Deut. 28:58-68).
>
> "'And all the nations shall say, Why has the LORD done thus to this Land? Why this great outburst of anger? Then the men shall say, Because they forsook the Covenant of the LORD....' (Deut. 29:22f).
>
> "Thus, the central image of this section of Rev. is a Covenant ratification ceremony (ch. 10), in which the Angel of the Covenant stands on the Sea and on the Land, lifting His right hand to heaven, swearing an oath and proclaiming the coming of the New Covenant... under 'the Lord and His Christ; and He will reign forever and ever' (Rev. 11:15)" (ibid p 225-7).

Foy Wallace (*The Book of Revelation*) concludes on this vision, "It was therefore in harmony with all the facts, scriptural and historical, that the mighty cavalry... was the immense Roman army which marched against Jerusalem… resulting in all the desolation foretold by Daniel and depicted by the Lord in pointing [to] the fulfillment." (ibid p 200).

Bruce Metzger says, "the overall intention of the sounding of the 7 trumpets is ... to bring people to repentance.... there is great emphasis on God's patience and mercy. Instead of total destruction, only 1/3 (9:18) or some other fraction of the whole is affected. The fraction is symbolic of the mercy of God. The calamity is not universal but leaves those who can learn from tragic events." (ibid p 66).

So I have here presented two interpretations of this chapter: the preterist view of a literal application of these symbols to Jerusalem in AD 70, and a figurative view of God's inward dealing with people and His called-out community at all times and in every place. But the good news is that Deut. 28 applied only to Israel. Its stipulations applied only to the Mosaic covenant that Yahweh made with Israel. It never applied to the Gentiles – the ethnic multitudes. With this final destruction of Jerusalem and Israel as a national entity, the curses of the Law ceased to exist. Paul explained this in Gal. 3:

> 10. **You see, however many people continue their existence from the midst of observances and works of Law** (= Everyone who lives by deeds based upon the Torah) **are continuously under a curse, for it has been and now stands written, namely that,**
>> **"A curse** (or: an adversarial prayer; imprecation) **[is settled] upon all** (or: [is] added to everyone) **not constantly remaining within all the things having been and standing written within the scroll of the Law** [= Torah], **in order to do them."** [Deut. 27:26]
>
> 13. **Christ bought us [back] out** (or: redeems and reclaims us out [of slavery] and liberates us) **from the midst of the curse of and from the Law, while becoming a curse** (or: accursed One) **for our sakes** (or: over our [situation])…
>
> 14. **to the end that the Good Word** (the Blessing) **pertaining to Abraham** (belonging to and possessed by Abraham; whose intermediary source is Abraham) **could within Jesus Christ suddenly birth Itself** (or: may from Itself, within Christ Jesus, at once come into being [and be dispersed]) **into the multitudes** (the nations; the ethnic groups; the Gentiles), **so that we** [note: "we" = the new "one" mankind] **could receive the Spirit's promise through the Faithfulness [of Christ]**
>> (or: to the end that we [all] may take in hand the Promise from the Breath-effect, through faith and trust; or: in order that we [Jew and Gentile] can lay hold of and receive the Promise – which is the Spirit – through that loyalty; [cf Isa. 44:3]).

Then, in Gal. 5:1 he admonishes them:

> **"For the [aforementioned] freedom, Christ immediately set us free** (or: [The] Anointed One at once frees us in, to, for and with freedom)! **Keep on standing firm, therefore, and do not again be habitually held within a yoke of slavery** (or: a cross-lever [of a pair of scales] whose sphere is bondage)
>> (or: Continuously stand firm, then, in the freedom [to which the] Anointing sets us free, and let not yourselves be progressively confined again by a yoke pertaining to servitude)!"

As J. Preston Eby has often said of such good news: "Aren't you glad!?" In Rom. 10:4, Paul put it this way:

> **"for you see, Christ [is] an end of Law** (or: for Christ [is] Law's goal and destiny; for [the] Anointing [is] termination from [the] Law; for Christ [was the] final act of [the] Law) **[leading] into the Way pointed out in fair and equitable dealings, and rightwised [covenant] relationships of justice in eschatological liberation, to, for and in everyone habitually trusting and believing**
>> (or: because Christ [entering] into the pointed-out Way – in everyone normally exercising faith with conviction, and with each person remaining loyal – [is; brings] Law's climax)."

Christ has made all things new (21:5, below). There is an entirely new arrangement (or: covenant): its realm is "within the midst of, and centered in, Christ," and its law is Love – God's love, dwelling with us – humanity dwelling in God (Acts 17:28). In fact, we have this beautiful affirmation, from Paul,

> "**Now [look], we have seen, and thus know and are aware, that to those habitually or progressively loving and giving themselves to God – to the folks being called and invited according to [the] purpose – He is constantly working all things together into good and is progressively working all humanity together into that which is advantageous, worthy of admiration, noble and of excellent qualities**" (Rom. 8:28).

Let us keep our present reality in mind as we continue studying the 1st century judgments that came upon Jerusalem.

Chapter 10

William Barclay refers to this section of Revelation as "a kind of interlude between the sounding of the 6th and 7th trumpets" (ibid p 54). Others agree with this perspective, and 10:1 does present a change in the scene from what John was seeing in 9:21. Yet is this a separate vision between the messages of these two trumpets; or is it another aspect of the 6th trumpet, giving us more information about what is involved in this message? Terry (ibid p 358) sees four things presented in this interlude: (1) the Strong Agent descending from "heaven" (10:1-7); (2) the eating of the little scroll (8-11); (3) measuring the temple of God (11:1-2); (4) the two witnesses (11:3-13). The 7th trumpet does not sound until 11:15, below. Beale sees this section as "an interpretative parenthesis…. put within the cycle of trumpets to connect the two halves of the Apocalypse together" (ibid p 520). He further sees chapter 10 as being "the introduction to the main content of the parenthesis in 11:1-13" (ibid). This interlude has been viewed as "covering the same period of time" as covered in chapters 8-9, above (Beale, ibid p 521). Simmons points out that, "At the conclusion of the 6th seal, there was an interlude consisting of a twofold vision…. Now, at the conclusion of the 6th trumpet, there is yet another interlude consisting of a twofold vision" (ibid p 203).

1. Next I saw another Strong Agent progressively descending (stepping down) **from out of the atmosphere** (or: sky; heaven) **– having been clothed with a cloud, and the rainbow upon His head, and His face as the sun, and His feet as pillars of fire**

Here John is observing action that comes from heaven (or: the sky) to the earth. This would also be the same as his observing the Star that had fallen from out of heaven (the sky), in 9:1, above. Wherever John's "location," he is in the realm of spirit and vision. The action in chapters 9 and 10 is in a different setting than the opening scenes of chapter 4.

John saw "the action" of this Strong Agent: **progressively descending** (literally: stepping down). The literal meaning is important. It calls to mind what Jesus said to Philip, in Jn. 1:51,

> "**I am presently saying to you folks, you will proceed seeing the heaven** (or: atmosphere; sky) **being one that is opened back up again, and 'God's agents repeatedly** (progressively; continuously) **ascending** (stepping back up again) **and habitually** (progressively; continuously; repeatedly) **descending** (stepping down)' [Gen. 28:12] **upon the Son of the Man** (or: Mankind's Son; the Son of humanity; the Human Son; = the Human Being; = the eschatological Messianic figure)."

We saw "a strong agent" in 5:2, above; now we see **another** One. The description of **another Strong Agent** in verses 1 and 2 is acknowledged by many to be a figure of Christ, similar to that presented in chapter 1, above. But let's look at the particulars given here:

a) "**Clothed with a cloud**": Barclay cites Ps. 104:3, "God makes the clouds His chariot." Recalling Nah. 1:3 ("the clouds are the dust of His feet"), Heb. 12:1, Mk. 13:26, and Prinzing's definition that, "literally a cloud is a visible mass of moisture suspended in the air… [and] it bespeaks of a people who have been lifted out of the debris of earth's corruption…," let us consider the likelihood that this figure represents the complete Christ – Jesus and His body. As to the cloud being the clothing of this figure, recall Paul's use of "clothing" as a figure of a body in 2 Cor. 5:1-4. We find, "**a Woman having been clothed** (cast around) **with the sun**" in 12:1, below. Here we see another picture of Christ, perhaps the corporate Christ, continually, or repeatedly, coming (descending) in "the dust of His feet," clothed with His body of sons and daughters. Marvin Vincent comments that the expression "a cloud" occurs seven times in this book, and that in all of them it is connected with the Son of Man. This symbol may also be an allusion to Ex. 40:34-38, where it could be said that a cloud clothed the Tabernacle:

> "Then a cloud covered the tent of the congregation, and the glory of Yahweh filled the Tabernacle…. The cloud of Yahweh [was] upon the Tabernacle by day, and fire was on it by night…"

In Lev. 16:2c, Yahweh told Moses, "I will appear in the cloud, upon the mercy seat," which is echoed in Mat.17:5,

> "**a cloud composed of light** (or: a cloud full of light; a cloud radiating light; a luminous cloud; an illuminated cloud) **suddenly brought shade upon them** (or: cast a shadow over them; overshadowed, or enveloped them). **And think of this! A Voice – from out of the midst of the cloud – progressively saying, 'This Man continues existing being My Son… Make it a habit to listen, to continue paying attention, and then to [really] hear Him** (implies: obey Him)!'"

The sense of the cloud "enveloping" them could be understood as "clothing" them. In 11:12, below, the two witnesses,

> "**heard a great** (or: loud) **Voice from out of the atmosphere** (or: sky; heaven), **repeatedly saying to them, 'You must climb up here** (or: ascend to this place).' **So they climbed up into the atmosphere** (or: ascended into the sky and heaven) **within the cloud**."

It could be that their ascent is into the same cloud that clothes the strong Agent, here. Poetic images involving clouds, and God's presence, are numerous in the OT. Ps. 18:11 is an example, "[He] made darkness his hiding-place (or: concealment) round about Him – His pavilion (or: booth), darkness of water, the thick clouds of the skies." Then there is Ps. 97:2, "Clouds and darkness [are] round about Him: righteousness (the righting deliverance of [His] way) and [right] judgment (or: justice; the effect of [His] decisions) [are] the basis and establishment of His throne" (MT with LXX, JM). Establishing God's presence by the symbol of a cloud is seen in Isa. 19:1a,

> "Yahweh rides upon a swift cloud, and shall come into Egypt…"

In Ex. 16:10, all the assembly of the sons of Israel, "turned towards the desert, -- and lo! – the glory of Yahweh appeared in the cloud."

b) "**The rainbow upon His head**": the rainbow in the cloud speaks of God's "covenant between [God] and the earth" (Gen. 9:13). This first setting of His bow in the cloud followed upon the judgment of the flood in Noah's day. Here too, it would seem to follow the judgments of chapter 9, but also, the bow was seen around the throne in 4:3, above, and this would suggest the thought that the throne (place of authority and ruling) is upon the Head, or IS the Head. For another look at "the bow which comes in a cloud," see Ezk. 1:26-28, with the vision of the throne and the "living beings." Prinzing associates the bow with "The Messenger of the Covenant" in Mal. 3:1. That the definite article "**the**" is used in speaking of "**the rainbow**," prompts Beale to consider it "an article of previous reference" (ibid p 524), thus providing a connection between 10:1, here, and 4:3, above.

c) "**His face as the sun**": see 1:16, above. We find this same description of the transfigured Jesus in Mat. 17:2, "**He was transformed** (changed in external form and appearance) **and His face radiated light, like a lamp, and shone like the sun.**" This can be seen as an allusion to Jn. 1:9,

> "**It was** (or: He was, and continued being) **the True and Genuine Light which** (or: Who) **is continuously** (repeatedly; progressively) **enlightening** (giving light to) **every person** (or: human) **continuously** (repeatedly; progressively; constantly; one after another) **coming into the world** (or: the ordered system of culture, religion, economics and government; or: the universe)
>
>> (or: It was the real Light, progressively coming into the world {organized system}, which is progressively enlightening {or: shedding light on} every human)."

In Jn. 8:12, Jesus said,

> "**I, Myself, am** (or: continuously exist being) **the Light of the world** [perhaps = the sun] (or: of the aggregate of humanity; of the ordered system; of the dominant cultural, political, economic and religious arrangements; of the universe; of 'the theater of history' – Walter Wink).
>
> **The one habitually and progressively following Me can by no means walk around** (= under no circumstances live his or her life) **within the darkness**
>
>> (or: the dim and shaded areas; the gloom and obscurity due to the lack of the Light of the Day; the [realm] of the shadows; [note: = ignorance; = that situation which existed before the Light came; or, could also refer to the dim condition within the holy place of the Temple, or to the darkness of death, blindness or the womb]),
>
> **but, to the contrary, he will progressively possess** (constantly have and hold) **the Light of 'the Life!'** (or: the light which is life; or: the Light from the Life.)"

Also, Paul spoke of Light shining forth, "**within the midst of our hearts, with a view to illumination of the intimate and experiential knowledge of God's glory – in Christ's face**" (2 Cor. 4:6). There is also the prophecy in Mal. 4:2, "the Sun of righteousness shall arise, with healing in His wings [Lamsa's rendering of the Peshita reads, 'healing upon his lips']."

d) "**His feet as pillars of fire**": similar to the description in 1:15, above, "**like bronze glowing in a furnace**," but here judgment is not emphasized (the bronze), rather it is God's essence: FIRE. The feet symbolize our walk on the Way – i.e., our daily living the cruciform Life as we follow Christ (Who IS the Way), walking the Path as we are led by the Spirit (Rom. 8:14). Beale (ibid p 525) cites Philo (*De Decalogo* 44), who paraphrases Ex. 19:18 "as 'the descent of a cloud which like a pillar stood with its foot planted on earth.'" Although the text does not state it, we can assume that there are two feet. As the feet represent the latter part, or end time, of the figure (*cf* the image in Dan. 2:28, 34), these two pillars of fire are His two witnesses upon the earth (11:5, below) – to bring His cleansing fire to the earth realm. When God led Israel by night in the wilderness it was by a pillar of fire (Ex. 13:21-22). Perhaps this speaks of His anointed leadership, protection and presence (as it was with Israel on their wilderness journey), via His two witnesses, who will lead the called-out communities through their dark night at that time (i.e., the 1st century), or, at any time. This idea is inherent in the proclamation of this Strong Agent in vss. 6-7, below. The overall description of this Agent calls to mind what Daniel saw when by the Tigris River (Hiddekel), in Dan. 10:5-6,

> "One Man clothed in linen. His waist girded with gold of Uphaz [perhaps = Ophir]; His body [was] like topaz (Tarshish-stone), His face like an appearance of lightning, His eyes like torches of fire, His arms and His feet [= legs?] like the sparkle of dazzling bronze, and the sound of His talking like the sound of a throng."

Jeremiah was set as a pillar of iron (Jer. 1:18). The overcomer in 3:12, above, is made a pillar in God's temple (His body). Rom 10:15, quoting Isa. 52:7, prophesies of these **feet**:

> "**How timely and seasonable [are] the feet of the folks continually bringing and announcing goodness** (or: the good news of ease and well-being)**: the good and excellent things!**"

Then in Eph. 6:15-16a Paul encourages us,

> "**sandaling the feet in readiness and in union with preparedness which comes from, has the character of and which belongs to the good news** (or: message of goodness and well-being) **of the Peace** (from the joining) – **within all situations** (or: in union with **all people**)…"

Finally, appropriate here is Ps. 119:59b, "let me turn back my feet to Your testimonies."

We see the symbolic action of a strong agent, along with a proclamation, in 18:21, below. We will also see, "**a bright, white cloud. And upon the cloud One like a son of man** (= a human; or: = the eschatological Messiah figure) **continually sitting, having a golden wreath upon His head**," in 14:14, below. That is an allusion to Dan. 7:13, where the LXX reads, "One progressively coming with the clouds of the sky (or: from heaven), AS a Son of humanity…" (JM).

An agent of Yahweh is frequently seen in the OT. Here is one example: in Gen. 22:15-17 we find, "And an Agent of [the] LORD (= Yahweh's Agent) called Abram the second time, out of the sky (or: heaven), saying, 'I have sworn by Myself, says [the] LORD (= Yahweh proceeds laying it out)… Surely, in continuously blessing I will progressively bless you…" (LXX, JM). *Cf* Jud. 2:1-3. In Acts 5:19 we read,

> "**during [the] night, an agent of [the] Lord** (= Christ's messenger, or an agent from Yahweh; or: = a person doing the Lord's bidding and then delivering His message) **opened the gates** (or: doors) **of the prison** (or: jail; place of being under guard). **Then, after leading them out**…"

We see in Scripture both symbolic visions (such as here in 10:1ff, and 18:21, below) and actual persons (such as in Acts 5:19 or in 22:8-9, below, in this *Unveiling*) from the realm of spirit, that are either a message, themselves, or are serving as God's agents to humanity.

James Stuart Russell points out that this Strong Agent who is speaking to John, in this chapter, is the same one that continues speaking to him in 11:1, below, and in 11:3 He says,

> "**I will continue giving to My two witnesses** (or: I will progressively supply for My two witnesses), **and they will proceed prophesying** (functioning as prophets)…"

Thus, he rightly concludes that this Agent "is no other than 'the Lord himself'" (*The Parousia*, Kingdom Publications, 1996, p 419).

Kaplan directs us to Heb. 1:1-3 as another view of what we see here, in 10:1,

> 1. **Long ago, in many parts** (or: fragments; = bit by bit) **and in much-traveled ways consisting of many turns and directions, God, having spoken to** (or: by; in; with) **the fathers – in** (= through; in [the words of]) **the prophets –**
> 2. **upon [the] last of these days spoke to us in a Son whom He placed** (or: sets) **[as; to be] Heir of all** (or: One who receives all humanity as an allotment; or: heir of all things) **through Whom He also made the ages**
>> (or: formed and constructed the various designated periods of time [which compose existence, as well as God's influence and activities]);
> 3. **Who, continuously being an effect of the radiance from**
>> (or: a result from a dawning and breaking forth of the bright light of the Day which is; a result of the outshining which is; an effulgence from) **the Glory and Splendor as well as an exact impress** (or: exact likeness as from a stamp or a die) **of His substructure**

(or: of His substance [that is] standing under as a foundation; which is the underlying support of His outward form and properties; or: from His assumed groundwork of the full expression [of His idea]) – **besides continuously bearing** (or: and while progressively carrying; and then repeatedly bringing) **the whole** (all things; everything and all existence) **by the gush-effect which is His power**

(or: in the result of the flow from the power which is Him; or: in the spoken declaration of, and which has the character of His power and ability) **through and by means of Himself – in producing a cleansing of the failures** (the misses of the target; the mistakes, errors and sins) **He at once seated Himself within [the] right part** (or: hand; = in union with an honored position and place of power) **of the Greatness centered and resident within high places.**

2. – and constantly holding in His hand a tiny scroll having been opened up. And He placed His right foot upon the sea, but the left upon the Land (soil; earth).

Now in this scene we have "**a tiny scroll**" (smaller than the one in ch. 5) and it is opened up. He is continuously holding it in His hand – which we later see is there for us to seize (take with our hands) and to devour. From the difference in size, as well as the difference in function, it would seem that this is a different scroll than the one in ch. 5. This one can be taken by a person, and is meant for someone to eat it and to digest its contents, and then, perhaps, deliver its message to "peoples and multitudes" (vs. 11). An open scroll signifies that its contents are available to be read, and considering that the sealed scroll reference in Dan. 12:9 meant that the writing pertained to the distant future, this open one meant that the time was near with regard to what the scroll said. Isa. 29:11 speaks of a sealed scroll signifying that it could not be read, in that condition. The scroll "**having been opened up**" speaks of the fact that its contents are revealed; the message from "heaven" is open both to the Strong Agent, and then, to John. This may be an allusion to Mat. 3:16,

"**Now upon being immersed** (baptized), **Jesus immediately** (straightway) **stepped back up from the water – and now look and consider! – the heavens at once opened back up again!** [or, with other MSS: the atmospheres were opened up to Him!] **Then He saw God's Spirit** (Breath-effect; Breath) **– as if it were a dove steadily descending – progressively coming upon Him.**" [cf Gen. 1:2]

The Unveiling that John received and wrote down has opened the heavens back up to us, again. What the scroll said is not important to the message of this vision. It is the scene that John sees, and the action that he is given to do, that are the message of this vision.

The figure of His stand also speaks of His complete, universal dominion – its all-inclusiveness. Noting Deut. 11:24 and Joshua 1:3 ("Every place on which the soles of your feet shall tread shall be yours"), the A. E. Knoch's *Concordant Commentary* says, "The planting of the messenger's feet on the sea and on the land is a token of possession." This figure is seen in a reference to Abraham's life, in Acts 7:5.

Upon Land (a figure of Israel or God's people, since "the land" is a figure of Israel throughout the OT and was a central figure in God's dealing with Israel where many of the prophesies were directed to "the Land;" see Walter Brueggemann, *The Land, Place as Gift, Promise and Challenge in Biblical Faith*, Fortress Press, 1977) and **upon the sea** (a figure of the masses of the remainder of humanity, the ethnic multitudes, the Gentiles) speaks to the universal dominion of God's kingdom that has now joined Jew and Gentile, circumcision and uncircumcision (Eph. 2:10-18). We are not told which **sea** it is, upon which He places **His right foot**; if it is the Sea of Galilee, then the setting would be Palestine, but if it is the Mediterranean, then this might indicate that the army coming from Rome is under His dominion. As Barclay points out, "sea and land stand for the sum total of the universe" (ibid). The setting, here, is outside of the temple and applies to the complete world of the Jews (Ex. 20:11a; cf Ps. 69:34). When

Yahweh was angry with His people (Isa.5:25) He said that He would call the far-off nations, and those nations would "roar against [Israel] like the roaring of the sea," while the Land (Israel) would have "darkness and distress" (5:30). Another picture is seen in Isa. 17:12-13,

"Alas! The booming of many peoples like the booming of the seas... and the rushing of nations! Like the rushing of mighty waters" (Rotherham).

The classic sea metaphor is Isa. 57:20, "But the lawless are like the sea, when tossed…" Close to our context in this vision is Lu. 21:25,

"there will keep on being signs: in sun and moon and stars… a constraint from [the] non-Jews (or: with a character of pagans; which is nations) **in the midst of a perplexity in which there seems no way out – [like being in the] roar and surging of a sea."**

Cf 13:1, 11, below.

The scroll "**having been opened up**" speaks of the situation of all that John has been seeing, and will yet see: an Unveiling; a Disclosure; a Revelation from and concerning Jesus Christ. This is the same message of which Paul spoke in Col. 1:26, concerning:

"**the Secret** (or: sacred mystery) **having been hidden away and remaining concealed away from the ages** (or: from [past] eons), **as well as away from the [past] generations, yet now is set in clear light in His set-apart folks** (or: is shown for what it is, for His sacred people)."

Because of this, we read of the situation of the new creation with its new arrangement,

"**now** (at the present moment), **being set in clear light so as to become visible** (or: manifested) **through the bringing to full light** (or: the full appearance in and by [the] Light) **of our Deliverer** (Savior; Rescuer), **Christ Jesus – on the one hand, idling down death** (or: The Death) **so as to make it unproductive and useless, yet on the other hand, illuminating** (giving light to) **life and incorruptibility** (the absence of the ability to decay) **through means of the message of goodness, ease and well-being**" (2 Tim. 1:10).

3. **Then He uttered a cry with** (or: by) **a great Voice, even as a Lion is roaring. And when He uttered a cry** (or: cried out), **the Seven Thunders uttered their own voices.**

We saw a similar cry, from the first "strong agent," in 5:2, above. This cry of **the great Voice** is, "**as a Lion is roaring**": Joel 3:16 reads, "And Yahweh shall **roar** from Zion." And then, in Amos 3:8, "The Lion roars – who will not fear? My Lord Yahweh **speaks** – who will not prophesy?" So here, again, we see the Lion of the Tribe of Judah. When He speaks, the Seven Thunders give their message, but John is not allowed to share this (vs. 4, below). The picture is a strong Messenger uttering a cry – and He has just descended from out of heaven. This sounds like 1 Thes. 4:16,

"**the Lord** [= Yahweh or Christ] **Himself will continue habitually descending** (or: repeatedly descend) **from [the] atmosphere** (or: heaven) **within the midst of** (or: in union with) **a shout of command, within the midst of [the] Chief Agent's** (or: in union with an original messenger's or a chief and ruling agent's) **voice, and within the midst of** (or: in union with) **God's trumpet** [note: figure of a message or a directive for action], **and the dead people within Christ** (or: in union with [the] Anointed One) **will continue raising themselves up first** (or: will one-after-another be standing up again in [the or their] first place)."

So this picture is of a coming of the Lord, a "**descent**" into the affairs of mankind; it is a picture of His taking dominion over the situation of humanity, and of the proclamation of a message. This word from Paul to Thessalonica calls to mind the words of Jesus in Jn. 5:25, 28-29,

"**Count on it, I am presently continuing to say to you folks that an hour is progressively** (or: presently in process of) **coming, and even now exists** (or: = is now here), **when the dead folks WILL be repeatedly hearing the voice of God's Son** (or: the Voice from, and which is, the Son of God), **and the ones hearing WILL proceed to be living**.… **Don't you folks be constantly**

> **amazed at this, because an hour is progressively** (or: presently; or: repeatedly) **coming within which all the people within the memorial tombs** (or: graves) **– will be continuously or repeatedly hearing His voice, and they will proceed journeying out: the ones doing virtue** (producing good) **into a resurrection which is Life** (or: of, from and with the quality of Life); **the ones practicing careless** (worthless, cheap, paltry, inefficient, thoughtless or mean) **things into a resurrection of evaluating for a decision** (or: a resurrection which is a judging)."

Scholars have assumed that what the 7 thunders uttered referred in some way to judgment (an obvious theme in this book), and have offered a variety of ideas concerning the meaning of the utterances. But "**their own voices**" (vs. 3) seem simply to be a response to the **cry** of the **great Voice** of the Strong Agent. Folks have suggested that **the Seven Thunders** are a reference to the seven voices of God in Ps. 29. There, in vs. 3, we read, "The voice of Yahweh is over the waters; the God of glory thunders." If this allusion is a key, then we could surmise that what the thunders said applied to the nations (which is what "the waters" usually signified, in Scripture). The last line of Ps. 29:3 reads, "Yahweh is over the many waters [i.e., nations]." In vss. 4-5 are three more statements about the voice of Yahweh: a) it [sounds; comes] with vigor; b) it [is filled with or comes] with honor; c) it [is] breaking the cedars of Lebanon. Then vs. 7 describes the voice of Yahweh as "hewing [with] blazes of fire." Indeed, this third point c), along with vs. 7, sounds like judgement, but points a) and b) call to mind His rescue of Israel in the Exodus story. And there are two more "voices of Yahweh" in this psalm:

> 8. The voice of Yahweh, it is causing the wilderness to travail (brings birth-pains – Rotherham)...
> 9. The voice of Yahweh, it makes the hinds travail [in birth] (causes the gazelles to bring forth—Rotherham) and He is stripping the wildwoods bare. In His temple everyone is saying, "Glory!"
> 10. Yahweh, He sat [enthroned] above the deluge (at the Flood – Rotherham), and Yahweh shall sit [enthroned as] King for the eon (unto times age-abiding – Rotherham).
> 11. Yahweh, strength shall He give to His people; Yahweh, He shall bless His people with peace (prosperity – Rotherham). (CVOT; Rotherham inserted)

So we see that the final voices of Yahweh cause birth of new life as He sits enthroned, and He gives His people strength and blesses them with peace and prosperity. These 7 voices, which thunder over all the nations, have a positive end in view: new birth, blessing and peace.

As with the definite article used in the phrase "the rainbow" (vs. 1, above), here the expression "**the 7 thunders**" references a specific, symbolic, group, and we do not find John asking who or what they are – he apparently understands the apocalyptic symbolism. In 14:2, below, John hears,

> "**a voice** (or: sound) **out of the atmosphere** (or: sky; heaven), **as a voice** (or: sound) **of many waters** [a figure of many nations], **and as a voice** (or: sound) **of a great thunder. And the voice** (sound) **which I heard [was] as lyre-singers, continuously playing their lyres** (or: harps)."

The "many waters" speaks of the many ethnic multitudes and nations, which sound like a "great thunder," which is probably used to speak of the volume of the sound that would be caused by a great multitude. And, it is a sound of singing and of playing music – a time of joy and rejoicing – as 14:3 explains. So our context may first pertain to 1st century Jerusalem and Judea (as we have seen, above), but the message of these visions also involves, and has ramifications for, all the nations, as well.

We first read of "thunders" (plural), in a logical connection with "lightnings," in 4:5, above:

> "**forth from out of the throne – lightnings and voices** (or: sounds) **and thunders repeatedly** (or: continuously) **proceed out**" – in the throne scene.

Next, in 6:1, with the opening of the first seal,

> "**one from out of the midst of the four living ones repeatedly saying, as a sound** (or: voice) **of thunder.**"

Notice that both of these instances are associated with, or are, "voices." The next time we find them is in 8:5, above, when the Agent throws fire from the altar into the earth, following the opening of the 7th seal,
> "**thunders and sounds** (or: voices) **and lightnings and shakings birthed themselves.**"

Here, in 10:3-4, is the third time that we find thunders in the Unveiling, and it is during the "interlude."

4. And when the Seven Thunders spoke (gave utterance), **I was about to be writing and I heard a Voice from out of the atmosphere** (or: heaven) **repeatedly saying, "You must seal** (or: = seal up and keep from being disclosed; place a seal on) **what the Seven Thunders uttered** (spoke)**," and "You may not write these things."**

Prinzing suggests a personal application to this directive:
> "The message of the 7 thunders could not be written down; each individual must hear it within himself, as God reveals the mysteries, the secrets which He would work into every life. 'The secret things belong unto the Lord our God: but those things which are revealed belong unto us...' (Deut. 29:29)."

Chilton rightly concludes that what the thunders spoke was meant for only John to hear. He goes on to suggest that what we should take from this is that God is not obliged to tell us everything (ibid p 263). But what is **sealed**, here, is small by comparison with all that is disclosed in this Unveiling, which John is told not to seal up in 22:10, below.

In "Living at Gilgal, part 3" ("The Shofar Letters") Larry Hodges shares,
> "It seems safe to assume that what the 7 thunders had uttered had to do with what the number 7 stands for symbolically – fullness, completion, perfection, maturity. John... was told... to seal up [what they said]. When a thing is sealed up, it becomes a mystery, a secret; it is not open. But we have hope given us, because the voice goes on to say, 'But in the days of the voice of the 7th angel (messenger), when he shall begin to sound, the mystery (which John had just created by sealing up what the 7 thunders had uttered) of God should be finished' – Rev. 10:7."

Job 38:25 speaks of, "Who has divided... a way for the lightning of the voices?" (Young). The Online Interlinear OT reads, "... a way for perception of sounds?" Poetically recalling the passage through the Red Sea (Ex. 14), Ps. 77:16-20 sets the ancient scene:
> "The waters saw You, and they travailed; indeed the abyss was disturbed. Thick clouds were made to storm down waters; the skies cast forth their voice; indeed Your arrows [= lightnings], they flew about. The voice of Your thunder was in the cyclone…. Your way was through the sea…. You guided Your people like a flock…"

Here, thunder is associated with deliverance.

In reference to Israel's bondage in Egypt, Ps. 81:7 instructs us,
> "You called in distress, and I liberated you; I answered you out of the concealment of the thunder [i.e., a dark thundercloud]."

So here, thunder is associated with concealment.

In 1 Enoch (Ethiopic Apocalypse, dated 2nd cent. BC to 1st cent. AD) we find the phrase: "the secrets of the thunder." Here is that section, 59:1-3,
> "In those days, my eyes saw the mysteries of lightnings, and of lights, and their judgments; they flash lights for a blessing or a curse, according to the will of the Lord of the Spirits. And there I saw the secrets of the thunder and the secrets of [how when] it resounds in the heights of heaven its voice is heard [in] the earthly dwellings. He showed me whether the sound of the thunder is for peace and blessing or for a curse…. After that, all the mysteries of the lights and lightnings

were shown to me [that] they glow with light for blessing and for contentment (or: satiation)." (*The OT Pseudepigrapha*, Vol. 1, Hendrickson Publishers, 1983, 1 Enoch, trans. by E. Isaac, p 40; brackets original)

In Jn. 12:28b-29 we find,

> "**Then a voice** (or: sound) **came from out of the midst of the heaven** (or: the sky; the atmosphere)**: 'I both bring** (or: brought) **glory to [it], and I will continue glorifying [it] again!' Hence the crowd of common folks, the [crowd] standing around and hearing [it], began to say that it had thundered. Others were saying, 'A messenger** (or: An agent) **has spoken to him'**."

When God speaks to an individual, that person can understand what is being said (as with John, in our text, above). But that message may not be meant for others to hear. Comparing Acts 9:7 with Acts 22:9 we may conclude that Jesus' voice to Saul was heard as a sound, but without understanding, by those who were with him on the road to Damascus. In 2 Cor. 12:4, Paul speaks of hearing,

> "**inexpressible gush-effects and utterances** (unutterable sayings and results of a flow; unspeakable results of inexpressible matters and declarations) **which are not being from out of existence** (or: which are not continuing from within the midst of being; or: which it continues being not right; or: for which there is no privilege or authority and which are not being allowed) **in a person** (for a human) **to at any point speak**."

A simple explanation, of why John was not permitted to write what the thunders uttered, is that what they said was not a part of what was being unveiled in this vision. It was not a part of the message-story that John was to pass on to the called-out communities. But the fact that the thunders spoke creates an "Amen" from God, concerning what **the Agent** signified by His **cry**.

5. And the Agent, Whom I saw standing upon the sea and upon the land, lifted up His right hand into the atmosphere (or: sky; heaven),

In vss. 5-7 we have a message, in the form of an oath sworn in union with God, from the Strong Agent: "**a time shall not longer be** (or: there will no longer be a delay, etc.), **but rather, within the days of the Seventh Agent.... God's secret is also completed** (reached its goal; finished; concluded; ended)..."
This is reminiscent of Yahweh swearing by Himself to bless Abraham (Heb. 6:13, 14). I suggest that this secret refers not only to the time of the end of the Mosaic age, but also to the promise made to Abraham and his Seed, and to the purpose of the ages, "Let Us make humanity in Our Image." I suggest that it applies to "the eager **expectation** of the creation," to the expectation for which creation was involuntarily subjected unto uselessness and pointlessness – i.e., to **the unveiling** of God's sons (Rom. 8:18-23).

Terry, Beale, D'Aragon and G.R. Beasley-Murray (*The New Bible Commentary, Revised,* W.B. Eerdmans Pub., 1970, p 1292) all, among others, point us to Dan. 12:7 as background for vss. 5-7, here, so let us call up this verse:

> "Then I heard the man clothed in linen (baddin) clothes, who was up above (over; up upon) the water of the river, and he lifted up his right [hand] and his left unto the sky (or: atmosphere; heaven) and swore an oath within, and in union with, the One continuously living on unto (or: into the midst of) the Age [of Messiah], that 'Unto a season of seasons, and half a season, within the midst of the [situation for] a dispersion to be completed (or: in union with [the] scattering being brought together to the goal and finished), they shall progressively come to know all these things, by intimate experience'" (LXX, JM).

Other LXX MSS read, 'Pertaining to a season... in consummating a scattering of [the] hand (= power, or, ability) of a people having been set-apart and sanctified (or: of [the] holy people).'

The CVOT (Heb. text) reads,
> "Until [the] era of [the] end.... [it is] for [an] appointed [time], [two] appointed [times] and half [an appointed time]. And when [the] shattering [of the] hand of [the] holy people [is] concluded, [then] all these things shall [have their] conclusion."

Another allusion has been considered by scholars: Deut. 32:36-43.
> "For Yahweh shall adjudicate His people and show Himself merciful over His servants when He sees that [the power of their] hand has departed.... I Myself put to death and I keep alive; I have transfixed, and I Myself shall heal, and there is no one who could reclaim from My hand! For I lift My hand to [the] heavens and declare: [As] I [am the] Living One for [the] eon, when I whet My flashing sword and My hand lays hold on judgment, I shall return vengeance... make repayment.... Be Jubilant, heavens, [together] with Him, and worship Him, all messengers of Elohim!.... a shelter shall He make for the ground of His people" (CVOT).

Cf Gen. 22:16; Isa. 45:23; Jer. 49:13; Amos 6:8, for places where Yahweh swore by Himself.

6. **and swore** (affirmed or promised with an oath) **within** (or: in union with) **the One continuously living on into the ages of the ages** (or: the Ages belonging to & pertaining to the ages; or: = the foremost of all the ages) – **Who framed** (created; founded; reduced from a state of disorder and wilderness) **the atmosphere** (or: heaven; sky), **and the things within it, and the land** (or: earth; ground), **and the things within her, and the sea, and the things within her – that a time shall not longer be** (or: that a period of time will not further continue being; that {a} time will not still exist; = there will be no delay; = there will be no longer a time of delay);

The description of **the One**, in the first clause, calls to mind Ps. 146:5-6.
> "Happy [is the person] who has the God of Jacob as his Help; His hopefulness is set on Yahweh, his God, Maker of [the] heavens and earth, the sea and all that is in them, the Guardian of truth for the eons, executing justice for [those] being exploited, Giver of bread to the famished, Yahweh, letting loose [those who are] bound, Yahweh, unclosing [the eyes of the] blind..." (CVOT; alterations, mine). *Cf* Neh. 9:6; Ex. 20:11.

If we take the view that this message applied to the time of the 1st century and to what God was doing in Israel at that time, then the finishing of this secret may have concluded in AD 70, with the destruction of Jerusalem. I suspect that the original recipients of this letter might have thought so. But there are yet ages to come in God's economy of the ages. Eph. 2:7 instructs us that God's purpose is,
> "**to the end that within continuously oncoming ages** (the indefinite time periods continually coming upon and overtaking [us]) **He may exhibit** (display) **the continuously transcending** (being cast beyond) **riches** (wealth) **of His grace and favor, in useful goodness** (beneficial kindness) **[flooding] upon us, within Christ Jesus** (or: in union with [the] Anointed Jesus)."

Paul refers to himself, using the word "**us**," as "**household administrators of God's secret**" (1 Cor. 4:1). Jude ends his letter with the phrase "**both now and on into all the ages** (eons; indefinite periods of time)!" So it behooves us to contemplate the compound phrase, here, "**on into the ages of the ages** (or: the Ages belonging to & pertaining to the ages; or: = the foremost of all the ages)." There is more to come, of which we have not been informed, except in such general statements as we have in Eph. 2:7.

The last clause of this verse has caused the confusion of interpreting it as speaking of the end of the existence of time. However, most all scholars agree that the correct understanding of the clause is something like the two paraphrases which I have parenthetically on offer: "There will be no longer a time of delay" before the sounding of the 7th trumpet, as vs. 7, below, indicates. This means that the last trumpet was about to sound, when John received this information. The clause has to do with the visions of this letter, and with the end of this present interlude we would see how the messages of these 7 trumpets conclude. Terry points out that "**a little time longer** (yet a short time)," of 6:11, above, "is about to end" (ibid p 360). The forty years of Jesus' generation have about run their course: God has given the unbelieving Jews of that period a time to change their thinking in regard to the coming of the Messiah. The Jewish rebellion is about to take the stage; the final act involving natural Israel is about to happen. As Deut. 32:35b forecasted, "a day of destruction [is] near (close at hand; about to touch them)" (LXX, JM).

Hab. 2:3 uses the verb form of the word for "time" in vs. 6, here. Its use, there, in the last clause, sheds light on its use here:
> "Because of that [i.e., vs. 2], [the] vision [is] yet pertaining unto an appointed season of a fitting situation (or: a fertile moment), and it will progressively rise up into a place of limit (a boundary; an extreme end), and not into emptiness or fruitlessness (not in vain, or to no purpose). If it [i.e., the vision] (or: He) should come after some time, you are to supportively remain under [the situation] and wait for it (or: Him), with endurance, because in progressively coming it (or: He) will proceed in arriving and be there, and can in no way delay (take added time)" (LXX, JM).

Cf Heb. 10:37-39. Mat. 25:5ff speaks to this situation:
> "**Now with the continued passing of time during [the; a] delaying of the bridegroom, they all became drowsy, nodded off, and then continued fast asleep. So, in the middle of [the] night, a shout** (or: cry) **had occurred, 'Look! The bridegroom! Be proceeding to now go forth into [the] meeting** (a moving from one place to participate in a face-to-face encounter with someone; [other MSS: unto his away-meeting])**!'**"

Beale (ibid p 546) suggests that proclamation, "there will be no delay," in this verse, is synonymous with the statement of 11:14b, below, "**The third woe is progressively coming swiftly**," and we concur.

7. but rather, within the days of the Seventh Agent, whenever he may be about to repeatedly sound a trumpet, God's secret (the secret, or mystery, of God or which pertains to God) **is also completed** (reached its goal and purposed destiny; finished; concluded; ended) **as proclaimed as good news to** (or: as He announced the message of goodness to) **His own slaves, the prophets** [other MSS: His own slaves, and the prophets].

Murphy sees this verse as relying "on the principle enunciated in Amos 3:7" (ibid p 110),
> "For My Lord Yahweh is not doing a thing without revealing His deliberation to His servants, the prophets" (CVOT).

This interpretation, of the last clause of vs. 7, here, supports the view that these visions are fulfillments of both OT and NT prophets, John, here, being one of these. By now it seems obvious that the first level of fulfillment applies to the final days of Israel's history, with insights given to the 1st century called-out communities of Christ concerning what will soon happen in Jerusalem.

The setting of this verse would seem to be the season (**within the days**) of which Dan. 12:7 spoke, so the proclamation of the Agent, here, is different from Daniel's prophecy. The 7th Agent is "**about to repeatedly sound a trumpet**," the 7th, or last, trumpet. The 7th trumpet is the final message from, and concerning, the old covenant. The context of this verse calls to mind Gal. 4:4,
> "**Yet when the effect of the filling of the time came, forth from out of a mission, God sent-off His Son, being Himself come to be born from out of a woman, being Himself come to be born under [the rules, authority and influence of] Law**..."

Paul says it this way, in Eph. 1:10,

> "**an administration, implementation and realization from a detailed plan of the effects of that which fills up the appointed seasons and fertile moments [designed] to itself bring back again all things up under one Head** (or: to unite all to the Source) **within and in union with the Christ: those things upon** [other MSS: within] **the heavens** (or: atmospheres) **and the things upon the land** (earth) – **centered in, within the midst of, and in union with, Him!**"

Peter put it this way,

> "**One being set in clear light and manifested upon [the] last part of the times** (or: of the [or: these] successive chronological time periods)" (1 Pet. 1:20).

Then, in 1 Pet. 4:17, he said,

> "**the fitting situation and fertile moment of the appointed season for the result of the judgment** (the effect of the evaluation and decision) **to begin from God's house.**"

Paul told Corinth,

> "**Now all these things went on progressively** (or: from time to time) **stepping together among those folks typically** (as examples), **and it was written with a view toward a placing [of them] into the minds of us: ones unto whom the ends** (= conjunctions; goals) **of the ages have come down to** (or: arrived at) **and are now face to face [with us]**" (1 Cor. 10:11).
>
> > [note: "the ends," plural, may describe a picture of a succession, where "one end" meets "another end," this latter being really the beginning of another indefinite time-period, stretched out like a rope; each rope in the time-line having "two ends."]

The author of Hebrews opens, in 1:2, with the phrase, "**upon [the] last of these days [He] spoke to us in a Son.**" Then in 9:26 (the chapter describing the fulfillment of the Day of Atonement), he says,

> "**upon a conjunction** (a joined destiny; a bringing of [two] ends together ["denoting the joining of two age-times" – E.W. Bullinger]) **of the ages, He has been and remains manifested** (has been brought to light and continues visible) **into a displacement of the failure** (from the error, sin and deviation from the target) **through the sacrifice of Himself** (or: through His sacrifice; or: by means of the sacrificial altar-offering which was Himself)." Cf Rom. 6:9-10.

In 1 Jn. 2:18, John is more specific,

> "**it continues being** (or: is progressively) **a last hour** (= an *eschaton* of the Day, or the closing moment [of the age])... **we constantly know by experience that it continues being a last hour** (= a closing moment [of the age])."

The time-setting of 10:7, here, speaks apocalyptically to the same time frames of these other NT witnesses.

This verse is not speaking of some judgment in our future, but is in the context of John's lifetime. Those who view this as pertaining to the future, and to some supposed "final judgment," must interpret the Greek word *mellō* in a sense that strays from its central meaning: **be about to; be on the point of**. This "time word" is used thirteen times in the Unveiling. We can see its central meaning, and sense its import, from what John said in vs. 4, above: he was "**about to** (*mellō*) **be writing**" when the Voice from the atmosphere stopped him from doing so. But this consistent, literal rendering does not fall in line with a futurist interpretation of this book. The "souls under the altar" in 6:9, above, were not going to have to wait a long time until, "**their brothers – those continually being about to** (*mellō*) **be killed, even as they [were] – would be fulfilled**" (6:11b). In 2:10, above, some were "**about to** (*mellō*) **experience** (or: to suffer; in which you are about to have sensible experience)." That happened then and there. Those in Sardis were to "**establish** (set fast) **the remaining things which were about to** (*mellō*) **die** (or: rot)" – 3:2, above. In 8:13, we read of, "**the three agents who are about to** (*mellō*) **be one after another sounding a trumpet.**" This same rendering fits the contexts of 12:4, 5, and 17:8, below – unless a futurist construct is placed upon those texts. We need to let the texts speak for themselves, especially on such an important interpretive term. Beale (ibid p 541) cites Mk. 13:7, 10 as evidence for a "future nuance" of *mellō*, and, indeed, anything that is described as "to be about to" is future from the time of the person speaking, but a distant future is in no way implied. But let us examine these verses in Mk. 13:

4. "Tell us, when will these things proceed in being? And further, what [is/will be] the sign whenever all these things may be ABOUT TO be progressively brought together and ended (or: concluding; or: finished together and brought to their purposed goal – their intended end and destiny)?"

5. So Jesus, giving a decided response, began to be saying to them, "Be continuously observing, and see to it [that] no one can lead you folks astray.

6. "Many folks will continue coming [depending or basing their authority] upon My Name, repeatedly saying 'I myself am' (or: saying that, 'I, in contradistinction to others, am he [or: the one]') – and they will successively be leading many folks astray (or: deceiving many).

7. "Yet, whenever you men may hear [the noise of] battles [nearby], as well as reports or rumors of wars [farther off], don't you folks be disturbed or alarmed, for it is necessary for it to happen, but nonetheless, [it is] not yet the end (the consummation; the closing act).

8. "For ethnic group (or: nation) will proceed being raised up upon ethnic group (or: nation), and kingdom upon kingdom. There will successively be earthquakes (or: shakings) in one place after another. There will continue being famines and times of hunger. These things [are] a beginning of 'birth pains.'

9. "So as for you folks, continue looking to (or: after) yourselves, for people will repeatedly give you over unto sanhedrins (the ruling councils, or courts, in the Jewish culture of that time), as well as unto synagogues (local religious and cultural centers). [There] you folks will be repeatedly beaten and severely whipped (or: lashed). Also, you will continue being caused to make a stand upon [the demand] of governors (rulers) and kings, in consequence of involvement with Me, [leading] into a witness and testimony to, and evidence for, them.

10. "Further, it continues necessary for the good news (the message of goodness, ease and well-being) to be publicly proclaimed into the midst of all the ethnic multitudes (unto all the non-Jews and the nations), first.

11. "Then, whenever they may repeatedly bring or progressively lead you folks, while in process of giving you over, do not continue anxious or filled with worry beforehand as to what you folks should be speaking. On the contrary, whatever may be given to and in you within that hour, continue speaking this. You see, you folks are not the ones then speaking, but rather, [it is] the Set-apart Breath-effect (or: Holy Spirit).

12. "And so, a brother will proceed giving over (delivering) [his] brother into death, and a father [his] child. Also, children will progressively rise up upon (or: repeatedly take a stand against) parents and even will proceed putting them to death.

13. "Furthermore, you will continue being people constantly hated, repeatedly regarded with ill-will by everyone (or: detached from all people) – because of My Name. Yet, the one enduring and remaining under [these situations] on into the conclusion [of these things] (or: unto the attainment of the goal; into the finished state of maturity; into the final act and end) will continue being kept safe (or: rescued; delivered; restored to health and wholeness; saved).

14. "Now whenever you folks may see 'the abomination of the desolation' (or: the detestable thing which results in a region becoming uninhabited, lonely and like a desert; or: the loathing and abhorrence which pertains to a wasted condition; [Dan. 9:27; 11:31; 12:11]) standing where it is binding not [to stand] (or: where it is not proper; where it must not) – let the one reading continue directing his mind and using his intellect [here] (= figure out what this means) – then let those within the midst of Judea progressively take flight, and continue fleeing into the mountains (or: hill country).

15. "But now for the one upon the housetop: let him not descend (step down), neither let him enter to pick up anything from out of his house.

16. "And for the one [having gone] into the field, let him not return (or: turn back) **unto the things [remaining] behind to pick up his cloak** (or: outer garment).

17. "Yet woe to (= it will be hard, perhaps even tragic, for) **the pregnant women, as well as for those still nursing [babies] in the midst of those days!**

18. "So you folks be continuously thinking and praying toward things going well, to the end that your flight (escape) may not occur (happen) **in winter** (or: in the rainy season),

19. "for those days will continue being pressure (tribulation; affliction; oppression) **the sort of which, [even] such a kind as this, has not happened** (occurred), **and could in no way have come to be, from [the] beginning of [the] creation** (= the bringing of order from out of chaos) **which God framed and founded, until now!** [Joel 2:2; Dan. 12:1; Lu. 21:22]

20. "And now – except [the] Lord cuts short (curtails; discounts) **the days – all flesh** (= people) **will not likely continue being kept safe or rescued. However, because of the chosen ones, whom He Himself picked out, He cuts short** (curtails) **the days.**

First of all, note the repeated use of the plural personal pronoun, which I have rendered "**you folks**." He meant those very disciples that were present with Him at the time of His speaking this. He tells THEM, "**Be continuously observing, and see to it [that] no one can lead YOU FOLKS astray**" (vs. 5). In vs. 7, "**whenever YOU MEN may hear**," and, "**don't YOU FOLKS be disturbed or alarmed**." A clear translation makes it obvious that His warnings and descriptions apply to His immediate listeners. Note, also, the cultural markers: sanhedrins, synagogues, folks on housetops (the roofs in that time/place were normally flat). The big question is vs. 10. Most will say that this was not fulfilled by AD 70! As a beginning, consider Acts 2:

5. **Now there were Jews permanently residing** (perhaps: staying) **in Jerusalem – well-received adult men who take hold well [on things]** (or: pious and circumspect adult males) **from every nation and ethnic group under the sky** (or: heaven).

8. "And so how are we ourselves now hearing – each one of us – in his own language and dialect, [the one] in which we were born?

9. "[There are] **Parthians, Medes and Elamites** [= portions of the Persian empire]; **even folks presently dwelling in Mesopotamia... both Judea, as well as Cappadocia... Pontus, as well as Asia** [= principally the kingdom of Pergamus, including Lydia, Mysia, Caria and Phrygia],

10. "**both Phrygia and Pamphylia; Egypt and the parts of Libya which is down toward Cyrene, as well as the temporary residents from Rome** (or: the repatriated Romans); **both Jews and proselytes** (converts to Judaism), **Cretans and Arabians** (or: Arabs) –

11. "**we continue hearing their speaking the magnificent things of God** (or: God's great deeds) **in our own tongues** (= languages)!"

Later, Paul made extensive travels:

"**with a view for** (in the purpose for) **me to have filled [the region] from Jerusalem even, around in a circuit, as far as Illyricum [with] the good news of, from, and concerning the Anointed One**" (Rom. 15:19).

He announced, in Col. 1:23, that "**the message of ease, goodness and well-being of which you hear** (or: heard) **[was] the [message] being heralded** (announced; publicly proclaimed and preached) **within all creation which is under the sky** (or: heaven)." This answers Mk. 13:10.

In Gal. 2:2 he reported,

"**I put up to them** (set back again for them; = submitted to them) **the message of goodness, ease and well-being, which I am habitually proclaiming as a public message within the multitudes** (or: among the nations and ethnic groups – non-Jews; Gentiles)."

Mk. 13:14ff gives descriptions of "the end" of which Jesus spoke, in 13:7. Those verses describe what happened in AD 66-70, which brought "the end." In Lu. 21:9 Jesus spoke of these same things that were soon to be coming, and then says, "…**but still the end** (or: the final act; the finished condition) **[is] not immediately**." Yet, in Lu. 21:20 He gave them the key to know when it would actually be the end:

> "**Now later, when you folks see Jerusalem being continuously surrounded by encamped armies, at that time realize and know from that experience that her desolation has drawn near and is now present**."

In Mk. 16:15, 20, we read,

> "**Then He said to them, 'As you are journeying on your way** (or: As you are traveling) **into all the ordered system** (the world of religion, culture and government; secular society), **you men make a public proclamation of the good news'**…. **Yet those men, in [their] going forth** (or: upon exiting [the area]), **made public proclamations of the Lord** (or: from the Lord; pertaining to the Lord) **everywhere**."

Russell comments,

> "[T]he phrase, 'all the nations'… is really equivalent to 'all the tribes of the land'…. What can be more evident than that the promise of Christ to be with His disciples to the close of the age, implies that they were to live to the close of the age? The great consummation was not far off; the Lord had often spoken of it, and always as an approaching event, one which some of them would live to see. It was the winding up of the Mosaic dispensation; the end of the long probation of the Theocratic nation; when the whole frame and fabric of the Jewish polity were to be swept away, and 'the kingdom of God to come with power.' This great event, our Lord declared, was to fall within the limit of the existing generation. The 'close of the age' coincided with the Parousia, and the outward and visible sign by which it is distinguished is the destruction of Jerusalem. This is the *terminus* by which, in the NT, the field is bounded. To Israel it was 'the end,' 'the end of all things,' 'the passing away of heaven and earth,' the abrogation of the old order, the inauguration of the new" (ibid p 120-1; emphasis original).

In Mat. 24:13-16, which is parallel to Mk. 13:7-14 (quoted above), we read,

> 13. "**Now [as to] the person remaining under [all this] and enduring unto [the] purposed goal** (or: into a final, destined act), **this one will be repeatedly rescued and delivered** (or: continuously kept safe).
>
> 14. "**Furthermore, this good news which pertains to the reign will be progressively publicly proclaimed within the whole inhabited area** (or: the Hellenistic world, as opposed to barbarian lands; or: = the Roman Empire) – **[leading] into a witness and evidence for all the ethnic multitudes** (or: unto a testimony among all the nations), **and at that point the purposed goal will proceed having arrived and continue here** (or: and at that time the final act will have progressively come, and its product will continue being here; or: and so then the destined end will be progressively arriving).
>
> 15. "**Therefore, whenever you men can see** (or: may perceive) **'the effect of the loathing and nauseating [event; condition; thing; situation] from the desolation**
>
>> (or: the result from the abhorring abomination associated with, or which causes, the devastation and abandonment; or: the resulting effect of the desecration, which is an act of ruining, forsaking and leaving uninhabited like a desert),' **that was being spoken through Daniel the prophet, standing 'within the midst of a set-apart place** (or: [the] holy place)' [Dan. 9:27; 11:31; 12:11] **– let the person presently reading continue to use his mind and intellect for the comprehension [of this]** (= figure out what this means!) –
>
> 16. "**at that time, let the people within the midst of Judea progressively escape** (flee; take flight) **into the hills and mountains**.

Of this passage, Max R. King explains,

> "'The end,' of which Christ spoke in His discourse on the future of Israel (Mat. 24:14), would come after the gospel was preached for a witness in all the world…. But when this desolation is *all* that is seen, the purpose of a complete desolation of *fleshly* Israel and their *earthly* city and sanctuary

is missed. Daniel was praying for Israel's *restoration*, not Israel's *annihilation*. Gabriel came to give Daniel understanding of the true, ultimate 'future of Israel.' There was to be another desolation far beyond the one experienced under the Babylonians. But out of this future, ultimate desolation would come the answer to Daniel's prayer. For what was Daniel praying in chapter 9? He was praying for that which he knew was imperative for Israel's restoration; namely, Israel's forgiveness.... desolation was not the final word.... desolation of Israel and Jerusalem (future to Paul's time) would result in the promised salvation of Israel. Israel's blindness would last 'until the fullness of the Gentiles be come in. And so all Israel shall be saved.... For this is my covenant unto them, when I shall take away their sin' (Rom. 11:25-27).... He saw this eschatological time of Israel's age-ending transformation as the fulfillment of God's covenant with Israel.... He (Christ, the coming Prince) confirmed the covenant with the many in that final week of consummation/restoration (Dan. 9:27)" (*The Cross and The Parousia of Christ, The Two Dimensions Of One Age-Changing Eschaton*, Writing and Research Ministry – The Parkman Road Church of Christ, 1987, p 333-4; emphasis original).

The immediacy of the events which Jesus described in Mk. 13 can be discerned in the manner in which He ended His discourse to those with him, in the final verses of that chapter:

> 35. **"Therefore you people continue being watchful and alert, because you have not seen and thus you folks are unaware of when 'the Lord of the House' is proceeding to come – whether [at] evening, or midnight, or [at] the crowing of the rooster, or early in the morning.**
> 36. **"Coming suddenly and unexpectedly, may He not find you folks continuing** (or: by habit) **fast asleep!**
> 37. **"Now what I am now saying to you people, I continue saying to everyone** (to all), **'You folks continue being watchful and alert'!"**

Col. 2:2 speaks of **God's secret**, so Paul's explanation should unpack vs. 7, here:

> "**being joined cohesively** (jointly knitted; welded together; literally: mounted together in copulation) **and united in love – even into all the riches pertaining to the state of having been brought to fullness whose source is comprehension into full, accurate, intimate and experiential knowledge of God's Secret: Christ**
> > (or: of the secret of the God who is Christ; or: the secret from God, which is [the] Anointing; [with other MSS: of the sacred mystery of the God and Father, in relation to the Christ {or: having its source in [the] Anointing; or: belonging to Christ}])."

Christ, and the Anointing of humans with His Spirit, IS the secret of God, and which came from God. This, of course, applies to the corporate Christ (Jesus and His body), as Paul widely instructs us. This IS the Gospel, which was, and is, "**proclaimed as good news to** (or: as He announced the message of goodness to) **His own slaves, the prophets.**" This is the message of the tiny scroll which John will be told to eat and digest so that he can prophesy to "**peoples and multitudes** (nations; ethnic groups) **and tongues** (languages) **and many kings**" (vs. 11, below).

Pertinent to our passage, here, are Paul's words in Rom. 16:25-26, 27a,

> "**Now by the One** (in the One) **being continuously able and powerful to set you steadfast** (to make you stand firm and settled) **in accord with** (or: corresponding to; in the sphere of; in line with) **my message of goodness and well-being – even the preaching and public heralding of the message of and from Jesus Christ – down from** (in accord with; in line with) **an unveiling of a secret** (or: a revelation and a disclosure of a mystery) **that had been being kept silent** (or: quiet) **in eonian times** (or: to [the] times [that would] pertain to the Age [of Messiah]), **but now is being brought to light and manifested, and through prophetic Scriptures, down from** (in accord with, on the level of and in line with) **a command of the eonian God**

(from the God Who exists through and comprises the ages; of God in relation to the ages; or: = from the God who created, inhabits, owns and rules the ages), **[which leads] into hearing obedience from faith as well as a humble listening and paying attention belonging to trust, pertaining to confidence and which comprises loyalty – suddenly being made known unto all the ethnic multitudes** (nations; Gentiles; pagans; non-Israelites) **– by God.**"

Jesus spoke of secrets (mysteries) to His disciples in Mat. 13:11,
> "**To you folks it has been given to intimately experience and insightfully know the secrets** (mysteries) **of the reign of the heavens** (or: the kingdom which is the heavens, which pertains to the heavens, and which emanates from the atmospheres)." *Cf* Mk. 4:11; Lu. 8:10.

Paul told the folks at Corinth,
> "**let a person** (a human) **continue logically considering** (or: measuring and classifying) **us as God's subordinates** (God's deputies; those under God's orders) **and house-managers** (or: administrators) **of God's secrets** (or: mysteries from God which require initiation for receiving; secrets which are God)" (1 Cor. 4:1).

In Col. 1:26-27, he said,
> "**the Secret** (or: sacred mystery) **having been hidden away and remaining concealed away from the ages** (or: from [past] eons), **as well as away from the [past] generations, yet now** (at the present time) **is set in clear light in His set-apart folks** (or: was manifested to His holy ones; is caused to be seen by His saints; is shown for what it is, for His sacred people), **to whom God wills** (or: at one point purposed; or: intends) **to make known by intimate experience, what [are] the riches of the glory of this Secret** (or: the wealth which has its source in this sacred mystery's manifestation which calls forth praise) **within the multitudes** (among the nations; in the Gentiles; IN UNION WITH the swarms of ethnic groups), **which is** (or: exists being) **Christ within you folks, the expectation of and from the glory**
>> (or: which is [the] Anointed in union with you people: the [realized] hope of the manifestation which called forth praise; or: which is [the] Anointing [and the Messiah] within the midst of you folks – the expectation which is the glory)."

We read in Col. 4:3 where he admonishes his listeners to,
> "**progressively praying** (speaking to having ease and goodness) **about us, to the end that God may open a door of the Word for us to speak the secret of the Christ** (or: may open a door pertaining to the message, for us to speak the mystery which has its origin in the Christ – the secret which is the Christ)."

And in 1 Tim. 3 we find this beautiful description:
> 16. **and so confessedly** (admittedly; with common consent and sameness of speech) **great is the secret** (or: mystery) **of the reverence** (the standing in awe of goodness, with adoration; the healthful devotion and virtuous conduct of ease, in true relation to God)**:**
>> **which is made visible** (manifested) **within flesh** (= a physical body),
>> **is rightwised** (set in equity and right relationship in the Way pointed out; eschatologically delivered and placed in covenant) **in spirit** (in union with Breath-effect),
>> **is seen by agents** (or: messengers),
>> **is heralded** (preached) **within multitudes** (among nations and ethnic groups),
>> **is trusted and believed within [the] world** (an ordered system; secular culture),
>> **is received back in good opinion and reputation.**
>> (or:
>> Who [some MSS read: God; others: He] was brought to clear light within flesh (= the natural realm); was shown righteous and just (= set in covenant) within spirit and attitude; was seen by agents; was proclaimed among Gentiles {non-Jews}; was believed within [the] world of society, religion, and government;

was taken back up again, within glory – a manifestation which calls forth praise!).

Another passage that we should consider, with regard to **God's secret**, is that of Eph. 3:
> 3. **that, in accord with an unveiling** (or: down from and in line with a revelation; in keeping with a disclosure), **the secret** (or: mystery) **was made known to me – even as I before wrote, in brief –**
> 4. **toward which [end] you, the folks continually reading** (or: habitually reviewing and recognizing; progressively gathering up knowledge), **are constantly able and continue with power to comprehend** (understand; apprehend) **my understanding** (insight; confluence of insights) **in the secret** (or: mystery) **of the Christ** (or: which is the Anointed One [= the Messiah]; from the Christ; with the character of the [Messiah]),
> 5. **which to other generations was not made known to the sons of mankind as it is now** (at the present time) **uncovered** (unveiled; revealed) **in spirit** (or: within a Breath-effect; or: in union with [the] Spirit) **by** (or: to; in; among) **His set-apart emissaries** (or: consecrated representatives that were sent forth from Him) **and prophets** (folks having light ahead of time),
> 6. (or, reading the phrase "in spirit" with the next phrase rather than the previous one:) **In spirit the nations** (the Gentiles; the ethnic multitudes; non-Jews) **are to continuously be joint-heirs and a Joint Body and joint sharers** (partakers; participants) **of The Promise – [along with the rest], resident within** (or: of the assurance in union with) **Christ Jesus through the good news** (or: the message of goodness, ease and well-being).

Note in vs. 3, here, that Paul was also given "**an unveiling**." Also, with the Unveiling given to John, here, having a large focus on "the End of the Old," note how Paul's unveiling (Eph. 3:6, above) presents the **good news** of "the Beginning of the New" in which,
> "**the nations** (non-Jews, etc.) **are to continuously be joint-heirs and a Joint Body and joint sharers of The Promise**!!!" – what GOOD news!

Jesus, Paul and the Unveiling all speak of **the secret(s)** (or: mystery{-ies}), and in all of them this term is equivalent to the concept of prophetic "fulfillment" of God's "**plan of the ages**" (Eph. 3:11). The secrets are now opened to us because Christ is risen and enthroned, which is the paramount fulfillment of all prophecy.

8. Then the Voice, which I heard from out of the atmosphere (or: sky; heaven), **is speaking again with me, and is saying, "Be going** (departing), **take** (or: receive with the hand; seize) **the tiny scroll – the one having been opened up within the Agent's hand, Who has taken a stand upon the sea and upon the land."**

This **Voice from out of heaven** (the same Voice that John heard in vs. 4, above), is speaking to John again, bringing personal instructions to him. It and various other voices play recurring roles of significance in this book. It behooves "the one having an ear to hear, [to] hear what the Spirit is saying to the called-out." Here John is told to participate in this vision: take the tiny scroll from the hand of the vision of the glorified, completed Christ, and then eat it. A.E. Knoch says that "The eating of the scroll correspond[s] to the digesting of its contents" (*Concordant Commentary on the New Testament*, Concordant Publishing Concern, 1968 p 393). Lee says that this means to receive it into one's being – echoes of Jeremiah (15:16) and Ezekiel (2:8; 3:1-3); Barclay concurs. We need to digest the message.

9. And so I went away toward the Agent, saying to Him to give to me the tiny scroll. And He is saying to me, "Take (or: Seize) **it and eat it down** (devour it)**: and it will proceed making your whole belly** (the hollow place; the cavity; the stomach and intestines; the innermost part; used of the womb) **bitter, but in your mouth it will continue being sweet as honey."**

John "**went away toward the Agent**." He enters deeper into the vision, leaving his prior position and location: he hears (vs. 8) and then he is to act. This is a pattern of obedience. This scene is an allusion to Ezk. 2:9 through 3:3,

> "And I saw, and behold, a hand was put forth toward me, and behold, in it was the roll of a scroll. Then He spread it before me, and it was written on both the face and the back; on it were written dirges, sad words and woe. Then He said to me: 'Son of humanity, eat what you find; eat this scroll, and go, speak to the house of Israel.' So I opened my mouth and He fed me this scroll, and said to me, 'Son of humanity, you shall feed your belly, and you shall fill your bowels with this scroll that I am giving to you.' So I ate it, and it was in my mouth like honey for sweetness" (CVOT).

In Ezk. 3:5 we learn that Ezekiel was being sent to the house of Israel, then in vs. 14 we see that the Spirit lifted him up (and he went in bitterness) to the exiles (vs.15), and was set as a "watchman unto the house of Israel" (vs. 17ff), to "give warning to them from [Yahweh]." That chapter ends with Yahweh saying, "The one who hears shall hear, and the one who forbears shall forbear, for they are a rebellious house." Our verse 9, here, (and then on through vs. 11, below) sounds like John is being given a commission of warning, similar to that given to Ezekiel. The next chapter, Ezk. 4, begins with Ezekiel being told to take a brick to represent Jerusalem, and then to "place a siege against it… construct an earthwork against it and set camps against it…" (Ezk. 4:2). The message is obvious: it is a warning that Jerusalem will be besieged by an enemy army. Its target is literal Jerusalem, the one situated and living on "earth." Kaplan points to the figure of a brick: something manmade, from the earth – the earthly people. Recall that the Tower of Babel was built of bricks (Gen. 11:3ff). Structures, like towers and walls, are hard, like Jerusalem's heart had become. This was not an organic symbol, like a vineyard; it represented their trust in their own defenses, which Ezekiel demonstrates to be futile. The similarity of the symbols in both texts (of eating a sweet scroll that brings bitterness) would seem to carry the same message: Jerusalem is about to be attacked. This happened in Jerusalem's past, and would happen again in its near future (that ended in its destruction in AD 70). Russell comments,

> "We infer, therefore, that in both the contents were *bitter*, for St. John, like Ezekiel, was the messenger of coming woe to Israel, and this very vision belongs to the woe-trumpets which sounded the signal of judgment" (ibid p 423).

Now Ps. 19:10 and Ps. 119:103 speak of God's judgments and His words as being sweet. In Jer. 15:16 he said,

> "Your words were found, and I have been devouring them; thus Your word becomes to me 'elation and rejoicing of my heart'; for Your Name is called over me, O Yahweh, Elohim of hosts!" (CVOT)

Heb. 6:5 uses a similar metaphor,

> "**tasting** (= experiencing) **a beautiful gush-effect of God** (or: an ideal result of the flow from God; or: God's fine speech; an excellent declaration pertaining to God; a profitable thing spoken, which is God) **– besides abilities and powers of an impending age**."

If the message that John was to prophesy (vs. 11, below) was itself to be a foretelling of doom, then we can see where it became a bitter thing to him. In 8:10-11, above, the message of the 3rd agent brought bitterness of wormwood in the waters. 11:2b, below, would seem to corroborate our conclusion here: Jerusalem was indeed destined to be "**given to the multitudes** (ethnic groups; nations), **and they will proceed treading the set-apart city** (or: the Holy City) **forty-two months**." The vision God gives us may be sweet, but the path through the "valley of the shadow of death" (the cross) which leads to the realization of the vision, is bitter. But that this scroll is described as a "**tiny scroll**" may be an indication that the period of destruction will be short – only three and a half years (**forty-two months** – 11:2b,

below). This period is described as "**travailing with birth-pangs, and being progressively tested and tried in the labor pains** (or: experiencing the touchstone) **to bring forth** (= to bear a child)" (12:2b, below, and we see there what comes of her giving birth!). So we must read on to see the resurrected Jerusalem, in 12:1, below, and at the end of our story. Another allusion for this scene is Mat. 26:26,
> "**And then at giving [them] to the disciples, He said, "You folks take [it]** (or: receive [this]). **Eat [it] at once. This is My body** (or: This is the body which is Me)."

10. **And then I took** (or: seized) **the tiny scroll from out of the Agent's hand, and devoured it, and it was sweet as honey within my mouth. And when I ate it, my belly** (hollow place, etc.) **was made bitter.**

The message of Christ's goodness, ease and well-being (the Gospel) is indeed sweet to His followers, but the cruciform Path that is involved in being a disciple requires the taking up of our own cross. This can be a bitter experience as it leads us into the death of our protected soul (Mat. 16:24-26). When John ate the tiny scroll, a part of the opened heavens was now inside him, a part of him (*cf* comment on 10:1, above). Beale points out that his "eating of the scroll signifies his identification with its message" (ibid p 550). In Ezk. 3:10, he was to take, and receive, God's words "into [his] heart and hear with [his] ears."

Jesus tasted the bitterness of what He knew was soon coming upon Jerusalem. In Lu. 19:41 He wept over her soon to be historic situation, and,
> 42. **then saying, "If you, even you yourself, knew by intimate experience or had discerned in this day the things [leading, moving or tending] toward peace** (or: a joining; or: = shalom; [other MSS: your peace])! **– but at this time it is** (or: has been) **hidden from your eyes –**
> 43. "**that days will proceed arriving upon you, and your enemies will be progressively setting up an encampment beside you and will continue casting up a mound beside [you and] a staked fortification** (or: rampart) **on** (or: next to) **you, and next will proceed to encircle and surround you, then continue bringing and enclosing pressure on you from every side!**
> 44. "**Later, they will proceed in dashing you to the ground and razing you, as well as your children within the midst of you – then they will continue not leaving stone upon stone within you – in return for what things? Because you do not know the season** (or: had no intimate or personal awareness so as to recognize the occasion; have no insights about the fertile moment) **of your visitation and inspection."**

For Himself, we read it said of Jesus, concerning the Path that led to His death,
> "**Who, instead of and in place of the joy** (or: in the position on the opposite side from the happiness) **continuously lying before Him** (or: lying ahead for Him), **remained under a cross – despising shame** (or: thinking nothing of [the] disgrace)" (Heb. 12:2).

There was sweetness in the revelation of God's purpose (which was written in the scroll of the Life of the Lamb), but His way is a way of bitterness that led Him "**to be a submissive, obedient One** (one who gives the ear and listens) **as far as** (or: to the point of; until) **death – but death of a cross** (torture stake)!" (Phil. 2:8b).

In Mk. 10:39, Jesus told His disciples,
> "**You folks will progressively drink the cup which I Myself am now progressively drinking, and you will also be progressively immersed in** (or: baptized with) **the immersion** (baptism) **which I Myself am now progressively being immersed, unto saturation** (baptized)."

11. **Then** (or: So) **He is** [other MSS: they are] **saying to me, "It presently necessitates you** (or: It is now binding [for you]) **to prophesy** (to exercise the function of a prophet) **again upon peoples and multitudes** (nations; ethnic groups) **and tongues** (languages) **and many kings."**

This verse should be taken as being in close association with the end of vs. 10, perhaps as an immediate response to John's bitter heart (or: inner cavity): **Then He is saying to me**..., or, **So He is saying to me**. John will **prophesy** to all these folks, while having the bitter knowledge of what is coming for them. Chapter 10 ends with John having this message within his life and being, and he is now instructed of the necessity to prophesy this word upon peoples and multitudes. Wallace suggests that, "John left the scene of these visions and became an active evangelist of many countries, among many peoples and tongues" (ibid p 210). We will see this symbolized in the scene of His two witnesses, in 11:3ff, below. Although understanding the 1st century import of these words which would be fulfilled in the destruction of Jerusalem, we can also discern the Pattern of the bitterness that comes with the cruciform life of His followers. Sorrow and weeping endures for the dark night of the soul before the joy comes in the morning of resurrection life (Ps. 30:5).

In Acts 9, Ananias also had a vision from the Lord, in which the Lord told him, regarding Saul,
> "Yet the Lord [= Christ] **said to him, "Be presently going, because this one is** (exists being) **a vessel of choice to Me** (or: a picked-out and chosen instrument by and for Me) **to lift up and carry My Name before** (in the presence of) **the ethnic multitudes** (or: nations; Gentiles) – **as well as [before] kings and [the] sons** (= people) **of Israel. For you see, I Myself will proceed underlining and pointing out** (or: plainly showing) **to him how many things it continues being binding and necessary for him to experience and be suffering – over [the situation of]** (or: for; on behalf of) **My Name**." (vss. 15-16).

So Paul's path and work were to be similar to those of John. Wallace here suggests that John would be a part of what "would fulfill Mat. 24:31" (ibid p 209).

The alternate MS readings of A and B, "they are saying," are older witnesses, but the TR reading, "**He is saying**" is more in concord with 10:9, above. Either reading gives the same message. Beale (ibid p 554) points out that the verb "**prophesy**" followed by the preposition *epi* is used 21 times in the book of Ezk., and 18 of those involve a proclamation of judgment. The common versions' rendering of *epi* as "about" (NRSV; NIV) is not so much wrong, as less precise. The KJV's interpretation, "before," gives the wrong picture (John need not be present to do what this verse states). The CLNT's rendering, "over," is a little better, but the literal, "**upon**," best carries the true picture: his words will come "**upon peoples**... etc." Those words of prophecy will have an effect (as we will consider in 11:3-12, below). Another interpretation of what was said to John, here, can be seen by what he said in 22:18a, below,
> "**I am continuously testifying** (repeatedly witnessing and giving evidence) **to** (or: in) **everyone [who is] habitually hearing the words** (or: messages) **of the prophecy of this scroll**..."

The remainder of the visions in the Unveiling would be at least a start of fulfilling the directive to John, here, for the Unveiling is, itself, a prophecy.

The broad and inclusive formulation of the words, "**peoples and multitudes** (nations; ethnic groups) **and tongues** (languages) **and many kings**," instructs us that this Unveiling will affect everyone, not just the Jews, or, Israel of the old covenant. It is the end of the old, and the beginning of the new – as we will continue to see as we move through the rest of the book. Terry points out that at this point John has not yet prophesied about what he is seeing, "He has only been receiving revelations" (ibid p 363).

At this point, Terry (ibid) also points us to 1 Jn. 2:8,
> "**Again**, (or: Once more) **I am writing to you an implanted goal** (impartation of the finished product within; inward directive) **new in kind and quality** (innovative and different in character), **which is true** (actual; real; genuine) **within Him, and within you** [other MSS: us], **that the**

>**Darkness is progressively being caused to pass by, and the True Light** (= Light of the new Day) **is already** (before now) **progressively shining and appearing.**"

The Darkness, referred to in this verse, likely referred to the shadows and darkness of the old covenant, prior to the coming of the Light of Christ (Jn. 1:4ff). Whereas the lampstand, in the temple, had been considered to be "the light of the world" of the Jews, now Christ and His body were the Light of the world (Mat. 5:14), and the light represented by the physical lampstand had become darkness:

>"**if your eye** [figure of one's point of view; world view; attitude towards others] **should continue being in a bad condition** (or: wicked; perhaps = diseased or cloudy; may suggest stinginess or being grudging), **your whole body** [figure for all of Israel] **will continue being** (will continuously exist being) **dark** (or: in the dark; **full of darkness**). **If, then, the light** [figure of the lampstand] **[which is] within the midst of you** [or, in the holy place of the temple] **is darkness** (or: continually exists being dimness and lack of the Light), **how thick [is] the darkness** (or: how great and extensive [will be] the obscurity and gloom of that area of shadows)!" (Mat. 6:23; brackets added).

But if the 1st letter by John, cited above, was written after the writing of the Unveiling and during the period of AD 66-70, the Darkness, here, might have referred to the judgment upon Jerusalem during that period. Even if it referred to the old covenant, John could have perceived its passing in what he was observing of the Jewish revolt and/or of Rome's conquest over the rebels.

Simmons (ibid p 210) calls to mind the intimation in Jn. 21:22-23 that John might live to see the coming of Christ (as symbolized here, in the Unveiling). He also points us to Mat. 16:28-29, and cites 2:5, 16, 25; 3:3, 11, above, along with 16:15; 22:7, 12 and 20, below, where Christ speaks of, "**continuously (repeatedly; habitually) coming to you** [as a group]," "**repeatedly (habitually) coming swiftly in you** (to you; for you)," or, "**until of which** [time or situation] **whenever I may arrive** (or, as a future: will proceed to be arriving)," etc. If Simmons is correct in these associations, then 2 Tim. 4:1 also may well refer to this "**arrival**" of the Lord:

>"**I am habitually giving thorough witness** (or: constantly testifying and showing evidence in every direction), **in the sight of God – even Christ Jesus: the One now being about to be progressively separating living folks and dead folks** (or: continuously making a decision about or judging living ones and dead ones) **down from** (in accord with; corresponding to; in the sphere of; in respect to; in line with; [other MSS: even]) **His full manifestation and His reign** (or: [with other MSS: and then] His added display as well as His sovereign kingdom activity)."

Chapter 11

1. **Next a reed like a staff** (or: rod) **was given to me, [and He was] presently saying,
   "Rouse yourself** (or: Arise; Awake) **and measure the temple of God** (God's temple, or dwelling), **and** (or: that is; namely) **the altar, and the folks continuously worshiping within it** (or: centered in Him; or: at the [altar]).

Terry rightly notes that, "Neither the temple, city nor witnesses of this chapter appear to John in vision, but all are presented as the word of the strong [agent]" (ibid p 368; brackets mine).

We find similar imagery in Ezk. 40-42. In Ezk. 40:3-7, we read of,
>"a man whose appearance [was] like the appearance of copper. In his hand [was] a twined cord of flax and a measuring reed... and he measured the width of the structure.... and he measured the threshold of the gateway.... then the anteroom..." (CVOT).

Following all the measuring done in those three chapters, which also describe the visionary temple and courts, we find in Ezk. 43:1-4 that he saw, "the glory of the God of Israel come from the east... and the Land was radiant with His glory.... The glory of Yahweh entered the temple... [and] filled the temple." Those chapters, and those leading up to chapter 47 with its vision of the "waters of life" streaming from the temple unto the Dead Sea, provide an instructive background to what these visions in the Unveiling are leading (chapters 21-22, below). That vision, in Ezk. 47, is also correlated with Zech. 13:1 (a fountain opened for dwellers of Jerusalem) and 14:8 (living waters flowing from Jerusalem), and then with Joel 3:18 (all Judah's channels flowing with water and a spring from the House of Yahweh), which give different pictures of the same things that are brought together in this Unveiling's finale.

Now there seems to be no break from the scene of ch. 10, above, but here someone gives John a reed which is like a **staff,** or a rod (vs. 1). This word "rod" was a unit of Jewish measurement, of about 6 cubits. It is a bamboo-like reed that often reached a height of 20 ft. So here again John is given personal instruction to participate in the vision: he must rouse himself and do some measuring. This action echoes Ezk. 40:3. It is used as a preparation for building or for restoration. "But here the meaning lies in preservation" (Barclay, ibid p 67). In 2 Sam. 8:2 we find a "measuring" for both death, and life:
> "He also defeated the Moabites and, making them lie down on the ground, measured them off with a cord; he measured two lengths of cord for those who were to be put to death and one length for those who were to be spared (kept alive)" (NRSV).

2 Ki. 21:13 uses the "line" for judgment:
> "I will stretch over Jerusalem the measuring line for Samaria, and the plummet for the house of Ahab; I will wipe Jerusalem as one wipes a dish, wiping it and turning it upside down" (NRSV).

Lam. 2:8 give a similar message:
> "The LORD determined to lay in ruins the wall of the daughter of Zion; He stretched the line; He did not withhold His hand from destroying..." (NRSV)

We find a repeated phrase in Isa. 28:10, "line upon line, line upon line" (Rotherham; KJV; NRSV; Young), where the noun is *qav*: "a *cord* (as connecting), especially for measuring; fig. a *rule*; also a *rim*, a musical *string* or *accord*" (Strong #6957). It is interesting that Isa. 28:9 asks rhetorically, "And whom would He cause to understand the message? Those who are [just] weaned from milk, just taken from the breasts?" – in other words, those who are still babies: the immature? No, the measuring for building and growth (28:10) comes to the mature, "Whom He would teach knowledge" (28:9a). It is fascinating, that instead of "line upon line," in vs. 10, the LXX has "expectation (or: expectant hope) upon expectation" following the imperative: "Be repeatedly receiving affliction (pressure; squeezing; ordeal; tribulation) upon affliction..." This would seem to speak to the context here, in the Unveiling. Affliction, followed by expectation (or: expectant hope).

Moving ahead in Isa. 28, after speaking of "laying in Zion a Foundation Stone" in vs. 16, vss. 17-18 state,
> "I will make justice the line, and righteousness the plummet (plumbline); hail will sweep away the refuge of lies, and waters will overwhelm the shelter. Then your covenant with death will be annulled, and your agreement with Sheol will not stand – when the overwhelming scourge passes through you will be beaten down by it" (NRSV).

Now Jer. 31:38-40 speaks of a future for Jerusalem, using the "measuring line" to speak of expansion:
> "The days are surely coming, says the LORD, when the city shall be rebuilt for the LORD.... And the measuring line shall go out farther, straight to the hill Gareb, and shall then turn to Goah. The whole valley of the dead bodies and the ashes [Gehenna?], and all the fields as far as the Wadi Kidron... shall be sacred to the LORD..." (NRSV; brackets added).

Likewise is Zech. 1:16,

"Therefore, thus says the LORD, I have returned to Jerusalem with compassion; My house shall be built in it, says the LORD of hosts, and the measuring line shall be stretched out over Jerusalem.... The Lord will again comfort Zion and again choose Jerusalem" (NRSV).

Paul spoke to this time in Rom. 11:23-26.

Since the temple (which includes the altar) is a type of the body of Christ, perhaps John is commissioned to check the state of the building against God's blueprints – to see if it has been built up,

> "**into [the] purposed and destined adult man** (complete, finished, full-grown, perfect, goal-attained, mature manhood) **– into** (or: unto) **[the] measure of [the] stature** (full age; prime of life) **of the entire content which comprises the Anointed One**
> > (or: which is the result of the full number which is the Christ; of the effect of the fullness from the [Messiah]; from the effect of that which fills and completes that which refers to the Christ; of the result of the filling from, and which is, the Christ)" (Eph. 4:13b).

Some see the altar here as the brazen altar of burnt offerings. Others see it as the golden altar of incense, since it is associated with the temple itself and those continuously worshiping with it. Whichever the case, these are put in contrast to the outer court – perhaps the court of the Gentiles/nations. Since this court is "**given**" to the nations/Gentiles/multitudes (vs. 2, below), and since these peoples could not enter the "outer court" of the temple (where stood the altar of sacrifice), we may conclude that it was the entire three-part temple that is being measured here. There were worshipers within both of the first two parts of the temple; those within the holy place (the location of the incense altar) would have been the priests, in the old system.

Just as John participated in the vision of the previous chapter (taking the scroll and eating it, then receiving personal information), here again, he is divinely "**given**" a measuring tool to participate in the vision. But his action in measuring these things is not recorded here. This measurement is a kind preliminary to an evaluation, leading to a decision (judgment) about what is measured. Paul gave thought to his own life and behavior,

> "**lest somehow, while proclaiming** (heralding; preaching; [note: at the games it means to announce the rules of the game and call out the competitors]) **to** (or: for) **others, I myself should** (can; may; would) **come to be one that does not stand the test** (or: is unproved or is without the approval which comes from testing; or: is disapproved and disqualified)" (1 Cor. 9:27b).

He was obviously aware of the testing of God's Fire, in regard to one's work on God's temple, as we in 1 Cor. 3:9-17, where, in vss. 13-15 he explains,

> "**each one's work will make itself to be visible in clear light** (or: will become apparent), **for the Day will make [it] evident** (show [it] plainly). **Because it is being progressively unveiled** (continually revealed) **within the midst of Fire, and the Fire, Itself, will test, examine and put to the proof** (or: prove by testing) **what sort of work each one's exists being. If anyone's work which he built upon [it] will remain, he will receive wages. If anyone's work will be burned down, he will incur a loss** (sustain the damage; forfeit [it]), **yet he himself will be saved** (rescued; delivered; healed and restored to health), **and as in this way – through Fire!**"

Paul's metaphor of building, in this Corinthian passage, may have foundations in the "four carpenters" of Zech. 1:20, the "man with a measuring line," in Zech. 2:1, and the figure of Zerubbabel "laying the foundation" and finishing the house, in Zech. 4:9. We can observe all these symbols coming together here in the grand, consummating Unveiling shown to John. At the same time there is a measuring to assure that the building is constructed "**according to the pattern**" (Heb. 8:5), and also a measuring for correction, where needed (or, destruction, when inappropriate materials have been used). Rotherham renders Jer. 30:11b,

"Though I make an end of all the nations whither I have scattered you, yet will I not make an end of you, but will chastise you in measure…" (Jer. 46:28 reads, "correct you in measure.")

Young renders the last clause, "I have chastised you in judgment;" CVOT: "I discipline you for judgment." The picture in Eph. 2 needs to be kept in mind:

> 19. **Consequently then, you folks no longer continuously exist being strangers** (foreigners) **and sojourners** (temporary residents in a foreign land), **but in contrast, you continually exist being fellow-citizens of those set apart to be sacred people** (or: folks residing together in a City belonging to, and composed of, the holy ones)**: even God's family** (or: household),
> 20. **being fully built as a house upon the foundation of the sent-forth representatives and prophets** (folks who had light ahead of time), **Jesus Christ continuously being a corner-foundation [stone] of it,**
> 21. **within and in union with Whom all the home-building** (all the construction of the house; the entire building), **being continuously fitted [and] progressively framed together** (closely joined together), **is continuously and progressively growing into a set-apart temple within [the] Lord:**
> 22. **within the midst of** (or: in union with) **Whom you folks, also, are continuously and progressively being formed a constituent part of the structure** (or: being built together into a house) – **into God's down-home place** (permanent dwelling) **within [the] Spirit** (or: in spirit; or: in the midst of a Breath-effect).

Added to this are the metaphors in 1 Pet. 2:5,

> "**you yourselves are, as living stones, continuously being erected** (or: progressively constructed and built up), **[being] a spiritual house** (a building with its source being the Spirit, with the characteristics of a Breath-effect), **into a set-apart priesthood to bear up spiritual sacrifices well acceptable in, by, to and with God through Jesus Christ**." Cf 3:12, above.

Although we do not see John measure the temple here, in 21:15-17, below, the agent who talked with John, "**was holding and continues having a measure, a golden reed, so that he may measure the City.**" This, of course was not the same city that we meet in vs. 2, below, but rather the city that Paul described in Gal. 24:26, "**the Jerusalem above is free, who is our mother.**"

In Ps. 39:4 we find, "Acquaint me, O Yahweh, with my end, and the measure of my days…" (CVOT). So the concept of "measure," can have more than one nuance. Here in 11:1, it can even have the sense of checking the proportions of what has been built, or, with regard to practices, the idea of social justice: Deut.25:15 sets out a principle,

> "A weight full and just shall you have; a measure full and just shall you have…"

Mic. 6:10 spoke against, "the scant measure," and Prov. 20:10 instructs us, "Diverse weights and diverse measures are both alike an abomination to Yahweh." Ps. 26:1-2 calls,

> "Judge me, O Yahweh…. Test me, O Yahweh, and try me; Do refine my innermost being and my heart" (CVOT).

Then Paul admonishes us,

> "**Keep on examining and making trial of yourselves, since you exist being in union with the confidence and faith** (or: within the midst of trust); **repeatedly test and assay yourselves so as to approve of yourselves and come to meet the desired specifications. Or are you not now fully aware nor presently recognizing yourselves, with accurate insight: that Jesus Christ constantly exists being within the midst of and in union with you people? – since you are surely not unable to stand the test, nor are you disapproved or disqualified!** (or: – except you are somewhat disqualified.)" (2 Cor. 13:5).

So, measuring can also have the idea of meeting the qualifications and passing His tests.

Another allusion to "measuring" may be to Yahweh's prophecy of judgment against Israel, and the house of Jeroboam. In Amos 7:7-9 we read,
> "Thus Yahweh shows me: And behold my Lord [is] stationed on a plumblined wall, and in His hand [is a] plumbline.... Behold Me placing a plumbline in the midst of My people Israel; I shall not continue to pass by them [any] longer. The high-places of Isaac will be made desolate, and [the grand] sanctuary of Israel shall be deserted..." (CVOT).

In our present vision, Christ is the measuring reed, and the plumbline. That which is aligned with Christ, and is filled with the "**measure of faith** (a meted amount of firm persuasion; a measured portion of trust; a [specific or allotted] ration of confidence and loyalty)" (Rom. 12:3b) will stand the test. We have similar imagery in 1 Enoch 61:1-5,
> "I saw in those days that long ropes were given to those agents.... 'Why have those hoisted these ropes and gone off?' And he said unto me, 'They have gone in order to make measurements.... These are the ones who shall bring measuring ropes of the righteous ones as well as their binding cords in order that they might lean upon the name of the Lord of the Spirits... These are the measurements which shall be given to faith and which shall strengthen righteousness. And these measurements shall reveal all the secrets of the depths of the earth, those who have been destroyed... So that they all return and find hope in the day of the Elect One. For there is no one who perishes before the Lord of the Spirits..." (ibid).

But the old temple, which rejected Christ's new arrangement, would be torn down (Lu. 19:44), for it was not aligned to the Plumbline by,
> "**grow[ing] up** (enlarge; increase) **into Him – the ALL which is the Head: Christ.... in accord with** (or: down from; commensurate to; in the sphere and to the degree of) **the operation** (operative, effectual energy) **within [the] measure of each one part, is itself continually making** (or: is for itself progressively producing and forming) **the growth and increase of the Body, [focused on and leading] into house-construction** (or: unto edification) **of itself within the midst of, and in union with, love** (full self-giving in an unambiguous urge toward union or reunion; acceptance)" (Eph. 4:15-16).

This present vision will take us to the sounding of the 7th trumpet (vs. 15, below) and the **great voices** in the **sky** (heaven; the atmosphere) "**continuously saying, 'The reign of the ordered System** (of the world of religion, culture, government and economy; or: of the realm of the religious and secular) **suddenly came to belong to our Lord and to the anointed of Him...**"

Following the pronouncements of vss. 15-18, we come to the subject of the temple again, in vs. 19,
> "**And then the Temple of God – the one within, or in union with, the atmosphere** (or: centered in the heaven) **– was opened and the ark of the covenant** (or: arrangement) **was seen within the midst of His Temple.**"

So it would seem that the temple that John has measured is a spiritual temple, and vs. 16 (which brings in again "**the twenty-four elders**") instructs us that John is still in the setting of chapter 4, above, not in the setting of the physical Jerusalem of the 1st century. Thus, we might surmise that the measuring of this temple has reference to the building of God's House in the new creation, with the new arrangement. This is the Temple into which Jesus entered (Heb. 9:4, 7, 11, 14-15, 24, 28; 10:19-22) as a Chief Priest in accord with the order and rank of Melchizedek. Through the Spirit (Heb. 9:14) He entered into the called-out folks, who are now the Temple of God, and sprinkled His blood (i.e., His Life) on their, and our, hearts. There was no need to measure the physical temple of 1st century Jerusalem, of which Jesus said,
> "**there can under no circumstances be a stone left or allowed to be upon [another] stone which will not be progressively loosed down to bring utter destruction**" (Mat. 24:2).

The last phrase, "**within it**" would have "**the temple**" as its antecedent. But the alternate rendering, "centered in Him (which could also be expanded to read, 'in union with Him')" would refer back to God as the antecedent: "those worshiping in God – i.e., in the Spirit." There is also the possibility of interpreting the phrase to mean "those worshiping at, or in the sphere of, the altar." This would be either "in prayer" (the incense altar) or "in the cruciform life" (the altar of burnt offerings). In Heb. 13:10 there is a comparison between the old and the new covenants, and it states,

> "**We continue having an altar from out of which those who continue habitually serving in the Tabernacle** (= those involved with the whole ceremonial economy) **do not have authority** (or: right; privilege) **to eat**." [cf 1 Pet. 2:9; Jn. 6:53-58]

These phrases could also signify that the people are a part of the temple, just as the altar is. So this listing may simply be meant to express the inclusiveness of the temple-as-people, who are to be measured. In 13:6, below, we see **His Tabernacle** (which in the Unveiling is equivalent to His Temple) defined as:

> "**those continuously tabernacling** (or: camping in tents; living in the Tabernacle) **within the atmosphere** (or: heaven)."

2. "**And the court** (unroofed enclosure; [used of the sheepfold in Jn. 10:1, 16]), **the one outside the temple, you must cast outside** (throw, or expel, out of doors), **and you may not measure her because it was given to the multitudes** (ethnic groups; nations), **and they will proceed treading** (advance by setting the foot upon) **the set-apart city** (or: the Holy City) **forty-two months.**

The "**court** (unroofed enclosure; [used of the sheepfold in Jn. 10:1, 16]), **the one outside the temple**" was the place where the people of Israel could come, bringing their offerings and sacrifices. It was the location of the altar of burnt offerings. The **temple** (*naos*), as signified here, was the holy place, and the holy of holies (cf the descriptions in Heb. 9:2-5). But historically, the "outer court" was a part of the Tabernacle (and later, the Temple) that enclosed the *naos* on all sides. There were divisions added within this court, during the period of Herod's temple, one of which was "the court of the Gentiles (nations; ethnic multitudes)."

The strange restriction about the **court** begs consideration: "**you must cast outside** (throw, or expel, out of doors), **and you may not measure her.**" This is judgment language. But remember, "judgment" is simply a decision that is based upon an evaluation of a situation. The Jewish leaders "cast out" of the temple (= they excommunicated) the person that Jesus had just healed:

> "**They decisively replied, and said to him, 'You yourself were wholly born within sins – and are YOU now teaching us?' And so they cast him out** (threw him outside)" (Jn. 9:34).

Consider Mat. 7:5, "**First extract** (cast out) **the rafter** (log; plank) **from out of your own eye**..." And then there is Mat. 8:11,

> "**Now I further say to you that many people from eastern lands, as well as western regions, will continue arriving. And they will one-after-another be made to recline [and dine] with Abraham and Isaac and Jacob, within the reign and sovereign rule of the heavens** (or: the kingdom of the atmospheres)."

This describes the ethnic multitudes (Gentiles; non-Jews) being grafted into Israel's olive tree (Rom. 11:17). It was the very 1st century time-frame leading up to this vision. But the next verse in Matthew 8 (vs. 12) speaks to our verse here:

> "**Yet the 'sons of the kingdom** (or: reign; = those who were in line to inherit the kingdom; or: = those who were supposed to manifest its reign and dominion)**' will be progressively thrown out into the external darkness** (external obscurity of the shadows). **There** [= outside the

banqueting building] **it will continue being 'the weeping and the grinding of teeth'** (or: The crying and the gnashing of teeth will continue being in that [outdoor] place, or situation)." [note: grinding/gnashing of teeth = either regret, or anger; or: it may be the place of the dogs (Samaritans) chewing on bones]

The prophetic action by Jesus, in Mat. 21:12 was set in the very courtyard which we are investigating here:

> "**Jesus entered into the Temple courts and threw out all the folks habitually selling [things], as well as those continuing in buying – as in a marketplace – within the Temple courts** (or: = and chased out all the vendors and shoppers from inside the Temple grounds)."

In Mat. 22:13-14 we read of an incident within the parable of the marriage of the King's Son (= the Messiah, and the eschatological messianic banquet). I suggest that the incident which was directed toward the Jewish leadership (*cf* Mat. 21:45) will be instructive to our vision, here:

> 13. "**At that point, the king said to the servants, 'Upon binding his feet and hands, you men throw him out into the darkness** (dim obscurity) **which is farther outside. In that place there will continue being the weeping** (or: lamenting) **and the grinding of the teeth.'**
>
> [comment: compare the binding of feet in Hos. 11:1-4, LXX:
>
> > 1. Because Israel [is] a young child, I Myself also love him, and I once called his children together from out of Egypt.
> > 2. The more I called them [to Me], the more they distanced themselves and kept away from My face (or: immediate presence). They sacrificed to the Baals, and then burned incense to the carved and chiseled images (= idols).
> > 3. And so I, Myself tied the feet of Ephraim together (i.e., restrained him; = hobbled him to keep him from wandering) [then] I took him up upon My arm – and yet they did not realize (or: know) that I had healed them.
> > 4. In the thorough ruin and destruction of humans I stretch out to them and lay [My hand] on them in binding ties (or: bonds) of My love.
> > And so I will be to them as a person slapping (or: striking) [someone] on his cheek, then I will look upon him (= either: keep an eye on him; or: give respect to him). I will prevail with him and then give ability and power to him. (JM)]
>
> 14. "**Now you see, many folks continue existing being called and invited ones, yet a few people [are also] chosen ones** (selected and picked out folks)**!**"
>
> [comment: notice the ironic inversion of this closing statement of the parable: here there were two sorts of people that were invited, the first group, then the second – which actually came to the feast; in this story, the one that was picked out (chosen and focused on) was also kicked out].

Then we have the parable of the unprofitable servant, Mat. 25:15-30. It ends (vs. 30),

> "**you men at once throw the useless slave out into the darkness** (dim obscurity and gloominess) **which is farther outside. In that place there will continue being the weeping** (or: lamenting) **and the grinding of the teeth.**"

As with the other "judgment" parables of Matthew, this most likely referred to the scribes, priests and Pharisees "losing their jobs" within God's reign, and being on the "outside" of His sovereign activities, of which we read in the book of Acts. And so here, in 11:2, some will go through hard times, while those chosen for the job will continue ministering, as we see in 11:3-11, below. Those "measured," here, are equivalent to those "sealed" in 7:1-8, above, and in 14:4b, below, this same category is called,

> "**the folks continuously following The little Lamb wherever He progressively leads** [other MSS: wherever He may habitually depart]. **These were** (or: are) **bought from humanity, a first-fruit in God** (by God; to God; for God), **even in** (by; with; for; to) **the little Lamb.**"

Those not "measured" are those who were not at that time ready for their "course finals" and did not at that point qualify in their evaluations: more course work needed to be completed. Since the folks represented by the outer court(s) are termed as being "**given to the multitudes**," it is obvious that God has already made a decision about the next phase of their journey. These may refer to those who were yet holding to the slave-girl (old covenant Jerusalem cultus and Law), and Paul said of their system, "**Cast out** (or: At once expel) **the servant girl** (the slave-girl; the maid) **and her son, for by no means will the son of the servant girl** (the slave-girl; the maid) **be an heir** (take possession of and enjoy the distributed allotment) **with the son of the freewoman**" (Gal. 4:30; Gen. 21:10). But Jesus experienced this being cast out, first:

> "**At the present time** (or: Now) **is an evaluation of and a decision pertaining to** (or: a sifting of and separation for; or: a judgment from) **this System** (or: this ordered arrangement; this world; this polity, culture and religion; or: this system of control and subjugation; or: the aggregate of humanity). **Now the Ruler** (the one invested with power; the leader; the chief; the ruler; or: the Original One; The Beginning One; the Prince) **of this System will be ejected outside**
> > (or: At this time the Chief of this world of culture, religion and government, the Originator and Controlling Principle of the ordered arrangement and universe, will be thrown out, [to the] outside [of it])" (Jn. 12:31).

Now in Jn. 6:37 Jesus said,

> "**All that** (or: Everything which) **the Father continues giving to Me will move toward Me to finally arrive here, and the person progressively coming toward Me I may under no circumstances** (or: would by no means) **throw forth from out of the midst** (eject; cast out) **[so that he will be] outside**."

Then Mat. 12:20b (quoting Isa. 42) presents the goal of His "casting out,"

> "**He [will] thrust-forth [the] separation-derived decision into a victory** (or: cast-out judging – unto victory)!"

And that Victory is given in 1 Cor. 15:54, "**The Death was drunk down and swallowed into Victory**," and those referred to in Matt. 12:20 shall also participate in this same Victory that we now possess, for,

> "**grace and joyous favor [is] in God** (or: by God) – **the One presently and progressively giving the Victory** (or: the overcoming) **to us** [i.e., to all humanity], **in us and for us through our Lord** (Owner; Master), **Jesus, [the] Christ**" (1 Cor. 15:57; bracketed comment added).

Also, we should keep in mind Rom. 11:1-5,

> 1. **I am asking, then, God does not thrust away His people, does He?** [*cf* Ps. 94:14] **Certainly not! For I myself am also an Israelite, forth from out of the seed of Abraham, of the tribe Benjamin.**
> 2. **God does not** (or: did not) **thrust away His people – whom He by experience intimately foreknew! Or have you not seen, and thus perceive, in [the passage of] Elijah, what the Scripture is saying as he is repeatedly encountering in God** (or: hitting on target when conversing with God), **concerning the sphere and condition of** (or: down against) **Israel?**
> 3. > "**O Lord** [= O Yahweh], **they kill Your prophets! They dig down under** (thus: undermine to demolish) **Your altars! And as for me, I was left under, alone** (or: I'm the only one left below), **and they continually seek** (are continuously trying to find) **my soul** (my breath; = they want to kill me)." [1 King 19:10, 14]
> 4. **To the contrary, what does the useful transaction** (the deliberative instruction; the oracle) **say to him?**
> > "**I leave down** (or: reserve) **to Myself** (for Myself; in Myself) **seven thousand adult males, those men who do not bend a knee to Baal.**" [1 Kings 19:18]
> 5. **Thus then, also, within the present season** (or: In this way, therefore, even in the current appropriate situation) **a destitute remainder** (or: a forsaken minority under the effect of lack; a remnant) **has been birthed** (exists) **down from** (in accord with) **a selection of grace.**

So with all this varied background for the symbol of "casting out the outer court," it behooves us to look for layers of interpretation.

A preterist interpretation of this verse (11:2) will see in it an allusion to the treading of the Roman army during the approximate forty-two months of the siege of Jerusalem in AD 66-70 (e.g., Simmons, ibid p 213). Historically, this is possibly correct. Isa. 64:10-11 spoke of Israel's history, but that was also a part of that to which Paul referred in 1 Cor. 10:11,

> "**all these things went on progressively** (or: from time to time) **stepping together among** (or: to) **those folks typically** (as examples; figuratively), **and it was written with a view toward a placing [of them] into the minds of us: ones unto whom the ends** (= conjunctions; or: goals) **of the ages have come down to** (or: arrived at) **and are now face to face [with us]**."

And Isa. 64 tells us,

> "Your holy cities are a wilderness; Zion is a wilderness; Jerusalem, a desolation. Our holy and our beautiful house… is burned with fire and all our pleasant things are laid waste" (vss. 10-11).

However, a viable alternative preterist view is given by Adam Maarschalk:

> "The Greek word used here for 'Gentiles' is 'ethnos, the counterpart of the Hebrew word 'goy' in the Old Testament. In the past, I simply assumed that this must be a reference to the Romans who helped destroy Jerusalem and the temple in 70 AD. I marked out 3.5 years from the time that Nero dispatched Vespasian as his war general (early 67 AD) until Vespasian's son, Titus, oversaw the burning of the temple in August 70 AD. **However, the Romans did not trample the city of Jerusalem for 42 months. They only trampled Jerusalem during the 5-month siege of Titus in 70 AD.** The Jews successfully kicked the Romans out of Jerusalem in August 66 AD, and they only managed to return to Jerusalem for a few days in November 66 AD when Cestius Gallus unsuccessfully attacked the city. For the next 3.5 years the Romans did not enter Jerusalem. During the 42 months before the Romans came, Jerusalem was indeed trampled, but it was by a different group of people. In early 68 AD Jesus ben Gamala, one of the former high priests, gave a speech in which he described what was happening to Jerusalem because of the Zealots:
>
>> "And this place, which is adored by the habitable world, and honored by such as only know it by report, as far as the ends of the earth, **is <u>trampled upon</u> by these wild beasts born among ourselves**" (Josephus, *Wars* 4.4.3).

So, according to this testimony, it was the Zealots who trampled Jerusalem, and they had a reputation for behaving like wild beasts. In what sense were they "Gentiles," though? Consider what [1] *The Universal Jewish Encyclopedia* and [2] *The Jewish Encyclopedia* say about the use of the word 'goy' in Scripture:

1. 'The Hebrew word goy (plural goyim) means "nation." In Biblical usage **it is applied also to Israel**: "Ye shall be unto Me a kingdom of priests, and a holy nation" (*goy kadosh*; Ex. 19:6).'

Source: 'Gentiles,' *The Universal Jewish Encyclopedia* (New York, NY: The Universal Jewish Encyclopedia, Inc., 1941); Volume 4, p. 533.

2. 'In the Hebrew of the Bible *goi* and its plural *goyyim* originally meant "nation," **and were applied both to Israelites and to non-Israelites** (Gen. xii. 2, xvii. 20; Ex. xiii. 3, xxxii. 10; Deut. iv. 7; viii. 9, 14; Num. xiv. 12; Isa. i. 4, ix. 22; Jer. vii. 28)."

Source: 'Gentile,' *The Jewish Encyclopedia* (New York, NY: Funk and Wagnalls Company, 1905); Volume 5, p. 615.

There were indeed multiple nations that trampled Jerusalem from the fall of 66 AD until the spring of 70 AD **when the Romans were not in the city**. Wikipedia gives this summary of those who fought the hardest against the Romans:

'During the Great Rebellion (66-70 CE) **the Galileans and Idumeans were the most adamant fighters** against Rome; they fought the Romans to the death when many Judeans were ready to accept peace terms.'

"Galilee was home to many Jews, but it was also associated with 'the Gentiles.' When Jesus departed to Galilee after John the Baptist was put in prison, Matthew said that this prophecy from Isaiah was fulfilled:

'The land of Zebulun and the land of Naphtali, the way of the sea, beyond the Jordan, **Galilee of <u>the Gentiles</u>**: The people who sat in darkness saw a great light, and upon those who sat in the region and shadow of death Light has dawned' (Matthew 4:15-16).

The three main Zealot leaders (Eleazar ben Simon, John Levi, and Simon Bar Giora) who orchestrated so much bloodshed in Jerusalem were not from Judea. John was from Gischala (Galilee) and Simon was from Gerasa (*Wars* 4.9.3), which at the time was one of the cities of the Roman Decapolis and today is in Jordan. By the time that Simon 'got possession of Jerusalem' in April 69 AD (*Wars* 4.9.12), he had an army of more than 40,000 people, including Idumeans, who he had gathered from the countryside. Eleazar took possession of Jerusalem even earlier, in late 66 AD. According to Wikipedia, he was likely from Galilee:

'Historical evidence of Eleazar arises in 66 CE, when he crushed Cestius Gallus' Legio XII Fulminata at Beit-Horon. Yet prior to this encounter, little is known about his early life and rise to power. **It can be inferred, however, from the geopolitical scene of ancient Israel in the first century CE, that he grew up in Galilee, the center of Zealotry.** Zealots were shunned by the High Priesthood in Jerusalem prior to the revolt. **This disunity with other sects of Judaism confined Zealotry to its birthplace in Galilee. Yet when the revolt broke out in 66 CE, the Galilean zealots fled the Roman massacres and sought refuge in the last major Jewish stronghold: Jerusalem.** Since Eleazar was placed in command of a large army of Jews in the battle against Cestius' Legio, he had already risen to a position of power in the priesthood prior to his military success.'

"In *Wars* 4.3.2-4, Josephus spoke of large multitudes from various regions that 'crept into Jerusalem' as the Jewish-Roman War was about to begin. Josephus said that 'the multitude that came out of the country were at discord before the Jerusalem sedition began' (see Revelation 6:4). He added:

'There were besides disorders and civil wars in every city; and all those that were at quiet from the Romans turned their hands one against another. There was also a bitter contest between those that were fond of war, and those that were desirous for peace… **[T]he captains of these troops of robbers**, being satiated with rapines in the country, **got all together from all parts, and became a band of wickedness, and all together crept into Jerusalem**… these very men, besides the seditions they raised, were otherwise the direct cause of the city's destruction also… Moreover, besides the bringing on of the war, they were the occasions of sedition and famine therein. There were besides these **other robbers that came out of the country, and came into the city, and joining to them those that were worse than themselves** …'

In *Wars* 4.9.10 Josephus says that John Levi of Gischala corrupted 'the body of the Galileans' in Jerusalem, who had given him his authority. Josephus went on to say of these Galileans that 'their inclination to plunder was insatiable, as was their zeal in searching the houses of the rich; and for the murdering of the men, and abusing of the women, it was sport to them…' The negative views that many Judeans had toward Galileans can be seen in the following Scripture verses: Matthew 26:73; Mark 14:70; John 1:46, 7:52….

"About a year into the Jewish-Roman War (66-73 AD), the Roman general Vespasian stated his strong suspicion that 'foreigners' had begun the war. Josephus then identified those foreigners and where they came from. It happened when Vespasian captured part of Galilee in the summer of 67 AD. He 'sat upon his tribunal at Taricheae, in order to distinguish the foreigners from the old inhabitants; **for those foreigners appeared to have begun the war.**' Some of those foreigners were from Hippos, which was 'a Greco-Roman city' in the Decapolis that was 'culturally tied more closely to Greece and Rome than to the Semitic ethnoi around' (Wikipedia). Josephus said that '**the greatest part of [those foreigners] were seditious persons and fugitives, who were of such shameful characters that they preferred war before peace.**' Most of the other foreigners were from Trachonitis and Gaulanitis, in the region of Batanea near Persia (*Wars* 3.10.10)." (https://adammaarschalk.com/2017/01/28/the-gentiles-trampled-jerusalem-for-42-months-revelation-111-2/ -- emphasis original)

This perspective will affect Maarschalk's interpretation of "the little beast" which we will first encounter in vs. 7, below. More of his research finds that "the headquarters of the Zealots were in Galilee," citing Robert Travers Herford (*Judaism in the NT Period*, The Lindsey Press, 1928 pp 66-67) in his blog, "An Overview of the Zealot Movement" (Pursuing Truth, adammaarschalk.com).

Yet we will also look for the figurative, spiritual understanding of the verse. There are two Jerusalem's in Scripture (e.g. Gal. 4:25-26), and so the preterist view sees this **set-apart city** (or: the Holy City) as the physical Jerusalem of the 1st century. But elsewhere in the Unveiling (21:2, 10; 22:19) this descriptive phrase refers to the New Jerusalem, and corresponds to the already present "**Jerusalem upon heaven** (or: a Jerusalem pertaining to and having the character and qualities of a superior, or added, heaven and atmosphere; or: Jerusalem [situated] upon, and comparable to, the atmosphere)," seen in Heb. 12:22ff. As we have been observing all through this work, there are multiple layers of interpretation to this apocalyptic literature. We should keep in mind, and continue looking for evidence of, the **blessing** and **happiness** that is promised to those "**constantly reading aloud** (or: retrieving knowledge from [it in the midst of an assembly]), **and those constantly hearing** (or: listening and paying attention to; = observing and obeying) **the words of the prophecy**" (1:3, above).

Here, in vs. 2, we see a separation being made: the temple and altar and the worshipers are by this measuring now separated from the rest of the city – even apart from the Holy (Set-apart) City, Jerusalem – or, from the rest of the temple complex. Simmons (ibid p 212) views the measuring of this group as corresponding to the sealing of the 144K in 7:3-4, above. We might consider this as correlating to the separation of the Manchild from the Woman, both of whom we shall see in chapter 12, below. If we see the figure of the Woman (12:1ff) as being Jerusalem of the 1st century, then a preterist interpretation of these scenes would fit – that this prophecy was referring to the events that concluded in AD 70, and the "**tread**[ing] **the set-apart city**" would refer to the soon destruction by the Romans, and so the **manchild** of 12:5 would first be Jesus, plus later, the called-out community that escaped Jerusalem. But if we see the Woman of chapter 12 as a type of the Bride of Christ (the Jerusalem which is above – Gal. 4:26), then these chapters can bear alternate interpretations, as well.

Considering this latter interpretation, let us now look ahead to 21:9-10, below,

"**And one of the seven agents – the ones holding** (having) **the seven shallow bowls: the ones being continuously full of the seven plagues – came and spoke with me, saying, 'Come here! I will proceed in showing you the Bride, the Wife of the little Lamb.' Next he carried me away, in spirit, upon a great and high mountain, and showed** (points out to) **me the set-apart** (or: holy; sacred) **city, Jerusalem, progressively** (or: habitually; or: presently) **descending out of the atmosphere** (or: heaven), **from God.**"

In these verses we see "the mother of us all," the Jerusalem above, continuously descending to those below, bringing life and light and healing to the nations. The Manchild would figure the Christ, the second Man, the last Adam (1 Cor. 15:44-48), or, it is a type of those at any point engaged in ministry to other folks who dispense from God's throne and participate in the activities of His reign.

But let us return to the last part of vs. 2: God always uses the multitudes (the nations) to tread His people as grapes. But this is always part of the purpose of His having a vineyard – to bring forth new wine. Yet there is the promise of Zech. 1:16, "I return to Jerusalem in compassions; My House (the temple) shall be built in it... and a tape shall be stretched out on Jerusalem." See also Zech. 2:1-5. But here, in 11:2, we have the situation where, "**The Lord** [= Yahweh] **will continue separating and making a decision about** (or: judging) **His people**," (Heb. 10:30b), and, "You have trodden down all them that err from Your statutes..." (Ps. 119:118). In Isa. 10 we see a picture of a similar scene where God used the nation of Assyria to judge His people,

> "And what will you do in THE DAY of VISITATION [note: much of today's "church" is presently seeking a "visitation" from the Lord], and in the desolation (vs. 3).... O Assyrian, the rod of My anger,... My indignation (vs. 5, 6). I will send him against a hypocritical nation [Israel], and against the people of My wrath will I give him charge, ... to tread them down like the mire of the streets... (vs. 11). Shall I not... so do to Jerusalem... upon Mt. Zion and on Jerusalem?" (vs. 12).

Isa. 5 deals with God's judgment of His vineyard. These things were literally fulfilled in times past, as well as in AD 70, but we can still see instruction for "His people" today. Recall Heb. 12:5b-11,

> "'**My son, do not be neglecting** (giving little care to) **the Lord's discipline** (education; child-training), **neither be exhausted** (= fall apart) **while being continually scrutinized or convicted** (exposed and put to the test; or: reproved) **by Him, for whom the Lord is loving** (urging toward reunion), **He is continuously and progressively educating** (or: child-training), **and He is periodically scourging every son whom He is taking alongside with His hands** (accepting; receiving).' [Prov. 3:11-12; cf Job 5:17; Ps. 94:12; Phil. 1:29].... **shall we not be continually placed under and humbly arranged and aligned by the Father of the spirits? And then we shall proceed living!** [cf Nu. 27:16; Eph. 6:2-3].... **Now on the one hand, all discipline** (instruction; child-training) **with a view to what is presently at hand, does not at the time seem to be joyous or fun, but to the contrary [is] painful and full of sorrow and grief; however afterwards, to, for, in and by those having been gymnastically trained** (= working-out while stripped of self-works) **through it, it is constantly and** [cf Jas. 3:18] **progressively yielding fruit which has the character and qualities of peace and harmony – which equates to fair and equitable dealings in rightwised relationships which are in line with the Way pointed out, and justice.**"

This principle should be remembered as we read through God's dealings with people, in this Unveiling.

It is easy to see the clause, "**given to the multitudes** (ethnic groups; nations)," as a reference to the Romans who would come to quell the Jewish rebellion, in the 1st century. This would be a fulfillment of Lu. 21:24,

> "**And so, folks will keep on falling by [the] mouth of a sword, and [others] will proceed being led captive into all the nations** (or: into the midst to unite with every ethnic group) **– and Jerusalem will continue being progressively trampled by and under pagans** (non-Jews; those of the nations) **until where they can** (or: should) **be fulfilled. And then there will progress being seasons of the ethnic multitudes** (or: fitting situations pertaining to the nations; or: occasions or fertile moments with regard to non-Jews)."

This calls to mind Isa. 63:18b, "our adversaries have trodden down Your sanctuary..."

A prophetic, spiritual application of this clause may be that it is an allusion to Rom. 11:17, the in-grafting of the ethnic multitude (nations; Gentiles) into the olive tree, "**until which [time]** (or: to the point of which [situation]) **the effect of the full measure** (or: the result of the entire contents; or: = the full impact and full compliment of forces) **from the nations** (or: of the ethnic multitudes; or: – which are the Gentiles –) **may enter in**" (Rom. 11:25b). With this view, we could see the two witnesses, below, as the multi-national (Jew plus Gentile) humanity of the called-out, prophetic communities, as they,

> "**smite** (strike) **the Land** (or: earth) **within every plague as often as they may will – if they intend** (purpose) **to**," and then lie, "**upon the broad place** (street; plaza) **of The Great City – whatever, spiritually, is normally being called** (or: named) **"Sodom" and "Egypt" – where also their Lord was crucified**" (11:6, 8, below).

We discussed this facet of the anointed ministry in chapter 9, above. We will investigate their ministry in greater detail, below.

Although John was not to measure the court outside the temple at that time, and even though the literal **set-apart city** was to be treaded down for 42 months, we have Zech. 2:1-5 that speaks of the new Jerusalem, which is above (*cf* chapters 21-22, below):

> "behold – a man with a measuring line in his hand… to measure Jerusalem…. [for] Jerusalem shall be inhabited as towns without walls for the multitude of humans and cattle therein; for I, says Yahweh, will be unto her a wall of fire roundabout, and will be the glory in the midst of her."

The time period of "**forty-two months** (3.5 years)" is the same period referred to in vs. 3, below, as **1260 days**, as well as the same **1260 days** in 12:6, below, and is equivalent to the "**a season, and seasons, and half a season**" mentioned in 12:14, below. We find the same phrase, "**forty-two months**," again in 13:5, showing that the events of chapters 11-13 all take place in this same eschatological time period. These parallel chapters occupy the same context, and perhaps the same scene on the stage. They are describing, from three different viewpoints, the intertwining of what is happening. As well as the allusion to Dan. 7:25 and 12:7, Nu. 33 lists forty-two journeys/encampments (vss. 5-49) of Israel's wilderness experience. Notice 12:14a, below, where the Woman is flown "**into the wilderness**." Beale reckons that Israel's wanderings in the desert was for forty-two years:

> "it appears that two years passed before Israel incurred the penalty of remaining in the wilderness for forty years" (ibid p 565).

But let us consider Dan. 12:7, which Simmons affirms to be prophetic of the war with Rome (ibid p 213),

> "The man clothed in linen…raised his right hand and his left hand toward heaven, and I heard him swear by the One who lives forever that it would be for a time, times and half a time [The LXX of the last phrase uses the same words as 12:14, below: "a season, seasons and half a season"], and that when the shattering of the power of the holy people comes to an end, all these things would be accomplished" (NRSV; brackets added). Dan. 7:25 has the same time words. *Cf* Dan. 9:24-27.

The time/season words in Dan. 12:7 do indeed correspond to the time/season words of these chapters in the Unveiling, and again, historically, I think that Simmons is correct. But just as Paul brought the historical death and resurrection of Christ on into the decades following the event, giving us a whole new understanding of those historical events, I suggest that the same applies here: there is another layer of interpretation, as we have discussed, above.

In regard to the ongoing application of the court being cast outside and not being measured, Prinzing (ibid) gives some interesting insights:

> "The application is two-fold. First, in speaking of our becoming the temple, He is dealing with our inner man, 'the hidden man of the heart.' 'For the Lord sees not as man sees; for the man looks on the outward appearance but the Lord looks on the heart' (1 Sam. 16:7). And so Jesus reproved the Pharisees, because they 'make clean the outside of the cup and of the platter, but within they are full of extortion and excess' (Mat. 23:25). And again emphasizing that it was not

the outward, but the inward that mattered, He said, 'Not that which goes into the mouth defiles a man, but that which cometh out of the mouth – this defiles a man.' Religion concerns itself with the measuring of the outward, the physical, the self-worth, the fame and success, etc. And they set standards for dress, and code of action, ignoring the fact that the outward is but a portrayal ground for the inward – and sooner or later all masquerades are stripped away, and we will be seen for what we are. In the measuring of the temple, altar and worshipper, the instruction was to place the emphasis upon the spiritual, not the natural.... Secondly, another application can be drawn – for the intense dealings of God are first upon the remnant firstfruits of the new creation order (the overcomer, which He is leading onward): these are being dealt with in ways and depths that the multitudes know nothing of. But the people of the court will carry on with their ministries and programs, often blessed by God for the realm in which they move, though they are totally ignorant of the 'wheel within a wheel,' of the separated walk of those who go on to worship in spirit and in truth."

So this picture is of a measuring (with all its nuances) of the temple, the casting out of the "outer court," and the trampling of the set-apart city. The following verses, and chapters, will help to clarify our understanding.

3. **"And I will continue giving to My two witnesses** (or: I will progressively supply for My two witnesses), **and they will proceed prophesying** (functioning as prophets) **a thousand two hundred sixty days, being clothed [in]** (or: cast around [with]) **sackcloth."**

Now we come to God's **two witnesses**. Much conjecture has been made as to who these two are, but we think the stress should be upon the fact that they are God's WITNESSES. In Deut. 19:15 we see God's principle set forth, "a matter shall be confirmed at (or: on) the mouth of **two witnesses**..." This topic came up during Jesus' earthly ministry. In Jn. 8:13, the Pharisees said to Him, "**You yourself are continuing to bear witness** (or: are now giving testimony) **about yourself! Your witness** (testimony) **is not true!**" In that same chapter, vss. 17-18, Jesus responds to them:

"**Yet even within your own Law it has been written that the witness** (testimony; evidence) **of two people** (humans; men) **is true** (or: exists being valid, genuine and real). **I, Myself, am the man now bearing witness** (or: habitually testifying; progressively giving evidence) **about Myself, and the Father – the One sending Me – is continuously bearing witness** (constantly testifying and giving evidence) **about Me.**"

So they saw only one man, Jesus, but He was TWO WITNESSES, because of the Father's presence in and with Him. Here, too, we should keep in mind that John was on Patmos, "**because of the testimony** (witness; evidence) **pertaining to and having the characteristics of Jesus Christ**" (1:10, above). It follows that what these two witnesses are proclaiming will be in concord with the life and message of their "heavenly" Witness, Jesus. Jesus, giving this Unveiling to John (*cf* the Prologue, above), was one witness and John was a second – but, in this, these both were symbols of His body. In 6:9, above, recall, "**the souls of the folks having been slaughtered [as in sacrifice] because of the Word of God** (or: God's message), **and because of the witness** (testimony; evidence) **which they were holding** (or: continued to have)."

We can see another example of this same type of situation in the ministry of the disciples in Mark 16:20. Jesus had been "**taken back up again** (or: was received again) **into the midst of the atmosphere** (or: sky; heaven)" (16:19), then in vs. 20,

"**Yet those men, in [their] going forth** (or: upon exiting [the area]), **made public proclamations of the Lord** (or: from the Lord; pertaining to the Lord) **everywhere – He continuously cooperating and working together, and repeatedly establishing** (setting on good footing) **the**

message (the Word; the thought; the idea) **through the consistently accompanying signs** (or: by means of the signs which continued attending as sequels)."

So now one can be alone here on the earth, and yet be two witnesses if the Lord (in the spirit, or in heaven) is working with him. To see "the Two Witnesses" as a figure of God's anointed ministry here seems consistent with the continual procession of figures which we have thus far seen in these visions. Dan Kaplan shared with me the following list of references which help explain the symbol of a "witness:"

Deut. 4:26, "I call the heavens and the earth **to witness** against you today…"

Jn. 5:36-37a, "**Yet I, Myself, constantly hold** (or: am continuously having) **the Witness** (or: the evidence) **[that is] greater and more important than [that] from John, for the works** (or: actions; deeds) **which the Father has given in Me** (to Me; for Me; by Me) – **to the end that I may bring them to the goal** (finish, mature and perfect them to their destined purpose) – **the works themselves which I am continuously doing** (performing; producing) **continuously bear witness** (testify; make claim; give evidence) **about Me, that the Father has sent Me forth with a commission** (as a Representative, or Emissary). **Also, the One sending Me, that Father, has borne witness** (has testified) **about Me.**"

In Acts 10, the following verses are instructive:

39. "**And we ourselves [are] witnesses** (or: folks who give evidence) **of all [the] things which He did** (and: performed; produced), **both within the country of the Judeans, and in Jerusalem – Whom also they lifted up and assassinated, hanging [Him] upon a wooden pole** (or: tree).

40. "**This Man God raised up on** (or: in; [D reads: after]) **[the] third day, and He gave** (or: gives) **Him to become visible within the midst –**

41. "**not among all the people, but rather among witnesses having been previously hand-picked and elected by God – in us** (or: to us) **who ate and drank together with Him, after the [occasion for] Him to stand back up** (rise again) **out from the midst of dead folks.**

42. "**And He passed along the directive for us to publicly proclaim, as heralds – to, and among, the people – and to certify at once, by personal evidence, and to give testimony as witnesses that this Man is and continues being the very One having been definitely marked out and specified by God [as] He who decides** ([the] Evaluator; a Separator for making decisions; Judge) **concerning presently living folks, and currently dead people.**

43. "**To this Man all the prophets continue bearing witness, giving testimony and presenting evidence: through His Name, everyone making it a habit to place their trust into Him and continue believing with [their focus] into the midst of Him is to at once receive a sending-away of mistakes** (a divorce from failures; a cancellation of errors; a forgiveness of sins; a flowing-off of deviations).**"**

44. **During the middle of Peter's still speaking these gush-effects and results of the flow** (or: declarations), **the set-apart Breath-effect** (or: the Holy Spirit; the Sacred Wind) **fell upon all the folks presently listening to and hearing the Logos** (the message; the Word). [note: this was the equivalent of a "Gentile Pentecost"]

Rom. 8:16, "**The same Spirit** (or: spirit; or: The Breath-effect Himself; or: This very attitude) **is constantly witnessing together with our spirit** (is continuously bearing joint-testimony to our spirit; is habitually co-witnessing for our spirit; is progressively adding confirming testimony and evidence in our attitude) **that we are, and continuously exist being, God's children** (ones born of God; children from God [not of the child-escort {Gal. 3:24}], by natural descent)."

Heb. 2:4 speaks of, "**God joining with added corroborating witness, both by signs and wonders and a full spectrum of** (or: various; multi-faceted) **powers and abilities, and by** (or: in) **divisions** (partings; distributions) **of set-apart Breath-effect** (or: of [the] Holy Spirit; from a sacred attitude), **corresponding** to His willing [it] and exercising His purpose." Then Heb. 10:15 affirms that, "**the set-apart Breath-effect** (or: Holy Spirit; Sacred Attitude) **is also habitually witnessing** (or: progressively attesting; periodically testifying) **to us, for us, in us and by us**."

Next, we have these examples from 1 Jn. 5:
> 8. **the breath** (or: spirit; Breath-effect) **and the water and the blood, and these three are [coming; proceeding] into the midst of the One** (or: exist [leading] into one [reality]; are existing into the one thing; or: = are in unison; or: = are in agreement, or are for one thing).
> 9. **Since** (or: If) **we are habitually receiving the testimony** (the witness; the evidence) **of humans** (or: from people), **the evidence of God** (God's witness; testimony from God; or: the testimony and evidence which is God) **is** (or: exists being) **greater, because it is God's testimony** (or: the witness which is God) **that He has testified** (given as evidence; witnessed) **and it now exists available as evidence** (or: testimony), **concerning His Son** (or: round about the Son which is Him; about the Son Who originates from Him).
> 10. **The person continuously and progressively believing** (or: keeping confidence and habitually putting trust) **into the midst of God's Son constantly holds** (or: has; possesses) **the testimony** (witness; evidence) [*p74* & A add: of God] **within himself; the one not believing in God** [A reads: the Son] **has made Him out to be** (or: has construed Him) **a liar, because he has not believed or put trust into the evidence** (testimony; witness) **which God has attested and affirmed concerning His Son** (or: shown as proof round about the Son from, and which is, Him).
> 11. **And so this is the evidence** (or: exists being the testimony, witness and attested affirmation)**: that God gives** (or: gave; grants) **Life pertaining to, and having the quality of the Age** (life whose source is the Age [of Messiah]; eonian life; Life of, for and on through the ages) **to, for and in us, and this very Life continuously exists within His Son** (or: is in union with the Son which is Him)**!**
> 12. **The one continually holding** (or: constantly having; progressively possessing) **the Son continuously holds** (constantly has; progressively possesses) **the Life**...

In this Unveiling, 1:5, above, described Him as, "**Jesus Christ, the faithful Witness** (or: reliable Evidence)," while 3:14 affirms Him as, "**The Amen** (The It-is-so), **the Faithful** (or: Trustworthy, Reliable) **and True Witness**."

These passages show the symbol of there being TWO witnesses, to affirm a matter, and the interaction of God being a second Witness, and providing corroborating evidence to the testimony of the earthly witness. Kaplan also pointed to the OT type of there being two cherubim as a part of the mercy seat in the Tabernacle, and then there being God's witnesses of the old and the new covenants (arrangements), the Word of God and the Spirit (Breath-effect) of God, and finally, Christ the Head and the body of Christ. The examples could be multiplied. So we should take time to ponder the significance of these players on the scene that John is hearing about. These two witnesses are not individual people, but rather they are figures, just as are "the temple" and "the outer court" and "the city." The next verse describes them as "**the two lampstands**," which is an allusion to 1:20b, above: the called-out, covenant communities. That there are two signifies the number of, or symbolizing, "witness," as seen above. Beale points out that their being killed (vs. 7, below) "is based on Dan. 7:21, where the last evil kingdom prophesied by Daniel persecutes not an individual but the nation of Israel" (ibid p 574). He notes that we see an individual woman (12:1ff, below) representing a corporate community within the context of this same symbolic time-period of three and a half years (ibid). As Smith has instructed us, numbers in the Unveiling represent ideas, not literal enumerations. We will also see, below, that the things which they do (the allusions to Moses and Elijah, vs. 6) they both do.

I love what Peter Hiett says in regard to the Biblical principle of two witnesses:
> "The gospel of Jesus involves a reasoned, systematic witness and a visionary, poetic, ecstatic witness. They are both prophetic, and both the testimony of Jesus...*logos* and *rhema*, principle and passion, mind and motion, reason and feeling, left-brained and right-brained, Baptists and Pentecostals, maybe even... male and female... two witnesses; one Jesus" (ibid p 142).

And we would add: a many-membered body, but one Spirit (1 Cor. 12:12; Eph. 4:4). In this same passage, Hiett points us to the picture in Acts 2:3, "**Then progressively dividing and self-distributing tongues – as if of fire – were seen by them, and He** (or: it; or: [one]) **sat down upon each one of them.**" I also like how he tied these verses of John 20 into this topic:

> 22. **And saying this, He suddenly blows on, and says to, them** (or: He breathes within [them], so as to inflate them [note: same verb as used in Gen. 2:7, LXX], and is saying to them), **"Receive a set-apart spirit!** (or: Get [the] Holy Spirit!; take the Sacred Breath!; or: Receive a sacred attitude),
> 23. **"If you folks should send away** (dismiss; allow to depart; forgive; pardon; divorce) **the mistakes** (sins; errors; failures) **of certain ones, they have been sent away for them** (or: have been and remain pardoned in them; have been dismissed or divorced by them). **If you would continue holding fast and controlling** (or: should keep on grasping and exercising strength; or: can restrain, hinder, hold back) **those of certain ones, they have been and continue being held fast and controlled** (seized; grasped; restrained).**"**

There is an ebb, and a flow, even as in the tides of the seas. There are contrasting times, as we read (and sing) in Eccl. 3:1ff. As Kaplan says, our very body is composed in corresponding parts, and this can be seen throughout creation. It is the Spirit of Life that orders both complimentary and contrasting witnesses which guide us on or path, and heal us in appropriate ways.

The verb of the first clause is in the future tense, a durative tense that speaks of continued action. Thus, we have, "**I will continue giving**." This can be pictured by Jesus' example of Him being the Vine that keeps supplying the Life-sap of the Vine to His branches so that they can produce His fruit (Jn. 15:1ff). The Strong Agent says that He will do the giving/supplying, so this is another key to the identity of this Agent: Christ. This calls to mind Jesus' instructions to His disciples in Mat. 10:19-20,

> "**you should not be anxious or overly concerned about how or what you should be speaking, for, what you should say will continue being given to you men – within that hour! You see, you, yourselves, are not the ones then speaking, but rather, [it is] the Spirit** (Breath-effect; Attitude) **of your Father repeatedly speaking within you**." (*cf* Mk. 13:11b)

We find a similar statement in Lu. 12:12,

> "**You see, the Set-apart Breath-effect** (or: Holy Spirit; Sacred Breath and Attitude) **will continue teaching you within that very hour what things it is necessary to say**."

The verb **giving** is not followed by a direct object, but since, "**they will proceed prophesying**," we can presume that at least part of what they are given will be the message from Christ, i.e., what to say. The parenthetical expansion of the clause may lend a clearer view of what is meant: "I will progressively supply for My two witnesses." This covers all potential needs that we might have.

Here in 11:3, these two witnesses "function as prophets." In Deut. 18:9 Moses is speaking to Israel concerning "when you come to the land that Yahweh your God is giving you..." In vs. 15 he prophesies about this time and situation, saying, "A Prophet from among you – from your brothers, LIKE ME – shall Yahweh your God raise up for you." While Israel was physically in "the Promised Land," they had many prophets. Yet when John the Baptist came, in enquiring who he was, and when John acknowledged "I am not the Messiah," the priests and Levites then asked him if He was Elijah, and he told them that he was not. So their next question was, "Are you THE PROPHET?" He replied, "No" (Jn. 1:20, 21). So after having had a history in which many prophets were sent to them, the Jews were still looking for THE PROPHET of whom Moses spoke. This Prophet would be their Messiah.

The agent Gabriel had appeared to Zechariah and had told him that he would have a son who he was to call John. He says of John, "**And so, he himself will continue advancing in His presence** (or: going forward in His sight) **– within and in union with a breath-effect** (or: wind) **and ability having the character and qualities of Elijah** (or: in association with Elijah's spirit and power; or: in an attitude and an ability which is Elijah [= God is Yah])..." (Lu. 1:17). In Matt. 17:10-13, we read,

> 10. **At this, the disciples questioned Him, in saying, "Why, in light of this, are the scribes** (the scholars; the experts in the sacred Scriptures) **constantly saying that it is binding** (necessary) **for Elijah to come first?"**
> 11. **So He, giving a decided answer, said, "Elijah is indeed progressively** (or: repeatedly) **coming, and then He will progressively move and reintegrate all men** (or: things) **away from where they have been placed** (or: put) **down, and from what has been firmly established.**
> 12. **"Yet, I am continuing in telling you men that Elijah already comes and they do not recognize** (or: fully know) **Him. But even more, they perform on Him as many things as they wish and intend.** (or: Elijah already came, and they did not recognize him, but rather, they did in him as much as they wanted.) **In this way** (or: Thus), **also, the Son of the Man** (= the Human Being; or: = the eschatological Messianic figure) **is progressively about to continue experiencing [things] by them, even suffering under them."**
> 13. **At that point, the disciples put it together that He spoke to them about John the Immerser** (or: Baptist).

In connecting Luke and Matthew, above, it would seem that it is the Spirit of God, working in God's anointed prophet, that is symbolized by the name "Elijah." Thus, also, I would say that Jesus associated Himself with this spirit of ministry in Mat. 17, above, when He said, "**In this way** (or: Thus), **also, the Son of the Man**..." In light of this, let us consider a literal translation of Mat. 11:13-14,

> "**For you see, all the Prophets and the Law prophesy** (showed light ahead of time) **until** (to the point of time up to; till the time of) **John. And so, if you now desire and continue purposing to welcome, embrace and accept [it; or: Him], the One being at the point of being at [His] periodical coming is Himself** (or: the person currently being about to be presently and progressively coming: this very one exists being) **Elijah.**"

These renderings use the Greek word "*autos*" as the intensive, in the first, or bold, version, and as the oblique, in the second, parenthetical, rendering of the last clause. Thus, it would seem that Elijah is the figure for God's Anointed, His Christ, as well as for His agent who announces His coming (e.g., John). But the term THE PROPHET (which John denied being) refers to THE CHRIST, both to Jesus when He ministered on earth, and to HIS BODY here in the Unveiling. As to this latter application, His body of followers, Jesus prophesied of these prophets which He would send, in Mat. 23,

> 33. "**[You] snakes! [You] offspring** (brood) **of vipers** (poisonous serpents)**! How can you flee and escape from the judging which has the qualities, character and significance of the valley of Hinnom** (= the sentence to the city dump [Greek: Gehenna; = the Valley of Hinnom]; the deciding which pertains to the waste depository of the city)**?** [*cf* Jer. 19:1-15]
> 34. "**Because of this – look and consider! – I, Myself, am continuing in commissioning and sending off to you people prophets, wise people and scholars** (scribes; theologians of the Law). **Of them, [some] you folks will proceed to be killing, and [some] you will proceed to crucify** (hang and put to death on stakes). **Further, of them [some] you people will continue severely whipping** (scourge; lash) **within your synagogues, and then you, yourselves, will continue pursuing and persecuting [them] from city to city** (or: town to town),
> 35. "**so that upon you, yourselves, can** (or: should) **come all [the] just** (equitable; rightwised) **blood being continuously poured out** (or: spilled) **upon the Land – from the blood of**

rightwised (just; fair; in-right-relationship) **Abel, until the blood of Zechariah, the son of Barachiah** (or: Baruch), **whom you people murdered between the Temple and the altar. 36. "Assuredly, I am now saying to you people, it will progressively move toward this point, and then arrive – all these things! – upon this generation!"**

In this verse it mentions that these are **clothed** in (or: cast around with) **sackcloth**. This was worn when one was mourning (Gen. 37:34), but was also a figure of repentance (Matt. 11:21; Jonah 3:8), and there is a definite sense of humiliation in Isa. 58:5, "... to bow down his head as a bulrush, and to spread sackcloth and ashes [under him]..." It also signified a time of trouble (Esther 4:1-3). Chilton points out: "the traditional dress of the prophets from Elijah through John the Baptizer, symbolizing their mourning over national apostasy (2 Ki 1:8; Isa. 20:2; Jonah 3:6; Zech. 13:4; Mat. 3:4; Mk. 1:6).... The two witnesses... represent the line of prophets, culminating in John the Baptizer, who bore witness against Jerusalem during the history of Israel" (ibid p 276). Simmons instructs us, "Typically, it was black (Rev. 6:12) and made from camel or goat hair (Mat. 3:4; Mk. 1:6)" (ibid p 215). It has been suggested that this figure of sackcloth speaks here of the two witnesses being yet in their mortal bodies (e.g., 2 Cor. 4:10-11; 5:1-4) as opposed to agents in glorified bodies (as seen at the tomb, following Jesus' resurrection, "**two adult men** {human males}, **in clothing that was constantly flashing and radiating beams of light**," Lu. 24:4b, and at His being caught up by the cloud, Acts 1:10b). It could also symbolize the nature of their ministry: judgment, to bring humility and a change of thinking and mourning to those to whom they ministered – as well as to foreshadow trouble. The term is used in Lu. 10:13b,

"**they would have long ago changed their thinking and altered their lives by turning [to God] – while [dressed] in sackcloth and continuing to sit in** (or: on) **ashes**." *Cf* Mat. 11:21. We should also note the "forty-two months" (vs. 2) and the "**1260 days**" (vs. 3 and in 12:6). These are all the same amount of time: three and a half years. Metzger says of this, "This period (three and a half years) is the traditional apocalyptic term of Gentile domination, derived from Dan. 9:27 and 12:7..." (ibid p 69). The period of their ministry follows the pattern of their Lord's, which many consider to be about the same length of time. That we see the same time period in 11:2, 3 and in 12:6 may indicate that these are parallel passages, giving different aspects of, or another presentation of, the same situation. This same period of time is stated in 12:14 as "**a season, and seasons, and half a season**." This latter is an echo of Dan. 7:25 and 12:7, and may well be the antitype of those two passages. In a personal conversation, Kenneth Earl pointed out that one half of a week is three and one half days, being equal to three and one half years since the 70 weeks of Dan. 9:24-27 equals 70 years that Jeremiah prophesied that Israel would be in captivity. Ken has shared that it was Jesus that "confirmed the covenant" in the "midst of the week," and His sacrifice "caused the sacrifice and the oblation to cease" [in God's economy] following His three and one half year ministry. Thus do we see the remainder of the 70th week (3 & ½ days = 3 & ½ years) fulfilled by His body, the "two witnesses," in what is described in chapters 11 and 12.

Those of a preterist persuasion view the second half of this 70th week, the final 3 & ½ years of Daniel's prophecy, as having been fulfilled when "God destroyed Judea and the city of Jerusalem in AD 67-70 by the invading Roman armies that came in" (John L. Bray, "The Millennium," p. 21). Also see "What Happened in AD 70?" by Edward E. Stevens, p. 9, under the section "Fulfillments Mentioned In Josephus" where he says, "Daily sacrifices ceased in the 'midst of the week' (i.e., after 3 & ½ years) – Dan. 9:27 (Wars 6:2:1);" Bray, in his booklet "The Rapture of Christians," p. 21, also quotes E. Hampded Cook from his book, *The Christ Has Come*, (1894), "... the surviving members of the Hebrew Christian church... hastily sought refuge in the wilderness, where for the whole duration of the war in Palestine – 1260 days, or 3 and ½ years – she remained, cared for by God."

The corporate ministry and function of witnessing (showing evidence and giving testimony) is seen again in 12:11, below, "**the word** (or: message; Word; Logos) **of THEIR witness** (evidence; testimony)." We read in Acts 1:8,

> "**you folks will progressively receive power and will continue taking to yourselves ability [at, or with, the] added, full coming of the Set-apart Breath-effect** (the Holy Spirit and Sacred Attitude) **upon you folks – and you will keep on being My witnesses** (those who testify and give evidence of what they have seen and experienced), **both within Jerusalem and within all Judea and Samaria... even as far as [the] end of the Land** (or: an extremity of the region, or a farthest point of the earth)."

This passage parallels the Olivet Discourse (Mat. 24, Mk. 13, Lu.21), where Jesus prophesied the destruction of Jerusalem.

4. **These are the two olive trees and the two lampstands** (= menorahs) **– the ones having made a stand** (or: been placed) **and are standing before** (or: in the presence of) **the Lord** [= Yahweh] **of the earth** (or: the Owner of the Land). [Jer. 11:16; Zech. 4:2-3, 11-14]

In this verse we come to "**the two olive trees and the two lampstands**" – each figure being "two witnesses" – that are a direct reference to Zech. 4. In that prophecy we see a fuller description. There also, the messenger rouses Zechariah (vs. 1). In vs. 2 we see that the lampstand has 7 lamps – sound familiar? This shows that this message concerns the 7 called-out communities in the Unveiling 2 and 3, but was a picture set in the tabernacle, in Zech. 4. Verse 3, there, says, "And two olive trees are over it, one on the right of the bowl [of the lamp] and one on its left." In our previous verse here, above, we are told that, "**they will proceed prophesying**," which is to say, they will be speaking God's Word. And seeing that our present verse refers to them as **lampstands**, we are reminded of Ps. 119:105,
> "Your Word [is a] lamp to my feet and a light to my path."

Also, Prov. 6:23,
> "For instruction [is] a lamp, and law [is] a light, and reproofs of admonition [are] a way [of/to] life."

Note Zech. 4:7 and 9 where Zerubbabel is a figure of the Anointed One, Christ: "And He shall bring forth the Headstone with tumults: Grace, grace to it!.... The hands of Zerubbabel laid the foundation of this house, and His hands SHALL COMPLETE IT!" Note that both "trees" of that vision are over (or: up upon) the lampstands, in the LXX of Zech. 4:3 – figuring the anointing being in the realm of heaven, or the spirit, that ministers the oil (i.e., the anointing) to the gathered assemblies.

In Zech. 4:11, he repeats the question as to who are these two olive trees. He is answered enigmatically in vs. 14, "These are the two sons of clear oil who are standing by the Lord of the entire earth" (CVOT). The conclusion seems obvious: these two witnesses are a figure of the anointed witness of, and from, His body – they are His anointed ones, His Christ – and here, in the Unveiling, they represent the WITNESS of the called-out communities. That they "**are standing before** (or: in the presence of) **the Lord**" signifies their authority in God's kingdom and tells us that **the Lord is present**. Mat. 18:20 informs us,
> "**You see, where there are two or three people that have been led and gathered together into My Name, I am there** (in that place) **within the midst of and among them**."

Being God's home, i.e., His temple, means "being in God's presence," where He resides. Recall the discussion of the lampstands in 1:20ff, above: the lampstand was located in the holy place – along with the "bread of the presence" (Ex. 25:30-31; 40:4; 1 Ki. 7:48-49).

Just as Zerubbabel and Joshua were historically involved with the building of the second temple, so are these two witnesses involved with the building of God's spiritual temple, Christ's body. Note the symbolism in Zech. 3:9, "the Stone [= Christ] which I have set before Joshua: upon One Stone are seven eyes… So I will take away the iniquity of the earth (or: that Land) in one Day."

Zech. 4:10b identified these eyes, "these seven are the eyes of Yahweh, running to and fro throughout all the earth (Land)." Here, in 4:5b, above, we have seven lamps defined as "the seven Spirits of God." The seven lampstands are seven covenant communities that are built upon the Headstone (Zech. 4:7), in and with Grace! The fullness of God's Spirit and Insights anoint His body, building it into His Temple. We can see this latter prophesied in Zech. 6:12b-13,

"Behold the Man! Branch (or: Sprout) is His name, and from His place He shall branch out (or: sprout), and He will build the Temple of Yahweh…. And He will sit and rule on His throne, and He will come to be Priest on His throne, and the counsel of peace shall come to be between the two of them." *Cf* 1:6; 5:10, above.

Just as these two are identified as **the two lampstands**, we are reminded, again, that Jesus told His followers, "**You folks, yourselves, exist being** (are) **the light of the ordered System** (the world of culture, religion, politics, government, and secular society; = the human sociological realm; or: the aggregate of humanity)" (Mat. 5:15). And Phil. 2:15b instructs us that,

"**you folks are continuously shining** (giving light; or: appearing; made visible by light) **as illuminators** (sources of light; or: luminaries) **within [the] dominating, ordered System** (or: centered in a world of secular culture, religion, economics and government; or: **in union with the aggregate of mankind**)." Note the solidarity expressed in this last phrase: "in union with.."

Paul's allusion, here, may be to Dan. 12:3,

"And the instructors (or: the intelligent; those who make wise; LXX: the folks putting things together) shall shine like the shining of the expanse (or: as the brightness of the atmosphere; LXX: of the firmament) – and they who bring (or: turn) many to righteousness (or, with Young: and those justifying the multitude; LXX: and from among the rightly-oriented fair and just folks of the many; or: even [coming] from the many rightwised folks) like the stars to times age-abiding and beyond (or: for the eon, and further; LXX: on into the Age, and yet still)."

The other side of the coin is the reference to the "olive tree" in Jer. 11:16 (and echoed in Rom. 11:17ff). There the context is judgment for Israel and Judah:

"What [right] has My beloved in My House, [when] she is executing [her evil] scheme?.... A flourishing olive tree, lovely with shapely fruit, Yahweh had called your name; but with the sound of a great din, He will ravage its leaves with fire and its branches will be smashed. Yahweh of hosts Who planted you has decreed evil against you due to the evil of the house of Israel and the house of Judah… by fuming [incense] to Baal" (Jer. 11:15-17, CVOT).

In the 1st century, judgment was coming to old covenant Israel while the witness from the new covenant Israel (composed of both Jew and Gentile – two witnesses) echoed the message of Jesus:

"**it continues being inadmissible** (not acceptable; = unthinkable) **for a prophet to be destroyed outside of Jerusalem! Jerusalem, O Jerusalem! – the one constantly killing off the prophets, and repeatedly stoning the people having been sent off as emissaries** (missionaries; representatives) **to her – how often** (how many times) **I wanted and intended to at once completely gather together and assemble your children, in the manner in which a hen [gathers] her own brood** (or: chicks) **under [her] wings, and yet you people did not want [it]! Look and consider this – your house** (or: House; = the Temple; or: household [a figure of the entire people]) **is being progressively left and abandoned** [other MSS add: {and} desolate – depopulated like a desert; *cf* Jer. 22:5] **to you people** (or: is habitually sent away because of you; or: is repeatedly forgiven for you folks)!" (Lu. 13:33b-35a).

So we can see nuances to two levels of interpretation for the figure of the "olive tree." Yet the main message is about the allusion to Zech. 4, and Christ's witness to Jerusalem through His body – both then and there, in the 1st century, and ever since throughout all nations. And keep in mind the continuity: Jer.

11 pictures "Israel and the house of Judah" as an "olive tree;" so does Rom. 11:17; and now here in the Unveiling we again have "olive trees." The religious system is still figuratively killing the witnesses (from within their ranks) that they oppose. David, in Ps. 52:8, described himself: "I [am] like a green (flourishing) olive tree in the house of God; I trust in the mercy of God, for times age-abiding, and beyond." And Ps. 92:13 reminds us that, "Those that are planted in the House of Yahweh shall flourish in the courts of our God."

The prophet Haggai references the two witnesses of Zech. 4, saying,
> "Yahweh stirred up the spirit of Zerubbabel the son of Shealtiel, governor of Judah, and the spirit of Joshua the son of Josedech, the high priest, and the spirit of the remnant of the People, and they came and did work in the House of Yahweh of hosts, their God" (Hag. 1:14).

This same prophet relayed the message that Yahweh would "fill this House with glory," and said that Yahweh proclaimed that, "The glory of this latter House will be greater than of the former… and in THIS place will I give peace (*shalom*)" (Hag. 2:7b, 9). I suggest that the "latter House" was a reference to the new covenant house: the body of Christ, God's Temple. The "peace" came by the blood of His cross (Col. 1:20; *cf* Eph. 2:15). Seeing that those two prophetic figures of Zech. 4 were, the one a member of the royal house, and the other a priest, Chilton connects these to the two witnesses here in the Unveiling, and concludes that they represent "the Spirit-inspired prophetic testimony of the Kingdom of priests (Ex. 19:6)" (ibid p 276-7). Riley discusses these two post-Exile prophets, and points out that by 516 BC, "the temple was completed: a high priest was again offering sacrifices and a new descendant of David was in power in Jerusalem. The two prophets envisioned the dawning of a new era" (*The River of God*, ibid p 209). He goes on to cite the final three vss. of Hag. 2, where we read,
> "Speak to Zerubbabel, governor of Judah, saying, I am going to shake the heavens and the earth [LXX adds: even the sea and the dry land]: I will overthrow the thrones of kingdoms and destroy the power of the kingdoms of the nations… In that Day, declares Yahweh of hosts, I will take you, Zerubbabel… My servant… and make you like a signet ring [LXX: seal], for I have chosen you" (vss. 21-23). *Cf* 7:3-8, above.

Riley continues:
> "Zechariah, for his part, foresaw a dual reign of ruler and priest. He had a vision of two olive trees that supplied oil…. 'these are the two anointed ones who stand by the Lord of the whole earth' (Zech. 4:14)… In this important vision, there are two anointed ones, two 'messiahs'" (ibid).

He earlier pointed out that, "Three offices were said to be anointed positions in Israel: the high priest, the king, and the prophets" (ibid p 206). In our present vision, the number "two" emphasizes that they are witnesses; the new arrangement in Christ has joined the earlier three "offices," or, "positions," into one, corporate, Anointed Body: the called-out communities. Recall 1 Jn. 2:20,
> "**You folks continue having the effects** (or: constantly hold and progressively possess the results) **of an anointing from the set-apart One** (or: the Holy One)."

5. **And if anyone is wanting or intending to harm or injure** (or: do injustice to) **them, fire is continuously** (or: repeatedly) **issuing** (or: proceeding) **out of their mouth and is one after another devouring their enemies** (or: adversaries); **and if anyone is intending** (wanting, willing) **to injure** (do injustice to; harm) **them, thus** (or: in this manner) **it is necessary for him to be killed.**

In vss. 5-6 there is a description of their ministry: **fire is continuously issuing out of their mouth**. They are not "dragons," but they minister the Word of God, Who is a consuming fire. God's word devours their enemies. Are people our enemies, or is it the carnal mind? We are instructed in Rom. 8:7 that,
> "**the result of the thinking** (disposition; thought processes; mind-set, outlook) **of the flesh** (= attention to Torah boundary-markers, custom and cultus; or: = the human condition) **[is; brings]**

enmity, alienation and discord [streaming] into God (or: hostility unto, or active hatred with a view to, God),"

Remember: we are dealing in figures here – symbols. It is the disposition of the flesh (the carnal mind) that is at enmity with God. This carnal mind (the one centered upon self and its interests) that wants to injure God's anointed ministry. The fire of God's Word will destroy these enemies (these carnal mindsets and interior strongholds) and will bring purification. Yet I would not say that their ministry might not have the same effect as Peter's words to Ananias and Sapphira (Acts 5). In vs. 6 are figures that represent the ministries (or: spirits; attitudes) of first Elijah (no rain) and then Moses (water changed to blood/every plague). This Prophet (One Body that has One **Mouth**, vs. 5) is The Prophet like unto Moses, which Moses foretold.

The allusion is to Nu. 16:35 when Korah, Dathan and Abiram rebelled against Moses' leadership, and from the appearance of the glory of Yahweh (vs. 19b), "there came out a fire from Yahweh and consumed the two hundred and fifty men that offered incense." And then, in 2 Ki. 1:10, 12,
> "Elijah answered… Now if I [am a] man of God, may fire descend from the heavens (or: skies; atmospheres) and may it devour you…. And fire descended from the atmospheres and devoured him and his fifty [men]."

In Mal. 4:5, Yahweh promised to send Elijah to Israel.

Another allusion may be to Isa. 11:4b,
> "He will smite the earth with the club (or: rod) of His mouth, and with the spirit of His lips shall He put the wicked to death" (CVOT).

Our text, here, is more like Jer. 5:14,
> "thus says Yahweh…. I will make My words in your mouth into fire, and this people [into] wood, and it will devour them." *Cf* Jer. 23:29; Hos. 6:5.

We saw in 9:17, above, "**And Fire, Smoke and Deity** (divine nature and character) **continuously issues forth from out of their mouths.**" It should be clear that this is metaphorical language. Jeremiah's dual commission was, "To pluck up and to break down, and to destroy and to demolish – [then] to build and to plant" (Jer. 1:10). We read of Yahweh's reign, in Ps. 97:3, "Fire is going before Him, and it sets His foes aflame round about. His lightning bolts illuminate the world; the earth (or: Land) sees and is travailing [*cf* 12:2, below]." The fire proceeding from **their mouth** is a variation of the metaphor of a sword proceeding from Christ's mouth in 1:16; 2:12, above, and 19:15, below. Recall what Jesus said, in Jn. 12:48,
> "**The person habitually displacing, disregarding, rejecting or setting-aside Me, and not progressively taking in hand and receiving or getting the effects of what I have gushed in speech** (the results of My sayings and declarations which flowed), **is constantly having that which is** (or: the One) **continuously evaluating, progressively deciding and repeatedly judging him: the WORD** (message; thought; idea; Logos) **which I spoke** (or: speak)! **THAT will continue to sift, separate, evaluate and make a decision about** (or: be judging) **him – within** (or: in union with) **the Last Day**."

In considering the temple, and its being separated for this measuring, Prinzing insightfully connects two passages: "'Can two walk together, except they be agreed?' (Amos 3:3). For 'what agreement hath the temple of God with idols?' (2 Cor. 6:16)." There is a definite separation due to the difference of vision, and thus a lack of agreement between His anointed body of followers in the earth and the City where their Lord was crucified (vs. 8b, below), the institutional church of His day. Not all are set with the same function; not all mature at the same time (1 Cor. 15:23). God is separating us from the idols within us, within the world's systems, and within the church systems.

The immunity from harm, during the course of their ministry, calls to mind Jesus' promise to His ministering disciples in Lu. 10:19b, "**nothing will proceed in any circumstance causing you folks harm** (or: wronging you or treating you unjustly)." In our text, here, Chilton concludes that "The two Witnesses, therefore, summarize all the witnesses of the Old Covenant, culminating in the witness of John" (ibid p 278).

The last clause of this verse may be an allusion to Heb. 10:28-29, since the historical witness of the called-out communities of the 1st century happened in the conjunction of the ages, when the earthly Jerusalem was being judged:

> "**Someone displacing** (setting aside; violating) **a custom of Moses** (or: Moses' Law) **is dying, apart from compassions, upon [evidence or testimony of] two or three witnesses. By how much worse punishment** (= heavier the sentence) **do you suppose he will be thought worthy and counted deserving: the one trampling down the Son of God, and considering the blood of the arrangement** (or: covenant) **common** (= profane) – **within which he was set-apart** (made sacred and holy) – **even insulting the Breath-effect of joyous favor** (or: Spirit of Grace)?**"

What is stated in vs. 29, here in Heb. 10, is what the Jewish leadership (i.e., those who did not accept Jesus as their Messiah, and the zealots like Saul of Tarsus) had done, and were at that time still doing (see vs. 8, below). But the risen Christ also said the following to one of His called-out communities,

> "**I am repeatedly** (habitually) **coming swiftly in you** (to you; for you) [again: you, singular], **and I will proceed waging war** (doing battle) **with them within the broadsword of My mouth**" (2:16, above).

It was **necessary** for the enemies of the cross to be killed, and for the center of that opposition to be destroyed (the temple, and Jerusalem). The old was being done away to make place for the new (2 Cor. 5:17b). But that was not the only reason. Their enemies were those who had taken the mark, nature and activities of the "beast" system (the injustice of the dominating systems of religion and Rome). They needed God's purifying fire (*cf* 14:10, below). But that the "fire issuing out of their mouth" was not to be perceived literally (especially in light of the new covenant arrangements and the teachings of Jesus), consider the situation in Lu. 9, where a Samaritan village had refused to receive them:

> 54. **Now, upon seeing [this], the disciples** [with other MSS: His apprentices] **Jacob** (James) **and John said, "Lord, are You now desiring that we should tell 'fire to come down from the sky** (or: from the atmosphere, or heaven) – **and so to seize and take them up so as to overcome and ruin' them, even as Elijah did?"** [2 Kings 1:9-16]
>
> 55. **Yet, being turned, He respectfully spoke a stern admonition to them** [later MSS add: and said, "You do not see or know of what sort of breath-effect (spirit; attitude) you are. For the Son of the Man does not come to destroy {the} lives (or: souls) of humanity, but rather to rescue, heal, save and restore to health and wholeness"]. *Cf* Jn. 3:17; 12:47b.

Now a few verses later, when sending out the 70, two-by-two, Jesus instructed them in Lu. 10:

> 10. "**But into whatever town or city you may one after another be entering – and they may not continue favorably welcoming and receiving you folks – after going out into its broad, open streets** (plazas or squares), **be at once saying,**
>
> 11. "'**Even the dust being caused to cling unto our feet – from out of your town – we are now in the process of wiping off for you people** (= with regard to you folks; [see note: ch. 9:5])! **Furthermore, continue knowing this by intimate experience, that God's reigning** (or: sovereignty; kingdom) **had drawn near and is close enough to touch** (= has arrived; = is accessible)!'
>
> 12. "**I am now saying to you folks, that within that Day it will be more able to hold up in** (or: endurable and bearable for) **Sodom than in** (or: for) **that town or city**."

Note the reference to Sodom, which we encounter symbolically in vs. 8, below.

When John the Immerser was questioned as to whether or not he was Elijah, he responded that he was not, and in Jn. 1:26b-27 directed them to the One that was coming after him, Who would baptize with the Sacred Breath-effect (Holy Spirit), vs. 33b. Mat. 3:11b records this incident with additional words:

> "**the One progressively coming close after me is** (exists being) **stronger than me** (or: I), **whose sandals I am not competent** (or: adequate) **to lift up and carry off. He, Himself, will proceed immersing** (baptizing) **you folks within the midst of a set-apart Breath-effect and Fire** (or: will repeatedly submerge you to the point of saturation, in union with [the] Holy Spirit, even to the permeation of a Sacred Attitude, as well as with [the] Fire).'

In Jn. 6:14, we see that people recognized concerning Jesus, "**This One is truly** (or: really) **The Prophet – the One periodically** (or: presently) **coming into the organized system** (or: the world of culture, religion and government)." *Cf* Jn. 7:40; Acts 3:22-23. The symbolic "two witnesses" here in the Unveiling represent the corporate "body" of "The Prophet." They do the works that He did: their words "immerse/baptize' folks in Holy Spirit and Fire.

Of historical interest is the "Community Rule" scroll, 1QS of the Qumran community, where in 8:4-10 we read:

> "When such men as these come to be in Israel, then shall... truly be established an 'eternal planting' (*Jubilees* 16:26), a temple for Israel, and – mystery! – a Holy of Holies for Aaron; true witnesses to justice, chosen by God's will to atone for the land and to recompense the wicked their due. They will be 'the tested wall, the precious cornerstone' (Isa. 28:16)... all of them knowing the Covenant of Justice... They shall be a blameless and true house of Israel... They shall be an acceptable sacrifice... ringing in the verdict against evil, so that perversity ceases to exist" (*The Dead Sea Scrolls, a New Translation*, HarperSanFrancisco, 1995, trans. by Michael Wise, Martin Abegg, Jr., & Edward Cook, p 137-8).

We are indebted to Beale (ibid p 585) for pointing us to this.

6. **These continuously hold** (or: have) **authority to close** (shut, lock) **the sky** (or: atmosphere; heaven), **so that it continues that it may** (or: can) **not shower rain [during] the days of their prophesying. And further, they continue holding authority upon the waters, to continuously turn them into blood; and to strike** (beat; impact) **the Land** (or: soil; earth) **within every blow** (or: wounding strike; impact; plague) **as often as they may will – if they intend** (purpose) **to.**

The **authority to close** (shut, lock) **the sky** is an allusion to Elijah in 1 Ki. 17:1; Lu. 4:25; Jas. 5:17. The **authority upon the waters, to continuously turn them into blood; and to smite** (beat, strike) **the Land** (or: soil; earth) **within every plague** is an allusion to Moses in Ex. 7:17, 19ff. These two prophetic abilities are combined into our "two witnesses" who each have the authorities of both Moses and Elijah. When Jesus was transfigured before Peter, Jacob (James) and John, in the high mountain,

> "**Elijah, together with Moses, was seen by them, and they continued being** (were existentially existing) **[there], continuing in conversation with Jesus.... then a cloud formed, progressively overshadowing** (casting shade upon) **them. Next a Voice sounded from out of the midst of the cloud, saying, 'This One is My Son, the Beloved One. Be habitually hearing, listening to [and thus, obeying] Him!'**" (Mk. 9:4, 7)

We will read of that same Voice and that same cloud in vs. 12, below. There is always a connection between heaven (or, our atmosphere) and earth (our physical environment). These in and of themselves are "two witnesses" for us. But in that vision, in Mk. 9, representatives of the Law and the Prophets were seen as witnesses to the new Exodus (Lu. 9:31 uses this word) which Jesus (the new Moses) was about to lead.

Wallace comments,

"The figurative phrase *to shut heaven that it rain not* signifies the restraining of civil powers to prevent and destroy the work of the witnesses. The power of the witnesses *over the waters to turn them to blood* and to *smite the earth with all plagues* were figurative descriptions of the calamities that would follow the testimony of the witnesses to the ultimate destruction of their persecutors" (ibid p 219-220; emphasis original).

This is a good figurative interpretation, but the allusion may be to Deut. 11:16-17 where Israel is admonished:

"Take heed to yourselves, that your heart be not deceived, and you turn aside, and then serve other gods and worship them, and so Yahweh's anger would be caused to burn upon you, and He would shut up the skies (or: heavens) that there should be no rain, and the soil (ground) would not yield her increase…"

This would bring famine – a "natural" distress and hardship for their existence. Beale sees this figure as "imagery of heavenly intervention" (ibid p 583). Jesus made reference to Elijah's ministry, in Lu. 4:

24. **But then He said, "The truth is, I am now saying to you people, that not one prophet is welcome or acceptable within His fatherland** (or: home territory; own country).

25. **"Yet, [based] on truth** (or: = in reality) **I am now saying to you folks, there were many widows during the days of Elijah, in Israel, when the sky** (or: heaven) **was shut and locked for three years and six months, so thus a great famine occurred upon all the land –**

26. **"and yet Elijah was sent to not one of them, except into Zarephath of the Sidon [territory], to a woman – a widow!"** [comment: vss. 26 and 27 speak of grace to the Gentiles]

As with Jesus' experience among His own (Jn. 1:11), the folks of "the Great City" (vs. 8, below) will resist the witness of these prophets. But what would be their message if not that of their Master? Paul wrote to Timothy (one among Christ's "witnesses") and in 2 Tim. 4 told him,

2. **Herald (Proclaim) the Word** (the idea; the message); **stand upon [it; or: It; Him] in season or out of season** (if the situation fits favorably, if the conditions are not favorable; whether convenient or not); **test and put to the proof; show further honor** (give higher value; assess greater worth; or, negatively: respectfully charge; strongly admonish; enjoin); **within every emotion which is long in arriving** (in all long-suffering patience which pushes anger far away), **and by teaching** (or: in union with instruction) **give aid, relief, comfort and encouragement as you call [others] to your side**.

3. **For you see, there will be an appointed season** (a situation; a fitting period of time) **when they will not continue holding up to themselves** (or: sustaining; holding themselves up in; or: putting up with; tolerating) **instruction** (teaching and training) **that is being continuously healthy and sound, but rather, they, habitually having their ear gratified by rubbing, scratching or tickling** (having their hearing titillated; or, as a middle: constantly procuring pleasurable excitement by indulging an itching) **will progressively pile and heap upon themselves teachers in line with and corresponding to their own rushing emotions,**

4. **and then, on the one hand, they will proceed to twist the ear** (or: the hearing) **and turn away from the Truth and reality, yet on the other hand, they will be progressively turned out** (have their [steps] turned out of [the Path] into a direction) **upon the myths** (fictions; legends; speeches; rumors; stories; tales; fables; things delivered by word of mouth).

The Unveiling speaks about this very "appointed season" and "situation" (2 Tim. 4:3, above) of which Paul wrote. The Word – Christ's message along with what Paul and the others were "given" to write – would be the very things that they would proclaim. Jesus spoke of the destruction of Jerusalem (Mat. 24; Mk. 13; Lu. 21) and gave dire warnings of woe to the scribes and Pharisees. His body, the "two witnesses," would naturally be prophesying the same message here in chapter 11.

The reference to **every blow/plague** is of course an allusion to the plagues brought upon Egypt (which is actually cited in vs. 8, below) as a prelude to the Exodus of Israel from Egypt. Those were done to

impact Pharaoh. So the setting here is placed into Israel's story. But keep in mind that this verse (11:6) is also symbolism. The "deliverance through threatened plagues" (they had the **authority** – the right and privilege, if they so desired), as a reference to Israel's exodus, now heralds the Deliverance brought by the Messiah, along with the appropriate "awards" (vs.18b, below) that will follow their testimony. The focus is on the Good News that they bring, not the plagues, or **impacting blows**. The plagues in Egypt were a prelude to the new creation at Mt. Sinai, when Israel became a nation, with a constitution (the Law). Verse 15, below, announces the preeminence of God's kingdom and Christ's reign (which Paul called "a new creation" in 2 Cor. 5:17). This verse is thus, also, an allusion to the deliverance brought by Christ in bringing humanity out of bondage. Note, also, where the Philistines' awareness of God's work in Egypt is noted, in 1 Sam. 4:7-8. By the descriptions of their **authority**, they represent both the Law and the Prophets, which was the Word which gave birth to the Messiah. Their witness and prophecy, which is the message of Christ, fulfill both the Law and the Prophets and so we have what Paul said in Rom.10:4,

> "**Christ [is] an end of Law** (or: for Christ [is] Law's goal and destiny; for [the] Anointing [is] termination from [the] Law; for Christ [was the] final act of [the] Law) **[leading] into the Way pointed out in fair and equitable dealings, and rightwised [covenant] relationships of justice in eschatological liberation, to, for and in everyone habitually trusting and believing**
>> (or: because Christ [entering] into the pointed-out Way – in everyone normally exercising faith with conviction, and with each person remaining loyal – [is; brings] Law's climax)."

We find "plague imagery," from Exodus, throughout the first six trumpets, below. We found the verb "to strike; to plague" in 8:12, above, and the noun "plague" in 9:20, above, so what is presented in those judgments may be associated with, or be another picture of, what the two witnesses are described as potentially doing here. Let us keep in mind that this picture is metaphorical, just as are the "two witnesses." In other words, their three-and-one-half-year ministry may correspond to the messages of the seven trumpets. Beale (ibid p 585-6) points out the repeated use of the verb for "killing" in 9:15, 18, 20; 11:5; and the word for "harming" in 9:10, 19 and 11:5. These examples may be a thread that shows continuity of the same theme of the tapestry given to John. Seeing the relationships of the parts lends insight to the meaning of the whole. But just as Paul wrote of,

> "**folks [who were] continuously existing being dead ones by** (or: to; with; in) **the results and effects of your stumblings aside** (offenses; wrong steps) **and failures to hit the mark** (or: mistakes; errors; times of falling short; sins; deviations)" (Eph. 2:1),

so should we understand the death and killing in this new covenant apocalypse. Yes, during the historical time-period (AD 66-70) that is the context of the Unveiling, folks physically died (even as did Ananias and Sapphira, in Acts 5), but the message of the Unveiling is spiritual and symbolic (1:1b, above). The old covenant, though spiritual (Rom. 7:14), focused on the flesh (e.g., purity codes, cultus of animal sacrifices, circumcision, etc.), but those old rules and categories passed away:

> "**the original things** (the beginning [situations]; the archaic and primitive [arrangements]) **passed by** (or: went to the side). **Consider! New things have come into existence** (have been birthed; or: It has become different, new things; or: He has been birthed and now exists being ones of a different kind, character and quality)" – 2 Cor. 5:17b.

Life in the reign of God and in the "new arrangement (covenant)" pertains to the Second Humanity, the *eschatos* (last) Adam which does not refer to the realm of the physical, but to the inner self, to motives, to attitudes, to relationships and to how we live. All these do, however, affect our physical lives. The New is reflected in the teachings of Jesus. E.g.:

> "**I, Myself, am now telling you folks not to at any point actively set yourself against, or take a counteractive or aggressive stand in opposition to, the bad situation**

(or: = participate in armed resistance against the miserable condition; = mirror the painful, insulting or laborious situation; or: = 'render evil for evil' in opposition to the evil or wicked person; = rebel or be part of an insurrection; = stand off an enemy)" (Mat. 5:39)

"**Be constantly loving your enemies** (urging toward reunion with, and accepting as persons standing on the same ground, those folks hostile to you; [comment: this could have applied to the Romans, as well as to personal enemies]), **and be habitually praying goodness over the people continuously persecuting you** (constantly thinking and speaking on behalf of the folks repeatedly pursuing you to have ease and well-being) **so that** (or: By this manner; This is how) **you folks can be birthed** (would come to be) **sons of your Father – the One within [the] atmosphere and in union with [the] heavens – because He is repeatedly making His sun to rise back up again upon bad** (evil; wicked; worthless) **folks as well as [upon] good** (virtuous) **folks, and He is habitually sending rain upon fair and equitable people** (those in right relationship; those within the Way pointed out; just ones; rightwised ones) **as well as [upon] unfair and inequitable people** (those not in right relationship; those not in the Way pointed out; unjust folks). **You see, if you should happen to love, accept, give yourself to, and participate with the ones constantly loving you folks, what wage or reward do you continue holding** (or: having)**? Are not also the tax collectors constantly doing the very same thing?**" (Mat. 5:44-46).

[note: tax collectors worked for the state (for either one of the provinces, or for the Empire) and were thus despised and considered outcasts of the local society, being perceived as both collaborating with the Romans and as getting money dishonestly through their business as a "tax-farmer," (someone who purchased from the state the right to collect official taxes, tolls, customs and dues: they made their money by adding on a percentage to the tax which they collected for the state), or by working for a "tax-farmer"]

"**Therefore, you folks will continuously exist being ones that have reached the purposed and destined goal: finished and completed ones; mature and perfected ones – in the same way as your heavenly Father** (or: your Father which has the qualities of, and is characterized by, the atmosphere) **constantly exists being One that is the goal and destiny: finished, complete, mature, perfect!**" (Mat. 5:48).

Could Christ's two witnesses do any less?

Prinzing speaks about this change as reflected in the pattern of the old:
"God said to Moses, 'Let them make Me a sanctuary; that I may dwell among them' (Ex. 25:8). Sanctuary – literally, a place set apart.... 'And it came to pass, that everyone which sought the Lord went out unto the Tabernacle of the congregation, which was without the camp' (Ex. 33:7).... 'Let us go forth therefore UNTO HIM without the camp...' (Heb. 13:13). And so there has been a going without the camp – beyond the forms of religion, beyond the symbol and ceremony, to be joined to Him in one Spirit.... 'In whom ye also are built together for a habitation of God through the Spirit' (Eph. 2:22)." Ray also quotes, appropriately, Ps. 23:4, "Your rod and Your staff – they comfort me" (ibid).

Since this measuring of the temple is also a figure of God judging the completeness and conformity to the Pattern, Ray continues, "Well Peter wrote, 'For the time is come that judgment must begin at the house of God... first begin AT US'.... Judgment – the correctional in-workings of God, begin AT, or literally, FROM, the House of God.... 'Because it is written, Be ye holy; for I am holy' (1 Pet. 1:16)." All of this was to begin at Jerusalem (Acts 1:8b).

In Num. 7:1, when the tabernacle and the altar (*cf* vs. 1, above) were dedicated, they were both anointed. Here, then, we have two "anointed ones" – the temple and the altar. Of what do these speak? Perhaps they are a figure of God's presence (recall that the temple is God's home among His people) and His attending judgments (the brazen altar represented judgment upon failure, deviation from the goal, sin). This was what the tabernacle signified in the wilderness: God's presence dwelling in the midst of Israel, and a cultic means of cleansing the people from the results of their failures. It is also a type of the spirit and life of sacrifice which characterize His Anointed. These are also His two witnesses: His Body and their life of sacrifice – laying down their lives for their friends (Jn. 15:13), just as He did.

Let us consider the last dependent clause, "**as often as they may will – if they intend** (purpose) **to**." Here the hypothetical, conditional conjunction, *ean*, comes before the verb (to will, intend and/or purpose), which, correspondingly, is in the subjunctive – the verb mood/mode of possibility. The message is this: they may NOT will, intend or purpose to do so. Consider Jesus, in Gethsemane, as recorded in Mat. 26:53,

> "**Or, are you continually imagining or supposing that I am not constantly able** (or: that I do not habitually have power) **to at once call My Father to My side for assistance, and He will right now place by Me** (or: furnish for Me; put at My disposal) **more than twelve legions** [= regiments; a legion was 6000 foot soldiers plus 120 on horse, plus auxiliaries] **of agents?**"

Did He use that ability and power to protect Himself and bring a plague upon those who came to arrest Him? Just as He submitted to the Father's will, we see the little animal/beast "**overcome** (or: conquer) **them, and then proceed in killing them**" in the next verse. Being joined to the Vine (Jn. 15:1ff), could they now say, with Jesus,

> "**On this account the Father continuously loves [us], because [we are] constantly placing** (or: repeatedly setting; or: progressively laying [down]) **[our souls]** (inner life or being; or: = the whole self), **to the end that [we] may take it in hand** (or: receive her) **again…. [We] constantly hold authority to place it** (lay it), **and [we] constantly hold authority from out of being to take it** (or: receive her; resume it) **again**"? (Jn. 10:17-18).

Jesus was "given" (as are these two witnesses) the ability that no one could take His life; as with these witnesses, none could take His life or harm Him until He had finished His testimony. These "two witnesses" are not in the old covenant, i.e., under Law, but are in the new covenant, i.e., under grace (Rom. 6:14). The Law has been turned on its head, and the transforming Fire that characterizes their words has the intent to "**mercy all mankind** (may make everyone, the all, recipients of mercy)!" (Rom. 11:32b). Here, on 11:6, D'Aragon (ibid p 481) points us to Mk. 9:23,

> "**Jesus said to him, "As to your 'if you continue having power and ability,' all things [are] possible to** (for; by; in; with) **the one habitually trusting** (or: progressively believing).**"
> [or, reading with A & other MSS: "About the 'if': you continue being able (having power) to trust (or: to believe). Everything (or: All) {is} endued with power for the one continuously trusting (or: progressively believing; constantly having confidence)!"]

He also insightfully cites Jn. 15:7,

> "**If you people can** (or: would) **remain** (abide) **within the midst of and in union with Me – and My gush-effects** (results of spoken words) **can** (would) **remain** [with *p*66 and others: and the flow of My declarations continues abiding) **within the midst of and in union with you – seek in petition** [other MSS: you will continue asking) **whatever you folks may habitually purpose** (constantly intend; repeatedly will; continuously want or desire), **and it will proceed coming to be in and among you folks** (or: will progressively occur for you; will continue being birthed by you folks; will habitually happen to you)."

Do you actually think that the two witnesses (i.e., the corporate, covenant community) would have forgotten these promises? Would these promises not have applied to His "two witnesses," the called-out covenant communities? We suggest that these folks were well aware of what our Father could do for them, and of the authority over the elements which had been given to them (as we saw in Jesus' life: calming the storm, stopping the flow of blood in healing a woman, etc.). They were His disciples: they had taken up their executions stakes in order to follow Him and to do the things which He did (Mat. 16:24-28; Jn. 14:12). So, "Would they have **willed** or **intended** or **purposed** to bring literal smitings and plagues upon those around them? Did Stephen, in Acts 7:60b?" Let us have the hermeneutic of taking into account the rest of the NT, and its message, as we unpack the Unveiling. In vs. 10, below, we see that they only **tested and examined** people. We are reminded of Heb. 4:12,

> "**You see, the Word** [in this situation: the witnesses' prophecy] **of God** (or: God's thought, idea and message; or: the expressed Logos from God; or: the Word which is God) **[is] living** (or: alive), **and active** (working; operative; energetic; at work; productive) **and more cutting above every two-mouthed sword, even passing through** (penetrating) **as far as a dividing** (or: parting; partitioning) **of soul and spirit** (or: of inner self-life and breath-effect), **both of joints and marrows, even able to discern** (separate; judge; decide) **concerning thoughts** (ponderings; reflections; in-rushings; passions) **and intentions** (notions; purposes) **of a heart** (= core of the being)."

7. **Now whenever they may complete** (finish; make an end of) **their witness** (or: testimony), **the little wild animal** (or: beast) **– the one repeatedly climbing up** (or: ascending) **out of the Deep** (or: the Abyss) **– will proceed making war** (or: do battle) **with them, and will progressively overcome** (or: conquer) **them, and then will proceed in killing them.**

Acts 7:52 may be an allusion that fits the second half of this verse:
> "**Which one of the prophets** (those who had light ahead of time and spoke before the people) **did your fathers not persecute and pursue? And they killed off those predicting concerning the coming of the Just One – of Whom you yourselves now became people who pre-commit and give in advance** (or: folks who **give-over** before, in front or **in preference**; or: ones who **abandoned** in time of need; people who [were] pre-paid), **even murderers: the very ones who received and took in hand the Law**."

Although Rome may have been an instrument, at times, it was Jerusalem who Jesus indicted:
> "**O Jerusalem, Jerusalem! The one repeatedly killing the prophets, and habitually stoning the people sent off with a mission to her**" (Mat. 23:37a). Cf Acts 7:57-58.

Here, Maarschalk interprets the figure of "the beast" as being the Zealots. See his blog: (https://adammaarschalk.com/2017/02/04/the-two-witnesses-killed-by-the-beast-revelation-113-13/).

In our comments on the previous verse we laid out some suggestions of why **the little wild animal** (or: beast) was able to overcome them. But let us consider this idea a bit more. It is to this sort of situation that Paul may have been speaking in Col. 1:24,

> "**I am at this moment continuing to rejoice within the effects of experiences and the results of my sufferings over your [situation] and on your behalf, and I am progressively filling back up in turn – so as in [His] stead to replace, supply and balance out, within my flesh** (or: = with the means of my natural situation) **– the deficiencies** (or: results from what is lacking; effects from need) **with regard to the pressures** (or: from the squeezings, tribulations and tight spots) **that pertain to the Anointed One** (or: that belong to and affect Christ; or: from the [Messiah]) **over [the situation of] His body, which is the called-out, covenant community** (which exists being the summoned-forth congregation – the ecclesia)
>> (or: Now I am progressively filled with joy – in union with the feelings coming from passion over you folks – and am habitually filling up again, to bring balance, the effects of what is lacking, resulting from the distresses of Christ – resident within my flesh – concerning His body, which is the invited-out assembly),"

As a further explanation of what Paul means by this, 1 Cor. 12:26 instructs our understanding of the relationship which we have with one another – including the Head of our corporate body, Jesus Christ:

"**whether one member is continuing to experience the effect of something, or constantly undergoes suffering, all the members continually experience the effect or the suffering together with [it].**"

In writing to the community in Philippi, Paul spoke metaphorically of the opposition that they would encounter, and of the experiences that they would have:

"**to you folks it is given** [note the "divine passive," here, which may unpack the meaning of the synonym in vs. 3a, above] **by grace** (or: He graciously was given in you people, as a favor for you people), **over the [issue] of, and on behalf of, Christ, not only to be progressively believing and habitually trusting into Him** (or: continuing faithful unto Him), **but further, also, to be repeatedly having sensible experiences over Him**

(or: to constantly experience feelings and impressions on behalf of Him; to habitually suffer and be ill used for His sake; to be continuously affected on account of the things pertaining to Him) –**constantly having the very** (or: continuously holding the same) **contest [as] in the public games** (or: race in the stadium; agonizing struggle in the gathered assembly) **such as you saw** (or: perceive) **within me and now are presently hearing in me** (or: and at this moment are repeatedly hearing [to be] in me)" (Phil. 1:29-30).

Then in 2 Thes. 1:4b-5, we hear Paul, again, where he speaks of:

"**all your pursuits** (or: chasings, persecutions and harassments) **and the pressures** (squeezings; constrictions; contractions; tribulations; oppressions; ordeals) **which you habitually have again** (or: sustain; hold up [in]; bear), **[which are] a display-effect** (demonstration) **of God's fair and equitable** (just; in accord with the Way pointed out) **deciding** (separating for an evaluation or a judging), **[leading] unto your being deemed fully worthy of God's kingdom** (or: of commensurate value, from God's reign and from the influence which is God), **over** (or: on behalf of) **which you also continue having sensible experiences** (or: normally feel emotions; or: repeatedly suffer)."

All these things came from the "beast," or, "little animal" nature within the adversarial people whom they encountered, or with whom they had regularly to deal. The NT epistles can flesh-out the symbolic pictures which we find here in the Unveiling.

The body of Christ dispenses and continues the work of Jesus Christ. When Jesus spoke to Peter concerning his following Him and feeding His sheep, He described the kind of **death** that Peter would experience, which would be "**bringing glory** (a manifestation which calls forth praise and a good reputation) **to God**," by figuratively describing Peter's future experience:

"**whenever you may grow old and decrepit, you will proceed stretching out your hands, and another will continue clothing and girding you, and will proceed carrying you where you are not intending** (willing)" and then He told Peter, "**Continue following Me!**" (Jn. 21:18b-19).

An illuminating phrase is used by Paul, in 1 Cor. 15, in which the noun **wild animal**, or, **beast** is joined to the verb "to fight; make war; do battle." I suggest that he is speaking metaphorically about conflict with people, in verse 32,

31. **Daily I am repeatedly facing death** (or: progressively dying)**! Brothers, [I swear** (or: strongly affirm)**] by my pride in you!** (or: Yes! On the basis of your own boasting, [my family]) – **which I continually possess, and hold within Christ Jesus, our Lord** (Owner; Master) –
32. **if I fight** (or: fought) **in accord with human [means, methods or purposes] with wild beasts in Ephesus, what [is] the benefit for or to me** (or: how am I furthered by it)**?**

In 2 Tim. 4 he again uses the animal metaphor:

16. **Within my first verbal defense no one happened to be beside me** (no one came along with me), **but rather, all forsook** (abandoned) **me – may it not be put to their account** (or: counted against them)!

17. **Yet the Lord took a stand beside me** (or: stood alongside in me) **– and He empowered me** (enabled me; gave me inward ability), **to the end that through me the message that is being heralded** (the contents of the public proclamation) **would be fully carried throughout with complete assurance, to full measure, and with absolute certainty, and so [that] all the ethnic multitudes** (nations; Gentiles; Goyim; non-Jews) **would** (could) **hear [it] – and I was dragged** (or: drawn) **from out of the mouth of a lion!**

18. **The Lord will continue dragging me away from every harmful act** (malicious or evil work) **and will continue delivering me into the midst of the reign and kingdom**...

Notice his attitude, in vs. 16: "may it not be put to their account or counted against them!" This is the attitude of His witnesses. Also consider the present tenses in the verbs of vs. 18. He entered the reigns of the ethnic multitudes (including Rome!), but was delivered until he had finished his course. These things were just what Jesus had predicted for His disciples:

> "**So as for you folks, continue looking to** (or: after) **yourselves, for people will repeatedly give you over unto sanhedrins** (the ruling councils, or courts, in the Jewish culture of that time), **as well as unto synagogues** (local religious and cultural centers). **[There] you folks will be repeatedly beaten and severely whipped. Also, you will continue being caused to make a stand upon [the demand] of governors** (rulers) **and kings, in consequence of involvement with Me, [leading] into a witness and testimony to, and evidence for, them. Further, it continues necessary for the good news** (the message of goodness, ease and well-being) **to be publicly proclaimed into the midst of all the ethnic multitudes** (unto all the nations), **first. Then, whenever they may repeatedly bring or progressively lead you folks, while in process of giving you over, do not continue anxious or filled with worry beforehand as to what you folks should be speaking. On the contrary, whatever may be given to and in you within that hour, continue speaking this. You see, you folks are not the ones then speaking, but rather, [it is] the Set-apart Breath-effect** (or: Holy Spirit)" (Mk. 13:9-11).

So while the dreams and visions that we encounter in Daniel symbolize hostile, dominating empires, let us consider a wider application to the term "little wild animal/beast" here in the Unveiling. In Ps. 22:12-13 we read, "many bulls have compassed me.... their mouths as a ravening and a roaring lion," and in vs. 16, "dogs have compassed me: the assembly of the wicked have enclosed me..." Note also the unbelieving Jews in Thessalonica who assaulted the house of Jason and certain others, as recorded in Acts 17:5-8.

And so now we see the entrance on the stage of **the little wild animal** (or: the little beast). Note that he is "**the one repeatedly, climbing up** (or: ascending) **out of the Deep** (the Abyss)." In 17:8 we read again about, "**The little wild animal** (beast)... [which] **is about to repeatedly climb up** (ascend) **out of the Deep**." The Greek is present tense, not future. Beasley-Murray remarks that, "He is spoken of as if well known..." (ibid p 1293). I think that we encounter this "beast nature," or "animal instinct," periodically climbing up out of the deep within us, and when it does, it kills the witness of God in our lives. But corporately, in the "macro-cosmic" application, whenever God's anointed servants come to a completion of what Father has assigned for them to do (figured by the 3 & ½ years), then the corporate beast that is within "**the peoples**" (vs. 9) will "**make war** (do battle) **with them, and will progressively overcome** (or: conquer) **them, and then will proceed in killing them**." Here they follow the pattern set by the Head, the "Sign," as in Lu. 2:34, "**Look and consider! This One continues lying down into the midst of a fall, and then a standing back up again, of many people within Israel – into a SIGN being constantly spoken in opposition to, and being repeatedly contradicted**." This Sign was our Pattern, and He pointed to, or spoke of, His body, His mature sons who are servants to mankind. A sign always points to, or announces, or identifies, something else – not itself. The first clause of this prophecy by Simeon is intriguing: "lying down into the midst of a fall [a figure of death] and a standing back up again [a figure of resurrection] of many people within Israel." We see this very thing in vss. 8-11a, below.

Terry (ibid p 370) sees the clause, "**making war** (or: do battle) **with them, and will progressively overcome** (or: conquer) **them**," as an OT echo, in the language of Dan. 7:3, 21, "four large wild beasts [were] coming up from the sea [of humanity]," and then a horn (figure of a king) of one of the beasts, "made war with the holy ones, and prevailed against them." The sea was often referred to as "the abyss," and Beale (ibid p 588) compares the Greek of the LXX in Dan. 3:7 to 11:7 in the Unveiling. Also, in Dan. 4:16, we read that "a beast's heart" was given to Nebuchadnezzar during the period of his judgment by God, and in 4:33, "he was driven from people and ate grass like an ox... until his hairs were grown like vulture's [feathers] and his nails like birds' [claws]." The idea, and similar phrasing of, "**making war**," found here, is also seen in 16:14; 17:14 and 19:19, below, suggesting a common theme on a common situation which is viewed from different perspectives.

Kenneth Earl said, "I want you to see that the death of the two witnesses is a part of the death of Christ." Is he speaking heresy here? Remember, the body of Christ is a part of the Christ. Rom. 8:17 informs us,
> "**we are continually affected by sensible experiences together – feeling together; receiving impressions, undergoing passion or suffering together – to the end that we may also be glorified together**
>> (or: can be given a shared appearance; would together receive a manifestation of that which calls forth praise; should be given a joint-approval and a joint-reputation; may be thought of and imagined together [in covenant relationship]),"

We with Him, and thus, He with us.

Recall our discussion of **the Deep**/Abyss in chapter 9, above. It is the same place/realm that we find here, and that we will encounter in 17:8 and 20:1 and 3, below. The metaphorical use should be applied here, for it is simply the deep recesses of the darkened human nature that becomes adversarial to the Light (Jn. 3:19), just as Jesus experienced in those of the scribes, Pharisees and priests – and those whom Paul encountered in Ephesus! The **little wild animal** (note the diminutive form – it is not something huge, but more like "the little foxes that spoil the vine" – Song 2:15) is not allowed to kill their witness until, "**they may complete** (finish; make an end of) **their witness** (or: testimony)." God is in control of the circumstances surrounding the work that He gives us to do. Only when we have finished our courses will we, "**be poured out as a drink offering**" (2 Tim. 4:6).

Here I am inserting a section from my commentary on 2 Thes. 2:1-12. We suggest that Paul's information, that he shared there, will illumine our present passage of the Unveiling:

> 1. **Now we are asking you, brothers** (= fellow believers; = family), **over [the subject of]** (or: concerning) **the presence of our Lord** (or: Master), **Jesus Christ, and our being gathered together** (or: being fully led together and assembling) **upon [the presence of] Him**
> 2. **in regard to this: you are not at any point to be quickly shaken** (tossed, as by the sea, or caused to totter, like a reed) **away from [your] mind** (mental senses of perception; the ability to be aware and reason; wits; intelligent understanding), **nor to be continuously alarmed** (caused to cry aloud from nervousness or excitement), **neither through a spirit** (or: a breath-effect; an attitude), **nor through a word** (or: a thought; a message; a verbal communication), **nor through a letter – as through us – as though the Lord's Day** (the Day of the Lord [= Yahweh or Christ]) **has been set in place** (placed in; made to stand in; has stood within so as to be here).

Now the "Day of Yahweh" was a term that figured a time of judging and hard times, in the Old Testament [e.g., cf Joel 1:15 and 2:1-2; Jer. 30:7; Amos 5:18; Zeph. 1:14-18]. It was obviously considered to be something to be alarmed about, and inwardly shaken. The term "presence" has more than one significance:

a) it can refer to His ongoing presence, via His Spirit (e.g., when two or three, or more, are gathered in His name, Matt. 18:20; it can refer to His solidarity and identity with His body, as Jesus stated in Matt. 25:35-40; it can refer to Him dwelling in His temple, John 14:20;

b) or, it can refer to His presence for a specific work, such as judging His people, or intervening in history to bring deliverance or rescue. He dwells in our atmosphere (heaven; sky) so He is ever present, and He is "continuously walking about within the midst of the seven golden lampstands (i.e., the churches)," and He walks with feet "like white brass (or: bronze; fine copper – a figure of His judging process) as having been set on fire in a furnace" and eyes "as a flame of fire" – Rev. 2:1; 1:14-15. But in 2:5 He says that He may come unto them and remove their lampstand. In Rev. 2:16 He threatens to quickly come to them and fight against them with the sword of His mouth. He threatened to come to Sardis as a thief (3:3).

We therefore suggest that Paul is differentiating between "the presence of our Lord, Jesus Christ, and our being gathered together upon His [presence]" – as being a habitual occurrence of the meeting together of His body in Thessalonica – and a special presence concerning the expected destruction of Jerusalem that Jesus foretold – "the Day of the Lord." This latter event was a time of shaking the heavens and the earth (Heb. 12:26), and it not only affected the Jews, but also the called-out communities of that period, as this letter suggests, and as we see from the letter sent from John to the 7 communities in 1st century Asia, as cited above. This letter was written prior to the Jewish revolt and the coming of the Lord in judgment via Rome.

3. **May no one at any point beguile or seduce you folks from a deception – not even down from one turn** (or: not according to one method; not in the sphere of a manner or disposition) – **because should not the standing away from** (the departure; the setting away; or: the rebellion; the revolt) **come first, and thus the human from the lawlessness – the person of failure**
    (some MSS: the Man who missed the mark – sinned; the human being with the qualities and character of error and mistake; [other MSS: the person owned by lawlessness or associated with illegal acts]) **be uncovered** (unveiled; revealed; disclosed): **the son of the loss** (= the person having the qualities of, or the character resulting from, the destruction),
4. **the one continuously occupying an opposite position** (or: constantly lying as the opposing counterpart) **and constantly lifting** (or: raising) **himself up over all** (or: upon everything) **being normally called God, or an effect of worship** (or: reverent awe), **so as to cause him to be seated – down into the midst of the temple of God** (or: God's dwelling place) – **continuously displaying himself, that this/it is God** (or: continuously pointing out that he himself is a god)?
5. **Do you not remember that, still being with you, I said these things to you?**

Historically, the revolt referred to in vs. 3 was the war of the Jews against the Romans, which ended in AD 70. Here I refer you to studies from the preterist viewpoint, such as:
    The Last Days According to Jesus – RC Sproul
    The Days of Vengeance – David Chilton
    The Parousia – James Stuart Russell
    The Cross and the Parousia of Christ – Max King
    The Perfect Ending for the World, and other works – John Noe ... to name just a few.

From the writings of Josephus, "the man of sin" has been identified by some writers as a historical person of that period and situation. But I suggest that it had a broader reference, both for them and for us: the estranged humanity within each of us, the false persona of the dying ego that is in bondage to the law of sin that works in our members (Rom. 7:23). That war indeed revealed this in all those that were involved in that war, on both sides, if you read that history. It was and is the estranged humanity "having the qualities of, or the character resulting from, the destruction" and loss which is due to Adam's sin.

Verse 4 characterizes every human being, before he or she has been regenerated, existentially resurrected into the life of Christ. Times of pressure, ordeal or conflict reveal our true condition: whether yet dead in trespasses and sins, or alive and laying down our lives for our friends.

In verse 3, the "standing-away from" can also have another interpretation: the called-out community (aka: church) "departing" from organized religion (whether the Jewish religion, of the time of Paul, or the Christian religion, of the ensuing centuries), and specifically, "departure and standing-away from" the Law. This separating reveals the life of God within His body, as well as the realm of death where the flesh wars against the spirit. Dan Kaplan has pointed out that there is only one other place where this Greek word is used in the NT, and that is in Acts 21:21 which speaks of the rumor that Paul had been teaching the Jews among the nations to stand away (revolt; apostasize) from Moses (i.e., the Law):

> **"Yet they have been orally instructed concerning you, that you are repeatedly** (or: habitually) **teaching all the Jews down through the ethnic multitudes** (or: nations; non-Jews) **an apostasy away from Moses, constantly telling them not to be circumcising [their] children, nor even to be living their lives** (continually walking about) **in** (by; with) **the customs."**

This may in fact have been the actual revolt, or, standing away from, of which Paul was here referring – the necessity to depart from the Law, as Dan Kaplan has suggested. When Paul made his defense to the crowd in Acts 22, he did not deny the rumor of 21:21.

6. **And now, you know** (have seen and are aware of) **the thing continuously holding down in a firm grasp** (detaining, restraining) **unto the [situation for] him to be uncovered** (unveiled; disclosed) **in his own fitting situation** (or: proper occasion; suitable season; fertile moment).

The word "know" is in the perfect tense of the Greek *oida*, which strictly means "have seen." Those of Thessalonica had seen that which Paul now describes as "holding down in a firm grasp (detaining, restraining)." It was so well known that Paul did not have to tell them who or what it was – unfortunately for us! It was a secret to those outside the called-out community, but those within had seen it and knew what he or it was. It was soon to be unveiled – at the right moment. The pronouns are masculine, so we normally translate this as "him/his." But Paul could have been referring to an object or a situation which in Greek was masculine, and thus have used the masculine pronoun. There is no way to be certain. Whether a man, or the inner estranged human, it was at that time soon to be uncovered. The "thing continuously holding down in a firm grasp (constantly restraining and detaining)" could well have been God, or, the body of Christ (the Perfect Man) – as suggested in the next verse.

7. **For the secret** (hidden purpose; mystery) **of the lawlessness** (pertaining to the condition of being without law; which is the unlawfulness; having the character of being violation of the Law; whose source is the contrariness to custom) **is already continuously working within** (operating; energizing), **[yet] only until the one** (or: man; [note: masculine article]) **continuously**

holding down in a firm grasp (detaining; restraining) **at the present moment can birth himself** (bring himself to be; = separate himself) **forth from out of the midst.**

Now the context would suggest that it is "the secret and hidden purpose of the lawlessness" to which Paul was referring in vs. 6 as having been veiled and covered – or hidden. The birthing "forth from out of the midst" could refer to the Christians leaving Jerusalem, just prior to its destruction. Or, it can refer to the Christ coming forth from the called-out body and unveiling the secret of that which is unlawful and contrary to custom. John saw this in the symbol of the woman birthing the man-child in Rev. 12. That, too, had multiple meanings:
a) Israel bringing forth Christ, or His body manifesting His life
b) The called-out folks departing the Jewish religion, or escaping from Jerusalem
c) the birthing of God's sons to deliver creation, in every time and place.

For our day, I suggest that the mystery and hidden purpose of "the lawlessness" is that "law of sin" to which Paul referred in Rom. 7. It is the law in our members that is contrary to the "law of the Spirit of life." Vs. 8 describes what happens when it is uncovered and revealed.

8. **And then** (at that time) **the lawless person** (the unlawful one; the one without law; the man who violates the Law; the person being contrary to custom) **will be uncovered** (unveiled; disclosed), **whom the Lord Jesus will take back up again** (or: lift up; reading *anaireō* with Nestle, Tasker & Concordant texts; Griesbach & other MSS read *analiskō*: consume, use up, expend) **by the Spirit** (Breath-effect) **of His mouth, and will deactivate** (render inoperative and useless; make inert) **by the manifestation** (the bringing of light upon and setting in full and clear view, causing an appearance) **of his** (or: its; or: His) **presence –**

Again, the application is both historical (Christ coming and judging literal Jerusalem, in AD 70), and also spiritual (Christ repeatedly coming and judging folks within His House, the called-out communities). He uncovers the false persona, our estranged human nature, and takes it back up again by the Spirit of His mouth; or with the other MSS, He consumes and renders it pure and restored. The Breath-effect of His mouth (whether breathing upon us, or speaking to us) is the manifestation of His presence. This, as in ch. 1, above, brings righteousness and restores the Way pointed out: justice, fair and equitable dealings, rightwised relationships.

Reading *anaireō*, we see that His Breath/Spirit takes the false and estranged back into Himself: restoration. Reading *analiskō*, we see purification and transformation. This manifestation of His presence comes both individually and corporately. The Christ event inaugurated the new creation in which He is habitually, or constantly, coming to us – dwelling in and among us, while we have been snatched up and seated with Him (Eph. 2:6) in the new heavens, the abode of the new human (earth).

9. **whose presence is continuously existing in correspondence to** (or: in line with; in the sphere of; on the level of) **the adversary's** (opponent's; or: satan's) **in-working activity** (or: is constantly in accordance with the operation of the "adversary," or, satan), **in all power** (or: within all ability) **as well as signs and wonders of falsehood** (or: which are a lie),
10. **and within every deception** (delusion; seduction) **of the injustice** (wrong; thing that is not the way pointed out and which is not right) **within the folks continuously or repeatedly being lost** (or: by the folks progressively destroying themselves) **in return for which** (or: in the place of which) **they do** (or: did) **not take unto themselves and welcomingly receive the love of, and from, the truth** (or: Truth's love; the Love which is Truth and Reality; or: an appreciation of and

affection for reality), **into the [situation for] them at some point to be suddenly delivered** (restored to health and wholeness; rescued; saved; restored to the original state and condition).

Now the "manifestation" in vs. 8 can also refer to the bringing light upon this "lawless person." Thus, vss. 9-10 can be read in two different ways:
a) following that which I just described above, seeing that it is Christ's manifestation and presence – meeting the inworking activity of the adversary, in its sphere, and on every level of its activity, within its signs and wonders of falsehood, and within each of its deceptions of injustice within the lost who are progressively destroying themselves, etc. Note that in the last clause of vs. 10 His work leads them "into the [situation for] them at some point to be suddenly delivered!"
b) seeing it as a manifestation of "the lawless person," either as an individual, historically, or as estranged humanity, we see that its presence corresponds to the working of the adversary within, which operates with its false power and lying wonders within deceptions of that which is contrary to the path of life. This causes folks not to receive or retain "the Love (God) which is Truth and Reality (Christ); or: an appreciation of and affection for reality." Nonetheless, the result is the same, as the last part of vs. 10 tells us: deliverance, rescue.

11. **And so, because of this, God is continuously sending to** (or: in) **them an in-working** (or: operation) **of wandering** (or: which is the source of being caused to stray; which has the character of error and deception) **into the [situation for] them to believe, and to trust, the lie,**
12. **to the end that all those not believing the Truth** (or: having conviction of or trusting the reality), **but rather approving and delighting in injustice** (inequity; the thing that is not right), **may** (or: can; would) **at some point be sifted, separated and decided about** (or: judged).

Verses 11-12 tell us of the intermediary judging of folks who are not presently a part of the called-out community. It is an echo of Rom. 1:24, which is a prelude to the period of sifting, separating and deciding by God as described here in vs. 12. This is an ongoing process, as vs. 11 says: He "is continuously sending to and in them an inworking (or: operation) of wandering." Here we see reference to the repayments noted in ch. 1:0, "squeezing and oppression, ordeal and trouble." As such things made the believers worthy of God's reign (1:5), so it will do in the sifting of these. Again, this applied to the situation in 1st century Thessalonica, and to all times and situations ever since. He is the same: yesterday, today, and on into the ages. (*Peter, Paul & Jacob, comments on 1 Pet., Phil., Col., 1 Thes., 2 Thes., 1 Tim., 2 Tim., Titus, Jacob (James)*, Harper Brown Pub. 2012 pp 138-141)
By placing this passage from Paul into its historical setting we can see why those of "The Great City" of vs. 8, below, killed the witness of the early followers of Christ. This should also help us to understand how the same situation was repeatedly happening in the centuries that have followed.

When the Messiah was rejected and killed, the curtain within the temple (that kept the innermost and holiest chamber of the temple closed off and dark, except when Yahweh's glory might light it) was ripped apart (Mat. 27:51; Mk. 15:38; Lu. 23:45) showing that the chamber was empty (the ark of the covenant had long before disappeared). Dan Kaplan has shared the insight that after the priest sewed the curtain back together again (for the next 30-some years they continued using the temple for the old covenant cultus, until the temple's destruction in AD 70), thus creating a figure of the abyss that was in the hearts of those not yet existentially indwelt by Christ. God's Light was gone, for it was the Word made flesh, the Christ; all that was left was the dead first Adam that Christ took to the grave. The temple became similar to the situation when the Philistines captured the ark (1 Sam. 4:10-22) and they came to realize that "the glory [was] departed from Israel." So it was, in 1st century Jerusalem. Yet the priests continued sitting in the temple, assuming that they were still the representatives of God, and this became an abomination that made them desolate (Dan. 12:11; Mat. 24:15), for there was now a new temple made of living stones, with a Priest in line with the order of Melchisedec (Heb. 5:10, *et al*). They represented the old, carnal nature that sits in the hearts of unregenerate humans, showing itself as being god, while not yet being a holy spirit. And so they, and others (like Saul, until he was transformed by Christ and became Paul) persecuted the Woman (Christ's bride, the called-out communities), as we will read in 12:1-17, below.

8. **And so their fallen dead body will be upon** [other MSS: And their fall will be into] **the broad place** (street; square; plaza) **of The Great City – whatever, spiritually, is normally being called** (or: named) **"Sodom" and "Egypt" – where also their Lord was crucified** (or: where their Lord, also, was hung on a pole: suspended and executed on a torture stake).

The statement, "**their fallen dead body will be upon the broad place** (street) **of The Great City**," implies the unity of their witness (notice the singular: **dead body**), and yet the plurality of this body (**their**…). If it was speaking of two individuals, it would have read, "their fallen dead bodies." In vs. 9, below, the text does use the plural, "**their bodies**," affirming a plurality of this symbol. That their bodies are on **the broad place** of the City shows that they will be a spectacle of shame – just as their Lord experienced the shame of the cross (Heb. 12:2) in this same City. "To deny proper burial was considered a great disgrace and insult to the dead" (Metzger, ibid p 70). Beale remarks that it,
> "emphasized by hyperbole that the true church will seem defeated in its role of witness… and will be treated with indignity" (ibid p 590).

Next, the prophecy must have been so enigmatic that the agent had to point out that this is a figure, for he says, "**whatever, spiritually, is normally being called** (or: named) **'Sodom' and 'Egypt.'**" The identity of the "City" is a figurative identity. We will now explore this enigma. Many interpreters have seen "**The Great City**" as a reference to Rome, but this does not fit the defining clause, "**where also their Lord was crucified**." So let up proceed to unpack this mysterious, compound description.

Sodom is spoken of in Judah (Jude) 7 as "**being given to fornication and outlandish prostitution, and then going away after different flesh** (= unnatural vice; or: = a different expression of alienation that was formed by the existing System)." 2 Peter 2:6 uses Sodom as an example for those about to be impious, irreverent, or ungodly. Gen. 18:20 says that "their SIN is exceedingly heavy." But Ezk. 16:48-50 gives an amplified picture,
> "By My life! says the Lord Yahweh, 'Sodom, YOUR SISTER, she and her daughters did not do WHAT YOU and YOUR DAUGHTERS have done! Look! This was the fault of Sodom, YOUR SISTER – pride (or: arrogance)! Gluttony and careless, tranquil ease were hers, and her daughters'; and that she did not support the house of the poor and the wretched. [*cf* Matt. 25:45]
> They were also haughty, and practiced depravity (abominations) before Me…'" (Fenton; Tanakh)

Note that her behavior made Jerusalem to be categorized as a sister of Sodom, in the Lord's eyes. Remember that a name speaks of one's character. I think we will see Jerusalem again, but called by a still different name, later on in this Unveiling.

In Jer. 23:11, 14 we find:
> "Indeed both prophet and priest, they are polluted; even in My House I find their evil, averring is Yahweh…. Among the prophets of Jerusalem I see a horrible thing: adultery and walking in falsehood. They reinforce the hands of evildoers so that no one turns back from his evil; to Me they have become like Sodom, all of them, and its dwellers like Gomorrah" (CVOT).

It should be clear, from these OT passages, that the City in this verse is 1st century Jerusalem.

The term "Egypt" speaks of what this country represented to Israel in all her history. It spoke of bondage. Thus, this Great City had become an oppressor, enslaving its citizens and subjects. Let us review a section of Jesus' critique of the rulers of Jerusalem, in Lu. 11:

42. "**But in contrast, tragic will be the fate for you Pharisees because you consistently give away one tenth** (or: habitually pay tithes) **from the mint and the rue, as well as every edible plant** (garden herb or vegetable), **and yet you folks are consistently bypassing the decisions which yield the justice and the love of God** (or: which have their origin in, and express the character of, God). **Now it was continuing binding and necessary to do these things, and not to bypass those things**....

44. "**Tragic will be your fate, you scholars** (theologians; scribes) **and Pharisees – the overly judging and critical folks**

> (*hupokrites*; or: those who put texts under close inspection to sift and separate and then give an answer, an interpretation, an opinion; or: those who live by separating things yet who under-discern; or: those who make judgments from a low view; or: those who under-estimate reality; or: perverse scholars who focus on tiny distinctions), **because you exist being as unseen** (or: = are unmarked) **memorial tombs** (= graves having the characteristics of Hades), **and so the people habitually walking around on top [of them] have not seen and so do not know** (= without realizing) **[it]!**" [note: contact with a grave rendered a person ceremonially unclean, according to their purity codes – thus, THEY made others unclean]

45. **Now a certain man of those versed in the Law** (a legal expert; a Torah lawyer and interpreter), **in giving a considered reply, is then saying to Him, "Teacher, in** (or: by) **constantly saying these things you continue invading our territory and outraging us by violating our rights – thus, insulting us, too!"**

46. **So He said, "Tragic will be the fate for you men versed in the Law** (Torah lawyers), **too, because you are constantly burdening people [with] cargos** (or: loads) **[that are] hard to bear** (= intolerable burdens), **and yet you folks are continuing to not even lightly touch the loads with one of your fingers!**

47. "**It will be so tragic for you, because** (or: It is so tragic among you, that) **you folks habitually build and erect the memorial tombs of the prophets, but your fathers** (or: forefathers; ancestors) **killed them off!**

48. "**Really** (or: Consequently; Accordingly then), **you folks exist being witnesses** (or: continuously are folks who testify and give evidence) **and you are constantly approving, thinking well of and giving endorsement to the actions** (deeds; works) **of your fathers** (and: forefathers), **because they indeed killed them off, and now you yourselves continue building the [memorial] houses** [other MSS: their tombs]**!**

49. "**That is why** (or: On account of this) **the Wisdom of God also said, 'As emissaries I will proceed sending off prophets and representatives unto them** (or: into the midst of them) **– and they will proceed killing off [some] from out of their midst, and then they will proceed to pursue** (chase; press forward [on] and persecute; [other MSS: banish]) **[others].'**

50. "**So thus, the blood of all of the prophets – that having been** [other MSS: being constantly or repeatedly] **poured out from the casting down** (the founding; the foundation; or: may = the conceiving) **of [the] ordered system** (world of culture, economy, religion and government) **– can** (or: would) **at some point** (or: suddenly) **be searched out to be required and exacted from this generation:**

51. "**from Abel's blood until the blood of Zechariah – the man losing himself** (or: perishing; being destroyed) **between the altar and the House – yes, I continue saying to you folks, it will progressively be sought out and exacted from this generation.**

52. "**Tragic will be the fate for you experts in the Law** (Torah lawyers), **because you lifted up and carried away** (or: lift up and carry off; took and remove) **the Key of the intimate,**

experiential, personal knowledge and insight. You, yourselves, do not enter [so as to experience and gain insight] and you hinder, block, prevent and forbid the folks periodically entering."

53. **And from there** (or: Then from that time and place), **upon His going out, the scribes** (scholars and theologians) **and the Pharisees began to fiercely keep on holding** (or: hemming) **[Him] in** (or: started to progressively bring dreadful entanglement on [Him]) **and to repeatedly get Him to speak without [His first] thinking** (literally: speak from the mouth) **concerning more things,**

54. **repeatedly lying in wait to ambush Him, constantly seeking to pounce on and catch** (or: trap) **something from out of His mouth** (= from His own words).

They practiced religious bondage for the common folks, and the Judaizers within Christianity have done the same things.

As Egypt was a "world power," it also carries the symbolic significance of "the world." Here then, "the set-apart City" has become characterized as being identified as "the world," or, "a world power." When Israel went down into Egypt, they received blessings at the hand of Joseph – who was a type of Christ. They were "in the world, but not of it." Yet notice Ex. 1:8, "Now there arose up a new king over Egypt, which knew not Joseph." Thus did the good times turn to bad, for Israel. I suggest that here, in chapter 11, we have a type of what would later become the institutional church (figured by the 1st century Jerusalem, in this historical metaphor) that "knows not Jesus." His teachings about doing "good" to, and blessing, one's adversaries seem to have been overshadowed by the supremacy of having "right doctrine." As in our passage here, they became persecutors of those who did not comply or conform.

The phrase "**where also their Lord was crucified**" establishes beyond a doubt that this Sodom and Egypt, where the two witnesses are overcome and killed, is the old covenant Jerusalem of the 1st century. It was a historical model of the spiritual counterpart, or application, in this new age where fundamentalist religions would continue to persecute and/or kill those who they deem to be adversaries. For an in-depth study of this reality, see *The Battle for God* by Karen Armstrong (Ballantine Pub., 2000) where she critiques the history of fundamentalism among Jews, Christians and Muslims. But for our present study, recall the words of Jesus in Lu. 13:33-35, cited in the discussion of vs. 4, above. As to the label, "**Egypt**," carrying the nuance of "bondage" (Ex. 13:3, *et al*, "you people came... out of the House of Bondage"), recall how Paul used this word to characterize the Law:

> "**for these women** [Sarah and Hagar] **are** (= represent) **two settled arrangements** (covenants; contracts; wills)**: one, on the one hand, from Mount Sinai, habitually** (repeatedly; continuously) **giving birth into slavery** (or: bondage) **– which is Hagar.** [*cf* Ex. 19:17 (LXX)]
> **Now this Hagar is** (= represents) **Mount Sinai, within Arabia, and she continuously stands in the same line** (or: keeps step in the same rank; marches in a column; walks or stands in a parallel row; or: is habitually rudimentary together; = corresponds to) **with the present Jerusalem, for she continues in slavery** (or: bondage) **with her children**" (Gal. 4:24b-25).

In the Gospels, Christ is seen as the new Moses, leading His people out of the bondage of the Law, so that they were no longer "under Law, but under grace" (Rom. 6:14). He came to set the captives free (Lu. 4:18).

Joel 3:18-21 speaks of the time of Christ, "when a spring from the House of Yahweh shall go forth [*cf* Ezk. 47].... [and] Egypt shall become a desolation... because of the wrong [done to the] sons of Judah when they shed innocent blood in their land. Judah shall be indwelt for the eon, and Jerusalem for generation after generation.... For Yahweh shall tabernacle in Zion [*cf* 21:3, below]" (CVOT; brackets added). The Egypt-metaphor, here in the Unveiling, which describes literal Jerusalem (figured as Egypt in Joel's prophecy) speaks of the coming judgment of literal Jerusalem in AD 70; the Jerusalem of Joel's prophecy speaks of the "heavenly Jerusalem/Zion" (21:2-22:5, below; Heb. 12:22-24; Ezk. 47:1ff).

We read Jer. 22:8, in regard to Yahweh's judgment of the house of Judah, centered in Jerusalem, and see that:
> "when many nations pass by this city [i.e., Jerusalem], and they say each one to his associate, 'On what [grounds] has Yahweh done thus to this GREAT CITY?' then they will reply, 'Because they forsook the covenant of Yahweh, their God, and they worshiped other gods and served them." *Cf* 14:8, 16:19; 17:5, 18, below.

Beale (ibid p 591) points us to the Sibylline Oracles where, in places, Jerusalem is referred to as a "**great city**" (5.154, 226 and 413; *The OT Pseudepigrapha*, ibid pp 396, 398, 403), during the period of Titus destroying Jerusalem, and Nero's career.

Another clue is found in Mat. 20:18-19,
> "**Look at this, and consider. We are progressively walking up into Jerusalem, and later, the Son of the Man** (= the eschatological messiah figure) **will proceed being turned over** (delivered and committed) **to the chief** (or: ranking) **priests and scribes** (scholars and experts in the Law), **then they will according to pattern proceed judging** (condemning) **Him to** (for) **death. Next, they will proceed turning Him over to the ethnic multitudes** (the nations; = foreigners) – **into [a situation] to ridicule, make fun of and mock, and then scourge [Him] with a whip, and finally to suspend and execute [Him] on a torture stake.**"

And again recall Lu. 13:33, "**it continues being inadmissible** (not acceptable; = unthinkable) **for a prophet to be destroyed outside of Jerusalem!**" We will read Christ's call to His people in 18:4, 8, below:
> "**Come out of her** (or: Go forth from out of her midst) **My people, so that you may not jointly participate with** (fellowship together with) **her sins** (failures; occasions of missing the mark), **and so that you may not receive from out of her plagues** (blows).... **she will proceed being burned down** (consumed) **within fire, because the Lord, the God evaluating and judging her, [is] strong!**"

This was to be a fulfillment of Isa. 64:10b-11a, "Jerusalem [is] a desolation: our holy and our beautiful house… is burned up with fire…" – because "the faithful city had become a prostitute" (Isa. 1:21). We read of this having happened in AD 70, to the literal city of Jerusalem and Herod's temple. But we also have 2000 years of the church's bloody history since that time. We can be instructed by reading of the judgment on Jerusalem and the death of Christ's followers, in the 1st century, but the message is also about the beast repeatedly climbing out of the abysses of the darkened hearts of estranged humans to slay Christ's witness in the world. We have seen more wars and more reports of wars as humans continue to kill humans in the name of God, fulfilling Jesus' words, "**everyone in the process of killing… folks off may [be] imagining** (supposing; holding the opinion of; thinking) **[themselves] to be proceeding in presenting an offering of sacred service to God**" (Jn. 16:2).

Metzger concurs that, "the ministry of the witnesses was exercised in Jerusalem" (ibid p 70), but the "allegory develops… to include the entire world" (ibid). As Peter Hiett says, "It is about *you* being a witness *now*" (ibid p 140; emphasis original).

In 1 Thes. 2, Paul addressed similar situations in Thessalonica and related them to what had been going on in Jerusalem and Judea:
> 13. **And so, on account of this, we ourselves also continuously give thanks to God by an unvarying practice** (or: incessantly; unintermittingly), **because in receiving** (or: taking to [your] side; accepting) **God's word and message, from a hearing from us at our side, you**

welcomingly accepted not a word of or from people (or: a human message), **but rather, according as it really and truly is, a word of God** (God's message; an idea from God; a thought which is God), **Which** (or: Who) **also** (or: even) **is continuously in-working** (being active; operating; energizing) **within and among you folks – those continuously trusting and progressively believing with loyalty.**

14. **For you, brothers** (= fellow believers), **were birthed** (or: were made to be) **imitators of God's called-out folks** (or: summoned forth communities) **– the ones within Christ being in Judea – because you also at one point experienced** (or: suffered) **the very same things by your own fellow-tribesmen, just as they also [did] by the Jews** (= the leaders of Judaism),

15. **even from those killing-off the Lord Jesus, as well as the prophets; even from those driving us out and continuously displeasing God, and from folks contrary to** (or: in opposition against) **all humans** (or: peoples).

Our current passage in the Unveiling was not an isolated incident.

9. **Then those out of the peoples – even from tribes and tongues and ethnic groups** (nations; multitudes; pagans; non-Jews) **– continuously see** (observe; cast a look upon) **their dead body three and one half days, and they will not proceed in releasing their dead bodies to be placed into a memorial monument or tomb** (= to be buried).

This seems to be an allusion to Ps. 79:2-3,
> "They have given the carcasses of Your servants as food for the flyer of the heavens, the flesh of Your benign ones to the wild animal of the earth. They have poured out their blood like water, around Jerusalem, and there was no one entombing them" (CVOT).

Simmons points out that, "Public display of corpses was a form of glorying in one's victory..." (ibid p 220) and cites 1 Sam. 31:9, 10 as an example from Israel's history:
> "They cut off [Saul's] head, stripped him of his gear and sent [messengers] to the land of the Philistines, round about.... and fastened his body to the wall of Beth-shan" (CVOT).

Such practices were forbidden in Israel's Law (Deut. 21:23; Josh. 8:29), but it was common among the Gentiles. Christ's body would have stayed on the cross had not the Jews objected and Joseph requested the body from Pilate. But AD 70 is testimony that the Jews were unable to keep this statute when slaughtered first by the Jewish rebels, and then by the Romans.

Peter had warned of such as this, in general terms, in 1 Pet. 4:

7. **Now the Goal** (or: the end; the final act; or: the finished Product; or: the completion of the plan) **of all people** (and: affecting all things) **has approached and is now near at hand and [He] is close enough to touch** (= has arrived)! **Therefore, you folks keep a healthy and sound frame of mind** (be sane and sensible) **and be sober** (be unintoxicated; i.e., be functional and with your wits about you) **into [a state, condition or realm] with a view toward having goodness and well-being** (or: into the midst of prayers).

12. **Beloved ones, do not repeatedly feel like strangers to the burning** (= the action of the Fire) **within and among you folks, which is habitually happening to you with a view toward your being put to the test** (or: which is repeatedly coming into being in the face of a proving trial for you; which is progressively birthing itself to an examination in you), **as though a strange thing or a foreign occurrence is repeatedly walking with you folks.**

13. **But on the contrary, keep on rejoicing and being glad to the extent or degree that you folks are continually participating with a common share in the effects of the experiences and the results of the sufferings of the Christ, to the end that, while continuously exulting and celebrating exceedingly, you folks can** (or: would) **also rejoice within the unveiling of His glory** (or: in union with the disclosure of His reputation; or: in the midst of the praise-inducing manifestation which is Him)!

The period of time, here, "**three and one half days**," is symbolic. It most likely corresponds to the other three and ½ time periods that we find in this section of the Unveiling. It may also be an allusion to Mat. 12:39-40,

> **39. So He, making a decided reply, said to them, "A good-for-nothing, worthless, base, knavish, grievously oppressive and wicked – even adulterous** (unfaithful and immoral) – **generation repeatedly seeks intently for a sign! And yet a sign will not proceed to be given to it – except the sign of Jonah the prophet.**
> **40. "You see, just as Jonah was within the midst of the belly of the huge fish** (or: sea monster) **[for] three days and three nights** [Jonah 1:17], **thus in this way will the Son of the Man continue being within the heart of the earth [for] three days and three nights.**

As to the description of the on-lookers: **the peoples – even from tribes and tongues and ethnic groups** (nations; multitudes; pagans; non-Jews), we find a list that fits this description among those in Jerusalem for the feast of Pentecost in Acts 2:9-10,

> "**Parthians, Medes and Elamites** [= portions of the Persian empire]; **even folks presently dwelling in Mesopotamia... both Judea, as well as Cappadocia... Pontus, as well as Asia** [= principally the kingdom of Pergamus, including Lydia, Mysia, Caria and Phrygia], **both Phrygia and Pamphylia; Egypt and the parts of Libya which is down toward Cyrene, as well as the temporary residents from Rome** (or: the repatriated Romans); **both Jews and proselytes** (converts to Judaism), **Cretans and Arabians** (or: Arabs)."

When we consider that this same group of "**peoples**... etc." may well be the same group referred to in 10:11, above (to which John was told that he must prophesy), John may have realized that this whole scene of the two witnesses would include him, in the very near future. It would have been like Jesus knowing what would soon happen to Him in Jerusalem, as He prophesied. And like Paul knowing that he would soon be poured out as a drink offering for the people. And like Peter being told how he would die. It all comes down to laying down one's life, or soul, for one's friends.

So we see the events following the figure of the death of the two witnesses, and their final end, begin to unfold. Their life and ministry show a certain parallel to that of Jesus, yet these are not allowed to be buried as Jesus was. Ken Earl suggested that those observing them wanted to make sure there was no plot by disciples to steal the bodies and claim that they, too, ascended as did Jesus. This interpretation sees this figure in literal fulfillment – and this might well have been the case in the 1st century setting, but we have no records of such. But the idea of shame, or that there were too many dead bodies (assuming an AD 70 scenario) seems more likely. What comes to mind is an allusion to Isa. 66:24 setting:

> "And they will go forth and see the corpses of the mortals who transgressed against Me, for their worm shall not die and their fire shall not be quenched, and they will become a repulsion to all flesh" (CVOT).

This would fit the aftermath of AD 70 Jerusalem, but not the situation of our verse here. However, one might speculate that, since those who killed the witnesses thought that they were serving God in doing so, they might have had this prophecy in mind, as well as the shame factor.

Yet how did this relate to the early called-out communities, and then to us as individuals who have been, or are being, grown throughout this age? What can we receive from this right now? Does the Lord use the little beast from within our personal Deep, as well as those people of the "beast system," to slay us (i.e., the false persona; the carnal and estranged self) so that resurrection life may ensue in place of our false ego? We live out His witness; we preach His anointed message; we destroy our inner enemies (crushing *satan*, our adversary, under our "feet" – i.e., in our personal walk with Christ – Rom. 16:20, as we follow Him, carrying our crosses – Mat. 16:24). Then suddenly, we are overcome by the little beast (from within, or from without – either of which affect us within). Those observing us could ask regarding us, "Can these bones live?" (Ezk. 37). Yet when the appointed time of death has been fulfilled, we hear the Voice within "repeatedly saying to [us], 'Climb up here, to this place!'" (vs. 12, below). And so we find ourselves on a higher place with new life and a greater vision from this new height.

The situation of vs. 9 may be that to which Jesus referred in Mat. 24:28, "**Wherever the carcass** (corpse) **may be, the vultures** (or: eagles) **will be progressively led together and gathered**."

10. **And so the folks continuously having a house down upon the earth** (or: the ones normally dwelling upon the Land) **are continuously rejoicing upon them, and they will continue being gladdened** (or: made happy) **and will proceed sending presents to each other, because these, the two prophets, tested and examined** (applied the touchstone to test the purity of the metal of) **those continuously having a house down upon the earth** (or: ground).

The subject of the first clause, "**the folks continuously having a house DOWN upon the earth**" does not refer to physical "earth-dwellers," but is a symbol: it designates those who have not yet existentially been born into His kingdom (i.e., His sovereign activities), and who are thus not yet seated with Christ in the heavenly realm (Eph. 2:6). *Cf* Hos. 4:1; Joel 1:2, 14; 2:1; Jer. 6:12; 10:18 for echoes of this imagery. It refers to those who have NOT been walking on the restrictive, cruciform Path, following the Anointing. They may not yet have even "**been made alive in Christ**" (1 Cor. 15:22). But Paul went on to instruct us that this happens, "**each person within the result and effect of his or her own class** (or: ordered place; appointed position [in line]; arranged time or order of succession; = place in a harvest calendar, thus, due season of maturity)" – vs. 23. We are not born into the same class, appointed position, or arranged time – either in the natural life, or, within His kingdom. To come to a better understanding of this phrase, here in vs. 10, we will take a diversion from our text to discuss a brief overview of the life-ways and callings within God's kingdom. Some are called to live a life of giving community and social support. This was apparently Jesus' calling, up to the time of His baptism by John, and the beginning of His ministry as God's Anointed One. His father, Joseph, was a craftsman (carpenter or stone mason). Peter and others were fishermen. Others were farmers or herdsmen, providing for the sustenance of their families and communities. If everyone became an evangelist, where would be the community? But most of humanity are "folks who have a house DOWN upon the earth," and are not necessarily "dwelling UP in the heavens" (the obvious contrasting metaphor) as a way of making a living, or as being a participant in Christ's reign.

Those of the multitudes – the world, including "the church world" or any religious setting – "**the ones… upon the earth** [realm]," are **made happy** by the fall and death of Christ's witnesses. The message of these prophets **tested and examined them** (vs. 10, below) – it weighed them in the balances and found them wanting of substance (i.e., the glory of Christ; Dan. 5:27) – and those thus tested were glad for the prophets to be gone. This verse can apply to the outward ministry to the called-out communities, and it now applies to people in general. Our self, which wants to save its life, is happy and wants to party when the heat of God's message to us is temporarily ended. The Word and the Spirit baptize us with Fire to test and examine the purity of the gold which He has placed within us. Our flesh always wants this to be over soon – and is glad when it appears to be so. But as we see, this is not the end of the story.

Christ's "**invitation to an above place** (upward call)" (Phil. 3:14) is to live in both realms at the same time, as we are called to be "**pressing forward, pursuing down toward** [the; or: an] **object in view** (a mark on which the eye is fixed)**: into the awarded contest prize**." Paul there identified this as coming to the place where we are, "**constantly holding things above and thus having all-surpassing value and superiority: that which pertains to and comes from the experience of the intimate knowledge of**

[our] Lord, Jesus Christ" (Phil. 3:8), and he continues on, in vs. 10, "**being a person that is being continuously conformed by** (being progressively brought together with the form of; being habitually configured to) **His death**." This sounds very much like the teaching from Jesus, to His disciples – and we will look at this, below. But this can only be done as the Spirit enables us – and this is a matter of God's choosing when He will do this for us. Furthermore, such a life only happens after we have been made alive in Christ. In 3:21, above, we read:

> "**To** (or: In; For) **the person who is habitually conquering** (repeatedly overcoming; normally victorious) **I will continue giving** [the right? the ability? the honor?] **to sit with Me within My throne, as I also conquer** (or: overcame and was victorious) **and sit with My Father within His throne**."

And in 2:26-27 Christ told them,

> "**And [to] the one habitually conquering** (repeatedly overcoming; progressively victorious)… **I will continue giving to him AUTHORITY** (privilege from out of Being) **upon the MULTITUDES** (the nations; the ethnic groups; the Gentiles), **and so he will continue shepherding** (i.e., feeding, tending and guarding) **them with a staff made of iron, as he is being continuously broken [like] pottery vessels,** [Ps. 2:8-9] **as I also have received from My Father**."

These verses, just quoted, speak to the ministry of the two witnesses (vss. 5-6, above). They overcame JUST AS Christ overcame: through death and resurrection. The little animal/beast that killed them is the same beast that killed Christ: the dominating collusions of religion and empire. As the liberating Shepherd's rod broke Him (note: He received it "from His Father"), they, too, received a breaking. And if they at some point struck the Land (vs. 6, above), it was with the Shepherd's rod, for the good of the sheep. Recall how David said, "Your rod and your staff! They **comfort** me" (Ps. 23:4b). In Isa. 11:4 it is said of Yahweh, "He will smite the Land with the rod of His mouth." These are corrective measures, as we read in Prov. 13:24, "He that keeps back his rod, hates his son." God loves the aggregate of humanity (Jn. 3:16). And in Micah 7:14 it is said, "O **shepherd** Your people with Your staff [rod], Your very own flock…" (Tanakh; brackets added).

So now, let us consider some of the things that Jesus said to His disciples, who were called to leave their professions and to follow His path. In Mat. 7:13-14, Jesus taught His followers,

> "**You folks enter at once through the narrow, restrictive and cramping gate**…. **for the gate is narrow, cramping and restrictive which is habitually leading off into the Life – and the path has been compressed and squeezed** [to where the traveler is pressed, encumbered]."

This is the Path of the disciple, the apprentice. He did not call all to follow this Path at this time, or even, necessarily, in this life. "The Life" is the Christ Life of cruciform, sacrificial living. He saves all, but are all called to follow the way of the cross? Peter was called to "shepherd" others (Jn. 21:15-22). It is the disciple/apprentice that is called to shepherd the multitudes. Are all called to "destroy their soul-life" (Mat. 16:25, "**whoever can loose-away and even destroy his soul-life** {the interior self} **on My account, he will continue finding it**")? He prefaced this statement by the qualifier,

> "**If anyone continues intending** (purposing; willing; wanting) **to COME ON BEHIND Me, let him at once deny, reject and disown himself, and then in one move lift up his execution stake** (pole for suspending a corpse; cross), **and after that proceed to be by habit continuously FOLLOWING after Me!**" – Mat. 16:24.

These requirements are not the speaking about "salvation," which comes as the "free gift of His grace." Neither is He is talking about a person's "final destiny," but about apprenticeship and about leaving things behind in order to come and be His disciple (student; learner; apprentice). Jesus began by calling only 12. At times He seemed to even discourage others, such as:

> "**Since** (of: If) **you continue desiring and intending to be mature and perfect** (= if you are serious about reaching the goal), **humbly proceed going your way, at once sell the things of your subsistence** (those things supporting you from your beginning and giving you authority; or:

your possessions and belongings; or: the things currently at your disposal), **and give [the proceeds] to the poor and destitute folks. Then you will continue holding and possessing treasure within the midst of heaven** (or: in [your] atmosphere). **After that, come here and be habitually following Me**" (Mat. 19:21).

This was not a general teaching, but a specific instruction for a specific individual. He was not talking about "works-based righteousness or salvation," but about following the cross-shaped Life of the Lamb. Not all believers are called to the same function in the body. Some are called to be the temple while the calling of others is to the outer court, or even (e.g., symbolically) to function as one of the twelve gates of the New Jerusalem, etc. Israel itself was called to be a special people, to be a light, a witness, to the nations. His kingdom is multifunctional; His reign is composed of different callings (kinds of service). Paul makes this clear in his discussion concerning "gifts" (more literally: grace-effects) in 1 Cor. 12. There, in vss. 29-30, he states:

"**[So you see that] not all [are] folks sent off on a mission** (representatives; envoys; emissaries). **Not all [are] those who have light ahead of time and speak it before others in public** (prophets). **Not all [are] people who teach** (teachers; instructors). **Not all [have] abilities or powers. Not all constantly hold** (habitually have or possess) **effects of grace which result in cures and healings. Not all habitually speak in multiple languages** (or: are constantly speaking by tongues; or: normally talk to tongues [figure of people groups of other cultures]). **Not all are continually interpreting** (or: habitually translating)."

In this life we all have different vocations (which means: callings). The training and education, or the skills and abilities, of one calling is not the same as another. Some are called, and birthed, to be a part of His firstfruits; others are chosen to be a part of the later harvest. Paul put it this way, in Rom. 9:

16. **Consequently, then, [it is] not of or from the one constantly exercising [his] will** (or: habitually intending or designing), **nor of the one constantly rushing forward** (or: continuously running or habitually racing), **but rather of, from, pertaining to and belonging to God, the One constantly being merciful**....

18. **Consequently, then, on whom He from time to time wills He is continuously merciful** (He constantly relieves from distress and misery). **Yet whom He from time to time wills** (intends; designs), **He continues progressively hardening.**

19. **You will ask me** (or: protest to me), **then, "Why, then, is He still blaming and continuing to find fault? For who has resisted** (stood against) **His intention** (the effect of His deliberated purpose and resolve) **and is yet still so standing?"**

20. **O human! On the contrary, even more, what** (or: who) **are you – the one habitually answering back to God** (or: disputing with God)**?**

"**The thing molded and formed will not proceed to be saying to the One molding and forming, 'Why do you make me thus?'**" [cf Isa. 29:16; 45:9; 64:8]

21. **Or does not the Potter hold authority or have a right pertaining to clay, forth from out of the same kneaded mixture to make the one a container** (a vessel; an instrument; a utensil) **into honor and value, yet the other into an un-honored one** (a worthless one; one without value; one deprived of privileges; or: = one for common use)**?**

22. **Now since God – habitually willing** (or: repeatedly intending) **to display and demonstrate inherent fervor, natural impulse, propensity and disposition** (or: teeming passion; swelling desire; or: anger, wrath and indignation), **and also to make known by personal experience His power and ability – in much long-suffering** (inner quietness; forbearance; pushing anger far away) **bears and carries** (or: brought forth and produced; or: enduringly supports while moving) **containers** (vessels; instruments; utensils) **of natural impulse** (belonging to a passionate disposition; displaying inherent fervor; from teeming passion and swelling desire; or: of anger; having the character of wrath; owned by indignation), **being folks having been fully outfitted, thoroughly prepared and made correspondingly adequate for loss** (or: having equipped,

adapted and adjusted themselves down into ruin, waste and destruction [of their well-being]), **and now continuing in this condition,**

23. **[it is] to the end that He could and would also at some point make known by intimate experience the wealth of His glory** (or: of His manifestation of that which calls forth praise; which pertains to His reputation) **upon containers of mercy** (instruments of mercy), **which He beforehand prepares into [being]** (or: made ready and provides into the midst of) **a manifestation of [that] glory**

24. **– even us, whom He calls, not only from out of the Jews, but further, even from out of the nations** (or: out of the ethnic multitudes, also; forth from the Gentiles, too).

As we observe in all of His creation, there is much variety in the expressions of His glory. Paul further instructs us in 1 Cor. 15:

39. **Not all flesh [is] the same flesh, but to the contrary, [there is] indeed one [flesh] of humans, yet another flesh of tamed animals, still another flesh of birds, and another of fishes.**

40. **And then [there are] supra-heavenly bodies** (bodies having the characteristics of that upon the dome of the sky), **and earthly bodies, but [they are] indeed different: the glory of the supra-heavenly [bodies is] one thing, while the glory of the earthly [is] different.**

41. **[There is] one glory of [the] sun, and another glory of [the] moon, and another glory of [the] stars, in fact star continues differing from star, in glory and splendor.**

42. **Thus ALSO** (or: In this way too) **[is] the resurrection of the dead people. It is habitually** (repeatedly; presently; one after another) **being sown within corruption** (or: in union with decay and ruin); **it is being habitually** (or: presently; repeatedly; one after another) **awakened and raised up within incorruption.**

43. **It is constantly being sown within dishonor** (in union with lack of value; in the midst of worthlessness), **it is being habitually** (or: repeatedly; constantly; one after another; progressively) **awakened and raised up within, and in union with, power and ability.**

44. **It is habitually** (continually; repeatedly; presently) **being sown a body having the qualities and characteristics of a soul** (a soulish body; or: = a body animated by soul; or: = a natural entity); **it is habitually** (repeatedly; constantly; presently; one after another) **being awakened and raised up a spiritual body** (a body having the qualities and characteristics of the Breath-effect; or: = a spiritual entity). **Since there is a soulish body** (or: = body animated by soul), **there also is** (or: exists) **a spiritual one** (or: = one animated by spirit).

[comment: note the germinal connection between the two – they are a progression of the same body]

We have taken this side trip in order to point out the complexity and diversity of the new creation. We should not judge these who "**are continuously rejoicing upon [the witnesses], and who continue being gladdened** (or: made happy) **and who proceed sending presents to each other**" because of the death of Christ's two witnesses – the witness of His called-out community. God has a plan for them, too. He will ultimately "**mercy all mankind** (may make everyone, the all, recipients of mercy)" (Rom. 11:32). They will come alive "in their own class, or order."

Here, in 11:10, "**having a house down upon the earth**" pictures those who mind the flesh realm (as Paul described some of those in 1 Cor. 3:1-3a – yet those fitting this description in Corinth, even though classified as "babies," were members of the called-out community and members of Christ's body). They are therefore often having "**enmity, alienation and discord [streaming] into God** (or: hostility unto, or active hatred with a view to, God)" (Rom. 8:6-7). This is why people resist God, even while believing in Him and being saved by Him. This was the picture often seen with Israel, though having experienced Passover and baptism in the Red Sea, still resisting Moses, or complaining, during their wilderness journey. An OT allusion to the reaction of the people over the death of the witnesses, here (but for a different reason), is the scene of Moses being on the mountain conversing with God, in contrast to the people having Aaron build them a golden calf and then having a party down below the mountain, below Moses' encounter with God.

Jesus told His disciples in Mat. 10:
> 17. **"So constantly hold your attention toward protecting yourself from humanity. You see, they will periodically be giving you folks over** (commit you) **unto [their] local city councils and courts, and then they will proceed scourging you with lashes and whips.**
> 18. **"Yet you men will also, on My account, be from time to time led** (or: brought) **before** (or: on [the stand to speak to]) **governors and kings, with a view to being a witness to them and providing evidence for them – as well as to and for and among the ethnic multitudes** (the nations; the non-Israelites; = the pagans).
> 22. **"And further, you folks will continue being hated, detached and regarded with ill-will by everyone – because of My Name…**
> 23. **"Now whenever they may continue chasing you or be repeatedly persecuting you in this [particular] city, proceed taking flight** (escaping) **into a different one, for, truly – I now say to you folks – you can under no circumstances complete the circuit of** (or: finish [visiting]) **the cities** (or: towns) **of Israel until the Son of the Man** (= the awaited Messianic figure) **should go** (or: comes; can come and then go).
> 24. **"A student is not over or above the teacher, nor [is] a slave over or above his owner.**
> 25. **"[It is] sufficient and enough for the student that he can come to be as his teacher, and the slave as his owner. Since** (or: If) **people call and surname the Sovereign** (Master and Sole Owner) **of the house** (the Householder) **'Beelzeboul'** [spellings vary; = lord of the flies, a Philistine deity], **how much rather** (or: more) **those of His household.**
> 26. **"So then, you men should not be made to fear them…**

The story being told in the Unveiling, concerning these two witnesses, echoes what this report from Mat.10 has said would happen. It was happening throughout that generation, and has continued on through the centuries, to this day, in many forms of persecution. It is important to see this passage of the Unveiling as a part, and a prophecy about, the greater whole. But keep in mind that a central message of this book is that the Lamb reigns, and God wins over the hearts and minds of humanity.

Chilton (ibid p 282) points us to a situation of those in opposition to a witness for the coming Christ: Herod's birthday party which ended with the beheading of John the Immerser (Mat. 14:3-12). He further points us to Herod becoming friends with Pilate (Lu. 23:12) and the sport made of their Messiah during the trials of Jesus and His crucifixion (Lu. 22:63-65; 23:8-12, 35-39), which led to the death of His witness (for three days!). Humanity is a "mixed bag." Although being part of the corporate *eschatos* Adam, we are all individuals, at the same time. We are all at different stages of life and growth, and produce at different levels of fruit (remember the 30-fold, 60-fold, 100-fold?). In Christ's kingdom it is not "us and them," or even "black or white," but One new Humanity (Eph. 2:15) which overcomes the duality of the old covenant (the "us-and-them" perspective), especially after it had become corrupted with Zoroastrianism (*cf* Riley, *River*, ibid p 202). Considering those who rejoice at the death of the witnesses, we should remember that Jesus said to those crucifying Him, "Father, forgive them, for they do not know what they are doing." We must keep in mind that these folks are part of those of whom Paul said, "**God encloses, shuts up and locks all mankind** (everyone; the entire lot of folks) **into incompliance** (disobedience; stubbornness; lack of being convinced), **to the end that He could** (or: would; should) **mercy all mankind** (may make everyone, the all, recipients of mercy)!" (Rom. 11:32). And we see in 21:3, below, that God has pitched His tent among these folks, to live among them, and the New Jerusalem continually descends to them, in order that the leaves of the tree of life can heal them (22:2, below).

Those who metaphorically dwell on the earth do not at that time have a vision, and, "When [there] is no vision a people become unbridled (let loose; cast off restraints and are made naked)" (Prov. 29:18; CVOT, Rotherham, Young). The picture here in 11:10 is just the opposite of 1 Cor. 13:6 which instructs us,

> "**[Love] does not continue to rejoice upon [seeing or hearing of] the injustice, nor is it happy about dishonesty, inequity, or lack of the qualities of the Way pointed out, yet it repeatedly rejoices with the Truth (or: takes delight together in Reality)."**

But let us keep in mind that Christ's message is Love ("unambiguous acceptance and the drive toward reunion with what has been estranged or demonized" – Paul Tillich), so the reaction of the witnesses would be a reproduction of 1 Cor. 13:7,

> "**[Love] continuously covers all mankind; it is habitually loyal to all humanity; it constantly has an expectation for all mankind; it is continuously remaining under and giving support to all people**
>> (or, since 'all' can also be neuter: It [i.e., unambiguous acceptance] progressively puts a protecting roof over all things; it is habitually trusting in, and believing for, all things; it is continually hoping in or for all things; it keeps on patiently enduring all things)."

And, as 1 Cor. 13:8 says, "**The Love** [i.e., God; Christ] (or: This unrestricted, self-giving drive toward reunion) **never – not even once – fails** (falls out or lapses; = becomes fruitless or ineffectual; [other MSS: falls down; collapses])." This is the Spirit of Christ, and 19:10, below, informs us that "the Breath-effect which is prophecy is **the witness** of, evidence for, and comes from, **Jesus**." This would have been the character of their prophetic **testing** of those around them. Although they might have prophesied judgment (as did Jonah to Nineveh), it will have a positive outcome (as it did for Nineveh). But the contrasting attitude is cautioned-against in 1 Jn. 3:12,

> "**not [living] like Cain. He was existing, and continued being, from out of the condition causing misery and hard labor** (the unprofitable attitude; the worthless mindset; the wicked intent; the toilsome situation; the sorry plight), **and so he slaughtered his brother. And on what score did he slaughter him? Because his works were gushed with misery and hard labor** (were wicked or evil; were toilsome; were unprofitable and worthless), **but those of his brother [were] ones in accord with the Way pointed out** (just ones; righteous ones; fair and equitable ones; rightwised ones)."

We are reminded that Isa. 26:9 tells us,

> "When Your judgments are in the earth, the inhabitants of the world learn righteousness" (NRSV).

Note the emphasis of this phrase, "**those continuously having a house down upon the earth**": it is used twice in this verse (two witnesses!) – so understanding their existential status is important. We would not consider these folks as being "spiritual." They are like those of whom Jesus spoke in Mat. 13:15,

> "'**For the heart of this people was made thick and fat, and thus has become impervious, dull and insensitive, and with the ears they hear heavily, and are thus hard of hearing, and they shut** (or: closed) **their eyes** (or: they squint their eyes), **lest at some time they might see with [their] eyes and should then be listening and hearing with [their] ears, and with the heart they could make things flow together so as to comprehend – and they might turn about! And so, I will progressively cure and heal them!**'" [Isa. 6:9-10]

Take note of "the divine passive" (i.e., the action by God) in the first clause of this verse in Matthew. And yet, and justly so, God was,

> "**not accounting to them** (not putting to their account; not logically considering for them; not reasoning in them) **the results and effects of their falls to the side**" (2 Cor. 5:19).

Now let us review the word rendered, "**tested and examined**." The parenthetical expansion gives the literal meaning: "applied the touchstone to test the purity of the metal of" (as a jeweler applies it to something made of gold to determine the percent of gold in the object, i.e., to determine the karat). We discussed its NT uses in the comments on 9:5, above. *Cf* Mk. 13:9-13 for a parallel to our present passage (11:3-10). There it predicts the persecution and "death" of Christ's "witness."

11. **Later, after the three and a half days, a spirit of Life** (Life's breath-effect or a spirit which is life) **from out of God entered within** [other MSS: into] **them and they stood upon their feet. And so** (a) **great fear fell upon the people continuing to be spectators of** (or: watching) **them.**

The end is an infusion of the Spirit of Life from God, and the finished product – the Last Adam (the completed body) – having done all, stands upon its feet. Here is an allusion to Eph. 6:13,
> "**and then accomplishing all** (achieving and effecting everything [the whole]), **to stand firm**."

This event is a figure of resurrection. We can see here an allusion to Ezk. 37:9-11a,
> "Then He said to me: 'Prophesy to the Spirit; prophesy, son of humanity, and you will say to the Spirit, Thus says my Lord Yahweh: Come from the four winds, O Spirit, and blow into these who were killed, so that they may live.' When I prophesied as He had instructed me, the Spirit came into them, and they lived and stood on their feet, a most exceedingly great assembly. Then He said to me: 'Son of humanity, these bones are the whole house of Israel'..."

The picture in Ezk. 37 and the description here, in vs. 11, both show that death is not the end. The end is life. Notice, also, that those in Ezekiel's vision represented "the WHOLE house of Israel." It calls to mind Rom. 11:26,
> "**So then, thus, in this manner and with this result: all Israel will progressively be delivered** (rescued, saved, made whole and restored to their original position [in the olive tree]), **according as it has been written,**
>> '**The One continuously dragging out of danger and drawing to Himself** (The Rescuer; The Deliverer) **will repeatedly arrive and be present from out of Zion; He will continue turning irreverence away from Jacob**'" (Isa. 59:20).

We read in Isa. 26:19,
> "Your dead shall live! Their carcasses shall rise! Awake and be jubilant, tabernacles of the soil!" (CVOT).

But the message of 11:11, here, is metaphorical: the witness of Christ will not fail, but will arise again and again. The laying down of life for another is the Seed of continued resurrection life for all. As with the Head, so with the body.

The work and witness has moved from the "little flock" to "the peoples." It was the expansion of the existential reign of God (His sovereign influence and activities) among the nations. This began in the book of Acts. So just who are these **peoples** (vs. 9)? Well, where were the witnesses slain and left lying? Was it not within "The Great City" (vs. 8) which we have already identified? Would it not be safe to assume that it would then be the citizens of this same city (the Jews of the 1st century; the carnal church and carnal humanity of subsequent times) who will be the ones who will observe and then celebrate? Remember that this letter and these visions were, and are, to the called-out, covenant communities – from the body's beginning to the present day.

The death of the witnesses, here, may be those referred to in 6:11b, above. The "**great fear**" calls to mind Acts 2:43, "**Now reverence, awe, respect and fear began to be birthed in every soul** (or: continued coming to be on every person), **and many miracles** (or: portents; omens) **and signs began occurring through the sent-forth folks** (the emissaries; the representatives)." The miraculous often brought fear. Even the failed attempt of exorcism by the seven sons of Sceva caused "**fear [to] fall upon them all, and then the Name of the Lord Jesus began becoming great and continued enlarging**"

(Acts 19:17b). Here Chilton points to the contrast of those who feared the Jewish leadership, sometimes referred to as "the fear or man": cf Jn.7:13; 12:42; 19:38 and 20:19 (ibid p 284). Ps. 105:38 records of the Exodus that, "Egypt was glad when they departed, for the fear of them fell upon them." Behind that fear was the fear of their God.

I am reminded of my university ethics class, where our instructor, Dr. John Wood, surprised us all when he said, "There is no respect without fear." Upon hearing this, my first thoughts were, no, I did not fear my parents or others whom I respect. But then he explained: as a boy he had such great respect for his grandfather that he "feared" doing anything that would (in young Wood's mind) cause his grandfather to ever think anything less of him, or cause his grandfather to be disappointed in him. With this explanation, I saw that I agreed, and that my own parents had placed the seed of "the fear of the Lord" in my own heart – not any sense of being afraid of my Father, but the kind of fear that Dr. Wood explained to us. There are different kinds of fear.

As an older adult, from inner, spiritual experience and many long conversations with, and listening to, our Father, over the years, I have come to see the wisdom of the fear of the Lord as a restraining factor for my immature years. But with the years and the existential knowing our Father, I came to realize that His perfect love never would change His opinion of me – no matter what I might do or not do. The knowledge of His perfect love cast out any fear of my own failure, knowing that I could never disappoint Him. His love is not performance-based.

12. **Then they heard a great** (or: loud) **Voice from out of the atmosphere** (or: sky; heaven), **repeatedly saying to them, "You must climb up here!** (or: Ascend at once to this place.)" **So they climbed up into the atmosphere** (or: ascended into the sky and heaven) **within** (or: in the midst of; in union with) **the cloud, and their enemies watched** (or: were spectators of) **them.**

The **great Voice** may well be an allusion to Jn.5:25,
> "**Count on it: I am presently continuing to say to you folks that an hour is progressively** (or: presently in process of) **coming, and even now exists** (or: = is now here), **when the dead folks WILL be repeatedly hearing the voice of God's Son** (or: the Voice from, and which is, the Son of God), **and the ones hearing WILL proceed to be living!**"

This, being set in figurative literature, might also be an echo of Paul in Rom. 6:5,
> "**For since we have been birthed** (have become) **folks engrafted and produced together** (or: planted and made to grow together; brought forth together; congenital) **in, by, to and with the result of the likeness of** (or: the effect of the similar manner from) **His death, then certainly we shall also continue existing [in and with the effects of the likeness] of The Resurrection**
> (or: which is the resurrection; or: from, and with qualities of, the resurrection)."

We have frequently cited Eph. 2:6, but I suggest that the picture here is the same as what Paul describes in 1 Thes. 4:16-17,
> "**the Lord Himself will continue habitually descending** (or: repeatedly descend) **from [the] atmosphere** (or: heaven) **within the midst of** (or: in union with) **a shout of command, within the midst of [the] Chief Agent's** (or: in union with a chief and ruling agent's) **Voice, and within the midst of** (or: in union with) **God's trumpet** [note: figure of a message or a directive for action], **and the dead people within Christ** (or: in union with an Anointing) **will continue raising themselves up first** (or: will one-after-another be standing up again in [the or their] first place). **Thereupon** (or: After that) **we, the presently living folks, the ones presently continuing to be left around, will – at the same time, together with them – proceed being seized and snatched away within clouds** (or: carried off by force, in union with clouds,) **into the midst of [the] air** (the atmosphere around us; [note: this would be in the earth's lower atmosphere, the

place where there is air]) – **into the Lord's meeting** (an encountering which is the Lord). **And thus** (in this way and manner) **shall we always continue being** (or: existing) **together with [the] Lord.**"

This picture of "**their enemies watched them**" is also a fulfillment of what was promised in 3:9, above, "**they will proceed worshiping in front of your feet and can know that I, Myself, love and accept you**," along with vs. 13b, below. Wallace considers this, along with the witnesses hearing the Voice, as, "the scene of victory; it is the apocalyptic picture of the triumph of the cause…" (ibid p 226). Terry points out that the witnesses heard the voice, but it does not say that those observing them did, and he compares this to the situation with the companions of Saul in Acts 9:7 (ibid p 374).

There is a fitting allusion, here, to Elijah's ascent into the atmosphere (2 Ki. 2:11), and an obvious allusion to their Lord's ascension in Acts 1:9, "**a cloud from underneath [Him] took and received Him** (or: He was at once hoisted on and fully lifted up, and even a cloud took Him in hand, from below)." It is a "glorification (an establishing of that which calls forth wonder and praise; an establishing of a reputation)" which aligns with what Paul wrote in Rom. 8:17b,

> "**we are continually affected by sensible experiences together – feeling together; receiving impressions, undergoing passion or suffering together – to the end that we may also be glorified together**
> > (or: can be given a shared appearance; would together receive a manifestation of that which calls forth praise; should be given a joint-approval and a joint-reputation; may be thought of and imagined together [in covenant relationship])."

This is also affirmed by 2 Tim. 2:11,
> "**You see, since we died together with [Him]** (or: For if we jointly die), **we will also continue living together** (or: proceed in jointly living; constantly co-live)."

Kaplan gave this synopsis of the Moses aspect of this passage: Moses led Israel out of Egypt and into the sea. This was Israel's corporate baptism unto the Law (1 Cor. 10:1-2), and represented their corporate death to the life that they were leaving behind. Paul uses this same baptism metaphor in Rom. 6:3-4a. When Moses led Israel out of the Red Sea, this was a figure of resurrection. In the Red Sea, Egypt died. So also, Paul instructs us in Rom. 6:4b-5 that, like Israel, we (now Jew plus Gentile, or, all of humanity, i.e., the second Humanity, 1 Cor. 15:47) have been raised up with Christ in His resurrection (each one in our own time – 1 Cor. 15:23a). Kaplan ended this with 1 Cor. 15:55, "**Where, O Death, [is] your victory** (or: overcoming)?" And so it is with Christ's "two witnesses." I suggest that what we have seen here in the Unveiling is a snap-shot of what Jesus said to His followers in Lu. 24:

> 47. **a change of mind and thinking – [proceeding, or, leading] into a flowing away of failures** (a sending away of mistakes; a forgiveness of sins; a divorcing of the situations of missing the target; an abandonment of guilt; a release from error) **– is to be proclaimed by heralds unto all the ethnic multitudes and nations** (or: the Gentiles; the non-Israelites), **beginning** (or: with folks starting) **from Jerusalem.**
> 48. "**You folks are witnesses of these things** (or: are people who can give evidence for these people).
> 49. "**And so, look and take note: I Myself am now progressively sending forth the Promise from out of the midst of, and from, My Father** (or: am out from within repeatedly sending forth My Father's promise, as an Emissary; [with other MSS: From where I now am, I now continuously send off the Promise, which is My Father]) **upon you people. So you, yourselves, sit down** (be seated) **within the City – until where** (or: which [situation] or: what [time]) **you can** (or: may) **clothe yourselves with** (or: enter within the midst of) **power and ability from out of the midst of exaltation** (or: height; elevation; perhaps: = on high).

The picture here in vs. 12 may correspond to what we read in 20:4-6, below, which ends with
> "**Blessed and happy and set-apart** (holy) **[is] the one holding** (or: having) **a divided part** (a piece) **within the first resurrection** (rising up) – **upon these the second death has no authority** (does not continue holding right or privilege; possesses nothing from the sphere of existing), **but rather, they will continue being priests belonging to God and to the Christ** (or: priests pertaining to God and the Anointed One; or: God's, even Christ's, priests; or: priests from God and Christ), **and they will continue reigning and exercising sovereign influence with Him a** [other MSS: the] **thousand years**,"

this last number being figurative, as all other numbers are in this book.

This passage has been a fulfillment of one aspect of what Jesus predicted in Lu. 21:
> 20. "**Now later, when you folks see Jerusalem being continuously surrounded by encamped armies, at that time realize and know from that experience that her desolation has drawn near and is now present.**
> 21. "**At that point, let the people in Judea progressively flee into the hill country and mountains; then let the people within the midst of her** [i.e., Jerusalem] **proceed departing out of that place, and don't let** (or: let not) **the folks in the country or the district continue coming** (or: going) **into her,**
> 22. "**because these are days of executing justice – of bringing about what is fair and right and of establishing what accords with the Way pointed out – with a view to have fulfilled all the things having been written!**
> 23. "**Tragic will be the situation for the women then being pregnant, and for the ones still nursing [babies] in those days. You see there will progressively be a great compressive force upon the Land, and inherent fervor bringing internal swelling emotion on this People.**
> 24. "**And so, folks will keep on falling by [the] mouth of a sword, and [others] will proceed being led captive into all the nations** (or: into the midst to unite with every ethnic group) – **and Jerusalem will continue being progressively trampled by and under pagans** (non-Jews; those of the nations) **until where they can** (or: should) **be fulfilled. And then there will progress being seasons of the ethnic multitudes** (or: fitting situations pertaining to the nations; or: occasions which have the qualities and characteristics of the pagans; or: fertile moments with regard to non-Jews).

Terry regarded this account about the two witnesses as concluding, "the fourfold picture of what we have entitled the second interlude (10:1-11:13)." He saw this section as picturing, "the work, power, suffering and glory of the founders of Christianity" (ibid p 374-5). He continued on to point out the use of the phrase, "in the last days," or a similar construction, found in Acts 2:17, Heb. 1:1 and 1 Pet. 1:20, as well as the statement of Heb. 9:26b,
> "**Yet now** (at this time), **once, upon a conjunction** (a joined destiny; a bringing of [two] ends together ["denoting the joining of two age-times" – E.W. Bullinger]) **of the ages, He has been and remains manifested** (has been brought to light and continues visible) **into a displacement of the failure** (from the error, sin and deviation from the target) **through the sacrifice of Himself** (or: through His sacrifice; or: by means of the sacrificial altar-offering which was Himself)." [*cf* Rom. 6:9-10]

To this we would add Heb. 9:28,
> "**so also, the Christ – being once borne** (or: carried) **close into the many** (or: being offered once unto and for the many) **to carry failures** (errors; sins mistakes; deviations; misses of the target) **back up again – will continue being made visible** (or: will be progressively seen) **forth from out of the midst of the second [place** (*cf* Heb. 9:3, 7 & 10:9; {comment: = the holy of

holies})] – **apart from failure** (apart from sin; apart from a sin offering; apart from error in attempting to hit the target) – **in those** (or: by those; to those; for those) **habitually receiving** (or: progressively taking) **from out of the midst of Him, [progressing] into a deliverance** (or: [leading] into a rescue; with a view to health and wholeness; into the midst of salvation)."

Notice the last clause of vs. 28, "**in** or **by** those **habitually receiving** from out of the midst of Him" – which refers, in part, to our two witnesses, and to His anointed body of followers ever since. Terry goes on to state that, "it is serious error of exegesis to maintain that the centuries of Christian history belong… to 'the end of the age,'" and concludes concerning this book,

"This Apocalypse depicts the end of the Old Testament cultus and the consequent beginning of the new kingdom of God among men…. Nothing is more firmly fixed in the common record of the synoptic gospels than the assertion of Jesus that the generation then living should not pass until all these things should be fulfilled" (ibid pp 375-6).

Chilton observes, "St. John draws an important parallel here… The ascension of the Witnesses is described in the same language as that of St. John's own ascension" (ibid p 284), in 4:1, 2a, above. *Cf* Ezk. 1:1b; 2:2; 3:22-24; etc. We should probably conclude that both were the same kind of ascension: into the realm of spirit. Both their death and their ascension are most likely metaphorical of the witness of the 1st century believers, as may well be 1 Cor. 15:52, which is set "**within, or in union with, the midst of the last or final trumpet**," which we encounter in vs. 15, below. We are reading a book of figurative language and symbols. But the prophecy is also timeless, for we have seen the death and resurrection of Christ's truth be repeated throughout the centuries (as has been experienced in personal situations by many of us in our own lives), and we will likely see it again, for the Prostitute continues riding the little animal (or: beast) – 17:3ff, below, and she has had many daughters.

Again, the **cloud** into which they ascend is most likely the same cloud that we saw in 10:1, above, and the same cloud experienced on the mount of transfiguration (Mk. 9:7; *et al*) where we find the same Voice, as well, along with both Moses and Elijah. In Ex. 19:9, Yahweh told Moses, "I [am] coming unto you in a thick cloud," and in vs. 16 we see that, "there were thunders and lightnings, and a thick cloud upon the mount, and the voices of the trumpet exceeding loud…" As stated above, this also might be an allusion to Elijah's ascension into the tempest (storm wind – the equivalent of a cloud) in 2 Ki. 2:11.

In line with the allusion to Moses is the part played by the "pillar of the cloud" as Israel came to the Red Sea, with the Egyptian army following after them. We see that in Ex. 14:19-20, that it went from its function of leading them and moved behind them so that it, "ultimately 'separates' Israel and Egypt in life and death….. exemplifying Yahweh's guidance and military protection as the ultimate distinction in mind between Israel and Egypt" (*Coming in the Clouds, An Evangelical Case for the Invisibility of Christ at His Second Coming*, Randall E. Otto, University Press of America, 1994 p 38). There, in vs. 20, we see where "it came between the camp of the Egyptians and the camp of Israel, and it was a cloud and darkness [to the Egyptians], but it gave light by night [to Israel]." This was part of what Moses said to Israel, "Yahweh shall fight for you, and you shall hold your peace" (14:14). In Ex. 16:10, at the time of providing them with "flesh" to eat, it records that when Israel gathered, looked toward the wilderness, "the glory of Yahweh appeared in the cloud." In 1 Ki. 8:10-11, at the dedication of Solomon's temple, "the cloud filled the House of Yahweh… the glory of Yahweh had filled Yahweh's House." With this association of the cloud with the temple, we are reminded of Jesus' words in Jn. 2:19,

"**Loosen** (or: Undo, and thus, destroy or demolish) **this Sanctuary** (Shrine; Divine Habitation; = the Temple consisting of the holy place and the holy of holies), **and within three days I will proceed to be raising it up**."

With the two witnesses being "the temple of God" (2 Cor. 6::16), this resurrection was an extended fulfillment of Jesus' prophecy. In Scripture, a cloud is usually a figure for God's presence and involvement in human affairs. It pictures heaven touching earth; the kingdom present and at hand. *Cf* the discussion of the cloud clothing in 10:1, above. There are other OT references that could be cited, as well as NT references, such as Mat. 24:30; 26:64, etc. We will see this cloud again in 14:14ff, below. But before we move on, we must at least mention the **cloud of witnesses**, in Heb. 12:1, some interpreters suggesting that this refers to the "witnesses" from those listed in Heb. 11. We will find those, again in Heb. 12:22-24 where we read of the "**Jerusalem-upon-the-heavens**," where we are,

> "**among ten-thousands** (or: myriads) **of agents and messengers** (people with a/the message): **[that is] in** (or: to) **an assembly of an entire people** (or: an assembly of all; a universal convocation) **and in** (or: to) **a summoning forth** (or: a called-out and gathered community) **of firstborn folks having been copied** (from-written, as from a pattern; or: enrolled; registered) **within [the; or: various] atmospheres** (or: heavens), **and in** (or: to; with) **God, a Judge** (an Evaluator and Decider) **of all mankind, even among** (or: to; with) **spirits of just folks** (or: breath-effects from those who are fair and equitable and in right relationship within the Way pointed out) **having been brought to the destined goal** (perfected; finished; matured; made complete), [*cf* Rev. 3:12; 21:1-2; Eph. 2:6; Phil. 3:20; Rev. 14:1-5; Ex. 4:22; Gal. 3:19] **and in** (or: to) **Jesus, a Medium** (or: an agency; an intervening substance; a middle state; one in a middle position; a go-between; an Umpire; a Mediator) **of a new and fresh** (young; recently-born) **arrangement**…"

We cited Jesus' ascension into the cloud in Acts 1:9, above, but Acts 1:11 gives a suggestive view of what this involved:

> "**This Jesus – the One being taken** (or: received; taken in hand) **back up away from you folks into the atmosphere** (or: the sky; heaven) **– will thus be periodically COMING and GOING, [in the] manner [in] which you gaze at Him progressively going His way into the atmosphere** (or: will in this way be continuing to go, [by] which [in] turning, you watched Him continue journeying into the heaven),"

My conflated rendering, "COMING and GOING" reflects the two basic means of the Greek verb, which is in the present tense, expressed here with the adverb "periodically" to contextually reflect the durative aspect of, in this case, repetitive action of the present tense.

The scene in our present verse (12) calls to mind Jesus' words in Jn. 12:

> 28. "**O Father, glorify Your Name** (bring glory and renowned reputation to your Name in a manifestation which calls forth praise)!" **Then a Voice came from out of the midst of the heaven** (or: the sky; the atmosphere): **"I both bring glory to [it], and I will continue glorifying [it] again!"**
> 29. **Hence the crowd of common folks, the [crowd] standing around and hearing [it], began to say that it had thundered. Others were saying, "A messenger** (or: An agent) **has spoken to him."**
> 30. **Jesus decidedly replied, and said, "This Voice has occurred not because of Me, but rather because of you folks** (= for your benefit).
> 31. "**At the present time is an evaluation of and a decision pertaining to** (or: a sifting of and separation for; or: a judgment from) **this System** (or: this ordered arrangement; this world; this polity, culture and religion; or: this system of control and subjugation; or: the aggregate of humanity). **Now the Ruler** (the one invested with power; the leader; the chief; the ruler; or: the Original One; The Beginning One; the Prince) **of this System will be ejected outside**
>> (or: At this time the Chief of this world of culture, religion and government, the Originator and Controlling Principle of the ordered arrangement and universe, will be thrown out, [to the] outside [of it]).

32. **"And so then I, if I should be lifted up from out of the earth, I will progressively drag** [note: drag as with, or in, a net; or: draw, as drawing water with a bucket, or a sword out of a sheath] **all mankind** (or: everyone) **to Myself."**
33. **Now He was saying this continuing to indicate, by a sign, by what sort of death He was progressively being about to be proceeding to die.**

Kaplan just reminded me of Micah 7:8, which is most appropriate here: "You must not rejoice against me, my enemy. Though I fall, I will rise; though I am sitting in darkness, Yahweh shall be light for me." A beautiful witness to His faithfulness. He further compared the cloud which led Israel through the wilderness to the Spirit leading God's sons, in Rom. 8:14. Thus, not only does the cloud represent God's presence, but it is a figure for the Holy Spirit. This calls to mind the figurative reading of Jesus' words to Nicodemus, in Jn. 3:8,

"**The Spirit** (or: Breath-effect, or, exhaled Breath; Attitude) **habitually breathes and blows where It** (or: He) **is presently intending** (willing; purposing), **and you continually hear Its** (or: His) **Voice, but yet you have not seen, and thus do not know, from what source It continuously comes, and where It progressively goes and habitually brings [things and folks] under [Its] control**."

The witnesses being agents of Christ's reign (or: kingdom), they most likely have, "**instead of and in place of the joy** (or: in the position on the opposite side from the happiness) **continuously lying before [them]** (or: lying in the forefront within [them]; lying ahead for [them]), **remained under a cross** (an execution pole for suspending a body) – **despising shame** (or: thinking nothing of [the] disgrace)," for they knew that,

"**God's kingdom** (or: the reign-and-dominion which is God; the expression, influence and activity of God's sovereignty) **is not** (or: does not exist being) **solid food and drink, but rather, eschatological deliverance into fair and equitable dealing which brings justice and right relationship in the Way pointed out** (being turned in the right direction; rightwisedness; also = covenant inclusion and participation), **peace** (and: harmony; = shalom) **and joy** (or: happiness; rejoicing) **within set-apart Breath-effect** (or: in union with and amidst a dedicated spirit and a sacred attitude; or: in [the] Holy Spirit)" (Rom. 14:17).

This may be the situation to which Jesus referred, in Mat. 24:30-31,

"**And at that time, the 'sign' which is the Son of the Man** (the Human Being; = the expected Messianic figure) **will be made progressively visible in union with heaven** (or: And then, He will be brought to light and made to shine: the Sign which is the Son with the Human qualities, centered within the midst of [the] atmosphere). **And at that point 'all the tribes of the Land** (or: earth) **will continue beating themselves** (= a figure of striking one's breast in grief and remorse; or: as when grain is being threshed; or: give themselves to wearisome toil; or: cut themselves off, as when harvesting grain),**'** [Zech. 12:10, 14] **and they will proceed in seeing for themselves 'the Son of the Man progressively coming and going, upon the clouds of the atmosphere** (or: sky),**'** [Dan. 7:13-14], **with power and ability, as well as much glory** (= many manifestations which call forth praise; an extensive good reputation)."

"**And then He will continue sending His agents** (messengers; folks with the message) **off on a mission 'with a great trumpet** (perhaps: = a large shofar; or: = a loud trumpet blast; [note: a figure of a publicly proclaimed message or instruction]),**'** [Isa. 27:13] **and they will progressively be fully** (or: additionally) **gathering together His picked out and chosen folks from out of the four winds – from [the] heavens'** (or: atmospheres') **extremities: until their farthest points** (= from the four quarters of the land, from one end of the sky to the other)**!**"

13. **And within that hour, a great shaking** (or: earthquake) **was birthed** (or: came to be; occurred) **and the tenth of The City fell** (or: collapsed), **and seven thousand names of humans** (= people) **were killed within the shaking** (quake), **and the remaining ones** (= survivors) **came to be terrified – and so they gave glory to the God of the heaven** (or: atmosphere; sky).

The phrase, "**within that hour**," shows that there is a direct correlation between the resurrection of Christ's witnesses and a shake-up of **The City**. Terry suggests that this is "The hour of the triumph of the witnesses, the last lingering hour of the sixth trumpet..." (ibid p 376). John referred to this hour in 1 Jn. 2:18,

> "**O undeveloped ones or folks of the age to be educated** (or: servants, little boys and little girls who might be hit in training and for discipline), **it continues being** (or: is progressively) **a last hour** (= an *eschaton* of the Day, or the closing moment [of the age]), **and according as you hear** (or: heard) **that an antichrist** (or: anti-anointing; that which is instead of, or in the place of, Christ or the Anointing) **repeatedly comes, even now many anti-anointings** (or: antichrists; many things or people taking the place of Christ or stand in opposition to the Anointing) **have been born and are here** (or: have come into existence and are at large), **from which fact** (or: whence) **we constantly know by experience that it continues being a last hour** (= a closing moment [of the age])."

This first spoke to what would soon come to historical Jerusalem in AD 70 – its political and economic destruction. But the metaphorical shaking of the old covenant religion (symbolized by "The City") is the main message. We saw this in the metaphorical shaking of the fig tree in 6:13. This was spoken of in Heb. 12:26-28a,

> "**Yet now it has been promised** (or: He has promised for Himself), **saying,**
>
> > '**Still once [more; or: for all] I am shaking not only the land** (or: earth), **but also the heaven** (or: atmosphere; sky).' [Hag. 2:6; Ex. 19:18; Joel 3:16-17]
>
> **Now the 'Still once [more; or: for all]' constantly points to and makes clearly visible the transposition** (transference; changeover; change of setting or place) **of the things being repeatedly shaken, to the end that the things not being repeatedly** (or: continuously) **shaken may remain.** [*cf* 2 Cor. 3:7-13] **Therefore** (or: Because of which), **continuously taking to our sides** (or: progressively receiving alongside) **an unshaken Reign** (or: Kingdom; Sovereign influence), **we are constantly holding grace and joyous favor**…"

D'Aragon comments that the "earthquake," is, "A symbol often used by the prophets for social or spiritual upheavals" (ibid p 481). *Cf* Isa. 2:19; Joel 2:10; Amos 8:8; Hag. 2:6; Mk. 13:8; and see 6:12, above.

Keep in mind that what was historical, and what spoke of a corporate shaking of people and systems, also has an individual application. God does bring shaking events into our individual bodies, our families, our social relationships, our economic situations and the political environments that influence our lives. Both literal earthquakes and literal storms can turn our lives upside down, or even cut them short. Amidst all of this we should take as our example **the remaining ones** (= survivors) of our present verse: "**they gave glory to the God of the heaven** (or: atmosphere; sky)," after coming to be **terrified** from all that had just happened. We should also see that this is the INTENT of all the "shakings." Considering that these folks, being mostly Jews, would have been familiar with the wisdom of their writings, where it says, "The fear of Yahweh [is the] beginning of knowledge" (Prov. 1:7), this should not surprise us. Terry comments that, "there is a notable change from the picture presented in 9:20-21" (ibid p 376). He compares it to the Roman centurion's response in Mat. 27:54. Beale (ibid p 603) points out a potential analogy with Nebuchadnezzar in Dan. 4:34, after having his "understanding/reason returned" to him following the judgment of 7 seasons of living like an animal of the field, where he was prompted to, "bless the Most High (the Supreme – CVOT)." The Old Greek reads, here, "Praise the Lord, God of heaven,"

(NETS), and the LXX, reads, "I… praise, greatly exalt and glorify the King of heaven." The phrase, "**the God of the heaven**," is normally used in the OT to express His sovereignty (e.g., Gen. 24:7).

When the witnesses are revived and take a stand, great fear fell upon "the observers." Our enemies may quake at our resurrection. Great shakings can be good! The result is a tithe of the City falls (of what else is 1/10th significant?). On the personal level, 1000 symbolizes our innermost being, our "holy of holies." 7 = fullness or completion. The old man of the heart has been totally killed by the shaking of our city. Everything that is left within us gives "**glory to the God of the atmosphere** (or: heaven)." On the corporate level, this symbolizes the total eradication of the presence, influence and rule of the flesh that has been targeted (the tenth of the city), i.e., anything produced by man and not God. Chilton notes that those that died here are, "the exact reverse of the situation in Elijah's day (1 Ki. 19:18)… 7 thousand remained faithful to the covenant" (ibid p 285). Here, this may represent a death of some aspect of the first Adam, or the removal of the old covenant thinking in our lives – just as the destruction of the 1st century temple ended the old covenant cultus from the Jewish community, and from those of Christ's followers who were trying to mix the old into the new. Remember: the setting of this apocalyptic scene is the set-apart City, which had come to be identified with blasphemous names, names of the world's centers of domination and corruption (Sodom, Egypt, and then, Babylon, below).

Wallace, taking the preterist view, sees the quake and the fractional part falling as meaning, "that the city and state and commonwealth of the Jews had come to an end," and with it representing one of Rome's ten provinces, "the part was put for the whole – Jerusalem representing Palestine… fell" (ibid p 227). He also interprets the 7 thousand "as a symbol of the perfect and complete," being a figure of, "the destruction of the Jewish commonwealth." Thus, we can find here an allusion to Isa. 29, prophesying the judgment of "the city [where] David dwelt." In that chapter **God** said, "**I will camp against you round about and will lay siege against you…. the multitude of your strangers shall be like small dust…. You will be visited by Yahweh of hosts with thunder, and with earthquake, and great noise, with storm and tempest, and the flame of devouring fire**" (vss. 3-6). The poetic language of Isa. 24:19-29 is quite picturesque:

> "The Land is utterly broken down; the Land is completely dissolved; the Land is moved exceedingly. The Land shall reel to and fro like a drunkard, and shall be removed like a cottage. Its transgression shall be heavy upon it; it shall fall and not rise again."

Then, in Ezk. 38:10-20 we read: "In that Day there shall be a great shaking in the Land of Israel…. the Land shall shake **at My presence**… and every wall shall fall to the ground." All this began happening at the death of Jesus, when He "**dismissed the Spirit**" (Mat. 27:50). In the following verse we find the curtain (veil) of the temple was torn and split in two, from top to bottom, "**and the ground was caused to shake** (or: the earth quaked) **and rock masses were split**" (vs. 51). There is another shaking in vs. 19b, below.

Here John finally sees the last **trumpet** being sounded. Is this merely the final one of the seven trumpets of this vision, or is the 7th trumpet the one which Paul referred to in 1 Cor. 15:52, "**within the midst of an instant** (or: in union with what is uncut and indivisible), **in a rapid sweep or blink of an eye, within, or in union with, the midst of the last or final trumpet**"? Many say no. But here Paul was speaking of not all sleeping (= dying) in vs. 51, then in the end of vs. 52 he says, "**And so we ourselves will keep on, one-after-another being changed** (or: progressively be made otherwise, altered and transformed)." Unpacking Paul's passage quoted above, 1 Thes. 4:14-17, we see where Paul speaks of those who did fall asleep, and "**we, the PRESENTLY living folks, the ones presently continuing to be left around**," (and thus, are not sleeping – vs. 15); this same scene is depicted here, in this passage of the Unveiling. There, in vs. 16, the Lord is descending from heaven (the atmosphere), "**within the midst of [the] Chief Agent's** (or: in union with an original messenger's or a chief and ruling agent's) **voice, and within the midst of** (or: in union with) **God's trumpet** [note: figure of a message or a directive for action], **and the**

dead people within Christ (or: in union with [the] Anointed One) **will continue raising themselves up first** (or: will one-after-another be standing up again in [the or their] first place)." Then, he continues on in vs. 17,

> "**we, the presently living folks… will – at the same time, together with them – proceed being seized and snatched away within clouds** (or: carried off by force, in union with clouds,) **into the midst of [the] air** (the air that we breathe in; the mist; the haze; the atmosphere around us; [note: this would be in the earth's lower atmosphere, the place where there is air]) **– into the Lord's meeting** (an encountering which is the Lord). **And thus** (in this way and such a manner) **shall we always continue being** (or: continue existing at all times) **together with [the] Lord**."

In both of these passages there is God's **Voice**, and His people are raised up into a **cloud**. Recall the picture of the glorified Christ **descending** in 10:1, above. We will later see the heavenly Jerusalem **descending** out of heaven (21:10, below). In this picture we see "His kingdom **having come**." (In vss. 11-12, above, we saw "the dead in Christ" arise!) This book is to the called-out, covenant communities, and is specifically about what they were experiencing, at that time (in the 1st century) and ever since, and about the things in which His communities will yet be involved. This is the 7th trumpet, the fulfillment of the messages: the kingdom of the world (the reigning of the governments, cultures, religions and societies of the ordered System) belongs to and is ruled by Yahweh – and more, as we will see in vs. 15, below!

Upon reflecting on the topic of the two witnesses in our present passage, Dan Kaplan shared with me the similarities that he observes between this picture and the one that is given to us in Gen. 37-47, the relationships and interactions between Joseph and his brothers, and the story that lands them all in Egypt. Between there and here is the story of Jesus, about whom we would point back to the envy which the scribes, priests and Pharisees exhibited, in the Gospel witnesses. For brevity, I will cite just one example: Mat. 27:18, "[Pilate] **had seen and was now aware that they** [the Jewish leadership] **committed Him** (or: handed Him over; surrendered Him; delivered Him up) **because of envy**." This was the root issue that Joseph's brothers had with him, and why they determined to get rid of him. His brothers were emotionally pained and tested because of the preference and special love which Jacob had given to Joseph. We suggest that the envy toward Christ had been transferred to His witnesses, and so – as with Joseph, and then with Jesus – they tried to get rid of this frustrating irritation that came at them through the fiery words of the two witnesses (Christ's prophetic body in Jerusalem). Thus, enter (stage left) the little wild animal (the beast – Rome?) that was able to do the job for them. And, like Joseph being figuratively killed (thrown in a pit: symbolic of a grave) and "**with a garment having been dipped in blood**" (Gen. 37:21; Rev. 19:13, below), Jesus was delivered into Roman hands to be killed (then placed in a grave), as Joseph was sold into Egypt, ending up in a prison cell.

And now consider the parallels of the final stories of these three:
  a) Joseph was raised from a figurative death to be in charge of a kingdom of the world and a blessing to Israel and to the nations. He "**loved [his] enemies** (urging toward reunion with, and accepting as persons standing on the same ground, those folks hostile to [him]), **and [he was] habitually praying goodness over the people continuously persecuting [him]** (constantly thinking and speaking on behalf of the folks repeatedly pursuing [him] to have ease and well-being)" (Mat. 5:44).
  b) Jesus was raised to God's throne and is in charge of God's kingdom, **forgiving His murders** and becoming a blessing to **the new combined humanity** of Gentile joined to Jew (Rom. 11:17; Eph. 2:15).
  c) Joseph forgave his brothers, telling them that "God sent me before you to preserve life…. To preserve you a posterity in the Land, and to save your lives by a great deliverance. So [it was] not you [that] sent me here, but God: and He has made me a father to Pharaoh and lord of all his

house, and a ruler throughout all of the land of Egypt." (Gen. 45:5b-8). In Gen. 50:20-21, Joseph said to his brothers, "you thought evil against me; God meant it unto good.... I will nourish you and your little ones. And then he comforted them and spoke kindly to them."

d) The two witnesses are raised up into the heaven (where, as overcomers, they reign with Christ). What do you suppose was their response to those who murdered them, and to those who rejoiced when it happened?

In Joseph's story, the "**woe**" was first for him, and later for his brothers (in their experiencing first the testing, and then remorse, along with having their sin exposed), when he confronted them. Kaplan also pointed to the interesting fact that Joseph later buried his father, Jacob, and then it was another Joseph who buried Jesus. The Scriptures are full of subtle analogies that can make themselves known to us, as we meditate upon them (Ps. 1:2).

We mentioned, above, how Stephen responded in regard to his murderers, after having given a testimony (witness) of Israel's history to them, and then being a witness that indicted them with the murder of Jesus (Acts 7): he essentially forgave them, asking the Lord not to lay that sin to their charge (vs. 60). Within that generation the Jewish leadership sponsored (e.g., with Saul and his cohorts) the continued killing of more of Christ's witnesses, including Peter, Paul and other of the sent-forth folks. Our story here, in 11:3-13, above, points both backward and forward. It has spoken to others who have been His "two witnesses" ever since. Kaplan ended his comments by citing Ps. 34:19,

"The pressures, squeezings, tribulations, ordeals and afflictions of the just folks (the righteous ones; those in the Path pointed out) [are] many, and yet the Lord will continue rescuing them (or: dragging them from danger) from out of the midst of all of them" (LXX, JM).

Barclay observes:
"The great interest of this passage lies in the fact that the unbelievers were won by the sacrificial death of the witnesses and by God's vindication of them. Here is the story of the Cross and of the Resurrection all over again. Evil must be conquered and men won, not by force but by the acceptance of suffering for the name of Christ" (ibid p 72).

14. The second woe departed (or: tragedy went away). **Consider! The third woe is progressively coming swiftly.**

This ends the second woe. Do you think that the three woes could correspond to the spirit, the soul and the body, for individuals? For the church of the 1st century, the three woes would have foretold three aspects of God's judgment on Jerusalem. Wallace suggests that, "The *woes* symbolize this devastation as a series of occurrences, executed in succession" (ibid p 226). This would fit the preterist view.

The phrase "**coming swiftly**" tells us that whenever God determines to invade history, there is usually a "suddenly." It can happen like a tornado, an earthquake or a hurricane. We find the third woe in 12:12, below.

15. Next the seventh agent sounded a trumpet, and great (or: loud) **voices of themselves came to be** (birthed themselves; occurred of themselves) **within the sky** (or: atmosphere; heaven), **continuously saying, "The reign of the dominating, ordered System** (of the world of religion, culture, government and economy; or: of the realm of the religious and secular; or: of the aggregate of humanity) **suddenly came to belong to our Lord** [= Yahweh or Christ] **and to the anointed of Him**

(or: The kingdom of the arranged system of our Lord and His Christ has come into existence; The sovereign influence pertaining to the aggregate of humanity, which belongs to our Lord and His

Christ, is birthed!; The rule as King, concerning the world, has come to be the possession of, and now has reference to, [Yahweh], as well as of, and to, His Anointed),
and so He will continue reigning (ruling as King) **on into the ages** (or: indefinite time periods) **of the ages** [other MSS add: So it is (Amen)]."

The **7th trumpet** is the last message: Christ, and His Lordship, which is what the "**great voices**" were "**continuously saying**." These were the voices of those who had been, "**jointly roused and raised up, and caused to sit** (= to be enthroned) **together within the things situated upon** [thus, above] **the heavens**" (Eph. 2:6) – they are the voices of the called-out and sent forth folks of the 1st century, and this is the message that they were proclaiming: "Christ rules! Jesus is Lord!" We will discuss this saying, and its parenthetical, optional renderings, below. It is the continued witness of those who were slain by the little animal (beast), in vs. 7, above, and vss. 11-12 describe what Paul stated in Eph. 2:6. We read a parallel statement in 12:10a, below, showing that these passages speak of the same Christ-event, from different viewpoints:

> "**Then I heard a great** (or: loud) **voice within the atmosphere** (or: sky; or: heaven) **repeatedly saying, "At the present moment** (or: Just now) **the deliverance** (the rescue; the return to the original state and condition; the health and wholeness; the salvation), **and the power** (or: ability), **and the kingdom** (or: reign; sovereign activities) **of our God was** (or: is) **birthed** (comes into existence; came to be), **also the authority** (privilege from Being) **of His Anointed** (or: which is His Christ; from His [Messiah])…"

This apocalyptic picture could also be referring to the situation of which Jesus spoke, in Mat. 24:31,

> "**And then He will continue sending His agents** (messengers; folks with the message) **off on a mission 'with a great trumpet** (= a loud trumpet blast; [note: a figure of a publicly proclaimed message or instruction]),' [Isa. 27:13] **and they will progressively be fully** (or: additionally) **gathering together His picked out and chosen folks from out of the four winds – from [the] heavens'** (or: atmospheres') **extremities: until their farthest points** (= from the four quarters of the land, from one end of the sky to the other)!"

The message quoted in the second half of this verse is the same message preached and taught by Christ's followers from the Day of Pentecost (Acts 2), on. This **gathering** began on the Day of Pentecost, and was continuing on through to the time of John's writing this book, and it has continued ever since, as Christ continues calling His firstfruits up into the cloud, or into His reign, by the message going into the four winds of our atmospheres – even to the farthest points. This message is still being proclaimed by those who have been brought to the figurative Mount Zion (Heb. 12:22, cited above). These are pictures of our present existence "in Christ."

This announcement was presented to John as an allusion to Dan. 7:13-14,

> "I was watching, within the midst of the night visions, and – consider this! – One as it were a Son of man (a Human), progressively coming with the clouds of the sky (or: heaven). And He came as far as the Ancient One of (or: from; pertaining to) the days, and He was brought face-to-face with Him. And now, the position of being in first place (the headship and the beginning rule; the dominion) was given to Him, along with the honor and sovereign influence (reign; kingship). Then all the peoples, tribe and language groups will continue performing as slaves to and for Him. His privilege out of Being (His right and authority) [is] a life-long privilege (an eonian or age-lasting authority of right) which shall not pass away, and His sovereign influence (reign; kingship) shall not be spoiled, ruined or caused to be lost by miscarriage or premature birth, throughout [its realm and sphere of influence]" (LXX, JM).

Gabriel's announcement to Mary, concerning Jesus in Lu. 1:32-33, seems to confirm that this passage in Daniel applied to Him:

> "**This One will proceed in being great** (or: a great One), **and He will continue being called 'Son of [the] Most High'** (or: a son of [the] Highest One), **and [the] Lord** [= Yahweh] **will proceed giving to Him the throne of David, His father** (= forefather; ancestor), **and He will continue reigning upon the house of Jacob – on into the ages. Furthermore, there will not proceed being an end of His reign** (or: sovereign influence and activity; kingdom; kingship)."

Verse 15, here, also echoes Dan. 2:34-35; 44-45. There, the head of gold is a figure of the Babylonian empire (vs. 38; *cf* Jer. 51:7); the silver chest/arms is the Medo-Persian empire; the bronze belly and thighs represent the Greek empire; the iron legs and feet speak of the Roman empire. Now views regarding the 4th kingdom vary, but the narrative seems to indicate an unbroken sequence of world powers, beginning with Nebuchadnezzar, until something "supernatural" occurs in vs. 34f, "till a stone severs itself, that is, not by hands." This language speaks of an act of God. We find that this Rock (or, Stone that the builders rejected) struck the statue on its feet (the 4th empire), and this act destroys the entire statue (successive systems of dominance). The fact that 4 empires appear as the visionary statue speaks to their world (four-directional) dominance. Thus, lesser historical kingdoms are not in view.

We may also hear another echo, here, from Obad. 21,
> "Then saviors (deliverers) will come up on Mount Zion to judge Mount Esau, and the kingdom will become Yahweh's."

The last clause of this verse, in the LXX has "the Lord" in the dative case, so it could read, "the sovereign influence (reign; kingship) will continue being by the Lord (or: for the Lord; in the Lord; with the Lord)." Micah 4:7b adds another witness: "And Yahweh will reign over them in Mount Zion, from henceforth on into the Age [of the Messiah]." We will reference Micah 4, again, and we find Zion playing a role in our story, in 14:1, below. Other OT allusions to God's/Christ's reign/kingdom abound. A NT verse that quotes Ps. 45:6-7 instructs us further:

> "**God [is] Your throne, on into the age of the Age, and the scepter of straightness [is] a scepter of His kingdom and sovereign activity**.
> (variant rendering, with other MSS: "Your throne, O God, and the staff of uprightness, [is the] staff of Your reign, unto the chief time period of the Age.)
> **You love and urge toward union with** (fully give Yourself to) **fairness and equity in rightwised [covenant] relationships within the Way pointed out** (or: justice; righteousness) **and yet you hate and detach from lawlessness. Because of this, God – Your God – anointed You with olive oil of extreme joy, at the side of** (or: = more than; = rather than) **Your partners** (or: associates; fellows)" (Heb. 1:8-9).

Now the first three kingdoms were already history, but vs. 35 says that the iron, the clay, the bronze, the silver and the gold were "broken to pieces at the same time," (NIV); "broken small together," (Young); "Then pulverized, as one," (CVOT); "broken in pieces at once," (Rotherham). Thus, this prophecy must have a significance other than something physical. The work of the "stone" is Christ,

> "**nailing it to the cross** (or: on the execution stake) **after Himself causing the sinking out and away of** (or: stripping off and away [of power and abilities]; putting off and laying away [of categories and classifications]; or: divesting Himself of) **the governments and the authorities** (or: the ruling and privileged folks or people of primacy). **And then He made a public exhibit, in a citizen's bold freedom of speaking the truth, leading them in a triumphal procession within it [i.e., the cross/suspension-pole]**" (Col. 2:15).

Recall 1:5, above, "**Jesus Christ.... the Ruler** (or: Prince; Leader, Beginner; Originator; One in first place) **of the kings of the earth**." The advent of the Anointed One and His work of the cross was the stone that smashed the power of the kingdoms of the world, and established the Kingdom of God within. Note in Dan. 2:35 that this Stone "became a huge mountain and filled the whole earth." The kingdom, reign and sovereign influence began as a stone and grew to become a huge mountain! This calls to mind the picture given in Isa. 9:7, "Of the increase of dominion (chieftainship – CVOT) and of prosperity (well-being – CVOT) there shall be no end" (Rotherham). The LXX reads: "**His position of being in first place** (the headship and the beginning rule; the dominion) **[will be] great, and of His peace from the joining, there is no boundary or limit**" (JM). This verse speaks of the throne of David and his kingdom, but these were a type of Christ and His reign within us, and His sovereign influence among us.

In Dan. 2:44 we see that God's kingdom crushes the kingdoms of the world, just as the **God of peace and joining**, through His body, crushes the adversarial spirit (*satan*) of those kingdoms under their feet (i.e., by the way they live, in their daily lives), (Rom. 16:20). Thus have we seen the call to be "overcomers," or, "conquerors," or, "victors." It was not the people or the kings of those kingdoms, but the carnal nature, the old humanity (1st Adam), the estranged aspect of the self in them, the adversarial spirit, that has to be crushed. And this is the work of Christ. But recall that Acts 1:1 speaks "**concerning everything** (or: about all the things) **which Jesus both BEGAN to continuously DO** (or: started to progressively make or construct) **and to habitually and progressively TEACH**." Remember also that He said to His disciples,

> "**It is certainly true, I am saying to you folks, the person habitually trusting and progressively believing into Me, the works** (actions; deeds) **which I Myself am constantly doing** (habitually performing; progressively making, constructing, creating, forming) **that one also will proceed doing** (performing; making; creating),..." (John 14:12).

Since the final of the three main feasts of Israel happened in the seventh month (Lev. 23:34), being the Feast of Tabernacles – could we say "the Feast of Tents," or "the Feast of His mobile Temple, His body"? – there is a symbolic connection with this 7th trumpet. The Day of Atonement, the second part of this Feast, involved TWO kids of the goats. One was sacrificed, the other – the scapegoat – bore the failures, iniquities and sins of Israel away from the camp and into the wilderness (Lev. 16). How Christ fulfilled this is discussed in Heb. 9 (for comments on that chapter, see, *John, Judah, Paul and ?, comments on First John, Second John, Third John, Judah (Jude), Hebrews, Galatians*, Harper Brown Pub., 2013 p 160ff).

Other roots of Rev. 11 are in the following:
> In Josh. 6:4, "Have seven priests carry trumpets [note that would be 7 trumpets]... On the 7th day march around the city 7 times with the priests blowing the trumpets." It was with the blowing of the trumpets that "the kingdom of Canaan" began to become the kingdom of the Lord's anointed people.
> Num. 10:2 says, "Make two [the number of witness] trumpets of hammered silver and use them for calling the community together, and for having the camps set out."
> In Lev. 25:9-10, "Then you will make the trumpet blast pass over all your land in the 7th month.... On the day of propitiatory shelters you shall make the trumpet pass in all your land. And you will hallow the year, the fiftieth year, and proclaim liberty in the land.... A jubilee year..."

Having discussed allusions and associations with regard to the first, bold rendering of the proclamation, let us now examine the notable optional renderings, and their implications:
> a) "The kingdom of the arranged system of our Lord and His Christ has come into existence."

This would speak of the arrival of God's kingdom, by reading the Greek genitive phrases "of our Lord and His Christ," as modifying the phrase "of the arranged system (*kosmos*)" which in turn modifies the subject, "kingdom." The "kingdom of the arranged system" is another way of saying, "the ordered reign," and it is the "arranged system" of how our Lord and His Christ both function and express sovereign influence – in the universe, and with/among/over people.

b) "The sovereign influence pertaining to the aggregate of humanity, which belongs to our Lord and His Christ, is birthed!" This would put the emphasis on the BIRTH of God's sovereign influence, as it pertains to the aggregate of humanity – in a way that corresponds to the new, unified humanity (Eph. 2:15), where there are no more cultural, race, class or gender differences in His new economy. Notice, also, that "the aggregate of humanity" can be read as "belonging to our Lord and His Christ."

c) "The rule as King, concerning the world, has come to be the possession of, and now has reference to, [Yahweh], as well as of, and to, His Anointed." This would be more in line with the bold rendering, except it expresses the genitive phrase (*tou kosmou*) as, "concerning the world," instead of, "**of the dominating, ordered System**," this latter expressing the character of human kingdoms and empires. This rendering also expresses the change in focus of God's rule, which now is not just focused on His symbolic example – Israel – but points to His possession of the world which now, in turn, has a new reference to Yahweh, through the advent of the Christ event.

We have presented the options for the somewhat ambiguous ending-phrase, first rendered: **our Lord** [= Yahweh or Christ] **and to the anointed of Him**. Scholars debate "Who is Who," here. We suggest that it can refer either to Yahweh and His Messiah, or to Christ and His anointed body. Both views are legitimate, here, both being true. The beauty is that we don't have to choose one rendering over the rest, but can simply meditate upon the nuances expressed by each one, as we realize that God is, and at the same time is becoming, All in all.

Hiett comments, "The seven trumpets comprise the seventh seal. At the seventh trumpet that great scroll from the throne of God is now entirely open" (ibid p 147). D'Aragon points to the verb being in the singular, in the last phrase, "**so He will continue reigning**," and comments: "The singular shows that the reign of God and that of Christ are one and the same" (ibid p 481). Zahnd cogently points us to the fulfillment of what Jesus told his disciples to pray for in Mat. 6:10a (*Sinners*, ibid p 186).

16. **Then the twenty-four elders** (or: old people) – **the people continuously sitting upon their thrones before** (or: in the presence of) **God – fell** (or: at once fall) **upon their faces and worshiped** (or: do obeisance to; began to worship in) **God,**

This verse brings us back to the throne scene of chapter 4, and our attention is called to "the universal church," to use Malcolm Smith's term, sitting upon their thrones. Note how they are "ruling and reigning with Christ": they show honor, reverence and deference to God (i.e., did obeisance, which was the oriental custom of the times)! They continuously give Him thanks and they acknowledge who He is and what He has done (vs. 17, below). He is the One who really reigns. He is the Head: the Alpha and the Omega. It might also suggest an end to hierarchal systems of sub-rulers: they leave their thrones as all people become, one-after-another, joined directly to the Vine, and each person is "led by the Spirit" (Rom. 8:14), being mature children (symbolized by the term "son," in the old patriarchal kinship system of biblical times).

17. **repeatedly saying, "We are continuously grateful** (thankful) **for You** (or: habitually give You thanks; repeatedly express the Goodness of Grace in You), **Lord** [= Yahweh] **God, the One of All Strength** (the Almighty/Omnipotent One), **the One continuously existing** (or: being), **even the One Who was continuously existing**, **because You have taken – so that You have in Your hand – Your great power and ability, and You reign** (or: began to rule as King by exercising sovereign influence)."

The personal pronoun, **You**, is in the dative case, and is the indirect object of the verb, **grateful/thankful**. The first parenthetical rendering is the more common English phrase, "we continuously give You thanks," which more formally would mean, "we give thanks TO You." These both say the same thing, in rendering the Greek. But a subtle nuance comes out which can express an even greater, heartfelt expression: that of gratitude that comes with insight and understanding of just what someone has done for us. Thus did I render the dative personal pronoun, "**for You**." It shows thankfulness for Who God really is, as well as for what He has done. It says that we are grateful to have Him as our God. It is saying, "we SEE You." The last option given for this phrase, "repeatedly express the Goodness of Grace IN You," has on offer the literal meaning from the Greek elements of the verb, *eucharisteō*, whose stem is *charis*, "Grace." The prefix, *eu-*, means "Goodness," ease and well-being. Here I rendered the personal pronoun in its "location" function, thus, "IN You."

The present tense of the verb shows that this is a constant way of life. The more normal description of God, as seen in 1:8, above, "**the One continuously being, even the One Who was and continued being, and the One presently and continuously** (or: progressively) **coming and going, the Almighty**," is changed, here. The picture of "coming and going" is missing – because the message of the new creation is His constant presence. The *parousia* came at Pentecost, and He never left – He just entered the "cloud" realm: a figure of the realm of spirit. He refers to the potential of His coming to the communities (chapters 2 and 3) in judgment, and we perceive that He came in judgment on Jerusalem, through the Roman army, in AD 66-70. But His presence never left creation or the covenant communities. Here, also, the emphasis is on His Strength (listed first in His description), and His continuous existence.

So the gathered communities (figured by the 24 elders) express their gratitude for Who He is, acknowledge His constant existence and strength, and then affirm why they are aware of all of this: **You have taken – so that You have in Your hand – Your great power and ability, and You reign**. What comfort; what confidence; and what peace this brings. Notice the rendering of the verb: have taken… have in Your hand. It is in the perfect tense (the action was done and completed in the past), with the results of the completed action carrying on into the present (have in… hand). The action happened at Christ's ascension, when He received (took in hand) the reign from "the Ancient of Days." What happened in AD 70 was merely evidence of what Jesus said after His resurrection (Mat. 28:18).

The scene is, once again, a symbol – which is an allusion to the ancient councils that would surround kings in their throne rooms. The picture here is that all authority belongs to Christ (Mat. 28:18). We saw in 4:10b, above, where they were acknowledging that their own victories were due to His Victory, by "**casting their wreaths** (symbols of victory or celebration) **before the throne**." There, that symbolic action was showing acknowledgement of God being the Creator – both of the original creation, and of the new creation. Here, in vs. 17, it is acknowledging His taking an active role in **reigning**, in His **power and ability**.

18. **Now the multitudes** (ethnic groups; nations) **were made angry** (became enraged; began to swell in passion; were gradually aroused and made impulsive) [Ps. 2:1], **and Your inherent fervor** (swelling arousal; impulse; wrath; anger; indignation; natural bent) **came** (or: comes; or: went), **and the season** (fitting situation; suitable circumstances; fertile moment) **for the dead folks to be sifted, separated, evaluated, decided about and judged, and then to give the wages** (or: reward) **to Your slaves: to the prophets and to the set-apart people, and to the ones continuously fearing Your Name – to the small** (= insignificant) **ones and to the great** (= important) **ones – and then to at once thoroughly spoil** (or: bring ruin throughout; cause decay through the midst; utterly destroy) **the folks continuously corrupting** (thoroughly spoiling, ruining, destroying and decaying) **the Land** (or: earth; soil).

What is the significance of this verse, where the multitudes are **made angry** (etc.)? Is this a response to, and then a result of, the world's kingdom becoming the Lord's, in vs. 15? Or was this just their natural, estranged state of being? Whichever, we see that God's inherent fervor also came, or it went (the verb means either one, and is in the "timeless" aorist tense). This is an echo of Ps. 2:1-9. The anger of the multitudes is also the result of their being subjected to vanity (Rom. 8:20). Furthermore,

> "**God's personal emotion and inherent fervor** (teeming passion and swelling desire; mental bent and natural impulse; propensity and disposition; or: anger, wrath and indignation) **is continuously remaining** (is now habitually dwelling and abiding) **upon**" the "**person now continuing being unpersuaded by the Son** (or: presently being constantly incompliant, disobedient or disbelieving to the Son; being repeatedly stubborn toward the Son)" (Jn. 3:36).

So is vs. 18 referring to that which has already happened and thus now exists, or is this in reference to a future event (viewed as past, or present, within this vision)? When His rule comes into our world, it does often make us (our flesh) angry and impulsive. Then His anger and impulse separates us for His decisions – often letting us reap our harvests (or, our wages). So in this scene we can see both the micro-cosmic view and the macro-cosmic view of what is, and of what will more fully be, as He deems necessary. There is no end to God's judgments, because they are His "course-correcting decisions" that are made on our behalf. He is ultimately "for us," but when His processes of transformation need to invade our path, He will momentarily be "against us." We see this characteristic in Isa. 54:8,

> "In effervescent wrath I concealed My face momentarily from you, yet with eonian benignity I have compassion on you" (CVOT). Rotherham reads: "In an overflow of vexation I hid My face for a moment…But with lovingkindness age-abiding have I had compassion on you."

Another witness is Isa. 60:10,

> "For in My vexation I smote you, but in My favor have I had compassion upon you" (Rotherham).

In the last part of this verse we have an example of sowing and reaping. Those who are continuously **spoiling the land** (or: the earth; or: = their own bodies) receive that which they have planted, as a harvest, upon themselves. But here, let us bring to the table what Paul said about sowing:

> "**God is not one to be sneered at** (to have a nose turned up at; to be scorned, mocked or treated like a fool), **for 'whatever a person is in the habit of sowing, this also he will reap,' because the person continually sowing into the flesh of himself** (= his estranged inner being), **will progressively reap corruption** (spoil; ruin; decay) **forth from out of the flesh** (= the estranged inner being);
>
> > (or: the one habitually sowing into the flesh [system], of himself will continue to reap decay from out of the flesh [system];)
>
> **yet the one constantly sowing into the spirit** (or: the Breath) **will be progressively reaping eonian life** (life having the characteristics of the Age [of Messiah]; or: life from the Age that lasts on through the ages) **forth from out of the spirit** (or: the Spirit; the Breath; that attitude)" (Gal. 6:7-8).

Now observe the sowing into the flesh realm: the reaping does not come from some other realm, but from this very SAME flesh realm – however one interprets the term, "flesh," (of which two interpretive examples are on offer in this verse: one's own "estranged inner being," or "the flesh [systems]" of religion or culture). This is not talking about an "after-death" reaping, but of a reaping right here in this life – as we can so easily observer abounding around us. The religious and cultural "broad-ways" continuously lead to ruined lives (Mat. 7:13).

Recall that Jesus said, in Jn. 12:31a,

> "**At the present time** (or: Now) **is an evaluation of and a decision pertaining to** (or: a sifting of and separation for; or: a judgment from) **this System** (or: this ordered arrangement; this world; this polity, culture and religion; or: this system of control and subjugation; or: the aggregate of humanity)."

It is only traditional eschatology that ASSUMES that these verses speak of some final judgment at some SUPPOSED end of human history. As Porgy said in the musical, "It ain't necessarily so..." The entire history of Israel speaks of judgment that came in their lives. After-death theories of retribution only came about when it seemed that there was no justice in this life (e.g., with the death of the Maccabees). They were inventions from human reasoning. Much speculation has been added to Heb. 9:27, but a literal and expanded rendering of the terms used can present a view that is different from tradition:

> "**And now, according to as much as it continues lying-away** (or: laid away; reserved-off; stored) **in** (or: with; for; to) **mankind** (or: people) **to die-away once, but after this a process of evaluating** (a separating and making a distinction to be a judging and determining; a deciding)."

"Evaluating and deciding" gives a different nuance than the emotionally-freighted term "judgment," as it is normally used in post-eschatological, or post-mortem, scenarios. Even the "decision" made about the "sheep and the goats" of Mat. 25, can have an AD 70 interpretation. The Jewish leadership was "cut off" from kingdom activities, while the disciples (sheep) moved right into the book of Acts. As in John 3:36, quoted above, we can look around and see the results of His decisions abounding even today. He has always meted out His judgments line upon line, age upon age. Thus do we constantly see His wrath "remaining; abiding." We can look to what happened to Israel (which things happened to them for us): He laid out the pattern in them. But, one might ask, what about the phrasing, "**the season** (fitting situation; suitable circumstances; fertile moment) **for the dead folks to be sifted, separated, evaluated, decided about and judged, and then to give the wages** (or: reward) **to Your slaves**"?

First of all, notice that John did not use the word "time (*chronos*)," but rather the word *kairos*, which primarily means "a season," (as in a particular time of the year), or "a fitting situation or suitable circumstances," or, as with animal husbandry, "a fertile moment." He was not referring to some imagined "end of time." Such seasons happened periodically, in Israel's history. The time for the **giving of wages** happened when a day's work was done in the parable of the day-workers (Mat. 20:1-16). This was indeed an "appointed period," as were Israel's appointed feasts, but they were associated with the agricultural seasons of the year. They were yearly events. No one who hires others to do a job waits until the end of their lives to pay or reward them. This theory of a "final judgment" or of a "final reward" is really nonsense – it does not align with what God has created or with what He has directed humans to culturally develop for a just life in this world. Will there be an accounting and a reckoning after we live this life? Certainly, for in a larger sense that will be the "end of our day" here. But there are ages that follow this one (Eph. 2:7), and there might well be more assignments for us to complete, with appropriate wages to be awarded again. This book repeatedly speaks of multiple ages. We need to change our thinking to accommodate a much larger picture for God's "**purpose of the ages** (a fore-designed aim, plan and object [which He is bent on achieving] of the unspecified time-periods) **which He formed** (forms; made; constructs; creates; produced) **within the Christ**" (Eph. 3:11).

Also, notice the semantic range of the word that is normally only rendered as "**judged**": **sifted, separated, evaluated, decided about and judged**. Not only this, "**the dead folks**" may be those who are,

> "**existing being dead ones by** (or: to; with; in) **the results and effects of your stumblings aside** (offenses; wrong steps) **and failures to hit the mark** (or: mistakes; errors; times of falling short; sins; deviations)" (Eph. 2:1),

and who are yet physically alive.

This passage is parallel to 20:4-15, below, which simply expands on this theme of judging, making decisions and giving wages.

The final clause: "**then to at once thoroughly spoil** (or: bring ruin throughout; cause decay through the midst; utterly destroy) **the folks continuously corrupting** (thoroughly spoiling, ruining, destroying and decaying) **the Land** (or: earth; soil)," speaks of particular judgments for particular situations, and may well be happening periodically, according to God's system of seasons. As we view our environments, in our day, we would like to see intervening decisions made to stop the spoiling and ruining of these environments. This could also apply to the "earth, soil" that is US! May our Father adjudicate those who are polluting our minds and ruining our health. Israel was directed to have care for their Land (which included animals and people), and Yahweh judged them when they did not do so. The very terms used (corrupting, spoiling, ruining, decaying, destroying) in both the offence and the judgment demonstrate a correspondence between the offense and the judgment. It is, once again, the principle of sowing and reaping. The reaping will also be in the appropriate sphere of one's existence: in "the flesh," as discussed above. But in one way or another, and at one time or another, we suggest that since God has been forming a new creation, that He will once again breathe the breath of Life into the dead flesh, as He did in the beginning. He is the Alpha and the Omega, the Beginning and the End.

19. **And then the Temple of God – the one within, or in union with, the atmosphere** (or: centered in the heaven) **– was opened** (or: was suddenly opened up), **and the ark of the covenant** (or: arrangement) [other MSS read: ark of the covenant of the Lord; or: ark from God's covenant] **was seen** (or: is seen) **within the midst of His Temple. Next lightning and voices and thunders and a shaking** (or: an earthquake) **and great hail were birthed** (came to be; occurred).

This presents **the temple of God** (the one within the atmosphere, or centered in heaven) **opened**. This is the "temple" composed of those "**caused [us] to sit together within the things situated upon** [thus, above] **the heavens**" (Eph. 2:6), which is the only temple now in existence. We are it! John sees the body of Christ, and sees it opened – a figure of being receptive and receiving to people. This is how Jesus left the literal temple (Matt. 27:51) when its veil was torn open from top to bottom – the holy of holies (figure of the core of our being) was open to all; no separation from people. And 2 Cor. 3:18 refers to us who, "**with unveiled face**" reflect the glory of Yahweh. In reference to John seeing this temple, Hiett concludes, "that's the temple he measured at the beginning of chapter 11…. within it – within *them* – is the lost ark of the testimony! The Church carried the testimony" (ibid p 150).

Paul's beautiful impartation in Eph. 1 certainly fits this verse:
>19. **And further, [I pray that you may know] what [is] the continually surpassing greatness** (or: the constant transcendence) **of His ability and power [being given] unto, and into, us – the people continuously believing, progressively trusting and constantly loyal – in accord with** (or: down from; corresponding to) **the operation** (or: in-working) **of force of His strength,**
>20. **which is operative** (or: which He exerted) **within the Christ** (the Anointed One), **awakening and raising Him forth from out of the midst of dead folks and then seating Him within** (or: = at) **His right [hand], within the things** (or: among the folks, places or realms) **situated upon the heavens**
>>(or: in union with the celestials; among the folks [residing] upon the atmospheres),
>21. **up over every primacy** (or: ruler; government; controlling effect; or: beginning; origin) **and authority** (or: right and privilege from out of being) **and power** (or: ability) **and lordship** (or: ownership), **as well as every name being continually named – not only within this age, but also within the impending one –**
>22. **and then placed and aligned all people in humbleness under His feet** [Ps. 8:6b; LXX]
>>(or: and arranges everyone in a supportive position by His feet), **and yet gives** (or: gave) **Him, [as] a Head** (or: Source; origin and beginning of a series) **over all humanity and all things, for the called-out community,**

23. **which [community] is His body, the result of the filling from, and which is, the One Who is constantly filling all things within all humanity** (or: humans)
> (or: which continues existing being His body: the resultant fullness, entire content and full measure of Him [Who is] progressively making full and completing all things in union with all things, as well as constantly filling the whole, in – and in union with – all people).

Because the temple is open, the ark of the covenant can now be seen; we can perceive what the Father is doing. The place of His manifested presence is now seen – His glory is now seen – within His body. The throne of God – the ark with the mercy seat and the cherubim – are now all manifested: in His body.

The **lightning, voices, thunders, shakings** (both heaven and earth) call us back to the scene of the throne again. The association of the tabernacle/temple with the throne scene is again established. Figures of God's presence (lightning, voices, thunders, shakings) are joined to the figure of His judgment: **great hail**. This reiterates in symbol what was just stated in vs. 18. Kaplan called to mind Ezekiel's first vision, noting the description of the living beings, there, as "**lightning**." The living beings of chapter 4ff, above, were also in the temple setting:
> "As for the likeness of the living ones, their appearance was like live coals of fire, burning up like the appearance of torches – the same went to and fro between the living ones – and the fire had brightness, and out of the fire went forth **lightning**. So the living ones ran, and then returned, like the appearance of a flash (or: streak) of **lightning**" (Ezk. 1:13-14; Rotherham). *Cf* Isa. 6:1-6.

Now we must keep in mind the key to these living ones, as given in Ezk. 1:5b, "They had the likeness of a **human**." Apocalyptic visions are not about some spiritual realm that is separate from the earth; they are about God's relationship with humans, and mostly about humans when they are living the life of one of the two Adams (1 Cor. 15:45), here on earth and its atmosphere (sky; heaven).

The vision of the seventh trumpet involved the tumultuous action of heaven upon the earth (the lightning and thunders) and a responsive shaking of the earth. But it also involved the voices of the message of Christ being proclaimed. As with the creation of Israel as a nation at Mt. Sinai (*cf* Heb. 12:18-21), we have environmental and spiritual shakings with the birth of the new creation (2 Cor. 5:17; Rev. 21:5). The journey continues. As someone recently said, "time is not running out, time is coming." The great **hail** and attending signs in the heavens announce the destruction and the end of the old arrangement (with Moses), but in Christ we look ahead, where, "**within the continuously oncoming ages** (the indefinite time periods continually and progressively coming upon and overtaking [us]) **He may exhibit** (display; point out; give proof of) **the continuously transcending** (being cast beyond; overshooting) **riches and wealth of His grace and favor, in useful goodness** (beneficial kindness)" (Eph. 2:7).

Thus ends the third vision. Some interpreters see this as the mid-point of the Unveiling, with chapters 12-22 covering the same territory, telling the same story, as chapters 1-11, but giving more details. (*cf* Beale, ibid p 622ff; Wallace pp 232-257) Folks have seen various patterns of 7 throughout the following section, from 12:1 through 15:4. These observations are valid, since there are patterns that can be seen woven into the entire tapestry that is presented from Gen. 1 through Rev. 22. Bullinger (*The Companion Bible*, p 1883) saw this next section as: a) 12:1-12, Woman, Child and Dragon; b) 12:13-13:18, Dragon and Two Beasts. Beale (ibid p 624) sees chapter 12 as one vision, "divided into three scenes: vss. 1-6, vss.7-12, and vss. 13-17." These, and other, constructs can be helpful to our perceptions of the internal literary connections and relationships, but we should keep in mind that they are only theoretical observations of what various people see in the text. The OT allusions, and the metaphors of the NT writers should be our foundational framework and building materials, as we reconstruct the messages of these visions, in our understanding. Notwithstanding, Terry provides cogent comparisons:

"As Joseph's second dream of the sun, moon, and stars bowing down to him was in the essential import only a repetition, under other symbols, of his first dream of the sheaves in the field (Gen. 37:5-11), and as Pharaoh's double dream of the kine [cows] and the ears was explained as but one in significance, but repeated unto the king twice... so the second half of this Apocalypse is another portraiture of the same great subject which has been set before us in the foregoing chapters.... In all this elaborate recapitulation, John follows the manner of the prophet Daniel, whose vision of the four beasts in chapter 7 is but another presentation of the same four kingdoms symbolized in Nebuchadnezzar's dream (chapter 2). Similar repetitions... appear in the apocalyptic portions of Zechariah and Joel, and constitute a notable feature of the biblical apocalypses" (ibid p 381; brackets added).

Metzger (ibid p 72) concurs, saying, in reference to the connection of chapters. 11 & 12,

"Chapter 11 of the book of Rev. concludes with references to judging the dead, rewarding the servants of God, and opening God's temple in heaven. Although this scenario would make a fitting end of the book, John... returns to an earlier stage and, so to speak, begins all over again. Chapter 12 can be characterized as a flashback..."

Chapter 12

1. **Next a great sign was seen within the atmosphere** (or: sky; or: heaven): **a Woman having been clothed** (cast around) **with the sun, and the moon down under her feet, and a wreath of twelve stars upon her head.**

This **great sign** is described in the manner to suggest its importance to the overall theme of the Unveiling.

The "**wreath of twelve stars upon her head**" immediately alerts us to the identity of the apocalyptic **Woman**: she is Israel. Israel was compared to a virgin and a bride in Jer. 2:32, and Jerusalem to a rejected girl in Ezk. 16:5 (whom Yahweh cleansed and made His wife). Paul picks up the same metaphor in Gal. 4:26 (comparing the old with the new), and then in Eph. 5:25-32; 6:16 (focusing on the new).

The "**travailing with birth-pangs**" of vs. 2, below, coupled with the **dragon** (a figure of Egypt: "Pharaoh, king of Egypt, the great dragon that lies in the midst of his rivers..." – Ezk. 29:3) taking a stand before the Woman, vs. 4, below, so that "**it may devour** (eat down; consume) **her child**" takes us back to the story that led up to Israel's Exodus, the time when Pharaoh gave orders to have the male children of Israel killed upon their birth. He told the Hebrew midwives:

"If it [be] a son, then you shall kill him.... Cast [him] into the river" (Ex. 1:16, 22).

We encounter a "**river**" coming from the dragon's mouth in vs 15, below. Kaplan has pointed out that Pharaoh was planting a seed that would in 80 (2X"40," the number of witness and testing) years bring a deadly harvest: the death of the firstborn of Egypt. In the time of the birth of the Christ, Herod was killing the young sons of Israel, and the new Moses (Jesus) had to flee out of the country with His parents, as had Moses, in the pre-Exodus story. I suggest that these are the stories behind the vision.

This Woman is located "**within the atmosphere** (or: sky; or: heaven)," and is an allusion to,

"'**Jerusalem upon heaven**' (or: in a Jerusalem pertaining to and having the character and qualities of a superior, or added, heaven and atmosphere; or: in Jerusalem [situated] upon, and comparable to, the atmosphere)" – Heb. 12:22. Cf Eph. 2:6, cited above.

Paul referred to her as, "**Jerusalem above... who is our mother**" (Gal. 4:26). We will see her again in 21:2, below: "**a new Jerusalem** (or: an innovative, different Jerusalem: new in character and quality),

progressively descending from out of the atmosphere (or: presently stepping down out of the midst of the sky; or: steadily stepping in accord, forth from heaven," and again, in 21:9b-10,

> "**the Bride, the Wife of the little Lamb…. the set-apart** (or: holy; sacred) **city, Jerusalem, progressively** (or: habitually; or: presently) **descending out of the atmosphere** (or: heaven), **from God**."

Paul also located us in this same sphere, in Phil. 3:

> 20. **You see, our citizenship** (result of living in a free city) **continues inherently existing** (or: continuously subsists) **resident within the midst of [the] atmospheres** (or: heavens), **from out of where we also continuously receive and take away in our hands from out of a Deliverer** (a Savior)**: [the] Lord, Jesus Christ,**
> 21. **Who will continue actively transfiguring** (progressively refashioning and remodeling; continuously changing the form of) **our body from the low condition and status** (or: the body of our humiliation) **[which is] joint-formed in, by and with the body of His glory, down from** (or: in accord with; in the sphere of; along the lines of; to the level of; following the pattern of; stepping along with; commensurate with; as directed by) **the inward operation** (in-working) **of the [conditions or situation for] Him to be continuously able** (or: with power) **also to humbly align The Whole to and in Himself** (or: to subject and subordinate all things for Himself).

The Woman represents those who have received, and have been "caught up" (1 Thes. 4:17) by, "**God's invitation to an above place** (or: the prize from, and which is, the upward calling from, and which is, the God) **within the midst of and in union with Christ Jesus**" (Phil. 3:14b).

The **twelve stars** echo Joseph's dream in Gen. 37:9-10 where Jacob interprets the eleven stars of the dream as representing his eleven sons (Joseph's brothers), which implies that Joseph was the 12th star. We find stars referenced as being "teachers/instructors" in Dan. 12:3b, and Paul uses stars metaphorically to represent those who are resurrected from the dead, in 1 Cor. 15:41b-42a,

> "**star continues differing from star, in glory and splendor** (or: for you see, [one] star is progressively carrying through and bearing apart in excellence from [another] star). **Thus also** (or: In this way too) **[is] the resurrection of the dead people**."

This number **12** relates to the twelve tribes of Israel, and is also seen with Jesus choosing twelve disciples. From this, many have seen the woman as a figure of Israel, and her child as representing Jesus, the Christ, and that is a valid layer of interpretation.

The Woman is, "**clothed with the sun**," which is a metaphor that calls to mind Mat. 13:43,

> "**At that time, the fair and equitable folks – who live in the pointed-out Way of right relationships, rightwised behavior and justice – will be progressively giving out light, as from lamps** (or: will shine forth from out of the midst), **in the same way as the sun, in union with the reign, and within the kingdom, of their Father**."

This may also be an allusion to Isa. 60:1,

> "Arise! Shine! For your Light has come and the **glory of Yahweh** has risen **upon you!**"

So this may suggest that she has been joined to Christ and is reflecting His glory (Jn. 15:4; 1 Cor. 6:17),

> "**continuously having** (holding; or: = bringing with it) **the glory of God** (God's glory; God's reputation; or: God's appearance), **her illuminator** (the cause of her light) **– like a most precious stone, as a jasper stone being continuously crystal-clear**" (21:11, below).

Prov. 4:18 instructs us with another clue:

> "But in contrast, the path of the righteous is as **the light of dawn** (or: bright light) – going on and brightening, on unto the stable part of the day" (Rotherham).

This could also be an allusion to Mat. 17:2,

> "**He was transformed** (changed in external form and appearance) **and His face radiated light, like a lamp, and shone like the sun. His outer garments also turned white – bright as the light!**" Cf Ps. 104:2, cited above, under 10:1.

Could her clothing be reflecting the radiance from the face of the Agent in 10:1, above, and be the effect described in 2 Cor. 3:18?

> "**we all, ourselves – having a face that has been uncovered and remains unveiled** [note: as with Moses, before the Lord, Ex. 34:34] **– being folks who by a mirror are continuously observing, as ourselves, the Lord's glory** (or: being those who **progressively reflect** – from ourselves as by a mirror – **the glory of [our] Owner**), **are presently being continuously and progressively transformed into the very same image, from glory into glory – in accord with and exactly as – from [the] Lord's Breath-effect** (or: from [the] Spirit of [the] Lord)."

And from Israel's history we recall,

> "But the **Sun** of Righteousness will shine forth to you with restoration on His wings, and you shall be brought out and sport like a bullock from the stall and tread down the wicked, for they will be dust under your feet..." (Mal. 4:2-3; Fenton).

Let us consider the symbol, "**the moon down under her feet**." In Joseph's dream, the moon represented his mother (Gen. 37:10). The idea of "under one's feet," suggests victory over something (e.g., Rom. 16:20), or the crushing of adversarial opposition (Gen. 3:15; also Josh. 10:24-26, "Come near, put your feet upon the necks of these kings..."), but now those have become her footstool (Ps. 110:1b). Here, the mother might be old covenant Israel that gave birth to the Messiah. The 1st century Jewish leadership was adversarial both to the Christ, and then to His apprentices. Our first introduction to the moon, Gen. 1:16 tells us, "Accordingly God proceeded to make the two great lights, the greater light as a ruler of the day, and the lesser light as a ruler of **the night**; likewise the stars" (Watts). The night represents **darkness** where one cannot see well. Christ was the Light that came to shine **in the darkness**; He brought the new Day. Paul put it this way, in 1 Thes. 5:5,

> "**you see, you all are sons of** (or: associated with and having the qualities of) **Light and sons of** (or: associated with and having qualities of) **Day! We are not of night, nor of darkness** (or: we do not belong to or have the characteristics of night)."

So here, we suggest, is another witness that the moon represented the old covenant and the Law, which the overcomer now has under her feet, having overcome death and the night through Christ. Again, quoting Paul in Rom. 6:14,

> "**you folks are not under Law** (or: do not exist being subject to [Torah] or custom), **but rather under Grace** (or: the Act which produced happiness, which was granted as a favor)."

In discussing those who wanted to remain under the Law and to continue its customs, Paul describes those practices in Gal. 4:10-11,

> "**You are for yourselves and in yourselves continuously watching closely and observing days** [e.g., sabbaths; days for fasting] **and months** (or: new moons) **and seasons** (or: appointed situations [e.g., feasts]) **and [sacred] years! I continue fearing for you, lest somehow I have, to the point of exhaustion, labored in vain** (for no purpose) **into you folks**."

The Hebrew word for "month" literally means, "new moon." The old covenant liturgical calendar was tied to the agricultural calendar – and both were governed by the moon: they were lunar calendars. The timing for all of their festivals was based upon the new moon. Having the moon under her feet meant that this "caught-up," resurrected Woman was no longer observing nor ruled by the festivals of Israel's history. For this reason, Paul spoke to this issue in Col. 2:

> 16. **Therefore, do not let anyone habitually pass judgment on you** (or: make decisions for you) **in [matters of] eating and drinking, nor in a part of a festival, or of a new moon, or of sabbaths** (= concerning [identity markers] or things that are of a religious nature or cultus),

17. **which things** (= cultic markers) **are a shadow of the things being about to be** (or: in regard to [what had been] the impending existence), **[which is] now, the body of the Christ**
> (or: and now the physical form is from, and belongs to, the [Messiah]; or: Yet the corporeal reality has the qualities of the Anointing; or: Whereas the corresponding embodiment of the idea, its mass and its substance [is] Christ; or: So then the body pertains to the [Messiah]; [note: A.T. Robertson views this construction, "the body," as the object which is casting the shadow; Vincent is similar; cf TDNT, VII, p 1039-40]).

18. **[so] let no one be acting as an umpire, or an arbiter in the public games, so as to decide down against you, or to disqualify you, in regard to the prize** (or: to award the prize [to you] unjustly – Eduard Lohse) – **in lowness of understanding, intellect, frame of mind and deportment, continuously wanting [you] also [to be] in ritual-relating to the agents**
> (or: constantly delighting in religious activity originating from the messengers [note: e.g., old covenant rituals]; or: repeatedly taking pleasure by cultic religious service about, or external worship of or through the "angels"), **while continuously stepping randomly and rashly into** (or: entering purposelessly, thoughtlessly or feignedly into; or: = being initiated into) **things which he has** [other MSS: he has not] **seen** [note: this may refer to being initiated into cultic secrets or mysteries], **progressively being made natural and instinctual by the inner senses and perceptions of his flesh**
> (or: habitually being puffed up under [the influence of] the mind of his flesh [= his natural abilities and conditions, or by his alienated self, or by the human nature that has been conformed to the System]),

19. **and thus not continuously getting strength from** (or: apprehending and becoming strong by) **the Head** (or: the Source), **from out of Whom all the body** (or: the entire body) – **being constantly fully furnished and supplied to excess with funds and nourishment, and progressively joined cohesively** (welded together; knitted and compacted together) **through the instrumentality of the joints** (connections; fastenings) **and links** (things bound together) – **goes on growing and increasing God's growth**
> (or: the growth of God; the growth having its source in God; the growth pertaining to God; the growth and increase which is God; or: the growth from God).

This word from Paul to Colossae is timely for our own day. The moon (and the moons of the old covenant) is under our feet (which gives another perception of Rom. 16:20). Yet (changing our perception to that of her standing, rather than being seated) she remains standing on the foundation of Israel's sacred writings, which include the "foundation" which is Christ (Isa. 28:16; 1 Cor. 3:11). Or, it speaks of her walk (how she lived her life): above the darkness of the night (the time of the moon, and its mere reflection of the sun's Light).

The Woman can also represent the corporate called-out body which brings forth Christ within it, or as Paul said,
> "**O my little children** (born ones), **with whom I am progressing, again, in childbirth labor** (travail; labor pains) **until Christ may be suddenly formed** (= until the Anointing would be at some point birthed) **within you folks!**" (Gal. 4:19).

A word on the "**wreath**" is in order. We saw it connected to "the Life" and faithful living in 2:10, above. In 3:11 we found that it was something to be "held-on-to." In 4:4 and 10 we observed that the old people had them, and in 6:2 the overcoming Christ-figure was given one. Then, turning to 2 Tim. 4:8, Paul instructed him:
> "**the winner's wreath of the Course having been pointed out** (the athlete's laurel wreath consisting of the rightwised relationship in fair and equitable dealings, and pertaining to the justice of right behavior on the course; or: = the wreath from covenant inclusion and participation)

continues laid away for me (or: is presently reserved in me), **which the Lord, the Fair** (Equitable; Just; Rightwising; [Covenant]) **Judge** [of the games], **will proceed to pay to** (or: award in) **me within the sphere of that Day – yet not only to me! ... but further, also, to all those** (or: in everyone) **being ones having loved** (urged toward union with; totally gave themselves to; unambiguously accepted) **His full appearance in Light** (or: the complete manifestation of Him; His fully bringing things to light; His full and accurate manifestation)."

Yet in 1 Thes. 2:19 he wrote,

"**For who** (or: what) **is our expectation** (or: expectant hope) **or joy, or shall continue being a crown** (victor's wreath) **of boasting and glorying in front of our Lord Jesus, in His presence, if not even you folks?**"

And in Phil. 4:1 we see this again,

"**Consequently, my brothers – loved ones and longed-for folks, my joy and winner's** (or: festal) **wreath – thus** (in this way) **you constantly stand within [the] Lord: [as or being] loved ones!** (or, as an imperative: be habitually standing firm in this manner: in [the] Lord!)."

So with these witnesses before us, can we not see that this Woman's victor's wreath is the fullness of God's people, figured in type by the twelve stars – the twelve tribes of Israel (which served as the "federal head" – or representative – of all humanity)?

We mentioned, above, Israel pictured as a woman in Ezk. 16. My friend Dan Kaplan pointed out that there, in 16:12 along with other ornamentations, Yahweh placed a "wreath of boasting upon [her] head" (LXX). So she was a figure, there, of the first phase of being Yahweh's wife. But like the literal Jerusalem (a figure of old covenant Israel who was unfaithful to her Messiah, and who Paul characterized as being in bondage with her children – Gal. 4:25)) that killed the prophets and the two witnesses, in chapter 11, above, Israel of Ezekiel's day "played the prostitute" (Ezk. 16:15). Isaiah also wrote of this, in Isa. 1:21. We will see her, again, in 17:4-5ff, below, with a Secret written upon her forehead: the Secret is that she is now titled, "Babylon the Great, mother of prostitutes." It is no surprise that when John saw her in that vision, he "**wondered** (marveled) **a great wonder** (or: [he] wondered, "[It is] a great marvel!")," in 17:6b. Like Isaiah, he wondered, "How can this be?" Had this woman been a figure of Rome, as many interpreters propose, he would hardly have wondered at it. But John does not marvel or wonder at the Woman here in 12:1. He knows her; he is a part of her. She is the redeemed Mt. Zion, the heavenly, New Jerusalem. She is Real, as compared to the shadow. She is the precious (*cf* 1 Cor. 3:9-17), as compared to the worthless. No dead prophets lie in her streets.

2. **And being pregnant** (continuously having or holding within the womb), **she is constantly crying** (or: repeatedly uttering a cry), **travailing with birth-pangs, and being progressively tested and tried in the labor pains** (or: experiencing the touchstone) **to bring forth** (= to bear a child).

She is described as pregnant, and **is constantly crying and travailing with birth-pangs** in order to bring forth, to bear her child. Here is an allusion to Gen. 3:16; bringing forth the Seed (3:15) would involve an increase of, "the pain, grief and the groanings of [her] pregnancy." During this season, she is also being tried and tested (experiencing the touchstone to determine her "metal;" [note: this word is used elsewhere, but translated "torment" in the KJV, e.g., Lu. 16:28]). The pregnant and travailing picture of the 1st century communities can be seen in this symbol. It is an allusion to Isa. 26:16-18b,

"O Yahweh, in distress they noted and sought You; they poured out a whispered prayer in Your discipline for (or: upon) them. Like a pregnant woman who is coming near to bear, who is travailing, who is crying out in her cramps, so have we become because of You, O Yahweh. We have been pregnant; we travail; yet, it is as though we bring forth wind...!"

But here, a Son is actually brought forth (vs. 5, below). In Isa. 21:3 (in a prophecy against Babylon and Arabia) he saw "a grievous vision" and, "therefore [were his] loins filled with pain: pangs [had] taken hold upon [him] as the pangs of a woman that travails..." Even when God is bringing something to birth, there is usually some pain. In Jer. 4:27-31, Yahweh said, "The whole land shall be desolate.... the whole city shall flee for the noise of the horsemen and bowmen.... (31) For I have heard a voice as of a woman in travail – the anguish as of her that brings forth her first child—the voice of the daughter of Zion..." Both Jerusalems (the one above, and the one called Sodom, Egypt and Babylon) were in travail, but for different reasons. Other examples of travail representing corporate distress can be seen in Jer. 6:24; 13:21 and 30:4-7 ("the time of Jacob's trouble"). For the 1st century, Paul instructed the folks in Asia Minor that,

> "**It continues binding and necessary for us to enter into the reign of God** (or: God's kingdom; the sovereign activities which are God) **through the midst of many pressures, squeezings, tribulations, afflictions and oppressions**" (Acts 14:22b).

She has been intimate with God, her Husband, and has received His seed. This child is the "Seed of the Woman" spoken of in Gen. 3:15; He is also Abraham's seed – the corporate Heir, according to Promise (Gal. 3:16). Note that in verses 6 & 11 we see the man-child referred to as the plural "**they**," the many-membered Christ. In Isa. 51:1 we see Israel as a mother; in Isa. 54:1 she is pictured as barren; in Isa. 66:8 it says, "As soon as Zion travailed, she brought forth her sons" (NAS). There is never just one situation or circumstance within our relationships with God. We are in individual paths, and in different seasons, just as a family is made up of different age-groups and even in overlapping generations. What we need to see are the patterns and the varied ways in which our Father directs our lives. We do not look at one another, but at Him, the Author and Finisher of our walk in His Trust (Heb. 12:2). We need to be aware of His presence throughout whatever He is birthing into our lives. The covenant communities are always to be giving birth to the Son in their lives, and the **birth-pangs** are the pressures, squeezings and persecutions that come in all areas of our lives. Both Jesus and His followers said that this would be the case for us. As with natural birth, at times we need to just breathe, and then comes the point when we must bear down and push. Paul's letters are full of references to the stresses in life.

Consider the parallels of this picture in ch. 12 to similar ones in Micah 4:8-13,
> "And as for you, Tower of the Flock, Hill of the Daughter of Zion, to you it will come – even the former dominion will come: the kingdom pertaining to the daughter of Jerusalem. Now why do you cry out loudly? Is there no king among you, or has your counselor perished, that agony has gripped you like a woman in childbirth? Writhe and labor to give birth, Daughter of Zion, like a woman in childbirth, for now you will GO OUT of the City, DWELL IN THE FIELD, and go to Babylon. There you will be rescued (or: delivered), there the LORD will redeem you from the hand of your enemies.... But they do not know the thoughts of the LORD, and they do not understand His purpose.... Arise and thresh, Daughter of Zion, for your horn I will make iron and your hoofs I will make bronze..." (NAS, modified).

Here in 12:6, below, we see that the woman takes flight "**into the wilderness**," similar to the Daughter Zion going out of the city "into the field." The wilderness is a place of testing: as with Jesus for 40 days, Moses for forty years, and Israel for 40 years. As with Israel, she too is nourished in the place of testing.

3. Then another sign was seen within the atmosphere (or: sky; heaven)**: and consider this! – a great fiery-colored dragon having seven heads and ten horns, and seven bands** (diadems; kingly ornaments) **upon its seven heads.**

The first thing to observe, here, is that what is described is "**another SIGN.**" It is a symbol that is pointing to a reality which it figuratively represents. It is a picture of the adversary of God's chosen; the opposition of His bride and of His anointed. I suggest that it is "**fiery-colored**" for the same reason that Peter described the trials and testing that the covenant communities were experiencing in similar terms:

> "**Beloved ones, do not repeatedly feel like strangers to the burning** (= the action of the Fire) **within and among you folks, which is habitually happening to you with a view toward your being put to the test** (or: which is repeatedly coming into being in the face of a proving trial for you; which is progressively birthing itself to an examination in you), **as though a strange thing or a foreign occurrence is repeatedly walking with you folks**" (1 Pet. 4:12).

It was probably from the same source from which Paul instructed the folks in Asia Minor (the same cities to whom the Unveiling was to be sent) to protect themselves;

> "**within all things and situations** (or: in union with **all people**) – **[be] at once receiving again** (or: taking back up) **the large oblong shield which is the Faithfulness** (or: of Trust; which has the quality of Faith; that belongs to Confidence and Assurance; from the Loyalty), **within which you will continue having power and be progressively able to extinguish all the fiery arrows of and from the worthless person**
>> (or: evil one; unsound and miserable situation; disadvantageous and unprofitable condition; malicious and depraved attitude; toilsome labor that is gushed with misery)" (Eph. 6:16).

But behind the immediate source (or, sources) of those fiery arrows may just be the One who sent the *seraphim* into Israel's camp (Nu. 21:6, 8) – yes, what KJV calls "fiery serpents" is the Heb. *seraphim*, "burning ones." Yahweh then told Moses to make a *seraph* of copper and put it on a pole for the people who were bitten by the *seraphim* could look at it and be healed. In the Gospels, Jesus referenced this incident concerning Himself, and the cross. Returning to the dragon's color, this may be either that it, too, was sent from God to test and try His people, or, that this may indicate that its appearance and color of fire signifies it as being a counterfeit of God, Who is Fire.

In the NT, the word **dragon** is used only in the Unveiling. But in the LXX, we find it used a number of times, so let us examine these. In Ex. 7:9, 10 and 12, where the Heb. uses the word "serpent," the LXX has the word "dragon." This is probably why vs. 9, below, gives multiple designations to this same character in our play. In Deut. 32:33, we have the statement, "their wine is the rushing passion of dragons." We find the term in Job 4:10; 7:12; 20:16; 26:13; 38:39; and 40:20. Job 38:39 speaks of dragons in the context of "hunting prey for the lions," then, the Lord asks a parallel question, "will you… satisfy the appetite of dragons?" So, this term was apparently used for a variety of wild animals. In Ps. 73 (MT: 74):13-14 we read of God shattering/crushing "the heads of the dragons," as the psalmist poetically rehearses Israel's Exodus. Ps. 90 (MT: 91):13 tells us, "On asp and cobra you will tread, and you will trample lion and dragon under foot" (NETS). And in Ps. 103 (104):26,"There ships travel, this dragon [MT: leviathan] that you formed to mock at him" (NETS). Isa. 27:1 is instructive for us here:

> "On that day God will bring his holy and great and strong dagger against the dragon, a fleeing snake – against the dragon, a crooked snake – and He will kill the dragon."

Jer. 9:11 tells us, "And I will render Jerusalem a settlement of migrants and a lair of dragons…" Jer. 27:8 uses the phrase, "like dragons before sheep." In Jer. 28:34, we read, "King Nebuchadnezzar of Babylon has devoured me… he has swallowed me like a dragon." Lam. 4:3 presents an unusual picture: "Indeed, dragons bared their breasts; their whelps sucked…" We quoted Ezk. 29:3, above, in connection with Egypt. Ezk. 32:2 confirms this connection,

> "Son of man, take up a lament over Pharaoh, king of Egypt… You were likened to a lion of nations, and you were like a dragon that is in the sea, and you were raising a horn against your streams…"

Then we have the delightful promise in Amos 9:3b,

> "even if they sink from my eyes to the depths of the sea, there I will command the dragon, and it shall bite them."

The final occurrence is Micah 1:8b, "she shall make lamentation like that of dragons, and mourning like that of the daughters of Sirens." (All LXX quotes from NETS).

As suggested above, in the comments on vs. 1, we suggest that the dragon is a figure for a world empire or a system of domination. Daniel saw them as four symbolic beasts in 7:2-8. There, in vs. 8 he noticed that one of the horns had, "eyes like the eyes of a human," and in vs. 17 it is explained to him that "these great beasts, which are four, are four kings which shall arise out of the earth (or: land)." Here, above, the **seven heads and ten horns, and seven bands** (diadems; kingly ornaments)" define an empire. The number 7 is, once again, symbolic. This **great fiery-colored dragon** represents human domination systems – first from Israel's story in Egypt, then on to the Babylonian, Persian, Greek, and finally the Roman Empire with its ten provinces (sub-kingdoms). The KJV usually renders the Heb. *tannin(m)* as "dragon," (although modern translations choose the word "monster"), and so we have in Jer. 51:34, "Nebuchadrezzar, the king of Babylon, has devoured me; he has crushed me… he has swallowed me up like a dragon…" The Heb. text of Isa. 51:9-10 recalls Israel's Exodus from Egypt and metaphorically refers to "the Arm of Yahweh" that "wounded the dragon" in order to make "a way for the ransomed to pass over." Chilton (ibid p 306) points out that the word *tannin* was used in Gen. 1:21, where, "God created great sea monsters (NRSV; Heb., *tannin*, = dragons)." So, the dragon is/was a creature of God's creation, but like the lion and other wild animals, it became a figure of a dominating system (or: kingdom; empire; religion) that could devour.

This **dragon** is specifically identified in vs. 9, below:
> "**the serpent from the very beginning** (or: the original, or ancient, serpent) – **the one being continuously called "slanderer"**
>> (one who thrusts something through [folks]; false accuser; separator; a "devil;" one who casts something throughout the midst [to cause division]) **and the adversary** (the opponent; the *satan*; [p47 and other MSS: one who stands in opposition; a counter-worker]), **the one continuously causing the whole inhabited area of the earth to wander** (or: that which causes straying; the one continually deceiving)."

The insertion of "serpent from the beginning" causes the reader's mind to go back to Eden, the Garden, and the temptation of the Woman. So here we are seeing the end of the story, the Seed of the Woman, the Man-child, with the serpent finally being cast out of the Garden, or "heaven." Recall that it was only Adam and Eve that were deported from Eden, in the Genesis story; the serpent remained there but was consigned to eating "dust," that of which the humans were formed. So here *satan*, loses its authority. Mark well the parenthetical expansion of "**the adversary**," and the expansion, "the opponent." The Greek word *satan*, is a transliteration of the Hebrew word that referred to any adversary or opponent. This term became personified and then mythological characteristics were added to it so that untrained readers bring to the term pagan ideas that have become traditional doctrine in the institutional churches. Riley explains:
> "The view that the good creation of the world would be attacked and defiled by spiritual forces that would impel its destruction was a doctrine of Persian Zoroastrianism.... Zoroastrianism had postulated two primeval but opposite principles, good and evil, and a final cosmic battle in which the forces of good, headed by a champion, the eschatological savior, would at the end of the age defeat the Devil, the demons, and his human followers.... Gnostic writers were the first to combine the dualism of Zoroastrianism with the Monad of Greek philosophy, producing a comprehensive religious worldview that was a direct precursor of Christianity" (*The River of God*, ibid pp 198, 214-15).

But what of the **7 heads**? Is there a correlation here to the 7 Asian communities, the places of *satan's* home and seat of operation (chapters 2 and 3, above)? It has always been institutional religion that has tried to kill what God was producing, just like Jerusalem was the one that killed all His prophets (Mat. 23:37). The organized religion of Christianity has indeed been a dragon to humanity – and one that has been totally divided (figured by the 7 heads), ruling in complete division. We will look at its offspring, the little wild beast with 7 heads and 10 horns, in the next chapter. Then it appears again in chapter 17, only there it is being ridden by the Great Prostitute (figure of Jerusalem in the 1st century; of the institutional churches and religions in the following centuries to this day). In chapter 17 the horns and heads are explained: the 7 heads are seven mountains, a figure of kingdoms, (vs. 9), and vs. 12 specifies that the 10 horns are 10 kings. We will discuss this later, but we suggest that this dragon in chapter 12 is the spirit and power behind the little wild beast of chapters 13 & 17, and of all domination systems. Simmons insightfully observes (ibid p 237) for the historical perspective,

> "In Daniel's series of visions concerning the world powers from the captivity to the coming of Christ, the number of heads, wings, horns, etc., all corresponded to various attributes of the nations described. For example, with the death of Alexander the Great, his empire was divided by his four generals Selucia (Syria), Ptolemy (Egypt), Lysirnicus (Greece), and Cassander (Asia Minor). These were represented by the four heads of the leopard-like beast of Dan. 7:6, and the four horns of the goat depicted in Dan. 8:8, 22."

He goes on to identify the 7 heads, here in the Unveiling, as, "the *imperial Caesars*," and the ten horns as the ten provinces of Rome.

The original 1611 version of the KJV included the Apocrypha. In a section called "The Rest of the Chapters of the Book of Esther," part of the 10th chapter (from a Greek text), vs. 7, records Mordechai (spelled Mardocheus, in this version) saying, "And the two dragons are I and Aman" (facsimile reprint, Hendrickson Pub., 2005). In other words, in their relationship with each other, he considered them both to be dragons!

4. And its tail is progressively dragging the third of the stars of the sky (or: heaven) **and casts** (or: it cast; it threw) **them into the earth** (or: onto the Land, or, ground). **And the dragon stood** (had made a stand) **before** (or: in the presence of) **the Woman – the one being about to bring forth** (= to give birth) **– to the end that whenever she may bring forth, it may devour** (eat down; consume) **her child.**

Whether the movement of the **tail** is purposely directed, or just the result of the dragon's movement, the outcome is the casting down of **1/3 of the stars from heaven** into the earth. Note the progressive action of the tail. It was not a one-time event. Now are these stars the agents which are the communities (1:16, 20, above)? Phil. 2:15, 16, tells us,

> "**so that you folks may come to be blameless ones, even unmixed** (artless and sincere) **children of God – unblemished** (flawless) **people in the midst of a crooked and distorted generation** (or: a twisted family which has been altered and turned in different ways so as to be dislocated), **within which** (or: among whom) **you folks are continuously shining as illuminators within [the] dominating, ordered System** (or: in union with the aggregate of mankind), **constantly holding upon** (or: keeping a good grip on and fully possessing) **Life's Word** (or: a message which is life; Reason, from Life; an idea with reference to Life; a laid-out thought that has the character of Life)..."

And Dan. 12:3, "And those teaching do shine as the brightness of the expanse, and those justifying the multitudes as stars..." (Young). God compared Abraham's future seed to the stars, in Gen. 15:5; 22:17, and Moses says, "Jehovah your God has multiplied you, and lo, you folks are today as the stars of the heavens, for multitude" (Deut. 1:10). Daniels' vision, in chapter 8, showed,

> "a little horn... and it grew great, even unto the host of heaven, and it cast down [some] of host and of the stars to the ground, and stamped upon them" (vss. 9-10).

In that vision, the little horn represented the power of a human kingdom.

In regard to Jerusalem's purging, we read in Zech.13:

"Awake, O sword, against my shepherd... smite the shepherd, and the sheep shall be scattered.... And I will bring the third part through the fire, and will REFINE them as silver is refined, and will TRY them as gold is tried: they shall call on My Name, and I will hear them; I will say, 'It is My people, and they shall say, Yahweh is my God" (vss. 7-9). *Cf* Hos. 2:23.
Verse 7b was quoted by Jesus in Mk. 14:27.

It could be that this primordial spirit casts down 1/3 of "spiritual Israel" from their place of being "seated together in heavenly places," which would be like the result of not abiding in the Vine (John 15), or, like "certain ones of the branches" that were broken out of the olive tree in Rom. 11:17. So is this referring to 1/3 of the tribes of Israel, or 1/3 of the covenant communities that became a) Judaized back into the flesh realm and food codes or purity codes, or b) cause to disintegrate as a community due to internal divisions or the removal of their lampstands, or c) refers to leaders of the communities that fail to remain connected to the Vine? The applications of this picture are not limited.

But the dragon had another purpose, for it "**stood** (had made a stand) **before** (or: in the presence of) **the Woman... to the end that whenever she may bring forth, it may devour** (eat down; consume) **her child**." This is an allusion to Pharaoh standing (i.e., making a ruling) concerning "every son that is born [to the Hebrews] you shall cast into the river" (Ex. 1:22). This recalls Peter's word about the one who thrusts-through folks (the devil) your adversary going about as a lion seeking whom it may devour (1 Pet. 5:8). Its purpose is to destroy God's Seed – both that Word sown within us, and the folks who compose God's Israel. Regarding the historic application of this verse, Simmons (ibid p 239) concludes:
> "In the present case, the great Dragon assumes the form of Rome, the world civil power; acting through Herod, its vassal, the Dragon tries to devour the Christ child..." (Mat. 2:11-18).

Note, here, that when it fails with the man-child (vs. 5), fails with the Woman (vs. 15-16), it then goes away after the remaining ones of her seed (vs. 17, below). Now consider that while the dragon and its agents, along with 1/3 of the "stars," are thrown out of heaven (the place of leadership; the realm of spirit; vs. 9, below) and into the earth, the Woman and 2/3 of the stars remain in the heavens, with the moon under their feet. This historic period was referred to by Jesus in Mk. 13:8-10,
> "**For ethnic group** (or: nation) **will proceed being raised up upon ethnic group** (or: nation), **and kingdom upon kingdom. There will successively be earthquakes in one place after another. There will continue being famines and times of hunger. These things [are] a beginning of 'birth pains.'**
> **So as for you folks, continue looking to** (or: after) **yourselves, for people will repeatedly give you over unto sanhedrins** (the ruling councils, or courts, in the Jewish culture of that time), **as well as unto synagogues** (local religious and cultural centers). **[There] you folks will be repeatedly beaten and severely whipped** (or: lashed). **Also, you will continue being caused to make a stand upon [the demand] of governors** (rulers) **and kings, in consequence of involvement with Me, [leading] into a witness and testimony to, and evidence for, them. Further, it continues necessary for the good news to be publicly proclaimed into the midst of all the ethnic multitudes** (unto all the non-Jews and the nations), **first**."

We see in this present scene (vs. 4), an allusion to the parable given by Jesus, in Mat. 21:38-39, and here the dragon takes the form of the Jewish leadership of Christ's day:
> "**Yet the vinedressers** (farmers; cultivators) **– upon seeing the son – said among themselves, 'This one is the heir! Come now! We should** (or: can) **kill him and then we can have his inheritance!' And so, upon taking hold of him, they threw him out – outside of the vineyard –and they killed [him]**."

5. **And so she brought forth a Son – an adult man** (or: male; masculine one) **Who is about to continuously shepherd all the multitudes** (ethnic groups; nations) **in the sphere of and with relying on the use of an iron staff** (or: rod). **Later, her child was snatched away** (seized and carried off by force) **toward God and to His throne.**

Here is an allusion to Isa. 7:14,
> "Therefore Yahweh Himself shall give a SIGN to you: Look! The young woman [LXX: an unmarried young woman; virgin; maiden; girl; cf 14:4, below] [is] pregnant, and is progressively bearing a son, and you will call his name Immanuel [meaning: God is with us]."

Another allusion is seen in Isa. 66:7,
> "That a woman hath brought forth before she travailed; that before her pangs came on, they are over and a male child born; who hath heard such a thing, or who hath seen the like?....That Sion should travail and bring forth her children, I Myself raised this expectation..." (*The Septuagint Bible*, Shekinah Enterprises, in the translation of Charles Thomson, 1808).

And then we have Micah 5:2-7a,
> "Yet you, Bethlehem... from you shall [One come] forth for Me to become the Ruler in Israel; yet His goings forth [are] from aforetime, from days eonian.... And He will stand and shepherd [them] in the strength of Yahweh... and they will dwell [securely].... And this [One] will be Peace.... Then the remnant of Jacob will come to be among the nations..." (CVOT).

The sign, here, points back to the birth of the Head, Jesus, and also points ahead to the birth of the rest of His Body, the body of Christ, for They are One. In Gal. 3:29, Paul made this connection clear:
> **"Now since you folks belong to Christ** (or: have [the] Anointing as your source and origin; or: So since you people have the qualities and character of Christ, and [are] that which is Christ), **you are straightway and consequently Abraham's Seed: heirs** (possessors and enjoyers of the distributed allotment), **down from, corresponding to and in the sphere of Promise!"**

That it is mentioned that He is "a masculine one" shows that He has the qualities and characteristics of an **adult male**. Thus, this does not refer to the birth of the baby Jesus, but to His being placed as a Son and declared so by His Father (Matt. 3:17) at His Jordan baptism. Being declared a Son meant that He had the authority of His Father. This answers to this corporate "man-child" being caught up **toward God** and toward **His throne** (figure for a place of authority). Furthermore, contrary to the rules of grammar, this adjective, "masculine one; male," is not in the masculine form (which would correspond to "son"), but is in the neutral (or: neuter) form – allowing it to be applied to either women or men. It could also be a subtle reference to the position of "eunuchs," as in Isa. 56:4-5,
> "For thus says Yahweh: To the eunuchs... [who] choose [that] in which I delight, and [are] holding fast to My covenant, I will give to them, in My house and within My walls, hand and name better than 'sons and daughters'... a name eonian which shall not be cut [off]" (CVOT).

God overcomes our places of being marred or maimed, distorted or ruined. This overall picture speaks to Christ's, and our, enthronement with His, and our, Father. The message to the called out communities is the same as that in 11:15, above: Christ reigns. He is beyond the reach of the dragon.

The dependent clause, "**Who is about to continuously shepherd all the multitudes** (ethnic groups; nations) **in the sphere of and with relying on the use of an iron staff** (or: rod)," is an allusion to Ps. 2:7b-9a. It also echoes 2:26b-27a, above. This is a symbolic announcement of the establishment of Christ's kingdom on earth – and the activities of the Good Shepherd (Jn. 10:2-16), and people, "**will continue listening to** (will habitually hear and pay attention to [implying: obey]) **My voice, and they** [other MSS: it; there] **will progressively become One Flock, One Shepherd**" (vs. 16). It will be when the Good Shepherd is "**continuing on his way upon [the track of] the lost one – until he can** (or: may) **find it**" (Lu. 15:4). It will be,

"**[A] time [when] He will proceed sitting down upon a throne which has the quality and character of His praise-inducing manifestation** (or: which has His glory as its source; or: which is His glory; or: which pertains to His good reputation). **And next, all the ethnic multitudes** (or: nations; people groups) **will be progressively collected and gathered together in front of Him, and then He will continue marking off boundaries and separating them from one another, just as the shepherd is habitually separating** [as in separate pens or groups] **the sheep away from the kids** (the immature goats)" (Mat. 25:31b-32).
[note: this is something habitually done; both groups are clean animals, were used in sacrifices, and are a part of the shepherd's herd]

Peter also spoke to this time, in 1 Pet. 5:4,

> 4. **and so, with the Chief Shepherd** (or: the Original and Ruling Shepherd) **[thus] being made visible** (being shown in clear light), **you folks will be bringing to yourselves – with care and kindly keeping – the unwithering and unfading wreath of the glory** (or: the enduring recognition of achievement which comes from this good reputation).

> > "It is the process implied in 5:3 [**progressively becoming beaten models** (types made by the strike of a hammer; examples) **for the little flock**] that makes the Chief Shepherd visible – in them, and now in us. The good reputation is that Christ is being observed in the lives of these folks. As they 'shepherd' their little flock, the Life which is Christ is being shown in clear light. And as Paul said in Phil. 4:1, the wreath, which signifies success in the metaphor of the stadium games, is actually the little flock that they are tending. It is 'the enduring recognition of achievement' in the lives now being lived in those whom they have been serving. It is Christ in them, the expectation which is the glory (Col. 1:27)" – *Peter, Paul and Jacob, comments 1 Pet., et al*, Harper Brown Pub., 2012, p 35).

As to the word "**snatched away**" in this verse, it is the same Greek word used in 2 Cor. 12:2, 4, and 1 Thes. 4:17. It is used of Philip in Acts 8:39 and of the Lord in Jn. 6:15. It is also used of OUR ministry to others in Jude 23, "**be continuously delivering** (or: repeatedly rescuing and saving, restoring to health and wholeness) **others, snatching them from out of the midst of the Fire**," which, I suggest, is something that God's agents do, at the appropriate time, in the situation described in 14:10, below. All of these instances happen here on our earth, or in our atmosphere/heaven.

Please take note of the work of this SON: **to continuously SHEPHERD ALL the ethnic multitudes** (people groups; nations) with **an iron staff**. This is the reward given to "the one continuously overcoming" in 2:26, 27, above, as we saw earlier. So the context is that of performing as a shepherd, which implies care, leadership, providing sustenance, and protecting the sheep (people groups). Note that this also implies that, "**all the multitudes** (ethnic groups; nations)" are SHEEP. But let us look at this figure of a **staff**, or, **rod**. We are familiar with the 23rd Psalm,

> 1. **[The] LORD** (= Yahweh) **continually shepherds** (habitually cares for and tends, repeatedly leads to pasture and constantly protects) **me [as a part of the flock], and He will continue causing me to lack nothing** (or: so, by habit, in not even one thing will He fail me, or come too late [for; to] me; or: and thus will He keep on causing me not to be in need of even one thing).
> 2. **Into a place of [the] tender shoot** (or: Into the midst of a verdant place), **there** (in that place) **He encamped me** (or: causes me to settle down in a tent); **upon water of rest** (or: at restful water; on a water of ceasing) **He nourishes and rears me.**

3. **He turned my soul around** (or: He turns upon my whole being; He restored my self-life; He turned-about my inner being)**: He leads and guides me upon the well-worn Path of the Way pointed out, in righted covenant-participation, because of and for the sake of His Name.**

4. **For you see, even if I may** (or: should; would; could) **be caused to journey** (travel; pass from place to place) **within the midst of a shadow of death** (or: death's shadow; a shadow, from death), **I will continue not being caused to fear bad [times]** (will not be repeatedly frightened by worthless [situations or people]; will not be habitually afraid of misfortunes, harmful [experiences] or base [schemes]), **because You are, and continue being, with me: Your rod and your staff – these, from a call to be at my side, give me aid and impart relief, encouragement and comfort** (these are paracletes to help me).

5. **You prepare a table** (= spread a meal) **before me right opposite the folks habitually afflicting me** (or: You make ready my table, in my sight, from within the midst of the people constantly bringing pressure against me and rubbing me the wrong way); **You anoint** (or: fatten) **my head in** (or: with) **olive oil, and Your cup is progressively** (or: continuously; repeatedly) **intoxicating – as the best** (as the most excellent, or strongest, [wine]).

6. **And thus, Your mercy and compassion will in itself continue eagerly pursuing in order to track me down – all the days of my life, and [this is for] the [situation; occasion] for me to continuously settle down and dwell within** (or: to be habitually residing centered in) **[the] Lord's** [= Yahweh's] **house on into a long duration of days.** (LXX, JM)

This should instruct us concerning the "SHEPHERDING" that is referred to here in the Unveiling. Both the Greek of the LXX, and the Hebrew of the Masoretic Text, use two different words for "rod" and "staff" in Ps. 23:4. The COVT renders "rod" as "club," which was shorter and used mostly for defense by shepherds; however, a survey of the use of the Heb. words shows some ambiguity in their use. In Micah 7:14 the prophet says, "Shepherd Your people with Your club, the flock of Your allotted inheritance…" And Yahweh answers in vs. 15, "As in the days of your going forth from the land of Egypt, shall I show him marvelous works." But let us consider more OT references that will shed light, beyond the context of Ps. 23. Passages from Israel's Exodus story will illumine our present context of Rev. 12. Moses was a shepherd when he had the "burning bush" experience. In Ex. 4:2-3,

"Now Yahweh said to him: 'What [is] this in your hand?' And he answered: 'A rod.' Then He said: 'Fling it to the ground.' So he flung it to the ground and it became a serpent (snake)…"

What a picture, and what does this say to us, in regard to vs. 9, below, where the dragon is called the ancient serpent (snake)? In Ex. 4:4, Moses is told to take the serpent by the tail (the most dangerous thing to do; refers symbolically to the last part), and the snake becomes a rod, again. In Ex. 4:17 he is told that it is with this rod that he "shall do SIGNS." Then, in Ex. 4:20, we learn that this same rod is now called, "the rod of God." Later, in Egypt, Aaron is instructed to take HIS rod (we now have two witnesses in Egypt using their rods to do signs), and "fling it before Pharaoh so that it may become a snake" (Ex. 7:9; LXX reads: dragon, in this passage), and in 7:12 we read that Aaron's rod "swallowed up" the rods of the Egyptian scribes and enchanters. This is a preview of "death being swallowed up in Victory," (1 Cor. 15:54b). It was this same rod (that now had within it the occult tools of the Egyptians) that Aaron was told to take and stretch out his hand over, and smite, the waters of Egypt (7:17-20), and "all the waters in the waterway were turned to blood." So we see that "the rod of God" was used for signs to bring deliverance. This is the picture behind 11:6, above, so we can see how this present vision parallels the "interlude" between the 6th and 7th trumpets, above.

In Micah 6:8-9, the rod is associated more with God's rule of the upright life:

"He has told you, humanity, what is good. What [is] Yahweh requiring from you, save [or: except] to do [right] judgment and love kindness [or: mercy] and to walk meekly with your Elohim [God]? The voice of Yahweh is calling to The City – and sagacity [or: wisdom] shall fear His Name – 'Hear the rod and [the One] Who appointed it" (CVOT; brackets added).

This very period of the shepherding reign that is referenced here in 12:5 of the Unveiling is an allusion to Isa. 11, where in vs. 4 we read,

> "He will judge the poor with righteousness and arbitrate for the humble of the Land with equity; He will smite the Land with the club of His mouth, and with the spirit of His lips shall He put the wicked to death."

The next few verses of that passage speak metaphorically of the new creation in which natures and characters have been transformed – which is prophetic of the Christ life of which we read here in the Unveiling's visions. In both Jer. 10:16 and 51:19 he speaks of Israel being "the rod (scepter) of His allotted inheritance."

The figure of **iron** spoke of strength, or of something hard: e.g., the yoke of iron, in Deut. 2:48, which spoke of God's judgment for Israel to "serve [their] enemies"… until the enemies destroyed them. Jeremiah was made to be "an iron pillar and a bronze wall against the whole Land" of Judea. It was used to speak of imprisonment "in darkness and in the shadow of death," or, of servitude, in Ps. 107:10, and in Isa. 60:17 it stood as a contrast to the increased blessings that God would bring His people.

The second statement, "**Later, her child was snatched away** (seized and carried off by force) **toward God and to His throne**," in one layer of interpretation speaks of Jesus' ascension into the clouds (Acts 1:9), following His ministry, death and resurrection. This clause has been seen as happening directly after the birth of her Son, in our present text. This is due to slavishly rendering the conjunction *kai* as "And." But this conjunction has a broader range, and often should be rendered, "**Later**," as I have here. Keep in mind that this is an apocalyptic vision, not a historical narrative. The conjunction could also be rendered, "Then," "And then," or, "And yet," and visionary time could accommodate Christ's literal ministry. But this "**Son – an adult man**," is a symbol. I suggest that it is better interpreted as a figure of the corporate Christ: Jesus and His body of witnesses. With this view, we have a direct tie-in with 11:11-12, above. This coming to the throne was the act that created the situation described in vs. 10, below:

> "**At the present moment** (or: Just now) **the deliverance** (the return to the original state and condition; the rescue; the health and wholeness; salvation), **and the authority, and the kingdom** (or: reign) **of our God was** (or: is) **birthed** (comes into existence; came to be), **also the authority of His Anointed** (or: His Christ; His anointed one)."

Paul referred to this "snatching-away" in Eph. 4:10,

> "**The One stepping down** (descending) **is Himself also the One stepping up** (ASCENDING) **far above** (back up over) **all of the heavens** (or: atmospheres; skies), **to the end that He would at once fill the Whole** (permeate and saturate everything; or: make all things full; bring all things to full measure and completion)."

Birth can be seen as a metaphor for resurrection (from the darkness of the womb to the light of the Day). Christ Himself was termed, "**a Firstborn forth from out of the midst of dead folks**" (Col. 1:18). When Jesus was baptized by John into the new way of thinking (*metanoia*), He was Anointed for ministry by the Holy Spirit descending upon Him, "**the heavens at once opened back up again**," and He was pronounced God's Son by the Voice from the atmosphere (Mat. 3:16-17). This was the beginning of another kind of birth for Him. Mat. 4 records what we might call the birth-canal experience (His wilderness testing), followed by spiritual midwife services (agents ministering to Him – Mat. 4:11), and then Lu. 4:14 tells us that Jesus returned from that experience "**within the midst of and in union with the power of the Spirit** (or: the ability which is the Breath-effect; the power from the Attitude)" and began His ministry. This was the birthing of Israel's Messiah into the public scene of Galilee. Furthermore, in Jn. 3:13, Jesus explains,

> "**no one has ascended** (or: stepped up) **into the heaven** (or: atmosphere) **except the One descending** (or: stepping down) **from out of the midst of the atmosphere** (or: heaven): **the**

Son of Mankind (the Son of the human; Humanity's Son; the Son of man) – **the One continuously being** (or: constantly existing) **within the midst of the heaven** (or: atmosphere)." Jesus ministered from His actual living within the sphere of "the midst of the heaven," i.e., within the atmosphere of God (*cf* Acts 17:28).

6. **Then the Woman fled** (or: takes flight) **into the wilderness** (or: desert; desolate place) **where she continues having, there, a prepared place from God** (or: a place having been made ready, from God), **to the end that THEY may continuously nourish her there one thousand two hundred sixty days.**

Now we see that the Woman **takes flight into the wilderness** into her **prepared place**. THEY (Christ and His corporate body – those snatched away in spirit to the place of authority) nourish their mother there for 1260 days. This THEY has been interpreted as those sent-forth folks, prophets, teachers and shepherds who comprise the male son, who have been caught up to a higher "place" (**God's throne**, vs. 5, above; Eph. 2:6) where they are enabled to **nourish** others. These would be the "saviors upon Mt. Zion" (Obad. 21).

Paul gave an expanded picture of the THEY who **continuously nourish** God's bride, here. In Eph. 4:
11. **And He Himself at one point gave** (or: gives; [*p*46: has given and it now exists as a gift]), **on the one hand, the folks sent off with a commission** (the representatives), **yet also those who have light ahead of time and speak it before others** (the prophets), **and on the other hand those who announce goodness and well-being and bring good news, and then the shepherds, and finally teachers** (or: the shepherds-and-instructors),
12. **facing and with a view toward the bringing down of the fresh and timely, for the preparation of the set-apart folks unto a work of attending service and dispensing, [leading] unto** (or: into) **construction** (house-building) **of the body which is the Christ** (or: from the Anointed One; or: the body formed by the Anointing),
13. **[to go on] until we – the whole of mankind** (all people) **– can** (or: would) **come down to the goal** (or: attain; arrive): **into the state of oneness from, and which is, The Faithfulness** (or: the unity and lack of division which has its source in trust, confidence, reliability, loyalty and fidelity), **even which is the full, experiential and intimate knowledge** (or: and from recognition; as well as pertaining to insight) **which is** (or: of; from; in reference to) **the Son of God, [growing] into [the] purposed and destined adult man** (complete, finished, full-grown, perfect, goal-attained, mature manhood) **– into** (or: unto) **[the] measure of [the] stature** (full age; prime of life) **of the entire content which comprises the Anointed One**
   (or: which is the result of the full number which is the Christ; of the effect of the fullness from the [Messiah], and which is, the Christ) –
14. **to the end that no longer would or should we exist being infants** (immature folks), **continuously being tossed by [successive] waves and repeatedly being carried hither and thither by every wind of the teaching within the caprice of mankind, in readiness to do anything with a view toward and leading to the methodical treatment** (or: the systematizing) **of The Wandering** (the straying; the deception).
15. **But continuously being real and true** (living in accord with reality and the facts) **within, and in union with, love** (or: centered in unambiguous acceptance; a full giving of ourselves with an urge toward union), **we can grow up** (enlarge; increase) **into Him – the ALL which is the Head: Christ** (or: [and] we would in love make all things grow up into Him Who is the head and source: [the] Anointed One)!
16. **– from out of Whom all the Body being continuously fitted and framed together and constantly being knit together and caused to mount up united through every fastening** (or: joint) **of the supply of rich furnishings** (or: completely supplied requirements) **in accord with**

(or: down from; commensurate to; in the sphere and to the degree of) **the operation within [the] measure of each one part, is itself continually making the growth and increase of the Body, [focused on and leading] into house-construction** (or: edification) **of itself within the midst of, and in union with, love.**

Beale sees the term "**place**" (*topos*) as a technical term for Jewish writers, suggesting that the term signifies a "protective sanctuary," and states that the LXX frequently uses this term to refer to the temple, the "holy **place**," and he instructs us that it is used "about 20 times" in 2-4 Mac., "with or without a qualifying adjective, [to refer to] the temple" (ibid p 648-9; brackets added). Since we are dealing with symbols and figurative language in this book, his arguments may have some merit. However, a survey of the word's use throughout the NT, and even in the Unveiling, reveals that the ordinary sense of the word is usually intended. And yet, considering the present scene of this vision, I concur that "protection" and "sanctuary" are nuanced in its use. In 12:8, below, the word is used with the sense of "position," or, "realm of authority/power." In vs. 14, below, it is referred to as, "**her place**." Thus, "position," or "realm of influence," may be nuances that we can unpack from its use here. Or, this may be an allusion to Ps. 91:1, "He that dwells in the secret **place** of the Most High – under the shadow of the Almighty will tarry, saying of Yahweh: my Refuge and my Fortress; my God, in Whom I will trust" (Rotherham). So, we can agree with Beale, that this is a "holy" **place** – "a place having been made ready, from God." In this "place," her "**life has been hidden so that it is now concealed together with the Christ, within the midst of God** (or: in union with God)" (Col. 3:3). In fact, Jesus may have been referring to this very **place**, in Jn. 14:2b-4,

> "**I am progressively passing** (or: traveling) **along to prepare and make ready a place in you** (or: for you; with and among you folks). **Even if I should journey on and prepare** (make suitable, fit and appropriate) **a place** (or: a spot; a position; a role) **in you folks** (or: with you; for you), **I am now presently** (or: progressively; repeatedly; habitually) **coming again, and then, I will progressively take you folks in My arms and receive you to Myself, directing you toward Myself so as to be face to face with Me, to the end that where I, Myself, am** (or: exist) **you folks also can continue being** (or: would ongoingly exist). **And to the place under, where I Myself am progressively leading the way** (or: where I am submissively going), **you have seen and know the Way** (or: path; road)."

That was the "**place**" of which Paul was speaking, in Col. 3:3, above.

In Acts 7:38 we read of, "**the called-out community which was our fathers within the desert** (which consisted of our ancestors in the desolate places of the wilderness)." In 1 Ki.17:1-16 and 19:3-8 we find Elijah (pertinent to the preceding context of chapter 11, above) fleeing into the wilderness to escape Jezebel. And, of course we recall how the younger Moses escaped into the wilderness because he had killed an Egyptian (Ex. 2:15). Then Heb. 11:37-38 presents a Club Med example,

> "**they went around** (wandered) **in sheepskins, in goat skins, continuously being behind** (being in want), **being constantly pressed** (afflicted), **habitually being held in the bad** (being maltreated) **– of whom the System** (the ordered arrangement; the world or culture, secular society, religions and government) **was not worthy – being continually deceived** (led astray; caused to wander) **in deserts and mountains and caves and the holes of the earth.**"

The 1260 days is the identical time period of the ministry of the 2 witnesses of chapter 11, above. It is also the same as the 42 months during which the Holy City (Jerusalem) is being tread under foot by the non-Jews (nations; multitudes). This may be another picture of the same situation, showing a different aspect of the ministry of God's sons to His bride, His people. Note also vs. 11, below, that they did not and do not love themselves (their souls; their inner lives) even to death. Just as Jesus overcame through death and resurrection, thus also do these (recall the resurrection of the 2 witnesses in 11:11-12, above).

Historically, this has reference to the Christians escaping from Jerusalem before its AD 70 destruction, but before that, Acts 8:1 tells us,

> "**Now on that day great persecution and pursuit occurred upon the called-out community [that was] within Jerusalem, so they were all – except for the sent-forth emissaries – dispersed and scattered as seeds down among the regions of Judea and Samaria.**"

Jesus had also suggested,

> "**Now later, when you folks see Jerusalem being continuously surrounded by encamped armies, at that time realize and know from that experience that her desolation has drawn near and is now present. At that point, let the people in Judea progressively flee into the hill country and mountains; then let the people within the midst of her** [i.e., Jerusalem] **proceed departing out of that place**" (Lu. 21:20-21).

The guiding allusion is to Israel's Exodus where they escaped from Egypt and entered upon their wilderness journey to the Promised Land. They were protected and were given provision for 40 years. It was through the ministries of Moses (leadership, water and food) and Aaron (priestly service to the nation) that they were "**continuously nourished.**" Metaphorically, for the 1st century communities, this spoke of their being outside the traditional religions, yet being constantly nourished by the Word and by the Holy Spirit being both within, and among, them. Many in our day have "**[gone] out** (or: should [have been] progressively going out) **toward Him – outside of the Camp – habitually bearing His reproach** (= the censure and disgrace which He bore; or: the insult which pertains to Him)" (Heb. 13:13), i.e., outside of traditional, institutional religions.

7. **Next a war** (or: battle) **was birthed** (broke out; came to be; arose) **within the atmosphere** (or: sky; or: heaven)**: the One, Michael** [the One in God's likeness]**, and His agents [went] to war** (or: to battle) **with the dragon. And the dragon did battle** (or: at once battles; = fought back), **as well as his agents,**

If we have been correct in interpreting these visions as allusions to Israel's exodus, and leading to their wilderness experiences, then this **war** would be an allusion to Israel's entry into the Land of the Promise, and the battle at Jericho. Crossing the Jordan River was a birthing from the wilderness into a land flowing with milk and honey. There, in Josh 5:13-15, we have a spiritual manifestation similar to Moses' "burning bush" experience:

> "when Joshua was at Jericho… [he] looked, and behold, a Man was standing in front of him with his sword drawn in His hand… He replied… 'I, as Prince of the host of Yahweh have now come'…. Then the Prince of the host of Yahweh replied to Joshua, 'Drop off your sandals form your feet, for the **place** on which you are standing, it is holy.'"

Our present picture may be an allusion to this incident. No more is said of this Man, but His self-identifying calls to mind Dan. 10:21.

Israel's birth from the desert and entry into the Land of Promise corresponds to the male Son being born and then being "forcefully carried away," up to God's throne (vs. 5). Joshua with his troops began to take the kingdoms of the Land for Yahweh; Jesus with His body of apprentices likewise began reigning with sovereign influence upon the earth. What follows in both cases is what we saw in 11:15, above: the kingdoms of the world (e.g., the city-state of Jericho, then; the Roman Empire, in John's day), coming under the influence of God's sovereign activities – the first, being described here being **a war/battle within the atmosphere** (or: heaven – the places of religious and political power that controlled people's environment).

The symbol, **Michael** – the name that means "the One who is like God" – has long been recognized as a figure of Christ. In Daniel's visionary cosmology, in his being informed by the "one in human form" (Dan. 10:18) who was speaking to Daniel, the figure Michael was termed as being Israel's Prince (Dan.10:21; 12:1). In other words, this apocalyptic figure represented Israel's Messiah. So His **agents**, here in vs. 7, are a figure for the body of Christ, His emissaries and called-out communities.

The dragon, in the setting of this vision, represents those who were in opposition to the Message of the Christ: that He is Lord; that He is Israel's Messiah. His **agents**/messengers – the sent-forth folks, prophets and teachers – were opposed first by the religious system of the Jews, and later by the political and religious system of Rome. Especially those in Asia Minor were confronted by the trade unions which required ritual worship of their patron deities, as well as the cult of Caesar-worship. Paul termed this battle as,

> "**[the] pulling down** (demolition) **of effects of fortifications** (or: strongholds; strongly entrenched positions [of the "Domination System" – Walter Wink, *Engaging the Powers*]), **progressively tearing down and demolishing conceptions** (concepts; the effects of thoughts, calculations, imaginations, reasonings and reflections) **and every height** (or: high position) **and lofty [attitude, purpose or obstacle] that is habitually lifting itself up against** (or: elevating itself up on so as to put down) **the intimate and experiential knowledge of God, and then taking captive every thought – one after another – and leading them prisoner into the hearing obedience of the Christ** (or: the humble attentive listening from the Anointed One; or: the submissive paying attention, which is the Anointing)" (2 Cor. 10:4b-5).

Reviewing Paul's terminology, here, we find that this is an inner battle to "take thoughts captive" – not to take people captive. By setting the battle in the atmosphere/heaven, John is relating to us the understanding that it is a "spiritual battle," not a war with other "beings." Paul made this clear in 2 Cor. 10:4a,

> "**for you see, the tools and weapons of our military service and warfare [are] not fleshly** (= do not pertain to our human condition; ["are not the weapons of the Domination System" – Walter Wink]), **but rather, [are] powerful ones and capable ones in God** (or: by God)."

Notice the final phrase that Paul used to give the sphere of activity: **in God**, and the means or instrument of our military service/warfare: by God. Keep in mind that we live in God; we are moved about by God; we have our existence in God – Acts 17:28. And, we will see how these **agents** of vs. 7 overcame the dragon and its agents, in vs. 11, below: "**because of the blood of the little Lamb, and** (or: even) **because of the word** (or: message) **of their witness** (or: from their evidence and testimony)." Those are the "weapons of our military service."

We can read about some of the early battles in the book of Acts; history records snippets of our continuing casting down of interior stronghold and corporate strongholds (*cf Engaging the Powers*, by Walter Wink). But in the realm and sphere of God, the battle was won via Christ's death and resurrection. From God's view (i.e., Christ's proclamation, on the cross), "It is finished." Here, Metzger concurs, saying of this, "Michael fighting the dragon is symbolic, representing the real victory won by the atoning death of Christ and the preaching of the gospel" (ibid p 74). This is why Eph. 6 instructs us that all we have to do is stand, while wearing the armor which is God, and we will be able to quench the fiery darts that people throw at us.

8. **and yet they were not strong** (or: had no strength), **neither was their place** (or: position) **any longer found within the atmosphere** (or: heaven; [comment: a symbol of a position of authority, control and dominion]).

This may seem surprising, when contemplating an opponent that has been characterized as a dragon: that it and its agents "**were not strong** (or: had no strength)." But this, of course, is in comparison to the risen Christ and His agents/apprentices. And it is wisdom to keep this in mind as we confront dominating systems of culture, government and religion. But just think of the next clause, "**neither was their place** (or: position) **any longer found within** [OUR] **atmosphere**." How, then, should we be viewing "city hall," i.e., whatever system of domination stands in opposition to life, freedom – and God' reign? What a message of victory and release this vision should trumpet to our hearts and minds! This proclamation of Christ's Victory is the Gospel: Good News – Christ has overcome and reigns within and among us! Jesus Christ is Lord!

We have seen a war in heaven between Michael and His agents and the dragon and its agents, and in the next verse, below, we find that the latter were thrown into the earth, but being here informed that no **place** for them any longer exists within the heaven (or: [our] **atmosphere**). Recalling Beale's suggestion that "**place**" had in some instances become a technical word for "the holy **place**," might this verse suggest that these folks no longer had a "place of influence" in God's temple, as the Romans had enjoyed with the Jewish authorities? On an individual level, when Christ is lifted up within us, and we are seated in His atmosphere (Eph. 2:6), there comes to be no **place** for the dragon and its messengers of gloom and doom, or its agents of strife and division. Recall what Judah said,

> "**For you see, some people came in unobserved, from the side – those having been previously written of old into this judgment** (or: people having from long ago been written into the effects and result of this decision)**: [to exist being] impious ones, people continuously changing the grace and favor of God into licentiousness, as well as repeatedly denying and disowning our only Sovereign and Lord, Jesus Christ**" (Jude 4).

Another layer of understanding, here, is that THOSE whom Jesus had characterized in Jn. 8:44 as,
> "**existing and having [their] being from out of, and having [their] source in, the ancestor who cast [an object] through [someone]** (or: the father, the devil; or: the father – the one thrusting [words or issues] through [folks/groups] and dividing them), **and [they were] habitually wanting** (willing; intending; purposing) **to be constantly doing [their] father's passionate cravings** (full-rushing over-desires),"

suddenly just had,
> "**God's reign** (or: the kingdom of God; the influence and activity from God's sovereignty) **progressively lifted up away from [THEM] and given to an ethnic multitude** (or: nation; people group; swarm of people) **consistently producing its fruit**" (Mat. 21:43).

When the temple in Jerusalem (which represented "heaven" – the place of God's throne) was destroyed, they no longer had a "place" for the old covenant sacrifice cultus, and the lampstand had been moved to be found in the 7 communities to which this letter was written. The ark, which had been lost to them, was now observed by John as being within these called-out communities – among the "Gentile" nations as it was when the glory departed in young Samuel's day (1 Sam. 4:21), but now being in a new covenant, with new branches grafted in (Rom. 11:17) to produce oil for it (Zech. 4:11-14),

> "two olive trees.... two olive branches... empty[ing] golden [oil] [into the lampstand].... These [are] the two sons of oil that stand by the Lord of the whole earth (or: Land)."

The "two witnesses" (Jew plus Gentile) were now being the One new Humanity (the last Adam) in Christ. They were now the corporate Michael, the new temple – the one in the "atmosphere" of the communities, in which God's Spirit had now taken up residence. It was now THEIR **place**. The New Jerusalem was seated with Christ, situated upon the heaven (again: Eph. 2:6; Heb. 12:22).

9. **And so thrown** (or: hurled; cast; tossed) **is** (or: was) **the great dragon, the serpent from the very beginning** (or: the original, or ancient, serpent) **– the one being continuously called "slanderer"**

(one who thrusts something through [folks]; false accuser; separator; a "devil;" one who casts something throughout the midst [to cause division]) **and the adversary** (the opponent; the satan; [*p*47 and other MSS: one who stands in opposition; a counter-worker]), **the one continuously causing the whole inhabited area of the earth to wander** (or: that which causes straying; the one continually deceiving). **It was** (or: is) **hurled** (thrown; cast; tossed) **into the earth** (or: Land), **and its agents were** (or: are) **thrown** (cast; tossed) **with it.**

Here is a key to interpretation which takes us all the way back to the Garden of Eden story in Gen. 3. This apocalyptic character (**the great dragon**) in our story has been directly identified with Eve's **serpent**, and we can likely assume, from this allusion, that it is the same **adversary** (spirit of opposition; Greek and Hebrew: *satan*) that we encounter in Job 1 and 2, and in Zech. 3. It is important to keep this statement in the context of the vision: the dragon represents in this story the same character that the serpent played in Eden's story (Gen. 3); this character is also **adversarial** to the Woman and her children (vs. 13b, below) and it represents those people (or groups) that **thrust things through** others and cause **division**. This character will be seen again in the next chapter where it and its beast-like systems and organizations seek to control humanity and lead them astray. The dragon-serpent-slanderer-adversary is not an ontological spirit-entity, but is a figure in God's story that represents that which tempts, deceives, **leads astray**, brings division, slanders and is adversarial to people. It is a symbol. We saw that its agents had a synagogue in Smyrna, in 2:9, and in Philadelphia, in 3:9, above, and that its throne (seat of power) and its dwelling place was in Pergamos, in 2:13, above. Those were the "heavens" out of which it was thrown. It was cast out of people (e.g., Lu. 10:17-19, below). It is the estranged ego within humans that loves only itself and seeks to control others. John called it that which is "anti-Christ" (1 Jn. 2:18, 22; 4:3). It is the distorted, selfish attitude that takes the place of the Christ-attitude that should be within us. It is the spirit/attitude that wants to exalt itself (Ezk. 28/Isa.14) and be like God by means of the Law (the knowledge of good and evil), instead of being birthed by God to be His child (Jn. 1:13)..

Because "**It was** (or: is) **hurled** (thrown; cast; tossed) **into the earth** (or: Land)," the folks in Rome could, "**trample and crush the adversary** (beat the opponent to jelly; shatter satan) **under [their] feet swiftly**" (Rom. 16:20). Jesus gave His apprentices the ability to accomplish what we read in vs. 9, here:

> "**So look, and realize – I have given to you folks the authority to habitually step on and trample snakes** (serpents) **and scorpions – as well as upon all the power and ability of the enemy** (or: the hostile or adversarial person) – **and nothing will proceed in any circumstance causing you folks harm** (or: wronging you or treating you unjustly)" (Lu. 10:19).

He made this statement following the report of their success over situations in people to whom His apprentices had delivered:

> "**Now the seventy** [other MSS: seventy-two] **returned with joy, one after another saying, 'O Lord, even the demons** (Hellenistic concept and term: = animistic influences) **are continually being subjected to us** (or: set under and arranged below for us) **within and in union with Your Name!' So He said to them, 'I continued gazing, contemplating and repeatedly watching the adversary** (opponent; enemy; or: satan) **suddenly falling – as lightning from out of the sky** (or: as lightning – from out of the atmosphere and heaven).'" (Lu. 10:17-18).

We find one allusion to this in the proverb against the king of Babylon (notice that this is an ancient domination system, as all empires were) in Isa. 14, where vs. 4b observes, "How has the oppressor ceased! The golden City ceased." Then vss. 10b-17 poetically and metaphorically instruct us:

> "Are you also become weak as we? [*cf* Rev. 12:8, above] Your pride is brought down to the grave… the worm is spread under you, and worms cover you. How are you fallen from heaven, O light-bearer, son of the morning! [how] you are cut down to the ground – [one] which had weakened the nations! For you said in your heart, 'I will ascend into heaven; I will exalt my throne

above the stars of God; I will sit also upon the mount of The Congregation, in the sides of the north; I will ascend above the heights of the clouds; I will be like the Most High!' Yet, you will be brought down to the grave (*sheol*), to the sides of the PIT (= the grave)! And the people that see you shall peer at you, and thoughtfully muse, [saying,] 'Is this the MAN that made the land (or: earth; region) to tremble and shook kingdoms... that made the land (earth; region) a wilderness, that did not open the house of his prisoners?'"

Ezk. 28 provides another allusion to a distorted human being (the Prince of Tyrus) brought low. Verse 2 opens with,

"Because your heart [is] lifted up and you have said, 'I [am] God (or: a god): I sit in the seat (throne) of God, in the midst of the seas;' yet you [are] a man (Heb.: *adam*), and not God, even though you set your heart as the heart of God."

Then, in vs. 7-10, it continues,

"I will bring strangers upon you, the terrible of the nations... they shall defile your brightness; they shall bring you down to the pit, and you will die the deaths of [those that are] slain in the midst of the seas... you [will be] a human (*adam*), and no god, in the hand of the person wounding you. You shall die the deaths of the uncircumcised..."

Verses 13-17 provide enigmatic grist for anthropological musings:

"You have been in Eden, the garden of God; every precious stone [was] your covering [note: a reference to the high priest's vestments].... You [are/were] the anointed cherub that covers and shelters... you were upon the holy mountain of God; you have walked up and down in the midst of the stones of fire [a possible allusion to the temple setting].... Your heart was lifted up because of your beauty, you have corrupted your wisdom by reason of your brightness: I will cast you to the ground; I will lay you before kings, so that they may look upon you..."

We see in these two examples a picture of the first Adam (all of us) in the state of estrangement, alienation and distortion. Just the kind of people that Christ came to deliver from such an ignoble existence. We, like Mordecai and Haman, became dragons. In Gen. 49:16-18 it was even foreseen by Jacob that Dan, although destined to "judge (or: adjudicate) his people, as one of the tribes of Israel," would "be a serpent by the way; an adder in the path that bites the horse heels so that the rider shall fall backward." Then Jacob makes an enigmatic statement, "I have waited for Your salvation-deliverance, O Yahweh!" Perhaps this was a plea to God, in our vernacular, "Help us, Lord!" But the main thing to take away, here, is how God casts down the proud, and often compares people to snakes (both John the immerser and Jesus did this, thus labeling the scribes and Pharisees).

Kaplan has pointed to Saul, in Acts 9, that he was **"still continuously inhaling and breathing** (or: in-spiriting and blowing [out]; animated with the spirit of) **threatening and murder** (or: slaughter) **into the midst of the Lord's disciples"** (vs. 1). But when confronted by the risen Jesus, **"with unexpected suddenness a light from out of the midst of the atmosphere** (or: sky; heaven) **flashed around him as lightning, and, having fallen upon the ground, he heard a Voice** (or: sound) **repeatedly saying to him, "Saul... Saul... Why do you continue pursuing and persecuting Me?"** (vss. 3-4). Dan understands Saul's experience as an example of what we read of here, in 12:9, happening to the **great dragon**. Saul had been on the road to Damascus, **"so that if he should be finding anyone being [a part] of** (or: belonging to) **the Way** (or: the Path), **he could lead [them] – both men and women – bound, into Jerusalem"** (vs. 2). In vs. 13, below, we see the dragon doing the same thing. But look what happened next to Saul. We find there, in vss. 17-18,

"So Ananias went off and entered into the house, and after placing [his] hands upon him, he said, "O Brother Saul! The Lord – Jesus, the One being seen by you on the road in which you were coming – has sent me with a mission so that you can look up and see again, and then you can be filled with [the] set-apart Breath-effect (or: [the] Holy Spirit; a consecrated attitude)**!" And immediately there fell off from his eyes [something] like scales**

(or: hulls; shells; rinds; incrustations; [Greek *lepris*; note: *lepra* is the word 'leprosy'; *lepros* is a leper]). **And so he looked up and could see again** (or: recovered his sight). **Next, after standing up, he was immersed** (or: baptized)."

The rest is history, as Saul becomes Paul. This gives us insight to how an adversarial spirit can be transformed into a sacred spirit within people. Paul later had this to say about himself as being one of the

"**failures** (those missing the target; sinners; outcasts), **of whom I myself exist being first** (or: am foremost). **But nonetheless, through this I was mercied, to the end that within me first** (= as the foremost case) **Jesus Christ may point out so as to publicly display every emotion which is long in arriving** (all long-suffering patience that pushes anger far away) **with a view to being an underline** (toward [being] a subtype; for a pattern) **of those about to be habitually believing** (or: progressively trusting, placing faith) **upon Him**" (1 Tim. 1:15b-16).

Paul experienced being,

"**progressively transformed** (transfigured; changed in form and semblance) **by the renewing** (or: in the making-back-up-new again) **of [his] mind** (of the mindset, disposition, inner orientation and world view) **into the [situation and condition for] [him] to be habitually examining in order to be testing and, after scrutiny, distinguishing and approving what [is] God's will** (design; purpose; intent)**: the good and well-pleasing, even perfect** (finished and complete)!" (Rom. 12:2).

An adversarial spirit can be transformed by the renewing of the thinking in a person, and in a corporate institution. Paul would later write, in 2 Tim. 2:

24. **Now it is continually binding for** (a constant necessity to) **a slave of [the] Lord not to be habitually fighting** (battling or contending), **but to the contrary [he/she] is to be gentle** (kind) **toward all, qualified, skillful and able in teaching, one holding up under poor conditions,**

25. **in accommodating meekness and with consideration constantly educating** (training; child-disciplining; instructing; correcting) **those habitually setting themselves in complete opposition or who offer resistance. May not God at some time give a change of thinking to them** (or: Would not God grant in them and supply for them a change of mind), **[directing and leading them] into a full and accurate experiential knowledge of Truth and reality?**

26. **And then they can sober up** (or: would come back to their proper senses) **from out of the adversary's snare** (or: forth from out of the midst of the trap of the person who thrusts something through folks or causes division) – **being folks having been [previously] captured alive under** (or: by) **him, into the will** (intent; design; purpose) **of that one** (or: that person).

Consider how in vs. 25a he says to deal with "those habitually setting themselves in complete opposition," in light of how Christ's followers are to overcome the dragons that they face in life (whether at work, or at home). The Fire of God (which we saw in 11:5, above, and will see again in 14:10, below) can transform a serpent into a seraph – and this can come in His "meekness, and with considerate educating."

10. **Then I heard a great** (or: loud) **voice within the atmosphere** (or: sky; or: heaven) **repeatedly saying, "At the present moment** (or: Just now) **the deliverance** (the rescue; the return to the original state and condition; the health and wholeness; the salvation), **and the power** (or: ability), **and the kingdom** (or: reign) **of our God was** (or: is) **birthed** (comes into existence; came to be), **also the authority** (privilege from Being) **of His Anointed** (or: which is His Christ; from His [Messiah]), **because our brothers' accuser** (person speaking against our members) **was cast down** (or: is hurled down) – **the one that was or is by habit repeatedly accusing** (speaking against) **them before** (or: in the sight and presence of) **our God, day and night."** [thus, the location is on earth, where there is day and night]

This is obviously parallel to 11:15, above, confirming the synchronous context of both passages. Paul gives us another look at the results, quoting Ps. 68:18 in Eph.4:8,

"**Going up** (or: Stepping up; Ascending) **into a height** (unto [the] summit) **He led** (or: leads) **captive a captive multitude** (or: He led 'captivity' captive). **He gave** (or: gives) **gifts to mankind** (or: for, in and among the humans; to humanity)."

So notice that what the **great Voice** in the **atmosphere** continued saying "**was** (or: is; – the timeless aorist tense) **birthed**" and happened all at the same time:
- a) **the deliverance** – i.e., the rescue, or our return to our primal condition in health and wholeness; the salvation [of humanity], i.e., the release and liberation from "slavery to failure"
- b) **the power** [of the Spirit] – or, the ability of God
- c) **the kingdom** – God's reign of sovereign activities and influence:
  "**eschatological deliverance into fair and equitable dealing which brings justice and right relationship in the Way pointed out** (being turned in the right direction; rightwisedness; also = covenant inclusion and participation), **peace** (harmony from the joining) **and joy within set-apart Breath-effect** (or: in union with and amidst a dedicated spirit and a sacred attitude; or: in [the] Holy Spirit)" (Rom. 14:17b).
- d) **authority: right and privilege from out of Being** which belongs to **His Anointed**; which is His Christ or which comes from His Messiah
- e) the **casting down** of our **brothers' accuser**, or, the person or institution that is speaking against our members.

Observe that **the accuser** did this "**day and night**" – signifying that this is here on earth, the place where there is day and night! Paul admonished his listeners to accomplish this very situation:
"**neither be folks constantly supplying nor repeatedly giving a place or position** (or: so don't go on allowing opportunity, a chance, or a room in which to expand) **for** (or: to) **the person who thrusts things through [folks or situations]** (or: the slanderer; the adversary; the accuser; the devil; or: that which casts [harm or division] through the midst of folks)" (Eph. 4:27).

Furthermore, this one speaking against the Body of Christ is doing so within God's presence, and in His sight. This may be an allusion to the adversary (*satan*) in Job chapters 1 and 2. It may be a reference to the situations that Jesus predicted for the disciples, in Mat. 10:17, 19,
"**they will periodically be giving you folks over** (commit you) **unto [their] local city councils and courts, and then they will proceed scourging you with lashes and whips**.... **whenever they may hand you folks over** (commit you), **you should not be anxious or overly concerned about how or what you should be speaking, for, what you should say will continue being given to you men – within that hour!**" Cf Acts 4:17, 21; 5:19ff; 6:11-14; 21:28ff; *et al.*

This is an allusion to the vision of Zech. 3:1-10 where, "the one that thrusts things through people (the one who brings accusations and division) stood at Joshua's right hand, to repeatedly be an adversary for him, and to continue occupying an opposite and opposing position to him" (vs. 2, LXX, JM). But now this accuser no longer enjoyed occupying that privileged "place" (vs. 8, above) as a priest in God's House. What we should see is that all of these players have their part to play in God's grand story of the ages. The negative was there in the beginning (in the Garden… in us) and we find it returning into God (Rom. 11:36) when it is cast into the symbolic, primordial Fire of God, Himself (20:10, below). The pond of Fire, there, is the same cauldron that we see in Mal. 3:2-3, where God sits and removes all the impurities from all that comes back into Him. More on this, below. Cf Job 1:9-6, 12 as analogous to both of these contexts. Another allusion may be to Jude 9,

9. **Yet Michael** (The One Who is like God), **the ruling agent** (the first, chief, or original messenger), **when making a distinction** (a discernment) **to the adversary** (or: the slanderer; the one who thrusts things through folks or situations, and thus causes divisions; the "devil"), **reasoned** (deliberated; spoke thoroughly; discoursed [as in using the Socratic dialectic method]) **concerning the body of Moses. He did not assume to bring a blasphemous or villainous**

judging upon [him] (or: to bring in addition a judging characterized by an abusive distinction or a slanderous decision; or: bring an added evaluating which hindered the light), **but rather, He said, "The Lord** [=Yahweh] **might hold you in added honor** (or: set a value upon you; put respect upon you; award you)."

"Several early church fathers, including Clement of Alexandria and Origen, said that Judah has here quoted the *Assumption of Moses*, and thus most commentators agree. This is an early first century Jewish work of non-canonical apocalyptic literature. Recall that Paul cites Hellenistic literature: Aratis, in Acts 17:28, quotes of Menander in 1 Cor. 15:33 and Epimenides in Tit. 1:12. But Paul also reinterpreted the story of Sarah and Hagar in Gal. 4. We saw Ezekiel and Jesus making other use of Sodom in the comments on vs. 6, above. The question then arises: should this non-Biblical story about Michael, Moses and the adversary be taken as cosmological or ontological reality, or like Paul's use of Greek plays and poetry – as a literary tool? I suggest that Judah is using this Jewish literature to make his point.

"For Michael (found in Dan. 10:13, 21; 12:1 and in Rev. 12:7 – both examples of apocalyptic literature: highly figurative and symbolic) I have parenthetically inserted the Hebrew meaning of the name, since we know so little about this character in those two stories. The eighteenth century Bible expositor John Gill says of this name, "By whom is meant, not a created angel, but an eternal one, the Lord Jesus Christ; as appears from his name Michael, which signifies, 'who is as God'" (John Gill's *Exposition of the Bible*, from BibleStudyTools.com).

"Also, I gave a translation of *arch-angelos*, "**the ruling agent** (the first, chief or original messenger)," to help us decipher this symbol in the story. Creation's first and ruling agent was Adam, in the Genesis story of creation. He was made in God's image – and thus was "like God" in form if not in character. So we have once again entered into God's story of humanity – not into a myth about "spiritual hierarchies" such as we find in dualistic pagan religions. In the figurative setting which forms the preamble to the book of Job, we find God "**making a distinction**" about Job to the adversary (Hebrew: *satan*), and "**reasoning** (deliberating; discoursing)" with the adversary concerning Job's character and situation. I suggest that this is a parallel image. The point of the picture which Judah is painting here is about "speaking respectfully of people" – especially leaders, and he is using this Jewish myth to do so. Michael "**did not assume to bring a blasphemous or villainous judging upon [him]**." Not blaspheme satan? No, not even this tool of God. Paul tells us to "Bless, and do not curse." Furthermore, the "**body of Moses**" most likely does not refer to his physical body any more than "the body of Christ" refers to His physical body in the writings of Paul. Here Judah uses it as a tool of his illustration. John Gill, in referring to this phrase in this verse, states, "it is best of all to understand it of the law of Moses, which is sometimes called Moses himself, [*cf* John 5:45; Acts 15:21; 21:21; 2 Cor. 3:15]; and so the body of Moses, or the body of his laws, the system of them; just as we call a system of laws, and of divinity, such an one's body of laws, and such an one's body of divinity" (Gill, ibid.).

"Now let us consider the word that Michael used. It is from *epi*, upon, and *timao*, to hold in respect, to honor, to value, to award – and thus you see the combined parenthetical amplification in the translation. It is also used in negative connotations, and thus can mean, to assess a penalty upon, or, to respectfully reprove, admonish or chide. But there is no reason not to keep the core meaning of the root: honor, value and respect –

especially in an honor/shame-based society such as we find in our first century contexts. Since this passage is contrasting Michael's actions to the negative actions of those who "came in unobserved," I chose the positive translation of *epitimao* – perhaps turning the *Assumption of Moses* account on its head" (*John, Judah, Paul & ?*, ibid p 78).

And more directly, Jesus Himself spoke explicitly about "**our brothers' accuser**," in Jn. 5:45b,

"**the one constantly accusing** (publicly speaking down against) **you people is** (or: exists being) **Moses, into whom you folks have put your expectation, and on whom you now rely**,"

by which He meant, "the Law." But in Christ's immediate circumstances, observe who wanted to "accuse" Him:

"**So they put a question to Him – to the end that they could accuse** (bring charges against and discredit) **Him**..." (Mat. 12:10).

"**And so, after standing up, the entire full count of them** (= the whole Sanhedrin and all assembled there) **led Him on to Pilate** [the Roman governor]. **Now [once there], they began to be progressively bringing charges and speaking down against Him, while accusing [Him]**..." (Lu. 22:1-2a).

We read in Dan. 6:4ff, that, out of envy of position, the presidents and princes of Babylon plotted to have Daniel killed. When this plot failed, vs. 24 instructs us,

"And so the king commanded and they brought those men which had accused Daniel, and they cast [them] into the den of lions..."

So, as we see, it is normally people who accuse people, or else it is their laws (as in Dan. 6) that does the work for them. We suggest that what the symbol, "**our brothers' accuser** (person speaking against our members)," was a figure of the Jewish leadership and their misuse of the Law. We saw this in the case of Jesus, and then with His apprentices, in the book of Acts. The historical reference was to the destruction of Jerusalem in AD 70; the spiritual reference was to the old covenant which had been distorted into a domination system, but what Paul said had a purpose, and had reference to an ultimate change of reigns:

"**Now Law and custom at one point entered in alongside** (or: intruded into the situation by the side) **to the end that the effect of the fall to the side** (or: so that the result of the offense and the stumbling aside) **would increase to be more than enough** (should greatly abound and become more intense). **But where the Sin** (the failure; the divergence and missing of the target) **increases** (or: abounded to be more than enough; becomes more intense) **THE GRACE** ("the act producing happiness, which is granted as a favor" – Jim Coram) **at once super-exceeds** (or: hyper-exceeded) **over and above, surrounding to excessive abundance and overflow, to the end that JUST AS the Sin** (the failure; the erroneous act; the deviation and digression which issued in missing the goal) **at one point reigned** (or: ruled as king; exercised sovereign sway) **within, and in union with, the Death, THUS SO** (or: in THIS way) **also the Grace and joyous favor would reign** (should rule as king; can exercise sovereign sway) **through an eschatological deliverance that created rightwisedness** (or: by means of being rightly-turned into an existence with equity in [covenantal] solidarity of right relationships which accord to the Way; through a liberating Justice-[expression]) **[which leads] into Life which belongs to, pertains to and has the characteristics of the Age** (or: eonian life; Life of the Age [of Messiah]; a life for the ages) **– through Jesus Christ, our Owner** (Lord; Master)" (Rom. 5:20-21).

The birth of Christ's reign, and the advent of the new covenant, cast down the reign which through the power of the Law had made sin to increase. Paul made this clear in Rom. 7:8-11,

8. **Yet the Sin** (or: the failure; the error; the mistake; the missing of the target; the deviation from the goal), **taking** (receiving; getting) **a starting point** (a base of operation; an occasion; a means of beginning) **through the implanted goal** (impartation of the finished product within; inward directive; commandment [to Adam, then to Israel]), **works** (or: worked) **down to effect and produce within me every full passion, strong impulse, over-desire and craving emotion**

upon things – for apart from Law (or: a custom; or: [Torah]) **sin** (error; failure; missing the target) **[is] dead** (or: [was] lifeless).

9. **Now I was at one time** (or: formerly) **habitually living apart from Law** (or: I was once alive, independent from custom and [Torah]); **yet, in connection with the coming of the implanted goal** (of the impartation of the finished product within; of the inward commandment and directive), **the Sin becomes alive again** (or: deviation, failure, error and the missing of the target revived and comes back to life), **but I die** (or: and I died; yet I die).

10. **Also, the implanted goal** (impartation of the finished product within; inward directive; commandment) **– the one [meant to lead] into Life – this was found by me** (for me; in me; to me) **[to be leading] into death.**

11. **For the Sin** (failure; error; the miss when shooting at a target; the deviation from the goal), **taking a starting point** (receiving an occasion and base of operation) **through the implanted goal** (impartation of the finished product within; inward directive; commandment [to Adam, then to Israel]), **completely makes me unable to walk the Path** (made me incapable to walk out [customs of the Law]; thoroughly cheats and deludes me, making me lose my Way; deceives me; [comment: reference to Eve in Gen. 3:13]) **and through it kills me off** (or: slaughtered me).

And in 1 Cor. 15:56, Paul affirms,

> "**Now the sharp point and stinger of** (or: the sting, thus, the injection from) **the Death [is] the Sin** (the mistake; the error; the failure), **and the power and ability of the Sin [is] the Law.**"

We suggest that it was the beast nature within estranged and distorted people that became a wild animal within them to rise up and kill the two witnesses in 11:7, above. It was the power and ability of the Law that rose up and killed their Lord, in the capital city of that same religious system.

Before moving on, let us consider the time statement that the "**great voice**" made, at the beginning of this verse: "**At the present moment** (or: Just now) **the deliverance… was** (or: is) **birthed** (comes into existence; came to be)." We find Paul using a synonym in 2 Cor. 6:

2. **for He continues saying,**

> "**At an acceptable season** (or: In an appropriate situation; For an agreeable *kairos*) **I fully hear and respond in regard to you, and within a day of deliverance** (on a day of health, restoration and salvation), **at your cry for help, I run to give aid to you** (I run with help for you)." [Isa. 49:8]

Consider! [It is] now (at this moment) **an especially acceptable season** (a fitting situation well-directed toward acceptance; a fertile moment of ease and face to face reception)!

Consider! [It is] now (at this moment) **a day of deliverance** (of health, rescue, safety, salvation and restoration to the wholeness of the original state and condition)!

Then in Eph. 3 Paul affirms:

10. **to the end that now** (at this present time), **in union with the highest heavens, God's greatly diversified wisdom** (or: the many-phased wisdom from God) **could be made known – through the called-out community – to the governments** (or: rulers) **as well as to the authorities and folks with privilege among those situated upon elevated positions**

> (or: made known through the summoned and gathered congregation: by the original members and the folks who have the right, that is, among the upper-heavenly folks;
> or: made known by means of the ecclesia with the founders and people having the privilege – in union with these celestial ones, within the midst of the things situated upon the atmospheres and among the folks [residing] upon the atmospheres),

11. **in accord with** (or: down from; corresponding to) **a purpose of the ages** (a fore-designed aim, plan and object of the unspecified time-periods) **which He formed** (forms; made; constructs; creates; produced) **within the Christ by our Lord and Owner, Jesus,**

12. **within, and in union with, Whom we continuously have the freedom of speech** (or: boldness, which comes with citizenship, to publicly speak the truth of a matter – without fear of reprisal) **and conducted access in the midst of trust** (confident reliance and loyalty), **through His faithfulness, trust, confidence and loyalty!**

We should conclude that the events in the vision of chapter 12 in the Unveiling were a present reality in the days of Jesus and in the days of Paul. Rom. 3:26 speaks in a similar vein:

> "**within the present season** (in the current fitting situation; in union with the current fertile moment), **for Him to be just** (or: One in covenantal solidarity that accords with fair and equitable dealings which comprise the Way pointed out) **and the One liberating, progressively turning in the right direction, making just and freeing from guilt while constantly placing in the Way pointed out which is righted, covenantal relationship** (or: The Right-wiser and Justifier of) **the person [issuing; being born] forth from out of the midst of Jesus' faithfulness**."

Let's consider some other interpretations of this verse. Malcolm Smith suggested that this event happened at the resurrection of Jesus (due to the completed work of Christ): "the heavens rejoiced, the church is now seated in heavenly places, and the devil has lost its authority" (ibid). But Jesus began "casting out" during His earthly ministry:

> "**Yet if I, Myself, in union with God's Spirit** ([being] within the midst of the effect of God's breath; in an attitude which is God) **am constantly driving** (or: casting) **out the demons** (the animistic influences; [a Hellenistic term]) **God's reign** (the kingdom from God; the sovereign rule which is God, and the influence of God) **has consequently preceded and come beforehand upon you people** (or: has really overtaken you folks and is now arrived and settled upon you)" (Mat. 12:28).

We also have the witness from Acts 10:38,

> "**Jesus, the One from Nazareth...went throughout repeatedly doing works bringing goodness, ease and well-being, as well as constantly healing all the folks being continuously held down under power** (tyrannized and oppressed) **by the one that casts things through folks** (the accuser, slanderer, adversary)**... because God was with Him**."

And in 1 Jn. 3:8b we read,

> "**Into this [situation] was** (or: is) **God's Son manifested and made visible, to the end that He would unbind** (loose; untie; destroy; disintegrate) **the works and actions of the adversary who casts things through the midst of folks**."

Ray Prinzing said,

> "We note that this 'war in heaven' is not spoken of until the man-child has been caught up to the throne, and begins to rule.... and now there is a further 'revelation of Jesus Christ,' as He is revealed in the triumph of HIS OVERCOMERS.... When the overcomers rise to take their place in His throne, it signifies that this processing is complete – they are fully born of God [1 John 3:9], their nature is HIS, their image is HIS, their holiness is HIS [Eph. 1:6-7; 2 Cor. 5:21]. And now there is naught that can accuse them – they have become ONE in the standard of His righteousness. No place is found any more for the accuser." (ibid; brackets added)

We suggest that there is a principle portrayed in vs. 7-10. It is that when one is caught up into the heavenlies, to the place of God's authority, that one is then able, "**at that present moment**," to cast the dragon from out of the heavenlies (realm of spirit) within himself, into the earth realm and take dominion over it within his own being. It is this personal catching up of one's spirit into union with God's Spirit (1 Cor. 6:17) that empowers him or her to overcome the serpent within the self (Rom. 7:15-23) or others, along with other spirits of its kind, to the end that they no longer have strength, and there is no longer a place found for them within the individual's atmosphere (heaven; realm of spirit). The war within the individual is Christ (the One in God's likeness) and His powers overcoming on our behalf, delivering us from our "first Adam" characteristics. This is symbolized by the figure of Michael and His agents (vs. 7).

There may be a time when this will happen in fullness for the corporate body of sons, but even in the "in part" state in which we now walk, I suggest that there are areas, figurative "cities" within the kingdom within us, in which we can see "**the adversary** (opponent; enemy; or: *satan*) **suddenly falling – as lightning from out of the sky** (or: as lightning – from out of the atmosphere and heaven)" (Lu. 10:18), even as,

> "**the seventy** [other MSS: seventy-two] **returned with joy, one after another saying, 'O Lord, even the demons** (Hellenistic concept and term: = animistic influences) **are continually being subjected to us** (or: set under and arranged below for us) **within and in union with Your Name!**'" (vs. 17).

Had *satan*, with this experience of the seventy, been completely cast out of every realm of heaven? No, only from out of the individuals over whom the seventy exercised the Lord's authority at that time. We later saw the system's adversarial spirit enter Judas' mind/spirit, in Lu. 22:3. We see a similar picture given by Paul in Rom. 16:20, where he prophesied that the community in Rome would soon crush *satan* under their feet. Paul spoke further, in regard to the whole creation, in Rom. 8:21-22,

> "**because even the creation itself will continue being progressively set free** (will be habitually liberated and constantly made free) **from the slavery of, and from, decay – even the bondage of deterioration which leads to fraying and ruin – [and released] into the freedom of the glory and splendor of God's children**
>> (or: into the liberty of the manifestation of that which calls forth praise from, and a good opinion which pertains to, God's born-ones; or: unto the freedom coming from God's imagination pertaining to God's children; or: into the midst of the freedom of the glory from the children [who] belong to God; or: toward centering in the liberty from the glory, which is God, [and] belongs to the children).
> **You see, we have seen, and thus know and are aware, that all the creation keeps on sighing, groaning or querulously moaning together, and yet progressively travailing together as in childbirth** (continues suffering common birthing pains) **until now** (to the point of the present moment)."

In 1 Tim. 2:5, Paul enigmatically pointed from primordial Eve (Gen. 3:15-16) to the apocalyptic Woman, here in chapter 12:

> "**she will be delivered** (rescued; saved; made whole and restored to her original state and condition) **through the Birth** (or: birthing) **of the Child – should they dwell** (abide) **within trust** (or: faith; faithfulness and loyalty) **and love** (acceptance) **and the results of being set-apart** (holiness; the quality of sacred difference), **with soundness of mind** (sanity; sensibility). **The Word [is] full of faith!** (or: Trustworthy [is] this message)."

But because Israel gave birth to Christ, the Man-child, she herself **will be delivered**, as we discovered in Rom. 11:

> 26. **So then, thus, in this manner and with this result: all Israel will progressively be delivered** (rescued, saved, made whole and restored to their original position [in the olive tree]), **according as it has been written,**
>> "**The One continuously dragging out of danger and drawing to Himself** (The Rescuer; The Deliverer) **will repeatedly arrive and be present from out of Zion; He will continue turning irreverence away from Jacob.**
> 27. "**And this [is] the arrangement for them from beside Me** (or: And this [will be] My covenant in, to and for them) **when I take away their failures** (deviations; sins; mistakes; misses of the target; shooting amiss of the goal)." [Isa. 59:20-21; 27:9]

Now Paul explains the temporary "dragon" relationship Israel had with the Christ-communities, at that time (before the she-dragon, Jerusalem, was cast down from her place in the heavens [i.e., her place as the priesthood in the Temple]), in the next two verses of Rom. 11:

> 28. **Corresponding to** (With respect to; In accord with; Down from) **the Good News** (the message of goodness and well-being), **on the one hand, [they were] ENEMIES** (hostile ones; ones regarded as enemies) **because of** (or: through; with a view to) **you folks; on the other hand, according to** (in accord with; down from; corresponding to) **the selection** (the choosing out; the election) **[they are] LOVED ONES, because of** (with a view to) **the fathers** (= the ancestors),
>
> 29. **for you see, the grace-effects and the calling of God** (or: because the results of God's joyous favor and invitation) **[are] void of regret and without change in purpose** (or: unregretted; not to be regretted afterward; are not subject to recall; = are never taken back).

So, "**our brothers' accuser** (person speaking against our members) **was cast down**." Now, other than it pursuing and persecuting the Woman (vs. 13, below), what does this mean for us? To Paul the answer was unveiled, and he bursts forth in Rom. 8:

> 34. **Who [is] the one habitually bringing commensurate evaluations or corresponding decisions** (or: constantly condemning and giving a verdict down against; or, as a future: will be separating by following the patterns so as to be indicting or passing sentence)**?**
> **Now Christ Jesus [is] at the same time the One dying, yet very much more being aroused and raised, Who also exists within God's right side** (at God's right hand or position), **Who also continuously hits on-target within** (or: falls in with the situation and addresses the concerns) **over our [situation and predicament] and on our behalf!**
>
> 35. **Who or what will be separating, dividing or parting us away from the Love of and from Christ** (or: the separation-overcoming acceptance which is Christ)**? Pressure** (squeezing; affliction; tribulation; oppression), **or confinement in a narrow, tight place** (distress; difficulty; trouble), **or pursuit** (the chase of persecution), **or famine** (or: hunger; deprivation of food), **or nakedness** (lack of sufficient clothing), **or danger** (peril; risk), **or sword?**

Those questions are rhetorical, for he continues, via an OT quote, that, Yes, we do have persecutions:

> 36. **Accordingly as it has been written,**
>
>> "**On Your account** (For Your sake; By reason of You) **we are progressively being put to death the whole day! We are logically considered** (accounted) **as sheep which belong to slaughter** (are associated with slaughter).**"** [Ps. 44:22] *Cf* 6:9-11, above.

But this is not the end of the story, for:

> 37. **But rather** (or: On the contrary), **within all these things we are habitually over-conquering** (we continue more than overcoming) **through the One loving, urging toward reunion with, and giving Himself to, us.**
>
> 38. **For you see, I have been persuaded and now stand convinced that neither death, nor life, nor agents** (or: messengers), **nor sovereignties** (rulers; those in prime position), **nor things being now here** (being placed within, at present), **nor things about to be** (impending, or about to consecutively come), **nor powers,**
>
> 39. **nor height, nor depth, nor any other or different created thing** (or: founded institution) **will be having power or be able to separate, divide or part us from God's Love** (or: from the acceptance from God; from the urge toward reunion, which is God; God's full giving of Himself to us) **which is within Christ Jesus, our Owner** (Lord; Master; Possessor).

And we see that this is the case, from vs. 11-17, below.

11. **And they at once overcame** (or: at some point conquer) **him** (or: it) **because of and through the blood of the little Lamb, and because of the word of their witness, as well as through the message**

from their testimony (that reason laid-out from the evidence, which is them) – **and they love not** (or: did not participate in union with) **their soul** (soul-life; inner selfhood) **even to** (or: until; as far as) **death.**

We should first keep in mind that this verse flows from, and is the result of, what is expressed in vs. 10. Beale suggests that it "summarizes the purpose of the whole chapter and especially vss. 7-12" (ibid p 663). This is where we see that they did not **love**, or, "participate in union with," **their souls**: a fulfillment of Mat. 16:24-26, denying the self and taking up the cross – destroying the soul for His sake. This verse presents the fact: the death of the Messiah (figured in, "**the blood of the little Lamb**"). It also presents the living out of the resurrected Life in Christ: "**the word of their witness**." Here is an allusion to 1:10, above, "**because of God's Word** (or: the message which is God; the thoughts and ideas from God) **and because of the testimony** (witness; evidence) **pertaining to and having the characteristics of Jesus Christ**."

In note 130, Beale (ibid p 664) cites the works of I.T. Beckwith (*Apocalypse*, 627) and M. Stuart (*Apocalypse* II, 259) as preferring, "a notion of means," in the prepositional phrases of *dia* with an accusative in the two prepositional phrases, within this verse, having this construction. Based on this, as confirming my own research on the use of *dia*, I have correspondingly conflated the renderings to reflect both nuances of the preposition, with the following implications:
    a) **because of the blood of the little Lamb** looks back to the cross, and the work of Christ
    b) **through the blood…** speaks to its ongoing effect in their lives
    c) **because of the word of their witness**, which says that their witness was a part of the cause of their victory
    d) **as well as through the message from their testimony**, which emphasizes the means and instrument of overcoming
    e) "that reason laid-out from the evidence, which IS them" expresses another meaning of *logos*, and renders the following phrase in apposition: i.e., their lives lay out and give evidence of God's reason: His "plan of the ages," and the Christ Event. They ARE (exist being) His witnesses.

The last phrase, "**even to** (or: until; as far as) **death**," is parallel to 2:10, above, "**be a faithful and reliable person until death**." In Acts 22:4, Paul explains: "**I – who quickly gave pursuit and persecuted this Way, to the extent of death**." This is an example of what vs. 11, here, is speaking. We also have a direct echo of 6:9, above:
> "**the souls of the folks having been slaughtered [as in sacrifice] because of the Word of God** (or: God's message), **and because of the witness** (testimony; evidence) **which they were holding** (or: continued to have)."

And then, in vs. 17, below, we see the dragon going after, "**those continuously keeping** (guarding; observing) **God's implanted goals** (inward directives) **and continuously holding the testimony of and from Jesus** (or: having the evidence about and possessing the character of Jesus)."

This is an obvious allusion to the death of the two witnesses, in 11:7, above, and to those such as Stephen, in Acts 7:1-60. It also picks up the thread in 5:6, above. We saw His blood again, in 7:14, above, where we read, "**they washed their robes** (uniforms; equipment) **and made them bright and white within the little Lamb's blood**." All of the whole life of the called-out communities stemmed from, "**the blood of the little Lamb**." And that **blood** issued forth from their proclamations about the Lamb: His death and now His life as Lord of lords and King of kings. That was their story; that was their song.

Seeing the "life of the covenant communities" portrayed in this symbol of vs. 11 calls to mind what John said in 1 Jn. 1:7b, where His blood may well be a figure for His Life:

> "**the blood of, from, and which is Jesus, His Son, keeps continually and repeatedly cleansing us** (or: is progressively rendering us pure) **from every sin** (or: from all error, failure, deviation, mistake, and from every shot that is off target [when it occurs])."

This may well be an allusion to the sprinkling of the blood on the altar and on the mercy seat on the Day of Atonement (*cf* Heb. chapter 9, in Israel's cultus-type, when all the sins of Israel for the previous year were cleansed away. We read in Heb. 10:19-22 how this applies to us:

> 19. **Therefore, having freedom, openness and boldness of speech which comes from being citizens, brothers, with a view to the Entrance of the set-apart places** (or: into the Pathway-into the midst, pertaining to the Holiest Place, which is the separated ones and which pertains to the sacred folks) – **within and in union with the blood of Jesus;**
> 20. **a Way** (Path) **which was done anew** (or: which He innovates and makes new in species, character or mode, within and in the midst) **for us and in us, recently slain and yet living, through the veil that is His flesh** – [*cf* Jn. 14:6; Rev. 5:6]
> 21. **along with a Great Priest [enthroned] upon God's House –**
> 22. **we can be continuously and progressively approaching with a true heart in union with full-assurance from the completed act of faithfulness** (or: centered within [the] full-carrying from [His] loyalty and fidelity), **the hearts having been sprinkled from a misery-gushed consciousness of what is evil or unserviceable** (or: a conscience in a bad condition), **and then the body having been bathed in and by clean water.**

It further reminds us of Jesus' words,

> "**No one continues holding** (or: having) **greater love** (urge toward reunion) **than this: that someone should place** (set; lay down) **his soul** (or: soul-life; inner being; self; person) **over [the situation or circumstances of]** (or: on behalf of) **his friends**" (Jn. 15:13).

This is also an allusion to 3:21, above:

> "**To** (or: In; For) **the person who is habitually conquering I will continue giving** [the right?] **to sit with Me within My throne, AS I ALSO conquer** (or: conquered) **and sit with My Father within His throne.**"

He also overcame through death; through not loving His life or soul. We can further hear an echo from the witness of John, the immerser,

> "**Look!** (Pay attention, see and perceive)! **God's Lamb** (or: the Lamb from God; the Lamb having the character and qualities of God; or, in apposition: the Lamb which is God), **the One continuously lifting up and progressively carrying away the Sin of the world, and removing the sin which belongs to and is a part of the System**
>> (or: habitually picking up and taking away the failure and error brought on by the organized system; progressively removing the falling short and the missing of the goal from the world of culture, religion, economy and government, society, and from **the aggregate of humanity**)!" (Jn. 1:29).

These folks had drunk from the Life of Jesus, for Jesus had given this stipulation in Jn. 6:

> 53. **Then Jesus said to them, "Most truly I am now laying out the arrangement for you people: unless you folks should at some point eat the flesh of the Son of the Human** (= the eschatological messianic figure), **and then would drink His blood, you are continuing not holding** (or: habitually having or presently possessing) **Life within yourselves!**
> 54. "**The person habitually eating My flesh and drinking My blood is continuously possessing** (habitually or progressively having) **eonian Life** (life derived from and having the qualities of the Age; age-enduring life), **and I, Myself, will proceed raising, resurrecting and standing him back up again in the Last Day,**
> 55. "**for My flesh is true** (real; genuine) **food, and My blood is true** (real; genuine) **drink.**

We suspect that not only was this same idea in the metaphor of the Vine and His branches (which drink of the "sap" of the Vine; Jn. 15:1ff), but also in the "cup" that He and His followers would drink:
> "**Do you now have power and do you continue able to drink the cup which I Myself am now progressively drinking…. You folks WILL progressively drink the cup which I Myself am now progressively drinking**" (Mk. 10:38-39).

We can see another layer, here: the allusion to and background of the lambs' blood on the doorposts which symbolized the overcoming of Israel over Egypt (the dragon) and which began their Exodus.

12. **Because of this, you atmospheres** (or: heavens) – **and the folks continuously tabernacling** (or: normally living in a tent; presently encamping) **within the midst of them – must continuously make yourselves glad** (keep or develop a good frame of mind; rejoice). **Woe to** (or: Alas for; A tragedy into) **the Land** (or: earth) **and the sea, because the slanderer** (separator; opposer; "devil;" the one who thrusts-through) **is** (or: was) **cast down to you, having great anger** (violent breathing; rushing passion), **knowing that he continues having a little season** (a small suitable place; a limited circumstance; a brief fitting situation).

The first half of this verse corresponds to 11:15a, 16 and 19, above. The worship of the 24 old folks is because God reigns and in 12:10 God's reign is birthed and the brothers' accuser lost its position in the heavens (i.e., the temple). In 11:19, the new temple (Christ's body; the covenant communities) is opened in heaven, and here they are called "**you atmospheres/heavens**." What was given as a snapshot view in 11:15-19 is here in chapter 12 presented step-by-step, in different but related figures. The heavens also represent the spirits of the people going through these experiences. They rejoice because Jesus is Lord. But their daily lives will still go through the **great anger** of the dragon through the persecutions of Christ's followers (in the book of Acts, and elsewhere in the NT) by the religious dragon/accuser (Jewish leadership and the Law), and then the collateral damage of Rome wasting Judea when quelling the rebellion. The second half of the verse corresponds to that persecution by the Jewish religionists (such as Saul and his friends). We will later find the beast (Nero) in Rome persecuting Christians, but the figure of the dragon is the spirit of the domination system that, like Saul, was filled with violent breathing and rushing passion (Acts 9:1) to wipe out this new "sect." The two witnesses are still in the city where their Lord was crucified, and the little animal (beast) will rush on them in great passion, and kill them, before the heavens can rejoice at their resurrection.

Here, in the first clause, we have an allusion to Isa. 49:13,
> "Be jubilant, heavens!... for Yahweh comforts His people, and He is having compassion on His humbled ones" (CVOT).

Deut. 32:43 proclaims,
> "Be jubilant, heavens, together with Him, and worship Him, all the messengers (agents) of God."

Then 1 Chron.16:31 reads, "Let the heavens rejoice…" Likewise is Ps. 96:11, "Let the heavens rejoice…" And Isa. 44:23 gives the reason: "Be jubilant, O heavens, for Yahweh has done it!" And Dan. 3:59 (LXX, Old Greek) instructs them, "Bless the Lord, you heavens…" Obviously, the address, "**you atmospheres** (or: heavens)," is a personification, but the casting-down of the dragon and its agents from their place of power in God's reign (i.e., the taking of the kingdom away from the Jewish leadership) was a cause for rejoicing and a "good frame of mind" in the realm of God's reign that had now passed to Christ's apprentices (the sent-forth folks and the covenant communities). But the Jewish slanderers and opposition made life on earth a **woe** for the Christ's apprentices.

This verse proclaims gladness and rejoicing to some, but **woe** (or: tragic situations) to others. It sets forth two realms of existence: heaven or earth. Now both realms are physically part of the same universe.

Heaven, or the sky, our **atmosphere**, was normally a reference to where there are clouds (as we saw in the Son of man vision, in Daniel). But it was a custom for the Jews to consider the rulers of the people (which when having no king of their own, was usually the priest class) as being their "heavens," and the symbol for that was the temple (which was supposed to be God's house among the people). Those who dwelled on **the Land** were the common people. If this symbolic dichotomy is still in play in this vision, then those now represented by the temple, or living in the heavens (the Jerusalem which is above, Gal. 4:26), would be the called-out communities. The **slanderer** (etc.) would be a figure of the Jewish persecutors of Christ's followers. The casting-down of the physical temple (the seat of the Jewish leaders' authority) in AD 70 would signal an end of their persecution of the Christ-community – both in Jerusalem and in Asia Minor, but it was a **woe** to the Land of Israel, those who continued in the old covenant religion. Furthermore, the adversarial spirit that was in the Jewish leadership, and its agents, was also in the domination system of Rome. This, it would seem, is the "third woe," spoken of, above.

Chilton (ibid p 318) understands **the Land** and **the sea** now to be the domain of the dragon, and cites chapter 13, below, which has "two great Beasts in the Dragon's image, arising from the Sea and the Land." Historically, this would speak of Rome coming by sea into Palestine as the Empire strikes back at the Jewish rebellion. At the same time, the dragon that called for the death of Christ continued bringing woe to the covenant communities. For a short season, those of the Jewish rebellion (during the time leading up to AD 70) would have been hostile to the Christ-community in Jerusalem (before they escaped to Pella), and following Jerusalem's destruction, there may have remained hostility to Christians in Asia Minor – but only for "**a little season**." We will see a description of this woe to the Land beginning with 13:1, below.

On another layer of interpretation, the folks who are "**tabernacling** within the **atmospheres** of the heavens" are a reference to the called-out communities, who ARE NOW the tabernacle, or, God's temple. Peter used this term concerning himself in 2 Pet. 1:13-14, "**as long as I continue existing within this tent-effect** (or: tabernacle)." We find that God will tabernacle with humanity, in 21:3, below, and where He is there is "heavenly life." The symbolic phrase here is a metaphor for living one's life, or dwelling, in the realm of God's reign; it is living in Christ; it is walking according to the Spirit (to use Paul's terms, Rom. 8:1). We who are seated with Christ in the heavens (or: in God's atmosphere) should be rejoicing in the resurrected life which we enjoy, and in the fact that He has overcome the dragon and its agents – no matter in which sphere of existence we had encountered them: the spiritual expressions in religion, culture, economics or government. We have cited a picture of this (Heb. 12:22-24), above. Paul says this another way, in Col. 3:

> 1. **Since, therefore, you folks were awakened and are raised up together in the Christ, be constantly seeking and trying to find the upward things** (or: the things being above), **where the Christ is** (exists being), **continuously sitting within the right [side]** (or: at the right [hand]) **of God.**
> 2. **Be constantly minding** (thinking about; setting your disposition and sentiments toward; paying regard to) **the upward things** (or: the things above), **not the things upon the earth,**
> 3. **for you folks died, and your life has been hidden so that it is now concealed together with the Christ, within the midst of God** (or: in union with God).

This would include those realms of heaven within us, individually, where these things have happened: we can rejoice and **make ourselves glad** in the Lord while keeping and developing "A GOOD FRAME OF MIND." But there is yet a woe to our lower realm, our land, our earth, because the adversary has been cast into this area of our life, and comes "down toward [us], having great swelling emotion and rushing passion." This is our personal dragon, be it old, distorted mind-sets, addictions, or anything that exalts itself against the knowledge of God (2 Cor. 10:5). So we should not be surprised to at times find ourselves in the grip of such inner feelings – until Christ within has our "earth" swallow up what is cast forth to envelope us as we go into a wilderness time (vss. 14 and 16, below). But we should take courage, for it has but **a little season** (or a small situation or suitable place and occasion) within which to work. Its end is sure.

13. **And when** (at the time that) **the dragon suddenly saw** (or: sees; perceived; observes) **that it is thrown** (was cast, thrust) **into the earth** (or: Land), **it pursued** (pursues, presses forward, runs swiftly to catch) **and persecuted the Woman who brought forth** (= gave birth to) **the Man** (or: male).

This verse reaches back to vs. 6, above, where, "**the Woman fled** (or: takes flight) **into the wilderness**," and then builds on 12b, above. Here we see an allusion to Pharaoh pursuing Israel as they left Egypt (Ex. 14). I conflated the two meanings of the verb (**pursued; persecuted**) since both are in view in the context of the vision. Saul and his associates stepped into history by pursuing Christians, as we read in the book of Acts. Others of the Jewish religion kept this up even after Saul's Damascus Road experience with the risen Jesus, and his call to be one of His sent-forth emissaries (Acts 9).

Continuing to view this passage historically, we can see that the Judaizers chased after the called-out communities, trying to overwhelm them with works of the Law: from circumcision to keeping the sabbath to celebrating the feasts (as well as keeping days, observing months, etc.). This was Paul's reason for writing both Galatians and Romans (as per Douglas A. Campbell, *The Deliverance of God*, 2009). The spirit of keeping codes and rituals continued on in many of the Jews who converted to Christianity – and so it has been to this very day, even among those who were never a part of the Jewish religion.

But what did Paul say, in addressing this unpleasant situation? In chapter 12 of his letter to the covenant community in Rome, he said,
> 14. **You folks keep on speaking well of** (or: repeatedly think goodness for; continue blessing) **the people consistently pursuing and persecuting you: be continuously blessing** (speaking well of [them] or thinking goodness for [them]) **and stop cursing** (or: you must not continue praying down on, or wishing anything against, [things, situations or people])!

Continuing on, in vss. 18b-19a he admonished them to:
> "**[live] being folks continuously at peace with all mankind** (or: in joined harmony in the midst of all people), **not being folks habitually getting justice for yourselves** (not maintaining what is right concerning yourselves; not avenging yourselves), **beloved ones, but on the contrary, you folks must yield the position held in anger** (or: give a place for [His] natural impulse, propensity, passion and personal emotion; give place to [His] intrinsic fervor; relinquish [your] right to anger or wrath), **for it has been written,**
> > '**In Me** (or: For and By Me; With Me) **[is] maintenance of justice**…"

Then in vss. 20-21, he gave examples:
> "**If your enemy** (the one hostile to you) **should perhaps be hungering** (or: continues hungry), **continue feeding him morsels** (supplying him with food); **if he may continue thirsting** (be constantly thirsty), **continue giving drink to him** (causing him to drink), **for while constantly practicing** (performing; doing) **this you will progressively pile on and heap up burning coals** (embers) **of fire upon his head.**" [Prov. 25:21-22]
> > [comment: the directives of feeding and giving drink correspond to what was to be done for brothers in Matt. 25:35, 40; the metaphor of heaping coals may correspond to Isa. 6:6 where a coal from the incense altar purged sin, so being put on his head may be a picture of purging his thinking; Wuest suggests this as supplying a needed source of fire for someone's home, meeting a desperate need – *Word Studies*, vol. 1, p. 220; as the first two are blessings, I suggest that this latter also is]

Do not be habitually conquered under (or: Stop being overcome by) **the worthless** (the bad of quality; the ugly and unsound; the evil), **but to the contrary, be constantly conquering** (overcoming; victorious over) **the worthless** (the unsound, the bad and the ugly; the evil) **[by being] in union with The Good One** (or: [a participant] within what is profitable; or: in the midst of virtue)."

[comment: this verse points to a positive interpretation of the burning coals in vs. 20]

Jesus included such situations in the "Beatitudes," in Mat. 5:

11. **"You folks are and continue to be happy** (and: blessed) **people! Now whenever people may denounce, reproach, heap insults on and persecute or chase you folks, and while continuously lying, may even say every bad thing** (spreading malicious gossip; [other MSS: every misery-gushed utterance]) **down against you – for the sake of Me,**
12. **be continuously rejoicing and repeatedly express extreme exultation, because your wage** (compensation; reward) **[is] much** (large; great), **within the heavens** (or: atmospheres [that surround you])! **You see, they persecuted the prophets before you in the same way.**

Now consider who the "they" were, in the last clause just quoted. "They" were the Jewish leadership of His day. Now concerning the historical situation to which this vision first applied, recall what Jesus said to His apprentices in Mat. 10:22-23,

"**And further, you folks will continue being hated, detached and regarded with ill-will by everyone – because of My Name. Yet the one remaining under [these conditions] and patiently enduring into a conclusion** (or: into an ending [of these events]; unto [the] final act) – **this one will habitually be rescued** (delivered; saved). **Now whenever they may continue chasing you or be repeatedly persecuting you in this [particular] city, proceed taking flight** (escaping) **into a different one, for, truly – I now say to you folks – you can under no circumstances complete the circuit of** (or: finish [visiting]) **the cities** (or: towns) **of Israel until the Son of the Man** (humanity's son; = the awaited Messianic figure) **should go** (or: comes; can come and then go)."

See, also, Mat. 24:9, where He was speaking about the time of the destruction of the Temple.

The dragon of "control and domination" was also incarnated in Rome, which, even after the destruction of Jerusalem and the quelling of its 1st century rebellion, from time to time continued to persecute the Christian movement. Both political regimes and religious institutions have been dragons of persecution all through history. John was writing of his own time, but the messages from these visions are, unfortunately, timeless. We live with it today. But our next verse gives hope.

14. **Then two wings of the Great Eagle** (or: Vulture) **were given to the Woman** (or: are given for the Woman), **to the end that she may progressively fly into the wilderness** (desert; uninhabited region) – **into her place – where** (in which place) **she is there continuously nourished a season, and seasons, and half a season** [Dan. 7:25; 12:7], **away from the serpent's face** (= its presence and ability to observe; = its influence).

This is an allusion to Ex. 19:4,

"You have seen what I did to the Egyptians when I bore you on vultures' [or: eagles'] wings and brought you to Myself" (CVOT; brackets added),

and, to Deut. 32:11-12,

"As an eagle [or: vulture] stirs up its nest, hovers over its fledglings [and] spreads its wings, taking one, bearing it on it pinions, Yahweh alone guided him [= Israel]..." (Rotherham; brackets added).

The primary background for this symbol is Israel's Exodus from Egypt. Here, the "Jerusalem which is above" (Gal. 4:26) is fleeing from both the dragon of the old covenant (the priests, scribes and Pharisees)

and the dragon which was Rome. For the Jewish Christians in the late AD 60's, the wilderness would have been any setting away from Jerusalem, which had been the traditional "world" of the old covenant. We read encouraging words concerning Yahweh that seem to fit this situation, in Ps. 103:5-7,
> "Who satisfies, with good, your age; your youth renews itself like an eagle; Yahweh is One who executes justice – yes, vindication for all the oppressed – Who made known His ways to Moses, His doings unto the sons of Israel."

And in Ps. 54:7, "For out of all distress has He rescued me." Then in Ps. 57:1b,
> "And in the shadow of Your wings will I take refuge, until the storm of ruin passes by."

Then, one of my personal favorites, Ps. 91:1, 4,
> "He that dwells in the secret place of the Most High will lodge under the shadow of the Almighty…. With His pinion will He cover you, and under His wings will you seek refuge; a shield and buckler is His faithfulness."

So this vision draws on Israel's rich history of God's protection and care.

The "**Woman**," Christ's bride continued to be forced to flee into the wilderness, outside of what came to be the institutional church, but the "earth" (the secular community) was found to be more loving and accepting than the dragon-riding woman of chapter 17. From the individual application, when the spirit is caught up to Christ's authority, it feeds and helps the soul through the dry periods.

This verse shows us that the called-out person and community are given the ability to enter the heavens, to fly (given wings of the Great Eagle, which is the figure of Christ, the Anointing, that face or aspect of the "living being" seen in chapter 4, above – what Paul Tillich calls the "new being"). At this stage of God's dealings with His people, we are taken to a place away from the serpent's face – and remember where satan's throne and dwelling place is: Pergamos (2:13, above), a part of the corporate institutional church. She (figure of those in Christ) is separated in this wilderness for the same time period specified in chapters 11, 12 and 13: for 3 and ½ years, or a season, seasons, and half a season. It is the figurative time period of the ministry of God's sons – both to her, and to those dwelling in "Sodom and Egypt" (11:3-8, above). But keep in mind that this is a **place** and a time of **nourishment** and of learning His ways. Paul spoke of this in Eph. 5:21, "**continually setting and arranging yourselves under** (placing yourselves in humble alignment; subordinating yourselves; being submissive) **so as to support one another, in respect for Christ**," and then a few verses later he gave these enlightening admonitions:
> 25. **O husbands, be constantly loving, and urging to unity with, [your] wives** (or: Men, continue giving yourselves for and accepting the women), **accordingly and correspondingly as the Christ also loved** (or: to the degree that, and commensurately as, the Anointed One loves and unambiguously accepts) **the called-out community, and gave Himself up** (or: commits and transfers Himself over) **in behalf of** (for the sake of; over [the situation of]) **her,**
> 26. **to the end that He may set her apart** (separate her; consecrate and make her holy), **cleansing** (purging) **[her] by the bath of the Water [that is] within a result of a flow** (or: in union with a gush-effect; or: in the midst of a spoken word, a declaration, or an utterance),
> 27. **so that He Himself could place beside Himself** (or: should present to and make to stand alongside in and with Himself) **an inwardly-glorious and honorable** (or: held in honor and high esteem; in-glorious-array; or: inwardly-reputable; centered-in-glory) **called-out community – [which] is continuously having neither spot** (or: stain), **nor wrinkle, nor any of such things, but to the contrary – to the end that she would continuously exist being set-apart** (holy; different from the 'ordinary and profane') **and flawless** (unblemished; or: unblamable).

Christ is the Husband of the Woman, and He will continue loving her the same way that He always has. As He has given her His wings, He had desired to use those wings as a hen to gather to Himself the Jerusalem of the 1st century (Mat. 23:27; Lu. 13:34 – and those references were to the context of what would be coming to historical Jerusalem in AD 66-70, and of what we read here in the Unveiling).

Numbers are significant in this book. It could have said that she was given "the wings of the Great Eagle," and we would have understood that a bird has two wings. The two wings are a reference to the two witnesses, as two is the number of witness in Scripture – Yahweh's witnesses (Acts. 1:8). This ministering body gives the Woman the gift of flying above adversarial circumstances in her life. Isa. 40:31 is a familiar vs., "But those who are hoping in Jehovah will regain power. They will mount up with wings like eagles..." (NWT). The NEB renders it, "but those who look to the Lord will win new strength, they will grow wings like eagles." Young reads, "But those expecting Jehovah pass [to] power, they raise up the pinion as eagles..." And the Tanakh says, "... shall renew their strength as eagles grow new plumes." These are varied renderings of a picture which expressed the truth in the prior vs. (29) of that context, that "He gives vigor to the weary, new strength to the exhausted" – a comforting promise. But these figures also suggest the ascending to a higher realm – one where there is nourishment for the spirit.

In our picture here in 12:14, we see that she can "**progressively fly**" (Greek present tense). When God births something new in us, this pattern will usually be followed and we will need to fly away from the serpent's face. Those who are a community where the serpent resides will always want to devour your child. Note also that she flies "**into her place**." This calls to mind the words of Jesus to His disciples in John 14:

> 2. **"Within My Father's house** (or: household) **are many abodes** (staying places; dwelling places; homes; rooms). **Now if not, I would at once tell you folks, because I am progressively passing** (or: traveling) **along to prepare and make ready a place in you** (or: for you; with and among you folks).
> 3. **"Even if I should journey on and prepare** (make suitable, fit and appropriate) **a place** (or: a spot; a position; a role) **in you folks** (or: with you; for you), **I am now presently** (or: progressively; repeatedly; habitually) **coming again, and then, I will progressively take you folks in My arms and receive you to Myself, directing you toward Myself so as to be face to face with Me, to the end that where I, Myself, am** (or: exist) **you folks also can continue being** (or: may and would ongoingly exist)."

Let's consider for a moment that the 1260 days of vs. 6 is called "**a season, and seasons, and half a season**" in vs. 14. Thus, this period of persecutions is for "seasons." It was for this same time period that Jerusalem was to be given to the nations for them to tread upon her (11:2, above). Luke 21 speaks of this situation,

> 24. **"And so, folks will keep on falling by [the] mouth of a sword, and [others] will proceed being led captive into all the nations** (or: into the midst to unite with every ethnic group) **– and Jerusalem will continue being progressively trampled by and under pagans** (non-Jews; those of the nations) **– until where they can be made full** (or: should be filled [up]; or: would be fulfilled). **And then there will progress being seasons of ethnic multitudes** (or: fitting situations pertaining to nations; or: occasions which have the qualities and characteristics of pagans; or: fertile moments from, and with regard to, non-Jews).
>> [D omits: seasons of nations; with other MSS: ... and then Jerusalem will continue existing being repeatedly trampled by nations up to the point where seasons of (or: appointed times from) nations can at some point be fulfilled or filled full]

Was this "seasons of nations (gentiles; non-Jews)" the period of three and a half years that lead up to AD 70, a season of the Romans who destroyed the Jews as a nation and as a religion? With the return of Christ in judgment upon the Jews (through the agency of the Romans), breaking out some of the branches of the olive tree (Israel, Rom. 11:17ff), what was left was the olive tree (the believers from the Jews), with the wild olive branches (the believing Gentiles) grafted into it, which came to be termed "the called-out community," the "little flock" to whom He gave the kingdom (Lu. 12:32). Historically, from the 1st century to the present, it has SEEMED primarily to be "**seasons of ethnic multitudes**," because the Christ-communities (made up of all ethnic groups – including Jews) did not have cultural markers (like circumcision; purity codes, etc.) that the Jews had maintained because of their Law. Perhaps this is due to what Paul instructed us in Eph. 2:11 concerning what had been separate categories, once known as "**uncircumcision**," i.e., the Gentiles, and, "**circumcision**," i.e., the Jews. These contrasting categories no longer exist in the "new creation" (2 Cor. 5:17); they have "passed away," and in God's relating to humans all people groups are now One New Humanity (the Second Humanity – 1 Cor. 15:47). He refers to the previous two categories as "The Both," in the following verses of Eph. 2, explaining how this change came to be:

> 13. **But now, within, in union with and centered in Christ Jesus, you – the folks once being far off** [i.e., the "uncircumcised" Gentiles] **– came to be near, immersed within and in union with the blood of the Christ**.
> 14. **You see, He Himself is our Peace** (or: continuously exists being our joining) **– the One making** (forming; constructing; creating; producing) **The Both** [i.e., Gentile and "circumcised" Jews] **[to be] one, and within His flesh is instantly destroying** (unbinding; unfastening; loosing; causing to collapse) **the middle wall of the fenced enclosure** (or: the partition or barrier wall)**: the enmity** (cause of hate, alienation, discord and hostility; characteristics of an enemy [that had existed between Jew and Gentile, because of the Law]),
> 15. **rendering useless the Law** (or: the custom; = the Torah) **of the implanted goals** (or: concerning impartations of the finished product within; from commandments; which was inward directives) **consisting in decrees** (or: prescribed ordinances), **to the end that He may frame** (create; found and settle from a state of wildness and disorder) **The Two** [Jew and Gentile] **into One qualitatively New and Different** [p46 & others: common] **Humanity** [the Last Adam – 1 Cor. 15:45] **centered within the midst of, and in union with, Himself, continuously making** (progressively creating) **Peace** (a joining);
> 16. **and then should fully transfer, from a certain state to another which is quite different, The Both – centered in, and within the midst of, One Body in God** (or: make completely other, while moving away from what had existed, and fully reconcile The Both, in one Body, **by**, **to**, with and for **God**), **through the cross – while in the midst of Himself killing the enmity and discordant hatred** ([between Jews and Gentiles]; or: killing-off the characteristics of enemies within [the previous Jew/Gentile dichotomy]).

In Gal. 1, Paul speaks of his experience of being separated from the old covenant that had first given him birth:

> 15. **Yet when God – the One marking off boundaries to separate and sever me from out of my mother's womb** (or: cavity; [comment: a figure of the religion of the Jews]), **and calling [me] through His grace and favor – thought well** (or: delights and takes pleasure)
> 16. **to unveil** (reveal; uncover; disclose) **His Son within the midst of me** (or: in union with me), **to the end that I in myself** (or: for myself; by myself; of myself) **would announce and proclaim the message of goodness, [which is] Him, within the ethnic multitudes** (or: may bring and tell the message of ease and well-being: Him [now] among the nations), **I did not immediately place myself back toward flesh and blood** (= present my cause up for the approval of other people; consult anyone; seek communication or advice from my race, kin or religion),
> 17. **neither did I go up into Jerusalem, toward those [who were] people sent off** (= to face and be with the commissioned representatives) **previous to me, but rather, I went off into Arabia, then later I again returned into Damascus.**

Sometimes an Arabian wilderness experience is exactly what is needed. It can aid in making a complete break with the past – as the Jerusalem covenant community of the 1st century had to do in order to leave behind what was being done away.

15. **Next the serpent cast** (or: spews) **water, as a river** (or: stream), **from out of its mouth, behind the Woman** (at the Woman's back; after the Woman) **to the end that it may cause her to be carried away by the river** (i.e., by its current).

Although it happened years ago, the memory is yet quite vivid for me of a particular incident when the Christian community, of which my wife and I were a part, was circulating rumors about our particular understanding of the effectiveness of the work of Christ's death and resurrection. She was asked to come before a group of women from a multi-denominational women's Bible study group. We knew that rejection awaited us at this meeting. It was on our way to the meeting when Lynda remarked that what the dragon of this vision cast out was a **river** of words that were meant to sweep her away. The words that came against us at that meeting had the venom that we expected. But the human empathy from other women of the group (not present at this "hearing"), along with other friends and members of Christ's called-out folks helped to swallow those words, and poured oil on our wounds. As our Father ordered our path, this action of the dragon would be repeated in other situations, along the Way.

The imagery of this verse may be an echo of Isa. 8:7-8,
> "Yahweh is bringing up over them the waters of the Stream... it will ascend over all its channels... it will pass on into Judah, overflow and pass... filling the width of your land, O Immanuel!" (CVOT).

Or, perhaps, Isa. 17:12,
> "Ah, the thunder of many peoples... like the thundering of the sea! Ah, the roar of nations... like the roaring of mighty waters!" (NRSV).

Jer. 46:8 is a probable allusion:
> "Egypt rises like the Nile, like rivers whose waters surge. It said, Let me rise, let me cover the earth, let me destroy cities and their inhabitants" (NRSV).

Or, there is Nah. 1:8, "in a rushing flood, He will make an end of His adversaries, and will pursue..."
These images would fit the situation for physical Jerusalem, in AD 66-70. Other examples can be cited.

Jesus warned about a flood that was to come upon that generation of physical Israel, and at the same time, upon those who in one way or another acclaimed Him Lord. He taught, in Mat. 7:

> 21. **"Not everyone constantly saying to Me, 'O Lord! Lord!' will proceed to be entering into the reign** (or: sovereign rule; kingdom; dominion, realm of action and activities) **of the heavens** (or: which has the character of, and emanates from, the atmospheres) **but rather, the one habitually performing the result or progressively producing the effect of the will, intent and purpose of My Father – the One within and in union with the heavens, and in the midst of the atmospheres – [will proceed entering].**
> 22. **"Within** (or: On) **That Day many will repeatedly say to Me, 'Lord! O Lord! do** (or: did) **we not prophesy in** (or: by) **Your Name? And do** (or: did) **we not cast out demons** (Hellenistic concept and term: = animistic influences) **in** (or: by) **Your Name? And do** (or: did) **we not perform many works of power and ability in** (or: by) **Your Name?**
> 23. **"And at that time I will repeatedly confess assuredly to them, 'I never came to know or became acquainted with you folks** (or: I not even once had intimate, experiential knowledge of you). **Those people habitually working** (performing; or: making a trade of; making a living in) **the lawlessness are now to go off to a space** (or: territory) **away, and proceed in giving way to Me and making room for Me.'** [Ps. 6:9]

> 24. **"Everyone, then, who continues obediently hearing these words** (thoughts; ideas; messages) **of Mine, and habitually does them** (or: acts on them), **will progressively be made to be and to become like an intelligent, considerate, thoughtful, prudent and sensible adult male, who builds** (or: built) **his house upon the rock-mass.**
> 25. **"And when the rain descended** (or: falls) **and the rivers came** (or: come) **[flooding] and the winds blew** (or: blow) **and lunged** (or: fall toward; lash against) **that house, it did** (or: does) **not fall, for it had been provided with a foundation and continued being established upon the rock-mass.**
> 26. **"And by contrast, everyone who continues hearing the words** (thoughts; ideas; messages) **of Mine and yet is not continuing in doing them** (or: acting on them) **will progressively be made to be and to become like a stupid, senseless adult male** (= an ignorant and careless builder) **who built** (or: builds) **his house upon the sand.**
> 27. **"And when the rain descended** (or: falls) **and the rivers came** (or: come) **[flooding] and the winds blew** (or: blow) **and lunged** (or: fall toward; lash against) **that house, it fell** (or: falls), **and its fall** (collapse) **was great."** [Isa. 28:14-18. Lu.6:46-49]

That house to which He referred was their Temple in Jerusalem.

We can observe that the attack comes from behind the Woman's back; she was already departing from the dragon's presence. This must be just before she takes flight as shown in vs. 14, otherwise, if she were flying above the earth, how could a flood be a threat to her? So here, in 15, she is yet earth-bound. But what is this river that the serpent casts out of its mouth? As with our own experience, I suggest that it was a stream of words which were spoken "behind her back." Paul experienced this, from both the Jews and the Judaizers, as well as from the economic sectors of the Empire. The institutional church of today (also the location of *satan's* headquarters) is noted for talking about others within their churches, or, in "other" churches. This is the work of the serpent, and its intent is to do damage to those of whom it speaks. In contrast, from out of Christ's true followers is to flow rivers of living water (Jn. 7:38). The world (including the church world) uses words to try to carry people away, or to cast them out, instead of bringing life and healing – and washing their feet. They want to put an end to those who they think are in error, or are what they consider to be a cult [see Gary Amirault's work, "Cults Calling Cults, Cults"]. So as you flee to the place God has prepared for you in the wilderness, know that the enemy will throw out a river of words against you, to try to carry or flush you away. It has always been this way.

The mouth was intended to speak the Word of the Lord. Moses was told, "I will be with your mouth, and will teach you what you will say" (Ex. 4:12). Deut. 8:3b told them that they should live, "on every utterance from the mouth of Yahweh." The prophets were supposed to speak the Word of the Lord, but in the situation recorded in 1 Ki. 22, vs. 23 informs us, "Yahweh has put a lying spirit in the mouths of all these prophets." David complained about the wicked person, saying, "His mouth is full of imprecation, with deceit and fraud; under his tongue [are] misery and lawlessness. He sits in ambush…" (Ps. 10:7-8a). In Ps. 35:21 David said, "they opened their mouth wide against me." Other examples could be listed, but this gives sufficient echoes to see the "mouth" as an instrument used for destruction. In 13:2, below, we see the **little animal** that has a **"mouth as a lion's mouth"** (*cf* 1 Pet. 5:8). In 13:5 we will see that **"a mouth, continuously speaking great things and blasphemies** (things that obscure the light; abusive slander; harm-avering misrepresentations) **was given to it**." Take note of the passive voice of the verb "**given**," which we will see again in 13:7. I suggest that these are other cases where it is "the divine passive," i.e., this is another picture of the antagonist that God has written into His story of the ages. The hero of the story is Christ, and then humanity (each one in his or her own class or group). The Second Humanity begins "the second half of life" on a journey of overcoming, through the blood of the Lamb and the message of its witness. But we are ahead of His story, at the moment, for beasts are yet to take the stage, for their time. As a preview of 16:13-14, below, we will see, "**out of the mouth of the dragon, and out of the mouth of the little wild animal** (creature; beast), **and out of the mouth of the false prophet – three unclean spirits** (or: impure attitudes), **as frogs – for they are spirits** (or: breath-effects; attitudes) **of demons** (a Hellenistic concept and term: = from animistic influences), **continually doing** (making; constructing; performing) **signs – which are continuously going out** (marching forth) **upon the kings of the whole inhabited land**…"

This is another example of the "**river** (or: stream), **from out of its mouth**," in our present verse. It is the same theme of the same story, that, like the parables of the kingdom as given by Jesus, tell the same thing, or side-stories, from different points of view, adding nuances to the plot.

As a practical example of daily living, Jacob spoke to our topic in the 3rd chapter of his open letter:

5. **Thus also, the tongue is a little member of the body, and yet is continuously making a loud, confident declaration or a great boast – consider how great a forest a little fire progressively sets ablaze** (or: lights up)!
6. **Well the tongue [is] a fire; [its fuel is] the System of injustice**
(or: the ordered and decorated but dominating world of secular culture, religion, politics and government which is unjust; or: the aggregate of humanity having the character of the absence of what is right; or: The tongue, also, [is] fire: the world of disregard for what is right).
The tongue is placed down within our members, continuously spotting (staining; = defiling) **the whole body, and repeatedly setting on fire the wheel of birth** (or: of coming into being; of production; from successive generation and descent; = the cycle of the origin [of life], or of generation; the wheel of *genesis*), **as well as being continuously set on fire by** (or: under) **the garbage dump** (the depository of refuse; Greek: *Gehenna* – the Valley of Hinnom).
7. **For every nature – both of wild animals and of flying creatures, both of creeping animals and of those in the salt sea – is continuously being restrained** (tamed) **and has been restrained by the nature of man** (the human nature).
8. **But the tongue – an unruly** (un-restrainable; other MSS: unfixed; unstable; restless), **worthless** (ugly; bad; malicious; unrefined; harmful; base) **[member], full of death-bearing venom – no one of humanity is able to subdue, restrain or tame.**
9. **With it we continuously speak well of** (or: speak a good word about; bless) **the Lord** [other MSS: God] **and Father, and with it we constantly curse** (pray down upon) **those men having been born "according to** (down from and corresponding to) **God's likeness."** [Gen. 1:26-27]
10. **Out of the same mouth is continuously coming forth blessing and cursing** (or: negative wishing; adversarial prayer). **My brothers, there is no need** (or: it is not necessary; it ought not be) **for these things thus to be repeatedly birthed** (or: to keep on happening in this way).
11. **A spring** (or: fountain) **is not continuously bursting forth the sweet and the bitter** (or: cutting and pricking; [*p*74: salty]) **out of the same hole** (or: opening).
12. **My brothers, a fig tree is not able to produce olives, nor a grape-vine figs, neither brine to produce sweet water.** (Jas. 3:5-12)

May we not be dragons, or, "devils," – 1 Tim. 3:11, "**Women** (or: Wives) **[of the community], similarly, [should be] serious** (dignified with majestic gravity, inspiring awe), **not devils** (or: adversaries; women who thrust things through folks)," and then we read in Tit. 2:3, "**not folks who thrust-through or hurl [a weapon, or something hurtful] through [someone]** (or: not devils nor slanderous adversaries which bring division and hurt)." I have cited these examples in order to show how what is put forth in apocalyptic vision, here in the Unveiling, was put in straightforward admonition by other NT writers. They are all speaking of the same things.

The metaphor of the mouth is used elsewhere in Scripture. In Ps. 18 David spoke of the "sorrows of death encompassing [him]," but in vs. 8 he speaks of "fire out of [Yahweh's] mouth," from out of His temple (*cf* 11:5, above). In 1:16, above, and 19:15, below, the risen Christ is pictured with a sword (figure of His Word) coming out of His mouth, and in 2:16 He spoke of using it on those who had a hateful doctrine, unless they change their minds and ways of thinking.

Paul referenced the Torah in Rom. 10:8, bringing a word of encouragement:
"**The result of the flow** (the gush-effect; or: the saying; the declaration; that which is spoken; the speech) **is** (or: exists) **near you – within your mouth and within your heart!**" [Deut. 30:11-14]

16. **So then the Land** (or: ground; earth) **ran to the aid of** (or: runs and helps) **the Woman, and the Land** (ground; earth) **at once opened** (or: opens) **up her mouth and swallowed** (or: swallows; gulps down) **the river which the dragon cast** (or: casts) **out of its mouth.**

This may be an allusion to Gen. 4:11, where the ground/earth/land "opened her mouth to receive [Cain's] brother's blood." The same poetic phrase, "her mouth," is used here, as was there. The intent of the dragon was indeed to slay her sister, as she had her Messiah. Again following the Exodus story, we are reminded in Deut. 11:4 how Yahweh "made the water of the Red Sea to overflow" the horses and chariots of Egypt, and in vs. 6 how "the earth opened her mouth and swallowed [folks]." Then in Nu. 16:1-33, we read of Yahweh's judgment on Korah, Dathan and Abiram, where "the earth opened her mouth and swallowed them..." God has always caused some sort of interaction between people and our environment, the earth. We should be instructed by this. Here, in vs. 16, we have a metaphor for God's using His creation, or, perhaps His people, to protect His communities. We are not told what form this metaphor of "**the Land**," or, "the ground/earth," took in rendering **aid** to **the Woman**. The ambiguity allows the picture to be applied to many situations of persecution. Since "The earth is Yahweh's" (Ps. 24:1), we can conclude that "[her] help comes from Yahweh" (Ps. 121:2).

So the land (or: earth) runs **to the aid of the** fleeing **Woman**. It opens its **mouth and swallows the river** which the dragon casts out of its mouth. What does this mean? In the OT the land was a figure for Israel, God's true people. Perhaps here this is a figure of God's true children who absorb all this talk to keep it from spreading, and run to the aid of this persecuted Woman (i.e., those of the community who are being slandered and wounded by negative criticisms, etc.) It can also be a figure of the "earth realm" and those who dwell there, and this is a picture of the many ways in which humanity has helped God's people despite how various "organizations" have persecuted them. Human kindness has been seen all through history.

This picture could be an echo of Isa. 59:19,
"And they from the west shall fear (or: revere) the Name of Yahweh, and from the rising of the sun, His glory; for a foe shall come like a rushing stream: [the] Spirit of Yahweh will make him flee, a breath of Yahweh driving it on" (CVOT; Rotherham).
Some folks have seen here an allusion to the imagery of Jer. 47:2,
"Behold, waters [are] ascending from the north, and they become an overflowing torrent; they shall overflow the Land and its fullness, [both] city and the dwellers in it" (CVOT).
The image could apply to physical Jerusalem in AD 70, or to those persecuting the called-out folks both then, and ever since. Dan. 9:26 (LXX, Theodotion) prophecies this:
"And after the sixty-two weeks, an anointing will be destroyed, and there is no judgment in it. And it (or: he) will destroy the city and the sanctuary along with the leader who is to come. And they will be cut off by a flood..." (NETS).
In Lu. 17, Jesus referenced the flood that Noah experienced:

> 26. **"Also, correspondingly as** (just as; accordingly as) **it was birthed** (happened; occurred) **within the days of Noah, in this way** (thus) **it will also progress being – within the days of the Son of the Man:**
> 27. **"they were eating, they continued drinking, they kept on marrying, they were habitually given** (or: taken out) **in marriage – until which day Noah at one point entered into the ark, and then the down-washing** (flood; cataclysm) **suddenly came and at once destroyed them all."**

Matthew places this statement in the Olivet discourse, Mat. 24:37-39. There, he continued on, speaking somewhat ambiguously, giving parallel examples of how the days of the Son of Man would come to be:

> 40. **"At that time two folks will continue being within the midst of the field: one man is being taken in hand** (seized) **and drawn to the side, and yet one man is repeatedly left alone to flow on his way** (or: continues on pardoned [with his debts] forgiven; or: is being sent away, allowed to continue relaxing while permitted to depart).
> 41. **"Two women are continuing to grind grain into meal and flour, within the mill** (or: in the midst [of working] the millstone)**: one woman is being taken in hand** (seized) **and drawn to the side, and yet one woman is repeatedly left alone to continue [in her work]** (or: pardoned; sent away; forgiven; etc., as in vs. 40).
> 42. **"Therefore, you folks stay constantly awake, be ever alert, and continue watchful, because you have not seen, nor do you thus know, in what sort of day your Owner** (Lord) **is in the habit of coming** (or: for what kind of day your Master repeatedly comes)."

The "two women" may refer to the "two women" to which Paul referred in Gal. 4:22-31. Our present vision of the Woman, here in chapter 12, can be interpreted as pertaining to BOTH of these women, on different levels of interpreting this vision.

On a personal level, our "flesh" sometimes absorbs and swallows up what the enemy may try to cast against our soul – what is termed our "defense mechanisms." The symbol of an overwhelming flood is common in the OT.

> Ps. 42:7, "All your waves and your billows have gone over me."
> Ps. 32:6, "the rush of great waters" shall not come near the psalmist.
> Ps. 124:4, "Then the water had overwhelmed us, the stream had gone over our soul."
> Isa. 43:2, "When you pass through the waters I [will be] with you, and through the rivers, they shall not overflow you..."

This figure can be of persecution, or just of hard times.

Paul informed us, in 2 Tim. 4:16-17,

> "**all forsook** (abandoned; [other MSS: were forsaking and abandoning]) **me – may it not be put to their account** (may it not be counted against them)**! Yet the Lord took a stand beside me** (or: stood alongside in me) **– and He empowered me** (enabled me; gave me inward ability).... **so [that] all the ethnic multitudes** (nations; Gentiles; non-Jews) **would** (could; may) **hear [it] – and I was dragged** (or: drawn) **from out of the mouth of a lion!"**

Paul does not say who dragged him to safety, but the "divine passive" of this picturesque speech instructs us that our Lord was behind it.

17. **And so the dragon was enraged** (is angered; swells with agitation of soul) **upon the Woman and went away** (or: goes off) **to make war** (do battle) **with the remaining ones** (the rest; those left) **of her seed** (= offspring) **– those continuously keeping** (guarding; observing) **God's implanted goals** (impartations of the finished product within; inward directives) **and continuously holding the testimony of and from Jesus** (or: having the evidence about and possessing the character of Jesus).

This scene ends with the dragon breaking off the pursuit of the Woman (the Bride) and turning its efforts against the remaining ones of her seed (those who are truly born from above, and are a part of the corporate Seed, but who are not yet caught up to God's throne – they are yet subject to the dragon's attacks). The Woman and the Man-child are now in a place beyond the reach of the dragon, but the others will follow them "in their own orders" (1 Cor. 15:23). On a personal level, these **remaining ones** might be a symbol for the areas of our interior "land" that have not fully died, existentially, as we carry our execution stake in following Him, and have not yet been fully purified (e.g., bits of raw ore still in the smelting pot). They might be things of the first Adam nature that have not yet,

> "**come down to the goal** (or: attain; arrive at; meet accordingly; meet down face-to-face)**: into the state of oneness from, and which is, The Faithfulness** (or: the unity of, that belongs to and which characterizes that which is faith; or: the lack of division which has its source in trust, confidence and reliability, has the character of and is in reference to the loyalty and fidelity), **even which is the full, experiential and intimate knowledge which is** (or: of; from; in reference to) **the Son of God, [growing] into [the] purposed and destined adult man** (full-grown, goal-attained, mature manhood) – **into** (or: unto) **[the] measure of [the] stature** (full age; prime of life) **of the entire content which comprises the Anointed One**" (Eph. 4:13).

Or, put another way, they are areas of our lives that have not yet fully,

> "**[grown] up** (enlarge; increase) **into Him – the ALL which is the Head: Christ!**" (Eph. 4:15b).

For all these things, as the Lord told Paul,

> "**My grace is continuously sufficient in you, for you see, ability** (or: the [other MSS read: My] power) **is habitually brought to its goal** (or: finished; perfected; matured) **within the midst of weakness** (or: in union with lack of strength and infirmity)" (2 Cor. 12:9a).

By this statement in vs. 17, the vision clearly identifies two separate groups. It is possible that the Woman and the Man-child are being presented as the leadership of the communities or the sent-forth folks (e.g., Peter, Paul, etc.), the folks with higher profiles within the Empire who would have been the natural targets both for Judaism and Rome. This concluding remark of the vision may be forward-looking, speaking to the lesser-known folks, or the next generation(s) that would follow. The dragon did not disappear here, but goes after other folks. Simmons offers the following on this verse:

> "The remnant (rest) of the woman's seed is the church among the Gentiles. The persecution against the Mother Church in Palestine having failed, the church in the provinces soon came under wrath, particularly in Asia, to whom the Revelation is addressed" (ibid p 251).

The first application of the message of this vision would have been for the early called-out, covenant communities. With the vision being written prior to the destruction of the Jewish society, we suggest that the Dragon (a figure of an adversarial spirit) of this vision was first the Jews who pursued the called-out communities and persecuted her seed, and second, the Judaizers who opposed Paul's good news. Following the destruction of the Jewish nation, this same spirit of control and domination (which had been in the Jewish leadership in Jerusalem and was also incarnated in the Roman Empire that had crushed Jerusalem) continued on, under Nero, and thus do we see the little animal (the little wild beast), in the next chapter, having a form (being conformed to the image of its "lord") similar to the Dragon: 7 heads and 10 horns.

Having seen Egypt and Israel's Exodus repeatedly being alluded to in this vision, it is possible that these are once again in the background here in vs. 17. As an allusion, the dragon can here represent Egypt, in Israel's story, having failed in its pursuit of Israel under Moses, and then it continues playing a role in Israel's history on throughout the OT. Also, the dragon is later seen in Babylon, then Persia, and then in Herod's kingdom, at the birth of Jesus, later to come in the form of Rome. The spirit of control and domination is seen in every political, economic, educational, and religious system that mankind has created. It came into the Christian religion when it became institutionalized. As our brother, Stacy Wood, said, "The Judaizers won [in the Christian religion]" (from a private conversation). The two women continued on unto our present day. One historical reappearance of this dragon was in the harlot church that brought about the Spanish Inquisition. Another was in the Protestant persecutions of the Anabaptists, and such as Michael Servetus (condemned by Catholics and Protestants alike, he was burned at the stake in Geneva as a heretic by order of the city's Protestant governing council). The church leadership also persecuted the mystics, such as Madame Jean Guyon. It sent crusaders to kill Muslims. It sent priests to the new world, who killed or enslaved native peoples. It produced the concept of "manifest destiny" that convinced Americans that it was God's will to take Native American lands and, if not killing them outright, to destroy their cultures. It's a bloody history.

Dan Kaplan reminded me of what Paul had written about the two women in Gal. 4. We have those same two women here in the Unveiling. Paul referred to them there as "two covenants" (vs. 24) and "two mountains" (Sinai, vs. 25, and the Jerusalem which is above, vs. 26, which in Heb. 12:22 is identified as Mount Zion). The Woman we've been reading of here in chapter 12 is the "Jerusalem which is above" (Gal. 4:26). The Jerusalem "that [then] was" (Gal. 4:25), in Paul's allegory, took the form of the dragon, here. But let Paul describe it for us, in that context:

> 28. **Now we, brothers, down from** (or: corresponding to; in the sphere of) **Isaac, are children of Promise** (or: ones-born of [the] Promise). [This corresponds to the Man-child, caught up to "heaven"]
> 29. **But nevertheless, just as then, the one being born down from** (in accordance with; corresponding to; on the level of) **flesh** [figuring the old covenant, and the Law (Sinai)] **was CONSTANTLY PURSUING and PERSECUTING the one down from** (in accordance with; corresponding to; in the sphere of) **spirit** (or: Breath-effect), **so also now.** [i.e., the DRAGON was pursuing and persecuting the new covenant communities]
> 30. **Still, what does the Scripture yet say?**
> "**Cast out** (or: At once expel) **the servant girl** (the slave-girl) **and her son, for by no means will the son of the servant girl** (the slave-girl) **be an heir** (take possession of and enjoy the distributed allotment) **with the son of the freewoman.**" [Gen. 21:10]
> 31. **Wherefore, brothers, we are not children of a slave-girl** (a servant girl), **but, to the contrary, of the freewoman**.

The flesh always rushes passionately against the Spirit (Gal. 5:17; *cf*. Rom. 7:23; Jas. 4:1-2). The "servant girl" (1st century Jerusalem, i.e., Judaism, or, the Law), which gave birth to those "after the flesh" (Gal 4:23), was cast out of heaven (vs. 9, above, symbolized by the dragon), for the dragon was not to be "an heir" along with "the sons of the freewoman." The "heavenly Woman" is now seated together with Christ in the "heavenly" realm: the spirit (Eph. 2:6). We will meet the other woman again in chapter 17, below, where she is "**sitting** (or: seated) **upon a crimson** (or: scarlet) **little wild animal** (or: beast)" (17:3), representing the collusion between the Jerusalem leadership and Rome. Recall Jn. 11:

> 47. **Consequently, the chief** (or: ranking) **priests and the Pharisees gathered [the] Sanhedrin** (= convoked a council of the leaders of the Jewish religious and political culture), **and they began to say, "What are we presently doing, seeing that this man is repeatedly doing many signs?**
> 48. "**If we let him go on in this way, they will all progressively put trust** (will continue believing) **into him, the Romans will proceed to come, and they will progressively take away both our place and our nation** (= political station, culture and corporate ethnic identity)."
> 53. **Therefore, from that day they deliberated and consulted together to the end that they should kill Him.**

This was the dragon-woman, riding the authority of the beast Empire which tried to do away with what God had birthed into His new creation. This dragon was of the same image as the wild animal (beast; little creature) that we will meet in 13:1, below: it had 7 heads (complete division of leadership in the completed form of the ancient serpent) with 10 horns (the power of the Law: the 10 commandments) and 7 diadems (complete control over the people, ruling as kings, "lording it over them" – 1 Pet. 5:3). It had come short of the glory of God and was not in His image. (I owe these correlations to a discussion with my friend Dan Kaplan.) Nonetheless, those "**continuously holding the testimony of and from Jesus**," need not worry, for Jesus told His followers,

> "**And you see, [it is] upon this: the rock mass** (or: bedrock) **[that] I will progressively be constructing and building up My house – the called-out community. And even gates of [the] unseen** (or: gates of an unseen place; [= boulders on the entrances of graves; = {the prison} gates of the 'house of death'; or: the bars enclosing the realm of the dead]) **will not continue bringing strength down against it** (or: will not proceed to be coming to their full strength in relation to it; or: will not continue overpowering it or prevail in resisting it)" (Mat. 16:18).

That Rock mass (or: bedrock; a figure of the corporate Christ) was the "Stone which was cut out of the mountain (Sinai) without hands, that broke in pieces the iron, the bronze, the clay, the silver and the gold" – i.e., the dominating kingdoms of the ancient world (Dan. 2:45) – which, after striking the multi-metal image, "became a great mountain (an apocalyptic figure of a Kingdom: the heavenly Zion) and it filled the whole earth" (Dan. 2:35). This is basically a preview of the ending of the story.

A word about the phrase, "**God's implanted goals** (impartations of the finished product within; inward directives)," is in order, since this is the first occurrence of the noun, *entolē*, in this letter. Instead of rendering it in the traditional English terms, such as, "commandment, precept, edict, decree, ordinance, or order," which are all legalistic terms, in English, I chose to give the rendering from the Greek elements of the word, which in my view better aligns with God's relationship with us in the new arrangement, or, the new covenant. The Greek word is from *en-*, which means within, inner, or, inward, and *tolē*, which is a form of the word *telos*: goal; finished product; end in view (*cf* Strong). I included the more traditional meaning "directives" to assist my readers in associating the traditional with my new rendering. In human affairs, when a boss or an army officer gives someone a directive, or an order, he or she implants in the mind of the employee or soldier the goal, or the finished product, of what he or she wants this person to do. He or she imparts the information, and the listener takes that into himself. But in the new arrangement, God leads us (Rom. 8:14) and puts His principles into our hearts (into the core of our being) and trains us as children, and then friends and brothers. Through His Word, and through the Spirit's leading, we now have His goals imparted into us, and the "DNA" of the finished product (ourselves in His image) is implanted within us. Yes, they are "inward directives," but the legal element is missing, since He calls us "friends," and "sons."

18. [other MSS: And it was placed (set; made to stand) upon the sand of the sea.]
    With these MSS, this statement would be tied to the end of chapter 12. However, the older MSS readings (reading the verb in the 1st person, instead of the 3rd) should open chapter 13, below. I offer Griesbach's text [racketed here, (reading with later MSS, which Young and Williams also follow)]. Furthermore, in all the MSS the verb is passive, while in chapter 12 the dragon was anything but passive: it was quite active. Also, it has been John that has been "acted upon" throughout these visions. Therefore, find another reading of vs. 18 below, just before 13:1.

Chapter 13

This next chapter will reach back to 11:7, recap the little animal's activities there, and then recap the period covered by 12:13-17. What will be seen are images based upon Dan. 7, and on the four beasts of that vision. All the animals/beasts are symbols of the dominating systems which come from the hearts of human beings that have been estranged from a living relationship with our Father. They are branches that did not stay connected to the Vine, our Tree of Life. Therefore, in this state of being, they are antichrists: their spirits are in opposition to, and are in the place of, Christ. Like Nebuchadnezzar in Dan. 4:16, "a beast's heart [has been] given to [them]." In 1 Jn. 2:18-19 we first read this term, and here we read of the setting (which, incidentally, was in the 1st century):

> 18. **O undeveloped ones or folks of the age to be educated** (or: servants, little boys and little girls who might be hit in training and for discipline), **it continues being** (or: is progressively) **a last hour** (= an *eschaton* of the Day, or the closing moment [of the age]), **and according as you hear** (or: heard) **that an antichrist** (or: anti-anointing; that which is instead of, or in the place of, Christ or the Anointing) **repeatedly comes, even now many anti-anointings** (or: antichrists; many things or people taking the place of Christ or stand in opposition to the Anointing) **have been born and are here** (or: have come into existence and are at large), **from which fact** (or: whence) **we constantly know by experience that it continues being a last hour** (= a closing moment [of the age]).
>
> 19. **They came** (or: come; go; or: went) **out from us, but they were not existing out of us** (or: they were not [a part] of us), **for if they were out of us, they would have remained with us; but [this was] to the end that they may be manifested** (caused to appear) **that they are not all out of us or from us.**

John goes on to define an antichrist in 1 Jn. 2:22,

> "**This person is the anti-anointing** (or: anti-anointed person; the one taking the place of and being in the opposite position of the anointing and of Christ): **the one habitually denying** (contradicting; saying, "No," about) **the Father and the Son.**"

He gives another example, further describing an antichrist, in 1 Jn. 4:3,

> "**and every spirit** (influence; attitude; breath) **which is not habitually speaking in accord with** (speaking like; or: avowing; confessing) **Jesus is not out of** (does not originate in) **God. And this [spirit, expression, or speech which is not in accord with Jesus] is of the anti-anointing** (or: that which pertains to the antichrist; from something in the place of Christ) – **which you folks have heard that it is constantly** (repeatedly; habitually) **coming, and now** (or: presently) **exists within the controlling ordered System** (or: is in the world of religion, economy, government and culture; or: has being in the realms of the secular and the religious) **already** (before now)."

His final description (and these four verses are the only places in the NT where we find the actual term) is found in 2 Jn. 7,

> "**Since many wandering-astray folks** (or: many who lead astray; many deceivers) **went out into the ordered System** (world of religion, secular culture, economics and government) – **those not continuously speaking like** (saying the same thing as; confessing) **Jesus presently coming in flesh** (= a physical body; or: = in [their] inner self): **this is the person wandering astray, even the one in opposition to Christ** (the one instead of, or in place of, Christ; the antichrist; or: the anti-anointing)."

Can you see why John used the diminutive form of the word "animal" in the Unveiling? They are simply people, and the systems or empires that they create – i.e., the spirits or attitudes or mindsets that are strongholds within these people or systems that at one level or another govern political, economic or religious organizations. They are what Paul referred to as, "the first Adam." In Paul's day, they were seen in the Jewish zealots that wanted to get rid of him (Acts), and in the Judaizers who opposed his message of grace (Galatians).

Terry suggests,

"We should keep in mind that in all this prophetic symbolism we have before us *the Roman empire as a persecuting power*. This Apocalypse is not concerned with the history of Rome.... The beast is not a symbol of the *city of Rome*, but of the great *Roman world power*..." (ibid p 393-4; emphasis original).

As cited earlier, Maarschalk presents a compelling argument for the "beast" being the Zealot movement, citing many references from Josephus (https://adammaarschalk.com/2017/04/09/who-was-the-beast-five-clues-long-island-conference-presentation/).

18. **And I was placed** (set, made to stand) **upon the sand of the sea,**

As you can see from the first words of vs. 1, below, this textual reading of 12:18 seems most reasonable, and Beale concurs (ibid p 681). It tells us that in this next vision, John was in the same "earth" realm as the wilderness that he had just viewed in the previous vision, but now he has been transferred to a beach setting, most likely the Mediterranean.

1. **and then I saw** (or: perceived) **a little animal** (a little, wild creature or beast) **progressively climbing up** (or: repeatedly ascending) **from out of the midst of the sea, having ten horns and seven heads, and ten bands** (diadems; kingly ornaments) **upon its horns, and blasphemous names** (or, names [other MSS: a name] of slander, abusive speech and light-hindering injury) **upon its heads.**

Beale (ibid) rightly points out that the conjunction, "**and**," at the beginning of the verse, introduces the next vision, and is not telling us what happens next, after 12:17. This chapter is parallel to the 2 witnesses' ministry, and to the vision of chapter 12. The imagery of the dragon in chapter 12, above, and now of a seven-headed, small wild animal arising from the sea would have likely called to mind both OT references (in those familiar with the Hebrew Bible) or what scholars have called "combat myths" that appear "in many cultures, ancient and modern, [which take] many forms" (Borg, ibid p 282). Borg continues,

"The archetypal plot is a story of cosmic conflict between good and evil.... Commonly the evil power was imaged as a dragon or sea monster or primeval serpent" (ibid).

He points us, first of all, to OT references:

Ps. 74.13b-14a, "You broke the heads of the sea monsters in the waters, You Yourself bruised the heads of the dragon" (CVOT). *Cf* Gen. 3:15
Ps. 89:9-10a. "You are Ruler over the swelling sea... You crushed Rahab..."
Isa. 30:7, "Egypt is vanity... I have called her Rahab..." Ps. 87:4a, "I shall mention Rahab..."
Isa. 27:1, "Yahweh shall visit with His sword upon the dragon, the fugitive serpent, even upon the dragon, the tortuous serpent, and He will kill the monster which is in the sea." (CVOT)
Isa. 51:9b, "Are You not It, the Hewer of Rahab, the Wounder of the monster?" (CVOT)
Ezk. 29:3, "Thus says my Lord Yahweh: Behold, I am against you, Pharaoh, king of Egypt, the great monster, reclining in the midst of its waterways..." (CVOT)
Job 7:12, "Am I the sea, or the [sea] monster?" (CVOT)
Job 9:13b, "the helpers of Rahab prostrate beneath Him" (CVOT)
Job 26:12, "By His power He stilled the sea, and by His understanding He shattered Rahab... His hand pierced the fugitive serpent."
Job 41:1, "Can you draw on the dragon with a fishhook?" (CVOT)

Such imagery would have been familiar to John's readers. We should note from Israel's Scriptures, cited above, that the OT does not present a "combat myth," but the sovereignty of Yahweh over His creation. As Rahab was a metaphor for Egypt, so these images in chapter 13 are likely references to Rome, or to some aspect of the Roman Empire, or to some "system of domination." Beale (ibid p 682-3) suggests that "The depiction of the two beasts in chapter 13 is based in part on Job 40-41," and notes that,

"Without exception the imagery of the sea monster is used throughout the OT to represent evil kingdoms who persecute God's people."

We have now come to the third view of the specific time: 3 and ½ years, or 42 months (vs. 5, below). This symbolic number is an echo from Dan. 7:25 which speaks of the fourth beast, "speaking words against the Most High," and wearing out the set-apart folks, "until a season, seasons and half a season" (LXX). Observe that John is not called up to heaven, but is placed upon the earth, or sand. This picture is of what is going on upon the lower realm, the earth realm. Call to mind that the term "sand of the sea" was used to refer to the seed of Abraham in Gen. 22:17, and to Jacob's seed in Gen. 32:12. But it was also used to refer to the host of the armies which came to fight against Israel in Josh 11:4. So John is no longer in the heavenlies, but is brought to the multitudes of the earth, or the Land. Is he figuratively standing with Israel, the sand, as he faces the sea, which figures the rest of humanity, or a mixture of ethnic groups? A. E. Knoch makes a good observation here that the sea of this vision is equivalent to the abyss, above, in 11:7 (ibid p 396). Beale notes that governors from Rome repeatedly came by sea to Ephesus, and so, "Roman ships literally seemed to be rising out of the sea as they appeared on the horizon off the coast of Asia Minor" (ibid p 682). We saw in the study of chapter 9 that there is a direct association between the sea and the abyss in the OT. Could the figure of the abyss then also be extended to represent humans, in apocalyptic literature? In Isa. 57:20 we read,

> "But the UNJUST will continue being tossed and caused to surge and swell, like waves, and will not be able to rest or stop" (LXX, JM)

Isa. 17:11-12 compares the noise of "many peoples" and "the nations" as the "thundering of the sea," and "the roaring of many waters." We see these waters defined as, "**peoples and crowds** (mobs) **and multitudes** (nations; ethnic groups) **and tongues** (languages)" in 17:15, below.

Both Barclay and Knoch see the two beasts (here, and in vs. 11ff, below) as associated with Dan. 7:3-7, which is probably the origin of these figures, and they agree that this first beast in the Unveiling is a composite of the four beasts which come up out of the sea in Daniel. Knoch notes that if you total up the number of the heads of the beasts in Dan. 7, you get 7. And the total number of horns there, is 10 (ibid).

Barclay, on the other hand, sees the beasts in Dan. 7 as symbols of the great empires that held sway in that part of the world during the time of Daniel. He says that "the beast like a lion with an eagle's wings stands for Babylon; the one like a bear stands for Media; the one like a leopard with four wings stands for Persia; and the fourth stands for the empire of Alexander the Great.... John's picture in the Revelation puts together in one beast the features of all four" (ibid p 88). He sees the 7 heads and 10 horns as representing the rulers and emperors of Rome. Both Barclay and Malcolm Smith point out the oppression of the "Caesar worship," and how the strength of Rome, combined with the organization of this state religion, persecuted the Christians. At that time, those who would not worship Caesar were ruined. Smith points out that if the working class did not offer incense to the patron god of their craft, they would lose their jobs and come to economic ruin (ibid).

Terry points out that the two beasts in this vision are contemporaneous, "and the second is a mere satellite of the first, exercising the authority of the first beast as if in his immediate presence" (ibid p 392). Beale posits that, "people in Asia Minor thought of whatever came 'from the sea' as foreign and whatever came from the land as native" (ibid p 682; cf Dan. 7:3). This may give us a clue to the identity of the second little animal, below. In connection to the similarities between the descriptions of the dragon in 12:3 and the little animal, here, Chilton suggests that, "The connotations of heads and horns are the same in both the Dragon and the Beast, but they refer to different objects" (ibid p 327). The little animal was the incarnation of the adversarial opposition that began in Judaism, continued in the Empire, and has been perpetually produced in human institutions, ever since. But here, let us look at another view, a second layer of interpretation, from Ray Prinzing:

> "The sea bespeaks the mass of humanity, out of which rises the bestial systems which have placed their mark upon 'ALL, both small and great, rich and poor, free and bond.' The fact is every creature bears this mark of the bestial nature, until such a time as the cross cancels out the old Adamic nature [= estrangement], and we were born anew with the nature, and conformed to the image, of The Son.... Either we will express the character of God, or the character of the bestial system of this world.... Not only is the bestial mark stamped upon the nature of man, to influence his thinking, and his handiwork, but we live under the mark of the beast by living in this commercialized world order" (ibid; brackets added).

He goes on to contrast the life of Christ while in this world, saying,

> "The name, nature, character of the beast touches every facet of our natural life. Yet Jesus had no trouble with this, and He instructed the people to 'Render to Caesar the things that are Caesar's, and to God the things that are God's' (Mark 12:17).... [In Matt. 17:27] He used the money system to pay the tribute of the system.... He did not rebel against that society, for such rebellion would have defiled Him, having partaken of the world's spirit of rebellion. He gave the system its due, and therefore was free of any obligation to it." Prinzing also goes to the Dan. 7:3-7 context and notes that "The lion 'was made to stand upon the feet as a man, and a man's heart was given to it.' This indicates the beast's approach to reason and humanity... secularism and humanism..." (ibid; brackets added).

Then he cites Paul in 1 Cor. 15:49,

> "**And correspondingly as we bear and wear the image of the dusty person,** [*p*46 adds: doubtless] **we can and should** [B reads: will] **also bear and wear the image of the supra-heavenly One** (or: belonging to the One having the quality and character of the finished and perfected atmosphere; or: from the fully-heaven [sphere]; of the added-sky person)."

With these perspectives in mind, let us continue this chapter. First, the word normally translated "beast" is in the diminutive form, thus do I add the descriptive "little." Even though we might see this system as fierce and fearsome, God refers to it as "a little wild animal." Note also that it is "**progressively climbing up** (or: repeatedly ascending)" out of the sea of humanity. It is not hard to observe this in people and organizations or political entities, from day to day.

In the 7 heads there may be the figure of division of leadership, which led to slow progress made in human institutions, and on our own path. If this interpretation is correct, then the figure would be of "complete division" among the leaders of societal structures. The 10 horns represents all the power that humanity has in its control. But, in the religious aspect of this animal nature, recall that 10 was a unit of measure for the holy of holies in the tabernacle (corresponding to the in-most part within us). "10" symbolized the Law, which was meant to "govern" ancient Israel, before she chose to have human kings (1 Sam. 8). The "**ten bands** (diadems; kingly ornaments)" on its horns speaks of its position of rule and domination. This wild animal is a picture of world domination systems, throughout human history. Maarschalk's understanding of these heads (in terms of the beast being the Zealots) are summarize here:

> "The family dynasty of 'Hezekiah the Zealot' (killed in 47 BC), who Josephus called 'the head of the robbers' (Wars 1.10.5); included 'Judas the Galilean' (Acts 5:35-37), his three sons, his grandson (Menahem), and Eleazar ben Jairus (Menahem's cousin), who led the final rebel holdout at Masada until AD 73; referenced in Revelation 13:1, 3; 17:3, 7, and 9-11" ("Who Was the Beast," ibid p 11).

The **blasphemous names** upon the heads symbolize the fullness of idolatry, as these heads – the concepts, thinking, character of the beast-like, estranged nature – are identified and worshiped as gods (vs. 12, below), and are given the leadership and recognition within humanity which really belongs to God. We see the same description on the little animal in 17:3, below, as it supports the Prostitute, and, if we look ahead to 17:3-17, we see more about this animal. The Great Prostitute (Jerusalem gone astray, or the false or apostate church – see Isa. 1:21, "How has the Faithful City become a prostitute...") – rides this little wild beast. Thus can we see the 7 heads of this beast potentially correlated to the 7 churches, of chapters 2-3, above, having gone astray by coming together with human systems and governments. In chapter 17 we will see that "the 7 heads are 7 mountains where the woman is sitting on them, and they are 7 kings (17:9). The woman was riding on the back of the Roman Empire, using its power and authority for its own means, then later upon the back of the Zealot's rebellion. These 7 churches have become 7 figurative kingdoms which are divided from each other, yet are part of the same system. Keep in mind that the number 7 symbolizes a representation of the complete or total picture of the subject matter. After the destruction of Jerusalem, in AD 70, the organized systems of Christianity came on board of this beast of Rome again, under Constantine.

Here it will be wise to bring Paul's unveiling into our picture:
> **you folks must at some point, for yourselves, enter within** (or: clothe yourselves with) **the full suit of armor and implements of war** (panoply; the complete equipment for men-at-arms) **which is God** (or: which comes from and belongs to God), **in order for you to be continuously able and powerful to stand** (or: to make a stand) **facing toward the crafty methods** (stratagems; schemes; intrigues) **of the adversary**
>> (or: = which throw folks into dualism with divided thinking and perceptions; or: from the person that throws something through the midst and casts division; or: from the slanderer who accuses and deceives; or: that have the quality of [what is commonly called] the "devil"),
>
> **because for us the wrestling is not against** (toward; with a view to) **blood and flesh** (= physical bodies), **but rather against** (toward; i.e., "face to face" with) **the beginning controls and rules**
>> (or: original rulings; or: rulers and controllers; governments; those things or people in first position; the beginning things or people; the original ones; the princes) **and face to face with the rights and privileges** (or: liberties to do as one pleases; or: authorities; or: aspects from out of existence), **with a view to the strengths of the System** (or: strengths of the ordered arrangement; or: universal powers of domination; the world's strong-ones; or: the strengths from the aggregate of humanity) **of this darkness** (realm of shadows, gloom and dimness; [comment: = ignorance]), **facing** (toward; or: with a view to) **the spiritual aspects** (or: breath-effected attitudes; or: conditions and qualities of a spirit) **of the worthlessness**
>> (the badness of conditions; the unsoundness and miserableness; the wickedness and depravity; the evil and malice; the disadvantageousness; the unprofitableness; the thing that brings toilsome labor and a gush of misery) **among those situated upon elevated positions**
>> (or: situated within the 'heavenly' positions or places; positioned in union with the 'heavenly' folks; among the folks [residing] upon the atmospheres)."
>>> [note: this verse could be speaking about the ruling authorities of the religious world of ignorance, with its now worthless sacrifices, or, about the political system of darkened strength which was currently in power, bringing bad situations; Walter Wink, in *Engaging the Powers*, uses the phrase "against suprahuman systems and forces" for part of this verse] (Eph. 6:11-12)

We have a balanced view of our existential situation in 1 Jn. 5:19-10,

"**We have seen and thus know that we are continuously existing from out of the midst of God, yet the whole ordered System** (or: the entire realm of the religious and the secular) **is continuously lying outstretched** (lying as asleep, idle or dead; reclining) **within the gush of misery** (within the disadvantageous, laborious and worthless situation; within the sorry plight; in union with wickedness and evil; in the midst of the misery-gushed [attitude and existence]), **yet we have seen and thus know that God's Son has arrived and is continuously here, and He has given thorough understanding to the end that we would constantly know by experience the True One, and we constantly exist within and in union with the True One: within His Son, Jesus Christ. This One is the True** (Real) **God, and Life pertaining to and having the qualities of the Age** (or: life having its source in the Age [of Messiah]; eonian life; Life of, for and on through, the ages)."

As we consider the "little animals" in this chapter, we can be informed by a post from Arthur Eedle:

THE WELLSPRING 36. LIONS EATING GRASS?

"[We] find the following in Isa. 65:25, **'The wolf and the lamb shall feed together, the lion shall eat straw [hay?] like the ox, and dust shall [still] be the serpent's food. They shall not hurt nor destroy in all My holy mountain,' says the LORD.** So what was the Lord conveying when he caused Isaiah to write these lines? The solution requires an investigation of the Scriptural use of animals to describe human behavior. Let us start with the best known example of all. **'The next day John saw Jesus coming toward him, and said, "Behold! The Lamb of God who takes away the sin of the world!"'** (Jn. 1:29) **'He was oppressed and He was afflicted, yet He opened not His mouth; He was led as a lamb to the slaughter, and as a sheep before its shearers is silent, so He opened not His mouth'** (Isa. 53:7). The Isaiah reference explains John the Baptist's use of the figure.

"Thinking further of Jesus' passion, we turn to Ps. 22:12-13. **'Many bulls encompass me, strong bulls of Bashan surround me; they open wide their mouths at me, like a ravening and roaring lion.'** Who are these bulls roaring like lions? It doesn't take much ingenuity to recognize them as the Jewish leaders. Furthermore, in verse 16 we read, **'Dogs are round about me; a company of evildoers encircle me; they have pierced my hands and feet.'** The figure now changes to dogs, the epithet Jews used when referring to Gentiles, in this case the Romans who were crucifying Him.

"We are now ready to apply this figurative principle to Isa. 11:6, **'The wolf shall dwell with the lamb, the leopard shall lie down with the young goat, the calf and the young lion and the fatling together; and a little child shall lead them.'** Something amazing and rather wonderful is happening in God's holy mountain, where all true believers dwell. Whereas throughout the last 2000 years members of God's Church have so often been at each other's throats, so that Paul had to say, **'If ye bite and devour one another, take heed that ye be not consumed one of another,'** (Gal. 5:15) now a new state of peace, compassion and gentleness is observed, whereby those who *had* been of wolverine tendency are now observed to be reconciled to the lambs who had been attacked, and those who had once possessed the vicious nature of leopards and lions now have their bestiality drawn, and the 'young goats and calves' no longer have any fear of them. Furthermore we are told that **'a little child leads them,'** reminding us that Jesus said, **'Unless you become as little children, you will by no means enter the kingdom of heaven'** (Mat. 18:3). Perhaps Jesus was thinking of these words in Isaiah when He was speaking.

"Now we are ready to understand the next verse in Isa. 11, **"The cow and the bear shall graze; their young ones shall lie down together; and the lion shall eat straw like the ox."** Those who had 'devoured and consumed one another,' as depicted by bears and lions, have now been taken through the fires of God's refining discipline, and become gentle, no longer desiring to consume and destroy brethren for not walking according to their rigid theologies. Erstwhile bears and lions have become as tame and docile as though they were lambs and calves. A good example of this is in the life of Saul of Tarsus, a man whose mission could be described as that of a roaring lion seeking whom he may devour. But after his Damascus Road experience, he became as a little lamb, and his letters are full of love and compassion. His bestial venom had been drawn….

"We shall not be looking for lions and bears eating grass in the Kingdom…. And so all these figurative passages, using animals to depict human behavior, are speaking of God's elect, and the attainment of His great purpose to have a glorious Church, redeemed, purged, refined, cleansed, like little children, in the image of God's Son, the Lord Jesus" (Brief postings of interest from Arthur Eedle, arthur@prophetictelegraph.co.uk, 17 July 2017)

Eedle further reminds us of Mat. 10:16,
"**Now look, and really see this situation: I, Myself, am now sending you folks off – being emissaries on a mission – as sheep within the midst of [a pack of] wolves! Therefore, habitually come to be thoughtful, prudent, cautious and discreet** (or: = wary and on the alert; = observant, decisive and timely) **– as the snakes [are]; and yet [still] unmixed** (pure; = without negative characteristics added) **– as the doves [are]**."

2. **Then the little animal** (little wild creature or beast) **which I saw was and continued to exist like a leopard, and yet its feet [were] as a bear's, and its mouth as a lion's mouth. Next the dragon gave its ability and power, its throne, and great authority and license** (or: as well as great right and privilege from out of its being) **to it** [i.e., to the little wild animal].

Let us consider a cogent perception of this first beast's place in 1st century Palestine, as unpacked by Adam Maarschalk:
> "In Daniels' vision, the lion represents Babylon (Dan. 7:4), the bear represents Medo-Persia (Dan. 7:5; 8:20), and the leopard represents Greece (Dan. 7:6; 8:21-22). In John's vision these same animals are listed in reverse order, referring to Greece, Medo-Persia and Babylon, respectively. As John saw the beast of his own time period, he also looked back into Israel's history and first saw the kingdom which had most recently held dominion over Israel – Greece….
> Greece/Macedonia was the kingdom which had held dominion over Israel as recently as 323 BC – 142 BC. The Greek language was dominant in the Roman Empire, and was the language into which the Septuagint was translated and the language in which most of the New Testament was written." ("The Beast Empowered By the Dragon" https://adammaarschalk.com/2017/02/11/the-beast-empowered-by-the-dragon-revelation-131-2/).

Maarschalk also points out that this "beast" has the primary characteristic (was like) "a leopard," i.e., its conformation, or "body," was a representation of Greece, or Hellenism, which dominated the culture and character of the Empire of John's day. His article include an insightful summary from Mark Mountjoy (New Testament Open University; January 24, 2017):
> "The Zealots correspond to the leopard traits of the beast. As thorough-going Hellenists they warred against each other just like Alexander's generals fought tooth and nail after he died. Leopards hunt at night and are swift and stealthy. The Sicarii correspond to the bear traits. The small knife they carried and were infamous for (and even named after) came from Persia (the

bear). Unlike the Zealots (who were swift and prone to infighting), the Sicarii were slow and, after the initial wins in Jerusalem, retired to Masada for the duration of the war. I would say that John Gischala and his initial leadership of the beast corresponds to the Babylonians. His boast about the Romans being unable to fly over the walls of Jerusalem even if they had eagle's wings (Wars 4.3.1:121-127) makes one think of Nebuchadnezzar's pride for the grand architecture and gardens of Babylon. And John Gischala, (like Belshazzar) went into the Holy Place and used God's utensils and the priestly oil and wine in a sacrilegious way (Wars 5.13.6:562-565)."

However exact the historical conclusions of Maarschalk and Mountjoy may be (and I think that they are), what we need to keep in mind is that those of 1st century Palestine were but examples of the ever-present existence of the "spirit" of control and of domination systems (*cf* Walter Wink, *Naming the Powers*), from Cain to Pharaoh to the kings of Israel to the empires in Daniel... *ad infinitum* to our present day. This is the "take away" message for us from this passage.

Observe that "**its mouth** [is] **as a lion's mouth**." By this sign we see a counterpart of the Lion of Judah speaking to His called-out. This mouth speaks words that are anti-Christ from the system that speaks "in place of Christ." The **dragon** (the adversary, the serpent) gives its **ability, power and authority** to this little wild animal. Thus, the false church rides upon the authority of the dragon just as the priests in Jerusalem rode upon the authority and power of Rome. Here, too, the words of this organized system have power to tear and devour.

But let us not forget the clues regarding the **dragon's** (the serpent's, the adversary's, *satan's*) **throne**: The risen Christ said that it was in Pergamos (2:13, above). It had gathering places (*synagogues*) in Smyrna (2:8, above) and Philadelphia (3:9, above). This dragon spirit was even working within the called-out communities!

The **mouth** also devours. The psalmist in Ps. 80 recalled,
> "You have brought a vine out of Egypt; You cast out the heathen, and planted it... it filled the Land.... Why have You broken down her hedges?... the wild **beasts** of the field **devour** it. Return, we beg You, O God of hosts: look down from heaven, and see, and visit this vine... [it is] burned with fire.... Let Your hand be upon the Man of Your right hand, upon the Son of man [whom] You made strong for Yourself... quicken us, and we will call upon Your Name. **Turn us** again, O Yahweh, God of hosts, cause Your Face to shine, and we shall be saved." (vss. 8, 9, 12, 13, 14, 16-19).

The metaphors concern Israel: their deliverance from Egypt, their history, and then the plight of their past, and their plea to God for deliverance and restoration, once again. The story described in this psalm is echoed again in the 1st century. Jerusalem would be burned again, "at the rebuke of His countenance" (Ps. 80:16) at His parousia of judgment in AD 70. This time the little **wild beast** would be the Zealots, and then Rome. But even in His coming in judgment (Mat. 24:7-44), Mat. 24:37b informed His apprentices that concerning all that He had described in that chapter, "**thus** (in this same way) **will progressively be the presence** (*parousia*) **of the Son of the Man**." Judgment was coming to physical Jerusalem through this **little animal** (Zealots; Rome), in that generation (Mat. 24:34). But this was the necessary passing away of the old so that the new could come (2 Cor. 5:17). God created the dragon, and in His time, He will "catch [the] dragon with a fish hook and put a halter around its nose" (Job 41:1, LXX). And for, "**each person within the result and effect of his or her own class** (or: ordered place; appointed position [in line]; arranged time or order of succession; = place in a harvest calendar, thus, due season of maturity)" (1 Cor. 15:23), "**all Israel will progressively be delivered** (rescued, saved, made whole and restored to their original position [in the olive tree])" (Rom. 11:26), as the psalmist prayed (Ps. 80:19).

We can learn from the repetitive pattern of deliverance-exile-deliverance-exile, in Israel's history, that God has lots of dragons in His rivers and seas. Some are home-grown (the little animal on the Land, vs. 11, below, represented by the behemoth in Job 40:15), but behind all of these that will appear again and again through our history, is the spirit of a dragon that is the object of Isa. 54:16,

> "Behold, I have created the smith that blows the coals in the fire, and that brings forth an instrument for his work; and I have created the WASTER to DESTROY."

In Hos. 13:6b-8, Yahweh says to Israel,

> "They were satisfied, and their heart was lifted up – because of this they forgot Me. Therefore am I become to them as a lion—as a leopard by the way do I watch. I will fall upon them as a bear bereaved, and will rend asunder the enclosure of their heart – that I may devour them there, like a lioness. The wild beast of the field shall tear them in pieces. It has utterly destroyed you, O Israel!" (Rotherham)

Behind everything we find God, because He is God. He uses kings and governments to do according to His plans. In Isa. 44:28 He called Cyrus, ruler of Persia, "My shepherd… he shall perform all my pleasure." Then in Isa. 45:1 we read, "Thus says Yahweh to His anointed, to Cyrus, whose right hand I have held to subdue nations before him…" Christ's *parousia* (presence; being alongside) was among the Zealots and Romans in Jerusalem, in AD 70. In Amos 3:6 we find,

> "Shall a trumpet be blown in the City, and the people not be afraid? Shall there be evil in a city, and Yahweh has not done it?"

Terry sees this first "beast" as representing the Roman Empire (ibid p 393). Metzger concurs (ibid p 75). Others view it as being the Emperor, Nero, due to vs. 3, below, and the legend, following Nero's death, that he would be resurrected and reclaim his throne. Barclay interprets the 7 heads as 7 Roman emperors (ibid p 89). Verse 17, below speaks of, "**imprinted mark-effect** (engraving; carve-effect) **or the name of the little animal, or the number of its name**," and vs. 18 instructs us that, "**the number of the little animal… is man's number** (or: [the] number of mankind; a number pertaining to humanity; a man's number)." The parenthetical expansion gives renderings that indicate either the number refers to "a man," and thus, possibly to Nero, or "[the] number of mankind [man was created on the 6th day, in the Genesis story] or a number pertaining to humanity." These have been the historical interpretations, but I think that Maarschalk, above, is a better reading of the text. Whatever John may have meant, with regard to the 1st century, the more general reading of the Greek phrase would better speak to the following centuries, as they read this vision. As Ray Prinzing perceived, quoted above, there was given to us a "beast" nature that became our "false persona" (to quote John Gavazzoni). It is obvious that the beastly spirit, personified in these visions as a dragon, works through humans who act like wild beasts. That spirit of domination gives its power and ability to the institutions that it creates. But Prinzing often quoted Ps. 76:10,

> "Surely the wrath of man shall praise You; the remainder of wrath You will restrain."

3. **And one of its heads was as having been slaughtered unto death, and yet the impact and blow of its death** (or: its death-blow; or: the plague from its death) **was cured** (or: tended; treated), **and later the whole Land** (or: earth) **followed after the little animal with fascinated wonder and admiration.**

As usual, we have an allusion to OT texts,

> "You broke the heads of the dragons in the waters; You broke the heads of Leviathan…" (Ps. 74:13b-14a).
> "Are You not the One that has cut Rahab [figure of Egypt], [and] wounded the dragon?" (Isa. 51:9).
> "He shall hurt [strike at – Tanakh] you [in the] head…" (Gen. 3:15, CVOT).

Just what does the first statement mean? Of what is it a symbol? We are not told, so the ambiguity leaves interpreters guessing. It has been considered to be a parody of the death and resurrection of Christ. It might be considered to be the antithesis of the death and resurrection of the two witnesses (11:7-12, above). We set out with an introduction of this chapter, above, with the statements of the antichrists found in 1 and 2 Jn. The dragon represents the counterpart and false image of the Spirit of God. Instead of generating Life, it causes death. This little animal from the sea (i.e., from the nations surrounding Judea and Jerusalem) is a symbol of the incarnation of the dragon which takes the role of all that is anti-Christ. It was observed in the Jewish leaders who turned Jesus over to Pilate, to have Him killed, and in that same leadership that tried to silence Christ's witnesses, following the Day of Pentecost. It was in those such as Saul, in Acts 9; Agrippa killed James, in Acts 12:1-3; it was in the silversmiths and the whole city of Ephesus, in Acts 19; and then in those who intended to kill Saul/Paul, in Acts 21:31, and in the Jews who vowed neither to eat nor drink until they had killed Paul, in Acts 23:12. With this history in mind, I suggest that **one of** the little animal's **heads** was the Judaism of Jerusalem, in the 1st century. Judaism was **slaughtered unto death**, in AD 70, but that "plague" **was cured**, and Judaism continued on in the Diaspora. It even came back with the Bar Kokhba Revolt against Rome, in AD 132-135.

Maarschalk makes a cogent suggestion here:
> "That head was Menahem, who achieved victories at Masada, came into Jerusalem as a king, and became the leader of the Zealots, only to be killed about one month later…. About a month after the Jewish-Roman War officially started…. The beast's wound quickly began to heal when the Zealots achieved a surprise victory against [the Syrian general] Cestus Gallus about two months later, in Nov. 66 (*Wars* 2.19.1-9)" ("Overview" ibid pp 30, 31).

He traces the Zealot movement back to Hezekiah who resisted Rome and Herod in 47 BC, listing the "heads" of the movement up to the time of the Zealot rebellion. (https://adammaarschalk.com/2017/03/16/revelation-133-and-the-wounded-head-of-the-zealot-movement/)

"**[And] later the whole Land** (or: earth) **followed after the little animal with fascinated wonder and admiration**," can refer to the fact that Judaism (or, as per Maarschalk, the Zealot rebellion against Rome) survived **the impact and blow of its death**, which was the destruction of an individual, or of Jerusalem and their temple. The "**whole Land**" refers to all the Jews who did not accept Jesus as their Messiah, and followed first after the Zealots, then later, after rabbinic Judaism with its adjustments in which the Torah study replaced the temple and its sacrifice cultus. Or, the phrase referred to those who approved of the Zealot's war. Josephus' *Wars of the Jews* gives ample evidence that the Zealots' behavior fit the description of a "beast" as much as Rome did. This is, of course, painting with very broad strokes.

What of the other six heads? We need not try to fit something historical into every detail of the vision. Remember, 7 is a symbolic number. Maarschalk (ibid) sees these as other generals in the rebellion. The message here is that a part of the little animal, the one that was centered in Jerusalem, received a "death-bow," but that head was tended, treated and a new leadership emerged among the Zealots. If we read the picture as speaking of the domination system that had happened in Second Temple Judaism, perhaps this was speaking of the demise of the temple: there was no longer a priesthood: it died; there was no longer a system of "little animal" sacrifices. There was no longer a central tithe reception center (as the temple had been), so they could not hire the craft of scribes. But the whole of the people of Israel still stood in awe of the Empire, and rightly so.

Now Barclay and preterist scholars such as R. C. Sproul (in, *The Last Days According to Jesus*) see this "beast" as a reference to Nero, and the "Nero resurrected" legend. Matthew Henry says, "Some think that by this wounded head we are to understand the abolishing of pagan idolatry, and by the healing of the wound the introducing of the popish idolatry..." Halley followed this line of thinking noting that "Rome fell in AD 476. But, in the Name of Christ, and by the aid of the Church, Rome came to life again..." Smith sees the wounded head as symbolic of all the nations having been smitten at the cross, but they are still here. We offer these alternate views as a contrast to what we have presented, above. Terry gives some historical perspective:

> "The heads of a symbolic beast are best understood as the chief seats of power and dominion.... the wounded head of this Roman beast is a reference to some temporary loss of power in one of its many seats of authority. According to 13:14 it was a 'stroke of the sword' by which the wound was given, indicating that it was some military conquest (cf 6:4)" (ibid p 394).

He goes on to cite the example of the Parthians overrunning all of western Asia and Palestine, resulting in Rome having no rule or authority of those areas for a full year. In regard to Terry's reference to the sword, in vs. 14, below, consider Who else has a sword, as we've noted, in 1:16 and 2:16, above, and in 19:15, below.

When Paul gave admonitions to Titus, in the first chapter of his letter he described circumstances and situations that shed light on our study of this "little wild animal,"

> 10. **You see, many folks, especially those from out of the Circumcision** (= the Jews), **are insubordinate ones** (not submitted to the arrangement; un-subjected to the order), **empty, vain and profitless talkers, even seducers of the intellect** (deceivers of the mind; people who mislead thinking),
> 11. **who it continues necessary to repeatedly muzzle** (gag; or: reign them in), **who are habitually turning-back whole households** [i.e., into the Law cultus of Judaism] (or: = constantly upsetting entire families), **repeatedly teaching things which it is binding not to [teach]: a "grace" of ugly** (deformed; disgraceful) **profit, gain or advantage!**
> 12. **A certain one of them, their own prophet** (= poet), **said, "Cretans [are] always liars, worthless little wild animals** (little beasts of bad quality), **inactive and idle bellies** (= unemployed gluttons)."
> 13. **This witness** (or: testimony [of the poet Epimenides]) **is true. Because of which case and cause, be repeatedly cross-examining them abruptly while cutting away [at the case] and bringing the question to the proof, so as to test and decide the dispute and expose the matter – to the end that they can be sound and healthy within the Faith and in union with trust and loyalty,**
> 14. **not habitually holding to** (having [a propensity] toward; heeding and clinging in the direction toward) **Jewish myths** (or: fictions; or, possibly: oral traditions) **and to implanted goals** (impartations of a finished product within; inward directives; commands) **whose source and origin is people** (or: human commandments) **[thus] continually being twisted and turned away from the Truth** (or: reality).

So you see, apocalyptic literature and visions were not the only genres to employ rhetoric with metaphors of little wild animals, or beasts. But since visions are usually portrayed with a certain amount of ambiguity with regard to possible interpretations, perhaps the intent was that they were not supposed to represent just one thing; the applications were to be open-ended so that they could fit many different situations in life and history.

In 1 Cor. 15:32 Paul speaks of his exposure to furious hostility within people by using the figure, "**I fight** (or: fought) **in accord with human [means, methods or purposes] with wild beasts in Ephesus**." You see, Ephesus (especially with its Jewish population) may have been another "head" of the animal. Peter makes an interesting remark of such folks,

> "**But these, as irrational** (wordless; unreasoning) **living ones** (or: animals), **being creatures of instinct having been born unto capture and then corruption** (decay; ruin), **within which**

things – being continuously ignorant – they are constantly blaspheming (speaking slander, insult and abusive speech; injuriously vilifying; or: hindering the Light) **within their corruption** (decay), **and they will be progressively ruined** (spoiled; caused to decay; corrupted), **being folks habitually wronging themselves** (or, reading as a passive: being wronged; suffering injustice)" (2 Pet. 2:12-13a).

Jude 10 is similar. In the OT, Jer. 10:14 records, "Every man is brutish in [his] knowledge." Then in vs. 21, "For the pastors are become brutish..."

Even today, people try to slay some facet or branch of the beast system – some social or political evil, e.g. – and just when they think it dead, someone comes along and attends to it, "heals it," and revives it. Congress brings the issue up in another bill! And we, through our religious works of the flesh, try to slay one of the heads of the estranged self within us, and because it is not God's time for this self to be destroyed, its "death-wound" is healed, and it bites us again! There always comes a time when God will deal with this beast. It is His work.

Just as Eve wondered after the deception of the serpent, humanity wonders after the power and image of the beast system in each of its seven mountains (kingdoms of society: religion, politics, education, the arts, economy, media and science – this 7-mountain concept has been presented by Lance Wallnau). As God's chosen people worship Him for giving His power to Christ, so the carnal mind worships the dragon because it is the power behind the beast systems. As those who receive Christ receive the One Who sent Him, so those who receive the estranged system receive the spirit of that system. And we have the saying, "We can't fight city hall... or the government... or denomination headquarters...!" But the carnal human is yet fascinated by himself, and by what he perceives that this carnal mind can do. Having cited a concept through Lance Wallnau (from hearing him speak via a webinar), I just visited his website, and lifted this opening quote from his home page: "A philosophy of life that works is one that gives perspective or purpose to the irritations that we encounter." We need to view all of life through the lens of Christ, and our Father, in order to have perspective concerning His purposes in our lives.

4. **And so people** [*p*47, 2344, *pc* read: it] **worshiped** (or: worship; do obeisance to; bow down to kiss the feet of) **the dragon because it gave** (or: gives) **authority to the little animal; and so they** (or: people) **worship the little animal, saying, "Who** (or: What) **[is] like the little animal** (the little creature or beast)**? And who** (or: what) **is able** (continuously has power) **to do battle** (or: wage war) **with it?"**

People tend to worship power, thinking to attract some power to themselves if they align themselves with some manifestation of power, or with the spirit that gave power to that specific manifestation. The spirit (the dragon) behind the manifestation (the animal) is often either religious (e.g. whatever particular religion one is admiring) or political (whatever organization one adheres to, whether a governmental empire, or an economic entity). Our tendency is to join what we think we can't fight. The worship consists of compliance to its demands, or attributing to it our admiration (for its reputation), or submission to it, out of fear of what it could do to us. Worship does not always manifest in religious clothing: it can simply be in the desire to be part of the "in" group, the intellectually discriminating and savvy group, or the "moral majority."

The first question may be an allusion to Ex. 15:11, "Who is like to you among the gods, O Yahweh?" Isa. 40:18 asks, "To whom, then, will you folks liken God? or what likeness will you people compare unto Him?" *Cf* Ps. 35:10; 71:19; 86:8; 113:5. The question here, in vs. 4, asks of humans or of human domination systems that comparison which should be asked of God. It is idolatry. Micah 7:18 gives the appropriate question:

"Who [is] a God like unto You, that pardons iniquity and passes by the transgression of the remnant of His heritage? He does not retain His anger for an age, because He delights in mercy."

Cf 18:18, below, where this question is asked concerning the "great City." D'Aragon sees this question as, "a parody of the honors paid to the Lamb (5:9)..." (ibid p 484).

Fear is at the core of the second question. Both questions display a lack of personal, experiential knowledge of God. It calls to mind the fear that Israel had of Goliath (1 Sam. 17:11). The question, here, also suggests that someone may WISH to do battle with this animal that has the **authority** of, and from, the **dragon**, but its apparent power seems too strong to resist. In the NT folks held back from acclaiming Jesus as Lord, for fear of the Jewish leadership (e.g., Jn. 7:13; 9:22; 19:38; 20:19). The Jewish leadership feared another head of the little animal: Rome (Jn. 11:48ff).

In the first parenthetical expansion, I added to the verb, **worshiped** (which is in the timeless aorist tense), the meaning, "do obeisance to," along with the basic cultural sense of the verb ("bow down to kiss the feet of") within the times and cultures involved in this Unveiling. Such worship usually involved an icon, an idol or some other representation of that which people "worshiped." "Worship" can be a way of showing allegiance or praise. Terry instructs us,
> "Pliny's letter to Trajan evinces the extent to which the worship of the emperor's image was required in the provinces (Pliny, *Epist.,* Bk. 10, epist. 96). See also Tacitus, *Annals*, bk. 15.29, 74" (ibid p 395).

The alternate MSS readings of 3rd persons, singular (for the 1st verb in the 1st clause) would have the **little animal** (of the last clause of vs. 3) worshiping the dragon. This would change the picture: the people (third clause) worship the **little animal**, as the **little animal** worships the **dragon**. This could be a parody of people worshiping Christ as Christ (in His earthly ministry) worshiped the Father by His faithfulness to the Father's will. The picture of the bold rendering has people worshiping both the dragon and its material manifestation (the animal) that came from out of the ethnic multitudes (the sea). In our alienated state of being (before being re-joined to the Vine) we will worship almost anything.

We want to again turn to Maarschalk:
> "Why does Revelation 13:4 apply to Israel so much better than it could possibly apply to Rome? Here's what we see when we look at the big picture:
> 1. The beast would be recognized as a victor of war. "*Who is able to make war with him?*" (Rev. 13:4).
> 2. The beast would then receive authority to continue for 42 months and overcome the saints (Rev. 13:5-7).
> 3. The beast would then be captured and killed by the sword (Rev. 13:10).
> 4. The beast would ultimately end up in the lake of fire (Rev. 19:20) and the birds would be filled with the flesh of his followers (Rev. 19:21).
>
> If we examine any historical overview of the Jewish-Roman War (AD 66 – AD 73), what will we see? Who started out victorious but ended up in misery and defeat? Was it Rome, or was it Israel? The reality is that Rome was embarrassed at the beginning of the war, but was thoroughly victorious in the end. Israel shocked everyone at the beginning with its victories, but was brutally destroyed in the end. Israel, not Rome, followed the pattern outlined above" ("Who Can Make War with the Beast?" https://adammaarschalk.com/2017/07/14/who-can-make-war-with-the-beast-revelation-134/)

5. **Then a mouth, continuously speaking great things and blasphemies** (things that obscure the light; abusive slander; harm-avering misrepresentations) **was given to it. Authority to act** (or: to make or do; to produce) **[for] forty-two months** [other MSS read: to make war 42 months; another early MS reads: to do what it wills 42 months] **was also given to it** (or: And so, a right from out of Being was allowed for it to suddenly form, construct and create [over a period of] forty-two months).

In today's vernacular, instead of using the metaphor of being **given** a "**mouth**," we might term it as being given a "platform" from which to proclaim our message. The first statement assumes the giver to be the dragon, the spirit of the system, as in vs. 2, above. D'Aragon describes the grammar, here, as, "The 'theological' passive" (ibid). Here, it would be set in contrast to the "divine passive," of 9:1, above. However, Beasley-Murray interprets the grammar here as a "divine passive," by saying, "Note that, although the dragon gave the beast his authority over the earth, the real permission for his blasphemous utterances and deeds, and even the duration of his reign, comes from God; see also vss. 7, 10, 14, 15" (ibid p 1295-6). Stern concurs, citing Isa. 45:6-7; Job 1:12; 2:6 (ibid p 828). Beale interprets from the first clause, here, that, "The beast's authority is expressed in his speech" (ibid p 695). He also sees God as the "ultimate source" for the little animal's authority, from, "the decreed time limit," stating that, "Only God... sets times and seasons" (ibid).

John does not tell us what the **great things** are, but if we view this little animal as Rome, then we might safely assume that it is speaking about Caesar, or, the Empire. This phrase comes from Dan. 7:8b, where "a little horn" of the beast of that vision had, "eyes like the eyes of a human, and a mouth speaking great things." *Cf* Dan. 7:11, 25; 11:36. It is likely that this system of domination was speaking things that intimidated the masses and instilled fear. In the following centuries, the institutional church preached the great doctrine of endless torment and the concept of "hell" which was foreign to both the OT and the NT. These teachings **blasphemed** the character of God, and "obscured the Light" of Christ as being the Savior of all humanity (e.g., 1 Tim. 4:10; *cf Hope For All; Ten Reasons God's Love Prevails*, by Gerry Beauchemin, 2018). Verse 6, below, informs us at to whom the **blasphemies** were directed.

During the 1st century, and ever since, the called-out, covenant communities were, and have been, frequently slandered and verbally abused. "Harm-avering misrepresentations" were brought against Jesus, and the book of Acts, along with Paul's letters, show us that Judaism (the dominant religion of Jerusalem and Judea) continued this same practice. The Caesar cult, and trade union religions, verbally abused and misrepresented Christ's followers in the other parts of the Empire.

Saul (Acts 9:1ff) received **authority to act** from the Sanhedrin in Jerusalem. Later, Judaizers from the Jerusalem church followed Paul's work among the Gentile followers, trying to discredit him and his revelation of the Good News of God's grace. The same thing has happened ever since. The dominant sect will always endeavor to discredit all who do not join it, or who refuse to submit to its "leadership." Also, their organization-based "authority" allows them to act by excommunicating, or by smearing the reputation of those who would stand against, or disagree with, that organization.

And further, do not the systems of our culture, our political organizations, our governments, and our entertainment industries, have a **mouth**? Consider how we like to talk; note our worship of the media. Ponder the produce from education, the arts, religion... Humans are constantly speaking "great things" and "blasphemies." The political and religious systems are believed to be needed in order to have "**authority to act**." Church systems in our day preach that you must be "under [their] authority," "under [their] covering" in order to do anything. Thus the dragon gives this wild animal (which is not domesticated or disciplined in the Lord's house) its "**authority to act**, to construct (and has not this spirit built buildings and kingdoms ever since it attempted to construct the tower at Babel), to produce and to do."

The phrase, "**forty-two months**," should be seen, here, as a symbol of limited persecution that is tied-in with the events described in 11:2 (the treading down of the holy City) and 12:6, 14 (the flight of the Woman into the desert), above, and so here it would be helpful to review the comments on those passages. What we read here applies to what was written there. Numbers in this book are ideas. A landmark type for beast-like persecution was the three and a half years of AD 66-70 where a domination system (the Zealots' war) filled Jerusalem. This imagery is based on the time themes in Dan. 7 and 9. Again, as Maarschalk has pointed out, it was the Zealots and the Sicarii who occupied and defiled Jerusalem for this time period (ibid).

6. **So it opened** (or: at once opens) **its mouth unto blasphemies** (injurious slander) **toward God, to blaspheme** (misrepresent and hinder the light of) **His Name and His Tabernacle: those continuously tabernacling** (or: camping in tents; living in the Tabernacle) **within the atmosphere** (or: heaven).

The first clause is an echo of Dan. 7:25,
> "And he will continue speaking words against the Highest One and will progressively mislead (or: continue causing to stray; [other MSS: wear down]) the holy ones of the Highest One and will continue having the opinion and expect to change seasons and law (or: appointed situations and custom), and it will be progressively given into his hand until (to the extent of) a season and seasons and half a season" (LXX, JM).

We can also see an allusion to Ps.73:9,
> "They set their mouths against heaven, and their tongues range over the earth" (NRSV).

This may also be that which Paul described:
> "**the human from the lawlessness – the person of failure: the son of the loss, the one continuously occupying an opposite position** (or: constantly lying as the opposing counterpart) **and repeatedly lifting himself up over all being normally called God or an effect of worship, so as to cause him to be seated – down into the midst of the temple of God – continuously displaying himself, that this/it is God** (or: continuously pointing out that he himself is a god)" (2 Thes. 2:3b-4).

Keep in mind that these dragons and little animals operate and manifest through people, as well as through institutions and empires. Jesus spoke of one, in Jn. 17:12b, "**except the son of loss** (the son of the dissolution, or, destruction; = the person having the qualities and characteristics of loss and dissolution or destruction), **so that the Scripture could and would be fulfilled**."

Or, this may be an allusion to Mat. 24:
> 15. "**Therefore, whenever you men can see** (or: may perceive) '**the effect of the loathing and nauseating [event; condition; thing; situation] from the desolation**
>> (or: the result from the abhorring abomination associated with, or which causes, the devastation and abandonment; or: the resulting effect of the desecration, which is an act of ruining, forsaking and leaving uninhabited like a desert),' **that was being spoken through Daniel the prophet, standing 'within the midst of a set-apart place** (or: [the] holy place)' [Dan. 9:27; 11:31; 12:11] **– let the person presently reading continue to use his mind and intellect for the comprehension [of this]** (= figure out what this means!) –
> 16. "**at that time, let the people within the midst of Judea progressively escape** (flee; take flight) **into the hills and mountains**...

This referred to the 1st century layer: that of the Zealots, and then Rome, occupying the temple. It is parallel to Lu. 21:20-21.

God is first to be named as the object of the little animal's **blasphemies**, and specifically, to "misrepresent and hinder the light of **His Name**." A person's name signifies not just one's identity, but what people think of the person. So when one's name is slandered it has a negative effect on his or her character and reputation. When one's name is misrepresented, it gives folks the wrong impression and a false idea of what he or she is like. When this animal system speaks against God's Name the result can be people turning from God, not trusting Him and believing wrong things about Him. Traditional Christianity has probably been the worst offender at slandering God's reputation by painting Him as a fiend who will torture most of humanity for ever – and ever (a contradiction in terms – how could there be something more than "forever"?). But the main fault for this has been faulty translations of the original languages of the Scriptures. Probably what runs a close second place as a reason for people not liking the God of institutional Christianity is the "flat" reading of the texts: reading everything literally, with no thought to the rhetorical devices used by the authors such as hyperbole and metaphor. Vying for second place is the quoting of verses out of context and "connecting the dots" of our favorite, "cherry-picked" verses that we use to construct our doctrines. More could be said here, but we will move on.

The Name of God had a very special place in Israel's history, in their religion and in their culture (these last two being existentially linked together). The third commandment that God gave to Moses was, "You will not take the Name of Yahweh, your God, in vain" (Ex. 20:7a). A person's name was intrinsically tied to and equated with the person. So to "injuriously slander" God's Name, is to do this to Him.

Here, **His Tabernacle** is defined as, "**those continuously tabernacling** (or: camping in tents; living in the Tabernacle) **within the atmosphere** (or: heaven)." The term "tabernacle" takes John's listeners back to the early times of Israel's history, the times before there was a temple, and specifically to Israel's creation as a nation, at Sinai, and the Exodus wanderings when the tabernacle was first constructed. In other visions in the Unveiling, the context has been, and will be again, the Temple. Might this be a clue that the "first little animal" speaks specifically in the realm of, or in terms of, the "first covenant" that created Israel, in relation to the "new covenant" that replaced the first? We read in Heb. 8:6-8,

> 6. **But now He has hit the mark of a thoroughly carried-through public service, even by as much as He continues being a Medium** (an agency; an intervening substance; a middle state; one in a middle position; a go-between; an umpire; a Mediator) **of a superior** (stronger and better) **arrangement** (covenant; settlement; disposition) **which has been instituted** (set by custom; legally [= by/as Torah] established) **upon superior** (stronger and better) **promises!**
> 7. **For if that first one was being unblamable** (without ground for faultfinding; beyond criticism; satisfying), **a place of a second one would not have continued to be sought** (looked for).
> 8. **For continuously blaming** (finding fault and being dissatisfied with) **them, He is saying, "'Consider! Days are progressively coming,' says the Lord** [=Yahweh], **'and I shall progressively bring an end together** (a conclusion of its destiny; or: a joint-goal) **upon the house of Israel and upon the house of Judah with a new arrangement** (a different covenant; an innovative disposition)…"

This new covenant focused on a different Name: the Name of Jesus. The head of the beast representing Judaism did not recognize the name, Jesus, as Christ's followers did. In Acts 3:6, Peter said to the lame beggar, "**Within, and in union with, the Name of Jesus Christ the Nazarene, start walking, and then keep on walking about** (around)!" In Acts 4:1-3a, we see the beginning of the push-back:

> "**Now during their continued speaking to the people, the chief** (or: ranking) **priests, the officer of the Temple guard** (= the Controller/Commander of the Temple), **and the Sadducees stood near them, in opposition, and at last took a stand upon [the scene], being progressively annoyed, exasperated, vexed through and through, and in a thoroughly worthless and knavish attitude because of their continuing to teach the people, and to be**

> bringing down the announcement and be fully proclaiming in [the case of] Jesus (or: in union with Jesus; in the sphere [or: authority] of Jesus) **the resurrection from out of the midst of dead folks. And so they thrust [their] hands on them and they were placed into custody** (in ward)…"

The next morning, as we read in Acts 4:18,

> "**And so, after calling them, they ordered [them] to cease making any utterance at all, as well as to terminate teaching anywhere, on [the authority or basis of] the Name of Jesus**."

When Saul was confronted by the Voice and the Light, on his way to Damascus, he wanted to know,

> "**Who are You, Lord** (or: Sir; Master)**?**"

The answer came with the identification by a Name:

> "**Now He replied, "I, Myself, am Jesus... Whom you continue pursuing and persecuting!**"

It is significant that He did not say, "I am the Lord," or, "I am Christ (or: the Messiah)." (Acts 9:5). He responded with His Name. Later, Paul would write,

> "**For this reason, God also lifts Him up above** (or: highly exalted Him; elevates Him over) **and by grace gives to Him** (or: joyously favors on Him) **the Name – the one over and above every name! – to the end that within The Name: Jesus!** (or: in union with the name of Jesus; in the midst of the Name belonging to [Yahweh-the-Savior]), **every knee** (= person) **– of the folks upon the heaven** (of those belonging to the super-heaven, or [situated] upon the atmosphere) **and of the people existing upon the earth and of the folks dwelling down under the ground** (or: on the level of or pertaining to subterranean ones; [comment: note the ancient science of the day – a three-tiered universe]) **– may bend** (or: would bow) **in prayer, submission and allegiance, and then every tongue** (= person) **may speak out the same thing** (should and would openly agree, confess, avow and acclaim) **that Jesus Christ [is] Lord** (Master; Owner) **– [leading] into [the] glory of Father God** (or: unto Father God's good reputation; [progressing] into a manifestation which calls forth praise unto God [our] Father)!" (Phil. 2:9-11).

In Rom. 2 we find a seminal statement that should shed light on our present passage:

> 23. **You who are boasting in law** (or: [the] Law [= Torah]; or: a law), **through the transgression of** (stepping across the line of; stepping to the side of; deviating from) **the Law, you are constantly dishonoring** (devaluing) **God,**
> 24. **for according as it has been, and stands, written [in the Tanakh** (Hebrew Scriptures)**], "Because of you, God's NAME** [Yahweh?] **is continuously being blasphemed** (vilified; misrepresented; slandered; given a false image which hinders the Light) **among the ethnic multitudes** (nations; non-Jews; Gentiles)." [Isa. 52:5; Ezk. 36:20]

So Paul is suggesting that, as in days of Israel's history, the Jews' behavior was the cause of God's Name being "vilified," etc. What I described, above, as having happened within organized Christianity was a repeat of what had happened in Judaism. The culprit in 13:6, here, may be another "head" of the little animal: the alienated human nature, aka, the first Adam. Everyone has been the same – both the former Jew, and the former Gentile. We have all missed the goal (which is: being in the image of God). But there is no condemnation, and 2 Cor. 5:19 tells us that He is not holding our transgressions against us, for the Garden story instructs us that through disobedience humanity (*cf* Rom. 5:12) lost its access to the Tree of Life. Being apart from this life left us "dead in trespasses and sins" (Eph. 2:1): we could only act like brute beasts.

The next object of blasphemy is presented as: "**His Tabernacle: those continuously tabernacling** (or: camping in tents; living in the Tabernacle) **within the atmosphere** (or: heaven)." This symbol is a figure of the body of Christ, God's temple (1 Cor. 6:19; 2 Cor. 6:16). Where they are living (i.e., in the **atmosphere**; heaven) is described by Paul in Eph. 2:6 and in Col.3:1, and is also seen in Heb. 12:22-24. Here, we can recall Jesus' words to His followers, in Mat. 10:

> **24.** "**A student** (or: disciple) **is not over or above the teacher, nor [is] a slave over or above his owner.**
> **25.** "**[It is] sufficient and enough for the student** (or: disciple) **that he can come to be as his teacher, and the slave as his owner. Since** (or: If) **people call and surname the Sovereign** (Master and Sole Owner) **of the house** (the Householder) **'Beelzeboul'** [spellings vary; = lord of the flies, a Philistine deity], **how much rather** (or: more) **those of His household.**

What this little animal (in the Jerusalem head and by the Zealot anr Rome heads) did to our Sovereign, it also did to those of His household. Our next verse (7a, below) speaks of this, echoing 11:7, above. There may also be an allusion to 11:1, "**and the folks continuously worshiping within it**." We can also look ahead to 21:3, below,

> "**Consider! God's tent** (the Tabernacle of God) **[is] with mankind** (the humans), **'and He will continue living in a tent** (dwell in a Tabernacle) **with them, and they will continue being** (will constantly exist being) **His peoples, and God Himself will continue being with them**."

With the tabernacle having been replaced by the temple, in Solomon's day, and it having been a symbol for "the heavens" (God's dwelling place; His throne being the ark in the holy of holies), Wallace presents a different take on this verse, viewing the blasphemies as coming from the emperor, and therefore, "The phrase '*them that dwell in heaven*' referred to the Jewish authorities, and signified the emperor's purpose to bring to end the Jewish state" (ibid p 292). In symbolic literature, there will always be different interpretations of the symbols. The OT is our main source for keys to interpret them, but even there we are confronted with layered meanings of the texts. Our main concern, here, is to find the application that can edify us and shed light on current situations that affect our lives. The rest is primarily history lessons.

7. Next it was (or: is) **given to it to wage war** (or: was allowed to do battle) **with the set-apart folks** (holy people; sacred one) **and to overcome them. And authority was given** (or: Then right and privilege from out of its being was allowed) **to it upon every tribe and people and tongue and multitude** (nation; ethnic group).

The first statement is an allusion to Dan. 7:21, where it speaks about a "horn" (figure of a king/ruler) of the fourth beast (most likely, a figure of the Roman Empire), "made war with the set-apart folks (the sacred people), and was strong, with a view to (toward; face-to-face with) them" (LXX, JM). The second statement is an allusion to Dan. 7:14, where dominion (Old Greek: authority – NETS) over people, nations and languages was given to "[one] like a Son of man." We should keep in mind that the Roman Empire had complete dominion over, "**every tribe and people and tongue and multitude** (nation; ethnic group)" within the Empire's reach. So we can see the political head of this little animal as Rome, in the period of AD 66-70. It overcame the "set-apart folks" known as the Jews, and it destroyed Jerusalem. But we will consider other layers of interpretation, as well. Many interpreters see this text in Dan. as a reference to Antiochus Epiphanes's persecution of Israel in the days of the Maccabees. As mentioned, above, visions can have multiple applications, as did the history of Israel (consider Paul's use of allegory in Gal. 4). We must keep in mind that we are reading texts of an ancient culture, so we must not put our modern interpretive constructs on them to suit our purposes.

However, again turning to Josephus, we find that there were multiple factions competing dominance among the Jewish rebels. Citing Martin Hengel (*The Zealots* pp 290-298), Maarschalk states, "According to Hengel, [1] Judas of Galilee, [2] Menahem, and [3] Simon Bar Giora were all Messianic pretenders… [the latter two] marched into Jerusalem like kings, were both regarded by their followers as kings…" ("Overview" ibid p 30). Many Jews killed other Jews.

The first clause reaches back to 11:7, to this same little's animal's overcoming of the two witnesses. It also reaches back to shed light on 12:7, showing that the "agents" of the dragon, there, is pictured here as a little animal. The "**set-apart folks**," here, are "**the remaining ones** (the rest; those left) **of her seed** (= offspring)," in 12:17, above. Governments have throughout history "**waged war with [God's] set-apart folks**." We saw this beginning to happen with the death of Stephen, in Acts 7:58-60, and in Acts 8:1, we read,

> "**Now on that day great persecution, pursuit and** [D adds: pressure] **was birthed** (occurred) **upon the called-out community [that was] within Jerusalem, so they were all – except for the sent-forth emissaries** (representatives) [D*& 1175 add: who alone remained in Jerusalem] **– dispersed and scattered as seeds down among the regions** (or: territories) **of Judea and Samaria**."

So here we see the Judaism head of the little animal. The Judaizers followed Paul all the way to Galatia, and very likely, throughout Asia Minor, and probably on to Rome. Judaism was adversarial to the Christ movement when it was within their "world," as we have seen, above. Through their leaders and synagogues, they had control over the "God-fearers" from the Gentiles. But their blasphemy against Christ was at the same time blasphemy against God. And they persecuted the Christ-followers (as with the case of Saul).

Hitler's Germany is an example that still touches us today. Since the establishment of the Zionist state of modern "Israel," the culture/religious/political conflicts and terrorism from both sides has been an ongoing plague in the Middle East. God has "set-apart" many ethnic groups to show forth the many aspects of His glory in creating them, giving them special wisdom and insights that "modern man" would do well to consider. But without rebirth into the higher consciousness and knowledge of Christ, the greed that has infected and poisoned the estranged heart (of "modern humans") sees these other cultures as either being in the way of their progress and of their gaining more, or as sub-humans that are only to be used or destroyed, or as a military/terrorist threat. They have not known that "everything is in relationship with everything" (Richard Rohr, Daily Meditations, 09/13/16).

An important insight into the manifestations of these animal incarnations is noted by Hiett (ibid p 167-8). He states,

> "In 1950 the great Dutch theologian Hendrik Berkhof wrote a seminal book entitled *Christ and the Powers*, in which he argued that Paul saw the principalities and powers as structures of earthly, human existence, 'social facts,' 'ideologies,' and 'nations' (Herald, 1962, 1977, first pub. Nijkerk, 1952)."

Hiett also rightly points out that, "Everything the beast does is allowed or granted to him" (ibid).

Recall that this is happening during the 42 months (vs. 5, above) that the witness of Christ is happening (11:2-3, above), and while Christ is being proclaimed and demonstrated, the beast system with Babylon on board (chapter 17, below) – the mystery of iniquity (2 Thes. 2:7) – battles against God's anointed. Let us consider this passage in 2 Thes. 2:7-10, along with my comments on those verses:

> 7. **For the secret** (hidden purpose; mystery) **of the lawlessness** (pertaining to the condition of being without law; which is the unlawfulness; having the character of being violation of the Law; whose source is the contrariness to custom) **is already continuously working within** (operating; energizing), **[yet] only until the one** (or: man; [note: masculine article]) **continuously holding down in a firm grasp** (detaining; restraining) **at the present moment can birth himself** (bring himself to be; = separate himself) **forth from out of the midst.**
>
> "Now the context would suggest that it is "the secret and hidden purpose of the lawlessness" to which Paul was referring in vs. 6 as having been veiled and covered – or hidden. The birthing

"forth from out of the midst" could refer to the Christians leaving Jerusalem, just prior to its destruction. Or, it can refer to the Christ coming forth from the called-out body and unveiling the secret of that which is unlawful and contrary to custom. John saw this in the symbol of the woman birthing the man-child in Rev. 12. That, too, had multiple meanings:
a) Israel bringing forth Christ, or His body manifesting His life
b) The called-out folks departing the Jewish religion, or escaping from Jerusalem
c) the birthing of God's sons to deliver creation, in every time and place.

"For our day, I suggest that the mystery and hidden purpose of "the lawlessness" is that 'law of sin' to which Paul referred in Rom. 7. It is the law in our members that is contrary to the 'law of the Spirit of life.' Vs. 8 describes what happens when it is uncovered and revealed."

8. **And then** (at that time) **the lawless person** (the unlawful one; the one without law; the man who violates the Law; the person being contrary to custom) **will be uncovered** (unveiled; disclosed), **whom the Lord Jesus will take back up again** (or: lift up; reading *anaireō* with Nestle, Tasker & Concordant texts; Griesbach & other MSS read *analiskō*: consume, use up, expend) **by the Spirit** (Breath-effect) **of His mouth, and will deactivate** (render inoperative and useless; make inert) **by the manifestation** (the bringing of light upon and setting in full and clear view, causing an appearance) **of his** (or: its; or: His) **presence –**

"Again, the application is both historical (Christ coming and judging, in AD 70), and Christ repeatedly coming and judging within His House. He uncovers the false persona, our estranged human nature, and takes it back up again by the Spirit of His mouth, or with the other MSS, consumes and renders pure and restored. The Breath-effect of His mouth (whether breathing upon us, or speaking to us) is the manifestation of His presence. This, as in ch. 1, above, brings righteousness and restores the Way pointed out: justice, fair and equitable dealings, rightwised relationships.

"Reading *anaireō*, we see that His Breath/Spirit takes the false and estranged back into Himself: restoration. Reading *analiskō*, we see purification and transformation. This manifestation of His presence comes both individually and corporately. The Christ event inaugurated the new creation in which He is habitually, or constantly, coming to us – dwelling in and among us, while we have been snatched up and seated with Him (Eph. 2:6) in the new heavens, the abode of the new human (earth)."

9. **whose presence is continuously existing in correspondence to** (or: in line with; in the sphere of; on the level of) **the adversary's** (opponent's; or: satan's) **in-working activity** (or: is constantly in accordance with the operation of the "adversary," or, satan), **in all power** (or: within all ability) **as well as signs and wonders of falsehood** (or: which are a lie),
10. **and within every deception** (delusion; seduction) **of the injustice** (wrong; thing that is not the way pointed out and which is not right) **within the folks continuously or repeatedly being lost** (or: by the folks progressively destroying themselves) **in return for which** (or: in the place of which) **they do** (or: did) **not take unto themselves and welcomingly receive the love of, and from, the truth** (or: Truth's love; the Love which is Truth and Reality; or: an appreciation of and affection for reality), **into the [situation for] them at some point to be suddenly delivered** (restored to health and wholeness; rescued; saved; restored to the original state and condition).

"Now the 'manifestation' in vs. 8 can also refer to the bringing light upon this 'lawless person.' Thus, vss. 9-10 can be read in two different ways:

a) following that which I just described above, seeing that it is Christ's manifestation and presence – meeting the in-working activity of the adversary, in its sphere, and on every level of its activity, within its signs and wonders of falsehood, and within each of its deceptions of injustice within the lost who are progressively destroying themselves, etc. Note that in the last clause of vs. 10 His work leads them "into the [situation for] them at some point to be suddenly delivered!"
b) seeing it as a manifestation of 'the lawless person,' "'either as an individual, historically, or as estranged humanity, we see that its presence corresponds to the working of the adversary within, which operates with its false power and lying wonders within deceptions of that which is contrary to the path of life. This causes folks not to receive or retain 'the Love (God) which is Truth and Reality (Christ); or: an appreciation of and affection for reality.' Nonetheless, the result is the same, as the last part of vs. 10 tells us: deliverance, rescue" (*Peter, Paul & Jacob*, Jonathan Mitchell, Harper Brown Pub., 2012, p 140-1).

Thus it is evident that the aim of the "beast" is a religious aim, and thus its war (vs. 7, here) is religious and spiritual, for its words are against those in heaven (the spiritual realm; and the folks living in the atmosphere). We suggest that, "**those continuously tabernacling** (or: camping in tents; living in the Tabernacle) **within the atmosphere** (or: heaven)," of verse 6, are the same ones called "**the set-apart (holy) folks**," here. These are set-apart within "**every tribe and people and tongue and multitude** (or: nation; ethnic group)."

Paul spoke of an interior battle within himself, as he personified the first Adam, in Rom. 7:23,
> "**yet I constantly see** (or: observe) **a different principle** (or: law), **within my members, [which is] by the Law** (or: custom; or: [= Torah]) **repeatedly taking the field to wage war against my mind** (or: warring in opposition to, and in the place of, the law of, and which is, my mind), **and repeatedly taking me prisoner and leading me into captivity within the principle** (or: in union with the Law) **of the Sin** (the failure; the error; the miss of the Target; the deviation from [Torah-keeping]) **– the one continuously existing** (or: now being) **within my members."**

The "**authority**" given to the little animal is from the spirit of the domination system which is adversarial to us. This is only relative authority, but even Nebuchadnezzar (Dan. 4:26) confesses that "the heavens [figure for God] do rule." And as we have seen in the story of Job, although satan (the adversary; opponent) was an instrument of the actual destruction, Job only recognized God as the One who gives and takes (Job 1:21). Further, satan (the adversarial spirit) received its commission, authority and **restrictions** from God in that situation (Job 1:12; 2:6). Consider Rom. 8:20,
> "**For you see, the creation** (or: that which was formed, framed and founded) **was placed, arranged and aligned under subjection in the empty purposelessness** (or: subordinated to vanity and by futility; made supportive to fruitless nonsense: in worthlessness, for nothingness), **not voluntarily or willingly** (from out of [its] being), **but rather because of** (through; on account of; for the sake of) **the one** (or: the One) **placing [it] under and arranging [it] in subjection** (or: in supportive alignment) **– based upon an expectation** (or: expectant hope) "

So ultimately, it is God Who gives both the dragon and the beast their authority, and it is done with His purpose in view. Jesus spoke to the "little animal" that was represented by Pilate, and told him,
> "**You were** [other MSS: continue] **holding no authority at all** (or: in even one thing) **down on** (or: against; with regard to; in the sphere of) **Me, except that it is existing having been given to you from above**" (Jn. 19:11).

8. And all those continually dwelling upon the earth (or: Land) **will proceed worshiping it – concerning which folks, their name has not been written within the scroll of** (or: which is) **"The Life of** (or: pertaining to) **the little Lamb"** – **the One having been slaughtered from a casting-down of**

[the; an] ordered arrangement (or: on account of [the] establishing of [the] world of culture, religion, government and economics; or: from [the] world's founding; or: from a disrupting, down-casting of [the] aggregate of humanity).

Simmons reads the first clause as being "inhabitants of Palestine." He continues,
> "The worship rendered is not emperor-worship *per se*, but Roman allegiance, and praise and adulation for the carnage wrought against the church. It is the voice of the mob and high priests crying, 'If you let this man go, you are not Caesar's friend; whosoever makes himself a king speaks against Caesar.... We have no king but Caesar.' (Jn. 19:12, 15)" (ibid p 260).

This is a preterist view, and presents a historical setting for this verse.

The idea of "**name... written within the scroll**," may be an allusion to Dan. 12:1b, "Now in that era your people shall escape – all [those] found written in the scroll" (CVOT). In regard to those who do not have their name in this particular scroll, we find David praying that his adversaries be cursed, using this metaphor:
> "Let them be wiped [out] from [the/a?] scroll of life, and let them not be written with [the] righteous" (Ps. 69:28; CVOT; bracket additions, mine).

This might simply be a poetic way of David asking God to destroy his enemies. In other words, it was probably speaking to David's current situation and his adversaries' present lives. The next verse (29) reveals David asking for present help.

In a pronouncement of "woe" to certain lying prophets, Ezekiel is told to tell them that God is against them, and He says,
> "And I will proceed stretching out My hand upon the prophets that see false [visions] and that divine lies: they shall not continue being engaged in the instruction and training of My people, nor shall they continue enrolled in the register of the house of Israel, and they will not proceed to enter into the Land of Israel – and through that they will come to know that I, Myself, [am] the Lord" (Ezk. 13:9; LXX).

This was not a promised eschatological judgment, but something that He would do then and there – similar to the warnings that the risen Christ proclaimed in chapters 2 and 3, above.

Those who dwell, spend their time, lives, thoughts, desires and affections upon the "earth realm" – the material – will be the ones who "worship" the beast, in any time or culture. Paul gave admonition in Col. 3 that urged living life in the kingdom, or as put here, "**tabernacling** (or: camping in tents; living in the Tabernacle) **within the atmosphere** (or: heaven)," (vs. 6, above). In that letter, Paul said,
> 2. **Be constantly minding** (thinking about; setting your disposition and sentiments toward; paying regard to) **the upward things** (or: the things above), **not the things upon the earth,**
> 3. **for you folks died, and your life has been hidden so that it is now concealed together with the Christ, within the midst of God** (or: in union with God).

Paul gave his own life as an example of living in "**eschatological deliverance into fair and equitable dealing which brings justice and right relationship in the Way pointed out, peace and joy within set-apart Breath-effect**" (i.e., in God's kingdom/reign, Rom. 14:17), when he said in Phil. 3:14,
> "**I am continuously pressing forward, pursuing down toward** [the; or: an] **object in view** (a mark on which the eye is fixed): **into the awarded contest prize of God's** (or: the award which is God's) **invitation to an above place** (or: the prize from, and which is, the upward calling from, and which is, the God) **within the midst of and in union with Christ Jesus**."

What he described in both passages, cited here, is the exact opposite of "**continually dwelling upon the earth**." In Phil. 3:20, Paul made it plain:

> "**You see, our citizenship** (result of living in a free city; or: commonwealth-effects; political realm) **continues inherently existing** (or: continues humbly ruling; continuously subsists; repeatedly has its under-beginning) **resident within the midst of [the] atmospheres** (or: heavens), **from out of where** (or: which place) **we also continuously receive and take away in our hands from out of a Deliverer** (a Savior; One restoring us to the health and wholeness): **[the] Lord** (or: a Master), **Jesus Christ**."

We find this present situation further described in Heb. 12:22-24. But those of whom John writes here have not yet existentially entered into this citizenship. This is symbolically described here as, "**their name has not been written within the scroll of** (or: which is) **'The Life of** (or: pertaining to) **the little Lamb'**." These folks are still living as the first Adam, so they will proceed to worship the current manifestation of power and authority (e.g., in the 1st century: Judaism or the Roman Empire or the Zealots). This description is an echo of 3:5, above, but there it did not yet speak of it as being a book of "The little Lamb's life." Still, that book spoke of a "**scroll of The Life**." What Life? The Life of the little Lamb who laid down His own life for His friends (humanity – Jn. 15:13); it was a cruciform Life. So the scroll spoken of here is the ledger of those who have been existentially raised up to sit with Christ in the realm of the atmospheres, or the heavens: Eph. 2:6. It records them (i.e., their names are written in it) as present residents of the "Jerusalem upon the heavens" (Heb. 12:22). We find that these are current members of Christ's body, His bride, and these descend from the heavenly atmospheres to minister Life and deliverance/healing to the rest of mankind (21:9-10, 24; 22:2, below). This book/scroll, is a symbol of those who are joined to the Vine (Jn. 15:1ff) and have the Life of its sap flowing through them and producing His fruit (Gal. 5:22-25). It is the record (in God's heart and mind) of His apprentices, who have followed His qualifying remarks in Mat. 16:24-26. And, as Paul says in vs. 25 of that passage in Gal. 5,

> "**Since** (or: If) **we continue living in and by spirit** (or: for [the] Spirit; to Breath-effect; or: with attitude), **we also can habitually advance orderly in line in regard to, or amidst, elementary principles** (or: [observing] rudimentary elements), **in and by spirit** (or: for [the] Spirit; by Breath-effect; with attitude; or: = walk in rank following [the footsteps] behind the Spirit)." [cf Rom. 4:12]

So we have described those who are not yet participants in the little Lamb's Life, by describing the opposite sphere of existence. Not having this life within them, they have no choice but to worship the only things that they were given eyes to see – which is that which is figured by the little animal, here. They are yet as Paul described in Eph. 2:1, "**continuously existing being dead ones by** (or: to; with; in) **the results and effects of your stumblings aside** (offenses; wrong steps) **and failures to hit the mark** (or: mistakes; errors; times of falling short; sins; deviations)." They have yet to be "born again" into the Life of Christ.

Now the **little Lamb** is phrased here as, "**the One having been slaughtered from a casting-down of [the; an] ordered arrangement**." Just to what this refers is debatable. Did this refer to the destruction of the "life in the Garden of Eden"? Was this Adam (who was a TYPE of Him Who is about to be – Rom. 5:14, and who was NOT DECEIVED – 1 Tim. 2:14) – knowingly giving himself to be slaughtered by receiving the fruit from His bride who had by eating just entered into the state of dying? Or was the casting down His inevitable death sentence? Was this rather referring to the actual death of Jesus? This is not necessarily a time statement, but rather a cause statement. It was the very casting down of the ordered arrangement of the old covenant (the Law, the priesthood, the animal sacrifice cultus, the Temple, the nation of Judea) in and by the rejection of their Messiah that brought on the slaughtering of the One who came to redeem them.

Let us consider the first parenthetical expansion, "on account of [the] establishing of [the] world of culture, religion, government and economics." This interprets the participle, "establishing," like the casting down of a foundation of a building. Rendering the preposition, "on account of," which could also be rendered, "from the occasion of," or, "from the fact of," presents the idea that in "establishing a new world of a new society, this little Lamb was slaughtered.

Another view of this enigmatic phrase is, "from a (or: [the]) world's founding." This could refer to Gen. 1, or to the founding of the nation of Israel, at Mt. Sinai. Reading it as an allusion to the creation story in Genesis, this statement could be considered prophetic: the slaughtering of the little Lamb was purposed from the very founding of the universe. Reading it as a reference to Sinai and the founding of Israel as a nation, it could be that with the inauguration of the sacrificial cultus which began with Israel's Exodus, God's Lamb was destined to be Israel's atonement.

Reading *kosmos* as, "[the] aggregate of humanity," instead of either "an ordered system," or, "a world," we are taken back to the Garden of Eden story, and humanity's "disrupting, down-casting" into an estranged, dying state of existence – separated from the Tree of Life (= separated from the Vine), and the nourishment from the trees in the Garden.

D'Aragon (ibid) points to Jn. 17:5 where Jesus makes a statement that has an enigmatic, apocalyptic ring:
"**So now You Yourself, O Father, glorify** (bring a good reputation and a manifestation which calls forth praise to) **Me alongside Yourself** (or: with the presence of Yourself) **in, by and with the glory** (good reputation; manifestation which calls forth praise) **which I was having** (or: used to hold) **and continued holding at Your side and in Your presence, before the universe** (or: world and system of culture, society, economy, religion and government) **is continuing to have being** (or: which I was constantly possessing before the aggregate of humanity continued to exist with You)."

We have a picture of the little Lamb slain in 1 Pet. 1:18-20,
> "**having seen, and thus knowing, that you folks were not unbound and released by a ransom of corruptible things** (things that are perishable and subject to spoiling)… **but rather by Christ's precious blood** (or: in valuable blood, which is [the] Anointed One; with honorable blood of anointing; by costly blood from [the Messiah]) **– as of a flawless** (unblemished) **and spotless Lamb: being One having been foreknown** (previously known by intimate experience), **indeed, before [the] casting down**
>> (as of material for a foundation: founding; as of seed in a field: sowing; as of seed of a man: conception [cf Heb. 11:11]; as in throwing something down: overthrowing; as in battle = slaying; in politics: abandoning [a measure]; of debts: paying down by installments;) **of [the; or: an] ordered System** (world; universe; a particular order or arrangement of things; or: = the aggregate of humanity), **yet One being set in clear light and manifested upon [the] last part** (or: final; [p72 and others read plural: last things, circumstances or aspects]) **of the times** (or: of the [or: these] successive chronological time periods) **because of you folks**."

Here we should mention that the RSV and the NRSV (and the RV mg) erroneously connect the phrase "from the foundation of the world" (as they render it) with, "everyone whose name has not been written." This decision may be based upon 17:8, below, but that verse is missing the phrase, "of the Lamb that was slaughtered." Fortunately the NRSV has a footnote that reads, "Or: *written in the book of life of the Lamb that was slaughtered from the foundation of the world.*" As Beasley-Murray says, "Nevertheless, the word order is decidedly against this [i.e., the RSV's] interpretation…" (ibid p 1296; brackets added). In the Greek text, the phrase, "**from a casting-down of [the; an] ordered arrangement**," follow directly after the perfect participle, "**having been slaughtered**." (note: CLNT, Young, Rotherham, Nyland all read with the order of the Greek text).

Before moving on, consider the appositional reading, "the scroll **which is** the Life of the little Lamb." A name represents a person, and in this case, a person's life. This scroll is a symbol: it points to and represents something. It represents the Life of the Lamb: how He lives; what He does; the existence He has. This is just another way of saying, "These folks are dwelling (abiding; remaining) in Me, the Vine; those others are not yet joined to Me, and thus are not producing My fruit. They can only worship their own domination system – that is all that they see, at this point."

9. **"If anyone continues having an ear, let him hear.**

This is what Jesus said to the multitudes, when He was speaking concerning John the immerser,
> "**Let the person now having ears to continue hearing, continue listening and hearing** (or: = pay attention)!" (Mat. 11:15).

He said the same thing in Lu. 8:8, after presenting the parable of the sower. It was a way of calling one's audience to pay attention, and to ponder what has just been presented. This statement, here, is also an echo of chapters 2-3, above, and reminds us that He is still speaking to the called-out communities. The listener/reader should be constantly hearing what the Spirit continues to say to folks. But in the context of the first listeners who were hearing this Unveiling read to them, John would have been alerting them to pay attention to what he had been describing: it applied to them and their lives, in Asia Minor, in the 1st century.

It is also possible to read vs. 9 as a way of introducing the enigmatic words of the following verse.

10. **"If anyone** (or: a certain one) **[is; is destined] into captivity, into captivity he is repeatedly** (continuously; presently) **departing** [Griesbach's text adds συναγει, so would read: If anyone is continuously gathering (bringing together) a captive host, into captivity he is proceeding to undergo]. **If anyone** (or: a certain one) **is continually killing with a sword, it is necessary for him to be killed with a sword. The patient and persistent endurance** (or: the steadfast, humble and supportive remaining-under) **and the reliability and faith of the set-apart ones** (or: trust and loyal confidence of the holy folks) **continually exists here."**

We have here what seems to be parenthetical to the narrative, and we see that it is made up of two quotations – Jer. 15:2, where Jeremiah tells the folks that such as are for death will go forth unto death; such as are for the sword will go forth unto the sword; such as are for famine will go forth to famine; and such as are for captivity will go forth unto captivity. What God decrees will happen, and in Israel's history, it did. Then Matt. 26:52 is quoted. In the Garden of Gethsemane Jesus tells Peter to, "**Turn away** (= Return) **your knife** (or: sword) **into its place. You see, all those taking [up] a knife** (or: sword) **will proceed in destroying themselves in union with a knife** (or: sword)." Jer. 43:10-11 may also be the focus of an allusion in vs. 10, here. There, when the Judean leadership had decided to seek refuge in Egypt from the threat of Babylon (contrary to God's warning against this, through Jeremiah), God told Jeremiah to tell them,
> "I will send Nebuchadrezzar, the king of Babylon, My servant…. And when he comes, he will smite the land of Egypt [and deliver] such [as are] for death to death; and such [as are] for the sword to the sword."

Since the book of Daniel has been a backdrop for the stage settings here in the Unveiling, my friend Dan Kaplan pointed out that it is a book that is set in the "**captivity**" of the Jews. Daniel was one of those who was destined to go into Babylonian captivity. In Dan. 6 we find him going into further captivity: the lion's den. But Daniel had "**patient and persistent endurance** (or: the steadfast, humble and supportive remaining-under) **and the reliability and faith of the set-apart ones** (or: trust and loyal confidence of the holy folks)," and he survived that ordeal unscathed. However, his accusers were then put into that same lion's den and did not survive (Dan.6:24). It was God that sent captive Judea as captives into Babylon. First-century Judea found themselves once again captive under Rome. But amidst all that, the Deliverer came, and in Eph. 4 we read this Good News:

8. **For this reason He** (or: it) **is constantly saying,**

"**Going up** (or: Stepping up; Ascending) **into a height** (unto [the] summit) **He led** (or: leads) **captive a captive multitude** (or: He led 'captivity' captive). **He gave** (or: gives) **gifts to mankind** (or: for, in and among the humans; to humanity)." [Ps. 68:18]

9. **Now** (or: Yet) **this "He went up** (ascended)**," what is it if not** (or: except) **that He also** [other MSS add: first] **descended** (stepped down) **into the lower parts** (or: the under regions) **of the earth** (or: which is the land; or: from the Land; or: of the ground)**?**

10. **The One stepping down** (descending) **is Himself also the One stepping up** (ascending) **far above** (back up over) **all of the heavens** (or: atmospheres; skies), **to the end that He would at once fill the Whole** (permeate and saturate everything; or: make all things full; bring all things to full measure and completion).

The statement about "**continually killing with a sword**" sounds like being at war, or perhaps it refers to The Jewish rebellion. Simmons cites the Jewish historian,

"Josephus reports that ninety-seven thousand Jews were taken captive and either sold or made to work in the Egyptian mines in consequence of the war with Rome" (ibid p 262, citing Josephus, *Wars of the Jews*, 6.9.2.3).

The contexts of Jer. 15 and 43 were ones of judgment. Jude 4 also speaks of a judgment,

"**For you see, some people came in unobserved, from the side – those having been previously written of old into this judgment** (or: people having from long ago been written into the effects and result of this decision)**: [to exist being] impious ones, people continuously changing the grace and favor of God into licentiousness, as well as repeatedly contradicting, saying, "No," to or about, disclaiming, denying and disowning our only Sovereign and Lord** (or: Supreme Ruler and Owner), **Jesus Christ** [= Messiah].

We want to comment on the clause in this quote: "**those having been previously written of old into this judgment** (or: people having from long ago been written into the effects and result of this decision)." We suggest that this is speaking of "predestination" only in the sense that the decision was made by God in the Garden of Eden. This clause describes the predicament of humanity, the condition of those existing outside the life of Christ. It once applied to everyone. The covenant communities have been "called-out" of that death into union with the Messiah.

Verse 10, here, may also be a prophetic warning to those incarnating a dragon spirit, as well as to those who align themselves with its manifestations (the little wild animals). Isa. 33:1 comes to mind:

"Woe, devastator… When you come to end devastation, you shall be devastated! When you have culminated dealing treacherously, they shall deal treacherously with you" (CVOT).

We also read in Gen. 9:6, "Whoever sheds the blood of a human, by a human his blood shall be shed…"

Situations and environments of captivity and of the use of the sword were seen in Israel's history; patient endurance and faith were needed as seen in Heb. 11:35b-38. Let us review those situations again:

"**Yet others were beaten to death with rods** (or: drummed upon), **not receiving** (or: accepting; taking) **toward** (or: with a view to) **themselves** (= refusing) **the releasing-away** (liberation; setting free from bondage or prison) **so that they may hit the target of** (or: attain) **a superior** (stronger and better) **resurrection.** [1 Ki. 17:17-24; 2 Ki. 4:18-37; Acts 22:24-25; *cf* Phil. 3:8-15]

> **But different ones took a trial** (or: received a test) **of mockings** (scoffings), **and of scourgings, and further, of bonds and imprisonment** (= put in chains and thrown in jail). **They were stoned, they were cut in two with a saw, they were put to the proof** (tried; tested), **they passed away in a slaughter** (or: by murder) **with sword, they went around** (wandered) **in sheepskins, in goat skins, continuously being behind** (being in want; being in the rear), **being constantly pressed** (squeezed; afflicted), **habitually being held in the bad** (being maltreated; having it bad) – [*cf* 2 Ki. 2:13 (LXX): Elijah's mantle a sheepskin – Denton] **of whom the System** (the ordered arrangement; the world or culture, secular society, religions and government) **was not worthy** (was not of equal value) **– being continually deceived** (led astray; caused to wander) **in deserts and mountains and caves and the holes of the earth** (or: ground)."

The first half of vs. 10 may refer to trouble ahead for either the Jews, or for the called-out communities. In the generation following the resurrection of Christ, the called-out communities certainly experienced hard times. During the period of the AD 66-70 rebellion, it was the Jews who suffered. But what can we take from this for our day and situation?

Prinzing appropriately quotes 2 Cor. 10:4-5 here,
> 4. **for you see, the tools and weapons of our military service and warfare [are] not fleshly** (= do not pertain to our human condition; ["are not the weapons of the Domination System" – Walter Wink]), **but rather, [are] powerful ones and capable ones in God** (or: by God), **[focused] toward [the] pulling down** (demolition) **of effects of fortifications** (or: strongholds; strongly entrenched positions [of the "Domination System" – Walter Wink, *Engaging the Powers*]),
> 5. **progressively tearing down and demolishing conceptions** (concepts; the effects of thoughts, calculations, imaginations, reasonings and reflections) **and every height** (or: high position; high-effect) **and lofty [attitude, purpose or obstacle] that is habitually lifting itself up against** (or: elevating itself up on so as to put down) **the intimate and experiential knowledge of God, and then taking captive every thought – one after another – and leading them prisoner into the hearing obedience of the Christ** (or: the humble attentive listening, which comes from the Anointed One; or: the submissive paying attention, which is the Anointing).

Verse 5 of this quote identifies the realm of our "wrestling" (*cf* Eph. 6:12): "conceptions, effects of thoughts, calculations, imaginations, reasonings, reflections," in other words, "every thought." 12:11, above, put our victory this way: "**because of and through the blood of the little Lamb, and because of the word of [OUR] witness, as well as through the message from [OUR] testimony** (that reason laid-out from the evidence, which is [US]) **– and [WE] love not** (or: did not participate in union with) **[OUR] soul** (soul-life; inner selfhood) **even to** (or: until; as far as) **death.**"

We find the last statement of this verse repeated (in another situation) in 14:12a, below. In both contexts, the "**set-apart ones** (or: trust and loyal confidence of the holy folks)" are present. In the present context of "captivity" and "killing," D'Aragon comments: "Such a surrender to God's will is the secret of the patience and serenity of the saints" (ibid).

11. **Next I saw another little wild animal** (little creature or beast), **progressively stepping up out of the midst of the Land** (or: earth; territory; region; soil), **and it had two horns like a little lamb, yet it was, and continued, speaking as [the; a] dragon,**

S. MacLean Gilmour states:
> "According to ancient tradition there were 2 monsters, Leviathan dwelling in the sea and Behemoth on the dry land" (ibid p 961).

In vs. 11 the scene changes and "**another little wild animal**" takes the stage. This one originates from "**the Land**" (or: the earth; the soil). Here the figure changes but portrays the same thing. The land, earth, soil speaks once again of humanity, for Adam was made of the soil of the earth. This is the same land or earth into which we are to pray for His kingdom/reign to come.

However, there is another aspect of the term "**the Land**," and that is that it may be used geographically, i.e., to identify a territory or region, and it sometimes bears a political connotation and represents both a given political territory and the people who live there. An example of this use of "the land" as a metaphor for "people" is found in Jer. 22. In vs. 2-3 the figure for the people is "the city" – Jerusalem; the figure for God's people is changed in vs. 18 where Yahweh says, "Son of man, the house of Israel is to me become dross...;" then in vs. 24 He says, "Son of man, say unto her, 'Thou [art] **the land** that is not cleansed...'"

Another example is Hos. 1:2, "Go, take to you a wife of prostitutions and children of prostitutions, for '**the land**' is verily committing prostitution rather than following Yahweh" (CVOT). In Hos. 4:3 we have, "Therefore '**the land**' shall mourn..." In Joel 2:18, "Then Yahweh will be jealous for His 'land' and He will spare His 'people.'" See also Joel 3:2 and Zech. 3:9. Ezk. 14:13 makes the point well, "Son of man, when '**the land**' sins against Me by trespassing grievously..."

Thus, I see two possible applications for the figure of "the land" in vs. 11: 1) humanity, the Adamic nature; and 2) the people that are the focus of the context, i.e., in a particular territory or region. Since the figure of the sea is more general, I lean toward this second application, especially considering the religious nature of the little animal which steps up out of it, and how it "repeatedly makes the land ... **worship** the first little animal" (vs. 12, below) which ascends from the sea.

This second animal has characteristics "**like a little lamb**," but it speaks "**as a dragon**." Does this call to mind the figure of a wolf in sheep's clothing (Matt. 7:15)? Paul spoke to this situation in Acts 20:29-30,

> "**Now I myself have seen and am aware that, after** (or: with) **my spreading forth as dust and ashes** (= going away, so as to be out of reach), **heavy** (= burdensome and oppressive) **wolves** [i.e., little animals] **will enter into the midst of you folks – folks by habit not sparing** (or: treating with tenderness or forbearance) **the flock, and men from among you yourselves** (= from your own community) [i.e., from your Land, or territory] **will of themselves proceed standing up, repeatedly speaking things having been thoroughly turned and twisted** (things that are distorted and not straight), [i.e., speaking 'like a dragon'] **to progressively drag away the disciples behind (thus: after) themselves**." (brackets added)

Note that this animal has "**two horns like a little lamb**." Its power is similar to, or a counterpart of, the power displayed by the lamb nature, but its speech (message) betrays it as anti-Christ. It describes a ministry that looks like true Christianity, but its message will be,

> "**teachings about and pertaining to, or which are, demons** [note: a Hellenistic concept and term: = animistic influences], **or, instructions and training which come from animistic influences** [= pagan religions]" (1 Tim. 4:1).

The two horns figure a counterpart of the "two witnesses," (chapter 11, above) and vs. 13, below, shows how it will perform "**signs and wonders of falsehood** (or: which are a lie)," (2 Thes. 2:9). Recall that this "**the secret** (hidden purpose; mystery) **of the lawlessness [was] already continuously working**" in Paul's day (2 Thes. 2:7). Metzger comments, "With a grim parody John describes the beast as having 'two horns like a lamb' – that is, it has taken on the guise of God's chosen one, yet 'it spoke like a dragon' (13:11)." Simmons points out that, "A horn is a symbol of strength, authority, and power (Ps. 89:24). It is also used to portray rulers or kings (Dan. 8:20, 21; Zech. 1:18, 21)." He further suggests that since its horns are like "a little lamb," that this symbolizes its religious character, specifically the temple cultus of sacrifices, suggesting that these

> "**two horns**" may refer to "the high priest and Sanhedrin… the ruling ecclesiastical powers in Jewry; armed with a system of courts through the synagogue, the high priest and Sanhedrin were able to extend the arm of their power beyond the territory of Palestine throughout the empire…" (ibid p 263-4).

We see in the next verse that this second little animal, "**is continually exercising** (doing, performing, executing) **all the authority of the first little animal**," which would fit the Jerusalem leadership operating in the power of Rome. Terry decided that, "this second beast is but a satellite of the great power denoted by the first beast" (ibid p 397). Rather than seeing this second animal as religious, Terry suggests that it refers to, "the provincial governments of Judea and Palestine" by governors, such as Pilate, who had, "the authority of Rome, as exercised by him in the crucifixion of Jesus" (ibid p 398). Both interpretations place the setting of our drama in 1st century Palestine.

These two "little wild animals (beasts)" may be an allusion to Ezk. 34:1-6 where Yahweh brings charges against the "shepherds of Israel" who "feed themselves" and "do not feed the sheep." In vs. 5 He explains,

> "And so My sheep were scattered, because there were no shepherds; then they became food to, and for, all the LITTLE WILD ANIMALS (beasts) of the field" (LXX, JM).

Verse 6 continues their plight, that, "there continued not existing (or: there kept on not being) the one habitually searching [them] out," which is in stark contrast to Lu. 15:4-6 and Jn. 10:1-16. In Mat. 9:36, Jesus viewed the multitudes of His day as being like those of Ezk. 34:5-6. In Mat. 10:6 He sends the twelve to "the lost sheep of the house of Israel." Mat. 23 lays the blame for this situation, and the soon-coming "Woes," at the feet of the scribes and the Pharisees.

Chilton (ibid p 336) viewed this "Land Beast" as "arising from within Israel itself." He (as do D'Aragon and Gilmour) further points to 16:13, below, to associate this little animal with the "False Prophet" (e.g., it speaks "as a dragon") and also cites 19:20, below, where we have just two figures operating together, "**the little wild animal** (beast) **was pressed and caught** (or: is arrested), **and with him the false prophet** (the lying prophet) – **the one that did** (or: who does) **the signs in his presence** (or: before him)." Then he quotes Mat. 24:5, 11,

> "**You see, many people will be coming, upon [association with; the basis of, or, the supposed authority of; on the reference to] My name, one after another saying, 'I, myself, am the anointed one** (or: the Christ),' **and they will be leading astray and deceiving many people…. Also, many false prophets will proceed in being raised up and they will be progressively leading many folks astray, deceiving them and causing them to wander.**"

As we opened the comments on this chapter, above, we would here point to all of these manifestations as being anti-Christ. Chilton goes on to quote Cornelis Vanderwaal (*Search the Scriptures*, Vol. 10, 1979 p 89): "In Scripture, false prophecy appears only within the covenant context," and then points us to Deut. 13:1-5 (ibid). Next he points us to Gen. 3:1-6 where we encounter a "beast of the field" that was a false prophet (*Cf* 12:9, above). Paul addressed contemporary situations along this line as we read in 2 Cor. 11:

> 3. **Yet I continue fearing lest somehow, as the serpent thoroughly deceived** (or: seduces; fully deludes) **Eve within its capability for every work** (its cunning ability in all crafts and actions; its readiness to do anything), **the results of directing your minds should be decayed** (could be ruined; would be spoiled or corrupted) **away from the singleness [of purpose] and simplicity [of being] – even the purity – which [focuses us] into the Christ** (or: [leads] into the Anointing).

4. For if, indeed, the person periodically coming is habitually preaching (proclaiming) **another Jesus – whom we do not preach – or, [if] you folks are continuously receiving a different breath-effect** (or: are repeatedly laying hold of a spirit or attitude that is different in kind and nature) **which you did not receive, or a different "good-news"** (a message of ease and wellness which is different in kind and character) **which you did not welcome and accept, are you repeatedly holding back from [him] in an ideal way?** (or: you folks are beautifully putting up with and tolerant of [it]! [other MSS: were you finely holding back from {it}?])....

13. **For such folks [are] false emissaries – fraudulent and deceitful workers – constantly changing their outward fashion and transforming themselves into emissaries of Christ.**

14. **And no wonder** ([it is] no marvel or cause for astonishment), **for the adversary** (opponent; *satan*) **itself is repeatedly changing its form and outward fashion** (transforming itself) **into a messenger of light** (or, as a passive: is from time to time being transformed and changed in its outward expression into an agent from [the] Light).

15. **Therefore, [it is] no great thing if its attending servants and dispensers also repeatedly change their form and outward fashion** (or: are habitually transformed) **as attending servants of fairness and equity** (dispensers of the way pointed out; = ministers of the covenant) **– whose finish** (or: end in view; finished product; attained goal; consummation) **will proceed in being in accord with, along the line of, to the level of and corresponding to their works and actions** (or: = their outcome will constantly be what they reap from their deeds).

D'Aragon (as well as Gilmour), however, sees this second little animal as, "a personification of the Antichrist of the religious sphere, embodied in pagan priesthood, which endeavored to draw all men to the cult of the emperor" (ibid p 484). Beale (ibid p 707) calls this second little animal, "the state's ally."

Beale suggest that the reason for the "**two horns**," instead of 7, like the little Lamb of chapter 5, is that it, "is to mimic the two witnesses, two lampstands, and two olive trees of 11:3-4" (ibid). He further conclude that, "this imagery and background suggest deception within the covenant community itself" (ibid p 708). *Cf* 2:14, 15, 20, above. This may also be an allusion to the imagery of Dan. 8:3-7.

This little animal is the system of religion (basing this determination on its association with being the "false prophet," and its focus on "worship" in vs. 12) which is the counterpart of the true body of Christ. It exercises all the authority of the first little animal (just as the body of Christ exercises all the authority of Jesus, the Head of the body), and leads "the Land" (God's people) in a worship which is in actuality a worship of the first little animal (an incarnation of the spirit of a dragon), and not a worship of God. This is also a worship of the little animal within man (soul worship; worship of man's will; worship of feelings and emotions; worship of the intellect and the ego), but yet it is a worship of the dragon who gave the first little animal its power, ability and authority (vs. 2). Keep in mind from chapter 17, below, that the false, prostitute church rides upon this anti-Christ power-and-authority structure. Beware of the wolf that appears as a sheep (or, as a representative of the little Lamb). But, as with the false-accusers in Dan. 6, God has a plan for false prophets. We find both those with the "beast nature" and those who "prophesy falsely" put into God's purifying, cleansing, transforming Fire (which is Himself) in 19:20, below.

Concisely stated, Maarschalk gives this definition of this Land beast:
> "**A beast from the land:** the false prophets (collectively) who worked with, and on behalf of, the Zealots/Sicarii; this beast was later called "*the false prophet*"; referenced in Revelation 13:11-17, 16:13, 19:20, and 20:10" ("Who Was the Beast," ibid p 11).

12. **and it is continually exercising** (doing, performing, executing) **all the authority of the first little animal** (or: little wild beast) **within its presence** (before it; in its sight), **and it repeatedly makes the**

Land (or: forms the earth) **and those dwelling in her, to the end that they would** (or: may) **worship the first little animal** (little creature or wild beast) **whose death-blow was cured** (or: treated).

When a person, or a social entity, has the **authority** of a parent, or a sponsoring social entity, he, she or it will **continually exercise** it. If Terry's suggestion, above, is correct, this second little animal is operating as a satellite of the parent organization (such as Rome). We might also view this new one as a "second generation" animal that will operate the same programs of the original one. This is the dark contrast to the Light operating in Christ's apprentices, His body, as seen in the book of Acts. They did what they did "in the presence" of Christ. The operation of this second little animal is within the realm (perhaps Empire) of the first animal that arose from the sea of humanity. Simmons interprets this:
> "To exercise all the power of the first Beast before him signifies the power given the Jews to conduct an inquisition with the blessing and approval of Rome. As demonstrated in the book of Acts, the Jews were always eager to accuse Christians to the civil authorities (Acts 13:50; 14:2, 5, 19; 17:5; 24:1)" (ibid p 264).

He further interprets **worship** as, "probably best understood in terms of admiration and allegiance.... they worshipped it because Rome represented their best and only hope against the church" (ibid). Wallace held the view that this second beast was an, "instrument of the first beast, enforced his will, exercising an authority not his own, but was derived solely from the superior beast number one, the Roman emperor." He interprets the **Land** (earth) as "the provincial governments," and **those dwelling in her** as "the people who were under their political rule" (ibid p 297). Chilton (ibid p 337) read this situation as, "The Jewish leaders... joined forces with the Beast of Rome." He then cites R.C.H. Lenski,
> "As the first beast is the agent of the dragon, so the second beast is the agent of the first beast. 'All the authority' makes the second beast the complete agent of the first" (*The Interpretation of St. John's Revelation*, Augsburg Pub. House, 1943, 1963, p 404).

Chilton goes on to see a contrast between this beast operating in the **presence** of the first beast, with "the function of the true prophet, who stood 'before [*the face of*] the Lord,' in God's presence... (1 Sam. 1:22; 2:18; 1 Ki. 17:1; *cf* Nu. 6:24-26; Hos. 6:2; Jonah 1:3, 10), just as the seven Trumpet-angels are said to 'stand before God' (8:2)" (ibid; brackets original). As to prophets being called "angels" (literally, "agent" or "messenger"), Chilton points us to the following passages:
> "The LORD, the God of their ancestors, sent persistently to them by His messengers (Heb. *malak*: agent; messenger; traditionally rendered "angel," elsewhere).... but they kept mocking the messengers (*malak*; LXX: *angelos*) of God, despising His words, and scoffing at His prophets, until the wrath of the LORD against His people became so great that there was no remedy" (2 Chron. 36:15-16, NRSV)

> "Then Haggai, the messenger (*malak*) of the LORD, spoke to the people..." (Hag. 1:13, NRSV).

> "See, I am sending My messenger (*malak*) to prepare the way before me..." (Mal. 3:1, NRSV).

Stern comments: "Non-futurists see this beast as symbolizing organized, institutional religion enforcing **worship** of **the first beast**" (ibid p 828). Beasley-Murray suggests that this, "seems to indicate that this figure represents the priesthood of the cult of the emperor. It is later called 'the false prophet'" (ibid p 1296), and Gilmour concurs (ibid p 961).

So on offer, here, is a variety of interpretations. What we should take away is the principle of multi-tiered domination systems that both operated in the past, and on through history to our present day. We see them in action composing all "seven mountains" of human organization. Some mountains require religious obeisance, while others require that dues or taxes be paid. Behind them all is the dragon-spirit of the first Adam, the carnal human that feeds on the "dust" of which humanity was formed (Gen. 3:14; 19).

13. **And it is continually making** (doing; constructing; performing; producing) **great signs** (wonders; miracles; marks; inscriptions), **to the end that it may** (or: that it would) **even repeatedly make** (a) **fire to continuously** (or: repeatedly) **descend from out of the atmosphere** (or: sky; or: heaven) **into the Land** (or: earth) **within the presence of** (in sight of) **the people** (or: humans).

The calling down of fire "**from out of the atmosphere** (sky; heaven)" is an echo of 1 Kings 18:24-39; the one that answered by fire was the true God. It is also an allusion to 2 Ki. 1:10, 12, where Elijah called for fire to come from the sky and consume the soldiers that came for him. Prior to Elijah's day, we read in Lev. 10:1-2 that Nadab and Abihu "offered strange fire before Yahweh… and there went out fire from Yahweh, and devoured them." *Cf* Nu. 16:35. There is also Amos 1:3-2:5, where the passage ends with Yahweh warning of sending a fire upon Judah, "and it shall devour the palaces of Jerusalem." *Cf* 20:9b, below.

But here we have something more like what Paul described in 2 Thes. 2 concerning "**the lawless person**," which can be either an individual or a corporate entity. Paul spoke both eschatologically and apocalyptically in vs. 8 of this passage, and then continued:

> 9. **whose presence is continuously existing in correspondence to** (or: in line with; in the sphere of; on the level of) **the adversary's** (opponent's; or: *satan's*) **in-working activity** (or: is constantly in accordance with the operation of the "adversary," or, *satan*), **in all power** (or: within all ability) **as well as signs and wonders of falsehood** (or: which are a lie),
> 10. **and within every deception** (delusion; seduction) **of the injustice** (wrong; thing that is not the way pointed out and which is not right) **within the folks continuously or repeatedly being lost** (or: by the folks progressively destroying themselves) **in return for which** (or: in the place of which) **they do** (or: did) **not take unto themselves and welcomely receive the love of, and from, the truth** (or: Truth's accepting Love; the Love which is Truth and Reality; or: the urge to union which is Reality), **into the [situation for] them at some point to be suddenly delivered** (restored to health and wholeness; rescued; saved; restored).
> 11. **And so, because of this, GOD is continuously sending to** (or: in) **them an in-working** (or: operation) **of wandering** (or: from straying; which has the character of error and deception) **into the [situation for] them to believe, and to trust, the lie,**
> 12. **to the end that all those not being faithful to the Truth** (or: believing and trusting the reality), **but rather approving and delighting in injustice** (inequity; the thing that is not right), **may** (or: can; would) **at some point be sifted, separated and decided about** (or: judged).

Of course vs. 11 of this passage clearly instruct us as to Who is behind all this, with vs. 12b giving the purpose of God's plan.

Beale (ibid p 708) sees in this "an ironic echo" of Moses' **signs** in Ex. 4:17, 30; 10:2; 11:10, noting also Ex. 7:11, that Pharaoh's magicians also performed signs "in like manner" – for a while. Paul referenced this situation as relevant to his own time of the "last days" (of the old covenant – 2 Tim. 3:1) when he said,

> "**Now, in the manner which Jannes and Jambres took a stand in opposition to** (or: resisted and opposed) **Moses, thus, also, these are continually taking a stand in opposition to** (opposing and resisting) **the Truth and reality**… **But they will continue making no further progress** (not be cutting a passage forward) **upon more [folks], for their mindlessness** (madness; lack of understanding) **will be quite evident** (in clear visibility) **to all, even as the [madness] of those [two, i.e., Jannes and Jambres] came to be. Yet you, yourself, follow closely beside me: in the teaching, by the instruction and with the training; in the leading, by the guidance for conduct; in the purpose**…" (2:Tim. 3:8-10a).

Philip encountered such a person in Samaria, Simon the sorcerer/magician (Acts 8:9ff), as did Paul, in Acts 13:8 (Elymas, the sorcerer). As a result of Paul's preaching in Ephesus,

> "**a considerable number of the folks practicing the meddling arts** (acts or works concerning [other folks]; things that work around [nature or people]; or: = sorcery or magic arts), **after bringing together the scrolls, began burning [them] down** (= up) **in the sight of all** (or: before everybody)" (Acts 19:19)

So such things were not all that unusual in the 1st century. But we should keep in mind that this, in our present verse (13), is something seen in a vision composed of symbols. Calling down fire from the "heaven" would symbolize evoking the power of the ruling authorities (in the 1st century, either Jerusalem, i.e., temple or Sanhedrin authority, or Rome: political authority). Over-awing demonstrations of power before the dominated populace would be effective for controlling the people, enforcing whatever form of "worship" (vs. 12) was intended by the little animal and its underlings. We see in vs. 14, below, that all this was intended to "**continually lead astray** (cause to wander; deceive)."

But the spirit evoking this kind of behavior was seen even in Jesus' apprentices: Jacob (James) and John wanted to call down fire from heaven on folks that were not receiving Jesus, in Lu. 9:54, but Jesus responded to them,

> "**He respectfully spoke a stern admonition to them** [later MSS add: and said, 'You do not see or know of what sort of breath-effect (spirit; attitude) you are. For the Son of the Man does not come to destroy {the} lives (or: souls) of humanity, but rather to rescue, heal, save and restore to health and wholeness']" (Lu. 9:55).

Jesus prophesied about this situation, here in the Unveiling, which was to come in that 1st century generation (Mat. 24:34), that during the conjunction/overlap of the old covenant age and the new covenant age,

> "**false christs** (or: false anointings; phony anointed ones; = counterfeit messiahs) **and false prophets will one after another be raised up, and they will continue giving** (presenting; = performing) **great signs and miracles** (amazing things; wonders) **so as to continuously mislead** (deceive; cause to wander; lead astray) – **if able** (if in [their] power; or: since [it is] possible) – **even the picked out and chosen folks**" (Mat. 24:24).

2 Peter 1:1 gives a similar warning:

> "**Yet false prophets also birthed themselves** (or: Now of themselves folks who pretended to have light ahead of time, or who had false knowledge and spoke before folks, came to be) **among the People – as also false teachers will continue existing** (or: being) **among you folks, ones who will proceed to stealthily introduce** (or: will continue bringing in alongside or smuggling in) **destructive choices** (or: destructive sects, schools or ways of thinking; sets of principles or courses of action marked by, and which pertain to, loss or destruction) **even repeatedly contradicting or denying** (disowning; disclaiming) **the Sovereign Owner** (or: Absolute Master) **having purchased them, continuously bringing swift loss, ruin or destruction upon themselves**."

Jesus also warned folks about metaphorical little animals, in Mat. 7:15,

> **Constantly apply yourselves to holding off the false prophets – whatsoever ones that are habitually coming to you folks in clothing belonging to sheep** (= disguised as sheep; pretending to have the covering or appearance of sheep), **yet inside they are ravenous, savage wolves.**"

In light of 11:5, above, and the fire being a symbol of "God's true word," this little beast is a person or an organization that pretends to be a representative or agent of God. Dan. 11:30-37 is a potential source for this echo.

Now Peter wrote metaphorically of a fire that would result in praise, honor and glory as it caused Jesus Christ to be unveiled within them, even though, and while, they were experiencing persecutions:

> "**within which [season] you folks are presently feeling constant joy and happiness and are continuing to rejoice exceedingly – though for a little while, at present, since it continues being binding and necessary, being pained** (distressed) **within various tests** (or: ordeals) **to put you to the proof. [This is] to the end that the examined and tested approval of your faith – [being] of much greater value and worth, and more precious, than of gold that constantly loses itself away despite being progressively tested and examined through FIRE – might be found [progressing] into praise** (approval) **and glory** (or: a good reputation) **and honor** (value) **within an unveiling of Jesus Christ**" (1 Pet. 1:6-7). *Cf* 1Cor. 3:13-17.

In addition, some Jews in Rome affirmed to Paul concerning the Christ movement,

> "**Indeed, you see, concerning this sect** (= denomination; chosen opinion; heresy), **it is personally known to us that it is continuously being spoken against and contradicted everywhere**" (Acts 28:22b).

Here is where we would be well advised to focus on Paul's words in Rom. 8:28,

> "**Now [look], we have seen, and thus know and are aware, that to those habitually or progressively loving and giving themselves to God – to the folks being called and invited according to [the] purpose**
>
>> (or: for, in and with the people progressively experiencing participating acceptance in, unambiguous love for, and the urge toward union with, God – in, with, by and for the people being invited down from an advanced placing, congruent with a design and corresponding to a before-placing and a prior setting forth)
>
> **– He is constantly working all things together into good and is progressively working all humanity together into that which is advantageous, worthy of admiration, noble and of excellent qualities,**
>
>> [with other MSS: Yet we know that God is continuously joining everything together (or: working together with everything) into goodness by those continuously loving God...]"

14. It also continually leads astray (causes to wander; deceives) **those** [other MSS read: Mine] **who are continuously dwelling upon the Land** (or: earth), **because of the signs which it was** (or: is) **given to it to perform** (or: allowed to do, make or construct) **in the presence of** (before; in sight of) **the [first] little animal** (little creature or wild beast). **[It is] constantly saying – to those habitually dwelling upon the Land** (or: territory; earth) **– to make** (or: construct) **an image** (likeness; resemblance; an icon) **to** (or: for) **the little animal** (little wild beast) **which continuously has the blow of** (holds the impact, wound and plague from) **the sword, and yet lives** (or: yet sprang to life).

Notice that this animal "**leads astray**, deceives." Also consider the alternate reading which inserts the word "Mine." The setting is that of sheep, God's people, who are "**dwelling upon the earth/Land**," and not in the heavenlies, who are caused to wander by false shepherds and systems. They correspond to "**the remaining ones** (the rest; those left) **of her seed**" in 12:17, above. Keep in mind that they are led astray "**because of the signs**" which the little animal **was given** to **perform**. In vs. 13 we are told that these "great signs" were such "that it may even repeatedly make fire to continuously (or: repeatedly) descend from out of heaven..."

So here we see that the context would have been 1st century Judea, the **Land** (that of which Mat. 24 referred), but it is also a type for the "called-out covenant groups" of the new order (such as the 7 communities to which this Unveiling was written). This lying wonder will appear to be "the fire of God" descending from heaven. If it is truly the fire of God, then it will consume the "sacrifice, and the wood, and the stones (the altar, i.e. that part of yourself upon which your life is offered), and the dust (the carnal Adam within), and... the water (our very life-source)" (1 Ki. 18:38). If these elements are still remaining after the fire supposedly falls upon us, then I think we should suspect that is was not the fire of God, but, "**great signs and miracles so as to continuously mislead** (deceive; cause to wander; lead astray) **– if able** (if in [their] power; or: since [it is] possible) **– even the picked out and chosen folks**" (Mat. 24:24b). To do this it will have to be something that really looks like God, in the minds of the people. Taken metaphorically, we have probably seen such things in so-called "miracle meetings" (which some of us have personally observed) or at times on Christian television. The false prophets continued in existence throughout history. But where there is a counterfeit, the implication is that the real exists.

Observe that where in vs. 13 the "sign" of fire descending was, "**within the presence of** (in sight of) **the people**," here, we see that these **signs** are also, "**in the presence of** (before; in sight of) **the [first] little animal**." So both the people and the first little animal are on the stage with the second little animal that is presently **performing**. These are the counterparts of the "two witnesses" of chapter 11, above. Dare we conclude that today's counterpart (on the religious "mountain") is the denominational headquarters and the local congregations? Or (on the political "mountain"), in the USA, Washington DC and the state governments? Or, the United Nations and the member countries? The 1st century picture of Rome and Judea is a pattern that reached back in history to Babylon and Egypt, but projects forward through history on to our own time. The two little animals represent two levels of domination, and are together a type of stratified dominion systems. They operate congruently, often simultaneously. Unfortunately, more and more, today, it is literal fire (explosives) that one country (or people group) rains down on another country (or people group).

The next thing that this second animal does is to tell those who dwell in the "earth realm" to construct an image – a resemblance – of the first animal. Our whole society – including the "church" – is obsessed with "image." This calls to mind the scene with Aaron and the children of Israel (who, incidentally, did not want to approach near to God, but wanted a go-between) and the construction of the "golden calf." Aaron made an image of a little animal. Ponder the fact that Israel was "living" down at the bottom of God's mountain, while Moses was up in the mountain receiving instructions from Yahweh. Two realms of living; one up in the clouds; the other on the Land. This particular animal of which Aaron made an image was one that was worshiped in Egypt. It corresponds to the animal-idol which "climbed up from" the hearts and minds of humanity – the sea, in vs. 1, above. Thus was this image a corruption of the Truth; it adulterated their adoration of God with something from the religions of the world. This happened in the "church age" when Constantine adulterated Christianity with elements from pagan religions. It has continued to happen to where the "church" is a reflection and image of the world systems (and particularly, today, the entertainment industry, or corporate economic entities). Likewise, business and corporations can reflect the same worship of image and forms, exploiting both men and women through their advertising as they exalt the flesh-orientation of our cultures. Professional sports can often call to our lower nature as we embrace violence of human against human. Film and television portray heroes and heroines as simply being better at violence than the "bad guys," and constantly promote an "us" and "them" mindset. Instead of being transformed into the image of Christ, by the renewing of our minds (Rom. 12:2), we are, "**constantly conforming ourselves to** (or, as passive: being repeatedly molded by, fashioned for or patterned together with) **this age**." We become what we behold or worship. So let us,
> "**having a face that has been uncovered and remains unveiled** [note: as with Moses, before the Lord, Ex. 34:34] **– be folks who by a mirror are continuously observing, as ourselves, the Lord's glory** (or: be those who progressively reflect – from ourselves as by a mirror – the glory of [our] Owner), **presently being continuously and progressively transformed into the very same image, from glory into glory – in accord with and exactly as – from [the] Lord's**

Breath-effect (or: from [the] Spirit and Attitude of [the] Lord [= Christ or Yahweh])" (2 Cor. 3:18, modified for a present admonition).

The making of, "**an image** (likeness; resemblance; an icon) **to** (or: for) **the little animal**," takes us back to the book of Daniel, again; this time to chapter 3. It is the story of Nebuchadnezzar's golden image to which the "people, nations and languages" were to "fall down and worship." It does not say that the image was of himself, so it probably represented his kingdom (e.g., Dan. 4:30). And like vs. 15b, below, whoever did not fall down and worship the image would be killed, by being "cast into the midst of a burning fiery furnace" (Dan. 3:1-6). The rest is history. Once again, it is the estranged, dualistic Adam nature that desires worship of the work from people's creations, and sometimes, of other people. "In Germany they worshiped Hitler [and their own race, country, etc.]. And communism is more than politics; it's a religion" (Hiett, ibid p 171; brackets added).

15. **And it was given to it** (or: So it was granted for her) **to give spirit** (breath; a spirit) **to the image** (or: icon) **of the [first] little animal** (little wild beast) **so that the image** (or: icon) **of the little animal can both speak and can cause** (or: make it; arrange) **that whoever would not worship the image of the [first] little animal would** (or: should) **be killed.**

To begin, let us consider the indirect object of the verb of the first clause: "**to it**," or, "for her." The passive subject to which, "**it was given**," is the second little animal, the antecedent in vss. 11-13. The Greek word of "little animal" is neutral, or neuter, so my bold rendering is "**to it**." But the personal pronoun is in the feminine form (with no feminine antecedent), and so I also offer, "for her." The question arises, is this a subtle, enigmatic reference to Israel, who was often portrayed as a woman? Is John indicating the leadership in Jerusalem by referring to this second little animal as a "her"?

Spirit, or "a spirit," is **given** to the image by this second little animal. This idol may be an allusion to Gen. 2, where God blew His breath (spirit) of life into His image that He has formed, then, "placed him in His garden-temple (Gen. 2:7-8); and the first thing we see the Image doing is *speaking*, naming and defining the creation ..." (Chilton, ibid p 341; emphasis original). In our day, does this perhaps picture the practice of saying that something is "The Holy Spirit" when in fact it is actually an expression of the animal nature from within us? Or is it "giving life" to a system, giving it ability to **speak**, just as the first animal, above, was given a mouth? This spirit of **the image** also enables the image to cause results. Whichever, the result is now the **worship** of the very **image** (which defines "idolatry"), and those who will NOT worship this image are to be killed (cut off from fellowship – remember, this is symbolism, although in the 1st century it may have resulted in actual death). Thus, power is given to the image: "**the image** (or: icon)... **can both speak and can cause** (or: make it; arrange)." As noted in the comments on the previous verse, "images" are used throughout our current culture and society. These images have power – and the intent of their power is to control and bring conformity. Resist it, and its aim will, one way or another, be to **kill** your influence, your voice, or you. But there is simultaneously another imaging going on:

> "**because those whom He foreknew** (whom He knows from previous intimate experience), **He also marked out beforehand** (determined, defined and designed in advance) **[as] copies** (joint-forms) **of the image** (material likeness; portrait; mirrored image) **of His Son** (or: He previously divided, separated and bounded conformed patterns from the image of His Son) **into the [situation for] Him to be** (or: to continually exist being) **the Firstborn among, within the center of, and in union with many brothers** (= a vast family of believers)!" (Rom. 8:29).

This word from Paul is the fulfillment of the decision made in Gen. 1:26. The counterfeit, as described here, in vs. 15, is something that is actually anti-human: animalistic.

In history, this picture takes us back to Daniel and the worship of the golden image of Nebuchadnezzar, as we noted, above. The underlings of the king were "the accuser of the brethren" (Dan. 3:8; Rev. 12:10, above). Similar situations would also have confronted the early called-out with the rise of Caesar-worship (the imperial cult), but it can also speak to all forms of idolatry in our lives. Beale rightly notes a, "transtemporal nature of chapter 13" (ibid p 711). In the 1st century, refusal to offer incense to the image of the patron deity of the trade unions could bring economic ruin to the citizens of Asia Minor: they could be barred from doing business. We are not told the reason, but we have the reference in 2:13, above, to Antipas suffering capital punishment. Yet we are not told of mass executions for failure to worship particular images. We must keep in mind the symbolic nature of this vision and not seek literal interpretations, if the text does not so indicate. Beale (ibid p 714) points out that the texts of chapters 2-3, above, do not indicate that all seven communities would experience the same things. This may also be seen in the opening statement of Heb. 12:4,

> "**You folks do not yet resist** (or: did not as yet take a stand down against, or fully put in place opposition) **as far as blood** (= to the point of bloodshed; or, as a figure: = to the depth of your soul-life)…"

And then, there is the admonition in Heb. 13:3,

> "**Be habitually reminding yourselves of those in bondage** (or: the bound ones; the prisoners), **as having been and now remaining bound together with [them]. [Take thought] of those maltreated** (or: those continually being held by the bad or in the worthless), **as being yourselves also within a body** (or: as it were even being the same – in union with [that] body)."

16. **And so it is continually making** (causing; forming) **all** (everyone) **– the little** (small; = insignificant) **ones and the great ones, the rich ones and the poor ones, the free ones and the slaves – to the end that they could** (would; may; [some MSS: it will]) **give to them an imprinted mark-effect** (an engraved work; emblem; result of sculpting; carve-effect [note: same root from which we get the word "character"]) **upon their right hand, or upon their foreheads,**

Observe that the verb "**making**" can also be translated "causing," or "forming." Two ideas are presented in these options: a) "making" as "enforcement" of a decree: "forcing" and "causing" compliance; or, b) "forming," as in constructing a perception for needed compliance, or creating a mindset that is conformed to the purposes of the system. The noun "**imprinted mark-effect**" can also be translated "sculpture," or, "an engraved work," each of which would be a representation of the system's image.

By using polar terms of **little – great; rich – poor; free – slave**, this verse shows that this image affects the entire society. Thus, "**it is continually making/causing everyone… to the end that they could/would give to them an imprinted mark-effect**." The "**they**" in this verse would be those of the "body" of this anti-Christ system, the world of society, religion, economy, education, politics and government. The MSS reading, "it will," is a referent to the "image of the little animal." A prime example is the fashion world of our day. To be "in" with the fashion trends one must wear the clothes and accessories which display the proper current "image." But a not quite so obvious example is the inward conformity – although this results in behavior which can be observed. Paul instructed us,

> "**the result of the thinking** (mind-set; effect of the way of thinking; disposition; result of understanding and inclination; the minding; the opinion; the thought; the outlook) **of the flesh** (= the human condition or the System of culture and cultus; or: = outward Torah ceremony) **[is; brings] death**" (Rom. 8:6a).

The "mark-effect" could even be the "image" of what is the accepted form of "praise and worship," or of tradition-based "sacraments," of the various religious groups of our day. Our society displays its marks, its images and logos, in the physical and the soulish arenas, as well.

The **mark-effects** in this verse call to mind the words of Jesus, in Jn. 10:7, and again explains in vs. 9, "**I Myself am the Door** (or: Gate; Entrance); **if anyone should enter in through Me he will be constantly kept safe and protected** (made whole; rescued; delivered; saved)..." In vs. 7, there, He related being the Door to "**the Door for the sheep**," but in vs. 9 He related it to being "**kept safe, protected and delivered**." This metaphor of His being the Door may be an allusion to Ex. 12:7, where the blood of the lamb was to be used to make a mark upon "the two door jambs and on the lintel" of each house. The lintel represented the head of a person, while the jambs could be a symbol of the hands. We saw the fulfillment of this in Jesus on the cross: blood on His head from the crown of thorns; blood on His hands from the nails. In both situations, it was for deliverance and safety (as we also saw in Jn. 10:9). So what we have here, in 13:16, is the system's counterfeit, to keep folks employed and fed within its dominating arrangements. This is an allusion that reaches all the way back to Yahweh setting a "mark," or, "sign," on Cain, in Gen. 4:15b. That situation was for his protection:

> "And Shehmaa appointed a sign for Qen, that no one finding him would slay him" (*The Israelite Samaritan Version of the Torah*, Wm. B. Eerdmans Pub., 2013, trans. by Benyamim Tsedaka).

The **hand** is a figure for what a person does: work; activity. The **forehead** is a figure for the mind: how one thinks; what mindset he has; her character; one's identity. Jesus used a similar metaphor in Mat. 5:29-30,

> "**So if your right eye is habitually a bait-stick which entraps you, immediately tear it out and throw it away from you!.... Also, if your right hand is habitually a bait-stick which entraps you, at once cut it off and throw it away from you!**"

If our works and mind conformed to the image of the little animal, this is anti-Christ, or "in the place of Christ." Verses 17-18, below, give more details about this mark-effect, and 17:5, below, gives another, specific, example of a corporate figure with its own identification written on its forehead. Recall the "**blasphemous names**" on the heads of the first little wild animal in 13:1, above. These identity or ownership marks (or, in our day, "membership" or "loyalty" marks, emblems or bumper stickers) are a negative contrast to the "seal marks" of figurative Israel, in 7:3-8, above (see comments there), and of the 144 thousand in 14:1, below: those, "**having His Name, and** (or: even) **His Father's Name, having been written upon their foreheads**." These in chapters 7 and 14 will be seen again, in 20:4, below. *Cf* 3:12, above, and its bookend, 22:4, below.

This "mark-effect" also has an allusion that reaches back to Ex. 13:9,

> "And you will come to have this as a sign on your hand and between your eyes for remembrance that the law of Yahweh may be in your mouth; for with a steadfast hand Yahweh brought you forth from Egypt" (CVOT). *Cf* Deut. 6:6-8; 11:18.

The dedication of the firstborn of men and animals, described in Ex. 13:12-16 concluded:: "It shall be as a **mark** on your hand or frontlets (**symbol** – Tankh) between your eyes" (vs. 16a, ESV). The Jews took this literally and attached phylacteries containing portions of Scripture to their foreheads and arms. But is this Jewish mark and symbol perhaps used here to associate the little animal with the Zealots?

17. **even to the end that a certain one would continually be unable** (or: not anyone would be continually able) **to buy or to sell if [he or she is] not the one continuously having the imprinted mark-effect** (engraving; carve-effect) **or the name of the little animal, or the number of its name.**

The "**imprinted mark-effect, or the name of the little animal, or the number of its name**" all speak of having the identity of, and/or being possessed by, the little animal. And again, the name represents the character, and signifies that the little animal owns such as have these identifying effects of the mark. Instead of being given the Father's name, they are given the name of (or: membership in) the little animal.

In this way, they become the body of the little animal. The slaves in the 1st century were often marked with their owner's mark.

> "One of the ways a ruler impressed his sovereignty most vividly on the mind of his subject was by issuing coins bearing his image and title. Throughout the Roman Empire, every transaction of buying and selling, if it involved the transfer of money, meant handling imperial coins. Around the head of the emperor on a coin were titles, including in some cases references to his being divine and worshipful. It is such coins that John refers to as bearing the mark of the beast, without which 'no one can buy or sell' (13:17)" (Metzger, ibid p 75-76).

However, Maarschalk presents this information:

> "**No one may buy or sell:** The Zealots minted their own coins beginning in AD 66 to represent their independence from Rome and discontinued the use of other coins in Jerusalem, at Masada (60 miles away), and perhaps elsewhere; some were labeled 'For the Redemption of Zion'; referenced in Revelation 13:17" ("Who Was the Beast" ibid p 12)

The **number of its name** is derived from the total of the numeric values of each of the letters in the name, since "the ancient peoples had no figures and the letters of the alphabet did duty for numbers as well" (Barclay, ibid p 100). Mounce (NIV Study Bible, ibid p 1940) notes here that "Riddles using numerical equivalents for names were popular" in that time.

To not be able **to buy or to sell** signifies that one cannot participate in that society, and if living in a city, could go hungry. It would also imply that only those who have the mindset of, or membership in, the animal society will be able to successfully function within that society. It is the thinking of the "business world" that one must step on others in order to climb the ladder of success. The "religious world" has its own mindset, to which one must show allegiance if he or she is to "make it" in that world. One must above all have the right doctrines (the forehead) and do the right things while not doing what they prohibit (the hand) if one is to receive the denominational "stamp of approval" and thus be able to function in that religious environment. In our present world all transactions are done with numbers that are attached to our names and identities.

However, if one does not receive the mark-effect of the little animal, he or she can still buy from the Lord – 3:18, above. Here we should consider this hyphenated, compound noun, **mark-effect**. This literal rendering comes from the –ma ending of this form of the noun. This ending signifies that the noun is expressing the effect or the result of that which the noun is signifying. In other words, someone might put a "mark" on us, yet we would not necessarily experience or live-out the effect of that mark. But parents often mark, or mar, their children, and these children can live their whole lives with the effect(s) of that mark/mar – unless they are healed, delivered, or are born-back-up again (Jn. 3:7) and existentially come to the place where, "**[It is] no longer I, but it is Christ continuously living and alive within me**" (Gal. 2:20).

But the fact is, we have all had the mark of the dragon-serpent which brought death to humanity within the Garden experience. Paul explains that because of Adam's disobedience, death spread unto all humanity, giving all the "mark" of death, and dying (Rom. 5:12). The dragon and its little animals and icons are a culture of death, and in 2 Cor. 1:9a Paul informed us: "**we ourselves had held and continued having, within ourselves, the result and effect from a decision of the Death** (or: from a judgment which meant death; or: the considered decision and insightful response in regard to death)." But the Good News is that Christ has been lifted up on the cross, and then exalted from the grave to sit enthroned upon the heavens (5:6, above), and He has raise us up in Him, and so we are instructed in Rom. 6:

5. **For since** (or: You see, if) **we have been birthed** (have come to be) **folks engrafted and produced together** (or: planted and made to grow together; brought forth together; congenital) **in, by, to and with the result of the likeness of** (or: the effect of the similar manner from) **His death, then certainly we shall also continue existing [in and with the effects of the likeness] of The Resurrection**

        (or: which is the resurrection; or: from, and with qualities of, the resurrection),

6. **while constantly knowing this by intimate experience, that our old, former humanity is crucified together** (or: was simultaneously and jointly impaled and put to death on an execution stake) **with [Him], to the end that the body of the Sin** (the body belonging to the failure; the corporal manifestation that pertains to the deviation; the group of people [Adam] who missed the target) **could and would be rendered useless and inoperative** (idled-down to be unproductive; made null, inactive and unemployed), **for us to no longer continually be a slave to the Sin** (or: perform as a slave in the failure, for the Sin, or by deviating and thus missing the goal)....

8. **Now since we died** (or: if we die) **together with Christ, we are continuously believing** (relying; trusting) **that we shall also continue living together in Him** (by Him; for Him; to Him; with Him)....

11. **Thus you folks, also, be logically considering** (accounting and concluding) **yourselves to exist being dead ones, indeed, by the failure to hit the target** (or: in the Sin; or: to the deviation), **yet ones continuously living by God** (in God; for God; to God; with God), **within Christ Jesus, our Owner**.

And so now we have what Paul describes in 2 Cor. 1:9b,

"**to the end that we may not exist being ones having put trust and confidence upon ourselves, but to the contrary, upon the God Who is continually** (habitually; periodically; repeatedly; or: presently) **awakening and raising up the dead ones!**"

As Paul said in Col. 3:

9. **Do not keep on** (or: Stop) **lying unto one another! [Be] folks at once stripping off from yourselves** (undressing yourselves from; or: go out and away from) **the old humanity** (the old human; = the old Adam; [= <u>the little animal **mark-effect, name and number**</u>]), **together with its practices,**

10. **and then [be] suddenly clothing yourselves with the new one, the one being continuously** (or: repeatedly; habitually; progressively) **renewed** (made back up new again, in kind and character) **into full, accurate, added, intimate and experiential knowledge and insight which is down from and corresponds to the image** (an exactly formed visible likeness) **of its Creator** (of the One framing and founding it from a state of wildness and disorder).

Or, as he said in Eph. 4:24a,

"**enter within** (or: clothe yourselves with) **the new humanity** (or: the Person that is different and innovative in kind and quality) **– the one in accord with and corresponding to God** (or: the person at the Divine level)..."

Even today the economic and political systems within which we live impose upon us "marks" of their systems in order for us to participate in our own culture and society. But here, once again, is the Good News: His reign is not of this ordered system of domination (Jn. 18:36), and even though Jesus said, "**I Myself also send them forth as emissaries** (representatives) **into the prevailing system of culture, religion and government**" (Jn. 17:18b), He also said, "**They do not exist from out of the System** (world of society, religion or politics) **as a source or origin**" (Jn. 17:16a). And despite all that our present little animal or its image rage against us,

"**JUST AS the Sin** (the failure; the erroneous act; the deviation and digression which issued in missing the goal) **at one point reigned within, and in union with, the Death, THUS SO, also,**

the Grace and joyous favor would reign (should rule as king; can exercise sovereign sway) **through an eschatological deliverance that created rightwisedness [which leads] into Life which belongs to, pertains to and has the characteristics of the Age** (Life of the Age [of Messiah]; a life for the ages) **– through Jesus Christ, our Owner…. for [our] sin** ([our] failure; [our] missing of the target) **will not continue exercising mastery** (or: You see, deviation from the goal shall not exert ownership and rule as [our] lord), **for [we] are not under Law, but rather under Grace** (or: the Act which produced happiness, which was granted as a favor)" (Rom. 5:21; 6:14; brackets a modification of the personal pronoun, on 6:14).

18. **Here is Wisdom! The one having a mind** (intellect; intelligence) **must calculate** (compute by pebbles) **the number of the little animal, for it is man's number** (or: [the] number of mankind; a number pertaining to humanity; a man's number)**: his number [is] 666** [MS C: 616].

The final message of this vision opens with the proclamation to John, "**Here is Wisdom!**" We find this attribute, also mentioned together with a "**mind**," in 17:9, below, and it gives more information about the **little animal**:

"**Here [is] The Mind** (intelligence; intellect)**: the one continuously having** (holding) **Wisdom** (or: Here [is] the mind [which] has wisdom)**: The seven heads are seven mountains**…"

. Let us note: "**The one having a MIND** (intellect; intelligence) **must calculate the number of the little animal**…" The call of the Spirit is to use your mind in this matter, and to actually calculate the number. The number is already given to us, so in this case to "calculate" or "compute" would not mean to total, but rather to "figure out what this means." But for those who shun the use of the mind in considering "spiritual" matters, here is an imperative from the Spirit to use your **mind**. It is wisdom to do so. It would also suggest that Wisdom is present in considering what may be thought of as negative, or worldly, matters. Paul spoke repeatedly concerning **wisdom**, and it is essential to have it when dealing with any incarnation of these little animals. But how do we attain this gift? Paul inform us:

"**Christ [is] God's power and ability, as well as God's wisdom**" (1 Cor. 1:24) Cf 1 Cor. 1:30.
"**Christ, within Whom are all the hidden treasures of the wisdom and knowledge**" (Col. 2:3).
In Col. 4:5 he admonishes us to, "**Be habitually walking about within wisdom**," and in Eph. 1:16-17 is "**speaking and thinking toward [folks] having… a spirit of wisdom and unveiling**." So with John being pointed to wisdom in these vision, we are reminded that Paul also speaks of, "**God's greatly diversified wisdom…[being] made known – through the called-out community – to the governments** (or: rulers; sovereignties; chief ones) **as well as to the authorities and folks with privilege among those situated upon elevated positions**" (Eph. 3:10). So the communities to which John was sending this Unveiling had a function to perform, in relation to these little animal systems that were persecuting and/or dominating them. They were to reflect God's "exceedingly varied" **wisdom** to these manifestations of the dragon. We will encounter Gods judging, below, but we would be advised to keep in **mind** how Paul spoke of His deciding activities, in Rom. 11:33,

"**O, the depth of [the] riches and wisdom and intimate, experiential knowledge and insight of God** (or: from God)**! How unsearchable the effects of His decisions** (the results of the judgments and evaluations from Him), **and untrackable His ways** (paths)."

Now Paul said this right after saying, "**that He would mercy all mankind**" (vs. 32).

Much has been made of the number 666, but I suggest that it is simply "**mankind's number**" – its identity, its mindset, it character – expressed in three-part fullness, representing the spirit, soul and body of a human, or, as Knoch says, "the summit of all man's efforts." Barclay says, "If we take Nero in Latin and give it its numerical equivalent, we get: N = 50; E = 6; R = 500; O = 60; N = 50. The total is 666…. In Hebrew the letters of Nero Caesar also add up to 666. There is little doubt that the number of the beast stands for Nero..." (ibid p 102). Beale (ibid pp 718-728) challenges the validity to this approach of interpretation, opting for interpreting this number in the same manner as other numbers in this Unveiling: metaphorically. Many take 666 as a symbol for humanity's imperfection – each digit falls short of the perfect number 7. Prinzing shared these insights: "The beast symbolized the flesh, the world, the devil. Its name bespeaks of its nature, its character. And its number depicts it reaching its full expression" (ibid). In other words, this is a symbolic representation of mankind (created on the 6th day) that has not yet entered into God's rest (the 7th Day). That picture is seen in Heb. 3, recounting Israel's wilderness experience, in 7b-8,

> "Today, if you could (or: can) **hear His voice, you would not be hardening your hearts, as in the incitement to bitter feelings** (or: the being exasperated and provoked; or: = the **rebellion**) **down from the day of putting to the proof by ordeals in the desert**."

To "harden one's heart" is to enter into the estranged realm of ourselves (the 1st Adam) that is represented here in chapter 13 of the Unveiling as, "**the little animal**." It represents a lack of trust – both of God and of others; it incarnates an absence of love. Heb. 3:12-14 speaks to this condition with an exhortation:

> **12. Exercise sight** (Be continuously observing), **brothers, [so] there shall not once be in any of you folks a bad, useless or misery-gushed heart** (a heart causing labor, sorrow or pain) **of unfaithfulness** (or: from disloyalty, disbelief or distrust; or: the source and character of which is an absence of faith and trust), **in withdrawing** (or: standing away and aloof; separating or revolting) **from the living God.**
> **13. But rather, be habitually calling yourselves alongside – entreating, admonishing, encouraging, bringing relief and helping each other – daily, concerning** (or: in accord with) **each day**... **so that not any one from the midst of you folks may be hardened by a deception of failure** (or: in treachery from a miss of the target; with seduction of sin; by cunning in regard to error; by deceit relating to a mistake).
> **14. For we have been born partners of the Christ** (or: we have come to be associates and participants who partake of the Anointed One and commonly hold the Anointing) **with the result that we are now in a binding partnership with Him, since surely we can fully hold in our possession – so as to retain firm and steadfast – the Origin of the substructure to the point of completion of the intended goal**
>> (or: if indeed, unto [the condition or state of] maturity, we would fully hold in our possession, so as to retain firm and steadfast, the beginning [position] with regard to the substance, essential nature and basis [of the new reality] – as well as the rule of that [which was] put under, as a standing for support).

Note the first clause of vs. 12 in this quote: it speaks to the condition of the heart (and recall in Dan. 5:21, how Nebuchadnezzar's heart was made like the "heart" of a beast), and of a withdrawing from God. Then vs. 13 warns of "deception of failure, or from a miss of the target (etc.)," which, apart from Christ, is the human predicament. But vs. 14 lays out the solution to mankind's beast-like condition, which Heb. 3:17 describes as, "**carcasses [that] fell in the wilderness**." Then, Heb. 4:3-4, 6 proclaim,

> "**For we, those at this point believing and trusting, are progressively entering into the rest** (or: the stopping).... **For He said in a certain place concerning the seventh, thus, 'And God rested in the seventh day from all His works'** [Gen. 2:2].... **there continues being left remaining [for] some folks to enter into it**."

This "rest," this place of being, is in Christ, where we live above the "little animal" realm, in restored relationships (the Way pointed out).

As to this number, 666, being used to identify a specific person (such as one of the Caesars), Beale notes that, "There is no evidence of any other number in the book being used in such a way. All the numbers have figurative significance and symbolize some spiritual reality..." (ibid p 721). In fact, take note of the number in the very next verse (14:1): 144,000. That number is an echo of those "**calculated**" in 7:4-8, above, both of these being figures of a corporate group. Understanding the word *anthropos* in this verse in a generic sense, as "humanity," and 666 being a collective number, "**man's number**," is, "consistent with 13:1, which affirms that the beast has its earthly origin in the sea of fallen humanity" (Beale, ibid p 724). Note the use of the same word, *anthropos*, in 21:17, below, "(a) **human's measure**." The form or the word is the same, both there and here. There *anthropos* qualifies "measure;" here it qualifies "number." Beale (ibid p 723) also sees this verse functioning as a call to the reader's attention concerning what has just been said in vss. 11-17, just like vs. 9, above, "employs the metaphor of hearing" to function the same way regarding what was said in vss. 1-8, above. Repetitions of rhetorical devices are scattered throughout this book. We may have an allusion in this number to the measurements of the image in Dan. 3:1, "whose height [was] six score cubits [and] the breadth thereof six cubits." Chilton points to Goliath, the champion of the Philistine army. His height is recorded in 1 Sam. 17:4; it was "six cubits and a span."

As we consider the possible renderings, "**man's number** (or: [the] number of mankind; a number pertaining to humanity; a man's number)," we have observed that the term can have a reference to humanity, as a whole, and not just be a symbol of a particular individual (e.g., Nero, etc.), as has often been the interpretation. Although the #666 has strong MS support, an important MS, C, reads 616, of which B. Metzger (*A Textual Commentary on the Greek NT*, 2nd Ed, UBS, 1994 p 676) informs us that Irenaeus made mention of this reading, and, "According to Tischendorf's 8th ed., the numeral 616 was also read by two minuscule MSS that unfortunately are no longer extant.... the Latin form Nero Caesar is equivalent to 616."

With this in mind, let us consider, again, the subject of this verse: **the little animal**. My friend Dan Kaplan brought to this text a correlation from Peter's experience in Acts 10, so let us review this passage and consider the meaning of the "little animals" in Peter's vision, when he was on the housetop:

> 10. **But he became very hungry – almost ravenous – and began desiring to at once taste** (= eat) **[something]. Now during their being in the midst of preparing [a meal], an ecstasy happened** (an out-of-place state of being was birthed [*p*45 reads: came]) **upon him,**
> 11. **and he is now – as a spectator – watching the sky** (or: heaven; the atmosphere) **– having been opened up – and in the process of descending [is] some container, like a large, fine linen sheet** (or: sail-cloth; bandage), **being gradually but progressively lowered down onto the ground** (or: Land; earth) **by [its] four corners** (extremities; origins; beginnings),
> 12. **within the midst of which were continuing under [the directive, or, power] of [their] origin all the four-footed animals, as well as creeping things** (perhaps: insects; reptiles) **of the ground** (or: land; earth) **and flying creatures of the sky** (or: atmosphere; heaven).
> 13. **Then a voice was birthed to him** (or: occurred, [directed] toward him), **"After getting up** (or: Upon arising), **Peter, slaughter** (or: sacrifice) **and then at once eat [it]!"**
> 14. **But Peter said, "Not even one [of those], Sir** (or: Lord; Master; or: = Yahweh?), **because I never eat** (or: ate) **all [that is] common** (= what is not set-apart as food for Israelites and is forbidden by the dietary rules of the Law) **and unclean** (meaning: ceremonially unclean)!"
> 15. **Then again, a voice, forth from a second [one, saying] to him: "You are not to continue making, or considering, common [the] things which God cleansed** (or: cleanses) **and made** (or: makes) **clean!"** [*cf* Mk. 7:18-19]
> 16. **Now this happened on a third [time]** (or: So this occurred three times), **and immediately the container was taken back up again, into the sky** (or: the atmosphere; heaven).

What Peter objected to, in this vision, was based upon the Jewish food code: he recognized that the "little animals" in the sheet were unclean, and not to be eaten, according to the Law. The symbolism in the vision would later be interpreted as a reference to "people" that the Jews considered to be "unclean," and this would involve another purity code: Jews were not supposed to enter the home of a Gentile, or to eat with them. Acts 10, and the chapters following, expand the issue, leading to the Jerusalem church becoming aware that Gentiles are included in this new participation of the Spirit. But let us hear Peter explain the matter to the household of Cornelius:

> 28. **Thus he affirmed to them, "You folks continue well versed [in the fact] and are well aware of how illicit and inappropriate** (forbidden by [our] Law and contrary to [our] established order) **it is for an adult man [who is] a Jew** (or: is of the Jewish culture) **to be intimately joined to, or to regularly come to** (or: visit and associate with), **a man from another race. And yet God pointed out and demonstrated to me not to continue saying [that] even one human [is] common** (= socially or ceremonially unhallowed or defiled) **or unclean**…

Let the last statement by Peter, in vs. 28, sink in. This should also be our mindset regarding humanity: none are common or unclean. Later, as Peter continued addressing them,

> 44. **During the middle of Peter's still speaking these gush-effects and results of the flow** (or: declarations), **the set-apart Breath-effect** (or: the Holy Spirit; the Sacred Wind) **fell upon all the folks presently listening to and hearing the Logos** (the message; the Word).
> 45. **Then the trusting** (full of faith) **folks from among [the] Circumcision** (= those of the Jewish culture and religion) **who came with Peter "stood out of themselves" in shocked amazement that the free gift of** (or: which is) **the set-apart Breath-effect** (the Holy Spirit) **had been poured out upon the nations** (the ethnic multitudes; the non-Jews) **as well,**
> 46. **for you see, they kept on hearing them continuously and repeatedly speaking with tongues** (in languages; by ecstatic glottal utterances) **and repeatedly magnifying** (speaking great things about) **God.**

Note the reaction and surprise of Peter's companions, in vs. 45. You see, "unclean animals" (from Peter's vision) were being gifted with God's Holy Spirit. But what was the reaction in Jerusalem? Acts 11 gives us the picture:

> 1. **Now the sent-forth folks and the brothers** (= fellow believers or members of the brotherhood) **who were down throughout Judea heard that the ethnic groups of the nations** (the non-Jews; Gentiles) **also welcomingly received and embraced the Logos of God** (or: the Word which is God; the message from God; God's thought, idea and reason).
> 2. **So when Peter went up into Jerusalem, the men from among [the] Circumcision** [note: i.e., the Jews adhering to the Jewish culture and religion: these may or may not have been a part of the called-out community] **continued their evaluation [of propriety] for a complete distinction and separation [between Jews and non-Jews], and so began taking sides against him to make a cleavage, contending and debating the issue with him.**

This is a typical reaction from a religious beast: little animals only want to accept their own, or those who in conformity join them. Peter explained to the group why he had done this, and concludes:

> 16. **"At this I was reminded of the results of the flow and the gush-effects** (or: words spoken) **by the Lord, as He was repeatedly saying, 'John, indeed** (or: for his part), **immersed in water, yet you yourselves will be immersed** (baptized) **within the midst of set-apart Breath-effect** (or: in [the] Holy Spirit).'
> 17. **"Since, therefore, God gave** (or: gives) **to them the equal free gift as also to us, when** (or: in) **believing and putting their trust upon the Lord, Jesus Christ – who or what [am] I? Was I able to cut off or hinder God?!"**

The reasons for including this incident, here, are: a) little animals in visions can simply represent people; b) what was once a "little animal" can be transformed when God determines to have His Breath-effect (His Holy Spirit) "fall" on a person or on a system. With God, all things are possible (Mat. 19:26). In all ages and in each environment humans come face to face with individual "little animals," and with corporate "little animals." Nero was obviously "a little animal" in "a little animal empire." They are all part

of God's plan of the ages. But the central message of this Unveiling is that the little Lamb reigns, so we need not fear or lose hope. Jesus told His followers,
> "**Within the System** (dominating and controlling world of culture, religion, economy and government; or: among and in union with the aggregate of humanity) **you normally have pressure and stress** (or: continually have squeezing; repeatedly have tribulation and oppression), **but nonetheless, be confident and take courage! I, Myself, have overcome and conquered the System** (dominating world; organized arrangement of religion and society; aggregate of humanity) **so that it stands a completed victory!**" (Jn. 16:33).

So ends the vision of the little wild animals that populate the sphere of the earth/Land.

Chapter 14

1. Later I saw this – so consider! The little Lamb [is; was] standing (or: having made a stand) **upon Mount Zion** (or: the mountain, Zion), **and with Him [are] one hundred forty-four thousand: folks continuously having His Name, and** (or: even) **His Father's Name, having been written upon their foreheads.**

The allusion in this opening view, presented to John, reaches back to Ps. 2:6,
> "Yet I have been established king under, and by, Him, upon Mount Zion, His set-apart mountain" (LXX, JM).

Also seen here is an echo of Isa. 2:
> 2. And it will come to pass in the latter days, the Mountain of Yahweh's House shall be set up, established and stand firm on the summit (or: as the Head) of the mountains... and all the nations will stream unto it.
> 3. .... For from Zion shall go forth a law (or: instruction), and the word of Yahweh (or: the message about Yahweh) from Jerusalem.
> 4. He will judge between the nations and arbitrate for (or: be umpire to) [the] many peoples...

Then in Dan. 2:35b, "And the stone that struck the image became a great mountain, and it filled the whole Land (or: territory; earth)." That mountain was explained by Daniel as God setting up a kingdom/reign that will "stand for the ages" (Dan. 2:45). Isa. 11:9 gives the promise, "They will not hurt, nor destroy, in all My holy Mountain; for you see, the land (or: Land; earth) is filled with the knowledge of Yahweh, as the waters form a covering to the seas." Both Paul, and the Unveiling, call this "a new creation." The little Lamb and His apprentices are the Firstfruits of many harvests that will come on through the ages – as folks plant their lives (the Life of the little Lamb) in the hearts of the oncoming generations. We also hear the witness of 1 Pet. 2:6,
> "**I am progressively setting** (placing; laying) **within Zion a chosen** (picked-out), **precious** (held in honor and value) **cornerstone lying at the extreme angle**..."

Now we encounter either another vision or another scene in the larger vision which preceded this scene. It stands in stark contrast to the subject of the previous chapter. It represents the new realm: the reign of God. The figure that opens this chapter is Jesus (the **little Lamb**; cf Jn. 1:29, 36) and His followers – His body. These 144,000 are undoubtedly the same figure as those that were sealed in 7:3-8, above. They are overcomers, since they have **His Name and His Father's Name** (which is either the same Name, or they have a double identity) written upon their foreheads (3:12, above). Perhaps it signifies that they have both the character of a Savior and of a Father. We also see in vs. 5, below, that they are without blemish – they have Christ's righteousness (the Lamb without blemish) from being joined to the Vine (Jn. 15:1ff) and are one with Him (1 Cor. 6:17; Jn. 17:21, 23), and the process of growth has been completed; they are a new creation with nothing of the old estranged creation left (2 Cor. 5:17). But more than this, having their Names on our faces means that we now have their identities. We now reflect their glory (2 Cor. 3:18). This may also be an allusion to Ezra 2:61-62, where qualification for the priesthood required a man's name to be in the genealogical records. But in the new arrangement (covenant), Jn. 3:7 requires another birth, and Rom. 8:14 characterizes this as being led by God's Spirit (cf also Heb. 5:5-6; 7:14-17 and Rom. 2:28-29). When you are dwelling on Mt. Zion (see Heb. 12:22, quoted under vs. 2, below) you can say, with Paul, that you no longer live, but it is Christ that lives in you (Gal. 2:20). You can also say, with Jesus, "**The one having discerned and seen me has seen, and now perceives, the Father!**" (Jn.14:9b). The last phrase of this verse is also an allusion to the headdress of the chief priest, in Ex. 39:30,

> "They also made the holy insignia blossom [or: burnished plate of the holy crown; {or: frontlet for the holy diadem}] of pure gold and wrote on it a writing like engravings of a seal: Holy to Yahweh"(CVOT; brackets: Rotherham; { }'s: Tanakh).

So this picture is also of His making us, "**priests in** (or: by; for; with) **His God and Father**" (1:6, above). These names also equate to the "**new name**" of 2:17, above. We find this same group in, and comprising, the New Jerusalem, in 22:3b-4, below,

> "**And God's throne – even the little Lamb's – will continue being** (or: existing) **within Her [i.e., the City], and His slaves will continue rendering sacred service to Him, and will constantly see His face, and His Name [is; or: will be] upon their foreheads**."

This "new name" is an allusion to Isa. 62:2b,

> "And you shall be called by a new name, which the Mouth of Yahweh will name."

And in Isa. 62:4 it is said, "But you shall be called, 'My delight is in her'…" In Isa. 62:12b, "And you shall be called, 'Sought out, a City not forsaken.'" Then in Isa. 65:15b we read, "And His servant will He call by another name." In Jer. 3:17, we are told, "At that time they will call Jerusalem, 'The throne of Yahweh.'" And in Ezk. 48:35 it says, "And the name of the city from [that] day [on will be]: Yahweh-[is]-there" (CVOT).

Zion is associated with being the location of the Temple (a figure of the body of Christ), e.g., Ps. 2:6, "I will pour a libation on My King, on Zion, My holy mountain" (CVOT). Also Ps. 132:13, "For Yahweh has chosen Zion; He yearns for it as His dwelling place." It is a symbol for the destination of God's people as they seek Him, "They go from rampart to rampart till each appears before God in Zion" (Ps. 84:7). It is associated with Jerusalem in Ps. 48:1-2, "Great is Yahweh... in the city of our God, His holy mountain; lovely of undulation, the elation of the entire earth is Mt. Zion... the town of the great King." Then there is Obad. 17, "Yet in Mt. Zion deliverance shall come to be, and it will be holy." And Obad. 21 promises, "And SAVIORS shall come up in Mt. Zion, to judge the mount of Esau, and the kingdom shall become Yahweh's" (a phrase similar to 11:15, above). Is this present picture, in 14:1-5, a picture of "saviors" on Mt. Zion? I suggest that it is, for they have the treasure of The Savior within their earthly vessel (jars of clay – 2 Cor. 4:7), and they minister the deliverance of Christ to those around them.

Zion was also used as a figure for Israel as a people, e.g., "Zion shall be redeemed with judgment, and her converts with righteousness" (Isa. 1:27). And Isa 33:5, "... He has filled Zion with judgment and righteousness." In Isa. 28:16 it says, "I lay in Zion, for a foundation, A STONE, a tried stone, a precious corner, a sure foundation..." – an obvious reference to Christ, the little Lamb. Recall that mountains are a prophetic term for kingdoms, or realms of dominion and reign, so Mt. Zion is a figure for the kingdom, reign and sovereign influence of God (and of the heavens – which is a parallel metaphor, as seen in Matthew's Gospel).

What we have, here, is a symbol of the corporate body of Christ, the composite of all His called-out, covenant communities. We will see more details in the following verses. But we saw them as Christ's witnesses (11:3-12, above), as the Woman in the heavens (12:1, above), and her corporate Son caught up to God's throne (12:5), and as the agents battling with the dragon (12:7, 11). These visions are giving different pictures of the same subjects, seen in different functions and from different views. What we see, here, is a direct contrast to the little wild animals of chapter 13. Zion, here, is described as the New Jerusalem of chapter 21, below (and 3:12, above), which has descended to minister life and healing to the ethnic multitudes (chapters 21 and 22). This picture is synonymous with "**the Jerusalem above is** (continues being) **free, who is** (or: which particular one continues being) **our mother**" (Gal. 4:26).

We find another witness in 4 Ezra (dated the late 1st century AD).
"I, Ezra, saw on Mount Zion a great multitude, which I could not number, and they all were praising the Lord with song. In their midst was a young man.... He is the Son of God, whom they confessed in the world" (2:42-43, 47).
"But He will stand on the top of Mount Zion, and Zion will come and be made manifest to all people, prepared and built, as you saw the mountain carved out without hands. And He, My Son, will reprove the assembled nations for their ungodliness..." (13:35-37; trans. by B. Metzger, *The OT Pseudepigrapha*, Vol. 1, ibid p 552).

2. **Then I heard a voice** (or: sound) **out of the atmosphere** (or: sky; heaven), **as a voice** (or: sound) **of many waters, and as a voice** (or: sound) **of a great thunder. And the voice** (sound) **which I heard [was] as lyre-singers, continuously playing their lyres** (or: harps).

Consider again their location: Mt. Zion. Yet their **voice** is heard from out of the **atmosphere**/heaven. So if they are on Mt. Zion, yet their voice was heard as the sound of many waters (= the voice of many agents of 5:11, above; see also 1:15, above, for another picture of this corporate Lamb – they have His Name, they have His voice) out of heaven, then I think that we can conclude that this is also a "figurative Mt. Zion" and not a geographic location on earth. In Heb. 12:22-24 we see another description of this group in the same location, and here it is said,

22. **But to the contrary, you folks have approached so that you are now at Mount Zion – even in a city of a continuously living God; in "Jerusalem upon heaven"**
(or: in a Jerusalem pertaining to and having the character and qualities of a superior, or added, heaven and atmosphere; or: in Jerusalem [situated] upon, and comparable to, the atmosphere) – **also among ten-thousands** (or: myriads) **of agents and messengers** (people with a/the message)**:**
23. **[that is] in** (or: to) **an assembly of an entire people** (or: an assembly of all; a universal convocation) **and in** (or: to) **a summoning forth** (or: a called-out and gathered community) **of firstborn folks having been copied** (from-written, as from a pattern; or: enrolled; registered) **within [the; or: various] atmospheres** (or: heavens), **and in** (or: to; with) **God, a Judge** (an Evaluator and Decider) **of all mankind, even among** (or: to; with) **spirits of just folks** (or: breath-effects from those who are fair and equitable and in right relationship within the Way pointed out) **having been brought to the destined goal** (perfected; finished; matured; made complete), [*cf* Rev. 3:12; 21:1-2; Eph. 2:6; Phil. 3:20; Rev. 14:1-5; Ex. 4:22; Gal. 3:19]
24. **and in** (or: to) **Jesus, a Medium** (or: an agency; an intervening substance; a middle state; one in a middle position; a go-between; an Umpire; a Mediator) **of a new and fresh** (young; recently-born) **arrangement** (covenant; settlement; a deposit which moves throughout in every direction; a placing through the midst; a will and testament), **and to and in blood of sprinkling, and to One continuously speaking something superior to** (or: stronger and better than) **Abel.** [*cf* Mat. 17:1-5; Rev. 21:1-2; 9b-22:5; Jn. 4:21; Ps. 46:4; 132:13; Isa. 28:16; 33:5]

The mention of **lyres** (or: harps) takes us back to 5:8, above (the **twenty-four elders**, or older folks), and points us ahead to 15:2, "**the folks** (or: those) **continually overcoming** (being progressively victorious; presently conquering) **– from out of [the power and influence of] the little wild animal** (creature;

beast), **and from out of [the nature of] its image**... **holding God's lyres** (harps)," which obviously is tied to chapter 13 (the animals) and here (the lyres).

The compound, descriptive phrases, "**as a voice** (or: sound) **of many waters, and as a voice** (or: sound) **of a great thunder**," are closely echoed in 19:6, below, that also came from "heaven" (19:1), i.e., the realm of spirit or God's reign (perhaps an allusion to "the tabernacle of David"). In 19:4 they are in the same setting as the 24 elders and 4 living ones (a temple setting in chapter 4), as we also see in our next verse, here. There, in chapter 19, all this comes from the great prostitute having been judged (19:2). The great multitude that is singing and playing **lyres**, here, may be rejoicing at the proclamation in vs. 8, below, concerning the fall of this same Babylon, and the corrective measures that follow. This all recalls the song of Moses and Miriam (Ex. 15), following the "fall" of Egypt, in the Exodus story.

3. **And they repeatedly sing a new** (strange) **song before the throne, and in the presence of the four living ones and the old folks** (or: elders). **And no one was able to learn the song** (or: ode) **except the one hundred forty-four thousand – those having been bought from the Land** (or: earth).

The idea of a "**new song**" finds echoes in Ps. 33:3, and Ps. 40:3 proclaims, "He has put a new song in my mouth: praise to our God; many shall **see** and **fear**, and shall **trust** in Yahweh." The purpose of this new song, expressed in the second clause of Ps. 40:3, is the same as we have in the Unveiling, in 5:9, 14:2, and 19:6. *Cf* Ps. 144:9; 149:1. The new song in Isa. 42:10 celebrates the arrival of the messianic promises declared in vss. 1-8 of that passage. There, the "new song" was to declare "His praise" as He spoke to them of "the new" that would be "sprouting," so,
> "Let the inhabitants of the crag raise shouts of triumph; from the top of the mountains let them cry aloud [and] let them render (or: attribute) glory to Yahweh; then let them tell forth His praise in the coastlands" (vss. 11b-12).

The idea of a "new song" was a recounting or a celebration of new acts of God.

They sing an ode **before the throne and in the presence of the four living ones and the elders** – an echo of the scene in chapter 4, above, and thus what we have is another view, or picture, of the same situation: the little Lamb on Zion is also the slain Lamb on the throne (5.6, above). That these singers are the 144K is made clear, here in vs. 3, where we are told that they are the only ones **able to learn** to sing it. This is parallel to the overcomer receiving a "new name" in 2:17, above, "**which no one has seen, so as to know, except the one presently receiving it**." I suggest that here in 14:1-5 we have another picture of those (the four living ones and the 24 elders) singing a "**new song**" in 5:8-11, above. The throne room scene there is the same place as the Mt. Zion scene, here, as seen in the OT quotes under vs. 1, above. The ability **to learn** comes to us the same way that it came to Christ:
> "**Even though continuously being a Son, He learned to listen, pay attention and act on it** (or: the giving of the ear in hearing from below, and then to obey) **from the things which He experienced** (or: what happened to Him [both the good and the bad])" (Heb. 5:8).

I included the alternate meaning, "strange," to give the sense of how different this "song" would be to those who are not yet capable of learning it. The way of the cross, the *cruciform* life, seems indeed strange to the person living in the little animal realm.

The final clause, "**those having been bought from the Land** (or: earth)," are the same ones referred to in the next verse as, "**These were** (or: are) **bought from humanity**." This is an echo from 5:9, above. Paul spoke with this verb in 1 Cor. 6:19b-20,

"**And further, you are not folks belonging to yourselves** (or: Also then, you people do not exist from yourselves), **for you people were bought, as at a marketplace: [there was] value and honor involved in the price** (or: [you are] of value)
> (or: = for you were bought and paid for; or: for from a valuable price you folks were bought at market).

By all means then, glorify God (bring a good reputation to God; manifest that which calls forth praise to God) **within your body** (or: within the midst of the body which you folks are)!"

1 Cor. 7:23 opens with the same words as 1 Cor. 6:20a, but ends with:
> "**Do not continue becoming slaves of humanity** (or: Do not repeatedly come to be slaves of people)." *Cf* 2 Pet. 2:1.

The Greek clauses of vss. 3 and 4, here, are very close to what we find in 5:9, above. All three of these verses are universal references: "from out of every tribe, tongue, people and nation (5:9); from the earth (14:3); from humanity (14:4)." As we will see, in the next verse, these are a "FIRST-fruit" that represents the Harvest from which it was taken.

4. **These are those who were** (or: are) **not stained** (polluted, contaminated) **with women, for they are** (or: exist being) **virgins. These are the folks continuously following The little Lamb wherever He progressively leads** [other MSS: wherever He may habitually depart]. **These were** (or: are) **bought from humanity, a firstfruit in God** (by God; to God; for God), **even in** (by; with; for; to) **the little Lamb.**

They are disciples (apprentices and followers) and have come to Him outside the camp (Heb. 13:13), outside the city, and are thus not contaminated with women (a figure of the "strange woman" of Prov. 2:16; 5:20; 6:24; 7:5; 20:16; 23:27; the contamination would come from participation in the prostitution with Babylon [seen below, in vs. 8] or any of her daughters, 17:5, below). The contamination could involve the leaving of their first love (e.g., like those in Ephesus, 2:4, above), or could refer to the prostitution with Jezebel in Thyatira (2:20-22, above), or it could speak of Judaizing with the Jews which were a synagogue of satan in Smyrna (2:9, above) – all this would be contamination. But these are the same ones to which Paul referred in 2 Cor. 11:2b,
> "**I myself joined you folks in marriage to one husband, to make a pure virgin** (= unmarried girl) **to stand alongside in the Christ**."

We find the term "virgin" used metaphorically in 2 Ki. 19:21 referring to the whole of Israel, and this verse uses the city, Jerusalem, in the same way:
> "This is the word that Yahweh has spoken concerning [Sennacherib]: The virgin daughter of Zion laughs you to scorn; mocks you. The daughter of Jerusalem wags her head after you."

We find this same verse in Isa. 37:22. Jer. 14:17b uses the term in a similar way, "For with a grievous injury the virgin, the daughter of My people, has been injured." Then in Jer. 18:13 we find the term explicitly applied to Israel: "A very horrible thing has the virgin, Israel, done!" And in Jer. 31:4, Yahweh promises, "Again will I build you, and you shall be built, you virgin, Israel..." Jer. 31:21 implores, "Return, O virgin of Israel." Lam. 1:15 sounds much like 11:2b, above, "Yahweh has trodden the virgin, the daughter of Judah, [as] in a winepress." Then Amos 5:2 records a dirge in which he states, "The virgin Israel lies forsaken on her soil (or: land)." These should be sufficient witnesses to confirm the meaning of the symbol in our text, here. These folks are Christ's called-out congregations. *Cf* also Lam. 2:13.

Upon reading our first draft, here, Kaplan pointed me to how God had washed Israel as she came through the Red Sea (Paul refers to it as her "**baptism unto Moses… in the sea**," 1 Cor. 10:2), which Ezk. 16 alluded to (see, under vs. 8, below). So she was a virgin, and Yahweh implanted His Seed (the Law) within her at Mt. Sinai. This was a shadow of Lu. 1:35,

> "**A set-apart** (or: holy) **breath-effect** (or: a consecrated wind; or: sacred spirit and attitude; [The] Holy Spirit) **will continue coming upon you, and a power** (ability; or: [the] Power) **which has its source and origin in** (or: which pertains to; or: which has the qualities and characteristics of; or: which is) **[the] Most High will continue casting a shadow upon you… the Set-apart One** (or: holy thing) **being progressively generated and born will continue being called God's Son** (or: a son of God; 'Son of God')."

This was the first phase of what Jer.31:31 spoke of as the "new covenant," continuing in vs. 33 saying, "I will put My law (or: instruction) in their inward parts, and write it in their hearts…" The putting of that "law/instruction" is the implanting of Christ within His **virgins**, just as with Mary, in Lu. 1, and Christ's bride/body, in 2 Cor. 11:2b, above, which is the second phase, as Heb. 8:10 attests, and Heb. 10:22 gives witness:

> "**the hearts having been sprinkled from a misery-gushed consciousness of what is evil or unserviceable** (or: a joint-knowledge full of annoying labor; a conscience in a bad condition), **and then the body having been bathed in and by clean water**."

Heb. 10:19 instructs us that this is, "**within and in union with the blood of Jesus**." With the birth of the **man-child**, 12:5, above, the Head came first, and then the "body." 1 Pet. 1:23 speaks of us,

> "**having been born again** (been regenerated; been given birth back up again), **not from out of a corruptible** (or: perishable) **seed that was sown, but rather from an incorruptible** (imperishable) **one: through God's continually living and permanently remaining Word**,"

just as Mary was. God's presence makes our "earth" holy, set-apart (Ex. 3:5). Mary was "overshadowed" by God's Spirit, just as the waters were in Gen. 1:2, and then as in Gen. 1:3 He said, "Let there be Light," so with Mary (she gave birth to the Light of the world), and so with us (now we are the light of the world – Mat. 5:14a). In both cases,

> "**the God suddenly saying** (or: the God Who once was saying), **"Light will shine forth** (give light as from a torch; gleam) **from out of the midst of darkness** (dimness and shadiness; gloom and the absence of daylight)!" **[is] the One who shines forth within the midst of our hearts, with a view to illumination of the intimate and experiential knowledge of God's glory – in a face of Christ**" (2 Cor. 4:6).

This was, as Paul put it in Gal. 1:16, "**to unveil** (reveal; uncover; disclose) **His Son within the midst of me**/us." Here, in 14:4, we are reminded of Isa. 7:13-14,

> "Therefore, the LORD (= Yahweh) Himself will give a Sign to you folks. Look [for it] and consider! The **virgin** (*parthenos* – the same word as here, in 14:4) shall conceive in the womb, and she shall bring forth (bear) a Son, and you shall call His Name, Emmanuel [Heb. = God-with-us]" (LXX, JM).

But let us consider another key to their identity: "**These were** (or: are) **bought from humanity, a firstfruit in God** (for God; to God; by God)…" This takes us to Jacob (James) 1:18,

> "**Being purposed** (intended; willed), **from being pregnant He gave birth to us** (brought us forth; prolifically produced us) **by a Word** (in a collected thought; for an expressed idea; with a message) **of Truth and from Reality – into the [situation for] us to be** (or: to continuously exist being) **a specific** (or: a certain; some) **firstfruit of His created beings** (or: of the effects of His act of creating; or: from the results of the founding and creation which is Himself; [other MSS: of the Himself-creatures])."

In the same chapter (31), where Jeremiah refers to Israel as a virgin, we find the term "firstborn" (vs. 9b) used to describe Ephraim, which came to be used to designate the northern tribes. "Firstborn" is used in the same way as "firstfruit" – in figurative descriptions they are virtually synonymous.

The concept of "firstfruit" reaches back to Israel's history, and is a subject of their Law that is worthy of its own study. The firstfruit of everything belonged to Yahweh, the Owner of all. Israel's Law of the offerings provided symbolic means of offering back to God what had come from Him and what belonged to Him. He received, via the offering cultus, the first part of the harvest, and an important point for our present context is that a "firstfruit" implied and represented the whole harvest – i.e., the rest of the crop from which the first ripe grains were taken and waved before Yahweh (Lev. 23:10-17). The statement by Jacob (James), above, may be implying that those who in this life are joined to the Lord are the "firstfruits" of His ultimate Harvest of All. An interesting linguistic point is that this term "firstfruits", in Greek, is *aparchē*, which is formed by prefixing the preposition *apo* (from) to the noun *archē* (beginning; origin; leader; ruler; etc.). Notice that the "-o" is dropped from the preposition when this is done. A rule of Greek grammar is that when a preposition ending in a vowel comes right before a noun that begins with a vowel, the final vowel of the preposition is dropped, so you would have (in this case), *ap archē*, which would read, "from a/[the] beginning. The MSS p47, Aleph, and others, give this second reading, here in vs.4. This might have been influenced by the LXX of Ps. 73[74]:2, "Remember the congregation (literally, the synagogue; the gathering-together) which You purchased from [the] beginning (*ap archē*)" (JM). So the p47, Aleph, etc., phrase in 4b, here, could read, "These were bought from among humans, from [the] beginning, by God."

The descriptive statement, "**These are the folks continuously following The little Lamb wherever He progressively leads**," clearly identifies this symbol of 144K as being the body of Christ, the followers of Jesus. A response was made to Him in Mat. 8:19,

"**Later, one scribe** (scholar; theologian; Law expert) **approaching [Him] said to Him, Teacher, I will follow you wherever you may be now departing** (or: are about to go off)!'"

Then, in Mat. 10:38 He instructed folks:

"**Furthermore, he who is not habitually taking his cross** (execution-stake; hanging-pole) **and then constantly following after** (behind) **Me, is not suitable for Me** (worthy of Me)."

And in 1 Pet. 2 we find echoes of both vss. 4 and 5, here, and a quote of Isa. 53:

21. **for into this you are called** (or: were invited), **because Christ also experienced [this]** (or: suffered) **over you folks** (or: for your sakes), **leaving continuously below** (or: behind) **in you** (or: with and for you) **an underwriting** (a writing under which you are to write or copy; hence: a pattern; a model) **to the end that you could** (or: would) **follow-on in the footprints of Him**
22. "**Who does not make a mistake** (Who did not perform failure; Who does no sin; Who does not construct failure to hit the target), **nor is** (or: was) **deceitful bait** (fraud; guile) **found in His mouth;**" [Isa. 53:9]. *Cf* Mk. 8:34; Lu. 9:57.

The present participle which describes these folks' actions and life-way should be noted: **continuously following**. This does not speak of a "decision for Christ" made at an altar, or anywhere else. It speaks of "keeping up with Christ," "**wherever He progressively leads**". Christ is not static; He is progressively leading humanity to a place in Him that is different from where it has been, or is now. He progressively leads us on our own path (sometimes "through the valley of the shadow of death" – Ps. 23). This corresponds to Rom. 8:14,

"**as many as are being continuously led by God's Spirit** (or: habitually brought or conducted in [the] Breath-effect which is God; progressively driven along with an attitude from God), **these folks are God's sons,**"

so Paul identifies this figurative group of 144K as "sons of God." Notice that Paul also uses the present tense, "continuously led; habitually brought in a Breath-effect; progressively driven along with an attitude from God." That rather covers it. It is the folks who are actively joined to the Vine that are with the little Lamb on Mt. Zion.

Another identifying description is that they are: "**a first-fruit in God** (by God; to God; for God)." We discussed "firstfruit," above, but I want to point out the qualifying dative phrase that follows: **in God**. There is no expressed preposition in the text, so we look to the context to determine the function of the noun case. On offer are four potential readings. In Greek grammar, this first rendering is of the function called the "locative," or, "local dative." It locates where these folks are. What comes to mind is Col. 3:3,
> "**you folks died, and your life has been hidden so that it is now concealed together with the Christ, within the midst of God**."

Now as you observe in the parenthetical expansion, this phrase could also be an "instrumental dative," and thus would be rendered: "by God." This means that God was the source of our becoming His "firstfruits." It is like saying that He is our Dad, and we are His kids. He produced us. The Vine grew us as a branch, out of Itself (Jn. 15:1). Which brings us to the last phrase where we have a similar situation of, "**in** (by; with; for; to) **the little Lamb**." God worked, and keeps on working, through Christ. Notice that I included in this phrase another option of the dative: "with the little Lamb." "With" simply gives us another nuance of our relationship to Christ. We are "with Him" on Zion. But we are also "in Him," i.e., "in Christ." Yet it was His work on the cross, and His resurrection, that made us firstfruits "by Him, for Him, and to Him."

4 Ezra 2:36-40 provides commentary that might apply to this passage:
> "Flee the shadow of this age; receive the joy of your glory; I publicly call on my Savior to witness. Receive what the Lord has entrusted to you and be joyful, giving thanks to Him who has called you to heavenly kingdoms. Rise and stand, and see at the feast of the Lord the number of those who have been sealed.... Take again your full number, O Zion, and conclude the list of your people..." (ibid p 527).

5. **And falsehood was not** (or: no lie is) **found within their mouth, for they are** (or: exist being) **without blemish** (are flawless, blameless and without defect; [some MSS omit: **for**]).

Also, the "little flock" (Lu. 12:32) of 144K who are associated with the little Lamb are termed "**without blemish**." This was a qualification for a lamb that could be used as a sacrifice (*cf* Heb. 9:14). These are those who would lay down their lives for their friends (Jn. 15:13). The only way someone could do this is by dwelling in the Vine that IS Love, because, "**apart from** (or: separated from) **[Jesus] [they] continue having ability and power to do** (make; construct; create; form; perform; produce) **nothing!**" (Jn. 15:5b). Jesus pointed the way for us in Jn. 15:10,
> "**Whenever you may** (or: should) **observe, watch over, guard and keep in view My implanted goals** (impartations of the finished product within; inward directives; interior purposes and destinies), **you will continue remaining** (abiding; dwelling) **within the midst of, in union with, and centered in My love, acceptance, fully giving of Myself, and urge toward reunion**."

Of these same folks it is said that "**falsehood is not found in their mouth**," what they speak is the true "good news." It was prophesied of their Lord, "nor was deceit in His mouth" (Isa. 53:9). These have been conformed to His image. In Eph. 4:25, Paul instructed folks:
> "**Wherefore, upon at once putting the false away** (or: being folks having at one point set the Lie off) **from yourselves** [as clothing or habits], **you folks be continuously speaking Truth and Reality**."

These folks are set in contrast to the one who speaks falsely: "**the false** (lying) **prophet**" (16:13, below). Witness to this is found in 1 Jn. 2:21, that, "**every lie is not forth from the Truth** (or: all falsehood is not [coming] from Reality)." Jesus spoke to those who fit this contrast, in Jn. 8:44,
> "**You folks, in particular, are** (exist and have your being) **from out of, and have your source in, the ancestor who cast [an object] through [someone].... Whenever he/it may be**

speaking the lie, he/it is continuing speaking from out of his own things – because he/it is (or: continues existing being) **a liar, and its father**."
So to have no falsehood or lie in one's mouth means that such a person is not speaking as an adversary, or as one who thrusts words or accusations through another person.

The last description of these folks, "**without blemish** (flawless, blameless and without defect)," is found elsewhere in the NT, in letters written to folks of the called-out covenant communities:

"**He chose us out** (or: selects and picks us out) **within Him, and in union with Him… to continuously be set-apart ones** (or: to progressively exist being sacred and dedicated people) **and flawless folks** (people without blemish or stain; blameless ones) **in His sight and presence** (or: in the midst of the sphere of His gaze) **in union with, and centered in, Love** (unrestricted acceptance with participation)" (Eph. 1:4).

"**that He Himself could place beside Himself… an inwardly-glorious and honorable called-out community… being set-apart and flawless**" (Eph. 5:27).

"**that you folks may come to be blameless ones** (those without defect), **even unmixed** (unblended; artless and sincere) **children of God – unblemished** (flawless) **people in the midst of a crooked and distorted** (as having been misshaped on the potter's wheel) **generation** (or: a twisted family which has been altered and turned in different ways so as to be dislocated), **within which** (or: among whom) **you folks are continuously shining** (giving light; or: appearing; made visible by light) **as illuminators** (sources of light; or: luminaries) **within [the] dominating, ordered System** (or: centered in a world of secular culture, religion, economics and government; or: **in union with the aggregate of mankind**)" (Phil. 2:15). [cf Dan. 12:3]

"**through His death, to place you folks alongside, down before Him and in His sight: set-apart** (holy) **folks and flawless** (unblemished; blameless) **ones**" (Col. 1:22).

"**be eager to be found [being] spotless folks and flawless ones in Him** (or: with Him; for Him), **in peace and in union with harmony from the joining**" (2 Pet. 3:14).

"**Now in and by** (or: with; to) **Him being powerful and able to keep and guard you folks from stumbling and from harm, and then to stand you flawless and blameless in the presence of His glory**" (Jude 24).

With all these witnesses, it is beyond doubt that the folks described in vs. 1, above (the 144K), ARE the called-out, covenant communities (such as those to whom this unveiling was written).

6. **Next I saw an agent** (or: messenger; a person with a message [other MSS: another agent, or messenger]) **continuously flying within mid-heaven, having eonian good news** (or: a message of goodness, ease and well-being pertaining to the ages and having the character and quality of the Age [of the Messiah]), **to proclaim the good news upon those situated** (or: habitually sitting down) **upon the Land** (or: earth), **and upon every multitude** (nation; ethnic group), **tribe, tongue, and people,**

As Jesus used parable after parable to describe the same subject, e.g., the kingdom, or the coming judgment upon the scribes and Pharisees, so here we see the Lord using different pictures to describe the same thing, just from different views. We suggest that vs. 6 is describing the 144K as agents, or messengers, preaching "**good news pertaining to the ages**." They are evangelists, pictured as "an agent/messenger **flying within mid-heaven** (i.e., in the realm of spirit and within the midst of the atmospheres of the world)." The **agent** is a symbol of the "people with the message" of Christ, Who, as the Anointed Savior, is, "**the same yesterday and today and on into the ages**" (Heb. 13:8). The location of the messenger's flight is "**within mid-heaven**," which we suggest speaks of the realm of people's minds, where the listener receives the message. Put into the symbolism of the temple complex, the mid-heaven is the holy place: the first chamber of the sanctuary, where the priests ministered and offered up prayers for the people. It was the location of the Light of the world (the 7-branched lampstand)

and the bread of Life (the 12 loaves of the presence, representing the 12 tribes). Light, bread and offering of thanksgiving were the elements that dispersed the Message of the Life of the Lamb – Who was "lifted up" for us in the first heaven, the outer court (location of the bronze altar of sacrifice, and the laver of water, for cleansing).

This message goes to "**every multitude** (nation; ethnic group), **tribe, tongue, and people**." We saw this same, all-inclusive group in 7:9, above,
> "**A vast crowd** (great multitude), **which no one was able to number, from out of every ethnic group** (or: nation) **– even of tribes and of peoples and of tongues** (languages) **– standing before** (in the sight of) **the throne... having been clothed with bright white robes**..."

That picture, in 7:9, showed us the result of the **proclaiming** done by this "corporate" **agent**, here. In the present scene, these folks are still living **upon the Land** (or: earth), and have not yet entered into the holy place of the temple (a figure of "heaven"), which is before the throne (in the holy of holies). Verse 6, here, shows the process; we saw the destiny of humanity in 7:9, above. Just as 7:9, above, followed directly after the sealing of the 144K of 7:4-8, so this picture in 14:6-7 follows the second presentation of the same 144K in 14:1-5, above. We see here the same thread that we had seen earlier, in the broad tapestry of God's reign in action. In the Unveiling, we see a continuation of the book of Acts, but it is presented in apocalyptic imagery instead of historical narrative. This is a picture of what Paul described in Eph. 3:9,
> "**to illuminate all people** (give light to everyone) **[as to] what [is] the execution of the detailed plan and household administration of the secret** (or: mystery) **pertaining to that having been hidden** (concealed) **away, apart from the ages** (or: disassociated from the [past] periods of time), **within the midst of God – in the One forming and founding** (framing, building and settling from a state of disorder and wildness; creating) **all things** (the Whole; everything)."

Paul put this in perspective, in Tit. 1:2-3,
> "**an expectation** (or: expectant hope) **of and from eonian life** (life having the quality and characteristics of, and its source in, the Age [of Messiah]; life for and throughout the ages) **which the non-lying God** (the God without falseness) **promised – before eonian times** (prior to the times belonging to the ages). **Now He manifests** (or: brought into clear light) **His Logos** (His Word; the Thought from Him; the Reason, Idea, communication and expression from Him; the discourse pertaining to Him; and the message which is Him) **in Its** (or: His) **own seasons, fitting situations and fertile moments within** (or: in the midst of) **a proclamation by a herald – which I, myself, was made to trust and believe – down from, in accord with and corresponding to a full arrangement** (or: a setting-upon; a complete disposition; a precise placing in order; an injunction) **of and from God, our Savior.**"

This gospel was not just for the Jews, it included all peoples, as both Peter and Paul discovered. This is the message of goodness which the true called-out folks were given to spread into the whole world, as Jesus instructed His followers, in Mat. 28:19-20, and again, in Acts 1:8,
> "**you folks will progressively receive power and will continue taking to yourselves ability [at, or with, the] added, full coming of the Set-apart Breath-effect** (the Holy Spirit and Sacred Attitude) **upon you folks – and you will keep on being My witnesses** (those who testify and give evidence of what they have seen and experienced; and later: martyrs; = you will continue telling about Me), **both within Jerusalem and within all Judea and Samaria... even as far as [the] end of the Land** (or: an extremity of the region, or a farthest point of the earth)."

7. **repeatedly saying in a great** (loud) **voice,**
> "**You people should reverence** (or: Be respecting and fearing) **God, and give glory to Him** (or: grant Him a reputation; give a good opinion in Him), **because the hour of His deciding**

(judging; judicial process; making-distinction-between) **came** (or: went; comes), **and you must worship the One making** (the Maker; the One constructing and forming) **the atmosphere** (or: sky; heaven) **and the earth** (or: land; ground) **and the sea and springs of water."**

The message began with the admonition that people should "**reverence** and fear **God**," which Prov. 9:10 tells us is "the starting point (beginning; commencement) of Wisdom," and which Prov. 14:27 instructs us is "a fountain of life." **Giving glory to Him** has been characteristic of those surrounding His throne in the previous visions, but now we also see that one of the reasons for giving this glory is because "**the hour of His deciding** (judging; judicial process; making-distinction-between) **came** (or: went; comes)." We will see in vs. 8 that the focus of His **decisions** is the fall of Babylon the Great.

The apparent ambiguity in the rendering: **came** (or: went; comes) is due to the fact that the verb means either to come or to go, and the tense, here, is aorist – which can be either a simple past tense, or a simple present, in English. The perspective of the reader, in regard to the historical fall of Jerusalem (vs. 8, figuratively called Babylon), would be the deciding factor. Those who read or heard this Unveiling prior to AD 70 would read/hear it as a simple present: His deciding comes. Those after AD 70 would read it as a simple past: His judging came (or: went). Folks reading this today can infer a timeless message about God's reign: His evaluating, deciding and judging always comes. But, it always comes "to pass." The effects are never permanent – only He is permanent, as are we, through being in Him.

The concept of **worship** should be understood in light of the context of the sphere of His judging: on the Land/earth (i.e., on Babylon, in the next verse, and on the little animals in the upcoming chapters), and in light of the audience relevance: everyone in the 1st century worshipped either Yahweh, Christ, Caesar, or pagan deities. This was a period of transition into the new age, with the new arrangement between God and humanity. Few at that time understood the magnitude of this change of arrangement (or: change of covenant). Notice that these folks were called and instructed (the verb is in the imperative voice) to worship the Creator: a very basic concept of God, to which all could relate. They should cease worshipping Caesar, the trade union deities, pagan deities, etc. This corporate messenger needed to **repeatedly** tell folks this, for it was a new concept to most of humanity at that time. Only the Jews worshipped just One God. This was "Reality 101." It informed the readers/listeners that this One God was "the Maker" of all that exists. There were not separate "**sea** gods" or "gods of **springs of water**."

Also take note that no specific rituals, religious markers, or requirements are mentioned here. These folks proclaim a situation that was described in Jn. 4:23,
> "**an hour is progressively coming – and now exists** (or: is; is being) **– when the true** (real; genuine) **worshipers will proceed to worship** (or: will habitually give worship to) **the Father within spirit and Truth** (or: in breath and reality; centered in the midst of [the] Spirit and a Fact; in union with attitude and genuineness, or actuality), **for the Father is also constantly seeking after such folks** (habitually searching out such ones as this; continuously looking for and trying to find lost ones to be this kind) **– ones presently by habit worshiping Him!**" Cf Acts 14:15-17.

8. **And then another, a second agent** (or: messenger), **followed, repeatedly saying,**
> "**It fell** (or: It falls)**! Babylon the Great fell** (or: falls), **because it has caused all nations** (all ethnic groups and multitudes) **to drink out of the wine of the strong passion** (violent breathing) **of her prostitution** (or: = idolatry; or: sexual acts contrary to the Mosaic Law)."

This was a word to that 1st century generation that the destruction of Jerusalem was about to happen. Notice the tense of the verb, the aorist, again: **It fell** (or: It falls)! The good news to us is that no matter what oppressive, controlling, corrupt system, organization or government arises to make us captive, the

Word of the Lord is, "It falls! Babylon the Great falls!" Babylon is the symbol, taken from Israel's history, used to signify that the leadership in Jerusalem had taken on the character of a domination system. But, once again, let us remember that when His judgments are in the earth (Isa. 26:9) the peoples learn righteousness (which is Christ). We find Peter, who was residing in Jerusalem, using this cryptic appellation in 1 Pet. 5:13a, "**The jointly-chosen** (selected-together) **called-out community** (assembly; congregation; ecclesia) **within Babylon constantly embraces and greets you folks**..."

In Ezk. 16:1-2, Yahweh said to Ezekiel, "Son of man, cause Jerusalem to know her abominations." Then he is instructed to say to Jerusalem,

> "Your birth and your nativity [was] of the land of Canaan; your father [was] an Amorite, and your mother a Hittite... in the day you were born your navel was not cut, neither were you washed... No eye pitied you... you were cast out in the open field.... Then when I passed by you and saw you polluted (or: trodden under foot) in your own blood, I said unto you, [when yet] in your blood, 'Live!' I caused you to multiply... [you] waxed great: [your] breasts are fashioned and your hair is grown – and yet you [were] naked and bare. Now when I passed by you... your time [was] the time of love [= marriageable age], and so I spread My skirt over you, and covered your nakedness. Yes, I swore unto you (= gave you my oath) and entered into a covenant (or: arrangement) with you [= married you], and you became Mine. Then I washed you with water... I thoroughly washed away your blood from you and I anointed you with oil. I clothed you... decked you with ornaments.... And your renown went forth among the heathen for your beauty: for it [was] perfect, through my comeliness, which I had put on you... But you trusted in your own beauty and played **the prostitute**... on everyone that passed by..." (vss. 3-15).

Ezk. 16:26 extends her fornications to the Egyptians; vs. 28, to the Assyrians; in vs. 29 they extend from "the land of Canaan unto Chaldea." The allusion of, "**all nations** (all ethnic groups and multitudes)," is to this chapter in Ezk. We saw "all nations" attending the Passover festival in Jerusalem, in Acts 2:5b, "**from every nation and ethnic group under the sky** (or: heaven)." *Cf* Acts 2:8-11. Prostitution and fornication are often metaphorical: they meant unfaithfulness to Yahweh, through involvements with other nations. As we will see in chapter 17, below, 1st century Jerusalem had the same failures, for there it is riding the little animal of Rome.

Verse 7 ended with an admonition to worship The Creator (The Word, Jesus, Who is Lord of All). This is the gospel's answer to the worship of the beast-system, spoken of in chapter 13, above, and vs. 8, here, explains that this Babylon system "**has caused all nations** (all ethnic groups and multitudes) **to drink out of the wine of the strong passion** (violent breathing) **of her prostitution**." This seems to be an all-inclusive statement. Babylon is a figure for the spirit of idolatry and the spirit of that which is in place of God and Christ, which has been, or is, upon every culture and in every age. In our local study of this, Mark Austin pointed out that in their drinking (participating) of her prostitution, they were really drinking wrath (God's inherent fervor and swelling passion) to themselves, thus the phrase, "**the wine of the strong passion** (violent breathing; also: = wrath) **of her prostitution**."

Another thought in the translation "strong passion" is the emphasis on the seduction of the system's passions which entangle the fool, "For the lips of a strange woman [= one that is not the true wife] drop as an honeycomb, and her mouth is smoother than oil; but her end is bitter as wormwood, sharp as a two-edged sword" (Prov. 5:3-4).

Isa. 1:21 reveals, "How has the Faithful City become a prostitute! – it was full of judgment; righteousness lodged in it; but now murderers." Verse 1 of that same chapter states, "The vision of Isaiah the son of Amos, which he saw concerning Judah and Jerusalem." In vs. 10 he goes so far as to call them Sodom and Gomorrah (recall the phrase used of Jerusalem in 11:8, above). Ezk. 23 speaks of the prostitutions of Samaria and Jerusalem, who were sisters (vss. 2 & 4). Verse 30 refers to "whoring after the heathen [nations], and because you are polluted with their IDOLS!" Basically, the prostitution involved departing from God's law and covenant so as to take up the ways of the world and become involved in their religions and idols. As to the "**wine**," in 17:6, below, John was given a picture of the same woman (which Isaiah and Ezekiel described) and he sees her "**drunken with the blood** [i.e., they were now murderers, as in Isa. 1:21] **of the saints, and with the blood of the witnesses of Jesus**." And Jesus, in Mat. 23:35, speaking to the Jews says, "**That upon you may come all the righteous blood shed upon the Land** (or: earth; soil), **from the blood of righteous Abel unto the blood of Zacharias**..."

The Christians of the 1st century could well have seen these figures in this Unveiling as referring to the leaders of the Jews, and thus, to Jerusalem. Today, we can see that since that time the history of the institutional church has been a parallel to both Israel of the OT and the Jewish leadership in the NT. The call in 18:4 below, to "**come out of her, My people**" applied physically to the Christians needing to flee Jerusalem before AD 70, but I suggest it has applied to Christians ever since, in their spirits and in their thinking – if not physically, at times – to come out of whatever situation or environment could be symbolized as Babylon. To participate in prostitution involves cohabiting with a spirit other than God – be it a spirit of religion, or any other spirit of the world. "**Adulterers and adulteresses** (= Folks unfaithful to Christ or God as your husband)! **Have you not seen, and are you not aware, that the System's friendship** (the affection whose source is this world of religion, culture, economy and government) **is a source of enmity with God** (or: hostility and hatred with regard to God; [Aleph reads: exists being alienation to God])?" (Jas. 4:4).

The phrase, "**It fell** (it falls)! **Babylon the Great fell** (falls)," here in vs. 8, was spoken of literal Babylon in Isa. 21:9, "Fallen! Fallen! is Babylon, and all the images of her gods are smashed to the ground!" In Isa. 13:19 he prophesied of ancient Babylon, "And Babylon, glory of kingdoms, proud splendor of the Chaldeans, shall become like Sodom and Gomorrah: overturned by God" (Tanakh). Jeremiah devotes chapters 50 & 51 to Babylon, and there we see many parallels to the figurative use of the name Babylon in this Unveiling. In 51:6-8 it is described as "a cup of gold... in the hand of Yahweh, making drunk all the earth..." In Zech. 2:7 we see, "Ho! Zion deliver yourself – you that dwell with the daughter of Babylon" – an echo seen in 18:4, below. We will speak more of Babylon in chapters 17 and 18, below.

9. **And another, a third agent** (or: messenger), **followed them, repeatedly saying in a great voice, "If anyone keeps on worshiping the little animal, and its image, and is progressively receiving an imprinted mark upon his forehead or upon his hand,**

Here we see another message, symbolized by another agent coming on stage, and this one ties in with chapter 13: the **worship** of **the little animal**, **its image** and **its mark**. Those who become involved with such will now have to drink a different wine: "**the wine of God's rushing emotion** (strong passion; anger)" (vs. 10, below). This also explains the imperative of "worshiping God," in the previous verse, as a direct contrast to worshiping the little wild animal, on this scene.

We should mark well the present tense of the verbs in this warning: **keeps on worshiping**; **progressively receiving**. This does not speak of a one-time event, but rather of a lifestyle. We should also consider the setting of this scene: it is a message of warning, such as those given to historical Israel by its prophets. The **third agent** does not act as a judge, but warns the people of the facts of what will happen if they keep on giving allegiance to the little animal (most likely the first animal of 13:1, above). By progressively receiving **an imprinted mark** upon one's mindset or thinking (figured by the **forehead**), eventually one's character, personality and world-view will be that of the little wild animal. Such folks would come to have a beast's image, instead of bearing the image of God. Corrective measures (therapy; treatment; purification – a burning-off of one's field: cf under vs. 11, below) will have to be undergone in order for this person to be healed and transformed to bear the image of God and reflect His glory (2 Cor. 3:18). The figure of a mark **upon one's hand** speaks to what a person does, how he or she performs or the kind of work they do. Jesus gave a similar admonition using hyperbole to describe the situation presented here in vss. 9-11. In Mat. 5 He gave warning regarding what greed, envy or lust (figured by the eye, which is just below the forehead, and directed by one's thinking) would lead a person to, and to what inappropriate or illegal actions (figured by the hand, as here) would lead:

> 29. **"So if your right eye is habitually a bait-stick which entraps you, immediately tear it out and throw it away from you! You see, it constantly brings things together for benefit and advantage in** (for; to) **you folks that one of your members should loose itself away** (may destroy itself; could come to be lost), **so that your whole body should not be thrown into the Valley of Hinnom** (Greek: *Gehenna* – the city dump [= to dishonor you by giving no burial; to treat you as a criminal]). [*cf* Jer. 31:38-40]
>
> 30. **"Also, if your right hand is habitually a bait-stick which entraps you, at once cut it off and throw it away from you! You see, it constantly brings things together for benefit and advantage in** (for; to) **you folks that one of your members should loose itself away** (may destroy itself; could come to be lost), **so that your whole body should not go off into the Valley of Hinnom** (*Gehenna* – the city dump outside Jerusalem)."

While in these two verses Jesus spoke of literal, physical judgment (crucifixion by the Romans and having one's body not buried, but simply dumped in the Valley of Hinnom) that could come upon the lawless or the rebels, our passage here in 14:9-11 speaks of corrective spiritual measures brought about that puts a person in the presence of the little Lamb, His agents, and the transforming, purifying Fire which is God Himself – as seen in the next verse.

10. **"he or she will also proceed drinking out of the wine of God's rushing emotion** (strong passion; anger) **– of the one having been mixed undiluted within the cup of His inherent fervor** (natural bent; impulse; indignation; wrath). **And he will proceed being examined** (scrutinized with the touchstone to test his "mettle") **within Fire and Deity** (or: in union with Fire, even Divine qualities) **in the presence of** (before; in the sight of) **the set-apart agents** (sacred folks with the message; holy messengers), **and in the presence of** (before) **the little Lamb."**

Jesus spoke of this time in Mat. 13:

> 40. **"Therefore, just as the weeds** (darnel) **are periodically collected together and are normally burned down** (or: up) **in a fire, thus will it be within the conclusion** (the combined final act; the joining of all parts and aspects to one end and goal) **of the age** [other MSS: this age].
>
> 41. **"The Son of the Man will progressively send off His agents** (messengers; folks with the message) **as emissaries, and they will continue gathering together out of His kingdom** (collect and cull out of His reign) **all the snares and things which entrap, as well as the folks habitually producing** (or: doing; constructing; practicing; creating) **the lawlessness.**
>
> 42. **"Next they will continue throwing them into the furnace** (oven; kiln) **of The Fire** [note: a figure of being dealt with in, and by, God; *cf* Mal. 3:2-4]**: 'the weeping** (crying and lamentation) **and the grinding of teeth' will continue being in that situation** (or: place).
>
> 43. **"At that time, the fair and equitable folks – who live in the pointed-out Way of right relationships, rightwised behavior and justice – will be progressively giving out light, as from lamps** (or: will shine forth from out of the midst), **in the same way as the sun, in union with the reign, and within the kingdom, of their Father. Let the person having ears to hear continue listening and be constantly hearing!"**

Paul may also have been speaking of what is apocalyptically described here, when in 2 Thes. 1 he wrote:
> 6. **since in regard to a person who observes the Way pointed out – a rightwised person – [it is right] in the presence of God** (or: if [it is], after all, the right thing with and beside God [= on God's part]), **to repay pressure** (or: squeezing and oppression; ordeal; trouble) **to those continuously pressuring** (squeezing; oppressing; troubling) **you folks,**
> 7. **and to** (or: for; in) **you – the folks being continuously pressed – relaxation** (ease; a relaxing of a state of constriction; relief), **together with us, within the midst of the uncovering** (the unveiling; the laying bare; the revelation; the disclosure) **of the Lord Jesus from [the] atmosphere** (or: sky; heaven), **along with agents of His power** (or: with His agents of ability) –
> 8. **within a FIRE, of flame** [with other MSS: in union with a blaze of fire] **continuously giving justice** (or: repeatedly imparting the effects of fair and equitable dealings from out of the way pointed out, while maintaining equity from what is right) **among** (or: for; in; with; to) **those not knowing** (or: perceiving) **God, even among** (or: for; in; with; to) **those not continuously listening to or paying attention and obeying the message of goodness and well-being, which is our Lord, Jesus** (or: which comes from and pertains to our Master and Owner: Jesus).
> 9. **These certain folks who will proceed paying the thing that is right** (incur justice, fairness and equity)**: ruin pertaining to the Age [of Messiah]** (or: an unspecified period of ruin or destruction; or: ruin for an age; eonian destruction having the character of the Age; or: life-long ruin) **[coming] from the Lord's face** [= the Christ's or Yahweh's presence], **even from the glory of His strength** (or: spreading from the manifestation which calls forth praise regarding, and having the character of, His strength) –
> 10. **whenever He may come and go, to be made glorious within** (to be glorified in union with; to have repute centered in) **His set-apart folks** (holy and sacred people), **and to be wondered at** (marveled at; admired) **within all the folks believing in that day, seeing that our testimony** (or: evidence), **[being placed] on you, was believed** (received with faith) **and is trusted.**

Cf 2 Thes. 2:1-12 for another allusion to our present vision.

Verses 10 and 11 figuratively describe what God's indignation, anger and strong passion are. In a book of symbols and figurative language there is no reason to suddenly assume that this passage is literal. In the books of the prophets in old covenant times, the wrath and anger were expressed literally, and we saw people killed, cities destroyed, God's people judged by heathen nations and taken into captivity. We saw a literal, historical destruction of Jerusalem by the Romans, and the burning of the temple, in AD 70. But those who were killed, died. Unless we want to say that the smoke of their testing arising "**on into ages of the ages**" was really for those 3 & ½ years that Jerusalem was under siege, I think that we need to seek the Lord for "**a spirit** (or: breath-effect; attitude) **of wisdom and revelation** (unveiling; uncovering; disclosure) **within the midst of a full and accurate experiential and intimate knowledge of Himself**
> (or: in a full realization of Him; or: within and in union with His full, personal knowledge; or: centered and resident within an added insight from Him, and which is Him)" (Eph. 1:17).

So let us examine the words and phrases in these verses.

The figure of "**drinking out of the wine**" speaks of participating in something that has an effect upon you. In vs. 8, it signified participating in the strong passion of her prostitution (idolatry), which effected a departure from God and an entering into her sins. It caused a drunkenness, a stupor, to come upon the peoples – they could not think clearly, and were led astray like the fool. This figure speaks of participating in His corrective judging – which leads to purification and transformation. The "**mixed undiluted**" signifies a severe dealing. Ps. 75:7-10 describes His judgment as "a cup full of foaming wine mixed with spices; He pours it out, and all the wicked of the land (or: earth) drink down to its very dregs..." Isa. 51:1-

19 describes this as calamities: "... ruin and destruction, famine and sword." But does it end with this destruction? Consider the next verses, 20-23,

> "Your sons have fainted.... they are filled with the wrath of Yahweh... therefore hear this, you afflicted one, made drunk – but not with wine: This is what your Sovereign Yahweh says, your God who defends His people, 'See, I HAVE TAKEN OUT OF YOUR HAND the cup that made you stagger; from that cup, THE GOBLET OF MY WRATH, you will NEVER DRINK AGAIN...'"

So, with this example, we see that God's cup of wrath here in chapter 14, also, will not last forever, but there comes an end, never to be repeated. In Jer. 25:15-38, the "cup filled with the wine of My wrath" was specified as, "the sword I will send among them," in vs. 16. Jerusalem and the towns of Judah were the first of "the nations" who were to drink out of this cup. His wrath was death and captivity (not endless torment!). This was fulfilled, and came to an end.

It happened again, to another generation, with the fall of Jerusalem in AD 70. His judgments have always happened in this life. Recall John 3:36, regarding the person disobedient (or: unpersuaded; incompliant) to the Son: "**the WRATH of God is presently and continuously remaining** (abiding; dwelling) **upon him**." That means it is right here, and right now. We can look around us at those not yet persuaded or obedient to the Son, and observe how His wrath (really, a swelling passion of His love) is continuously dwelling upon them, and they do not see His Life, at this time. Is it now the sword? Sometimes. Sometimes it is the bondage to drugs, alcohol, abuse, inward strongholds, etc. But this is not that last that we will see of these folks who experience the scrutiny and examination in His **Fire and Deity**. We find them again in 15:2, below, after they have progressively overcome from having been in the midst of the power of the little animal (the beast-like creature), having come out from under the character of its image, and from out of the influence and identity of the number of its name. It takes the purging Fire of God's character and influence to remove the dross in the smelting process (Mal. 3:2-3).

So just what is this picture of being "**examined** (scrutinized with the touchstone to test his 'mettle')"? This is a word which the common translations render "tormented." The Greek word is *basanidzō*: "to apply the lapis Lydius, or touchstone; thus: to test, examine closely, scrutinize; to try the genuineness of a thing; to rub metal on the touchstone."

The idea of examination by torture is an invention of man, not God. But the most accurate determination of the meaning of a word is from it use, so let us examine some NT contexts:

> Matt. 8:6, "Lord, my boy is prostrate in the house, a paralytic, terribly suffering (*basanidzō*)." The boy was discomforted by the ailment. Here, the KJV renders this word "tormented."

> Matt. 14:24, "... in the midst of the sea, being slammed (NIV: buffeted; KJV: tossed – *basanidzō*) by the waves, for the wind was contrary." Here the disciples are being put to the proof by a contrary storm, and it is within this trying situation that Jesus comes to them, walking upon and being an overcomer over, the lake. The Lamb is in our situation, here, as well, presenting Himself to those within this hard situation. The same situation is recorded in Mark 6:48 where the KJV says that they were "toiling" (*basanidzō*) in rowing.

> 2 Pet. 2:8, speaking of Lot being distressed by the filthy lives of lawless people, it "tormented (*basanidzō*) his righteous soul" (NIV; KJV reads "vexed"). This was a mental and an emotional stress and discomfort, not what we would call torture, as folks often paint the picture here in Rev. 14:10-11.

In 9:5, above, we saw that this word was used of the pain of a scorpion sting. In 11:10, above, the preaching of the two prophets brought irritation (*basanidzō*) to those hearing them. Then in 12:2, above, we saw the pregnant woman "tormented" (*basanidzō*) by the pain of childbirth – and as with the disciples, it is a Godly one that is being tried and tested.

In all of these instances, it is the ordinary hassles and discomforts or pains of our daily lives that are used to try, test, examine and scrutinize our "mettle." Why do we imagine it to be more for those in this situation which is symbolically described, here? It will be severe, but will it necessarily be more severe than how God's wrath was poured out in the past? In the late 1st century Christian writing, *The Didache*, we read a teaching that speaks of "examination" (although using a Greek synonym) that is a "woe" for someone who accepts alms or charity when pretending to be in need:

"Habitually give to everyone that asks anything of you, and do not demand [it] back (or: = do not make any counter-demands), for it follows that the Father constantly wills and intends to repeatedly give to all from out of His own grace-effects (= that His goods be shared with everyone). Happy and blessed is the person habitually giving according to (along the lines of) this imparted directive and implanted goal; for it follows that he or she is guiltless (or: blameless). Now alas (or: A woe): to and for the person receiving something, he or she will continue guiltless; yet the person not habitually having [real] need [yet] having constantly [received; taken] will proceed giving a cause or paying the penalty (or: = called to account) as to why he took (or: received [it]) and for what (= with what results). Now coming to be in confinement, he or she will continue being scrutinized and **examined** concerning which he or she performed (or: practiced), and 'he shall not leave from there until he has paid back the last penny [of illegitimately received alms]'" (1:5, parenthetical paraphrases: Aaron Milavec, 1989). *Cf* Mat. 5:26

This teaching, from the *Didache*, gives an example – in the negative part – of a person who is living and acting with the character and identity of a little animal, instead of the Human (the first Adam, instead of the Last Adam). All of us must stand under the scrutiny of Christ's corrective, or rewarding, judgment.

Now let us examine the phrase "**Fire and Deity**." God manifested Himself as fire to Moses in the burning bush (note: the bush was not destroyed, but the ground was MADE HOLY – Ex. 3:5). He was a pillar of fire to lead Israel by night in the wilderness (Ex. 13:21, 22, *et al*). He appeared as tongues of fire on the Day of Pentecost (Acts 2:3). Consider these other witnesses:

"**For even OUR GOD** [is] **a continuously** (or: progressively) **all-consuming FIRE**" (Heb. 12:29).

"**He will proceed immersing** (baptizing) **you folks within Holy Spirit and FIRE!**" (Matt. 3:11).

We suggest that the figure of fire in this verse is a symbol for God Himself. But what about the word, **Deity**? The Greek word is *theion*, the neuter form of *theios*, which means "Divine, Deity, the Divine Nature, or of and from God." Now the physical element is sulphur, "that is, divine incense, since burning brimstone was regarded as having power to purify and to avert contagion" (Vincent). But here we see an immersion into God's Nature and His Character. It is the second death that will end with resurrection Life: a transformed existence in Him.

The picture is one of Divine cleansing and purification. This is judgment, a decision regarding those who need the cleansing from the mark, the character and identity of the beast system, in all its manifestations. Some tie this in with the judgment of Sodom and Gomorrah in Gen. 19:28, or like Edom in Isa. 34:8-10, but neither of these areas are still burning, and Jude 7 uses the former as an example of eonian judgment (or: "**fire pertaining to the Age** [i.e., the Age of Messiah]).

In Ezk. 16:53 God speaks of "[bringing] back their captivity, the captivity of Sodom and her daughters, " and in vs. 55, speaking to Jerusalem, "When your sisters Sodom and her daughters shall return to their former estate, then you and your daughters shall return to your former estate." Jerusalem was restored after her Babylonian captivity. She stands as a witness for others.

Returning to the Unveiling, here in 14:10, note the environment of this examination – "**in the presence of** (before; in the sight of) **the set-apart agents** (sacred folks with the message; holy messengers), **and in the presence of** (before) **the little Lamb**." This picture calls to mind Jn. 5:
> 22. "**for neither is the Father presently** (progressively; constantly) **separating and making a decision about** (evaluating; judging) **anyone, but rather, He has given all sifting and decision-making in the Son** (or: has granted all judging by the Son; has handed over all evaluating of issues to the Son),
> 23. "**to the end that everyone** (or: all mankind) **may continuously be honoring the Son** (or: would habitually value, and constantly find worth in, the Son), **correspondingly as they may be continually honoring the Father**... Cf Mat. 16:27

Who do these "**agents**" represent? Notice that the phrase "**set-apart agents**" can also be rendered: "sacred folks with the message; holy messengers." I suggest that this is speaking of the called-out communities who have been seated together with Christ in the heavenlies (Eph. 2:6), right here on earth. Notice my comment that is inserted in vs. 11: day and night are representations of time elapsing on earth, as the earth turns. The setting was described in vss. 6-7, "**those situated** (or: habitually sitting down) **upon the Land** (or: earth), **and upon every multitude** (nation; ethnic group), **tribe, tongue, and people**.... **must worship the One making** (the Maker; the One constructing and forming) **the atmosphere** (or: sky; heaven) **and the earth** (or: land; ground) **and the sea and springs of water**." Both idolatry (worship of the little animal and its image) and true worship were happening in the same place and at the same time: here on earth. In this book of visions, it was specifically the Land of Palestine/Israel.

Recall that **fire** proceeds out of the mouths of the **two witnesses** in 11:5, above. Then Obadiah 17 speaks of deliverance on Mt. Zion, and in vs. 18 says that "the house of Jacob SHALL BE A FIRE, and the house of Joseph A FLAME, and the house of Esau [figure of the flesh] for stubble, and they shall kindle in them and devour them" (cf 1 Cor. 3:12b). This is a figure of the work of the set-apart agents here in 14:10. We see them spoken of again in Jude 23,
> "**be continuously delivering** (or: repeatedly rescuing and saving, restoring to health and wholeness) **others, snatching them from out of the midst of the Fire; be repeatedly extending compassionate mercy in reverent fear, while hating and radically detaching from even the garment having been stained** (or: spotted) **from the flesh** (= the alienated human nature; = the self that was formed and controlled by the System)."

Yes, when the Spirit indicates that the work of the Fire is complete, we snatch them out of their situations and in compassion extend love, grace and mercy (Rom. 11:32b).

We see another picture of these folks in Heb. 1:7, where we have a quote from the Psalms:
> "**He is the One making His agents** (messengers; folks with the message) **spirits** (or: Breath-effects), **and His public servants a flame of fire.**" [Ps. 104:4]

This is an example of Hebrew parallelism – the second line being a restatement of the first, but in a different figure; the figure is a reference both to the priests, as "public servants," and to the called-out community, figured as the lampstand in the Tabernacle, in 1:20 above, and referencing Acts 2:3 – there being "tongues as if of fire" burning on the lamps in the one case, and upon the people in the second case; the agents speak a message of words that are "spirit," the effect of the Breath. Then, in Heb. 1:14,

"**Are not all people public-serving Breath-effects** (or: spirits; winds), **being sent forth unto attending service because of those folks being about to progressively inherit deliverance** (or: receive the allotment of salvation, health and wholeness)**?**"

So we, being one spirit with the Lord (1 Cor.6:17) we are His "public-serving Breath-effects" being sent forth to serve others with the life of Christ, the fruit of love. We are characterized as His "flame of fire."

But some of these agents will,

> "**hand over such a man, with the adversarial [spirit]** (or: by the opponent; or: to *satan*), **into a loss of the flesh** (or: an undoing and destruction of this [estranged human nature]; a loss of [his "dominated existence" – Walter Wink]) **– to the end that the spirit may be saved** (rescued; delivered; restored to health, wholeness and its original state and condition): **within the midst of and in union with the Day of** (or: in this day from, or, which is) **the Lord**" (1 Cor. 5:5).

Another example is 1 Cor. 3:13-15 where we see that God's fire does not destroy a person,

> 13. **each one's work will make itself to be visible in clear light** (or: will become apparent), **for the Day will make [it] evident** (show [it] plainly). **Because it is being progressively unveiled** (continually revealed) **within the midst of Fire, and the Fire, Itself, will test, examine and put to the proof** (or: prove by testing) **what sort of work each one's exists being.**
> 14. **If anyone's work which he built upon [it] will remain, he will receive wages** (pay; compensation).
> 15. **If anyone's work will be burned down, he will incur a loss** (sustain the damage; forfeit [it]), **yet he himself will be saved** (rescued and delivered; healed and restored to health; returned to his original state and condition), **and as in this way – through Fire!**

Peter admonishes us, in 1 Pet. 4:

> 12. **Beloved ones, do not repeatedly feel like strangers to the burning** (= the action of the Fire) **within and among you folks, which is habitually happening to you with a view toward your being put to the test** (or: which is repeatedly coming into being in the face of a proving trial for you; which is progressively birthing itself to an examination in you), **as though a strange thing or a foreign occurrence is repeatedly walking with you folks.**

Another aspect of the environment of the "**Fire and Deity**" (later seen as the "lake or pond of Fire and Deity" in 20:10, below) is the presence of **the little Lamb** (Who is the Anointed Savior, "**Jesus Christ: the same yesterday and today and on into the ages**" – Heb. 13:8). Consider that it does not say that they are before "the judge," or in the presence of "the king," but that they are with **the little Lamb**. As with the serpent on the pole in the wilderness (Num. 21:9; Jn. 3:14), all they will have to do is look to the Lamb that paid the price for their sins, and they will be healed. In Isa. 45:22, Yahweh gave the command: "Turn toward Me and be saved." Arthur Eedle instructs us concerning this verse, "The Hebrew text shows a **double imperative**. In other words we are presented with a **double command**" (The Wellspring #23, 5 June 2017). This experience in the Fire and Deity is Christ dragging them to Himself (Jn. 12:32). We should also remember what Jesus said of Himself and of His purpose, in Jn. 3:17,

> "**For God does not send forth His** [other MSS: the] **Son as an Emissary, or Representative, into the world** (or: System; aggregate of humanity) **to the end that He should continuously separate and make decisions about the world** (or: would at some point sift and judge the System, or the aggregate of humanity), **but to the contrary, to the end that the world would be delivered**
>> (or: that the System could be healed and made whole; that the ordered arrangement should be restored to health; that the aggregate of mankind may be saved – rescued and re-established in its original state): **through Him!**"

We see another application to the Nu. 21/Jn. 3:14 connection in 2 Cor. 3:18, as WE behold Him and are being transformed:

> "**But we all, ourselves – having a face that has been uncovered and remains unveiled** [note: as with Moses, before the Lord, Ex. 34:34] – **being folks who by a mirror are continuously observing, as ourselves, the Lord's** [= Yahweh's or Christ's] **glory** (or: being those who progressively reflect – from ourselves as by a mirror – the glory of [our] Owner), **are presently being continuously and progressively transformed into the very same image, from glory into glory – in accord with and exactly as – from [the] Lord's Breath-effect** (or: from [the] Spirit and Attitude of [the] Lord [= Christ or Yahweh])."

Considering the context of 2 Cor. 3, this may refer to the transformation from the glory of Moses, into the glory of Christ; or, it may be speaking of a from-time-to-time transfiguration from the glory of humanity into the glory of the Anointing, on an individual basis.

11. **And so the smoke of** (or: from) **their examination and testing by the touchstone continually ascends on into ages of the ages** (or: indefinite time-periods which comprise the ages). **And those continually worshiping the little animal and its image – and if any one continually receives the imprinted mark** (carve-effect; emblem) **of its name – they, continually, are not having rest day and night** [comment: day and night are representations of time elapsing on earth; cf Heb. 4:1-16].

It speaks here of this going on "DAY and NIGHT." In other words, since it also happens at night they will have **no rest** from the dealing of God, in this situation. This phrase speaks of the situation on earth, and the ages speak of time. The rotation of the earth also creates the sense of time. It is the earth itself that is the location and the environment of their judgment. In Mal. 3:1 we see that "the Lord, Whom you seek, shall suddenly come to His temple." Remember that these visions in the Unveiling have corresponded to the Tabernacle/Temple shadow. Mal. 3:2, 3 says, "for He is like A REFINER'S FIRE, and like fuller's soap; and He shall sit AS A REFINER and purifier of silver: and He shall purify the sons of Levi, and purge them as gold and silver.... And I will come near to you to (for) judgment" (vs. 5). The point of the fire is purification and refining. He will burn out our pride and our wickedness; they "shall be stubble: and the Day that comes shall burn them up" (Mal. 4:1).

That "**the smoke... ascends on into ages of the ages** (or: indefinite time-periods which comprise the ages)" shows that this is an ongoing process for all humans that continue being born during the ages to come (cf Isa. 34:9-10, "night and day... unto an age-time... unto generations... unto a long time..."). Everyone needs this process, and it has been happening ever since God came to dwell among us. Humanity is God's great opus, and His testing of His work continues on until all are in His image.

Verses 10 and 11 may also be allusions to Heb. 6:4-8, and thus be applied to believers or followers of Christ that turned back to Judaism or to some other religion (vs. 6). Note that the ground was very fertile, and had been producing good crops (vs. 7):

> 7. **For you see, a piece of land** (or: ground; soil; = a field; or: a territory) **which is drinking** (= soaking in) **the rain often coming upon it, and producing vegetation** (pasture; produce) **fit for and useful to them through whom it is habitually being cultivated, [is] also continuously sharing in and partaking of a blessing from God;**
> 8. **but when repeatedly and progressively bearing forth thorns and thistles [it is] disqualified** (worthless; unable to stand the test [for planting a new crop]) **and [is] close to** (or: near) **[the] curse** (or: a down-prayer and a corresponding wish against [the situation] is at hand), **the end** (the resultant situation) **of which [the thorns, briars, thistles and the field is] into [a time of] burning** (or: = the field ends up being burned off).

Here we will quote from my comments on these verses, in *John, Judah, Paul and ?*,

"The first thing to keep in mind is that the subject of this metaphor is "**a piece of land**," or, a field, Greek: *gē*. The present crop of thorns and thistles – which will be burned off – is not the subject.

"It is the ground, the land, which correlates to the people of vss. 4-6. This field (= these people) had drunk in "**a blessing from God**." It (= this group) was good soil and had produced crops "**fit and useful**" to the Farmer (a figure of God; *cf* John 15:1; Jacob [James] 5:7). However, it is now bringing forth useless crops. What is to be done? To sow seeds in among all those thorns and thistles would be to waste the seeds, the effort, and the time (a whole season of potential growth). The time-honored agricultural practice is to burn off an area of land to clear it of weeds, grasses, etc. that would be competition to the crop that folks wanted to grow. The ash from the burned plants adds both nutrients and mulch to the soil, and an ideal situation is the result.

"The word **curse** is *kat-ara*. *Ara* is a prayer, or a wish. *Kata* has the basic meaning of "down," and the extended meanings of "corresponding," or "against," (among others). My parenthetical expansion presents optional renderings that help to give insight to this word that is ordinarily rendered just "curse." Our author may be referencing the situation described in Gen. 3:17-19. There, in the LXX, the same word *gē* (soil; ground; land; territory) is used to describe Adam, and a strengthened form of the same word is used for "curse." Furthermore, we have the identical phrase "**thorns and thistles**" given as the resulting produce of the soil/land in that judgment. So the folks who are "falling aside along the way" (vs. 6) have returned to the situation and condition from which they had been rescued. They were living as though the Messiah had not yet come – even as those who were of the ethnic multitudes (the Gentiles) and did not know Yahweh. Their condition was the same situation as the plight of humanity: ugly and worthless "fruit."

"During the ministry of Jesus to Israel, many folks came to Him and partook of His teachings, healings and miracles, and then later fell away and returned to their former way of life. John the baptizer spoke of the Holy Spirit baptizing folks with fire, garnering the grain but burning up the worthless part of the dead plant (Lu. 3:16-17). The dead plant (chaff) was a figure of the old covenant religion and existence which brought forth the Seed (the Messiah). But this metaphor by John was also a prophecy that would be fulfilled with the Romans burning Jerusalem in AD 70. Our author here (writing before AD 70) may have had this prophecy in mind, or the prophecy given in the figure of the destruction of Jerusalem as the burning of Babylon (Rev. 17:16).

"But during that first century generation, many were allured by the Judaizers and the Gnostics. These folks would also fit the descriptions given here in our text. With all of these possible applications, we need to keep in mind that this "judgment" has a positive end in view for the subject of the metaphor: the piece of land (a time-honored figure for Israel in the OT), the field, the territory. These folks would receive a new planting of the Word, and would again produce good fruit by the Spirit of God. Isa. 26:9b makes a profound statement:
> "For when Your judgments are in the earth, the inhabitants of the world learn righteousness" (NRSV)
> "For Thy judgments bring men light, till very pagans learn the right" (Moffatt)
> "For as a light will Your judgments be to the earth; the dwellers of the habitance will learn righteousness" (CVOT)
> "When your judgment dawns upon the earth, the world's inhabitants learn justice" (The New American Bible).

The Hebrew word for "earth" used in this Isaiah verse is *erets*, which also means "land." So this verse can be either specific as referring to Israel as the land, or general, as a matter of principle.

In the first clause, both Moffatt and the CVOT draw upon the LXX" (Harper Brown Pub., 2013, p 130-40).

Another allusion, here, may be to Ps. 17:
> 3. You assay (test, so as to find proof concerning) my heart (the core of me); You visit and watch over, to inspect and to guard, by night; You burn and purge me (or: set me on Fire), and thus, injustice (lack of right; absence of what has been pointed-to) is not found within me – so that my mouth would not speak of or babble about the works of the people (the actions from humans; the deeds pertaining to the peoples). (LXX, JM)

12. **In this place is** (or: Here exists) **the persistent and patient endurance** (the steadfast, humble remaining-under for support) **of the set-apart folks** (or: from the saints) – **the people continually keeping watch upon** (guarding, observing, having custody over) **God's implanted goals** (impartations of the finished product within; inward purposed directives and inner destiny) **and the faith of Jesus**
> (or: the trust pertaining to Jesus; the loyalty belonging to Jesus; the faith which belongs to and comes from Jesus; the conviction which is Jesus; the reliability of and from Jesus).

So in this environment of Fire and Deity is the place for the persistent and patient endurance of His saints – as we deal with these folks and rescue them, when the work is done. Peter refers to these situations and says that we should not be surprised "at the burning within and among you..." (1 Pet. 4:12), and Paul says that no trial comes to us "except those which are part of the human situation" (1 Cor. 10:13, Barclay translation).

We are all the same – none are righteous, no, not one – all have gone astray. We all need the same purifications. All souls (= people) are God's (Ezk. 18:4); Christ covered (1 Pet. 4:8) and washed away the sins of the whole world (1:5, above; Ezk. 16:9; 1 Cor. 6:11; 1 Jn. 1:7; 2:2). Therefore, we must be baptized in Holy Spirit and Fire now (Mat. 3:11), or be tried with Fire and Deity, later.

Traditionally, vs. 12 has been separated off from vss. 9-11 and thus it has been made to be an enigmatic, stand-alone statement that left the reader wondering what John meant. Various attempts to solve that seeming enigma have been offered, over the centuries since John penned this vision, but by including it within the context of the previous three verses it eliminates the supposed "enigma," and enlightens the whole passage. The purpose of this observation is not to explain the setting, context or purpose of these four verses, but is to simply point out that vs. 12 points back to vss. 9-11, instructing us that "**In this place**" – i.e., the place of the examination and testing of the person who is "**continuously worshiping the little wild animal and its image**" (vs. 9, and note the present tense of the verb) – "**is** [the very place of] **the persistent and patient endurance** (the steadfast, humble remaining-under for support) **of the set-apart folks**, and **from** the saints." We can also observe that "**this place**" is "in the presence of the set-apart agents and in the presence of the little Lamb" (i.e., Christ), in vs. 10. Said another way, "this place" is a place of "Fire and Deity (or: Divine qualities; Greek: *theion*)," and it is where **the set-apart folks** do their work – which takes **persistent and patient endurance**.

Now let's look at these people described as, "**the people continually keeping watch upon**, guarding, observing and having custody over **God's implanted goals**, His impartations of the finished product within, as well as His inward purposed directives and inner destiny." These are the folks that "have the message" (vs. 10b, above) and are in the presence of those who bear an animal's image (vs. 9, above) instead of God's image. The **set-apart folks** in this verse are **the set-apart agents** of 10b, above. As God's transforming Fire (God Himself) and His Divine qualities do their work on the folks bearing the mark and image of the little animal, the sacred messengers (the called-out, covenant communities) are there to inform them about God's goals and inner destiny for them that He is presently writing upon their hearts. Their work is to instruct them about the impartation of the finished product (Christ in them, so that they will bear God's image) which is the result of God's Fire. The listeners and viewers, by the message of the sacred folks in their presence, are in the process of being transformed by the renewing of their minds so that they, too, will have their Father's name written in their foreheads (vs. 1, above).

This whole picture which John was observing is a reflection from Mal. 3 where Yahweh is described as being "like a refiner's fire" (vs. 2b). There, Malachi is instructed that Yahweh will "sit as a refiner and purifier of silver [note: the touchstone – vs. 10, above – was used to grade precious metals]: and He shall purify the sons of Levi, and purge them as gold and silver that they may offer unto Yahweh an offering in righteousness" (vs. 3). The setting in Mal. 3 was Judah and Jerusalem (vs. 4), just as it is in this book of Unveiling. See my article, "The Location of the Lake of Fire," below, following this commentary.

Our calling is to offer "**persistent and patient endurance**" while giving "steadfast, humble remaining-under [the situations which, and the people whom, we encounter] for SUPPORT" of their needs. We are His agents (or, vessels) of mercy (Rom. 9:23). It is in the very place of their experiencing the fire of His love. But people do not usually recognize it as an expression of His love. All they know is the pain, the sorrow, the regret, the loss, etc. So this is why our Father has brought them into our presence: to be tended and informed by us, His agents.

Heb. 12 ends with the reminder that "**our God is a consuming Fire**" (vs. 29). When we understand that He sends the burning into our field with the purpose of cleansing it of competing weeds (Heb. 6:7-8), we should also realize that a farmer does not then throw away a field that he has just burned off. No, he now plants a new crop of Good Seed into it. All of the pictures and metaphors are given to us to teach us His ways for this life. It is here that we need His "course adjustments" and "dross removal." But of course, if it doesn't happen in this life, He is the same for the ages as He was yesterday and is today (Heb. 13:8). He will always be "the Anointed Savior (Christ Jesus)," and in the ages to come we will be there for folks, exhibiting His grace and mercy to them and informing them to "just look at the little Lamb, and be healed." If we can imagine the scene in Jerusalem on that historic Day of Pentecost that is described in Acts 2, we will see 120 people gathered together and it will look like a lake of fire. Verse 3 instructs us that, "**progressively dividing and self-distributing tongues – as if of fire – were seen by them, and He** (or: it; or: [one]) **sat down upon each one of them**." They had become human lampstands: the light of the world. Above, 1:20 figuratively pictured the called-out, covenant communities as lampstands, and then 2:1 informs us that the resurrected Christ is "**continuously walking about within the midst of the seven golden lampstands**," i.e., within the communities of His body. This visionary scene in the Unveiling is an allusion to Dan. 3:25 where One like the Son of God was seen "walking in the midst of the fire" with the three Hebrew men. My wife, Lynda, added this observation:

> "When they were thrown into the fire, it didn't destroy them, it DELIVERED them! The fire burned off their bonds and set them free.... This is a manifestation of sons with THE SON. There was no smell of smoke or burning... the Word says that when we lose our life, we actually FIND IT. God would have us see the whole; His all-embracing beauty that leads us into a radiant Hope! His intent is not to destroy, but to save. This is the liberty that sets all of creation free. It is the Anointing (Christ) fire of His HOLY Spirit, burning away the dross of those things which have 'fallen short' of HIS GLORY!" (emphasis original)

She then recalled Ps. 12:6,
> "The little thoughts and messages (*logia*) of and from [the] Lord [= Yahweh] are harmless, acceptable and pure thoughts (messages; ideas; little Words): [they are] silver having been purified and refined by fire, tested and put to the proof (and thus, approved) in the Land and for the earth – one having been, and being, cleansed and purified seven times" (LXX, JM).

Note that the perfect participle in the final clause of this verse is singular, and so it is referring to the Land and the earth.

13. **Next I heard a Voice out of the atmosphere** (or: sky; heaven), **saying,**
    "Write: 'From the present moment (from this time; from now; henceforth) **the dead ones [are] blessed** (happy) **folks – those continuously dying within the Lord!'" "Yes, indeed,"** the Spirit continues saying, **"to the end that they may rest themselves from out of their wearisome labor** (travail; toilsome exhaustion), **for their works** (actions; deeds) **are continually following together with them."**

    > [Sinaiticus & p47 omit ναι, "yes, indeed," so an alternate rendering would be: "Happy {are} the dead ones – those continuously dying in the Lord! Henceforth, the Spirit says that they may rest, for their actions follow with them."]

This speaks of **those dying within the Lord** as being **blessed** and **happy** (two meanings of the same Greek word). Depending upon which text we follow, one could say either that this **blessed** and **happy** condition, or state, originated in that "**present moment**," and we can assume that this is a result of the work of the little Lamb. Or it says that **the dead** folks which are **dying in the Lord** are **happy**, and **henceforth the Spirit says that they may rest**. Whichever, if the "dead folks" are "**happy ones**" it indicates a state of feeling, of awareness, no longer a state of sleep such as some would believe. If these may "**rest**," I suggest that they have entered a sabbath condition, into the promised rest of Heb. 4:1-11. This could also be an allusion to Wis. 4:7, "Now though a just and righteous person should come to an end early (reach his destiny prematurely), he or she will continue being in rest" (LXX, JM). Their rest after "**wearisome labor** (travail; toilsome exhaustion)" follows the example of their Master, i.e.,

> "**our Lord Jesus Christ's act of faithfulness** (the process of the trust; the work from the loyalty), **wearisome toil of love** (the beating and cutting off involved with the acceptance, and with the urge toward union; the burdensome labor from the total giving of the self to [others]) **and persistent patient endurance from expectation, in front of our God and Father**" (1 Thes. 1:3).

However, rather than this being an existential pronouncement, or an ontological description, we should probably read this statement metaphorically – as with all the other symbols and figures in the Unveiling. We, the living (in Christ) are those who have died and been buried in Him (Rom. 6:2-8), and we are blessed and happy because we continue living with Him (Rom. 6:8b). So let us recall what Jesus said, in Jn. 11:25-26,

> "**Jesus said to her, "I am the Resurrection** (or: the standing back up again; the Arising) **and the Life. The one progressively believing and habitually putting trust into Me, even if he may die-off** (or: die-away), **will continue living** (or: will proceed being alive)! **And further, everyone** (or: all mankind) **– the person presently living and progressively trusting-and-believing into** (or: regularly experiencing convinced faith into the midst of; being constantly faithful unto) **Me – can by no means** (or: may under no circumstances) **die-off** (or: die-away), **on into the Age [of Messiah].**"

It seems best to actually quote from Rom. 6, here:

> 3. **Or are you continuing to be ignorant that as many of we who are immersed** (or: were at one point soaked or baptized) **into Christ Jesus are immersed** (or: were then baptized) **into His death?**
> 4. **We, then, were buried together** (entombed together with funeral rites) **in Him** (or: by Him; with Him), **through the immersion into the death, to the end that just as Christ was roused and raised forth from out of the midst of dead folks THROUGH THE GLORY of The Father** (or: which is the Father), **thus also we can walk around within newness of life.**

5. **For since** (or: You see, if) **we have been birthed** (have become; have come to be) **folks engrafted and produced together** (or: planted and made to grow together; brought forth together; congenital) **in, by, to and with the result of the likeness of** (or: the effect of the similar manner from) **His death, then certainly we shall also continue existing [in and with the effects of the likeness] of The Resurrection,**
6. **while constantly knowing this by intimate experience, that our old, former humanity is crucified together with [Him], to the end that the body of the Sin could and would be rendered useless and inoperative for us to no longer continually be a slave to the Sin,**
7. **for you see, the One at one point dying** (or: the person at some point experiencing death) **has been eschatologically released and rightwised away from the Sin.**
8. **Now since we died together with Christ, we are continuously believing** (relying; trusting) **that we shall also continue living together in Him** (by Him; for Him; to Him; with Him).

Paul also said, in Phil. 1:21, "**to be dying [is] gain** (advantage; profit)." And here can be tied-in his words in 1 Thes. 4:14, the encouragement that, "**since we habitually believe that Jesus died and then arose, thus** (in this manner) **also, through Jesus, God will continue** (or: be repeatedly and progressively) **leading together with Him the folks being made to sleep.**" No matter on which level we take these words, they are a blessing, and as we experience them, we will be happy.

This **Voice** comes as an apparent interjection into the scene just described, above. That scene described a "second death" experience for those who had been marred by the thinking and environment of the domination system, and the allurement of their own love-starved, inner cravings (Jas. 1:14). These folks are dying to the beast influences and alien characteristics, and since being within the midst of Fire and Deity, they are "**dying within the Lord.**" Yes, "**[It is] fearful** (a fear-inspiring [experience]) **to suddenly fall-in – into hands of a continuously living God**" (Heb. 10:31), and indeed, "**[there is] a certain fearful taking** (or: receiving) **in hand from out of a separation for a decision, leading to a judging, and a zeal of Fire being about to be continuously and progressively eating** (or: consuming) **the hostile folks** (the ones under the circumstance of being in an opposing position)" (Heb. 10:27), but we have been given our Father's perspective:

> "**He is continuously bringing [things; situations] together** (progressively collecting unto profitability) **– unto this: to mutually partake of His set-apartness** (or: to take by the hands together, share and mutually receive from the holiness and sacredness which is Him). **Now on the one hand, all discipline** (instruction; child-training; education) **with a view to** (or: face to face with) **what is presently at hand, does not at the time seem to be joyous or fun, but to the contrary [is] painful and full of sorrow and grief; however afterwards** (or: subsequently), **to, for, in and by those having been gymnastically trained** (= working-out while stripped of self-works) **through it, it is constantly and** [cf Jas. 3:18] **progressively yielding fruit which has the character and qualities of peace and harmony – which equates to fair and equitable dealings in rightwised relationships which are in line with the Way pointed out, and justice** (also: = from covenant inclusion and participation)" (Heb. 12:10b-11).

We find a correlating "beatitude" formula in 19:9, below:
> "**And then he is saying to me,**
>> '**Write: "Blessed** (Happy) **ones [are] the folks having been called** (the summoned ones; those being invited) **into the wedding supper** (meal) **of the little Lamb."**'"

Now that pronouncement follows 19:3, below, where we read,
> "**And so the smoke from her goes on rising up on into** (or: progressively ascends into the midst of) **the ages of the ages** (or: crowning time-periods of the ages; indefinite eras which comprise the ages),**" – which corresponds to vs. 11, above, in our present chapter.

Then another "beatitude" is found in 20:6, below, that fills in the picture even more:
> "**Blessed and happy and set-apart** (holy) **[is] the one holding** (or: having) **a divided part** (a piece) **within the first resurrection** (rising up) – **upon these the second death has no authority** (does not continue holding right or privilege; possesses nothing from the sphere of existing), **but rather, they will continue being priests belonging to God and to the Christ** (or: priests pertaining to God and the Anointed One; or: God's, even Christ's, priests; or: priests from God and Christ), **and they will continue reigning and exercising sovereign influence with Him**…"

This further describes the work of the "agents" of vs. 10, above: "exercising sovereign influence (or: ministering Christ's reign) through being priests to those who are undergoing God's testing in the purifying Fire of Himself.

Since "**their works are continually following together with them**," we might conclude that these works have survived the fire and must be of the quality of gold, silver or precious stones (1 Cor. 3:12). We may also have an allusion, here, to Paul in 1 Tim. 5:
> 24. **The failures** (shortfalls; errors; mistakes; deviations; sins) **of some people are obvious** (portrayed before the public), **continually proceeding into a separation and then a decision which leads into judging, yet also, for certain** (or: with some) **folks, they are normally following upon** (or: after; = they have not yet caught up with them; or: they are habitually accompanying [them]).
> 25. **Similarly, the beautiful acts** (the excellent deeds; the fine and ideal works) **are obvious** (portrayed before the public), **and yet the ones habitually holding otherwise** (having [acts or deeds] in a different way) **are not able to be continuously hidden.**

We find an echo in 22:12, below, of the ideas presented here, and by Paul,
> "**Consider this! I am continuously** (or: habitually; progressively; repeatedly) **coming quickly** (swiftly), **and My wage** (reward for work; compensation; recompense) **[is] with Me, to give back** (give away; render; pay) **to each one as his work is** (= what he deserves)."

Observe the present tense of continued or habitual action in the verb "coming." Rewards and corrections are each ongoing events within His present reign – nothing waits for some imagined "final end." This statement in 22:12 is followed by another "blessing formula" in 22:14,
> "**Blessed** (Happy) **folks [are] the ones** (folks; people) **continually washing their garments** (equipment; [other MSS: continually doing His implanted, inner goals]), **to the end that their authority** (or: right out of Being; privilege) **will continue being over** (or: upon) **the tree** (pole) **of The Life, and they may at any point enter into the City by the gates**."

We know from Heb. 12:22 that this is a present situation, for we have come to, and are presently at, this City. It is all about here, and now. The future takes care of itself, as it continuously comes to us.

Before moving on, we should note what Beale calls a "ground clause" or, "the logical basis" (ibid p 768), because it is introduced by the conjunction, "**for**." The sense is that they are happy and blessed, and now they may **rest**, "because" (or: grounded upon the fact that) their **works** and deeds "**are continually following together with them**." We might say that they reap a harvest from what they have sown. Paul spoke of this in Gal. 6:
> 7. **Do not be continually led astray** (or: Stop being caused to wander and being deceived); **God is not one to be sneered at** (to have a nose turned up at; to be scorned, mocked or treated like a fool), **for "whatever a person is in the habit of sowing, this also he will reap,"**
> 8. **because the person continually sowing into the flesh of himself** (= his estranged inner being), **will progressively reap corruption** (spoil; ruin; decay) **forth from out of the flesh** (= the estranged inner being);

(or: the one habitually sowing into the flesh [system], of himself will continue to reap decay from out of the flesh [system];)

yet the one constantly sowing into the spirit (or: the Breath) **will be progressively reaping eonian life** (life having the characteristics of the Age [of Messiah]; or: life from the Age that lasts on through the ages) **forth from out of the spirit** (or: the Spirit; the Breath; that attitude).

Of great importance in Paul's words, here, is the source, or ground, from which one will reap who sows into the flesh: his or her harvest will be corruption, in the realm of flesh. This applies individually and corporately (especially as seen in the corruption of the "flesh system" in AD 70). Again, it is about the here and now – or else in some sort of flesh of one's next existence (to be determined by our Father). Verses 14-20 present a new section which pictures One like a son of man sitting on a cloud, and two separate harvests that are parallel, but with some differences. Terry sees them as distinct visions (ibid p 410). Beale (ibid p 770) regards this section as the 6th vision (of a series begun at 12:1, above) that will be followed by a 7th section (15:2-4, below). Barclay viewed 14-20 as depicting judgment in two metaphors that were familiar to Jewish thought (ibid p 115). Beasley-Murray interprets vss. 6-20 in accordance with the six agents that make appearances on the stage of one vision, which he terms "the day of wrath" (ibid p 1297). D'Aragon's assessment is similar, seeing this section as "the proclamation of imminent judgment (ibid p 484-5). Bullinger concurs with these last three scholars, keeping all of chapter 15, below, as a separate vision (*The Companion Bible*, p 1903), in contrast to Beale.

Let us examine how the two harvests compare (as per Terry, ibid):
    a) both have actors in the atmosphere (cloud/temple in heaven)
    b) both have a harvesting tool (sickle)
    c) both involve "another agent" that gives a command "in a great voice" to reap/gather
    d) both agents come from the temple complex
    e) both crops are ripe for harvest
    f) both harvests are reaped, with the grapes going to the wine press.

The question that addresses us: Is this apocalyptic repetition, with both describing the same event (similar to Hebrew parallelism), or are these contrasting harvests that depict different messages?
Both harvests are allusions to Joel 3:13, in a context of judging "all the nations from round about" (vs. 12),
    "Send forth the sickle, for the harvest is ripe. Come, tread, for the wine-trough is full…," and then, in vs. 14, "For near is the day of Yahweh in the vale of decision!" (CVOT)

14. And then I saw, and look: a bright, white cloud. And upon the cloud One like a son of man (= a human; or: = the eschatological Messiah figure) **continually sitting, having a golden wreath upon His head and a sharp sickle** (instrument for cutting off, cropping and harvesting) **in his hand.**

The allusion, here, goes back to Jesus, in Mat. 24:30b,
    "**they will proceed in seeing for themselves 'the Son of the Man progressively coming and going, upon the clouds of the atmosphere** (or: sky),**' with power and ability, as well as much glory.**"

Both there (in Mat. 24) and here (in 14:14) are allusions to Dan. 7:13-14, "the Son of man coming with the clouds." Chilton suggests that the cloud here, in vs. 14, is the same cloud as seen in 10:1, above, and says, "Let the Beasts do their worst – the Son of Man has ascended in the Clouds and received everlasting dominion over all peoples and nations!" (ibid p 371). The fact of it being "**a bright, white cloud**" may signal an allusion to Mat. 17:5,
    "**While [Peter] was still speaking, a cloud composed of light** (or: a cloud full of light; a cloud radiating light; a luminous cloud; an illuminated cloud) **suddenly brought shade upon them** (or: cast a shadow over them; overshadowed, or enveloped them)."

We can also recall His departure, in Acts 1:9. "**He was suddenly exalted** (or: raised upon [them]; lifted up to a higher status), **and then a cloud from underneath [Him] took and received Him** (or: He was at once hoisted on and fully lifted up, and even a cloud took Him in hand, from below)." That John saw Him sitting, here, suggests that His throne is in the midst of our atmosphere. His *parousia* (presence) is with us.

In Mk. 4:29, Jesus said,
> "**Now at the time when the fruit may give from its side** (or: whenever the crop should commend, hand over, and deliver up [the grain]; = be ripe), **he at once progressively sends forth the sickle, because the harvest has stood at hand and provides itself** (or: the reaping has taken its place at the side; or: the harvest is present and stands ready)."

In Mat. 9:36-38, Jesus said to His followers,
> "**Now upon seeing the crowds, He felt deep feelings, tender affection and compassion about them....At that point He then says to His disciples, 'The harvest** (matured crop) **[is] indeed vast** (much; huge), **and yet the workers** (= the harvesters) **[are] few. Therefore, urgently ask – even beg – the Owner** (or: Master; Lord) **of the harvest so that He would thrust out workers into His harvest.'"**

It would seem that He was connecting the crowds to the harvest, and thus, the "harvest" is a metaphor for gathering folks into His reign. In Jn. 4:35-38 He put it this way:
> "**At that point He then says to His disciples, 'The harvest** (matured crop) **[is] indeed vast** (much; huge), **and yet the workers** (= the harvesters) **[are] few. Therefore, urgently ask – even beg – the Owner** (or: Master; Lord) **of the harvest so that He would thrust out workers into His harvest.... I, Myself, sent you men off as commissioned agents** (or: representatives; emissaries) **to be constantly harvesting** (or: reaping)…"

We will consider, below, the judgment-oriented uses of "the harvest" in the OT, but the way Jesus seems to have used the metaphor, this would seem to be a positive, Christ-oriented (kingdom) application which had a 1st century context – one that these quotes of Jesus seemed to be imminent to His time, and urgent for His followers. In the parable of the sower, in Mat. 13, He locates the time of the harvest at the end of the old-covenant age, "**[the] harvest is [the] bringing of the parts together to one destined end** (or: a combined final act; a purposed consummation; a putting together of the final product; a joining of all aspects into the fruition of the goal) **of an age**" (vs. 39).

The One on the cloud is unmistakably a harvester, for He is holding a **sickle**. It may be symbolically significant that this word is used 7 times in this passage about harvesting. And 1:7, above, indicates that this image is of Christ, the Son of man. The **golden wreath upon His head** tells us that He is an Overcomer (3:21, above; 17:14, below), and in Jn. 16:33 Jesus informed us to,
> "**be confident and take courage! I, Myself, have overcome and conquered the System** (dominating world; organized arrangement of religion and society; aggregate of humanity) **so that it stands a completed victory!**"

15. **Next, another agent** (or: messenger; person with a message) **came forth out of the Temple, repeatedly crying out in a great voice to the One sitting upon the cloud,**
> "**You must send Your sickle and You must reap** (gather in the harvest), **because the hour to reap comes** (or: came), **because the harvest of the Land** (or: earth) **is dried** (parched; withered; thus: = ripened)."

That this agent comes out of the Temple (the body of Christ) is symbolic of the people of the covenant communities who call to Christ to bring in the harvest, as Jesus instructed His disciples to do in Mat. 9:38 (Chilton, ibid p 372-3). His **sickle** is a figure for His servants, His "instruments," {as was Paul, '**a vessel**

of choice to Me (or: a picked-out and chosen **instrument** by and for Me) **to lift up and carry My Name before the ethnic multitudes** (or: nations; Gentiles; non-Israelites)" – Acts 9:15} and the rest of us, who are to be, "**containers or instruments of mercy**" (Rom. 9:23).

Let us now consider Joel 3. It follows Joel 2:32, "And it will be that everyone who shall call on the Name of Yahweh shall escape, for in mount Zion and in Jerusalem deliverance shall come to be, just as Yahweh says; and among the survivors are those whom Yahweh is calling." Then ch. 3 begins:

> "For behold, in those days and in that season, when I shall TURN BACK the captivity of Judah and Jerusalem, I will also convene ALL THE NATIONS, and bring them down to the Vale of Jehoshaphat. And I enter into judgment with them there concerning My people, even My allotment Israel, whom they disperse among the nations..." (vss. 1-2, CVOT).

Then in vss. 12-17,

> "All the nations shall rouse and ascend to the Vale of Jehoshaphat (the valley where Yah judges), for there will I sit to judge all the nations from round about. Send for the sickle, for the harvest is ripe, come, tread, for the wine trough is full, the wine vats run over, for great is their evil. Throngs, throngs in the vale of decision! For near is the day of Yahweh in the vale of decision! Sun and moon are somber, and stars gather their brightness, and Yahweh shall roar from Zion, and from Jerusalem shall He give forth His voice, and heavens and earth shall quake. Yet Yahweh is a refuge for His people, and a stronghold for the sons of Israel. And you shall know that I am Yahweh, your Elohim (God), tabernacling in Zion, My holy mountain, and Jerusalem shall come to be a holy [city], and aliens shall pass in her no longer" (CVOT; additions, mine).

Now let us bring here what Heb. 12:22a unpacks for us:

> "**you folks have approached so that you are now at Mount Zion – even in a city of a continuously living God; in Jerusalem upon heaven'**..."

The verb, "**have approached... you are now at**," is in the perfect tense. The action happened in the past as a completed action, and now exists in that completed state. Here the writer is affirming what Joel said in 3:17, just quoted: "I am Yahweh, your Elohim, **tabernacling** in Zion, My holy mountain, and Jerusalem..." With the coming of the kingdom at the advent of the Messiah in the 1st century (as this verse in Heb. 12 affirms), we now see and understand that of which Joel foretold. We saw that Peter affirmed this in Acts 2:16.

The language and figures in Joel are similar to those here in this chapter, and Joel's passage speaks of Jerusalem's restoration, which literally may have first referred to the post-exile period. Now here, in the Unveiling, we see Jerusalem once again in a judgment cycle in the time of the early called-out, covenant communities. But we also now see the reality of Joel's shadow: it is the heavenly Zion, the spiritual Jerusalem, from which Christ roars as the Lion of the tribe of Judah, and gives forth His voice, shaking both heaven and earth – the temple and the people (Heb. 12:26). Now He is a stronghold for "the Israel of God" (Gal. 6:16); now we are His tabernacle/temple, and "the heavenly Jerusalem" IS a "holy city," as Joel 3:17 prophesied. Will the multitudes (nations) yet again be judged in a figurative "valley of decision"? I think that this has periodically been happening.

In John's day, it was the time for the Son of man to, "**send [His] sickle and [He] must reap** (gather in the harvest), **because the hour to reap comes** (or: CAME), **because the harvest of the Land** [Israel; Palestine] (or: earth) **is dried** (parched; withered; thus: = ripened)." So what happened in the 1st century, in the context of God's reign? First of all,

> "**Now from the days of John the Immerser until right now, the reign and dominion of the heavens** (or: sovereign rule of the kingdom of the atmospheres) **is itself continuously pressing** (or: is progressively pressing and forcing itself) **forward with urgency, and those urging and**

pressing forward [toward the goal] are one after another grasping it and then drawing it up [to themselves]" (Mat. 11:12).

We read how this "**pressing forward**" happened in the book of Acts, and also in Paul's letters. We observe in this Unveiling how the little Lamb reigns and how the multitudes gather before Him, in praise and allegiance. We will see more of this in the following chapters. But immediately following Jesus' ministry and teaching, we have the fulfillment of the Day of Pentecost (Acts 2) which was traditionally celebrated on the 6th day of the 3rd month, following the barley harvest in the 2nd month. We suggest that the grain harvest, here in vss. 15-16, symbolized people's entry into Christ's kingdom in what is recorded in the book of Acts. It extended for that entire generation (40 years), until the harvesting of the grapes, seen below, in AD 70.

16. **And so the One continuously sitting upon the cloud cast** (or: thrusts) **His sickle upon the Land** (or: earth) **– and the Land** (or: earth) **was reaped!**

We find a prediction of this in Mat. 3:12,

"**Whose winnowing fork** (or: shovel) **[is] within His hand, and He will proceed thoroughly cleaning up** (clearing, scouring and cleansing) **His threshing floor and then will progressively gather** (bring together) **His grain into the storehouse** (granary; barn), **yet the chaff** (straw and husks) **He will continue completely burning, in an inextinguishable Fire.**"

We should note concerning the "chaff," that it was the part of the plant that produced the grain, just as Israel produced the Messiah. It does not represent something bad, but something that is no longer needed, and will not be eaten or used to plant the next crop. The chaff represents the Law and the old covenant, in this picture. Personally, it represents the first Adam, within us – the hay and stubble that will not survive God's Fire. We came here via the first Adam, but it is that non-nourishing, non-Christ part of us that must be destroyed (Mat. 16:24-25a). Now Jesus speaks of another burning in Mat. 13:30, but this is something inserted into us: weeds that were never a part of us (or of His planting):

"**Allow** (or: Leave) **both to continue growing side by side until the harvest, and within the season of the harvest I will proceed to be telling the reapers, First gather the weeds together and bind them into bundles for the purpose of burning them down. But progressively gather the wheat** (or: grain) **into my barn** (storehouse)."

Again, Jesus further explained,

"**[the] harvest is [the] bringing of the parts together to one destined end of an age, but the harvesters** (reapers) **are agents** (messengers; folks with the message)" (Mat. 13:39b).

From a preterist viewpoint, we could see that "the harvest is [the] bringing of the parts together to one destined the end (*sun-teleia*: 'denoting the joining of two age-times, i.e., the closing time of one leading on to the other' – Bullinger; or: the conjunction)" of the old covenant age, with the consummation of the new age of the Messiah. Jesus spoke this before the conclusion of the Jewish age. With this view in mind, we can also see that "**the good SEED are the sons of the kingdom**" (Matt. 13:38), and this would fit the situation of the first harvest (vss. 14-16, above), for it is a dry, grain crop, and it is the figure of Christ, "coming in the clouds," who is in charge of this reaping of the Land (or: earth) here, in vs. 16. This would also be Christ protecting His called-out folks, calling them to go out of Jerusalem before the coming destruction – a harvesting, a coming out of her (18:4, below). With a harvest, there were multiple activities, each with different ends in view. There was both death, and resurrection.

Again, "**these things happened to them** [literally, in AD 66-70] **as types and were written for OUR admonition**" (1 Cor. 10:11), into whom, I suggest, the end of our age arrives. When any one of us reaches our ripe, mature age in Christ, I suspect that He comes and harvests us – either figuratively or literally. The Land is a figure of Israel, God's specific people, and is still a figure for we who have been grafted into their olive tree (Rom. 11:17).

17. Next another agent came out of the Temple [which is] resident within the atmosphere (or: within the midst of the heaven), **he, too, having a sharp sickle.**

Here we have a two-part sign: two harvests which happen on earth, but are done from the atmosphere above the earth, among the clouds. The **Temple** is also involved, so this second agent from the temple would be a figure representing Christ's body, the ones through whom the Son of man will be working, as they do the harvesting of the grapes, in the next verse. The **agent** in this verse is representative of the two witnesses, of chapter 11, above. We have God's implements of harvesting, just like Eph. 6:11 speaks of us having God's whole suit of armor. But we will see, in the next verse, that we do not act on our own, but we wait for the word to act – which may come from another member of the body who has a different gift, and different "authority" (*ex-ousia*): "right from out of Being."

Micah 4:13 speaks of a different kind and aspect of harvest, but it shows God's people being involved in the activity: "Arise and thresh, O daughter of Zion...," and Isa. 41:15 speaks of Jacob, where Yahweh tells him, "I have constituted you a threshing sledge... you shall thresh mountains... make hills like trash."

18. Then another agent, having authority upon the Fire, came forth out of the altar and uttered (or: utters) **a sound by a great outcry to the one continuously holding the sharp sickle,**
> **"You must send your sharp sickle and you must gather** (pick) **the clusters of the Land's** (or: earth's) **vineyard** (grapevine), **because her grapes are in their prime** (are at the peak of ripeness)."

Observe that we have an agent from the altar (which was outside the temple), who has the "**authority upon the Fire**." Is this fire the same fire that we saw earlier in this chapter – the Fire and Deity? Or, is this the same agent that threw fire into the earth, in 8:5, above? Does this symbol represent the cooperation in God's economy between the crushing and the fiery purging? This "authority" concerning fire was seen with the gifting of the two witnesses, and their use of this fire, in chapter 11, above. The allusion may also be to Isa. 6:6-7, where the "burning one" (*seraph*) took Isaiah's iniquity away, using a live coal (burning ember) from the altar.

The vineyard is a figure of His people, and particularly this allusion is to Israel, in the OT, where it is frequently used. Ps. 80:8, "You caused a vine to journey from Egypt... and you planted it." Isa. 5:7 informs us, "The vineyard of Yahweh of hosts [is the] house of Israel..." The grape harvest was at another time of the year from the barley and wheat harvests. The care of a vine dresser is seen in the last comment, "**her grapes are in their prime** (are at the peak of ripeness)." This is not normally an observation aimed at destroying the vineyard, but of the owner's investment in it, as we see in Jas. 5:7,
> "**Be patient** (long-tempered; long-passioned; slow to rush; or: Have long-term feelings and emotions, with anger pushed far away), **then, brothers, during the continuance of the Lord's** [= Yahweh's, or, Christ's] **presence and His being alongside. Consider! The worker of the land repeatedly receives** (takes out into his hands from within) **the precious fruit of the land, being patient** (slow to rush and with long-term feelings; with anger far from him) **upon it, during the continuance where it can receive 'an early as well as a latter** (or: late) **rain.'"**

The OT quote in the last clause, here, implies the purpose of these rains: "that you may gather in your corn and your wine and your oil" (Deut. 11:14).

But to get wine, grapes must be crushed. We receive the wine of the new covenant in His blood because He was "bruised for our iniquities" (Isa. 53:5). He drank the cup that the Father gave Him to drink (Mat. 26:29, 42). But recall that Jesus said to His disciple, "You shall indeed drink of the cup that I drink of; and with the baptism that I am baptized with shall you be baptized" (Mark 10:39). Those figures spoke of His cross. His disciples are to also take up their crosses. Judgment BEGINS at the house of God (His temple; His people; 1 Pet. 4:17). Most commentators understand the harvesting of the vineyard as a figure of judgment, as Joel 3:13, above, indicates: "for the wine trough is full, the wine vats run over, for great is their evil." With the vineyard metaphor historically tied to Israel, one can connect the dots to see this as a harvesting Jerusalem (the place of Jewish leadership) in judgment, in AD 70. But let us consider another line of interpretation.

The Feast of Ingathering (or: Tabernacles; Coverings; Lev. 23:34), in the 7th month of the Jewish calendar, was the final, yearly celebration in Israel's religious/agricultural calendar, within which was the Day of Atonement (Sheltering; Covering) which Jesus fulfilled (as described in Heb. 9). It followed the grape harvest which happened in the 6th month. The 7th month also began the plowing and the beginning of sowing the new crops of wheat and barley, which continued into the 8th month which also brought the fall rains (*Holman Bible Dictionary*, 1991, pp 486-7). Joel 2:21-27a proclaimed hope for Israel:

> "Fear not, O Land; be glad and rejoice, for Yahweh will do great things. Be not afraid, you beasts of the field, for the pastures of the wilderness will sprout... a tree will bear its fruit; fig and vine will give their strength. Be glad, sons of Zion... for He will give you.... a former rain and a latter rain, as formerly. The threshing sites will be full of grain, and the vats will overflow with grape juice (or: new wine) and oil.... Then you will eat and eat and be satisfied.... You will know that I [am] within Israel..."

This would describe the period at Ingathering, since it includes the grape harvest. So with this allusion in mind, we could conclude a positive meaning for this section of the vision. J. Preston Eby reaches this conclusion:

> "The winepress is not evil but good. The Son of man did not come to destroy grapes, but to obtain grape juice. He did not come to squash men and destroy them in a winepress so that their blood will be squeezed out of them in some horrible judgment and execution. He came instead to bring forth a *life-flow* from them so that the new wine of the kingdom can be poured out as a drink offering and a transforming, life-giving power to all men everywhere!" (Kingdom Bible Studies: From the Candlestick to the Throne, Part 173).

Seasons and cycles are an inherent part of God's plan of the ages. Times and seasons have always regulated agricultural economies. Both OT and NT employ metaphors from this lifestyle to instruct us about our Father's dealings with us. One season ends, and another begins, just as the planting of the fields comes after the year's final harvest – of the grapes. But the burning off of a field (Heb. 6:8b), means that the field is ready to be planted again – and the subject of this metaphor is "the field," a "piece of ground," not the thorns and briars that overgrew it. Fire does not destroy the field, it cleanses it. The squeezing of the grapes is the means to produce the New Wine for the New Wineskins (Lu. 5:37-38). The destruction of Jerusalem was the discarding of the old wineskin; the covenant communities (which began as a part of Jerusalem) became the New Wineskins. When Jesus ministered in the 1st century, Hos. 10:1 was the situation: "Israel is a ravaged vine" (Tanakh); "... a regressing vine" (CVOT). Jer. 48:32b-33 proclaimed,

> "A ravager has come down upon your fig and grape harvests.... I have put an end to wine in the presses, no one treads [the grapes]..." (Tanakh).

Likewise in Isa. 16:10b, "No more does the treader tread wine in the presses – the shouts I have silenced" (Tanakh). Jesus came to a fig tree and found leaves (which indicated that at least firstfruit or immature fruit should have been there), but he found no figs (Mk. 11:13). There was no fruit from the leadership of the Jews (Mat. 3:8; 21:43). Following this particular thread, the grape harvest here in 18-20 would not seem to apply to physical Jerusalem of the 1st century, for it had no fruit.

To have wine, the grapes must be pressed. In Jn. 16:33 we saw that, "**Within the System** (dominating and controlling world of culture, religion, economy and government; or: among and in union with the aggregate of humanity) **you normally have pressure and stress** (or: continually have squeezing; repeatedly have tribulation and oppression)." Eby pointed us to Acts 14:22 as an echo for our present context:

> "**It continues binding and necessary for us to enter into the reign of God** (or: God's kingdom; the sovereign activities which are God) **through the midst of many pressures, squeezings, tribulations, afflictions and oppressions**."

In the 1st century, both the new covenant communities, and then in the late 60's, Jerusalem (and the Jewish leadership) experienced treading, pressure and squeezing. God had a positive plan for all of it. But Jesus had given a "sign" of a new wine, a figure of a new arrangement/covenant, which did not require the growing of grapes, nor their harvest or crushing. It was at a wedding, in Cana of Galilee (Jn. 2:1-11). This new wine required "new wine-skins" (Mat. 9:17; Lu. 5:38).

19. **And so the agent cast** (or: thrusts) **his sickle into the Land** (or: earth), **and picks** (gathers) **the vineyard of the Land and he casts [it; them] into the great wine-press** (trough; tub) **of God's strong passion** (rushing emotion; or: anger).

One interpretation of this **agent** is that this one represents Rome, in their judgment of Jerusalem in AD 70. The meaning of it having come, "**out of the Temple [which is] resident within the atmosphere**" (vs. 17, above) is that this judgment came from God's throne, fulfilling the prophecy given by Jesus (Mat. 24; Lu. 21; Mk. 13). We can take away the insight to see God behind everything that comes into our lives. As Job said, "Though He may slay me, yet will I trust Him" (Job 13:15a). "Shall we receive good at the hand of God, and shall we not receive evil?" (Job. 2:10). "Shall there be evil in a city, and Yahweh has not done it?" (Amos 3:6b). Trust and knowing God are the source of these extreme statements. Paul said of the passing of the old and the coming of the new:

> "**Yet further, all these things [are]** (or: the Whole [is]) **forth from out of the midst of God – the One transforming us to be completely other [than we were]**
>> (or: bringing us into another place or state of being; changing us to correspond with other [perceptions and conceptions]; altering us to be conformed to another [person]; changing us from enmity to friendship; reconciling us) **in Himself** (or: with Himself; by Himself; to Himself; for Himself), **through Christ, and giving to us the attending service of, and the dispensing from, the transformation [for folks] to be other [than before]**" (2 Cor. 5:18).

Thus, with the wine-press being "**of God's strong passion**," and that it was "trodden outside of the City [i.e., Jerusalem]," vs. 20, and that this is a huge harvest of the vine, and with this "vine" producing such a vast amount of "**blood**," the preterists see this figure being applied to the judgment which God brought upon the Jews at the close of that age. By this vision the called-out communities of the 1st century would have been warned about what was coming: a good harvest for them; bad news for the Jewish leadership and Jerusalem. "The treading of grapes was a common OT figure for the execution of divine wrath (see Isa. 63:3; Joel 3:13)" (Mounce, *NIV Study Bible*, ibid p 1941). Lam. 1:15b put it this way,

> "The Lord has trodden the daughter of Judah as in a wine press."

The Tanakh reads Isa. 63:4, "For I had planned a day of vengeance – and My year of redemption arrived!" (punctuation, mine). In the Christ Event(s), there was both salvation and judgment. In the physical destruction of Jerusalem, there was the spilling of a lot of blood. In the spiritual realm of the New Jerusalem, there was a mighty outflow of the "wine" of the Spirit from the pressured called-out folks. Both concurrent events were the results of **God's strong passion** (rushing emotion; or: anger).

20. **Then the wine-press** (or: trough) **was trodden** (or: is trod as a path) **outside of the City, and blood came** (or: comes; goes) **forth from out of the trough** (or: wine-press) **up to the horses' bridle – from a thousand six hundred stadia** (a fixed standard of measure; a racecourse; a stadium).

The **wine-press** is OUTSIDE the City. In 11:2, above, it IS the City that is trodden. Does this indicate "phase two" of His judgment process? Each in their own order? It was literally outside the City where He suffered. Prinzing wrote, "First it was written of our Redeemer, 'I have trodden the winepress alone; and of the people there was none with me' (Isa. 63:3). And then He apprehends unto Himself an 'election of grace,' a firstfruits, who are drawn 'forth therefore unto Him without the camp, bearing His reproach' (Heb. 13:13). And now the great 'winepress experience' faces all creation – warring fiercely against all impurity, treading out the self-will and rebellion of man" (ibid).

> "Now all the ends of the world shall remember and turn unto the Lord: and all the kindreds of the nations shall worship before You. For the kingdom is the Lord's: and He is Governor among the nations." (Ps. 22:27-28)
>
> "For God has allowed us to know the secret of His plan, and it is this: He purposed in His sovereign will THAT ALL HUMAN HISTORY shall be CONSUMMATED IN CHRIST, that everything that exists in Heaven or earth shall find its perfection and fulfillment in Him" (Eph. 1:9-10, Phillips)

It has been pointed out that 1600 stadia is the approximate length of Palestine, from north to south. This would be a figure that all of God's people must eventually drink of His cup. The distance, 1600 stadia, is literally about two hundred miles. Though exaggerated, as is characteristic of apocalyptic literature, it also informs us that it is describing a relatively small, localized scene – a limited setting. It is the Land of Israel, into which the agent of vs. 19 "**cast his [harvesting] sickle**" in order to "**gather** (pick) **the clusters of the Land's vineyard**" (vs. 18). It was a harvest of judgment upon Jerusalem (**the City**, vs. 20). The volume of blood that came from the wine-press (**up to the horses' bridle**) creates a picture of many people being slaughtered – which happened when Rome destroyed "the City" in AD 70.

Jesus had pointed out how the scribes "sat in Moses' seat" and had come to dominate the people. We read in Mat. 23:4,

> "**they habitually tie up and bind heavy loads** (or: burdensome cargos), **and then constantly place [these] as an addition upon the shoulders of people** (or: mankind) **– yet they, themselves, are not willing to budge or put them in motion with their finger** (or: = to 'lift a finger' to help carry them)!" (cf Lu. 11:46, where He identified them as "experts in the Law")

In regard to the judgments pictured in Revelation, Borg suggests that,

> "we find the same twofold focus that marks so much of the Bible as a whole: radical affirmation of the sovereignty and justice of God, and radical criticism of an oppressive domination system pretending to be the will of God. The domination system that John indicts is a subsequent incarnation of the domination system that existed in Egypt [cf 11:8b, above, "**The Great City – whatever, spiritually, is normally being called 'Sodom' and 'Egypt' – where also their Lord was crucified**"] in the time of Moses and then within Israel itself in the time of the classical prophets. It is the same domination system that Jesus and Paul and the early Christian movement challenged" (ibid p 291-2; brackets added).

In our local study, Mark Austin saw in this chapter a correlation with Ps. 1. In vs. 1-3 we have the description of the righteous: those 144K on Mt. Zion with the Lamb. In vs. 4-6 we have a picture of the judgment of the unrighteous (those not yet in Christ): like chaff, driven by the wind (spirit); unable to stand in the judgment; sinners (those missing the mark) not yet able to be part of the congregation on Mt. Zion with the sprits of just folks having been perfected in Christ. Mark also pointed out that in Ps. 1:6 it is the WAY of the ungodly, i.e., their PATH and their way of life, that shall perish.

Something to remember, when considering both of these harvests, is that these harvests are the intended goal of both crops. We plant and cultivate in order to harvest. So does God. As we consider this chapter, from vs. 6 through vs. 20, 6 agents take the stage. Symbolically, the number 6 is humanity's number, as we saw above, and may be a figure of the human involvement in this passage. Verses 6-13 present the Good News and the judgment of symbolic Babylon. It is possible that vss. 14-20 present pictures of this same subject matter, with vss. 17-20 giving more details on the judgment of Babylon/Jerusalem. What happened in Jerusalem, in AD 70, is a prophecy of what God will eventually (in His own time and season) do when religious oppression or domination systems become fully "ripe," in His view. He is the SAME: yesterday, today and on through the Ages.

However, J. Preston Eby presents a viable argument against this picture of the grape harvest being figurative of people being killed in battle, and against the term "**blood**" being a reference to literal blood. Remember, this is a book of symbols. Here, Eby says, "It's not about a war, my friend, it's about THE HARVEST!" (ibid). He cites Jn. 6:53 as an example for "blood" being a figure for "life" or Spirit:

> "**unless you folks should at some point eat the flesh of the Son of the Human** (the Son of man; = the eschatological messianic figure), **and then would drink His blood** (or: since you would not eat the flesh which is the Human Being, and further, drink His blood), **you are continuing not holding** (or: habitually having or presently possessing) **Life within yourselves**."

Then he says this about the blood and the distance of "**from a thousand six hundred stadia**,"

> "The blood flows to the horse bridles for a distance of sixteen hundred furlongs. Now sixteen hundred furlongs are equal to about one hundred and eighty five miles, which is approximately the distance from Dan to Beersheba — the length of the land of Israel. So in type it represents a life-flow that reaches not just to mount Zion, nor to the temple on mount Moriah, nor to the capital city of Jerusalem, nor to the land of Judah, but unto *all the Lord's people* from one end of His "land" unto the other!" (ibid).

Here, I would also point out the figurative number "1000," that we saw in the plural in 5:11, 7:4-8, 11:13, 14:1, 3, and will see in 21:16. In the singular we find it in 11:3, 12:6, 14:20, and 20:2-7. All of these contexts can be seen as references to God's people and things of His Spirit. It has also been noted (Terry, ibid p 413) that 1600 is 40X40, 40 being the number of testing or judgment (Gen. 7:12; Nu. 14:34). Next, note the literal meaning of **stadia**: a racecourse (but could be used to refer to a stadium, which surrounded a racecourse). This calls to mind Paul's use of this word to symbolize one's life in following the Lord. 1 Cor. 9:24,

> "**those progressively running, on the race-course within a stadium, are indeed all progressively running** (or: constantly and repeatedly racing), **yet one normally** (= each time) **grasps** (takes; receives) **the contest prize** (victor's award)? **Be habitually running** (progressively racing) **so that you folks can** (may; would) **seize and take [it] down in your hands!**"

Was the use of this term a subtle reference to Paul and his use of the term? See his use of the metaphor of "running" in 1 Cor. 9:26, Gal. 2:2, 5:7, Phil. 2:16 and then, in Heb. 121:1b,

> "**we can and should through persistent remaining-under** (or: relentless patient endurance and giving of support) **keep on running the racecourse** [Gal. 5:7] **continuously lying before us**."

Eby also pointed out that a fluid literally coming up to a horses bridle would make it impossible for the horse to remain on its feet. He sees here the horse as a symbol of the strength of the flesh, and Dan Kaplan pointed out that a horse would fit the category of a little animal. Miriam sang, "the horse and his rider has He thrown into the sea" (Ex. 15:21). *Cf* 15:3, below, and "the song of Moses" (Ex. 15:1ff). Taking these thoughts together, we may have a picture of the life of the Spirit of Christ overwhelming the power of the little animal, throughout the Land (i.e., in all of its inhabitants). However we wish to view the grape harvest, it is a positive event!

This next chapter, 15, functions as an introduction to the pouring out of the shallow cups of God's passion (chapter 16).

Chapter 15

1. **Next I saw another sign in the atmosphere** (or: sky; heaven) – **great and wonderful** (marvelous): **seven agents continuously holding the last seven plagues** (impacts; blows; strikes), **because within them God's strong passion** (or: rushing emotion; or: wrath) **is** (or: was) **brought to its goal** (has been brought to its purpose; is completed; is finished; was ended; has accomplished its destined aim).

In Lev. 26:21, Yahweh instructs Israel, "Yet if you folks walk contrary to Me, and will not obediently listen to Me, I will bring seven times more plagues upon you – in accord to your mistakes, failures and sins." Terry (ibid p 414) also points us back to the similar scene in 8:1-2, where we see 7 agents with 7 trumpets. The 7th plague, blow or impact (16:17-21) brings the fall of Babylon, proclaimed in 14:8, above. These visions are one double-edged theme (the victory of Christ; the fall of Babylon-Jerusalem) that is interwoven and interlocked in a movement toward the goal: the New Jerusalem (21:2ff) and the making of all people anew (21:5), and then the presentation of the Bride (21:9ff), i.e., the covenant communities of Christ.

Here is another set of sevens. It could be that these are thus described to indicate that this is another view of what is happening with the seven trumpets (= messages), above. The idea of 7 is repeated in the phrase "**last 7 plagues**" – or the completeness of the "blows, impacts, strikes and smitings" that were to fall on that generation, "**because within them God's strong passion** (or: rushing emotion; or: wrath) **is** (or: was) **brought to its goal** (has been brought to its purpose; is completed; is finished, was ended; has accomplished its destined aim)." But as we take an overview of this scene, we see echoes of Exodus in the plagues brought against Egypt through the rod of Moses. Recall the purpose of those plagues as given by Paul in Rom. 9:17,

"**For the Scripture is saying to Pharaoh that,**
'**Into this itself** (or: For this very thing) **I roused you forth** (I awakened and stirred you to come out), **so that I may** (or: would) **display and demonstrate in you My power and ability, so that My Name would be thoroughly proclaimed** (preached and published far and wide) **within all the land** (or: in the entire earth).'"

The completion of God's strong passion would of necessity be a part of the "PLAN of the ages" (Eph. 3:11, Diaglott). "And this is in harmony with God's MERCIFUL PURPOSE for the government of the world when the times are ripe for it – the purpose which He has cherished in His own mind of restoring the whole creation to find its one Head in Christ; yes, things in heaven and things on earth, to find their one Head in Him" (Eph. 1:9-10, Weymouth).

Let us see if we can find a purpose statement here, in chapter 15. I would suggest that vs. 4, below, points the way:

"**O Lord** [= O Yahweh], **who may by no means** (or: who may in no way) **fear You and glorify** (bring good reputation to) **Your Name? Because [You] only** (alone; without accompaniment) **[are] appropriately pious, sanctioned, and benign** [Vat. 2066 reads: Set-apart (Holy)]. **Because the multitudes** (nations: ethnic groups) **WILL continue arriving, and they WILL**

> **continue worshiping in Your presence** (in Your sight; before You). **Because the results of Your rightwising act and the effects of the eschatological deliverance which is You** (effects of Your fairness and equity, just decrees and decisions; actions according to the Way pointed out, results of justification, actualization of justice and rightwising of relationships) **are manifested** (or: were brought to light; were made to appear)."

In 16:9, below, we will see the purpose again stated, though unfulfilled at that time, "... **and they did** (or: do) **not CHANGE THEIR MINDS** (their way of thinking) **to give Him glory** (or: to have a good opinion of Him)." The same idea is repeated in 16:11. God's judgments are always brought to cause humanity to change their minds, have a paradigm shift and then return to Him. But for this to happen the kingdoms of this world must first be broken; Babylon must fall. In looking at the present scene beginning in 15:1, we need to discern the concept, idea and message which "seven agents holding the last seven plagues" presents to us.

If we take the preterist position on this vision, we will have to come to the conclusion that this vision is in the context of the fulfillment of judgment prophesied against Jerusalem, and that these agents poured out their shallow cups during the period of AD 68-70. The fall of Babylon (a figure of corrupt Jerusalem, "which then was" – Gal. 4:25), which we see in the latter part of this current vision, was a figure of the fall of Jerusalem. God made a conditional promise to Israel at Mara, under the old covenant, in Ex. 15:25-26,
> "There He made for them a statute and a judgment, and there He probed them, for He said: IF you shall hearken, yea hearken, to the voice of Yahweh your Elohim (God) and do what is upright in His eyes, and give ear to His instructions and observe all His statutes, then all the illnesses which I placed on the Egyptians I shall not place on you, for I am Yahweh, your Healer" (CVOT).

But again, in the 1st century we see that they did not keep the "IF," and these bowls echo the "illnesses" which He placed on the Egyptians. Moses prophesied of Israel's demise in Deut. 4:26-28,
> "I call heaven and earth to witness against you this day: that you folks shall soon utterly perish from off the land whereunto you go over Jordan to possess it.... and Yahweh shall scatter you among the nations..."

But even here Moses gives a promise of restoration, in vs. 30-31, "When you are in tribulation, and all these things are come upon you, even in the latter days, if you turn to Yahweh your God and shall be obedient unto His voice, (for Yahweh your God IS A MERCIFUL GOD), He will not forsake you..."

So this is the "back story" to God's **strong passion**. His strong passion is that of a Father's love for His children. The Greek word is *thumos*, which comes from *thuō*, which means "to rush." The noun refers to an emotion of the mind or soul that can make a person rush into action, or have "strong passion." This can be positive, as in making love, or rushing to give aid or rescue; or, it can be a negative emotion, such as "anger," or it's extreme, "wrath." Correction must come, when a child goes astray, but consider the Lord's motive:
> "**for whom the Lord** [= Yahweh] **is LOVING** (urging toward reunion and acceptance), **He is continuously and progressively educating** (or: disciplining; child-training), **and He is periodically scourging every son whom He is taking alongside with His hands** (accepting; receiving)." (Heb. 12:6; cf Prov. 3:11-12; cf Job 5:17; Ps. 94:12; Phil. 1:29)

This is a vision of God's loving passion, for we see in Heb. 12:7, "**as to sons is God Himself continuously bringing [discipline and child-training] to you**." Let us keep in mind that here John calls what he sees, "**great and wonderful**." They have a **goal, purpose and destiny** that is Good News to humanity, for this dealing with His people in the 1st century demonstrates that He will do the same for all, for Paul instructs us that Christ's **goal** was, "**to the end that He may frame** (create; found and settle from a state of wildness and disorder) **The Two into One** [i.e., Jew and Gentile; circumcision and uncircumcision – Eph. 2:11-15a] **qualitatively New and Different** [p46 & others: common] **Humanity centered within the midst of, and in union with, Himself, continuously making** (progressively creating) **Peace and Harmony** (a joining; = shalom)" (Eph. 2:15b).

Heb. 12:9b instructs us, "**To a much greater extent, shall we not be continually placed under and humbly arranged and aligned by the Father of the spirits** (or: the Progenitor of breath-effects and Mentor of attitudes)**? And then we shall proceed living** (or: progressively live)!" [*cf* Nu. 27:16; Eph. 6:2-3]. Verses 2-4, below, present the outcome of the ministry of "**the seven agents' seven golden bowls** (or: shallow cups)" that we see, in vs. 7, that one of the four **living ones** gave to the 7 agents.

2. **And I saw as it were a glassy** (crystalline) **sea having been mixed with Fire, and the folks** (or: those) **continually overcoming** (being progressively victorious; presently conquering) **– from out of [the power and influence of] the little wild animal** (creature; beast)**, and from out of [the nature of] its image, and from out of [the identity of] the number of its name – standing** (or: having made a stand) **upon the glassy** (crystalline) **sea, continuously holding God's lyres** (harps).

The **glassy, crystalline sea** is the same stage setting that we saw in 4:6, above, and so we know that this corresponds to the holy place, before God's throne (the ark of the covenant, with its mercy seat) in the midst of the temple. This describes the realm of the Spirit, or heaven, within and among His covenant communities (which are His temple). These folks have been enabled to "walk, actually **stand**, on water." It is calm (God's peace is in them, to arbitrate in their hearts – Col. 3:15) with no tossing waves as are those not yet joined unto the Lord. Notice that the sea has been **mixed with Fire** (a figure of God). This is a picture of humans having had God mixed into their lives. We saw a picture of this same place and these same people (**in the presence of the little Lamb**, on His throne) in 14:10, above, but there it just described the environment of those who had been marked by the little animal (the contrarian nature of the false persona – the lost and estranged human identity). But now we see them having been enabled to **overcome**, through the mixing in of His Fire and Deity – their baptism in the Holy Spirit and Fire is complete, and now they **stand** in Christ (Eph. 6:13).

It is God Himself, and His holy Nature that made them "progressively victorious" **from out of [the power and influence of] the little wild animal** (its religion, society, culture, economics and government). They were by His Grace released **from out of [the nature of] its image** (the image of the earthy – 1 Cor. 15:49), and set free **from out of [the identity of] the number of its name** (a reference back to 13:17, above)! This scene is an allusion to Israel's victory over the little animal of Egypt, after they crossed the Red Sea. It also points to the victory of both martyrs and survivors over the little animal of Rome, or the Zealots, and further on to the remnant communities on through history to this present day, where they are still opposed by the little animal spirit of Orthodoxy and the heresy hunters.

Now they participate in making music with the twenty-four old folks of 5:8b, above. The orchestra of **lyre**-players has grown. Terry (ibid p 415) sees this as an allusion to Israel's victory song, in Ex. 15:20, that was "accompanied with the sound of tambourines." They sing odes (vs. 3, below), like the 144, 000 in 14:3, above, but here it is the song of the two covenants (Moses and the little Lamb) that probably recount the tales of the old and praise the glory of the new. They are the rebuilt Tabernacle of David (which was the type in which musical instruments were introduced as a part of praise before the presence of Yahweh) which had fallen down into ruin (Acts. 15:16).

As noted above, being in the presence of the little Lamb and the transforming power of His fiery Deity (14:10-11) brings **continual overcoming** within a person. Recall that the little Lamb is **within the midst**

of the throne (5:6, above). The testing and the overcoming always happens in His presence – the presence of the One who is a continually consuming Fire. In that throne scene, the little Lamb was standing. This brings to mind the vision that Stephen had as he was facing his final testing, being stoned to death by the little beast of Jerusalem's religious leaders (Acts 7:55-60): he saw Jesus standing at the right hand of God.

3. **And they repeatedly sing the song** (or: ode) **of Moses, God's slave, as well as** (or: even) **the song** (or: ode) **of the little Lamb, saying,**
> **"O Lord** [= O Yahweh], **The All-Strong** (Omnipotent, Almighty) **God, Your acts** (works) **[are] great ones, and wonderful ones** (marvelous ones)! **The King of the nations** (multitudes, ethnic groups; [Sinaiticus* & p45 read: King of the ages])! **Your ways** (roads, paths) **[are] just ones** (fair and equitable ones in accord with the Way pointed out) **and true** (or: real) **ones!**

We have allusions to OT passages here:
> "The works of Yahweh are great..." (Ps. 11:2a).
> "Wonderful (Marvelous) are Your works..." (Ps. 139:14).
> "Look and consider! I am contracting a covenant; before, and in the presence of, all your people I will do marvelous things" (Ex. 34:10).
> "Consider! I, Myself, repeatedly strengthen [the] thunder and habitually form (construct) wind and spirit, continually proclaiming (announcing) unto humans (people) His Anointed One, while constantly forming morning and mist, and then climbing up upon the high places of the Land (or: earth) – The Lord [= Yahweh], the All-Strong [is] a Name for Him!" (Amos 4:13, LXX, JM).

In vss. 3 & 4 we see this praise figured by an ode, a song. Note that this is one song – one ode – which is referred to as the song of Moses AND the Little Lamb. The song is the same for both of them, for Moses prefigures Christ. This is a symbol of the Law which was fulfilled through Christ, the Lamb which is God and Who takes away the sin of the world. It is a message of deliverance and salvation. This song affirms what God does (His acts are great, wonderful and right). His ways, the paths He ordains for humanity, are "just paths" and true roads (ways of reality). Who [implying no one] can but fear Him and eventually bring glory to His Name? The insight and perception displayed by this ode of praise and affirmation (their witness to the world) has been gained through the experience of having His purifying Fire mixed into their being, and into the reality upon which they stand. Their lives are proof, and are offered as evidence (witness) that the little animals of the domination systems can be overcome – people can become freed from all addictions. As Paul said, in Gal. 5:1, "**for freedom we have been set free.**"

Notice that they recognize that God is, "**The King of the nations** (multitudes, ethnic groups; [Sinaiticus* & p45 read: King of the ages])!" The alternate MS readings may have been either a scribal error, or a scribal attempt to make the proclamation more general. Naming God as "King of the nations" is harder to accept – it is too close and personal for the person with the 1st Adam thinking! But King of the ages would also be true. The statement is probably a quote of Jer. 10:6-7,
> "O Yahweh, You [are] great, and Your Name [is] great in mastery (or: might). Who would not revere (or: fear) You, O King of the nations? ... There is NONE like unto You!"

It also takes faith, trust and understanding to affirm that "**[His] ways [are] just and true.**" Humanity (and even Job!) has long questioned this. Theologians and philosophers have given this a name: *theodicy*. But those who have come through His Fire and His transforming deliverance know the reality of this affirmation.

4. **"O Lord [= O Yahweh], who could not by all means** (or: who would not in any way; = will not really) **reverence or fearfully respect You and glorify** (bring good reputation to) **Your Name? Because [You] only** (alone; without accompaniment) **[are] appropriately pious, sanctioned, and benign** [other MSS: Set-apart (Holy)]. **Because all the multitudes** (nations: ethnic groups; [other MSS: all people]) **WILL continue arriving, and they WILL continue worshiping in Your presence** (in Your sight; before You). **Because the results of Your rightwising act and the effects of the eschatological deliverance which is You**
> (effects of Your fairness and equity, just decrees and decisions; actions according to the Way pointed out, results of justification, actualization of justice and rightwising of relationships) **are manifested** (or: were brought to light; were made to appear)."

This verse echoes Ps. 86:9-10,
> "ALL the nations and ethnic multitudes – as many as You made – WILL continue arriving and WILL continue worshiping in Your presence (in Your sight; before You), O Lord! And they WILL constantly bring glory and a good reputation to Your Name, because You are Great, even constantly doing wonders and forming marvels; You are the only God: the Great One!" (LXX, JM)

And then, Mal. 1:11b,
> "My Name has been, and stands, glorified, with a good reputation, among the ethnic multitudes and nations; and in every place incense is brought and offered to My Name... My Name [is] Great among the nations and ethnic multitudes, says the LORD [= Yahweh], [the] All-Strong" (LXX, JM).

Verse 4 gives us three "**Becauses**." They are all because of Him. Nothing is mentioned in this ode of the works of a human, or even of His set-apart folks. It is because HE is the **only One** Who is "**appropriately pious, benign and sanctioned**" by God's natural laws. Here I conflated three meanings of the word *osios*. It is because of Him that **all the multitudes** (all the nations; all ethnic groups; or: ALL people) **WILL continue arriving**, and they **WILL worship** in His **presence**. The alternate MS reading, "all people" says the same thing. None are left out. What a promise! I have emphasized the strength of the future indicative by putting the word "**WILL**" in all caps. It WILL happen, according to this declaration. It is because of and through the work of Christ that God's **rightwising act and the effects of the eschatological deliverance ARE MANIFESTED**, brought to light and made to appear. Remember that this is also the song of Moses – there is a continuity portrayed here. They are acts of deliverance and justification – but they are also acts that are a prelude to a walk in the wilderness, a time of existential cleaning and healing.

The words **results** and **effects** express the plural *–mata* ending of *dikaiōmata*, which I have rendered "**rightwising act**" and "**eschatological deliverance**" and which, in the parenthetical expansion, can also be rendered: fairness and equity, just decrees and decisions; or: actions according to the Way pointed out, results of justification, actualization of justice and rightwising of relationships. This broad semantic range of meanings constitutes a compilation of the insights of linguists, lexicographers and scholars. If one meditates on each meaning, a much broader understanding of the Christ Event will emerge.

Notice the final verb, **are manifested**, which is in the aorist (the fact tense), passive (i.e., God has manifested this)! They were "brought to light" through the coming of the Messiah, His death and resurrection, but further, they were "made to appear" in and through the called-out communities – like those we see in vs. 2, above, and in 14:1, above. We saw them all through the book of Acts, and they appeared in the NT letters. They have been manifested all through history, and continue so, today.

Terry (ibid) points out that vss. 2-4 are a literary feature that "corresponds to the introduction of the multitudes… around the throne (ch. 7), which was brought in between the opening of the 6th and 7th seals, and just before… the 7 trumpets of woe."

5. **Later, after these things, I saw, and the Temple** (Divine habitation; sanctuary), **which equates to the Tabernacle of the Witness** (or: whose source and origin was the tent of testimony and evidence), **was opened up within the midst of the atmosphere** (or: centered in, and in union with, heaven),
6. **and the seven agents – those continuously holding the seven plagues** (impacts; blows) **– came out of the Temple, being clothed with bright, clean** (unsoiled, pure) **linen** [other MSS: *lithon*, stone], **and having been girded around the chests** (or: breasts) **[with] golden girdles** (belts; sashes).

We are not told how long it was between John's hearing the ode in vss. 3-4 and what he now sees here, but that previous scene and performance occupied some time before this next scene takes the stage. The reason for this opening phrase is not given, we simply observe it. Perhaps John was being given time to take in, and/or write, what he had just seen and heard. This may be why we are given understanding a little at a time, so that we can absorb it and "walk it out." The setting definitely corresponds to Israel, and the number 7 is an allusion to Lev. 26:14-39, with the repeated phrase, "7 times," in vss. 18, 21, 24, and 28, are echoed in the 7 seals, the 7 trumpets and 7 shallow bowls here in the Unveiling. Also, note the references to "My covenant" throughout Lev. 26. So the focus of our present passage of the Unveiling continues to be Jerusalem and Judaism of the 1st century AD.

In verses 5-6 we return to the main vision, and the setting is the Temple. Verse 5 refers to it as **the Temple** (or: Divine habitation; sanctuary) **which equates to the Tabernacle of the Witness**, again tying it to the types with Moses, David and other figures of the OT. We find the phrase "tabernacle/tent of witness/testimony" in the LXX version of Ex. 29:10, 11. In it was kept the "two tablets of witness" (Ex. 31:18, LXX). The "witness/testimony" is of God's plan of the ages that was built into the "pattern that [had] been shown to [Moses] on the mountain" (Ex. 25:40, LXX). *Cf* Acts 7:44 (these two NT examples show that both Luke and John were using the LXX, not the Tanakh). Heb. 8:5 is another witness:

> "**an example** (underlying copy; the effect of something shown from under) **and by** (or: in; with) **a shadow of the folks upon the heavens**
>
> > (or: of the super-heavenly ones; or: of the things pertaining to completely heavenly places and things; or: of [things or situations] from the One [resident] upon the atmosphere), **just as Moses had been managed** (or: instructed)…"

Heb. 9:11 expands this thought,

> "**So Christ, after suddenly coming to be present at [our] side [as] a Chief** (or: Ruling; Ranking) **Priest of the good things happening** (or: of virtuous people being birthed; [with other MSS: pertaining to impending excellent things]), **by means of the greater and more perfect** (more matured, complete and destined) **Tabernacle not made by hands – that is, not of this creation**…"

Here, again, we see that it is now **OPENED up, and is within the midst of the atmosphere** (this ties in with 11:19, above). So we have a picture of continuity, from one age/arrangement to the next, and yet the change in the arrangement is seen by its being "**opened up**." In the old order, access to it was only given to the priests – it was not open to the people.

The alternate rendering, "whose source and origin was the tent of testimony and evidence," affirms that the old covenant Temple was generally patterned after the wilderness Tabernacle. But at the new level of the new covenant, the new temple, Christ's corporate body, had its source in the Temple of the old covenant, just as the new situation of Israel's olive tree (Rom. 11:17) – old branches that believed, plus newly engrafted Gentile branches – had its source in the Root (Rom. 11:18). Furthermore, this new temple included "**the testimony/witness of Jesus**," (1:2, 9; 12:17; 19:10).

We should also observe, through the alternate renderings, that THIS temple is both "centered in" and "in union with" "heaven," i.e., it is aligned with God's reign and purposes. That the agents **come out of the Temple** (as in 14:15, 17, above) would signify that they are PRIESTS, and that they represent God's temple and His throne. Note the definite article, "**the**," before "**seven agents**" and "**seven plagues (impacts; blows).**" This use (grammatically called "an article of previous reference") tells us that John was seeing the same agents that he previously saw in vs. 1, above.

We also see the figure of the overcomer, the "**bright, clean linen**" (3:4, above). These agents are a part of His Body. That there are 7 in this vision signifies that they represent the complete, or entire, body of covenant communities (figured by the 7 communities to which this letter was written). All members have a part in the ministry.

I included the alternate reading, *lithon*, in vs. 6 because it is found in two important MSS, plus other witnesses. However, there is just one Greek letter that differentiates between the two readings: *linon* and *lithon*. We have no other instance in the Unveiling of a stone, or stones, being clothing for individuals – unless it would here be signifying a high priest, or an allusion to Ezk. 28:13, "every precious stone [was] his covering." But we do find the City so described, in 21:11ff, below.

The bold reading would suggest that these agents were priests, by the "**bright, clean** (unsoiled, pure) **linen**," and the "**golden girdles**" (*cf* 1:13, above: the description of the Son of man). Once again, they are figures, or symbols, for those of the called-out communities who are identified in 1:6, above, as "**a kingdom: priests in** (or: by; for; with) **His God and Father.**" *Cf* Ex. 28:39. We might also have an allusion to 2 Thes. 1:5-8a,

> "**[This is] a display-effect** (result of pointing-out; demonstration) **of God's fair and equitable** (just; in accord with the Way pointed out) **deciding** (separating for an evaluation or a judging), **[leading] unto your being deemed fully worthy of God's kingdom** (or: of commensurate value, from God's reign and from the influence which is God).... **to repay pressure** (or: squeezing and oppression; ordeal; trouble) **to those continuously pressuring you folks, and to** (or: for; in) **you – the folks being continuously pressed – relaxation** (ease; a relaxing of a state of constriction; relief), **together with us, within the midst of the uncovering** (the unveiling; the laying bare; the revelation; the disclosure) **of the Lord Jesus from [the] atmosphere** (or: sky; heaven), **along with agents** (or: messengers) **of His power – within a fire, of flame continuously giving justice...**"

There is also Jude 14-15,

> "**Behold, the Lord** [=Yahweh] **came** (or: comes and goes) **within His set-apart myriads** (or: in union with innumerable holy multitudes, which are Him), **to form a separation** (or: make a decision; perform a sifting and a judging) **which corresponds to and falls in line with all people** (to the level of everyone), **and to test** (or: search thoroughly) **the irreverent folks concerning all their irreverent works which they irreverently did, and concerning all the hard things which irreverent outcasts** (folks in error; sinners; failures; folks who make mistakes and miss the target) **spoke against Him.**"

7. **Then one out of the four living ones gave** (or: gives) **to the seven agents seven golden bowls** (or: shallow cups) **continuously brimming** (being full) **of the strong passion** (rushing emotion; or: fury; anger) **of the God Who is continuously living on into the ages of the ages** (or: from God, the One continuously living [and proceeding] into the [most significant] eons of [all of] the eons).

This verse reaffirms the "throne room" setting, for one of the **four living ones** is on the scene. We last saw the **living ones** in 6:1-8, as they called forth the four horses. So this vision may be an echo of that section of the Unveiling. This one gives the **shallow, golden cups** of God's strong passion to the 7 agents. Another picture of the living ones is Ezk. 1, and there, in vs. 28, above them is the "appearance of the likeness of the GLORY of Yahweh." From this we would infer that the strong passion which is to be poured out is associated with, or has its origin in, the glory of God – and it will bring Him glory and praise. We should also note the small containers that hold God's **strong passion** (rushing emotion; or: fury; anger). His corrections are measured, and are in small doses. Other than in relations to this vision, this word for "**bowl**/shallow cup" is only use elsewhere in the Unveiling in 5:8, above, "**shallow bowls being continuously brimming full of incenses**." We find this same word used, in the LXX, in association with the bronze altar of burnt offerings in Ex. 27:3; 38:23; Nu. 4:14 and multiple times in Nu. 7, referring to gifts given by the people at the dedication of the sanctuary. It is used in Zech. 14:20, "saucers in front of the altar," in a context that also speaks of holy "cauldrons [i.e., larger vessels] in Jerusalem," in the larger context of "holiness." Zech. 9:15 uses this word in a context of drinking. So temple and the altar of sacrifice, together with an association with holiness, may be the allusions to which the symbol of the **golden, shallow bowls-saucers-cups** are pointing, in this vision of God's **strong passion**.

The rendering "**cups**" calls to mind the words of Jesus, although he used another word for cup,
> "**You folks will progressively drink the cup which I Myself am now progressively drinking, and you will also be progressively immersed in** (or: baptized with) **the immersion** (baptism) **which I Myself am now progressively being immersed, unto saturation** (baptized)" (Mk. 10:39).

This was in reference to Christ's **passion** of the cross. So we should contemplate the setting of this vision as being that of the sacrifice cultus which had the goal of removal of failure, error and the missing of the goal (or: sin): deliverance, cleansing and rescue! This fits the parallel of the metaphor that we saw in 14:10-11, above. Verse 8, below, will expand on this same theme.

Adam Maarschalk adds his witness concerning the covenantal imagery in this passage:
> "There are several reasons why it's valid to say that Israel was the target of the seven seals, trumpets, and bowls…. **Those seven-fold judgments of Leviticus 26 were reserved for Israel alone. They weren't for both Israel and Rome**. So it follows that when the fifth bowl judgment was poured out "*on the throne of the beast*," it was Israel, not Rome, which experienced that darkness and pain. It was Israel that represented the kingdom of the beast. **If the fifth bowl was poured out on Rome, then the bowls were only a six-fold judgment on Israel and "a one-fold judgment" on Rome**, but that's not the case. Leviticus 26 was completely, not partially, fulfilled" ("Who Was the Beast?" ibid pp 2-3; emphasis original).

8. **And then the Temple was made full of smoke from out of God's glory, and from out of His power** (or: ability) **and no one had power** (or: was able) **to enter into the Temple until the seven plagues** (impacts; blows; strikes) **of, or from, the seven agents would** (or: can) **be brought to their purposed goal and completed.**

The first clause is an allusion to Isa. 6:4, as we see that **the Temple is "made full of smoke from out of God's glory, and from out of His power**." When the six-winged burning one of Isa. 6:2-3 said that "All the earth (or: Land) is filled with His glory," vs. 4b records that, "**the House** [= the temple] **was filled with smoke**." In Ex. 40:34-35, when Moses had finished the work of the Tabernacle, "the cloud covered the tent of appointment, then the glory of Yahweh filled the tabernacle, so that Moses was unable to enter into the tent of appointment, for the cloud tabernacled (resided as in a tent) on it, and **the glory** of Yahweh **filled the tabernacle**."

We see a similar situation with the dedication of the Temple in 1 Kings 8:10-12. There,
> "the cloud filled the house of Yahweh so that the PRIESTS could not stand to minister because of the cloud: for the glory of Yahweh had filled the house of Yahweh. Then spoke Solomon, 'Yahweh said that He would dwell in thick darkness.'"

Here in the Unveiling, in 15:8, where it says that "no one was able (or: had power) to enter into the Temple," it should be understood that this would refer to those serving as priests, as in 1 Kings 8, above. It should also be clear that this scene in the Unveiling involves the Temple, His body, being filled with the glory of God. We must be filled with His glory in order to administer His decisions upon humanity.

Thus we see that the outpouring of His strong passion is also a part of the manifestation of His glory. This was the case when Yahweh delivered Israel out of Egypt – it brought Yahweh a name among the nations. Joel 2:2 speaks of this as "A day of darkness and of gloominess, a day of clouds and thick darkness, [yet] as the morning spread upon the mountains – a great and strong people." Now Peter, in Acts 2:16, referred to the outpouring of the Holy Spirit on the Day of Pentecost as being "that which was spoken by the prophet Joel." It began with a manifestation of His glory, but later there was also His judgment, in AD 70. All these things also happened in the 1st century with a view to our admonition, as well as to those upon whom "the ends of the ages" had come down to meet.

The **seven plagues**, or blows/impacts, like the seven trumpets, had a **purposed goal** which Mal. 3:2-3 described as the purification of the sons of Levi, as Yahweh's "Agent/Messenger" would sit "like a refiner's Fire, and like fullers' soap," as "a refiner and purifier of silver... purging them as gold and silver so that they may offer unto Yahweh an offering in righteousness (or: justice)." Levi was the tribe from which the priests arose. Malachi is of course using these metaphors in accord with his day, so they are old covenant metaphors. Understanding the seven agents/messengers as the body, or corporate representation, of the Messiah, we can conclude that they are agents of refining and purification, and that this is the goal of their ministries. Mal. 3:3 calls to mind 1 Cor. 3:12-17. If this correlation is correct, then one aim for these shallow bowls is purification of the called-out communities, with regard to their works – whether or not they are of value for building the temple – 1 Cor. 3:16-17. It is also an aspect of deliverance, healing and salvation (1 Cor. 3:15b). Another level, or application, of these plagues (blows; impacts) is precisely the tribe of Levi in 1st century Jerusalem and Judea, as the Olivet discourse of Jesus is fulfilled, in AD 70. As with the plagues in Egypt, there was both darkness and light; there was destruction and deliverance. We will observe that the seven bowls of God's passion, in the next chapter, closely correspond to the seven trumpets, above. This may be an example of "apocalyptic repetition" which gives the same message as the previous vision, while adding details and/or broadening the applications.

Chapter 16

1. **And I heard a great Voice out of the Temple, saying to the seven agents,**
> **"You must go** (depart) **and you must pour out the seven bowls** (shallow cups; saucers) **of God's strong passion** (fury; rushing emotion; anger) **into the Land** (or: earth; region)."

So now the action begins, and the agents are dispatched **out of the Temple** to pour out **God's strong passion** out of their shallow cups, **bowls** or saucers into THE LAND. Once again, this can also be translated "the earth," but this message was first written to a specific people about specific events in a specific "**Land**" (Palestine), or territory. We who read this letter can apply the principles to our times or to other events in history since AD 70, realizing that He is the same yesterday (in OT times), today (in the 1st century), and on into our ages. He can, and I believe that He does, judge us as well. Let me here note the term "shallow cup" or "saucer." This is a picture of a small measure, thus a limited dealing. The term "Land" was often an OT term applied to the people of Israel. We can see God's rushing emotion poured out on Jerusalem through the rebellion of the Zealots and the carnage done by them against those who did not support the rebellion or were considered Roman collaborators, then later through the Roman army – on a first level of interpretation – but let us also look for a positive end of this "move of God."

The figure, "**pour out**," may be an allusion to Ps. 69:24,
> "Pour out Your swelling, inherent fervor upon them, and let the rushing strong-passion and fury of Your swelling, inherent fervor seize them and take them down" (LXX, JM).

Or, Jer. 10:25, "Pour out Your rushing strong-passion upon the ethnic multitudes that have not known You…" And then, Ezk. 14:19, "Or also, [if] I continue sending added (or: successive) death upon that land, and I will continue pouring out My rushing strong-passion upon it…" Zeph. 3:8 prophesies,
> "Because of this, remain under, endure and wait for Me, says [the] Lord [= Yahweh], unto a Day of My rising up into the midst of a Witness (or: a testimony; evidence). For this reason and purpose, the effect of My decision and the result of My judging [will come] into the midst of gatherings of ethnic multitudes (or: nations): to welcome and take in kings to pour out upon them all swelling, inherent fervor of rushing strong-passion. Because of that, all the Land (or: territory; earth) will continue being correspondingly used up and fully consumed (spent) in a Fire from My zeal (or: in union with Fire of My jealousy)" (LXX, JM).

2. **Then the first one went forth and poured** (or: at once pours) **out his bowl** (or: cup) **upon the Land** (or: ground; earth; territory) **– and a bad and malignant, festering wound** (or: ulcer) **came to be upon those people having the imprinted mark** (engraving; carve-effect) **of the little wild animal** (creature; beast), **even upon those continuously worshiping its image** (or: likeness).

The first bowl/cup/saucer is now poured out **upon the Land** (etc.). This location, the sphere targeted by the cup, corresponds to the judgment of the first trumpet (8:7, above) which also came upon the Land. Compare the 6th plague upon Egypt in Ex. 9:9-11. Now look at the curses and punishments that were to come upon GOD'S PEOPLE if they were disobedient. Deut. 28:27, "Yahweh shall smite you with the boil of Egypt, with piles, with eczema, and with the itch from which you cannot be healed" (CVOT). Then in vs. 35, "Yahweh shall smite you with an evil boil… from the sole of your foot and unto your scalp." Can we see now upon whom these plagues were sent? It was upon the Jews of the 1st century. Yet, it was also figuratively upon the institutional church throughout history, and in our day, as well. Yes, the organized church has the imprinted mark of the little carnal animal. Its institutions looked and function just like the kingdoms of the world and the institutions of the social systems, and today they are even acknowledged to be run like big business – for efficiency, and control, and to comply with the government (the beast upon which it rides), of course. The Jews did the same with Rome, and the Zealots acted like beasts towards many of their own people.

The **bad and malignant, festering wound** that came upon the **people** who have had the **imprinted mark** is a figure of all the physical and emotional wounding that the church systems inflicted upon its members and upon those it considered to be heretics. The first cup brings forth the fruit of the nature of those animal systems that took control of the people. Once the fruit is seen (the festering wounds and malignant ulcers) the tree can be recognized (Mat. 7:16). The symptoms declare the disease.

Although this may seem to be harsh, it is really a blessing. Once we recognize the disease, we can apply the right treatment. The cure is in "**the blood of Jesus Christ**" (1 Jn. 1:7). By the "stripe" or "bruise" of the cross, we can be healed (Isa. 53:5b) as we abide in Him (Jn. 15:1ff). Job's final testing was the ulcers in his flesh (Job 2:7). But as we saw with Job, it was for his ultimate good. The shallow saucers have a positive purpose. The boils, or ulcers, in Egypt had in view the deliverance of Israel. The threatened boils of Deut. 28 had in view Israel's correction. Physical illness often has the effect of turning one's thoughts to the Lord – for healing, or for a change from the way one has been living. Often, the beast way of thinking or acting leads to physical illness or deterioration. It always leads the soul into darkness.

3. **Then the second one poured** (or: at once pours) **out his bowl** (or: cup) **into the sea – and it came to be blood as of a dead person, and every living soul within the sea died.**

This corresponds with the first plague in Egypt, Ex. 7:17-21. Compare also Rev. 8:8-9, the 2nd trumpet. This was also part of the power of the Two Witnesses, in 11:6, above. So what we have here is another vision which parallels chapters 8 & 11. We have another place where **everyone died**:

> "**You see, Christ's love** (urge toward accepting reunion; full giving of Himself to [us]) **continuously holds us together. [We are] deciding** (discerning; judging) **this: that** [some MSS add: since] **One Person** (or: Man) **died over** [the situation of] **all mankind** (or: for the sake of all); **consequently all people died** (or: accordingly, then, all humanity died)" (2 Cor. 5:14).

This may first be an allusion to the predicament of humanity: the death of the 1st Adam (Rom. 5:12) where as the result of one offense, death spread throughout humanity; and then to the solution that we just read in Paul's 2nd letter to Corinth: in the death of the Messiah (the One Person), all humanity was taken into His death. This was the second death for humanity. Paul put this predicament-solution-goal another way in Rom. 11:32,

> "**For you see, God encloses, shuts up and locks all mankind** (everyone; the entire lot of folks) **into incompliance** (disobedience; stubbornness; lack of being convinced), **to the end that He could** (or: would; should) **mercy all mankind** (may make everyone, the all, recipients of mercy)!" (Rom. 11:32).

Paul then relates this to His judgments, in Rom. 11:33b,

> "**How unsearchable** (inscrutable) **the effects of His decisions** (the results of the distinctive separations, judicial awards, judgments and evaluations from Him), **and untrackable** (untraceable) **His ways** (paths; roads)."

Things are not always as they first seem, especially to our natural reasoning.

The sea is often a figure for the masses of humanity. Here, the first application of this symbol was the mixture of Judeans, Galileans, Idumeans and other ethnic groups of the AD 66-60 Judean rebellion.

4. **Then the third one poured** (or: at once pours) **out his bowl** (or: cup) **into the rivers** (or: streams) **and into the springs** (or: fountains) **of the waters – and they became blood.**

This same plague, of water **becoming blood**, affects not only the sea (the multitudes), but also all waters and the sources of water (cf Ex. 7:17-19). This echoes 8:9-11, the 3rd trumpet, which also draws a distinction between "the sea" and "the rivers and springs." The "source of life" now brings death. This sea is not yet a glassy sea, but is a sea where souls die (from lack of the pure Water of Life, the Word of God), and where you find the blood of the slain and wounded. This sounds like many a church and parachurch group. The first meaning pointed to, and foretold, the dead who were slain by the Romans under Titus. This negative interpretation also applies to the institutional church, through the centuries, which both literally and figuratively killed those who differed from its doctrines or were not submissive to its practices.

But in the new creation with its new covenant we are called to drink Christ's blood (Jn. 6:53-56; Mat. 26:28). Once again, we can discern two levels of interpretation.

5. **And I heard the Agent of the Waters saying,**
   "You are continually a Just One (a Righteous One; One Who observes the way pointed out), **the One continuously existing** (or: being), **even the One Who was continuously existing, the appropriately pious, sanctioned, benign One, because You suddenly evaluate and judge** (or: made a decision; judged) **these,**

The **Agent of the Waters** (the one in charge of bowls 2 & 3?) interjects praise in vs. 5 and 6, which compares to the praise of 15:3-4, above. Terry observes, "As the angel [agent] of a church is but a figure for the church itself, so *the angel [agent] of the waters* is but a personification of the waters themselves" (ibid p 419; emphasis original; brackets added). This proclamation may be an allusion to Ps. 19:9b, "The judgments of Yahweh are truth; they are righteous altogether" (CVOT).

The praise that burst onto the stage was **because** God "**suddenly evaluated and judged these**" – notice that God's decision was focused upon a specific group; it was just and a response to Israel's misdeeds, which is what Yahweh had done all through Israel's history.

6.   **"because they poured** (or: pour) **out [the] blood of the set-apart folks and of the prophets, and You gave** (or: give) **them blood to drink: they are deserving [this]!"** [*cf* Lu. 11:50-51]

Who was it that poured out the blood of the set-apart folks and the prophets? Lu. 11:49-51 tells us,
   49. **"That is why the Wisdom of God also said, 'As emissaries I will proceed sending off prophets and representatives unto them** (or: into the midst of them) **– and they will proceed killing off [some] from out of their midst, and then they will proceed to pursue** (chase; press forward [on] and persecute; [other MSS: banish]) **[others],'**
   50. **"So thus, the blood of all of the prophets – that having been** [other MSS: being constantly or repeatedly] **poured out from the casting down** (the founding; the foundation; or: may = the conceiving) **of [the] ordered system** (world of culture, economy, religion and government) **– can** (or: should; would) **at some point** (or: suddenly) **be searched out to be required and exacted from this generation:**
   51. **"from Abel's blood until the blood of Zechariah – the man losing himself** (or: perishing; being destroyed) **between the altar and the House – yes, I continue saying** (or: am now saying) **to you folks, it will progressively be sought out and exacted from THIS GENERATION.**

And it was exacted, in AD 70. *Cf* Mat. 23:34-37, where vs. 35 refers to "**all [the] just** (equitable; rightwised) **blood being continuously poured out** (or: spilled) **upon the Land.**" Observe the corporate, national and historical focus of Jesus' words in Lu. 11, above. He was speaking of His present time.

We also have a direct answer as to who did this in 17:6, below,
   "**Then I saw the woman [Babylon], being continuously drunk from out of the blood of the set-apart folks and from out of the blood of the witnesses of Jesus.**"
Cf 14:8, above, and vs. 19, below. And again, Lu. 13:34, "**O Jerusalem, Jerusalem, which kills the prophets and stones them that are sent unto you**..." Thus it is THESE, the Jews of 1st century Judea (then later the false church of the centuries which follow), to whom He gives blood to drink: they are deserving. We should realize that this literal fulfillment of Jesus' words primarily affected only Judea and Jerusalem, the religious symbol and representative of the old covenant. The Diaspora Jews were only indirectly affected, through the loss of the temple in Jerusalem.

7. **Then I heard the Altar saying,**
   "Yes indeed, O Lord [= O Yahweh], **the All-Strong** (Omnipotent; Almighty) **God, Your decisions** (separations; judgings) **are true and real ones, and fair** (equitable; just; right) **ones."**

This message gives the echo of praise and affirmation which comes from the **Altar**. Does this correspond to the earlier scene of the altar, in ch. 6:9-11, in the opening of the 5th seal, where John heard the cry, "**Until when** (How long)..." from the souls (or: people) **under the altar of burnt-offering**? Are they also seeing what John is seeing, and now that they see the plan further unfolded they say, "**Your decisions** (judgings) **are true ones and real ones, and fair** (equitable; just right) **ones**"? Are they thus a part of the "**cloud of witnesses** (or: martyrs)" that encompass us (Heb. 12:1)? Or, is this an allusion to 8:3-5, above, which would correspond to the altar of incense. Whichever, the **altar** is a part of the Temple, His body.

Note the punctuation of judgment by these repeated, though varied, refrains of praise. Perhaps Malcolm Smith is right in this series of visions being a kind of cosmic opera.

8. **Next the fourth one poured** (or: at once pours) **out his bowl** (or: cup; saucer) **upon the sun – and it was given to him to burn the people** (the humans; mankind) **in Fire.**

Verses 8 and 9 present the pouring of the **fourth** cup, or saucer. The **sun** was also targeted in 8:12, above, when the 4th trumpet sounded. There it brought darkness, but here the result is men being burned in **Fire** with **great heat** (vs. 9, below). This seems to echo 14:10, above: those being tested with Fire and Deity in the presence of the set-apart agents (His body) and of the little Lamb.

This may be an allusion to Ex. 10:21ff, where Moses was told to "stretch forth his hand toward heaven." There, the result was darkness in all the land of Egypt. Here it was as though the earth was drawn closer to the sun, or that the earth was turned into a burning desert – which would suggest an allusion to Israel in the wilderness, but without the Cloud of God's presence as their shelter. Here, it is the intensification of His Fire for purification (Mal. 3). This foreshadows the later metaphor of, "**the lake** (or: basin; artificial pool; marshy area) **of the Fire: the one continuously burning within the midst of [the] Deity**," (19:20ff, below). In Ex. 9:22-24, Moses stretched forth his hand to heaven, and this time the plague was "hail, and Fire mingled with hail" with the "Fire running along the ground."

9. **And so the people** (the humans) **were burned [with] great heat, and they blasphemed** (spoke insultingly of; slandered; misrepresented; vilified; hindered the Light of) **the Name of God – the One having authority upon these plagues** (blows; impacts; strikes) **– and they did** (or: do) **not change their minds** (their way of thinking) **to give Him glory** (or: to have a good opinion of Him).

Those being burned have spiritual insight: they recognize the source of this plague, for they blaspheme "the Name of God," not *satan* or the devil. The setting for these plagues and blows is right here on earth – this is the realm of their impacts. There is sure enough here to make one feel as though he is in the fire, from time to time, but this is a special dealing from God that, like His traditional dealing with Israel, came upon Jerusalem through a foreign power as the final dealing with them as a people group separate from the rest of humanity. You see, through the blood of their Messiah, God demolished the prior categories of Jew and Gentile (circumcision and uncircumcision) making of the two "people groups" to be "one new humanity" (Eph. 2:11-17). This happened at the end of the old covenant age when the new age, the new creation and the new arrangement (the covenant of His laws written in our hearts, in the core of our beings) was being birthed through the called-out, covenant communities. He came in this plague, "sitting as a Refiner of silver and of gold, purifying the sons of Levi (i.e., the priesthood and religious leaders)," as predicted by Mal. 3:2-3, and they felt the **great heat** of His intimate presence among them.

Now I wonder, in this blaspheming "the Name" (either Yahweh, Jesus or one of His other Names), are they simply using the Name of the Lord in vain, as we often hear these days – when things don't go peoples' way? Is this burning plague like the "fiery trial" that Peter spoke of in 1 Pet. 4:12? Are these fiery trials – that Peter tells us we should not be surprised at – the same as the testings that are "common to humanity" of which Paul speaks, in 1 Cor. 10:13? Or, is this specifically the burning of the physical temple and Jerusalem during the siege by Rome? However we interpret this vision, they do not change their way of thinking so as to give glory to Him. But again, from the statement here in vs. 9, it seems that this was God's intent: that they WOULD change their thinking concerning Jesus as their Messiah, so as to **"to give Him glory** (or: to have a good opinion of Him)." We saw similar responses in 9:20-21, above. Compare 2:21, above, spoken to the covenant community of Thyatira. Following the earthquake in 11:13, above, some did then give glory to Him. But here they do not seem to be responsive to "**God's useful kindness** (benevolent utility) **and abruptness** (sheer cutting-off; rigorous severity)" (Rom. 11:22).

10. **Next the fifth one poured** (or: at once pours) **out his bowl** (or: cup) **upon the throne of the little wild animal** (creature; beast) – **and its kingdom** (or: reign) **came to being made dark** (or: had been darkened), **and they were biting their tongues from the painful labor** (misery; travail; hard toil),

This plague (blow) may correspond to the 5th trumpet. See the comments on that in 9:1-11, above, which may simply be the same corrective measures which are seen from a different perspective.

From the pouring of the 5th cup/bowl/saucer, we see **the little animal's** "**kingdom being made dark**," the target having been its **throne**. Now in 13:2, above, we saw that the dragon (a figure of *satan*, i.e., the adversarial spirit of opposition) gave its "**throne and authority**" to this **little animal**. Recall that this "throne" (seat of power) was located in Pergamos (2:13, above). Of course all of this is metaphor and symbol. To try to read these figures literally will be to distort the apocalyptic nature of this letter. The little animal's reign/kingdom/realm is within the midst of God's people, and vice versa. Any system or organization that is crafted by the mind of the "beastly" expression of people will have the character and qualities of a little wild animal. This spirit of the dragon also reaches into the seats of the nations, so Rome (which is probably represented by the 4th beast, in Dan. 7:7-8) could also have been indicated here, with its own beast system (the animal nature and way of acting). Also, if we consider again 11:7, above, we see that this repeatedly climbs up out of the abyss of the human nature (carnal, beast-like attitudes and responses). We further see it, today, even in the "literal interpretations" of the Law and the prophets – which caused the Jews to reject Jesus as the Messiah, and then to persecute the called-out community. But the contents of this cup brought darkness (ignorance; lack of vision and understanding) to this Pharisaical or Zealot kingdom, and soon destroyed it. We see the roots of this judgment in 8:12, above, the 4th trumpet. Darkness continued as an environment for the Zealot rebellion and the Roman Empire, and then, later, for the "church" which it later created. Ezk. 32 gives a lamentation for the fall of Egypt, and in vss. 7-8 symbolically states,
> "I will extinguish you: I will cover the heaven and make its stars dark; I will cover the sun with a cloud, and the moon shall not give her light. All of the light of the light in heaven I will make dark over you, and set darkness upon your land, says the Lord God."

Now as to **biting their tongues**, recall the Jewish "beast" response to the preaching of Stephen:
> "**Well now, while progressively hearing these things, they were being progressively sawn in two in their hearts** (= emotionally ripped and cut to the core so as to be filled with rage), **and**

so they began and continued to grind and gnash [their] teeth on him (= at his words) **with noises as of a wild animal eating greedily**" (Acts 7:54).

Their religion had also brought "**painful labor**," for Jesus said that they bound heavy burdens upon the people (Mat. 23:4). Today there is much darkness in many of the churches, for they do not see the light of God's grace and thus do they heap heavy burdens of religious works or prohibitions upon those who are ignorant of God's Word, and people still gnash their teeth in self-guilt, while the misery of carnal programs requires hard toil and great physical and emotional support to keep them going. We still see the "us versus them" attitude toward folks who read the Scriptures differently from particular "daughters" of Jerusalem (aka, Babylon). Having moved away from engaging in physical persecution (in the "enlightened" countries), we still have emotional, political and sometimes economic persecution of those whom the "orthodox" consider to be "heretical."

Rome was already "dark," so the kingdom that was **made dark** was the religious hierarchy, first of the Jews, in the 1st century, then the Zealot rebellion, and later the stratified system of organized Christianity, in the following centuries. The "**biting their tongues**" may be an allusion to the Jewish leadership having the "kingdom" taken from them (Mat. 21:43), their missing out on the Messianic banquet (Mat. 25:1-12), and their being determined to be "unprofitable servants," and losing their job (Mat. 25:28), ending up having this decision made concerning them:

> "**And now, you men at once throw the useless slave out into the darkness** (dim obscurity and gloominess) **which is farther outside. In that place there will continue being the weeping** (or: lamenting) **and the grinding of the teeth**" (Mat. 25:30).

Following AD 70, this was their situation, and condition. They were unprofitable to God's reign, and were the "foolish virgins" of Israel that ended up being broken out of their own olive tree (Rom. 11:17). If it seems hard to see this interpretation of the Jewish leadership in the 1st century being figured by this symbol of the **little animal's kingdom**, consider Acts 8:1, 3,

> "**Now on that day great persecution, pursuit and** [D adds: **pressure**] **was birthed** (occurred) **upon the called-out community [that was] within Jerusalem, so they were all – except for the sent-forth emissaries** (representatives) [D*& 1175 add: who alone remained in Jerusalem] – **dispersed and scattered as seeds down among the regions** (or: territories) **of Judea and Samaria**.... **Now Saul began devastating, then continued laying waste and bringing havoc to, the called-out community, repeatedly making his way into and invading one house after another. Constantly dragging away and pulling along both men and women by force, he routinely handed [them] over into prison** (or: transferred and committed [them] to a jail)."

See Maarschalk's comments on this verse, cited in 15:7, above.

11. **and they blasphemed** (abusively slander; hindered the light of; vilify) **God with reference to the atmosphere** (or: heaven's God; the God of the atmosphere; God, Who is heaven; the God from the sky) **from out of the midst of their painful labor and from out of their festering wounds** (ulcers), **and did not** (or: do not) **change their mind** (their way of thinking) **from out of their works** (or: actions).

This shows that they are still hurting from the 1st plague (festering wounds – some of which are received "in the house[s] of [our] friends," Zech. 13:6), and again, they appropriately blame God, Who is indeed the source of this trouble, i.e., their judgment. Their **blasphemy** echoes vs. 9, above. Still, they do not change their way of thinking nor have a paradigm shift from their **mindset of works**! Their hands are imprinted with the mark of the beast system; they work like the world. Thus, the judgment must continue to come upon them so that they may learn the true righteousness (Isa. 26:9), that of the Christ who, apart from works, joins them to Himself. Like the Exodus plagues on Egypt, these seven last plagues (or:

blows) intensify as they move forward. We see the same, unchanged reaction to these plagues in vs. 21b, below. This calls to mind Heb. 6:6,

> "**after falling by the side** (or: falling aside along the way), **[they are] powerless and unable to be repeatedly renewing again into a change of mind: [they are] continuously suspending back up** (or: hanging on a pole; crucifying) **again in, with, to, for and by themselves the Son of God, and [are] constantly exposing [Him] to public shame/disgrace**."

But Heb. 6:7-8 uses an agricultural metaphor to show that even though they need to have their "Land" burned off, to remove the competing thorns and thistles, the burning is not their end. A farmer burns off his field in order to enrich the soil with the ash, and then replant in this productive soil once the competing vegetation has been removed. Paul put it this way,

> "**Now [look], we have seen, and thus know and are aware, that to those habitually or progressively loving and giving themselves to God – to the folks being called and invited according to [the] purpose – He is constantly working all things together into good and is progressively working all humanity together into that which is advantageous, worthy of admiration, noble and of excellent qualities**" (Rom. 8:28).

All things, means all things! All that we read in the Unveiling is "according to [His] purpose," and is being worked INTO good: that which is advantageous, worthy of admiration and which has excellent qualities. This is how we who know God are to view all things: TO US, to our view and perception, He is working all humanity together into goodness, which is God, Himself. All ends in Him (Rom. 11:36).

12. **Next the sixth one poured** (or: at once pours) **out his bowl** (or: cup) **upon the great river Euphrates, and its water was** (or: is) **dried up, to the end that the way** (road, path) **of the kings – the ones from the risings of [the] sun** (or: = the east) **– may be prepared** (made ready).

The 6th plague begins with **the water of the Euphrates River** being **dried up to prepare the way** (road; path) of **the kings from the rising of the sun**. The figure here is tied to the following two verses. But just as in a natural waterway drying up, the frogs appear from the mud, which are representative of unclean spirits (or: attitudes – effects of the breath of the dragon, for they come from its mouth – or words, for words are also spirits, which came out of the mouth of its mouthpiece, the false prophet) and animistic (spirit) influences, termed "*demons*" in the Hellenistic culture and religions of that time. This figure of a "**false prophet**" (vs. 13, below) is also an echo of Jezebel in Thyatira (2:20, above).

The drying up of a river means that the Land has experienced a draught – there has been a severe lack of the water of life upon humanity. Famine is usually a result, and so folks look to other geographic areas to bring in the sources of life – here, the kings from the east. But when kings come, so does domination, control and loss of freedom. The allusion may be to Jer. 50:38, in a passage that speaks of Babylon's destruction, "A drought against her waters that they may dry up!" Isa. 11:15 also employs the metaphor of a blow upon important rivers:

> "Then Yahweh will drain the tongue of the sea of Egypt, and wave His hand over the Stream (or: River, i.e., the Euphrates) with the vehemence of His wind (or: Spirit), and He will smite it into seven wadis (or: streams), and one will tread it in sandals" (CVOT; parentheses added).

Cf Jer. 51:35-37. In Zech. 10:11 we find, "All the shadowy depths of the waterway will be dried up; the pride of Assyria will be brought down." The imagery, here in vs. 12, is a foreshadowing of destruction. The "many waters" upon which Jerusalem sat (17:1, below) was the many nations that comprised the Roman Empire – upon which she rode, for both economy, protection and place of being as a nation (Jn. 11:48). Chilton viewed **the kings from the rising of the sun** literally, as "thousands of these very troops [that] actually did come from the Euphrates," citing Philip Carrington, *The Meaning of the Revelation* (1931), that these would be reinforcement for Titus (Chilton, ibid, p 408; brackets added). *Cf* Isa. 10:5-6.

Now Barclay (ibid p 128) points out that the drying of the Red Sea, then later of the Jordan River, were divine acts which gave exit from the armies of Egypt, and then access into the land of promise (Ex. 14:21; Josh. 3:17). Barclay instructs us,
> "Herodotus tells us (1:191) that when Cyrus the Persian captured Babylon he did so by drying up the Euphrates... he temporarily deflected the course of the river into a lake. The level of the river dropped and in the end the channel of the river through Babylon became a road" (ibid p 129).

Both the Jews and the Christians would have been aware of this history and the meaning of the symbol: it signified conquest – which we now know of as the history of the fall of Jerusalem in AD 70. Foy Wallace makes similar statements, saying, "The drying of the river... symbolizes obliterating all deterrents to the hordes overrunning Judah and besieging Jerusalem..." (ibid p 341). The Euphrates River was the boundary-line of Israel on the northeast. In Isa. 8:5-8, the flood season of this river is compared to the king of Assyria, "... and he shall come up over all his channels, and go over all his banks; and he shall pass through Judah..." In Isa. 41, 44, 45 and 46 we are informed about the victory of Cyrus, and Persia, overcoming Babylon, which lead to Israel's release from captivity in Babylon. But here, in the Unveiling, Jerusalem has become the new Babylon, and now Titus (Rome) is raised up to destroy Jerusalem which has killed all God's prophets (vs. 6, above; Lu. 11:50-51), and bring release to the called-out, covenant communities – the resurrected "Israel of God" (Gal. 6:16) which is composed of olive branches of both Israel and the Gentiles into one new tree of Life: the continuation of the Root (Rom. 11:17-18), the new Jerusalem upon the heavens (Heb. 12:22).

Witness Lee, in *The Recovery Version* of the NT, points out that "the plagues of both the sixth bowl and the sixth trumpet are related to the same river, the Euphrates." When considering the 6th trumpet in 9:13-21, above, we noted that the loosing of the four agents which were bound upon "the great river" resulted in the coming of a great army. But recall that, in the particulars of the imagery there, this judgment was from the Lord, and its purpose was stated in vs. 20, "**so that they may NOT worship the demons** (Hellenistic concept and term: = animistic influences) **and the idols** (forms)." Giving importance to demons has been a weak point in the lives of God's people ever since the introduction of this concept into Jewish cosmology, from Persian Zoroastrianism (*cf* Riley ibid). Idolatry ran through the entire history of ancient Israel, as a nation.

So the preterists see John as having been given a symbol of the over-run of Jerusalem. It puts an end to their worship, as the first covenant was terminated. It is a picture of the destruction which was to come to Babylon, which we see later in this vision. But note the paradox: it is a figure of forces coming from where literal, historical Babylon once was – when they overthrew Jerusalem – to now overthrow Jerusalem which had become another Babylon. Literally, it is the pagan world destroying the Second Temple world of the Jews, ending their age. In relation to the called-out, the message for us is the same. Whenever God's "Faithful City" becomes a harlot (Isa. 1:21), God removes the protection and brings judgment. "Babylon is allegorical of the idolatry that any nation commits..." (Metzger, ibid p 88). When God's correction comes, it is a positive event for humanity. Israel was a seed that needed to fall into the ground and die, so that it (represented in its Messiah) could be resurrected and bring forth much fruit (Jn. 12:24).

13. **And I saw – out of the mouth of the dragon, and out of the mouth of the little wild animal** (creature; beast), **and out of the mouth of the false prophet – three unclean spirits** (or: impure attitudes), **as frogs**

Now we come again to **the dragon**, the **little wild beast**, and the **false prophet** which speak forth **unclean spirits**, or express "impure attitudes." These **unclean spirits** (attitudes and breath-effects that have not been washed in the blood of the little Lamb) come **out of the mouth**. The figure is of words spoken or a message given which have the dragon or a lie, from the beast nature in mankind, as their source. I suggest that these parallel the dragon and the two "**beasts**" of chapter 13, above, and are in fact the same as are described there. The dragon, the little animal and the false prophet are symbols of **spirits** that have not yet been **cleansed**. These figures represent the work of our adversary, the estranged carnal mind of those who still are existentially "**dead in trespasses and sins**" (Eph. 2:1), and symbolize the rise of "many false prophets" of which Jesus spoke in Matt. 24:11. Keep in mind that John is here being shown things by signs: they are figures, representative pictures. Thus "the false prophet" is a sign representing the rise of "many false prophets," in the 1st century, and ever since. That they appear **as frogs** is to remind the reader that this picture still relates to the plagues in Egypt (the 2nd plague there, Ex. 8:2-7). In that situation, the land was over-run with frogs. From Lev. 11:9-12, 41-47, we learn that frogs fall into the category of being "unclean," as far as their dietary laws were concerned. So here they are a symbol for what was considered **unclean**, in the old covenant. We read in Mat. 12:34,

> "**You see, from out of the midst of the effect of the excess from the heart's surrounding abundance, the mouth is continually speaking.**"

Then, in Mat. 15, Jesus instructs us:

> 18. "**Yet the things constantly emerging and flowing forth out of the mouth are continually coming forth from out of the midst of the heart**
>> (the core of the individual; the self as a whole, at its deepest level, which is the individual's animating and driving force [note: I owe these last phrases to Marcus Borg, *The Heart of Christianity*]) – **and those things continually make the person contaminated, defiled, ceremonially unclean and common.**
>
> 19. "**For example, from out of the heart** (the core of our being) **habitually come forth worthless reasonings** (wicked designs; considerations having a bad quality; miserable and laborious dialogues and arguments), **murders, adulteries, fornications and prostitutions, sexual immoralities** (fornications; prostitutions), **thefts, false testimonies** (or: false presentations of evidence), **blasphemies** (malicious slanders; abusive misrepresentations).
>
> 20. "***These*** **continue being the things that are making the person contaminated** (unclean; defiled; common) – **yet to eat a meal with unwashed hands does not make the person common, contaminated or unclean!**"

Remember, everything in this vision is a symbol, a figure that represents a reality in our existence and in our world. In the quotes from Mat. 15, above, we see Jesus speaking in plain speech about what is unclean and impure. The vision is representative of real spirits and attitudes within social and political organizations (figured by the dragon {the spirit of empire or domination systems}), religions, trade unions, etc. (the little animals within the empire) and mouthpieces for the animal organization, or the government (false prophets; today, often: the media). We will see these three elements cleansed, in 20:10, below. We can see a correlation with 9:17-19, above, in the 6th trumpet.

Does this speak of the Land of Judea (or: today's "church") being over-run with false prophets, folks with the character of "little animals," or those who operate with the spirit of **the dragon**? The result here in the Unveiling is war. History attest to this in 1st century Palestine, and then one faction battling another faction in churches down through history, ever since! John elsewhere said "**many false prophets have gone** (or: come) **out into the ordered System** (world of societal culture, government, economy and religion) **and continue there**" (1 John 4:1). The prophecy of Jesus had already come true. God's involvement in all of this may find an echo in 1 Ki. 22:19-22, according to the prophet Micaiah (see below). We find 2 Thes. 2 giving further evidence for this:

> 11. **And so, because of this, God is continuously sending to** (or: in) **them an in-working** (or: operation) **of wandering** (or: from straying; which has the character of error and deception) **into the [situation for] them to believe, and to trust, the lie,**
>
> 12. **to the end that all those not being faithful to the Truth** (or: believing and trusting the

reality), **but rather approving and delighting in injustice** (inequity; the thing that is not right), **may** (or: can; would) **at some point be sifted, separated and decided about** (or: judged).

Terry suggests that **the false prophet** is "but another name for the second beast, out of the land (13:11)" (ibid p 421). Maarschalk presents a good excursus on this topic:

Jewish False Prophets Working with the Zealots

"In *Antiquities* 20.8.6, Josephus wrote the following about numerous false prophets who deceived the Jews during the time of the Procurators Felix (52-58 AD) and Festus (59-62 AD):

> 'These works – that were **done by the robbers** – filled the city with all sorts of impiety. And now **these impostors and deceivers** persuaded the multitude to follow them into the wilderness, **and pretended that they would exhibit manifest wonders and signs, that should be performed by the providence of God.** And many that were prevailed on by them suffered the punishments of their folly; for Felix brought them back, and then punished them. Moreover, there came out of Egypt about this time to Jerusalem one that said he was a prophet, and advised the multitude of the common people to go along with him to the Mount of Olives…'

In *Wars* 2.13.4-6, Josephus wrote about various false prophets and deceivers who worked to persuade the people to revolt against the Romans and who killed those who refused to revolt:

> 'There was also another body of wicked men gotten together… **These were such men as deceived and deluded the people under pretense of Divine inspiration, but were for procuring innovations and changes of the government; and these prevailed with the multitude to act like madmen**, and went before them into the wilderness, as pretending that God would there show them the signals of liberty… for **a company of deceivers and robbers got together, and persuaded the Jews to revolt**, and exhorted them to assert their liberty, **inflicting death on those that continued in obedience to the Roman government**, and saying, that such as willingly chose slavery ought to be forced from such their desired inclinations; **for they parted themselves into different bodies, and lay in wait up and down the country, and plundered the houses of the great men, and slew the men themselves, and set the villages on fire; and this till all Judea was filled with the effects of their madness.** And thus the flame was every day more and more blown up, till it came to a direct war.'

In *Wars* 6.5.1-2, Josephus talked about how, when the temple was burned down, the number of people killed in that blaze was especially high because so many people listened to the words of a false prophet. Josephus also revealed that this false prophet was one of **many** false prophets **who had been hired** by the Zealots to control the people and keep them from fleeing from their control:

> '**A false prophet was the occasion of these people's destruction**, who had made a public proclamation in the city that very day, that God commanded them to get upon the temple, and that there they should receive miraculous signs of their deliverance. **Now there was then a great number of false prophets suborned [hired] by the tyrants to impose on the people**, who denounced this to them, that they should wait for deliverance from God; **and this was in order to keep them from deserting**' (*Wars* 6.5.2)" ("Who Was the Beast?" ibid p 9; emphasis original).

14. – **for they are spirits** (or: breath-effects; attitudes) **of, or which are, demons** (a Hellenistic concept and term: = from animistic influences), **continually doing** (making; constructing; performing) **signs – which are continuously going out** (marching forth) **upon the kings of the whole inhabited land, to assemble them** (bring them together) **into the battle** (combat, war) **of that great Day of the All-Strong** (Omnipotent) **God.**

Now in regard to the "**spirit of a demon**" coming out of the mouth of **the false prophet**, go to 1 Kings 22:19-23. The setting there is the same as the one here, "Yahweh sitting on His throne" (vs. 19), and Yahweh wanted to persuade Ahab that he may go up and fall (= defeat and death) at Ramath-Gilead. Then we have this interesting situation,

> "And there came forth a spirit, and stood before Yahweh, and said, 'I will persuade him... I will go forth and I will be A LYING SPIRIT in the mouth of all his prophets'.... Now therefore, behold YAHWEH hath put a lying spirit in the mouth of all these your prophets, and Yahweh has spoken evil concerning you."

Rotherham renders vs. 22, "I will go forth and BECOME a spirit of FALSEHOOD, in the mouth of all his prophets." Notice my expanded conflation, "**spirits which are demons**." This renders the genitive case as apposition, giving a description, or definition, of what kind of "spirit, breath-effect, or attitude" that John, and his readers are to understand that these **frogs** represented, in this symbolism. Paul Tillich has more than once defined the term *demon* as representing that which distorts truth and reality, and the *demonic* as a reference to something/someone who has been distorted from what it was created to be.

Observe that these spirits are continually performing signs. Recall 13:13-15, above, and the "great wonders" of the second beast. Jesus said, concerning the Pharisees, and the Jewish leadership,

> "**A good-for-nothing, worthless, base, knavish, grievously oppressive and wicked – even adulterous** (unfaithful and immoral) **– generation repeatedly seeks intently for a sign! And yet a sign will not proceed to be given to it – except the sign of Jonah the prophet**" (Mat. 12:39).

So beware of following after signs, and those who purportedly perform them.

Another interesting situation is in Ezk. 14:7-11, speaking of any man of Israel who,

> "breaks away from Me and turns his thoughts upon his fetishes... and then goes to the prophet to inquire of Me through him, I, Yahweh will respond to him directly.... And if a prophet is seduced and does speak a word [to such a person], IT WAS YAHWEH WHO SEDUCED THAT PROPHET; .... the punishment of the inquirer and the punishment of the prophet shall be the same" (Tanakh).

Both the KJV and Lamsa use the word "deceived" for "seduced" in this verse.

Paul warned of this situation in 1 Tim. 4:

> 1. **Now the Spirit is explicitly saying that within subsequent seasons** (in fitting situations and on appropriate occasions which will be afterwards) **some of the faith will proceed standing off and away [from the Path, or from the Community]** (or: some people will progressively withdraw from this conviction and loyalty), **habitually holding toward wandering and deceptive spirits** (or: straying and seducing breath-effects and attitudes) **and to teachings of demons**
>   (to teachings about and pertaining to, or which are, demons [note: a Hellenistic concept and term: = animistic influences]; or: to instructions and training which come from animistic influences [= pagan religions]),
> 2. **within perverse scholarship of false words**
>   (or: in association with overly critical hairsplitting of false messages; in the midst of gradually separated interpretations of false expressions; or: in union with deceptive decisions by speakers of lies)...

The "**the kings of the whole inhabited land**" will be seen again in 17:16-17, below. Simmons explains,

> "The kings of the earth [land] are Herod and the rulers of the Jews who lifted themselves up against Christ and the church" (ibid p 306; brackets added).

We see Peter, John and those with them quoting Ps. 2:2 in Acts 4, where they applied the phrase to Herod, Pilate, etc.:

> 26. **'The kings of the land took a stand, and the rulers** (or: the leaders; the officials) **were gathered together at the same [place]** (or: = joined forces upon the same [purpose and intent]) **– down against the Lord and down against His Anointed One** (or: the Christ which was Him).' [Ps. 2:1-2]
> 27. **"For in truth** (actuality) **both Herod and Pontius Pilate, together with ethnic multitudes and [the] People of Israel – [coming] upon** (= against) **Your set-apart Servant Jesus, Whom You anointed – were gathered together** (thus: were made to join forces) **in this city**
> 28. **"to do whatever** (or: as many things as) **Your hand and Your counsel** (purpose; plan; intent; design) **previously marked out the bounds for and limited beforehand to be happening** (to come to be; to occur).

Although we see the 1st century interpretation as the first level of understanding, all of these symbols, including "the kings" are representative of the domination systems ever since that time, and all over the globe. We see these situations in politics, in businesses and industries, in education, in entertainment, in media, etc. We seldom find the fruit of the Spirit within these systems. Rather, we find the image of God normally distorted by greed and lust for power.

Notice that it is "**spirits** (or: breath-effects; attitudes) **of, or which are, demons** (a Hellenistic concept and term: = from animistic influences)" that "**are continuously going out**." What was the purpose of their going out "**upon the kings**"? It was "**to assemble them** (bring them together) **into the battle** (combat, war) **of that great Day**." So here we see that the coming together for war was incited by these "attitudes from animistic influences." Curiously, this is one of only three places where this word, or its cognate (in 9:20), is used in the Unveiling. The other place is in 18:2, below. From traditional theology and eschatology, one would expect this book to be rife with these terms. As noted in the text of the verse, this term has its origin in the Hellenistic culture and religion. The *TDNT* defines *demon* as an "animistic influence." This idea comes from pagan religions and world views. Webster defines animism as, "The old hypothesis of a force (*Anima mundi*, soul of the world) immaterial but inseparable from matter, and giving to matter its form and movements; the attribution of spirit or soul to inanimate things." Such beliefs often gave rise to polytheism. From contact with the religions of Egypt, Persia and Greece, the Jews had come to accept an animistic world view, and tended to think of creation in this dualistic way. Jesus, and the writers of the NT made no recorded attempts to change this pervasive ontological-attitude. I recommend Walter Wink's exhaustive work that includes this term: *Naming the Powers*. This term would have been familiar to John, and so he employs it to designate adversarial, or negative, **spirits** (or: attitudes) that can influence people whose lives are not "**hidden with Christ, within the midst of God**" (Col. 3:3).

Dan Kaplan has pointed us to Mat. 12, again, perceiving a reference to corporate Israel (specifically the Jewish leadership of Jesus' day) in Jesus' instruction in vss. 43-45 concerning unclean spirits:

> 43. **"Now whenever the unclean spirit** (or: unpruned attitude; unpurged breath-effect; foul wind) **should come forth** (or: go out) **away from the person, it normally passes through waterless places, continuously seeking a resting place – and it continues finding none.**
> 44. **"At that point, it proceeds to say, 'I will proceed turning back into my house from where I came** (or: moved) **out.' And, upon coming, it is then finding [it] continuing being unoccupied** (being unemployed, and thus, at leisure) **and having been swept clean with a broom – even having been put in orderly arrangement and decorated!**
> 45. **"At that time it continues journeying on its way, and then proceeds taking along with itself seven different spirits** (attitudes; breath-effects; winds) **more good-for-nothing and useless** (base, wicked, knavish, grievously oppressive and evil) **than itself, and upon entering, it settles down and continues dwelling there in the house. So the last [circumstances] of**

> that person becomes progressively worse than the first ones. Thus in this way will it also proceed being with (or: for; in; to) **this good-for-nothing and wicked generation."**

Take note of Jesus' own application to the then-present generation of the Jews in Palestine in the last sentence of this teaching. Notice the apocalyptic number of "7 different spirits" in vs. 45. Jesus came to cleanse the house of Israel, and God's House (the Temple), and He did so by submitting to their spilling of His blood. But they refused His work of the cross and persecuted His followers, and so by AD 70 their last situation was worse than what it was before.

So what is the, "**great Day of the All-Strong** (Omnipotent) **God**"? Here are some OT verses which may inform us about this phrase:

> "Howl! For the day of the LORD is near; it shall come like havoc from Shaddai [traditionally: 'the Almighty']" (Isa. 13:6, Tanakh).
>
> "Now look! An incurable Day of the Lord is repeatedly (or: progressively; or: presently) coming: [a day] of rushing emotion and swelling passion to lay the inhabited land desolate (a wilderness), and to loose-away (or: destroy) the people who fail to hit the target (the failures; those who shoot off-target; the sinners; the deviators; those who err from the goal) from out of the midst of it" (Isa. 13:9, LXX, JM).
>
> "Blow a horn in Zion; sound an alarm on My holy mount! ... For the day of the LORD has come! It is close – a day of darkness and gloom; a day of densest cloud spread like soot over the hills; a vast, enormous horde…" (Joel 2:1-2a, Tanakh).
>
> "Woe to those yearning for the day of Yahweh! …. It [will be] darkness and not light…" (Amos 5:18, CVOT).

So it was usually a reference to God's judgment upon Israel. Chilton and Terry both suggest that this was what Jesus referred to in Mat. 22:7, "**So the king inwardly swelled with fury and was made to teem with anger. And then, sending his soldiers he destroyed those murderers and set their city in flames.**" *Cf* Lu. 19:27.

15. "**Consider! I continually** (or: repeatedly; or: presently) **am coming as a thief! The one continually watching** (or: in wakeful vigilance) **and keeping guard upon his garments [is; will be] blessed** (or: a happy person), **to the end that he may not be continually walking about** (or: roaming; = living his life) **naked so that they may continually see** (or: observe) **his indecency** (condition of being without proper form, shape or character; shame; ungracefulness)."

Here the speaker is obviously Christ. He inserts into this vision a warning to the called-out of 1st century Asia Minor, but this word still speaks to us as history rolls on, and He continues coming to us. In 2:5, above, He told Ephesus, "**I am continuously** (repeatedly; habitually) **coming to you** [as a group]," and in 2:16 informed Smyrna, "**I am repeatedly** (habitually) **coming swiftly in you** (to you; for you)." To Thyatira He said, "**what you have** (hold) **you must get into your power** (be strong in; lay hold of), **until of which [time or situation] whenever I may arrive.**" He gave the message of "arriving **as a thief**" to the community in Sardis (3:3, above) and following His message to Philadelphia, in 3:11, proclaimed, "**I am repeatedly** (habitually; constantly) **coming and going swiftly** (or: = progressively coming soon)!"

A similar picture is given by Jesus in Mat. 24:

43. "**Yet you are progressively coming to know that by experience** (or, as an imperative: Now be personally knowing that, through normal experience), **because if the householder had seen and known in what sort of watch** (= which of the watches) **[of the night] the thief is normally coming, he would have kept awake, remained alert and kept watchful, and then he would not let** (permit) **his house to be dug through.**

44. **"Because of this, you yourselves progressively come to be ready and prepared as well, because at an hour for** (= about) **which you are not normally thinking** (imagining; supposing; = expecting), **the Son of the Man** (= the eschatological Messiah figure) **is normally** (or: repeatedly; or: presently) **coming.**

Paul, in 1 Thes. 5:2, warned,

"**for you yourselves are accurately aware** (know exactly from having seen) **that a day of, from and which is the Lord** [= Yahweh] **thus continually comes** (is habitually and repeatedly coming and going; is presently coming) **as a thief in a night** (or: within [the] night)."

The day of Yahweh was a term that figured a time of judging and hard times, in the OT; cf Joel 1:15; Jer. 30:7; Zeph. 1:14-18.

In regard to, "**walking naked**," we recall 2 Cor. 5:1-4, where in vs. 3 Paul instructs them,

"**being folks at some point entering within and clothing ourselves** (or: being dressed, also), **we shall not continue** (or: proceed) **being found naked**."

In 3:18a, above, we read,

"**I continue advising you** [singular] **to buy from Me gold having been refined** (set ablaze) **forth from out of fire, to the end that you may become rich; and white garments, to the end that you may clothe yourself and the shame** (disgrace) **of your nakedness may not be manifested** (brought to light; caused to appear)."

In Rom. 13, Paul gave these admonitions:

12. **The night advances, and the day has approached and is presently near. We should put, then, the acts of the Darkness** (works from the realm of the shadows) **away from ourselves** (or: = ignorance; that which was before the light arrived), **and clothe ourselves with the instruments** (tools; weapons; implements; [some MSS: works; deeds]) **of Light.**...

14. **but rather, you folks must clothe yourselves with** (or: enter within and put on) **the Lord, Jesus Christ, and stop** (or: do not continue) **making forethought** (constructing provision; planning ahead) **into excessive desires of the flesh** (= into rushing upon emotions from the inner self; = into the setting of feelings and longings upon something oriented to the System).

Nakedness is first encountered in the Garden of Eden (Gen. 2:25; 3:7, 10-11). In Gen. 3:21, God clothed Adam and Eve, covering their nakedness. In Ezk. 16:7 Yahweh described Jerusalem as being naked when He passed by her, and in vs. 8 He "covered [her] nakedness," then in vs. 22 reminds her of the nakedness of the days of her youth that she has forgotten, "in all [her] abominations and prostitutions." In Ezk. 16:37-40 He promises to "gather all [her] lovers… and [He] will uncover [her] nakedness unto them…. and [He] will also give [her] into their hand" to be stoned and thrust-through with the sword. In 17:16, below, we find, "**the ten horns which you saw** (or: see) **– even the little wild animal – these will continue hating** (detaching from) **the Prostitute, and [she] being made desolate** (having been laid waste), **they will also proceed making her naked…**" This, in the next chapter, is an echo of Ezk. 16. We see the first mention of the upcoming "gathering" in vs. 16, below.

However, we should not stop at Ezk. 16:40, but read the rest of that chapter. Following her judgment, because she broke the covenant with Yahweh (vs. 59b), He told her,

"Then I Myself will call to mind (remember) My covenant (arrangement) – the one with you, in [the] days of your infancy – and I will proceed causing to rise up in you (or: with you; for you; to you) an eonian covenant (an arrangement with the character and quality of the Age [of the Messiah]; a covenant which is the Age [of the Messiah])" (Ezk. 16:60, LXX, JM).

His judgments are never the end for people, they bring us to the goal of our existence. When the cleansing (1 Jn. 1:7b) is completed, His love covers us (1Pet. 4:8), and we are enabled to follow Paul's admonition in Rom. 13:12, 14, above. All of these messages were to the called-out communities, and the visions are meant to inform those of the 1st century – and we, in the following centuries, continue learning from them.

16. **And He** [Aleph reads: they] **gathered** (or: assembles) **them together into the place being called, in the Hebrew, Armageddon** [= the hill of Megiddo; some MSS: Mageddon].

In verse 14, above, the spirits go out to assemble the inhabitants of the land to go to war. Compare 13:5-7, above, where the 1st beast is given a "mouth" and then makes war with the set-apart folks (this is also seen in 11:7, above). The verb **gathered** (or: assembles – the aorist tense) **together**, or "synagogues," has no expressed subject. It is simply the 3rd person form of the verb. The Nestle-Aland text, Westcott and Hort, Griesbach, and TR (i.e., most MS witnesses) all read the verb singular ("**He**"). Only MS Aleph reads it plural, "they." The reading "they" (which some translations follow) would see vs. 15 as parenthetical (the NEV puts it in parentheses) and read vs. 16 as picking up where vs. 14 left off, with its plural subject. Thus, the Aleph reading could be a scribal adjustment to the text, to accord with vs. 14. The only difference between the singular and plural forms is the final vowel of the verb. But the reading, **He**, has Christ or God (vs. 15) as the antecedent subject, and thus the One arranging this battle as with the situation in 1 Ki. 22, cited above.

What about this **gathering** (for war) at **Armageddon**? Barclay (ibid p 132) tells us that it is the Plain of Esdraelon, which was part of the highway from Damascus to Egypt. It was a great battle field from the ancient times to the time of Napoleon. It was where Barak and Deborah defeated Sisera (Jud. 5:19-21), where Ahaziah died (2 Kings 9:27), and where Josiah was killed in a battle with Egypt (2 Kings 23:29-30). This verse is an allusion to Israel's history, locating the subject matter of the "bowls" in a context of the judgment of Jerusalem, in AD 66-70. But we will not see what was to happen here until it is discussed as Gog and Magog in 20:8-9, below. The prophet Zechariah presents an interesting picture in chapter 12:
> "Behold, I will make Jerusalem a bowl of reeling for the peoples all round. Judah shall be caught up in the siege upon Jerusalem, when all the nations of the earth gather against her….In that day I will make the clans of Judah like a flaming brazier… like a flaming torch… They shall devour all the besieging peoples… Jerusalem shall continue on its site…. In that day I will all but annihilate all the nations that came up against Jerusalem. But I will fill the House of David and the inhabitants of Jerusalem with a spirit of pity and compassion, and they shall lament to Me about those who are slain… the wailing in Jerusalem shall be as great as the wailing at Hadad-rimmon in the plain of Megiddon" (vss. 2-11, Tanakh).

The situation and context of this Zech. 12 pronouncement remains ambiguous, and need not concern us here, but an allusion to it is obvious, here in vs. 16. The House of David could be seen by John as pointing to Christ and His body – for we see them involved as agents in this present vision. Zechariah continues in the next chapter in what seems to be pertinent to the 1st century, and to what develops in the Unveiling, below:
> "In that day a fountain shall be open to the House of David, and the inhabitants of Jerusalem, for purging and cleansing. In that day, too – declares the LORD of Hosts – I will erase the very names of the idols from the Land; they shall not be uttered and more. And I will also make the 'prophets' and the 'unclean spirit' vanish from the Land" (Zech. 13:1-2, Tanakh).

His **Fire and Deity** (14:10, above), i.e., the "lake of Fire," below, is the instrument of "erasing the names of the idols" (the name and mark of the "beast") from the minds and actions of humanity.

17. **Next the seventh one poured** (or: at once pours) **out his bowl** (or: cup) **upon the air – and a great voice came** (or: goes) **forth from the Temple of the atmosphere** (or: heaven) [other MSS: out of the temple from the throne; other MSS: out of the temple of God], **from the throne, repeatedly saying, "It has come to be** (or: He has been birthed; It has come into existence; It has occurred)!"

We come to the last of the last blow, the 7th plague. It is a blow upon **the air**, and would seem to be a counterpart of the 4th plague in Egypt, which was a grievous swarm, perhaps a mixture of insects – since the Heb. root, there, shows that they were mixed (Bullinger). The LXX calls them "dog flies," and the CVOT renders it "a heavy mixture of flies" (Ex. 8:24). This might be pointing to the aftermath of the AD 70 battles, and the proliferations of dead bodies (*cf* Isa. 66:24). Notice that most of these plagues are directed at the flesh. But here, the symbol of "**the air**" may refer to the atmosphere, and may be pointing out that the reign of the heavens – inaugurated by the death and resurrection of Jesus (and His departure into the air, in the midst of a cloud, in Acts 1:9-11) – "has come into existence," or, that results of its presence "have occurred."

Next **a great voice**, or message, comes **from out of the Temple** (His body) and proclaims, "He has been birthed," (there is no personal pronoun expressed as the subject of the verb). This **great voice** may be describing the message proclaimed by Christ's followers that He is the Firstborn from among the dead. Or, it can be rendered, "**It has come to be**," or, "It has happened (occurred)!" No explanation of this statement is given in the text. We could infer that this speaks of the fulfillment of a prophecy, of God's plan, perhaps referring back to vs. 1: the ending or completion of God's strong passion and fury. Perhaps this is an echo of Jesus' cry on the cross, "It is finished," which Rabbi Dick Reuben says is what the priest would say when the atonement sacrifice was completed. We can also relate this to the **great voices** during the sounding of the 7th trumpet (11:15, above) saying, "**The reign of the dominating, ordered System** (of the world of religion, culture, government and economy; or: of the realm of the religious and secular; or: of the aggregate of humanity) **suddenly came to belong to our Lord** [= Yahweh or Christ] **and to the anointed of Him**..."

We should not forget another "pouring out," as prophesied by Joel,
> "Then I will progressively give back to, for and in you folks, in place of the years... [consumed by] the great power (= empire; army) which I sent forth into the midst of you.... And so you people shall progressively come to fully know that I, Myself, continuously exist (am) within the midst of Israel – even I, Myself: the LORD your God, and there exits none except Me – and in no way will My people continue being ashamed, on into the Age. And so, after these things, it will continue existing (or: progressively be). Then I will continue progressively pouring out from My Spirit, upon all flesh..." (Joel 2:25, 27, 28; LXX, JM)

Recall that Peter applied this passage to the pouring out of the Holy Spirit in the 1st century, in Act 2:16-21. God's pouring out was correction, cleansing and giving new life. This period birthed the new age with the new arrangement between God and humans, which act formed the new creation.

18. **Then lightnings and voices and thunders came to be** (occurred), **and a great shaking** (= an earthquake) **came to be** (occurred), **such as had not come to be** (or: did not happen) **since** (or: from which [time]) **the humans came to be** (or: mankind was birthed) **upon the Land** (or: ground; earth) – **a shaking** (quake) **of such magnitude, so very great!**

This "saucer-pouring" is attended by **lightnings**, **voices** and **thunders** and **a great shaking**. This is an echo of Ex. 19:10-20 when Yahweh came down on Mt. Sinai. There it was all the people who shook (trembled, vs. 17), including Moses (Heb. 12:21), at the presence of God. So this figure shows that the Lord has come in this "plague," for these are signs of His presence and His dominion (figured by His throne: see 4:5, above). We are told in 1 Thes. 4:17 that,
> "**Thereupon** (or: As a next step) **we, the presently living folks, the ones presently continuing to be left around, will – at the same time, together with them – proceed being seized and snatched away within clouds** (or: carried off by force, in union with clouds,) **into the midst of**

[the] AIR (the air that we breathe in; the atmosphere around us; [note: this would be in the earth's lower atmosphere, the place where there is air]) – **into the Lord's meeting** (an encountering which is the Lord). **And thus** (in this way) **shall we always continue being** (or: continue existing at all times) **together with [the] Lord**."

So if the Lord was present in the AIR in this plague, perhaps there was a "catching up" at this time – as some preterists believe. Perhaps this happens each time He comes. The **air** could also be a figure for the realm of the spirit, in the lowest heaven which touches the earth. The **great shaking** echoes Heb. 12:

> 26. **Whose voice shook the land at that time. Yet now it has been promised, saying, "Still once [more; or: for all] I am shaking not only the land** (or: earth), **but also the heaven** (or: atmosphere; sky)." [Hag. 2:6; Joel 3:16-17]
> 27. **Now the "Still once [more; or: for all]" constantly points to and makes clearly visible the transposition** (transference; changeover; change of setting or place) **of the things being repeatedly shaken, to the end that the things not being repeatedly** (or: continuously) **shaken may remain.** [cf 2 Cor. 3:7-13]
> 28. **Therefore, continuously taking to our sides** (or: progressively receiving alongside) **an unshaken Reign** (or: Kingdom; Sovereign influence)...

Cf above: 6:12; 8:5; 11:13, 19. Also: Mat. 24:7; 27:54; 28:2. The shakings are signs of the change from the old to the new.

19. And the Great City came to be [divided] into three parts, and the cities of the nations (multitudes; ethnic groups) **fell, and then Babylon the Great** (or: the Great Babylon) **was called to mind** (or: is remembered) **in the presence of** (before; in the sight of) **God, to give to her the cup of the wine of the strong passion** (rushing emotion; fury; anger) **of His inherent fervor** (natural impulse; mental bent and disposition; personal emotion; indignation; wrath).

This may be an allusion to Isa. 51:17,

> "Rouse yourself! Rouse yourself! Arise, Jerusalem! You who have drunk from the hand of Yahweh a [or: the] cup of His fury; the goblet-cup of tremoring you have drunk..." (CVOT).

Ezk. 23 prophesies against the prostitution of Samaria and her "younger sister," Jerusalem (vs. 4b). In vss. 31-33, Yahweh says,

> "You have walked in the way of your sister; therefore will I give her cup into your hand... You shall drink of your sister's cup deep and large... with the cup of astonishment and desolation..."

The City's falling apart "**into three parts**" is an echo of the other fractional judgments, seen above, but is also prophetic of the divisions that happen to her daughters, in the coming centuries. The City was once a unity, but it is now fragmented, representing its dualistic and fragmented view of God and creation.

Verses 18-20 picture the fall of Babylon (figure of Jerusalem in the 1st century, and of the organized systems of religion and political powers in the following age) and her "daughters" (the cities of the multitudes, nations and ethnic groups which also become a figure for church "denominations"). Chilton rightly makes the observation:

> "Another indication that the Great City is Jerusalem is the fact that St. John distinguishes her from the cities of the Gentiles [nations], which fell with her" (ibid p 416; brackets added).

Don K. Preston explains,

> "It is critical to understand that the word 'remembered' is a covenantal word. The word translated remembered is used some 37 times in the OT.... It is significant that in Rev. the judgments portrayed as coming against 'Babylon' are covenantal judgment directly from the Torah (Lev. 26; Deut. 28-30; Deut. 32), which is called the Song of Moses. Significantly, the Song of Moses is

about Israel's last days, when Israel herself would become like Sodom (32:20-32)" ("Objection Overruled!" in *Fulfilled! Magazine*, Vol. 12, Issue 1 pp 17-18).

Preston, in this same article, says, "Sebastian Smolarz illustrates the point that in 86 of the 91 occurrences of the word harlot in the OT, the reference is to either a literal wife that committed adultery (violating the marriage covenant), or, Israel as the wife of YHWH that violated the marriage covenant (*Covenant and the Metaphor of Divine Marriage in Biblical Thought*, Wipf and Stock, 2011 p 8)." *Cf* 17:1-5, below.

This 7th shallow cup also equates to the "**cup of the wine**" of the **strong passion of His inherent fervor**. The visionary act of "pouring out" is a figure for an experience of those upon whom such is poured. It corresponds to 14:10-11, above, "**the wine of God's rushing emotion and strong passion**," which was explained as being scrutinized with the touchstone (= tested) in Fire and Deity (= God and His Divine Character) within the presence of His set-apart agents (His body) and in the presence of the Lamb. There we saw that they could behold the Lamb, and "at length, when [they] can or may turn towards the Lord, the veil shall be taken away from around [them]. And the Lord is the Spirit, and where the Spirit of the Lord [is, there is] FREEDOM! And [so] all, with unveiled face[s], BEHOLDING the Lord's glory in a mirror, are progressively being TRANSFORMED [into] the same image, from glory to glory, even as from the Lord [Who is the] Spirit." (2 Cor. 3:16-18) Thus it will be with all who are cast into His presence. Judgment, yes. Transformation, YES!

Once again, carefully consider the semantic range of "**inherent fervor**," and do not automatically call to mind human anger or wrath. His ways are above ours. If He is Love, then His "natural impulse" is Love. If He is full of mercy, then His "mental bent and disposition" will be mercy, when the corrective measures have done their job. If He is gracious, thus also will be His "personal emotion." This Unveiling is about coming to know our Father, and our Lord, Jesus Christ. Like a good Father, His anger is against human violence and injustice, but the wrath is enacted in Love, which never fails (1 Cor. 13:8).

20. **Then every island fled** (took flight), **and the mountains** (or: hills) **were not** (or: are not) **found,**

These islands and mountains are figures of kingdoms, which we previously discussed in 6:14, above. They are not found because they have been absorbed into the kingdom of our Lord and His Anointed (11:15, above). The little Lamb has overcome the world. We find a similar, more extensive and inclusive statement in 20:11, below,

> "**Next I saw a great bright, white throne, and the One continuously sitting upon it from Whose face the Land** (or: ground; earth) **and the atmosphere** (or: sky; heaven) **flee** (or: at once fled). **And a place is not found for them** (or: And then no position was discovered by them or found in them)."

This is figurative of the departure of the old creation that was simultaneous with the emergence of the new creation, of which Paul spoke in 2 Cor. 5:17. The righteous (figured by its white color) throne pictures God's kingdom having been established in justice through the coming of the Messiah, and the old order (the old covenant and temple cultus that governed Jerusalem and all the synagogues of the Diaspora) was taken away through the establishment of the new order that is union with Christ Jesus.

> "'**Consider! I am arriving to do** (form; make; create) **Your will** (purpose; intent; resolve), **O God!**' – **He is habitually** (or: progressively; or: presently) **taking back up the first, so that He could make the second** [*cf.* ch. 9:28] **to stand** (or: that He may place and establish the second)" (Heb. 10:9).

21. **and hail, great** (large) **as weighing a talent** (about 70 pounds), **is continuously coming down** (descending) **out of the atmosphere** (or: sky; heaven) **upon the people** (the humans; mankind). **And**

the men blasphemed (abusively slander; misrepresented and hindered the light of) **God from out of the midst of the plagues** (or: blows; impacts) **of the hail, because Her plague** (blow) **is exceeding great.**

This brings an end to this 7th plague (the last blow upon Jerusalem). Hail was a part of the 7th plague in Egypt, too. There it smote human and beast and every herb of the field, and broke every tree of the field (Ex. 9:25). Here the impact is spoken of only coming upon people, but being huge (approximately 100 #'s). The idea is devastation and ruin. This echoes reference to the day of the Lord in Ezk. 13:1-16, where an overflowing downpour and hail are sent because they had not "gone up into the gaps, neither made up the hedge for the house of Israel to stand in the battle in the day of the Lord.... because they beguile My people, saying 'Peace,' and there is no peace..." Verse 13, there, repeats this idea, "and hailstones in My fury – to consume" (Young).

In Josh. 10:11 great hail came upon the enemies of Israel, so that more died by the hailstones than died by the sword. Isa. 28:2 threatens Ephraim with "a tempest of hail and a destroying storm." Ezk. 13:11-13 speaks of God's judgment against Israel by "an overflowing shower in My anger, and great hailstones, in fury to consume!" Hailstones were a part of God's pleading with people in the context of the prophecy against Gog, in Ezk. 38. So once again, we see the symbols of the OT used in these visions. The message here would have been a warning of the coming destruction of Jerusalem, and a calling to mind of God's judgments in Israel's history. Josephus gives the following report of Rome's siege of Jerusalem:
> "The engines that all the legions had ready prepared for them were admirably contrived... those that threw stones were more forcible and larger.... Now the stones ... were of the weight of a talent [100 #'s].... The blow they gave was no way to be sustained..." (*Josephus, Complete Works*, Kregel Pub., 1960, *Wars of the Jews*, v.6.3, p 557, William Whiston trans.; brackets added).

In a taped teaching, Lynn Hiles points out that those stones would likely have been limestone, from the local terrain, and their light-tan, whitish color flying through the air may have indeed looked like huge hailstones.

This chapter ends with a response from the people being judged by the blows and impacts of these plagues. It is similar to the response to the 4th plague (vs. 9) and to the 5th plague (vs. 11). Here they blaspheme God because of this great smiting by hail. It is what we, today, would call "natural disaster." But again, those of that day recognized God as the cause of such disaster. And so, let us keep in mind the words of Heb. 12:11, "Now ALL DISCIPLINE, indeed, for the present is not seeming to be a thing of joy, but of sorrow. YET SUBSEQUENTLY it is rendering the peaceable fruit of righteousness TO THOSE EXERCISED THROUGH IT" (CLNT; emphasis added). We must remember that "all His ways [are] JUDGMENT... Just and upright [is] He" (Deut. 32:4). And, in Heb. 12:9 we are asked,
> **"To a much greater extent, shall we not be continually placed under and humbly arranged and aligned by the Father of the spirits** (or: the Progenitor of breath-effects and Mentor of attitudes)**? And then we shall proceed living** (or: progressively live)**!"** [*cf* Nu. 27:16; Eph. 6:2-3]

Paul told the called-out in Corinth that "**If anyone is corrupting the temple of God, God will be ruining him**" (1 Cor. 3:17). Earlier in that same chapter (vs. 3) he had called them fleshly, carnal, and said that they were living in accord with the rest of humanity. Like the seven called-out communities in this book, they had some problems. It is typical for all called-out communities. But above we have pointed out God's ways, "which are judgment." And Peter reminds us that "[it was then] **the era** [for] **the judgment to begin from God's house**..." (1 Pet. 4:17). The judgment of these 7 plagues came to what had been "God's house," His people, the Jews (and recall that He came to His own, and His own did not receive Him – John 1:11 – although they were forgiven of this from the cross), and now their house is left to them desolate (Matt. 23:38).

But like the fractional judgments of this book, in Rom. 11 we note that it was only "**some of the branches**" that were broken out of the olive tree (the true Israel that brought God's anointing to humanity), and now other branches are being grafted in among that remnant and have become joint participants of the root and fatness of that tree (Rom. 11:17). The message of these 7 shallow cups is a message for the covenant communities. It happened first to the natural, but it will also happen to us – and has happened periodically throughout history.

> "His judgments do not save us, but they condition and prepare us to receive HIM who is our Salvation. They cause us to turn to the Lord in repentance, and we find He has been drawing us to Himself through it all" (Prinzing, ibid).

Paul wrote,
> "**you were saddened and made anxious down from and in correspondence to God**... **For you see, the anxiety, sadness and pain down from, in the sphere of, in line with and in correspondence to God continuously works, habitually effects and progressively produces a change in thinking and frame of mind: [in turn, leading] into a deliverance and wholeness of health** (a rescue and restoration to the original state and realm; salvation) **void of regret and without change in purpose. Yet the anxiety, sadness, pain and sorrow which belongs to the world** (that comes from secular society, and the organized System of religion, culture, economy and government) **is continuously working down the production of death** (or: is in line with repeatedly and progressively bringing about death)." (2 Cor. 7:9-10).

Sorrow that comes "down from" (the Greek is *kata*) God comes via His judgment. His Word, including His Word of judgment, does not return to Him void – Isa. 55:11 – "but will accomplish what [He] desire[s] and achieve the purpose for which [He] sent it."

> "But while the wrath of God is love's severity, yet it remains purest love, seeking the ultimate good for creation, and so it continues to apply the strokes of chastisement. Repentance will come, but how great is the need for the in-working of His judgments, until that submission comes" (Prinzing, ibid).

We should keep in mind that these 7 blows (impacts; strikes; plagues) were a picture of God's complete "**inherent fervor** (natural impulse; mental bent and disposition; personal emotion; indignation; wrath)" – 7 being the idea of a complete cycle. This also "finished" His "wrath" (15:1, above). We can see it fulfilled upon Jerusalem in AD 70, but this in turn becomes a type, a pattern, and a message to all who read this prophecy.

Chapter 17

1. **Next one of the seven agents – the ones holding the seven bowls – came and spoke with me, saying,**
   > "**Come here! I will proceed showing** (pointing out to) **you the effect of the judgment** (the result of the administering of justice; the effect of the judicial decision and equitable sentence) **of the Great Prostitute – the one continuously sitting upon the many waters,**
2. > "**with whom the kings of the Land** (or: earth) **commit** (or: committed) **prostitution** (or: fornication) **– and those continually dwelling down upon the Land** (or: earth) **[that] are** (or: were) **made drunk from out of the wine of her prostitution.**" [note: see Isa. 1:21; comment: prostitution can be a symbol of idolatry]

These verses inform us that this is a continuation of the previous vision, since it is **one of the seven agents** of chapter 16 who comes and speaks with John, and thus makes him more than a passive observer: John interacts with the vision. The agent comes to show John the next scene in the vision: **the judgment of the Great Prostitute**, and of those who participate with her. This chapter "amplifies the 6th and 7th bowls" (Beale p 847).

Wallace makes some insightful observations:
> "These remaining chapters of the apocalypse surround only two opposite figures – the old apostate Jerusalem in contrast with the New Jerusalem, the Victorious Church of Christ.... The 17th & 18th chapters must be considered as one – for the announced judgment upon the Harlot by the angel at the beginning of ch. 17 was suspended by the vision of the Harlot" (ibid p 363-4).

The term **prostitute**/harlot is a familiar symbol/figure in the OT. God calls Nineveh a harlot in Nah. 3:4, "the well-favored harlot, the mistress of witchcrafts, that sells nations through her prostitutions..." Isa. 23:16, 17 call Tyre a harlot, and we have noted Isa. 1:21 calling "the Faithful City (Jerusalem)" the same, while Ezk. 16:15 says that she "played the harlot." So both Jerusalem as well as heathen cities were termed the prostitute in the OT. Jerusalem was characterized thus by turning away from Yahweh to the gods of the nations. The question is, which city is being figured by this woman who is seated upon **the many waters**, and upon **the little wild animal** (vs. 3), here in the Unveiling? Some have said it was Rome of the past; others see her as Rome of the future. The preterists understand her to be Jerusalem of the 1st century. We see in 18:4, below, that she is someone from whom John's listeners were to separate themselves:

> "**Come out of her** (or: Go forth from out of her midst) **My people, so that you may not jointly participate with** (be a partner with; fellowship together with) **her sins** (failures; occasions of missing the mark), **and so that you may not receive from out of her plagues** (blows)."

The mention of "plagues" is a reference to destruction. It was Jerusalem that was destroyed, in AD 70.

The allusion of "**many waters**" looks back to Jer.51:13, identifying the prostitute as Babylon, but the figure is explained here in vs. 15, below: "**The waters which you saw** (or: see), **where the Prostitute continually sits, are peoples and crowds** (mobs) **and multitudes** (nations; ethnic groups) **and tongues** (languages). This suggests that she,
> "had her commerce with all the nations of the Roman empire and derived her revenues from them. She would not even hesitate for the sake of gain to make Jehovah's temple 'a house of merchandise' (Jn. 2:16)" (Terry, ibid p 427).

Chilton (ibid p 424) points out that the descriptive phrase, "**many waters**," was used of the 144K in 14:2, above, and of those praising God in 19:6, below, and thus we can see that this is also a figure of covenant people – which in turn points to these waters being those over whom Jerusalem dominated and from whom received support. With regard to Nineveh and Tyre being termed harlots/prostitutes, Chilton notes that these are, "the only two cities outside of Israel that are accused of harlotry... both [having] been in covenant with God... (1 Ki. 5:1-12; 9:13; Amos 1:9); Nineveh was converted under the ministry of Jonah (Jon. 3:5-10)" (ibid n 2; brackets added).

We find Israel accused of "playing the harlot" in Jer. 2:20 and 3:1, then in 3:3 she is described as having, "a whore's forehead." Hos. 9:1 proclaimed, "Rejoice not, O Israel... for you have gone a whoring from your God; you have loved a reward (= prostitute's pay) upon every threshing floor." Chilton notes that Solomon's temple was built upon what had been David's threshing floor (2 Chron. 3:1). He further states that, "the action of grinding at a mill is a Biblical image of sexual relations (Job 31:10; Isa. 47:2; Jer. 25:10)" (ibid p 426). *Cf* Ruth 3:2-9.

The clause "**with whom the kings of the Land** (or: earth) **commit** (or: committed) **prostitution**" is language from Isa.23:17, "and has allusion to a widespread commerce resembling that of ancient Tyre" (Terry ibid p 427). The indicted collusion here may be an echo of Acts 4:

> 26. **'The kings of the land took a stand and the rulers** (or: the leaders; the officials) **were gathered together at the same [place]** (or: = joined forces upon the same [purpose and intent]; or, perhaps: = as one) **– down against the Lord and down against His Anointed One** (or: the Christ which was Him).**'** [Ps. 2:1-2]
> 27. **"For in truth both Herod and Pontius Pilate, together with ethnic multitudes and [the] People of Israel – [coming] upon** (= against) **Your set-apart Servant** (or: holy Boy) **Jesus**...

Jerusalem reached out to all of the Diaspora, and Israel's history involved political alliances:

> "Thus, Hosea decries Israel's political compacts with the Assyrians, stating, 'Ephraim has hired lovers' (Hos. 8:9; cf 2:1-7)" (Simmons, ibid p 316).

Ezk. 16:25 says of Jerusalem,

> "You built your mound at every crossroad; and you sullied your beauty and spread your legs to every passerby, and you multiplied your harlotries" (Tanakh).

The next clause, "**those continually dwelling down upon the Land**," has two possible referents:
> a) people not joined to Christ, and thus not existentially "dwelling" in the "heavens" as a part of His body, the called-out communities;
> b) businessmen of Judea (the "Land") who, through connections with the leaders of Jerusalem, were profiting from trade with foreign governments or with others within the Empire.

The clause, "**made drunk from out of the wine**," is a figure of excess or over-abundance. It "went to their heads," figuratively speaking. The opposite condition is seen in the contrast given by Paul:

> "**stop being made drunk** (or: Do not be continuously made intoxicated) **by wine, within which exists the disposition of one having no hope of safety** (dissipation and ill health; desperation), **but rather be continuously or repeatedly filled full in spirit** (within [the] Spirit; within the midst of [the] Breath-effect; in the sphere of attitude; in union with [the] Breath)' (Eph. 5:18).

3. **And he carried me away, in spirit** (or: within [the] Spirit; in union with a Breath-effect), **into a desert. And I saw a woman continuously sitting** (or: seated) **upon a crimson** (or: scarlet) **little wild animal** (or: beast), **[which was] continuously loaded** (freighted) **with names of blasphemy** (which hinder light; of injurious, abusive slander; or: from a misrepresented image), **having seven heads and ten horns.**

The description, "**carried away in spirit**" may signify that he was transported in the vision. The alternate renderings, "within, or, in union with, [the] Spirit or a Breath-effect," emphasize the sphere of what John is seeing, and the means of his being brought to the next scene of the "play." It also affirms that what he is describing came from God. It is similar to what he said in 1:10, above.

What is the significance of the setting being **a desert**? In Israel's history, the desert was a place of testing (Nu. 13-14). It was there that God led her "these 40 years in the wilderness, to humble you and to prove you, to know what was in your heart" (Deut. 8:2). It was a place where there was no fruitfulness (Jer. 2:2ff). It was in the desert that Jesus was tested by the devil (Mat. 4:1-11). In fact, it was there that the devil showed Him all the kingdoms of the inhabited land (Mat. 4:8). I wonder if He saw these as a seven-headed animal, for "**He was constantly being WITH the little** (small) **wild animals**" during His 40 days in the wilderness. This setting corresponds, but in contrast, to the place where the "heavenly" woman fled from the dragon, in 12:14-16, above. By collusion with Rome, Jerusalem had become one with the current domination system. When Christianity became institutionalized, it also joined with Rome, in the 4th century, and once again rode the little animal system. This system took the called-out communities into a spiritual desert. God's Israel was no longer a watered garden (22:1-2, below; Isa. 58:11; Jer. 31:12).

The **names of blasphemy** show the character of this animal. The parenthetical expansion of the term offers us a broader view of what these names meant. The literal meaning of the phrase, from the Greek elements of the word, and in apposition, is: "which hinder light." This would mean that the domination system obscured the Light of Christ and the true knowledge of God. Another use of the word blasphemy (which itself is a transliteration of the Greek letters, not a translation of the word) signified "to speak harm; injurious, abusive slander" – a frequently used tool of the system. The "traditions of the elders" had been, "**habitually invalidating** (depriving of lordship; making void of authority) **the Word of God** (God's thought and idea; the message from God)" (Mk. 7:13), and did not yield the fruit of the Spirit, but rather distorted God's truth and reality. This had happened before. Yahweh said to Israel, "I had planted you a noble vine, wholly a right seed. How then are you turned into the degenerate plant of a strange vine unto Me? …. A wild ass, used to the wilderness…" (Jer. 2:21, 24). This is why Jesus repeatedly stood against the scribes and the Pharisees.

The final rendering on offer is reading the phrase as an ablative which would inform us that the character and identity of their ordered theology presented God "from a misrepresented image" of God. It was one that laid heavy burdens upon people (Mat. 23:4). Later manifestation of this little animal would center around a doctrine from *demons*: the terror of eternal torment by a merciless god – a blasphemous image imported from foreign religions. In accord with the 7 heads of this little animal, a number that spoke of fullness and completeness, this system did not have just one blasphemous characteristic but was **loaded**, or freighted (implying commerce), with these names. It had a complete reputation for hindering the light, slandering its opponents and misrepresenting the reality of God.

Roman emperors tended to assume the titles and positions of deity. In the Scriptures, blasphemy also represents an attitude of disrespect, especially toward God. In Matt. 12:32, Mark 3:29 and Lu. 12:10, we see that blasphemy against the Holy Spirit (i.e., against God) shall not be pardoned nor forgiven – one must pay the penalty for this: judgment. Thus do we see here in chapters 17 and 18 that the woman who associated herself with the blasphemous beast is judged, and in 19:20, below, the beast also is judged.

Blasphemy happened to Paul in Rom. 3:8 and in 1 Cor. 4:13; 10:30. In Titus 3:2 Paul admonishes them "**to be in the habit of speaking injuriously of** (blaspheming; slandering; defaming) **no one**." In 1 Tim. 1:20, speaking of Hymeneus and Alexander, Paul says,
> " **whom I gave over** (or: commit; commend; transfer; handed along; deliver) **to the adversary** (or: entrust and render as a yield to be matured in and with the opponent; or: pass along to and deliver by this *satan*) **to the end that they would be child-trained, educated and disciplined with a view toward maturity, [so as] not to constantly blaspheme** (speak abusively; malign, defame or slanderously vilify; give a false image or misrepresent in a way that hinders the Light)."

Michael would not even blaspheme *satan*, as recorded in Jude 9. In 1 Tim. 6:4 Paul warns that there may be some in the called-out community who may come without sound words, but rather with morbid questionings and controversies, out of which is being birthed envy, strife, BLASPHEMIES, etc. So, with this in mind, I suggest that there is a connection between these "names of blasphemies" and the carnal, "beast" nature within people "**within which also you formerly walked, when you lived in these things**" (Col. 3:7). But we also see this in the called-out communities, and thus the admonition in Eph. 4:31,
> "**So let every bitterness, swelling negative emotion** (inherent fervor; or: natural propensity, disposition and impulse; or: wrath), **enraged impulse, clamorous outcry, and blasphemy** (slanderous, abusive or light-hindering speech; malignment, vilifying defamation) **be at once**

lifted up and removed from you folks, together with all worthlessness (that which ought not to be or is of bad quality; malice; ugliness; depravity) **and keep on becoming kind folks**..."

The particular color **crimson**/scarlet calls to mind Isa. 1:18 where Israel's sins were thus described, just before the lament of vs. 21, where Judea and Jerusalem were characterized as being a prostitute. This color may signify blood that the system of dominance had shed, and it may speak to the wine with which the kings had become drunk. But we may also gain insight from God's admonition in Isa. 1:17, "Learn to cause goodness; seek justice; relieve the oppressed and make happy those that have been soured; bring justice to the orphan and contend for the widow." In vs. 18b He lays out hope in regard to their scarlet and red sins: "as snow, they shall be white… they shall become as wool."

The figure of "**a crimson** (or: scarlet) **little wild animal**" calls us back to the "**fiery-colored dragon**" of 12:3 and the **little wild animal** that is described in 13:1, above, that was given the throne and authority of the dragon. The **woman** of vs. 1-2, above, receives support from this little wild animal (the domination system) which in the 1st century was the Roman Empire, and then, for a time, the Zealots. This pattern of prostitution with ruling powers has been observed down through the following centuries.

4. **The woman also had been clothed [with] purple and crimson** (scarlet). **And having been adorned** (overlaid; gilded) **with gold and precious stones and pearls, she is continuously holding in her hand a golden cup** (goblet) **[which] is continuously loaded** (freighted; brimming) **with abominations** (detestable things) **and the unclean things** (impure aspects) **of** (from) **her prostitutions.**

The woman is wearing the colors of the little wild animal system. Jerusalem now reflects Rome. Later, the institutional church reflected the image of secular kingdoms, even having its own militant arms and orders. She is obviously not poor. Here we see the Jewish privileged class in luxury. Recall the parable in Lu. 16:19 where Jesus portrayed the Jews as "a rich man which was clothed in purple..." This is God's people depicted as being in association with the world systems and wearing their clothing instead of the righteousness of God. The **precious stones** and fine garment answered to the high priest's vestments. The **golden cup** represents the experience **of her prostitutions** (note the plural) which she holds out for the rulers of the Land to receive from her. Those experiences (the figure of the **cup**) are the extreme opposite of being set-apart, sacred and holy. Her religion defiles rather than purifies. We see her named, in the next verse, and we see in Jer. 51:7,
> "Babylon [was] a golden cup in Yahweh's hand, making the entire earth drunk; the nations drank of her wine; therefore the nations are raving mad."

Yahweh chided Jerusalem in Jer. 4:30-31,
> "And you, [who will be] devastated, what are you doing that you clothe yourself in scarlet (or: crimson), that you ornament [yourself with] ornaments of gold, that you amplify your eyes with pigment? [It is] for futility… they seek your soul. A sound like one in travail I hear, distress like [a woman] bearing a firstborn. [The] sound of the daughter of Zion, gasping for breath… before killers!" (CVOT).

We may also see, in her adornment, allusions to Adam in Ezk. 28:13 (and there, a reference to Eden, Gen. 2:11-12) and to the passage of Isa. 54:11-12 where Yahweh promises to later, "embed your stones with fair colors (or: in antimony) and lay your foundation with sapphires… make your windows with agates and your gates of carbuncles (fiery-red stones) and all your borders of pleasant (or: delightful) stones." Cf 21: 11, 18-21, below, and Isa. 60:10-11. We read in Ezk. 5:11-12 Yahweh speaking against Jerusalem,
> "because you have defiled My Sanctuary with all your abominations, even I Myself also shall hack down, and My eye shall not spare. A third of you shall die by plague… consumed by famine, a third shall fall by a sword… a third shall I toss to every wind."

Paul admonished the called-out communities to **adorn** themselves differently, in 1 Tim. 2:
> 9. **Likewise, women to habitually adorn and arrange themselves in an ordered and arranged system of proper behavior and descent clothing: with modesty, so as to be unseen** (or: as having downcast eyes), **and soundness of mind** (sanity and sensibility), **not in braids** (or: inter-weavings) **and in golden ornaments, or in pearls or expensive garments,**
> 10. **but rather – what is suitable** (proper; fitting; becoming) **in** (or: for; to) **women giving instruction on reverence for God** [note: refers to women who taught "God-fearers" in synagogues, to prepare these folks for conversion] **– through good works and virtuous actions.**

His gender specific, and culturally relevant words are appropriate for a generalized, corporate contrast to the prostitute, here described. Also note the contrast in Peter's admonitions in 1 Pet. 3:2-4,
> 1. **Likewise** (In like manner)... **if any are habitually unpersuaded by the Word** (or: uncompliant or disobedient to the message; unconvinced with the thought, reason or idea), **they will continue being profited** (will progressively receive advantage; or: will proceed in being acquired as gain) **without a word** (or: message; reason), **through the behavior** (or: conduct; way of life) **of the wives** (or: women),
> 2. **being eyewitnesses of** (or: looking upon and observing) **the pure behavior** (or: way of life; conduct) **of you folks – which is turned upward in reverence, respect and [sacred] fear and awe –**
> 3. **whose world must not consist of the external adornment – of braiding or interweaving or struggling with [the] hair and [the] placing-around of gold ornaments, or of dressing up** (putting on garments) **–**
> 4. **but to the contrary, [it should consist of] the hidden person** (concealed humanity; cloaked personality) **of the heart, within the incorruptible and imperishable quality of the gentle and still** (at ease; restful; quiet) **spirit** (or: attitude; disposition; or: Breath-effect), **which is** (or: continually exists being) **of great value and very costly in God's sight** (= view, or, perspective).

As to "**abominations** (detestable things) **and the unclean things** (impure aspects)," we read Ezk. 5:11-12, cited above. Jesus spoke to this situation in Mat. 23:
> 25. "**How tragic is the fate in you people – scribes and Pharisees: overly-critical interpreters! For you folks are habitually cleansing the outside of the cup and of the fine side dish – yet inside they continuously contain a full load from snatching** (plunder; pillage; = the fruits of forceful greed) **and lack of strength** (or: self-indulgence).
> 26. "**Blind Pharisee, first cleanse the inside of the cup and of the fine side dish – so that its outside can also come to be** (be birthed) **clean!**
> 27. "**Tragic will be the fate of you Law scholars and Pharisees – you who recite a front of your own opinions and answers! [It will be] because you continue closely resembling whitewashed** (i.e., plastered with lime) **tombs** (grave sites), **which indeed, from outside, continue being made to appear in the prime of beauty, for a time – yet inside they contain a full load of bones of dead folks, as well as every uncleanness.**
> 28. "**In this way you, yourselves, also on the one hand are continually made to outwardly appear to people [to be] just** (fair, righteous, in right relationships, and in accord with the way pointed out) **– yet inside you continuously exist being men glutted and distended, full of opinionated answers** (or: perverse detail-oriented scholarship; hyper-criticism and judgmentalism; well-sifted wicked interpretations) **and lawlessness** (= practice which is contrary to the Law [Torah]). *Cf* Mk. 7:1-23.

These words have hit the mark on through history, and still apply today. The Good News comes in listening to, and abiding in, Christ so that we do not fall into the same snare (*cf* Rom. 11:18-26).

5. **And upon her forehead, a name having been written:**
   A MYSTERY (A SECRET; a matter that to gain the knowledge of which initiation is necessary) –
   BABYLON the GREAT: The <u>Mother</u> of the Prostitutes and of The Abominations (Detestable Things) **of The Land** (or: from the earth).

Before considering the specifics regarding the meaning of "**Babylon the Great**" (an allusion to Dan. 4:30), we would like to remind you of 11:8, above, "And their fallen dead body will be upon the broad place of **The Great City** – whatever, spiritually, is normally being called 'Sodom' and 'Egypt' – WHERE also THEIR LORD was CRUCIFIED." So Jerusalem already has some symbolic/spiritual names applied to her. We should not miss that this **name**, signifying both identity and nature, was written on **her forehead** (*cf* Jer. 3:3), in contrast to the Name of the Father written on the foreheads of the 144K, in 14:1, above. The latter symbolically comprises the Christ, while the former is a manifestation of the antichrist (that which is instead of, and in the place of, and is resistant to, Christ). Again, the forehead is a symbol for one's thinking and mindset – it is another name corresponding to the little wild animal upon which she rides: she has taken the beast's identity and is the property of this little wild animal. She has become the bride of the beast, set in contrast to the Bride of the little Lamb, seen in 19:9bff, below.

Here John is told that the city's name is "**secret**," or, "a mystery" – something that only those initiated into the meaning of the Jewish symbols of OT apocalyptic literature would understand – and they would know first of all that it DID NOT refer to the literal city of Babylon (either past or future): this name is a "mystery." Wallace observes that in vs. 16 the beast hated the Harlot. But the beast of the 1st century was the Roman Empire, so it would make no sense that the Roman Empire hated Rome (if this was the city meant by this figure). Thus the Harlot was of necessity some other city. However, it is historically clear that there was indeed animosity between the Roman Empire (the beast, or little wild animal), and Jerusalem. This description may suggest a reference to that of which Paul spoke in 2 Thes. 2:7,
> "**the secret** (hidden purpose; mystery) **of the lawlessness** (which is the unlawfulness; having the character of being violation of the Law) **is already continuously working within** (operating)."

This secret was the darkness from out of which the secret of, from, and which is, Christ was made to spring forth (2 Cor. 4:6), as a Seed from out of the soil (*cf* Col. 1:26, 27; 4:3; 1 Cor. 2:7; 4:1; Eph. 1:9; 3:3, 9: 5:32; 6:19). Beale notes that the word **secret**, or, 'mystery,' "occurs in the Greek OT with an eschatological sense only in Dan. 2:18-19, 27-30, 47 LXX…" (ibid p 858).

In Jer. 2, the Word of Yahweh tells him, "Go and cry in the ears of Jerusalem (vs. 2)…. Israel was holiness unto Yahweh (vs. 3)…. when upon every high hill [the place of the pagan idols] and under every green tree you wandered, playing the harlot" (vs. 20). See also Jer. 3:1, 6 & 8.

Ezk. 16:2 reads, "Son of man, cause Jerusalem to know her abominations." Then note vs. 15, "But you… become a prostitute…" And in vs. 26-29 it shows that she engaged in prostitution with Egypt, Assyria and even Babylon, and vs. 35 begins Jerusalem's judgments. Compare vs. 16, below, with Ezk. 16:36-41,
> "Then I will hand you over to your lovers [the Gentile nations], and they will tear down your mounds and destroy your lofty shrines. They will strip you of your clothes and take your fine jewelry and leave you naked and bare. They will bring a mob against you, who will stone you and hack you to pieces with their swords. They will burn down your houses…"

Ezk. 16:44 states, "like mother, like daughter." The subtitle of the woman here in vs. 5 proclaims, "**The MOTHER of the Prostitutes**." And again consider the story of the "Two Sisters" in Ezk. 23. There we see a similar judgment being prophesied against the "Faithful City" – which had become a Prostitute. And then Hos. 1:2 records that "the land is verily committing prostitution rather than following Yahweh." *Cf* Hos. 2:1-5.

So it would seem from these passages that, based upon OT symbolism and characterizations by the Lord, Jerusalem is a prime choice for being the one who is here figured as "The Great Prostitute."

In Gal. 4:22-31, Paul spoke of "the Jerusalem which now is" as being "in slavery with her children." How was 1st century Jerusalem in slavery? First of all, she was an occupied country, so in that sense she was a slave to Rome. And in Rom. 6:16 Paul says, "Are you not aware that to whom you are presenting yourselves AS SLAVES unto OBEDIENCE, his slave you are, whom you are obeying, whether of Sin into death, or of Obedience into righteousness?" (CLNT) By rejecting her Redeemer, Jerusalem remained a slave to sin.

What is said here of the figure of Jerusalem was said of the literal city Babylon in Jer. 51:6, "Flee from Babylon! Run for your lives! Do not be destroyed because of her sins." *Cf* vss. 2, 4, above; 18:4, below. And then Jer. 51:13, "You who live by many waters and are rich in treasures..." *Cf* vss. 1, 4, above; 18:10-13, below. The Jewish Christians would therefore understand the symbolic message about the Babylon here in the Unveiling. They would know to flee out of Jerusalem, for destruction was coming.

Now some think that Jer. 51 means that the Babylon here in chapter 17 is literally a city called Babylon. But please note vs. 15, below, where an explanation of the FIGURE of the "**many waters**" is explained, that these waters "are peoples, and crowds, and multitudes and tongues." If the waters are symbolic, why should we not conclude that the name "Babylon" is also symbolic? Peter, being in Jerusalem, uses this name in the same way that John did here. 1 Pet. 5:13 says, "Greeting you is **the church in Babylon**, chosen together with you, and Mark, my son." This letter from Peter is "to **the SCATTERED** (dispersed)." The same word "scattered" is used in Acts 8:1 where Luke records the reason for this scattering,

> "**Now on that great day great persecution was birthed upon the called-out community [that was] WITHIN JERUSALEM; so they were ALL – EXCEPT for the sent-forth emissaries** (representatives) **– dispersed and SCATTERED as seeds down among the regions of Judea and Samaria**."

This would suggest that the emissaries (including Peter) stayed in Jerusalem. In fact MSS D* & 1175 insert after **emissaries**, the clause, "who alone remained in Jerusalem." So it was from Jerusalem (now significantly referred to as Babylon) that Peter wrote his first letter to those who had been dispersed by the persecution that was happening in Jerusalem. This salutation in 1 Pet. 5:13 also came from Mark, who was also living in Jerusalem (see Acts 12:12).

This woman can also be found in the allusion to Jezebel and "her children" in 2:20-23, above. The spirit of the Prostitute was not only in apostate Judaism, but continued on within the called-out communities, on down through the centuries – and is very active in our day.

6. **Then I saw the woman, being continuously drunk from out of the blood of the set-apart folks and from out of the blood of the witnesses of Jesus, and seeing her I wondered** (marveled; was awestruck [with]) **a great wonder** (or: astonished perplexity; or: I wondered, "[It is] a great marvel!").

John records that when he saw **the woman** that he "marveled" or "**wondered**." He did not wonder about the beast, but about the woman. There seems to be a sense of surprise in Isaiah's words, "How becomes a Prostitute the town that was faithful Zion" (1:21, CVOT, reading with the LXX). In Isa. 5:7b, Yahweh remarks concerning Israel, His vineyard,

"I remained and waited for him to produce justice, but he produced lawlessness, and [I saw, or found] not fairness, equity or right relationships in the Way pointed-out, but in contrast, a cry!" (LXX, JM).

Here we are told that this woman is **drunk "from out of the blood of the set-apart folks and from out of the blood of the witnesses of Jesus."** This is an allusion to 11:3ff, above. We have previously pointed out Jesus' words in Matt. 23:34-36 "that upon YOU may come all the **righteous blood** shed upon the Land..." Also Lu. 13:33-35, "Jerusalem... which **kills the prophets**..." We find this thought reiterated in 18:4, below,

> "**And within her was** (or: is) **found blood of prophets and of set-apart folks – even of all those having been slaughtered upon the Land.**"

Connecting this with the witnesses of Mat. and Lu., the identity of the woman is unmistakable.

Acts 7:52 shows Stephen denouncing Jerusalem's abominations,

> "**Which one of the prophets** (those who had light ahead of time and spoke before the people) **did your fathers** [D* reads: those men] **not persecute and pursue? And they killed off those predicting concerning the coming of the Just One** (the Fair, Equitable, Right One that is in rightwised relationships of the Way pointed-out) **– of Whom you yourselves now became people who pre-commit and give in advance** (or: folks who **abandoned** in time of need; people who [were] pre-paid), **even murderers.**"

Here, we also recall Mat. 27:25, "**Then, giving a decided reply, all the people said, "His blood [is] upon us** (or: [be splattered] on us; = the responsibility for his death falls on us), **and upon our children!**"

Now call to mind how the institutional church persecuted those it considered to be heretics, in the last 1750 years (especially such times as the Spanish Inquisition). Religious wars, ethnic genocides and radical terrorism by fundamentalist religions have smeared blood around the globe – and usually because of greed for wealth and power (the mindset of the little animal, upon which they still sit). In the "less primitive" (?), modern cultures, the killing is social, reputational, economic, and relational, where some religious pundit pronounces, "Farewell, Heretic (fill in the name)" and attempts to dismiss those who hold views that run counter to what is deemed "orthodox" by the religious "in crowd." And we still marvel and sit in wonder that such esteemed institutions could be characterized as a prostitute, by God. Religion has been one of the primary proliferators of hate – and often for purportedly ethical, theological or moral "causes." To keep up appearances, this woman often kills her wounded, as well. And we continue to marvel at it all.

7. **And the agent said to me,**
> "**Why do** (or: did) **you wonder** (marvel; are you awestruck with astonished perplexity)**? I will proceed declaring to you the secret of the woman and of the little wild animal [which is] continuously bearing her aloft, [and] which has the seven heads and the ten horns.**

The **agent** is surprised that John does not understand the picture which he has just seen, so he or she proceeds with an explanation. This calls to mind Jesus expressing surprise that His disciples did not understand a parable that He had just given to them (e.g., Mat. 15:16). But as Paul informed us, **secrets** must be revealed by an unveiling of our spiritual perceptions. Also note that it is not just "the woman" of which he or she is to **proceed** in **declaring the secret**: it concerns her AND **the little wild animal** which has the **7 heads and 10 horns**. Each of these parts are important pieces of the puzzle. We may wonder why John had to have **the secret of the little wild animal** explained to him, but this is probably so that John's listeners would hear the explanation and its connection to 13:1ff, above.

8. **"The little wild animal (beast) which you saw was existing, and does not exist** (is not), **and is about to repeatedly climb up** (progressively ascend) **out of the Deep, and to repeatedly lead under** (or: go away; [other MSS: then it progressively withdraws]) **into loss** (or: destruction). **And those continually dwelling down upon the Land** (earth) – **whose names have not been written upon the little Scroll of THE LIFE from [the] casting-down** (foundation) **of [the] world** (ordered system; or: aggregate of humanity) – **will continue wondering** (marveling), **continually observing** (beholding) **the little wild animal, that it was continuously existing** (it was), **and it does not exist** (is not), **and it will proceed being present** (exist alongside).

Now let us look at **the little wild animal**, with its 7 heads and 10 horns, and which **repeatedly ascends** from **out of the Deep**. We saw it at work against the "**two witnesses**" in 11:7, above – and the location was Jerusalem. We saw it rise up out of the sea of humanity in 13:1-7. We are given more specific information in vss. 9-17, below, but as a preview to help us understand this verse:
> The 7 heads are 7 mountains (vs. 9).
> The 7 heads are 7 kings (vs. 10).
> The 10 horns are 10 kings (vs. 11).
> These 10 have one opinion, thought or resolve, and submit to the corporate animal (vss. 13, 17).
> These 10 do battle with the little Lamb (vs. 14), but are overcome by Him.
> They finally lay waste the Prostitute and burn her (vs. 16).

The fact that this **little wild animal repeatedly climbs up out of the Deep** (the depths of humanity) should alert us to a perception that its habitual activity is from its power and ability, or from its authority (the right and privilege, from out of its existing), or from its having been directed to do so. Such an observation suggests that it a) has a purpose to fulfill, b) is part of a plan, or c) that it is part of the needed environment for what humanity is to learn during our "school of earth experiences" (Hannah Hurnard), i.e., the reason for our journey through the Valley of the Shadow of Death (Ps. 23).

We observe from 20:1-3, below, that God is able to direct an agent to capture, overpower and imprison **the little animal**, called "the old serpent, the one who/which thrusts things through folks, and the adversary." We also observe, in 20:7 that it is released from prison for a short mission, then is returned to its origin (Fire and Deity) in 20:10 (cf Rom. 11:36). So, we can understand and rest at ease that God controls this negative spirit (just as we observe His control of *satan* in Job 1 and 2) and that He uses it for His plan of the ages. Isa. 54:16 informs us that Yahweh "created the waster to destroy [things]," and that it is "an instrument for His work." The adversary (devil; serpent) is compared to the work of a blacksmith who creates useful tools in his forge (Isa. 54:16a).

We can also observe this spirit periodically climbing up within social structures and domination systems (that are all creations of the human mind and spirit in those who collectively give rise to these ideas), as we contemplate and follow human history. If we can accept the Garden of Eden environment as a metaphor for the complexity of human nature, as well as being a story of the creation of a person, then we may be able to see that the serpent (*satan*; the "devil") normally works through people or social structures, and within the natural world (as we observe in Job's story), and thus has a valid part of the human story. It was created to be our adversary, but is meant to be overcome, harnessed and used, under the direction of the Holy Spirit. Paul did this in 1 Cor. 5:5. God used an agent of the adversary to work with His grace to keep Paul from being lifted up with pride from all that he had been given (2 Cor. 12:7). Overcoming this adversarial spirit is what Paul referred to in 2 Cor. 10:5,
> "**progressively tearing down and demolishing conceptions** (concepts; the effects of thoughts, calculations, imaginations, reasonings and reflections) **and every height** (or: high position; high-effect) **and lofty [attitude, purpose or obstacle] that is habitually lifting itself up against** (or:

elevating itself up on so as to put down) **the intimate and experiential knowledge of God, and then taking captive every thought – one after another – and leading them prisoner into the hearing obedience of the Christ**."

Christ cast down the old system, the old covenant and the old God-to-humanity arrangement (2 Cor. 5:17) in order to "found and establish" the NEW (*cf* 21:5, below).

Now in 18:9-10, below, the kings of the Land, who have committed prostitution with her and have indulged with her, lament and grieve for her as they distance themselves from her, observing her burning in judgment. Then the merchants of these kingdoms also mourn at their loss of business, as recorded in the remainder of chapter 18. Our next view of this animal is in 19:19-20, below, where it and the kings of the Land (with their armies) are gathered together to make war against Him that sits upon the white horse, in the atmosphere (or: heaven). So this is the story line, which in Christ has already been completed. The preterist view sees this animal to be the Roman Empire of the 1st century, but I suggest that it is also a type of all the governments (empires; domination systems) upon which the institutional "church" rides in the centuries that follow.

As with Rome and its ten provinces, the **ten kings** (vs. 12, below) are associated with the ten toes of the image in Dan. 2:31-45. Those toes are a part of the 4th and final kingdom shown in Nebuchadnezzar's dream, as iron mixed with clay. Those ten toes represent the 10 provinces of the Roman Empire. It is the kingdom of God which destroys these kingdoms – the work of the cross of Christ. His death and resurrection were figured as the Stone which struck the image in the dream – and this happened in the time of the 4th kingdom, the Roman Empire. That Stone, which grew into a great mountain (= a kingdom) and filled the whole earth, began as the Rock upon which He is building His called-out, covenant community (Mat. 16:18).

The 7 mountains/kings (vss. 9-10, below) are considered to be the first 7 Roman emperors, the 6th one (the one that "is" or then existed, vs.10, below) being Nero. Recall our study in 13:18, above, where the number of the "beast," being 666, was associated with Nero. Also recall Maarschalk's view that this represented the leaders of the Zealots. With this overview in mind, let us return to vs. 3 and observe that the agent carried John away "in spirit." This should indicate to us that what he was to see would also be "in spirit." Just as Jerusalem was "spiritually called Sodom and Egypt" (11:8, above), John is now given a picture of a **City** (vs. 18, below) which is given another "spiritual" name: **Babylon**.

Although we have seen the historical fulfillment of this vision as being Jerusalem riding the power of the Roman Empire in the 1st century, we can also understand that the symbolic blasphemous names had their application to this same spiritual beast in the centuries that followed, with the "church" (the organized, hierarchal institution, as contrasted to "the called-out, covenant communities") becoming institutionalized. It then replaced Jerusalem as being the "woman" now riding it. After the demise of Rome, the church-institution itself became a power and incorporated the structure of human government that remains unto this day, and instead of being a community united in love, it is now completely divided (the 7 heads now internalized), with many heads and power centers. Is there not a name, given by these organizations, upon each head? The spirit of division continued from the very start when carnal people within the communities started to place their association and identity with one man or another:

> 12. **Now I am saying this because each of you is habitually saying, "I, myself, am indeed [a follower] of Paul," yet [another], "I myself belong to Apollos," and [another], "As for me, I [am] of Cephas' [group]," but [another], "I, myself, [am] from Christ."**
> 13. **Christ has been parted and remains divided into fragments!** (or, as a question: Has Christ been fragmented into divided parts?)" (1 Cor. 1)

Today we have Catholics, Eastern Orthodox, Lutherans, Presbyterians, Baptists, The Assembly of God, Four Square, etc., and some attach the title "Pauline" to the name of their church, or call it, "Christ's Church of [Anytown]." The names tend to be exclusive in some way, and thus exclude other groups, and are divisive. They "misrepresent and hinder the light" (*blasphēmeō*). We still have the same spirit that Paul found in Corinth – Jerusalem indeed has many daughters (vs. 5, above) – and Christ's uninformed bride rides upon these various systems of organization, as well as, historically, upon many civil governments. The history of the institutionalized "church" has been of those "continuously drunk from out of the blood of the set-apart folks, and from out of the blood of the witnesses of Jesus" (vs. 6, above). No wonder John was amazed at what he saw. The castigation of those who differ in their doctrines from what is considered to be "orthodox," or the traditions of the "fathers," has been an integral part of the story of the organized "church." Sadly, we find this same spirit in the leadership of many local congregations and parachurch groups. It is the spirit of "us and them." It is the spirit of "domination."

Here again (vs. 5, above) we have a name written in the forehead, showing identity and mindset. It is a symbolic name, called a "**mystery**," making it clear that it is not to be taken literally. In contrast, the "mysteries of the kingdom" were to be revealed only to disciples, or followers, of Christ (Matt. 13:11), and Jesus spent three years initiating them into those mysteries. Paul referred to himself as a steward "**of the mysteries of God**" in 1 Cor. 4:1. It was he who made the most frequent use of this word in the NT. Jerusalem of the 1st century was this "Babylon the Great," but after the destruction of the mother, her daughters – which eventually became many denominations – continued to be drunk from the blood of His set-apart ones, as well as of those from other religions. All the earth has become drunk from religion. Wars are to this day fought from a mindset of a union of religion and government. Saul exemplified this spirit of 1st century Jerusalem; the crusades of the "church" in the middle ages embodied it; and today we see it in the terrorism of the jihad. The little beast comes from deep within all of us, and in the history of humanity it repeatedly ascends out of this **Deep** (vs. 8).

In the narratives of the Gospels, we saw how the Jewish leadership of the 1st century used the Romans to slay Jesus. Then there was the parallel case in 11:7, above, where the two witnesses were killed by this same little animal: prophetic of the history of the institutional church as it rode this beast. It is this system of domination and control upon which the institutional "church" rides, and which leads its people into **loss and destruction**. It was the leadership in Israel which caused all the sheep to be lost (*cf* Ezk. 34), but this condition brought the true Shepherd onto the scene. Let us bring Him into the scene of Israel's lost daughters, to bind the wounded of today's "churches," and to give light to those who sit in darkness.

Now what about the statement where those who are **earth-bound in their citizenship**, who were **not written upon the little Scroll of The LIFE** of the little Lamb in this age (or in this present life)? *Cf* discussions of this symbolic phrase in 3:5 and 13:8, above, and in 20:15 and 22:19, below. This calls to mind the language of Acts 13:48b, "**And so they trusted and believed – whoever were folks having been set and arranged into an eonian life** (or: into life which has its source and quality from the Age [of Messiah])," which seems to point to God's plan concerning,
> "**each person within the result and effect of his or her own class** (or: ordered place; appointed position [in line]; arranged time or order of succession; = place in a harvest calendar, thus, due season of maturity)" (1 Cor. 15:23a).

But how are we to understand the following compound phrase, "**from [the] casting-down** (foundation) **of [the] world** (ordered system; or: aggregate of humanity)"? We discussed this same phrase in 13:8, above, and its use here logically applies to the same time or situation. So there is apparently a direct association between the slaying of the little Lamb (13:8), and the "**names have not been written upon the little Scroll**." Paul used the phrase in question, in Eph. 1:4,

"**He chose us out** (or: selects and picks us out) **within Him, and in union with Him** [F, G: for or in Himself] **before [the]** (or: prior to a) **casting down** (or: a laying of the foundation; a conception) **of [the] ordered system** (world; universe; cosmic order; or: human aggregate), **[for] us to continuously be set-apart ones** (or: to progressively exist being sacred and dedicated people) **and flawless folks** (people without blemish or stain; blameless ones) **in His sight and presence**."

This sounds very similar to vs. 8, here. Jesus used the phrase in Jn. 17:24b, when speaking to the Father concerning:

"**My glory** (the appearance of My manifestation which calls forth praise; manifest Presence), **which You have given to Me as a possession because You loved** (accepted; fully gave Yourself to) **Me before [the; a] casting-down of [the; a] universe** (or: tossing down of a world; or: [the] founding of an organized system; a sowing [as seed] or [impregnating] of [the] aggregate of humanity; founding of [the] system of culture and society; or: a casting corresponding to and in agreement with an ordered disposition of [the] Dominating System)."

Lu. 11:50 speaks of,

"**the blood of all of the prophets – that having been** [other MSS: being constantly or repeatedly] **poured out from the casting down** (the founding; the foundation; or: may = the conceiving) **of [the] ordered system** (world of culture, economy, religion and government)."

If we understand the noun, **casting down**, as "establishing, or, founding," the reference may be to the creation of Israel as a nation, at Mt. Sinai, and to the scrolls that listed the names of the tribes of Israel (and later, the genealogical records), along with a second allusion to membership in the new creation (2 Cor. 5:17), for now we,

"**are and continue being [a] letter** [= a scroll of the LIFE] **– being one having been written** (inscribed; imprinted; engraved) **within [our] hearts; one progressively being experientially known and continuously read** (or: periodically recognized and experienced again) **by all people**" (2 Cor. 3:2; brackets added).

This may also be an echo of 7:4-8 and 14:1, above: being **sealed** answering to being "**written upon the little Scroll**," here.

Or, understanding the same noun in its negative, or destructive, sense: it may be a reference to the casting out of humanity from the Garden of Eden, the death of which Paul speaks in Rom. 5:12 (the result of Adam's disobedience), or perhaps it is echoing the symbolic stories in Isa. 14:4-23 (the setting, there, being Babylon), or Ezk. 28 that used Edenic imagery in regard to Tyre, where in each parable the "Adam" (or, "humanity") symbols were cast down.

On yet another level, when "**the Ruler** (the one invested with Power; the Leader; the Chief; the Original One; the Beginning One; the Prince) **of this System [was] ejected outside** (cast out)" (Jn. 12:31b), in His burial He took the all of Israel and its whole world (cultural and religious system) to the grave. If one died, all died (2 Cor. 5:14b). There had to be a death and a burial (a "casting-down" of the old) before there could be a resurrection (a "founding and an establishing" of the new). This symbolic phrase has multi-vectors, pointing in different directions – depending upon the contexts to which it is applied. These two interpretations can also be seen in Heb. 4:3, where it speaks,

"**with regard to the works** (actions; deeds) **– being born** (or: brought into existence; caused to happen or occur) **from [the] casting down** (or: laying of a foundation) **of an ordered system** (or: of [the] world; or: namely, of the works born from cosmic conception [from the usage of *katabolen* with *spermatos* in Heb. 11:11]; thus: of works generated from conception of a world or of the aggregate of humanity).

These folks **wonder** as they **observe** that this little wild animal **was existing**, and **presently** (at that time in the 1st century) **did not exist**, and yet was destined to **exist "alongside"** (when Constantine made Christianity the state religion). This is an echo of 13:3, above, "**one of its heads was as having been slaughtered unto death, and yet the impact and blow of its death** (or: its death-blow) **was cured** (or: tended; treated)." Here, Kaplan pointed to another level of application, a spiritual analogy in regard to the old, carnal "beast-nature" within us: it was in existence in our past, but with its death (in Christ) it no longer exists. Yet, from time to time (to keep us humble, as with Paul?) it seems to appear and "be alongside" us again [cf Rom. 7:4-24; "**Consequently I keep on finding the principle** (or: this law) **in me – in the person normally willing** (purposing; intending) **to habitually do** (perform; produce) **the ideal** (the beautiful; the fine) **– that in me** (or: with me; for me) **the worthless** (the ugly; the ignoble; the base; the evil) **is constantly lying close by**" – 7:21]. The next verse, below, gives further instruction concerning this little wild animal.

9. "**Here [is] The Mind** (intelligence; intellect)**: the one continuously having** (holding) **Wisdom** (or: Here [is] the mind [which] has wisdom)**: The seven heads are seven mountains, where the woman continuously sits upon them,**

To understand this we must consider its meaning in the 1st century as it applied to the called-out communities of that time. If we see that this little beast was Rome, with its 7 heads which are 7 mountains (figure of the Empire), and the 7 kings (vs. 10) being the succession of emperors in that time – the one that then existed would have been Nero, the 6th (five had fallen before him) – then I think this passage becomes a little clearer. Vespasian followed, but he only "remained a little while." Simmons takes a different view, seeing the two symbols (the Woman; the Beast) being, "one is *political*, the other *demographic;* both are *enigmatical*," also pointing out that Jerusalem is also situated upon 7 hills: Zion, Acra, Moriah, Bezetha, Millo, Ophel and Antonio (ibid p 322 and n 4). He argues that if the 7 heads were a figure of Rome one would not need wisdom or **the mind** to understand the symbology. He notes that, "The description of the woman is far more consistent with Jerusalem's relationship to *Asia* than to the city of Rome. Rather than interpret the mountains geographically, the better view is to interpret them *demographically*, as population centers of the ancient world, not the topography of the land." He further points out that, "In prophecy, mountains and hills generally represent nations, peoples and governments (Ps. 68:15, 16; Isa. 41:15, 16; Jer. 3:23; 51:25; Dan. 2:35)" (ibid p 323; emphasis original). Along with Simmons' objections to the more popular interpretation is the principle noted throughout the Unveiling: numbers are symbols, and the pictures are figurative, not literal. If the "many waters" upon which she sits is a symbol, and if the woman is a symbol, then so also should the mountains be a symbol, or, figurative. Simmons' view is supported by Maarschalk's research, for Simmons' *political* symbol.

Borg notes that, "from antiquity, Rome has been known as the city built on seven hills or mountains" (ibid p 277). One reading of vs. 10, below, makes further identifying references to these seven mountains also being representative of seven kings (read: Caesars). So, the mountains upon which the woman was sitting may have indicated Rome, but this does not mean that the woman is a symbol of Rome; rather, she is supported and operates by the power and authority of Rome. Take note, in vs. 16 below, that,

"**And the ten horns which you saw** (or: see) **– even the little wild animal – these will continue hating** (detaching from) **the Prostitute, and [she] being made desolate** (having been laid waste)**, they will also proceed making her naked and will progressively eat her flesh** (= physical form) **and then they will proceed burning her down in a fire**."

This clearly shows that the woman and the "little wild animal" upon which she was sitting (vs. 3, above) represent separate entities. Rome did not hate itself. The Zealots hated those Jews who did not support the rebellion (Maarschalk). But the woman now looks a lot like Rome and is described as clothed with that which was identified with the Empire. "But these seven heads of the beast no more represent literal mountains than do the seven heads of the dragon in 12:3.... Rather do mountains symbolize seats of power and political and governmental resources" (Terry ibid p 431).

10. **"and they** (or: there) **are seven kings: five fell, the one is** (exists), **the other one came not as yet, and when he may come it is necessary for him to remain** (abide) **a little while** (briefly).

As you see, there are two ways of reading the Greek of the first clause. The verb **are** is third person, plural, with no subject expressed. So, in English, we supply either **they** or "there." Either is correct. Terry and Simmons opt for "there," since kings have been represented by "horns," not by heads, and the seven heads of the dragon (12:3) were not given as seven kings. But vs. 12, below, mentions 10 kings (using the symbol of horns). D'Aragon simply states that, "Since the Beast represents the Roman Empire, the seven heads must represent emperors... The number seven is possibly symbolic, embracing all the emperors..." (ibid p 487). Simmons points out that "These kings do not reign contemporaneously, but successively. We conclude they belong to Imperial Rome" (ibid p 324). Terry lists the 5 kings as Julius Caesar, Augustus, Tiberius, Caligula and Claudius, and concludes, "The one then reigning was Nero, the sixth of the list, and the other, the seventh, had not yet come when this book was written" (ibid). Galba was the successor to Nero, who reigned for 7 months (68-69).

The phrase, "**a little while** (briefly)," may be an allusion to Dan. 7:12,
> "As for the remainder of the animals, their authority was caused to pass away; yet a lengthening of life [was] granted to them until the stated [time; situation] and season."

Beale (ibid p 870) agrees that, "Nero serves as a good illustration of the text's idea." The little animal is any embodiment of the flesh-oriented nature, and is a spirit of opposition and domination. That spirit is symbolically characterized as a dragon, as we saw above, and it gives rise (in people and systems) to expressions as little wild animals – creatures that are not subject to reason nor are they responsive to God's Spirit, except as He uses them as His tools, and as it were, in His hands. When this spirit is expressed through people, we get what Peter described:
> "**these, as irrational** (wordless; unreasoning) **living ones** (or: animals), **being creatures of instinct having been born unto capture and then corruption** (decay; ruin), **within which things – being continuously ignorant – they are constantly blaspheming** (speaking slander, insult and abusive speech; injuriously vilifying; or: hindering the Light) **within their corruption** (decay), **and they will be progressively ruined** (spoiled; caused to decay; corrupted), **being folks habitually wronging themselves**" (1 Pet. 2:12).

Maarschalk suggests that these 7 "kings" were "the family dynasty of Hezekiah the Zealot." The seventh one was Menahem, who claimed to be the Messiah and was killed in the temple at Jerusalem by Zealots, in AD 66 ("Overview" ibid p 17).

11. **"And the little wild animal which was existing, and does not exist, it is also itself [the; an] eighth, and is** (exists) **out of the seven, and progressively leads under** (or: habitually goes away) **into loss** (destruction; state of being lost).

Here, it speaks of this entire **little animal** as being "**itself [the; an] eighth**" and as "**existing out of the seven**." If we see this enigmatic verse as giving us an "idea," then what is the significance of it being "the eighth"? As the Scriptural week consisted of seven days, the eighth day would be the beginning of a new week. Thus the number 8 has come to be seen as signifying "a new beginning." So in our present context, it would then seem that this beast (who is of the same spirit or nature of the seven – symbolizing the complete beast) has a new beginning. If this thinking is correct, then we can see where the beast of the institutional "church" age is prophesied to come into being.

Traditional preterist interpretation looks to pin the eighth one on a successor of Nero, one of the Caesars. This would have been appropriate for John's listeners, in the 1st century. Simmons points to the word [the] not being in the text before the word **eighth**, and concludes that this one is "*an* eighth king... he is *contemporaneous* with the sixth king, and not successor to the seventh" (ibid p 326; emphasis original). Beale observes that, "an eighth king is not a literal quantitative referent to an actual eighth king in a historical order of succession from the seven preceding kings. Rather, 'eighth,' like 'seven,' has a figurative meaning" (ibid p 875).

However, another layer of interpretation can understand this **eighth** one to simply be of the same spirit of the **seven**, but a new manifestation of the adversarial dragon spirit that is repeatedly incarnating in domination systems. We can observe, from history, how these **little wild animals progressively lead** everyone **into loss**, and how they themselves **habitually go away into destruction**, and **lead** people **under** a state of being lost. This final phrase can be an allusion to Dan. 7:11b,
> "I looked until the beast was slain, and his body destroyed and then was given to the burning flame."

All beast systems eventually have an end and exit the stage of human history. Some last longer than others. Here, the mention of the number 8, which also has been associated with resurrection (Christ arising on the 8th day; the arising of the new week), may point to future manifestations of the domination spirit that repeatedly inhabits human beings. The natural man usually displays the counterfeit of the real: the Second Man (1 Cor. 15:47). We might also have an allusion to Eccl. 11:2, here: "Give a portion to seven, and also to eight, for you know not what evil shall be upon the Land." Also, Mic. 5:5b speaks of "seven shepherds, and eight overlords of humanity." These successive beast systems may be allusions to Nebuchadnezzar's dream, in Dan. 2, where successive empires were variously depicted by an image of those empires within the one human image.

Another reading of the first clause may indicate that the second verb phrase, "**and does not exist**," speaks to it being a non-entity: it has no ontological existence of itself. Rather it is a domination system or a psychological construct that is created by estranged human minds and is placed upon societies. We have a similar statement about demons, cited above, where the LXX text reads:
> "This is a people that ... offer[s] sacrifices in gardens, and burn[s] incense on bricks to the demons – which things DO NOT EXIST" (Isa. 65:3; JM).

12. **"And the ten horns which you saw are ten kings who do not yet receive a kingdom, but they are continually receiving authority AS kings [for] one hour with the little wild animal.**

The 10 **horns**, at that time being first representative of the 10 provinces of the 1st century Roman Empire, would be prophetic of the "provinces" – later known as "denominations" – of the organized "church" system in the next age, in which we now live. At the time of the Unveiling, they had "**not yet received a kingdom**." Ten represented a real number of those provinces but also is a symbol for, "the *totality* of those allied or subject kings who aided Rome in her wars both on Judaism and Christianity" (Terry ibid p 433; emphasis original). They had no independent sovereignty, but were subsections of the Empire. Ten is also another figure, or idea, of the division within institutional Christianity that would develop in the following centuries. Before the Reformation they would have been representative of the regional bishops. They did not then receive separate kingdoms, but "**they are continually receiving authority AS kings**" – and this the bishops did have. Later, the denominations assumed the same authority, and today some individual "churches" are like little kingdoms, where in some denominations (and in some independent churches) the "pastor" has the final say on church matters. We have known one such person who considered himself as being like a CEO.

The short space of time, "**one hour**," emphasizes the transitory character of those who function as "sovereigns" within their individual "kingdoms." This could be an allusion to the transitory reigns of the majority of Israel's kings, especially when they became politically involved with pagan nations (e.g., Egypt). Metaphorically, bad situations that may be presently "ruling" our lives, because of their collusions with domination systems, will come to an end – as history marches on. All domination systems **receive [their] authority** because of being involved **with the little wild animal** that resides within unloving, self-centered people and organizations.

13. **"These continually hold** (or: have) **one opinion** (or: thought; resolve), **and they continually give their power** (or: ability) **and authority to the little wild animal.**

But what of their holding **one opinion**, one thought or one resolve? Was this not in regard to **giving their power and authority** to the beast system? In other matters there have always been disagreements and opposing resolves between different groups, whether they were political or religious in nature. But the one opinion has always been: to support the system; to support the denomination; to support the local structure. Terry rightly proposes that in this vision these kings "represented the same power that was symbolized by the beast out of the land, in 13:1-7," above (ibid). Simmons sees them represented in the 10 horns with 10 crowns, in 13:1, above (ibid p 326). They are integral parts of the "body of the beast" system that has been infused with the spirit of the dragon. Simmons further comments: "The Beast exists only in the abstract and relies upon the provincial governments to carry its purpose into effect" (ibid). This can also be applied to controlling "church" denominations that embrace the spirit of domination. Viewing the 1st century setting from Maarschalk's presentations, we could deduce that each of the successive leaders of the Zealots gave everything that they had to the Zealot Rebellion.

14. **"These will proceed waging war** (or: do battle) **with the little Lamb, and the little Lamb will progressively overcome** (subdue; conquer) **them because He is LORD of lords and KING of kings, and the ones with Him are CALLED ONES and CHOSEN ONES and FAITHFUL ONES** (or: trusting folks; people filled with faith; loyal ones)."

And so thus do we have these of the dominating system, the world – be it political or religious, make **war with the little Lamb** and with those who are **WITH Him**: with Him in spirit; with Him in their being His will; with Him in His reign/kingdom/activities. Those with Him also have one resolve, one thought: "Your kingdom come! Your will be done!" – here, on earth. And so it will be, for this verse tells us that He **"WILL overcome them, because He IS Lord of lords and King of kings."** His reign and kingdom will overcome the systems and organizations of the world. The first clause echoes 12:7, above, and the rest of the verse is a reprise of 11:15 and 12:11, above, speaking to the same events in those previous visions. This calls to mind Jude 14-15:
> "**Behold, the Lord** [=Yahweh] **came** (or: comes and goes) **within His set-apart myriads** (or: in union with innumerable holy multitudes, which are Him), **to form a separation** (or: make a decision; construct a distinction; perform a sifting and a judging) **which corresponds to and falls in line with all people** (to the level of everyone), **and to test** (or: search thoroughly) **the irreverent folks concerning all their irreverent works** (activities; deeds) **which they irreverently did, and concerning all the hard things which irreverent outcasts** (folks in error; sinners; failures; folks who make mistakes and miss the target) **spoke against Him.**"

We will see this acted out in chapters 19 and 20, below. Here the announcement proclaims the Lamb's success, which is the main theme of the Unveiling – it is Good News. This is an apocalyptic Gospel.

The **called, chosen** and **faithful ones** who are with Him are the same ones that John saw in 14:1-5, above. They are the same ones of whom Paul spoke in Rom. 8:

28. **"Now [look], we have seen, and thus know and are aware, that to those habitually loving God – to the folks being called and invited according to [the] purpose**
> (or: for, in and with the people progressively experiencing love for God – in, with, by and for the people being invited down from an advanced placing, congruent with a design and corresponding to a before-placing and a prior setting forth) – **He is constantly working all things together into good and is progressively working all humanity together into that which is advantageous, worthy of admiration, noble and of excellent qualities,**
> [with other MSS: Yet we know that God is continuously joining everything together (is habitually working together with everything) into goodness by those habitually loving God...]

29. **"because those whom He foreknew** (whom He knows from previous intimate experience), **He also marked out beforehand** (determined in advance) **[as] copies** (joint-forms) **of the image** (material likeness; mirrored image) **of His Son** (or: He previously divided, separated and bounded patterns of the image of His Son) **into the [situation for] Him to be the Firstborn among, within the center of, and in union with, many brothers** (= a vast family of believers)!

30. **" Now [in fact, consider this]: those whom He at one point before-marked-out** (or: designates beforehand; [A reads: knew from prior intimate experience]), **these He also at once called** (or: calls; invited), **and whom He called** (or: calls; invites), **these He also in one stroke rightwised by an eschatological deliverance** (or: makes and sets right, frees from guilt and liberates from bondage, while making them fair and placing them in [covenant] relationships in the Way pointed out). **Now further, those whom He rightwised** (or: liberates and turns in the right direction; or: = included in covenant), **these He also instantly glorified**
> (or: makes of reputation which calls forth praise; gives a splendid appearance; gives honorable thoughts and imaginations; clothes with splendor)."

15. **Then he is saying to me,**
> **"The waters which you saw** (or: see), **where the Prostitute continually sits, are peoples and crowds** (mobs) **and multitudes** (nations; ethnic groups) **and tongues** (languages).

Now this can speak of the Roman Empire, in the literal fulfillment, and is "suggestive of the many and extensive affiliations of Jerusalem with the mixed populations of the Roman Empire" (Terry ibid p 434). Isa. 17:12 speaks of, "the noise of many **people**... like the noise of the seas and the rushing (or: tumult) of **nations**... like the rushing (tumult) of abundant **waters**." *Cf* Acts 2:5-10. This is also an allusion to Babylon (Jer. 51:13), but the Secret (Mystery) was that Jerusalem had become another Babylon, as suggested above. Simmons (ibid p 327 n 9) cites Philo who described the "pervasiveness of the Jews":
> "[The nation was] not contained as every other nation was by the circuit of the one region which was allotted to it for itself, but... spread over the whole face of the earth; for it is diffused throughout every continent, and over every island, so that everywhere it appears but little inferior in number to the original native population of the country" (Philo Judaeus, *De Legatione Ad Gaium*, XXXI; Yonge Ed.; brackets added).

Simmons further notes that, "in virtually every place Paul journeyed in the ancient world, Jews were there who opposed and persecuted him.... The city and temple were supported by contributions of first fruits sent by Jews from Asia, Egypt, Europe and every corner of the empire" (ibid p 327-8). He also points to the "telling accusation" that we see in Acts 21:27-28, which, "was brought *not* by dwellers of Jerusalem, but Jews dwelling in Asia" (ibid; emphasis original):
> "**So as the seven days were being about to be concluding, the [fanatical and extremist religious] Jews from the Asian [district], upon catching a view and gazing upon him** [i.e., Paul] **in the midst of the Temple complex, began pouring [themselves into the midst],**

> together with [the] whole crowd, to mix and stir up confusion – then they laid [their] hands on him, repeatedly crying out, 'Men! Israelites! Come help [us]... now (Run immediately to our cry)! **This man is the person who is constantly teaching all people everywhere against the People** [= Jews or Israelites] **and the Law and this** [Concordant text adds: holy] **Place! Still more than this, he also brought Greeks into the Temple complex and has thus made this set-apart and sacred Place common** (= profane, contaminated and defiled)!'"

Now these **waters** can also speak of her daughters, and the whole world of the age which has followed the old-covenant, Mosaic age, in the figurative application. Just as Rome laid Jerusalem waste and made her naked, ate her flesh and burned her down in fire, so also have the daughter religions warred against the various power systems of the historic "church," history being filled with religious wars which are a progressive, figurative fulfillment of vs. 16, below. Kingdoms against religions have filled history with carnage. Even in our day, one Christian faction wages media battles against another, or against all others. So even yet, "**Christ is parted**!" (1 Cor. 1:13).

But NOTE! This has been, and yet is, God's will and purpose, "**UNTIL God's Words shall be completed**!" (vs. 17, below). Have we seen the finished perfection of His Words? In one sense, yes (and here the full preterists agree): it was all finished in AD 70, upon whom came the end of the Mosaic age. Yet there is still further application, for Scripture speaks here in the Unveiling of "the ages," of "the ages of the ages," and in Eph. 2:7 of "the ages to come." Many presume that these are idioms descriptive of eternity, but these are clearly "time" words, and speak of multiple ages which both begin and end: of ages past (Eph. 3:5) as well as of future ages to come, and thus do we have a plurality of ages in God's program.

16. "**And the ten horns which you saw** (or: see) **– even the little wild animal – these will continue hating** (detaching from) **the Prostitute, and [she] being made desolate** (having been laid waste), **they will also proceed making her naked and will progressively eat her flesh** (= physical form) **and then they will proceed burning her down in a fire**.

The **ten horns**, representing the ten provinces of the Roman Empire, comprise **the little wild animal**, just as the ten provinces comprise the Empire. As stated above, this verse confirms that **the Prostitute** is not the same as **the little wild animal** with the seven heads and **ten horns**. There is collusion, and **the Prostitute** is being supported by the beast, but the two are distinct. Chilton notes: "The destruction of the Harlot by her former 'lovers' is inexplicable apart from the hypothesis that she is Jerusalem" (ibid p 439 n 19). The number 10 in this figure may be a veiled reference to the "feet" (having 10 toes) of Nebuchadnezzar's dream (Dan. 2:33): the place and the time when the "Stone [that] was cut out without hands [i.e., this was not the work of humans, but of God]... struck the image upon his feet... and broke them to pieces." This did not refer to striking a literal kingdom any more than it meant that the stone was literal. Rather, it referred to the destruction of the "domination systems" that the statue of successive empires represented, for the next verse states that,

> "the iron, the clay, the brass, the silver and the gold, were broken to pieces together, and became like the chaff of the summer threshing floors; and the wind (or: Spirit) carried them away, so that no place was found for them. And the stone that struck the image became a great mountain [figure for God's kingdom: Dan. 2:43-45] and filled the whole Land/earth" (Dan. 2:35).

Thus, when Christ (the Stone) came, Jesus said, "**I, Myself, have overcome and conquered the System** (dominating world; organized arrangement of religion and society) **so that it stands a completed victory**!" (Jn. 16:33). He was not speaking of having conquered the literal Roman Empire, in a literal, physical way. He was speaking of Spirit and Life, for His words were Spirit and Life (Jn. 6:63).

He overcame by the Spirit of Life, which was also the Spirit of Resurrection. Thus do we have Paul proclaim in 1 Cor. 15,
> "**The Death was drunk down and swallowed into Victory** (or: overcoming)!" [Isa. 25:8]
> "**Where, O Death, [is] your victory** (or: overcoming)**?**
> **Where, O Death, [is] your stinger** (sharp point; sting; goad; spur)**?**" [Hos. 13:14;
> note: TR reads "O Unseen (Hades)" in the second line, following the LXX and Heb.]....
> **But grace and joyous favor [is] in God** (or: by God) – **the One presently and progressively giving the Victory** (or: the overcoming) **to us, in us and for us through our Lord** (Owner; Master), **Jesus, [the] Christ!**" (vss. 54b, 55, 57).

You see, Jesus told Pilate,
> "**My kingdom** (My sovereignty; the realm and activity of My reign and activity; My reign as king) **is not from out of this System** (world of organized government, culture, economics or religion) **as its source or origin. If My kingdom** (or: reign, realm and sovereignty) **were from out of this System, as a source or origin, My subordinates** (those under My orders) **would have been progressively contending, struggling and fighting, to the end that I could** (or: would) **not be commended, committed or given over to the Jews** (= religious authorities)." (Jn. 18:36).

This is also why His kingdom/reign is termed "**the kingdom/reign of the heavens**" in Matthew's Gospel, and why He said, "**God's reign** (kingdom; royal rule; sovereign influence and activity) **continually exists inside you folks** (or: is on the inside of you people; or: = within your community)."

Terry interprets this verse as, "a vivid apocalyptic portraiture of the terrible judgments inflicted on Jerusalem by the Roman armies" (ibid p 434). Mat. 24:15, speaks to her **desolation**,
> "**Therefore, whenever you men can see** (or: may perceive) '**the effect of the loathing and nauseating [event; condition; thing; situation] from the desolation**
>> (or: the result from the abhorring abomination associated with, or which causes, the devastation and abandonment; or: the resulting effect of the desecration, which is an act of ruining, forsaking and leaving uninhabited like a desert),' **that was being spoken through Daniel the prophet, standing 'within the midst of a set-apart place** (or: [the] holy place)' [Dan. 9:27; 11:31; 12:11]..."(cf Mk. 13:14)

In Lu. 21:20, Jesus lays it out:
> "**Now later, when YOU FOLKS see Jerusalem being continuously surrounded by encamped armies, at that time realize and know from that experience that her desolation has drawn near and is now present**."

The figure of **making her naked** may be an allusion to Yahweh's judgment of Judah and Jerusalem, in Jer.13:26-27,
> "So I Myself also have stripped off your skirts over your face, that your dishonor may be seen: your adulteries and your neighings [Jer. 5:8], the lewdness of your prostitutions... Woe to you Jerusalem! You are not clean!" (CVOT)

Or, possibly to Lam. 1:8-9,
> "A sin Jerusalem sinned... all who glorified her... have seen her nakedness... Her uncleanness is in her skirts.... She has come down..."

Then in Nah. 3:4-5,
> "All because of the many prostitutions of the Prostitute.... Behold Me against you... I will roll your skirts over your face and I will show the nations your nakedness, and kingdoms your dishonor."

Hos. 2:10 prophesies, "And now will I uncover her lewdness, in the sight of her lovers, and none shall deliver her out of My hand." God always did these thing through foreign nations which performed as His tools of judgment. Cf Isa. 47:2-3; Ezk. 16:37-41; 23:22-30.

Jer. 4:30 speaks to the whole picture:

"And you, who will be devastated, what are you doing that you clothe yourself in scarlet, that you ornament yourself with ornaments of gold? .... [your] lovers will despise and reject you..."

The picture "**progressively eat her flesh** (= physical form)," calls up the picture of the end of Jezebel, in 2 Ki. 9:36, "dogs shall eat the flesh of Jezebel." Israel considered Gentile nations (i.e., those not in covenant with God) as being dogs (cf Mat. 7:6a; 15:26). Mat. 24:28 makes an enigmatic statement that might explain our text, here:

"**Wherever the carcass** (corpse) **may be, the vultures** (or: eagles) **will be progressively led together and gathered**."

Some have suggested that the "eagles" were a reference to the eagles on the head of the Roman army's standards.

The last clause, "**they will proceed burning her down in a fire**," is an allusion to Ezk. 16:41, "And they shall burn your houses with fire... and cause you to cease from playing the Prostitute..." Being burned is picked up again, in 18:8b, below. Barclay comments here:

"This is the punishment for the most heinous sin (Lev. 20:14), and above all the punishment for the daughter of a priest who has been guilty of sexual immorality (Lev. 21:9) (ibid p 149).

This, of course, happened to Jerusalem in AD 70. But let us keep in mind the history of animosity between secular governments and the institutional church. All domination systems of governments and religions have through time tried to destroy the little Lamb's Bride – the called-out covenant communities. And on both corporate and individual levels, it has always been that,

'**the flesh [system or nature] is constantly rushing passionately down upon** (or: against) **the spirit** (or: Breath-effect), **and the spirit** (or: Breath-effect) **down on** (or: against) **the flesh [nature, or, system of religion], for these things are constantly lying in opposition to each other** (lying set to displace each other)" (Gal. 5:17).

But, Paul makes it clear in Rom. 8:8 that,

"**People being in union with, or centered in, flesh** (= the alienated human condition; or: = the religious system involving flesh sacrifices, Torah boundary-markers/customs) **have no power and are not able at any point to please God** (or: to fit or adapt to God; or: to be content with God)."

17. "**For God gave** (or: gives) **into their hearts to do His opinion** (thought; resolve; purpose), **even to form** (make; do) **one opinion** (thought; resolve), **and to give their kingdom to the little wild animal** (beast) **UNTIL God's Words** (the Words of God; the thoughts and messages from God) **shall be completed** (finished; ended; perfected; brought to their purposed and destined goal).

The message of this verse echoes Paul in Rom. 9:17,

"**For the Scripture is saying to Pharaoh that,**

'**Into this itself** (or: For this very thing) **I roused you forth** (I awakened and stirred you to come out), **so that I may** (or: would) **display and demonstrate in you My power and ability, so that My Name would be thoroughly proclaimed** (preached and published far and wide) **within all the land** (or: in the entire earth).' (Ex. 9:16)."

In Rom. 9:20, Paul quotes Isa. 29:16,

"**The thing molded and formed will not proceed to be saying to the One molding and forming, 'Why do you make me thus** (or: did you create and construct me this way)?'"

Then in vs. 21, he continues, "**Or does not the Potter hold authority or have a right pertaining to clay, forth from out of the same kneaded mixture** (effect of uniform mixture)...?" His rhetorical question may be an allusion to Isa. 45:9b, "Shall the clay say to its potter, What are you making?" In Isa. 64:8, Isaiah's affirmation to Yahweh is, "We [are] the clay, and You [are] our Former." We also have the witness of Prov. 21:1,

> "Like rillets (channels) of water [is the] king's heart in the hand of Yahweh; wherever He desires, He redirects it" (CVOT).

More specific to our text, here, is Lu. 21:22,

> "**These are days of executing justice – of bringing about what is fair and right and of establishing what accords with the Way pointed out – with a view to have fulfilled all the things having been written** (or: for all that is written to be fulfilled)!"

Jesus put it in these words, in Mat. 23:

> 35. "**so that upon you, yourselves, can** (or: should) **come all [the] just** (equitable; rightwised) **blood being continuously poured out** (or: spilled) **upon the Land – from the blood of rightwised** (just; fair; in-right-relationship) **Abel, until the blood of Zechariah, the son of Barachiah** (or: Baruch), **whom you people murdered between the Temple and the altar.**
> 36. "**Assuredly, I am now saying to you people, it will progressively move toward this point, and then arrive – all these things! – upon this generation!**

This Unveiling to John is affirming Jesus' prophecy. All these witnesses proclaim God's sovereignty, and His involvement in the affairs of humanity.

God even brings "unity" to these kings so that they, "**form** (make; do) **one opinion** (thought; resolve)," i.e. "**to do His opinion** (thought; resolve; purpose)," which was to judge Judah and Jerusalem and to destroy the temple. This works out by all 10 provinces' will submitting to the Emperor's will, i.e., "**give their kingdom to the little wild animal** (beast)," in support of Rome's war to suppress the Jewish rebellion.

Israel's judgments from God had historically been His bringing surrounding nations against a straying people, so that they would cry out to Him for deliverance. See the story in Judges, for examples of this, and read Israel's prophets to see God's same program in action. This passage and chapter 18, below, speak to Dan. 9:24-27. The last clause, "**God's Words** (the Words of God; the thoughts and messages from God) **shall be completed** (finished; ended; perfected; brought to their purposed and destined goal)." has reference to the end of the old covenant age and the destruction of the temple, along with all the genealogical records of who were Levites, thus excluding any more priests from being confirmed. This all is the "**completion**," the "bringing to their purposed goal" of everything pertaining to the age of the Law. Those kings would unite (as part of the Roman suppression) against 1st century Jerusalem and Judea, but this was only **UNTIL** God's goal of ending that age was accomplished.

We saw Christ's warning of impending judgments of His followers in His letters to the 7 communities, in chapters 2 and 3, above. He is the same: yesterday, today and on through the ages (Heb. 13:8).

18. "**And the woman, which you saw, is the Great City – the one continuously having a kingdom** (or: reigning with dominion) **upon** (over) **the kings of the Land** (region; earth)."

We saw the phrase, "**the Great City**, in 11:8, above, where it was figuratively applied to "Sodom and Egypt," which the text interpreted this as being, "**where also their Lord was crucified.**" So this provides us with another clue that the agent is speaking of physical Jerusalem of the 1st century. Josephus also called Jerusalem "that great city" in *Wars*, vii.8.7. The phrase is used of Jerusalem in Jer. 22:8. "The destruction of Rome had no eschatological significance, but the fall of Jerusalem did; it was the eschatological event marking the consummation of the ages" (Simmons, ibid p 330). It was *"The End of the Old, and The Beginning of the New."* In Lu. 19:41-44, "Jesus wept over Jerusalem, not Rome" (ibid).

The question is, when did Jerusalem ever **have a kingdom**, or hold dominion, upon the kings of the land (or: earth)? The participle "have" is in the present tense, which I have thus rendered "**continuously having**." Was this true of Jerusalem in John's day? Wallace explains this in the following manner:
> "The last statement of vs. 18 'which reigneth over the kings of the land' did not refer to the empire of the Caesars, nor the city of the emperors. The word 'reign' here denoted a dominion. The 'earth,' as defined at the beginning and later repeated, referred to the LAND of Judea, inclusive of Palestine. The city of Jerusalem was the royal city where the kings of Judah reigned. The phrase 'the kings of the earth' was used in the sense of Acts 4:26-27: 'The kings of the earth stood up, and rulers were gathered together against the Lord and against His Christ. For of a truth against thy holy child Jesus, whom thou have anointed, both Herod and Pontius Pilate, with the Gentiles and the people of Israel, were gathered together.' These 'kings of the earth' were of Judah, and Jerusalem was the capital city of the land, standing in the same relation to these 'kings of the earth' as Rome sustained to the emperors. The second psalm represents Jerusalem as ruling with a rod of iron over 'the kings of the earth' who had set themselves against the Lord's anointed One. In the *Wars*, Book 3, Sect. 3,5, Josephus adds that 'the royal city Jerusalem was supreme, and presided over all neighboring country as the head does over the body'" (ibid p 375).

Terry concurs, stating that, "the latter part of the verse should be translated *which has dominion over the kings of the land*." He further views, "the latter half of the Apocalypse (chapters 12-22) [as] in the main a repetition of the first half (chapters 1-11) under different symbols..." (ibid p 434; emphasis original). Here, he also affirms,
> "If the beast is the Roman Empire, the harlot must be something else than the city of Rome. Or it cannot be said that the emperors of the chief princes of the empire hated Rome or ever sought to destroy [it].... Rome is only incidentally connected with this... This revelation is not particularly concerned with the fall of the Roman Empire as such, but only as it rises and passes from view as an instrument used by the Almighty to accomplish what his own wisdom and counsel determined to have done" (ibid p 435-6; brackets added).

The visionary symbol of, "**a woman continuously sitting** (or: seated) **upon a crimson** (or: scarlet) **little wild animal** (or: beast)" (vs. 3, above) is now explained as a City that is having dominion over "**kings of the Land**." Selina O'Grady offers historical insights into this era and region on "How religion uses empire and empire uses religion..." (*And Man Created God, A History of the World at the Time of Jesus*, St. Martin's Press, 2012). They needed each other.

So how about the figurative aspect of this verse? Has the visible "church," the historic system of this age – which followed the age ending in AD 70 – held sway or exercised dominion over the kings of the earth? I think history answers an emphatic, "Yes!" Borg instructs us,
> "An earlier generation of scholars.... thought that John's communities were facing a major outbreak of persecutions ordered by the emperor Domitian.... More recently, however, scholars have concluded that there is little historical evidence to support the claim that there was major persecution in the time of Domitian.... Nevertheless, there are clear indication that it is not simply Rome-as-persecutor but Rome-as-*empire* that accounts for John's indictment of Rome as the incarnation of the dragon, the ancient seven-headed monster that plunges the world into chaos.... Because that empire was the then-contemporary incarnation of the 'domination system' that has marked so much of human history" (ibid p 284-286; emphasis original).

Teachers such as Malcolm Smith connect the figure of Babylon in the Unveiling with the historic figure of Semiramis, wife of Nimrod in Gen. 10:10 and 11:9, and history (or, legend) has it she reigned as queen over Babylon for 102 years. Her title was "The Queen of Heaven," and she is credited with being the mother of heathen idolatry which worshiped female gods, and later, the female form (as in our current culture). Nimrod is supposed to have met her when she ran a brothel. Where it says that she is "drunk with the blood of the saints," Smith suggests that this is a spirit that is out to destroy the life of God's people. He sees in this figure the spirit that sits on the backs of governments, yet which is also the spirit of religion, which Christianity also has embraced. (ibid)

George Hawtin also taught on this subject, and in his booklet entitled "Mystery Babylon," he makes the following comments:
> "It is spiritual Babylon that separates Christian from Christian, destroying unity and dividing purpose, and making all speak a different language... making them foreigners and strangers, none speaking intelligibly to the other....
> "The spirit of Babylon goes much deeper than sects and denominations. It is a mystery the spirit of which seems to be deep-rooted in the heart of man.... you will find it in your heart, if you look close enough....
> "We must have the name Babylon erased from our foreheads by the mind of Christ and a new name written there, even the name of the City of God....
> "The kingdom of God comes not with observation. It is only Babylon that can be observed....
> "To have the name of God in the forehead is to have the mind of Christ. Therefore to have the name Mystery, Babylon, in the forehead is to have the very mind of this mysterious system that loves the visible and loves to point to some earthly thing and say, 'This is the tower that leads to heaven'....
> "Mystery Babylon... is... something so deep-seated that Christians are unable to think except in terms of 'established orders... creeds, assemblies, doctrines, meetings, communions, baptisms, programs... preachers, missionaries, tracts, healings, gifts, personal work... church buildings... etc.,'....
> "'He that is joined to a harlot is one flesh...' (1 Cor. 6:16). You have been joined by the carnal mind to this woman so long, that you don't know how you can live without her.... 'Beware lest any man spoil you... after the traditions of men...' (Col. 2:8)."

On this chapter Ray Prinzing has the following to say:
> "The word 'Babylon' means: confusion. It matters not which segment of the world's institutional structures we consider, be it economic, political or religious, there is one word that can be written across the whole: CONFUSION. It is the MIXTURE of good and evil that brings such confusion. So interwoven is truth with error, helping others while building a kingdom for self, good works that are a blessing to many, while fostering one's own name and reputation, that it is difficult to know which is right and which is wrong....
>
> "This system has catered to, excited and serviced all the lust of the flesh. 'For all that is in the world, the lust of the flesh, and the lust of the eyes, and the pride of life, is not of the Father, but is of the world' (1 John 2:16). Men have worshiped at the shrines of desire – desire for fame, fortune, pleasure, etc. God has used this as a means of EXPOSING ALL THAT IS IN THEIR HEART. 'Out of the heart of men proceed evil thoughts, ADULTERIES, fornications...' (Mark 7:21). When desire and opportunity meet, that which is within shall be manifested....
>
> "Gen. 11 gives the record of how people found a plain in the land of Shinar and proceeded to build a city and a tower, but God intervened, confounded their language, and scattered them.... The Heb. word for 'confound' used here is *balal* meaning: to mix, to mingle, and thus literally, to mix self in. The more self-centered each man became, with his own expression, the less they could communicate with others, so frustration took over, and they left off building and went, every one, their own way... Self seeks to be surrounded with ease and prosperity.... [then] men come to this next expression of self, 'let us build us a city and a tower'.... concurrent with the building

comes the thought, 'let us make us a name'.... [the next thought being;] self-preservation, 'lest we be scattered'" (ibid; emphasis original; brackets added).

Ray appropriately cites Dan. 4:30, the statement of Nebuchadnezzar as he was walking about the royal palace, "Is not this great Babylon that I have built for a royal dwelling by my mighty power and for the honor of my majesty?" Knowing about the foolishness of this statement, we might not actually say such a thing, but we are made of the same dust that he was. And for us, too, pride goes before destruction (Prov. 16:18).

The contrast of the woman here in chapter 17 to the woman in 12:1ff, above, and chapters 21-22, below, is the same contrast offered by Paul in Gal. 4:22-31, which was between the "**slave-girl**" and the "**freewoman**" (vs. 31). It was between the then "**present Jerusalem**" (vs. 25) and "**the Jerusalem above**" (vs. 26). It was between "**the one... born down from flesh**" and "**the one... from... Promise**" (vs. 23). Efforts to fit the woman of chapters 17-18 into a future, literal construct beyond AD 70 are misguided and groundless. Only the symbols continue. The prophecies of Daniel (such as the metal image of Dan. 2) pointed through consecutive world empires (from Daniel's time, on) that are easily seen fulfilled in the 1st century. Rome was the fourth metal (iron, then iron mixed with clay) of Dan. 2, and then of the fourth beast of Dan. 7, which in turn is the scenario from which chapter 17 is a development, through allusions. As noted above, the Stone that figuratively demolished the concept and power of dominion (from Nebuchadnezzar to Rome) was the Christ, whose 1st century comings (recall the repetitive aspect of the present tense of the participle in 1:8, above, and elsewhere) and continued presence among us accomplished all this. Chilton comments, in regard to this chapter, "When Israel was faithful to God... the world was at peace; when Israel broke the Covenant, the world was in turmoil" (ibid p 443). Barclay cites R.H. Charles quoting Ps. 76:10a, "Even the wrath of men is made to praise God," and then Barclay ends his comments on this chapter:
> "The truth behind this is that God never loses control of human affairs. In the last analysis God is always working things together for good" (ibid p 149). Amen!

Chapter 18

This chapter does not introduce a new subject, but continues the picture of the fall of the Prostitute, whose stage mask is Babylon. Everett F. Harrison (*The Wycliffe Bible Commentary*, Moody Press, 1962, 1990) notes that "Most of the chapter is occupied with a description of the wealth of the city, the merchandise which is brought here for sale, and the grief of the merchants, who have been made rich by this traffic, as they look upon the city now being made desolate by fire..."

1. **After these things I saw another Agent progressively descending out of the atmosphere** (or: sky; heaven), **continuously having great authority** (or: privilege from out of Being), **and the Land** (or: ground; or: earth) **was lighted** (illuminated) **by His glory** (or: His manifestation which called forth praise; or: the splendor which was Him).
2. **Then He uttered** (or: suddenly utters) **a cry in a strong voice, repeatedly saying,**
    "**She falls** (She fell)**! Babylon the Great falls** (fell) **and becomes** (became; comes to be; is birthed) **an abode** (dwelling) **of demons** (or: animistic influences) **and a confine** (ward, prison, a place of keeping watch over) **of every impure attitude** (unclean spirit) **and a preserve** (cage; a guard-house) **of every unclean and hated** (or: rejected-from-lack-of-value) **bird and animal,**

John is now seeing another vision, or another "act" in God's cosmic "play." So what he is seeing is a sign, and we should ask what this sign represents. It is the descending of an **Agent** that has "**great authority**" and "**glory**." Jesus, in Matt. 28:18, said, "**All authority** (or: Every right and privilege from out of Being) **is** (or: was at once) **given to Me within heaven and upon the earth** (or: in sky and atmosphere, as well as on land)!" Jn. 5:26b-27a makes quite a statement (by Jesus) on **authority**:

> "**He gives in the Son** (or: to the Son) **to be continuously holding** (or: constantly having) **Life within Himself, and He gives in Him** (or: to Him; by Him) **authority** (or: the right; the privilege; or: out of [His] essence and being) **to be habitually separating and deciding** (to be constantly sifting and evaluating; to continuously do [the] judging)…"

Or, Jn. 10:17b-18,

> "**I Myself am constantly placing** (or: repeatedly setting; or: progressively laying [down]) **My soul** (inner life or being; or: = the whole self)… **I Myself continue putting** (placing; setting; laying) **it away from Myself. I constantly hold authority** (continuously have the right and hold the 'position'; or: continue possessing privilege from out of the midst of Being) **to place it** (lay it), **and I constantly hold authority from out of being** (continuously possess the right, forth from [My] existence; = am in the authoritative position) **to take it** (resume it) **again. This implanted goal** (purposed impartation of the finished product within; inward directive and destiny) **I received from** (or: at) **My Father's side**."

And there is Jn. 17:2,

> "**Correspondingly as You give** (or: gave) **to Him right, privilege and authority from out of Being concerning all flesh** (= people) **to the end that everything** (or: each one; all, male or female) **which You have given to Him, to them He will continue giving eonian life**."

All this is what we would call, "**having great authority**." This just might be the same **Agent** that we encountered in 10:1, above. That One also "**uttered a cry with** (or: by) **a great Voice**" (10:3, above).

The phrase, "**progressively descending out of the atmosphere** (or: sky; heaven)," calls to mind Jn. 3:13,

> "**No one has ascended** (or: stepped up) **into the heaven** (or: atmosphere) **except the One descending** (or: stepping down) **from out of the midst of the atmosphere** (or: heaven)**: the Son of Mankind** (the Son of the human) – **the One continuously being** (or: constantly existing) **within the midst of the heaven** (or: atmosphere)."

And, Jn. 3:31b, "**The One continuously coming** (or: habitually going; repeatedly coming and progressively going) **forth from out of the midst of the heaven** (or: the atmosphere) **is, and constantly exists being, above upon all people** (or: up over upon all things)." Then in Jn. 6:38a, Jesus said, "**I have stepped down to this level** (or: descended), **away from the heaven** (or: the atmosphere)…"

We suggest that what John saw here was a figure of the coming of the Lord spoken of in Lu. 21:27,

> "**And at that point** (or: time), **they will keep on seeing** (or: perceiving) '**the Son of the Man** (= the Human Being; = the eschatological messianic figure) **progressively coming within the midst of a cloud**,' [Dan. 7:13-14] **with power and much glory** (or: with ability and a profound reputation; or: along with power and a manifestation which calls forth praise)."

Recall that Jesus made this statement of 21:27 following Lu 21:20-23,

> 20. "**Now later, when you folks see Jerusalem being continuously surrounded by encamped armies, at that time realize and know from that experience that her desolation has drawn near and is now present.**
>
> 21. "**At that point, let the people in Judea progressively flee into the hill country and mountains; then let the people within the midst of her** [i.e., Jerusalem] **proceed departing out of that place, and don't let** (or: let not) **the folks in the country or the district continue coming** (or: going) **into her,**
>
> 22. "**because these are days of executing justice – of bringing about what is fair and right and of establishing what accords with the Way pointed out – with a view to have fulfilled all the things having been written** (or: for all that is written to be fulfilled)!

23. "Tragic will be the situation for the women then being pregnant, and for the ones still nursing [babies] in those days. You see there will progressively be a great compressive force upon the Land, and inherent fervor bringing internal swelling emotion on this People.

This was the notice by Jesus that corresponds to "**Come out of her, My people**" that we will see in vs. 4, below. And we further suggest that John is seeing what Paul spoke of in 1 Thes. 4:16,

"**because the Lord** [= Yahweh or Christ] **Himself will continue habitually descending** (or: repeatedly descend) **from [the] atmosphere** (or: heaven) **within the midst of** (or: in union with) **a shout of command, within the midst of [the] Chief Agent's** (or: in union with an original messenger's or a chief and ruling agent's) **voice, and within the midst of** (or: in union with) **God's trumpet** [note: figure of a message or a directive for action]…"

Marvin Vincent, in commenting on vs. 1, above, directs us to Ezk. 43:2,

"And behold! the Glory of the Elohim of Israel comes from the way of the east [= the sun's rising]. And His Voice is as the sound of many waters [Rev. 1:15]. And the earth is enlightened by His glory" (*Vincent's Word Studies in the New Testament*, Vol. 2, Hendrickson Pub, 1985).

This brings us to the expression of vs. 1, "**the Land was lighted** (illuminated) **by His glory** (or: His manifestation which called forth praise; or: the splendor which was Him)**.**" John saw this happen, but what does this part of the scene mean? Is it an allusion to Jn. 1:4-5, 9?

4. Within It (or: Him), **life was continuing and progressively existing**

(or: In It was life [as a source]; [Aleph, D and other witnesses read present tense: In union with it there continues being life; Life progressively exists within the midst of It]).

And the life was continuing being, and began progressively existing as, the Light of mankind (or: Furthermore, the Light progressively came to be the life known as "humanity," and was for human beings; or: Then the life was existing being the light from the humans).

5. And the Light is constantly shining in the dim and shadowed places, and keeps on progressively giving light within the gloomy darkness where there is no light (or: within the midst of the obscurity of The Darkness where there is no light of The Day; or: = in the ignorant condition or system). **And yet the darkness does not grasp or receive it on the same level.**

9. It was (or: He was, and continued being) **the True and Genuine Light which** (or: Who) **is continuously** (repeatedly; progressively) **enlightening** (giving light to) **every person** (or: human) **continuously** (repeatedly; progressively; constantly; one after another) **coming into the world** (or: the ordered system of culture, religion, economics and government; or: the universe)

(or: It was the real Light, progressively coming into the world {organized system}, which is progressively enlightening {or: shedding light on} every human).

Jesus expanded this understanding in Jn. 8:12,

"**Jesus therefore again spoke to them** [i.e., to those whom He had just been teaching, in vs. 2, or at a later time], **saying, "I, Myself, am** (or: continuously exist being) **the Light of the world** (or: of the cosmos; of the ordered system; of the dominant cultural, political, economic and religious arrangements; of the universe; of 'the theater of history' – Walter Wink). **The one habitually and progressively following Me can by no means walk around** (= under no circumstances live his or her life) **within the darkness, but, to the contrary, he will progressively possess** (constantly have and hold) **the Light of 'the Life!'** (or: the light which is life.)" *Cf* Jn. 9:5; 11:9; 12:46; 1 Tim. 6:16.

Light represents knowledge and understanding. The message of this Agent proclaims the fall of Jerusalem and its control over the people of Israel through the Law. This "illumination" by God's **glory** (which is Christ, and then Christ in His firstfruits, i.e., His called-out communities who are now the Light of the world – Mat. 5:14) may look back to the coming of Christ in the Gospels, then in the book of Acts, and now here, in the Unveiling. The Light that shines in the darkness into which Jesus came in order to illuminate the Land of Israel, and then the rest of the world, through His body, is the Good News which we proclaim. Some doubt that this Agent represents Christ, but reading the last phrase as apposition seems to indicate that it does: "His manifestation which called forth praise: the splendor which was, or is, Him."

The proclamation of vs. 2, above, echoes Isa. 21:9,
> "Behold this! Coming [is a] chariot [with] men! A pair of horsemen!
> And he is responding and saying: She has fallen! Babylon has fallen!" (CVOT)

But we also see this pronounced concerning the "house of Israel" in Amos 5:1-2,
> "The virgin of Israel is fallen; she shall no more rise; she is abandoned... forsaken on her Land."

Here, (in 18:1, above) we have, in apocalyptic visionary-figure, a presentation of the coming of the Lord with judgment upon Jerusalem. He descended in the Chief Agent's (Christ's) Voice with a proclamation of the sentence of Babylon (a symbol for Jerusalem). The description of her condition after her fall (vs. 2) is in symbolic terms which paint a picture of a ruined and uninhabited city. We find the imagery of "**every unclean and hated** (or: rejected-from-lack-of-value) **bird and animal**" in Isa. 13:21,
> "Yet desert-beasts will recline there, and their houses will be full of owls; ostriches will tabernacle there, and hairy [goats], they shall dance there. Desert-howlers... and wild jackals in its places..."

Now in Jer. 9:11 another key is seen: "I will make Jerusalem into [rubble, or, assault] mounds: a habitation of wild jackals." Jer. 50:39 speaks of Babylon in the same terms of Isa. 13:21, and Jer. 51:37 reprises Jer. 9:11. Babylon became a figure for Jerusalem when the latter existed in a condition that required God to send Israel into exile, which for the people was like being in a desert. Exile was a way of cleansing the Land from the sins of the people. It was seen in the symbol of the "scapegoat" that, on the Day of Atonement, was sent into the wilderness to remove the people's sins from the camp of Israel (Lev. 16:8, 10, 26). God's "judgments" are always to cleanse, to cover (the meaning of the Hebrew word "atone") and to remove from us the impurities from our existence (just as the refining process removes that which is not gold – Mal. 3:2-3).

The unclean and hated birds are the vultures looking for rotting flesh. But this was also a code word for the Roman army, with its eagles on their standards. Their camps were the **abodes** of "demons," the animistic spirits of Hellenistic culture, which attended their Hellenistic world view and emperor worship. Jerusalem was no longer a city of Yahweh's purity. This same, specific term, "**an abode** (dwelling)," is used in only one other place in the NT, applying to the exact opposite situation:
> "**within the midst of** (or: in union with) **Whom you folks, also, are continuously and progressively being formed a constituent part of the structure** (or: being built together into a house) – **into God's down-home place** (place of settling down to dwell; abode; permanent dwelling) **within [the] Spirit**" (Eph. 2:22).

It had been set forth for Jerusalem to be as Paul described in Eph. 2, and as we read in Ps. 76:2,
> "Salem became His abode; Zion, His den" (Tanakh), but things changed.

Note that it "**becomes** (became; comes to be; is birthed; [note: aorist indefinite tense])" this way – it was not that way before! Before, it was the holy city, Jerusalem. Simmons concurs: "The cities of the Gentiles could not *become* the habitation of devils for they were ever and always such. [This]... speaks to the fact that she was once free from these defilements..." (ibid p 332; brackets added).

A verse that is often overlooked, in regard to the coming of Christ, is in the context of Jesus being led to Caiaphas the **chief priest**, where the **scribes** and the **elders** were assembled (Matt. 26:57). Note what Jesus says to THEM, in vs. 64,

> "**Jesus is then saying to him, 'You yourself are saying [it]** (or: are [so] saying)**! Moreover, I am now saying to YOU people, from now** (this present moment) **on YOU folks will proceed to be seeing 'the Son of the Man** (= Adam's son; the eschatological Messiah figure; the representative human) **continuously sitting at the right [hand]' of the Power, and 'progressively coming** (or: repeatedly coming and going) **upon the clouds of the atmosphere** (or: sky; heaven).'" [Dan. 7:13; Ps. 110:1]

Because Jesus said this, we believe that it happened when He came as John saw in the prophetic vision described in this chapter: those folks actually saw Him – in the same manner that Stephen saw Him, and later Saul heard Him, on his way to Damascus.

Of what is this description a figure? Keep in mind that her identity is reaffirmed in vs. 24 as the place where "was found [the] blood of prophets and of set-apart folks – even of all those having been slaughtered upon the Land," and that Jesus spoke this of Jerusalem in Matt. 23:29-38.

Borg insightfully comments,
> "'Babylon the Great' is not a code name simply for Rome [here I would say, "Jerusalem," but I concur with the point he makes]; it designates all domination systems organized around power, wealth, seduction, intimidation, and violence. In whatever historical form it takes, ancient or modern, empire is the opposite of the kingdom of God as disclosed in Jesus…. In this context, John's portrait of Rome [or: Jerusalem] means, Do not betray the vision of Jesus and accommodate yourself to empire, for it is the beast" (ibid pp 288-289; brackets added).

3. **"because all the multitudes** (nations; ethnic groups) **have drunk** [other MSS read: fallen] **from out of the wine of the strong passion of her prostitution, and the kings of the Land** (earth) **commit** (committed) **prostitution** (fornication; = idolatry) **with her, and the merchants** (those who travel by sea for trade) **of the Land** (earth) **are** (or: became) **rich from out of the power** (or: ability) **of her headstrong pride and wanton luxury** (or: reveling)."

For the expression, "**have drunk** [other MSS read: fallen] **from the wine of the strong passion of her prostitution**," see the comments on 14:8, above. The imagery compares to Jer. 25:27, 29-30,
> "Thus says Yahweh of hosts, God of Israel: Drink and be drunk, and then vomit and fall [so] that you cannot arise, because of the sword that I am sending between (or: among) you…. For look and see! In the city over which My Name is called, I [am] starting to bring evil and calamity… For I [am] calling a sword on all the dwellers of the Land, declares Yahweh of hosts…. Yahweh shall roar from [the] height, even from His holy habitation He shall give [forth] His voice; He shall roar mightily over His homestead; He shall answer [with a] vintage-shout, like those who tread the winepress, to all the dwellers of the Land."

In Jer. 51:7 we read, "Babylon [was a] golden cup in Yahweh's hand, making the entire Land drunk; the nations drank of her wine… [and] are mad!" God used Babylon to bring judgment upon Israel. But, cf Jer. 51:37.

The last part of this verse brings up, "**the merchants** (those who travel by sea for trade) **of the Land** (earth)." Why would this class of society become "**rich from out of the power** (or: ability) **of her headstrong pride and wanton luxury**"? This would seem to be outside of the charge of idolatry, which was often an OT charge that was symbolized by prostitution (opening themselves to the influence of other religions, as we saw in OT references, above). It was about profit. Merchants were getting **rich** from unjust dealings with the common people. It became economic oppression. This cultivated **headstrong pride** among Jerusalem's elite. **Wanton luxury** describes excess, and unfair advantage. This may be one of the reasons that Paul spoke as he did concerning the "fondness for money," in 1 Tim. 6:

9. Yet those wanting and determining to be rich are continually falling in – into a trial and a trap and many senseless and hurtful strong passions (many over-desires void of understanding and bringing weakness; disadvantageous wants and needs), **which things habitually swamp those people, sinking them to the bottom, into ruinous corruption** (or: destruction) **and loss,**
10. for a root of all the bad things (the worthless qualities; the injurious situations; the poor craftsmanship; the ugly personalities; the malicious desires) **is the fondness of silver** (= love of money; = covetousness) **of which some, habitually extending and stretching themselves out to reach, are caused to wander off** (or: were led astray) **away from the faith and they pierce themselves through with a rod and put themselves on a spit** (or: they run themselves through, stabbing themselves all around) **for** (or: in; to; with; by) **many pains.**

In Mat. 21, Jesus famously addresses the commercial issues that merchants in Jerusalem, and perhaps the priest class, had set up:
12. Next, Jesus entered into the Temple courts and threw out all the folks habitually selling [things], as well as those continuing in buying – as in a marketplace – within the Temple courts (or: = and chased out all the vendors and shoppers from inside the Temple grounds), **and then He turned upside down the tables of the money-exchangers, along with the chairs and benches of the people continually selling the doves and pigeons.**
13. And He proceeds saying to them, "It has been written,
  'My house will continue being called a house of prayer (speaking, thinking or acting, with a view toward goodness and well-being),'** [Isa. 56:7; cf Targum Zech. 14:21]
 yet you folks habitually make it a den of bandits (or: a highwaymen's cave)**!"** [Jer. 7:11-15]
 [note: here he implicitly invokes Jeremiah's prophecy of destruction]

The incident recorded in Jn. 2:13-17 reports Jesus saying, in vs. 16,
 "**Stop making** (or: Do not habitually make) **My Father's House a house of merchandise** (a merchant's store; a market place; a house of business)!"

Yahweh had a controversy with Judah, in Hos. 12:2ff. In vs. 7 He call Judah, "A trader (or: merchant; trafficker) who uses false balances (or: scales of deceit): he loves to overreach and exploit." Jacob (James) writes "**to the twelve tribes who are to be constantly rejoicing within the scattering**" in AD 47-48, and in his first chapter brings the following charge to them:
3. Your gold and silver have been corrupted with poison (or: corroded and covered with oxidation), **and their venom** (or: corrosion) **will proceed being unto you a witness** (or: evidence) **and will progressively eat your flesh** (= the enslaved and alienated self; = the human nature that has been molded by and conformed to the System) **as fire. You folks pile up a treasure hoard in the midst of last days!**
4. Consider and look to the workers' pay (wage; hire) **– that having been withheld by you which belongs to those mowing your farms – which constantly utters** (or: shouts) **a cry, and now the outcries and shouts of those gathering in the harvest have entered into the ears of the Lord of hosts** (= Yahweh of Armies)**!**
5. You folks live a soft life in delicate luxury (or: You self-indulge) **and take excessive comfort and live in wanton pleasure upon the land. You nourish your hearts in the midst of** (or: = fatten yourselves up for) **a day of slaughter!**
6. You oppose fairness, equity and justice, while you degrade the way pointed out; you murder the fair and equitable person…

In his first general epistle, John wrote an admonition about not getting caught up in the over-desires that permeated life in the Empire, in the areas of society, politics, culture, business or religion. He used the word commonly rendered "world" (which is better rendered, "system," or, "ordered arrangement;" it does not mean "earth," or, "the planet") to cover these categories, and in chapter 2 advises:

> 15. **You folks should not be habitually loving** (as indicative: are not normally accepting; as imperative: Stop constantly seeking reunion with) **the world** (secular realm and the controlling ordered arrangement of culture, religion, economy and government), **neither** (or: not even) **the things within the world** (ordered system of domination). **If anyone is in the habit of** (or: keeps on) **loving the world** (ordered system of religion, or of secular society), **the Father's** [other MSS: God's] **Love** (or: the love which the Father has; the Love which is the Father) **does not exist within him,**
>
> 16. **because everything within the world** (ordered but dominating System of the secular and the religious) **– the flesh's over-desire**
>
>> (full passion of the alienated human nature; lust of the estranged self; earnest wants of the false persona that was conformed to the System), **and the eyes' over-desire, and the arrogant ostentation** (haughty, presumptuous or pretentious egoism) **pertaining to living** (= the biological and sociological life we live), **is not out of the Father as a source** (or: does not proceed from the Father), **but rather is continuously forth from out of the world** (the ordered System of society, culture and religion),
>
> 17. **and the world** (ordered System of religion, society, culture, economy and government) **is progressively** (or: constantly; repeatedly) **being caused to pass along** (pass by; pass away), **as well as its over-desire** (full passion; earnest wants; lust), **yet the person constantly doing** (or: performing) **God's will** (intent; purpose; desire) **remains** (abides; dwells) **on into the Age** (= the time and sphere characterized by the Messiah).

As we see from these epistles, the merchants and leadership of Jerusalem were not the only ones who had to guard against the desires of the flesh. We learn in Prov. 11:1 that, "Deceitful (false) scales are an abhorrence to Yahweh," *Cf* Prov. 16:11; 20:23. Jacob (James) 4:4 put it straight to folks, showing the character of their unloving behaviors:

> "**O adulterers and adulteresses** (= O people unfaithful to Christ or God as your husband)! **Have you not seen, and are you not aware, that the Domination System's friendship** (the affection whose source is this world of the controlling organization's religion, secular culture, economy and government) **is a source of enmity with God** (or: hostility and active hatred with regard to God; [Aleph reads: exists being alienation to God])? **Whoever, then, may have been made to want** (to intend; to purpose) **to be the Domination System's** (or: organization's; world's) **friend is continuing to be established** (habitually set down; progressively rendered or constituted) **[as] God's alienated and hostile person.**"

In *Peter, Paul & Jacob*, my "Comments on Jacob" offers the following on Jas. 4:4,

> "Keeping in mind that Jacob was writing a general letter to those scattered among, and influenced by, other cultures, he may have referred to personal immoral behavior among the called-out communities. Yet, these folks would also be aware of Isa. 1:21, "How has she become a prostitute, a town [= Jerusalem] faithful? Full of [right] judgment [was] Zion. Righteousness, it was lodging in her, yet now, murderers!" (CVOT). Israel committed adultery by turning to the false gods of paganism. This may have been that to which Jacob was here referring.
>
> "Through Constantine, the "church" became very friendly with the political System, and then with pagan religious systems, as Christianity became the state religion, and this blending led to the darkness of the Middle Ages. It set up a church system that was at enmity with the love of God, and thus, with God Himself. As codex Aleph reads, it became "alienation to God." The last sentence of vs. 4 applies today as it did back then: friendship with the institutional church, or with

a political system, and their systems of domination, control and governmental stratifications demonstrates a lack of being reconciled to God and sets us in a stance that is alien to the heart of God. Instead of the unification that is in Christ, it creates an "us-and-them" mentality and view of humanity" (ibid p 235).

Trade with "those who travel by sea for trade" meant involvement with "the nations," and this of itself was not a bad thing. But it was an avenue of entry, into Jerusalem's practices, for the ethos of the nations. Human nature tends toward self-centeredness, and absence of love, in one's "business" dealings. For this reason, Paul addressed this issue in Eph. 4:

> 17. **This, then, I am continually laying out** (saying) **and giving evidence of within the Lord: no longer are you folks to be continuously walking [your path]** (i.e., conducting yourselves; adjusting your behavior) **according to the way that the nations** (the multitudes; the non-Israelites; the Gentiles; the ethnic or special or pagan groups) **are continuously walking around** (behaving) **– within the empty purposelessness of their mind,**
> 18. **being folks having been, and still yet being, darkened in** (or: by) **the divided thought and the thing passing through the mind, having been and continuing being alienated** (estranged) **away from the Life of God – through the ignorance continuously existing** (or: being) **within them [and] through the petrifying** (becoming stone; callousness; = insensitivity from dulled perception) **of their heart,**
> 19. **which certain people, being folks having ceased to feel pain** (being insensible, dulled or callous), **gave themselves over** (transferred, committed and abandoned themselves) **to outrageous behavior** (excessive indulgence; wantonness; licentiousness), **into every unclean performance** (work, trade, business or labor of impurity) **in greed** (always wanting more; covetousness; schemes of extortion; = wanting more than one's due, in disregard for others).

We see a classic example of Jerusalem's condition in the parable given by Jesus in Lu. 16. Now observe in vs. 14 that, "**Now the Pharisees, habitually being inherently fond of silver** (= money-lovers), **were listening to all these things**." The parable opens in vs. 19, with a stark contrast:

> 19. "**Now there was a certain rich man, and he was in the habit of dressing himself with purple fabric and fine linen** (a shiny white cloth made from bleached flax; used in Egypt for wrapping mummies; = costly garments) **while daily enjoying himself and being in a good frame of mind – [being simply] radiant** (or: [living] splendidly and magnificently).
> 20. "**Now in contrast, there was a certain destitute man named Lazarus, who, having been sorely wounded, had been flung [down] and cast [aside]** (or: having been afflicted with sores and being ulcerated, was normally placed) **in the proximity of and [facing] toward the large portico** (gateway and forecourt) **of his [house].**

Deut. 15:7 had given instruction to this situation:

> "In case there should be among you a needy person, one of your brothers within one of your gates in your land… you shall neither make your heart rigid nor shut your hand from your needy brother… open your hand to him…"

The rich in Israel, and in Jerusalem, had failed to do this – as Jesus suggests by this parable aimed at the Pharisees.

4. **Next I heard another Voice from out of the atmosphere** (sky; heaven), **repeatedly saying, "Come out of her** (or: Go forth from out of her midst) **My people, so that you may not jointly participate with** (be a partner with; fellowship together with) **her sins** (failures; occasions of missing the mark), **and so that you may not receive from out of her plagues** (blows; impacts),

Wallace comments,

"The voice from heaven introducing vs. 4 was a call to the faithful saints to depart from the doomed city before the calamity struck. It is manifestly parallel with the Lord's exhortation in Matt. 24:15-16 for his faithful disciples to flee Jerusalem when the signs of the impending destruction appeared. The same call was spiritually applied by Paul to the Corinthians (2 Cor. 6:14-18), beseeching them to cut all the ties that would bind them to heathenism or in any way maintain affiliation with the heathen world and its temple of Belial. Its derived or applied meaning was to abandon all that both Judaism and heathenism represented..." (ibid p 379)

He further states, "The extensive traffic in thirty articles specified by John represented the affiliations of the Jewish capital with all the heathen world.... There was no source of revenue from the heathen world not included in the coalition between Jerusalem and the merchants of the earth, as described in vs. 15-16..." (ibid p 381)

The fall of Jerusalem was something that was in process for many years, as her moral condition became worse and worse, until "in one day" – the Day of the Lord – "her plagues, i.e., her blows from the Roman army" arrived (vs. 8, below). Verse 4 makes it clear that she had been the residence of God's people, but He calls them out so that they will not participate in her sins, and thus receive from out of her plagues (the coming judgment). This call echoes from Israel's history,

"Come forth from Babylon! Hasten away from the Chaldeans!... Yahweh has redeemed His servant Jacob!" (Isa. 48:20; CVOT)

Then speaking of the redemption of Jerusalem (in vs. 9b), Isa. 52:11 calls out,

"Withdraw! Withdraw! Go forth from there! Do not touch the unclean! Go forth from her midst! Be pure, you bearers of the vessels of Yahweh!" *Cf* Ezra 1:7-8; 5:14-15; Jer. 50:8; 51:6, 45. Also,

"We would have healed Babylon, yet she would not be healed. Forsake her! And let us go, each one to his land, for her judgment touches the heavens and it is lifted unto the skies" (Jer. 51:9).

But now, Jerusalem answered to the figure of Babylon, and Jesus' admonition in Mat. 24, cited by Wallace, above, and His words recorded in Lu. 21 ring with urgency to those followers of Christ then living in Jerusalem (who would also likely hear of the Unveiling from the called-out communities is Asia Minor) so they knew to escape from Jerusalem so as not to feel the impact of the city being struck. We should note, here, that God calls His people to escape the destruction of the City, and of the temple. The judgment was against the corrupt religious system, not the people. The Jewish rebellion and Jerusalem's destruction were facts of human history and people did die during that war, but the significance of this domination system being brought down was a matter of God's reign and sovereign activities which brought "The End of the Old, and the Beginning of the New," which was a matter of the realm of spirit.

Now this call has continued to sound, down through the centuries, even to this present day. Each generation has had to deal with, and some eventually come out of, this Secret Babylon that rides the beast (domination systems) in every country, religion and century. We must all hear this call. And then, as many "come-outer" groups have said, we must have Babylon purged out of ourselves lest we build her anew. Viewing this historically, Simmons observes,

"The great struggle of the early church was to separate Christianity from Judaism.... There was a tendency to keep many of the dietary and ceremonial laws... also a tendency in some to bind these laws on the Gentiles.... Paul's teaching of a complete severance... was a cause of his persecution and arrest" (ibid p 333). *Cf* Acts 21:20-22, 28.

The author of Hebrews gave a similar call, in 13:12-13,

"**Jesus also suffered** (and/or: had experiences of His bodily senses and emotions) **outside of the gate** [*p46* and others: the Camp]**, so that He may set-apart** (or: would make holy and sacred) **the People through His own blood**. [comment: this was a fulfillment of the Day of Atonement: Lev. 16:27] **Now then, we can keep on coming out** (or: should be progressively going out) **toward Him – outside of the Camp – habitually bearing His reproach** (= the censure and disgrace which He bore; or: the insult which pertains to Him). [*cf* Heb. 11:26; 1 Pet. 4:12-14,17]

This was a call to participate in His sacrifice, and also to leave Judaism (or: religion), and thus to bear the same reproach and insults that He bore; it is also a call to bear away from them the mistakes and failures of others – John 20:23. The change in seasons, the coming of the new age with its new message of Good News, was destined to inhabit a greater context. It was necessary to leave old paradigms, for the old was passing away (2 Cor. 5:17). Jesus illustrated this in a parable in Lu 5:

> 36. **Now He also began telling an illustration to them** (or: a parable directed at them), **"No one is ripping** (or: tearing) **a patch from a new cloak** (or: outer garment) **[and] proceeding to sew [it] on an old cloak! Now if he does, he will proceed both tearing the new one, and the patch from the new one will not continue sound together** (being in symphony; = matching) **with the old one.**
> 37. **"Furthermore, no one normally puts just-made, new wine into old wineskins** (skin bottles). **Now if he does, the fresh, new wine will progressively burst and tear the wineskins, and it will proceed being spilled out, and also the wineskins will continue destroyed.**
> 38. **"To the contrary, freshly-made, new wine [is] drained into and stored in different, new, wineskins** (used-for-the-first-time, or renovated, skin bottles), **and then both are preserved.**

The Potter had made a vessel (Israel), yet in HIS hands, "the vessel which He was making with clay was ruined in the hand of the Potter, and so He turned back and made it into ANOTHER vessel (= a new creation)" (Jer. 18:4). We will see this "another," new vessel as the NEW Jerusalem, below. But first, the old one had to be destroyed, back into malleable clay, to then be reworked on His potter's wheel.

5. **"because her sins** (failures) **are glued together** (joined; adhered so as to be heaped, built or piled) **as far as the atmosphere** (or: sky; heaven). **And God remembers** (called to mind) **her unjust effects** (injuries done; misdeeds; unjust acts; ill-gotten gains; things contrary to the way pointed out).

Note how her **failures** (sins) adhere so as to be **heaped** or built "**as far as the atmosphere** (or: sky; heaven)." This is an echo of Gen. 11:4. We should also observe that this chapter focuses on the judgment of the woman, not the little wild animal. It is the City where "**their Lord was crucified**" (11:8, above). Here God calls to mind her acts that are contrary to the way pointed out, and the unjust effects of these acts. Now it is payday – her harvest has come – and she receives double of what she sowed (vs. 6, below). The first clause of this verse is an allusion to Jer. 51:9, where it is said, "her judgment reaches unto heaven, and is lifted up to the skies."

It will be instructive to recall, here, the literal meaning, and thus concept, of the word "**sin**." In both Hebrew and Greek it literally meant: fail to hit the target. This could be a mistake in aiming, or an error in releasing the arrow. But behind all this is implicit an attempt to hit the target. Justice and equity to others was one of Israel's "targets." The Law had laid this all out. Thus, that this verse addresses her "**glued together**" mound of **sins**, or, "failures to hit the target," it becomes evident that God is once again, as in her history, bringing judgment to His people (Heb. 10:30). And as usual, it is focused on the capital city, Jerusalem.

That "**God remembers**" is a covenant term. He is acting in covenant, remembering Deut. 28:15ff – the curses and judgments of that contract with Israel. Israel, too, was supposed to remember: Ex. 13:3; 20:8; 32:13; Nu. 15:39-40; Deut. 8:2, 18; 9:7; 24:9, 18; Josh.1:13; Jud. 8:34. He was making an end of the old arrangement (covenant).

6.   **"You folks** (or: Let people) **give back and pay to her** (render for, or restore in, her) **as she also** (even as she) **paid** (or: pays; etc.), **and double to her doubles** [other MSS: double the doubles] **according to her works** (acts). **In the cup which she mixes** (blended), **mix** (blend) **double for her.**

It may seem strange that I rendered the opening imperative, "**You folks give back and pay.**" This is because the verb is a plural directive. This is missed by the common rendering, "Give to her..." Following the continued imperative in vs. 7, below, we do not come across another imperative until vs. 20. Between there are descriptions of her past situation and the reactions to this judgment by other people. The imperative of vs. 20 is,

> "**Continue well-minded** (mentally at ease with a healthy attitude) **on her, O Atmosphere** (Heaven) – **even the** (or: that is, those) **set-apart ones and the envoys** (sent-forth folks) **and the prophets – because God decided and executed** (or: evaluates and judges; makes a distinction by separating) **YOUR evaluation of her.**"

Now the alternate, parenthetical, rendering of this second person, plural imperative, "Let people," is viable, and may simply be God's pronouncement being carried out by "people." There is no expressed subject for this imperative, so I have supplied two that may be implied. I tend toward, "**You folks,**" due to the next imperative that breaks into the narrative in vs. 20, cited here. What comes to mind is Paul's declaration in 1 Cor. 6:2-3,

> 2. **Or have you not seen so as to know that the set-apart folks** (the saints; the holy, sacred people; the different-from-the-profane folks) **will proceed to sift, separate, evaluate and decide about the organized System** (the world of culture, religion and government; or: secular society)? **So since** (or: if) **within the midst of, among and in union with you folks the world System is to be habitually** (progressively; repeatedly) **evaluated and judged, are you people unworthy or unfit in regard to deciding about very trivial controversies**
>
> > (or: not of equal value to the smallest standards by which to sift and evaluate; or: of [holding the] least tribunals or places for court)?
>
> 3. **Have you not seen so as to know that we shall continue sifting, separating, evaluating and making decisions about agents** (or: will continue judging messengers) – **why not, indeed, the affairs and business matters of everyday life?**

This seems to describe the covenant communities' participation in kingdom business – here and now. This is why,

> "**He jointly roused and raised** (or: suddenly awakens and raises) **[us] up, and caused [us] to sit** (or: seats [us]; = enthroned [us]) **together within the things situated upon** [thus, above] **the heavens**" (Eph. 2:6).

This situation was apocalyptically described by Jesus in Mat. 19:28,

> "**So Jesus said to them, "It is true** (or: Truly; Amen) – **I am now laying it out and saying to you men – in** (in union with) **the Rebirth** (Birth-back-again) **when the Son of the Man** (or: = the eschatological messianic figure; or: the Human Being) **would** (or: should; may) **sit upon the throne of His glory** (or: of his reputation and manifestation which calls forth praise; which is His assumed Appearance), **you yourselves – the folks following Me – you also will be habitually sitting down upon twelve thrones** (or: seats) **repeatedly separating-out [issues], evaluating and making decisions for, or administering justice to, the twelve tribes of Israel.**"

The same situation was further described by Jesus in the parable of the sheep (Jesus' followers, who hear His voice: John 10:3, and who are led by Him: Rom. 8:14) and the kids in Mat. 25:34,

> "**Come here, you folks having received words of ease and wellness from My Father! At once come into possession of the inheritance of, and enjoy the allotment of,** [the period of, place of, or realm of] **the reign** (or: kingdom; activity of sovereignty) **having been prepared and made ready from a founding** (or: a casting down) **of a system.**"

May the Spirit lead us into the proper interpretation of this imperative.

What about the severity of the judgment: "**pay to her** (render for, or restore in, her) **as she also** (even as she) **paid** (or: pays; etc.), **and double to her doubles**... **mix** (blend) **double for her**"? In the last clause it states that the **mix** is to be in her own "**cup which she mixes**," so there seems to be a sense of equity and that she shall "reap what she has sown." But why the **doubles**? This comes from Jer. 16:18, a judgment spoken against Israel,

"I will first repay double for their depravity and their sin, because they have profaned My Land..."
Then, in Jer. 17:18, Jeremiah asks of God,

"Let my persecutors be ashamed... Bring on them a day of evil; break them [with] a double breaking."

The cup that she mixes could also refer to the way she has made her dealings. She was one whose Law said that she should not steal, but in Rom. 2:21, Paul says such folks, "**You, the one constantly preaching** (proclaiming; heralding), **"Do not steal," are habitually stealing!**" In Ex. 22:4, the Law was:

"If the theft is found... whether bull or donkey or flockling, he shall repay double."

Since the destruction of Jerusalem was the final judgment upon Israel, as a nation, and was an old covenant kind of judgment, it was the final **payment** for her cup that was full, as vs. 24, below, affirms: "**within her was** (or: is) **found blood of prophets and of set-apart folks – even of ALL those having been slaughtered upon the Land**." The idea of "**double to her doubles**" is most likely for rhetorical effect: hyperbole.

7.   "**As much as she glorified** (or: glorifies) **herself and indulged** (lives in proud luxury), **so much give to her examination** (testing) **by the touchstone and mourning** (grief; sadness; sorrow), **because within her heart she is continually saying, 'I continually sit as a queen, and I am not a widow; I may by no means see mourning** (grief; sadness; sorrow; misery).'

This pronouncement calls again to the parable of the rich man in Lu. 16:25, where the decision for correction takes the form of a reversal:

"**But Abraham said, 'Child** (or: My boy; Born one; or: Descendant), **be reminded that within your life** (or: lifetime) **you took away** (or: received from; or: got in full) **your good things** (or: the good things that pertain to you; the good things that had their source in you), **and Lazarus likewise the bad things** (the [experiences] of poor quality; the worthless things; the harmful and injurious [treatments]; the [conditions] as they ought not to be). **But at the present time, here he continues being called alongside and given relief, aid, comfort and consolation, yet you yourself continue being given pain.**"

Here, CHILD suggests that Abraham (addressed by the rich man as "father," in vs. 24) recognizes the one in flames as an Israelite, while, Lazarus is a figure of the Gentiles (the ethnic multitudes). Notice, though, that he did not use the word, "son," which would indicate a mature man, one in the place of "sonship." This man represented the same level of development that "kid" did in the parable of the "sheep and the kids," in Mat. 25. Bringing **the touchstone** back on stage directs us back to 14:10, above: the **examination** and purification within the midst of Fire and Deity. This would suggest that this Woman has taken the mark of the little animal. This dealing from the Lord calls to mind Ps. 137:8,

"O daughter (= one having the characteristics) of Babylon, who is to be destroyed; happy is the one rewarding you as you have served us."

Considering that, "**she glorified** (or: glorifies) **herself and indulged** (lives in proud luxury)," further brings up the image of the rich man in Lu. 16:19, "**he was in the habit of dressing himself with purple fabric and fine linen** (a shiny white cloth made from bleached flax; used in Egypt for wrapping mummies; = costly garments) **while daily enjoying himself and being in a good frame of mind – [being simply] radiant** (or: [living] splendidly and magnificently)."

Where she positioned herself for leadership, **sitting as a queen** – as did Jezebel in the days of Elijah, and her counterpart in the covenant community (Thyatira, 2:20, above), calling herself a prophetess and a teacher – she now encounters death, mourning and famine (vs. 8, below). The "**mourning** (grief; sadness; sorrow)" will be the loss that she must undergo. In Lu.19:41 Jesus wept over Jerusalem, then in vss. 43-44 describes her utter destruction. The "grief and sorrow" that would be experienced by Jerusalem answers to His parables which end with certain ones "**weeping and grinding their teeth**." Consider the following situations:

    a) Mat. 8:12, "**the 'sons of the kingdom** (or: reign; = those who were in line to inherit the kingdom; or: = those who were supposed to manifest its reign and dominion)' **will be progressively thrown out into the external darkness** (external obscurity of the shadows)..."

    b) Mat. 13:42, "**the folks habitually producing** (or: doing; constructing; practicing; creating) **the lawlessness... will continue thrown into the furnace** (oven; kiln) **of The Fire**..."

    c) Mat. 13:50, "**within the destined conclusion of the** (or: = that) **age: the agents** (messengers) **will be constantly going forth and will be progressively marking off boundaries for the worthless and disadvantageous folks or circumstances** [to remove them] **from out of the midst of the fair and equitable folks or situations, and then will continue casting them into the furnace** (oven; kiln) **of The Fire**..."

    d) Mat. 22:11-13, "**a person there who had not put on wedding apparel**.... [will be] **thrown out into the darkness** (dim obscurity) **which is farther outside** [of the wedding celebration – a figure for being active in the Messiah's reign]..."

    e) Mat. 24:51, the **worthless slave** (Israel), "**will proceed being cut in two** [hyperbole for: severely punish; or, metaphor: cut him off from employment] **and then he will proceed being put with the perverse, opinionated scholars who have all the answers and are hyper-critical and overly judgmental**..."

    f) Mat. 25:30, "**the useless slave will be thrown out into the darkness** (dim obscurity and gloominess) **which is farther outside**..."

In each of these illustrations, after God's judgment, they **wept** and **ground their teeth** because of the loss of their position, or because they were ejected from the party. This is what happened when Jerusalem was destroyed in AD 70. All those parables in Matthew were prophetic of what was going to happen, as Jesus described specifically in the "Olivet Discourse" (Mat. 24 and Lu 21). When in God's plan it is time to depose dominating leaders, God removes them from their position and begins His cleansing and transforming process on them. It is not usually a fun time, but it has a good outcome. As we read in Dan. 4:37, "those that walk in pride He is able to abase." The statement, "'**I continually sit as a queen**," is an allusion to Isa. 47:7-9,

"You said, 'I shall be a lady (or: mistress) unto times age-abiding'.... Now, therefore, hear this, you 'Lady of pleasure' who dwells securely, who said in her heart, 'I [am] and there is no one besides; I shall not sit a widow, nor know loss of children.' Yet, there shall come to you – both in a moment, in one day – loss of children and widowhood..."

Jerusalem had Isa. 54:5 that she took as a promise to her, "Your Maker [is] your husband..." But the previous verse had spoken of a previous widowhood. So we can suppose that the Jewish leadership of Jesus' day may have felt that all this would not come again, just as they asserted to Jesus, "**we have served as slaves to no one at any time**" (Jn. 8:33), but indeed their history spoke otherwise. But the words of Micah 3:9-12 rang true in 1st century Jerusalem,

"[The] heads of the house of Jacob, and princes of the house of Israel... abhor justice and pervert all equity. They build up Zion with blood, and Jerusalem with lawlessness. The heads thereof judge for a bribe, and the priests thereof teach for hire… and say, 'Is not Yahweh among us? No evil can come upon us!' Therefore shall Zion – for YOUR SAKE – be plowed as a field, and Jerusalem shall become heaps…"

But let us keep Isa. 54:7-8 in mind, as we inquire for understanding of God's judgments:

"For a small moment have I forsaken you; but with great mercies will I gather you. In a little wrath I hid My face from you, for a moment. But with age-lasting kindness will I have mercy on you, says Yahweh, your Redeemer."

8.   **"On account of this, in** (or: within; on) **one day her plagues** (blows) **will progressively arrive: death, mourning** (grief) **and famine. And she will proceed being burned down** (consumed) **within fire, because the Lord** [= Yahweh], **the God evaluating and judging her, [is] strong!**

Just as the rich man's harvest was this fire (Lu. 16:24ff), so it is hers: **she will proceed being burned down** (consumed) **within fire**. The phrase, "**in** (or: within; on) **one day**," is an allusion to Isa. 47:9, cited above. The one day is the "day" of judgment. Historically, this came true in AD 70. It happened just as Jesus predicted that it would. At times there are literal fires, but more often it is the "fiery trials" of which Peter spoke in 1 Pet. 4:12, or it may be the testing of our works and activities, of which Paul spoke in 1 Cor. 3:12-15. And, as Jesus said, "**everyone shall be salted with Fire**" (Mk. 9:49).

Under the Law, the arrangement was that if Israel walked contrary unto Yahweh, there would be judgment, as laid out in Lev. 26:25-26, 29-32,

"I will bring a sword upon you…. I will send the pestilence among you…. [break] the staff of your bread [= famine]…. You shall eat the flesh of your sons and daughters…. I will make your cities waste…. I will bring the Land into desolation…"

Josephus, in *Wars of the Jews*, V, 12.3.4, gave details of such things happening in Jerusalem, during the Roman siege. Paul spoke to the topic of the Lord's coming on "the Day of the Lord," as "a thief in the night," in 1 Thes. 5:2-3, where,

"**sudden, unexpected ruin** (destruction) **is presently standing upon them, just as the birth-pang for the pregnant woman, and they may by no means flee out or make an escape.**"

We saw in 17:16, above that it was the complete little animal (figured by the 10 horns) that "**burned her down in a fire**," but here we are informed that the Empire is but an "instrument for His work" (Isa. 54:16), and that it is **God evaluating and judging her** through Rome. Yes, He cannot be opposed: He is **strong**. *Cf* Isa. 50:34. Paul instructs us that He is:

"**the One continuously operating** (effecting; energizing) **all things in accord with** (or: down from; in line with; in correspondence to; following the pattern of) **the deliberated purpose** (intent; design; plan) **of His will** (or: resultant decision of His resolve; effect of His desire)" (Eph. 1:11).

9.   **"And the kings of the Land** (earth) **– those committing prostitution** (or: acts of fornication) **with her and indulging** (living in proud and wanton luxury) **– will proceed weeping and lamenting** (smiting or cutting themselves in wearisome labor) **upon** (over) **her when they may be observing** (or: seeing) **the smoke of her burning,**

Here, in vss. 9-11, we see the sorrow of the kings of the Land (historically, the provincial kings such as Herod, Agrippa, Festus, Albinus, Florus, etc.; and today, whoever in the system who watches a profitable enterprise crash) as they lament lost revenues. The **kings of the Land** were not "covenant people," but were a part of the Empire, so the interactions – both political and economic – between them and Jerusalem were characterized with the OT imagery of employing a Prostitute. Were it not for their loss of commercial gain, it would be unlikely for kings to weep and lament over the death of a prostitute. But this symbolism, taken from Yahweh's repeated characterization of Israel interacting outside of covenant, in Israel's history, speaks to how this Woman had received the mark of the animal system.

The **smoke of her burning** has long been seen as an allusion to Gen. 19:28, especially with the name Sodom being used to describe Jerusalem, in 11:8, above. But in the Genesis text it was Abraham that observed, "the smoke of the country…as the smoke of a furnace."

10. **"while standing away, at a distance, on account of the fear of her examination** (testing) **by the touchstone, repeatedly saying, 'Woe, tragic is the fate of the Great City! Babylon, the strong city! Because in one hour your evaluating and judging came!'**

Yes, when people fall, those who had been associates, but did not really love them, will **distance** themselves, fearing to be implicated, or in some way to be drawn in to the **examination** by those who are charged in the offense, or whatever caused the fall. They will shake their heads and say how "**woeful and tragic**" is the situation. They will be amazed at how **the strong city** (state, country, enterprise or individual) could come to ruin – and just be glad that it was not them.

So how did the rulers of the other provinces take the fall of Jerusalem? We could research Josephus for answers, but that is not our purpose here. Here we want to receive the message from this historical occurrence. Jesus used the word **Woe**, or "tragic," in Mat. 11:21,
> "**Tragic will be your fate, Chorazin! Tragic will be your fate, Bethsaida! Because if the powers and abilities being birthed and happening within you had taken place in Tyre and Sidon, long ago they would in sackcloth and ashes** (= humility and regretful sorrow) **have changed their minds and way of thinking, and would have turned to God.**"

He said this, "**to censure and reproach the character and reputation of the cities within which most of His powers and abilities happened**" (vs. 20), and yet they had not changed their thinking. The same was true of Jerusalem, and thus are we reading of her here. In Mat. 18:7 He used this same expression referring to, "**the System**," with its "**bait-laden traps and snares**," and proceeded to warn the people about the things that can lead them to crucifixion and then have them end up in Gehenna, the city dump. But an insightful reading of the text can observe a veiled warning concerning the Jewish leaders and the fate of Jerusalem, which also had not changed its thinking.

The downfall suddenly came. **In one hour** the Roman army came. In a relatively short war, it put down the Jewish rebellion. This was her "**evaluating and judging**," by God, as we saw indicated, above. Isa. 66:24 had been fulfilled:
> "And they shall go forth and look upon the carcasses of the men that have transgressed against Me, for their worm shall not die, neither shall their fire be quenched. And so they shall be an abhorring unto all flesh."

That is a picture of Gehenna, the dump outside of Jerusalem, to which Jesus referred in Mat. 18:8-9.

11. **"And the merchants** (sea traders) **of the Land** (or: earth) **[are] continually weeping and mourning upon** (over) **her, because no one continues buying their cargo** (merchandise) **any longer:**

Could **the merchants** referred to here be the same ones of whom Jesus said that they had made His Father's house "a house of merchandise"? (John 2:16) Alain Decaux, in noting that many Jews lived in Asia Minor (the first recipients of this Unveiling), instructs us:
> "Flavius Josephus gives an account of the favorable treatment the Romans granted them: the TRADE that they practiced drew the Jews closer to them; they more often spoke Greek or Latin

than the indigenous peoples did... strong Jewish communities [were] able to claim their rights and [were] unafraid to appeal local decisions by the Roman authority. They even obtained exoneration from common charges. If a dispute set them in opposition to the native population, most of the time the Romans found in favor of the Jews... we see pagans and Jews living on good terms... the customs of the Jews ended by seducing them" (*Paul, Least of the Apostles, The Story of the Most Unlikely Witness to Christ*, Pauline Books and Media, 2006 p 90-91; emphasis and brackets added).

Today, we can see this as a good thing. But with regard to God's plan to end the old age and change the arrangement of God-to-human, and human-to-God, relations (as Jesus unveiled in John 4:21-24, and Paul unveiled in 2 Cor. 5:17 and in Eph. 2:11-16) it was necessary to have the Temple destroyed, and the Jerusalem leadership ended. Although this was a cause for **weeping and mourning** for **the merchants**, we have seen that "weeping may endure for the night" (Ps. 30:5), the joy of God's New Day came in the morning of the New Age. And we can be sure that, in time, the merchants and sea traders got over it.

12. **"a cargo of gold, and of silver, and of precious stones, and of pearls, and of fine cotton, and of purple, and of silk, and of scarlet** (crimson), **and every aromatic** (thyme or citron) **wood, and every ivory utensil** (or: vessel), **and every utensil** (vessel) **[made] out of precious wood** [other MSS: stone] **and of copper** (or: bronze) **and of iron and of shining marble,**
13. **also cinnamon** [grown in Arabia & Syria] **and amomum** [fragrant white vine from India], **and incenses and essential oil** [aromatic juices from trees; used for anointing] **and frankincense** [from Mt. Lebanon and Arabia], **and wine and olive oil, and the finest flour, and grain and cattle and sheep and horses and four-wheeled chariots** (carriages; coaches), **even bodies and souls** (or: = lives) **of people.**

Verses 12-13 list the kinds of merchandise that will no longer be listed in Dow Jones. Note that they are primarily luxury items, not just wheat and barley as in 6:6, above. And note the last item listed: **souls of people**. She made money from peoples' lives. We also see merchandising of people's "souls" today. Gary Sigler has mentioned the distinctions between the principles of Babylon and the principles of the Kingdom: in Babylon it is "buying and selling;" in the Kingdom it is "receiving and giving."

The specification of the kinds of trade commodities echoes Ezk. 27:12-22 that was set in the lamentation for the fall of Tyre. John's listeners would have perceived the point of this well-known referent. The point here is that Jerusalem, the "great City," was no mean commercial center (so Simmons, ibid p 342). The destruction of Jerusalem did not affect just the Temple, but the entire economy of Judea and would have had far-reaching consequences for all of Palestine. Those wholesale suppliers who imported these goods and services to Jerusalem lost a large market. Slave trade, **the bodies and souls of people**, was also taken into consideration, here. Simmons insightfully points us to Nah. 3:15-17 as an example of where "Merchants of this sort are often portrayed negatively in the scriptures, like locusts eating the substance of other peoples, denuding the land" (ibid).

Alfred Edersheim instructs us concerning the commercial status of 1st century Jerusalem,
"In these streets and lanes everything might be purchased: the production of Palestine, or imported from foreign lands – nay, the rarest articles from the remotest parts. Exquisitely shaped, curiously designed and jeweled cups, rings and other workmanship of precious metals; glass, silks, fine linen, woolen stuffs, purple and costly hangings; essences, ointments, and perfumes as precious as gold; articles of food and drink from foreign lands – in short, what India, Persia, Arabia, Media, Egypt, Italy, Greece and even the far-off lands of the Gentiles yielded, might be had in these bazaars. Ancient Jewish writings enable us to identify no fewer than 118 different

articles of import from foreign lands, covering more than even modern luxury has devised" (*The Life and Time of Jesus the Messiah*, Wm. B. Eerdmans Pub. Co., Vol. 1, 1953 p 116).

14. **"And the fruit season** (or: autumn; ripe fruits) **of your soul's earnest desire** (yearning) **went away** (passes away) **from you, and all the fat** (sumptuous) **things and the bright, shining things destroyed themselves** (became lost; perished) **from you, and no longer may you by any means find** [other MSS: will they continue finding] **them.**

This seems inserted to poetically encapsulate this change of state as the passing away of the fruit season (with its normal expectation for a harvest of goods) of their soul's earnest desire. Self will no longer be gratified. It is a loss of all sumptuous things, and of bright, shiny toys. They have lost them, and cannot find them! Is the Lord indicating shallowness here?

But more than this, as with the earlier sacking of Jerusalem and the removal of the temple's gold utensils and vessels to Babylon (*cf* Dan. 5:2-3), the Jews no longer had the physical treasures and the gold that adorned Herod's temple. Now even the golden lampstand and the gold from the altar of incense were gone. Jerusalem was a wasteland by comparison to her former glory. There would be nothing to draw trade to her any more.

At yet another level, the fig tree had dried up (6:13, above; Mk. 11:12-21; Lu. 13:6-9): no more would it see a **fruit season**. No longer would the Law produce anything or be an avenue for merchandise, as Jesus had found the temple courts to be. Jesus spoke of this season in Mat. 24:

> 32. **"Now learn the [point of the] illustration** (parable) **from the fig tree: Whenever its branch may already come to be tender** (= in bud), **and the leaves can progressively produce and sprout out, you normally know by experience that the summer [is] near.**
> 33. **"You folks, yourselves, in this way – whenever you men may see and can perceive all these [aforementioned] things – be also then knowing that it is near** (at hand, close enough to touch), **[come] upon the gates** (or: doors)!
> 34. **"It is true** (Amen; Truly; Count on it), **I now say to you folks, that this generation can by no means pass by until all these things can happen** (should occur; may come to be).
> 35. **"The heaven and the earth** (or: The atmosphere and sky, as well as the land,) **will pass on by, yet My thoughts and words** (or: ideas and messages) **can by no means pass on by.**

The "heaven" that was to pass away was the Temple leadership; the "earth" that was to pass away was the people, as a nation.

15. **"The merchants of these things – those becoming rich from her – will proceed standing away at a distance, because of the fear of her testing** (examination) **with the touchstone, continually weeping and mourning,**

Verses 15-19 focuses on the commercial associates of this city. They distance themselves from her "for **fear**" of what is happening to her. They mourn their losses. They are amazed at so much wealth being destroyed, leaving her as a desert. The transportation industry is also affected (vs. 17, below).

The comment about **distancing** themselves from her **because of the fear of her testing** (examination) is repeated from vs. 10, above. The same reasons suggested there apply here. The words of Jesus come to mind:

> "**Now again** (or: Furthermore), **I continue saying to you folks, it is easier for a camel to squeeze through a needle's eye** (hole) **than for a rich, wealthy person to enter into God's reign** (or: kingdom influence and sovereign activities)" (Mat. 19:24).

Obviously, a big part of **the merchants'** world had come to an end, just as it did for the Jews.

16. **"saying repeatedly, 'Woe, tragic is the fate of the Great City – the one being clothed in fine cotton and purple and crimson** (scarlet), **and being overlaid** (gilded; adorned) **in gold and precious stone and pearls – because in one hour so much wealth** (so great riches) **is** (or: was) **laid waste** (made desolate; made as a desert).'

The last clause tells the story of their view of this **tragic fate** of Jerusalem: "**so much wealth** (so great riches) **is** (or: was) **laid waste** (made desolate; made as a desert)." Jesus spoke to the desolation of the temple in detailed terms of its extent:
> "**Under no circumstances may be left here stone upon stone, which may not by all means be loosed down** (dislodged and torn down)" (Mk. 13:2b).

The emphatic phrase, "**in one hour**" repeats the same descriptive phase of vs. 10b, above, showing of what her "**evaluating and judging**" entailed: it was her desolation. In Mat. 23:37-38 Jesus pronounced:
> "**O Jerusalem, Jerusalem! The one repeatedly killing the prophets, and habitually stoning the people sent off with a mission to her**... **Your House is progressively left [to be] a wilderness** (desert; desolate place) **for you people** (or: is now abandoned to you)." *Cf* Jer. 22:5

17. **"And every navigator** (helmsman; one who steers), **and everyone repeatedly** (habitually) **sailing upon a place, and sailors** (ship men; seamen; mariners), **and as many as are continually working the sea, stand** (or: stood) **away at a distance,**
18. **"and, continuously observing the smoke of her burning, they were crying out, repeatedly saying, 'What [exists] like the Great City?'**

This may be another allusion to the fall of Tyre, in Ezk. 27:26-33,
> "Your rowers have brought you into many waters; the east wind has broken you in the heart of the seas. Your riches, your wares, your merchandise, your mariners and your pilots... sink into the heart of the seas on the day of your fall.... the mariners... stand upon the land... and cry bitterly. They cast up dust upon their heads.... and weep for you... and lament over you: What (or: Who) [is] like Tyre.... When your wares went forth... you enriched the kings of the land (or: earth)..."

The repetitions in the commercial theme of this passage is typical of apocalyptic imagery, and falls in line with the redundancy in the visions which we have already seen, above. Like the merchants in vss. 15-16, above, they are moved by economic loss, not compassion, as is emphasized in vs. 19b, below. International shipping was the focus of their concern.

19. **"And they cast dust** (loose earth) **upon their heads, and were uttering cries, continually weeping and mourning, repeatedly saying, 'Woe, tragic is the fate of the Great City in which all those having ships in the sea became rich from out of her valuable merchandise** (or: preciousness; estimated worth; imputed value), **because in one hour she was laid waste** (made like a desert).'

We saw in the comments on vs. 16, above, the **casting dust on their heads** was part of the allusion to Ezk. 27. The **weeping and mourning** is continued apocalyptic repetition. As with the end of vs. 16, above, the cry of these is also that, "**she was laid waste** (made like a desert)." We also have, here, a third repetition of the phrase, "**in one hour**." Thus, we have an emphasis of the suddenness, and the time-limit, of God's judging of her. It is like the Lord's describing His coming to folks as being "**like a thief**" – suddenly, and without warning (3:3; 16:15, above; 2 Pet. 3:10; 1 Thes. 5:2; Mat. 24:43).

The merchants of Jerusalem and Judea had far-flung trade interactions that included shipping companies. When Jerusalem fell, the entire Empire was economically affected. From a historical perspective, O'Grady instructs us:
> "[The] great churn of gods and religions was powered by trade and the city. Cities and towns were booming along the trade routes that threaded together four empires – Rome, Parthian (formerly Persian), Kushan and Chinese…. People were on the move as they had never been before, and as they would never be again until Victorian times…. In the absence of constant warfare, there was money to spend… merchants… plodded with thousands of heavily laden camels through deserts, or risked shipwreck and pirates, to bring silk from China, frankincense and myrrh from Southern Arabia, spices and pearls from India, and pomegranates and rugs from Parthia to people who were discovering the delights of luxury goods…. The ancient world was undergoing a period of globalization every bit as dislocating and traumatic as our own" (ibid pp 2-3).

The fall of Jerusalem, in AD 70, had a widespread effect.

20. **"Continue well-minded** (mentally at ease with a healthy attitude; thoughtfully considerate for good) **on her, O Atmosphere** (Heaven) **– even the** (or: that is, those) **set-apart ones, the envoys** (sent-forth folks) **and the prophets – because God decided and executed** (or: evaluates and judges; separates for distinction) **your evaluation of her** (or: the effect of a judgment pertaining to you folks and the decision-result from you folks, from out of her)."

Suddenly we have an imperative inserted into the narrative description of the City's ruin. Now the focus changes to **heaven**, our **Atmosphere** – personified here, in direct address – and the **set-apart folks** who continuously, consciously inhabit God's Atmosphere. It further names **the envoys**, or, the "sent-forth folks," and **the prophets**. This is us, His Temple out of which His agents have been sent with the cups, or bowls, or saucers of His Passion. They, representing the whole spectrum of the called-out communities, while living in the realm of spirit (the heavenlies – Eph. 2:6), are told to "**Continue well-minded**" at what has happened (the old is passing away; behold the new has come) to this Great City. This opening imperative about our attitude and disposition toward **her** speaks to a greater depth of our thought-life than is commonly rendered, "Rejoice." It means to "habitually be mentally at ease with a healthy attitude," and always be "thoughtfully considerate for good." The root of the verb means "to be careful and considerate." Prefixed to this is the particle *eu-* which means "goodness, ease and well-being." Remember, "**to us** [that is, we whose eyes have been unveiled to see God's purpose and plan that is operating through Christ] **He is constantly working all things together into good**" (Rom. 8:28).

The personification of the Atmosphere/Heaven, calls to mind Yahweh addressing Israel, metaphorically, in Isa. 1:2, "Hear, O heavens, and give ear, O earth…" In. Jer. 6:19 we read similarly, "Hear, O earth…" Micah 6:2 presents Yahweh saying, "Hear, O you mountains, Yahweh's controversy; also [hear] you strong foundations of the earth: for Yahweh has a controversy with His people…" The explanation in vs. 20, here, of to whom He is speaking, comes clear by the three-fold designation: the Atmosphere, or Heaven is the new leadership in His kingdom who are His, a) **set-apart** agents b) that function as **envoys** and c) are **prophets**. This imperative is followed by the proclamation that compares to 11:15, above, but now it is a time of judging, as presented in 11:18, above.

Now it is **THEIR** judicial process that is going on. Recall what Paul said concerning the called-out communities, in 1 Cor. 6:2,
> "**Or have you not seen so as to know that the set-apart folks** (the saints; the holy, sacred people; the different-from-the-profane folks) **will proceed to sift, separate, evaluate, decide**

> **about and JUDGE the organized System** (the world of culture, religion and government; or: secular society)**?**"

They – **the set-apart ones, the envoys and the prophets** – did the evaluating and made the decision about the Woman on the little animal; **God carried it out** through His instruments on the earth. This rendering of the final clause, "**your evaluation of her** (or: the effect of a judgment pertaining to you folks and the decision-result from you, from out of her)," seems strange, but it is accurate. The CLNT renders this, "God judges by passing your sentence upon her." Note the alternate renderings, offering the personal, plural pronoun first as a possessive, **your**, then as a genitive of association, "**pertaining to you folks**," and finally as an ablative, "**from you folks**." All of these options fit the context. This prepositional phrase modifies the noun *krima*, and having the *–ma* ending signifying an effect, or a result: a **decision** reached by evaluating, or, a decision-result. Or, "**the effect of a judgment**." So this picture places the called-out community as an actor in this play, operating from Christ's throne (the Mercy Seat in the holy of holies, i.e., the innermost part of the heavenly Temple, which is Christ's body). The communities are overcomers in Christ, and are seated with Him (3:21, above). The bottom line of this final clause is that God, with whom we are joined in Spirit (1 Cor. 6:17) gives us the job of evaluating this Woman, and then coming to a decision about what He should do in her case. Is this an allusion to Jas. 5:16b?

> "**A petition** (prayer) **from a person within the Way pointed out** (of a fair and equitable person; of one in right relationship; of a rightwised and rightly aligned man; from a just one) – **which progressively works inwardly and itself continuously creates energy from union – constantly exerts much strength.**"

This is part of what Paul meant in 1 Cor. 3:9,

> "**For we are God's fellow-workers** (or: we are co-workers of and from God)."

Paul gave us an example of this, in 1 Cor. 5:3, 5,

> "**For I myself, indeed, continuing being absent – in the body – yet continuously being present alongside – in** (or: by; with) **the spirit** (or: Breath-effect; or: attitude) **– have, as being present, already sifted, evaluated and decided about the man thus working down to this effect....** [you are] **to hand over such a man, with the adversarial** [spirit] (or: in the adversary; by the opponent; or: to satan), **into a loss of the flesh** (or: an undoing and destruction of this [estranged human nature]; a loss of [his "dominated existence" – Walter Wink]) **– to the end that the spirit may be saved** (rescued; delivered; restored to health, wholeness)**: within the midst of and in union with the Day of** (or: in this day from, or, which is) **the Lord**"

This may be an allusion to Ps. 149:4-9,

> "For Yahweh… is making the humble beautiful with salvation. May the benign ones be joyous in [this] glory…. To execute vengeance on [the] nations; corrections of folks; to bind their kings….
> To execute a written judgment against them. This [is the] honor of all His benign ones." (CVOT).

The LXX of these last two statements reads: "To create (form; produce) in and among them an effect of a written decision (or: sentence). This glory is for and in all His devout, pious and sanctioned folks" – JM.

Jesus spoke of this situation in Mat. 19:28,

> "**I now am saying to you men, In the rebirth – when the Son of the Man** (mankind's Son; = Adam's son; [or: the eschatological messianic figure]; or: the human) **can sit upon the throne of His glory** (or: the throne of his good reputation and manifestation which calls forth praise) **– you yourselves, the ones following Me, will continue sitting down – even you, upon twelve thrones** (or: seats; chairs) **– continuously separating [issues], making decisions and administering justice for the twelve tribes of Israel.**"

Mat. 23 is filled with His criticism of Jerusalem's leadership, predicting their fall, and Mat. 24 gives further description of what would soon happen. He made an **evaluation** of them in 23:33,

> "**[You] snakes! [You] offspring** (brood) **of vipers** (poisonous serpents)**! How can you flee and escape from the judging which has the qualities, character and significance of the**

> **valley of Hinnom** (= the sentence to the city dump [Greek: *Gehenna*; = the Valley of Hinnom]; the deciding which pertains to the waste depository of the city)**?**"

Jesus was no false prophet, this literally came true in AD 70.

We suggest that the key to interpreting this verse is 11:3-12, above. These visions in the Unveiling are inter-locked, intertwined. Recall that these **Two Witnesses** responded to the upward call, "**climb up here**," and then "**they climbed up into the atmosphere** (or: ascended into the sky and heaven) **within** (or: in the midst of; in union with) **the cloud**," in 11:12. That was likely a "**cloud of witnesses**" (Heb. 12:1), and their destination was described in Heb. 12:22-24 as **Mt. Zion**, "**Jerusalem-upon-heaven**." Furthermore, we see from 11:3 that they were **prophets**, just as these who are addressed as such here, in 18:20. In 11:6 they functioned like the ministries of Elijah and Moses, "**holding authority**" upon the skies and the Land, and in fact, they brought the **plagues**, as did Moses. They were a figure of God's agents within the City where their Lord was crucified: Jerusalem, figured here as Babylon. Between their ministry and ascension, the little animal killed them, as they followed their Lord to their crosses. They did the works that He did, as He ministered through them, then they laid down their lives for their friends. They may have been the "souls under the altar" in 6:9, above, for that altar of burnt offerings, in the outer court, is equivalent to the cross of Christ. But during their ministry, they "**sifted, separated, evaluated and decided about the organized System**," and it was from the authority of "**[their] evaluation of her**" that "**God decided and executed [their] decision**." It was thus, "**the effect of a judgment pertaining to [them]**." Also, during the time of their prophesying, it was "**the decision-result from** [them]."

The final phrase, in the parenthetical expansion, "**from out of her**," can have at least two interpretations:

a) She has grown rich by unjust means, even while taking the lives of the **set-apart folks** and the **prophets** (vs. 24, below), so her unjust gain would be taken from her; her conquerors would strip her bare. Considering the emphasis on merchants and shipping trade, in vss. 11-19, above, we suggest that Jesus' story of the "unmerciful servant" in Mat. 18 may have currency here:

> 32. "**At that point, after calling him** [i.e., the first slave] **to himself, the owner proceeds saying to him, 'O worthless and wicked slave! I cancelled that entire debt for you, since you begged and entreated me.**
> 33. "'**Was it not of necessity binding [on; for] you, also, to dispense mercy to your fellow slave, just as I myself also dispensed mercy to you?'**
> 34. "**So, internally swelling with indignation and anger, his owner handed him over** (committed him) **to 'the people who to test folks'** (literally: those who apply the touchstone to determine the grade, and to show the quality, of fine metals) **until where [the occasion or situation develops that] he could** (or: would) **pay back all that continued being owed.**
> 35. "**My heavenly Father** (or: My Father, Who inhabits, and can be compared to, the atmosphere) **will be progressively dealing with you folks in this same way** (or: will continue doing to you men in like manner), **too, if each person does not release and forgive his brother** (and let things flow away for him), **from your hearts.**" [*cf* 5:7; 6:12, above; Eccl. 28:2ff]

b) This destruction would be the first phase of removing from her both guilt and the effect of her sins. It would be the cleansing and purifying work of God's Fire and Deity, as in 14:10, above. For this, the Atmosphere, or Heaven, would be "**thoughtfully considerate for** [her ultimate] **good**." Even though now broken out of her olive tree (Rom. 11:17), she could yet be grafted back in again (Rom. 11:23ff). When this happens the allusion of this verse will be to Isa. 44:23, "Sing, O you heavens… for Yahweh has redeemed Jacob…" or Isa. 49:13, "… for Yahweh has comforted His people, and will have mercy upon His afflicted."

21. **And then, one strong agent lifts** (took up; carried away) **a stone as great as a millstone, and casts** (or: cast) **[it] into the sea, saying,**

> **"Thus, by violence** (or: impetuous motion) **Babylon the Great City will be cast** (thrown) **and can by no means any longer be found** (or: be yet found).

The scene now turns back to focus on Babylon's destruction, and John sees on stage a cameo appearance of **one strong agent** who **lifts up and carries away** a stone, "**as great as a millstone**" into the sea, intimating that the inhabitants of Jerusalem and Judea will be dispersed into the chaos of the Gentile nations of the ethnic multitudes. Describing the action as **by violence** and **casting/throwing** indicates that Jerusalem's demise will be by war and destruction. The **great millstone** metaphor, as well as showing the great "ripple effect" of the splash from casting down Babylon, also suggests that this system snared some of the little ones of whom Jesus spoke in Matt. 18:6. The strong agent may be the same one seen in 5:2 and 10:1, above, thus representing the continuity in the themes of these visions. Chilton suggests that the symbol of the millstone signifies the ceasing and removal of productivity (ibid p 460).

Taking into consideration the part played by the set-apart folks, etc., in the previous verse, Mat. 21:21 comes to mind:
> "**So Jesus, giving a decided reply, said to them, "Truly** (It is so; Depend on it; Amen), **I am now saying and laying it out for you, if you can continuously hold trust** (or: if you folks should constantly have faith) **and would not be affected by some separating factor passing through your act of discerning or judging, leading you to hesitate, doubt, or completely question your decision, [then] not only will you men do [what I did] to the fig tree, but further, you can also say to this mountain range** (or: hill country; mountain), **'Be uplifted, and then be flung** (cast) **into the midst of the lake** (or: sea)!' **It will progressively come to pass** (It will proceed in birthing itself and happening)."

Keep in mind that, in prophetic language, a mountain was a figure for a kingdom, and the sea represented the masses of humanity. Jesus may have had Judea and Jerusalem (or: Israel) in mind, because He said this in response to the withering away of the fig tree (vss.18-20).

This symbolic act echoes Jer. 51:63-64, where Jeremiah gives a scroll to Seraiah and tells him to "bind a stone" upon the scroll and "cast it into the midst of the Euphrates," and then proclaim, "Thus shall Babylon sink and shall not rise from the evil that I will bring upon her." This image may also be a reflection from the Egyptian army being destroyed by the Red Sea as it pursued Israel. Recall 11:8, above, and the insinuation of Jerusalem as being a modern Egypt.

22. **"And so, a sound** (voice) **of lyre-players/singers and of musicians and of flutists and of trumpeters may by no means be heard in YOU any more** (yet; further), **and every technician** (craftsman, artist) **of every trade** (craft; art) **may by no means be yet** (any longer) **found within YOU. And a sound of a millstone may by no means be yet found in YOU,**
23. **and a light of a lamp may by no means any longer shine within YOU; and a voice of a bridegroom and of a bride may by no means any longer be heard in YOU, because YOUR merchants were the great ones of the Land** (or: earth) **because all the multitudes** (nations) **were** (are) **deceived** (led astray; caused to wander) **in YOUR employment of drugs** (sorcery; enchantments)."

In vs. 22-23 we see a description of a dead city – no life or activity. No more entertainment or professionalism. No grinding of grain – a figure both of food production as well as of the process of teaching the Word and giving "meal offerings." In AD 70 it was literal famine; since then it has been times of a "famine of hearing the Word of the Lord" (Amos 8:11).

The lack of there being the light of a lamp speaks of there being no light in this city any more, and calls to mind His warning to the called-out community in Ephesus: that unless they repent and do the first works, He would come swiftly and remove their lampstand out of its place (2:5, above). His warnings and prophecies of judgment were not just to Jerusalem and Judea, but also to the called-out.

Notice that in these two verses it changes from a narrative to a monologue spoken TO the Woman. To highlight this, I put the "YOU's" and "YOUR" in upper case. We must keep in mind that this is still a letter sent to the followers of Christ in Asia. But the message was also to Jews and Judaizers in the Diaspora, as well. This affected everyone, for as Edersheim pointed out, above, trade relations spread from Jerusalem throughout the Empire, and beyond.

This pronouncement echoes Jer. 25:10, a message to Judah and Jerusalem,
"I will take from them the voice of mirth, and the voice of gladness, the voice of the bridegroom and the voice of the bride; the sound of the millstones, and the light of the candle." *Cf* Ezk. 26:13
The picture in all these verses is that of a loss of prosperity and joy (*cf* Terry, ibid p 439). *Cf* Jer. 7:34; 16:9. The accusation, "**because YOUR merchants were the great ones of the Land**," may be an allusion to the overthrow of Tyre, "whose merchants [are] princes," in Isa. 23:8. Their prior position is no longer significant.

Mentioning, "**YOUR employment of drugs** (sorcery; enchantments)," calls to mind the prediction of Babylon's fall in Isa. 47, where in vs. 9 we read of her coming "bereavement and widowhood" that suddenly would "come on [her] despite [her] many enchantments and countless spells." Nineveh was also condemned, "because of... [being] the mistress of witchcrafts, that sells nations through her prostitutions, and families through her witchcrafts (or: enchantments)" (Nah. 3:4). Do we find a correlation of this to some of the Jews, in Acts 13:6?
> "**Now after going through the whole island up to Paphos, they found a certain man – a magus** [note: originally of the Persians, Medes and Babylonians as priests and wise men, magi specialized in the study of astrology and enchantment and were often employed as official spiritual advisers; some were sorcerers] **[and] a false prophet – a Jew named Bar-Jesus** (son of Jesus)."

Simmons (ibid p 345) points us to Acts 19:13-14 where we read of "**wandering** (or: periodically roving; habitually vagabond) **Jews – being practicing exorcists** (folks who exacted or administered oaths; people who pronounced incantations)," and also to Mat. 23:15 where Jesus says of the Pharisees,
> "**you habitually go around the sea and dry [land] to make one convert** (proselyte), **and whenever he may become** (should be birthed) **[one], you proceed making him a son of the valley of Hinnom** (= a person having the character and qualities of a city dump, or a part of a refuse depository [Greek: *Gehenna*]) **twice as much as yourselves**."

Was this, perhaps, that to which Paul referred, in 1 Tim. 4:7, "**you must constantly refuse and avoid** (excuse yourself from) **profane and old-womanish myths**"? Or to, in Tit. 1:14, "**holding to** (having [a propensity] toward; heeding and clinging in the direction toward) **Jewish myths**"? Especially in our day, these admonitions from Paul should be heeded. Strange cosmologies, often taken from Gnostic texts, are currently found in fringe groups of Christianity. Obscure statements from Genesis and enigmatic meanings of certain Hebrew words have spawned a new esoteric mysticism of dualism, and once again we have what Paul spoke of in 2 Tim. 4:3f,
> "**For you see, there will be an appointed season** (a situation; a fitting period of time) **when they will not continue holding up to themselves** (or: sustaining; holding themselves up by and in; or: putting up with; tolerating) **instruction that is being continuously healthy and sound, but rather, they, habitually having their ear gratified by rubbing, scratching or tickling will progressively pile and heap upon themselves teachers in line with and corresponding to**

their own rushing emotions, and then, on the one hand, they will proceed to twist the ear (or: the hearing) **and turn away from the Truth and reality.**"

The word for **employment of drugs** (sorcery; enchantments) is found together with the accusations of **the prostitutions of Jezebel**, in 2 Ki. 9:22 (LXX – there designated as 4 Reigns/Kingdoms), the latter being a symbolic reference to the idolatry (Baal worship) which she introduced into Israel. *Cf* 2:20, above. Isa. 57:3-7 ties sorcery with prostitution:

> "But as for you, come closer, you sons of a sorceress, you offspring of an adulterer and a harlot…. On a high and lofty hill you have set your couch; there, too, you have gone up to perform sacrifices" (Tanakh).

24. **And within her was** (or: is) **found blood of prophets and of set-apart folks – even of all those having been slaughtered upon the Land** (or: earth).

Cf Mat. 23:34-38; Lu. 13:33-34; and here is Acts 7:51-53, where Stephen recounts it to the Jewish leaders:

> 51. "**'Stiff-necked** (= Obstinate and proud) **men' and 'people uncircumcised in hearts and ears!'** [Ex. 32:9; Lev. 26:41]
> **You yourselves are ever repeatedly falling in opposition against** (or: are always by habit resisting and clashing with) **the Set-apart Breath-effect** (or: the Holy Spirit; Sacred Attitude)! – **as your fathers** (or: ancestors), **so also you folks!**
> 52. "**Which one of the prophets** (those who had light ahead of time and spoke before the people) **did your fathers** [D* reads: those men] **not persecute and pursue? And they killed off those predicting concerning** (or: bringing down the announcement in advance about) **the coming of the Just One** (the Fair, Equitable, Right One that is in rightwised relationships that accord with the Way pointed out) – **of Whom you yourselves now became people who pre-commit and give in advance** (or: folks who **give-over** before, in front or **in preference**; or: ones who **abandoned** in time of need; people who [were] pre-paid), **even murderers:**
> 53. "**the very ones who received and took in hand the Law – [leading] into [situations] thoroughly arranged and fully set in order by [His] agents and messengers – and yet you people did not observe it, maintain it, keep it or guard it!**"

In this verse, as well as seeing this picture as representing Jerusalem, let us also recall the history of "the organized church." What occurred before occurred again, and again, and again. And if it was not a physical killing, it was character assassination, being called heretics, or "injurious rumors" (blasphemies), which practices characterize the organized system, or the self-appointed defenders of "orthodoxy," etc.

As we think about the "then-present" Jerusalem, recall Paul's words in Gal. 4:22-31. In vs. 25 he says that "**Hagar stands for Mt. Sinai in Arabia, and she corresponds to the present Jerusalem, for she and her children are slaves.**" In vs. 24 he had said "**These two women stand for two covenants.**" The in vs. 30 he says, "But what does scripture say? '**Drive out the slave-girl and her son, for the slave-girl's son will not be allowed to share the inheritance with the free woman's son.**'" (Barclay translation).

So as "Hagar represents the covenant which had its beginning on Mt. Sinai, and which bears children destined for slavery" (vs. 24, Barclay), and this corresponds to the pre-AD 70 Jerusalem, we can see that not only was Jerusalem destroyed in AD 70, but also so was the covenant that had its beginning on Mt. Sinai. God was here casting out the slave-girl and her seed (the legalism derived from the Law). But as we consider the end of Jerusalem, the "type," and the apostate church-system, the "anti-type," let us remember the words of Jesus in Matt. 21:31b,

> "**I am now saying and laying it out for you that the tax** (or: tribute; toll) **collectors** (or: tax farmers; businessmen who bought the contract to collect taxes for the government) **and the prostitutes are constantly preceding you men into God's reign** (or: the kingdom of God; the sovereign activity of God)!"

He was speaking then of literal prostitutes, and to literal chief priests and elders of literal Judea. Let us heed His warning to them, lest we become proud of our enlightenment and supposed position (Rom. 11:21). As we consider the anti-type in our day, let us realize that those who have played the spiritual prostitute may also come to Him. As we see that Babylon (Jerusalem) was burned in fire, let us remember that "EVERYONE will be salted with fire" (Mark. 9: 49), and the context of this statement was "the Gehenna of fire" of vs. 43-48. Gehenna was the city dump just outside Jerusalem. What Jesus was speaking of here in Mark 9 actually happened to Jerusalem, as prophesied by the Agent to John here in the Unveiling, as well as recorded in the history written by Josephus. But note that "everyone" will be salted with fire – or "baptized" in fire, as John the baptizer put it (Lu. 3:16b).

Chapter 19

1. **After these things I heard – as it were a great voice of a large crowd – folks in the atmosphere** (or: heaven; sky) **repeatedly saying,**
> "**Hallelujah** (Praise Yahweh)**!: the Deliverance** (Salvation; Rescue; Healing) **and the Glory and the Power** (or: Ability) **of, from and which is our God!**

The opening phrase, "**After these things**," points back to chapter 18: the proclamation of Babylon being cast down. 19:1-6 are really a continuation of the previous chapter, giving praise to God for what was just described in 18:2-24, and providing a segue to the announcement of the marriage of the little Lamb and His Wife, vs. 7, her clothing, vs. 8, and the call to the marriage supper, vs. 9, followed by the King of kings, Lord of lords, on the white horse, and those with Him. All of this is cause for **praise to Yahweh**! He is the cause for what was just described, and for what is to follow. It is all a part of His plan of the ages.

This section begins with praise from **a large crowd** (the cloud of witnesses – cf Heb. 12:1) – praise to **God Who IS** our Salvation and **Deliverance**; **Yahweh** is also our **glory** as well as our **power** and ability. There is no verb following the exclamation "**Praise Yahweh**!" so I used the colon to join the following phrases to this exclamation, indicating them as being descriptive of Yahweh, our God. It recalls Ex. 15:2 and Ps. 118:14, "Yahweh is my strength and might; He has become my deliverance (salvation)," and Ps. 62:2, "Truly He is my Rock and Salvation." This **great voice in the atmosphere** was also heard in 11:15, above.

The word commonly translated "**Hallelujah**" is not a translation, but a transliteration of the Greek: *allēlouia*. I kept the common rendering because of tradition, but the literal meaning is, "**Praise Yahweh**." This same Greek word is used, in the LXX, in Ps. 104:1; 105:1; 106:1; 110:1; 111:1; 112:1; 113:1; 114:1; 115:1; 116:1; 117:1; 118:1; 134:1; 135:1; 145:1; 146:1; 147:1; 148:1; 149:1; 150:1. This word is used four times in 19:1-6, here in the Unveiling. So this should give us an idea of Who is being referred to as God, in the Unveiling. The name "Yahshua" (one Hebrew spelling of the Greek, "Jesus") means Yah (short for Yahweh) is Salvation, or, the Savior, etc. With all this in mind, I rendered the genitive/ablative form *tou theou* (**God**) as "**of, from**," ending with an appositional rendering, "**which is our God**." The **Deliverance** is God's deliverance; it comes from God; and most astoundingly, it IS in fact God. When God acts, the very action IS God. Our very Salvation IS God Himself entering into history, into our situations, and into

US! Remember, God IS Spirit (Breath-effect). When we received the effect of His Breath, in Gen. 2:7, He Himself entered into humanity. The **great voice** of the **large crowd** is in this one short imperative, or exclamation, followed by the statement, proclaiming both the plan of the ages and the Good News that came in Jesus Christ. The man Adam is "**the image and glory of God**" (1 Cor. 11:7).

The message from this **large crowd** may be an allusion to 1 Chron. 29:10-11 where king David is recorded as having pronounced a blessing (spoke words of goodness) concerning Yahweh, in the presence of the called-out community (*ekklēsia*):
> "Blessed (Spoken well of; An Idea of Goodness, Ease and Well-being; A laid-out message of blessing) are You, O LORD (= Yahweh) God of Israel, our Father, from the age unto the Age. In and by You, O Lord, [is] the greatness and the power and the boasting and the victory and the strength! Because You continue with dominion as Master of all things and all people within the atmosphere (heaven) and upon the Land (or: earth)..." (LXX, JM)

2. **"Because His judgings** (decisions and administrations of justice; judicial processes; separations and evaluations according to the Way pointed out) **[are] true ones and fair** (equitable; just; rightwised) **ones, in that** (for) **He judged** (or: judges) **the Great Prostitute – anyone who was spoiling** (ruining; corrupting) **the Land** (or: earth) **within** (in union with) **her prostitution** (or: fornication; = idolatry) **– and He restored a rightwised situation of equity in fairness for** (or: avenges; vindicates; executes the right for) **the blood of His slaves from out of her hand."**

Observe that the praise is because of **His judgings** of the Prostitute, the once-faithful City – which included "anyone" who was habitually spoiling and ruining the Land (a figure of His people) with her idolatry and pagan influences. The spoiling of the land by prostitution with the gods of the nations via their religions was a continual problem with Israel of old. These decisions and administrations of justice **"restored a rightwised situation of equity in fairness for** (or: avenges; vindicates; executes the right for) **the blood of His slaves from out of her hand**." His processes of judging bring restoration of what is right and "in accord with the Way pointed out" – and this Way is Christ. And when the results His judgings – these decisions (note the plural) – come, the people of the domination systems learn what is right (Isa. 26:9). Furthermore, recall that,
> "The judgments of Jehovah are true, they have been righteous – together. They are more desirable than gold, yes, than much fine gold; and sweeter than honey, even liquid honey of the comb. Also – Thy servant is warned by them, 'In keeping them is great reward.'" (Ps. 19:9-11; Young) *Cf* Ps. 119:137.

Deut. 32:43 gave a forecast of this action by God:
> "Continue well-minded (mentally at ease with a healthy attitude; thoughtfully considerate for good), O heavens, together, and in association, with Him, and let all messengers (agents, folks with the message) of, and from, God do obeisance to Him, and in Him! Continue well-minded (mentally at ease with a healthy attitude; thoughtfully considerate for good), O nations, along with His people, and let all sons of God internally strengthen themselves in Him! Because He will progressively decide concerning, and have right done for (habitually conduct legal proceedings on the behalf of), the blood of His sons. Then He will proceed to render what is right from the way pointed out, and will progressively recompense corresponding justice to (or: award back what is right, in the proper place and situation, from among) the folks that are adversarial or alienated (hostile, feuding; acting with disfavor) and will also continue making corresponding recompense to and among the folks with ill-will (people who love less, esteem less, detest or hate [others]). And then the LORD [= Yahweh] will progressively purge and cleanse the Land of, and which is, His people" (LXX, JM).

In regard to this call to praise, Chilton (ibid p 469) observes that Jerusalem's passing is not to be mourned: "God's will is to be performed on earth as it is performed in heaven."

This pronouncement with a view to the judging of **the Great Prostitute** is expanded by a dependent clause that opens with the relative pronoun, "**anyone who**." This could also be understood as, "whatever," showing that the judging applied not just to Jerusalem, but also to **anyone**, or, whatever, **was spoiling, ruining or corrupting the Land**; "the Land" being a figure of "the people" of Judea, Palestine or the Empire. In this letter, it would certainly include the *Diaspora*, the Jews dispersed into other countries that followed the lead of the Jerusalem leadership in persecuting and killing **His slaves**. The effects of His decision on Jerusalem affected Jews everywhere, and likewise the ones that they had been persecuting. We find a criticism of Israel in Isa. 59:14 that had applied in her history, and in human dealings throughout human history:

> "So [right] judgment is turned away backward, and justice is standing far off; for truth stumbles in the square, and [what is] correct cannot enter" (CVOT).

Also, there is Amos 5:7, "You…turn justice to wormwood, and hurl righteousness to the ground" (Tanakh). *Cf* Isa. 10:1-4, where in vs. 3 we read, "And what will you folks do in the Day of visitation, and in the desolation…?" Jer. 7:7 explains how it will be if they execute justice without oppression, and do not follow other gods (vss. 5-6): "Then I will cause you to dwell in this place, in the Land that I gave to your fathers…" *Cf* Ezk. 22:6, 7; Zech. 7:8-13; Ps. 82. For the same reasons given in these OT references, Jerusalem was destroyed in AD 70. In Lu. 18:2-5, Jesus tells a story of a woman who is persistent in seeking justice from a judge who did not fear God nor respect people, yet being wearied of her troubling him, he finally gave the woman justice. This is put in a "how much more" comparison with God, in vs. 7, using rhetorical questions:

> "**Now [think about it]! Would** (or: Should) **not God by all means make the situation right** (or: do that which will bring the fairness, equity and justice) **for His picked out and chosen people – those constantly crying, or calling, out to Him day and night? And thus, does He continue pushing anger far away and is He repeatedly long before rushing with passion upon them?**"

The last clause of vs. 2 has traditionally been understood by rendering the verb as "avenges" or "vindicates" with the main nuance being punitive judgment. But such a view is normally seen as a simple "getting even" with her for what she had done, without considering the positive aspect, also inherent in the verb, "**restored a rightwised situation of equity in fairness for**," or "executes the right for," which are within its semantic range. These latter renderings express the nuance of purpose: restoration and a return to equity, the absence of this latter state being that of which the prophets had historically accused Israel. There was more to the fulfillment of Mat. 24 and Lu 21 than just the tearing down of the temple and the destruction of Jerusalem. The new age, with its new arrangement, brought the fairness and equity that is inherent in God's reign, or kingdom. This reign/kingdom does not have an Israelite on the throne, but God Himself, in Christ and within His body. This is an allusion to the time of God being Israel's King, prior to Israel becoming a kingdom, beginning with Saul. This is the only way to have **rightwised situations of equity in fairness**. Human kingdoms are always void of this, as the story of Israel and the history of the beastly kingdoms which surrounded her amply display.

We should also observe that the AD 70 judgment of Jerusalem was characteristic of, and the last in the line of, Israel's judgments (which was normally carried out by dominating kingdoms or empires from among the nations), ushering in the end of the Mosaic age. It was an act that arose from the Jewish leadership breaking the Law (e.g., shedding **the blood of His slaves**, the prophets of the past, and the sent-forth folks of the 1st century), thus terminating that covenant, as described in Deut. 28. But **the**

blood of His slaves was a part of His blood (for they were His body and were to drink the cup that He drank – Mat. 20:23; Mk. 10:39), and as Paul said in Col. 1:24,
> "**I am at this moment continuing to rejoice within the effects of experiences and the results of my sufferings over your [situation] and on your behalf, and I am progressively filling back up in turn – so as in [His] stead to replace, supply and balance out, within my flesh** (or: = with the means of my natural situation) **– the deficiencies** (or: results from what is lacking; effects from need) **with regard to the pressures** (or: from the squeezings, tribulations and tight spots) **that pertain to the Anointed One** (or: that belong to and affect Christ; or: from the [Messiah]) **over [the situation of] His body, which is the called-out, covenant community** (which exists being the summoned-forth congregation – the ecclesia)."

Like His, their blood was not shed in vain. Ps. 116:15 declares,
> "Precious, valuable and honored – in the sight and presence of [the] LORD (= Yahweh) – [is] the death of His devout and loyally benign folks" (LXX, JM).

This pronouncement against the Great Prostitute may be an allusion to Jezebel in 1 Ki. 16:29-34; 18:4, 13; 21:1-16, ending with 2 Ki. 9:7 where Elisha anointed Jehu to be king of Israel, and told him,
> "Thus speaks Yahweh, God of Israel.... You will strike down the House of Ahab, your master; thus will I avenge the blood of My servants the prophets and the blood of all the servants of Yahweh at the hand of Jezebel."

3. **Then a second time they have said, "Praise Yahweh** (Hallelujah)**!"**

Chilton (ibid p 469) quotes E.W. Hengstenberg in regard to this Hebrew phrase, "Hallelujah," that was transliterated into Greek:
> "[The] preservation of the Hebrew word, as in the case also of *Amen* and *Hosanna*, serves like a visible finger-post to mark the internal connection between the church of the NT and that of the Old" (*The Revelation of St. John*, vol. 2, Mack Pub. Co., p 238).

And so the smoke from her goes on rising up on into (or: progressively ascends into the midst of) **the ages of the ages** (or: crowning time-periods of the ages; indefinite eras which comprise the ages).

The narrative of this verse shows that although her judgment came in one hour (18:10, above), the burning continued **on into the ages** (it is the burning that causes the smoke, this latter being a result and an indicator of the process going on). This brings a second witness of praise to Yahweh. For 1st century folks, they saw the end of Jerusalem, and thus the end of the old covenant and system of worship as the slave-girl (Gal. 4) was cast out. But the burning and evidence of this end continues on into the next ages, a witness that it is no longer an outward religion, but rather a relationship with God "in spirit and truth/reality" (Jn. 4:23, 24). This picture is an allusion to Isa. 34:8-10:
> "You see, [it is] a day of [the] Lord's (= Yahweh's) deciding and judging, and a year of recompense from (or: pertaining to) Zion's judging. And so her valleys (or: ravines) shall be turned into pitch, and her Land into sulphur (Greek *theion* – deity; the divine nature) and her Land (territory; region; soil) shall be as pitch continuously being burned, night and day [compare this figure to the lake of Fire, here in the Unveiling]. And it shall not be quenched, on into the midst of the Age-time (or: for a lifetime; unto THE time-period), and her smoke will go up, above: it shall be made progressively desolate on into the midst of her generations" (LXX, JM; brackets added).

The "sulphur" is a figure for divine activity upon the people, purifying them. In the natural, sulphur fights disease and is a purgative. This burning is a part of the answer to Jesus' prayer on the cross,
> "**O Father, let it flow away in them** (or: send it away for them; forgive them), **for they have not seen, so they do not know or perceive, what they are now doing**" (Lu. 23:34).

With God's forgiveness comes the flowing away from us of the results from our mistakes and sins. He sends away our guilt and shame, and the Fire of His presence purifies us. Note the reference to "her generations" in Isa. 34:10, above. God's judgments do not bring an end to people, but to situations and conditions OF people.

The "crowning time-periods" may relate what Paul referred to as, "**the continuously oncoming ages** (the indefinite time periods continually and progressively coming upon and overtaking [us])," in Eph. 2:7, that continue moving to the goal of God's plan of the ages (Eph. 3:11). Rendering the last phrase, "indefinite eras which comprise the ages," offers us another literal understanding of the Greek phrase. The term "**age**" means an indefinite period of time. It originally referred to a person's lifetime.

Mal. 4 predicted "the coming Day [that would be] consuming like a stove... which shall not leave to them root or bough. Yet [the] Sun of righteousness will radiate... [with] healing in Its wings.... And he will restore the heart of the fathers to the sons and the heart of the sons to their fathers..." (vss. 1-2, 5). Judgment? Yes. Blessing? Yes!

4. **Then the twenty-four elders** (old people) **and the four living ones fall** (or: fell) **down and worship** (or: did obeisance, kissing toward) **the God continuously sitting upon the throne, repeatedly saying,**
   "Amen (Make it so; So be it). **Praise Yahweh** (Hallelujah)!"

Verses 4-5 show us that we are still in the setting of chapter 4, above, in the presence of God's throne, and the message (**Voice**) **from the throne** (vs. 5, below) continues to be that we should be **habitually praising God**. Note that it is **the God** who is **continually sitting upon the throne**, and this God was revealed to be the slain little Lamb, in 5:6, above.

The 24 **elders** have frequent parts in this cosmic drama: cf 4:4, 10; 5:5-8, 11, 14; 7:11-13; 11:16-18; 14:3, above. This is their last appearance on stage. This scene/figure reveals that those who live their lives in the atmosphere of the little Lamb, the God that is ruling from His throne within His Temple (that being both the universe of creation, and the called-out community/individual, which is His body) affirm (say **Amen** to) God's will in His dealings with humanity, and give Him praise for enacting His will. The **four living ones** may be a figure of the spiritual aspect of the totality of creation, or God's kingdom (the number 4, significant of the 4 directions, or "everywhere") and each of the 4 faces (expressions, presence and identity) may signify a) humanity, along with b) the spirits or realms of heaven/sky (eagle: realm of spirit), and c) sacrifice, burden-bearing and food production (calf: realm of the incarnated service), along with d) government/society (lion: realm of public service, defense and leadership); cf 4:7, above. All of these are subservient (**do obeisance**) to the Lordship of Christ, even though humans are called to reign with Him over "the fowl of the air and over every living thing that moves upon the ground" (Gen. 1:28). And so, the message to, and from, all creation is, "**Praise Yahweh!**" (Ps. 150:6).

The proclamation from these elders and living ones is considered an allusion to Ps. 106:48,
   "Blessed be Yahweh, God of Israel, from one age even unto another (or: from the eon, and until the Eon). And then all the people will say, 'Amen! [LXX reads: Let it come to be! Let it come to be!] Praise Yah!'" (Rotherham; additions mine; cf the context of vss. 42-48 of this psalm).

5. **And a Voice from out of the throne came forth, saying,**
   "Habitually praise our God, all His slaves – even the people continually fearing, revering and respecting Him – the small ones and the great ones."

This **Voice** comes from Christ (figured by **the throne**, for it is the little Lamb that is within the midst of the throne, 5:6a, above; *cf* 3:21, above). We heard this same **Voice** in 16:17, above, when He said, "**It has come to be!**" Here, Christ is again pointing us to God, the Father, as He did in Jn. 20:17, "**I am progressively stepping back up again** (or: now ascending) **toward My Father – even the Father of you folks – and My God: even [the] God of you people!**" This incident may be an apocalyptic way of fulfilling that to which Paul referred in 1 Cor. 15:28,

> "**Now whenever the whole** (or: all things) **may be completely supportively-aligned in Him** (or: subjected/appended to Him; subordinately sheltered and arranged for Him), **then the Son Himself will also continue being supportively aligned to, fully subjoined for and humbly attached under as an arranged shelter in, the One subjecting, appending and sheltering the whole in Him** (or: attaching all things to Him), **to the end that God can be all things within the midst of and in union with all humanity** (or: may be everything in all things; or: should exist being All in all; or: would exist being everything, within the midst of everyone)."

Here, with reference to those "**fearing Him – the small ones and the great ones**," Vincent refers us to Ps. 115:13, "He will bless those who fear Yahweh, the small and the great alike;" and then in reference to, "**Habitually praise our God...**" he point us to Ps. 134:1, "Lo! Bless Yahweh, all you servants of Yahweh..." (Rotherham) *Cf* Ps. 22:23. The idea of habitual praise of God is because of what He has done, and what He habitually does, and what He will continue doing. A similar construction to the imperative of the 1st clause, here, is found in 2 Chron. 20:19, in the LXX:

> "Then the Levites from among the sons of Caath, and from among the sons of Core, stood up to continue praising [the] Lord (= Yahweh) God of Israel, in a great (loud) voice, unto [the] height" (JM). *Cf* 1 Chron. 16:36b.

The compound phrase, "**the small ones and the great ones**," is rhetoric for the totality of society – every social and economic strata is included. Here, Chilton (ibid p 472) sees Him as calling out to His brothers (Rom. 8:28; Heb. 2:11-12) in this admonition.

6. **Next I heard as a voice of a large crowd, and as a sound of many waters, even as a sound of strong thunders saying,**
    "**Praise Yahweh** (Hallelujah)! **Because the Lord** [= Yahweh] **our God, the Almighty, reigns!**
7.   **We should** (or: may) **continually rejoice** (be glad; be full of joy), **and we should continually celebrate** (exult), **and we should** [other MSS: we will continue to] **give the glory to Him, because the wedding** (marriage festival) **of the little Lamb came** (arrived and happened; or: comes) **and His Wife made** (or: makes) **herself ready** (prepares herself).**"**

Take note that the **large crowd** has "**a voice**" – one voice: His Voice, as it is described in Dan. 10:6b, "like the sound of a multitude." The sound of the wings of the living ones in Ezk. 1:24 was, "like the sound of many (or: mighty) waters, like the voice of Shaddai (the Breasted One; traditionally, and LXX: the Almighty; CVOT: Him Who Suffices), a tumult like the din of an army camp" [*Cf* Ezk. 43:2]. The first clause of the proclamation (vs. 6) echoes both Ps. 93:1 and 99:1, "Yahweh reigns!" We saw this described in 11:14-15, above. The verb "**reigns**" is in the aorist tense, rendered here as a simple fact (as does the CLNT). Beale (ibid p 931) suggests rendering it as an ingressive aorist, "has begun to reign," citing 11:15, 17, above, but this seems unnecessary and out of sync with OT witnesses.

Verses 6-7 has the "cloud of **witnesses**" (Heb. 12:1, and then in vs. 22-24, "the heavenly Jerusalem" which is "an assembly of an entire people, a called-out of first-born folks... and, Jesus...;" also note that their voice is the same as the Son of man, in 1:15, above) again giving praise, and now we learn that it is because **God reigns** (functions as King), and **the wedding of the little Lamb came**, and **His Wife** has

made herself ready. So we see the demise of Yahweh's wife, Jerusalem of the old covenant, and now the presentation of the **Wife** of the **little Lamb** – His called-out community, which he called out of the religions of the world. We will see this bride in 21:2 & 10, below, figured as the "new" Jerusalem (called "**the Jerusalem which is above**" by Paul in Gal. 4:26), as she now descends out of the atmosphere (the place of her encounter with the Lord, 1 Thes. 4:16-17), which, I suggest, was the time and place of the marriage. The descent of Christ in 18:1, above, focused on the judgment of the old; the descent of His Wife focuses on blessings for the earth, as God/the Lamb brings in the new order, the new age, as we see in 21:5,

> "**And then the One** (or: He [who is]) **continuously sitting upon the throne said,**
> '**Consider this! I am presently making all things new** (or: habitually creating everything [to be] new and fresh; progressively forming [the] whole anew; or, reading *panta* as masculine: I am periodically making **all humanity** new, and progressively, one after another, producing and creating **every person** anew, while constantly constructing all people fresh and new, i.e., continuously renewing **everyone**)!'" [Isa. 43:19; 65:17-26; 2 Cor. 5:17]

Now we also see the reason for the celebration: the marriage festival. In Isa. 54:1-8 it says, "Begin singing, you barren and childless.... 'For your Maker is your husband.... the LORD (=Yahweh) calls for you – and as new wedded wives who displease,' says your God – 'for a moment sent off, but called back with great pity. In quick anger My face I had hid for a moment, but now with a lasting affection I cherish,' says the LORD, your defender." (Fenton) This gives us a reference point for the figure of God's people being His Wife, and in relation to Him as in a marriage.

Ezk. 16:7 -14 gives another picture, "... I am spreading My hem over you and am covering your nakedness. And I am swearing to you and entering into a covenant with you [= marriage]... and you are becoming mine. Then I am washing you with water.... rubbing you with oil. I am clothing you..." (brackets added). Then Hos. 2:19-20 tell us, "And I have betrothed you to Me to the Age.... and you have known Jehovah" (Young). So here in chapter 19, we see that the marriage metaphor was one that was a familiar one to Israel. Paul takes it up, applying it to the called-out communities, in Eph. 5:23-33,

> "**because a husband exists being a head of** (or: is a source with reference to) **the wife as also** (or: even as) **the Christ [is] Head** (or: Source) **of the called-out community**..."

Marriage symbolism is often seen in the gospels. There is the **marriage feast** in Matt. 22:2-13 with the subject of **wedding apparel**, in vss. 10-11. Mark 2:19 speaks of the "**sons of the wedding hall**" and the **bridegroom**, and then John 3:29 remarks about the "**friend of the bridegroom**." Paul picks up the same metaphor in 2 Cor. 11:2, speaking of his having already "**joined**" that called-out community "**in marriage to one husband, to make a pure virgin to stand alongside in the Christ**." He uses this figure to describe the relationship between Israel and the Law in Rom. 7, noting that when the Husband dies, "she has been RELEASED... **from the Husband's Law**" (vs. 2). The husband-wife symbolism began with Adam and Eve, and continues throughout the entire Bible. God is portrayed to us as Family, and the central theme is union. We saw this same Wife in 12:1, above, who was adorned with the heavenly wreath and was pregnant with God's corporate Son. That was a picture of the results of the consummation of the marriage: she became "**the mother of us all**" (Gal. 4:26). So this scene in chapter 19 is a flashback. We saw the called-out folks impregnated in Acts 2:2, where the wind of God's Spirit filled His new house (His new Temple), His new Adam (Gen. 2:7).

In regard to Jerusalem of old, recall God's words to her in Jer. 3:14-15,

"Return, you apostate sons, urges Yahweh, for I am become your Husband... and I will give you shepherds according to Mine own heart, who will feed you with knowledge and discretion" (Rotherham).

Another promise to her is in Isa. 62:4-5,
"No more shall men call you Forsaken, no more shall your land be called Desolate.... for the LORD delights in you and to Him your Land is wedded ... and your God shall rejoice over you as a bridegroom rejoices over the bride" (NEB). *Cf* Hos. 2:16-20.

So here, we have a new bride (wife) and a new covenant (arrangement), in a new creation where everything, and everyone, is being made new (21:5, below). And Yahweh, through the death and resurrection of Jesus the Messiah, has – together with us – been transformed into being a symbolic little Lamb surrounded by 144,000 sheep to whom He is now joined in union. "The union of one believer with Christ is a representative of all such unions of all time" (Terry, ibid p 441). The last clause, "**His Wife made** (or: makes) **herself ready** (prepares herself)," looks forward to the next verse where ""**it was given** (note the 'divine passive') **to her that she may clothe herself**." The preparation spoken of here is an allusion to 7:13-15, above:

"**These – the ones having been clothed** [note the divine passive] **with the bright, white robes** (or: uniforms; equipment).... **These**... **washed their robes** (uniforms; equipment) **and made them bright and white within the little Lamb's blood**."

This, in turn takes us back to 1 Jn. 1:7b,
"**the blood of, from, and which is Jesus, His Son, keeps continually and repeatedly cleansing us** (or: is progressively rendering us pure) **from every sin** (or: from all error, failure, deviation, mistake, and from every shot that is off target [when it occurs])."

Paul expressed this as being God's work or action upon us:
"**for you see, God is the One habitually operating with inward activity, repeatedly working within, constantly causing function and progressively producing effects within, among and in union with you folks – both the [condition] to be habitually willing** (intending; purposing; resolving) **and the [situation] to be continuously effecting the action, repeatedly operating to cause function and habitually setting at work so as to produce – for the sake of and over the pleasing good form and the thinking of goodness in delightful imagination**" (Phil. 2:13).

Compare Paul's admonition to Christ's wife in Eph. 6:11-18 with what is written of Yahweh, in Isa. 59:17,
"So He shall proceed putting on eschatological deliverance into the Way pointed out, with justice, fairness and equality as body-armor (like a coat of mail), and the helmet of salvation (rescue into wholeness) on His head; then He shall proceed putting on garments of a maintaining or of a defending from the position of what is right, as clothing, and shall continue wrapping Himself in zeal as in a robe" (conflation of LXX, CVOT and Tanakh, JM)

8. **Then it was** (or: is) **granted** (or: given) **to her to the end that she may clothe herself with bright and clean fine cotton** (or: she may cast bright, pure, fine linen around her) **– for the fine cotton** (or: linen) **represents the effects of right relationship and equity in the life of the Way pointed out**
(or: the results of being rightwised; the actualizations of justice; consequences of justice rendered from being turned in the right direction; the effects of having been eschatologically delivered and placed in the Path pointed out; or: the just acts or awards) **of the set-apart folks** (pertaining to, and on behalf of, the saints; from the sacred people; belonging to, and characterizing, the holy ones).

The background of this picture is found in Ezk. 16:8-13, which we noted above. It was a symbolic story of Yahweh marrying Israel. Along with the other descriptions of her "clothing" being decorated and her being given ornaments, note vs. 10 where she was clothed "with badgers' skin." Both KJV and Young give this rendering, which to us might not seem complimentary, but it is the same word that was used in Ex. 26:14 and 36:19 describing the material used for making the covering of the Tabernacle. In Nu. 4:4-6, the covering of badgers' skins were used to cover the veil and the ark of the testimony, when the camp of Israel moved forward. This symbolic association of Israel with the Tabernacle should not be missed.

This verse gives the picture of how she makes herself ready (vs. 7 above): it is by **clothing herself** with Christ (Rom. 13:14), her righteousness (1 Cor. 1:30) – figured by the **bright and clean fine cotton** (or: pure fine linen). This symbol answers to being clothed in a white garment, and is associated with the overcomer in 3:5, above. This picture, in vss. 7-9, is what Paul was speaking of in 2 Cor. 11:2,
> "**for I continue with hot zeal** (eager vehement passion) **concerning you in** (or: with; by) **God's fervent zeal** (an eager vehement passion which is God), **because I myself joined you folks in marriage to one husband, to make a pure virgin** (= unmarried girl) **to stand alongside in the Christ**."

You see, our being **joined to the Lord** (1 Cor. 6:17) is being **married** to Him, being "**one spirit**." This is in direct contrast to having been joined to the Harlot (the old Jerusalem of chapter 18, figuring the old covenant religion that had become distorted and polluted – filled with dead people's bones, Matt. 23:27) and thus having become "**one flesh**" with her (1 Cor. 6:16). The judgment of Harlot Jerusalem was seen in Paul's metaphor of the olive tree in Rom. 11:17 (unbelieving branches being broken out). The wild branches being grafted in are an echo of Zech. 2:10-11, where it says "And MANY NATIONS shall be JOINED to the Lord in THAT DAY, and shall be My people..."

An allusion to Isa. 61:10 can be seen here:
> "I will greatly rejoice in Yahweh; My soul shall exult in My God; for He clothes Me with garments of salvation; with (or: in) a robe of righteousness He wraps Me, as a bridegroom adorns himself with priestly beauty (or: a turban; a chaplet), and like a bride bedecks herself with her jewels and finery" (Rotherham, CVOT, Tanakh).

For the word "righteousness," the LXX uses *dikaiosunē* (eschatological deliverance… justice, etc., as in Isa. 59:17, quoted above)

Recall the attire, in 15:6 above, of the seven agents who come from the Temple (i.e., this symbol means that they are a part of, or represent, the Temple): "**clothed with bright, clean** (unsoiled, pure) **linen**." In the various visions, we suggest that the metaphors for "agents," "temple" and "city" are all involved with or represent the same existential entities: the called-out, covenant communities. Like Paul's metaphors concerning the husband and wife, in Eph. 5, here in John's visions it is about Christ and the called-out. Note in vs. 14, below, "**the armies in the atmosphere** (or: heaven) **– ones having been clothed with** (invested with; entered within) **clean** (or: pure) **bright, white fine cotton**." Cf 3:4, 5, 18, above, for association with the "overcomer; victor," and the called-out communities to which this Unveiling was sent. All of these examples are references to such as those to whom Paul advised in Rom. 13:12
> "**We should put, then, the acts of the Darkness** (works from the realm of the shadows; actions that belong to dimness and obscurity) **away from ourselves** (or: take off and put away the deeds pertaining to darkness; = ignorance; that which was before the light arrived), **and clothe ourselves with the instruments** (tools; weapons; implements; [some MSS: works; deeds]) **of Light** (or: The Light)."

And in Rom. 13:14, he put it this way:
> "**you folks must clothe yourselves with** (or: enter within and put on) **the Lord, Jesus Christ**."

Gal. 3:27 instructs us:
> "**as many of you folks as were immersed into Christ, at once clothed yourselves with Christ** (or: were plunged into so as to be enveloped by then saturated and permeated with Anointing – or, the Anointed One – instantly entered within and put on [the] Anointing)."

Let us now consider the explanation given for the significance of **fine cotton**: "**the fine cotton** (or: linen) **represents the effects of right relationship and equity in the life of the Way pointed out.**" I want to highlight the *–mata* ending of this plural noun that I have first rendered "**the effects of**..." This nuance is critical to our understanding of what is being said. Our clothing, our being prepared as Christ's Wife, are the **effects** of what Christ has done in us, and what we are in Him. The root idea of the noun *dikaiōmata*, which is a part of the *dikē* (way pointed out; justice; etc.) word family, has a broad application in the semantic range as seen in the words that compose this family. My first rendering, here, gives the core meaning, but translators have seen other meanings in the varying contexts where it has been used. Here are some of these on offer that seem to be possible fits to this context:

    a) the results of being rightwised (i.e., turned in the right direction – i.e., towards Christ)
    b) the actualizations of justice (God's bringing His justice into human history, righting the human situation)
    c) consequences of justice rendered from being turned in the right direction (the justice of God's right act of "righting" creation and humanity)
    d) the effects of having been eschatologically delivered and placed in the Path pointed out (i.e., what has happened from Christ rescuing us, giving us life, and placing us into His Way)
    e) the just acts or awards (i.e., the acts of the communities which are the result of being transformed by their being in Christ; or, the awards that are a harvest of abiding in the Vine – Jn. 15:1ff, etc.)

Some commentators see in this verse the human acts of vengeance or retribution, but these connotations seem out of place in a wedding dress. God has purified us, not punished us. We see a cognate of this word in the negative situations referenced in 18:5, above: "**her unjust effects** (injuries done; misdeeds; unjust acts; ill-gotten gains; things contrary to the way pointed out)." This contrast, in the life of the Prostitute, describes the fruits of Israel prior to the Christ Event, and His work of eschatologically rightwising people. The picture, in the previous chapter, of old Jerusalem being judged is the **effect** of her having been taken to the grave with Christ. The path into the Life of the Age of the Messiah is through death and resurrection. The "fine bright, pure, fine linen around her" is a figure of resurrection life. Christ is our righteousness (1 Cor. 1:30b), and we are transformed to become what He IS (2 Cor. 3:18). Paul also said in Rom. 5:17b,

> "**much more, rather, will the peoples** (= the masses of humanity) **– in continuously receiving and seizing upon** (taking in hand) **the surrounding superabundance** (encircling, extraordinary surplus and excess) **of the Grace and of, from and which is the gratuitous gift of the liberated Rightwisedness** (of the solidarity in fair and equitable treatment; from the placement in right [covenant]-relationship in the Way; of the justification and freedom from guilt while being turned in the right direction and made right) **– continue reigning** (or: ruling as kings) **within and in union with Life through the One, Jesus Christ.**"

Then in the next verse, he continued:

> "**through one just-effect and the result of one right act which set [all humanity] right and in accord with the Way pointed out** (through the result of one act of justice, equity and solidarity; through a single decree creating rightwised relationships; through one effect of rightwising which turns [people] in the right direction) **[it comes] into ALL MANKIND** (all humanity; all people; = the whole race) **[bringing them] into a setting right of Life and a liberating rightwising from Life [including them in covenant community]**" (vs. 18b).

We find this situation spoken of in Isa. 61:11b,

> "Thus will the LORD cause eschatological deliverance into the Way pointed out (justice, equity and rightwised relationships) and gladness (a leap for joy which results from rejoicing exultation)

to progressively rise up before (in the sight and presence of) the ethnic multitudes (the nations)" (LXX, JM).

This was the work of Christ that now adorns us.

The genitive phrase that ends this verse, and that modifies the noun that we just considered, presents us with some ambiguity that is worthy of our focus: **of the set-apart folks**. On offer are three additional renderings that all also fit the context, and perhaps amplify our perceptions of this verse:

> a) pertaining to, and on behalf of, the saints (this sees the action or rightwising and delivering as being done by Christ)
>
> b) from the sacred people (this would say that the fruit is being produced by the communities)
>
> c) belonging to, and characterizing, the holy ones (these express functions of the genitive of possession, and the descriptive genitive, describing the set-apart folks).

All of this lends insight to the importance of the "wedding garment" in Mat. 22:11-13.

9. **And then he is saying to me,**
> **"Write: 'Blessed** (Happy) **ones [are] the folks having been called** (the summoned ones; those being invited) **into the wedding supper** (meal) **of the little Lamb.'"**

He also is saying to me,
> **"These are the true Words of** (or: real thoughts and messages from) **God!"**

This tells us that we are blessed to be able to participate in this celebration, and thus in its reality, and then affirms the truth and reality of what has just been said. The term **"blessed folks"** is frequently used in the "sermon on the mount" in Matt. 5, and calls to mind "Blessed is the man.." in Ps. 1, repeating it in many other psalms. This phrase is used in the Unveiling in 1:3, 14:13; 16:15; 20:6; 22:7 & 14, as well as in this chapter. It is easy to see why Ray Prinzing titled his book on Revelation "... *A Positive Book.*"

In Matt. 22:2-14 we have the parable of the King's Son's wedding. Jesus spoke this as a warning to the Jewish leadership, pointing out that it was just those who were "invited" who were the ones who refused to attend, and who then, "**forcibly taking hold of his slaves, insolently violated their human rights and then killed [them]**." So "**the king inwardly swelled with fury and was made to teem with anger. And then, sending his soldiers** (troops), **he destroyed those murderers and set their city in flames**" (vs. 7). This is a clear reference to AD 70. In Matt. 8:12 Jesus says this in another way,

> "**Yet the 'sons of the kingdom** (or: reign; = those who were in line to inherit the kingdom; or: = those who were supposed to manifest its reign and dominion; [this is a reference to Israel])' **will be progressively thrown out into the external darkness** (external obscurity of the shadows). **There** [= outside the banqueting building] **it will continue be 'weeping and grinding of teeth'** (or: The crying and the gnashing of teeth will be in that [outdoor] place, or situation)."
> [note: grinding/gnashing of teeth = either regret, or anger]

No wonder those called to this wedding here in chapter 19 are termed "blessed and happy folks." Another parable portraying the Jewish leadership as missing out on the Messianic banquet is the parable of the wise and foolish virgins, in Mat. 25:1-12. They were all waiting for the Bridegroom [figure of the anticipated Messiah] to come. Their foolishness caused them to miss out on the kingdom activities (the Messianic banquet) that the Spirit was doing through Christ's followers, as we find recorded in the book of Acts. They were invited, as was all of Israel, but the lamp of the old covenant was going out (vs. 8) – there was no longer light in their lamps (or, figuratively, in the lampstand of their temple). Christ came as the Light that was shining in the darkness of the old covenant Israel. They did not receive His Light, and their lamps held the fading light of a previous day. This was a parable of missing out on what God was doing, while others had been included in His reign at that time. The same message is found in Lu. 14:15ff, where one of the Pharisees said to Jesus, "**Whoever will continue eating bread** (= a meal) **within God's reign** (kingdom; royal rule) **[will be] happy, blessed and fortunate**," and then Jesus presented them with the parable of the great supper, where those invited made excuses for not coming,

> "**So the owner** (lord; master) **said to the slave, 'At once go out into the roads and fenced areas** (or: hedgerows; boundary walls), **and at once compel** (force; oblige) **[them] to come in, so that my house may be filled to capacity!'** [comment: a figure of Gentile inclusion] **You see, I am now saying to you folks that not even one of the adult men of those having been invited will proceed in having a taste of My dinner**" (vss. 23-24). [cf Isa. 25:6-12 – messianic banquet]

That John was told to write this indicates that this was a message specifically to the seven communities in Asia Minor. The invitation for participation in the Messiah's presence was a "**witness to you people [concerning] these things [being imposed] upon the called-out communities**" (22:16, below). And notice that in 22:17, both the **Spirit** and the **Bride** present the invitation to everyone. They are "**continuously saying, 'Be repeatedly coming!'**" This banquet lasts for the Age of the Messiah.

Recall Paul's words in Rom. 8:30,

> "**Now [in fact, consider this]: those whom He at one point before-marked-out** (or: designates beforehand; [A reads: knew from prior intimate experience]), **these He also at once called** (or: calls; invited), **and whom He called** (or: calls; invites), **these He also in one stroke rightwised by an eschatological deliverance** (or: makes and sets right, frees from guilt and liberates from bondage, while making them fair and placing them in [covenant] relationships in the Way pointed out). **Now further, those whom He rightwised** (or: liberates and turns in the right direction; or: = included in covenant), **these He also instantly glorified**
> > (or: makes of reputation which calls forth praise; gives a splendid appearance; gives honorable thoughts and imaginations; clothes with splendor)."

The second statement, "**These are the true Words of** (or: real thoughts and messages from) **God**," is echoed in 21:5b, below: "**Write, because these words are dependable** (or: faithful; reliable) **ones and true ones** (ones full of faith and realities)." These affirmations of what is written in the Unveiling call the listener to an awareness of the seriousness and reality of what is being spoken and presented. They are a rhetorical device similar to how Jesus would say, "Amen, amen (or: Count on it; Truly). They affirm that what is being said is coming from God.

10. **And so I fell before his feet to worship him, and he is saying to me,**
    > "**See and perceive! No!** (= Don't do that!) **I am your fellow-slave and [am] from among your brothers** (or: = even belonging to [a group of] your fellow believers) **– the ones constantly holding** (having) **the witness of** (or: the testimony pertaining to, and the evidence about) **Jesus – Kiss face-to-face with** (or: do [your] obeisance to) **God! You see, the evidence of** (or: testimony pertaining to; witness about) **Jesus is the spirit of The Prophecy** (or: For the Breath-effect which is prophecy is the evidence for, and from, Jesus)."

John records his response to all that he has seen and heard, and his reaction to the agent calls to mind the scene of Peter, James and John on the mount of transfiguration, with Jesus. John is overwhelmed with all of this and returns to the practice of the old flesh covenant of worshiping by falling at a person's feet, and thinking that a person in the realm of spirit should be worshiped. But the messenger corrects him, explaining that "**I am your fellow-slave and [am] from among your brothers** (or: = even belonging to [a group of] your fellow believers) **– the ones constantly holding** (having) **the witness of** (or: the testimony pertaining to, and the evidence about) **Jesus**." Obeisance is only to be given to God, and Jesus explained that this is to be done in spirit and in truth – not in physical practice (John 4:21-24). We see a parallel incident in 22:8-9, below.

In Acts 9:12 we read, concerning Saul, "**within a vision** (the effect of something seen) **he saw an adult man named Ananias coming in and putting [his] hands upon him so that he can look up, and see again**." So it was not unusual for John to be seeing a man who was functioning as the Lord's agent in this vision, just as Ananias was seen by Saul. Then, in Acts 16:9, Luke informs us that,

> "**during one night, a vision** (or: sight; effect and result of something seen) **was seen by** (or: in) **Paul:** [D adds: as it were] **a certain Macedonian man was standing** [D adds: before him] **and calling him to his side for assistance, and repeatedly saying, 'After crossing over into Macedonia, run to us with aid, in response to our cry for help!'**" [note: this was a call to come to Europe]

We saw that "**the ones constantly holding** (having) **the witness of** (or: the testimony pertaining to, and the evidence about) **Jesus**" functioned as prophets, in chapter 11, above. In Heb. 1 we find,

> 7. **And then, on the one hand, to the agents** (messengers; folks with the message) **He is saying,**
>
> > "**He is the One making His agents** (messengers; folks with the message) **spirits** (or: Breath-effects), **and His public servants a flame of fire.**" [Ps. 104:4]
> > [comment: this is an example of Hebrew parallelism – the second line being a restatement of the first, but in a different figure; the figure is a reference both to the priests, as "public servants," and to the called-out community, figured as the lampstand in the Tabernacle in Rev. 1:20, and referencing Acts 2:3 – there being "tongues as if of fire" burning on the lamps in the one case, and upon the people in the second case; the agents speak a message of words that are "spirit," the effect of the Breath]

You will note that here I translated the definite article before the word prophecy, "**The Prophecy**." We suggest that the agent was referring to the entire Unveiling here, calling it "The Prophecy." The spirit of the entire prophecy is a witness of Jesus, or the testimony pertaining to Jesus – and His purpose of the ages. But there is another possible allusion in the agent referring to "The Prophecy." On the Day of Pentecost, Peter, in Acts 2:16ff, referenced Joel 2:28-32. There are also the prophecies of Ezk. 39:29 and Zech. 12:10 that can be applied to our present context. The "pouring out of His Spirit upon the house of Israel" was another way of speaking of the coming of the Age of the Messiah.

The parenthetical alternate rendering of the last clause gives the Greek a different rendering: "For the Breath-effect which is prophecy is the evidence for, and from, Jesus." This reading understands the definite article being used emphatically, so it is not translated into English. Note the last prepositional phrase that offers alternate functions of the genitive case: "for, and from, Jesus." This picture calls to mind what Jesus said about His Father being a second witness for Him, in Jn. 5:

> 36. "**Yet I, Myself, constantly hold** (or: am continuously having) **the Witness** (or: the evidence) **[that is] greater and more important than [that] from John** (or: the greater testimony compared to the one that John gives), **for the works** (or: actions; deeds) **which the Father has given in Me** (to Me; for Me; by Me) **– to the end that I may bring them to the goal** (finish, mature and perfect them to their destined purpose) **– the works themselves** (or: these same actions) **which I am continuously doing** (performing; producing) **continuously bear witness** (testify; make claim; give evidence) **about Me, that the Father has sent Me forth with a commission** (as a Representative).
> 37. "**Also, the One sending Me, that Father, has borne witness** (has testified) **about Me**...

11. **Then I saw the atmosphere** (or: sky; heaven), **having been opened – and consider! A bright, white horse. And the One continually sitting upon it being constantly called "Faithful** (Full of Faith; To Be Trusted; Trustworthy; Loyal) **and True** (or: Real)**," and He is continuously judging** (making decisions and evaluations) **and battling** (making war) **in eschatological deliverance** (within equitable dealings; in justice, fairness and righted relations which accord with the covenantal Way pointed out).

Wallace call this chapter "The Vision of Victory":
> "There is a striking analogy between these scenes of the church emerging in victory from the period of persecution... and the deliverance of Israel from Babylonian exile, described by Ezekiel in the closing section of his prophecy from the 36th to the 39th chapters. The nation of Israel was comforted, and their release was described in terms of a figurative resurrection; and the return to their homeland was pictured as a 'new heaven and a new earth' (Isa. 66:2). The closing chapters of Rev. from ch. 19 to 22 follow the course of Ezekiel's apocalypse of Israel returning from the 70 years of exile, but here the church was seen emerging from the period of persecution. The symbols are similar, and the parallel is evident" (ibid p 386).

In his blog, Brian Zahnd gives an excellent overview of this scene:
> "First we must remember that all of Revelation is communicated in theatrical symbol — *all of it!* Locusts that look like horses with human faces, women's hair, and lion's teeth.
> An army of two million soldiers riding lion-headed horses that breath fire and belch sulfur.
> A red dragon with seven heads in the heavens that sweeps away a third of the stars with its tail.
> A seven-headed beast from the sea with the body of a leopard, the feet of a bear, and the mouth of a lion.
> "An angel in the sky with a giant sickle who reaps all the grapes of the earth and puts them in a winepress that generates a river of blood for two hundred miles. These are all symbols! None of them are literal! Just as Jesus riding a flying white horse wearing a blood-drenched robe with a sword protruding from his mouth is a *symbol*. The question is, what is John communicating to us with his creative symbols?

> "To begin with, the rider on the white horse is called Faithful and True, and his name is The Word of God. John is not depicting a literal event in the future, but giving us a symbolic reality about the present — John is depicting the glorious triumph of the Word of God (Jesus Christ). The one called The Word of God is not riding the red horse of war, but the white horse of triumph. Jesus doesn't overcome evil by war, but by his word. This is how Jesus wages his righteous war. Jesus doesn't wage war like the murderous beast of Rome; Jesus wages war as the slaughtered Lamb of God" (brianzahnd.com, War of the Lamb, May 8, 2017).

The first thing that John saw, in this next vision, was **the atmosphere** (or: sky; heaven), **having been opened**. Jesus had this same experience:
> "**Now upon being immersed** (baptized), **Jesus immediately** (straightway) **stepped back up from the water – and now look and consider! – the heavens at once opened back up again!** [or, with other MSS: the atmospheres were opened up to Him!] **Then He saw God's Spirit** (Breath-effect) **– as if it were a dove steadily descending – progressively coming upon Him**" (Mat. 3:16). [*cf* Gen. 1:2]

We suggest that John was seeing a vision similar to what Jesus saw. It was the beginning of the new creation; the situation of the new arrangement; it was the entrance of God's kingdom coming on stage. We find here language similar to the opening clause in Ezk. 1:1b.

In 3 Macc. 2 we observe the same phrase describing the Rider, here, used by Simon the high priest in praying to Yahweh, the "King of heaven" (vs. 2), saying, "And You are surely **faithful and true** to your word" (vs. 11; *The OT Pseudepigrapha*, Vol. 2, ibid p 519, trans. by H. Anderson). *Cf* 21:5 and 22::6, below.

We saw this same "actor" on the stage in 6:2, above. This vision would seem to be either another version, or an expansion of the earlier snap shot: **the One** (Christ) on the **white horse**. We saw the white cotton/linen in vs. 8, above, and its association with 3:4-5, above, and we will see that those who "**continued following Him**" in vs. 14, below, are also on white horses and are "**clothed with** (invested with; entered within) **clean** (or: pure) **bright, white fine cotton**," as well. The idea of purity in these figures is readily apparent, but from vs. 8 we also see that by being clothed in white and mounted on white horses, this Rider and His armies represent:
    a) right relationship, equity and justice in the life of the Way pointed out
    b) rightwised covenant inclusion – that is their ultimate goal
    c) eschatological deliverance – that is what these armies bring, based on the blood of the Lamb
    d) from 3:4-5, above, we understand these folks to be overcomers
    e) our conclusion must be that they have a positive, redemptive, rightwising motive and purpose.
Let's consider the description of this Rider, from this verse, on through vs. 16:
    a) He is **called Faithful** (Full of Faith; To Be Trusted; Trustworthy; Loyal) **and True** (or: Real): this means that He can be relied upon, and is genuine; He is not imaginary or a lie. *Cf* 1:5, and 3:14, above; 2 Tim. 1:12; Jn. 14:1.
    b) He is **continuously judging**, which means that He is constantly evaluating human situations and is then making decisions – He does not wait until our life is over, or until some imagined "end of history!" His metaphorical riding forth is not a one-time event in history.
    c) He is **continuously making war in eschatological deliverance**, which is a symbolic picture, referencing 12:7-11, above, of the ongoing work of the cross and resurrection, as folks continue being born, grow and are in need of His deliverance and transforming power. He battles injustice "within equitable dealings; in justice, fairness and righted relations which accord with the covenantal Way pointed out;" this is covenantal activity (ending the old and beginning the new).
    d) **His eyes are a flame of fire** (vs. 12, below; recall 1:14, above – this is the same One)
    e) **Upon His head are many diadems** (vs. 16: King of kings). Does this mean that He is in fact the real ruler of all kingdoms? Or, is this a symbol of His having conquered the kingdoms of this world, and now exercising unseen control over human history? *Cf* Mat. 28:18, and ponder this.
    f) He, too, being Himself an Overcomer, **has a name which no one else knows** – as do all overcomers (2:17, above), thus showing His solidarity with us.
    g) He has **a garment that has been dipped in blood**: either the blood of His enemies, or the blood of His own sacrifice, which latter captures the souls (the soul is in the blood) of His enemies. As Israel's final sacrifice which fulfilled the Day of Atonement (*cf* Heb. 9:1-28; 10:20), He cleansed the entire camp of Israel (the whole People) – a figure of cleansing all mankind (Acts 10:15b; 11:9; and in 11:18b, "**God also gave** {or: gives} **to the non-Jews** {the ethnic multitudes of the nations} **the change of mind** {or: change in thinking} **[which brings one; or, leads] into Life!**").
    h) His Name is called "**The Word of God**" – a reference to John 1:1ff, and more, *cf* below.
    i) **A two-edged broadsword repeatedly issues forth from His mouth** (see Heb. 4:12), so He battles with His words, as we see in Eph. 6:17, "**the Spirit's sword – the one being God's gush-effect** (or: which is the result of the flow from God; the one existing [as] a result of a flux or an effect of a continuous movement, the source of which is God; or: which is a spoken Word of God; or: that being an utterance or declaration which is God)," which we, too, are to use.
    j) **He shepherds the nations with an iron staff** (*cf* 2:27, above – the overcomers)

k) He continually treads the wine vat of the strong passion of God's internal swelling fervor – His wrath (recall that this wrath presently dwells upon the uncompliant – John 3:36 – and so is their current situation).

l) His garment and thigh have the inscription, "King of kings & Lord of lords" – an echo of Mat. 28:18, "**All authority has been given to Me in heaven and on earth**."

He also has a following: **the armies** (plural – does not say how many) **of the atmosphere** (or: heaven). Recall the soldier's equipment that we are admonished to wear, Eph. 6:10-17. This is a picture of Christ and His body – us, the called-out communities.

So what did this picture speak to the 7 churches in the 1st century? That Christ and His body, the called-out community, has overcome and will fulfill the purposes of God. This figure shows that Christ is active, on the move and involved. He is overcoming in all situations. He is the One whom we can trust – He is real. He brings the reality of His kingdom into our earth, riding triumphantly through the midst of our being – as well as throughout the earth realm. He constantly judges us, correcting our path to be in accord to "the Way pointed out." His sword (Word) "**penetrates as far as a dividing** (parting) **of** [our] **soul** [from our] **spirit**... **to discern [the] thoughts** (in-rushing passions) **and intentions of** [our] **hearts**" (Heb. 4:12). And all this is "**shepherding**" His sheep.

The last clause of this verse echoes Ps. 96:13,
> "He repeatedly comes to evaluate, make decisions about, and judge the Land (or: earth; territory). He will progressively evaluate and decide concerning the inhabited area in eschatological deliverance and a righting of situations into justice and equity of the Way pointed out, even rightwising peoples within His Truth, and in union with His reality" (LXX, JM). *Cf* Ps.72:2.

Also, Jer. 23:5,
> "Look, and consider! Days are progressively coming, says [the] LORD (= Yahweh), and I will proceed causing to stand up (or: I will raise up) in (or: for) David a just and rightwised rising-up (or: dawning), then a King will continue reigning and He will progressively take notice, perceive and cause things to flow together with understanding, and then will progressively form and create the effect of justice and eschatological deliverance (rightwised existence in the Way pointed out) upon the Land (or: earth; territory; soil)" (LXX, JM).

12. And His eyes [are] [other MSS add: as] a flame of fire; and upon His head [are] many diadems (kingly bands), **having a name having been written** [other MSS: having names written, and a name] **which no one knows except Himself**,

These **eyes** were seen by John in 1:14, above, so this is the same One, the risen Christ, who first spoke to John. *Cf* Dan. 10:6. He is the One that is "**continuously walking about within the midst of the seven golden lampstands** (the called-out covenant communities – 1:20-2:1b, above)." And because His eyes are "**the seven spirits of God**" (5:6b, above), "He will not proceed in making decisions or judging according to the reputation, the appearance, or what 'seems' to be the case, nor will He test or put to the proof according to the thing that is, or was, said or what is, or was, reported" (Isa. 11:3, LXX, JM).

The "**many diadems** (kingly bands)" are symbolic of His being King and Lord of many kings and lords of the earth. *Cf* 11:15, above, and the contrast to the 7 diadems on the dragon (12:3). These may also be an allusion to the seven horns (figures of the strength of the completeness of kingdoms or governments) on the little Lamb, in 5:6, above.

The statement that only He knows the Name that is written upon His head calls to mind Jn. 17:26, "**I made Your Name intimately known to them – and I will continue making It experientially known.**" Only intimacy of the marriage relationship and personal unveiling brings the *gnosis* (intimate, experiential knowledge) that reveals His Name (character, personality, true identity). The **name** is His "**Name, the one new in character and quality** [other MSS: and the new name]" (3:12, above). *Cf* 2:17, above. The names given in vss. 13 and 16, below, are separate titles, not to be confused with the special name referred to in this verse. Jesus said, in Lu. 10:22,

> "**All mankind and All things were given over and transferred to Me by, and under, My Father, and yet no one is in constant, intimate, experiential knowledge of Who the Son is** (exists being), **except the Father, nor Who is the Father, except the Son – and whomsoever the Son is now wanting and continuing intending to at some point unveil** (uncover; reveal; disclose) **[Him].**" *Cf* Mat. 16:16-17.

This corresponds to 14:3, above, where only that specific group could learn "the new song." Experience and intimacy are key to "knowing." Beale (ibid p 957) observes, "The names in 3:12 and in 19:12 are different metaphorical ways of saying the same thing." 1 Jn.3:1b also lends insight here:

> "**the System** (the world; the realm of the secular and religious; the ordered arrangement of culture, religion, economy and government) **is not habitually having experiential or intimate knowledge of us** (does not know or have insight into us), **because it did not know** (or: it does not have an intimate, experiential knowledge of) **Him.**"

In 1 Cor. 8:3, Paul instruct us:

> "**Now if anyone is continuously or habitually loving** (urging toward reunion with; fully giving oneself to) **God, this person has been personally and intimately known by God and continues under the experience of His knowledge** (or: this One has been intimately known by him [i.e., by the one progressively loving God])."

This corresponds to Jn. 10:4b, "**the sheep progressively follow him, because they have been acquainted with and recognize his voice.**" And Jn. 10:27-28a,

> "**My sheep are constantly hearing and listening to** [implying: obeying] **My voice, and I Myself am progressively** (or: continuously) **knowing them by intimate experience, and they are progressively** (or: habitually) **following Me, and I Myself am continuously giving eonian life** (age-enduring life; life having the qualities and characteristics of the Age [of Messiah]; a life from, of and for the ages)…"

This corresponds to 14:1-5, above. A possible background for this concept of an unknown name, because it is a new name, may be Isa. 65:15,

> "For you see, you folks will leave behind your name for a glut (or: unto full disgust) among (or: to; with) My picked-out and chosen ones, and [the] Lord shall progressively lift you folks up and take you back, again (or: do away with you), yet by, with, to, for and among those continually performing as slaves to, for, in, with and by Me, a Name new in quality and character will continue being called, which shall continue being spoken well-of, blessed, and laid out with goodness, ease and well-being, for they will constantly speak well of (lay out words of goodness concerning) the True and Real God" (LXX, JM).

In Isa. 62:2 we read of Jerusalem, "Then you will be called by a NEW name, which the mouth of Yahweh shall specify."

The other MSS reading would suggest that the "names" were written upon the **diadems**, which might refer to the various kingdoms or realms over which He reigns. *Cf* Ps. 110:6. Perhaps it is a reference to the many names that Israel attributed to God by attaching a quality or characteristic to the abbreviated name, Yah. Perhaps this is an allusion to Heb. 7:2 and the order of Melchisedec: "**King of the Way pointed out** (King of fairness and equity; King of Justice and Righteousness; King of Rightwised

Relationships; also: = King of covenant living)," and, "**King of Peace and of Harmony from the Joining.**" In Isa. 62:3, 5 we observe that it is written concerning Zion and Jerusalem, "Then shall you become a crown of adorning, in the hand of Yahweh, and a royal diadem, in the hand of your God…. And with the elation of a bridegroom over [his] bride, [so] will your God be elated over you."

The "Odes of Solomon," dated as early as the late 1st century, presents what may be Jewish-Christian thought from the early spread of Christianity. Ode 42:8-9, 20, use language similar to our context, with allusions to the OT:
> "Like the arm of the bridegroom over the bride, so is my yoke over those who know Me. And as the bridal feast (or: bed; couch; chamber) is spread out by the bridal pair's home, so is my love by those who believe in Me…. And I placed My name upon their head, because they are free and they are Mine" (*The OT Pseudepigrapha*, Vol. 2 ibid p 771).

13. **and having been clothed** (or: cast around) **with a garment having been dipped in** (immersed; [other MSS: sprinkled with]) **blood** (or: dyed with blood), **and His Name is being called "The Word of God** (God's *Logos*; The Message from God; The Idea which is God; The Expression about God).**"**

The first clause may be an allusion to Lev. 8:30, the consecration of the priests:
> "Moses took some of the anointing oil and some of the blood which was on the altar and spattered it on Aaron, on his garments and on his sons and on his sons' garments with him; so he hallowed Aaron, his garments and his sons and his sons' garments with him" (CVOT).

But the allusion may reach back farther, to Gen. 37:31, where Joseph's ornamented tunic was, by his brothers, dipped in the goat's blood, after they sold him into slavery. That OT incident may be a foreshadowing of Jesus' treatment by His brothers, before He, too, became Israel's Savior.

Another possible allusion is to the grape harvest, which can have a dual application: the blessings of new wine from the vine, and a metaphor for judgment – the crushing of the grapes. The OT reference is Isa. 63:1-7,
> "'Who is this, suddenly birthing Himself (or: coming to be) alongside from out of the midst of Edom [CVOT reads: humanity; from Heb.: *adom*], [with] garments dyed red, from Bosor [Heb.: vintage]? – in this manner, seasonably ripe and timely in His set equipment (or: lovely, fair and beautiful in a kingly/priestly long robe/apparel), in bodily force, with strength? – I am thoroughly laying it out and progressively discoursing concerning eschatological deliverance (a rightwising unto the Way pointed out, with the justice, fairness and equity of righted covenant inclusion) and a rescuing (a restoring, saving) deciding (or: judging). Why are Your garments dyed red, and Your items of apparel [dyed] as from a trodden wine trough full or [what] continued being trampled?'
>
> "[Yahweh answers] 'Being filled from continued trampling down – and no man from among the nations (ethnic multitudes) continues being with Me – I trampled them down in My rushing emotion, and then I crushed them in pieces as soil and brought down their blood into the ground. For you see, a Day of Reward (giving or paying back in turn; recompense) came upon them, and a year of liberating release continues being present, alongside (at hand).
> Then I looked around, and there was no helper; and so I paid attention and reflected on [the situation], and no one continued taking hold on the other side, to assist. And so My arm rescued them and drug them to safety. Then My rushing emotion and passion took a stand upon [the situation] and attended [to it], and in My internal swelling fervor (or: natural impulse; anger) I trampled them down, and brought their blood into the ground.'

"I remembered the Mercy of, and from, the LORD (= Yahweh) – the excellences of, and gracious acts from, [the] LORD (= Yahweh) – within all the things in which He continually rewards us and repeatedly pays us back. [The] LORD (= Yahweh) [is] a good Decider (Evaluator; Judge) for, and in the midst of, the House of Israel; He repeatedly brings upon us, and provides for us, corresponding to His Mercy, and according to the abundance of His eschatological Deliverance (rightwising treatment of justice which accords to the Way pointed out)" (LXX, JM).

As we consider the mixed message of this passage, we see that Yahweh's decisions bring both judgment and blessings, the latter always following the former. A possible correlation to the red garments in Isa. 63:1, above, is that part of the covering of the Tabernacle was constructed of rams' skins dyed red (Ex. 25:5; 26:14; 35:7 – 39:34). We will consider Paul's connection between garments and the Tabernacle (Tent), below. The prophet wondered about and questioned what he saw, yet knew that what he was laying out for us was Yahweh's ultimate, eschatological deliverance and righting of situations. The treading of a wine trough was the whole purpose for having a vineyard, but the harvest meant a cutting off (from the vine) and a trampling of the grapes. The Day of Reward was the reward of the harvest – a blessing. Eschatologically it meant a "year of liberating release." But the cup of blessing (1 Cor. 10:16) comes from a casting into the wine trough. The old must be harvested; the new comes with another season. But all the same, Christ's followers are called to take up their execution stakes and follow His path – and for the same reason. Our crushing sheds forth His Lifeblood. Others drink the blessing, just as we did. It is a continuous journey. But the prophet realized that Yahweh "repeatedly brings His mercy upon us" (*cf* Rom. 11:32). The OT pattern that we observe was intended for, and resulted in, good (Rom. 8:28). For more on this metaphor, see the discussion on 14:18-20, above, and on vs. 15b, below.

In discussing this verse with my wife, Lynda, she mentioned Jesus' first sign, in Jn. 2:1-11. There He passed over the normal process of crushing grapes, then the time in the wineskin for fermenting the juice. The Water of Life became the best wine. So here we should look for the new wine of the new covenant, where old metaphors are transformed to show forth the glory of God in the Face (character) of Jesus Christ (2 Cor. 4:6). Lynda also mentioned the need for new wineskins (Mat. 9:17): we need new creation in Christ, with its corresponding new world view and its new applications of old metaphors, as we saw with Jesus and Paul. Jesus symbolized the cluster (Isa. 65:8) that was crushed to bring us the new wine, He has, in the picture in this verse, been bringing forth new wine in and for others by walking through us in His wine trough. Wine is a symbol of celebration (Jn. 2:1-11) and of bringing joy (Ps. 104:15), which in turn is a figure of God's reign (Rom. 14:17b). The cup of the wine in Mat. 26:27-29 represented His life-blood of the new arrangement (covenant) and the celebration of His Father's reign.

We find Paul using the metaphor of being "**clothed**," in 2 Cor. 5:1-4,

"**if our house, of the tabernacle which is pitched on the land, would at some point be dismantled** (or: that whenever our house, which is this tent upon the earth, should be loosed down), **we constantly have** (continuously hold; presently possess) **a structure** (a building) **forth from out of the midst of God**.... **we are continuously groaning, utterly longing and constantly yearning to fully enter within and to CLOTHE upon ourselves** (to dress upon ourselves) **our dwelling-house** (habitation) **– the one [made] out of heaven** (or: the one from, or made of, atmosphere).... **to fully enter within and to ADD CLOTHING upon ourselves, to the end that the mortal** (or: this mortal thing) **may be drunk down and swallowed under** (or: by) **The Life**." *Cf* 1 Cor. 15:54b.

With these metaphorical insights from Paul, let us apply them to Christ, Who was symbolically clothed with the Life of the Spirit (the Anointing to be the Messiah), or as Dan Kaplan says, "He was clothed with the Father: with His Nature and Character," so that when we see Him, we see the Father (Jn. 14:9). That was also the clothing of being humanity's Chief Priest (Heb. 7-9), that would have been "spattered" with His own blood, as He sprinkled our hearts (Heb. 10:19-22).

The **Name** that is **being called** has an apocalyptic significance, just as did the other names that were called, in 11:8, 12:9 and 16:16, above. The Figure bearing this Name can be understood from the five functions of the genitive case that are on offer:
- a) The Word of God – a reference to all the uses of this phrase in the OT
- b) God's *Logos* – bringing to mind Jn. 1:1, 14, and the multiple implications which *logos* contains
- c) The Message from God – Christ is the Message, the Good News, the announcement of the goal of the ages, and the way to victory
- d) The Idea which is God – Christ is what God had in mind, from the beginning: the Human expressing what God IS
- e) The Expression about God – Christ expresses and reveals God's character and personality.

This name also points back to vs. 9, above, and 21:5, below, while connecting to the "**the faithful Witness**" of 1:5, along with 6:9-10, and 20:4. This is a picture of Christ overcoming by His Word. Verse 15, below, implies His Word in action, and connects that metaphor with that of our picture here, in vs 13.

14. **And the armies in the atmosphere** (or: heaven) – **ones having been clothed with** (invested with; entered within) **clean** (or: pure) **bright, white fine cotton – continued following Him upon bright, white horses.**

Armies in the atmosphere (they have been caught up into the clouds, with the Lord; *cf* 1Thes. 4:17), or in the heaven (place of leadership; position of ruling), riding **bright white horses**, is a picture of overcomers, as we saw in 6:2, above. Like that One, they go forth conquering in the righteousness of eschatological deliverance, bringing people and situations into alignment with the Way pointed out. They bring justice and equity; they bring that which is right and fair. They are priests from the heavenly (resurrected) Temple on the spiritual mount Zion. They ride out from Jerusalem-upon-heaven (Heb. 12:22-24). Do not lose track of the fact that this picture is a symbol. It is representative. Those with Christ are His holy messengers, His set-apart and sent-forth agents (12:7-8; 14:10b, above). The horses are symbols for victors. They overcame by the blood of the little Lamb, and the word of their testimony (12:11, above). Paul described this group in 2 Cor. 10:3-6a,

> 3. **For though habitually walking about and ordering our behavior within [the] flesh** (= in a physical body; or: = in the human condition), **we are not waging warfare** (or: performing military service) **in correspondence and accord to flesh** (= on the level of estranged or enslaved humanity, or in line with human condition; or: = in the sphere of old covenant Jewish reasonings),
> 4. **for you see, the tools and weapons of our military service and warfare [are] not fleshly** (= do not pertain to our human condition; ["are not the weapons of the Domination System" – Walter Wink]), **but rather, [are] powerful ones and capable ones in God** (or: by God), **[focused] toward [the] pulling down** (demolition) **of effects of fortifications** (or: strongholds; strongly entrenched positions [of the "Domination System" – Walter Wink, *Engaging the Powers*]),
> 5. **progressively tearing down and demolishing conceptions** (concepts; the effects of thoughts, calculations, imaginations, reasonings and reflections) **and every height** (or: high position; high-effect) **and lofty [attitude, purpose or obstacle] that is habitually lifting itself up against** (or: elevating itself up on so as to put down) **the intimate and experiential knowledge of God, and then taking captive every thought – one after another – and leading them prisoner into the hearing obedience of the Christ** (or: the humble attentive listening, which comes from the Anointed One; or: the submissive paying attention, which is the Anointing),
> 6. **even continuously holding [them] in a ready state and prepared condition to support fairness and equity, while maintaining rightwised relationships from out of the Way pointed out, for every mishearing** (or: hearing-aside; setting of our attention to the side; or: disobedience)...

We were informed in 17:14b, above, concerning those with Christ, that, "**the ones with Him are CALLED ONES and CHOSEN ONES and FAITHFUL ONES** (or: trusting folks; people filled with faith; loyal ones)." They are the same ones that we saw with the little Lamb in 14:1, above. The picture described here is of the same group: the called-out covenant communities. The One on the white horse, described in vss. 11-13, above, is the little Lamb of 17:14a, above. By the description of their clothes we see that they are the overcomers of 3:4-5, 18. They have the same clothing (figure of social rand, station and function) as the Lamb's Wife (vss. 7-8, above). They are clothed like the 24 elders, in 4:4, like the martyrs in 6:11, and like the great multitude before the throne, in 7:9, 13 and 14.

15. **Also, a sharp two-edged broadsword repeatedly goes out** (issues forth; proceeds) **from His mouth, to the end that in it He would bring a blow to** (or: could touch; should strike) **the multitudes** (nations; ethnic groups). **And then He will continue shepherding them with an iron staff. Furthermore He is continually treading, [as on a path],** (or: trampling) **the tub** (the wine vat) **of the wine of the strong passion of the internal swelling fervor** (natural impulse; mental bent; personal emotion; or: indignation; wrath) **of the All-Strong** (Almighty) **God.**

We saw the same picture of "**a sharp two-edged broadsword repeatedly [going] out from His mouth**" in 1:16, above, so this is another witness that what John saw here is the same risen Christ. The allusion in the first sentence of our present verse is to Isa. 11:4, but let us read a bit of that context for a clearer picture of what John observed:

> "And then (or: So) a staff (or: shoot; rod) will progressively come forth from out of the root of Jesse, and a blossom (or: flower) will continue climbing up from the root, and a Breath-effect of (or: [the] Spirit from, and which is) God will continue fully resting (keep on having a fixed place of rest) upon Him.... He will not have the habit of deciding according to the repute, the opinion or what seems to be the case, neither will He proceed in testing or putting to the proof in accord to (or: from the sphere of) the report or the saying [about the case]. But to the contrary, He will habitually administer judging for a humble one (or: make evaluations, deciding with a view to [the] person of low position) and will continue putting to the proof and testing the humble and low folks of the Land (or: from the soil or ground; who are earth)....
> So He will progressively touch (or bring a blow to; strike) [the] Land (soil; ground; earth) with the Word of His mouth (or: in the Message from His mouth), and in union with a Breath-effect (or: in a Spirit) through [His] lips He will proceed lifting up (taking back again; or: doing away with) an impious person (a shameless and irreverent one), and He will continue existing with (or: in) eschatological deliverance (rightwising fairness and equity of righted relationships in the Way pointed out; justice and rightwising) tied around His waist (or: loins), and [His] sides wrapped and bound with Truth and by Reality. And then a wolf will continue being fed together with a lamb and a leopard will rest again (or: rest back) with a kid, and a young calf and a bull will graze together with a lion, and a little infant (or: child) will progressively lead them" (Isa. 11:1-2a, 3b-6, LXX, JM).

Cf Isa. 49:1-3, where Israel is described as having had his "mouth made like a sharp sword."

Thus we see that the allusion of **bringing a blow to**, or touching, **the multitudes** comes in a passage that ends with a transformation of the character of creation, and peace between former adversaries. It comes in a context of eschatological deliverance, where the Isa. 11 passage continues with good news (e.g., vs. 9a, "they shall not hurt nor have power to destroy anyone on My set-apart mountain"). Isa. 11:9b-10 instructs us that,

> "the whole, all together, [are] to experientially know the LORD, just as much water fully covers a sea, and in that Day there will be the Root of Jessie, even the One progressively rising up to rule (or: to begin) nations (ethnic multitudes; Gentiles): upon Him nations (ethnic multitudes; Gentiles)

will place [their] expectation, and His full rest will continue being a state of honor (or: of value)" (LXX, JM).

The risen Christ does battle using His Word. Like us, He does not battle against flesh and blood, but against the strongholds in people's minds, bringing deliverance to them. The blow delivered by the Spirit of His mouth divides between soul and spirit within the core of us (Heb. 4:12). It "touches us," and we are never the same again. Now observe: with that "touch" "**He will continue SHEPHERDING them with an iron** (i.e., strong, not to be resisted) **staff**." That staff (from the root of Jesse, i.e., the Messianic Anointing) brings correction to a straying sheep (Lu. 15:4-7; He follows after them UNTIL He finds them), and it also defends the flock from adversaries. *Cf* 2:27; 12:5, above; Ps. 2:9.

> "This is the kind of war that is symbolically depicted in Revelation with a rider on a white horse called The Word of God who wears a robe drenched in his own blood and wages a righteous war with a sword coming from his mouth. This is not a literal war, this is a symbolic war. This is not a future war; Christ is waging this war right now. I know Christ is waging this war right now because I am among those who have been slain by the sword of his mouth and raised again to newness of life! Jesus slays me. He slays me with his divine word. And in slaying me, he sets me free. This is salvation. John the Revelator is showing us how Jesus saves the world, not how Jesus kills the world" (Zahnd, War of the Lamb, ibid).

"The last half of the verse is an echo of 14:19-20, q.v., above, and Isa. 63:1-6, quoted, above, in the comments on vs. 13. This is apocalyptic repetition. It emphasizes that the Overcomer brings the intended harvest that creates the new wine for the marriage of the little Lamb with His Wife. His **continual treading** brings out the best of us, and "**the strong passion of the internal swelling fervor** (natural impulse; mental bent; personal emotion; or: indignation; wrath) **of the All-Strong** (Almighty) **God**" is indignation against injustice, and even wrath against our participation in the prostitution of idolatry (in all of its forms), but it is also an expression of His passionate love for Humanity. His "natural impulse" is love for the aggregate of humanity (Jn. 3:16). Let us recall a few witnesses from the OT:

Isa. 19:22 (LXX, JM),
"And so [the] Lord (= Yahweh) will smite and wound (or: strike down with a fatal blow) the Egyptians, and then shall completely heal them – and thus they will be fully turned back toward (or: face to face with) [the] Lord (= Yahweh). Then He will listen unto them and thoroughly heal them."

Hos. 5:14-6:4 (LXX, JM),
"Because of this, I Myself am like (or: exist being as) a panther to (or: for; in) Ephraim, and like a lion to (or: for; in) the house of Judah: thus I Myself will tear, and then journey on; I will take (grasp in [My] hand; seize), and there will be no one to be rescuing and dragging [folks] out of [My grasp].
I will journey on and return into My place until they will be caused to disappear, AND THEN they will search for My face, and seek My presence. Within the midst of (or: When encompassed with and joined to) their pressure and affliction they will seek Me early and come to Me before the dawn, repeatedly saying, 'Let us go our way and return to [the] Lord (= Yahweh) our God, because He Himself tore [us], and yet He will heal us. He will smite and wound (or: strike down with a fatal blow), and then He will bind us and bandage the wound. After two days He will make us sound and healthy; within (or: on) the third day we shall stand back up again from out of the midst (or: will be raised forth again) and then we will live before Him – in His sight and presence – and we will have insight (*gnosis*) and intimately know by experience! Let us press forward and run to intimately experience and know the Lord (= Yahweh) firsthand: we will find Him ready and

prepared – like the early morning (or: as the dawn), and then He will come to us (or: for us; in us) – like [the] early and latter rain to and on the Land (or: in the earth).'"

Hos. 11:1-4 (LXX, JM),
"Because Israel [is] a young child, I Myself also love him, and I once called his children together from out of Egypt. The more I called them [to Me], the more they distanced themselves and kept away from My face (or: immediate presence). They sacrificed to the Baals, and then burned incense to the carved and chiseled images (= idols).
And so I, Myself tied the feet of Ephraim together (i.e., restrained him; = hobbled him to keep him from wandering) [then] I took him up upon My arm – and yet they did not realize (or: know) that I had healed them. In the thorough ruin and destruction of humans I stretch out to them and lay [My hand] on them in binding ties (or: bonds) of My love.
And so I will be to them as a person slapping (or: striking) [someone] on his cheek, then I will look upon him (= either: keep an eye on him; or: give respect to him). I will prevail with him and then give ability and power to him."

Then in Hos. 11:8-9, Yahweh says re: Ephraim,
"My heart is turned for a change within itself, My change in care and interest is jointly stirred and excited: I will not do or perform in accord with (or: to the degree of) the inherent fervor of My hard-breathing passion – I will not leave Ephraim down within the midst of the [situation] to be wiped out of the midst, because of the fact that I Myself am God, and not human, a Set-apart One within your midst!" (LXX, JM)

Ps. 7:11 (LXX, JM),
"God [is] a fair and just evaluator and decider (or: judge), as well as a Strong One who takes a long time before breathing hard and rushing into passion. He is not one who is constantly bringing on anger from inherent fervor (or: passionate wrath) every day."

Isa. 48:9 (LXX, JM),
"For the sake of My own Name and Reputation, I will point out, show and demonstrate the fury of my rushing passion (or: wrath), and then will bring upon you My inner glory – to the end that I will not destroy you out of the midst."

16. **And upon His garment and upon [His] thigh He has a Name having been written:**
   "King of kings and Lord of lords."

We saw this same title in 17:14, above. This is apocalyptic duplication, for emphasis. Upon His blood-drenched **garment** were the titles of His sovereign position, and His identity as Owner and Master (or, **Lord**) of all human lordship and ownership. Paul used this same compound title of Christ in 1 Tim. 6:15b-16a,

> **"The Happy and Only Able One** (only Powerful One; alone Potent One)**: The King of those reigning as kings, and Lord** (Master; Owner) **of those ruling as lords, the Only One continuously holding and having possession of immortality**…"

This may be an allusion to Deut. 10:17, "For Yahweh your God [is] God of gods and Lord of lords." This vision in the Unveiling seems intent on repeatedly identifying Christ with Yahweh. In Dan. 2:47, Nebuchadnezzar affirmed to Daniel that, "your God [is] a God of gods and a Lord of kings." The idea in this compound title was seen in 11:15, above, and is also likely an allusion to Ps. 2:2-8. What also comes to mind is 1 Cor. 15:25,

"**For it is binding and necessary for Him to be continuously reigning** (ruling as King; exercising sovereignty) **until which [time or situation]** (or: until where) **He would put** (or: may place; could set) **all the things that have or hold ruin** (or: the enemies) **under His feet**."

Ps. 46:10-11a echoes this picture:

"Relax and know that I [am] Elohim (God); I shall be exalted among [the] nations; I shall be exalted in [the] earth (land; soil). Yahweh of hosts [is] with us..." (CVOT; parentheses mine).

Chilton (ibid p 488) points us to 2:7, 11, 26-28; 3:5, 12, 21, above, where the called-out communities are called to conquer and overcome, even as He overcame. This vision is also a reprise of the Rider in 6:2, above.

But why was this **Name** written upon His **thigh**? The word is used only here, in the NT. It had significance in the OT as the location on another person under which one swearing an oath or a covenant to him was to place his hand (Gen. 24:2, 9; 47:29). So it speaks to the idea of covenantal commitment or promise to do His will. It was also the typical location where a sword was worn (Ex. 32:27; Judg. 3:16, 21). We read in Ps. 45:

2. Grace with joy-producing favor [that is] youthful, well-formed, proper and seasonable, in and with fine, ideal beauty – at the side of, and in contrast to, the sons of the People (or: the humans) – was held forth (made to project from; made prominent so as to stand out) on your lips. Because of this, God spoke goodness, ease and well-being to (or: blessed) you, on into the midst of the Age [of Messiah].

3. Proceed in girding your sword upon your thigh, O able and powerful one, in (or: with) your well-formed, proper youthfulness and in (or: with) your fine and ideal beauty.

4. Next stretch tight and bend [the bow] and continue greatly prospering and reigning (exercising sovereign influence); on account of truth (or: reality), mild gentleness (or: humble meekness) and eschatological deliverance into the Way pointed out, in rightwised relationships of justice, and then your right hand will continue leading and guiding you wonderfully, on your journey.

5. O able and powerful one, your arrows (darts; missiles) are sharpened [and are] in the heart of the kings' enemies (hostile ones); peoples shall one-after-another (or: progressively) fall down under you.

6. God [is] your throne (or: Your throne, O God [is]) on into the midst of an indefinite time of the Age [of Messiah]. A staff of upright straightness and equity [is] the staff of your rule and reign (sovereign influence and activity).

7. You love (accept and drive for union with) eschatological deliverance in the Way pointed out, with rightwised, just relationships, and you hate lawlessness. Because of this, God, your God anoints you with olive oil of great joy and exultation, at the side of, and in contrast to, your partners and companion participants. (LXX, JM)

Gen. 32:25 records Jacob's thigh being touched during the night of wrestling with a Man. This was the time of Jacob's name being changed to Israel. Elsewhere in this Unveiling, **garments** spoke of a person's condition, or position. Here, its symbol, when combined to the idea of **a Name** and **a thigh**, may indeed speak of Christ's enthronement and new Name, as we saw in 3:12, above.

Hiett observes:

"[In] AD 312, the emperor Constantine confessed Christ as 'King of kings and Lord of lords.' By the end of the fourth century, most of the Roman Empire was at least nominally Christian" (ibid p 227).

17. **Next I saw one Agent** (or: person with a message) **standing in the sun. And he cried with a great voice, repeatedly saying to all the birds continuously flying in mid-heaven,**
   "Come! Be gathered together into God's great supper (meal taken at evening),

The setting and manner of proclamation here echoes the same situation of 18:1, above. There, "**the Land** (or: ground; or: earth) **was lighted** (illuminated) **by His glory**," which is exactly what **the sun** does, so we can see the correlation between these two scenes. Both pictures represent, "**The life [that] was continuing being, and began progressively existing as, the Light of mankind. And the Light is constantly shining in the dim and shadowed places, and keeps on progressively giving light within the gloomy darkness where there is no light**" (Jn. 1:4b-5a). This may also be an allusion to Mal. 4:2,
   "Yet [the] Sun of righteousness will radiate for you [who] fear My Name, and healing [will be] in Its wings" (CVOT).
In Gen. 1:16 the sun (the greater luminary) was to rule the Day, a figure of "the Day of Christ."

The calling of **all the birds** is an allusion to Ezk. 39:4b, "I will give you unto the ravenous birds … to be devoured." Beale (ibid p 965) notices that both of these announcements are associated with birds (*cf* 18:2b) and judgment, and that since the language is similar, the association must be intended. While chapter 18 narrates the fall of Babylon, this second will narrate the fall of the false prophet (i.e., the false message) and of the little animal (the domination system that supported the Prostitute). In the realm of God's reign, the two go down together. Historically, Jerusalem was destroyed prior to the eventual fall of Rome. Perhaps this is why John was shown these two events in separate visions. But from God's view, from the perspective of the ages, the one soon follows the other. Both are now ancient history to us, yet the spiritual principle continues: religion is usually associated with and depends upon human systems of domination (whether physical or social-emotional-economic). The message to us is that both will fall – all in God's time and plan.

The detail that the birds are "**continuously flying in mid-heaven**" points us to vultures (or, eagles: the symbol of the Roman army, and now, curiously, to America), or other birds of prey that we normally see in continuous flight, in the midst of the sky, searching for dead, or living, flesh. We saw this same phrase in 8:13, above:
   "**I saw and heard one vulture** (or: eagle; [Aleph with Maj. text, *Koine* proper; Maj. text, Andreas: agent; messenger]), **constantly flying within mid-heaven, repeatedly saying by a great voice, 'W**oe (or: Tragic will be the fate)**! W**oe (or: Alas)**! W**oe (or: Tragedy)**!'**…"
Ezekiel's vision, concerning the judgment upon Gog (ch. 39; *cf* comments below, on this prophecy), had a specific purpose:
   "So shall they know that I [am] Yahweh, and my holy Name will I MAKE known in the midst of My people Israel, and will not allow My holy Name to be profaned any more – So shall the nations KNOW that I [am] Yahweh, Holy in Israel" (Ezk. 39:7b-8; Rotherham; emphasis mine).
Note the emphasis on Christ's Name in vss. 11-16, above.

In Mat. 24:28, Jesus said,
   "**Wherever the carcass** (corpse) **may be, the vultures** (or: eagles) **will be progressively led together and gathered**."
As with this prophecy by Jesus, we find that the judgment for disobedience to the old, Israelite covenant was, "Your carcass shall be food for all birds of the sky (heaven)…" (Deut. 28:26).

Our present vision (ch. 19) now changes, and John sees a picture of a meal that is in stark contrast to the wedding supper. In vss. 11-16 we saw the triumphant Christ with His armies, and the battle is described in the metaphor of His treading the wine vat. Now we see the results of this battle: the vultures are called in, implying that there is nothing but dead bodies (or: flesh) of that which God has determined to destroy. Even their horses are dead – an echo of the Egyptian army in the Red Sea. This part of the vision is analogous to vs. 15, above.

"**God's great supper**," is an echo of vs. 9, above, but a contrast. Beale (ibid) rightly observes that "judgment [the righting of a situation] is but the other side of the coin of salvation" (brackets, mine). Both judgment and deliverance happen in this life to bring correction and release in this life. His decisions for us in the "next life" will be that of a Father who loves us. I am here reminded of a recent connection that Richard Rohr made (in his Daily Meditations) of two verses:

> "**For thus God loves** (fully gives Himself to and urges toward reunion with) **the aggregate of humanity**" (Jn. 3:16a).
> "**Who or what will be separating, dividing or parting us away from the Love of and from Christ**?" (Rom. 8:35a).

For all of us, this second supper (which, for us, is the work of His death and burial), which strips the 1st Adam's flesh (the carnal thinking) from us, must come in conjunction with, or prior to, the first supper of vs. 9. Death and resurrection are "two sides of the same coin." The judgment on Pharaoh and Egypt was the initiation of the liberation from slavery for Israel. Now it is the liberation from the slavery to the Law, for religion brings spiritual slavery (Gal. 4:21-5:18).

This same picture is used in Ezk. 39:17-20,

> "And you, son of man, thus says Yahweh God; Speak unto every feathered fowl, and to every beast of the field, 'Assemble yourselves, and come; gather yourselves on every side to My sacrifice... even a great sacrifice upon the mountains of Israel, that you may eat flesh and drink blood.... of the princes of the earth...'"

As this prophecy presented the victory of God for Israel, so these similar images present the victory of Christ over the world and false religions and systems of domination. Here the picture projects into the ongoing ages of the future, as did the vision in Daniel, where the Rock – that struck the feet of the statue and brought it to the ground – became a mountain and filled the whole earth. We should also keep in mind the facts of Israel's great feasts. They involved eating the flesh of slain animals. Those feasts fed the priests and the people. Viewed as types for the spiritual pictures that are also generated, here in the Unveiling, we should be advised to look for a similar purpose in God's decisions, for which the religious folks prefer the term "judgments." Our judgments (the death of our "animal" nature as fertilizer for the birth of our God nature, *theosis*) feed the new man of the heart.

18. "**so that you may eat kings' flesh and military commanders'** (commanders of 1000 men; tribunes) **flesh, even the flesh of strong ones, and the flesh of horses and of those sitting on them; both flesh of all free ones and of slaves; even of little ones and of great ones.**"

The historical view understands this description as a metaphor for the carnage resulting from the destruction of Judea and Jerusalem, ending in AD 70. The Romans did their worst, and all levels of the Judean society were destroyed. No class or condition of people were able to withstand the assault. The description in Ezk. 39:17-20 gave more details, but this verse gives a clear picture. The death of the horses may be an allusion to the Egyptian army drowned in the Red Sea while following after Moses and Israel. The mention of "tribunes" shows that the Romans also lost lives during the long siege. Simmons rightly points out:

> "It is important to make the connection here with the battle of Gog and Magog [*cf* Ezk. 39], because this again demonstrates how the book of Revelation is not in chronological order. In chapter twenty, when loosed from the Bottomless Pit, Rome goes forth to gather the nations that

are in the four quarters of the earth [or: land; may refer to the Roman Empire], 'God and Magog,' together for battle (Rev. 20:7)" (ibid p 357-8; brackets added).
He rightly observes that the manner of portrayal in these visions is "to emphasize the end of the various actors.... The themes progress toward a climax and appointed end, but not in chronological order" (ibid).

But what does it say to us today? First, that Christ is continually making decisions, judging and making figurative (spiritual; non-carnal) war with individuals by speaking His Word in righteousness (vs. 11), dealing with and rightwising each person in his or her own order, in the procession of life – and that He repeatedly does this as the occasion and His purposes demand. *Cf* 2 Cor. 10:4. During His wrestling with us, as He overcomes our defenses, He is at the same time "**progressively [dragging]** [note: drag as with, or in, a net; or: draw, as drawing water with a bucket, or a sword out of a sheath] **all mankind** (or: everyone) **to [Himself]**" (Jn. 12:32). But secondly, we can see the result: dead FLESH! And then He calls in the flesh-eaters of the atmosphere (where they continuously fly in our minds or in the psychological atmosphere of our environments) – the realm of spirit – and they pick the bones clean until there is no more FLESH (thoughts or actions that are adversarial to His Spirit – Rom. 8:4-8). And then, one could say to us, "Can these bones live?" (Ezk. 37:1-14). This is the baptism with Fire and Holy Spirit.

Terry (ibid p 446) calculates six kinds of flesh in this verse, but does not state how he divides these categories. Six, being generally accepted as the Biblical number for humanity, would speak symbolically to the observation that it is primarily humans that are being affected, here. If we classify **military commanders**, **strong ones** and **those sitting on** [the horses] as one kind of flesh (military folks), then those, together with the flesh of horses (perhaps symbolic of military prowess), provide one couplet that is followed by two couplets that each contrast the social stratifications which generally made up 1st century society. This seems to be an emphatic way of saying that the entire society is being dissolved – as was the case in Jerusalem, AD 70. On a spiritual level of interpretation, this could speak to Christ, and His reign within us, completely annihilating all fleshly resistance to His rule within us.

19. **And then I saw the little wild animal** (creature; beast), **and the kings of the Land** (or: earth), **and their armies, having been gathered** (assembled) **to make the war** (or: do the battle) **with the One continually sitting upon the horse, and with His army.**

Verses 19-21 reiterate this battle, vs. 20 giving specific information to the destiny of **the little wild animal** (beast – introduced in 13:1-8, above) and the false prophet (equivalent to the second beast of 13:11-15). The gathering for battle was seen in 16:13-16, above, when the 6th cup was poured out. In 16:13 the dragon (the adversarial spirit of opposition) was mentioned along with the little beast and the false prophet. Here, in chapter 19, it is only the beast and false prophet that are cast into the lake of Fire (God), as we will read in vs. 20. We do not see the devil cast there until vs. 10 of the following chapter – and yet there, too, it follows a description of a battle.

Witness Lee connects this battle with the Valley of Jehoshaphat in Joel. 3:9-16, and with Zech. 14:2-3 and 12-15 (NT, Recovery Version, notes). Recall that Peter connected the latter verses of Joel 2 with what happened on the day of Pentecost (Acts. 2:16-20), so it would not be historically unreasonable to connect what is described in Joel 3 with what happened about 40 years after the day of Pentecost, or as Jesus said, on "this generation."

Gary Demar connects the prophecy of Zech. 14 to the events surrounding Jerusalem's destruction in AD 70. But I suggest that what has been may well be again, and Yahweh will again, from time-to-time, roar out of the heavenly Zion, and utter His voice out of the New Jerusalem, and then the atmosphere (heaven) and the earth (humanity) will shake again – Joel 3:16.

Of vss. 11-21, James Stuart Russell says,
> "This magnificent passage is descriptive of the great event which occupies so prominent a place in NT prophecy, the Parousia, or coming in glory of the Lord Jesus Christ. He comes from heaven; He comes in His kingdom; 'on his head are many crowns;' He comes with His holy angels; 'the armies of heaven follow him;' He comes to execute judgment on His enemies; He comes in glory.... It must be remembered that it is a poem rather than a history that we are now reading; a drama, rather than a journal of transactions.... If we examine the prophetic discourse on the Mt. of Olives we shall find the same order of events. It is immediately 'after' the great tribulation that the sign of the Son of man appears in heaven.... coming in the clouds of heaven with power and great glory (Matt. 25:29). The scene represented in this vision is that very event. The Lord Jesus is 'revealed from heaven with his mighty angels, in flaming fire taking vengeance on them that know not God...' (2 Thes. 1:7, 8)." (*The Parousia*, Kingdom Publications, 1996 [1887] pp. 510-511)

Russell does, however, give consideration to the possibility that the whole scene of the great battle and the victory of Christ may "be properly conceived as taking place in the spirit, not in the flesh... [since this] follows the allusion to the marriage supper of the Lamb, an event which is certainly supposed to take place in the spiritual and eternal state" (ibid p 512-13). With this thought I concur, for in AD 70 we do not see Rome defeated – that comes later in history. But the called-out communities of the 1st century could take courage that even if they saw Rome destroy Jerusalem and the physical temple, it was only the beginning for the active influence of Christ in the new creation.

Verse 21, below, ends with a recap of vs. 18, above, bringing in the **birds**, again. But we will see that those who were "**killed off**" by Christ's mouth-sword (His Word) were simply termed, "**the remaining ones** (the rest; the ones left)." Now this would be a reference to "**the kings of the Land** (or: earth), **and their armies**," that came to "**make war** (or: do battle)" with Christ. Thus, we have a picture of Christ as the total Overcomer in the conflict. In vs. 20 we will see the **animal** system, and the **false prophecy** system being removed from power and influence. Christ defeats ALL opposition. This is simply more apocalyptic redundancy that dramatically pictures the central message of this Unveiling: Christ reigns, despite all opposition.

This verse is probably an allusion to Ps. 2:2,
> "The kings of the earth (or: land; region) stood side by side, and the rulers gathered together, against the Lord and against his anointed" (NETS; expansions, mine).

But recall God's response to this:
> "He who resides in the heavens (atmospheres) will laugh at them..." (Ps. 2:4a, NETS; expansion, mine).

And what will He do next?
> "Then He will continue speaking [i.e., using the sword of His mouth] to them, in His swelling passion, inherent fervor, and natural impulse (or: temperament; disposition)..." (Ps. 2:5a, LXX, JM)

This confrontation was not just about ending the old, Mosaic Law, or about the destruction of the temple which ended animal sacrifices, or about the destruction of Jerusalem, in AD 70. It is also a message that declares God's and Christ's sovereignty, which also demonstrates the non-existence of what theologians erroneously term, "free will." Where is the free will of humans in the picture that is being described for us, here? Humans have a will, but it is not free until Christ sets people free (Jn. 8:32, 36; Rom. 6:18, 22; 8:2; Gal. 5:1): only God's will is free.

Simmons points out that,
> "This is the same gathering together to make war as depicted in Rev. 16:14, 17:14 and 20:8" (ibid p 358).

If we keep in mind that we are reading about the same event, or portrayal, in each of these chapters, then the Unveiling comes into clearer view. They each supply added information by describing the same message with different pictures. Jesus did this same thing when teaching about the reign (kingdom) of God. Beale states that this present verse (19:19) "essentially duplicates the wording used in 16:14 and 20:8…" (ibid p 967). This whole scene is an allusion to Ezk. 39, and 38:2-9 together with 39:2 show us that it is God that is doing the "**gathering**."

> "I will turn you back… and will cause you to come up… upon the mountains of Israel" (Ezk. 39:2).

Here, in 19:19 above, the definite article before the word "**war**/battle" may be significant. It is not referring to just "any" war, but to the decisive one. In the historical setting, we may see the siege of Jerusalem as the "final battle" which ended Jews being separate from Gentile; which eliminated any one "nation" or "people group" as being favored above all others (*cf* Eph. 2:15). In the "kingdom/spiritual" setting, this "battle" was won by the resurrection of "the Word made flesh."

> "**Himself causing the sinking out and away of** (or: stripping off and away [of power and abilities]; undressing [them of arms and glory]; putting off and laying away [of categories and classifications]; or: divesting Himself of) **the governments and the authorities** (or: the ruling folks or people of primacy, and the privileged folks). **And then He made a public exhibit, in a citizen's bold freedom of speaking the truth, leading them in a triumphal procession within it [i.e., the cross/suspension-pole]**" (Col. 2:15).

Cf Zech. 14:2m, as well as Zech. 14:12-15, and the turn of events in 14:16,
> "And it will come to be that everyone left of all the nations coming against Jerusalem, will also go up, as often as year by year, to worship the King, Yahweh of hosts, and to celebrate the festival of booths (tabernacles)" (CVOT; expansion, mine).

With God, the End is always also a Beginning. His mercy endures for the ages. As you ponder this verse in Zech., keep in mind which Jerusalem Paul would have had in mind (Gal. 4:26). I suggest that John would also have seen it as the "New Jerusalem," which we will see in chapters 21-22, below. This has been happening ever since the resurrection of Christ, and it is still happening today.

20. And yet the little wild animal (beast) was pressed and caught (or: is arrested), **and with him the false (lying) prophet – the one that did** (or: who does) **the signs in his presence** (or: before him), **in which he led astray** (or: he deceives) **the folks taking the imprinted mark** (carve-effect) **of the little wild animal, and continually worshiping its image; while living, the two were cast** (or: the two, continuing to live, are thrown) **into the midst of the lake** (or: basin; artificial pool; marshy area) **of the Fire: the one continuously burning within the midst of [the] Deity** (or: the basin of the fire being repeatedly kindled, or being constantly on fire, through union with Divine Nature). [Rom. 11:36]

The message is clear, which is the same message throughout this book: Christ is triumphant. Here it is not the Prostitute that is killed, but **the little wild animal** upon which she rode. In this scene, the little beast and the kings of the Land are not gathered against the City, but against the One sitting upon the horse (vs. 11, above). So historically, I suggest that this represents Rome's persecution against the called-out, in the period following the destruction of Jerusalem. But as Malcolm Smith repeatedly said of this book, "Things are not always what they seem to be – the Lamb rules." So this is a prophecy of the end of the little wild animal (the fourth kingdom of Dan. 2:34-35; 43-45; 7:3-27). The animal and the false prophet represent government (dominion systems) and religion. But also recall, here, Maarschalk's view that this little animal represented the Zealots, and the false prophet was their mouthpiece for keeping other Jews in line with their rebellion against Rome. In either interpretation, neither of them can stand against the Rider on the white horse, nor against His army. That is the message of hope: Christ reigns!

The doing of the deceptive "signs," by the false/lying prophet may be an allusion to the Exodus where Pharaoh's magicians, Jannes and Jambres, "withstood Moses" (2 Tim. 3:8).

That the leadership of Judea (the false prophet) was associated with Rome (the beast) is clearly shown in Acts 4:27,
> "**For in truth** (actuality; reality) **both Herod and Pontius Pilate, together with ethnic multitudes and [the] People of Israel – [coming] upon** (= against) **Your set-apart Servant** (or: holy Boy) **Jesus, Whom You anointed – were gathered together** (thus: were made to join forces) **in this city**,"

but we see that this was all a part of God's plans, for vs. 28 continues:
> "**to do whatever** (or: as many things as) **Your hand and Your counsel** (purpose; plan; intent; design) **previously marked out the bounds for and limited beforehand to be happening** (to come to be; to occur)."

The dependent clause (set off with dashes) that immediately follows the figure called, "**the false** (lying) **prophet**," is given to describe this character in the play. It was not just any "false prophet," but a specific one that played a part in the story of the Unveiling. It (using a neutral pronoun: this could be a "he" or a "she" in the drama) "**did** (or: who does; the aorist [fact] tense) **the signs in his presence** (or: before him), **in which he led astray** (or: he deceives) **the folks taking the imprinted mark** (carve-effect) **of the little wild animal, and continually worshiping its image**," and this calls us back to 13:13-16, which tells us that its power and its character is that of a little animal, a beast. Recall that this one was "**progressively stepping up out of the midst of the Land** (or: earth)" – 13:11, above – and this tells us that it came from the lower human nature (earth, a figure of the flesh, rather than of spirit) of people. If the English term "**Land**" – rather than "earth" – is used, then we have a more specific reference to the Jewish religion, for "Land" was an OT symbol of Israel, and geographically indicated Palestine. Recall that it had "**two horns like a little lamb**" (two being the number of "witness," in the Law; "lamb" being a symbol for the sacrificial system of the temple cultus), but it "**continued speaking as [the; a] dragon**" (the Jewish leadership was adversarial to Christ, and Jesus told them that their source, i.e., their spiritual father, was "the devil" – Jn. 8:44). An example of the scribes and Pharisees making the Law and the Prophets false, or, a lie, is seen in the confrontation in which Jesus spoke boldly to them, in Mk. 7:
> 8. "**Abandoning** (Sending off; Divorcing; Letting go) **the implanted goal** (impartation of the finished product within; inward directive) **of and from God, you folks continuously keep a strong hold on the traditions of and from men.**"
> [some MSS add: – baptisms (= ceremonial washings) of pots (pitchers, jugs) and cups, and you are constantly doing many other similar things of this sort]
> 9. **Further, He went on to say to them, "You men keep on beautifully** (adroitly) **setting aside God's implanted goal** (impartation of the finished product within; inward directive and purposed destiny) **so that you can keep and maintain your tradition…"**

And in Mat. 15:6-7a, He said to them:
> "**And thus you people at once invalidate** (make void of authority; cancel and make of no effect) **God's idea, word and message through your tradition! [You] perverse scholars who in micro-scrutinizing make decisions from a low position!**

Because they rejected Jesus as the Promised One of the Prophets, the Jewish leadership became the collective "false and lying prophet." The symbol here may be an allusion to passages such as Jer. 29:23,
> "[It is] because they committed decadence in Israel… and spoke the word of falsehood in My Name, which I did not instruct them… averring [is] Yahweh" (CVOT).

Our present verse is a metaphor for God cleansing falseness from the leadership of His people. Religion has spoken lies about God, making Him appear cruel in His judgments. All these folks, who in the name of God have taken on the mark of an animal, in their thinking and in their actions, must be purged in His Fire and Deity. No matter how large a "ministry" or a following; no matter how ancient their traditions or how aged their "orthodox" dogmas, they have spoken lies about God's character. They, collectively (like the scribes, Pharisees and priests before them), have been "**the false** (lying) **prophet**." Riley (*The River of God*) traces out how pagan teachings crept into Judaism, then were passed on to Christianity:

> "Yet sometime in the 2nd millennium BCE, a revelation was made to a priest and prophet, Zoroaster, that would enter the River of God nearly a thousand years later and become one of the foundations on which Christianity would be based. According to Zoroastrian doctrine, there was only one true God, who was opposed by a nearly equal and opposite Devil.... The very idea of a fiery hell was Zoroastrian (and Greek); it shows up in Israelite texts only after the Exile.... Visible here quite easily is one form of a combination of Greco-Roman and Zoroastrian dualism... A form of that combination lies at the base of Christianity" (ibid pp 197-8, 202).

Isa. 9:15b is just one other example,

> "The prophet teaching falsehood: he is the tail [of the beast]" (Rotherham; brackets mine).

Zech. 13:2b, 3b spoke of addressing such situations:

> "Moreover, also, even the prophet and the spirit of impurity will I cause to pass away out of the Land.... For falsehood have you spoken in the name of Yahweh" (Rotherham).

The problem has been misuse of position and authority, while absorbing the thinking of the religions of other little animals (kingdom; empires; philosophies). Their words, and their teachings, need to be purified (1 Cor. 3:12-15), to be as Yahweh's words (utterances):

> "The words (utterances; sayings) of Yahweh are words that are pure [unadulterated], [as] silver, refined in a crucible of earth: purified 7 times" (Ps. 12:6, Rotherham; expansion, brackets: mine).

Much philosophy and many dualistic, pagan doctrines have polluted God's Word. In God's time, He will "**press, catch, seize and arrest** (stop)" those who are a part of "**the false and lying prophet**," and it will be said, "Well, so much for their 'free will.'"

In the book of Job we have his three "friends" spouting the conventional wisdom of their day, but when Yahweh shows up and confronts them, He says to Eliphaz, "My anger is hot against you and your two associates because you [did; do] not speak concerning Me what is rightly so (or: the thing that is right), like My servant Job [has done]" (42:7b; CVOT / Rotherham). In like manner, Jesus told His listeners,

> "**You hear** (or: heard) **that it was declared.... Yet I, Myself, am now telling you folks**..." (Mat. 5:38a, 39a).

It was not that what was said in Ex. 21:24, i.e., what they had "heard," was wrong or not "fair," but it applied to a human form of justice, and did not represent the true picture of a God of mercy and love (e.g., Rom. 11:32). The teachers of the Law had not grown up in their understanding of God's ways. Consider this sampling of invectives given by Jesus, in Mat. 23:

> 13. "**And so, tragic will be the fate for you, scribes** (scholars; theologians; Law experts) **and Pharisees – [you] overly critical and perverse folks who make decisions from a low point of view! – because you consistently shut and lock up the reign of the heavens in front of mankind**....
>
> 15. "**It will be a tragic fate for you, scribes and Pharisees – perverse scholars who live by separation and have all the answers! Because you habitually go around the sea and dry [land] to make one convert** (proselyte), **and whenever he may become** (should be birthed) **[one], you proceed making him a son of the valley of Hinnom** (= a person having the character and qualities of a city dump, or a part of a refuse depository [Greek: Gehenna]) **twice as much as yourselves**....

23. "**O the tragic fate by** (or: for; with) **you folks – scholars, theologians and experts in the Scriptures and [the] Pharisees – [you] under-discerning folks who live by close inspection of minor details: [it is] that you habitually give away a tenth** (or: tithe back) **from the mint and the dill and the cummin, and yet you abandon and let flow away the weightier** (= more important) **matters of the Law** [= Torah]**: the justice** (equity; fairly evaluated decisions), **the mercy, and the trust**...

24. "**Blind 'guides and leaders' of the way: constantly filtering and straining [out] the gnat, yet habitually gulping** (drinking; swallowing) **down a camel!**....

33. "**[You] snakes! [You] offspring** (brood) **of vipers** (poisonous serpents)**! How can you flee and escape from the judging which has the qualities, character and significance of the valley of Hinnom** (= the sentence to the city dump [Greek: Gehenna]; the deciding which pertains to the waste depository of the city)**?** [cf Jer. 19:1-15]

Read Yahweh's critique of the "shepherds of Israel" as presented in Ezk. 34. There, in vs. 22, Yahweh promises to save His flock so that they will no longer be a prey to those shepherds, and One like David will properly shepherd them. Verse 25 promises "an arrangement (covenant) of peace, from a joining," saying that He will "remove worthless (unsound, misery-gushing, malevolent) little animals (beasts) away from the Land" (LXX, JM).

We read a more neutral presentation of the old situation, which had to come to an end, in Heb. 10:1a,

"**You see, the Law** (= Torah), **holding a shadow of** (having shade from) **the impending good things** (virtues; excellent, agreeable or useful qualities or results) **– not the very image of or the same reproduced likeness from those transactions** (results of executing or performing; effects of practices)."

John put it this way,

"**the Law was given through Moses, yet grace and truth are birthed** (or: joyous favor and reality came to be) **through Jesus Christ**" (Jn. 1:17).

A shadow can distort the true image of an object. Darkness can deceive one's perceptions of a situation. The Light came to dispel the darkness, and to reveal God's Reality.

Now let us consider God's decision of what they must experience: **the lake of the Fire: the one continuously burning within the midst of [the] Deity**." For this phrase, see the discussions on 9:17 and 14:10, above. But here we want to call your attention to the fact that this, too, is an apocalyptic symbol; a figure; a metaphor. Wallace remarks that, "The lake of fire was not literal any more than the beast was literal" (ibid p 397). Note the expansion on the work commonly rendered "lake." The semantic range of the Greek word includes: "basin; artificial pool; marshy area." This may, indeed, correspond to the "brazen laver" just outside the holy place of the Tabernacle. Instead of it being literal water, for cleansing and purification, the apocalyptic image is a basin of fire, which means this is not a cleansing that a priest does, but one that God does – with Himself and His divine Nature. To supplement our perception of this strange image, on offer is the following short inquiry into this topic:

LOCATION of the LAKE of FIRE

The Unveiling presents The Lake of Fire as "**the second death**," or, death to "death and the grave (hades)" which are cast into it. Preston Eby's study on this subject (and he may have been quoting of Ray Prinzing) says that, "either we now take up our cross and follow Him as He immerses us in His Holy Spirit and Fire, or, upon the results of His judging, we will be cast into His Fire" (a paraphrase). In the end, everybody dies this second death (the death to death; the death to minding the flesh) because everyone is "salted with Fire" (Mark 9:49). But those who overcome in union with Him now will not be hurt by this process (2:11, above) – and I suspect that these folks are the agents who are present with those being tested in the Fire and Deity (14:10, above).

I also noticed that this purging time in chapter 14 is described right after the description of those who follow the Lamb (vss. 1-4), and that setting is Mt. Zion. Just as many scenes in the Unveiling are suggestive of the temple, and it is our current view that Babylon is a figure of Jerusalem, it makes us wonder about the setting for "the lake of the Fire and Deity." Isa. 29 describes Yahweh's judgment upon Jerusalem as His visiting it "with thunder and earthquake, and great noise with storm and tempest, and **the flame of devouring fire**" (vs. 6).

In Isa. 30:33 the setting is Tophet (Hebrew: altar; this was another name for the valley of Hinnom, which later, in Greek, became Gehenna) and it says "the BREATH of Yahweh, like a stream (valley; brook; wadi) of brimstone (sulphur; deity, *theion*, in LXX), consumes it." And in Isa. 31:9 we see that it speaks of Yahweh, "whose **Fire is in Zion**, and **His furnace in Jerusalem**." Recall that Heb. 12:22 tells us that we have come to, and are presently at (perfect tense), Mount Zion, unto the city of the living God, the heavenly Jerusalem.

Then in Isa. 33:5 we see that "He has filled Zion with judgment and righteousness," which shows the association of the two. And in vs. 11 He says that they "will conceive chaff and bring forth stubble [something easily burned; shades of Obad. 18, "The house of Jacob shall be a fire, and the house of Joseph a flame, and the house of Esau for stubble"]: YOUR breath, as fire, shall devour you." Then 35:14-15, "... Who among us shall dwell with the devouring fire? Who among us shall dwell with eonian burnings? He that walks righteously and speaks uprightly..."

Next we see Isa. 34:9-10,
> "And the streams thereof shall be turned into pitch, and the dust thereof into brimstone (sulphur; deity, in the LXX) and the land thereof shall become burning pitch. It shall not be quenched night nor day; the smoke thereof shall go up unto the Age: from generation to generation..."

Note that "night and day" are here on earth – as are "generation to generation."

The **second death**, which is described in 20:14, below, as "**the lake of the Fire**," equates to what Jesus referred to in Mat. 25:31-46 as the "**age-lasting** (or: eonian) **fire**" that was prepared for the devil (the adversary; the person who thrusts something through another) and his agents (vs. 41). This we see fulfilled in Rev. 19:20 and in 20:10. But we should also recall that in our Matthew passage it is the goats (literally: kids – the immature), those who did not recognize Christ in Jesus' brothers (family members, vs. 40), that did not minister to Him when He (in them) was hungry, thirsty, a stranger, naked, sick or in prison. Now although these kids were clean animals (goats were used in sacrifices to the Lord, and Christ as our atonement would have been symbolized as a goat, or kid, not a lamb), they were just "kids," i.e., immature folks who were producing no fruit of the Spirit (love for their sisters or brothers in need). Thus they are judged and to go forth "into correction for an indefinite period of time (or: eonian pruning – which switches the metaphor)." The Greek word for correction in this verse is *kolasis*, and is an agricultural term that means to prune, or correct the growth of a vine or tree. The obvious meaning is that this fire is designed to cause better growth which will produce more and better fruit.

We suggest that this lake of Fire experience is the same experience that John the baptizer spoke of when he said that Jesus would dip, or immerse, you "**within Holy Spirit and Fire**" (Lu. 3:16).

This fire is meant to burn out any cowardice, unbelief, abominable things, and that which would cause us to murder, be involved in prostitution, sorcery or idolatry, or to be false and a liar (as listed in 21:8, below). It is also meant to remove the adversary from us, rid us of false prophesying, and free us from being agents of the beast nature – all the things that would keep us from living the Christ Life, figured here by being "**written in the scroll of The Life**" (20:15).

Is there any connection between the figure of the lake of the Fire here in the Unveiling, and the figure of "the Gehenna of fire" used by Jesus in the gospels? We know that, literally, Gehenna is the Valley of Hinnom which is located to the southwest of Jerusalem, and which had become the city dump in Jesus' day. Refuse from the city, as well as bodies of criminals who were considered unworthy of burial, were dumped there to be burned. With all that decaying organic material, there were plenty of worms in the area anywhere the fire was not burning. This was the scene from which Jesus took this metaphor. Gehenna is used twelve times in the NT: 7 times in Mat.; 3 times in Mk.; once in Lu.; and once in Jas.; notice it is not found in Paul. It is first used in Mat. 5:22 where Jesus is making a comparison to the Law regarding the act of murder (vs. 21),

> "**However, I, Myself, am now saying to you people that EVERYONE, who – from internal swelling or agitated emotions of his natural disposition, or from the fruition of his mental bent – is habitually being impulsive or intensely angry to his brother** (= fellow member of the society) **will be held within the decision** (or: held under the control of the crisis or the judging of the local court). **Now whoever may at some point say to his brother, 'Raca** (an Aramaic word of verbal abuse: contemptible imbecile; worthless good-for-nothing; senseless empty-head; brainless idiot; blockhead)**!' will be held within** (and thus: accountable to) **the Sanhedrin** (the ruling Jewish council). **Yet whoever may at some point say, 'Inept moron** (Stupid scoundrel; Despicable fool; You perverse idiot)**!' will be held within** (and thus: accountable to) [placement] **into the [part of] the Valley of Hinnom which pertains to the fire** (i.e., the incinerator for refuse in the dump outside of Jerusalem)."

Note here that all the offences are against another human being; they all led to judgment and punishment by a human court; they were misdemeanors that were relatively on a par with each other. But they all came from attitudes or spirits that were contrary to love – and they needed to be cleansed out of people.

Keep in mind that the context of this saying is the "Sermon on the Mount," which was directed, first of all, to His disciples (Mat. 5:1), teaching the principles of the Kingdom (and in this case comparing them to a more serious crime in the Law: murder). Can we believe that Jesus is saying that, in the Kingdom which He is proclaiming, one can be sent to what institutional Christianity calls "eternal fire (or: hell)" for calling someone "stupid"? Is that the "good news"? In vs. 20 He had just been giving a qualification for entering into the reign of the heavens: to have a right relationship with folks that exceeded the relationship and fairness exhibited by the scribes (scholars; theologians) and the Pharisees (practitioners and experts of the Law). He was in this sermon describing the characteristics of what Paul referred to as "**the upward call in Christ Jesus**." He was presenting a narrower and more restricted path, in comparison to the broad highway of the Law and 2nd temple Judaism, which only led to destruction.

But as none can keep the Law, other than Christ, so also none can have super-abounding rightness, except for the Christ who lives within us. As another example, let us look at Mat. 5:29-30 where we see two more occurrences of "Gehenna." These involve "**looking at a woman to lust for her**" (vs. 29), and **stealing** (vs. 30). The first is an inward thought; the second an outward act. In both of these infractions the judgment is "**the whole body being cast into the**

city dump (Gehenna)." Did Jesus mean this literally? The Valley of Hinnom was a dishonorable place in which to end. It happened literally to criminals of that day.

In discussing these verses in our local gathering, Mark Austin suggested that the phrase "the whole body" may be a veiled reference to "the body of Israel" in that day. This was the end of the body politic of the Jews, in AD 70.

Was Jesus merely reiterating the Law? Did He mean that one should literally wrench out an offending eye or chop off one's own hand, if he was failing when being tempted? If so, then this is not really good news that Jesus is bringing to us. Most rational individuals will realize that Jesus was using hyperbole here: a figure of speech. He meant to get rid of those situations in which a person's weaknesses were causing him to fail. Paul addresses the same problem, as he discussed it in Rom. 7. But if Jesus' admonition, graphic as it is, is a figure of speech, then why do we suppose that failure to follow His admonition would result in a literal judgment of being cast into a literal "eternal lake of fire"? And if we are being literal, Gehenna is no longer burning – as you can see for yourself if you tour literal Jerusalem today. The lake of the Fire, spoken of in the Unveiling, is also a figure, a symbol. Again, it is called the second death in 20:14. The first death brought us into this realm of the physical life here on earth, and thus we were "**dead by and in trespasses and sins**" (Eph. 2:1); we were blind, living in the darkness of the Unseen; some of us were whited graves, full of dead people's bones (Mat. 23:37). But the second death is death to the first death (both of which are figurative, in these contexts).

The next use of the Greek "Gehenna" is in Mat. 10:28. Who were those who "are killing the body, yet are not able to kill the soul"? The Romans, the Sanhedrin, murderers. Who is He telling us to fear in the next statement? Who can "destroy the soul, as well as the body, in Gehenna"? Well, God could. Is He telling them to fear God? God can destroy the body in many ways. He uses the figures of Gehenna and the "lake of the Fire," to describe destroying the soul (the false, estranged ego, or, persona). Consider how He put it in Matt. 16:24-25,

> "... **let him deny himSELF, and take up HIS CROSS, and follow Me: for whosoever may be wanting to save his soul shall continue DESTROYING IT** [via the broad path]. **Yet whoever should be destroying his soul** (i.e., the self; the selfish ego) **on My account shall continue finding it**."

We destroy our souls by submitting to His baptism of Fire, here and now; this is taking up our crosses. But let us consider another interpretation of Mat. 10:28, from a study by the author:

> "We see that the result of judgment by the person who has the power to kill in such a manner that it effects the 'soul' also has the power to throw the entire person into the Valley of Hinnom (*Gehenna*), just like in the above examples. Who had that power? The Roman Prefect over Judea (at this time, Pilate). He could not only kill you, but also ruin your reputation and the perception of your character (your 'soul'), and also affect the lives of your family, as they might also be considered to be enemies of the Empire. This person (Pilate) killed Jesus, and for many Jews this made it hard for them to accept a 'crucified Messiah.' For them His reputation (soul) was destroyed. Remember, Jesus was speaking to an honor/shame-based society. Honor, for oneself and for one's family, was everything. Being killed just meant that your life on earth was ended (which eventually happens to everyone); being killed as a criminal meant being considered as an outcast of society with people remembering you as being a shameful person who was without honor. Your life would come to be considered as having had no value.

"Crossan informs us about Roman crucifixion with its customary lack of burial in his book, *Who Killed Jesus*, (HarperSanFrancisco, 1996). In his chapter on 'Burial,' he explains,
> 'The hierarchy of horror was loss of life, loss of possessions, loss of burial, that is, destruction of body, destruction of family, destruction of identity. For the ancient world, the final penalty was to lie unburied as food for carrion birds and beasts' (ibid p 160).

He quotes Tacitus (*Annals* 6.29) who said, 'a man legally condemned forfeited his estate and was debarred from burial' (ibid p 161). Crossan goes on to say,
> 'Lack of proper burial was not just ultimate insult, it was ultimate annihilation in the ancient Roman world. There would be no place where the dead one could be mourned, visited, or remembered…. It was precisely that lack of burial that consummated the three supreme penalties of being burned alive, cast to the beasts in the amphitheater, or crucified. They all involved inhuman cruelty, public dishonor, and impossible burial…. In the case of crucifixion, it presumes that the body was left on the cross until birds and beasts of prey had destroyed it' (ibid p 161).

Crossan also points us back to Deut. 21:22-23, where we read in vs. 23b,
> 'for [one] being hung [is under] a malediction of Elohim, and you shall not defile your ground that Yahweh your Elohim [is] giving to you [as] an allotment' (CVOT).

"This lends comprehension to the warning that Jesus gave in regard to having one's body end up in the city dump (the Valley of Hinnom, or, *Gehenna*) – the place where the Romans would ultimately deposit the human remains of one that was crucified. Crossan quotes Martin Hengel's comment (*Crucifixion*, p 88) that,
> 'In this way [the crucified person's] humiliation was made complete. What it meant for a man in antiquity to be refused burial, and the dishonor which went with it, can hardly be appreciated by modern man' (ibid p 163; brackets mine)"

(from the author's study: "Where Jesus Gave Warning of Judgment").

Mat. 18:9 is a repetition of Mat. 5:29, and Mark 9:43, 45 & 47 tell us about the same. But Matt. 23:15 makes His use of Gehenna as a figure of speech quite obvious. His is speaking of the Pharisees proselytizing, and in so doing making the proselytes "**twice as much a son of Gehenna as yourselves**" (Weymouth). The term "son of Gehenna" is "A Hebraism which equals Gehenna's people" (Bullinger), or, "folks having the qualities and characteristics of the city dump, full of dead people's bodies, and destined for shameful ruin." This is answered by what Jesus said to them in vs. 33 of this same chapter,

> "**O serpents, O generation of vipers! How can you be fleeing from the judgment of Gehenna?**"

That generation was on the "broad path which leads to destruction." It happened to them in AD 70. But what does this say to us? Perhaps just that all who have the character which Jesus describes as "serpent" are destined for the purification process. Those who receive the serpent's words and thoughts (its seeds) must endure the judgment which will burn over their fields (Heb. 6:7-8). Those who are serpents have the identity of the beast nature – the mark of the beast.

Now consider the use of this word as found in Jas. 3:6,
> "**Well the tongue [is] a fire; [its fuel is] the System of injustice** (or: the ordered and decorated but dominating world of culture, religion, politics and government which is unjust; or: The tongue, also, [is] fire: the world of disregard for what is right).

> **The tongue is placed down within our members, continuously spotting** (staining; = defiling) **the whole body, and repeatedly setting on fire the wheel of birth** (= the cycle of the origin [of life], or of generation; the wheel of genesis), **as well as being continuously set on fire by** (or: under) **the garbage dump** (the depository of refuse; Greek: Gehenna)."

If one has the nature of Gehenna (i.e., is one of Gehenna's people), "**out of the heart the mouth speaks**" (Mat. 12:34). Obviously James is speaking figuratively. We must see Gehenna as a figure, but not as a figure of an eternal place of punishment.

> "When you pass through the waters, with you I AM, or through the rivers, they shall not overflow you – WHEN YOU WALK THROUGH FIRE, you will not be scorched, and a flame shall not kindle upon you, For I – Yahweh, am your God, the Holy One of Israel, ready to save you." (Isa. 43:2, 3)

He does take us through the Fire, but He is there ready to save us even while we are within the fire, as the three Hebrews in the furnace found out (Dan. 3). The fire delivered them from their bonds, and ended in God being glorified. All things return to the Fire, for,

> "**From out of the midst of Him, and then through the midst of Him, and then INTO the midst of Him [are] ALL THINGS**" (Rom. 11:36).

Being seated with Him in the heavenlies there are no more outcries, and no more religious works, painful toil to try to please God, or misery due to our failures and mistakes: Mat. 11:28,

> "**So everyone come here, toward Me! – all those constantly weary and exhausted from toil and labor, as well as folks having been caused to carry a load, and continuing burdened down – and I, Myself, will refresh you and cause you folks to rest**."

These conditions exist now, in Christ, but we need to see that all this is true in the context of the City (21:2), and apply at this point to God's people (21:3), and the overcomer (21:7). 21:8 points out those who yet need the work of the baptism in the Spirit and Fire (the second death), and 22:15 tells us that these folks are outside the City (New Jerusalem), whose gates are never closed (21:25). [This ends the study, "Location of the Lake of Fire"]

"Fire and Deity" (vs. 20, above) is an allusion to Ezk. 38:22, in reference to Gog and the land of Magog,
> "And I will proceed judging him with (or: in; by) death and with (in; by) blood and in torrential, flooding rain and hailstones. Then I will rain Fire and Deity (the Divine Nature) upon him, and upon all those with him, as well as upon many nations (ethnic groups) with him" (LXX, JM).

Notice the association of "natural" calamities, and then the intrusion of God Himself (Fire and Deity) into the situation. Again, this is a picture of a "baptism" with, and in, "the Holy Spirit and Fire" (Lu. 3:16).

The part about the "**little animal**" is likely an allusion to Dan. 7:9b-111,
> "After this I beheld, and lo! A fourth beast, dreadful and terrible.... And I beheld till the thrones were set and an Ancient of days was seated.... His throne was a flame of fire.... A river of fire rolled before Him.... I looked then... until the beast was slain and destroyed, and its body given to be burned with fire" (*The Septuagint Bible*, [LXX] trans. by Charles Thomson, circa early 1800's, Shekinah Enterprises).

An indicator that the setting of this verse was here on earth, and in this life, is seen in the present participle: this happened (in history) to these two figures of the drama, "**while living**." God's history of judgment upon nations is clearly seen in the OT. It happened there and then. AD 70 was just another example. On an individual basis, it happens to us here, and now. We will discuss this further when we come to 20:11, below.

21. **And the remaining ones** (the rest; the ones left) **were killed off in the broadsword coming out of the mouth of Him who is continuously sitting upon the horse. And all the birds were fed until satisfied from out of their flesh.**

This looks like an allusion to Isa. 11:4b-5,
> "He will strike the Land (or: earth; soil; = the flesh of people, and their circumstances) with the club of His mouth, and with the Spirit of, and from, His lips. Righteousness will be a belt for His waist, and faithfulness, a belt for His loins."

Paul spoke of this in 2 Thes. 1:7b-8,
> "**within the midst of the uncovering** (the unveiling; the laying bare; the revelation; the disclosure) **of the Lord Jesus from [the] atmosphere** (or: sky; heaven), **along with agents of His power** (or: with His agents of ability) – **within a fire, of flame** [with other MSS: in union with a blaze of fire] **continuously giving justice** (or: repeatedly imparting the effects of fair and equitable dealings from out of the way pointed out, while maintaining equity from what is right) **among** (or: for; in; with; to) **those not knowing** (or: perceiving) **God, even among** (or: for; in; with; to) **those not continuously listening to or paying attention and obeying the message of goodness and well-being, which is our Lord, Jesus.**"

Then in 2:8 of this same letter, he said,
> "**And then** (at that time) **the lawless person** (the unlawful one; the one without law; the man who violates the Law; the person being contrary to custom) **will be uncovered** (unveiled; disclosed), **whom the Lord Jesus will take back up again** (or: lift up; [reading *anaireō* with Nestle, Tasker & Concordant texts; Griesbach & other MSS read *analiskō*: consume, use up, expend]) **by the Spirit of** (or: the Breath-effect from) **His mouth, and will deactivate** (render inoperative and useless; make inert) **by the manifestation** (the bringing of light upon and setting in full and clear view, causing an appearance) **of his** (or: its; or: His) **presence.**"

As mentioned, above, **the remaining ones**, or, "the rest," means "**the kings of the Land** (or: earth), **and their armies**" (vs. 20). Here it does NOT say that **THEY**, while living, are cast into the Fire. The point is that God has removed the political and religious systems of domination (beast and prophet) in His new creation. The **broadsword coming out of His mouth** speaks of the message of the Good News that takes all humanity to the grave, with and in Him (2 Cor. 5:14b, "**[We are] deciding** (discerning; judging) **this: that** [some MSS add: since] **One Person** (or: Man) **died over [the situation of] all mankind** (or: for the sake of all); **consequently all people died** (or: accordingly, then, all humanity died"). Remember, we are reading apocalyptic imagery, not historical narrative. The sword is not literal, and thus, neither are the deaths of all these folks, nor their flesh, nor the birds. It is a picture of the Overcomer (Christ) overcoming those who have been deceived into tribal, dualistic thinking. It is the overcoming of the false ego and the perception of separated existence.

Why are we told, in vs. 21, that "**all the birds were fed until satisfied**"? This is an echo of Ezk. 39:11-20. Is this to emphasize the abundance of flesh that needs to be consumed? May it imply that there will come an end to the need for these flesh-consumers? To aid in understanding the bird symbol, I am inserting here a short meditation about part of a parable about birds that eat seeds:

What Do the Birds Represent?

When Jesus explained the parable of the sower, He interpreted the first section – (Mat. 13:4) of the seed falling on the path, or alongside the road, and the birds coming and eating the seeds – in verse 19, where the birds are explained as symbolizing what is commonly translated "the evil one." Now this is a correct translation, however, the Greek word here, *ponēros*, has a much wider range of meaning and application than just "the evil one" or, "the wicked one."

In Christian tradition, we often hear a second level of interpretation that "the evil one" refers to the devil, or *satan*. The next step is to apply all or part of the common myth or traditional theology about the devil (or, *satan*) to the context where we find the word *ponēros*.

So in Mat. 13:19, due to these Christian traditions, we then begin to picture some dark spirit operating in the heart of the person whose "soil" is like the trodden path. *Satan* is lurking there, gobbling up the seeds of the Word (or, the message of the kingdom), so that it will not take root in his heart. Wow! What a picture: *satan*, the devil, feeding on the Word of God! Now that is quite a thought – if that be the case.

But let us look at the context of what prevents other seeds from being productive, when landing on the other types of soil. The hindrance in the "**rocky soil**" is the pressure and tribulation, along with persecution (vs. 21). The hindrance in the soil overgrown with "**thorns**" is "**the anxiety (care; worry; concern; distraction) of the age** [other MSS: this age], **and the seductiveness and deception of the riches and wealth [involved]**" (vs. 22). Now both of these hindrances are the common situations that we all face in life. They are not necessarily the work of a primordial dark spirit that is working against the kingdom of God. They are simply aspects of the environment into which we have been born.

So why should we presume that the soil which is downtrodden has the devil working in its heart? By choosing the other meanings of *ponēros* in translating verse 19, I perceive a situation which is more in line with the hindrances of vss. 21 and 22. Thus, my translation:

"**Concerning everyone constantly listening to and hearing the Word of the sovereign reign and activities** (or: the thought, idea and message of the kingdom) **and yet continuing in not understanding** (being unable to have things flow together unto comprehension)**: the worthless person or the disadvantageous circumstance** (or: the one who brings pain and misery through hard labor; the malevolent and wicked man; the evil one; or: the difficult and wearisome situation) **is repeatedly coming and is habitually snatching up what has been sown** (scattered as seed) **within his heart – this is the one sown alongside the path or road.**"

Now here are conditions to which we all can relate. We see a person whose heart has been downtrodden and is now hard. The message cannot penetrate him to where he can understand it. Perhaps he is like the one prophesied about by Isaiah, quoted in Mat. 13:15,

'**For the heart of this people was made thick and fat, and thus has become impervious, dull and insensitive, and with the ears they hear heavily, and are thus hard of hearing, and they shut** (or: closed) **their eyes** (or: they squint their eyes), **lest at some time they might see with [their] eyes and should then be listening and hearing with [their] ears, and with the heart they could make things flow together**

> **so as to comprehend – and they might turn about! And so, I will progressively cure and heal them!'** [Isa. 6:9-10]
> (or: ... and they squint their eyes! At some point should they not see with [their] eyes, and continue listening so as to hear with [their] ears, and thus understand in the heart? And then they can turn around, and I will continue healing them!')."

The "**worthless person** (*ponēros*)" may be his associate who mocks such ideas about Christ and the kingdom of God. The "disadvantageous circumstances (*ponēros*)" may be the atheistic education in which he was reared, or his drug-addiction, or her domestic abuse, or the years of poverty.

Such things, I suggest, fit better with the contexts of the other soil conditions. The birds represent adverse conditions and situation encountered in this life. If Father has not yet plowed up our downtrodden heart-paths, our associates or our environments can rob us of His words of life.

So as we consider other levels of spiritual interpretation concerning "**all the birds**" here in the Unveiling, we may want to look beyond dualistic traditions that were spawned from superstitions inherent in the animism of pagan religions. *Cf* Jer. 12:9

Note, again, in our present verse, that the remaining ones are killed with the sword of His mouth: His Word. This speaks of Christ and His body ministering the Word. It is the Word that brings an end to the beast system and to false religion. It is the Word that delivers us from false concepts, feelings of guilt or any other mental/spiritual stronghold. In 20:9, below, we see this same event described by a different metaphor: "**Then fire descends** (or: came down) **from God, out of the atmosphere** (or: sky; heaven), **and devours them** (eats them down)." Although this probably had prophetic reference to things of the 1st century, I see a need of the same in our day, too. This is why He is continually, or repeatedly, doing battle in righteousness, bringing eschatological deliverance to the world of mankind. Wallace observes:
> "As the birds devour the carrion, the truth consumes every form of error..." (ibid p 398).

In contrast to the Jewish thought of some in the 1st century, Metzger observes,
> "It is noteworthy that the victory is won by Christ's word alone without any military help from the faithful. This picture contrasts sharply with other apocalypses of the period and, in particular, with the War Scroll of the Qumran sect" (ibid p 92).

This fact echoes 12:11, above, and applies to the same situation:
> "**And they at once overcame** (or: at some point conquer) **him** (or: it) **because of and through the blood of the little Lamb, and because of the word of their witness, as well as through the message from their testimony** (that reason laid-out from the evidence, which is them) – **and they love not** (or: did not participate in union with) **their soul** (soul-life; inner selfhood) **even to** (or: until; as far as) **death**."

Zahnd gives cogent warning against drawing a literal interpretation of this chapter, saying, "A *Left Behind* theology of Revelation turns the Lamb into a beast" (*Sinners*, ibid p 173; emphasis original).

Chapter 20

We ended chapter 19 with the war between the Rider on the white horse, including His army, and the little beast, along with the false prophet and the kings of the Land. John now sees a new vision, but this one seems to follow the last in sequence, for vs. 10, below, lets us know that now the devil is cast into the lake of Fire and Deity where the little beast and the false prophet were cast, in 19:20, above. So this chapter is simply a continuation and development of the previous section. This next vision contains numerous symbols, and should be read through the lens of apocalyptic imagery. These symbols include: a) a chain, b) the Deep (the Abyss), c) the dragon-serpent-devil-*satan*, d) a key, e) locking, f) sealing, g) a little animal (beast), h) resurrection, i) life, and j) 1000 years. It begins with k) an apocalyptic "Agent" in l) the atmosphere (sky; heaven). To come to a legitimate interpretation, we must look for the figurative meanings that the author intends.

In verses 1-3, we have the devil arrested, but not yet put in the Fire with the other two. It is subdued and restrained within the Deep (the Abyss), to end its job of deception for the symbolic period (?) of 1000 years. It was the power behind the little wild animal and the false prophet (the two little beasts of chapter 13), but Yahweh was not through with it yet – there was apparently more work for it to do – so it will be released from its cage, for a little while, in order for it to finish its work, and then be returned to the primeval Fire (God), where it will be joined by death and the Unseen (*Hades*), vs. 14, and those who were not placed within the scroll of The Life (vs. 15). So what does all this mean? Let us begin our quest to discover what these things "unveil" for us.

1. **Next I saw an Agent progressively descending out of the atmosphere** (or: sky; heaven), **continually holding** (or: presently having) **the key of the Deep** (or: the abyss) **and [there was] a great chain upon His hand.**

We suggest that the **Agent** of this verse is a figure of the corporate Christ which has **the keys** of God's Kingdom, or, Reign (1:18; 3:7; 9:1, above; Mat. 16:19; Lu. 11:52; Isa. 22:22), which includes the realm signified by the symbol of the Deep (see the discussion on this topic in 9:1ff, above). The Agent is **continually holding** (or: presently having) **the key**, which is one of those that Christ gave to His followers. This Agent (the resurrected, corporate Christ) also holds "**the keys of, and pertaining to, the Death and of, and pertaining to, the Unseen** (*Hades*; *cf* 1:18, above)," and is **progressively descending**, just as is "**the set-apart** (or: holy; sacred) **city, Jerusalem**," in 21:10b, below. This is why Paul could make use of *satan* (literally: the adversary) to teach folks not to blaspheme (1 Tim. 1:20), and why the called-out folks in Rome could crush *satan* (their particular adversary) under their feet (Rom. 16:20). Remember the theme of this book: the little Lamb rules! Pagan Christianity in our day does not see *satan* as God's negative tool (Isa. 54:16), and in a dualistic mindset, many of its members continue "fighting the enemy," and "doing spiritual warfare" to try to defeat *satan* and "overthrow its kingdom" (which is non-existent). We have seen only two kingdoms in this book: God's and the world's (or: humanity's). The serpent, *satan*, is a negative tool in the hands of God (*cf* Job 1 and 2), easily bottled up at any time, as we see here in vss. 1-2.

We observe, in the next verse, that the **great chain** is for the purpose of **binding the dragon**, that **primeval serpent**. The adjective **"great"** suggests that this adversarial spirit of domination is either very large, or very strong. But as we observe in the next verse, it is no match for the **Agent**.

Saul was a great adversary to the early followers of Christ, until the risen Jesus turned him around from that path. Later, Saul's former Jewish associates, while continuing the persecution of the called-out folks, then turned against him (who was now known as Paul), and became his adversaries. Just as the Jewish leadership was the Adversary to Jesus, they continued as the Adversary to His followers. Ezk. 19:1-9 presents a lamentation for the princes of Israel. In this apocalyptic story, the leaders of Israel are portrayed as a young lion that devoured people, so the nations caught it and brought it **in chains** into the land of Egypt. The mother lion took another of her whelps and made him a young lion, and it did the same as the first lion. So the nations took him in their "pit," and brought it **in chains** to Babylon, so that his voice should no more be heard upon the mountains of Israel. This lamentation may inform the scene that we are now investigating. The **chain** may be an allusion to Judah (Jude):

6. **Besides that, those agents** (or: folks having or bringing a message) **not guarding** (keeping watch over; maintaining) **the beginning of themselves** (or: the rule of themselves), **but to the contrary, after leaving away from** (= abandoning) **the personal dwelling place** (one's own abode or habitation), **He has guarded, kept watch over and maintained under gloom** (or: thick darkness) **by imperceptible** (or: in unobservable, but effecting-all) **bonds, with a view to a judging** (a sifting and a separation for evaluating; a making of a distinction and a deciding) **of a great Day** (or: pertaining to or whose source is a great day; or: which is [the] great Day).

Because of "transliteration" (instead of "translation") of the Greek *angelos* and rendering its plural "angels" instead of "**agents**" or "folks having or bringing a message," and due to non-canonical fanciful stories of "angels," this verse has been turned into mythology in traditional interpretations because of reading sections of The Assumption of Moses and the Book of Enoch into the text of Judah which we are now investigating.

But another interpretation is viable, which reaches back into the canonical story in the book of Genesis. We suggest that those "**agents**" were the ones that were given dominion over the earth (Gen. 1:26) and had a "**personal dwelling place** ([their] own abode or habitation)" in Eden. These were Adam and Eve. They did not guard "**the beginning of themselves** (or: the rule of themselves)," but "**to the contrary, after leaving away from the personal dwelling place [Eden]**" God "**has guarded, kept watch over and maintained [them; = humanity, their corporate body] under gloom** (or : thick darkness) **by imperceptible bonds**."

We find Jesus coming "**to publicly proclaim, as a herald, to** (for; among) **captives a release and liberation**" (Lu. 4:18) and to be "**constantly shining in the dim and shadowed places, and keeping on progressively giving light within the gloomy darkness where there is no light** (or: within the midst the obscurity of The Darkness where there is no light of The Day; or: = in the ignorant condition or system)" (John 1:5a). But like these of whom Judah speaks,
> "**mankind loves the darkness** (or: the people love the dimness of obscurity and gloom; or: the humans loved the realm of the shadow) **rather than the Light, for their works** (deeds; actions) **were continuing to be bad ones** (unsound ones; wicked ones; laborious ones; toilsome ones that created bad news; wrongful ones)" – John 3:19.

Notice that God "**maintained**" and "**kept watch over**" these folks "**with a view to a judging of a Great Day**" – which we see at the cross of Jesus, the beginning of the Day of the Lord. He took the judgment of humanity upon Himself and gave us His life. But not everyone has yet been existentially given birth into this new creation, for as Paul said, it is "**every person in his own class and order**" (1 Cor. 15:23). Humanity cannot see their bonds, for they are "**imperceptible**" (Greek *a-idiois*: not-seen; un-perceived).

A parallel passage is 2 Pet. 2:4,
> 4. **For since** (or: if) **God did** (or: does) **not spare agents** (or: folks having a/the message) **– but who at one point were** (or: are) **straying from the goal** (or: when failing to hit the mark; at missing the target; upon committing error) **– but rather gave** (or: gives) **them over into an act of judging – of being repeatedly pruned** (cut back for correction), **while being constantly watched over, kept, maintained and protected – giving [them] the experience of Tartarus** [Hellenistic mythological term and concept: the subterranean world; *cf* LXX, Job 40:15 (the marshlands and wild areas around the Jordan River) and 41:23 (the caverns and lower parts of deep waters and the abyss)] **in dark, gloomy pits** (caves; caverns) [other MSS: in ropes (or: chains; bands; cords); = in bondage].

The clause "**gave them over into an act of judging – of being repeatedly pruned** (cut back for correction)" calls to mind Rom. 1:24. The description of their resultant state of being in Rom. 1:25-32 expands upon 4b, above. This has been the story of unredeemed humanity. But the Light has come:

> "**It was** (or: He was, and continued being) **the True and Genuine Light which** (or: Who) **is continuously** (repeatedly; progressively) **enlightening** (giving light to) **every person** (or: human) **continuously** (repeatedly; progressively; constantly; one after another) **coming into the world** (or: the ordered system of culture, religion, economics and government; or: the universe)
> (or: It was the real Light, progressively coming into the world {organized system}, which is progressively enlightening {or: shedding light on} every human)" – John 1:9.

(*John, Judah, Paul & ?*, Harper Brown Pub., 2013 pp 75-76)

2. **And He seizes** (or: put a power-hold on) **the dragon, the primeval** (ancient; original) **serpent, who is a false accuser and the adversary** (or: one who thrusts things through to harm or cause division, and is the opponent; a devil, even *satan*), **and He binds** (or: bound) **it** (or: him) **"a thousand years."**

In the visions that begin in chapter 12, there seems to be a link between the dragon, the sea beast and the land beast, whom we have potentially identified through the previous chapters. The beast from the sea was a figure of the Roman Empire, and the one from the Land played the religious part of the story, representing the Jewish leadership (chapter 13, above). The dragon is a figure of the domination systems of societies, the adversarial spirits that control and kill. Cultural entities tend to embody this spirit and are a part of God's purpose of the ages, but there come times where He cuts these entities off and subdues their power. That is the picture that we see here. Observe that this fierce **adversary and false accuser** is easily overcome by the **Agent** in this scene, and is **bound** by Him. This calls to mind the work of Jesus, when He spoke metaphorically of "binding the strong man," in Mat. 12:29. Recall what Jesus said to His followers, in Mat. 16:

> 19. "**I will continue giving to you the keys** [note: = means of locking or unlocking] **which have their origin and source in the reign and activities of the heavens**
> > (or: which pertain to and have the characteristics of the kingdom of the heavens; or: which belong to the sovereignty from the atmospheres; or, as a genitive of apposition: the keys which are the sovereign reign of the heavens). **And so, whatever you can** (or: may; should) **bind upon the earth will continue being [something] having been bound, and still remaining bound, within the midst of the heavens** (or: in the atmospheres). **Also, whatever you can** (or: may; should) **loose upon the earth will continue being [something] having been loosed** (unbound; untied), **and remaining free of bonds, within the midst of the heavens** (or: in the atmospheres)."

We suggest that this informs this passage of vss. 1-3, and that of 7-10, below. The action of the Agent, here, presents another picture of what we saw in 12:7-9. There the dragon was cast "into the Land (territory; earth; soil)" – i.e., the realm of natural humanity; the Land-earth-soil there, we suggest, corresponds to **the Deep** (vs. 3, below). This may correlate to Jesus casting the animistic influences (*demons*) into the swine, which in turn took them into the sea (figure of the Deep, in that incident; *cf* Mat. 8:28-32; Lu. 8:26-35). The disciples did the same thing as our apocalyptic Agent, here, and then reported it to Jesus, in Lu. 10:

> 17. **Now the seventy** [other MSS: seventy-two] **returned with joy, one after another saying, "O Lord, even the demons** (Hellenistic concept and term: = animistic influences) **are continually being subjected to us** (or: set under and arranged below for us) **within and in union with Your Name!"** [comment: 70 in Judaism = "the non-Jewish nations" – Bruce Chilton]

18. **So He said to them, "I continued gazing, contemplating and repeatedly watching the adversary** (opponent; enemy; or: satan) **suddenly falling – as lightning from out of the sky** (or: as lightning – from out of the atmosphere and heaven).

19. **"So look, and realize – I have given to you folks the authority to habitually step on and trample snakes** (serpents) **and scorpions – as well as upon all the power and ability of the enemy** (or: the hostile or adversarial person) **– and nothing will proceed in any circumstance causing you folks harm** (or: wronging you or treating you unjustly).

Paul described what we have in 20:2, showing its ultimate purpose, in Eph. 4:8-10,

8. **For this reason He** (or: it) **is constantly saying,**

"**Going up** (or: Stepping up; Ascending) **into a height** (unto [the] summit) **He led** (or: leads) **captive a captive multitude** (or: He led 'captivity' captive). **He gave** (or: gives) **gifts to mankind** (or: for, in and among the humans; to humanity)." [Ps. 68:18]

9. **Now** (or: Yet) **this "He went up** (ascended)**," what is it if not** (or: except) **that He also** [other MSS add: first] **descended** (stepped down) **into the lower parts** (or: the under regions) **of the earth** (or: which is the land; or: from the Land; or: of the ground)**?**

10. **The One stepping down** (descending) **is Himself also the One stepping up** (ascending) **far above** (back up over) **all of the heavens** (or: atmospheres; skies), **to the end that He would at once fill the Whole** (permeate and saturate everything; or: make all things full; bring all things to full measure and completion).

There may also be allusions, here, to Ezk. 32:18; 28:8; 31:16.

We see again this enigmatic "**a thousand years**." Remember, numbers in this book are ideas, not literal enumerations, and in between the first and final events of this vision we see an unspecified number of thrones where the souls of the martyrs for Jesus – and those of the resistance who refused to worship the little beast or to take its mark – live and reign with Christ for "a thousand years." This metaphorical "time" is at first glance apparently concurrent with the dragon's imprisonment, and this is all associated with what is called "the **first resurrection** (rising up)" (vs. 5-6, below). But Simmons (ibid p 369-376) has pointed us to the grammatical structure of the "thousand years" phrase in this passage. Here (vs. 2) there is no definite article ("the") modifying the phrase, but it is used in vs. 3 ("the thousand years"), which is a referential use of the article, pointing us back here, to vs. 2. The same symbol is used, in the two verses, to refer to the same feature of the vision. In vs. 4 we find the basic phrase (without "the") "**a thousand years**," again. If that same symbol was referring to its use in vss. 2-3, then it should have read "the thousand years" (some later editors added "the" to the phrase – apparently assuming that this is how the text should have read: an interpretation that was probably aimed at clarification). So vs. 4 is apparently using the "thousand years" symbol in a new situation, and thus the two uses are not necessarily concurrent. Simmons concludes that there must be "two separate thousand year periods… contemplated by the text" (ibid p 374). But this seems to be interpreting the symbol as a literal time period. However, it seems that he is correct in differentiating the uses of the "thousand years" symbol. In vs. 5 we find the definite article ("the") with the phrase, again. This referential use would point back to "a thousand years" of vs. 4. The pattern is: a, the, a, the. When we come to vs. 6, the MS evidence "is almost evenly balanced" (Metzger, *A Textual Commentary on the Greek New Testament*, 2nd Ed, ibid p 687) between the definite article ("the") being present and absent before "thousand years." In vs. 7, "the" appears again before the phrase. There, the topic is, "**the adversary** (*satan*) **will proceed being loosed from out of its prison**," a referential use pointing back to vs. 2, here. Before making any conclusions about this textual pattern of the articles, let us expand our investigation of the symbol, "**thousand years**."

The teaching by the institutional church about a "millennium" (i.e., this figure of "**a thousand years**") is primarily based upon this chapter, but the views of what is meant by "a thousand years" vary. There are three main views:

> 1. Amillennialism: basically that 1000 yrs. is a figure of speech, or a symbol, like other numbers in this book; that Christ and His church are presently reigning in His kingdom, which is a spiritual kingdom – one not of this "world." The present form of God's kingdom will be followed by Christ's "return to earth," then there will be the "general resurrection," the "final judgment" and Christ's continued, "literal, physical reign" over the perfect kingdom on this new earth, in an "eternal state" of this new existence.
> 2. Premillennialism: views the 1000 yrs. as literal, and that Christ will physically return to earth and set up a physical kingdom which will begin the 1000 yrs. So, following "the final resurrection," the "last judgment," and the renewal of the literal heavens and the earth, this "future, temporal/earthly kingdom" will merge into the "eternal kingdom," and the Lord will reign "forever" on this new earth.
> 3. Postmillennialism: The world, i.e., the aggregate of humanity, will at some point be turned to Christ which will inaugurate a long period of peace and prosperity, termed the "millennium." This "future period" will come to an end with Christ's "second coming," followed by the "resurrection of the dead," the "final judgment," and the "eternal state of existence."

In these three short doctrinal abstracts, I have put various "theological" and "doctrinal" concepts in quotation marks, as being pertinent to these doctrinal views. Each of these doctrinal positions is futurist, placing this "event" in the future.

The Preterist view is generally amillennial in that it sees the 1000 years as a symbol, and there are also varieties of preterism in the field of eschatology. Most of these view this passage as completely figurative, and have come to the conclusion that the term "1000 years" is not a literal period of time. But for the most, they apply this passage to the 1st century, which is now history for us. "Partial Preterists" may see this particular chapter as yet a future event, at the "end of the ages." Except for the amillennialists, all other points of view see this as happening some time in history – the question is at which point.

If we consider "the kingdom of God within [us]" – the microcosm, so to speak – we can see personal applications for the pictures in this passage. In this application of the vision, the Agent progressively (or: continually) descending in vs. 1 is Christ, Who comes down into the "Deep," the Abyss within us, and there binds the dragon within so that it can no longer lead us astray or deceive us through deceptive thoughts and perceptions (as the serpent was portrayed as acting, in the Garden of Eden story). This dragon is an apocalyptic image of the beast nature which ascends out of this Deep (11:7, above) within each of us in order to slay the witness of Jesus in our lives. But here we see that Christ will repeatedly descend, as needed and progressively deeper, within us, to bind it and to resurrect the witness into the realm of the heavenlies (11:11-12, above).

The number 1000 is a figure derived from 10 X 10 X 10. The aspect of years signifies that this applies to the realm of time and our life, here on earth. The only thing used as a type and a shadow from the OT, to give us the key to understand this symbol, is the dimensions of the Holy of holies, in the Tabernacle (itself being a type of the body of Christ). It measured 10 X 10 X 10. We first heard of this correlation through the teaching of Malcolm Smith. The "1000 years" is a figure of the dwelling place of God within us during the ages. It speaks of the "length and width and height" of "the depths of God" (Eph. 3:18; 1 Cor. 2:10b). It is a figure of the kingdom of God, and thus do we see the phrase in vs. 4, below, "**they live and reign** (or: lived and reigned) **with the Christ** (the Anointed One) **one thousand** [other MSS: the thousand] **years**." Simmons comments,

"As a large number, one-thousand uses *quantity* to describe *quality*. For example, an empire of a thousand years suggests more than its length or duration, it implies its *greatness*" (ibid p 365).

Jean-Pierre Ruiz simply states,

"The period of a *thousand years* is symbolic both here and in vss. 4-7..." (*The New Oxford Annotated Bible*, Oxford Univ. Press, 2001, NT p 445 n 20.2-3).

Cf Deut. 7:9, "a thousand generations." And then there is Ps. 91:7, "A thousand shall fall at your side..." We can observe the intended hyperbole in Ps. 50:10b, "For every beast (or: animal) in the forest [is] Mine, and the cattle upon a thousand hills (or: mountains)." 2 Pet. 3:8 is a classic verse that shows the metaphorical and enigmatic use of this number, indicating that it is really speaking of the Day of the Lord, or, the realm of God's reign:

"**let it not continue unnoticed, escape your detection, or be hidden from you – beloved ones, one Day beside the Lord [is] as a thousand years, and yet a thousand years [is] as one Day**."

Kaplan also brought to the table some good OT references that shed light on this topic. Speaking of the new Day of the new creation (or: God's reign), Isa. 60:19-20a, 22a, instructs us,

"No longer shall the sun be your light by day... But Yahweh will become your light eonian, and your Elohim your beauty. No longer shall your sun set.... The smallest shall become a thousand." (CVOT).

Then in Ps. 84:10a we read:

"Better [is] a Day, in Your courts, than a thousand..." "This speaks of a Day of reigning" (Kaplan).

Kaplan points to the sense of endless duration that Scripture portrays:

"O Yahweh, You Yourself have become our Habitation (or: dwelling place) in generation after generation. Ere the mountains were born and You travailed [with the] earth and [the] habitance: from age unto age You are God. You turn a mortal back to crushed dust, and then say, 'Return, you sons of Adam (or: humanity),' for a thousand years, in Your eyes [are] as yesterday... or [as] a watch in the night..." (Ps. 90:1-4; CVOT, Rotherham).

He then noted that no one in the OT was recorded as living to 1000 years. One thousand speaks of fullness, which is only attained in God's realm and reign – the sphere of God's greatness, i.e., in Christ. He further suggested the symbol of 1000 being parallel to the term "many." In 1:15, 14:2, 17:1, and 19:6, above, we see "many waters;" in 5:11 we have "many agents/messengers;" in 10:11, "many peoples;" in 19:12, "many crowns." This also calls to mind Heb. 2:10, "many sons," which corresponds to the 144 thousand of 7:5-8 and 14:1, above, and the "many abodes (dwelling places)" – our Father's house – of Jn. 14:2. This symbol sets the scene of "extensiveness," and "completeness," which eventually involves "THE MANY" of Rom. 5:15, 16, 19; as well as "many" in Rom. 8:29; and 12:4, 5, 20. Keep in mind: numbers, in the Unveiling, are ideas.

The dragon, taken figuratively, is for a little time loosed within us in order to fester up all ungodliness within us so that God's Fire can devour any remaining unrighteousness yet in our "land/soil/earth." This is the process of deliverance, purification and sanctification, and Christ is the Agent Who knows when the dragon needs to be loosed, and thus used for God's purposes in our lives. Recall that an agent of *satan* WAS GIVEN to Paul – another "fruit of the spirit;" adversity (?) – "lest [he] should be lifted up by the transcendence of the revelation" (2 Cor. 12:7, CLNT). So we have here a picture which tells us that God, through Christ as the Agent, has complete control of the devil, or, *satan*, i.e., any spirit of adversity or opposition: in ourselves, and in others. This is an important part of "the gospel," the GOOD NEWS.

Note how I translated vs. 2-3: it does NOT say here that He bound, or **binds** (aorist tense) it "for" a thousand years, because there is no preposition or conjunction in the Greek text. The binding and the casting into the Deep are each metaphors associated with the figuré "1000 years," which signifies our innermost being, our holy of holies – the place from where Christ reigns, and the infinite source within us where God imprisons our adversary, until it is time for it to be transformed in the Consuming Fire, which we will see pictured in vs. 10, below.

At this point we are presented with a picture of the positive side of the situation, and in vs. 4 we see thrones, and the Overcomers sitting upon them. These are the same ones noted in 12:11, above, who "**overcame** [the dragon] **because of the blood of the little Lamb, and** (or: even) **because of the word** (or: message; Word; Logos; laid-out expression) **of their witness** (evidence; testimony) **– and they love not** (or: did not love) **their soul** (soul-life; inner self; personhood) **even to** (or: until) **death**."

Now authority to judge is given to them and these LIVE and REIGN WITH Christ, seated with Him in His throne (3:21, above) – and His throne (figured by the Mercy Seat on the Ark) is in the sphere of the 10 X 10 X 10, the holy of holies, the place where He speaks to us. In Ex. 25:22 we see, "And I will meet with you there, and will speak with you from off the propitiatory (mercy-seat – Young), from between the two cherubim, which are upon the ark of the testimony" (Rotherham). This is the "1000 years" kind of reign: as we live with Christ, in His presence in the Holy of Holies, in the heaven within us. It is a figure for God's kingdom and the Age of the Messiah (eonian Life).

This living and reigning with Christ (both within, now, and outwardly as He directs us) IS the FIRST (or: foremost) RESURRECTION (vs. 5, below). The rest of the dead folks, being yet dead, are not living within this realm yet. When the "1000 years" (this realm in Christ – the body of the Anointed One, the full stature in Christ) are finished, matured and brought to the attainment of the goal, then (vs. 3, below) they will loose *satan* (an adversarial spirit) from within in order to bring about a consummation upon the whole land (specifically, the land of Israel – the called-out community) where the Fire can descend from the heaven within them (the Lord roaring out of Zion, His body – Joel 3:16; Amos 1:2) and devour the enemies of His people's spirits (vs. 9, below). With this overview, let us continue reading.

3. **Then He casts** (or: threw) **it** (or: him) **into the Deep** (or: abyss) **and He closes** (or: shut; locked) **and seals** (or: stamped with a seal) **over upon it** (or: him), **to the end that it** (or: he) **can no longer** (or: would not still) **deceive** (lead astray; cause to wander) **the multitudes** (the nations; the non-Israelites; the ethnic groups), **until the thousand years may be ended** (finished, completed, perfected; brought to the destined goal; can have its purpose fulfilled). **After these [events; things], it is necessary for it to be loosed [for] a little time.**

Again, notice the complete control that the Agent (Christ) has over the "devil" and "*satan*." This message must not be missed. Such spirits are OUR adversaries (1 Pet. 5:8), not God's. They are His tools. This picture is an echo of 12:9, above, where the dragon was cast out of "heaven" (the realm of our spirits) and into our earth. The Deep (abyss), was another term for the sea: a part of the earth realm.

Being **cast into the Deep** (the abyss) is only a temporary situation and location. We find its final place and end, or goal, in vs. 10, below. So why is it locked-away for this relatively short "time," or in the presence of this cubic (10 X 10 X 10) sphere of existence? Why not put it directly into "**the lake** (or: basin; artificial pool; marshy area) **of the Fire and Deity** (or: which is Fire, even Divine Nature)"? We actually have a precedence for such an action in Jesus' wilderness testing in Mat. 4. There, the "**examiner**" (vs. 3; note its function), that is called "one who thrusts [something] through a person; the devil" (vs. 5), proceeds to bring the tests, trying to **deceive** and trap Jesus, and then (vs. 11) we find that, "**the opponent** (the adversary; the one who had been thrusting [Him] through) **progressively flowed away from Him** (or: proceeded to divorce Him; presently abandoned Him)." Lu. 4:13 adds this important detail:

"**upon concluding and bringing all [of the] test and examination to its goal, the adversary** (the through-thruster) **withdrew and took a stand away from Him, UNTIL an appointed season** (or: a fertile moment; a fitting, convenient or opportune situation)."

What does this mean to us? We suggest that these symbols are saying that as we inhabit Christ's reign (the sphere of His presence in our "holy of holies" – the dwelling place of God within us) and are seated with Him in His atmosphere (the heavenlies – Eph. 2:6), Christ seals up our inner adversary so that it "**can no longer** (or: would not still) **deceive [us]** (lead [us] astray; cause [us] to wander)." The **thousand years** is a symbol of the situation that Paul referred to in Col. 3:3,

> "**you folks died, and your life has been hidden so that it is now concealed together with the Christ, within the midst of God** (or: in union with God)."

When we are awake to this, and conscious to this reality, the opponent is locked and sealed within our Deep, until Christ has no further use for it in this form, then it will be transformed and purified in Himself, Who dwells within us.

Another layer of interpretation can be observed in the symbol of **the Deep** representing the masses of humanity: **the multitudes** (the nations; the non-Israelites; the ethnic groups). This would have told the called-out communities that when "Abiding in Jesus" (Jn. 15:1ff; another allusion of "a 1000 years") the dragon is removed from their communities, and restrained. "*Satan*" is under their feet, in this situation. And furthermore, it is restricted from interfering with their outreach to **the multitudes**. Even within the ethnic multitudes its influence will be **sealed** so that it cannot mix **deception** into the proclaiming of the Good News.

But as night follows day, seasons change and we all come into further testing as God uses the examiner as a tool of further purification on this journey into the depths of the Father. Even though the "*demons*" were subject to the disciples, they experienced failure when Jesus was taken by the Jewish authorities. Recall that the serpent was not cast out of the Garden of Eden. It is a part of us (the Garden was a metaphor for us) until its work is done. We will not see it, nor the tree of the knowledge of good and evil, in the New Jerusalem garden (chapter 22, below). Our journey ends in a Garden that has been made new (21:5, below). In Christ, the serpent is hung on the pole (Nu. 21:8-9; Jn. 3:14).

Simmons insightfully observes,
> "The release of the Dragon is manifested in the form of the Beast that rises from the Bottomless Pit (Rev. 11:7; 17:8)" (ibid p 366).

We will come to its being "**loosed [for] a little time**" in vss. 7-9, below. That "little time" is associated with our brief time on this earth; the realm of our "flesh,"

> "**All flesh [is] like grass** (or: vegetation), **and all its glory [is] like a flower of grass** (of vegetation): **the grass is caused to dry out and wither, and the flower falls off**" (1 Pet. 1:24).

4. **And I saw thrones – and they sit** (or: sat; are seated) **upon them, and judgment-effect** (decision-result; judicial process and verdict) **is given by them** (or: authority to judge was given to them; decisions and separations are made by them) **– and souls** (inner lives) **of those being ones having been cut with an axe** (= beheaded) **because of the testimony** (witness; evidence) **of** (or: pertaining to and on behalf of; from; which is) **Jesus, and because of the Word of, from, and which is God – even those** (or: also the ones) **who do not** (or: did not) **worship the little wild animal** (or: beast), **nor its image, and do not** (or: did not) **take** (or: receive) **the imprinted mark** (engraving; carve-effect; result of sculpting) **upon their forehead and upon their right hand – and they live and reign** (or: lived and reigned) **with the Christ** (the Anointed One) **a thousand** [other MSS: the thousand] **years.**

The scene develops, and John records what he saw. The setting has evolved beyond the scenes 4:4, and 5:9-10, and of the little wild animals of chapter 13, above, and the picture presented is that of the called-out communities that have been, "**jointly roused and raised** (or: suddenly awakens and raises) **up, and caused to sit** (or: = enthroned) **together within the things situated upon** [thus, above] **the heavens**" (Eph. 2:6). These do not have **the imprinted mark** (= identification; sign of ownership; character) in their thinking (**forehead**) or action (**right hand**) that is associated with the beast (**little wild animal**) systems of the world. These **souls** (= people) are now enthroned, and even though they had been beheaded, now "**they live and reign** (or: lived and reigned) **with the Christ**" in the setting symbolized apocalyptically by the phrase "**a thousand years**," and which Paul described as being "**upon the heavens**

> (or: in union with the full, perfected heavenlies; or, although neuter: among those comprising the complete and perfected heavenlies; in union with the celestials; among the folks [residing] upon the atmospheres) **within and in union with Christ Jesus**" (Eph. 2:6).

The first clause presents an allusion to Dan. 7:9, and the last clause alludes to vss. 18, 27,
> "I was perceiving until thrones were situated, and [the] Transferrer of Days sat [down].... Yet the saints of [the] supremacies shall receive the kingdom, and they shall safeguard the kingdom unto the eon.... And the kingdom and the jurisdiction and the majesty of [the] kingdom under the entire heavens [will be] granted to the people of [the] saints of the supremacies. Their kingdom [is an] eonian kingdom, and all [other] authorities shall serve and hearken to them" (CVOT).

What we read in Ps. 122:3-5 suggests the setting, here:
> "Jerusalem! that has been built a true city all joined together as one; whither have come up the tribes of Yah, a testimony to Israel, to give thanks unto the Name of Yahweh; for there are set thrones for justice; thrones for the house of David" (Rotherham). *Cf* 4:4, above.

Another allusion is to Mat. 19:28,
> "**So Jesus said to them, "It is true** (or: Truly; Amen), **I now am saying to you men, In the rebirth – when the Son of the Man** (mankind's Son; = Adam's son; [or: the eschatological messianic figure]; or: the human) **can sit upon the throne of His glory** (or: the throne of his good reputation and manifestation which calls forth praise) **– you yourselves, the ones following Me, will continue sitting down – even you, upon twelve thrones** (or: seats; chairs) **– continuously separating [issues], making decisions and administering justice for the twelve tribes of Israel.**" *Cf* Lu. 22:30

Likewise, Paul refers to this same situation in 1 Cor. 6:2a,
> "**Or have you not seen so as to know that the set-apart folks** (the saints; the holy, sacred people; the different-from-the-profane folks) **will proceed to sift, separate, evaluate and decide about the organized System** (the world of culture, religion and government; or: secular society; or: = the Roman Empire)**?**"

We saw the beginning of this in the book of Acts, which in turn was a manifestation of Mat.25:34, 46b.

The "**souls** (inner lives) **of those being ones having been cut with an axe** (= beheaded) **because of the testimony** (witness; evidence) **of** (or: pertaining to and on behalf of; from; which is) **Jesus**" are those seen in 12:11, above, and 6:9-11, above. These were the same ones to whom John addressed this letter, in 1:9-10, above, "**I, John, your brother and joint-participant** (or: sharer of common-being/partnered-existence) **within the pressure** (squeezing; affliction; tribulation; oppression) **and kingdom... because of God's Word** (or: the message which is God; the thoughts and ideas from God) **and because of the testimony** (witness; evidence) **pertaining to and having the characteristics of Jesus Christ.**" An allusion can also be seen to 12:5, above, with the symbol of the corporate "manchild," "**an adult man** (or: male; masculine one) **Who is about to continuously shepherd** (tend and protect) **all the multitudes** (ethnic groups; nations) **in the sphere of and with relying on the use of an iron staff** (or: rod). **Later, her child was snatched away** (seized and carried off by force) **toward God and to His throne.**"

Recall mention of this as an award of the overcomers in 3:21, above. This present scene is tying all these threads together in this wonderful spiritual tapestry.

The functions of people sitting on thrones has other OT allusions:
"O Elohim, bestow Your [right] judgments on the king, and Your righteousness on [the] royal son; may he adjudicate Your people with righteousness…" (Ps. 72:1-2a; CVOT)
"He will judge the poor with righteousness and arbitrate for the humble of the Land with equity…" (Isa. 11:4a; CVOT).
"Behold, [according] to righteousness a King shall reign; as for chiefs, [according] to [right] judgment shall they control. A Man will be like a hiding place [from the] wind; and a place of concealment [from the] storm…" (Isa. 32:1-2a; CVOT).

Paul made reference to these in 2 Tim. 2:11-12a,
"**You see, since we died together with [Him]** (or: For if we jointly die), **we will also continue living together** (or: proceed in jointly living; constantly co-live); **since we are continuously remaining under for support** (or: if we continue patiently enduring), **we will also continue reigning** (performing royal activities and influence) **together with [Him]**…"

He also said that we would, "**continue reigning** (or: ruling as kings) **within and in union with Life through the One, Jesus Christ**" (Rom. 5:17b).

Some interpreters have viewed the **thousand years** as a symbol denoting a long, though indefinite period. It is seen as the eon, or age, or ages, which begins with what John saw in 19:11-16, above, and then continues until the fulfillment of 1 Cor. 15:25. We suggest that this symbol is a figure for "eonian Life," or, "the Age of the Messiah," the "new creation," which has nothing to do with "time." But it happens "in time," i.e., during our life here on earth.

Paul spoke of the **living and reigning**, mentioned here, as an already realized situation:
"**Since, therefore, you folks were awakened and are raised up together in the Christ** (or: If, then, you are aroused and raised with the Anointed One), **be constantly seeking and trying to find the upward things** (or: the things being above), **where the Christ is** (exists being), **continuously sitting within the right [side]** (or: at the right [hand]; = at the place of receiving, and in the place of honor and the power) **of God**" (Col. 3:1). *Cf* Rom. 6:5

Jesus also spoke of this situation, in Jn. 17:24,
"**Father, I continue purposing and intending** (or: willing; wanting) **that those also, whom You have given to Me and that I now possess, would continuously exist being with Me where I, Myself, am** (continuously exist being)…"

Take note that Jesus did NOT say, "where I, Myself, WILL be." He was referring to a sphere of existence, and to a relationship, that Jesus was THEN demonstrating, and which His disciples would also experience upon the advent of His Holy Spirit coming upon them in the new creation, on the Day of Pentecost (Acts 2).

5. **But the remaining** (the rest) **of the dead ones do not** (did not) **live until the thousand years may be caused to reach the purposed and destined goal** (or: would be finished, concluded or ended). **This [living and reigning with Christ is** (or: This thousand years represents)**] the first resurrection.** (or: The first rising up [is] this:)

The last verb of the first statement should be first considered, to determine which meaning of its semantic range best fits the context. We have chosen as the best reading, which concords with the symbolism of what we have seen in regard to "the thousand years," as being: "**may be caused to reach the purposed and destined goal.**" This is a passive aorist, subjunctive. The **thousand years**, being a figure for the reign of the called-out communities, with Christ, is characterized in the second statement of this verse as being "**the first resurrection.**" This is a spiritual standing up out of the previous condition of, "**continuously existing being dead ones**" (Eph. 2:1). The **first resurrection** is also described as our new situation and condition, in Eph. 2:6.

So this **thousand years**, this "reigning with Christ," will continue until it has been **caused to reach the purposed and destined goal**: the bringing-to-life of all of humanity, through the work of the called-out communities (or: the remaining part of the first Adam being resurrected to be a part of the life-giving Spirit of the last Adam (1 Cor. 15:45, 48); or: the completion of the birth of the Family, which is God, that has been born from above by the Jerusalem which is Above, who is our mother – Gal. 4:26). As this ministry of Life continues, individuals of "**the remaining** (the rest) **of the dead ones**" will be given the Breath-effect, and will themselves come to be Life-engendering spirits – until the goal of "All within all" has been reached. So we read in 1 Cor. 15:25-27a, 28,

> "**For it is binding and necessary for Him to be continuously reigning** (ruling as King; exercising sovereignty) **until which [time or situation]** (or: until where) **He would put** (or: may place; could set) **all the things that have or hold ruin** (or: the enemies) **under His feet. [The] last holder of ruin** (or: enemy; quality having ill-will) **being progressively brought down to idleness** (made unemployed and ineffective; rendered useless and unproductive) **[is] the Death** (or: Death, a last enemy, is being presently nullified and abolished). **For you see,**
> > '**He completely arranges, humbly aligns and then appends and puts under shelter all humanity** (or: subjoins, supportively arranges in subordination, and brings under full control, all things) **under His feet** (= as supporting forces in His kingdom)'" [Ps. 8:6]….
> **Now whenever the whole** (or: all things) **may be completely supportively-aligned in Him** (or: subjected/appended to Him; subordinately sheltered and arranged for Him), **then the Son Himself will also continue being supportively aligned to, fully subjoined for and humbly attached under as an arranged shelter in, the One subjecting, appending and sheltering the whole in Him** (or: attaching all things to Him), **to the end that God can be all things within the midst of and in union with all humanity** (or: may be everything in all things; or: should exist being All in all; or: would exist being everything, within the midst of everyone)."

We who are joined to the Vine are now where He is, and partake of the Life of the Sap (Spirit) of the Vine; this is the **first resurrection**. We are the **thousand years**, another figure for the Age of the Messiah.

The other **thousand years** is the sphere and existence of the dragon spirit of domination and control (the ages, or living, apart from the Vine; being dead in failures and sin). It is bound and imprisoned by the **thousand years** of liberation, healing and restoration in Christ. They are contrasting spheres of being: heaven, and earth.
Terry observes,

> "Nothing is said, either here or in vss. 12 and 13, of a rising up from the dust of the earth or a resuscitation of mortal bodies…. The word *resurrection* is here no more to be pressed into a literal significance than the words *thrones* and *books* and *lake of fire*, but *the first resurrection* is expressly shown in the context to be a *living and reigning with Christ*" (ibid p 452; emphasis original).

Wallace points us to Ezk. 37:1-14 (which, incidentally, leads us into the Ezk. 38-39, in vss. 8-10, below) as an example of "a figurative or spiritual resurrection" (ibid p 404ff) where, being in captivity, Israel had described their situation: "Our bones are dried and our hope is lost (our expectation has perished); we are cut off from our parts (we have gotten ourselves severed)" – vs. 11b. Their resurrection (of the valley of dry bones) was a figure of their release from captivity. Jerusalem of the 1st century was still in figurative exile, now under the dominion of Rome. "Taking Israel out of the land of their captivity and bringing them back to their own land was called a resurrection. They were in the grave of captivity in Babylon, yet they were a living people.... When the Jews were **converted** to Christ under the gospel, it was **the receiving** of them '**as life from the dead**'" (Wallace, ibid p 406-7, citing Rom. 11:15b).

Mark well John's definition: **This [living and reigning with Christ is** (or: This thousand years represents)**] the first resurrection**. It is the Age of Messiah; it is "eonian Life in Christ."

6. **Blessed and happy and set-apart** (holy) **[is] the one holding** (or: having) **a divided part** (a piece) **within the first resurrection** (rising up) – **upon these the second death has no authority** (does not continue holding right or privilege; possesses nothing from the sphere of existing), **but rather, they will continue being priests belonging to God and to the Christ** (or: priests pertaining to God and the Anointed One; or: God's, even Christ's, priests; or: priests from God and Christ), **and they will continue reigning and exercising sovereign influence with Him the** [other MSS: a] **thousand years.**

This corresponds to 2:11b, above, where the overcomer is not hurt from **the second death**, and also to 1:6 which states that He has made us (or: made "of us," reading with C) **a kingdom: priests** (or: a **priesthood** – other MSS) for God. *Cf* 5:10, above. The overcomer has been "baptized within Holy Spirit and Fire (Lu. 3:16); she/he has been baptized "with the baptism that [Christ was] baptized with" (Matt. 20:22); she/he has renounced self, picked up his/her cross (figure of the death of the estranged soul) and has followed the Lord (Matt. 16:24-25). *Cf* 14:13, above. Now she/he is "**holding** (having) **a divided part** (a piece) **within the first resurrection** (rising up). Paul gives the best commentary on this new situation, in Rom. 6:
> 4. **We, then, were buried together in Him** (or: by Him; with Him), **through the immersion** (baptism) **into the death, to the end that just as** (or: in the same manner as) **Christ was roused and raised forth from out of the midst of dead folks THROUGH THE GLORY of The Father** (or: which is the Father), **thus also we can walk around** (or: we also should likewise conduct ourselves) **within newness of life** (in union with life characterized by being new in kind and quality, and different from that which was former).
> 5. **For since we have been birthed** (have become; have come to be) **folks engrafted and produced together** (or: planted and made to grow together; brought forth together; congenital) **in, by, to and with the result of the likeness of His death, then certainly we shall also continue existing [in and with the effects of the likeness] of The Resurrection**
>> (or: which is the resurrection; or: from, and with qualities of, the resurrection),
> 6. **while constantly knowing this by intimate experience, that our old, former humanity is crucified together with [Him], to the end that the body of the Sin** (the corporal manifestation that pertains to the deviation; the group of people [Adam] who missed the target) **could and would be rendered useless and inoperative** (made null, inactive and unemployed), **for us to no longer continually be a slave to the Sin,**
> 7. **for you see, the One at one point dying has been eschatologically released and rightwised away from the Sin**
>> (or: set in the Way pointed out, away from the Failure; turned in the right direction, away from the deviation and missing of the target; placed into equity and right relationships,

away from error; = has been delivered and moved away from The Sin, and has been brought into participation in covenant relationship).

8. **Now since we died together with Christ, we are continuously believing** (relying; trusting) **that we shall also continue living together in Him** (by Him; for Him; to Him; with Him)....

10. **for what He died He died for the Sin** (or: by the Failure; in the deviation; to the Sin; with the Error) **once for all [time and people]** (or: at once and only once); **yet what He lives** (or: Yet [the life] which He continues to live), **He continues living in God** (for, to, by and with God).

11. **Thus you folks, also, be logically considering** (reckoning, accounting and concluding) **yourselves to exist being dead ones, indeed, by the failure to hit the target** (or: in the Sin; or: to the deviation), **yet ones continuously living by God** (in God; for God; to God; with God), **within Christ Jesus, our Owner** (or: in union with [the] Anointed Jesus, our Lord and Master).

He gives further commentary on this in 1 Cor. 15:

42. **Thus also** (or: In this way too) **[is] the resurrection of the dead people. It is habitually** (repeatedly; presently; one after another) **being sown within corruption** (or: in union with decay and ruin; in perishability); **it is being habitually** (or: presently; repeatedly; one after another) **awakened and raised up within incorruption** (non-decayability; imperishableness).

43. **It is constantly being sown within dishonor** (in union with lack of value; in the midst of worthlessness), **it is being habitually** (or: repeatedly; constantly; one after another; progressively) **awakened and raised up within, and in union with, power and ability.**

44. **It is habitually** (continually; repeatedly; presently) **being sown a body having the qualities and characteristics of a soul** (a soulish body; or: = a body animated by soul; or: = a natural entity); **it is habitually** (repeatedly; constantly; presently; one after another) **being awakened and raised up a spiritual body** (a body having the qualities and characteristics of the Breath-effect; or: = a spiritual entity). **Since there is a soulish body** (or: = body animated by soul), **there also is** (or: exists) **a spiritual one** (or: = one animated by spirit).

45. **Thus also** (or: In this way also), **it has been written, "The first human** (or: man), **Adam, came for existence** (or: was birthed) **into [being] a living soul"** [Gen. 2:7]; **the Last Adam into [being] a continuously life-making** (life-engendering; life-creating; life-giving) **Spirit** (or: Breath-effect; Attitude).

46. **Nevertheless, the spiritual [is] not first, but rather the one having the qualities and characteristics of a soul** (the soulish), **then afterwards, the spiritual** (that pertaining to and having the qualities of Breath-effect and Attitude).

47. **The first human** (person; man) **[was/is] forth from out of the earth** (land; ground; soil; dirt), **made of moist soil and mud** (or: having the quality and characteristics of moist dirt that can be poured); **the Second Human** (Person; Man; [other MSS add: {is} the Lord]) **[is made] out of heaven** (or: [is] from [the] atmosphere and sky; [p46 reads: {is} spiritual]).

[note: the phrases describing the materials, or the origins, of the two humans are parallel in the Greek MSS from which I have given the bold rendering]

48. **As [is] the person made of and having the character and quality of moist soil or mud** (or: pourable dirt), **of such sort also [are] the people [who are] made of and have the character and quality of moist soil or mud** (soil-ish folks); **and likewise, as [is] the Heavenly Person** (or: the one made of and having the quality and character of the supra-heaven), **of such sort also [are] the supra-heavenly people – those made of and having the quality and character of the supra-heaven** (or: the finished and perfected atmosphere, or the added sky).

49. **And correspondingly as we bear and wear the image of the dusty person,** [p46 adds: doubtless] **we can and should** [B reads: will continue to] **also bear and wear the image of the supra-heavenly One** (or: belonging to the One having the quality and character of the finished and perfected atmosphere; or: from the fully-heaven [sphere]; of the added-sky person).

Notice vs. 49b, "we **can** and **should** also bear and wear the image of the supra-heavenly One." That means here, and now. Jesus adjusted Martha's perception of both "the Last Day," and "the Resurrection," saying,

> "**I am the Resurrection** (or: the standing back up again; the Arising) **and the Life. The one progressively believing and habitually putting trust into Me, even if he may die-off** (or: die-away), **will continue living** (or: will proceed being alive)!" (Jn. 11:25).

Christ is the Age, the 1000 years, the new creation, the Resurrection, the Rebirth (Mat. 19:28), the Life.

Note the expansion on the word **no authority**: nothing from the sphere of existing. The noun *exousias* literally means "from out of being/existing." These "**blessed and happy and set-apart**" folks that possess the reign (or sovereign influence) of the heavens (Mat. 5:3) ARE **the first resurrection** (rising up). They are those to whom John sent this letter (1:6, above). Paul wrote to Titus,

> "**down from and corresponding to His mercy, He delivered us** (or: He saves, rescues and restores us to the wholeness and health of our original condition) **through a bath of and from a birth-back-up-again** (or: [the] bathing of a regeneration; note: can = a ritual immersion pool of rebirth) **and a making back-up-new** (of a different kind and quality) **again from a set-apart Breath-effect**
>> (or: of a renewal and renovation whose source is [the] Holy Spirit; or: a set-apart spirit's creating or birthing [us] back-up-new-again; a renewal which is a holy attitude)" (3:5b).

Resurrection, here in the *Unveiling*, is a symbol. "The fact that they had to be told that it was a resurrection is proof that it was used in an unusual sense of the word; it was a figurative, metaphorical use..." (Wallace, ibid p 416).

Chilton goes on to say, "The first resurrection... is our re-creation in His image, our participation in His Resurrection.... The First Resurrection is taking place now. Jesus Christ is reigning now (Acts. 2:29-36; Rev. 1:5). And this means, of necessity, that 'the Millennium' is taking place now as well" (ibid p 518). Malcolm Smith again concurs, saying that the 1st resurrection "takes place in our spirits when we are born again."

Prinzing notes a different Greek word that is often translated "arose," "raised up," or "awaken." This word is "*egeirō*," and is used in Matt. 27:52-53, "**Later, the memorial tombs** (graves) **were opened up, and many of the bodies of the set-apart** (holy; sacred) **people – of the folks who had fallen asleep and continued sleeping – were aroused** (awakened) **and raised up!**" – the graves may have metaphorically referred to their bodies. Recall Jesus' calling the scribes and Pharisees "whitewashed tombs" (Mat. 23:27). Other places where this word is used are,

> "And that, knowing the time, that NOW it is high time to 'awake' (*egeirō*) out of sleep..." (Rom. 13:11)
> "Therefore it says, 'AWAKE (*egierō*), O sleeper! and arise (stand up) **from out of the dead ones, and Christ will shine upon you**'" (Eph. 5:14)
> "**If then you were RAISED** (*egierō*) **together with Christ... For you died, and your life has been hidden with Christ, within God**" (Col. 3:1, 3).

He also cites Rom. 8:6, "**to be carnally minded IS DEATH; but to be spiritually minded is LIFE and peace**," and says, "This is the working of the first death... to mind the things of the flesh..."

We can also consider Rom. 5:12,

> "**Because of and through this** (or: Therefore; That is why), **just as through one man** (or: So it is that, even as through the act or agency of one person,) **The Sin** (or: the failure, miss of the target and deviation from the goal) **entered into the aggregate of humanity** (ordered system of

religion, culture, society and government; or: world; cosmos), **and through The Sin** (failure; the mistake; the miss of the target; the deviation) **The Death [also], in this way The Death thus also passed through in all directions** (or: came through the midst causing division and duality; went throughout) **into all mankind** (or: into the midst of humanity; or: to all people), **upon which [situation, condition, and with the consequential result that] all people sin** (or: everyone failed, missed the target, fell short of the goal; or: all make mistakes and deviate from the path)."
Here Prinzing says, "The second death is prepared to purge out and burn away all sin and its results.... Death came as an enemy... Now God makes DEATH OVERCOME ITSELF. It is by death that death is rendered powerless..." (Heb. 2:9, 14, 15).

The following section of vss. 7-15 seems to recapitulate the description of the judgment and battle described in 19:11-21, above.

7. **Then, when the thousand years may be caused to reach the purposed and destined goal** (or: would be finished, completed or ended) [other MSS: after the thousand years], **the adversary** (*satan*) **will proceed being loosed from out of its prison** (his place of being watched and guarded),

This is phase two: the believer's progressive purification and transformation. Our inner adversary (the wise serpent within our garden of self) must do further work. When the sap of the Spirit is flowing, this inner little animal is watched and guarded, and we produce the fruit of the Vine (the Spirit's fruit). But, as Jesus instructed us, even the branches that are bearing fruit need seasonal pruning and cleansing (Jn. 15:2b). During this process, sometimes "all hell breaks loose" and we produce thorns and thistles, instead of fruit, or we build on His house with wood, hay and stubble. But, as we read in vs. 9, below, He is faithful to send His Fire to the situation (*cf* Jn. 15:6; 1 Cor. 3:13-15; Heb. 6:7-8). This happened to Paul, as he shared in 2 Cor. 12:

> 7. **And now, in the excess of the unveilings** (or: with the transcendence of the revelations; by the extraordinary amount and surpassing nature of the disclosures), **through this [situation] and for this reason – so that I could not be progressively exalted** (or: would not continue being overly lifted up [in myself or by others]) **– something with [its] point in [my] flesh is given in me** (or: an impaling-stake for the human nature was given for me; or: a thorn to the natural realm, and a splinter by alienated humanity, was assigned to me): **an agent of** (or: a messenger from) **the adversary, to the end that he** (or: it) **could** (or: should; would) **repeatedly beat me in the face** (or: slap me on the ear) **with his** (or: its) **fist.**
>> [comment: this personification of the irritation may well be metaphorical and may refer to his social or cultural-religious situation]
> 8. **I called the Lord** [Christ or Yahweh] **alongside for relief, ease and comfort, and entreated [Him] three times over** (or: about) **this, so that he** (or: it) **would** (or: should) **at once stand away and withdraw from me,**
> 9. **and yet He has said to me – and His declaration stands, "My grace is continuously sufficient in you** (or: My joyous favor is constantly adequate to ward [it] off for you), **for you see, ability** (or: the [other MSS read: My] power) **is habitually brought to its goal** (or: finished; perfected; matured) **within the midst of weakness** (or: in union with lack of strength and infirmity)." **Most gladly, therefore, I will rather continue boasting within the midst of and in union with weakness, to the end that the ability of the Christ** (or: the Anointed One's power) **can pitch its tent** (or: should tabernacle) **upon me** (or: = set up residence upon me during this transient life and journey; perhaps: = fulfill the type of the Feast of Tabernacles with me; or: = be my house from heaven; [*cf.* 2 Cor. 5:1])!

Jesus, in speaking of **the adversary**, said,

"**You folks, in particular, are** (exist and have your being) **from out of, and have your source in, the ancestor who cast [an object] through [someone]** (or: the father, the devil; or: the devil father; or: the father – the one thrusting [words or issues] through [folks/groups] and dividing them), **and you are habitually wanting** (willing; intending; purposing) **to be constantly doing your father's passionate cravings** (full-rushing over-desires). **That one was existing being a murderer** (a killer of humanity) **from [his/its] beginning** (or: from [the] start; from [its] origin; or: from headship, chieftainhood, government or rule), **and he/it has not stood and does not now stand within the Truth** (or: it had not made a stand in union with reality), **because truth is not** (openness and reality does not exist) **within him** (or: it). **Whenever he/it may be speaking the lie, he/it is continuing speaking from out of his own things – because he/it is** (or: continues existing being) **a liar, and its father** [note: either the father of the lie, or of the liar]" (Jn. 8:44).

It is **the lie**, spoken within, or entering into our hearts like a spear-thrust, that **deceives** us, and others (vs. 3, above; vs. 8, below). Observe the connection that Jesus made between this **adversary** and the Jewish leaders to whom He spoke this verse. "YOU FOLKS have your source in the ancestor who cast [an object] through [someone]…" This adversary is within people (Mat. 16:23).

In regard to the 1st century, historical context, this verse may refer to Rome "being loosed" against Jerusalem in AD 66-70, following the reign of the called-out folks during that period. Simmons sees "the Dragon and Satan in the book of Rev. [as] symbolic references to Imperial Rome" (ibid p 379). Or, it may refer to the persecutions of the called-out communities by the Jews during the generation that led up to the Jewish rebellion, which ended in AD 70. Keep in mind that **the adversary** is an adversarial spirit that has been pictured here as a dragon, but which also operated through the two little animals (Rome, and the Jewish opponents of Christianity in the 1st century).

Before beginning the following section of verses 8-10, the reader will be better informed by first reading Ezk. 38-39, to which these verses allude. Those two chapters use different metaphors for the destruction of the same enemy (Gog): a sword in 38:21; fire in 38:22 and 39:6. By now, our readers should be familiar with multiple pictures of the same topic.

8. **and it** (or: he) **will continue going forth** (or: progressively come out) **to deceive** (lead astray) **those** [other MSS: all the] **nations** (multitudes; ethnic groups) **within the four corners of the Land** (or: territory; or: earth) – **"Gog and Magog"** [Ezk 38:2] – **to gather them together into the battle** (or: war): **their number [being] as the sand of the sea.**

In vss. 7-9 we see that the battleground (vs. 9, below) where the adversary musters its forces is the Beloved City (another name for Jerusalem): the literal city in AD 70 (the historical interpretation), but now in the bride of Christ (21:9-10, below; the second, and later, level of interpretation: the first followers of Christ and then the following generations). This corresponds to 12:13-17, where the dragon goes after the Woman who had birthed "the manchild." On the personal application, it is the adversary gathering enemies within our land (our earth nature) to attack our soul (the bride of our spirit). But thank God for His Fire (9:b, below)! All of that within us which has the mark (character) of the estranged human (the beast) will be devoured.

This scene in our ongoing drama is a recap of 16:13, 14 and 16, above. This is apocalyptic redundancy, not a different battle. It is setting the message of God's corrective measures in the context of Israel's prophets, and in relation to how God dealt with Israel, in the past. Her ancient story is being re-enacted in the Unveiling to speak first to her 1st century situation, but also to speak a message for her daughters, in the following generations. This is why we receive a blessing for reading her history (1:3, above).

As with Yahweh's dealings with Pharaoh (Rom. 9:17), Ezk. 38:23 declares God's purpose here, as well,
> "Thus I will magnify Myself and sanctify Myself, and I will become known in the eyes of many nations. Then they will know that I [am] Yahweh!" (CVOT)

Notice that Ezk. 39:7 locates the place of these events:
> "I shall make known My holy Name in the midst of My people…" (CVOT)

That was in both literal Jerusalem, in the 1st century, and in Christ's called-out covenant communities who had been grafted-in among the believing branches of Israel's olive tree (Rom. 11:17). We suggest that the events here described are an allusion to Ezk. 38-39, but it does not correspond completely: there are multiple layers of application in the drama. Rome was the little animal that destroyed literal Jerusalem, but before that it had the leadership of Jerusalem (Secret Babylon) riding on its back, which took on the role of "Gog, riding Magog" in its attacks on the New Jerusalem (the covenant communities that were called out of Babylon). The imagery is of an enemy attacking God's People, and then being destroyed (vs. 9, below).

9. And they ascended (or: climb up) **upon the breadth of the Land** (or: territory; earth) **and came around the encampment** (or: surround the fortress) **of the set-apart** (holy; sacred) **folks, even the Beloved City** [other MSS: even the city of the set-apart ones]. **Then fire descends** (or: came down) **from God, out of the atmosphere** (or: sky; heaven), **and devours them** (eats them down).

Observe that they had to **ascend** – they had to climb up on Mount Zion to attack her (*cf* Ezk. 38:9, 16). But they also came **upon the breadth of the Land** (a figure of God's People: the two Jerusalems of Gal. 4:25, on each application of the imagery). The Jews persecuted the Christians throughout the Empire; later Rome conquered all of Judea. The language also has an allusion to Hab. 1:6, where the Chaldean armies were described as coming against Israel, and to Isa. 8:7-8. But vs. 9, here, also echoes Deut. 23:14, "For Yahweh, your God, walks in the midst of your **camp** to deliver you, and to give up your enemies before you. Therefore shall your camp be holy…" The term "camp" is frequently found in the records of Israel's wilderness journeys (*cf* Nu. 5:3-4; 31:19). But Christ was the new Moses, leading His followers out of Jerusalem and into the wilderness of the Greco-Roman world. So now we see them camping in tents (*cf* the imagery of God living in a tent among His People, again, in 21:3, below) – temporary dwellings, no longer in a physical temple or structure.

The "**set-apart** (holy; sacred) **folks**" had been a term for Israel, but now it referred to the called-out folks of the covenant communities in Christ (5:8-9; 13:7-10; 12:14, above). The **Beloved City** was a term for the OT Jerusalem (Jer. 12:7; Ps. 78:68; 87:2-3; 122:6; Isa. 66:10; Zeph. 3:14-17), but is now the New Jerusalem (3:12, above; 21:2, 10, below). Thus can we see dual applications of the imagery on the stage.

The **fire descending from God** is an allusion to Elijah's history, in 2 Ki. 1:10-14, and to the two witness ministry in 11:5, above. This is a picture of God defending His People and overcoming their opposition. It graphically demonstrates, once again, that the little Lamb reigns. This picture alludes to Ps. 11:5-7,
> "The Lord (= Yahweh) [is] in His set-apart temple… His throne [is] in the atmosphere (heaven)….
> He will rain down snares: Fire and Deity upon folks that deviate and miss the target…" (LXX, JM).

Paul said to those in Thessalonica,
> "**you also at one point experienced** (or: suffered) **the very same things by** (or: under) **your own fellow-tribesmen, just as they also [did] by** (or: under) **the Jews** (= the religious leaders of Judaism)…. **But inherent fervor** (or: swelling passion; teeming desire; or: anger; wrath; agitation of soul) **advances upon them unto a purpose** (or: on into [the] final act; or: in the end; on into the midst of a destined goal)" (1 Thes. 2:14-16).

This scene in vs. 9 may be that of which Paul spoke in 2 Thes. 1:6-8,

"**[it is right] in the presence of God** (or: if [it is], after all, the right thing with and beside God [= on God's part]), **to repay pressure** (or: squeezing and oppression; ordeal; trouble) **to those continuously pressuring** (squeezing; oppressing; troubling) **you folks,
and to** (or: for; in) **you – the folks being continuously pressed – relaxation** (ease; a relaxing of a state of constriction; relief), **together with us, within the midst of the uncovering** (the unveiling) **of the Lord Jesus from [the] atmosphere** (or: sky; heaven), **along with agents of His power** (or: with His agents of ability) **– within a fire, of flame continuously giving justice** (or: repeatedly imparting the effects of fair and equitable dealings from out of the way pointed out, while maintaining equity from what is right) **among** (or: for; in; with; to) **those not knowing** (or: perceiving) **God, even among** (or: for; in; with; to) **those not continuously listening to or paying attention and obeying the message of goodness and well-being, which is our Lord, Jesus**."

Max R. King observes,
"It is apparent that Satan's end-of-the-age assault against the church was under God's control, serving to magnify the triumph of Christ and the utter defeat of Satan. The identifying of the antichristian forces of the short period of intense tribulation should be relatively simple in light of the background struggles that characterized the gospel missions of the early church" (ibid. 235). Chilton says, "God is now with the Church, and it is the Church's opponents who will be shattered…" (ibid p 525). Terry concurs that, "The *city* is the new Jerusalem" (ibid p 455). Simmons agrees that, "'beloved city' referred to Jerusalem, but [is] appropriated and applied here to the church" (ibid p 385). We are now in the new creation. These applications are no doubt true, but so is the other side of the coin: God bringing the Romans against physical 1st century Jerusalem.

10. **And so the devil** (slanderer; accuser; one who thrusts-through or causes division), **the one continuously deceiving them** (repeatedly leading them astray) **is cast** (or: was thrown) **into the lake** (or: basin; artificial pool; marshy area) **of the Fire and Deity** (or: which is Fire, even Divine Nature) **where the little wild animal and the false prophet also [are; presently exist]. And they will be examined and tested by the touchstone day and night, on into the ages of the ages**
(or: – the place where even the small beast and the lying prophet will also experience hard situations [that lead] into the indefinite time periods of the eons).

When the work is complete, the one who has been thrusting us through, our accuser and adversary, will be thrown into **the lake of Fire and Deity** and thus be transformed and caused to ascend back into God (Rom. 11:36). God will test and examine the transformation of the devil, as well as our beast-like qualities and the prophetic which speaks falsely within us – using the touchstone until it tests out pure gold. "The fining pot is for silver, and the furnace for gold: but Yahweh tries the heart" (Prov. 17:3). It is only the **Fire and Deity** of God that is able to purge out both **deception** and the **deceiver** from our hearts. Its words were placed there in the Garden, bringing the death of deception into all humanity (Rom.5:12). And touching the historical perspective, the **devil-slanderer** was the Jewish leadership that cried for the Romans to **thrust** nails and a spear **through** Jesus. And now came their time for Christ to return in judgment, through the Fire that burned Jerusalem in AD 70. Jesus spoke of this, concerning the Jewish leadership of His day, in Mat. 25: 41, 46,
"**'[You] folks having been brought under the curse, continue proceeding on your way, away from Me, into the eonian fire**
(or: fire for an undetermined period of time; the fire which comes with the Age [of Messiah]; the fire pertaining to and having its source in the Age; the age-lasting fire; the fire having the quality and characteristics of the Age) **– the one having been prepared and made ready in** (or: by; with; for) **the person who thrusts [something] through [folks]** (the

adversary; one who casts [something] through the midst and causes division; the 'devil') **as well as in** (or: by; with; for) **his agents** (messengers).... **And so, these folks will continue going off** (or: coming away) **into an eonian pruning**
> (a lopping-off which lasts for an undetermined length of time; an age-lasting correction and rehabilitation; a pruning which brings better fruit and which has its source and character in the Age; a cutting off during the ages)..."

Maarschalk, interpreting this little wild animal (beast) as the Jewish Zealots, remarks:
> "The primary message and agenda of the Zealots was war. They persecuted those who threatened that agenda or wouldn't go along with it. The Zealots stood in total opposition to the message of Jesus, the new covenant, and the kingdom of God. They were determined to maintain, build, and spread their own kingdom. They were extreme nationalists, but ironically they destroyed their own nation and region fighting for that ideal" ("Who Was the Beast?" ibid p 11).

The reason that the **examination** and **testing** lasts **on into the ages of the ages** is because folks continue being born, throughout the ages. Each one comes with the old Adamic nature and self; each needs the **deceiver** as a sparring partner to strike him or her in the face – as did Paul. As with Jesus in the wilderness testing, each person needs to face the tests that this inner **thruster** will bring. What happened in Jesus and Paul needs to happen within each individual, as the One smelting and purifying our gold and silver sits, until He sees His reflection in the molten metal that He has placed within us.

As we noted above, **day and night** signifies that this is happening right here, on earth – as "the world" turns. Again, keep in mind that this situation described in this verse, and the three players, are all apocalyptic symbols for our inner being, and all that is within us. Remember that Paul admonished wives not to be "**devils**" (1 Tim. 3:11). In 2 Tim. 3:2-3, he warned that,
> "**the people** (the humans; mankind) **will continue being folks that are fond of themselves** (self-loving; selfish).... [and that they will be] **without natural affection, unwilling to make a treaty** (implacable; not open to an agreement), **devils** (adversarial slanderers; folks who throw or thrust something through people to hurt or cause divisions)..."

It is for this reason that such folks will also be "**cast** (or: thrown) **into the lake of the Fire**" (vs. 15, below), for purification and cleansing from this adversarial spirit that does not love. When we understand the figures and symbols in this passage, the message becomes quite plain. It was written to, and about, people: US! This verse is a recap of 14:10, above: those who still have the "beast" influence in their works and thinking. Viewing this picture in its apocalyptic, timeless nature, we can perceive that this is also a recap of 19:17-21, above. It is all saying the same message: "**Indeed, everyone** (all humanity) **will be salted** (seasoned and preserved) **in** (with; by) **fire!**" (Mk. 9:49).

11. **Next I saw a great bright, white throne, and the One continuously sitting upon it from Whose face the Land** (or: ground; earth) **and the atmosphere** (or: sky; heaven) **flee** (or: at once fled). **And a place is not found for them** (or: And then no position was discovered by them or found in them).

This vision is, like those before it and those after it, a figurative picture that represents an idea – that of God's reign (the throne), His omnipotence (His face, and thus, the awe that accompanies His presence), and the effect of His manifested presence (the "fleeing" of the creation in its prior existence and character). What follows is a scene of evaluations and decisions (a situation of judging) made by the **One continuously sitting upon [the throne]**. It has traditionally been assumed (erroneously, we suggest) that this is a picture of "the last judgment," but we should first of all take notice that it does not say that this is a "last judgment." Here I will cite John Noē, "First, what does the Bible say about a 'final judgment' or 'last judgment'? The answer is, NOTHING! Neither expression is used in Scripture, and for good reason" (*The Creation of Evil, Casting Light into the Purposes of Darkness*, East 2 West Press, 2015 p 39; emphasis original).

The setting is here on **earth**, but the scene is the disappearance of the old "heaven and earth" (Jewish indicator of Israel's universe: the temple – God's house among them – was its 'heaven' and the earth/land was a figure of its people, or the land of Palestine) that existed under the Sinai arrangement. So this picture is set in the new creation of which Paul spoke in 2 Cor. 5:17. Here John saw a visionary picture of the new situation described there by Paul, where "**the original things** (the beginning [situations]; the archaic and primitive [arrangements]) **[had] passed by** (or: went to the side)." Here, John saw the old pass from the scene: "**And a place is not found for them** (or: And then no position was discovered by them or found in them)." There is no more **place or position** for the Law, or things of the old Mosaic covenant, or a distinctive "place" for Israel, in the new arrangement, in which we have,

"'**a new** (new in nature; different from the usual; better than the old; superior in value and attraction; new in quality) **atmosphere** (or: sky; or: heaven) **and a new Land** (or: earth)' [Isa. 65:17; 66:22], **for you see, actually, the first** (former; preceding; earlier) **atmosphere** (or: heaven) **and the first** (former, preceding) **Land** (or: earth; soil; ground) **went away** (or: moved off, and passed away), **and the sea does not exist any longer**" (21:1, below).

Allusion to Ps. 102:25-27, Isa. 51:6 may be in view with this description of the passing of the old. We find similar pictures in 2 Pet. 3:7, 10 and 12. For more on that passage, see, *Peter's Encore and Later Paul*, Harper Brown Pub., 2016.

Now we come to the "**great bright-white throne**," scene of vss. 11-15. The color white speaks of purity. This calls to mind David's musings of Yahweh's judgments in Ps. 19,

"The results of [the] Lord's decisions (the judgment-effects from [Yahweh]) [are] true (valid; real; dependable; genuine), having come from what is right (just; fair) and now doing justice upon the same: more desired above gold and much precious stone; sweeter, above and beyond honey and honeycomb" (9b-10; LXX, JM).

We saw this same One sitting upon a **white** horse, in 19:11, above.

When we come before Him who **sits** upon His **throne**, both our heaven and our earth (our whole world) flee as we are humbled before His mercy, grace and love. There is no place for either our earth-nature, nor our spirit or will, when we are judged by Him (when He makes a decision concerning us). He gives us a new heaven (a renewed spirit: "Create for me a clean heart, O Elohim, and RENEW with me an established spirit" – Ps. 51:10, CVOT) and a new earth (a new creation, the Second Man – 21:1, below; 1 Cor. 15:47).

The literal fulfillment of the earth and the heaven fleeing happened with the termination of the Jewish "world" at His *Parousia* in AD 70. Simmons comments, "the heavens and earth stand for a system ordered and ordained of God… symbolic of the covenantal system embodied in fleshly Israel and the Mosaic law" (ibid p 390). God's pattern is "first the natural (that which pertains to the first Adam, the soul life; the arrangement for literal Israel), and afterward that which is spiritual" (1 Cor. 15:46). We are now in the afterward. We are in the new creation with the new arrangement where Jew and Gentile are "**one new humanity**" (Eph. 2:15). In the sphere of God's reign, the history of the first Adam came to a close with the end of literal Israel's history (the end of all the previous ages, with the Christ event and the coming of the new). The first humanity died with Christ:

"**[We are] deciding** (discerning; judging) **this: that** [some MSS add: since] **One Person** (or: Man) **died over [the situation of] all mankind** (or: for the sake of all); **consequently all people died** (or: accordingly, then, all humanity died). **And further, He died over all humanity** (over [the situation] of, and for the sake of all) **to the end that those living may** (or: could; would) **no**

longer live for themselves (to themselves; in themselves; by themselves), **but rather for** (or: in; by; to; with) **the One dying and then being awakened and raised up over them** (over their [situation]; for their sakes), **so that we, from the present moment** (or: from now) **[on], have seen and thus know** (or: perceive; or: are acquainted [with]) **no one on the level of** (or: in the sphere of; in correspondence to) **flesh** (= the estranged human nature; = the self enslaved to the System), **if even we have intimately, by experience, known Christ** ([the] Anointed One) **on the level of flesh** (or: = in the sphere of estranged humanity; or: = in correspondence to a self oriented to the System), **nevertheless we now** (in the present moment) **no longer continue [thus] knowing [Him or anyone]**" (2 Cor. 5:14b-16).

This was the decision made about humanity at "the great white throne judging" that happened with the resurrection and enthronement of Christ. Note that in the realm of His reign and judging, "**all people, all humanity, died**" when He (as the First Adam, First Humanity) died. The scene described in our present passage of the Unveiling is referred to in Heb. 9:27,

"**And now, according to as much as it continues lying-away** (or: laid away; reserved-off; stored) **in** (or: with; for; to) **mankind** (or: people) **to die-away once, but after this a process of evaluating** (a separating and making a distinction to be a judging and determining; a deciding)."

The book of Hebrews was written prior to the closing acts of the age (in AD 70) which terminated the Law and Israel as a nation. Chapter 9 of the book of Hebrews speaks of the Day of Atonement where Jesus entered the new, spiritual, temple (the second humanity – 1 Cor. 15:47) and cleansed His throne (the mercy seat in the holy of holies) with His blood. For a fuller discussion of this, see *John, Judah, Paul & ?*, and the section, *Comments on Hebrews*, Harper Brown Pub., 2013.

There may be an allusion in this scene that reaches back to the vision in Dan. 7:9-14, which is relative to the judgment of the fourth beast, there. Ezk. 1:26-28 may also be in view, and we are also taken back to 4:2 and 5:7, above. In Simmons' view, "The timing of the judgment is therefore firmly established at the end of the Mosaic age when Christ came in the glory of his Father with the holy angels (Mat. 16:27, 28; 24:3, 34; 25:31-46)" (ibid p 389). An allusion to Isa. 6:1 has also been seen. But note there that the setting was "the temple," which connects us, again, to the setting of Heb. 9.

12. **Then I saw the dead folks – the great ones and the little ones – standing before the throne. And little scrolls are** (or: were) **opened up. And then another little scroll is opened up, which is of** (or: the one pertaining to; belongs to; or: from) **The Life. And the dead ones are judged** (were evaluated) **from out of the things having been written within the little scrolls, according to their works** (down from their actions; on the level of their deeds).

This vision simply gives us a picture of standing before God's judging, using the figure of people standing before an earthly king to receive his decisions. This scene is parallel to the proclamation in 11:18, above. Since sin was taken away on the cross, this judgment is simply a decision that accords with a person's works (vss. 12, 13), and they will be tried by fire (vss. 14, 15). Now let's see what Paul had to say regarding the judgments of one's works in 1 Cor. 3:

13. **each one's work will make itself to be visible in clear light** (or: will become apparent), **for the Day will make [it] evident** (show [it] plainly). **Because it is being progressively unveiled** (continually revealed) **within the midst of Fire, and the Fire, Itself, will test, examine and put to the proof** (or: prove by testing) **what sort of work each one's exists being.**

14. **If anyone's work which he built upon [it] will remain, he will receive wages** (pay; compensation).

15. **If anyone's work will be burned down, he will incur a loss** (sustain the damage; forfeit [it]), **yet he himself will be saved** (rescued and delivered; healed and restored to health; returned to his original state and condition), **and as in this way – through Fire!**

Now notice the important qualifier concerning this judgment. It is: "**according to their works** (down from their actions; on the level of their deeds)." It is NOT, "according to one's decision for, or against, receiving Christ as their Savior." It is NOT, "according to whether or not one was baptized – the right way, into the right group, etc." It is NOT, "according to one's doctrines or to whether or not one is a 'believer.'" This describes a decision that is based upon how one lives, or lived, and upon what a person does/did. Using Paul's metaphor, above, it is an evaluation of whether these "works" were profitable, or worthless, and then a decision is made to **save** the person, **through His Fire**, as we have seen, above. All will we done "on the level of their deeds," or, "down from (*kata*) their actions." We saw this in the metaphor of burning off the field, to clear the weeds and brambles, in Heb. 6:7-8.

There seems to be a correlation between **the little scrolls** (peoples' lives) of the last clause, and **another little scroll**, "**which is of** (or: the one pertaining to; belongs to; or: from) **The Life**." Notice the definite article of the phrase, **The Life**. This has reference to the Christ Life. There is a comparison being made. The metaphor is: how does/did your actions and works align with the Life of Christ? Did/do your deeds bear God's image? Is there more purification needed? When tempering a tool or a weapon in a forge, the smith takes it from the fire and looks at the color of the metal as it is cooling, after having been plunged into water or oil. It usually requires multiple returns to the fire, and then the tempering water/oil, to achieve the desired temper. Viewing this "white throne" evaluation as a one-time event misses the whole point of its purpose.

Let us consider what is meant by, "**the dead ones are judged** (were evaluated)." Recall, above, that the setting of this evaluation is "earth," and is coming from the location of "the temple." Keep in mind that the phrase, "**the dead ones**," is a symbol. This is NOT literal; it is part of an apocalypse. Was this decision first made upon those who Jesus said,

> "**continue closely resembling whitewashed** (i.e., smeared or plastered with lime) **tombs** (sepulchers; grave sites), **which indeed, from outside, continue being made to appear in the prime of beauty, for a time – yet inside they contain a full load of bones of dead folks, as well as every uncleanness**" (Mat. 23:27)?

That description meant that those scribes and Pharisees were "dead people." Paul referred to humanity as a whole as being people,

> "**continuously existing being dead ones by** (or: to; with; in) **the results and effects of your stumblings aside** (offenses; wrong steps) **and failures to hit the mark** (or: mistakes; errors; times of falling short; sins; deviations)" (Eph. 2:1).

The pure decision, concerning humanity that was dead in the first Adam (Rom. 5:12), came at the cross and the resurrection. Each of us was included in that "judgment," and each one existentially experiences it "**within the result and effect of his or her own class** (or: ordered place; appointed position [in line]; arranged time or order of succession; = place in a harvest calendar, thus, due season of maturity)" (1 Cor. 15:23). In 1 Tim. 5:6 Paul referred to one, who, "**while continuing being alive** (or: [though] living), **she is dead** (or: she has died)." The Unveiling is a book of symbols and figures. We must not import literal interpretations into this drama, or tapestry. Paul also used this metaphor in Col. 3:16,

> "**And you folks – continuously being dead ones within** [other MSS: by] **the results and effects of falls to the side, and in** (or: by) **the uncircumcision of your flesh** (= physical bodies or national heritage; or: = estranged human nature and alienated self) **– He makes** (or: made) **alive together: you** [other MSS: us] **jointly together with Him, gracing us, granting joyous favor to us** [for; in] **all the effects of the falls and stumbling to the side** (= false steps)."

Brian Zahnd has written a book whose very title reveals the nature of the One who judges humanity from His great white throne: *Sinners in the Hands of a Loving God; The Scandalous Truth of the Very Good News*, Waterbrook 2017.

13. **And the sea gives** (or: suddenly gave) **[up; back] the dead folks within it, and death and the Unseen give** (or: = the grave gave) **[up; back] the dead folks within them. And they are judged** (evaluated) **according to their works** (in correspondence with their actions; in line with their deeds).

We first of all offer the "Collective Body View" of some Preterists, on this verse: it is "The collective body of old covenant Israel [that] was raised out of covenantal death into the new covenantal life of Christ" (Ed Stevens, "Fulfilled Magazine," winter 2017 p 15). This fits with a 1st century AD interpretation of the Unveiling – verses 5 (above) and 13 are seen in that context. The "Unseen" (*hades*) is a "Synonym for [the] grave only, not a place in the unseen realm" (ibid p 13).

Here in the Unveiling, **the sea** is a figure of humanity (or Palestine, in the 1st century), just as it is in 13:1, above, from out of which the first little animal comes. The picture of humanity would be of the releasing those that are dead by, and in, trespasses and sin (Eph. 2:1). **The Unseen** (*hades*) where all who are dead exist and even the realm of death, or the power of death, itself released those imprisoned within them. This was effected by the cross and the resurrection of Christ. And as 1:18b, above, instructs us, the risen Christ,

> "**constantly holds the keys of, and pertaining to, the Death and of, and pertaining to, the Unseen**
>
> > (or: continues having the keys, which are Death and Hades [= *sheol*; perhaps: "the grave"]; habitually possesses the keys from the Death and from the unseen "realm/state of the dead"; keeps on holding the keys belonging to death and shadowy existence)."

Although "the Unseen" was commonly used as a phrase to denote either "the grave" or "the realm of those who have physically died," remember, again, that here in the Unveiling it is used in a metaphor. Jesus was sent, "**into the midst of those sheep having been destroyed, the ones that belong to the house of Israel**" (Mat. 15:24). Being "destroyed (or: lost)" was a figure for being dead. Jesus was speaking metaphorically. In the parable of the prodigal, the father said, "**this one – your brother – was existing being dead, and now he comes to life; and was one having been lost and destroyed – and now he is found!**" (Lu. 15:32b). He said (Lu. 19:10), "**the Son of the Man** (= the eschatological messianic figure; = Adam's son) **came to seek after, and then to save, deliver and restore what is existing being lost and destroyed.**" Jesus spoke somewhat enigmatically in Jn. 5:

> 25. "**Count on it** (Amen, amen), **I am presently continuing to say to you folks that an hour is progressively** (or: presently in process of) **coming, and even now exists** (or: = is now here), **when the dead folks WILL be repeatedly hearing the voice of God's Son** (or: the Voice from, and which is, the Son of God; or: the voice of the Son, Who is God), **and the ones hearing WILL proceed to be living!**
> 26. "**You see, just as the Father continuously holds** (or: constantly has) **Life within Himself, thus also, He gives in the Son** (or: to the Son) **to be continuously holding** (or: constantly having) **Life within Himself,**
> 27. "**And He gives in Him** (or: to Him; by Him) **authority** (or: the right; the privilege; or: out of [His] essence and being) **to be habitually separating and deciding** (to be constantly sifting and evaluating; to continuously do [the] judging), **because He is a son of mankind** (= because He is human – a member of the human race [= Adam's Son]; or: = because He exists being the eschatological Messiah).

28. "**Don't you folks be constantly amazed at this, because an hour is progressively** (or: presently; or: repeatedly) **coming within which all the people within the memorial tombs** (or: graves) **– will be continuously or repeatedly hearing His voice,**

29. "**and they will proceed journeying out: the ones doing virtue** (producing, making or constructing good) **into a resurrection which is Life** (or: of, from and with the quality of Life); **the ones practicing careless** (base, worthless, cheap, slight, paltry, inefficient, thoughtless, common or mean) **things into a resurrection of separating and evaluating for a decision** (or: a resurrection which is a judging).

Note that in vs. 25 He said that "**an hour… even now exists** (= was THEN here)." If we hear Him with apocalyptic ears, we will see that He was speaking figuratively. In Jn. 12:31a He told them,

"**At the present time** (or: Now) **is an evaluation of and a decision pertaining to** (or: a sifting of and separation for; or: a judgment from) **this System** (or: this ordered arrangement; this world; this polity, culture and religion; or: this system of control and subjugation; or: the aggregate of humanity)."

It was the period, or season, for the sifting and evaluation that was the end of that Age, in the 1st century.

In Mat. 16:18-19, Jesus informs us about His "**house – the called-out community**":

"**And even gates of [the] unseen** (or: gates of an unseen place; [= boulders on the entrances of graves; = {the prison} gates of the 'house of death'; or: the bars enclosing the realm of the dead]) **will not continue bringing strength down against it** (or: will not proceed to be coming to their full strength in relation to it; or: will not continue overpowering it or prevail in resisting it). **I will continue giving to you the keys** [note: = means of locking or unlocking] **which have their origin and source in the reign and activities of the heavens. And so, whatever you can** (or: may; should) **bind upon the earth will continue being [something] having been bound, and still remaining bound, within the midst of the heavens** (or: in the atmospheres). **Also, whatever you can** (or: may; should) **loose upon the earth will continue being [something] having been loosed** (unbound; untied), **and remaining free of bonds, within the midst of the heavens** (or: in the atmospheres)."

Can we then surmise that because "**death and the Unseen give** (or: = the grave gave) **[up; back] the dead folks within them**," that the called-out community was involved in this? Were the keys given here in Mat. 16:18 the same keys spoken of in 1:18b, above? If we conclude that who John saw in the vision of chapter 1, above, represented the "corporate Christ," i.e., Jesus and His body (recall in 1:16, 20; 2:1, etc., the agents were in His hand), then these may indeed be the same keys. He came,

"**to publicly proclaim, as a herald, to** (for; among) **captives a release and liberation** (a letting go away) **and to** (for; among) **blind folks a seeing again** (a recovery of sight), **to send away with a mission those having been shattered by oppression, in a state of release and liberation**" (Lu. 4:18).

Paul states concerning Christ, in Eph. 4:8 (citing Ps. 68:18), that,

"**Going up** (or: Stepping up; Ascending) **into a height** (unto [the] summit) **He led** (or: leads) **captive a captive multitude** (or: He led 'captivity' captive)."

Jesus instructed us,

"**the person habitually trusting and progressively believing into Me, the works** (actions; deeds) **which I Myself am constantly doing** (habitually performing; progressively making, constructing, creating, forming) **that one also will proceed doing** (performing; making; creating), **and he will progressively be doing greater than these, because I Myself am progressively journeying** (traveling; going from this place to another) **toward** (or: facing) **the Father**,"

In all that He does, "**we are God's fellow-workers** (or: we are co-workers of and from God; we exist being co-workers who belong to God)" (1 Cor. 3:9). In Mat. 10:8, Jesus commissioned His disciples to serve people in a wide range of ways,

"**Be constantly serving, curing and restoring to health** (or: giving attentive care to and treatment for) **those who are habitually weak, feeble and inadequate. Habitually be rousing and raising up dead people. Be continually cleansing lepers** (scabby folks). **Make it a habit to cast out demons** (Hellenistic concept and term: = animistic influences). **You folks receive** (or: received) **freely** (as a gift; = without cost), **[so] give freely** (as a gift; = without charge)."

This verse could be taken either literally, or metaphorically, according to how they were "**being continuously led by God's Spirit**" (Rom. 8:14), and according to the situation and need.

14. **Next the Death and the Unseen** (or: = the grave) **are cast** (or: were thrown) **into the lake** (or: basin; artificial pool) **of the Fire** (or: the marshy area where there is fire). **This is the second death: the lake of the Fire** (or: the basin which is the fire).

When one stands before the throne of God, not even death itself (having been conquered by Christ) can hold on to one who had before been captive to it. The situation in Paul's day was described in Rom. 8:35-39. Death (vs. 38) can no longer separate folks from God's love. So now, here in vs. 14, we see that **the Death** and **the Unseen**, having completed their appointed works, are now returned to the source, and we have the death of **the Death**. Athanasius of Alexandria gave a brief overview of how this worked, from his perspective on the Incarnation:

"The Word [Jn. 1:1] perceived that corruption could not be got rid of otherwise than through death; yet He Himself, as the Word, being immortal and the Father's Son, was such as could not die. For this reason, therefore, He assumed a body capable of death [Jn. 1:14], in order that it, through belonging to the Word Who is above all, might become in dying a sufficient exchange for all, and, itself remaining incorruptible through His indwelling, might thereafter put an end to corruption for all others as well, by the grace of the resurrection.... Naturally also, through this union of the immortal Son of God with our human nature, all men were clothed with incorruption in the promise of the resurrection. For the solidarity of mankind is such that, by virtue of the Word's indwelling in a single human body, the corruption which goes with death has lost its power over all.... He has come into our country and dwelt in one body amidst the many, and in consequence the designs of the enemy against mankind have been foiled and the corruption of death, which formerly held them in its power, has simply ceased to be. For the human race would have perished utterly had not the Lord and Savior of all, the Son of God, come among us to put an end to death" (*On the Incarnation*, 9, www.saintmartin.com; brackets added).

Paul referenced this situation in 1 Cor. 15:26, referring to **the Death** (personified) as being, "**[The] last holder of ruin** (or: enemy; quality having ill-will) **being progressively brought down to idleness** (made unemployed and ineffective; rendered useless and unproductive)," or: "Death, a last enemy, is being presently nullified and abolished." This verse presents a picture of what wrote in 1 Cor. 15:54b, in quoting Isa. 25:8, "**The Death was drunk down and swallowed into Victory** (or: overcoming)!" This verse proclaims the Victory of Christ.

When judgment comes, whether in this life (for our Father continuously makes decisions about us here, too – Heb. 12:9, when we are in subjection to the Father of spirits, we LIVE) or when we die, if our names are not yet recorded in heaven (Lu. 10:20) He baptizes us in the lake of **THE FIRE**, to cleanse and purify us – and our God is this consuming Fire (Heb. 12:29).

This judgment of Fire was discussed in 14:10-11, above. There we noted that this time of testing is where there is "day and night," an expression of time and it carries on, not in "eternity," but on into indefinite time periods of the ages – according as He deems necessary and helpful – and 21:8, below, gives another description of all who have "their part" in this experience:

"**the timid** (in cowardly) **folks and for faithless ones** (in unbelieving people) **and for or by abominable, disgusting folks, and for or in murderers, and for or with prostitutes and for or by sorcerers** (users of drugs) **and for or by idolaters and for, in or by all the liars** (the false ones)..."

Now keep in mind that Jesus said that prostitutes and tax collectors would get into the kingdom before the religious folks (the theologians, the priests and elders) – Mat. 21:31. It simply may mean that since they know their need of Christ more than the self-righteous one, then they won't have such a long treatment in God's purification process.

The second death, which is described here as "**the lake of the Fire**," equates to what Jesus referred to in Mat. 25:31-46 as the "**age-lasting** (or: eonian) **fire**" that was prepared for the devil and his agents (vs. 41). This we see fulfilled in 19:20 and 20:10, above. But we should also recall that in our Mat. 25 passage it is the goats (literally: **kids** – the immature), those who did not recognize Christ in Jesus' brothers (family members, vs. 40) when He was hungry, thirsty, a stranger, naked, sick or in prison – and did not minister to Him in them – that needed His Fire. Now although these kids were clean animals (goats were used in sacrifices to the Lord, and Christ, as our Atonement, would have been symbolized as a goat, or kid, not a lamb), they were just "kids," immature folks who were producing no fruit of the Spirit (love for their brothers in need). Thus they are judged and, in Mat. 25:46, go forth

"**into an eonian pruning**

(a lopping-off which lasts for an undetermined length of time; an age-lasting correction and rehabilitation; a pruning which brings better fruit and which has its source and character in the Age; a cutting off during the ages)" – which switches the metaphor, from Mat. 25:41. The Greek word for correction is *kolasis*, and is an agricultural term that means to prune or to correct the growth of a vine or tree. The obvious meaning is that this fire is designed to cause better growth which will produce more and better fruit (i.e., care for those in need).

We suggest that this "lake of Fire experience" is the same experience that John the baptizer spoke of when he said that Jesus would dip, or immerse, you "**within Holy Spirit and Fire**" (Lu. 3:16). This fire is meant to burn out any cowardice, unbelief, abominable things, and that which would cause us to murder, be involved in prostitution, sorcery or idolatry, or to be false and a liar (ch. 21:8). It is also meant to remove the adversary from us, rid us of false prophesying, and free us from being agents of the beast nature – all the things that would keep us from living the Christ Life, figured here by being "written in the scroll of The Life" (vs. 15, below). It is the same Fire that we find in 1 Cor. 3:15,

"**If anyone's work will be burned down, he or she will proceed in incurring a loss** (sustaining the damage; forfeiting), **yet he himself or she herself will be saved** (rescued and delivered; healed; restored; made whole; kept safe), **and as in this way – through Fire!**"
[*cf* 1 Cor. 5:5, below; Job 2:6, LXX]

He does take us through the Fire, but He is there ready to save us even while we are within the fire, as the three Hebrews in the furnace found out (Dan. 3). The fire delivered them from their bonds, and ended in God being glorified. All things return to the Fire, for,

"**Because, forth from out of the midst of Him, then through the midst of Him** (or: through means of Him), **and [finally] into the midst of Him, [is; will be] the whole** (everything; [are] all things)" (Rom. 11:36).

We can also see Heb. 6:7-8 (the field being cleared of weeds and brambles, in order to be re-sown with good Seed) as applicable to the priest, scribes and Pharisees of 1st century Jerusalem – or, the Zealots during AD 70. Paul had described Israel, according to the flesh, as those "whose is the sonship and the glory and the covenants and the legislation and the divine service and the promises" (Rom. 9:4, CLNT).

Would not Heb. 6: 4, 5 & 6 describe the same thing? And yet, that is not the end of the field, or piece of ground (which is the subject of the metaphor), as we read:

> "**the end** (the resultant situation) **of which [the thorns, briars, thistles and the field is] into [a time of] burning** (or: = the field ends up being burned off)" (vs. 8).
>
> [comment: this is a time-honored agricultural practice for preparing a field for planting a crop – the competition has been removed and the ground has been enriched by the ash]

Now there is another view of the Second Death that my friend Dan Kaplan shared with me years ago. Call to mind Eph. 2:1, where Paul said that we all were,

> "**continuously existing being dead ones by** (or: to; with; in) **the results and effects of your stumblings aside** (offenses; wrong steps) **and failures to hit the mark** (or: mistakes; errors; times of falling short; sins; deviations)."

So that was the first death (and it was not a physical death – obviously). We quoted from Rom. 6 above, under vs. 6, in regard to the resurrection. But it bears repeating here, with regard to the Second Death:

> 3. **Or are you continuing to be ignorant that as many as are immersed** (or: were at one point soaked or baptized) **into Christ Jesus are immersed** (or: were then baptized) **into His death?**
> 4. **We, then, were buried together in Him** (or: by Him; with Him), **through the immersion into the death, to the end that just as Christ was roused and raised forth from out of the midst of dead folks THROUGH THE GLORY of The Father** (or: which is the Father), **thus also we can walk around** (conduct ourselves) **within newness of life.**
> 5. **For since we have come to be folks engrafted and produced together in, by, to and with the result of the likeness of His death, then certainly we shall also continue existing [in and with the effects of the likeness] of The Resurrection**
> 6. **while constantly knowing this by intimate experience, that our old, former humanity is crucified together with [Him], to the end that the body of the Sin could and would be rendered useless and inoperative, for us to no longer continually be a slave to the Sin,**
> 7. **for you see, the One at one point dying has been eschatologically released and rightwised away from the Sin.**
> 8. **Now since we died together with Christ, we are continuously believing** (relying; trusting) **that we will also continue living together in Him** (by Him; for Him; to Him; with Him)....
> 11. **Thus you folks, also, be logically considering yourselves to exist being dead ones, indeed, by the failure to hit the target** (or: TO the deviation), **yet ones continuously living by God** (in God; with God), **within Christ Jesus, our Owner.**

Now add to this what Paul said in 2 Cor. 5:14b,

> "**One Person** (or: Man) **died over [the situation of] all mankind** (or: for the sake of all); **consequently all people died** (or: accordingly, then, all humanity died)."

You see, Christ is the Second Death for all humanity. But He is also the transforming Fire of Mal. 3:2-3, Who purifies all of us.

15. **So if anyone is not found** (or: was not found) **written within the scroll of** (or: which is) **The Life, he is cast** (or: was thrown) **into the lake of the Fire** (or: the artificial pool having the character and quality of the Fire; the marshy area from the Fire; the shallow basin, where there is fire).

For a person to be **not found written within the scroll of** (or: which is) **The Life** means that this one has not been "abiding in the Vine" (Jn. 15:1ff) and still has the influence and identity (mark) of the little animal nature controlling his or her mind and actions (14:10, above). This verse is a promise that all mankind will at some point be purged of the fleshly disposition (the carnal mindset) and cleansed from the effect of listening to the adversarial spirit that came from partaking in legalism (law) and dualistic, tribal thinking (us versus them). They will be "salted with Fire" (Mk. 9:49) and baptized (Lu. 3:16) in Holy Spirit, or a set-apart Attitude, and Fire (God).

Dan Kaplan views this "lake of the Fire" as a symbol of the "brazen altar" in the tabernacle/temple setting. This is the place of the sacrifice of the little Lamb (the place of Israel's sin offering) which represented the people being offered to God, the place where the priests, representing Israel, would eat His flesh (Jn. 6:53). Kaplan sees this as corresponding to the cross of Christ. This began the journey of humanity into the holy place (the place of the lampstand which represented the called-out groups, the twelve loaves of bread that represented Israel, and the altar of incense) which led into the holy of holies (Heb. 10:19-22): the place of God's throne (the mercy seat; Rom. 11:32) and being enthroned with Christ (Eph. 2:6; figured by the two grasped-ones – the cherubim). We have seen these symbols in the preceding chapters. This apocalyptic vision represents those who are not the "firstfruits," but are the harvest itself (i.e., all humanity) being returned into God (Rom. 11:36).

On this final section of chapter 20, James Stuart Russell writes:
> "Like the other catastrophes which have preceded it, it is a solemn act of judgment... The Seer now resumes the narration which had been interrupted by the digression respecting the thousand years, taking up the thread which was dropped at the close of vs. 4. We are therefore brought back to the same standpoint as in the first and fourth verses. This catastrophe naturally and necessarily belongs to the same series of events as have been represented in the vision of the harlot city, and falls within the prescribed apocalyptic limits, belonging among the things 'which must shortly come to pass'....
> "It is the great consummation, or one aspect of it, towards which all the action of the Apocalypse moves.... In the catastrophe of the 7th trumpet it is declared that 'the time of the dead, that they should be judged, is come,' etc. (ch. 11:18); and in the catastrophe of the 7 mystic figures we see 'a WHITE cloud, and on the cloud one sitting, like unto the Son of man' (ch. 14:14), corresponding with 'the great WHITE throne, and him that sat on it,' in the passage now before us..." (*The Parousia*, ibid p 523-4)

As pointed out above, the last part of this chapter, vs. 11-15, is often thought of as "the final judgment." This is a common phrase from institutional Christian teachings on eschatology (the study of "last things," or "the time of the end of the, or an, age") and the word "final" is normally used to indicate a judgment at the end of human history. But, again, the text does not say that this is "the final (or, last) judgment," so such a concept of "final" should not be "read into" the text. A judgment can bring an end to something, like the judgment of Jerusalem in AD 70 brought an end to the Jewish temple and to the nation of the Jews, at that time. It ended an age, but the new age was at the same time just beginning. And further, we ask, Do we see the idea of a final judgment set forth anywhere in the types and shadows of the OT? No. What we see are repeated judgments, or periodic judgments, according to God's purposes in any given time or situation. Was the judgment of Egypt final, when God delivered Israel? No, Egypt continued as a nation. It was final only for those who actually died a physical death – and in reality, most everyone does physically die – and only in the sense of a physical death. We see judgments of cities and kingdoms (e.g., Sodom; the kingdoms represented by the image in Nebuchadnezzar's dream; the economy of natural Israel destroyed in AD 70). We see individuals judged and killed – but do these hold a figure for a "final judgment"? No. This concept is foreign to the Scriptures.

In Matt. 10:15 Jesus speaks about Sodom and Gomorrah in comparison to how cities or villages or houses which do not receive the disciples or hear their words would be judged – and the context is 1st century Israel. Note the word "**more**" (suggesting a variation in degree in the sentences), and that the judgment was ENDURABLE:

"Assuredly – I now say to you folks – it will proceed being more ENDURABLE in the land of Sodom and Gomorrah, in a day of separating and deciding, than in THAT city (or: it will be MORE supportable for the land of Sodom and Gomorrah, in a day of judging, than for that town)!" His comparison is saying that in the upcoming judgment on Judea, the results that happened in AD 70 would be worse than what happened in Sodom, etc. But nowhere does it speak of a "final judgment."

In the chapter, "Mercy Triumphs over Judgment," under a section titled, "Jurgen Moltmann: The Universality of the Cross and the Necessity of Judgment," Bradley Jersak examines "Moltmann's Critique of the Traditional Doctrine of Judgment." In regard to both the medieval and modern versions, Jersak states:

> "Moltmann rejects both versions as being rooted in the Egyptian *Book of the Dead* and such non-Christian sources [citing Moltmann's The Final Judgment, p 569]. He argues that the traditional doctrine of judgment falls short of being 'Christian theology' because it does not ultimately serve Life and actually bleeds terrible ecological, psychological, sociological, and political consequences into our world. As such, our doctrine of judgment needs to be Christianized. It needs to represent God as revealed in Jesus Christ. How so? For Moltmann, salvation is not exclusive because it does not depend on a particular(ist) formula for relationship with God, but on what God in Christ accomplished effectually through the Cross" (*Her Gates Will Never Be Shut; Hope, Hell, and the New Jerusalem*, Wipf & Stock, 2009 p 147; brackets added).

And so the "cosmic opera" continues. J.S. Russell approaches chapter 21:1-22:5 with the following words,

> "This vision is the last of the series, and completes the mystic number 'seven.' It is the grand finale of the whole drama, the triumphant consummation and climax of the apocalyptic visions. It stands in striking antithesis to the vision of the harlot city; it is new Jerusalem in contrast to the old; the bride, the Lamb's wife, in contrast with the... adulteress whose judgment has passed before our eyes....
>
> "We now find ourselves surrounded by scenery so novel and so wonderful that it is not surprising that we should be in doubt where we are. Is this earth, or is it heaven? Every familiar landmark has disappeared; the old has vanished, and given place to the new: it is a new heaven above us; it is a new earth beneath us. New conditions of life must exist, for 'there is no more sea.' Plainly we have here a representation in which symbolism is carried to its utmost limits..." (*The Parousia*, ibid p 525, 527)

Now in the following chapter we will see that John is once again carried away, in spirit, upon a great and high mountain. This is an echo of Ezk. 40:2, where the hand of Yahweh brought Ezekiel, in vision, to "a very high mountain on which there seemed to be the outline of a city..." In Ezk. 48:30-35 the gates of the city are listed, each one corresponding to one of the tribes of Israel (clearly echoed in the picture we have here, in 21:14, below). Verse 35, there, ends, "And the name of the city from that day on shall be 'Yahweh Is There'" (corresponding to 21:3, below). This is also seen in Ezk. 37:27, "My dwelling-place shall be with them..." More references to the OT could be listed, but it is clear that this vision has its roots in the prophecies of the OT. But for now, let us consider the verses themselves.

Chapter 21

1. **Then I saw "a new** (new in nature; different from the usual; better than the old; superior in value and attraction; new in quality) **atmosphere** (or: sky; or: heaven) **and a new Land** (or: earth)," **for you see, actually, the first** (former; preceding; earlier) **atmosphere** (or: heaven) **and the first** (former, preceding)

Land (or: earth; soil; ground) **went away** (or: moved off, and passed away), **and the sea does not exist any longer.**

This is a clear allusion to Isa. 65:17, "I create new havens and a new earth; and the former things shall not be remembered, or come to mind..." Cf also Isa. 66:22. Here we should ask, Is this a vision of the recent past, the present, or the future? John Noē offers a guideline for studying such a vision as this: "Eschatology (the study of last things / the end times) is all about the change of covenants, not a future change of cosmos" (ibid p 271 n 2). The vision shown to John was a picture of what existed in his day, with the coming of the new arrangement (or: covenant) in Christ. This vision still applies to our own day. Eschatology in Scripture does not address the concept of an end of human history or an end of the physical creation. It speaks of the end of Israel's Mosaic age, or the age of the Law, which is now history.

Peter made mention of this same situation in 2 Pet. 3:
> 13. **Yet we, according to** (or: down from and in line with) **the effect and result of His promise, are habitually receptive toward fresh skies and continue with expectation, face to face with atmospheres new in kind and quality** (or: keep an opinion with regard to new heavens) **and a land** (or: soil; ground; earth) **new in kind and quality, within which [situations; conditions] a rightwising eschatological deliverance** (or: righted existence of living in covenant relationships of the fairness which accords with the Way pointed out; liberated participation in the justice and equity of the new arrangement) **is presently and permanently settled down** (is continuously dwelling and at home).

> "Peter and his listeners were by habit **receptive toward** the new creation and the new covenant arrangements where they had been "**made alive together by** (or: joins us in common life with, for and in; [p46, B: within; in union with]) **the Christ.... and He jointly roused and raised** (or: suddenly awakens and raises) **[us] up, and caused [us] to sit** (or: seats [us]; = enthroned [us]) **together within the things situated upon** [thus, above] **the heavens within and in union with Christ Jesus** (Eph. 2:5-6). They were now **face to face with atmospheres new in kind and quality** that presented them with **fresh skies** and kept them with opinions that were shaped by the new heavens (i.e., the rule of Christ via the Spirit, in the kingdom of the heavens – as Jesus described in His parables). And God's **rightwising, eschatological deliverance** (the work and resurrection of Christ) is constantly resident within this new world of the Second Humanity – the resurrected existence that is the life of the ages which has **settled down** and continuously dwells within Christ." (*Peter's Encore & Later Paul*, ibid p 56)

Simmons comments here:
> "The imagery of a new heavens and new earth is derived from the book of Isaiah where it had both mediate and immediate application. In its immediate, historical application, the new heavens and earth was a poetical description looking to the restoration of Israel to its land after the captivity in Babylon; however, in its mediate, plenary application and significance, the new heavens and earth looked to the Messianic age and kingdom" (ibid p 396).

The joyful flourishing of Christ's kingdom was described in terms of the wilderness being glad and the desert rejoicing and blossoming as a rose, where waters break out and steams flow in the desert, with no lions or ravenous beasts (Isa. 35:1-10). Isa. 11:6-9 speaks figuratively of the absence of hurt and destruction by describing wolf, leopard, lion, and bear no longer eating sheep and cattle: a transformed creation. Yet Isaiah was not writing about animals, but about people and nations having their characters transformed, because "the Land (or: earth) shall be full of the knowledge of Yahweh" (vs. 9b). Consider the figurative language in Isa. 2:2,

"And it shall come to pass in the last days [that] the mountain [a figure of a kingdom] of Yahweh's house [His temple; His people] shall be established in the top of the mountains [figure for the kingdoms of the world], and shall be exalted above the hills – and ALL nations shall flow unto it."

Mark well the cataclysmic language of a re-ordering of land masses. They spoke of a new Land/earth, which was a figure of God's reign and kingdom being established as we saw in 11:15, above.

A very revealing use of "heavens and earth" is found in Isa. 51:15-16,

"Yet I am Yahweh, your God, who split (or: divided) the sea [a reference to passing through the Red Sea, at the Exodus from Egypt]... Therefore I put My words in your mouth, and with the shadow of My hand have I covered you: to plant the heavens and to lay the foundations of the earth – to say to Zion, 'You are My People'..."

Verse 16 – the putting of His words in them – speaks of His giving them the Law, as Mt. Sinai. He created them as a nation, there. The symbolic language of "planting the heavens" and "founding the earth" refer to establishing them as a nation, and making Israel His People. This was the former "heavens and earth" that passed away – in AD 70.

What John saw was a whole new world. Paul spoke of this new, ordered system in 2 Cor. 5:17,

"**Consequently, since someone [is] within Christ** (or: So that if anyone [is] in union with [the] Anointed One; or: And as since a Certain One [was] in Christ), **[there is] a new creation** (or: [it is] a framing and founding of a different kind; [he or she is] an act of creation having a fresh character and a new quality)**: the original things** (the beginning [situations]; the archaic and primitive [arrangements]) **passed by** (or: went to the side). **Consider! New things have come into existence** (have been birthed; or: It has become different, new things; or: He has been birthed and now exists being ones of a different kind, character and quality)."

As Terry points out (ibid p 460), "This renovation, as Heb. 12:26, 27 shows, involves a removal or passing away of that which is old and shaken." The cross and then the destruction of Jerusalem in AD 70, "shook heaven (the temple and the priesthood) and earth (the people and their place in God's economy)." The statement that, "**the first** (former; preceding; earlier) **atmosphere** (or: heaven) **and the first** (former, preceding) **Land** (or: earth; soil; ground) **went away** (or: moved off, and passed away)" speaks of passing away of the arrangements under the old, Mosaic covenant (Heb. 8:7-8; 9:1). This is a symbol of the end of the temple/priesthood cultus (Jn. 4:21), and the end of Israel as a nation (AD 70). It represents the death of the first Adam (or: of our "old humanity" – Rom. 6:6) when humanity was buried with Christ, as mentioned above. The old creation was still groaning when Paul was writing Rom. 8:22. Note that in Rom. 8:23 Paul puts himself and the called-out communities (those possessing the firstfruits of the Spirit) as being in solidarity with the rest of humanity that was still groaning, until the placement in the Son would also be unveiled to them. He was one with them. They were all "one body."

Another example of apocalyptic destruction (in Noah's day) was cited in 2 Pet. 3:6 where, "**the ordered System** (world of culture and relationships) **of that time destroyed** (or: lost) **itself, being washed down** (inundated; deluged) **by water**." Now it was not the physical earth that was destroyed, but people and their cultures. Peter then compares this to the "fire" that was about to come upon Jerusalem, on,

"**A** [note: not "The"] **day of separating for deciding** (or: with the character of evaluating for judging), **as well as of loss, ruin or destruction which pertains to the irreverent humans** (or: of people devoid of reverential awe toward God)" (vs. 7b).

Having seen that this is a book of signs and symbols, we should not start putting a literal interpretation on this vision. The figure of "**the sea does not exist any longer**" should be an immediate clue. What this is saying is that there is no longer a distinction between God's people and the great "sea of humanity" which had been the non-Israelites, or Gentiles. He has broken down the "middle wall" and made of the two "**one new humanity**" thus give peace, from the joining, to the tossing waves of the sea (Eph. 2:14, 15). Isa. 57:20 used this same simile, "the **lawless** are like **the sea**, when tossed, for it cannot rest; its waters toss out mire and dirt." As all humanity was included in the first man, Adam, so all humanity is included in the Last Adam, the Second Man, the Lord from heaven (1 Cor. 15:45-47).

In regard to the final clause, "**the sea does not exist any longer**," Borg remarks,
> "The sea as home of the ancient monster [*cf* 13:1, above], from which empire after empire ascended, is gone" (ibid p 289; brackets added).

In Christ there is no empire, for all are brothers (Rom. 8:29b). All serve one another (Mat. 23:11; Jn. 13:5, 14). This picture may be an echo of the destruction of Babylon where in Jer. 51:36b we find the symbolic language, "I will drain her sea and dry up her fountain." All of this points to the end of the old, and the beginning of the new.

2. **Next I saw the set-apart** (or: holy) **city, a new Jerusalem** (or: an innovative, different Jerusalem that is new in character and quality), **progressively descending from out of the atmosphere** (or: presently stepping down out of the midst of the sky; or: steadily stepping in accord, forth from heaven), **[coming] from God, being prepared** (having been made ready) **as a bride, being arranged** (having been set in order; adorned; decorated) **for** (or: by) **her man** (husband; a male person of full age and stature).

This picture follows the Isaiah text (65:17) quoted above, alluding to Isa. 65:18b, which explains the previous verses in both texts:
> "Because I Myself am presently, progressively making (forming; constructing; producing; creating) Jerusalem [to be] a result of exceedingly glad rejoicing, and My people a well-minded attitude that is mentally at ease, healthy and thoughtfully considerate for good" (LXX, JM).

The "new heavens and the new earth" of vs. 1, above, are in fact this **new Jerusalem**, described as "**the bride**" in vss.9b-10, below. Also, Isa. 61:10 spoke to this situation:
> "For He clothes me with garments of salvation (or: deliverance), in a robe of righteousness (LXX: a well-minded attitude that is mentally at ease, healthy and thoughtfully considerate for good); He clads me like a bridegroom adorned with priestly attire (or: a turban); like a **bride** ornamented with her jewels (or: bedecked with her finery)."

And now we see that what John saw was what Paul referred to in Gal. 4:26, "**the Jerusalem which is above**." We see the same picture in Heb. 12:22-23,
> "**you folks have approached so that you are NOW at Mount Zion – even in a city of a continuously living God; in 'Jerusalem upon heaven'** (or: in a Jerusalem pertaining to and having the character and qualities of a superior, or added, heaven and atmosphere; or: in Jerusalem [situated] upon, and comparable to, the atmosphere)... **an assembly of an entire people** (or: an assembly of all; a universal convocation) **and in** (or: to) **a summoning forth** (or: a called-out and gathered community) **of firstborn folks having been copied** (from-written, as from a pattern; or: enrolled; registered) **within [the; or: various] atmospheres** (or: heavens)... **spirits of just folks** (or: breath-effects from those who are fair and equitable and in right relationship within the Way pointed out) **having been brought to the destined goal** (perfected; finished; matured; made complete)."

Heb. 11:16 speaks of those of the past, both prior to and within the old Mosaic covenant:
> "**Now they are continuously stretching themselves out in order to touch a superior** (stronger and better) **one: this is one belonging to the superior-heaven** (or: that is, pertaining to the One upon the atmosphere; or: this exists being one from the added, superimposed heaven)."

What is described here in 21:2 is exactly that to which those passages in Hebrews refer. This **New Jerusalem** is "**the city continuously having the foundations – whose Craftsman** (or: Technician; Artisan) **and skilled Worker for the people** (or: Producer; Architect) **[is] God**" (Heb. 11:10). The particular Greek word **new**, that is used here, signifies that it is "an innovative, different Jerusalem that is new in character and quality," and corresponds to the "**new atmosphere and new earth**" of the previous verse. This City answers to "**the greater and more perfect** (more matured, complete and destined) **Tabernacle not made by hands – that is, not of this creation**" that pertains to "**a New and Different Arrangement** (an innovative disposition and covenant that is new in kind, quality and character)" (Heb. 9:11, 15). This City houses,

> "**an administration, implementation and realization from a detailed plan of the effects of that which fills up the appointed seasons and fertile moments [designed] to itself bring back again all things up under one Head** (or: to gather everything around the main point and sum it all up in unity; to unite and return all things to the Source) **within and in union with the Christ: those things upon [other MSS: within] the heavens** (or: the atmospheres) **and the things upon the land** (earth) **– centered in, within the midst of, and in union with, Him!**" (Eph. 1:10),

where we are "**jointly roused and raised up, and caused to sit** (or: = enthroned) **together within the things situated upon** [thus, above] **the heavens**" (Eph. 2:6). Paul spoke further about this City:

> "**Consequently then** (or: Thereupon), **you folks no longer continuously exist being strangers** (foreigners) **and sojourners** (folks being or living beside a house; temporary residents in a foreign land), **but in contrast, you continually exist being fellow-citizens of those set apart to be sacred people** (or: folks residing together in a City belonging to, and composed of, the holy ones): **even God's family** (members of God's household), **being fully built as a house upon the foundation of the sent-forth representatives** (or: emissaries) **and prophets** (folks who had light ahead of time), **Jesus Christ continuously being a corner-foundation [stone] of it**" (Eph. 2:19-20).

In Phil. 3::20 he proclaimed:

> "**You see, our citizenship** (result of living in a free CITY; or: commonwealth-effects; political realm) **continues inherently existing** (or: continues humbly ruling; continuously subsists; repeatedly has its under-beginning) **resident within the midst of [the] atmospheres** (or: heavens), **from out of where** (or: which place) **we also continuously receive and take away in our hands from out of a Deliverer** (a Savior; One restoring us to the health and wholeness of our original state and condition): **[the] Lord** (or: a Master), **Jesus Christ**."

John saw a City that is a figure of the new covenant, the children of promise (Gal. 4:23, 24, 28). That it is **progressively descending** speaks to us of the character of the called-out communities: although seated with Christ in the heavenlies (Eph. 2:6), this company takes the form of a servant, as does our Lord, and descends to minister to those living in the earth realm, to bring life to the dead, healing to the sick, freedom to the prisoners, and inclusion to the outcasts. Although **adorned** as a **bride**, she is God's tent (vs. 3, below):

> "**within the midst of** (or: in union with) **Whom you folks, also, are continuously and progressively being formed a constituent part of the structure** (or: being built together into a house) **– into God's down-home place** (place of settling down to dwell; abode; permanent dwelling) **within [the] Spirit** (or: in spirit; or: in the midst of a Breath-effect and an attitude)" (Eph. 2:22).

Through her, God is manifested among humanity, and now all humanity are God's people – and He is their God, as we see in the next verse. What a picture! The "descending" of the New Jerusalem may be a part of what Jesus enigmatically spoke to Nathaniel, in Jn. 1:51, "**you will proceed seeing the heaven** (or: atmosphere; sky) **being one that is opened back up again, and 'God's agents repeatedly** (progressively; continuously) **ascending** (stepping back up again) **and habitually** (progressively; continuously; repeatedly) **descending** (stepping down)' [Gen. 28:12] **upon the Son of the Man.**"

The phrase "**set-apart** (or: holy) **city**" echoes Isa. 48:2, and Isa. 52:1 admonishes, "Put on your beautiful clothes, Jerusalem, the holy city…. Shake yourself from the dust, and arise…" The picture of a **bride** echoes Paul in Eph. 5:25-32 where he ends his thought on the husband-bride relationship by saying,
> "**This secret** (or: mystery) **is great** (= important), **but I am speaking unto** (or: into; with a view to) **Christ, even** (or: and; as well as) **unto** (or: into; with a view to) **the called-out community** (or: the called-out person; or: the summoned-forth covenant assembly)."

3. **And then I heard a great voice from out of the throne** [other MSS: atmosphere; heaven] **saying, "Consider! God's tent** (the Tabernacle of God) **[is] with mankind** (the humans), **'and He will continue living in a tent** (dwell in a Tabernacle) **with them, and they will continue being** (will constantly exist being) **His peoples, and God Himself will continue being with them** [some MSS add: their God].'**

The **great voice** may be the same one heard in 19:1, above. The MSS vary, some reading "**from out of the throne**," others reading "from out of the atmosphere/heaven." The symbols are similar, and present the same message, as we have seen throughout the Unveiling. The throne is the place of rule, in God's kingdom; His throne is in "heaven," figured by the mercy seat in the Tabernacle (in the innermost chamber), which itself represented "heaven" (the sphere and realm of God) on earth.

In Israel's history, **God's tent** (the Tabernacle of God) was where He lived among Israel during their wilderness journeys, following the Exodus. It was associated only with Israel, under the old covenant, or, arrangement. Now things are different. The old arrangement has passed away (died with the death of their Messiah). Now there is a new arrangement where His Tabernacle is "**with mankind** (the humans)." This is because it is a new creation (2 Cor. 5:17) in which God's People now include Israel plus the ethnic multitudes (or: the Jews together with the Gentiles/nations – Eph. 2:11-22). Now everyone is included.

An allusion to Lev. 26:11-12 is seen here, which Paul quotes in 2 Cor. 6:16
> "**For, you see, WE** [other MSS: you folks] **continuously exist BEING** (we/you are) **a temple of [the] living God, just as God said,**
>> '**I will proceed to make My home and will continue walking about within and among them** (= I will habitually reside, as in a house, and live My life within and among them), **and I will proceed existing being** (or: I will continue being) **their God, and they will proceed existing being** (or: will continue being) **My people'.**"

So the same thing that was said to Israel, when they were created to be a nation, with their own, special "heaven and earth," is now said to the new creation – the "**WE**" (Jew plus Gentile) of 2 Cor. 6:16a.

The allusion can also be seen pointing to Ezk. 37:26-28 (in the same chapter that we saw, above, had application to the visions here). There we read,
> "And I will set and progressively establish My set-apart (holy) [chambers; places; things] within their midst, on into the Age (or: the indefinite time). Then My Tabernacle (settled and established tent) will continue existing (being) among them, centered in them, and I will continue being God to them (or: a God for them and with them), and they will continue being My People" (LXX, JM).

Jer. 31:33 is referenced in the phrase by the MSS that add "their God" to the end of vs.3, above:

"For this is the covenant… averring [is] Yahweh, 'I will I put My law within them, and I shall write it on their heart; I will become their Elohim (God), and they shall become My people'" (CVOT). Solomon could not comprehend how this could be (2 Chron. 6:18). But Yahweh had plainly laid this out in Ex.29:44-46. This was promised again, in Zech. 2:10-11, where the prophet adds,

"And MANY NATIONS shall be joined to Yahweh in that Day, and shall be My People."

Then, in the next verse, he says further, "And Yahweh… shall choose Jerusalem again." But Paul opened the promises up to everyone, in Rom. 8:14, saying,

"For as many as are being continuously led by God's Spirit (or: habitually brought or conducted in [the] Breath-effect which is God; progressively driven along with an attitude from God), **THESE FOLKS are God's sons** (these continuously exist being sons of God; or: = these are folks who have the character and qualities of God)."

The clause, **"He will continue living in a tent** (dwell in a Tabernacle) **with them,"** is represented by a Name that was given in Isa. 7:14, "you will call His name Immanuel," and repeated in Isa. 8:8, where He is momentarily addressed, "O Immanuel!" Then the meaning of this name is spelled out in Isa. 8:10 that concludes with, "For with us is El (God)." The fulfillment of Isa. 7:14, which was quoted in Mat. 1:23, is explained as a reference to the birth of Jesus. And Jesus said of Himself,

"You see, where there are two or three people that have been led and gathered together into My Name, I am there (in that place) **within the midst of and among them"** (Mat. 18:20).

The **tent** in which God **will continue living** is His new, inclusive humanity. Paul used the tent metaphor is 2 Cor. 5:1-2,

"if our house, of the tabernacle which is pitched on the land, would at some point be dismantled (or: that whenever our house, which is this tent upon the earth, should be loosed down), **we constantly have** (continuously hold; presently possess) **a structure** (a building) **forth from out of the midst of God: an eonian house** (a house having the qualities and character which pertain to the Age; a house for the ages) **– not made by hands – resident within the heavens** (or: in union with the atmospheres). **For you see, even within this one we are continuously groaning, utterly longing and constantly yearning to fully enter within and to clothe upon ourselves** (to dress upon ourselves) **our dwelling-house** (habitation) **– the one [made] out of heaven** (or: the one from, or made of, atmosphere; the [dwelling-house, or habitation] from out of the midst of [the] sky)."

Paul's words, here, can be taken corporately (signifying "the body of Christ," God's Temple, or Tabernacle), or have an individual application. Corporately, here in the Unveiling, the temple has expanded to be the City that John saw, "descending out of heaven, or, the atmosphere" (vs. 2, above) – the same location of "**our dwelling-house**" to which Paul just referred – and thus we see in vs. 22, below, that this City has no temple (the "Tabernacle/Temple" of the old covenant was destroyed, or, "**dismantled**," as Paul puts it; cf Jn. 4:21). In 2 Per. 1:13, Peter used the same metaphor, in apparently a personal application, "**as long as I continue existing within this tent-effect** (or: tabernacle)…"

We should not miss this important promise: "**God Himself will continue being with them.**" We saw this previously in 7:15b, above. No, He is not taking people off to the sky somewhere; His plan has always been for Him to be with, among and within humans. He blew Himself into humanity when He first created us (Gen. 2:7). He came as a Wind and filled with Himself the firstfruits of His new creation, His second humanity, in Acts 2:2-4. We have further clarification of all of this in 1 Jn. 4:

13. **Within this we are continually knowing by experience that we are constantly remaining** (dwelling; abiding) **within the midst of, and in union with, Him and He Himself within us, because He has given to us from out of His Breath-effect** (or: Spirit; Attitude).

14. **And we have gazed upon this public situation, and are repeatedly testifying** (giving witness and evidence) **that the Father has sent forth** (dispatched as a Representative) **the Son – [the] Savior of the world** (or: Deliverer of the ordered and controlling System of religion and secular society; Restorer of the universe; or: the Rescuer and Healer of all humanity).

15. **Whoever may speak in accord** (confess; avow; say like words; say the same thing; agree) **that Jesus exists being God's Son** (or: is continuously the Son which is God), **God continuously dwells** (abides), **remaining in him, and he himself within God.**

16. **And we have come by intimate experience to know and have believed, trusted and are convinced of the Love which God has** (or: holds) **continuously within** (or: among) **us. God exists continually being Love** (God is Love), **and the person continuously remaining** (dwelling; abiding) **within, and in union with, the Love, is continuously remaining** (dwelling; abiding) **within, and in union with, God – and God constantly dwells** (remains) **within the midst of him and abides in union with him.**

4. **"And He will continue anointing** (or: progressively smear or repeatedly wipe away) **every tear from their eyes. And the Death will no longer continue existing** (or: the death shall proceed being no more) **– neither will mourning** (sadness; grief), **nor an outcry, nor hard work** (painful toil; misery) **continue existing any longer** ([they] will continue being no more), **because the FIRST THINGS went** (or: passed) **away."** [cf 2 Cor. 5:17]

This verse presents a challenge to our understanding, so we will be tempted to ask: Is this view of **the Death** a literal statement amidst all the symbols of these visions? Or is this also a figure? The answer is: It is an apocalyptic vision; it is symbolism. Note the definite article before the word Death. It is **the Death** of, and from, "**stumblings aside** (offenses; wrong steps) **and failures to hit the mark** (or: mistakes; errors; times of falling short; sins; deviations)" of which Paul spoke in Eph. 2:1. It is the Death of which he spoke in Rom. 8:6,

> "**For the result of the thinking** (mind-set; effect of the way of thinking; disposition; result of understanding and inclination; the minding; the opinion; the thought; the outlook) **of the flesh** (= the human condition or the System of culture and cultus; or: = outward Torah ceremony) **[is; brings] death, yet the result of the thinking** (mind-set; disposition; thought and way of thinking; outlook) **of the spirit** (or: the Spirit; the Breath-effect; the Attitude) **[is; brings] Life and Peace**."

Now, in contrast, the nouns of the following clause do not have the definite article before them. Once we live in Life and Peace (i.e., in Christ; in the reign of God) **mourning, outcries, hard work** (recall: His yoke is easy) do not "**continue existing any longer**," or, "[they] will continue being no more." This announcement is about spiritual things. They are not referring to the natural world or the physical universe.

Another clue is in the last clause, "**the FIRST THINGS went away**." This is the echo of 2 Cor. 5:17, quoted above. It is picture of being "in Christ," which IS the new creation of which Paul spoke. What went away was the 1st covenant, together with the Law, the Aaronic priesthood, the sacrifices, the worship in religious activities, the "holiness laws" of "clean and unclean" purity codes, the separation of a chosen people-group from the rest of humanity, the observance of days or weeks, circumcision and ritual purity, etc., etc. For freedom Christ has set us free (John 8:36; Gal. 5:1) from the bondage to ritual and religion. John Gavazzoni shared with me a connection that he had made between what is described here and the words of Jesus, concerning the Jewish leadership of the 1st century and those who then rejected Him. In Lu. 13 Jesus spoke to the situation that would soon come to them:

> 23. **Now at one point, someone said to Him, "Sir** (or: Master; Lord), **[I wonder] if [only] a few are proceeding in being saved**
>> (or: if few are progressively being rescued; if the folks presently being healed and made whole are a small number)**?"**

So He said to them,

24. **"You folks be continually struggling and constantly exerting yourselves vigorously even to the point of agonizing, as contestants in the public games, to at once enter through the narrow door** (or: cramped entry), **because many people – I now tell you – will continue seeking to enter, and yet they will not continue having strength.**

25. **"From [the point or time] where the master of the house** (or: the owner and lord of the house; the householder) **may get up and lock off** (close and bar) **the door** (or: entry), **and then you folks should begin to stand outside and to repeatedly knock [at] the door** (or: entry), **repeatedly saying, 'Sir** (or: Master; Lord; [other MSS: Sir, sir! {or: Lord, Lord!}]), **open up to us** (or: for us)!' **And then, giving a decided reply, he will proceed in declaring to you folks, 'I have not seen, and thus do not know, you people. From what place are you?** (or: I am not acquainted [with] whence you are [come]!).'

26. **"At that point you will begin to be saying, one after another, 'We ate and drank in front of you** (in your sight)! **Also, you taught in our town squares** (plazas; broad streets)!'

27. **"And yet, he will continue declaring, 'I am now saying to you, I have not seen, and thus do not know, from where you are. Stand off away from me, all [you] workers of injustice**
> (laborers in that which is not right; unfair workmen; folks whose actions do not accord with the Way pointed out; workers void of rightwised relationships)!'

28. **"Whenever you may** [other MSS: will] **see Abraham, Isaac and Jacob – as well as all the prophets – within the midst of God's reign** (or: sovereign activities and influence; kingdom), **yet you yourselves, one after another, being thrown outside, the weeping and the grinding** (or: gnashing) **of the teeth** (= the sorrow and regret) **will be [out] there, in that place.**

29. **"Not only that, people will continue arriving from eastern regions and western territories, as well as from [the] north and [the] south, and they will proceed in being made to recline back at a meal, within God's reign** (kingdom; sovereign projects and programs).

30. **"And so – now think about this – there are last ones who will proceed in being first ones; and there are first ones who will regress to being last ones."**

Although their place of preeminence in God's reign, that of being "first ones," would pass away from them, take note that in vs. 30 Jesus said that even though they would "regress to being last ones," this implies that they, too, will at some point enter into the new creation of God's present reign of the new arrangement. In Mat. 21:31 Jesus put it this way:

> "**Jesus said, "That's right** (You got it; Amen)! **I am now saying and laying it out for you that the tax** (or: tribute; toll) **collectors** (or: tax farmers; businessmen who bought the contract to collect taxes for the government) **and the prostitutes are constantly PRECEDING YOU men into God's reign** (or: the kingdom of God; the sovereign activity of God)!"

In Christ, in the realm of spirit, God **anoints** and wipes away tears (a figure of sorrow and grief), for we now have joy and expectation. We saw this in 7:17b, above,

> "**And God will continue anointing** (or: wiping and smearing) **every tear shed from out of their eyes.**" *Cf* Isa. 65:19.

Isa. 60:20b spoke of this situation: "Your days of mourning will be finished up."
The picture has reference to Christ's deliverance of humanity from bondage and exile. Recall Israel's lament, when in Babylon (Ps. 137:1). But this proclamation in the Unveiling echoes Isa. 35:10,

> "And the ransomed of Yahweh, they shall return, and they will enter Zion with jubilant [song]… And affliction and sighing will flee" (CVOT). *Cf* 7:15-17, above; Isa. 51:11.

In Him, joined to the Lord, death ceases to exist: John 11:26,

> "**And further, everyone** (or: all mankind) **– the person presently living and progressively trusting-and-believing into** (or: regularly experiencing convinced faith into the midst of; being

constantly faithful unto) **Me – can by no means** (or: may under no circumstances) **die-off** (or: die-away), **on into the Age [of Messiah]**."
And there is no more mourning for we see in Lu. 4:18 that He came to "**heal the brokenhearted**."

> "God has wiped away our tears, for we are partakers of His First Resurrection. One striking evidence of this is the obvious difference between Christian and pagan funerals: We grieve, but not as those who have no hope (1 Thes. 4:13). God has taken away the sting of death (1 Cor. 15:55-58)" (Chilton ibid p 547).

In fact, Paul assures us that in Christ, "**The Death was drunk down and swallowed into Victory** (or: overcoming)!" (1 Cor. 15:54; Isa. 25:8). Then he goes on to say that we have already been given this Victory, in God, and by God:

> "**But grace and joyous favor [is] in God** (or: by God) – **the One presently and progressively giving the Victory** (or: the overcoming) **to us, in us and for us through our Lord** (Owner; Master), **Jesus, [the] Christ!**" (1 Cor. 15:57).

The late 1st century book, *The Fourth Book of Ezra*, speaks of, and echoes, this same situation:

> "The root of evil is sealed up from you, illness is banished from you, and death is hidden; hell has fled and corruption has been forgotten [fn x: Syr.; Lat.: 'Hades and corruption have fled into oblivion'], sorrows have passed away, and in the end the treasure of immortality is made manifest" (8:53-54, trans. by B.M. Metzger, *The OT Pseudepigrapha*, Vol. 1, ibid p 544).

Being seated with Him in the heavenlies there are no more outcries, and no more religious works, painful toil to try to please God, or misery due to our failures and mistakes. Recall Mat. 11:28,

> "**So everyone come here, toward Me! – all those constantly weary and exhausted from toil and labor, as well as folks having been caused to carry a load, and continuing burdened down – and I, Myself, will refresh you and cause you folks to rest**."

These conditions exist now, in Christ, but we need to see that all this is true in the context of the City (vs. 2, above), and they apply, at this time, to God's people (vs. 3), and the overcomer (vs. 7, below). Then vs. 8 points out those who yet need the work of the baptism in the Spirit and Fire (the second death), and 22:15, below, tells us that these folks are outside the City (New Jerusalem). In Him, the "**first things**" have gone away. Later in this chapter we see that this community gives Light to the world (vs. 23-24; cf Mat. 5:14) and is inclusive, allowing the multitudes of the ethnic groups (and religions?) enter into the City (vs. 24-26) to participate in all that she is, and to be transformed. This is heaven, the realm of spirit, and is continuously being brought to earth and being made available – through the Spirit of Christ – to all humanity. Verses 1-4 have led up to the overarching proclamation in our next verse:

5. **And then the One** (or: He [who is]) **continuously sitting upon the throne said,**
    "**Consider this** (or: Look, and see)! **I am presently making all things new** (or: habitually creating everything [to be] new and fresh; progressively forming [the] whole anew; or, reading παντα as masculine: I am periodically making **all humanity** new, and progressively, one after another, producing and creating **every person** anew, while constantly constructing all people fresh and new, i.e., continuously renewing **everyone**)!" [cf 2 Cor. 5:17]

This is the same One of 20:11, above, "**the One continuously sitting upon [the pure throne] from Whose face the Land** (or: ground; earth) **and the atmosphere** (or: sky; heaven) **flee** (or: at once fled)." Because the old ones fled away, He had to create new ones. They fled because, "**He has made the first** (or: former) **'old,'**" (Heb. 8:13). It involved, "**the transposition** (transference; changeover; change of setting or place) **of the things being repeatedly shaken**" (Heb. 12:27). This is a new beginning; a new economy; a new covenant. This One sits upon "**God's – even** (or: and) **the little Lamb's – throne**" (22:1, below).

Notice the Greek present tense in the first clause of the proclamation: it is an ongoing and progressive work of Christ. God is "**presently making all things new** (or: habitually creating everything [to be] new and fresh; progressively forming [the] whole anew)." But then look at the verb tenses in vs. 6, below, "**They have come into being** (been born; come to be) **and stand accomplished** (are produced)!" Here we have the perfect tense; in Christ it stands a completed work, referring to His people. The various other MSS read the verb in different persons (1st and 3rd), but they are all in the perfect tense. This does not refer to a future event.

Here, Metzger points out,
> "[T]he present tense also suggests that God is continually making things new here and now (compare 2 Cor. 3:8; 4:16-18; Col. 3:1-4)" (*Breaking the Code* ibid p 99).

An important point in this verse is that the form of the word **all** serves both as a neuter gender, and as a masculine. I gave the all-inclusive neuter rendering first: **all things**. But equally important is the masculine rendering, given in the second half of the parenthetical expansion:
> "I am periodically making **all humanity** new, and progressively, one after another, producing and creating **every person** anew, while constantly constructing all people fresh and new, i.e., continuously renewing **everyone**."

What a promise; what an adventure we are experiencing. We clay pots (2 Cor. 4:7) were, "marred in the hands of [our] Potter." So our condition was His fault (and plan), and "so He [is] making it another vessel (pot), as it seems good to [Him]" (Jer. 18:4). This is an internal process for God, because,
> "**For you see, within the midst of and in union with Him we continuously live** (or, as a subjunctive: could be constantly living), **and are constantly moved about and put into motion** [passive voice], **and continue existing** (experiencing Being)" (Acts 17:28).

Or, as Paul put it elsewhere, we are all passing "**through the midst of Him**" (Rom. 11:36). We can't get away from him, nor can He get away from us (as if He would ever want to!). And so, we read Paul saying in 2: Cor. 5:18, 19, 20,
> "**Yet further, all these things [are]** (or: the Whole [is]) **forth from out of the midst of God – the One transforming us to be completely other [than we were]**.... **as that God was existing within Christ** (God was and continued being in union with [the] Anointed One) **progressively and completely transforming [the] aggregate of humanity** (or: world) **to be other [than it is]**.... [and thus], **We are constantly begging and urgently asking, on behalf of Christ** (or: for Christ's sake)**: 'Be fully transformed in, be correspondingly altered by, be changed from an enemy to be a friend with, be reconciled to, and be altered to be another [person] by, God!'**"

A conclusion by Beale seems appropriate here: "The book portrays an end-time new creation that has erupted into the present old world through the death and resurrection of Christ and through the sending of the Spirit at Pentecost" (ibid p 175).

This verse echoes Jesus in Mat. 19:28, "**In the rebirth – when the Son of the Man** (mankind's Son; = Adam's son; [or: the eschatological messianic figure]; or: the human) **can sit upon the throne of His glory**," and Acts 3:21,
> "**times of a movement away from all things that have been firmly put down, set and established and until the periods of successive events which occur in passing moments, moving all mankind away from having been placed and positioned down as well as from the state or condition of all things that had been determined from an indefinite period of time** (or: from a [particular] age) **– of which things God spoke** (or: speaks) **through [the] mouth of His set-apart prophets** (those sacred folks who spoke light ahead of time)."

See the article, "What is the Timeframe of Acts 3:21?," at the end of the comments on this book, below. The "movement away from all things that have been firmly put down, set and established (*apokatastasis*)" was the movement from the Law of Moses, the old arrangement/covenant that for Israel had long been established. It was an old wineskin, with old wine. The new arrangement/covenant, which Jesus compared to "new wine," needed a new vessel to contain it. In Mat. 9 He told folks;

> 16. **"Now nobody normally puts a patch of unshrunk cloth upon an old outer garment. You see, its filling-effect** (i.e., the pre-shrunken patch which fills in the hole) **is progressively pulling up away from the outer garment, and the split-effect** (tear; rip; rent) **progressively becomes worse.**
>
> 17. **"Neither are people normally draining fresh, recently made, new wine into old skin-bags** (bottles), **otherwise the skin-bags are constantly bursting** (being torn open), **and then the wine is constantly being spilled out and the skin-bags continue being destroyed** (ruined). **To the contrary, people normally drain fresh, just-made, new wine into skin-bags having a new character and quality – and both continue being preserved.**

This was the reason that He needed to make a new creation: a new heaven (temple) and a new earth (transformed, resurrected people). Now the blended covenant communities were the new temple, and the one new humanity was the new "earth."

Next He is saying [to me],

> **"Write, because these words are dependable** (or: faithful; reliable) **ones and true ones** (ones full of faith and realities)."

God reminds John to write these words down, because they are Faithful words, and True words, a reference to 19:11, above. He is constantly (or: repeatedly) making ALL THINGS new in kind, new in quality. What is left outside of this statement? These proclamations of good news are, of themselves, "full of faith and realities" of the new creation – His new, inclusive, People; His household and its life-giving arrangements. The background of this idea can be seen in Isa. 43:19,

> "Behold, I [am] doing a new [thing]; Now it is sprouting... I am placing a Way in a wilderness, Tracks in desolation" (CVOT).

And there is the passage in Isa. 65:17-25, where he spoke of, "creating new...creating Jerusalem... etc."

6. **Then He said to me,**

> **"They have come into being** (been born; come to be) **and stand accomplished** (are produced) [Concordant Gr. Text reads, with Sinaiticus: I have become (been born)!; Griesbach reads γεγονε: It has been done; Rotherham simply says: Accomplished; Barclay, Young, Beck, NASB, NKJV, Amplified all read w/Griesbach; Weymouth, Williams, Wuest, Robertson & Vincent read w/the Nestle-Aland & Metzger Text, γεγοναν (3rd. per. pl.)]! **I am the Alpha and the Omega: The Beginning** (Origin; Source; Headship; First Principle) **and The End** (The Goal; Consummation; The Final Act; The Finished Product; The Destiny; The Purpose).
>
> **"To him who is continuously thirsty, I, Myself, will continue giving from out of the spring of the Water of the Life, as an undeserved** (free) **gift** (or: As for Me, I will freely, gratuitously, be repeatedly giving from the midst of fountain of the water from the Life).

Here we have three variant readings, each one well attested in different manuscripts. Since we have no way of knowing which one represents the original, let's consider each one:

> a) 1st person singular: "I have become," or, "I have been born." The CLNT reads, "I have become the Alpha and the Omega, the Origin and the Consummation." If we see here the terms "Alpha and Omega" as referring to the whole plan of the ages – all of that which is "**from out of**

Him and through Him and [back] into Him," (Rom. 11:36) – then we can see this as a statement of Him being "**All in all**" (1 Cor. 15:28).

b) 3rd person singular: "It has become (come to be; been done; been birthed)." This could refer to the completion of His plan ("Accomplished," as Rotherham reads), similar to the statement of Jesus on the cross, "It is finished." Here, then, we would be seeing the "goal" from God's point of view – it is a finished work! Or, it could read "He has been born," referring to the Messiah – implying the work of Christ.

c) 3rd person plural: "**They have come into being** (been born; come to be)." This is the preferred reading of the more recent critical texts. This phrase could have as its antecedent the last sentence of vs. 5, and thus it is the faithful and true words that have "come to pass." Or perhaps, that the "**first things passed away** [and]... **all things [have become] new!**" This could then refer to the arrival of the New Order. Yet another interpretation would come from rendering this phrase "**They have been born**." We could then see this as parallel to 12:1-5, above, referring to the birth of the "corporate manchild" and their ascension to the throne.

The next statement is pregnant with possibilities:
> "**I am the Alpha and the Omega: The Beginning** (Origin; Source; Headship; First Principle) **and The End** (The Goal; Consummation; The Final Act; The Finished Product; The Destiny; The Purpose)."

The first phrase is a repetition of 1:8, above. The second phrase is found in Isa.41:4, "I, Yahweh, the First and the Last: I [am] He (or: I am He who is)!" The context is expanded in Isa. 44:6, "Thus says Yahweh, King of Israel, and his Redeemer, Yahweh of host: I [am the] First, and I [am the] Last..." Isa. 48:12 reads, "Hearken to Me, Jacob, and Israel, My called; I [am] He, I [am the] First; Indeed I [am the] Last." The combined statements are an allusion to 1:4b, above,
> "**the One continuously existing** (or: unceasingly being; Who continuously IS), **even the One Who was, and continued being, and the One Who is continuously** (or: repeatedly; habitually; progressively) **coming or going**."

The expanded options for **The Beginning** need little comment, but the semantic range is food for thought. Origin and Source can be seen, as well as End are seen by Paul in Col. 1:16,
> "**within Him was created the whole** (or: in union with Him everything is founded and settled, is built and planted, is brought into being, is produced and established; or: within the midst of Him all things were brought from chaos into order) – **the things within the skies and atmospheres, and the things upon the earth** (or: those [situations, conditions and/or people] in the heavens and on the land); **the visible things, and the unseen** (or: unable to be seen; invisible) **things: whether thrones** (seats of power) **or lordships** (ownership systems) **or governments** (rulers; leadership systems; sovereignties) **or authorities – the whole has been created and all things continue founded, put in order and stand framed through means of Him, and [proceeds, or were placed] into Him** (or: = He is the agent and goal of all creation)."

Take note of Paul's apocalyptic form of speaking of Christ in this verse to Colossae.

The options for **The End** present us with a number of trails to follow:
a) **The End**: Christ is the End of the old creation, of the old covenant, of the old humanity.
b) The Goal: God is the Goal toward which everyone and all things are moving; God is their Destiny (Rom. 11:36). Paul expressed another aspect of the goal in 1Cor. 15:21-22,
> "**For since through a person** (or: a human; or: humanity) **[came] death, through a Person** (or: a Human), **also, [comes] resurrection of dead people. For just as within Adam all humans keep on** (or: everyone continues) **dying, in the same way, also,**

within the Christ, all humans will keep on being made alive (or: in union with, and within the midst of, the Anointed One, everyone will one-after-another be created with Life)."

d) The Consummation: Christ is the Consummation of the previous age of the Law, and the Consummation of each age thereafter (Rom. 10:4).

e) Christ is the Final Act of the plan of the Ages. All things are summed up in Him. In Eph. 4:6, 10 we read:

> "**[There is] one God and Father of all humans – the One upon all people and [moving] through all people, and within the midst of all humanity and in union with all people and all things.... to the end that He would at once fill the Whole** (permeate and saturate everything; or: make all things full; bring all things to full measure and completion)."

f) Christ is the Finished Product of God's creation: the Last (*eschatos*) Adam. In speaking of the called-out folks, Paul says of the covenant community, in Eph. 1:23,

> "**which [community] is His body, the result of the filling from, and which is, the One Who is constantly filling all things within all humanity** (or: humans)
>
> > (or: which continues existing being His body: the resultant fullness, entire content and full measure of Him [Who is] progressively making full and completing all things in union with all things, as well as constantly filling the whole, in – and in union with – all people)."

g) God is the Destiny of all humanity and all creation. All things end their journey in Him. (Rom. 11:36).

h) Christ is the Purpose of all creation. Note the all-inclusiveness of Col. 3:11,

> "**Christ [is] all, and within all**
>
> > (or: Christ [is] all humanity, and within all mankind; or: Christ [is] everything or all things, and within everything and all things; [note: the Greek is plural, and is either masculine, signifying "mankind," or neuter, signifying all creation, in these phrases])."

Now let's look at the final statement of vs. 6, which is an echo of 7:16, 17, above. This metaphor, which is based on Isa. 55:1,

"Ho! All [who are] thirsty! Come (or: Go) to the water!.... without price!"

Then in Zech. 14:8 we read, "living waters shall flow forth from Jerusalem." These are metaphors for life. From 22:1, below, we see that this water of the life flows forth from out of God's throne (the great white throne!), and this same offer is presented in 22:17. Jesus has prophesied about this **Water** in Jn. 7:37-38,

> 37. **Now within the last day – the great one – of the feast** (or: festival), **Jesus, after having taken a stand, stood and then suddenly cries out, saying, "If ever anyone may continue being thirsty, let him be habitually coming toward** (or: face to face with) **Me, and then let the person continuously trusting and progressively believing into Me be constantly** (habitually; repeatedly) **drinking!** [cf Isa. 12:3; 55:1]
>
> > (or: let him be progressively coming to Me and keep on drinking. The person habitually being faithful unto Me,)
>
> 38. "**Just as the Scripture says, 'Rivers** (or: Floods; Torrents) **of living water will continuously flow** (or: gush; flood) **from out of the midst of His cavity** (His innermost being or part; or: the hollow of his belly; [used of the womb])."" [cf Isa. 58:11; Ezk. 47:1; Joel 3:18; Zech. 13:1; 14:8]

The temple which Ezekiel saw is the Temple which is the body of Christ. In Ezk. 47 he saw waters which issued out from this Temple and became a river (vs. 5). Actually, vs. 9, in the Heb., tells us that it became "two rivers," figuring the "two witnesses" that are His body:

> "And it shall come to pass, that EVERY LIVING SOUL that swarms whithersoever the rivers shall come SHALL LIVE, and the fish [= people] shall become a great multitude; for these waters have come thither that THEY may be healed, so shall EVERYTHING LIVE whithersoever the river comes" (Rotherham; emphasis added).

Note that 47:8 tells us that,

> "These waters are going forth unto the region toward the east, and shall go down unto the WASTE PLAIN, and shall enter the sea [the Tanakh reads "the sea of foul waters (i.e., the Dead Sea)], unto the sea being led forth, then shall the waters [i.e., the Dead Sea] be healed" (Rotherham; brackets and emphasis added).

So now we see where the river of life is going (to the dead), and what it will do (give life)! And EVERYTHING will LIVE, as a result of God's free GIFT: His grace; His Life! What a picture of life from death.

The Greek word *dorean* is both the accusative singular, and means "a free gift," and also the adverb form, meaning "freely." From the syntax I went with the former (as does Wuest), but many render it as the latter. Christ is here doing what He told His disciples to do: "Freely you received; freely give" (Matt. 10:8).

Recall Jesus with the Samaritan woman (one considered "unclean" in that time):

> "**If you had seen, so as to be aware of and now perceive God's gift** (*dorean*)**, and Who is the One presently saying to you, '[Please] give [some] to me, to drink,' you would ask** (or: make request of) **Him, and He would give living water to you**" (John 4:10).

This same word is used as an adverb (freely) by Paul in Rom. 3:24,

> "**while being folks presently and progressively being made right, freed from guilt, placed in solidarity within the Way pointed out, and continuously set in right relationship** (or: being [all] one-after-another delivered and rightwised; being ones habitually turned in the right direction; being [all] presently justified [by covenant inclusion]) **freely** (as a gift; gratuitously) **by His grace** (or: in His favor; with His grace; by His gratuitous act which brought joy) **through means of the process of a release-from-an-enslaved-condition and a liberating-away-from-imprisonment, which is resident within Christ Jesus** (or: by the setting-free which is centered in [the] Anointed Jesus; or: through the redemption that is union with Jesus [the] Messiah)."

Here in the Unveiling, a second witness is given when this offer made in 21:6 is repeated in 22:17. The call is made to all – even to those in the "Dead Sea" (a figure of the grave – this is where the "life" of the Jordan River ended in dead waters). The picture is clear: Life is offered to those who are without life – those who are dead.

7. **"The one habitually being victorious** (or: progressively overcoming) **will proceed inheriting** (acquiring by lot) **these things, and I will continue being a God for him** (in him; to him) **and he will continue being a son** [Griesbach reads: the son] **for Me** (in Me; to Me; with Me; by Me).

This verse could be interpreted to be speaking of Christ, "**the One**," instead of those of the covenant communities. Jesus spoke of Himself as having **overcome** the dominating system (Jn. 16:33). In this case, Ps. 2:7-8 may be in view: "He has said to Me, My Son [are] You; I, today, have begotten You. So ask of Me, and I shall give [the] nations [as] Your allotted inheritance."

This proclamation about **being victorious** recalls the promises at the close of each of the seven letters in chapters 2 and 3, above. This would then identify this passage as pertaining to the called-out communities in Asia Minor... and beyond. It is another message to "**the overcomer**." We saw them in 14:4, above: "**These are the folks continuously following The little Lamb wherever He progressively leads**." We saw them again, in 20:4, they "**live and reign** (or: lived and reigned) **with the Christ** (the Anointed One) **a thousand years**." The promise of **inheriting** brings to mind Rom. 8:17,

> "**Now since children** (or: Yet if ones born by natural descent), **also heirs** (possessors and enjoyers of an allotted inheritance; those who hold sway over the allotted portion)**: on the one hand, God's heirs, on the other, Christ's joint-heirs if so be** (or: provided) **that we are continually affected by sensible experiences together – feeling together; receiving impressions, undergoing passion or suffering together – to the end that we may also be glorified together**
>> (or: can be given a shared appearance; would together receive a manifestation of that which calls forth praise; should be given a joint-approval and a joint-reputation; may be thought of and imagined together [in covenant relationship])."

Paul also expressed the idea of our being heirs in his letter to Galatians. There, in 3:29, he affirms:

> "**Now since you folks belong to Christ** (or: have [the] Anointing as your source and origin; or: So since you people have the qualities and character of Christ, and [are] that which is Christ), **you are straightway and consequently Abraham's Seed: heirs** (possessors and enjoyers of the distributed allotment), **down from, corresponding to and in the sphere of Promise!**"

He further explains this in 4:7 where he terms it, "**an heir** (a possessor and an enjoyer of the distributed allotment) **through God** [other MSS: God's heir through Christ]." What does this mean? Our minds can explode with the words and concept found in 1 Jn. 3:1-2,

> "**You people at once consider** (or: look and perceive) **what kind of** (what sort of; what unusual, foreign or exotic) **love** (or: acceptance) **the Father has given to** (or: in; for) **us, which we now have as a gift, to the end that we can** (or: would) **be called God's children! And we are.... and yet it has not yet been made visible** (or: it is not yet apparent or manifested) **what we will proceed in being**... **[Yet] we know [that] folks like to Him** (like-ones to Him; ones like Him; people resembling Him) **we will be existing, because we will continue seeing and will be progressively perceiving Him just as** (according and exactly as; in the manner that) **He constantly exists** (or: He is)."

In the new creation, the new arrangement, or in the sphere of "the atmosphere (or: heaven)," the concept of being "God's children" is not the same as it meant in the old creation, or the old arrangement (covenant). What this means had not yet been made visible to John. He could only surmise that we would exist being as "ones like Him." This was not an expectation that was held by those of the old covenant. But the Hellenist culture (into which Christianity exploded in the 1st century) would better understand this, for they had been educated with the Greek literature of the past, where some heroes, though living tragic lives, joined the family of the "gods" in the atmosphere. In his *First Apology 21*, in the middle of the 2nd century, Justin Martyr defended the Christian faith to the Roman emperor, Antonius Pius, by saying, "We introduce nothing new beyond those who you call sons of Zeus" (Gregory J. Riley, *One Jesus, Many Christs*, HarperSanFrancisco, 1997 p 71). But this was not understood by the Greeks or Romans to be open to just anyone. Riley explains,

> "But as the message [about Jesus] reached outside of Palestine and into the larger gentile world, it was the central story of the career of Jesus as hero, the story most familiar to the culture at large, that gave it a hearing, and it was its call for EVERYONE to follow and reap the rewards that the heroes alone had once obtained that gave it such wide appeal" (ibid p 207-8; brackets and emphasis added).

God had long before prepared the ground of the Greco-Roman world to receive the message of the risen Christ. Paul cited "**certain of the poets**" (the Cilician poet Aratus 315-240 BC; and Cleanthes 331-233 BC) that said, "**You see, we are also a family of the One**" (Acts 17:28).

"**I will continue being a God for him**" repeats an OT promise made to Abraham (Gen. 17:7f), then it is expanded to include His people, in Zech. 8:8. "**He will continue being a son for Me**" was made first concerning Solomon (2 Sam. 7:14) and applied to David later, in Ps. 89:26f. Here we see another confirmation of the continuity between the old and new covenants, even though everything has changed.

8. **"Yet for the timid folks** (in the cowards having shrinking palpitations) **and for faithless ones** (in unbelieving or disloyal people; [TR, & Peshita add: and failures/sinners]) **and for or by abominable, disgusting folks, and for or in murderers, and for or with prostitutes and for or by sorcerers** (users of, or enchanters by, drugs) **and for or by idolaters and for, in or by all the liars** (the false ones)**: their portion [is] within the lake** (or: their [allotted] part [is] union with the basin; the share from them [is] in the artificial pool; the region pertaining to them [is] centered in the marshy area) **continuously burning with Fire and Deity, which is the Second Death."**

Now we have an antithesis of vs. 7. There are two immediate inheritances here: one is blessing (vs. 7), the other is correctional judgment for transformation (vs. 8). The indictments of vs. 8 are stronger, but the comparison of these two verses to the scene described in Mat. 25:31-46 seems obvious. Those described in vs. 8 receive the same penalty as those of Mat. 25:41 & 46a. Yet the "crimes" of those in Mat. 25, at first glance, seem much less serious – they are failures of "omission." The kids (immature goats, i.e., the Jewish leadership) failed to show love to Christ's family members during the generation that followed the coming of Jesus as the Messiah.

These in vs. 8, however, are timid folks, unbelievers, faithless ones, murderers, etc. Those in Matt. 25 were just immature and unaware. Do both "groups" receive the same judgment? Both are cast into Fire. But the nature of the judgment in Mat. 25:46 is *kolasin aionion*, age-lasting pruning; pruning and correction of growth for an unspecified period of time. And what have we seen to be the nature of fire? It transforms, purifies and causes what is being burned to ascend into the atmosphere. These are thrown into the very midst of God (Fire and Deity). This is really a blessing for them. It is exactly what our Father has been doing with us, as His Fire burns within us, and as we walk through adversarial conditions and circumstances in this life. As Peter said,

> "**Beloved ones, do not repeatedly feel like strangers to the burning** (– the action of the Fire) **within and among you folks, which is habitually happening to you with a view toward your being put to the test** (or: which is repeatedly coming into being in the face of a proving trial for you; which is progressively birthing itself to an examination in you), **as though a strange thing or a foreign occurrence is repeatedly walking with you folks**" (1 Pet. 4:12).

As here in 21:7-8, so in Mat. 25: one group inherits the kingdom; the other inherits chastisement, correction and pruning to produce His fruit (Love). And since both the kids and the sheep were part of the Shepherd's herd, in Mat. 25, we suggest that vs. 8 here is a description of the Jewish leadership and zealots of the 1st century. Paul, as Saul, had been one of them. Fire and Deity rained down upon them in AD 70. They were "children of Gehenna" (Mat. 23:15). Chilton quotes J.P.M. Sweet (*Revelation* 1979) in regard to vs. 8, "'the list belongs, like similar lists in the epistles, to the context of baptism, the putting off of the "old man" and putting on of the new' (*cf* Gal. 5:19-26; Eph. 4:17-5:7; Col. 3:5-10; Tit. 3:3-8)" (ibid p 550). That is what this baptism of Fire is all about! It is not "punishment," but cleansing, purification and pruning with the goal of the Spirit's fruit as its aim. Remember Mal. 3:2b-3,

> "He [is] like a refiner's Fire, and like fullers' soap. And so He shall sit [as] a refiner and purifier of silver; and He shall purify the sons of Levi, and purge (or: purify) them as gold and silver, so that they may offer unto Yahweh an offering in righteousness."

Chilton (ibid) points us to the references here in the *Unveiling*, where each category named in this verse is found elsewhere in the book. Listing them is impressive; they appear throughout the Unveiling:

> **for the timid** (in the cowardly) **folks**: all these do not "run the race or compete in the games" (Paul's athletic metaphor for a focused life in Christ – 1 Cor. 9:24) and so they are not overcoming or victorious, because they are too timid to "enter the contest."
> **for faithless ones** (in unbelieving or disloyal people): 2:13, 19; 13:10; 14:12.
> **for failures/sinners**: 5:8; 8:3-4; 11:18; 13:7, 10; 14:12; 18:20; 19:8.
> **for or by abominable, disgusting folks**: 17:4-5; 21:27 (note that location, in vs. 27, below: it is outside the City, but not in a pagan "hell;" these are those who partook of the "golden cup," in 17:4; *cf* Mat. 24:15).
> **for or in murderers**: 13:15; 16:6; 17:6; 18:24. *Cf* Mat. 23:37; Acts 7:52 (the Jewish leadership).
> **for or with prostitutes**: 2:14, 20-22; 9:21; 14:8; 17:2, 4-5; 18:3; 19:2.
> **for or by sorcerers** (users or formulators of drugs): 9:21; 18:23; 22:15. *Cf* 18:2.
> **for or by idolaters**: 2:14, 20; 9:20; 13:4, 12-15. *Cf* 18:2, "**abode of every impure attitude** (unclean spirit)."
> **in or by all the liars** (the false ones): 2:2; 3:9; 16:13; 19:20; 20:10; 21:27; 22:15. *Cf* Jn. 8:44.

Who are all these folks that comprise this list? They represent a cross-section of humanity: the "lost" folks whom the Good Shepherd will, in time, find (Lu. 15:4-7) and transform (Rom. 12:2). In this "cosmic opera" (Smith's term for the Unveiling) they provide the dark, contrasting backdrop for each scene of the play. Simmons (ibid p 404) points us to Mk. 8:38-9:1, which should be read together as part of the same discourse:

> "'**Furthermore, whosoever may be ashamed of or embarrassed because of Me and My messages** (Words; Thoughts; Ideas) **within the midst of this adulterous and erring** (failing; mis-shooting; sinful; deviating) **generation, the Son of the Man** (or: the son of mankind; the Human) **will also continue being ashamed of and embarrassed because of him – whenever** (at the time that) **He may come within the midst of His Father's glory** (or: in a manifestation which calls forth praise for His Father) **along with the set-apart agents** (or: holy messengers; sacred folks with the message).' Then He continued saying to them, '**Truly** (or: Assuredly; Amen), **I am now saying to you folks that there are certain ones** (or: some) **of those standing here who under no circumstances can taste** (may test by sipping; = experience; partake) **of death until they can** (should; may) **see God's kingdom** (God's reign and influence as King; the sovereign activity which is God) **being present, having already come within the midst of power and ability.**'"

These folks, who might be ashamed or embarrassed, would be the **timid**, or cowardly, in that 1st century honor/shame-based society. Much in this list has to do with actions, works or deeds. We read in Jn. 3:19 that,

> "**Now this continues being the** (or: So there continues being the same) **process of the sifting, the separating and the deciding** (the evaluating; the judging), **because the Light has come** (or: has gone) **into the world** (the aggregate of humanity; the ordered system and arrangement of religion, culture and government; or: the system of control and regulation), **and yet the humans love the darkness** (or: the men [= the leadership] love and fully give themselves to the dimness of obscurity and gloom; or: mankind loved and moved toward union with the shadow-realm) **rather than the Light, for their WORKS** (deeds; actions) **were continuing to be bad ones** (unsound ones; wicked ones; laborious ones; toilsome ones that created bad news; wrongful ones)," *Cf* 1 Cor. 3:13.

The last category listed, "**all the liars** (or: false ones)," was a theme addressed in 1 John:

> "**The person who keeps on saying, 'I have come to know Him by experience,' and yet is not habitually keeping** (observing) **His implanted goals** (impartations of the finished product within; inward directives), **is a liar** (exists being one who speaks falsehood) **and God's Truth** (the

Reality of God; the Genuine Actuality which is God) **is not** (or: does not exist) **within this one**" (2:4).

"**Which one is** (exists continuously being) **the liar, if not the person habitually denying** (repeatedly disowning; constantly contradicting), **[saying] that Jesus is not the Christ** (the Anointed One [= Messiah])**? This person is** (exists being) **the anti-anointing** (or: anti-anointed person; the one taking the place of and being in the opposite position of the anointing and of Christ)..." (2:22).

"**If anyone may up and say, 'I am constantly loving God,' and yet may be habitually hating** (or: would keep on regarding with ill-will or detaching from) **his brother, he is a liar** (he exists being a false one)" (4:20a).

"**the one not believing in God** [A reads: the Son] **has made Him out to be** (or: has construed Him) **a liar, because he has not believed or put trust into the evidence** (testimony; witness) **which God has attested and affirmed concerning His Son** (or: shown as proof round about the Son from, and which is, Him)" (5:10b).

Kaplan pointed us to Isa. 28:15-18, where the people of Jerusalem had "made **a lie** their refuge." Speaking to them, Yahweh says,

"For you say: 'We have contracted a covenant with Death, and with the Unseen (*sheol*) we have made a public treaty: The overflowing scourge, when it passes, it shall not come on us, for we have made **a lie** our refuge, and in **falsehood** we are concealed....' [Yet] your covenant with Death will be annulled, and your public treaty with the Unseen shall not stand firm..."

Here, John may have "categories" or "religious groups" in mind, as well as individuals. We can discern these categories as potentially targeting the unbelieving Jews, or the unbelieving pagans. Paul may have been thinking along these same lines when he wrote Tit. 1:15-16,

"**To the pure folks, everything [is] pure** (or: All things [are] clean for, with and in the clean ones). **Yet to** (or: for; in; with) **those having been stained and remaining defiled** (corrupted; polluted), **and to** (or: for; in; with) **faithless people** (those without trust; unbelieving ones who lack loyalty), **nothing is pure or clean – but rather, their mind, as well as the conscience, has been – and now remains – stained, defiled and corrupted. They are repeatedly adopting the same terms of language, and habitually making confession and avowing to have perceived and now know God, YET they are constantly contradicting and denying** (repudiating; disowning; refusing) **[this] by the** (or: their) **WORKS** (in the actions and things done), **continuing being detestable** (abominable), **incompliant** (stubborn; disobedient; unpersuasive) **and disqualified** (disapproved; rejected after trial) **with a view toward every good work** (excellent and virtuous activity)."

Recall that "**the Second Death**" (here, in vs. 8: "**burning with Fire and Deity**") was mentioned in 2:11, above, and it is those mentioned here in vs. 7, above, who will not "**be injured or harmed from the midst of the second death**," but it does not say that they will not experience it! The "gold, silver and precious stone" of 1 Cor. 3:12 experienced the same Fire as did the "wood, hay and stubble" – but the former survived the Fire unhurt, while the latter "**experienced loss**" (3:15) even while being "**saved, delivered and healed**" by that same Fire. Paul made a similar list in 1 Cor. 6:9-10, and then a list in Gal. 5:19-21 where he categorizes them as,

"**the WORKS** (actions; deeds) **of the flesh [religion]** (or: = whose source and origin are the estranged human nature; or: pertaining to the flesh [system, or, nature]; or: = whose results and realm are the self in slavery to a system)."

In Eph. 5:3-5, he ends the list showing what it is that folks who practice such things are missing:

"**[A person with such behavior] is not now holding enjoyment of an inheritance** (does not currently continue having use of an allotted gift from someone who has died) **within the Christ's and God's reign or sphere of sovereign activity** (or: in union with the kingdom of the Anointed One [= the Messiah], as well as of God; or: centered in the royal influence from the Christ, and from God; [*p46*: within the reign of God])."

This is like the Jews who missed out on the manifestations of God's glory, in the book of Acts. Beale (ibid p 1061) points out that Israel and Judea had been accused of three of the items of our list here in vs. 8. Jer. 3:9-10 declares,

"And yet her **prostitution** came to nothing, and she committed adultery with the tree (or: wood) and the stone [= idolatry]. Then in all these things **faithless** (treacherous; not-staying-with-the-covenant) Juda did not return to Me from out of her whole heart, but only in **lying** (by falseness and with pretense)" (LXX, JM).

We would be advised to consider the corporate application (the Jewish leadership in Jesus' day, along with possibly the Zealots who fomented the Jewish wars, and the synagogue resistance in the Diaspora), keeping in mind that all the vices listed here in vs. 8 are SYMBOLS, as well.

It is noteworthy that this list of unredeemed humanity (here, in vs. 8) comes into the SAME dealing of God that the little animal, the false prophet and the adversarial spirit also undergo (above: 19:20; 20:7-10). That is because all those things, that these three symbols represent, are within us – until he cleanses us from them. It is the place where the "kids" had to endure a period of "pruning" (Mat. 25:41, 46). But this is not the end. Hos. 13:14 gave a promise:

"From the grip of the Unseen I shall ransom them; from Death I shall redeem them."

The **second death** is the end (i.e., the death) of **Death** for those who are processed by it. Paul spoke of this in 1 Tim. 1:10, referring to the work of Christ:

"**our Deliverer** (Savior; Rescuer), **Christ Jesus – on the one hand, idling down death** (or: The Death) **so as to make it unproductive and useless, yet on the other hand, illuminating** (giving light to) **life and incorruptibility** (the absence of the ability to decay; un-ruinableness) **through means of the message of goodness, ease and well-being**."

The work of Christ was complete, but each of us enters into it existentially, and experientially, as we are born into this life, and are processed by this life. On the cross, all humanity was "**immersed** (or: at one point soaked or baptized) **into Christ Jesus: [was] immersed** (or: baptized) **into His death**" (Rom. 6:3). Christ's death was the "second death" – the death to the realm of "sin and death." But He did not die "instead of us," He died as us, on our behalf, and took us with Him into that second death. It is pictured here as "**Fire and Deity**." Although the work of Jesus, on the cross, was "finished," all humanity must go through the purification of His presence, and Parental correction (Heb. 12:2-11). But, as with Christ, His purifying fires can yield a joy that is set before us, for we know the outcome, because:

"**We, then** (or: consequently), **were buried together** (entombed together with funeral rites) **in Him** (or: by Him; with Him), **through the immersion** (baptism) **into the death, to the end that we can walk around** (or: we also should likewise conduct ourselves and order our behavior) **within newness of life**" (Rom. 6:4).

God's Divine Nature (**Deity**) is Love. The Fiery experiences that He takes us through in this life, and perhaps, the next (?), are expressions of His Love. It is for the love of gold that a refiner puts the gold ore in the fire: to remove all that is not gold. This second death is so that we no longer will "**let the Sin continue reigning** (or: allowing the failure, the mistake, or the deviation from the goal to continue on the throne ruling as king) **within our mortal body**," and would "**stop constantly placing our members** (or: body parts) **alongside** (providing and presenting them) **[as] tools** (or: instruments) **of injustice** (disregard for what is right; activities discordant to the Way pointed out); **but rather, at once place**

ourselves alongside for disposal to God (or: stand yourselves with God, at [His] side; by and in God, present yourselves; set yourselves alongside [each other], for God)" (Rom. 6:12-13).

Richard Rohr makes an astute observation:
> "But the core value and transformative truth of initial God experience is still there, right beneath the surface, in many people who were "baptized in both fire and Spirit," which is Jesus' baptism (Matthew 3:11b) as distinguished from John's mere water baptism. If we would be honest, many Christians belong to the ritual and moral religion of John more than the fire religion of Jesus, which is based in living experience" (Daily Meditations, 01/25/17).

That is the existential reality of which vs. 8, here, is speaking.

The process of being put into **the Second Death** is to bring about the fulfillment of 1 Cor. 15:26, 28,
> "**[The] last holder of ruin** (or: enemy; quality having ill-will) **being progressively brought down to idleness** (made ineffective, useless and unproductive) **[is] the Death** (or: Death, a last enemy, is being presently nullified and abolished)....
> **Now whenever the whole** (or: all things) **may be completely supportively-aligned in Him** (or: subjected and appended to Him; subordinately sheltered and arranged for Him), **then the Son Himself will also continue being supportively aligned to, fully subjoined for and humbly attached under as an arranged shelter in, the One subjecting, appending and sheltering the whole in Him** (or: attaching all things to Him), **to the end that God can be all things within the midst of and in union with all humanity** (or: may be everything in all things; or: should exist being All in all; or: would exist being everything, within the midst of everyone)."

It is the death within us that needs to die. That death is like the weeds that an adversary over-sowed in our field (Mat. 13:24-30). This second death symbol calls to mind the process of ridding the field of weeds, thorns and thistles, in Heb. 6:7-8, freeing it, so that the rich soil can be sown with Good Seed, once again. Dan Kaplan commented on this:
> "Thorns and thistles are the imitations of the real life giving words. The old man Adam and his seed that was in him produced in him after his/its kind: doubt, fear, unbelief, worry, cares of life, hate, strife, malice, envy, false witness, division, deception, murder. This death-producing flesh and the carnal mind that produces these seeds needs to die."

Terry makes insightful comments at this point, regarding interpreting these visions:
> "But we shall miss the great purpose of John's Apocalypse if we presume to treat these seven last visions of triumph as [only] a literal record of historic events…. It is an ideal picture of what the Messiah is and what he does during the whole period of his reign; not [just] of any one particular event of his coming" (ibid p 463; brackets added, as our view).

I like Ken Nichols' take on this verse:
> "I read the list in 21:8 like this:
>> the timid (or, cowardly) folks – those who are still afraid of God (listed first [intentionally?] as this represents SO many people);
>> and for faithless ones (in unbelieving people) – those who continuously doubt God's love for them;
>> and for or by abominable, disgusting folks – those who feel dirty and unclean (guilty) before God;
>> and for or in murderers, -- those who have committed heinous crimes and believe they cannot ever be forgiven;
>> and for or with prostitutes – those who have done such things that their self-worth and worth before God are shattered;

and for or by sorcerers (users of drugs) – those stuck in addiction, to substances or worldly power, who do not know how to get free;

and for or by idolaters – those who still place other things ahead of God, such as money, or have misplaced devotion, say to a church or a preacher;

and for, in or by all the liars (the false ones) – those who lie to themselves and everyone else that all is fine between them and God, but still, in their heart, they feel far from Him.

"They need to confess this truth, and discover the underlying issue (likely one of those above) that is keeping them 'distant.'

"Of course, I'm not saying that's exactly what John had in mind when he wrote that, but viewing it through the compassion of Christ (and isn't that part and parcel with the fire of God), this is what I see. Everyone who still needs 'refinement' to realize God's true character of goodness and love and how God sees them as precious children, no matter what the world, religion or they themselves have told them.

"I think this death is 'thrown into the fire' because that's where it happens. God 'defeats' this death by birthing again all those who die in this fire - who finally 'give in' and allow God's love to renew them and give them their true identity in Him. This death is the 'last enemy,' meaning to me that once you get through this time, you (hopefully) never go back to 'adversarial' (Satanic) thinking like those things listed above. This is how 'those who lose their life will find it.'

"I'm also sitting here thinking on the 'Book of Life' again. It says all those not found in the book are cast into the fire. They have not yet found their TRUE life. They have not yet passed from death (2nd) unto life (ontologically in Christ, yes, they have but not in their own minds). One writes themselves into the book of life, when one realize their true self, their true source OF life, and oneness with that source" (from a personal email).

Zahnd cites Heb. 10:31, "It is a fearful thing to fall into the hands of the living God," and then explains: "And no doubt it is. In the hands of God, there is no place to hide. We have to be honest with ourselves. In the hands of God, we can no longer live in the disguise of our lies. In the hands of God, we have to face ourselves. And that can be terrifying. When the prodigal son returned home and fell into the arms of his father, I'm sure the boy felt afraid. We can tell by how he immediately speaks of his unworthiness, 'I am no longer worthy to be called your son.' This wayward son has fallen into the hands of his father; his fate is in his father's hands... and he is afraid. But there is no better place to be! This gracious father in Jesus's parable is given to us as a picture of our heavenly Father! When the prodigal son fell fearfully into the hands of his father, forgiveness, healing and restoration began. Just because the prodigal son felt fear as he fell into his father's hands doesn't mean he had anything to fear FROM his father. In his father's hands was the only safe place to be. It was in the far country that the prodigal son was in danger, not in his father's hands. When we fall into the hands of the living God, we are sinners in the hands of a loving God" (*Sinners in The Hands of a Loving God*, ibid p 19-20; emphasis added).

Let us also consider the metaphorical use of "fire" that we find in Ps. 65 in the LXX (66, in MT):

Unto the Goal (Into the midst of the Finished Product, the Completed End in View)
An Ode, which is a Psalm pertaining to Resurrection

1. Let all the Land (or: territory; earth) shout aloud to God (for God; with God)!

2. O now sing to and play stringed instruments at length for (or: in) His Name! You folks give glory to (supply a good reputation for; present a manifestation which engenders praise of; render an assumed Appearance in) His praise!

3. You people say to God, "How awesome (respect-engendering) [are] Your works (accomplishments; deeds; actions)! Centered in (or: In the midst of) the magnitude (great extent; mass) of Your power and the greater amount of Your ability, Your hostile folks (folks who hate) will repeatedly lie concerning You (deal falsely with You)."

4. Let all the Land (or: earth) at once collectively do obeisance to and in You, and then at once collectively make music to, for and in Your Name.

5. Come and see the works of, and from, God: awesome (respect-engendering) in desired plans above, and centered in designed purposes beyond, the sons of the humans.

6. He is the One progressively turning-together, altering and changing the sea into dry land: "In a river, they will proceed going through on foot!" There, in that place, they will progressively be put into a good, healthy frame of mind with a disposition of well-being and ease [being set] upon Him,

7. [that is,] on the One continuously ruling (being master) in union with (in the midst of) the exercising of His power and ability of (or: pertaining to; from) the Age: His eyes are constantly looking upon and attentively observing the ethnic multitudes (the nations); let not those habitually provoking or embittering continue lifted up within themselves.

8. O ethnic multitudes (nations), be habitually speaking well of (saying good things about; blessing) our God, and make heard the voice of the praise of Him:

9. Who is the One placing (setting) my soul (inner life) into Life, not giving my feet into a surge from a rolling swell (a wavering or tottering).

10. Because You, O God, tested and proved us (made a trial to assay, discern and then approve us). You purged and purified us in Fire, as the silver is repeatedly purged and purified (refined).

11. You brought us into the snare; You set squeezing pressures (ordeals or distressing trials and afflictions; tribulations) upon our back;

12. You mounted people upon our heads: we went through Fire and Water, and then You led (brought) us out of the midst [of it] into an upward-life (breath-again; re-animation; an again-soul; a person-again). (JM)

Notice the praise accorded to God for the purifying work of the "Fire" upon Israel, in this Psalm. That is our pattern for interpreting these Fire scenes in the Unveiling.

9. **And one of the seven agents – the ones holding** (having) **the seven shallow bowls: the ones being continuously full of** (or: brimming with) **the seven plagues – came and spoke with me, saying, "Come here! I will proceed in showing you the Bride, the Wife of the little Lamb."**

Now the scene changes. John is approached by **one of the agents** who had the **shallow bowls** (even though full, and brimming, shallow bowls do not hold great contents). He comes to show John **the Bride, the little Lamb's Wife**. What happens next (vs. 10, below) is the spiritual transport that will show John the symbol of this Bride-Wife. John once again is personally brought into the midst of the vision. To do this he must go with **the agent** who will **proceed to show** John the next vision. In 17:1 we read,

> "**one of the seven agents – the ones holding the seven bowls – came and spoke with me, saying, 'Come here! I will proceed showing** (pointing out to) **you the effect of the judgment** (the result of the administering of justice; the effect of the judicial decision and equitable sentence) **of the Great Prostitute**…"

We should not miss this detail of John's escort to the next vision. Agents of judgment (specified by being ones who held the seven bowls) are also agents of revelation and disclosure. This present scene reaches all the way back to chapter 15:5-6 and 16:1ff, where we saw that these agents were ministers of the Temple (they symbolized priests, the called-out folks). The scene in vs. 9, above, reached back to the purifying scene, with the agents present, in 14:10ff. We are seated together with Christ (Eph. 2:6) and participate in all aspects of Christ's reign.

We know from the culture of the Jews, in the 1st century, that betrothal was more serious that it is in our day, and so a "bride" was in almost the same position, socially, as being a "wife." But these, again, are symbols, here. The description "**Bride**," suggests a new relationship, while the term "**Wife**" suggests a marriage in the past, and an established relationship. The word "bride" (*numphē*) is used in relation to Christ only in Jn. 3:29, in the Gospels; it is not used at all in the Epistles or Acts, and is used in the Unveiling only in 18:23, 21:2, 9, and in 22:17. The word "wife" (*gunē*) is normally rendered as "wife" only here, and in 19:7, above, in this book. All other occurrences of this word, in the Unveiling, are normally rendered "**woman**," which is the other common meaning of the word. So I suggest that in this symbolic setting, the choice of terms indicates that this "woman" is a recent wife to the little Lamb, but now has an established place in His household and kingdom. The new "woman" has replaced "the old woman." Paul discussed the significance of this in Rom. 7:1-6, where in vss.3b-4, discussing their freedom from the relationship with the Law, they were free to marry Christ:

"**if the husband** [Yahweh] **may die** [in Christ's death], **she is free** (she exists in a state of freedom) **from the Law** [= Torah], **not to be an adulteress, pertaining to her becoming [a wife] for** (or: to) **a different man** (or: a different husband). **So that, my brothers** (= fellow covenant-believers), **you folks also were made dead to the Law** (or: were put to death by the Law [=Torah] and with the Law), **through the body of the Christ, [proceeding] into the situation to become [the wife] for** (or: to; in; with) **a different One – in** (to; for) **the One being roused and raised forth from out of the midst of dead folks – to the end that we may bear fruit by God** (or: produce a harvest in, for, to and with God)."

This is the central reason for her to be called the New Jerusalem, with a new covenant relationship with God. She is Yahweh's/Christ's new Wife (now composed of former Israelites and former Gentiles).

Beale (ibid p 1062) sees 21:9-22:5 as a recapitulation of the preceding section of chapter 21. He insightfully points us to the following correlations, which readily become apparent:
    a) 21:2 corresponds to the same scene in 21:9-11, which expands on 21:2;
    b) 21:3 is given further details and descriptions in 21:22-24 and in 22:3;
    c) 21:6 looked back to 21:1 (a new creation, in both verses).
    d) Then we find 21:8, above, revisited in 21:27, below.

As Terry puts it (ibid p 465; brackets added), "So, after the manner of apocalyptic repetition [and Hebrew parallelism], the seer now proceeds to take up the last preceding vision (21:1-8) and expand it with manifold details..." This should help us track the scenes as they open, below. In vs. 6, above, we read, "**They have come into being** (been born; come to be) **and stand accomplished** (are produced)." And now we have the vision of new Jerusalem (21:10- 21:5).

Simmons points out the sequence of these visions: "[The] marriage of the bride follows the destruction of the fleshly Jerusalem (Rev. 19:1-7)," and cites the parable of the king "burning their city" in Mat. 22:7-8, and says, "Before Isaac could inherit, the son of the bondwoman was cast out (Gal. 4:21-31)" (ibid p 405). Beale notes that in this verse John "hears" that he will see **the Bride**, and then (vs. 10, below) he is shown "**the set-apart** (or: holy; sacred) **city, Jerusalem**."

10. **Next he carried** (or: carries) **me away, in spirit** (or: in the midst of a Breath-effect), **upon a great and high mountain, and showed** (points out to) **me the set-apart** (or: holy; sacred; [TR adds: and great]) **city, Jerusalem, progressively** (or: habitually; or: presently) **descending out of the atmosphere** (or: heaven), **from God**

Now John is brought, in spirit, to a **great** and **high mountain**. This picture is an echo of Ezk. 40:1-2 where Ezekiel is brought into Israel in "visions of God," and is "set down upon a very **high mountain**." That vision came to him AFTER Jerusalem "was smitten" (vs. 1), just as the present vision which John sees follows the vision of its destruction in 19:1-7, above. This mountain would be "Mt. Zion... the City of the Living God, the Heavenly Jerusalem" (Heb. 12:22), and the **city** is the one of which it is said that Abraham,

> "**continued taking with the hand from out of** (or: reaching in and receiving, then taking away from within) **the City continuously having the foundations – whose Craftsman** (or: Artisan Technician) **and skilled Worker for the people** (or: Producer; Architect) **[is] God**" (Heb. 11:10).

This city comes "**from God**," because God is the one who "crafted" it. As Paul put it,

> "**we are** (continually exist being) **the effect of what He did** (or: His creation; the thing He has constructed; the result of His work; His achievement; His opus; the effect of His Deed)" (Eph. 2:10a).

This action of the City answers to what Jesus taught His disciples to pray: "**Make Your reign and kingdom COME...upon earth**" (Mat. 6:10).

The present scene is parallel to 17:1, 3, as cited in the comments on vs. 9, but here the setting involves the counterpart to the Prostitute: the "**holy**," heavenly, or spiritual, **Bride** of Christ, symbolized by the set-apart, heavenly/spiritual City, New Jerusalem. As Beale points out (ibid p 1064), this parallelism to chapter 17 is a strong indicator that the City pictured here should also be seen as a symbolic picture. Here John is taken to **a great and high mountain**; back there he was taken to "**a desert**." This "high mountain" is a figure of "the atmosphere; heaven" where, symbolically, the "clouds" of God's "presence" often rest. It portrays the very opposite of the desert of trials and tests – e.g., Israel in the wilderness journeys, following the Exodus; Jesus' testing following His passing through the Jordan River, upon His baptism by John; the Woman flying into the desert, in 12:14, above.

It is important to note that John had to be "**in spirit**" in order to see this City. As with Paul, whose good news came by revelation, one must have his or her eyes and face unveiled (2 Cor. 3:18) to see "**the Jerusalem above**... **who is** (or: which particular one continues being) **our mother**" (Gal. 4:26). As my wife, Lynda, commented here: "Only in spirit (Life) can we see the 'set-apart.'"

We see that the present tense is used in the verb, **descending**, for it is **progressively, habitually** (and presently) doing so. This marks the character of the called-out communities. The importance of this can be seen in the fact that this action, described here, is being stated for the second time in this passage (*cf* vs. 2, above). Although already seated with Christ in the atmosphere (Eph. 2:6) it habitually descends to those yet living on the earth (the flesh realm) to minister Life to them. We see in vs. 25, below, that her gates are never shut to them.

The TR addition, "and great," modifying "**city**" has led interpreters to the conclusion that "the great city," in the Unveiling, is Jerusalem. Here in 21:2, 10, it is the New Jerusalem; but in 11:8, 14:8 and 16:19, the descriptive phrase refers to the "old" Jerusalem, the one that was "**in slavery** (or: bondage) **with her children**" (Gal. 4:25). The fact that this heavenly city is called a NEW Jerusalem emphasizes that its parallel counterpart, "Secret Babylon," is the "old" Jerusalem. Paul contrasted the allegorized two women (Sarah and Hagar) in Gal. 4:24, "**these women are** (= represent) **two settled arrangements** (covenants;

contracts; wills)**: one, on the one hand, from Mount Sinai, habitually** (repeatedly; continuously) **giving birth into slavery** (or: bondage) **– which is Hagar**." So the real issue between the two women seen in the Unveiling, is the two covenants (arrangements). As the book of Hebrews trumpets, "the new is better" (e.g., Heb. 8:6-8). In the OT patterns, the older child was, counter-culturally, seldom selected by God; the younger (newer) one was chosen to be a type, a foreshadow, of the new arrangement that was to come: the one of "spirit and truth" (Jn. 4:23-24). Hiett puts it this way, "The great city is a harlot redeemed, a bride in love.... The New Jerusalem is the creation of *God*" (ibid p 258-9; emphasis original).

Paul took this theme up in 1 Cor. 15:
> 45. **Thus also** (or: In this way also), **it has been written, "The first human** (or: man), **Adam, came for existence** (or: was birthed) **into [being] a living soul"** [Gen. 2:7]; **the Last Adam into [being] a continuously life-making** (life-engendering; life-creating; life-giving) **Spirit** (or: Breath-effect; Attitude).
> 46. **Nevertheless, the spiritual [is] not first, but rather the one having the qualities and characteristics of a soul** (the soulish), **then afterwards, the spiritual** (that pertaining to and having the qualities of Breath-effect and Attitude).
> 47. **The first human** (person; man) **[was/is] forth from out of the earth** (land; ground; soil; dirt), **made of moist soil and mud** (or: having the quality and characteristics of moist dirt that can be poured; soilish); **the Second Human** (Person; Man; [other MSS add: {is} the Lord]) **[is made] out of heaven** (or: [is] from [the] atmosphere and sky; [*p46* reads: {is} spiritual]).

The action of the City's descent in this verse, coupled with what the agent in vs. 9b informed John that he was about to see, is well stated by Zahnd as "the marriage of heaven and earth" (*Sinners*, ibid p 187).

11. **– continuously having** (holding; or: = bringing with it) **the glory of God** (God's glory; God's reputation; or: God's appearance; or: the opinion from God; the manifest presence, which is God), **her illuminator** (that which gives her light; the cause of her light) **– like a most precious stone, as a jasper stone being continuously crystal-clear,**

We see here an allusion to Isa. 60:1, 2b,
> "Arise... For your light has come, and the glory of Yahweh is radiant upon you.... Yahweh shall be radiant upon you and His glory shall be seen over you." *Cf* Isa. 60:19b.

A similar allusion is Isa. 58:8,
> "Then your light shall burst through early, like the dawn, and your healing and wholeness will spring up quickly. And so your eschatological deliverance and justice will go before you, while the glory of Yahweh (or: Yahweh's reputation and manifestation which induces praise) will continuously wrap around and cloak you" (LXX, JM).

Another fascinating picture is found in Zech. 2:5,
> "And so I, Myself, will continue being for her, says [Yahweh], a city wall of Fire round about [her], and with a view to glory (or: even unto a manifestation which evokes praise) will I continue being (existing) within the midst of her" (LXX, JM).

Both vs. 11 and these OT pictures speak of God's intimate presence with His Bride. All that He is simply radiates on her, and then from her to where she, herself, appears as a flawless jewel (*cf* Mal. 3:17).

Consider the parenthetical expansion of the phrase, "God's glory." The Greek word *doxa* can also mean "appearance," or "opinion," which creates a "reputation." Or, (reading the form of the noun, "God," as an *ablative*), this can speak of her having received, "an opinion **from** God" about her. It can also refer to God's "manifest presence," or, the form of the word "God" in the phrase can be read as *apposition*, so that it would read, "the glory which is God." In Ezk. 43:2, we find "the glory of God" personified and approaching the temple from the east. There, His voice is compared to "many waters" and "the Land shone with His glory." Then in 43:5, "the glory of Yahweh filled the house (temple)." This sounds like scenes from the Unveiling, and the Bride is His house. So the glory of God is Christ, the presence of God Himself. Beasley-Murray observes that the **glory** which the City has is "**as a jasper stone, crystal-clear**," and comments, "i.e., it has a glory like that of the Creator, whose appearance is also stated to be like a jasper (4:3)" (ibid p 1307).

The Bride – the set-apart, heavenly Jerusalem – **continuously has**, or holds, "**the glory of God**." This is a statement of present fact and reality. We are containers of God's glory – for "**Now we presently and continuously hold** (have and possess) **this treasure within containers** (jars; pots; vessels; equipment) **made of baked clay** [e.g., pottery; bone ware] **so that the transcendence of the power may habitually originate its existence in God**" – 2 Cor. 4:7. Paul had just explained that,

> "**the God suddenly saying, 'Light will shine forth** (give light as from a torch; gleam) **from out of the midst of darkness** (dimness and shadiness; gloom and the absence of daylight)!' [is] the One who shines forth within the midst of our hearts, with a view to illumination of the intimate and experiential knowledge of God's glory – in a face of Christ**
> > (or: [is] He Who gives light in union with our hearts, [while] facing toward an effulgence and a shining forth which is an intimate knowing of the praise-inducing manifestation whose source and origin is God, and which is God, [while] in union with face to face presence of Christ [other MSS: Jesus Christ])" (2 Cor. 4:6)

We saw this "heavenly Woman" in 12:1, above, where instead of twelve gates (vs. 12, below) she had twelve stars, as a wreath, upon her head.

God's glory, like Christ, was often hidden in the OT, appearing in shadows. In Ex. 16:10 it appeared in "the cloud" in the wilderness, and in Ex. 24:16-17 we find that "the glory of Yahweh tabernacled over Mt. Sinai.... Now the appearance of the glory of Yahweh was like a devouring fire..." Later it "filled the Tabernacle (figure of the body of Christ)" as the cloud covered the "tent of the congregation" (Ex. 40:34-35). We have seen that devouring fire here in the Unveiling.

In Ezekiel's vision of the Living Ones, in chapter 1, we see "an atmosphere, as sparkling ice [terrible crystal – Rotherham] in appearance, stretched out over their heads, upward" (vs. 22); and "above the atmosphere, which is over their head, as the appearance of a sapphire stone, is the likeness of a throne. And on the likeness of the throne is a likeness of a human [a figure of Christ] on it, upward" (vs. 26); "It is the appearance of the likeness of the glory of Yahweh" (vs. 28) – CVOT.

Many seek to see His glory as though it is something separate from Himself, and they seem to be unaware that He has given His glory (Christ – the "Man" of 1 Cor. 11:7) to His called-out community. In Jn. 17:22, Jesus said to the Father, "**I, Myself, have given to them** (or: in them), **and they now possess, the glory** (the notion; the opinion; the imagination; the reputation; the manifestation which calls forth praise) **which You have given to Me, and which I now possess**." It is we who should be showing forth the shining forth of Him from within our hearts. He is the ultimate manifestation of God's glory. Recall Paul in 2 Cor. 3:18,

> "**But we all, ourselves – having a face that has been uncovered and remains unveiled** [note: as with Moses, before the Lord, Ex. 34:34] **– being folks who by a mirror are continuously observing, as ourselves, the Lord's** [= Yahweh's or Christ's] **glory** (or: being those who progressively **reflect** – from ourselves as by a mirror – the glory and reputation of [our] Owner), **are presently being continuously and progressively transformed into the very same image, from glory into glory – in accord with and exactly as – from [the] Lord's Breath-effect** (or: from [the] Spirit and Attitude of [the] Lord [= Christ or Yahweh])."

In our discussion about those in God's Fire and Deity, in 14:10, above, we suggested that the "agents; folks with the message" who, along with the little Lamb, were present with those in the Fire, were the folks of the called-out communities: His body; His bride. Here we see those folks as this City that is reflecting the glory of God. As those in the Fire behold that glory, they, too, are being "continuously and progressively transformed into the very same image" of Christ. This, of course also applies to those in vs. 8, above. But a larger view of the transformation "**from glory into glory**" may be the covenantal change, for earlier in this same chapter of 2 Cor. 3, Paul explained:

> **7. Now since** (or: if) **the attending service of the Death** (or: the dispensing of provision from death; the serving of provisions and support, which is the death) – **being one that has been formed by a beaten impression of types and the outlines of patterns that exists as engravings within letters and the effects of written texts chiseled on stones – was birthed and came into existence within glory** (in a manifestation which called forth praise and with a good reputation), **so that the sons of Israel came to be continuously unable** (or: habitually having no power) **to intently gaze into the face of Moses, because of the glory and manifestation which came from his face – which [glory] was being progressively unemployed so as to be brought down to having no work, to be ineffective and nullified –**
> **8. how shall not rather the attending service and dispensing of the provision of the Spirit** (or: which has its source in the Breath-effect; marked by, pertaining to and being the effect of the spirit and attitude) **continue being within glory** (existing in the midst of a manifestation which calls forth praise; being centered on and in union with a good reputation and with imagination)**?**
> **9. For since** (or: if) **the attending service and dispensing of the corresponding evaluations and commensurate decisions which follow the pattern** (or: separations for condemnation; judgments which are down-decisions against folks) **[had] glory, to a much greater degree does the attending service and the dispensing of the eschatological deliverance into fairness and equity in rightwised relationships** (or: righteousness from covenantal inclusion: that which corresponds to the Way pointed out, and which turns us in the right direction) **progressively surround and continuously exceed in glory** (or: habitually overflow with a manifestation which calls forth praise and brings a good reputation)**!**

Paul also spoke of this in Col. 1:27,
> "**the riches of the glory of this Secret** (or: the wealth which has its source in this sacred mystery's manifestation which calls forth praise) **within the multitudes** (among the nations; in the Gentiles; IN UNION WITH the swarms of ethnic groups), **which is** (or: exists being) **Christ within you folks, the expectation of and from the glory**
> > (or: which is [the] Anointed in union with you people: the [realized] hope of the manifestation which called forth praise; or: which is [the] Anointing [and the Messiah] within the midst of you folks – the expectation which is the glory)."

Seeing that **God** is **her illuminator** (that which gives her light; the cause of her light), we can relate to Paul's words in Eph. 5:14,
> "**Let the sleeper** (the person continuously down and being fast asleep) **be waking up, continue rousing, and then stand up** (arise) **from out of the midst of the dead ones, and the Christ will continue shining upon you** (progressively enlightening you)!"

Receiving Christ's light is resurrection from the dead! What Paul said to them was an example of Ps. 119:130, "The revelation and manifestation (or: unfolding and exposition) of Your words and ideas continuously gives light and progressively illuminates, and will progressively cause the infants to understand" (LXX, JM). Kaplan observes that, "The City presents to us the Beauty of God, and thus, when we perceive this vision, it stirs up our imagination and spiritual insights so that when we see this

City (Christ's body) manifesting Him, we also see the Father (Jn. 14:9). God's presence will invade the graves within us,"
> "**And you see, [it is] upon this, this rock mass** (or: the bedrock), **[that] I will progressively be constructing and building up My house – the called-out, covenant community. And even gates of [the] Unseen**
>> (or: double-winged doors of an unseen place; the openings or orifices which are unseen {e.g., entrance of a womb}; gateways or entrances from the Unseen; [= boulders on the entrances of graves; = {the prison} gates of the 'house of death'; or: the bars enclosing the realm of the dead])
> **will not continue bringing strength down against it** (or: will not proceed to be coming to their full strength in relation to it; or: will not continue overpowering it or prevail in resisting it)" (Mat. 16:18b).

12. **continuously having a great and high wall, having twelve gates, and upon** (or: at; or: on top of) **the gates twelve agents** (messengers), **and names** [Sinaiticus adds: of them] **having been inscribed** (engraved; imprinted) **upon [them], which are the names of the twelve tribes of the sons of Israel:**

From 21:12 through 22:5, the descriptions of the City are based on the vision in Ezk. 40-48. The reader would do well to review those chapters in order to better appreciate the apocalyptic images that we will encounter in this next section of the Unveiling.

This verse correlates to the twelve stars seen on the Woman in 12:1, above; the sealing of the twelve tribes of Israel in 7:4ff, above; and all the way back to Joseph's dream where the "eleven stars" represented his eleven brothers (Gen. 37:9-10). The figure of a city represents a people, not physical structures. The **great and high wall** is a symbol for the protection for those whose lives have, "**been hidden so that [they are] now concealed together with the Christ, within the midst of God** (or: in union with God)" (Col. 3:3). This may be an allusion to the time of Israel's freedom from Babylon, and their return to rebuild the walls of that ancient city (Neh. 2:17). Nehemiah said that doing so would end their being a "reproach" among the surrounding nations, and within the Persian Empire. The burned gates and broken walls were a witness of Jerusalem's previous defeat and destruction. The **high wall** (note the singular: a continuous wall surrounding the city) is certainly **great**, for in vs. 17, below, we learn that it is "**one hundred forty four** (does that number sound familiar?) **cubits**," which would be approximately from 216 to 225 ft., if taken literally. This gives the reader some perspective of the picture that John was seeing. We read in Isa. 26:1, "Look, a strong city, and he will make our salvation [safety; security] its wall and outer wall" (NETS; brackets added).

The **twelve agents** (or: messengers) that were "**upon**, or, **at**, or, **on top of**" the **twelve gates** may have allusions to a number of OT situations. Here, Lynda points out that the number 12 is a figure that is representative of Divine government. The first would be Gen. 3:24, in the apocalyptic symbol of "the cherubim" (plural),
> "And so at one point He cast Adam out, and caused him to proceed settling down and continue dwelling off in a place opposite, and instead of, the paradise (garden; orchard) of pleasure, delight and luxury. Then He stationed the cherubim (transliteration of the Heb.: folks having been grasped), along with the burning (or: flaming) sword – the one that is continuously twisting, turning and progressively changing – to continuously watch over, guard, keep secure, maintain and preserve the Way (path; road) of, from, pertaining to, and which is, the Life" (LXX, JM).

Those cherubim were characterized as "burning ones" (Hebrew: *seraphim*) in the temple vision of Isa. 6. The flaming sword of Gen. 3:24 calls to mind what we encounter while walking the Way of Christ, "**the Word of God** (or: God's thought, idea and message; or: the expressed Logos from God; or: the Word which is God) **[is] living** (or: alive), **and active** (working; operative; energetic; at work; productive) **and more cutting above every two-mouthed sword, even passing through** (penetrating) **as far as a dividing** (or: parting; partitioning) **of soul and spirit** (or: of inner self-life and breath-effect), **both of joints and marrows, even able to discern** (separate; judge; decide) **concerning thoughts** (ponderings; reflections; in-rushings; passions) **and intentions** (notions; purposes) **of a heart** (= core of the being)" (Heb. 4:12).

The next allusion may be Isa.62:6a,
"On your walls, Jerusalem, I appoint those keeping watch – all the day and all the night" (CVOT).
And then there is Ezk. 41:25, where the image is the Temple doors:
"On them, on the doors of the Temple, [were] made cherubim (grasped ones) and palms…"

The "**names of the twelve tribes of the sons of Israel**" being "**inscribed upon the gates**" is a direct echo of Ezk. 48:31-34, which go on to list on which sides of the City each tribe is named. Four groups of three tribes are each associated with one of the cardinal directions. We find the apocalyptic term **thousand** in Ezk. 48:35a, "Round about, eighteen thousand" (Rotherham). The Tanakh gives this gloss: "The circumference [shall be] 18,000 [cubits]." In vs. 16, below, we find a different number, 12 thousand for each of the four sides (totaling 48,000) and this difference in numbers should tell us that neither of these apocalyptic visions are meant to be taken literally. The remainder of that verse states, "And the Name (or: a name) of the City, from that Day on, [will be] Yahweh-is-There" (CVOT). So Christ's presence (Christ in you, the expectation of glory) defines the City. Kaplan adds:
"Israel is representative of the Father, and Israel's twelve sons are a figure of 'the sons of God.'
Thus, these twelve gates represent God's sons (Rom. 8:14)."
But even as the twelve gates symbolize corporate Israel, each individual gate represents an individual tribe, and each name on each gate was originally an individual son of Jacob. O'Donohue suggests, "Individuality is the only gateway to spiritual potential and blessing" (ibid p 81). Each gate did not have the name "Israel," or even, "Jerusalem." We experience the holy corporately (as did Israel during the Exodus), but we enter it individually, as members of a body. Jesus identified Himself at the Door (or: **Gate**; Entrance) in Jn. 10:9. But, like Reuben, the eldest son of Jacob, Paul identifies God's Son as, "**the Firstborn among, within the center of, and in union with many brothers** (= a vast family of believers)!" And so, it follows that each one of us is a door, a gate, of the City. Christ's solidarity, and identity, with His brothers was clearly portrayed in the parable of the sheep and the kids, in Mat. 25. In vs. 40 he proclaims, "**Upon such an amount** (or: = To the extent) **that you did** (or: do) **and perform(ed) [it] to** (or: for) **one of these belonging to the least of My brothers** (used collectively: = the members of My family; or: = those of My group or brotherhood), **you did and perform [it] to and for Me!**"

The **twelve agents**/messengers, and the twelve gates that are identified by the names of the twelve tribes of Israel, compose the first half of the picture of "twenty four elders" in 4:4, above. The second half of this encompassing twenty four is seen in the "**twelve names of the twelve emissaries** (sent-forth folks; representatives) **of, and from, the little Lamb**" – vs. 14, below. Chilton (ibid p 555) points us to Eph. 2:19-22,
"**Consequently then** (or: Thereupon), **you folks no longer continuously exist being strangers** (foreigners) **and sojourners** (temporary residents in a foreign land), **but in contrast, you continually exist being fellow-citizens of those set apart to be sacred people: even God's family** (members of God's household), **being fully built as a house upon the foundation of the sent-forth representatives** (or: emissaries) **and prophets** (folks who had light ahead of time), **Jesus Christ continuously being a corner-foundation [stone] of it…. continuously and progressively being formed a constituent part of the structure** (or: being built together into a

house) – **into God's down-home place** (place of settling down to dwell; abode; permanent dwelling) **within [the] Spirit**."

13. **from the east** (a rising) **three gates** (or: gateways; portals; vestibules; structural entry-forecourts); **from the north three gates; from the south three gates; from the west** (a sinking) **three gates.**

The four sides and four directions noted here speak figuratively of the layout of camp of Israel in the wilderness (Nu. 2:2-25), and has reference to both "the four quarters of the world" (Matthew Henry), and the four living ones before the throne, seen in chapter 4, above.

Chilton (ibid p 555) points out the repeated use of the preposition "**from**," suggesting (from Sweet, *Revelation*) that this may be an allusion to Isa. 49:11-12,
> "I will make all My mountains a way (road; path), and My highways shall be raise up. Behold, these from afar shall come, and behold, these from the north and from the sea (= the west), and these from the land of the Sinim ['probably China,' Rotherham, note e]" (CVOT).

Simmons comments: "The first covenant had been marked by a particularism; the new is marked by universalism. The gospel is for all men (Mat. 28:19)" (ibid p 407). This also calls to mind Lu. 13:29,
> "**people will continue arriving from eastern regions and western territories, as well as from [the] north and [the] south, and they will proceed in being made to recline back at a meal, within God's reign** (kingdom; sovereign projects and programs)."

Kaplan has shared:
> "The three pearls on each side correspond to '**the Way** (or: Path), **the Truth** (the Reality) **and the Life** (or: = I am the way to really live). **No one is presently going to, or progressively coming toward, the Father, except through Me** (through means of Me, or, through the midst of Me)' – Jn. 14:6, These, in turn, correspond to the new attitude/spirit, soul and body of the new creation – our new heaven and earth. Every gate is the same way into God's glory. As the wall is around Jerusalem, so is God around His people. The City is a picture of being complete in Him. These gates are figures of entrances, echoing what Jesus said in Jn. 10:7, '**I tell you, and it is certainly true, I Myself am the Door for the sheep** (or: the sheep's Gate and Entrance).'"

Because of the enormous size of this symbolic City, there are comparatively MANY ways to enter her, and from every direction. She is like a giant vortex, or funnel, that will draw in and receive all humanity. Verses 12 and 13 should be seen together, where the word **gates** is used six times. Between here and 22:14, below, we find it used five more times. It is obvious that this symbol is considered to be important. The NT uses two Greek forms that are commonly rendered "gate." The form used in the Unveiling has the semantic range given in the parenthetical expansion on its first use, here in vs.13, above: gateways; portals; vestibules; structural entry-forecourts. The stunning declaration in vs. 25, below: **shall by no means be closed** (or: under no circumstances be locked) **by day**. Coupled with this is the surprising proclamation which follows: **night will not be** (or: not continue existing,) **in that place** (or: and you see, there will not be night there). So the reality is: these gates will never be closed. This same word was used in Lu. 16:20, the place where Lazarus was laid down, in that parable, and which turned out to be his place of entry into that which the City, here, represents. As given in the parenthetical expansion of Mat. 16:18b, cited above, the same word that is rendered here as a "gate" of the City was used as the "entrance" of a womb. Since this City is a symbol for the Lamb's Wife, the City (the called-out covenant communities) may be a metaphor for the place of spiritual conception, and then birth into God's realm of sovereign activity (or: kingdom). *Cf.* Gal. 4:26; Jn. 3:3-7.

Jesus, using the other form of the word normally rendered "gate," spoke of two different gates:

> a) "**wide [is] the gate and spacious** (roomy, free, open) **[is] roadway habitually leading off into the loosing-away of loss and destruction** (or: demolition)."
>
> b) "**the gate is narrow, cramping and restrictive which is habitually leading off into the Life – and the path has been compressed and squeezed** [to where the traveler is being pressed and encumbered]."

He advised entering by this second gate. (Mat. 7:13-14; cf Lu. 13:24) We suggest that these two gates spoke of passing into the two Cities that are symbolically presented in the Unveiling.

14. Also, the wall of the City continues having twelve foundations, and upon them twelve names of the twelve emissaries (sent-forth folks; representatives) **of, and from, the little Lamb.**

John observed 'upon" the **foundations** of this NEW Jerusalem, "**twelve names of the twelve emissaries** (sent-forth folks; representatives) **of, and from, the little Lamb.**" This symbol explains and identifies the origin of this City. It is "founded" upon the small group that Jesus called to follow Him, and the number "**twelve**" is a reference to the twelve disciples with whom He started out, and again displays the concept of "Diving government" (Lynda). It was into this foundational group that He would gradually implant the revelation of who He is, and of what they would begin to build:

> "**And you see, [it is] upon this, this rock-mass** (or: the bedrock) **[that] I will progressively be constructing and building up My house – the called-out community**" (Mat. 16:18).

Peter referred to this in 1 Pet. 2:5 where he told his listeners:

> "**you yourselves are, as living stones, continuously being erected** (or: progressively constructed and built up), **[being] a spiritual house** (a building with its source being the Spirit, with the characteristics of a Breath-effect)."

Then Paul spoke of Jesus together with His followers as "one body" with many members, calling this composite "Christ," in 1 Cor. 12:12. Yet in 1 Cor. 3:11 he instructs us,

> "**no one can** (or: continues able to; is having power to) **lay another foundation** (or: to place or set another foundation [Stone] of the same kind) **beside** (or: in addition to and distinct from) **the One lying** (or: continuing being laid)**: which is** (continues being) **Jesus Christ** (Jesus [the] Anointed One; = Jesus, [the] Messiah)."

Christ is the Head of the "body;" He is also its Source. Yet, among the ethnic multitudes, Paul said,

> "**For we are God's fellow-workers** (or: we are co-workers of and from God).... **I lay** [other MSS: have laid] **a foundation** (or: laid a foundation [Stone]), **yet another is progressively building a house upon [it]**" (1 Cor. 3:9, 10).

We saw "people" as being an integral part of God's building, and City, in 3:12, above,

> "**The one habitually conquering** (repeatedly overcoming so as to be the victor) **– I will continue making** (forming; constructing; creating; producing) **him [to be] a pillar** (or: column) **in My God's Temple, and he** (or: it) **may nevermore** (by no means any more) **come** (or: go) **out** (outside), **and I will proceed to write upon him My God's Name, and the name of the City of My God: 'The New and different Jerusalem.'**"

Reference to this is found in Eph. 2:19-22 where the foundation of the called-out communities are "**the emissaries** (representatives) **AND the prophets.**" Furthermore, by joining the twelve tribes of Israel (figure of the old covenant), with the twelve **emissaries of the little Lamb** (representative of the new covenant), this City represents the joining and peace spoken of in Eph. 2:14,

> "**You see, He Himself is our Peace** (or: continuously exists being our joining and harmony) **– the One making** (forming; constructing; creating; producing) **The Both [to be] one, and within His flesh** (= physical being; or: = system-caused crucifixion) **is instantly destroying** (unbinding; unfastening; loosing; causing to collapse) **the middle wall of the fenced enclosure** (or: the

partition or barrier wall): **the enmity** (cause of hate, alienation, discord and hostility; characteristics of an enemy)."

The "**Both**" to which Paul referred in this verse were the **Circumcision** (the Jews; Israel) and the **Uncircumcision** (the Gentiles; the ethnic multitudes of the nations), as he mentioned in Eph. 2:11.

In Rom. 11:17, 24, Paul gave a metaphor of what is seen in this City:

"**Now since some** (or: if certain ones) **of the branches are broken off** (or: were at one point broken out of [the tree]), **yet you yourself, being a wild olive tree of the field or forest, you are** (or: were) **grafted in within** (or: among) **them, you also came to be** (are birthed; are become) **a joint-participant** (a partner taking in common together with; a co-partaker) **of the Root and of the Fatness** (= sap) **of The Olive Tree** (or: of the oil of the olive).… **For since you yourself were cut out of the olive tree [which is] wild** (of the field or forest) **by nature, and then to the side of nature** (perhaps: = outside of, or contrary to, nature) **you are** (or: were at one point) **grafted in – into a fine** (beautiful; cultivated; GARDEN) **olive tree – to how much greater an extent** (or: for how much rather) **will these, the ones in accord with nature, proceed in being engrafted into their own olive tree!**"

As noted, above, part of the picture is an echo of Paul in Eph. 2:19-20,

"**being fellow-citizens of those set apart to be sacred people** (or: folks residing together in a City belonging to, and composed of, the holy ones): **even God's family** (members of God's household), **being fully built as a house upon the foundation of the sent-forth representatives** (or: emissaries) **and prophets** (folks who had light ahead of time), **Jesus Christ continuously being a corner-foundation [stone] of it** (or: there being an extreme point and head of the corner, or, capstone/keystone: Jesus Christ Himself)."

This City is a picture of the completed building – composed of "**The Both**," Jew and Gentile – to which Jesus referred in Mat. 16:18, above. In Eph. 2:15 Paul called this new creation "**one new humanity**," where ethnic and cultural identities and differences disappear.

To the twelve tribes on the gates, above, plus the twelve emissaries mentioned here (a total of 24), allusion has been seen to 1 Chron. 24:3-19, where the names of twenty-four chiefs, or governors, of the sanctuary are listed. Then in 1 Chron. 25 we find twenty-four orders of singers.

In the Dead Sea Scroll 1QS8 we find similar metaphors that speak of,

"twelve laymen and three priests who are blameless…," and, "When such men as these come to be in Israel, then shall the society of *Yahad* truly be established, an 'eternal planting' (*Jubilees* 16:26), a temple for Israel, and – mystery! – a Holy of Holies for Aaron; true witnesses to justice… They will be 'the tested wall, the precious cornerstone' (Isa. 28:16) whose foundations shall neither be shaken nor swayed…" (lines 1-8; *The Dead Sea Scrolls, A New Translation*, trans. by Michael Wise, Martin Abegg, Jr. & Edward Cook, HarperSanFrancisco, 1996, p 137).

15. And he who is speaking with me was holding and continues having a measure, a golden reed, so that he may measure the City – even her gates and her walls:

Now we see the agent who had been talking with John enter into the scene with **a golden reed to measure the city**. Gold being a figure for the attributes of God, Witness Lee saw this as being "measured according to the divine nature." There is no mention or figure of her being "found wanting" in this picture (Dan. 5:27). It calls to mind what Paul spoke of in Eph. 4:13 of coming,

"**into the state of oneness from, and which is, The Faithfulness** (or: the unity of, that belongs to and which characterizes that which is faith; or: the lack of division which has its source in trust,

confidence and reliability, has the character of and is in reference to the loyalty and fidelity), **even which is the full, experiential and intimate knowledge** (or: and from recognition; and of discovery; as well as pertaining to insight) **which is** (or: of; from; in reference to) **the Son of God, [growing] into [the] purposed and destined adult man** (complete, finished, full-grown, perfect, goal-attained, mature manhood [= the Second Humanity]) – **into** (or: unto) **[the] measure of [the] stature** (full age; prime of life) **of the entire content which comprises the Anointed One**
> (or: which is the result of the full number which is the Christ; of the effect of the fullness from the [Messiah]; from the effect of that which fills and completes that which refers to the Christ; of the result of the filling from, and which is, the Christ)."

We should observe the contrast, here, to the situation described in 11:1-2. There John was given an ordinary measuring reed and was instructed to measure only the temple, and not even the temple courts. There it also described a time of the City being "**tread**" upon by the ethnic multitudes. Our present vision is of the "prepared" Bride, and it is measured by "heaven's" standards.

Ezk. 40-47 are full of such measurements. Zech. 2:1-2 presents us with a similar picture, where the prophet sees "a man with a measuring line in his hand.... to measure Jerusalem." Zech. 2:6 gave God's call for the captive Jews to "flee from the land of the north," saying, "Deliver yourself, O Zion, that dwells with the daughter of Babylon" (vs. 7). That was echoed in 18:4, above, having a literal fulfillment just prior to AD 70 where Christians heard the call to leave physical Jerusalem before its destruction. But in our present chapter we see the City into which we have been called, and of which we are a part. Returning to Zech. 2:10-11a, we find what we read about in vs. 3, above:

> "'Sing and rejoice, O daughter of Zion: for, lo, I come, and I will dwell in the midst of you,' says Yahweh. And then many nations shall be joined to Yahweh, in that Day, and shall be My people."

16. And the City is lying (or: is continually being laid) **square** (four-angled; four-cornered), **and her length [is] even as much as the width. And he measured** (or: measures) **the City with the reed upon twelve thousand race-courses** (stadiums; fixed standards of measure): **her length and width and height are equal.**

That the City is "**lying square**" corresponds to the four cardinal directions specified in vs. 13, above. Wallace suggests that this shape, "was a Greek term used to denote perfection in any form" (ibid p 440). This shape is an allusion to Ezk. 45:2-3,

> "And there shall be from this a holy precinct five hundred by five hundred **square** all around.... and in it shall be a holy precinct, holy of holies" (NETS).

The measure has the symbolic number **twelve** modified by the figurative word "**thousand**," as we have considered, above. Taken literally, "The city measures fifteen hundred miles... in height" (Metzger, ibid p 100). We should with this information lose all doubts of the picture in the chapter being symbolic.

The "**twelve thousand race-courses**," speaks of the fact that this city is built of individual races run (or: lives lived): "Do you not know that those running in a race-course (or: stadium) all indeed run... thus run, that you may obtain" (1 Cor. 9:24, Diaglott). Then there is Heb. 12:1,

> **after at once putting off from ourselves all bulk and encumbrance** (every weight; all that is prominent; or: getting rid of every arrow point within us) **and the easily-environing** (skillfully-surrounding; well-placed encircling) **failure** (sin; error; mistake; shooting off-target; missing of the point), **we can and should through persistent remaining-under** (or: relentless patient endurance and giving of support) **keep on running the racecourse continuously lying before us** (or: lying in the forefront within us; or: lying ahead, among us)."

And, of course, there is Paul in Phil. 3:14-15a,

"**I am continuously pressing forward, pursuing down toward** [the; or: an] **object in view** (a mark on which the eye is fixed)**: into the awarded contest prize of God's** (or: the award which is God's) **invitation to an above place** (or: the prize from, and which is, the upward calling from, and which is, the God) **within the midst of and in union with Christ Jesus. Therefore – as many as [are] people who are mature** (ones who have reached the goal, being finished and complete) **– we should constantly be of this frame of mind** (have this attitude and opinion; think this way; be minding and paying attention to this)."

Another thing that we can note from these measurements is the aspect of equality. No member is higher than another. Furthermore, the **equal** dimensions calls to mind the equal dimensions of the holy of holies, in the Tabernacle, and again in the Temple (1 Ki. 6:20). With Paul declaring that WE are God's Temple (2 Cor. 6:16), with these cubic dimensions it would seem that WE are, in fact, the new Holy of holies. We read in Heb. 9:8 that,

"**the Way** (Path; Road) **of the set-apart places** (or: of the separated ones; **pertaining to the sacred folks**; of the Holies) **[was] not yet to have been manifested** (caused to appear; brought to light) **while the first tabernacle is having a standing**."

This can be seen with two applications:

a) Jesus is "the Way," but He could not be manifested until He had taken the "first way," the old covenant temple cultus, to the grave. *Cf* Jn. 4:21; 1 Sam. 4:21-22.

b) The Way "pertaining to the sacred folks" (the called-out, separated folks) could not be caused to appear while the old covenant had a standing – i.e., had a position in God's economy.

This is what Paul spoke of in Col. 1:26,

"**the Secret** (or: sacred mystery) **having been hidden away and remaining concealed away from the ages** (or: from [past] eons), **as well as away from the [past] generations, yet now** (at the present time) **is set in clear light in His set-apart folks** (or: was manifested to His holy ones; is caused to be seen by His saints; is shown for what it is, for His sacred people)."

That the three dimensions are given (where else is a city thus described in Scripture?) suggests an allusion to the three-fold dimensions that we find in Eph. 3:18-19,

"**may you folks be fully powerful and thus act out of strength to grasp** (receive down for yourselves; take possession of so as to comprehend), **together with all the set-apart folks** (saints; holy ones), **what [is] the width and length and height and depth, and thus to know – and gain insight by intimate experience – the love of, from, and which is, the Christ [that is] continuously transcending** (overshooting; being thrown over and beyond; surpassing) **personal experiential knowledge and insight, so that you folks would be filled unto all the effect of the fullness of God and the result of the filling from God**."

Paul spoke similarly in Rom. 8:39,

[neither] height (effect of being high), **nor depth** (or: deep places), **nor any other or different created thing** (or: founded thing; institution) **will be having power or be able to separate, divide or part us from God's Love** (or: from the acceptance from God; from the urge toward reunion, which is God; God's full giving of Himself to us)."

And as he exclaims Rom. 11:33, "**O, the depth of [the] riches** (wealth; resources) **and wisdom and intimate, experiential knowledge and insight of God** (or: from God; which is God)!"

As to its shape and size, Metzger says,

"The city measures fifteen hundred miles in length, in breadth, and in height (21:16). But how can a city be a cube? The description is architecturally preposterous, and must not be taken with flat-footed literalism. In ancient times the cube was held to be the most perfect of all geometric forms" (*Breaking the Code*, ibid p 100-1).

In Ezk. 40:5 we read that, "its breadth was equal to the reed, and its elevation was equal to the reed" (NETS). Dan. 2:35 described a kingdom that became a "mountain" that filled the whole Land. A City that was this high would have been like a "mountain."

17. **And he measured her wall: one hundred forty four cubits –** (a) **human's measure, which is an agent's [measure].**

Once again, the number 12 again (in the 144; *cf* 7:4-8 and 14:1, 3, above) comes on stage. **One hundred forty four** is the "square" of the "twelve tribes," and fits with a "square City." As with the multiples of 144 X 1000, Kaplan sees here the multiplication of the fullness of Israel in the measure of the City's walls. He goes on to explain that this number represents the composite new olive tree of Rom. 11:17, where the wild (Gentile, ethnic-nation) branches grow together with the believing branches of the Jews as the all-inclusive tree of Life. That the number 12 is so apparent throughout the Unveiling is evidence that this City and its walls include, and point to, the fullness of Israel. In Rom. 11:23, Paul instructs us, concerning the unbelieving ones of Israel, that, "**God is able** (capable; is constantly powerful) **to graft them back in again**," and so, in the end (as pictured by this glorious City), "**all Israel will progressively be delivered** (rescued, saved, made whole and restored to their original position [in the olive tree]), **according as it has been written,**
> '**The One continuously dragging out of danger and drawing to Himself** (The Rescuer; The Deliverer) **will repeatedly arrive and be present from out of Zion; He will continue turning irreverence away from Jacob**'" (Rom. 11:26).

Note that the agent's measure is also a human's measure. In this we may have a hint at the "agent" being identical with "a human" – at least in visions. What is on earth is a reflection of what is in heaven (a common aspect of Greek cosmology that those of the Hellenistic culture would understand), and agents in "heaven," or, the atmosphere, may have once been, or still be, human (see 19:10, above, and 22:9, below). The **cubit** is an ancient unit of measurement, based on the forearm length from the middle finger tip to the elbow bottom, of a human male. It was an approximate length, based upon what they would have considered to be the size of an average man. It was a point of reference, not an exact length, except where "cubit rods" were used – but the length of them varied in different times and cultures. Here it is figurative reckoning, and it again speaks to us of the human element of this "heavenly City."

Ezk. 40 opens with visions from God, where he is shown "the structure of a city." In vs. 3 he saw "a man whose appearance was like the appearance of bronze (or: copper), with a flax-cord in his hand, and a measuring reed – and he was standing in the gate." The association between the one who measures, and that of being human, may be a visionary key. As we saw above, in 1 Pet. 2:5, Scripture makes people analogous with stones (the building material of large structures, in John's day). John, the Immerser, informs us that, "**God continues able** (or: constantly has power) **to at once raise up** (or: awaken) **children to Abraham** (or: for Abraham; in Abraham) **from out of these stones!**" (Mat. 3:9).

The word **human** is used only here and in vs. 3, above, in this chapter. Its use here may be pointing back to God's Tabernacle being with humans. Again, the picture of this City joins "heaven" and "earth." It thus joins "spirit" with "the material."

18. **And that which was built within her wall is jasper, and the City [is] pure** (clear; clean; cleansed) **gold like pure** (clear, clean) **crystal** (or: glass),

Verses 18-20 list the gemstones and jewels out of which the city is built. This calls to mind Mal. 3:17, "... in that day when I publicly recognize [and] openly declare them to be My jewels..." (Amplified OT), and,

Isa. 54:11-12, "O afflicted one... I will set your stones in antimony, and lay your foundations with sapphires. I will make your pinnacles of agate, your gates of carbuncles, and all your wall of precious stones." Paul referred to himself and those at Corinth as being, "**God's building** (or: construction project; structure, or act of building)," in 1 Cor. 3:9, and as His temple, in vs. 17. They were also the builders, together with God, and in vs. 12 he said that they should build upon the foundation with "**gold and silver [with] precious** (valuable) **stones**."

Precious stones start out as ordinary minerals, until heat and pressure turn them into jewels, in their "earth experience." The gold breastplate of the high priest had 12 jewels, each one engraved with one of the names of the 12 tribes (Ex. 28:15-30). The City, here, (into which the precious stones were set) is "**pure gold**." The fact that the gold is described as "pure," tells us that these folks had been with the Refiner (Zech. 13:9; Mal. 3:2-1) – all impurities have been removed. This figure also says that it is God Himself who holds these stones together and gives them form and structure. They dwell in Him. As Paul said,

> "**for you see, Christ's love** (urge toward accepting reunion; full giving of Himself to [us]) **continuously holds us together**" (2 Cor. 5:14a).

"**And that which was built within her wall is jasper.**" We saw in 4:3, above, that God's appearance is like jasper. The New Jerusalem bears the appearance of God. Witness Lee (*The Recovery NT*) observes that with the city being of gold that is like clear glass, it would be transparent, and he refers us to 2 Cor. 3:2 that we are letters that are being read by everyone. With 10b and 11b, above, describing the whole City as being "**like a most precious stone, as a jasper stone being continuously crystal-clear**," it is expected that **the wall** and **the City** would also have the same description, here.

The descriptions of Solomon's temple shed light on the symbolism we have in our present passage. *Cf* 1 Ki. 6:19-30, where most everything was overlaid with gold. In fact, reading all of 1 Ki. 6-7 will be instructive for understanding vss. 19-20, here, for there is obvious correlation between the two passages.

19. **and the foundations of the wall of the city are ones having been set in order** (made a system and are a world; or: arranged as the aggregate of humanity; or: adorned) **with every precious stone.**
    The first foundation: jasper; the second, sapphire (or: lapis lazuli); **the third, chalcedony; the fourth, emerald;**
20. **the fifth, sardonyx; the sixth, sardius** (or: carnelian); **the seventh, chrysolite** (or: topaz); **the eighth, beryl; the ninth, topaz** (or: peridot); **the tenth, chrysoprasus; the eleventh, hyacinth** (jacinth); **the twelfth, amethyst.**

The picture given here, with these twelve gem stones set in the twelve foundations, presents us with the breast-plate of the high priest being placed upon little Lamb's "**twelve emissaries** (sent-forth folks; representatives)" (vs. 14, above), suggesting the priesthood of Christ's followers (1:6, above). Ex. 28:17-20 gives the original description of that breastpiece. That these foundations correspond to the stones worn by the high priest may imply OT imagery as foundational to this city. That breastpiece, being made of the same materials, and having the same square form of the City, of which we read here, points to the holiness of this city, and to its function as a temple where Yahweh lives. Where in the old arrangement only the priests could be in the temple, and only the high priest in the holy of holies, now God's presence is accessible to all, as Heb. 10:21-22a instructs us, "**with a Great Priest [enthroned] upon God's House** (or: the house from God) **we can be continuously and progressively approaching**" God.

The phrase, "**having been set in order** (etc.)," is the plural form of the same perfect participle used to describe the Bride, in vs. 2b, above. It is a cognate of the word *kosmos*, so it speaks of an ordered arrangement of a new "world." Wis. of Sol. 18:24a says of the high priests garment, "You see, upon [the] long, full-length robe was the whole ordered system (or: aggregate of humanity; *kosmos*)" (LXX, JM).

The king of Tyre, in Ezk. 28:12-19, was "full of wisdom and perfect in beauty." He was "in Eden, the garden of God... of **every precious stone** was your covering.... until perversity was found in you... [and] I cast you upon the earth.... unto times age-abiding." Here in chapter 21 we have a picture of humanity restored to Eden, for that passage in Ezk. 28 speaks of the "casting out" of humanity from the Garden (Gen. 3). The poetic imagery of that ruler of Tyre called him "an anointed cherub that covers" and said that he "walked up and down in the midst of the stones of fire"(vs.14) – all of which is temple imagery and priesthood imagery, intimating Adam's function in the proto-temple (the Garden). In a parallel portrayal, the "prince of Tyre" is put in the role of Adam, in Ezk. 28:1-10. There it says of him, "Because your heart [is] lifted up, and you have said, 'I [am as] God; I sit in the seat of God – in the midst of the seas; yet your [are] a man [Heb. *adam*], and not God" (vs. 2). In vs. 7 he is told, "Behold, I will therefore bring strangers upon you – the terrible of the nations... against the beauty of your wisdom, and they shall defile your brightness." Then vs. 10 concludes, "You will die the deaths of the uncircumcised..." The following dirge against the king of Tyre, states, "Your heart was lifted up because of your beauty; you have corrupted your wisdom by reason of your brightness; I will cast you to the ground; I will lay you before kings, that they can look at you" (28:17). This was played out in literal Jerusalem (a figure of the first Adam, God's son – Lu. 3:38b – as was Israel, Ex. 4:22) in AD 70. What we see in our present passage of the Unveiling is the resurrected Last (*eschatos*) Adam, and His Bride, with the glory and beauty restored.

Another allusion of all these precious stones significantly calls us back to the areas outside Eden, to where the four rivers flowed, in Gen. 2:10-14. There was gold in Havilah, as well as the pearl (or: bdellium) and the onyx stone. This present picture is another hint of humanity's return to Paradise (2:7, above). Recall Jesus' words on the cross, in Lu. 23:43,

> "**Truly it is so** (or: Count on it!)**... I am now saying to you** (D adds: Be of good cheer and take courage)**... Today** (This very day) **you will proceed being** (continue existing) **with Me within the midst of Paradise** (= in the Garden [note: used in the LXX for the Garden of Eden in Gen. 2:8])!"

Then there are Paul's words in 2 Cor. 12:3-4,

> "**I have seen and know such a person** (man; human)**... that was snatched away** (seized and taken) **into the Paradise and heard inexpressible gush-effects and utterances** (unutterable sayings and results of a flow; unspeakable results of movement and flux; inexpressible matters and declarations) **which are not being from out of existence** (or: which are not continuing from within the midst of being; or: which it continues being not right; or: for which there is no privilege or authority; which are not being possible; which are not being allowed) **in a person** (to mankind; for a human) **to at any point speak**."

Having our eyes opened through the symbolism in the Unveiling, we can now look back with understanding at the symbolism concerning the beginning of humanity's journey, from Garden to Garden. Consider the number four, in Gen. 2:10, compared to the use of "four" in our visions in the Unveiling. It speaks of universal outreach and inclusion. The gold of Gen. 2:11-12 is reflected in this Garden City that we are here seeing described. Why is it mentioned that there is "the pearl" (CVOT) there? Did this point us to the gates of our present City? Was it indicating that there would be multiple entrances back into the "heavenly," or spiritual, Eden? And why is one of the rivers the Euphrates (vs. 14), which is normally associated with Babylon? Was this a clue that the human journey would include a passing through Babylon? The onyx stone is representative of the gems that make up the foundation of the City, which no longer has any trace of Babylon, or the Euphrates, but once again has the Tree of the Life, and the River of Life flowing through it. All that is listed in Gen. 2 is prior to Adam's expulsion in Gen. 3. God had already prepared the materials that he would eventually find, in Havilah, and that he then would use to build God's habitation (1 Cor. 3:9-17).

Now in 22:1-3, below, we have mention of a tree of Life, a river, and the curse. We see here the Omega, while the Genesis story gives us the Alpha. The last two chapters of the *Unveiling* present the End of the epic human drama that began in Genesis, while at the same time presenting the Beginning of the New story. History has been recording the human adventures in the new Age of the Messiah, even though Christ's kingdom was still only seen in a thread of first-fruit lives of individuals, and Babylon was once again rebuilt in the 4th century, wearing a mask of Christianity while continuing to kill its prophets, just as the old Jerusalem had done. All of the Scriptures, both the "Hebrew Scriptures" and the "Christian Scriptures," speak, ultimately, of just two humans:
> "**The first human** (person; man) **[was/is] forth from out of the earth** (land; ground; soil; dirt), **made of moist soil and mud** (or: having the quality and characteristics of moist dirt that can be poured; soilish); **the Second Human** (Person; Man; [other MSS add: {is} the Lord]) **[is made] out of heaven** (or: [is] from [the] atmosphere and sky; [*p46* reads: {is} spiritual])" (1 Cor. 15:47).

The fourth vision of 4 Ezra shows the seer a woman. In 10:7 he speaks to her of "Zion, the mother of us all, [being] in deep grief and great humiliation." This book is dated in the late 1st century, so the author may be referring to the results of AD 70. Later in this vision, we read:
> "While I was talking to her, behold, her face suddenly shone exceedingly, and her countenance flashed like lightning... While I was wondering what this meant, behold, she suddenly uttered a loud and fearful cry, so that the earth shook at the sound. And I looked, and behold, the woman was no longer visible to me, but there was an established city, and a place of huge foundations showed itself" (10:25-27; *The OT Pseudepigrapha*, Vol. 1, ibid p 546-7).

It is possible that the author was influenced by the Unveiling, but it demonstrates the currency of Jewish apocalyptic in that period.

21. **And the twelve gates [are] twelve pearls – each one of the several gates was [made] out of one pearl. And the broad place** (street; plaza; square) **of the City [is] pure** (clean, clear; cleansed) **gold, as a translucent crystal** (or: transparent glass).

Here we find that the gates are **pearls**, and vs. 12, above, told us that there is an agent upon each gate. Does this correspond to 1:20, above, where each covenant community has an agent? With each gate inscribed with the name of one of the 12 tribes, we suggest that entry into this City requires being grafted into Israel's olive tree (Rom. 11:16-17).

The pearl is formed when a painful grain of sand enters into the oyster. Entrance into the city is through pain and irritation being covered by His sufficient grace (2 Cor. 12:9), or through much pressures and tribulations (Acts 14:22). Lee (ibid) comments,
> "Pearls are produced by oysters in the waters of death.... This depicts Christ as the living One coming into the death waters, being wounded by us, and secreting His life over us to make us into precious pearls for the building of God's eternal expression. That the twelve gates of the city are twelve pearls signifies that regeneration through the death-overcoming and life-secreting Christ is the entrance into the city."

The pearl is also formed within the midst of the sea (a figure of humanity, at large) where everyone is exposed to the minor irritants of this life. Kaplan echoes Lee, pointing out that,
> "The pearl represents Christ's sacrifice through which everyone enters. These pearls recall 'the Pearl of great price' in Mat. 13:45-46, in which God is represented as selling all that He has (represented in the giving of His Son, and Himself, to humanity) in order to acquire it."

In the illustration of the "treasure hidden in a field" (Mat. 13:44), we see that God also "sold all that He had" and bought the whole field to get it. Keep in mind that in Mat. 13:38 Jesus explained that "**the field is the organized System** (the ordered arrangement; the world of religion, economy, culture and government; = the realm of society; or: the aggregate of humanity)." The significance of each gate being composed "**out of one pearl**," suggests that entry into the City came from only One pain, One death; that of the cross of Christ, whose wounds of the nails and spear were covered with the glory of resurrection.

The **broad place** (or: street; plaza) being clear gold speaks of a Godly walk (a walk which is composed of God, or lived by God in us) in which we are transparent – so that God can be seen in our lives, "... **to unveil His Son in me**..." (Gal. 1:16). Lee says concerning the life of the saints, "The divine nature of God is their pathway" (ibid). The word, which can be rendered "street," is in the singular. In this City, there is only one Way: Christ, or, self-giving love and unconditional acceptance of others. I first chose the meaning **broad place**, or, "plaza," or, "square," since this would speak of a meeting or gathering place, and its being "**pure**, clear, cleansed **gold**" could symbolize that they meet, gather or stand in God's Presence, and it is His nature that enables this unifying togetherness. The standing is on God; their way and path is God's. This may also be an allusion to Isa. 35:8-10,

"A highway (or: raised way/road), a clean one, will be (or: appear) there, and it shall be called the Highroad of Holiness (or: Sacred Way)... Thus shall travel the redeemed, and the ransomed of Yahweh shall return. They will enter Zion with joy (or: jubilant [song]) and with eonian rejoicing on their heads, while sorrow (or: affliction) and sighing will flee." (CVOT, Rotherham and Tanakh)

We find that the movement of the Christ-followers was first called "**the Way** (Path; Road)" in Acts 9:2; 19:9. 23; 24:22.

Beale notes that "**pure**, clean" modifies **gold**, "nineteen times in Ex. 25-39" (ibid p 1089). The allusion, here, is obvious. *Cf* 17:4; 18:12, 16, above. The word **crystal**, or glass, is used only here and in vs. 18, above, in the NT. The adjective, "made of crystal or glass," is found only in 4:6 and 15:2, above. The word **translucent**, or, transparent, literally means, "shine-through." So the quality of the **gold** (signifying God's divine nature) in this City is such that God's glory can shine through it, to be observed by those outside the City, and those within the City. The gold on the inner walls of Solomon's temple could only reflect the light (as the moon reflects the sun). Here, the light shines through both the standing and the walk (which comprise the life) of those who compose this City.

22. And yet I did not see an inner sanctuary [= the holy place, or places, of the Temple] **within her, for the Lord** [=Yahweh]**, Almighty** (All-Strong) **God, even** (or: also) **the little Lamb, is her inner sanctuary** (or: continuously exists being her sacred dwelling place and divine habitation).

Here, through the rest of the chapter, is summarized what Ezekiel described in chapters 40-43 of his prophecy. We need look no further for an additional fulfillment of those chapters. What is described in Unveiling chapter 21 calls to mind the statement we find in Hag. 2:7b-9,

"'And I will fill this House with glory,' says Yahweh of hosts. 'Mine is the silver, and Mine is the gold,' averring is Yahweh of hosts. 'Greater shall become the glory of this latter House than the former... And in this Place shall I give peace,' averring is Yahweh of hosts" (CVOT).

This new situation is also proclaimed by Jeremiah,

"And it shall come to pass... in those days, declares Yahweh, they shall say no more, 'The ark of the covenant of Yahweh.' Neither shall it come up on the heart, neither shall they remember it, neither shall they miss it, neither shall it be made any more. At that time shall they call Jerusalem, 'The Throne of Yahweh,' and there shall be gathered unto her all the nations – to the Name of Yahweh, to Jerusalem; and they shall walk no more after the stubbornness of their own wicked heart" (Jer. 3:16-17; Rotherham).

Now we see that Yahweh, figured here as "**the little Lamb**," is her inner sanctuary, her temple, her sacred dwelling place. This, of course, takes us back to John 17:21-23, our being one in the Father and in the Son; or, to John 15:1-10, the disciple abiding in the Vine. As we are a dwelling place for God, so is He a dwelling place for us (Acts 17:28). It should also be evident, here, that the little Lamb is the Husband of the Bride, and in this picture they are joined – One: "**Now the person continually joining himself** (or: being habitually glued in intimate union; in himself being continuously welded) **to** (or: in; with) **the Lord exists being one spirit** (or: one Breath-effect)" (1 Cor. 6:17). This is true marriage. The little Lamb together with His sheep. This City symbolizes the kingdom which it was the Father's good pleasure to give to His little flock (Lu. 12:32). He is the Head, and they are His body. We find an allusion to this City-temple in the words of Jesus, in Jn. 2:19-21,

> "**Jesus considered then responds to them, and says, 'Loosen** (or: Undo, and thus, destroy or demolish) **this Sanctuary** (Shrine; Divine Habitation; = the Temple consisting of the holy place and the holy of holies), **and within three days I will proceed to be raising it up.'** …. **Yet that One** (= He) **had been laying [things] out concerning, and speaking about, the Sanctuary which is His body** (or: the Divine habitation of the body belonging to, and which is, Him; the inner Temple pertaining to His whole corporeal and material substance)."

Metzger asserts,
> "There is no temple or sanctuary in the holy city, for in one respect, the city itself is all sanctuary. Its dimensions, being in the form of a cube, are like the Holy of Holies in the Mosaic tabernacle of old. The immediate presence of God is no longer in a reserved place… God is now accessible to all. The assurance that the city's 'gates will never be shut by day' (21:25) conveys the sense of perfect freedom of access and fellowship with God" (*Breaking the Code*, ibid p 102).

Following Beale's suggestion (ibid p 1091), I have rendered the genitive phrase in 3:12, above, as appositional: "**in the Temple that is My God**." This finds agreement in our present verse. As Jesus said in Jn. 4:26, **inner sanctuary** is "in Spirit and Truth (or: Breath-effect and Reality)," and being married to the little Lamb, His home is her home. We find this described in 1 Jn. 4:16b,
> "**God exists continually being Love** (God is Love), **and the person continuously remaining** (dwelling; abiding) **within, and in union with, the Love, is continuously remaining** (dwelling; abiding) **within, and in union with, God – and God constantly dwells** (remains) **within the midst of him and abides in union with him**."

And as Jesus prayed in Jn. 17:20-21,
> "**I am not now making a request about these only, but further about those habitually trusting and progressively believing into Me through their word** (or: message; what they lay out), **to the end that all mankind may** (or: everyone would) **continuously exist being one, correspondingly as You, O Father, [are] within the midst of Me, and I [am] within the midst of You – so that they, themselves, may and would also continuously exist being within the midst of Us, to the end that the aggregate of humanity** (the System: world of culture, religion and government; or: secular society) **can** (may; would) **continuously trust and progressively believe that You sent Me forth as an Emissary with a mission**."

This City began being built with the coming of Jesus. He told His disciples:
> "**You see, where there are two or three people that have been led and gathered together into My Name, I am there** (in that place) **within the midst of and among them**" (Mat. 18:20).

23. **Now the City continually has no need of the sun nor of the moon, to the end that they may** (should) **continually shine for, in, or on, her, for the Glory of God** (or: the Glory which is God; the imagination from God) **illuminates** (enlightens; gives light to) **her, and her lamp [is] the little Lamb.**

This is the realized fulfillment of Isa. 60:19-20,
> "No longer shall the sun be your light by day, nor shall the moon give light for brightness for you by night, but Yahweh will become your light eonian, and your Elohim (God) your beauty [LXX: your glory]. No longer shall your sun set, nor your moon be gathered in, for Yahweh, He shall become your light eonian, and your days of mourning will be finished up" (CVOT).

We find in Ezk. 43:
> "the earth (or: Land) was enlightened by His glory," vs. 2b, and,
> "the glory of Yahweh filled the House," vs. 5b (CVOT).

This equates **the little Lamb** (Christ) with **the glory of God**, once again, for He is what **illuminates her** – she no longer needs light from something (or, from some religious system) that is outside of her. Throughout this Unveiling, the marked association of the Little Lamb with Yahweh is evident. The genitive phrase can also be rendered appositionally, "the Glory which is God," which would describe His manifest presence. Also on offer is this phrase rendered as an ablative, with another meaning of *doxa*: "the imagination from God." When He gives us His imagination, our perceptions are expanded. We receive unveilings. Ps. 119:104-5 gives a practical application of this:
> "I ponder Your precepts [the LXX reads: From Your implanted goals and internal directives I send things together and comprehend], therefore I hate every false way. Your word [LXX: law; normal pattern; principle] is a lamp to my feet, a light for my path" (Tanakh; [LXX, JM]).

The lack of **need of the sun nor of the moon** is not a cosmological statement about her relationship to the physical universe. Such flat-footed literalism would completely miss the point of this apocalyptic language. This City is not a literal city; it is a People. The Light that illuminates her is God, manifested in the little Lamb (Jn. 1:4-5, 7-8),
> "**It was** (or: He was, and continued being) **the True and Genuine Light which** (or: Who) **is continuously** (repeatedly; progressively) **enlightening** (giving light to) **every person** (or: human) **continuously** (repeatedly; progressively; constantly; one after another) **coming into the world** (or: the ordered system of culture, religion, economics and government; or: the universe)
>> (or: It was the real Light, progressively coming into the world {organized system}, which is progressively enlightening {or: shedding light on} every human)" (Jn. 1:9).

Another layer of understanding this verse comes from Joseph's dream in Gen.37:9-10, where "the sun and the moon" represented Jacob and Rachel, Joseph's "father and mother." This symbol may be saying that this City no longer needs the light of the old covenant (the shadows from the "fathers"), nor a physical lineage, nor the Levitical priesthood, nor a physical temple to be the light of this new creation in Christ. Her "**lamp [is] the little Lamb**." Jesus said,
> "**I, Myself, am** (or: continuously exist being) **the Light of the world**
>> (or: of the cosmos; of the ordered system; of the dominant cultural, political, economic and religious arrangements; of the universe; of 'the theater of history' – Walter Wink).
>
> **The one habitually and progressively following Me can by no means walk around** (= under no circumstances live his or her life) **within the darkness** (or: the dim and shaded areas; the gloom and obscurity due to the lack of the Light of the Day; the [realm] of the shadows; [note: = ignorance; = that situation which existed before the Light came; or, could also refer to the dim condition within the holy place of the Temple, or to the darkness of death, blindness or the womb]), **but, to the contrary, he will progressively possess** (constantly have and hold) **the Light of 'the Life!'** (or: the light which is life.)" (Jn. 8:12).

Heb. 1:3 describes the Son as,
> "**continuously being an effect of the radiance from**

(or: a result from a dawning and breaking forth of the bright light of the Day which is; a result of the outshining which is; an effulgence from; an effect of an off-shining [light]-beam belonging to; or: a result of a reflection of) **the Glory and Splendor**..."

The Fourth Book of Ezra speaks of a similar situation:
> "no sun or moon or stars...or darkness or evening or morning... or noon or night, or dawn or shining or brightness or light, but only the splendor of the gory of the Most High..." (7:39-42; ibid p 538).

24. And so the multitudes (nations; people groups; ethnic groups; or: non-Jews) **will continue walking about** (i.e., living their lives) **by means of her Light** (through light from her). **And the kings of the Land** (or: earth) **continually carry** (bring; bear) **their glory** [other MSS adds: and honor] **into her.** [Isa. 60:1ff]

This picks up the theme of Isa. 60:3,
> "And nations will go to your light, and kings to the brightness of your radiance" (CVOT).

The LXX of this reads, "Then kings will continue journeying to (or: traveling in; passing along by) your light, and multitudes (ethnic groups; nations; Gentiles) to, in, by or with your brightness and shining" (JM). It is interesting that the very next chapter, Isa. 61, is what Jesus quoted in Lu. 4:19-20 and applied to Himself and to that time. Barclay (ibid p 216) calls these final verses of chapter 21 "a picture of universal salvation." Speaking of Yahweh's House, Isa. 2:2b predicted that "all nations shall flow unto it."

The promises made by Yahweh in Isa. 49 (whether to Israel, or to her Messiah) include, in vs. 6, "I will give You also for a light of [the] nations" (CVOT). The point being, that the Light that should arise from Israel would be FOR the nations, the ethnic multitudes that had been outside of Israel (Eph. 2:12-13). In a section of Isa. (49:1-55:13) which *The Jerome Biblical Commentary* (ibid p 375) terms, "Hymns to the New Jerusalem," Isa. 55:5 speaks of "a nation [where] they have not known you, they shall run to you, on account of Yahweh, your Elohim (God)" (CVOT). Isa. 56:6-8 speaks of,
> "sons of the foreigner.... I will bring them also to My holy mountain and make them rejoice in My House of prayer... for My House shall be called a House of prayer for all peoples, averring is my Lord Yahweh, Convener of the expelled of Israel: I shall convene more to him..." (CVOT).

Barclay says of Isa. 66:19, "It is Israel's task to declare God's glory among the Gentiles" (ibid p 217). Paul and others, ever since, have done this. Isa. 45:22 is explicit:
> "You peoples – those from the end of the earth – be at once fully turned and converted, upon Me!" (LXX, JM)

Zeph. 2:11 offers another beautiful picture that relates to our present context:
> "[The] LORD [= Yahweh] will be caused to progressively shine upon them and will continue being made to appear upon them, and then He will proceed to fully destroy all the gods of the ethnic multitudes (or: from the nations) of the earth. And so all the islands and coastlands of those ethnic multitudes (or: nations) will progressively, one-after-another, bow and prostrate themselves to Him, and in reverent homage will keep on kissing His feet or the hem of His garment – each one from out of his own place" (LXX, JM).

Later in his prophecy, Zephaniah describes what Yahweh would do that speaks to 21:8, above, and calls to mind Heb. 6:7-8 (the cleansing of the field, the soil),
> "Because of this, remain under [the situation], patiently giving support, [the] LORD [= Yahweh] continues saying and laying it out, unto a Day of My standing back up again, and resurrection into evidence (or: with a view to witness and for testimony) through which the effect of My evaluation and the result of My decision [leads] into a gathering together of ethnic multitudes (or: nations; people groups) – of the [situation] to receive and welcome kings into the midst in order, at some point, to pour out (or: forth) upon them all swelling passion of rushing emotion. On the basis of that, all the Land (or: soil; ground; earth) will progress in being correspondingly consumed within

the midst of (or: in union with) [the] Fire of My ardent affection (or: zeal; heated emotion), so that THEN (at that time) I will progressively alter, change and turn-about [the] tongue across (or: for) peoples, into its generation, with a view to [the situation for] all people to continuously (or: repeatedly) call upon the Name of [the] LORD [= Yahweh] – to perform as slaves to (or: for; in; by) Him, under one yoke" (Zeph. 3:8-9; LXX, JM)

So you see, they are to be cleansed, but for a positive purpose!

Now call to mind what Jesus said:

"**At once lift up My crossbeam** (or: the **yoke** which is Me) **upon you people, and instantly learn from Me, because I am mild-tempered** (gentle, kind and considerate) **and humble** (low) **in the heart, and 'you folks will continue finding refreshment and discovering rest in and for your souls** (the whole inner person; the mind, emotions and nerves).' [Jer. 6:16] **You see, My crossbeam** (or: the **yoke** which is Me) **is useful, well-fitting and kindly obliging, and My load** (the burden that is Me and which pertains to Me) **continues being light** (not heavy)" (Mat. 11:29-30).

We read of the Day of which Zephaniah spoke, above, in Zech. 14:9-11,

"Then Yahweh will come to be King over the entire earth (or: Land).... from the gate of Benjamin unto the place of the first gate.... and Jerusalem will dwell in serenity" (CVOT).

In *Testaments of the Twelve Patriarchs, The Testament of Asher, the tenth son of Jacob and Zilpah*, 7:3 makes a wonderful prediction (written 2nd century BC),

"You will be scattered to the four corners of the earth... until such time as the Most High visits the earth. He shall come as a man eating and drinking with human beings, crushing the dragon's head in the water. He will save Israel and all the nations" (*The OT Pseudepigrapha*, Vol. 1, ibid, trans by H.C. Kee, p 780).

Jesus made the association between a city and people, and of both being "light," in Mat. 5:14-16,

"**You folks, yourselves, exist being** (are) **the light of the ordered System** (the world of culture, religion, politics, government, and secular society; = the human sociological realm; or: **the aggregate of humanity**). **A city located up on a mountain** (or: situated on top of a mountain range) **continues unable to be hidden or concealed**.... **the lampstand**.... **In this way, let the Light, which you folks possess** (or: which has a source in you folks; or: which you people are), **shine in front of mankind** (before humans), **so that people can see your fine works** (or: the beautiful works that you are; the ideal acts which come from you folks) **and they can give glory to** (or: and [these deeds; or: these works of beauty] will bring a good reputation for) **your Father – the One in union with the atmospheres [that surround you folks]** (or: within the midst of the heavens)!"

Verse 24, here, presents a picture which can be seen from the beginning of Christ's called-out followers, on to our day. The **multitudes** – the nations, **all ethnic groups**, the non-Israelites – **walk about** (= live their lives) **by means of her LIGHT**. This light is The Truth; this light is The Way; this light is The Life; this light is Christ. He is "**The True Light, which, upon coming into the world, enlightens every person**" (John 1:9). And the called-out communities have been given the Light (Christ in us).

25. **Also, her gates shall by no means be closed** (or: under no circumstances be locked) **by day, for night will not be** (or: not continue existing,) **in that place** (or: and you see, there will not be night there).

Here we have an allusion to Isa. 60:10, where it says,

"Your gates shall be open continually; day and night they shall not be shut.... you shall call your walls Salvation, and your gates Praise."

Now since the gates are never closed by day, and there will be no night there, we can conclude that there will always be access to God's presence; always access to enter (= become a part of) the Bride. Night is caused by the earth turning away from the light. In this realm, there will no longer be a turning away; no longer a vacillating between light and darkness. There is also no longer any dependence upon creation (in this case, the sun) for life. Here God is the source for everything. The open gates present a symbol of peace and security. They also present the picture of continuous accessibility – there is no cut-off point.

Ps. 139:12 previews this, showing us that the context of this City is her place in Christ, for her life is hidden with Christ, within the midst of God (Col. 3:3), where there is no darkness (1 Jn. 1:5b). Here in this psalm, David has been speaking of his life and his relationship with Yahweh, and then he muses:
> "If I said, Surely darkness snuffed me up, and night is belted about me, even darkness is not darkening to You; and night, as day, is giving light: darkness [is] as light" (CVOT).

Such imagery points us away from the literal, and toward the figurative and spiritual. Within this City that comes from God (vs. 2, above) it is "the Day of Christ," where we are "**all are sons of** (= associated with and having the qualities of) **Light and sons of** (= associated with and having qualities of) **Day! We are not of night, nor of darkness** (or: we do not belong to or have the characteristics of night, nor to or of dim obscurity from shadows and gloom)" – 1 Thes. 5:5. Paul further admonishes folks concerning this new situation,
> "**As within [the] Day, we should** (may; can) **walk about** (= live our lives) **respectably** (reputably; decently; with good form; mannerly; presentably)..." (Rom. 13:13).

We, being a part of this City, have a mission to walk out, as we follow Him:
> "**We, on the other hand, being of Day** (belonging to and having characteristics of [the] Day; having [the] Day as our source), **can and should continuously be sober** (clear-headed), **putting on** (or: clothing ourselves with; enveloping ourselves in; entering within) **a breastplate of faith and love** (or: which is trust and acceptance urging toward union; from fidelity and a giving of self) **and, as a helmet, an expectation** (or: expectant hope) **of deliverance** (health and wholeness; rescue and salvation; restoration to our original state and condition), **because God Himself did not** (or: does not) **place or set us into anger** (inherent fervor; violent emotion; wrath; or: teeming, passionate desire), **but rather, into an encompassing of deliverance** (or: unto establishing a perimeter of safety; into making health and wholeness encircle [us]; into the forming of an encompassing salvation around [us]) **through our Lord, Jesus Christ**" (1 Thes. 5:8-9).

Peter spoke of this situation, where the City of glory descends to those below, calling them to his side to encourage them to continue,
> "**holding your beautiful behavior** (your fine and ideal turning yourselves back around) **among the multitudes** (the companies; the associations; the ethnic groups; the nations; the castes; the non-Jews, or, Gentiles), **to the end that, within what thing they are continually speaking down pertaining to you folks** (repeatedly speaking against you) **as of ones constantly doing the worthless and things of bad quality** (or: as of evildoers or criminals; as of those repeatedly creating bad situations or forming what not ought to be), **repeatedly looking upon and observing as eyewitnesses the outcome from the beautiful actions** (the fine deeds; the ideal and honorable works), **they may glorify** (or: give a good opinion of) **God, within a day of inspection and overseeing care**" (1 Pet. 2:12).

In 2 Pet. 1:19, he explains the Path and mission for this City,
> "**And so, we continue having the Idea which was spoken ahead of time in and as Light** (or: the prior-enlightened Thought and Reason; or: the Prophetic Word) **more confirmed** (established), **by, and in, which you folks continue doing beautifully** (performing ideally; producing finely), **while continuously holding toward** (= playing close attention to) **[it] as to a**

lamp continually shining within a parched place – until which [time or occasion] the Day may shine through and a light bearer [= a morning star] **may rise within your hearts**
> (or: constantly heeding, as to a lamp progressively making things appear in a dark, dingy or dirty place, until that the Day can dawn, and a light-bringer can arise in union with your core and innermost being)."

Paul describes the situation of this City descending into the midst of humanity, in Rom. 8:

18. **You see, I have come to a reasoned conclusion** (or: I am reckoning and logically considering) **that the effects of the sensible experiences – sufferings, impressions, passions or feelings – of the current season** (or: of the situation fitted to the present time) **[are] not equivalent** (are not of equal value or worth)**, [being] face to face with the glory** (or: [are] of insufficient weight when put in balance to the manifestation which calls forth praise as well as the reputation and good opinion) **which is progressively about to be disclosed unto us, and for us** (or: unveiled into our midst; revealed to and [enter] into us).

19. **For the looking away and watching with the head stretched forward alertly** (or: the peak expectation, premonition or intuitive opinion; or: = the concentrated and undivided focus) **of the creation is constantly receiving and taking away from out of the unveiling of God's sons**
> (or: = the uncovering and revealing of folks who have the character and qualities of God; or: the disclosure pertaining to the sons of God; or: the unveiling and revelation which belongs to God's sons; or, as an ablative: **the disclosure from God's sons**).

20. **For you see, the creation** (or: that which was formed, framed and founded) **was placed, arranged and aligned under subjection in the empty purposelessness** (or: subordinated to vanity and by futility; made supportive to fruitless nonsense: in worthlessness, for nothingness)**, not voluntarily or willingly** (from out of [its] being)**, but rather because of** (through; on account of; for the sake of) **the one** (or: the One) **placing [it] under and arranging [it] in subjection** (or: in supportive alignment) **– based upon an expectation** (or: expectant hope) **–**

21. **because** (or: that) **even the creation itself will continue being progressively set free** (will be habitually liberated and constantly made free) **from the slavery of, and from, decay – even the bondage of deterioration which leads to fraying and ruin – [and released] into the freedom of the glory and splendor of God's children**
> (or: into the liberty of the manifestation of that which calls forth praise from, and a good opinion which pertains to, God's born-ones; or: unto the freedom coming from God's imagination pertaining to God's children; or: into the midst of the freedom of the glory from the children [who] belong to God; or: toward centering in the liberty from the glory, which is God, [and] belongs to the children).

But outside of this place in God (i.e., outside the City, 22:15, below) there is still darkness in which people, the entire creation of humans about which Paul spoke, above, live their lives. This is why the City descends to them, to enlighten their darkness. As Paul said in Rom. 8:19, above, we are here so that those who are not yet born into God's reign can be, "**constantly receiving and taking away from out of the unveiling of** (and, the disclosure from) **God's sons**." The statement about **darkness**, here in vs. 25, is repeated in 22:5, below.

Peter Goodgame posted the following, excellent article, "Only An Entrance," on Facebook:
> "The Gates of the New Jerusalem will never be shut. This is a metaphor that symbolizes the unconditional love of God, demonstrating that His mercy is truly everlasting. There is no expiration date on God's eternal love and His offer of forgiveness through the blood of Jesus extends throughout space and TIME.

"Some think that the expiration date to receive salvation is marked at physical death, and there are many Scriptures that seem to uphold this, yet the love of God should compel us to dig deeper. So the question is, if the gates of the eternal city are open forever, but the opportunity for redemption has an expiration date, then what's the point? If there is a place in TIME when the final verdict is announced on every human soul that has ever existed, then what is the purpose for these open gates? If this is the case you would think that after Revelation 20 the gates would then be firmly closed with a loud BOOM that echoes throughout the universe, and then all the SAVED people would cheer, and all the DAMNED people would groan, right? But I wouldn't cheer for this, would you?

"The reality is that Revelation does not end with the apparent hopelessness of Revelation 20, but with an eternal optimistic invitation for ALL to enter into the gates and drink of the water of life. The Spirit and the Bride say, 'Come on in, its free!' (Rev 22:17). The Bride is BOTH the City and the Church: she is the redeemed who are the overcomers through Christ, whose names are written in the Book of Life, who have washed their robes in the blood of the Lamb.

"So who are THEY talking to? Who is outside the city? Why are the gates open? Is it an entrance, or simply an exit for the redeemed to go back and forth as they wish? Well if we dig deeper we will find that NOBODY who has entered the gates will EVER go out again. Here is what it says in Rev. 3:12 to set this up:
> 'Him that overcometh will I make a pillar in the temple of my God, and HE SHALL GO NO MORE OUT: and I will write upon him the name of my God, and the name of the city of my God, which is new Jerusalem, which cometh down out of heaven from my God: and I will write upon him my new name.'

"Did you catch that? The overcomers will NEVER leave the Temple, which means they NEVER leave the city, because the New Jerusalem is simply one big Temple eternally focused on the worship of God. Why would anyone want to leave the presence of Jesus? In fact Paul states in 1 Thes. 4:17 that we will never leave His side! This means that the ONLY purpose for the eternal city to have eternally open gates is to allow those outside to enter in whenever they are ready. So who is outside?

"Revelation 22:14-15, 'Blessed are those who wash their robes, so that they may have the right to the tree of life and that they may enter the city by the gates. Outside are the dogs and sorcerers and the sexually immoral and murderers and idolaters, and everyone who loves and practices falsehood.'

"The gates are eternally open, the invitation is eternally proclaimed, yet one must still be washed by the blood of the Lamb, be given a new Name, and find it in the Book of Life, in order to enter into the city. If these are the conditions, then certainly the opportunity to satisfy these conditions is also available, wouldn't you think? Or are the open gates merely MOCKING the wicked, manned by armed guards checking names on a list?

"So what else is outside the New Jerusalem other than the wicked?

"Revelation 21:5-8, 'And He who sits on the throne said, "Behold, I am making all things new." And He said, "Write, for these words are faithful and true." Then He said to me, "It is done. I am the Alpha and the Omega, the beginning and the end. I will give to the one who thirsts from the spring of the water of life without cost. He who overcomes will inherit these things [referring to the

New Jerusalem], and I will be his God and he will be My son. But for the cowardly and unbelieving and abominable and murderers and immoral persons and sorcerers and idolaters and all liars, their part will be in the lake that burns with fire and brimstone, which is the second death.'

"Note that key opening phrase: 'I am making all things new.' There are two things to be emphasized here. First of all, the verb 'make' is in the present, active, indicative tense. In other words, this is still a work in progress, even as the wicked suffer in the Lake of Fire. Yes, the old heaven and old earth have fled away but God's work continues! He is still continuing to make all things new. Secondly, God is making ALL things new. Yes, ALL! He doesn't destroy or cast away an old thing, or eternally preserve its old condition. He is making all things new.

"So how is this being accomplished? Well, as shown in the text above, there is FIRE outside the gates. The New Jerusalem is a heavenly reflection of the old Jerusalem. The New Jerusalem is the heavenly model and the old is the earthly copy. In earthly Jerusalem the fire outside the gates was maintained in the Valley of Gehenna to burn rubbish. It was also where wicked idolaters once sacrificed their sons in the fire to Moloch. Now we need to be very careful before we claim that God is burning or eternally punishing the wicked in a similar fire, in cruel imitation of Moloch, outside the gates of the New Jerusalem! I can't imagine a more terrible slander against the eternally loving character of God!

"No, heaven's no! That is NOT what is happening outside the gates of the New Jerusalem in the Lake of Fire! The Lake of Fire is not a place of divine retribution, it is the place where God is making all things new! Only NEW THINGS are allowed in the city, so it is ONLY outside where old is being turned into new. God is love. God is a consuming fire. God's wrath lasts for a moment (Psalm 30:5) but His mercy is everlasting.

"If those inside the gates never go out, and the only people outside the gates are the wicked, and the gates are eternally open, then what else can we conclude? Yes, through the destructive fire of His love God is making ALL THINGS NEW, and New Creations with New Names will be emerging out of the ashes to look up with hope to the open gates. They will awaken into their true identities and they will also find that they are quite a bit thirsty." (used by permission)

26. **And so they will continuously carry** (or: bring) **the glory** (or: reputation; notion; opinion; appearance; imagination) **and the honor** (or: value; worth; respect) **of and from** (or: which are) **the multitudes** (nations; non-Jews; ethnic groups) **into her.**

Just what is "**the glory and honor of and from the multitudes** (nations; ethnic groups)" that these multitudes will carry into the city? Gifts from the east were presented to Jesus when He was a young boy. What are the gold and spices that could be brought into this city? We can see in the types, as noted in Isa. 60, above, and of what the queen of Sheba brought to Solomon – and even how Israel took the gold of Egypt. But what do these foreshadow? It would seem that God has placed glory and honor within all nations and ethnic groups. He placed things of value within them, and it is these things (as well as the people, themselves) which they will contribute to the City, as they come into the Light. The phrase **the multitudes** can be rendered appositionally, thus, "the glory and the honor, which are the nations." In Isa. 66:12a, Yahweh says,

> "Behold, I shall stretch out peace over her like a stream, and the glory of the nations, like a watercourse overflowing..." (CVOT).

Speaking concerning Jerusalem, Tobit 13:11 proclaims,

"A bright light will shine to all the ends of the earth; many nation from far away will come to you, the inhabitants of all the remote parts of the earth to your holy name, also bearing their gifts in their hands for the king of heaven. Generations of generations will give joyful worship in you, and the name of the chosen one will last for the generations of the world" (NETS).
Hag. 2:2 proclaims that "the delight and precious things of all the nations shall come in."

We saw the phrase, "**the glory** (or: reputation; notion; opinion; appearance; imagination) **and the honor** (or: value; worth; respect)" in 4:9, 11 and 5:12, 13, above, where they were directed toward God and the little Lamb. These speak of those positive qualities that make us who we are, and these things are because of God dwelling within us, whether we recognize it, or not. They are brought to the City, because that is where God now lives. In Isa. 49:18b, we read of those whom Yahweh brings to Zion that she "shall clothe [herself]" with them, "as an ornament," and she, "shall tie them on as a bride does." A complete turn-around is seen in Isa. 49:17, "And soon you will be built by those by whom you were destroyed" (NETS). The City in this vision is the completeness of God's House, and Home. Although it may seem strange that Isaiah spoke of former strangers and persecutors building this new Jerusalem, consider what Paul said in 1 Cor. 3:9-17, where some folks brought and used worthless material that could not withstand His Fire. His plan of the Ages also involves muck, mire and the feeding of pigs (as we walk through the valley of the shadow of death – the Law, etc.), as a part of our journey. But, thankfully, His Fire cleanses everything, as we are immersed in His Spirit and Fire.

The entry of all these folks **into her** represents the results of what Jesus told His followers to do:
"**while going on your way, instruct and make disciples** (at some point enlist students and apprentices) **of all the ethnic multitudes** (the pagans; the Gentiles; the nations; the non-Israelites), **habitually immersing them** [i.e., the people (masculine pronoun)] (or: one-after-another [B & D read: at some point] baptizing them to the point of infusion and saturation)…" (Mat. 28:19).
Or, as we have in Mk. 16:15,
"**As you are journeying on your way into all the ordered system** (or into the midst of the aggregate of mankind: the world of religion, culture, government and secular society), **you men make a public proclamation of the good news** (or: herald the good message of ease and wellness) **to the entire creation** (or: in all the founded and civilized area that has been reclaimed from the wild)."

27. **And yet, under no circumstances may anything common** (or: can all profane, ceremonially unclean, contaminating or non-sacred [things]) **or the person continuously making an abomination** (or: producing a disgust-effect) **and a lie** (or: [the] false) **enter into her** [note: cf 22:14, below], **except the ones having been written** (or: those being engraved) **within the scroll of "The Life of the little Lamb"** (or: the little Lamb's scroll of "The Life").

This is, first of all, a promise that God will cleanse and transform people. He will change them from being **common and profane** to being set-apart, holy, sacred and precious. We find here an echo of Isa. 52:1,
"Put on your beautiful clothes, Jerusalem, the holy city! For the uncircumcised and unclean shall not again come into you any longer" (CVOT).
They must first have their hearts circumcised (Rom. 2:29), and "wash their robes" (7:14, above; 1 Jn. 1:7).

Nik Ansell makes an astute observation, here,
"In the final chapters of John's vision, we might expect to discover that the sinners, who clearly do not escape the apocalyptic judgment described in 18:1-20:15, are either in the lake of fire or have now been annihilated by it. But instead, we actually find them outside the city (Rev. 22:15).

Furthermore, this 'exclusion' is one that must be read in light of the fact that there is still a mission to the nations (Rev. 21:24; 22:2)" (Afterword; "Hell: The Nemesis of Hope?," in *Her Gates Will Never Be Shut*, by Bradley Jersak, ibid p 210).

This verse provides a clarification: only those **having been written within the scroll of the Life of the little Lamb** are able to enter her. First, again, it is a scroll of HIS Life, as well as being His "scroll of 'The Life.'" Next it would seem then, that prior to the multitudes of Gentiles entering in (with their glory and honor) that their names will have been written into this scroll, noting that they are now participating in the "Life of the Vine." We suggest that this scroll has names added to it on throughout the ages to come. We saw in 3:5, above, a connection between those whose names are enrolled in this **scroll** and the overcomers of the called-out community:

> "**And I will by no means blot out his name from the scroll of The Life** (= participation in the Christ, Who is the Life)."

This metaphor of "the scroll" is equivalent to Jesus' metaphor of the Vine, in Jn. 15:1ff. It speaks of existential membership in the mystical, or spiritual, community where the life of Christ flows through each member that composes Christ's body that live here as "the light of the world." This is a cleansed City that is void of dualism that produces the **lie**. It no longer has *satan's* throne within it (2:13, above). It no longer contains "the synagogue of *satan*" (3:9, above). The spirit of Jezebel (2:20, above), along with the doctrines of Balaam and of the Nicolaitans (2:14, 15, above), have been expunged from her. She is a symbol of those who are in union with God; she is a realm of existence that cannot be profaned or made to produce disgust-effects. She is immune to the serpent's lie. She represents the transformed and purified life where all has been made new. Entrance into her requires first being refined to have all dross removed (Mal. 3:2-3). For these reasons, she bares God's Name, Christ's new Name, and God's City's Name (3:12, above): New Jerusalem. The description of this City continues in the next chapter.

Chapter 22

1. **And he showed** (points out to) **me a clean, pure river of "water of, and from, life"** (or: Life's water; or: water which is Life), **bright** (resplendent, glistening, clear, sparkling) **as crystal** (clear ice), **continuously flowing** (issuing) **forth from out of God's – even** (or: and) **the little Lamb's – throne!**

Here we are caught back to Gen. 2:10,
> "Now a river continuously and progressively flows (journeys; proceeds) forth from out of the midst of Eden to continuously water and give drink to the Paradise (Garden; orchard). From that place it keeps on separating and marking off boundaries, dividing itself into four beginnings (or: sources; heads; headships)" (LXX, JM).

In *The Testament of Dan, the seventh son of Jacob and Bilhah* (2nd century BC), vs. 5:12 reads:
> "And the saints shall refresh themselves (or: rest) in Eden; the righteous shall rejoice in the New Jerusalem" (*OT Pseudepigrapha*, Vol. 1 ibid p 810, trans. by H.C. Kee).

We can see an allusion, here, to Ps. 46:4-6,
> "The effects of the sudden, onrushing torrents of the river (or: The rapid movements of the flowings from the river) continuously make well-minded and mentally at ease (or: progressively develop a glad frame of mind that is thoughtfully considerate for good in; keep on producing a healthy attitude for) the City of, and from, God; the Highest sets-apart and makes sacred His Tabernacle. God [is] resident within the midst of her (or: [resides] centered, and in union with, her); she will not be shaken, moved or caused to shudder. God will keep on helping her (or: will repeatedly give her aid; will constantly assist or rescue her) with, in and by [His] presence (or: with [His] countenance; [other MSS: facing morning by morning])" (LXX, JM).

Two verses in Zechariah also speak to this scene:
> "In that Day there shall come to be a fountain opened for the house of David, and for the dwellers of Jerusalem" (13:1, CVOT).
>
> "And it will come to be in that Day, [that] living waters shall flow forth from Jerusalem" (14:8, ibid).

But the strongest allusion is to Ezk. 47:1-12,
> "He brought me back to the portal of the House [= Temple], and behold: water coming forth from under the sill of the House, eastward... the water descended from underneath along the right shoulder of the House, south of the altar....a torrent which I was not able to cross.... These waters... enter the sea [note: a figure of humanity]... and the waters [there] are healed. It will come to be that every living soul that swarms wherever the watercourse is coming shall live, and there will be very many fish [comment: a figure of people – Mat. 4:19]... everything will live wherever the watercourse shall come.... By the watercourse along its shore on this side and on that side shall grow up every food tree. Its leaf shall not decay, nor shall its fruit come to an end; for [each of] its months it shall yield firstfruit, for its waters [are] they which go forth from the Sanctuary; its fruit will be for food and its leaf for healing" (CVOT; brackets added).

Note the purpose of this river that in Ezekiel's vision flows toward the Dead Sea (a figure of the "dead in trespasses and sins" that are outside of this City): it is to bring healing and life. That is God's purpose for humanity: judgment, which leads to healing and life.

This verse picks up the description of the City from 21:25, above. God's throne (vs. 3, below) resides within the City (just as the Ark was within the Tabernacle, which, in turn, was within the camp of Israel). Think of that! The throne of God is within His Bride, His people – within each of us! But why should we be surprised, since Jesus told us that His kingdom and reign are also within us. Yes, He dwells within the corporate body, the City, but also recall John 14:23,

> "**Jesus conclusively replies, and says to him, 'If anyone continues** (or: may be habitually) **loving, accepting, fully giving himself to, and urging toward union with, Me, he WILL continue constantly watching over so as to observe, guard, preserve and keep My word** (My thought, idea and message; what I laid out), **and My Father will continue loving, fully giving Himself to, and urging toward union with, him, AND, facing toward him, We will continue coming to him and will be progressively making** (constructing; forming; creating; producing) **a home** (an abode; a dwelling place; a place to stay) **with him** (or: at his side and in his presence).'"

If the Spirit dwells within an individual, then God dwells within him or her.

It is from the **throne** (the place where He rules and is Lord) that the river of "**water of, and from, life**" is **continuously flowing**. Recall this also from Jesus,

> "**Just as the Scripture says, 'Rivers** (or: Floods; Torrents) **of living water will continuously flow** (or: gush; flood) **from out of the midst of His cavity** (His innermost being or part; or: the hollow of his belly; [used of the womb])'" (John 7:38).

Joel also prophesied of this:
> "All channels of Judah shall flow with water, and a spring from the House of Yahweh shall go forth…" (3:18b, CVOT).

So the result is that which was described in Isa. 58:11,
> "Yahweh will guide you continually and He will satisfy your soul... invigorate your bones, and you will become like a well-watered garden, and like a flowing well of water whose waters are not defaulting" (CVOT).

Consider the symbol of "**a clean, pure river**." There is no "dirt" (earth; pollution from human flesh) within this flow. It is coming from the midst of a City that has been purified by the little Lamb's Life, and it is "**continuously flowing** (issuing) **forth from out of God's throne**." What could be cleaner, or more pure? It is not coming from some human hierarchy or religious organization (Secret Babylon). This river is also "**bright, as crystal or ice.**" It is precious, and it is clear – we can see the Life of this water, as we behold the face and image of Christ. The Light shines through It, and through US! We should also call to mind Jn. 4:14,

> "**Yet whoever may** (or: would) **drink from out of the water which I, Myself, will be continuously giving to him will not repeatedly become thirsty, on into the age, but further, the water which I shall constantly give to** (or: in) **him will progressively come to be within him a spring** (or: fountain) **of water, constantly bubbling up** (continuously springing and leaping up) **into a life having the source, character and qualities of the Age** (life of and for the ages; eonian life; = the life of the Messianic age)."

Consider the alternate genitive renderings: "Life's water; or: water which is Life." The connection between water and life, in human existence, is well known. These terms are frequently used metaphorically throughout the NT. Jesus came to give us water, and to give us Life.

The late 1st century author of *Odes of Solomon* offers in Ode 6,

> "For there went forth a stream, and it became a river great and broad; indeed it carried away everything, and it shattered and brought [it] to the Temple. And the restraints of men were not able to restrain it… it spread over the face of all the earth and it filled everything. Then all the thirsty upon the earth drank, and thirst was relieved and quenched. For from the Most High the drink was given" (vss. 8-12);
>
> "Everyone recognized them as the Lord's, and lived by the living water of eternity. Hallelujah" (vs. 18)" (*The OT Pseudepigrapha*, Vol. 2, ibid p 738-9; trans. by J.H. Charlesworth)

This calls us back to Isa. 35:7,

> "The parched sink of glowing sand will become a pond or a lake, and the thirsty [ground, or people] springs and fountains of water."

Also, Isa. 43:19-20, speaking to the future, while reflecting back to Israel's past wilderness journey:

> "Look, and consider: I Myself am progressively forming and producing things and situations that are new in kind and character… I will continue creating (building) a Road (Path; Way) within the midst of the desert (or: wilderness), and rivers within the midst of the waterless place…. because I gave water within the desert (wilderness) and rivers within the midst of the waterless place…" (LXX, JM).

He continues doing what He always has done, but now doing even more. *Cf* Isa. 41:18-20

His **throne** is within us (we are the City); the River of the "**water of life**" is therefore within us; "**the tree of life**" is then also WITHIN US (vs. 2, below) – and thus, the Garden of Eden is within us, and we are within it, for all this is WITHIN the City, which is the Bride of the little Lamb. Viewing this picture from another perspective, WE are all of the things described here: water of life; tree of life; place of God's throne. Our return to the Garden brings the end of the curse (vs. 3, below) and of the death attached to that curse. The road (Way) of the tree of the life was continuously watched over (guarded) by the cherubim (the living ones of Ezk. 1:5ff; 10:14) and by the flaming sword (the Word of His Fire) – Gen. 3:25. Walking the path where His Word pierces to the joints and the marrow, dividing our soul from our spirit, judging our thoughts and the intents of our heart (Heb. 4:12), is the Way to the Tree of the Life.

There is only one **throne**, and it is **God's** throne, as well as the **little Lamb's throne.** It is now also OUR throne, for He has seated us in it, together with Him (Eph. 2:6). This speaks of the union of which Jesus spoke in Jn. 17:21-14. And recall 3:21, above:

> "**To** (or: In; For) **the person who is habitually conquering** (repeatedly overcoming; normally victorious) **I will continue giving** [the right? the ability? the honor?] **to sit** (or: be seated) **with Me within My throne, as I also conquer** (or: conquered; overcome; overcame and was victorious) **and sit** (or: sat down) **with My Father within His throne**."

You see, this City is a symbol of the corporate 7-fold called-out communities of chapters 2-3, above. The risen Christ walks the Street of this City, just as He walked with Adam and Eve in Eden's garden, and as He continuously walks among the 7 lampstands (1:20; 2:1, above). Both in 3:21, above, and here, in 22:1, there is only ONE **throne.** This means that there is no "spiritual/heavenly" hierarchy. We are all Christ's brothers (Rom. 8:29b) – and if you can receive it, we are now all incarnations of the Father (He blew His life into us). Recall Paul's words, in 1 Cor. 4:15,

> "**in contrast** [you do] **not** [have] **many fathers** (or: parents), **because in one moment I myself fathered** (gave birth to; generated) **you people within and in union with Christ Jesus**."

This is because we no longer live, but Christ lives in us (Gal. 2:20), for you see, "**we died, and our life has been hidden so that it is now concealed together with the Christ, within the midst of God** (or: in union with God)" (Col. 3:3). If we "abide in the Vine" (Jn. 15:1ff), when they see us, they will see the Father. You know a tree, or a vine, by its fruit (the Spirit's fruit).

2. **Within the midst of her broad place** (plaza; square; street), **and on each side of the river, [is] a tree** (a wood; timber; a log; same word used in Gen. 2:9, LXX; figure for "the cross" in the NT) **of, and which is, life periodically producing twelve fruits, continually yielding** (or: giving away) **according to each month, and the leaves of the tree** (wood; timber) **[are given] for** (or: into) **service** (nurture, care; healing, cure or medical service; a body of household attendants) **of the multitudes** (nations; Gentiles; non-Jews; ethnic groups),

This description echoes Ezk. 47:7, 12, and may be an allusion to Dan. 12:5-7. As to the term "**tree of, and which is, life**," the term 'tree,' is singular in number but should be understood in a collective sense. Note the semantic range of the word in the parenthetical expansion, e.g., "a wood," which could refer to an orchard of a specific species of tree, or, "an aggregation of *dendra*, or trees, commonly called a *wood*, or *forest*" (Benjamin Wilson, *Emphatic Diaglott* p 816). The NWT renders it "trees of life." Or, it could refer to "timber," or, "a log." This scene is reminiscent of the Garden of Eden (Gen. 2:9): the tree of life is present here, **within the midst of her broad place** (plaza; square; street), and standing **on each side of the river**, perhaps a grove on each of its banks. Recall that the tree of life is said to be "**in the midst of the paradise of God**" (2:7, above), and eating of it is promised to **the overcomer**. So this City is also the New Paradise of God: the Garden of Eden of the New Creation. Visiting the *Odes of Solomon*, again:

> "And he took me to his Paradise, wherein is the wealth of the Lord's pleasure. I contemplated blooming and fruit-bearing trees…. Their fruits were shining… And a river of gladness was irrigating them…. Indeed, there is much room in your Paradise, and there is nothing in it which is barren, but everything is filled with fruit" (11:16, 23, ibid p 745-6).

The tree of life within us is continuously yielding fruit of life (i.e., fruit of the Spirit, the fruit of the Vine), according to the seasons in which we are living. The symbol, "**periodically producing twelve fruits**," can have a two-fold meaning: referring either to twelve crops of fruits (one each month), or, it is making a reference to the twelve gates and the twelve tribes. 4 Ezra 2:18-19 gives a picture of "twelve trees loaded with various fruits, and the same number of springs flowing with milk and honey, and seven mountains on which roses and lilies grow" (ibid p 527). These are visions of a Paradise, allusions to the Garden of Eden in Gen. 2. Wisdom was called a "tree of life" in Prov. 3:18, which is ironic when we recall that it was "the tree of the knowledge of good and evil" (a figure of the Law, that defined right and wrong) that was supposed to make a person wise (Gen. 3:6), but that was the Lie, from the serpent.

The **leaves of the tree** are available **for service** (or: nurture, care; healing, cure or medical service) of the multitudes: the nations, the ethnic groups, those who are not yet the Israel of God (Gal. 6:16). *Cf* Ezk. 47:12. As the semantic range of "service" shows, this word can also refer to "a body of household attendants." God's household is here to serve the ethnic multitudes that are outside the City. This availability of the leaves for the nations makes it clear that this is a scene that refers to "earth existence," not an imagined "far away heaven." This corporate tree, **which is life, periodically producing twelve fruits, continually yielding** (or: giving away) **according to each month**, is the true Israel (the olive tree of Rom. 11:17, the Second Humanity composed of Gentile grafted in and joined to Jew), as seen in Ps. 1:3,

> "And thus, he will continue existing, being like the tree [that] has been planted beside the divided-out paths of the waters (or: outlets of water through [the orchard]; or: rivulets of the waters that pass through), which will give (yield; = produce) its fruit in its season (or: fitting situation) and whose leaf (or: foliage) will not proceed to fall off. And so, everything that he should continue doing (or: all things – however much he can make or produce) will proceed to be thoroughly prospered (continuously led down an easy path, or along a good road)!" (LXX, JM).

This is a figure of the grace and provision which God supplies through His called-out communities.

The 1st or 2nd century, *Apocalypse of Abraham* echoes this scene, in 21:6,

> "And I saw there the garden of Eden and its fruits, and the source and the river flowing from it, and its trees and their flowering, making fruits, and I saw men doing justice in it, their food and their rest" (*The OT Pseudepigrapha*, Vol. 1, ibid, p 699, trans. by R. Rubinkiewicz).

We find the statement in *The Fourth book of Ezra*, 8:52, that, "Paradise is opened, the tree of Life is planted, the Age to come is prepared, plenty is provided, a City is built, rest is appointed, goodness is established and wisdom perfected beforehand" (ibid p 544). Beasley-Murray suggests that vs. 2, here, "supplies a pictorial counterpart to the prophetic song of 15:4," above, (ibid p 1308).

3. and every result of [something] having been placed or put down, or every effect of [something] laid down, deposited or established, will no longer continue existing. And God's throne – even the Little Lamb's – will continue being (or: existing) **within Her [i.e., the City], and His slaves will continue rendering sacred service to Him,**

God's **slaves** have His Name upon their foreheads (vs. 4, below; 14:1, above). They **serve Him** and **see His face** (vs. 4, below). This calls to mind Matt. 5:8, "**Those who are clean in the heart [are] happy and blessed, because they, themselves, will progressively see God!**" To "see" also means to perceive, comprehend and understand. Metzger points out that,

> "In antiquity, to see the face of the king... implied that one was granted an audience with the king, and an opportunity to present one's petition in direct personal conversation (Gen. 43:3, 5; Ex. 10:28, 29; and elsewhere).... also to enjoy a relationship of absolute trust and openness" (ibid p 103).

We should not miss the location of the opening clause of this verse: "**and every result of [something] having been placed or put down, or every effect of [something] laid down, deposited or established** (*katathema*) **will no longer continue existing**." This statement is a continuation of vs. 2 that speaks about, and expands upon, "the **care** of, and **service** to, **the multitudes**: the ethnic groups of the nations!" The nations no longer have "any result of what had been placed down, or established," upon them; nor does anyone else. It is a new creation; all things are being made new (21:5, above). Everything prior to the coming of the Messiah has passed away (2 Cor. 5:17).

Now due to the subject (*katathema*) of this first clause being commonly rendered, "curse," an allusion has been made to Gen.3:14-19, 23, as well as to the curses in the Law (e.g., Lev. 26; Deut. 26-28). However, the LXX does not use this word in those passages – or at all. Paul used a different word when he spoke of those "curses," in Gal. 3:13a,

> "**Christ bought us [back] out** (or: redeems and reclaims us out [of slavery] and liberates us) **from the midst of the curse** (*katara*: adversarial wish, prayer or declaration; imprecation) **of and from the Law.**"

Those OT passages, cited above, used the word *katara*, or a strengthened form, *epi-kataratos*, along with the cognate verb (*katara-omai*) of this second noun. But we no longer make the traditional assumption that *katathema* is a synonym of *katara*, nor that it is speaking about a "curse." Rather we suggest that this first clause is speaking about the situation of the new covenant, because it still holds true that,
"**however many people continue their existence from the midst of observances and works of Law** (= Everyone who lives by deeds and actions based upon the Torah [i.e., the old covenant]) **are continuously under a curse** (*katara*) " (Gal. 3:10), and if they do,

> "**people who in union with** (or: centered in; [remaining] within) **Law continue being liberated and rightwised, from grace** (or: placed in the Way pointed out and included in the new covenant of grace; being given an eschatological transformation, which is favor), **were at once discharged** (made inactive, idle, useless, unproductive and without effect; or: voided, nullified, exempted) **away from Christ – you at once fell out from [the grace and favor]!**" (Gal. 5:4)

And this would then apply to those who want to continue observing the feasts of Israel, which were works of the Law, or keep the sabbath or the "ten commandments," or any of the purity codes. It was likely concerning those who leaned in the Judaizing direction that in Rom. 12:14 Paul said, "**stop cursing** (*katara-omai*: you must not continue praying down on, or wishing anything against, [things, situations or people])!" We now live in this new situation, "the new creation," with its "new covenant/arrangement."

Now the word *katathema*, in our present passage, is used only here, in the NT. My editions of the LXX and my Greek Concordance of the LXX do not show it used in the LXX. As rendered above, its literal semantic range is: "a result [note the -*ma* ending of the word] of having been placed or put DOWN, or an effect of something laid down, deposited or established." Its antithesis would be *anathema*, which literally means "the result of setting or placing UP," and this latter word was originally used of "setting up" an offering to a deity (e.g., Lev. 27:28, "Now every set-up [offering] {*anathema*} which a person should set (or: place) up and dedicate to the Lord [= Yahweh]..." – LXX, JM). So what is the significance of this symbolic word used here in vs. 3, as it is used in conjunction with the description of this City, the New Jerusalem? We suggest that this may correspond to *apokatastaseōs* (found only in Acts 3:21, and discussed below, in the article following the comments on this *Unveiling*), which signifies "a movement **away from** what had been placed down and established." Thus, this new City does not have anything of what had previously been placed down and established in the old covenant or the Law given to Moses.

So the negation of *katathema*, used here in vs. 3, implies a new creation. The old arrangement no longer exists; there is a new covenant. Thus, the doom pronounced on "all the nations" (Isa. 34:2ff) is no longer in effect. This is because of the Christ event, along with the present reality that was stated in 21:3, above: God is dwelling here, among humans (i.e., all the nations). We read in Isa. 65:23b, "neither shall they continue to bear (or: produce) children into a curse (*katara*)" (LXX, JM), which also finds fulfillment in our present vision, due to no more *katathema* (no longer the old establishment, the old covenant or the Mosaic Law). My friend Ken Nichols concluded from this that, "It is the end of the establishment." This is the freedom of which Paul spoke in Gal. 5:1. In Col. 2:14 we observe that Christ was,

> "**anointing and wiping out the handwriting in the decrees** (bonds; bills of debt; ordinances; statutes) **put down against** (or: with regard to the effects of the thoughts or suppositions, and the results of the appearances of what seemed [to be], corresponding to) **us, which was continuing**

to be under, within and set in active opposition to us, and He has picked it up and lifted it from out of the midst, nailing it to the cross."

This clause in vs. 3, above, has traditionally been associated with Zech. 14:11,

"They will permanently settle down and dwell in her [Jerusalem], and there will not continue being the effect of something placed up as an offering to a deity (*anathema*), and Jerusalem will continue permanently settled confidently and fully persuaded" (LXX, JM).

This has been due to interpreters employing the secular use of the word *anathema*, missing its original religious connotation. But when *anathema* is properly understood, especially in its covenantal context with Israel, what Zech. 14:11 may be predicting is the abolishing of animal sacrifices, meal offerings and the entire OT priestly cultus, that were practiced in the old covenant Jerusalem. *Cf* Jn. 4:21-23. Heb. 10:26b affirms this:

"**there is no longer a sacrifice concerned with sins** (failures; etc.) **repeatedly** (or: continuously) **left behind** [D* reads: left around; = available for to use]."

As a contrast to the old covenant sacrifices (still happening when the book of Hebrews was written) that were repeated throughout each year, Heb. 7:27 instructs us concerning the work of Christ,

"**Who is not having daily necessity, just as the chief priests, to repeatedly offer up sacrifices over their own failures** (errors; sins) **before, and after that, those of the people. For this He performed just once** (once for all; on one [occasion]), **offering up Himself** [other MSS: bringing (or: carrying) Himself toward {God, or, us} (or: presenting Himself); *cf* Heb. 9:25-28]."

Gavazzoni has suggested another layer of interpretation for there being no more *katathema*. This layer would apply to the overarching "plan of the ages" and the observation that *katathema* began in the Garden of Eden, if not before. He pointed us to Rom. 8:20,

"**For you see, the creation** (or: that which was formed, framed and founded) **was placed, arranged and aligned under subjection in the empty purposelessness** (or: subordinated to vanity and by futility; made supportive to fruitless nonsense: in worthlessness, for nothingness), **not voluntarily or willingly** (from out of [its] being), **but rather because of** (through; on account of; for the sake of) **the one** (or: the One) **placing [it] under and arranging [it] in subjection** (or: in supportive alignment) – **based upon an expectation** (or: expectant hope)."

What we are told here in vs. 3, above, is that the expectation of our trajectory has arrived (in Christ) and that the prior placing "under subjection in the empty purposelessness" (Rom. 8:20) no longer exists – within the City. When writing this, in the mid-50's AD, Paul had not yet seen the full end of the old creation (consummated in AD 70), and so was still groaning (Rom. 8:23). Gavazzoni observes:

"The 'results of everything laid down' have to do with the results of the descent involved in creation (down from above), therefore an essential existential dis-connect occurred with its inherent 'results'... the results of its subjection to futility will be done away with by Him who 'is making all things new.' Maybe what is being said here involves the opposite of 'being born back UP again,' as opposed to being laid down, put down, or lowered. I hear, 'He that descended is the same also that ascended up far above all heavens, that He might fill all things' (Eph. 4:9-10). The descent of creation headed by the first Adam consummated in/by the descent of Jesus in the death of Jesus all the way 'into the lower parts of the earth' whereupon He, the Last Adam, went on in ascension to make all things new, leaving no results of 'the fall' to continue" (from a personal email).

Another allusion of this first clause may be to Rom. 6:5, 8, 11,

"**For since we have been birthed** (have come to be) **folks engrafted and produced together** (or: planted and made to grow together; brought forth together; congenital) **in, by, to and with**

> the result of the likeness of (or: the effect of the similar manner from) **His death, then certainly we shall also continue existing [in and with the effects of the likeness] of The Resurrection.... Now since we died together with Christ, we are continuously believing** (relying; trusting) **that we shall also continue living together in Him** (by Him; for Him; to Him; with Him).... **Thus you folks, also, be logically considering** (accounting and concluding) **yourselves to exist being dead ones, indeed, by the failure to hit the target** (or: in the Sin; or: to the deviation), **yet ones continuously living by God** (in God; for God; to God; with God), **within Christ Jesus, our Owner.**"

Death (Rom. 5:12) placed us down into the death of the 1st Adam, and the 2nd Adam took us down into the grave in His death, but that *katathema* no longer exists, because we have been raised up, in Him, so that we are now, "**the supra-heavenly people – those made of and having the quality and character of the supra-heaven** (or: the finished and perfected atmosphere, or the added sky)" (1 Cor. 15:48b).

J. H. Paton, in an article published in "The World's Hope," March 15, 1907, says of the bride in this passage,
> "She is there symbolized as the New Jerusalem (as the false church is called Babylon) and her twelve gates stand open for the corrupt, unsaved nations, who are outside of the city, to hear the invitation [of ch. 22:17] to wash their robes, eat of the tree of life, drink of the waters of life freely, and enter through the gates into the city. The gates are the way through the walls, and the walls are salvation. 'We have a strong city; salvation will He appoint for walls and bulwarks.' Isa. 26:1. Hence to be outside is the condition of those who are still lost – unsaved, and to come in through the gates is to be saved" (reprinted by Savior of All Fellowship).

Once again, in typical apocalyptic repetition, John affirms: "**And God's throne – even the Little Lamb's – will continue being** (or: existing) **within Her.**" We can draw at least three clear conclusions from this:
   a) The great, white throne (**God's throne**) is within the Bride, the called-out communities.
   b) Those who enter her gates, into the City, will stand before God's throne of grace (Heb. 4:16).
   c) The **little Lamb's throne** presents Christ slain, who forgives those who killed Him (5:6, above; Lu. 23:34).

The last clause includes the phrase, "**His slaves.**" This should be understood in its 1st century context. The term "slave" described an existential relationship to the one that "owned" him or her: his or her "lord." In Rom. 1:1 Paul referred to himself as a "slave of Jesus Christ." Here, in this *Unveiling*, John did the same (1:1, above). He and the risen Christ referred to His followers (the called-out communities) using this same term (1:1; 2:20, above). So we are being taken full circle in this clause, the rest of which ("**continue rendering sacred service to Him**") takes us back to "the sheep" and their service to Christ, in Mat. 25:35-40. We also see this "sacred service" encouraged by Paul, James, Peter and John, in their letters to the called-out.

4. and will constantly see His face, and His Name [is; or: will be] upon their foreheads.

Paul spoke of the goal (perfection; maturity) that is pictured in the vision of this City, in 1 Cor. 13:12-13,
> "**For you see, at the present moment we continue seeing and observing through means of a metal mirror, within the midst of an enigma** (the result of something obscurely expressed, hinted or intimated, giving an indistinct image), **but at THAT point, face to face. Right now I am progressively coming to intimately and experientially know from out of a part** (gain insight from a piece; be acquainted with a portion of the whole), **but thereupon I shall continue accurately knowing and recognizing, from full intimate experience and added insight, correspondingly as I am also fully and accurately known, by intimate experience. So at

the present time trust (or: faith; loyalty; trustworthiness), **expectation** (or: expectant hope) **[and] love** (unrestricted acceptance which overcomes existential separation – Tillich) **– these three – continue remaining and habitually dwell [with us], yet the greatest of these [is] the Love** ([God's] urge toward unambiguous, accepting reunion – Tillich; self-giving – Rohr).

You folks make haste to progressively run after and continuously pursue this Love!"

He wrote this prior to AD 70, when the old Jerusalem was still standing, and when Christ had not yet returned in judgment on the old city, fully terminating the old arrangement (or: covenant) and "the establishment," with its Law and temple cultus (*cf* Mat. 26:63-64; Mk. 14:62). When writing this first letter to Corinth, it is quite possible that he had not yet seen what was later revealed to him, as expressed in Eph. chapter 2, and in the second letter to Corinth, chapters 3-5, where in 3:18, he said,

"**But we all, ourselves – having a face that has been uncovered and remains unveiled – being folks who by a mirror are continuously observing, as ourselves, the Lord's glory, are presently being continuously and progressively transformed into the very same image, from glory into glory – in accord with and exactly as – from [the] Lord's Breath-effect**."

Unveilings were progressively happening during that period of the 1st century; as humanity grows in Christ, new unveilings continue to come from Him. He is the same, and does the same, on into the ages (Heb. 13:8).

John elsewhere said,

"**We have perceived, and thus know** (or: are aware) **that if it** (or: He) **should be** (or: whenever it {or: He} may be) **made visible, apparent and manifested, [then] folks like to Him** (like-ones to Him; ones like Him; people resembling Him) **we will be existing, because we will continue seeing and will be progressively perceiving Him just as** (according and exactly as; in the manner that) **He constantly exists** (or: He is)" (1 John 3:2).

Heb. 12:14 admonishes us,

"**You folks be continuously pursuing peace and joined-harmony with all mankind** (or: with everyone) **– as well as the process and resultant state of being different and set-apart** (or: sacredness; the sanctification; or: = the situation of being set aside for God's use), **apart from which not even one person will proceed in seeing** (or: continue perceiving) **the Lord**."

Jesus set forth a condition in which folks **will constantly see His face**:

"**Those who are clean in the heart [are] happy and blessed, because they, themselves, will progressively see God!**

(or: = The folks that have had the core of their beings made clean [are] happy people, in that they will continue to see God [in everything]!)" (Mat. 5:8).

He at one point said to His disciples,

"**You folks, yourselves, are already clean** (cleansed), **cleared and pruned ones through and because of the word** (laid-out message; thought) **which I have spoken to you** (in you; for you; among you)" (Jn. 15:3).

In Jn. 13:10 He had also told them, "**You men continue being clean folks**." And so, Jesus could say to Philip, "**The person having discerned and seen Me has seen, and now perceives, the Father!**" (Jn. 14:9). But as with the need for regularly having our feet washed (Jn. 13:10a; a figure of needing to be cleansed in our "walk" of daily living), we are instructed that, "**the blood of, from, and which is Jesus, His Son, keeps continually and repeatedly cleansing us** (or: is progressively rendering us pure)," (1 Jn. 1:7). O'Donohue observes, "The face is the threshold where a world looks out and a world looks in on itself. The face brings two worlds together" (ibid p 82).

The psalmist implored, "Shine Your face, and presence, upon Your slave; rescue and deliver (or: give health, restore and save) me in Your mercy" (Ps. 31:16; LXX, JM). Ps. 34:15-16 is quoted in 1 Pet. 3:12, "**[the] Lord's** [= Yahweh's] **eyes [are] upon** (= He looks with favor on) **[the] fair and equitable folks** (the rightwised ones; the just ones who walk in the Way pointed out), **and His ears [directed] into their request pertaining to need; yet [the] face of [the] Lord** [= Yahweh] (i.e., His countenance and posturing) **[is] upon** (= set against) **wrongdoers** (those constantly practicing worthless things, repeatedly constructing bad things or habitually doing evil)."

Ps. 34:17 continues, "The righteous cry out, and Yahweh hears, and from all their distresses He rescues them." An allusion in vs. 4, above, may be to Ps. 17:15,

"Now as for me, I will continuously be seen by Your face, in the midst of a rightwising, eschatological deliverance into union with the Way pointed out. I will be continuously fed until satisfied within the [situation for] Your glory to be made visible and to be seen" (LXX, JM).

Ps. 11:4 explained, "Yahweh [is] in His holy temple... His eyes are perceiving; His eyelids are testing [the] sons of humanity." And in Ps. 27:4 we find this desire: "One [thing] I have asked from Yahweh... that I may dwell in the House of Yahweh... to perceive the pleasantness of Yahweh" (CVOT). Then Ps. 42:2 proclaims, "My soul thirsts for God, for [the, or, a] living God! When will I come and appear before God?"

In the 2nd century BC text, *Testament of Zebulon, the sixth son of Jacob and Leah*, 9:8, we read:
"And thereafter the Lord himself will arise upon you, the light of righteousness with healing and compassion in his wings. He will liberate every captive of the sons of men... and every spirit of error will be trampled down. He will turn all nations to being zealous for him. And you shall see [God in a human form], he whom the Lord will choose: Jerusalem is his name" (*Testaments of the Twelve Patriarchs, OT Pseudepigrapha*, Vol. 1, ibid p 807; brackets original).

The last phrase, "**His Name [is; or: will be] upon their foreheads**," echoes 3:12, above, and specifically 14:1. This symbol speaks of both ownership (we belong to our Father; and Paul said in 1 Cor. 6:20, "**you people were bought: [there was] value and honor involved in the price** {or: [you are] of value}"). This phrase also speaks of identity. We know someone by their face. When folks see us, they should be seeing the Father. A name speaks of a person's character and reputation: these folks have God's character. This is like bearing the Father's image; our lives reflect His reputation. One bearing the name of his or her lord and master also carried the authority of their owner and lord. As an allusion to the OT, this signifies that these folks are priests in this City-temple. In Ex. 28:36-38a we see that,

"You will make a blossom of pure gold and engrave on it [like] engravings of a seal: Holy to Yahweh. You will place it on blue twine and it will come to be on the turban, on the forefront of the face of the turban shall it come to be. It will come to be on the forehead of Aaron..." (CVOT).

5. **And night will no longer continue existing. And so they continuously have no need of the light of a lamp, or even the light of the sun, because [the] Lord** [= Yahweh] **God will continue giving light upon** (or: will constantly illuminate) **them, and they will continue reigning** (performing as kings; having sovereign influence) **on into the ages of the ages** (or: the indefinite time periods of the eons).

At the beginning of this vision (21:1, above) we saw that, "**the sea does not exist any longer**," and we viewed this statement in the light of its symbolism. Then, in 21:4, we were informed that, "**the Death will no longer continue existing**." In vs. 3, above, we discussed the proclamation that the prior established situation "**will no longer continue existing**." Now, in vs. 5, we read, "**And night will no longer continue existing**." The predicate, in the Greek, is the same in each of these clauses that refer to four subjects which cease to exist. These are not to be taken literally, but symbolically. Here, **night** is symbolic of the time of darkness. This proclamation is a restatement of 21:25, above – cf comments there. It calls us back to the picture in 12:1, above, where our current City was depicted as a Woman who had "**the moon down under her feet**," which was figurative of having overcome "the lesser luminary" that was created "for rulership of the night" (Gen. 1:16, LXX). The next verse (1:17) explains that these were "to give light upon the earth, and to separate between the light and the darkness." The night of God's creative story was the time of darkness. Here, in vs. 5, this symbol tells us that there is no longer any darkness in the realm of existence (the new creation) that is being described, i.e., the New Jerusalem, the Bride of the little Lamb. It is "separated from the darkness" of the former age, the age of the Mosaic Law in the old creation which was formed at Mount Sinai, in the times of differentiation between people-groups, cultures and nations. Now, in God's plan for the ages, the new age arrived with the Messiah, and God joined all races and nations into being "**one new humanity**" – Eph. 2:11-22 – in His new, kingdom economy. Outside the City we find that things have not changed, and people are still being processed as they continue being born into the "earth" realm, as we see in vss. 11-15, below. This entire vision describes the here and now – in the realm of the called-out communities.

The description of this scene ends promising that **night will no longer continue existing**, and that God's slaves **will continue reigning**: the endless "Day of the Lord" will have come. Knowledge (light) will be direct from God, for "**God will continue giving light upon** (or: will constantly illuminate) **them**." This is a repetition of 21:23, above, and thus a repeated allusion to Isa. 60:19-20, along with an echo of John 1:9 – all begun with the first advent of Christ, which began the eschatological Day of the Lord. This is also an allusion to Ps. 36:9,

"For with You [is the] fountain of Life; in Your Light shall we see Light."

The *Apocalypse of Abraham* (ibid p 697) gives this description:

"In Your heavenly dwelling place (there is) an inexhaustible light of an invincible dawning from the light of Your face."

The lampstand imagery that presented a "temple" setting of the called-out communities (1:20, above) has now expanded to City-wide imagery in a picture of the fullness, beyond the shadowy environment within a limited structure and into the open Light of the New Day. Having "**no need of the light of a lamp, or even the light of the sun**," is a symbol for what Paul informed those in Corinth: "**we are habitually walking about** (= living our lives) **through faithfulness and trust** (or: faith; [His] loyalty) **not through perception of the appearance of external form**" (2 Cor. 5:7). John explained, in 1 Jn. 1:7,

"**Yet if we keep on walking about** (= continue living our life) **within the midst of and in union with the Light, as He exists** (or: is) **within the Light, we constantly have common being and existence** (or: hold common fellowship, participation and enjoy partnership) **with one another, and the blood of, from, and which is Jesus, His Son, keeps continually and repeatedly cleansing us** (or: is progressively rendering us pure) **from every sin** (or: from all error, failure, deviation, mistake, and from every shot that is off target [when it occurs])."

Those within this City are "**continuously led by the Spirit**" (Rom. 8:14). His **Light** gives them understanding; they do not need the knowledge (light) of the former creation/covenant. They have been moved from "**thick, dark storm-cloud, and murky, gloomy darkness** (or: the realm of nether gloom; the dark, shadowy quarter of dimness and obscurity)," of Heb. 12:18-21, to Heb. 12:22-24, and to the situation in Heb. 12:28,

"**continuously taking to our sides** (or: progressively receiving alongside) **an unshaken Reign** (or: Kingdom; Sovereign influence), **we are constantly holding** (or: progressively having; [other MSS: can be now having]) **grace and joyous favor, through which we are** [other MSS: can be] **continually serving, well-pleasingly, in God** (or: for God; by God; to God), **with modesty** (an unseen behavior and manner) **in taking hold easily of goodness and well-being, as well as discretion and awe as to what is proper**." [*cf* Jn. 1:17]

Paul described the former situation, in Rom. 5:14,

"**But nonetheless The Death reigned** (or: holds royal and kingly rule) **from Adam as far as and as long as Moses** [= Law], **even upon those not sinning** (failing to hit the target; deviating from the goal) **upon the result of that which is conformed to the stepping aside** (or: the transgression) **of Adam – who is, and continues being, a replication** (an impress; a pattern; a type; a prefigure) **of and from the One being repeatedly** (or: always; or: progressively) **about to [intervene].**"

Then he moves to our present reality:

"**For since by the effect of the fall to the side** (or: in the result of the stumbling aside; with the effect of the offense) **of the one The Death reigned** (or: reigns; rules as king) **through that one, much more, rather, will the peoples** (= the masses of humanity) **– in continuously receiving and seizing upon** (taking in hand) **the surrounding superabundance** (encircling, extraordinary surplus and excess) **of the Grace and of, from and which is the gratuitous gift of the liberated Rightwisedness** (of the solidarity in fair and equitable treatment; from the placement in right [covenant]-relationship in the Way; of the justification and freedom from guilt while being turned in the right direction and made right) **– continue reigning** (or: ruling as kings) **within and in union with Life through the One, Jesus Christ**" (Rom. 5:17).

Paul describe the transition in another way in 2 Cor. 3:

7. **Now since the attending service of the Death – being one that has been formed by a beaten impression of types and the outlines of patterns that exists as engravings within letters and the effects of written texts chiseled on stones – was birthed and came into existence within glory, so that the sons of Israel came to be continuously unable to intently gaze into the face of Moses, because of the glory and manifestation which came from his face – which [glory] was being progressively unemployed so as to be brought down to having no work, to be ineffective and nullified –**

8. **how shall not rather the attending service and dispensing of the provision of the Spirit continue being within, and in union with, glory?**

9. **For since the attending service and dispensing of the corresponding evaluations and commensurate decisions which follow the pattern [had] glory, to a much greater degree does the attending service and the dispensing of the eschatological deliverance into fairness and equity in rightwised relationships progressively surround and continuously exceed in glory!**

Notice that in Rom. 5:14, it spoke of the "reign" of the Death, and then in 2 Cor. 3:7 he termed the same situation as "the attending service of the Death." This presents a good, instructive contrast to the correlation of the set-apart folks "**reigning**," here in vs. 5, to the "**rendering sacred service**," in vs. 3, above. What Paul gave in teaching was presented to John in the context of all these visions in the Unveiling.

The verse ends with the promise that "**they**" – His servants of vs. 3 – will reign **on into the ages of the ages**. This is a paradox: **slaves reigning as kings**. But this was the message of Jesus: he who would be greatest (e.g., would reign) must be the servant of all (Mat. 23:11). Paul instructs us, in 2 Tim. 2:11b-12a,

"**You see, since we died together with [Him]** (or: For if we jointly die), **we will also continue living together** (or: proceed in jointly living; constantly co-live); **since we are continuously remaining under for support** (or: if we continue patiently enduring), **we will also continue reigning** (performing royal activities and influence) **together with [Him]**."

Of course, this also ties in with the overcomers of 3:21, above. Note the durative aspect of the future tense in these promises. Note also the parallels of "continue living together" and "continue reigning together." This reigning is what Jesus referred to in Mat. 25:46b, and is what continued in Acts 2, on unto this day. It is reigning as our Lord reigns: serving God through serving His brothers (humanity, corporate Adam); it is the cruciform life. Dan. 7:27 spoke of this Messianic situation:

"Now the reign and that which is out of Being (or: the sovereign influence and the right from out of existing with privileged authority), as well as the greatness (or: magnitude; majesty) of the kings that are down under the whole atmosphere (sky; heaven) [other MSS: of all the kingdoms under heaven] is given to set-apart folks of the Most High (or: was granted among [the] sacred people from [the] Highest). And so His reign [is] an eonian reign (a kingdom pertaining to the ages, and in relation to the ages), and all rulers, headships and dominions will continuously perform as slaves to Him, for Him and in Him, and will constantly pay full attention, submissively hear and obey [Him]" (LXX, JM).

All of this calls to mind God's original purpose for humanity, as stated in Gen. 1:28, along with Ps. 8:4-6.

In *Testaments of the Twelve Patriarchs* (ibid p 795), *Testament of Levi, the third son of Jacob and Leah* (2nd century BC), we find the following:
> "The heavens will be opened, and from the temple of glory sanctification will come upon him, with a fatherly voice, as from Abraham to Isaac, and the glory of the Most High shall burst forth upon him.... For he shall give the majesty of the Lord to those who are his sons in truth.... And in his priesthood the nations shall be multiplied in knowledge on the earth and they shall be illuminated by the grace of the Lord... In his priesthood sin shall cease and lawless men shall rest from their evil deeds, and righteous men shall find rest in him. And he shall open the gates of paradise; he shall remove the sword that has threatened since Adam and he will grant to the saints to eat of the tree of life. The spirit of holiness shall be upon them..." (18:6-12a).

These pictures calls to mind the blessing found in Nu. 6:24-27,
> "May Yahweh bless you and keep you; may Yahweh light up His face toward you and be gracious to you; may Yahweh lift His face to you and appoint peace for you. Thus they will place My Name over the sons of Israel and I Myself shall bless them" (CVOT).

Verse 5, here, ends the vision of the New Jerusalem, the Wife of the little Lamb. The rest of this chapter is the conclusion of the Unveiling. But before moving on, a brief review of the rhetorical devices where contrast that can be observed in the Unveiling may be helpful as an overview of some of the main threads of this verbal tapestry. Beale presents these (ibid p 1117-1121) and we offer something similar:

    a) the phrase, "the street of the city" that occurs in both 21:21, and 11:8 (the old Jerusalem)
    b) Babylon described with gold, precious stones and pearls; the New Jerusalem with the same
    c) the pure Bride in 21:2, 9; the Great Prostitute in 17:1-2; 18:9
    d) the kings of the earth in 17:16-18 compared to 21:24-26
    e) healing and life in 22:1-2 contrasted with the death of the set-apart folks in 17:4-5; 18:23
    f) the blessing of entering the new City, in 22:14, below; the call to escape Babylon in 18:4
    g) the phrase "It has come to be" in 16:17-18 compared to "They have come into being" in 21:6
    h) the names on the forehead in 17:5 contrasted to 22:4
    i) names in the book of the Life, 21:27; names not in the book of the Life, 17:8
    j) Babylon glorified herself, 18:7; the new Jerusalem reflects God's glory, 21:11, 23
    k) Babylon becomes an abode of demons, 18:2; the new City a dwelling of God, 21:3, 11, 22-23
    l) the realm of the spirit/atmosphere/heaven contrasted to the earth realm
    m) a little, slain Lamb, 5:6, contrasted to a lamb-horned beast that spoke like a dragon, 13:11

The letters to the 7 communities, in chapters 2 and 3, address the flaws yet present among them; the New Jerusalem presents these same communities as they appear when they reflect His image and His glory (21:1-22:5), instead of their own appearance and reputations. This book presents the end of the old amidst the birth of the new. The two Cities, set in contrast as antitheses, represent the "first Adam," and the "last Adam" of Paul's explanation (1 Cor. 15:45); the first City was "**sown a body having the qualities and characteristics of a soul**," the second City was "**raised up a spiritual body.... [which] should** [B reads: will continue to] **also bear and wear the image of the supra-heavenly One** (or: belonging to the One having the quality and character of the finished and perfected atmosphere; or: from the fully-heaven [sphere]; of the added-sky person)" (1 Cor. 15:44, 49). Beale (ibid p 1118, 1121) states that J.M. Vogelgesang (*Interpretation of Ezekiel in Revelation*, p 98-102, 112) "concludes that the New

Jerusalem is really a 'Babylon redeemed,'…. [and] also suggests that the various ways in which John extends facets of the Ezekiel 40-48 vision to include worldwide Gentile realities expresses a notion of universal salvation" (brackets added).

The Epilogue (22:6-21)

We will notice phrases and statements in this section which take us back to 1:1-3, above, and which also suggest allusions to Dan. 2:28, 29b, 45b:

> "But there is (exists) a God within the midst of [the] atmosphere (or: centered in, and in union with, heaven) habitually unveiling secrets (or: repeatedly revealing and progressively disclosing mysteries), and He has made known to king Nabuchodonosor **things which of necessity must** (it is binding to) **come into being** (be birthed; happen, occur) at an end of the days…. what things must happen…. and the dream is true (real), and the interpretation of it [is] trustworthy and reliable" (LXX, JM).

In some of the following verses, there is ambiguity as to who is doing the speaking, and scholars differ in their conclusions. We will endeavor to follow the text and suggest what seems to us to be the case as to who is the speaker.

6. **Then he said to me,**
    "These words (messages) **are faithful ones and true ones, and the Lord** [= Yahweh], **the God of the spirits of** (or: from) **the prophets, sent** (or: sends) **off His agent** (or: the person with a message from Him) **with a commission** (as an envoy) **to show** (point out; exhibit) **to His slaves things which of necessity must** (it is binding to) **come into being** (be birthed; happen, occur) **in speed** (swiftness, quickness, – so the Lexicons; but Wuest, Williams, Barclay, Lattimore, Beck, Goodspeed, NEB, Nyland translate this phrase: soon; others give: shortly).

This verse begins the Epilogue of the Unveiling. The first clause refers to the entire book, but it is also the concluding statement of the final vision (21:1-22:5). It also repeats 21:5b, above. The agent affirms to John that all that he has heard is **faithful** to the Truth, and they are **true** to the reality to which they point. These **words** and messages came from the risen Lord, who is **Faithful** and **True** (1:5; 3:7, above). The original audience is being encouraged to believe what they have heard, and to trust that the situations described are real. This also speaks to us as we apply what we have learned concerning 1st century situations, the inauguration of the new creation, our relationship to what has happened, and our applications to our own day. The phrase, "**the God of the spirits of** (or: from) **the prophets**," may be an allusion to *1 QH* 20.11b-13,

> "And I, the Instructor, have known You, O my God by the spirit which You gave me, and I have listened faithfully to Your wondrous counsel by Your holy spirit. You have opened within me knowledge in the mystery of Your insight, and a spring of [Your] strength […]" (*The Dead Sea Scrolls; A New Translation*, Michael Wise, Martin Abegg, Jr., & Edward Cook, HarperSanFrancisco, 1996 p 108-9; brackets original).

The speaker could be Jesus, since there are obvious links to chapter one here, but most likely the speaker is the same agent that spoke to John in 21:9, above, and who then carried him away to see the vision of the set-apart City that we just reviewed, who then came on the scene again in 21:15 and 22:1. There may also be an allusion, here, to Lu. 24:44-46,

> 44. **Now He says to them, "These [were] My words** (thoughts; ideas; or: This [is] My message) **– which I spoke to you folks, while yet being together with you – That it continues binding and necessary for all the things having been written within the Law of Moses, and in the Prophets and Psalms, concerning Me, to be fulfilled."**

45. **At that time He fully opened back up again their minds to be habitually making the Scriptures flow together** (or: to continue putting the Scriptures together so as to comprehend [them]),
46. **And then He says to them, "Thus is has been written** [other MSS add: and thus it continued binding] **[about] the Christ** (the Anointed One)**: He was to suffer, and then to rise** (or: stand back up again) **from out of the midst of dead folks – on the third day –**

The verb, "**sent off… with a commission**," is *apostellō*, and is a cognate of the noun that is commonly transliterated, "apostle." God sent this "person with a message" to show the visions **to His slaves**. Now the wording is somewhat ambiguous – to which agent is he referring? The infinitive phrase, "**to show to His slaves**" is identical to the one in 1:1, above, so this statement about "**His agent**" may refer to Jesus Christ.

Those who interpret the prophesies of the Unveiling as pertaining to our time, or to the future, see this verse as saying that when these things happen they will happen quickly, in swiftness. The preterists, and others, see this statement as saying that the agent was telling John that these things were soon to happen, in the 1st century. We have seen that they did, or at least one application of them did. The clause, "**things which of necessity must** (it is binding to) **come into being** (be birthed; happen, occur) **in speed** (swiftness, quickness)" exactly repeats the same dependent clause of 1:1, above. The parenthetical expansion and explanation about how different translators render the phrase "**in speed**" begins with the lexical meaning of the phrase, and then lists some folks who give an idiomatic rendering. The grammar of the Greek text of the Unveiling has often been criticized. Beale states, "Dionysius of Alexandria (d. AD 264-265) observed that John's 'use of the Greek language is not accurate, but he employs barbarous idioms…'" (ibid p 100). This book is ending where it started, or, this is apocalyptic repetition – to show emphasis. These phrases seem to expresses immediacy. Imminence, as related to what must "happen," is also seen in vss. 7, 10, 12 and 20, below. If we take into account Jesus' predictions about the destruction of the temple and of Jerusalem (Mat. 24; Lu. 21) and His statements that these things would happen in that 1st century generation, then an idiomatic rendering, "soon," or, "shortly," may best convey the author's intent. The writings of Paul would also seem to support this view.

As to the phrase "**the God of the spirits of** (or: from) **the prophets**," Lee states that this "indicates that these prophecies are related to those in the OT and the NT, all of which were spoken by the prophets in their spirits…. Hence, to comprehend these prophecies, we too need to be in our spirit under God's anointing" (ibid). This qualifying phrase affirms the connection between what has been spoken in this Unveiling and all the allusions that were made to the prophets in the OT. This compound phrase is composed of two genitive phrases, and interpreters have presented a variety of readings of the genitives, as well as a variety of interpretations of just what these "**spirits**" are. This could refer to the prophets' own spirits, or attitudes. It could be speaking of the "spirits" of their individual writings. A possible appositional reading of the first phrase could be, "The God that is the spirits of the prophets," the plural echoing "the seven spirits of God," or, it could be signifying that the "spirit" in which each prophet spoke, or wrote, was, in fact, God speaking through them. Rendering the second phrase as an ablative, this could be speaking of the spirits which came "from the prophets" through the reading of their words. Each prophet has a different "flavor." An objective genitive reading could suggest that God is the one owning, ruling over and inspiring these spirits. And also recall that Paul said,

> "**Also – [the] spirits and attitudes of the prophets are normally humbly aligned with [other] prophets, or, to [the] Prophets**
>> (or: breath-effects of those having fore-light are constantly subjected and subjoined to the arrangements [made] by [the] folks having fore-light)" (1 Cor. 14:32).

Then Peter instructed us that,

"**previously enlightened information** (or: prophecy) **was** (or: is) **not at any time brought by** (or: in; for; with) **[the] will** (intent; resolve; purpose) **of a human, but rather being continuously carried by** (or: swept along under [the influence of]) **[the] set-apart Breath-effect** (or: Holy Spirit), **people spoke from God** [with other MSS: God's set-apart (holy) folks speak]" (2 Pet. 1:21).

7. **"And consider this! I am continuously** (habitually; repeatedly) **coming quickly** (swiftly). **Blessed** (Happy) **[is] the one continuously keeping** (actively observing; watching over; preserving) **the words** (or: messages; thoughts and ideas) **of the prophecy of this scroll."**

This is a parenthesis, recording the words of Christ (*cf* 16:15, above). Noting that the verb in the first sentence is in the present tense, which denotes continuous, habitual or repeated action, and since He (Jesus is the speaker here) follows this verb with the adverb form of the noun "**quickly**," used also used in vs. 6, above, I suggest that His "**continuously coming quickly**" would apply to the period of the 1st century, as well as to other incidents connected with His habitual comings. This proclamation echoes 1:1, above, that applied to the entire of the content of this Unveiling:

"**that which continues necessary to come to be** (or: be birthed; happen) **in swiftness** (= speedily; or: shortly),"

as well as what we read in 1:3, "**the situation is close at hand** (or: for you see, the season, fertile moment and appointed occasion is near – close enough to touch)." He continues, in 1:7, to tell John, "**He is continuously** (or: presently; repeatedly; habitually; progressively) **coming with the clouds**." *Cf* comments on these verses, above. Below, in vs. 10, it is again emphasized: "**for the season** (fitting situation) **is progressively near** (or: continues existing close at hand). Verses 12 and 20, below repeat this same message; by now it should be clear that He was not referring to a far-distant future.

This habitual and repeated coming, proclaimed here, is the SAME as the comings spoken of in 2:5, 16, 25; 3:6, 11, above. Jesus told His disciples, in Mat. 10:23,

"**Now whenever they may continue chasing you or be repeatedly persecuting you in this [particular] city, proceed taking flight** (escaping) **into a different one, for, truly – I now say to you folks – you can under no circumstances complete the circuit of** (or: finish [visiting]) **the cities** (or: towns) **of Israel until the Son of the Man should come** (or: goes; can come and then go)."

Then in Mat. 16:27-28 He told them,

"**You see, the Son of the Man is presently about to continue progressively coming within the glory of His Father, with His agents** (messengers). **And at that time, He will proceed giving back** (recompensing) **to each one in corresponding accord with his practice, behavior and operation of business. It is so** (or: Truly), **I am now telling you men, that there are some** (or: certain ones) **of the folks presently standing here who under no circumstances can taste** (= partake of, or, experience) **death, until they can perceive and see the Son of the Man progressively coming in His reign** (or: within His kingdom; joined to His sovereign activities)."

And in Mat. 24:30, 34,

"**And at that time, the 'sign' which is the Son of the Man will be made progressively visible in union with heaven** (or: [the] atmosphere). **And at that point 'all the tribes of the Land** (or: earth) **will continue beating themselves** (= a figure of striking one's breast in grief and remorse; or: as when grain is being threshed; or: give themselves to wearisome toil; or: cut themselves off, as when harvesting grain),' [Zech. 12:10, 14] **and they will proceed in seeing for themselves 'the Son of the Man progressively coming and going, upon the clouds of the atmosphere** (or: sky),' [Dan. 7:13-14], **with power and ability, as well as much glory.... I now say to you**

folks, that this generation can by no means pass by until all these things can happen (should occur)."

Recall the conversation between Peter and Jesus, in Jn. 21:21-22,

> "**Peter, therefore, seeing and perceiving this one, says to Jesus, 'Lord** (Master)**, now what [of] this man?' Jesus then says to him, 'If I am intending** (willing; purposing) **him to continue remaining until I am progressively coming, what [is it; effect comes] toward you?'**"

Paul told those in Corinth,

> "**Now I forcefully declare this, brothers** (= family)**, the season** (fitting and appointed situation; fertile moment) **now exists being one that has been contracted** (drawn together so as to be shortened, curtailed and limited)!" (1 Cor. 7:29).

We read in 1 Pet. 4:7,

> "**Now the Goal** (or: the end; the final act; or: the finished Product; or: the completion of the plan) **of all people** (and: pertaining to and affecting all things) **has approached and is now near at hand and [He] is close enough to touch** (= has arrived)! **Therefore, you folks keep a healthy and sound frame of mind** (be sane and sensible) **and be sober** (be unintoxicated; i.e., be functional and with your wits about you) **into [a state, condition or realm] with a view toward having goodness and well-being** (or: into the midst of prayers)."

Then there is this illuminating passage in Jacob (James) 5:

> 7. **Be patient** (long-tempered; long-passioned; slow to rush; or: Have long-term feelings and emotions, with anger pushed far away)**, then, brothers, during the continuance of the Lord's** [= Yahweh's, or, Christ's] **presence and His being alongside. Consider! The worker of the land repeatedly receives** (takes out into his hands from within) **the precious fruit of the land, being patient** (slow to rush and with long-term feelings; with anger far from him) **upon it, during the continuance where it can receive "an early as well as a latter** (or: late) **rain."**
>
> 8. **You, too, be patient** (be slow to rush while maintaining long-term feelings; putting anger far away)**; establish** (place supports and make stable; firmly set) **your hearts, because the Lord's** [= Yahweh's or Christ's] **presence has drawn near** (has approached and now exists close to us).
>
> 9. **Brothers, do not be groaning down against** (or: sighing in relation to; or, may = complaining about or blaming) **one another, so that you may not be separated and have a decision made** (or: be put asunder, sifted, scrutinized and judged). **Consider! The Decider** (Sifter; Separator; Evaluator; Judge) **has taken a stand, and now continues standing before the doors.**

The message of this Unveiling speaks to all the things of these seven NT witnesses.

It would seem that Jesus has in mind the entire "**prophecy of this scroll**" of which He speaks a **blessing** for those continuously observing and preserving these "faithful and true" words. This repeats 1:3a, above. If you can see the prophecy of **this scroll** as applying to the historical events of "God's eschatological deed.... The salvation-occurrence" (Bultmann, ibid) which brought an end to the old covenant (the end of the "Jewish age") and which inaugurated the new covenant (which also began the next age, which is composed of the "cultivated olive" with the "wild olive" grafted in – Rom. 11:16-24) in the "second humanity" (1 Cor. 15:47) – the Last Adam; the New Creation; the New Man; "the Israel of God" (Gal. 6:16) – the Kingdom Age), and to His coming in judgment upon Jerusalem, and that these things happened to them for us and to unveil Christ and His body in their present reality, THEN we will live as blessed and happy folks! This scroll is about fulfillment and an ending of the old, and the birthing/resurrecting of the NEW. Understanding the words and the message of this Unveiling is understanding the Good News in Christ.

This pronouncement of being **blessed**, is one of 7 "beatitudes" in the Unveiling. The others are in: 1:3; 14:13; 16:15; 19:9; 20:6; and 22:14. Significantly, these 7 beatitudes give the Unveiling a fully positive theme.

8. **And I, John, [am] the person progressively hearing and seeing these things. And when I heard and saw, I fell down to do obeisance** (kiss toward; worship) **in front of the feet of the agent [who] is progressively exhibiting** (pointing out) **these things to me.**

This takes us back to the scene in 1:17, above, where John was similarly overcome and fell down, as well as 19:10, above. But here, he does not fall "as dead" as he did before the Lord, there. John was blessed because he had an ear to hear; he was blessed because his eyes saw (Matt. 13:15). What he had heard and seen gave rise to this physical expression of awe, respect and reverence – which was culturally appropriate in this situation. It would be commonly done in the presence of earthly dignitaries or persons of high office or social status.

9. **And he is saying to me,**
"**See! No!** (may =: Don't) **I am your fellow-slave, even of** (belonging to; from among) **your brothers – of** (or: belonging to and from among) **the prophets and of** (even from among) **those continuously keeping, observing and maintaining the words and messages of this scroll. Kiss face-to-face in, and with, God** (or: do [your] obeisance to God)**!**"

The opening interjection, "**See! No!**," may be an idiomatic way of saying, "Don't!" A few later MSS added an interpretive admonition "you should do," following the negative particle, which would mean: "Don't do that!" This may be a correct interpretation, but another reading might yield this interpretation: "Look at what you've just seen! No, you're missing the point, I've not presented all this so that you would continue in the old traditions. I'm one of your brothers! You now have face-to-face relationship with God!"

Here, and through vs. 11, it is the agent speaking. We saw this same admonition in 19:10, above. It is repeated here as a second witness that we are not to worship others, even if they appear to us from the realm of spirit. This agent points out that he is on the same level as John (folks only expressed reverence and worship to someone on a higher social level), and actually was a fellow-slave from the prophets of old, and one of the people that both keep and observe the words of this scroll. In other words, he was a part of "the whole family in the heavens and on earth" (Eph. 3:15, Young). He was a part of John's brothers and belonged to the group called "the prophets." We contemplate this as being a glorious role (that of being an "agent," or a "messenger") that awaits us when we pass from this life – at least we would love it to be so :)

This agent's identification of him/her-self is similar to what we saw in 6:11, above, so we may discern a possible connection to those, "**down under the altar of burnt-offering, the souls of the folks having been slaughtered [as in sacrifice] because of the Word of God** (or: God's message), **and because of the witness** (testimony; evidence) **which they were holding** (or: continued to have)," in 6:9, above. Or, as Paul says in 1 Cor. 3:5, we are all, "**attending servants and dispensers of [spiritual] provisions, through whom you folks came to believe and trust – even as the Lord** [= Christ or Yahweh] **gave** (or: gives) **to and in each one.**"

Some have understood the clause which follows "**of the prophets**" as being descriptive of this phrase, thus implying that the agent is referring to all those who are "**continuously keeping, observing and maintaining the words and messages of this scroll,**" of which he or she is part. The continuous action of the present participle indicates a habitual way of life. This may simply be another way of saying that he or she is a citizen of this new City.

Now since John's act of obeisance was culturally appropriate, what is the significance of this agent's refusal to allow John to do this to him (or: her)? A similar situation is found in Acts 10:25-26, where Peter rejects obeisance from Cornelius with the words: "**Get up** (or: Stand up; Rise)**! I myself also am the same as you – a human!**" Now Paul used this same word in 1 Cor. 14:24-25,

> "**Now if everyone may be prophesying, one after another, and some unbeliever** (person without faith) **or an ordinary uninstructed person may at some point enter, he is progressively being given the proof [of the situation], being exposed to convincing arguments, by everyone – [and] by everyone continues being sifted, sorted and held up so that a decision [regarding the situation] can come to him! The hidden things of his heart are now progressively coming to be set in clear light, and thus – falling upon [his] face – he will proceed to be doing obeisance to** (or: worshiping) **God, progressively proclaiming back [to you] that God is existentially within, essentially in union with, and is presently being among you folks!**"

So the act, in itself, was not wrong. Let us consider another situation which might enlighten our current verse. In Acts 14:8-10, when Barnabas and Paul were in Lystra, we read of Paul healing a lame man: after, "**seeing that he is progressively having faith pertaining to being healed**," Paul simply said to him, "**Stand up erect upon** (or: upright on) **your feet!**" Now consider the crowd's reaction to this event:

> "**upon seeing that which Paul did, the crowds lifted up** (elevated) **their voice in [the] Lycaonian language, repeatedly** (or: one after another) **saying, "The gods, being made to resemble humans, stepped down** (or: descended) **to us!**" (vs. 11).

The crowd was speaking from the common Hellenistic word-view throughout the Empire: there was a hierarchy of spiritual beings (agents, gods, demiurges, etc.) that comprised the "heavens," or the world of the gods. In our present verse, the agent/messenger is refuting this prevailing understanding of the universe. There is only One to Whom such respect and reverence is to be shown, and that is God. And all acts of reverence are to be those of "spirit and reality" (Jn. 4:23-24). Furthermore, God has raised us up to sit with Him in this sphere, and there is no hierarchy in God's reign. In this realm we are all brothers – as Paul affirmed in Rom. 8:29b – we are all one Family. The old paradigms have passed away; reality has now been unveiled and is being disclosed to the world. Paul addressed this topic in Col. 2:

> 18. **[so] let no one be acting as an umpire, or an arbiter in the public games, so as to decide down against you, or to disqualify you, in regard to the prize** (or: to award the prize [to you] unjustly – Eduard Lohse) **– in lowness of understanding, intellect, frame of mind and deportment, continuously wanting [you] also [to be] in ritual-relating to the agents**
>
>> (or: constantly delighting in religious activity originating from the messengers [note: e.g., old covenant rituals]; or: repeatedly taking pleasure by cultic religious service about, or external worship of or through the "angels"), **while continuously stepping randomly and rashly into** (or: entering purposelessly, thoughtlessly or feignedly into; or: = being initiated into) **things which he has** [other MSS: he has not] **seen** [note: this may refer to being initiated into cultic secrets or mysteries], **progressively being made natural and instinctual by the inner senses and perceptions of his flesh**
>
>> (or: habitually being puffed up under [the influence of] the mind of his flesh [= his natural abilities and conditions, or by his alienated self, or by the human nature that has been conformed to the System]),
>
> 19. **and thus not continuously** (or: terminating the continuum of) **getting strength from** (or: apprehending and becoming strong by) **the Head** (or: the Source), **from out of Whom all the body** (or: the entire body) **– being constantly fully furnished and supplied to excess with funds and nourishment, and progressively joined cohesively** (welded together; knitted and

compacted together; united and made to go together as in mounting for copulation) **through the instrumentality of the joints** (connections; junctures; fastenings) **and links** (things bound together, as by ligaments) **– goes on growing and increasing God's growth**
> (or: the growth of God; the growth having its source in God; the growth pertaining to God; the growth and increase which is God; or: the growth from God).

It is of interest that with the exception of 1 Cor. 14:25, which referred to someone who was not yet a part of the new covenant community, and of two OT quotes (Heb. 1:6 and 11:21), the word for **obeisance**, or, "worship," is completely absent from the Epistles of the NT. We find it very common in the Gospels and Acts, as well as repeatedly here in the Unveiling. But all of these are either during the time and situations of the old arrangement, or during the transitions between the ages, or, in the Unveiling, in contexts of OT allusions or contextual frameworks. In vs. 4, above, we saw that people in the City see God's face. For this reason, my bold rendering of the last clause, here, is, "**Kiss face-to-face in, and with, God.**" This is the literal meaning of the word (the verb: "to kiss," prefixed by *pros*: toward; in the direction of; face-to-face with), followed by the dative expression (in, with, to God). Heinrich Greeven informs us that for the Greeks this may have carried the idea of a "blown kiss to one of higher rank" (*TDNT*, Vol. 6, ibid p 759). Recall that in 2 Cor. 3:18 we are informed that, "**we all, ourselves – having a face that has been uncovered and remains unveiled** [note: as with Moses, before the Lord, Ex. 34:34] **– being folks who by a mirror are continuously observing, as ourselves, the Lord's** [= Yahweh's or Christ's] **glory**." We are in intimate relation to Him, as the Wife of the little Lamb. In 1 Jn. 1:1, 3, we find language of intimacy with Christ:

> "**The One whom we have listened to, and still hear; the One whom we have seen, and now yet perceive with our eyes** (or: in our eyes); **the One whom we gazed upon as a public spectacle** (as an exhibit in a theater) **and our hands handled** (felt about for and touched) **– groping around the Word of the Life.... The One whom we have seen, and still now see, and we have heard, and now continue listening to and hearing, we are also constantly reporting to you, to the end that you, too, may be continuously having common being and existence** (or: would be progressively holding partnership and participation) **with us. And yet, our common being and existence** (or: participation; fellowship; partnership; sharing) **[is] with the Father, even with His Son, Jesus Christ**."

Speaking of God, John speaks of "**the One within you folks**," in 1 Jn. 4:4, and then clearly states it in 4:12, "**If we are habitually loving** (urging toward reunion, acceptance and participation in) **one another, God constantly remains** (dwells, abides) **within us**."

Kaplan pointed out to me that "**observing and maintaining the words and messages of this scroll**" is an allusion to Gen. 2:15 where the metaphor was that of cultivating and maintaining (guarding; watching over; keeping charge of) the Garden (LXX).

10. **Next he is saying to me,**
   "**Do not seal the words of the prophecy of this scroll, for you see, the season** (fitting situation) **is progressively near** (or: continues existing close at hand). [Dan. 12:4, 9]

This clearly emphasizes the imminence of the prophecy's fulfillment: "**the season** (fitting situation) **is progressively near** (or: continues existing close at hand)." For this reason, John is told: "**Do not seal the words of the prophecy of this scroll**." This is in contrast to the command to Daniel to "conceal the words and seal up the book until the time of the end" (Dan. 12:4; *cf* Isa. 8:16). That was because the prophecy given to Daniel spoke of the distant future (approximately 500 years, according to Dan. 9:24-27); but because John's prophecy refers to the imminent future, he is instructed to keep the scroll unsealed. And observe that the Spirit had John write the last part of this verse using the present tense: "for the season (or: fitting situation) is **progressively NEAR** (or: continues existing close at hand)." What it spoke of concerned (first of all) the time of the 1st century, the Roman Empire, and the physical Jerusalem where our Lord was crucified. If John A.T. Robinson is correct in his pre-AD 70 dating of this *Unveiling*, then that time (along with those situations) was only a couple years away for John and his contemporaries. All of this began to happen during the days of John the Immerser, who immersed Jesus in the Jordan River. Following Jesus' testing in the wilderness, Jesus began publicly proclaiming the Good News in Galilee:

> "**The season and appointed situation has been fulfilled** (The fertile moment has been filled up and now continues full and is now ripe) **and God's kingdom** (the reigning and ruling of God as King; God's activity of exercising sovereignty) **has approached and is now near at hand and is close enough to touch** (= has arrived and is now accessible)! **You folks be progressively and continuously changing your thinking – change your perceptions, frame of mind, mode of thought and understanding; change your direction and turn back [toward God] – and be progressively believing while constantly placing your trust in the good news** (the message of goodness, ease and wellness)!" (Mk. 1:15)

Peter proclaimed the fulfillment of Joel's prophecy three and a half years later, on the Day of Pentecost (Acts 2:16-21). What has been disclosed here in the Unveiling corresponds to Daniel's prophecy about the "era of the end" (12:4, 9) and the "end of the days" (12:13) of the old covenant age. The Unveiling concerns the fulfillment of Daniel's prophecies, which spoke of what would "befall your people [Israel] in the latter days" (10:14) of that age. The ministry of Jesus inaugurated the new age of the Messiah. Dan. 9:26 predicted that the "Messiah shall be cut off," and then, "the city and the holy place shall be laid in ruins." Dan. 12:7 referred to this era as being "when the shattering of the hand of the holy people [Israel] is concluded" (CVOT). Rotherham renders this clause, "when the dispersion of a part of the holy people is brought to an end." The Tanakh reads, "when the breaking of the power of the holy people comes to an end." This all happened in AD 70. For Daniel, "the holy people" was a code name for Israel. The statement by the agent, here, was unambiguous: "**the season** (fitting situation) **is progressively near** (or: continues existing close at hand)." He was referring to John's day, in the 1st century.

In Mk. 13 (*cf* Mat. 24:15) Jesus made reference to Dan. 9:27, citing it in reference to what would happen at the time of the destruction of the temple, and what would be happening to His listeners during that period:

> "**Now whenever you folks may see 'the abomination of the desolation'** (or: the detestable thing which results in a region becoming uninhabited, lonely and like a desert; or: the loathing and abhorrence which pertains to a wasted condition; [Dan. 9:27; 11:31; 12:11]) **standing where it is binding not [to stand]** (or: where it is not proper; where it must not) – **let the one reading continue directing his mind and using his intellect [here]** (= figure out what this means) – **then let those within the midst of Judea progressively take flight, and continue fleeing into the mountains** (or: hill country)" (Mk. 13:14).

John was to send these messages and visions to the called-out communities (1:11, 19; 2:1ff, above; vss. 18-19, below) to let them know that what Jesus has prophesied was about to happen. This was a time for unsealing scrolls (5:1ff, above) and examining their contents (20:12, above). It was no longer of keeping secrets and mysteries hidden; it was a time of Unveiling (*cf* Rom. 16:25; 1 Cor. 14:6, 26; 2 Cor. 12:1, 7; Gal. 1:12; 2:2; Eph. 3:3). In Eph. 1, Paul prays for Asia Minor,

> **17.** to the end that the God of (or: pertaining to; or, reading the genitive as in apposition: Who is) **our Lord Jesus Christ, the Father of the Glory** (or: the founder and archetype of, and which is, this manifestation which calls forth praise), **might give** (suddenly impart) **to you folks a spirit** (or: breath-effect; attitude) **of wisdom and revelation** (unveiling; uncovering; disclosure) **within the midst of a full and accurate experiential and intimate knowledge of Himself**
>> (or: in a full realization of Him; or: within and in union with His full, personal knowledge; or: centered and resident within an added insight from Him, and which is Him),

> **18. the eyes of the heart of you folks** (= the insights and perceptions of the core of your [corporate] being) **having been and continuing enlightened** (or: now being illuminated into a state of enlightenment) **into the [situation for] you folks to have seen and thus perceive and know what is the expectation** (or: expectant hope) **of His calling** (or: from HIS calling; belonging to His summons; from the invitation which is Him) **and what [is] the wealth and riches from the glory** (or: of the imagination and opinion; pertaining to the reputation) **of and from the enjoyment of His lot-acquired inheritance within, in union with, and among the set-apart, sacred people** (the holy ones).

We, in the centuries which have followed, have seen figurative "Babylons" rise and fall, in relation to God's servants. The dominating, organized systems of religion have always been "close at hand." Other "beast" kingdoms and empires have come and gone; they are part of God's plan for those continually being born into the natural realm of earth, and vs. 11a, below, speaks to their conditions. Many have seen their respective encounters with the organization of religion as encounters with the Mystery: Babylon (especially from Luther, on: under the dominance of Secret Babylon's many daughters). And because this fitting SITUATION constantly exists, "**God's personal emotion and inherent fervor** (teeming passion and swelling desire; mental bent and natural impulse; propensity and disposition; or: anger, wrath and indignation) **is continuously remaining** (is now habitually dwelling and abiding) **upon**" these continuing situations (Jn. 3:36b). Thus, the call continues for those who have ears to hear, "Come out of her, My people." While proofing this passage, Lynda asks the rhetorical question in reference to this call: "Why? Because Babylon (confusion) represents abomination which pertains to a 'wasted condition' (i.e., religion, Law, dead works, etc.) and desolation."

11.   **"The one continuously acting unjustly** (unfairly; inequitably; contrary to the Way pointed out; also: = living out of covenant) **must yet** (or: still) **act unjustly** (unfairly; = apart from covenant); **and the filthy one must yet** (still) **be filthy; and the just one** (fair and equitable one; = the one in covenant) **must yet** (still) **do justice** (behave fairly and deal equitably in rightwised, covenant relationships); **and the set-apart** (holy) **person must yet** (or: still) **be set apart** (or: made holy)."

Just as vs. 10, above, was an allusion to Dan. 12:3 and 9, this verse is an allusion to Dan. 12:10, "Many will be purified and purged (be made white; LXX: tried by Fire), and be refined; and yet the wrong (or: wicked; LXX: lawless) will act wrongly, and none of the wrong shall understand. But the intelligent (knowledgeable) are understanding (or: will understand)."
Daniel's prophecy is an indicative statement about what will happen in the days of the end of the age, while the verbs, here in vs. 11, are all imperatives. This is why I added the word "**must**" before them. These are commands for all those who correspond to these various categories, and therefore are "**yet**," or, "still" to do these things. Now imperatives are often rendered with the auxiliary verb, "let." But considering the source of these imperatives, it seems a stronger auxiliary should be used: they **must** act according to their character or condition. This determinative verse, composed of imperative directives, has posed problems for interpreters who read them with an Enlightenment, modern or post-modern world view. Determinism is simply out of vogue. But if we are to correctly understand this verse, we must read it from the world view of 1st century Hellenism, combined with 1st century Judaism, for the Unveiling is a combination of both in its rhetorical framework. Both the author and his listeners viewed God as being in direct control of human events, as well as of the cosmos. The change from an indicative statement in Daniel's time, to a collection of imperatives, here, suggests both urgency and an understanding that the fulfillment of Daniel's prophecies are soon to be upon the nation of Israel, in John's time.

The rhetorical character of this verse presents us with two sets of imperative proclamations that are parallel, both of which must be interpreted in the same manner: as imperatives. Verses 8 and 9, above, should be seen as parenthetical: an incident that occurred between John and the agent which broke the flow of the information being given to John in vss. 7-8. The discourse to John picks up again in vs. 10, and vs. 11 is a continuation. Verses 6, 7 and 10 all express the immediacy of the fulfillment of what has been shown to John in the Unveiling, up to this point. It has been suggested (by Mounce, in Beale ibid p 1132) that vs. 11 is informing John that there is no longer any time for people to change their patterns of behavior – the fulfillment is that soon to happen. Verse 12, below, seems to reinforce this interpretation: the time of "**giving back** (paying) **to each one as his work is** (= what he deserves)" is at hand. Judgment is coming, and as Jesus said in Lu. 21:20-28,

> 20. "**Now later, when you folks see Jerusalem being continuously surrounded by encamped armies, at that time realize and know from that experience that her desolation has drawn near and is now present.**
> 21. "**At that point, let the people in Judea progressively flee into the hill country and mountains; then let the people within the midst of her** [i.e., Jerusalem] **proceed departing out of that place, and don't let** (or: let not) **the folks in the country or the district continue coming** (or: going) **into her,**
> 22. "**because these are days of executing justice – of bringing about what is fair and right and of establishing what accords with the Way pointed out – with a view to have fulfilled all the things having been written** (or: for all that is written to be fulfilled)!
> 23. "**Tragic will be the situation for the women then being pregnant, and for the ones still nursing [babies] in those days. You see there will progressively be a great compressive force upon the Land, and inherent fervor bringing internal swelling emotion on this People.**
> 24. "**And so, folks will keep on falling by [the] mouth of a sword, and [others] will proceed being led captive into all the nations** (or: into the midst to unite with every ethnic group) **– and Jerusalem will continue being progressively trampled by and under pagans** (non-Jews; those of the nations) **– until where they can be made full** (or: should be filled [up]; or: would be fulfilled). **And then there will progress being seasons of ethnic multitudes** (or: fitting situations pertaining to nations; or: occasions which have the qualities and characteristics of pagans; or: fertile moments from, and with regard to, non-Jews) [with other MSS: … and then Jerusalem will continue existing being repeatedly trampled by Gentiles up to the point where seasons of nations can at some point be fulfilled or filled full]….
> 27. "**And at that point** (or: time), **they will keep on seeing** (or: perceiving) '**the Son of the Man** (= the eschatological messianic figure) **progressively coming within the midst of a cloud,**' [Dan. 7:13-14] **with power and much glory.**
> 28. "**Now as these things are beginning to be progressively happening, at once bend back up** (or: stand tall and erect), **and then lift up your heads, because your setting-free** (the loosing-away and release of you folks from prison; your redemption from slavery) **is progressively drawing near!**"

With these things in mind, vs. 11 can be seen as another expression of imminent expectations for the events that had been shown to John.

Kaplan has pointed to the parenthetical expansions in the verse: first the reference to a person who is **continuously acting** "contrary to the Way pointed out." The Way pointed out is the path of justice, fairness and equity. One acting **unjustly** acts in a way that is contrary to the Way. The just way was that which was defined by the covenant. Therefore, someone that is behaving in an unjust way is "living out of – i.e., outside of – the covenant." In contrast to this, **the just one**, the person living "in Christ," is the person that is "the one that is in covenant." The Jews of the old covenant, or the new humanity within the new covenant, can behave in such a way that existentially they are "outside of the covenant" – separated from the Vine; overgrown with weeds and brambles; fallen out of grace (or, e.g., Rom. 11:17-22). Kaplan suggests that these negative behaviors, here in vs. 11, were the same situations to which Peter pointed:

> "**upon [the] last** (or: final [phases]) **of these** (or: the) **days mockers** (scoffers) **will continue coming and going – in mocking** (scoffing; deriding), **according to their own cravings**.... **Yet at the present time the heavens and the earth** (or: the atmospheres and skies, as well as the land), **by the same Word – having been collected and being stored up as treasure, by** (or: in; for; with) **fire – continuously exist, being constantly kept** (watched, guarded and maintained) **with a view to a day of separating for deciding** (or: with the character of evaluating for judging), **as well as of loss, ruin or destruction which pertains to the irreverent humans** (or: of people devoid of reverential awe toward God)" (2 Pet. 3:3, 7).

Next, Kaplan cites Paul's detailed list of these folks, in 2 Tim. 3:

> 1. **Now progressively come to know this and continue realizing it, that within [the] last** (or: final) **days hard seasons** (difficult occasions and situations; irksome, perilous or fierce seasons or situations that are hard to deal with; hard appointed periods) **will progressively set themselves in** (put themselves in place),
>
> 2. **for the people will continue being folks that are fond of themselves** (self-loving; selfish), **fond of silver** (= have affection for money or things of monetary value which makes them stingy), **empty pretenders, haughty and arrogant, blasphemers** (abusive slanderers; folks who defame with a false image; or: light-hinderers), **uncompliant and disobedient to parents, ungrateful, undutiful** (disloyal; without regard for divine or natural laws; malign),
>
> 3. **without natural affection, unwilling to make a treaty** (implacable; not open to an agreement), **devils** (adversarial slanderers; folks who throw or thrust something through people to hurt or cause divisions), **without strength** (without [self-] control), **uncultivated** (wild; untamed; ferocious; fierce), **without fondness for expressions of good or aspects of goodness** (or: without affection for good people; unfriendly; averse to virtue),
>
> 4. **pre-committers** (or: ones who give-over in advance, or who abandon), **rash** (reckless), **folks having been inflated with the fumes of conceit** (or: ones being beclouded in smoke), **pleasure-lovers** (ones fond of self-gratification) **rather than friends of God** (ones fond of God),
>
> 5. **continuously holding** (having) **a form of reverence** (virtue and pious awe) **yet being folks having refused, contradicted and now denying** (saying, "No," to) **its power and ability! And so, be habitually turning your steps in a direction away from these folks and avoid them,**
>
> 6. **for you see, forth from out of the midst of these folks are the people repeatedly slipping-in, into the houses,** (or: worming their way into households) **and habitually leading into captivity little women**
>
>> [note: this is the diminutive of "women," thus, perhaps: women of undeveloped character, ability, or inward stature. While the word for "woman" is feminine, the noun "little women" and the following participles are neuter – or neutral – so this rare word may be a figure for what was a cultural view for "feminine" aspects of all people, e.g., their feelings and emotions, or general receptive qualities]
>
> **– those having been piled on and now being heaped up with failures** (errors; misses of the target; deviations from the goal; sins), **being constantly, or from time to time, led by** (or: in; to) **various** (diverse; many-colored) **over-desires,**
>
> 7. **at all times** (or: always) **folks** [note: again a neuter, or neutral, participle] **that are constantly learning, and yet not at any time being able or having consistent power to come into a full, accurate experiential and intimate knowledge of Truth** (or: which is reality).

Verse 11, above, sets these folks in contrast to the called-out, covenant communities to which the Unveiling is to be sent.

Allusion to Ezk. 3:27b has been suggested: "The one who hears shall hear, and the one who forbears shall forbear, for they are a rebellious house" (CVOT). Verse 17, below, is a call to "**the one continuing to listen and hear**." Another suggested allusion is to Isa. 6:10,
> "Dull the people's mind, stop its ears, and seal its eyes – lest, seeing with its eyes and hearing with its ears, it also grasp with its mind, and repent and save itself" (Tanakh).

Jesus cited this passage with regard to the Jewish leadership, in Mat. 13:14-15.

Because situations similar to those of the 1st century repeatedly arise, and God's inherent fervor continues to live with them, we see that the conditions of those in this verse must also continue – it is part of their judgment. We might understand vs. 11 in the light of Judah (Jude) 4,
> " **For you see, some people came in unobserved, from the side – those having been previously written of old into this judgment** (or: people having from long ago been written into the effects and result of this decision)**: [to exist being] impious ones, people continuously changing the grace and favor of God into licentiousness, as well as repeatedly contradicting, saying, "No," to or about, disclaiming, denying and disowning our only Sovereign and Lord** (or: Supreme Ruler and Owner), **Jesus Christ** [= Messiah]."

From this we might conclude that some folks are currently undergoing God's judgment: to exist as they now do (*cf* Rom. 1:18-32; note there that the word "knowing" means to know by experience), while others are currently chosen at this time to be delivered out of this condition to be God's firstfruits of His new creation. Everyone has their own time for being born into the body of Christ (1 Cor. 15:22-23). But the harvest is now and ongoing: to have firstfruits is evidence that the entire crop is present. "**And so they trusted and believed – whoever were folks having BEEN SET and arranged into an eonian life** (or: into life which has is source and quality from the Age [of Messiah])." (Acts. 13:48b). We see contrasting situations in Judah (Jude) that may be parallel to our present text:
> 22. **And so, on the one hand, you folks be repeatedly extending compassionate kindness on some folks in order to relieve their misery and affliction** [other MSS read: put to the proof; expose; convict; reprove] **while continuously discerning, sifting and thoroughly separating so as to accurately decide [about their situation]**
>> (or: be continually showing mercy on some who are constantly undecided and continue wavering and doubting because of making divided judgment in or for themselves);
>
> 23. **yet on the other hand, be continuously delivering** (or: repeatedly rescuing and saving, restoring to health and wholeness) **others, snatching them from out of the midst of the Fire; be repeatedly extending compassionate mercy in reverent fear, while hating and radically detaching from even the garment having been stained** (or: spotted) **from the flesh** (= the alienated human nature; = the self that was formed and controlled by the System).

This situation now exists right here – else how could we be constantly snatching folks **out of the midst of the Fire** right now? This leads us to another layer of interpretation for vs. 11, above: The proclamation may indicate that the judgment that came upon Jerusalem in AD 70 did not mean that humanity would no longer continue with people of varied personalities, religions and worldviews, who might display polar opposites in the way they live their lives. The Unveiling is not about the end of time, the end of humanity or the end of nations and cultures. What changed was the coming of the Age of the Messiah and a call to a higher way of life. What this verse says is exactly what we have observed throughout human history, up to our present time. But now the True Light shines upon humanity, and His reign progresses, leading onward those who have been given eyes to see and ears to hear (Mat. 13:16). There is continued purpose for those within the City, and also for those that are still outside the City. The unjust cannot but do the same as they have done until Christ transforms them. The just folks have already been at least partially transformed and thus are to continue showing love and forgiveness to the unjust, and to wash the feet of the filthy. Those yet living in the jurisdiction and authority of the outer darkness will continue there until Christ "**changes [their] position** (or: transports [them], thus, giving [them] a change of standing, and transfers [them]) **into the midst of the kingdom and reign of the Son of His love**" (Col. 1:13).

The following verses (perhaps on through vs. 19, or the first part of 20), appear to be the words of Jesus, as in 1:8, above.

12.   **"Consider this! I am continuously** (or: habitually; progressively; repeatedly) **coming quickly** (swiftly), **and My wage** (reward for work; compensation; recompense) **[is] with Me, to give back** (give away; render; pay) **to each one as his work** (accomplishment) **is** (= what he deserves).

We have been programmed by tradition to think of this happening only at "the end of time," or at some "final" judgment. But He does not here say that this is the case. When He comes, He brings each one His pay. This is an allusion to Jer. 17:10,
> "I the LORD test the mind and search the heart, to give to all according to their ways, according to the fruit of their doings" (NRSV).

In the parable of the vineyard workers, their pay came at the end of their work day (Mat. 20:1-16). Here in vs. 12, we have an allusion to Jesus, speaking in Mat. 16:
> 27. "**You see, the Son of the Man** (or: mankind's son; or: = the Son of Adam; or: [the eschatological Messianic figure]; or: the Human Being) **is presently about to continue progressively coming within the glory** (the manifestation which calls forth praise) **of His Father, with His agents** (messengers). **And at that time, He will proceed giving back** (or: repaying; recompensing) **to each one in corresponding accord with his practice, behavior and operation of business.**
> 28. "**It is so** (or: Truly; Amen), **I am now telling you men, that there are some** (or: certain ones) **of the folks presently standing here who under no circumstances can** (or: may) **taste** (= partake of, or, experience) **death, until they can** (or: should) **perceive and see the Son of the Man** (mankind's son; = the eschatological Messianic figure; = Adam's Son) **progressively coming in His reign** (or: within His kingdom; joined to His sovereign activities)."

This sounds a lot like He was referring to the time of that 1st century generation, does it not? *Cf* 2:23b; 20:12-13, above.

He speaks now as the Rewarder, the One who pays humans **wages**, as in Heb. 11:6,
> "**Now apart from faith, trust, confidence and loyal allegiance, [one is] powerless** (or: unable) **to please [God] well. It is necessary and binding for the person habitually approaching God to believe** (to be convinced and trust) **that He is** (or: that He exists), **and that He habitually comes to be** (or: becomes) **the One who pays back wages** (or: gives away rewards) **to, in and for those folks repeatedly** (or: constantly) **seeking Him out** (or: seeking from out of Him)." [*cf* Rom. 14:23b; 2 Pet. 4:9]

Wisdom 5:15 states,
> "Now just and equitable folks continue living on into the midst of the Age, and their wage (or: reward) [is] in (or: within the midst of; in union with; centered in) [the] Lord."

Here Kaplan comments:
> "He puts us on His throne (3:21, above; Eph. 2:6); He gives us eonian life (e.g., Jn. 5:24, *et al*); He raises us up and gives us life:
>> '**You see, just as the Father is habitually** (repeatedly; constantly; presently) **raising up the dead folks, and is repeatedly** (continually; presently) **making [them] alive, thus also, the Son is habitually** (constantly; presently) **making alive which ones He is presently intending** (willing; purposing)' (Jn. 5:21).
>
> Also, what we sow is what we will reap (Gal. 6:7), and,

> '**because the person continually sowing into the flesh of himself** (= his estranged inner being), **will progressively reap corruption** (spoil; ruin; decay) **forth from out of the flesh** (= the estranged inner being);
>> (or: the one habitually sowing into the flesh [system], of himself will continue to reap decay from out of the flesh [system];)
>
> **yet the one constantly sowing into the spirit** (or: the Breath) **will be progressively reaping eonian life** (life having the characteristics of the Age [of Messiah]; or: life from the Age that lasts on through the ages) **forth from out of the spirit** (or: the Spirit; the Breath; that attitude)' (Gal. 6:8).

2 Jn. 8 advises,
> '**be continuously seeing to yourselves** (looking at yourselves), **to the intent that you people would** (or: may) **not destroy** (or: lose) **what we** [other MSS: you folks] **did** (produced; worked for), **but rather may receive back full wages**.'

In 3:11, above, Christ admonishes them,
> '**I am repeatedly** (habitually; constantly) **coming and going swiftly** (or: = progressively coming soon)! **You must be continuously strong in what you have** (or: you must constantly hold in your power that which you possess) **to the end that no one may take your winner's wreath** (your emblem of victory; or: your encirclement).'"

As we saw above, the decisions about pay and reward will be commensurate with what a person has done – whether good or ill. Also recall the message of the parable of the sheep and the kids, in Mat. 25: the wage was in accord with how each group had treated others.

The second half of this verse repeats 11:18b, above. The allusion is also to Isa. 40:9b-11,
> "You repeatedly bringing and presently announcing a message of goodness, ease and well-being (or: good news) to Zion, climb up at once upon a high mountain; you repeatedly bringing and presently announcing a message of goodness, ease and well-being (or: good news) to Jerusalem, lift up your voice with (or: in) strength. You folks lift [it] up – do not continue fearing! Say to, and in, the cities of Judah, 'See, and consider your God!' See, and consider [the] LORD [= Yahweh, in Heb. text]! [The] LORD progressively comes (or: repeatedly comes and goes) with strength, and [His] arm [is] with lordship (ownership, mastery and proprietary rights). See, and consider! His wage (or: reward for work; recompense) [is] with Him; and the work [lies] before Him (or: in His presence; or: in opposition to Him). He will continually tend and care for His flock, as a Shepherd, and will repeatedly (or: continually) gather together lambs in (or: with) His arm, and will repeatedly comfort and give aid to those pregnant or with young" (LXX, JM). *Cf* Rom. 2:4-9

What was written of Yahweh, in Isa.40, is spoken by Jesus, about Himself, here in the Unveiling. In Isa. 62:10-11 we read,
> "Continuously pass on (travel) through My gates... lift up out of [your] midst a signal unto the ethnic multitudes (nations)... Say to the daughter of Zion: Look and consider, your Savior has arrived and is present, and continues being at your side, continuously holding His own pay (or: reward), and His accomplishment (deed; work) before His face" (LXX, JM).

In response to Isa. 62:11b, quoted here, Kaplan remarks, "God invests in His people; i.e., WE are His pay, His reward." He further cited Gen. 15:1 where a word from Yahweh came to Abram: "You must not be fearing, Abram! I [am] your Shield, your exceedingly increased Reward" (CVOT).

13. **"I am the Alpha and the Omega, the First and the Last, the Beginning** (Origin; Source; Headship) **and the End** (Goal; Finished Product; Purposed Destiny).

This repeats 1:8 combined with 1:17 and 2:8, above, where He begins His instructions to John to send what he sees to the 7 called-out communities, addresses one of those communities, and then expands the expression in 21:6, which is repeated here: "the Origin and the Goal," or, "**the Beginning and the End**." *Cf* the comments of those verses, above. The formula here in vs. 13 expresses the same ideas that were stated in 1:4b, above. He is the Source and the destination toward which everyone and everything will be brought, because of God's "eschatological deed" in Christ. He comprises "The Finished Product" of the plan and purpose of the ages. He is **the Alpha and the Omega** that **Began**, and then **Ends**, the existential journey that is described in Rom. 11:36a,

> "**Because, forth from out of the midst of Him, then through the midst of Him** (or: through means of Him), **and [finally] into the midst of Him, [is; will be] the whole** (everything; [are] all things; or: = Because He is the source, means and goal/destiny of all things – everything leads into Him)!"

This is another allusion to Isa. 41:4; 44:6 and 48:12. "In this book, God and Christ tend to merge" (*The Interpreter's One-Volume Commentary on the Bible*, ibid p 968).

> "At the winding up of the whole scheme of revelation, He announces Himself as the One *before whom and after whom there is no God*" (Jamieson, Fausset, Brown, ibid p 1591; emphasis original). *Cf* Isa. 43:10b

Isa. 43:11 proclaims, "I, I [am] Yahweh, and there is no Savior apart from Me" (CVOT). Then Isa. 45:5 instructs Israel, "I am Yahweh, and there is none else; besides Me there is no God" (Rotherham).

And then, as to **the First and the Last**, there may be an allusion to 1 Cor. 15:

> 45. **Thus also** (or: In this way also), **it has been written, "The FIRST human** (or: man), **Adam, came for existence** (or: was birthed) **into [being] a living soul"** [Gen. 2:7]; **the LAST Adam into [being] a continuously life-making** (life-engendering; life-creating; life-giving) **Spirit** (or: Breath-effect; Attitude).
> 47. **The first human** (person; man) **[was/is] forth from out of the earth** (land; ground; soil; dirt), **made of moist soil and mud** (or: having the quality and characteristics of moist dirt that can be poured; soilish); **the Second Human** (Person; Man; [other MSS add: {is} the Lord]) **[is made] out of heaven** (or: [is] from [the] atmosphere and sky; [*p*46 reads: {is} spiritual]).
> 49. **And correspondingly as we bear and wear the image of the dusty person,** [*p*46 adds: doubtless] **we can and should** [B reads: will continue to] **also bear and wear the image of the supra-heavenly One** (or: belonging to the One having the quality and character of the finished and perfected atmosphere; or: from the fully-heaven [sphere]; of the added-sky person).

This self-identification affirms Who it is that is making the promise of vs. 12, above, and the blessing of vs. 14, below, and makes firm His involvement with the whole story of humanity, and with all of creation. This One transcends all the ages. He began all, and He finishes all. He both began and finished each age of the past, and will do the same with the present and with all future ages. He is "**the same yesterday and today and on into the ages**" (Heb. 13:8). This calls to mind Heb. 12:2, where we read of:

> "**Jesus, the Inaugurator** (First Leader; Prime Author) **and Perfecter** (*teleiōtēs*; Finisher; the Bringer-to-maturity and fruition; He who purposes and accomplishes the destiny) **of the faith, trust, confidence and loyal allegiance**."

Kaplan also called to mind Jn. 17:4,

> "**I Myself glorify** (or: brought a good reputation and a manifestation which called forth praise to) **You upon the earth** (or: the Land), **finishing and perfecting** (*teleiōsas*; bringing to its goal, purpose, destiny and fruition) **the Work** (the Deed; the Act) **which You have given to** (or: in; for) **Me, to the end that I could do** (or: would perform) **[it]**,"

as well as Jesus' proclamation in Jn. 19:30, "**It has been finished** (*tetelestai*; or: It has been brought to its goal and end), **and now stands complete** (having been accomplished, perfected, ended and now is at its destiny)!" Dan further pointed out the allusion to Zech. 4:9,

"The hands of Zerubbabel laid the foundation of this House, and his hands shall complete it" (CVOT).

The final noun, **the End** (*telos*), can also be rendered: the Finished Product. Here He may be speaking of the fullness of Himself as the corporate New Creation, or, the corporate Christ, or, the New Humanity. Another level of interpreting this is that this One is the Purposed Destiny of the Ages. As Kaplan suggests, there may also be an allusion, here, to 2 Tim. 4:7, where Paul says,

"**I have finished the race** (ended [*teteleka*] the racecourse; reached the goal of my contest; I have fought to the finish); **I have kept** (observed; watched over; guarded; kept in custody) **the faith, trust, confidence and loyalty**."

He knew that "**God is the One habitually operating with inward activity, repeatedly working within, constantly causing function and progressively producing effects within**" (Phil. 2:13). God was the Omega and the Finisher of Paul's course in life.

This verse reaches back to Gen. 1:1, and carries on through to Rev. 22:21. This book is an Unveiling of the whole plan and purpose of God, not just a description of its end. *Cf* comments on 21:6, above. Richard Rohr, in his Daily Meditation, "The Nature of Being," for 3/1/2017, observes:

"Alpha now matches Omega (see Revelation 1:8; 21:6; 22:13). Duns Scotus saw the Christ icon as the Alpha point, and Teilhard de Chardin saw Christ as the Omega point. History had a pattern, a trajectory, and a goal, which gave everything coherence."

On his 2/28/2017 post, Rohr quoted Catherine Mowry LaCugna:

"The God of Jesus Christ is, as Bonaventure put it, the *fontalis plenitudo*, the fountain overflowing with mercy and justice, and also the *telos*, the end and fulfillment of every creature" (*God For Us: The Trinity and Christian Life*, HarperSanFrancisco, 1991 p 399).

14. "**Blessed** (Happy) **folks [are] the ones** (folks; people) **continually washing their garments** (equipment; [other MSS: continually doing His implanted, inner goals and directives]), **to the end that their authority** (or: right out of and from Being; privilege) **will continue being over** (or: upon) **the tree** (pole) **of The Life, and they may at any point enter into the City by the gates.**

This verse speaks of a way of life, "**washing their garments**," or, with the other MSS, "continually doing His implanted, inner goals and directives." Both readings speak of the same reality: a way of life that is involved with what is not "clean" when they go out to those outside the City (vs. 15, below), to serve them – which is the goal which He has implanted in the hearts of His sheep: to minister to the needs of others (Mat. 25:35-36). This results in getting spots on our garments (Jude 23). It also calls to mind what Jesus said about the need for having our feet (the part of us that walks the path of earth, Mat. 10:14) washed (John 13:10).

The goal stated in this verse is to have **authority** (literally: right from out of being, or, from His Being) over/upon **the tree of The Life**. This is an echo of 2:7, above: a promise "**In and by the one** (or: To or for the person) **continuously overcoming** (habitually conquering; normally victorious)**.**" Those who live as described in the first half of the verse are those who (changing the metaphor) "abide/remain in the Vine" (Jn. 15:5). This gives them access to the City, as well, i.e., to the body of Christ. This ability to **enter into the City by the gates** is an echo from Isa. 62:10, 12, "Pass, Pass through the gates [LXX: Go through My gates].... [into] a City Not Forsaken" (CVOT; brackets added). An allusion may be seen to Isa. 26:2,

"At once disclose and open back up again [the] gates; let a people habitually keeping, guarding and maintaining the Way pointed out (rightwised justice and equity resulting from eschatological deliverance) and keeping, guarding and maintaining Truth and Reality at once come into the midst (or: enter)" (LXX, JM).

Also, Ps. 117:20,

"This [is] the Gate of the LORD; just and equitable (or: rightwised) folks will continually journey into the midst, in union with it" (LXX, JM). *Cf* 3:12, above; *Testament of Levi* 18:10ff, cited above.

John 10:9 tells us that His sheep "**will be habitually going in** (entering) **and going out** (exiting) [of the fold, vs. 1, which corresponds to the City, here] **and will continue finding pasture** (something to feed on)." In this last metaphor, Jesus is the door, while here in the Unveiling the gates are described as pearls: it was His pain (and death), and now ours as we follow Him, which transforms us into the pearl of resurrection life. We have access from having been placed within Him. We saw this happening in Act 2:47b,

"**Now the Lord** [= Christ or Yahweh] **kept on adding and placing toward [the goal; the City] the folks being from day to day rescued** (saved; delivered; made whole; restored)."

Entering the City is an apocalyptic way of saying what Paul described in Col. 1:13, which speaks of God,

"**drag[ing] us out of danger** (or: rescu[ing] us) **forth from out of the midst of the authority of the Darkness** (from Darkness's jurisdiction and right; from existing out of gloomy shadows and obscure dimness; = the privilege of ignorance), **and chang[ing] [our] position** (or: transported [us], thus, giving [us] a change of standing, and transferr[ing] [folks]) **into the midst of the kingdom and reign of the Son of His love**."

We would also suggest that the "pole" of **The Life** also represents the cross. That is the Key of the kingdom; it unlocks God's reign within us, and among us. Access to **the tree of The Life** (i.e., the Christ-Life) implies access back into the Garden of Eden: the Way of entry (Christ) has been restored (Gen. 3:24). It is because of this that, "**upon these the second death has no authority** (does not continue holding right or privilege; possesses nothing from the sphere of existing)" (20:6, above). Being sent out of the Garden was the 1st death; it was a result of the new sense of alienation and lack (a feeling of being naked and vulnerable), and thus a rift in humanity's relationship with God.

The environment outside the City (described in the next verse) is a picture of the world: the domination system within which the City has been placed, and in which the called-out communities live their lives. These are some of "**what things are presently existing**" (1:19, above). But 1 Jn. 1:7-9 applies to this ongoing situation, for His "blood continually and progressively **cleanses us** from all sin and failure." We are "**continually washing [our] garments**," as well as those belonging to other folks, **within His blood** (1:5; 7:14, above) and by a "**cleansing** (purging) **by the bath of the Water [that is] within a result of a flow** (or: in union with a gush-effect; or: in the midst of a spoken word, a declaration, or an utterance)" – Eph. 5:26.

15. "**Outside [are] the dogs and the sorcerers** (enchanters by drugs) **and the fornicators** (male prostitutes) **and the murderers and the idolaters and everyone continuously fond of** (being friendly to) **and constantly practicing** (making; doing) **falsehood** (deception; a lie).

Jesus equated dogs with the unclean nations (i.e., the non-Jews; specifically the Syrophenician woman), in Mark 7:26-28. *Cf* Mat. 15:21-28. Paul applied the term "dogs" to the "false circumcision" that betrayed the covenant by rejecting Christ, in Phil. 3:2,

"**Constantly keep your eyes on and be aware of the dogs** (= impudent, shameless or audacious people; scavengers without a master); **habitually be observing so as to take heed**

of worthless workers (craftsmen of bad quality; laborers who are not as they ought to be); **keep on seeing so as to continually observe and be aware of [the party of] the down-cision** (the mutilation; the maim-cision; the cutting-into; the sacrificial meat-hacking; the wounding or maiming; or: = folks who cut things down or off; [comment: a sardonic slur = the circumcision])."

The works described here apply to those that are outside the kingdom/reign/sovereign-actions, at this time. This first phrase may be an allusion to Deut. 23:18, "You shall not bring the wages of an unchaste woman (or: the fee of a prostitute), or the hire of a dog, into the House of Yahweh, your God." Jesus instructed His listeners, "**You folks should not give the set-apart** (holy; sacred) **things to the dogs, neither should you throw your pearls in front of the pigs**" (Mat. 7:6). "**Outside**" is the place of the "outer darkness" into which the Jewish leaders and their old covenant cultus were to be cast: Cf Mat. 8:12; 22:13; 25:30. This first reference was to these leaders of the 1st century being cast out of their position in the kingdom (God's reign and sovereign activities); the next was of a guest at a wedding who was not properly attired; the last was of a servant losing his job – all metaphors spoken about the scribes, Pharisees and priests: the 1st century leadership of their religion. Terry (ibid p 474) suggests that the "gnashing and grinding of teeth" of Mat. 22:13 was a reference to the dogs around oriental cities during that era. Beale (ibid p 1141) suggests a correlation between the symbol "dog" and those who have the mark of the beast (13:15-18, above). Peter spoke of those who turned back to their former religion by quoting the proverb, "**a dog turning about upon its own vomit**" (2 Pet. 2:22), so the use of this term in the Unveiling may be a reference to those who turned back to Judaism, or, to Judaizing. Another allusion may be to Ps. 59:1-6, 14, "they make a noise like a dog, and go round about the city." Harvey states that the reference to **dogs**, "was Jewish language for pagans… who persevered in the notorious sins of heathendom" (ibid p 841). The City, here, exists within the midst of the domination systems of the cultures of the earth, but Christ's kingdom is not a part of those systems (Jn. 18:36).

This verse may also be an allusion to Mal. 3:5, following the proclamation of the sending of His messenger (or: agent) of the covenant to purify and refine the Levites (Mal. 3:1-3), where the setting is "Judah and Jerusalem" (vs. 4). Verse 5 promised Yahweh's coming near to them "for judgment" against such as listed here, in vs. 15. But keep in mind the nation-specific aim of this judgment: Israel. It happened in AD 70.

The folks in this verse are awaiting the time of their "order; rank; class" (1 Cor. 15:23). The remaining categories of this verse are also listed in 21:8, 27, above, where we see that not only can they not, in that condition, enter the City, but "**their portion [is] within the lake** (or: their [allotted] part [is] union with the basin; the share from them [is] in the artificial pool; the region pertaining to them [is] centered in the marshy area) **continuously burning with Fire and Deity, which is the Second Death**." Now note the following:

    1. Gehenna (the valley of Hinnom), the city dump where purification fires continually burned, and worms ate rotting organic matter that was not burning, was just OUTSIDE the city of Jerusalem which existed in the 1st century. As the old Jerusalem of the old covenant was a shadow of the new (heavenly; "above;" spiritual) Jerusalem, so the Gehenna into which men could have been literally cast – after being killed, of course – is a shadow of God's purifying Fire which burns up our dead flesh (the character of the 1s Adam, "flesh" nature; or, as Paul put it in Rom. 8:7, "**the result of the thinking** {disposition; thought processes; mind-set, outlook} **of the flesh** {= attention to Torah boundary-markers, custom and cultus; or: = the human condition} **[is; brings] enmity, alienation and discord [streaming] into God** {or: hostility unto, or active hatred with a view to, God}").

2. These (presently in the lake of Fire, as described in 21:8, above) are "**constantly practicing (making; doing) falsehood (deception; a lie);**" are "**continuously fond of** deception." The list here in vs. 15 is similar to the list in Jude 4, 7, 8, 10-13, 15-16. Note that these in Jude 12 were "**twice-died**" (i.e., in the lake of Fire), yet they are here, and active, even in the called-out community (Jude 4). Yes, they are experiencing God's judgment (Jn. 3:36), which is typified by the judgment of Sodom and Gomorrah (Jude 7) – whose fire came swiftly, yet did not burn for long, for it was eonian fire: fire pertaining to that age (i.e., in time). Furthermore, above we saw that we are to be "**snatching them OUT of the Fire**" (Jude 23). In fact,

> "The house of Jacob [God's chosen people] shall be a fire, and the house of Joseph [figure of the headship of the Christ] a flame, and the house of Esau [figure of the estranged flesh] for stubble, and they shall kindle them and devour them; and there shall not be [any] remaining of the house of Esau .... and saviors shall come up on mount Zion to judge the mount of Esau; and the Kingdom shall be Yahweh's" (Obad. 18, 21).

Convenient of the Lord to have them so close to the City (figured by mount Zion in that text).

Rudolf Bultmann observes:

> "Now, as then, 'God's Wrath' pours out 'against all ungodliness and wickedness of men' (Rom. 1:18).... In reality 'wrath of God' means an occurrence, viz. 'the judgment of God.' God is He who 'inflicts wrath' (Rom. 3:5)' when the 'wrath of God' is said to be 'revealed' (Rom. 1:18), that does not refer to a didactic communication about it but to its becoming effective. When the 'wrath of God' is described (Rom. 1:18-32), it is shown to be identical with that which factually already takes place in the heathen world: abandonment to the 'lusts of their hearts' (vs. 24), to 'dishonorable passions' (vs. 26), to a 'base mind' (i.e., corrupted intent, vs. 28).... Rom. 1:18-32 means the judgment that is constantly taking place; so does Rom. 13:4f where governmental authority is called 'the servant of God to execute wrath (= punishment) on the wrong-doers'..." (*Theology of the New Testament*, Scribner & Sons, 1951 p 288-9).

We would be well-advised to apply Bultmann's conclusions from these Romans passages to the inherent fervor of God's judgment that we have encountered here, in the Unveiling. For an in-depth study on this topic, we suggest: *Just Paul, comments on Romans*, Jonathan Mitchell, Harper Brown Pub., 2014, 305 pages.

16. "**I, Jesus, sent My agent to bear witness to, and among, you people [about] these things [coming; being applied] upon the called-out communities** (or: to testify these things to, by or in you, over [other MSS: within] the assemblies). **I Myself am** (exist being) **the Root and the Offspring of** (Family from; Race which is) **David, The light-emitting** (Shining) **Morning Star**.

Now Jesus makes His identity clear and personally confirms the validity of the visions (just as He personally verified the activities of the called-out folks to Saul, on the road to Damascus) and gives confirmation that "**these things**" are to be "**witnessed upon the called-out communities**," or, His agent was "to testify these things to, by or in you folks, over the summoned-forth assemblies." The phrase, "**these things**" is a reference to the entire Unveiling, from 1:1 to 22:21. The awkwardness of the Greek text of this verse apparently prompted some MS scribes to change the preposition from "**upon**" to "**within.**" I have filled the ellipsis preceding this preposition by inserting "**[coming]**," or, "**[being applied]**," since the book is about things that would soon come, and the messages were intended, first of all, for the seven called-out communities in 1st century Asia Minor (*cf* chapters 2 and 3, above) . However, interpreters have suggested more extended meanings for the preposition "upon," each of which would make for different interpretations about the meaning of the clause (*cf* Beale, ibid pp 1143-46).

The visions of the Unveiling begin and end with the called-out communities, and pertain to the body of Christ that is in the earth. The alternate MSS reading, "within," solves the awkwardness and carries a potential intent which John may have had. The parenthetical alternative for the entire predicate reads the syntax differently: "to testify these things to, by or in you [the dative case], over [an alternate meaning of the preposition, instead of "upon"] the summoned-forth assemblies." In all cases, the covenant communities are the first target-audience to which Jesus sent His agent to bear witness and testify, through John sending the scroll, or codex, to them. The **witness** was to "come" **upon** them, or "be applied" **upon** them, and thus to have an effect. AD 70 had an effect upon all Christians and Jews: there was no longer a temple; Jerusalem was destroyed; the old passed away. The new age had fully come. There was no more "Jerusalem church." Antioch would become the new center, or "cradle," of Christianity, for that time. In vs. 18, below, we are informed that the witness of this book is a "**prophecy**," and Isa. 55:11 instructs us that His Word will not return to Him "empty" of what He desires: "it prospers in that for which [He] sent it." His Words come "upon" folks to accomplish what He intends. Since His words are spirit (or: Spirit), the Unveiling would be the Spirit coming upon them. The prophecies in the Unveiling came "from above," and were intended to come "**upon the called-out communities**."

The predicate, "**sent My agent**" contains an allusion to Mal. 3:1. In both Hebrew and Greek, the words for "agent" also mean "messenger," this latter being the common rendering of the Malachi text. In the Unveiling, these figures were frequently acting within the visions, so I have opted to more often use the term "agent," since they were representing God as well as bringing John messages. This predicate echoes 1:1, above, where John was told that God was, "**sending [Him] as an emissary** (or: representative), **through means of His agent** (or: messenger)."

Jesus continually exists as being both **the Root**, as well as **the Offspring of David**. The parenthetical expansion offers optional renderings of *genos*: Family, or, Race. These expand our potential interpretations of the phrase. The genitive form of "**David**" allows the prepositions "**of**" or "from," or (as apposition), "which is." **Jesus** proclaims that He **Himself** (the emphatic personal pronoun is used) is "**the Offspring of David**," which tells us of his natural lineage, as given in Mat. 1, yielding His legal right to be the King of literal Israel. It also provides a continuity of the "olive tree" (Rom. 11:17-18) where Paul tells us that we are, "**a joint-participant** (a partner taking in common together with; a co-partaker) **of the Root and of the Fatness** (= sap; = Spirit) **of The Olive Tree**," and that, "[we] **are not bearing** (supporting; sustaining; carrying) **The Root, but rather, The Root** [us]." Now if the reading is, 'I am the Root and Family from David," He would have been making a corporate statement, like saying that He was the Last Adam, or the Second Humanity (1 Cor. 15). The next offering is, "I am the Root and Race which is David," which would be like saying, "I am Israel," I am the corporate People to which the prophecies about David pointed. The expected Messiah was in fact a new Race of Being that had the prophetic code name, "David." An allusion can be seen to Isa. 9:7,

> "Of the increase of dominion [LXX: His beginning and rule {shall be} great] and of the peace (well-being; prosperity) there shall be no end or limit – upon the throne of David and upon his kingdom, by establishing it and by sustaining it with justice and with righteousness – from henceforth, even unto times age-abiding: the mixture of hot honor and affection (zeal) of Yahweh of hosts will perform this!"

Jesus brought up the topic of the Messiah, in regard to "Whose son is He," in Mat. 22:
> 42. "**How does it normally seem to you** (or: What do you folks now think and what is your view) **concerning the Anointed One** (the Christ; = the Messiah): **Whose Son** (or: Descendant) **is He?**" They, as a group, are replying to Him, "**David's.**"
> 43. **He then says to them, "How, then, is David – within and in union with [the] Spirit** (or: in spirit; in the effect of [His] Breath; in attitude) **– normally calling Him 'Lord'** (Master)**?, saying,**

44. "'[The] Lord [= Yahweh] said to my Lord (Master), "Be continuously sitting from out of (or: = at) My right-hand [parts] until I should place (or: put) Your alienated ones (or: folks filled with hate and hostility; enemies) down under Your feet'? [Ps. 110:1]
45. "Since (or: If), therefore, David is normally calling Him, 'Lord' (Master), how does He exist being His 'Son'?"

Notice that His listeners could not give a response, and Jesus did not give them an answer. Here, in 22:16, He gives the answer: it had to come via revelation (the Unveiling) – no amount of searching the Scriptures or natural reasoning could unveil the secret (Rom. 16:25b). Even His disciples had to have Him open the OT to see Him in its prophecies:

> "And so, beginning from Moses, and then from all the prophets, He continued to fully interpret and explain to (or: for) them the things pertaining to (or: the references about) Himself within all the Scriptures.... "Were not our hearts constantly burning as He continued speaking to us on the road (or: in the path; with the way) – as He continued fully opening up the Scriptures to (and: for; or: in) us?".... At that time He fully opened back up again their minds to be habitually making the Scriptures flow together (or: to continue putting the Scriptures together so as to comprehend [them])" (Lu. 24:27, 32, 45).

In *Commentary on the Whole Bible* we read: "*Root* of David, as being Jehovah; the offspring of David as man. David's Lord, yet David's son" (Jamieson, Fausset and Brown, ibid p 1591). This is why He possesses "**David's key**" (3:7, above): He IS the David of which the OT prophesied, in regard to the coming of the Messiah, the "Anointed One" – He is the One like a son of man, or, we could say, like David, "And to Him was granted jurisdiction and esteem and a kingdom, even that all the peoples and leagues and language-groups shall serve Him..." (Dan. 7:14, CVOT).

Saying this differently, the "**I AM**" is the source and the fruition of all things. Israel, symbolized in "David," is a figure of the body of Christ; the Firstfruit unto God; His "Firstborn" (Ex. 4:22); the Head and Source of all humanity, and of all of the universe. Not only is He the root and the fruit, He is the whole Tree. This phrase is a fulfillment of Isa. 11:1, 10, which speaks of the Root and stump, shoot or stem of Jesse:

> "Now a slip (young shoot; stick; staff) will progressively come (or: go) forth from out of the midst of the root of, and which is, Jesse.... And in that Day there will continue being a Root from (or: of) Jesse, even the One continuing in arising and progressively (or: repeatedly) standing up to constantly rule [the] nations (ethnic multitudes; Gentiles); upon Him nations (ethnic multitudes; Gentiles) will continue placing expectation, and His rest will continue being honor and of value" (LXX, JM).

Sirach (Eccl.) 47:22 proclaims, "Yet the Lord will in no way (or: never) abandon His mercy... And so He gives a remnant by (or: to; in) Jacob, and by (or: to; in) David a Root from out of the midst of him" (LXX, JM). In the *Testament of Judah, the fourth son of Jacob and Leah*, remarkable statements are made in this 2nd century BC work. 24:1-6 gives us:

> "And after this there shall arise for you a Star from Jacob in peace: And a man shall arise from my posterity like the Sun of righteousness, walking with the sons of men in gentleness and righteousness, and in him will be found no sin. And the heavens will be opened upon him to pour out the spirit as a blessing of the Holy Father. And he will pour the spirit of grace on you. And you shall be sons in truth, and you will walk in his first and final decrees. This is the Shoot of God Most High; this is the fountain for the life of all humanity. Then he will illumine the scepter of my kingdom, and from your root will arise the Shoot, and through it will arise the rod of righteousness for the nations, to judge and to save all that call on the Lord" (*Testaments of the Twelve Patriarchs*; *The OT Pseudepigrapha*, Vol. 1, ibid p 801).

The phrase "**The light-emitting** (Bright) **Morning Star**" can symbolize His being the Promise, and the Inauguration, of the New Day. It can also suggest that He is the Firstborn among many stars (Rom. 8:29;

8:14; Job 38:7). He is the reward of the overcomer (2:28, above). Peter relates the incident on the mount of transfiguration, and the Voice having been brought out of the atmosphere (heaven),

> "**And so, we continue having** (or: constantly hold) **the Idea which was spoken ahead of time in and as Light** (or: the prior-enlightened Thought and Reason; or: the Prophetic Word) **more confirmed** (validated; established; certain), **by which** (or: in which) **you folks continue doing beautifully** (performing ideally; producing finely), **while continuously holding toward** (= playing close attention to) **[it] as to a lamp continually shining within a parched place – until which [time or occasion] the Day may shine through and a light bearer** [= a morning star] **may rise within your hearts**
> > (or: constantly heeding, as to a lamp progressively making things appear in a dark, dingy or dirty place, until that Day can dawn, and [the] Light-bringer can arise in union with your core and innermost being)" (2 Pet. 1:18, 19).

This verse in 2 Peter both locates the Kingdom and clarifies the location of Christ: in the core of our innermost being. In fact, this being a "**star**," it gives the location of the "heavens" – in our hearts! It also is an echo of Num. 24:17, "A star shall come forth out of Jacob." God's people give birth to "stars." Cf Dan. 12:3. The symbol of the Morning Star may be an allusion to Lu. 1:78-79,

> "**because of our God's inner organs which are composed of mercy** (= His tender compassions which have the character and quality of mercy), **in union with and amidst which an upward performance and a rising** (= a daybreak) **from out of the midst of an exaltation** (or: from on high), **to at once 'shine upon the people continuously sitting within the midst of darkness** (the realm of the shadow and obscurity; dimness and gloom)' [Isa. 9:1] **– even within death's shadow; to cause our feet to be fully straight and to [walk] in correspondence to straightness, into the path** (way; road) **of peace.**"

17. "**And now the Spirit and the Bride are continuously saying, 'Be repeatedly coming!' Then let the one continuing to listen and hear say, 'Be continuously coming!' And so let the person constantly thirsting continuously come; let the one habitually willing at once receive Water of Life freely**"
> (or: "And so the Breath-effect and the Bride are constantly laying it out: 'Be progressively going!' Also, let the person now hearing say, 'Be progressively going!' Then, let the one repeatedly being thirsty habitually come and go. The person desiring and intending must at once take the Water from, and which is, Life for a free gift [to others]").

Now we see Jesus (the Bridegroom) speaking as "**the Spirit**," together with His **Bride** (the called-out). This also shows that it is Christ Who is speaking through the proclaiming of the good news BY the called-out folks. Bultmann addresses this thought:
> "[T]he salvation-occurrence continues to take place in the proclamation of the word. The salvation-occurrence is eschatological occurrence just in this fact, that it does not become a fact of the past but constantly takes place anew in the present.... Paul expresses this by saying that at the same time that God instituted reconciliation He also instituted the 'ministry of reconciliation' which is the 'message (literally 'word,' KJV) of reconciliation' (2 Cor. 5:18f). Consequently, in the proclamation Christ himself, indeed God Himself, encounters the hearer, and the 'Now' in which the preached word sounds forth is the 'Now' of the eschatological occurrence itself (2 Cor. 6:2)" (Rudolf Bultmann, ibid p 302).

Pause, and let this sink in!

We who hear are instructed to repeat the message, "**Be continuously coming!**" The statement is in the present imperative, and is singular. It is a directive, a command, which goes out to all humanity, but to each individual, personally. God says (and the Bride should be saying) "Come!!!" It is not a request, it is an order. All must eventually obey – He did not add, "if you choose to do so." What God commands all must ultimately do, "**For who** (which one; what) **has resisted** (stood against or in place of) **His intention** (the effect of His deliberated purpose and resolve) **and is yet still so standing?**" (Rom. 9:19b).

Who are those who are continuously thirsting? Once one drinks of Christ he does not thirst again (Jn. 4:14) because he has a spring of water (river of life) within him. So who are the thirsty? How about those just outside the City; those in the Fire. Since the salvation-occurrence, the gulf (Lu. 16:24) is bridged by Christ; old things have passed away, and behold all has become new.

> "And you will bail water with elation from the springs of salvation. And you will say, in that Day [the Day of the Lord], 'Acclaim Yahweh!'" (Isa. 12:3, 4, CVOT; brackets added)

This is the message, "Acclaim Yahweh (= Jesus: Yah Saves)," which we proclaim to them as we give to them the Water of Life (and thus, they live) freely (as a gift of His grace). "Ho, everyone who thirsts come to the waters, and he who has no money; come, buy and eat! come, buy wine and milk without money and without price" (Isa. 55:1); Jesus himself said, "He who comes to me shall not hunger; and he who believes in me shall never thirst" (Jn. 6:35).

The last half of this verse is a restatement of the promise made in 21:6b, above. This message began when Jesus first said it, in Jn. 7:37,

> "**Now within the last day – the great one – of the feast** (or: festival), **Jesus, after having taken a stand, stood and then suddenly cries out, saying, "If ever anyone may continue being thirsty, let him be habitually coming toward** (or: face to face with) **Me, and then let the person continuously trusting and progressively believing into Me be constantly** (habitually; repeatedly) **drinking!** [cf Isa. 12:3; 55:1; Jn. 4:10-14]
> (or: let him be progressively coming to Me and keep on drinking)."

Mark well the present tense in these commands: continuous and/or repeated action. The "**Water of Life**" is within the City, so this is an open, ongoing imperative to enter the City, for He has provided the Way, the Truth and the Life to all humans; to every person. But as we recall Ezekiel's vision of the waters, the water also goes out to the place of the dead, seeking the lost – until He finds them (Lu. 15:4). We may also have, here, an allusion to Israel's salvation history, during their wilderness wandering. In 1 Cor. 10:4, Paul instructs us,

> "**They all drank the same spiritual drink, for they kept on drinking from out of a spiritual bedrock** (or: cliff rock; rock mass) **– one continually following along behind** (or: progressively accompanying [them]). **Now the bedrock** (or: cliff rock) **was the Christ** (or: the rock mass was existing being the Anointing)."

Those who have been given ears to hear are now given the same work that the Spirit and the Bride are doing. This is parallel to what Paul said that God has done:

> "**placing within us the Word** (the Idea; the Reason; the message) **of the corresponding transformation to otherness** (or: the full alteration; the change from enmity to friendship; the conciliation)" (2 Cor. 5:19b).

Once again, we must continue to listen, and hear, what the Spirit is continuously saying (cf chapters 2 and 3, where this imperative is spoken to all seven of the called-out communities).

We should not miss the word "**freely**." Paul put it this way:

> "**For the [aforementioned] freedom, Christ immediately set us free** (or: [The] Anointed One at once frees us in, to, for and with freedom)! **Keep on standing firm, therefore, and do not again be habitually held within a yoke of slavery** (or: a cross-lever [of a pair of scales] whose sphere is bondage)

(or: Continuously stand firm, then, in the freedom [to which the] Anointing sets us free, and let not yourselves be progressively confined again by a yoke pertaining to servitude)!" (Gal. 5:1)

No longer is any sort of religion necessary in which we must "pay some dues." He requires nothing of us; Life is a gift, and is the only "sacrament" we need. In Rom. 3:24, Paul spoke of:

"**being folks presently and progressively being made right, freed from guilt, placed in solidarity within the Way pointed out, and continuously set in right relationship** (or: being [all] one-after-another delivered and rightwised; being ones habitually turned in the right direction; being [all] presently justified [by covenant inclusion]) **freely** (as a gift; gratuitously) **by His grace** (or: in His favor; with His grace; by His gratuitous act which brought joy) **through means of the process of a release-from-an-enslaved-condition and a liberating-away-from-imprisonment, which is resident within Christ Jesus** (or: by the setting-free which is centered in [the] Anointed Jesus; or: through the redemption that is union with Jesus [the] Messiah)."

Paul went on to speak of this grace in Rom. 5:15b-16,

"**you see, since by** (or: in) **the effect of the fall to the side** (the offense) **of the one THE MANY** (= the mass of humanity) **died, MUCH MORE** (= infinitely greater) **[is] the Grace of God** (God's Grace; favor which is God), **and the gift** (or: gratuitous benefit) **within Grace – a joy-producing act of Favor – by that of the One Man, Jesus Christ, surrounded** (or: encircles) **into encompassing superabundance** (extraordinary surplus and excess) **into THE MANY** (= the mass of humanity). **And further, [it is] NOT [with] the effect of the gush and flow of the gratuitous gift as [it was] through one missing of the target** (failing; deviating; sinning). **For you see, on the one hand, the effect of the decision and judgment** (result of the separating, evaluation and verdict) **[was] from out of one [failure and deviation, which led] into a commensurate effect of a decision** (a corresponding result of a negative evaluation which fell in line with the decision and followed the pattern which divided [us] down). **But on the other hand, the effect of the grace** (the product of the gratuitous favor and the resulting joyous benefit) **[is] from out of the effect of many falls to the side** (result of many stumblings-aside and offenses) **into the effect of a rightwising deliverance into covenant inclusion in the Way and making things right**

(the result of a liberating placing into right relationships within the Way pointed out; or: the effect of an act of justice; an effect of equity; a just award; or: a result of fairness, removal of guilt, and justification, while being turned in the right direction; an amendment of what was wrong; a just-effect; = the effect of covenant inclusion and participation)."

The City, described above, is an existential location and fountain of this freedom, because "**the Jerusalem above is** (continues being) **free, who is our mother**" (Gal. 4:26). As with the context of Gal. 4, Rom. 8:2 instructs us about being free: "**the principle and law of, from and which is the spirit and attitude of 'The Life within Christ Jesus' frees you away from the Law of the Sin and the Death.**" Cf 21:4, above.

The parenthetical alternate-rendering of the verse offers the other meaning of the imperative form of *erchomai*: Go! Instead of directing folks to come to the Spirit and the Bride, it can be instructing them to go to the river of Life, the source of which is now in the Garden-City. Also, folks are told to "take the Water from, and which is, Life: it is a free gift." The water is the source of Life, and is a symbol of Life: a flow. Cf comments on 22:1-2, above.

18. I am continuously testifying (repeatedly witnessing and giving evidence) **to** (or: in) **everyone [who is] habitually hearing the words** (or: messages) **of the prophecy of this scroll: If ever anyone**

should overlay (place upon; thus: add) **upon them, God will overlay** (impose; add) **upon him those plagues** (blows; impacts; strikes; smitings) **having been written within this scroll.**

This warning against altering the teachings of **this scroll** shows that the plagues written in this book were not just happenings of the 1st century, else how could they be later applied to those who add to the words of this prophecy? Those to whom this verse is referring are identified as those: "**habitually hearing the words** (or: messages) **of the prophecy of this scroll.**" We find identical phrasing in 1:3, above. This would be folks who are a part of the covenant communities to whom these messages were sent.

The idea of "**overlaying**," or "adding," would suggest obscuring or changing the meaning of the words though inserting extraneous doctrines into the text (e.g., like making the "lake of fire" into a place of eternal torment, instead of a cleansing and purifying process that is God Himself), or by applying the visions in a literal way to some future "end of time" scenario in the Middle East. It could also suggest the inserting of pagan concepts about the Unseen (calling it the "hell" of pagan religions) into the interpretation of the text, rather than letting OT and NT Scriptures interpret the symbols.

The allusions of this verse, and of the next, are to Deut. 4:2 (cf 2:14, above, for this context); 12:32 and 29:20. In the immediate contexts of each of those passages was idolatry – which is always a persistent temptation. The MT and the LXX both have 12:32 as the beginning of Deut. 13, which addresses the issue of false prophets. We are also reminded of Prov. 30:6,
   "Do not add to His words, lest He should correct you, and you be [proved] a liar."
These allusions continue the Unveiling's frequent correlations to OT judgments, which were the "root" of the judgment of AD 70.

Nonetheless, this warning should be seen as a positive promise: folks who do such things need the "impacts" and God's Fire to purge their thinking and their behaviors. Folks usually "place conditions upon" others in order to control the behavior of others. The "plagues," or, "smitings," will simply be a harvesting of what they have sown. These "strikes" would be along the lines of what was given by the resurrected Christ to the seven churches, in chapters 2 and 3, above. Adding to what has been written in the Unveiling would be like the thorns and thistles that were added to the productive field in Heb. 6:8, which was a reference to Judaism that added pagan ideas and Persian dualism into their religion, and the "field" of Jerusalem ended in being burned, in AD 70. All that is involved in God's cleansing and correction is Good News. It is the process of forming us into what was the initial purpose of creating humans: to make us in God's image. Sometimes this involves making us into another vessel (Jer. 18:4, 6).

19. **And if anyone should take away from the words of the scroll of this prophecy, God will take away his part from the tree of the Life, and out of** (or: forth from) **the set-apart City – of** (or: pertaining to) **the things being written within this scroll.**

This shows that one can be kicked out of the City, to the outside, where they may weep and gnash their teeth. This is a figure that applied to the Jews of the 1st century, as Jesus prophesied of their being cast into outer darkness and having regrets (weeping and gnashing teeth; Mat. 8:12, et al) – i.e., losing their place of leadership in the kingdom (figured here by the City). However, it can also apply to us,
   "**You people who in union with** (or: centered in; [remaining] within) **Law continue being liberated and rightwised, from grace** (or: placed in the Way pointed out and included in the new covenant of grace; being given an eschatological transformation, which is favor), **were at once discharged** (made inactive, idle, useless, unproductive and without effect; or: voided,

nullified, exempted) **away from Christ – you at once fell out from [the grace and favor]!**" (Gal. 5:4).

It was by partaking of the tree of the knowledge of good and evil (= the Law) that man lost his right to the tree of the life in the Garden (here: City). The letter kills; the Spirit gives life. So this verse is pointing back to Gen. 3:22-24; those who **take away from the words** recorded here will experience a "second death" – a second expulsion from God's Garden. This judgment calls to mind Rom. 11:18-22, where Paul speaks of believing branches being broken out of the olive tree into which they had been grafted. Taking away parts of God's Unveiling implies that one had not been "abiding in the Vine" (Jn. 15:6), and thus, "**they are constantly gathering** (or: leading) **them** [other MSS: it] **together [as in a bundle]. And then, they are normally throwing** (or: casting) [*p66* adds: them] **into the fire.**" It is interesting that in Jn. 15:5a Jesus made a self-identifying metaphorical statement that is parallel to vs. 16b, above: "**I, Myself, am the Grapevine.**"

In Mk. 4:24-25 Jesus gave the warning:

"**Habitually observe and take note of** (face, look at and regard; pay attention to) **what you folks are habitually listening to and hearing. With what measure, rule, or standard you folks habitually measure** (or: In the measure by which you repeatedly measure [people; situations; things] or measure out [to people]), **it will habitually be measured in or for you** (or: measured out to you).... **and from him who is not habitually possessing** (having and holding), **even what he normally possesses will also proceed being lifted up and taken away.**"

Fairness and equity, sowing and reaping, continue being part of the Way pointed out to us. Justice and rightwised living are a part of "righteousness, peace and joy in the Set-apart Breath-effect (Rom. 14:17)."

The warnings given here call to mind Gal. 1:8,

"**However, even if we – or an agent from the atmosphere or sky** (or: a messenger from out of the midst of heaven)**! – should ever bring or announce something as "good news"** (as the message of goodness; as being the evangel or gospel) **to you folks which is to the side of that which we announce** (or: is parallel to what we announced) **to you folks in the message of goodness, ease and well-being, let it be placed on the altar before the Lord** (set up as a result of a divine offering [i.e., to see if it is "accepted" by God, or "rejected," as Cain's was])."

In these two verses we see that if we add to God's program, He adds measures to correct us. And if we take something away from His grace, love, mercy and correction, He removes some privilege from us and restricts our life (like the pruning, in Mat. 25:46). But as He said in Gen. 1:31, it is all "very good."

20. **The One continuously testifying these things is saying,**

"**Yes, I am continuously** (or: habitually; repeatedly; or: presently) **coming quickly** (swiftly; promptly)**!**"

Amen (So be it; It is so; Count on it). **Be continuously coming** (or: repeatedly coming and going), **Lord Jesus!**

The identification of the speaker, "**The One continuously testifying**," calls us back to 1:2, above, "the testimony from [Messiah] Jesus."

This presses the point of vs. 12, above: He told them that He was swiftly coming; that He repeatedly does so. He had also affirmed this in vss. 7 and 10, above. This should impress us concerning its intended meaning: Soon! John answers affirmatively in return, "**Amen** (So be it; It is so; Count on it). **Be continuously coming** (or: repeatedly coming and going), **Lord Jesus!**" In all of our stresses and troubles, we usually – in our own words – say the same thing, meaning "Come right now and help me!"

And He does. This does not deny His constant presence with us, but it fits the apocalyptic genre of the Unveiling: picturing Christ coming in special times and ways, for incidental purposes as He sovereignly interacts with human history, guiding or intervening. Present, yet constantly coming, creates the apparent paradox of God. It is similar to our being in the midst of Him (Acts 17:28), yet Him being within us. John's response speaks in alignment with what He says that He is continuously, or repeatedly, doing.

21. **The Grace and favor of the Lord Jesus [is] with everyone** (or: all humanity; [other MSS read: ... with all of you; ... with the set-apart ones; ... with all the set-apart folks]). **Count on it** (or: It is so; Amen).

This is a typical closing of a 1st century letter, an epistolary postscript, and reminds us of Paul's letters. It echoes the greeting in 1:4, above. "**The GRACE and FAVOR of the Lord Jesus [is] with EVERYONE**" is the textual reading in the Nestle-Aland 27th edition of *Novum Testamentum Graece*. Note that there is no copulative (verb of being) in the text, and I supplied the normal "[is]" for such a statement. Others make this a blessing, or a benediction, using the form "[be]" as the copulative. The affirmation seems most in line with the free offer, given above: the one thirsting and willing to drink may come and drink of this grace and receive life! God's **grace** is here, **with everyone**!

Some Concluding Thoughts

In an article titled "A Society of Redeemers," published in The Morningstar Journal, Francis Frangipane says, "The character of God is connected to the cross.... The cross is not just a place where wounded people get healed; it's where wounded people become an offering for those who wounded them. The cross represents the perfecting of love in your life.... God is perfecting love in us.... He can only do that in a realm where injustice forces you to have to climb to the nature of Christ..." We would rather say, "Where injustice places you in a situation in which only Christ can lift you to His cross, to obtain His nature." But we love where, in this same article, Frangipane says, "To become like Jesus is our destiny." That is what it means to become an "overcomer," in this book. It is the work of Christ within us.

In this book we saw the Lamb as having been slain, yet now alive. But we want to go to another type. In Rom. 12:1 Paul says,

> "**Consequently, brothers, I am repeatedly calling you folks alongside to advise, exhort, implore and encourage you, through God's compassions to stand your bodies alongside** (or: to set or place your bodies beside) **[the] Well-pleasing, Set-apart** (Holy; Different-from-the-usual), **Living Sacrifice by God** (or: in God; for God; to God; with God), **[this being] your sacred service which pertains to thought, reason and communication** (or: your reasoned and rational service; the logical and Word-based service from you folks; or: = temple service)."

Here we see ourselves called to participate with the antitype of the scapegoat, on the Day of Atonement. In Ex. 16, when Yahweh was to "appear in the cloud, upon the Mercy Seat" (vs. 2), Aaron was to "take two KIDS of the goats for a sin offering..." (vs. 5), and "cast lots upon the two goats; one lot for Yahweh, and the other for the scapegoat. And Aaron shall bring the goat upon which Yahweh's lot fell, and offer Him as a sin offering. But the goat upon which the lot fell to be the scapegoat, SHALL BE PRESENTED ALIVE before Yahweh, to make an atonement (covering and cleansing) with Him, and to let him go for a scapegoat into the wilderness" (vs. 8-10). The scapegoat was "a living sacrifice," and Christ goes into the wilderness for us, bearing away the sins of the nation (a figure of the whole of humanity). But we also participate in the goat that was slain and offered up, for Paul tells us in 2 Cor. 4:10,

> "**[We are being folks] at all times continuously carrying around** (or: bearing about) **among the body Jesus' being put to death** (or: within [our] body the deadening, deadness and state of death, which comes from Jesus; or: within the midst of the body the dying associated with Jesus; or: the dying which is Jesus, in union with the body), **to the end that the life, also, of Jesus** (or:

so that also the life which comes from and is Jesus; or: so that Jesus' life) **can** (or: could; may; would) **be set in clear light and manifested, within our body** (or: in the midst of the body, which is us)!"

These are expectations for the covenant communities to live-out before the world that surrounds us.

And consider this: it was the little animal which killed the two witnesses in 11:7, above. It was also the religion of killing little animals (the Law through the instrument of the Jews) which sacrificed "Christ, our Passover" (1 Cor. 5:7). Is it not the "beast" nature of man which requires atonement for sin? The lost sheep of the house of Israel are a type of mankind lost in Adam. God became a sheep as we saw in 5:6, above, "**a little Lamb, as slain**..." He even became a Kid of the goats, "for a sin offering" (call to mind the kids of Matt. 25:31-46). And where the shepherds of Israel had not fed the flock, nor sought that which was lost (Ezk. 34:1-6), "... thus says Yahweh God: behold, I, even I, will both search [for] My sheep, and seek them out. As a Shepherd... so will I seek out my sheep, and deliver them..." (vss. 11-12). "Yahweh is my Shepherd..." (Ps. 23:1). And then we have Jesus, identifying Himself as Yahweh by saying in John 10:11 & 14, "**I AM the Good Shepherd**..." The Good Shepherd continually gives His life for the sheep. But remember that the overcomer is called to "**shepherd the nations** (ethnic multitudes)." Thus are we called to "**lay down [our lives] for [our] friends**" (John 15:13). And, "... **that [we] keep on loving one another – correspondingly as** (to the same degree as; in the same sphere as) **[He] loves [us]**" (vs. 12).

We have come full circle to "**standing our bodies alongside the Living Sacrifice**" (Rom. 12:1).

Just as we are branches, joined to the Vine, so all that He did we have been a part of; all that we do is really just Him being lived out in us. We produce His fruit. We work His works. We saw in the picture of Jerusalem descending from God, out of heaven, that God was within her (21:22), and that she has God's glory (21:11). This reveals and manifests the answer to the prayer of Jesus, "**That they all may be one; as You, Father [are] within Me, and I within You, that they also may be one in Us.... And the glory (manifestation which calls forth praise) which You gave to Me I have given to them.... I within them, and You within Me, that they may be perfected** (brought to the goal) **into One**..." (Jn. 17:21-23). This is the goal of the ages; this is why He is continually coming to us; this is why His grace is with everyone; this is why He is continually and progressively making all things new. All the events and processes that have been pictured for us in this *Unveiling* have one purpose in mind:

> "**An administration, implementation and realization from a detailed plan of the effects of that which fills up the appointed seasons and fertile moments**
> > (or: a dispensing of the entire contents of the opportune situations; [leading] into a house-law of the result from the full measure of the fitting situations and a management of the household of the complement of the seasons; into an administration of the full effect from the eras), **[designed] to itself bring back again all things up under one**
> **Head** (or: to gather everything around the main point and sum it all up in unity; to unite and return all things to the Source) **within and in union with the Christ: those things upon [other MSS: within] the heavens** (or: the atmospheres) **and the things upon the land** (earth) **– centered in, within the midst of, and in union with, Him!**" (Eph. 1:10).

> "The book of Revelation is not where the good news of the gospel goes to die. The book of Revelation is where the good news of the gospel finds its most creative expression. Through inspired dreamlike images John the Revelator dares to imagine a world where the nightmare of endless war finally succumbs to the peaceable reign of Christ. And I, for one, believe in the vision John saw" (Zahnd, War, ibid).

"Only that shall happen which has happened, only that occur which has occurred..." (Eccl. 1:9, Tanakh). Selah.

Zahnd also observed,

"Both Armageddon and New Jerusalem are symbols, but they are true symbols of very real alternative fates. The way of the Beast leads to Armageddon, while the way of the Lamb leads to the New Jerusalem.... Jesus' lamb-like kingdom is the saving alternative to the beast-like empires of the world [be they political or religious].... The book of Revelation doesn't anticipate the end of God's good creation; it anticipates the end of death-wielding empire.... Thus the drama of Revelation is cast as an epic conflict between the Lamb (Jesus) and the Beast (Rome) [with the woman of religion riding, and supported by, empire]" (*Sinners*, ibid pp 154-156; brackets mine).

John's *Unveiling* is a beautiful picture of Jesus, the risen and enthroned Messiah, bringing an end to the old covenant age while simultaneously inaugurating the new covenant age of God's presence living within the new City of the Second Humanity (1 Cor. 15:47) that is here, and now.

What is the Timeframe of Acts 3:21?

In Acts 3:21, Peter speaks of times, and of a situation of fulfillment:
> "**until times of a movement away from all things that have been firmly put down, set and established and until the periods of successive events which occur in passing moments, moving all mankind away from having been placed and positioned down as well as from the state or condition of all things that had been determined from an indefinite period of time** (or: from a [particular] age)."

What is the timeframe of this proclamation? Let us first note some common interpretations, but then read through the preceding context before arriving at an answer to this question.

The answer to the question that this study investigates will be in accord with how each person that asks it understands such phrases as, "the time of the end," the "end of the age," or "the consummation or conjunction of the ages," or, "the eschaton." What Peter said in this verse, and the context of his impromptu sermon, will normally be interpreted as belonging to one of these categories of eschatology. But let us consider his words and the situation when he and John came out of the temple area and into the portico, and then addressed the crowd of Jews that were reacting to the miracle of the healing of the lame man.

Acts 3:
> 9. **And so all the people saw [the man] continuously walking around and praising God.**
> 10. **Now they began to recognize him, and were fully perceiving that this man was the one customarily sitting for gifts of mercy** (alms) **at the Beautiful Gate of the Temple complex – and they were filled with wondered astonishment and ecstasy, being internally put out of their normal position of understanding things – upon the thing having stepped together with him** (= at what had happened to him).
> 11. [conflated with D:] **So as Peter and John proceeded going out, and with his continued going out with them, clinging** (firmly holding fast) **to Peter and John, the entire [crowd of] people – overawed and out of their wits – ran together to them at the portico** (or: porch) **normally called Solomon's Colonnade** [note: built on a remnant of the ancient Temple].
> 12. **Now Peter, upon seeing [this], gave a decided reply to the people: "Men! Israelites!** (or: Men of Israel!) **Why do you folks continue amazed with wonder upon this [occurrence;** or: **man]? Or, why do you continue staring and gazing intently at us – as if by our own power and ability or godliness** (religiousness; devout conduct; piety) **[we] had been making him to be walking around?**
> 13. **"The God of Abraham, of Isaac and of Jacob – the God of our fathers – brought glory** (a manifestation which calls forth praise) **and a good reputation to His Servant** (or: Boy) **Jesus, Whom indeed you folks turned over** (gave aside; [D adds: unto judgment]) **and renounced** (or: disown; denied) **before Pilate's face – [he] having decided to be releasing that One!**

The basis of Peter's explanation for the incident begins with a statement that Yahweh "**brought glory and a good reputation**" to Jesus – even though they (note plural pronoun: "you folks") had turned Him over and renounced Him before Pilate. We should observe here that Peter lays this action upon all the Israelites that were present – he is not just putting the blame on the Jewish leadership. All of the actions in the Christ Event will be seen to be corporate actions.

> 14. **"But then you yourselves renounced** (disowned; denied) **the set-apart and fair Person** (the holy and just One Who personified the Way pointed out; this consecrated and rightwised One), **and instead you demanded for yourselves an adult man [who is] a murderer – to be at once graciously surrendered to you, as a favor.**

Again, he emphasizes "you yourselves" as being the ones who "renounced, disowned and denied" **the set-apart and fair Person**. They had chosen a murderer to be released – someone who Peter here affirms to be guilty of sin, a breaker of the Law – as they disowned "the holy and just One Who personified the Way pointed out (i.e., God's justice and flawless observation of the Covenant)." They denied "this consecrated and rightwised One." So Peter is rehearsing current events – the context, so far, is only a couple months in their past. He has also laid out before them the guilt of their unjust act. There is blood on their hands.

> 15. **"So you folks killed-off the Inaugurator of the Life** (or: Life's Originator; this Author, Founder, Leader, Prince and Initiator of the Life) **– Whom God raised up out from among the midst of dead folks, of which and of Whom we ourselves are witnesses, and continue being both evidence and testimony.**

Here Peter does not lay the blame on the Romans, who were indeed the instrument (the beast upon which the Jerusalem leadership was riding – Rev. 17:3ff), but addressing these "men of Israel" he says, **"So YOU FOLKS killed-off the Inaugurator of the Life."** Notice that I translate the definite article that is in the Greek text. He is "the (or: 'this' – giving the article its original demonstrative function) Author, Founder, Leader, Prince and Initiator of **THE Life**." Peter is not pointing back to Genesis, but is speaking of "the Life of Christ," and "resurrection life" that Jesus brought to humanity. Jesus informed us in Jn. 10:10b, "**I Myself come so that they can progressively possess** (would continuously have; could habitually hold) **Life**," and in 10:28a, "**I Myself am continuously giving eonian life** (age-enduring life; life having the qualities and characteristics of the Age [of Messiah]; a life from, of and for the ages) **to and in them**," and then in 11:25a, "**I am the Resurrection** (or: the standing back up again; the Arising) **and the Life**."

Then in the second half of this verse Peter continues the same context of the Christ Event, pointing to the resurrection of Jesus, saying, "**Whom God raised up out from among the midst of dead folks**."

> 16. **"Consequently, by the faith from** (or: in the trust which has its source in; with the loyalty and reliability of) **His Name, His Name at once made this person firm, solid and stable – whom you now continue watching and gazing at, and have seen so thus know – and the faith, trust, loyalty and faithfulness that [is] through and by means of Him both gave and gives to him the entire allotment of whole and complete soundness... in front of you all!**

Peter now explains to the crowd that "**His Name**" had healed the man. It had happened "**by the faith from His Name**," or, "in the trust which has its source in His Name," and the healing came "with the loyalty and reliability of His Name." These different prepositional phrases represent the potential functions of the ablative-genitive case of the noun "faith/trust/etc." John was given further insight regarding His Name in the letter that he was to send the called-out community in Philadelphia, that through being joined to the Vine (Jn. 15:1ff), who IS The Overcomer (Jn. 16:33; *cf* 1 Cor. 15:54, 57), they would have written upon them, "**My God's Name, and the name of the City of My God: 'The New Jerusalem' – the one habitually descending from out of the atmosphere** (or: heaven), **from God – and My new Name**" (Rev. 3:12). Peter and John bore His Name, and all which that Name represents. We who also abide in the Vine also bear His Name. Selah.

All that had happened to the man (i.e., his healing) was "through and by means of [Christ]." The imparted "faith, trust, etc." had the effect of giving to him "**the entire allotment of whole and complete soundness**." This word is used only here in the NT. But a cognate is found in 1 Thes. 5:23 where Paul speaks of their, "**whole allotment** (= every part) **– the spirit, the soul and the body**." See also Jas. 1:4. These words are formed by adding the adjective "whole; entire" to the noun that means "an allotted share or possession." So Peter's choice of words in describing the man's gift of healing tells us something of what the Christ Event ushered-in. They were living in a sphere of having "the entire allotment," which in this case was manifested as "whole and complete soundness" of this man's body.

> 17. "**And so now, brothers, I have seen and so know that you acted and committed [it] in accord with and down from ignorance** (lack of knowledge) **– even as also your rulers** (chiefs; leaders) **[did].**

As Paul said in 2 Cor. 5:19b, that God is, "**not accounting to them** (not putting to their account; not logically considering for them; not reasoning in them) **the results and effects of their falls to the side** (their trespasses and offenses)," so here, Peter makes allowances for them, due to their "ignorance (lack of knowledge)."

> 18. "**But what God fully announced-down in advance** (or: before) **through the mouth of the prophets** (those who have light ahead of time and speak before people) **– [the situations which] His Anointed One** (or: Christ) **was to experience and suffer – He thus, and in this way, fulfilled.**

What they had done had actually acted-out what was foretold by the OT prophets concerning Israel's Messiah. It was a part of "the Way pointed out" – i.e., to lay one's life down for one's friend. And this is what Jesus did, for the whole world. Notice, again, that our context is still the Christ Event.

> 19. "**Therefore, at once change your way of thinking** (your frame of mind and point of view; [by customary use this implies: and return to Yahweh]), **and turn around toward [the situation for] your failures** (errors; times of missing the target; sins; deviations) **to be anointed out and wiped forth from your midst, so that seasons of cooling again, as well as fitting situations and fertile moments of refreshing could, should and would come from [the] face of the Lord** [= Yahweh or Christ],

With all this explained to them, Peter admonished them to "**at once change [their] way of thinking and [their] frame of mind and [their] point of view.**" As noted in the verse, by its customary use for Israel, this also meant that they should turn to Yahweh for His mercy as displayed in the Christ Event, for as Paul informs us,

> "**For you see, God encloses, shuts up and locks all mankind** (everyone; the entire lot of folks) **into incompliance** (disobedience; stubbornness; lack of being convinced), **to the end that He could** (or: would; should) **mercy all mankind** (may make everyone, the all, recipients of mercy)!" (Rom. 11:32).

Now Peter meant that these particular Israelites should do this right then and there. He goes on to instruct them to "**turn around toward [the situation for] their failures** (etc.) **to be anointed out and wiped forth from [their] midst.**" What would they gain from this, beyond their times of missing the target being washed away? His purpose clause that immediately follows gives us the answer: "**so that seasons of cooling again, as well as fitting situations and fertile moments of refreshing could, should and would come from [the] face of the Lord** [= Yahweh or Christ]." That would be an immediate response to the change of thinking and their focusing on their needy situation. Now lest Peter be misconstrued as preaching a form of "works righteousness," recall what Paul said about the entrance of faith and trust, which are in fact Christ Himself, entering into people:

> "**the faithfulness** (or: the trust and **faith**; confidence; loyalty) **[comes or arises] from out of the midst of, or from within, hearing, yet the hearing [comes] through a gush-effect of Christ, even through the result of a flow which is Christ** (or: through Christ's utterance; through something spoken concerning Christ; or: by means of a declaration which is anointed, or from Christ; through a word uttered which is Christ; [other MSS: God's speech])" (Rom. 10:17).

We should not miss the plural noun of which I have conflated three rendering: a) **seasons**; b) **fitting situations**; c) **fertile moments**. These offer us some of the nuances of the Greek *kairos*. But just how long would these seasons be? How many fitting situations would Yahweh send? When are the fertile moments of His sheep? It would appear that they were in one of these at that very moment – but the plural noun indicates that there would be more of them. So our eschatology might just need to be a bit open-ended. Of course, one could argue that these seasons and situations for those particular men to whom Peter spoke these words might have been "fertile" only until AD 70, as they were being invited to enjoy the "cooling and refreshing" of the movement of God's Spirit upon and among them, as we see recorded in the rest of the book of Acts, as well as in the other NT letters. But for the rest of humanity in the centuries that have followed, we have records of "seasons of refreshing" throughout the history of the "church." The metaphor, "**[the] face of the Lord** [= Yahweh or Christ]," speaks of His being present – and of their being in His presence. It is from His presence among and within us that these seasons, fitting situations and fertile moments "**come**."

> 20. "**and that He would send forth in** (or: to; for; with; by; among) **you folks the One having been handpicked beforehand to be ready and at hand, Christ** (= Messiah) **Jesus,**

Now this verse is a continuation of vs. 19 and is simply a further explanation of the "seasons, etc." of which he was referring, indicating that God, via His Spirit, would send the very Christ/Messiah to them whom they had just hung on a pole. Paul speaks to the same situation in 2 Cor. 3:16, "**Yet whenever the time should be reached when it** [= the heart] **can** (or: would; may; should; or: shall at some point) **twist and turn upon, so as to face toward, [the] Lord** [= Christ], '**the head-covering** (veil) **is progressively taken from around [the heart of Israel]**'" – and then they will behold him, as 2 Cor. 3:18 describes. This verse was speaking about the 1st century context that Peter was at that time addressing.

> 21. "**Whom indeed it continues necessary and binding for heaven to welcome, accept and embrace** (or: for [the] atmosphere to grant access, admit, receive and take to itself) **until times of a movement away from all things that have been firmly put down, set and established and until the periods of successive events which occur in passing moments, moving all mankind away from having been placed and positioned down as well as from the state or condition of all things that had been determined from an indefinite period of time** (or: from a [particular] age) **– of which things God spoke** (or: speaks) **through [the] mouth of His set-apart prophets** (those sacred folks who spoke light ahead of time).

Observe that this verse is a continuation of vs. 20. The "**Whom**" refers to Jesus, the Messiah. But what are we to make of the first clause? First of all, we must keep in mind that the relationship of Jesus to the heavens has a subordinate modifier that begins with "**until times**" – plural. Furthermore, Peter does not use the same word here that he used in vs. 19 (seasons, etc.), but uses a term to indicate "time" – the Greek *chronos*. Next, before unpacking this verse we should consider Peter's immediate reference to Israel's history and the prophecy that Moses gave concerning the Messiah that would come and would function as a Prophet; vs. 23 alludes to the fact that this Prophet would also rule Israel, and in connecting both vss. 22 and 23 to Christ, we should probably consider this as a reference to His enthronement. Recall that the resurrected Jesus told His disciples that, "**All authority** (or: Every right and privilege from out of Being) **is** (or: was) **given to Me within heaven and upon the earth** (or: in sky and atmosphere, as well as on land)!" (Mat. 28:18).

Just what is Peter referring to by his use of the word, "heaven"? Does this clause mean the Jesus must be kept somewhere away from the earth until these "times" come about? Here we should be instructed by traditional Jewish perception of the temple being God's house, and thus, by extension the temple was an eschatological term for "heaven" (which comes all the way down to earth, as does the sky and atmosphere – as indicated in the parenthetical expansion, above). In Isa. 51:15 Yahweh makes a reference to Ex. 14:21 (so, Bullinger), the Exodus, "I [am] Yahweh... that divided the sea." Then in 51:16,

> "Therefore have I put My words in your mouth [at Mt. Sinai] and with the shadow of My hand have I covered you [cleansing and atonement], to PLANT the HEAVENS, and to LAY THE FOUNDATIONS of the EARTH, and to say to Zion, 'You are My people.'"

The heavens and the earth were poetic language describing the priesthood, with its tabernacle cultus, and the twelve tribes of Israel, the people.

God's house, His temple, is now His body (1 Cor. 6:19; 2 Cor. 6:16). Yahweh told Moses to build a tent (the tabernacle) so that He could dwell among Israel (Ex. 25:8; *cf* Deut. 23:14a). In the new creation, as described in Rev. 21:1ff, we learn in vs. 3 that, "**Consider! God's tent** (the Tabernacle of God) **[is] with mankind** (the humans), **and He will continue living in a tent** (dwell in a Tabernacle) **with them, and they will continue being** (will constantly exist being) **His people, and God Himself will continue being with them**." Now Paul instructs us that this situation already exists, for,

"**since someone [is] within Christ** (or: So that if anyone [is] in union with [the] Anointed One; or: And as since a Certain One [was] in Christ), **[there is] a new creation** (or: [it is] a framing and founding of a different kind; [he or she is] an act of creation having a fresh character and a new quality): **the original things** (the beginning [situations]; the archaic and primitive [arrangements]) **passed by** (or: went to the side). **Consider! New things have come into existence** (have been birthed; or: It has become new things; or: He has been birthed and now exists being ones of a different kind, character and quality)" (2 Cor. 5:17).

The resurrection of Christ inaugurated the new creation, and that new tent in which God dwells is termed by Paul as God's temple – the called out, covenant communities. It is binding for these communities "**to welcome, accept and embrace, to grant access, admit, receive and take to itself**" for Rev. 2:1b informs us that He is constantly walking around amidst the communities, and Rev. 3:20 describes a situation in Laodicea where He was seeking admittance to their group. Jesus told His disciples, "**You see, where there are two or three people that have been led and gathered together into My Name, I am there** (in that place) **within the midst of and among them**" (Mat. 18:20). Paul instructs us that,

"**He jointly roused and raised** (or: suddenly awakens and raises) **[us] up, and caused [us] to sit** (or: seats [us]; = enthroned [us]) **together within the things situated upon** [thus, above] **the heavens within and in union with Christ Jesus**" (Eph. 2:6).

Many other examples could be given to demonstrate that Christ's presence is now here with, and within, us. But let us move on to the next word that has had much written about it and which most have put off into the future. It is the noun, *apokatastaseōs*, which is used only here in the NT. The verb form has a basic meaning: to set down or to place in correspondence to [something]. This word is qualified by the prepositional phrase *pantōn*, and then further qualified by the remainder of the verse. Although the noun phrase has been translated "restitution of all things" (KJV), and the NRSV renders the phrase "universal restoration," a close analysis of the elements of the Greek word yields potentially different understandings of what Peter meant by using this phrase amid a context that has been speaking of his own time.

This noun is composed of *apo-*, *kata-*, and *staseōs*. *Apo* signifies movement away from; *kata* has the basic meaning of down; *staseōs* means a placing or a setting. Here are the renderings on offer:

    a) **a movement away from all things that have been firmly put down, set and established**
    b) **moving all mankind away from having been placed and positioned down**
    c) **moving all from the state or condition of all things that had been determined**.

The first offer would refer to the firmly set down and established Law of the Mosaic Covenant: God was moving everything away from the Law of the old covenant. The second offer would refer to humanity's release from prison and resurrection from the dead. The third offer speaks to what was the human predicament that resulted from Adams disobedience. The movement was away from an existing situation. But this movement is not necessarily "back," as in restoration. The movement is into the new, which is the better (Heb. 7:19, 22; 8:6; 10:34; 11:35).

The form of the word "all" is both neuter and masculine, thus the rendering "all things" and "all mankind." Both readings work here. I have also offered an alternative to the rendering "**until times**": **until the periods of successive events which occur in passing moments**.

Taking all these renderings into consideration, the picture seems to be speaking of the Christ Event of the 1st century, rather than a future "universal restoration." This gloss of the NRSV, as well as the traditional "restoration of all things" (NASB), seems to inject a future time context that the Greek does not demand or even necessarily indicate. The plurality of "times" could well allude to the growth of the reign/kingdom in the figure of the Stone that "became a great mountain and filled the whole land/earth" (Dan. 2:35c). Paul uses a similar noun which proclaims the same truth, but that is based on the word *allos* (other), in 2 Cor. 5:19,

> "**God was existing within Christ** (God was and continued being in union with [the] Anointed One) **progressively and completely transforming [the] aggregate of humanity** (or: world) **to be other [than it is]**
>> (or: progressively bringing [the] ordered System into another level or state; repeatedly changing [the] universe to correspond with other [conditions; perceptions]; progressively altering [the] ordered arrangement of culture, religions, economy and government to be in line with another one; habitually and progressively changing [the] secular realm [of humanity] from enmity to friendship; reconciling [the] world [of mankind]) **in Himself, to Himself, for Himself and by Himself, not accounting to them** (not putting to their account; not logically considering for them; not reasoning in them) **the results and effects of their falls to the side** (their trespasses and offenses), **even placing within us the Word** (the Idea; the Reason; the message) **of the corresponding transformation to otherness** (or: the full alteration; the change from enmity to friendship; the conciliation)."

When Christ came, His ministry, death, resurrection and then the judgment of Jerusalem in AD 70 fulfilled all that had been written in the OT concerning Israel (Lu. 21:22). But His resurrection and enthronement began something new (2 Cor. 5:17; Rev. 21:5), and there are no definite indications (with the possible exception of 1 Cor. 15:24-28, depending upon how one interprets this apocalyptic language) that the new which Christ inaugurated and inhabits will ever end.

A parallel idea to this verse, and to this whole sermon, is described in Heb. 3:18-4:6 where the metaphor of Israel entering into the Promised Land is employed: moving from the wilderness wandering and desolation (which ended in the death of the unbelieving generation) into the Rest (Christ) flowing with milk and honey and vineyards (Christ, the Vine). In the book of Hebrews, they are exhorted not to return to the works of the Law, but to remain in the works of the Messiah and His better arrangement (or: covenant).

Continuing on with Acts 3:
> 22. "**Indeed, Moses said,**
>> '**[The] Lord [= Yahweh] God will proceed raising up for** (or: to; among) **you folks a Prophet from out of the midst of your brothers, as** (or: like) **me. You people will continue listening to His [words] and hearing** (= obeying) **Him in regard to** (or: in accordance with) **all things – as much** (or: as many) **as He may be speaking to you folks!**
> 23. '**So it will continue being [that] every soul** (= person) **which may** (or: should; or: will) **not listen to or hear** (= obey) **that Prophet will progress being completely brought to destruction** (or: ruin and loss) **from out of the midst of the People.'** [Deut. 18:15-16]
> 24. "**Now all the prophets also fully announced these days, from Samuel on, and as many as consecutively** (in order according to succession) **spoke.**

Here, again, following what is presented in vs. 21, we see that Peter is speaking of **THESE DAYS** (vs. 24), as being the things of which the prophets fully announced.

> 25. "**You yourselves are the sons of the prophets and of that which was thoroughly set in order and arranged through the covenant, which God fully arranged** (or: covenanted) **to, and with a view toward, your fathers** (= ancestors), **progressively saying to Abraham,**

> **'And so, within and in union with your Seed, all the families** (or: kinship groups; clans; tribes) **of the earth** (or: land) **shall proceed being blessed and will continue having words of goodness, ease and well-being spoken to and about them.'** [Gen. 22:18; 26:4]
>
> **26. "To you folks first, God, in raising up His Servant, sent Him forth continually blessing you and repeatedly speaking words of goodness, ease and well-being within the [situation for] constantly and progressively turning each one away from your misery-gushed situation of worthless conditions, laborious works, painful relationships, malicious deeds** (or: from these wicked plans as well as from the evil thoughts and dispositions of you people)."

In these last two verses, the context is Peter's time, but the quote of Gen. 22 and 26 speak of a durative future where God's blessings **will continue**, and now Peter reprises vs. 19, with a conclusion that describes their situation, conditions and activities ("misery-gushed" [a literal rendering], etc.). Note that he says that God "**sent Him forth**…" The entire passage speaks of the 1st century Christ Event, and specifically to the men to whom Peter was speaking. T. Everett Denton explains of vss. 24-26,

> "In vs. 24, just as he did in Acts 2:16ff, Peter… came right out and plainly told them that the days in which they – that generation – were living were the last days of prophecy…. This means that the days of that generation (not the days of our generation today) were the days of the fulfillment of all prophecy ever given (*cf* Lu. 21:22)" (*Pertinent Parousia Passages, Second-Coming Scripture Studies*, 2016 pp 35-36).

Richard Rohr has made an astute observation concerning our own day,

> "Christianity's efforts at evangelization will remain trapped in culture and fundamentalism until we ourselves are large enough to proclaim a cosmic notion of Christ" ("Daily Meditation," 7/9/17).

The 1st century was the time of "The End of the Old, and the Beginning of the New."

YOU WILL LOVE GOD

Deut. 6:4-6 presented Israel with this promise. We can observe how there were those who did love God, from reading the OT accounts. But the obvious fulfillment of this promise is seen in Israel's "Federal Head" and representative, her Messiah, and through Him all those who are joined to Him. But let us observe this promise, as recorded in the Septuagint (LXX):

> 4. **Listen, pay attention and hear, O Israel! [The] LORD** (= Yahweh), **your God, [the] LORD** (= Yahweh) **is** (continually exists being) **One.**
> 5. **And so, you** [singular; = you, as a people] **will keep on and progressively love** (urge toward reunion with, and have unambiguous acceptance of) **[the] LORD** (= Yahweh), **your God, out of** (from the midst of) **your whole thinking faculty** (or: thoughts and understanding that move through the mind; note: the normal LXX translation of Heb. *leb*), **and out of** (from the midst of) **your whole soul, and out of** (from the midst of) **your whole power and ability.**
> 6. **And thus, these effects of the flows** (these results of the sayings, speeches and things that are spoken) – **as much as I, myself, presently continue imparting as inner directives to you, and implanting as instructions for the goal, the purposed aim and the union-centered destiny for you, today – will continue being within** (in the midst of, centered in and in union with) **your heart, and within** (in the midst of, centered in and in union with) **your soul.**

In vs. 5, the verb "**love**" (*agapaō*) is not in the imperative mood, but in the indicative. It is a statement of fact, and thus is a promise, since the verb tense is future. This tense, in Greek, belongs to the group of verbs (along with the imperfect and the present) which are all "durative," meaning they express continued, repeated or progressive (or, "lineal") action. This was God's plan for humans, and Israel was to live out (embody) this relationship between God and humans, as instruction and enlightenment for the rest of humanity. How would this come about? Verse 6 gives the explanation. By means of the instruction (Torah) given through Moses, God would, "presently continue imparting as inner directives to you, and implanting as instructions for the goal, the purposed aim and the union-centered destiny for you, today – [and they] will continue being within (in the midst of, centered in and in union with) your heart, and within (in the midst of, centered in and in union with) your soul." I have expanded the meaning of the verb, *entellomai*, in rendering this clause. It is a combination on *en* (within; centered in; in union with) and the verb form of the word group of *telos*, (aim; purpose; goal; end; destiny). This verb is commonly rendered, "command." But what happens when an authority gives a subordinate a "command"? The authority speaks or writes the desired end, or goal, of this "command," and the subordinates internalize the directive as a goal to be accomplished. So what the authority does is "**impart**," or "**implant**," his words into the hearts of his subordinates so that they fulfill the purpose, aim and goal of those words. Does this remind you of God saying He would write His laws (instructions) on/in our hearts? Yes, it does.

But what was God's goal in imparting the words that Israel (note the corporate instruction) would love the Lord (Yahweh, in the Heb.)? Verses 5b explains that they would do this with their entire being and abilities, and vs. 6b explains that His goal for them would permeate their interior being. I suggest that when this inner directive and impartation enters the heart, His Word (*Logos*) will create a new heart to accomplish His aim. But what did it mean, that they will progressively love God? What is the "**love**" of which He speaks, here?

The noun that is related to the verb *agapaō* is *agapē*. Now Paul normally quoted from the LXX, when citing the OT, so when he wrote a short essay on *agapē*, he no doubt was familiar with the verb's use in our Deut. 6 text, above. But before we look at 1 Cor. 13, I want to share meanings of *agapē* extracted

from the writings of the theologian, Paul Tillich, in *Systematic Theology III*, pp 134-137 and *Perspectives on 19th and 20th Century Protestant Theology*, p 200:
> 1. the urge or drive toward reunion
> 2. the acceptance of the other one as a person
> 3. unambiguous love
> 4. the power of reunion with the other person as one standing on the same ultimate ground
> 5. unrestricted acceptance which overcomes existential separation, in spite of the estranged, profanized and demonized state of the object.

Richard Rohr has given an added definition of *agapē*: a drive to give yourself totally to something or someone.

We should not miss the dynamic quality that these two scholars give to the term, agape. Could this be explained by John's definition of the essence of God? He put it succinctly in 1 Jn. 4:16,
> "**God exists continually being Love** (God is Love, which is Unrestricted Acceptance, etc.)."

Then in the 19th vs. of this same chapter, he instructs us that,
> "**We ourselves are habitually loving** (or, as a subjunctive: can and should be constantly loving) **because He Himself first loved** (or: urges to reunion with) **us**."

So what does this *agapē* look like? Paul explained it in 1 Cor. 13:
> 4. **The Love** (or: This unrestricted acceptance, etc.) **is habitually even-tempered, taking a long time to be in a heat of passion** (is constantly long-enduring/suffering and patient; keeps on putting anger far away; continues slow to progress toward rushing emotions which cause violent breathing; continues passionately persevering unto the goal) – **it continues being usefully kind. The Love** (or: This urge toward unambiguous, accepting reunion and giving of oneself) **is not constantly boiling with jealousy and envy. The Love is not continuously bragging or "showing off" – it is not habitually being puffed up; it is not conceited or arrogant.**
> 5. **It is not repeatedly indecent in manner or behavior** (it does not continually display lack of [good] form, rudeness or improper demeanor); **it is not habitually self-seeking** (or: not constantly pursuing its own interests or rights); **it is not continually caused to be sharp [in response] nor aroused to irritation or upset emotions; it is not habitually keeping account of the worthless thing, nor logically considering something of bad quality, nor counting the injury.**
> 6. **It does not continue to rejoice upon [seeing or hearing of] the injustice, nor is it happy about dishonesty, inequity, or lack of the qualities of the Way pointed out, yet it repeatedly rejoices with the Truth** (or: takes delight together in Reality).
> 7. **[Love] continuously covers all mankind; it is habitually loyal to all humanity; it constantly has an expectation for all mankind; it is continuously remaining under and giving support to all people.**
>> (or, since "all" can also be neuter: It [i.e., unambiguous acceptance] progressively puts a protecting roof over all things; it is habitually trusting in, and believing for, all things; it is continually hoping in or for all things; it keeps on patiently enduring all things.)
> 8. **The Love** (or: This unrestricted, self-giving drive toward reunion) **never – not even once – fails** (falls out or lapses; = becomes fruitless or ineffectual; [other MSS: falls down; collapses]).

Now in Jn. 3:16, we are informed by John that God does all of this:
> "**For thus God loves** (*agapaō*: fully gives Himself to and urges toward reunion with) **the aggregate of humanity** (the universe; the ordered arrangement; the organized system [of life

and society]; the world), **so that He gives His uniquely-born** [with other MSS: the only-begotten] **Son...**"

God does unto humanity what He said that Israel would do to Him (which was accomplished in the Messiah, Israel's representative – the Second Humanity, the Last Adam, 1 Cor. 15:45, 47).

When we think of speak of "love," we tend to default into thinking in terms of *eros*, or of the affection of *philia*, in regard to that promise in Deut. 6 (or, even in John's or Paul's writings). We who have known God as our Father have had developed in us a filial love for Him,

> "**because God's love** (the urge toward reunion and the unambiguous, uniting acceptance from God; God's giving of Himself to [us]) **has been poured out in a gush and shed forth so that it now floods within our hearts, permeating the core of our being, through the Set-apart Breath-effect** (or: Holy Spirit; Sacred Attitude) **being given to us** (in us; for us)" (Rom. 5:5b; -- thank you, Art White, for tying this in here).

But this filial love for our Father (wonderful as it is) is not what seems really to be behind the idea of *agapē*. If we adopt Tillich's understanding of agape (and keep in mind that the verb form was used in the Deut. text), then God was saying that Israel will increasingly "accept Him," and will have an "urge toward union with Him," even to the point of having a recognized "standing on the same ground" (as per Tillich) as Him. This goes way beyond our "heart feelings for Him" (as important as those are!), which we later see w/David, in the psalms, and in the prophets. We will then be enabled to "love the aggregate of humanity (the world)" as He does, and do all that His "agape" does, for "God is Agape!" With our hearts "**joined to the Lord**" (1 Cor. 6:17), and our whole being "**dwelling/abiding in the Vine**" (Jn. 15:1ff), we will be able to have, "unrestricted acceptance of people which overcomes existential separation, in spite of their estranged, profanized and demonized state." In fact, by His indwelling Spirit, we will have, "the urge, drive and power of reunion with other people, as one standing on the same ultimate ground with them."

And then, the risen Christ will say,

> "**I am truly now saying to you folks, upon such an amount** (or: To the extent) **that you did** (or: do) **and perform(ed) [it] to** (or: for) **one of these belonging to the least of My brothers** (used collectively: = the members of My family), **you did and perform [it] to and for Me!**"

The lived-out expressions of *agapē* (e.g., 1 Cor. 13:7, above; also 1 Jn. 5:3) are "**loving**" God. The imparted, or implanted, ability for us to love God and to love others is the result of Christ making all things, and all people, new (Rev. 21:5). He makes our hearts new by coming into union with us, transforming us to be the very Love that He is – and this is the reality of being "**born back up again to a higher place** (or: brought to birth again; or: given birth from above)" (Jn. 3:3). By being "**born... from out of the midst of God**" (Jn. 1:13), we become His children, and we love because of His Love that gave birth to us. Thus it is our destiny: to **progressively love God** as He "unveils" Himself to us in and by His Spirit, in and by His creation, as well as in and by other people.

> "**We have seen and thus know that God's Son has arrived and is continuously here, and He has given thorough understanding** (input throughout the mind) **to the end that we would constantly know by experience the True One, and we constantly exist within and in union with the True One** (or: in the real [situation]; in the midst of Reality)**: within His Son, Jesus Christ. This One is the True** (Real; Genuine) **God, and Life pertaining to and having the qualities of the Age** (or: life having its source in the Age [of Messiah]; eonian life; Life of, for and on through, the ages)" (1 Jn. 5:20).

This was another *Unveiling* that was given to John, concerning Jesus Christ.